ANNUITY TABLE — Present Value of $1 to Be Received Annually for N Years Running

Years (N)	1%	2%	4%	6%	8%	10%	12%	14%	15%	16%	18%	20%	22%	24%	25%	26%	28%	30%	35%	40%	45%	50%
1	0.990	0.980	0.962	0.943	0.926	0.909	0.893	0.877	0.870	0.862	0.847	0.833	0.820	0.806	0.800	0.794	0.781	0.769	0.741	0.714	0.690	0.667
2	1.970	1.942	1.886	1.833	1.783	1.736	1.690	1.647	1.626	1.605	1.566	1.528	1.492	1.457	1.440	1.424	1.392	1.361	1.289	1.224	1.165	1.111
3	2.941	2.884	2.775	2.673	2.577	2.487	2.402	2.322	2.283	2.246	2.174	2.106	2.042	1.981	1.952	1.923	1.868	1.816	1.696	1.589	1.493	1.407
4	3.902	3.808	3.630	3.465	3.312	3.170	3.037	2.914	2.855	2.798	2.690	2.589	2.494	2.404	2.362	2.320	2.241	2.166	1.997	1.849	1.720	1.605
5	4.853	4.713	4.452	4.212	3.993	3.791	3.605	3.433	3.352	3.274	3.127	2.991	2.864	2.745	2.689	2.635	2.532	2.436	2.220	2.035	1.876	1.737
6	5.795	5.601	5.242	4.917	4.623	4.355	4.111	3.889	3.784	3.685	3.498	3.326	3.167	3.020	2.951	2.885	2.759	2.643	2.385	2.168	1.983	1.824
7	6.728	6.472	6.002	5.582	5.206	4.868	4.564	4.288	4.160	4.039	3.812	3.605	3.416	3.242	3.161	3.083	2.937	2.802	2.508	2.263	2.057	1.883
8	7.652	7.325	6.733	6.210	5.747	5.335	4.968	4.639	4.487	4.344	4.078	3.837	3.619	3.421	3.329	3.241	3.076	2.925	2.598	2.331	2.108	1.922
9	8.566	8.162	7.435	6.802	6.247	5.759	5.328	4.946	4.772	4.607	4.303	4.031	3.786	3.566	3.463	3.366	3.184	3.019	2.665	2.379	2.144	1.948
10	9.471	8.983	8.111	7.360	6.710	6.145	5.650	5.216	5.019	4.833	4.494	4.192	3.923	3.682	3.571	3.465	3.269	3.092	2.715	2.414	2.168	1.965
11	10.368	9.787	8.760	7.887	7.139	6.495	5.937	5.453	5.234	5.029	4.656	4.327	4.035	3.776	3.656	3.544	3.335	3.147	2.752	2.438	2.185	1.977
12	11.255	10.575	9.385	8.384	7.536	6.814	6.194	5.660	5.421	5.197	4.793	4.439	4.127	3.851	3.725	3.606	3.387	3.190	2.779	2.456	2.196	1.985
13	12.134	11.343	9.986	8.853	7.904	7.103	6.424	5.842	5.583	5.342	4.910	4.533	4.203	3.912	3.780	3.656	3.427	3.223	2.799	2.468	2.204	1.990
14	13.004	12.106	10.563	9.295	8.244	7.367	6.628	6.002	5.724	5.468	5.008	4.611	4.265	3.962	3.824	3.695	3.459	3.249	2.814	2.477	2.210	1.993
15	13.865	12.849	11.118	9.712	8.559	7.606	6.811	6.142	5.847	5.575	5.092	4.675	4.315	4.001	3.859	3.726	3.483	3.268	2.825	2.484	2.214	1.995
16	14.718	13.578	11.652	10.106	8.851	7.824	6.974	6.265	5.954	5.669	5.162	4.730	4.357	4.033	3.887	3.751	3.503	3.283	2.834	2.489	2.216	1.997
17	15.562	14.292	12.166	10.477	9.122	8.022	7.120	6.373	6.047	5.749	5.222	4.775	4.391	4.059	3.910	3.771	3.518	3.295	2.840	2.492	2.218	1.998
18	16.398	14.992	12.659	10.828	9.372	8.201	7.250	6.467	6.128	5.818	5.273	4.812	4.419	4.080	3.928	3.786	3.529	3.304	2.844	2.494	2.219	1.999
19	17.226	15.678	13.134	11.158	9.604	8.365	7.366	6.550	6.198	5.877	5.316	4.844	4.442	4.097	3.942	3.799	3.539	3.311	2.848	2.496	2.220	1.999
20	18.046	16.351	13.590	11.470	9.818	8.514	7.469	6.623	6.259	5.929	5.353	4.870	4.460	4.110	3.954	3.808	3.546	3.316	2.850	2.497	2.221	1.999
21	18.857	17.011	14.029	11.764	10.017	8.649	7.562	6.687	6.312	5.973	5.384	4.891	4.476	4.121	3.963	3.816	3.551	3.320	2.852	2.498	2.221	2.000
22	19.660	17.658	14.451	12.042	10.201	8.772	7.645	6.743	6.359	6.011	5.410	4.909	4.488	4.130	3.970	3.822	3.556	3.323	2.853	2.498	2.222	2.000
23	20.456	18.292	14.857	12.303	10.371	8.883	7.718	6.792	6.399	6.044	5.432	4.925	4.499	4.137	3.976	3.827	3.559	3.325	2.854	2.499	2.222	2.000
24	21.243	18.914	15.247	12.550	10.529	8.985	7.784	6.835	6.434	6.073	5.451	4.937	4.507	4.143	3.981	3.831	3.562	3.327	2.855	2.499	2.222	2.000
25	22.023	19.523	15.622	12.783	10.675	9.077	7.843	6.873	6.464	6.097	5.467	4.948	4.514	4.147	3.985	3.834	3.564	3.329	2.856	2.499	2.222	2.000
26	22.795	20.121	15.983	13.003	10.810	9.161	7.896	6.906	6.491	6.118	5.480	4.956	4.520	4.151	3.988	3.837	3.566	3.330	2.856	2.500	2.222	2.000
27	23.560	20.707	16.330	13.211	10.935	9.237	7.943	6.935	6.514	6.136	5.492	4.964	4.524	4.154	3.990	3.839	3.567	3.331	2.856	2.500	2.222	2.000
28	24.316	21.281	16.663	13.406	11.051	9.307	7.984	6.961	6.534	6.152	5.502	4.970	4.528	4.157	3.992	3.840	3.568	3.331	2.857	2.500	2.222	2.000
29	25.066	21.844	16.984	13.591	11.158	9.370	8.022	6.983	6.551	6.166	5.510	4.975	4.531	4.159	3.994	3.841	3.569	3.332	2.857	2.500	2.222	2.000
30	25.808	22.396	17.292	13.765	11.258	9.427	8.055	7.003	6.566	6.177	5.517	4.979	4.534	4.160	3.995	3.842	3.569	3.332	2.857	2.500	2.222	2.000
40	32.835	27.355	19.793	15.046	11.925	9.779	8.244	7.105	6.642	6.234	5.548	4.997	4.544	4.166	3.999	3.846	3.571	3.333	2.857	2.500	2.222	2.000
50	39.196	31.424	21.482	15.762	12.234	9.915	8.304	7.133	6.661	6.246	5.554	4.999	4.545	4.167	4.000	3.846	3.571	3.333	2.857	2.500	2.222	2.000

SOURCE: Robert N. Anthony and James S. Reece, *Accounting Principles*, 4th ed. (Homewood, IL.: Richard D. Irwin, 1979).

COMPOUND INTEREST RATE TABLE

Annual Percentage Rate

Number of Periods	1.00%	1.50%	2.00%	2.50%	3.00%	3.50%	4.00%	4.50%	5.00%	6.00%	7.00%	8.00%	9.00%	10.00%	12.00%	14.00%	16.00%	18.00%
						(Future Value of $1 – Principal Plus Accumulated Interest)												
1	1.010	1.015	1.020	1.025	1.030	1.035	1.040	1.045	1.050	1.060	1.070	1.080	1.090	1.100	1.120	1.140	1.160	1.180
2	1.020	1.030	1.040	1.051	1.061	1.071	1.082	1.092	1.103	1.124	1.145	1.166	1.188	1.210	1.254	1.300	1.346	1.392
3	1.030	1.046	1.061	1.077	1.093	1.109	1.125	1.141	1.158	1.191	1.225	1.260	1.295	1.331	1.405	1.482	1.561	1.643
4	1.041	1.061	1.082	1.104	1.126	1.148	1.170	1.193	1.216	1.262	1.311	1.360	1.412	1.464	1.574	1.689	1.811	1.939
5	1.051	1.077	1.104	1.131	1.159	1.188	1.217	1.246	1.276	1.338	1.403	1.469	1.539	1.611	1.762	1.925	2.100	2.288
6	1.062	1.093	1.126	1.160	1.194	1.229	1.265	1.302	1.340	1.419	1.501	1.587	1.677	1.772	1.974	2.195	2.436	2.700
7	1.072	1.110	1.149	1.189	1.230	1.272	1.316	1.361	1.407	1.504	1.606	1.714	1.828	1.949	2.211	2.502	2.826	3.185
8	1.083	1.126	1.172	1.218	1.267	1.317	1.369	1.422	1.477	1.594	1.718	1.851	1.993	2.144	2.476	2.853	3.278	3.759
9	1.094	1.143	1.195	1.249	1.305	1.363	1.423	1.486	1.551	1.689	1.838	1.999	2.172	2.358	2.773	3.252	3.803	4.435
10	1.105	1.161	1.219	1.280	1.344	1.411	1.480	1.553	1.629	1.791	1.967	2.159	2.367	2.594	3.106	3.707	4.411	5.234
11	1.116	1.178	1.243	1.312	1.384	1.460	1.539	1.623	1.710	1.898	2.105	2.332	2.580	2.853	3.479	4.226	5.117	6.176
12	1.127	1.196	1.268	1.345	1.426	1.511	1.601	1.696	1.796	2.012	2.252	2.518	2.813	3.138	3.896	4.818	5.936	7.288
14	1.149	1.232	1.319	1.413	1.513	1.619	1.732	1.852	1.980	2.261	2.579	2.937	3.342	3.797	4.887	6.261	7.988	10.147
16	1.173	1.269	1.373	1.485	1.605	1.734	1.873	2.022	2.183	2.540	2.952	3.426	3.970	4.595	6.130	8.137	10.748	14.129
18	1.196	1.307	1.428	1.560	1.702	1.857	2.026	2.208	2.407	2.854	3.380	3.996	4.717	5.560	7.690	10.575	14.463	19.673
20	1.220	1.347	1.486	1.639	1.806	1.990	2.191	2.412	2.653	3.207	3.870	4.661	5.604	6.727	9.646	13.743	19.461	27.393
22	1.245	1.388	1.546	1.722	1.916	2.132	2.370	2.634	2.925	3.604	4.430	5.437	6.659	8.140	12.100	17.861	26.186	38.142
24	1.270	1.430	1.608	1.809	2.033	2.283	2.563	2.876	3.225	4.049	5.072	6.341	7.911	9.850	15.179	23.212	35.236	53.109
26	1.295	1.473	1.673	1.900	2.157	2.446	2.772	3.141	3.556	4.549	5.807	7.396	9.399	11.918	19.040	30.167	47.414	73.949
28	1.321	1.517	1.741	1.996	2.288	2.620	2.999	3.430	3.920	5.112	6.649	8.627	11.167	14.421	23.884	39.204	63.800	102.967
30	1.348	1.563	1.811	2.098	2.427	2.807	3.243	3.745	4.322	5.743	7.612	10.063	13.268	17.449	29.960	50.950	85.850	143.371
32	1.375	1.610	1.884	2.204	2.575	3.007	3.508	4.090	4.765	6.453	8.715	11.737	15.763	21.114	37.582	66.215	115.520	199.629
34	1.403	1.659	1.961	2.315	2.732	3.221	3.794	4.466	5.253	7.251	9.978	13.690	18.728	25.548	47.143	86.053	155.443	277.964
36	1.431	1.709	2.040	2.433	2.898	3.450	4.104	4.877	5.792	8.147	11.424	15.968	22.251	30.913	59.136	111.834	209.164	387.037
38	1.460	1.761	2.122	2.556	3.075	3.696	4.439	5.326	6.385	9.154	13.079	18.625	26.437	37.404	74.180	145.340	281.452	538.910
40	1.489	1.814	2.208	2.685	3.262	3.959	4.801	5.816	7.040	10.286	14.974	21.725	31.409	45.259	93.051	188.884	378.721	750.378
42	1.519	1.869	2.297	2.821	3.461	4.241	5.193	6.352	7.762	11.557	17.144	25.339	37.318	54.764	116.723	245.473	509.607	1044.827
44	1.549	1.925	2.390	2.964	3.671	4.543	5.617	6.936	8.557	12.985	19.628	29.556	44.337	66.264	146.418	319.017	685.727	1454.817
46	1.580	1.984	2.487	3.114	3.895	4.867	6.075	7.574	9.434	14.590	22.473	34.474	52.677	80.180	183.666	414.594	922.715	2025.687
48	1.612	2.043	2.587	3.271	4.132	5.214	6.571	8.271	10.401	16.394	25.729	40.211	62.585	97.017	230.391	538.807	1241.605	2820.567
50	1.645	2.105	2.692	3.437	4.384	5.585	7.107	9.033	11.467	18.420	29.457	46.902	74.357	117.391	289.002	700.233	1670.704	3927.357
52	1.678	2.169	2.800	3.611	4.651	5.983	7.687	9.864	12.643	20.697	33.725	54.706	88.344	142.043	362.524	910.023	2248.099	5468.452
54	1.711	2.234	2.913	3.794	4.934	6.409	8.314	10.771	13.939	23.255	38.612	63.809	104.962	171.872	454.751	1182.666	3025.042	7614.272
56	1.746	2.302	3.031	3.986	5.235	6.865	8.992	11.763	15.367	26.129	44.207	74.427	124.705	207.965	570.439	1536.992	4070.497	10602.113
58	1.781	2.372	3.154	4.188	5.553	7.354	9.726	12.845	16.943	29.359	50.613	86.812	148.162	251.638	715.559	1997.475	5477.260	14762.381
60	1.817	2.443	3.281	4.400	5.892	7.878	10.520	14.027	18.679	32.988	57.946	101.257	176.031	304.482	897.597	2595.919	7370.201	20555.140

SOURCE: Federal Reserve Bank of New York, *The Arithmetic of Interest Rates*, pp. 26–27.

COMMERCIAL BANK MANAGEMENT

The IRWIN/McGraw-Hill Series in Finance, Insurance, and Real Estate
Stephen A. Ross
Sterling Professor of Economics and Finance
Yale University
Consulting Editor

FINANCIAL MANAGEMENT

Benninga and Sarig
Corporate Finance: A Valuation Approach

Block and Hirt
Foundations of Financial Management
Eighth Edition

Brealey and Myers
Principles of Corporate Finance
Fifth Edition

Brealey, Myers, and Marcus
Fundamentals of Corporate Finance
Second Edition

Brooks
PC FinGame: The Financial Management Decision Game
Version 2.0 DOS and Windows

Bruner
Case Studies in Finance: Managing for Corporate Value Creation
Third Edition

Chew
The New Corporate Finance: Where Theory Meets Practice
Second Edition

Grinblatt and Titman
Financial Markets and Corporate Strategy

Helfert
Techniques of Financial Analysis: A Modern Approach
Ninth Edition

Higgins
Analysis for Financial Management
Fifth Edition

Hite
A Programmed Learning Guide to Finance

Kester, Fruhan, Piper, and Ruback
Case Problems in Finance
Eleventh Edition

Nunnally and Plath
Cases in Finance
Second Edition

Parker and Beaver
Risk Management: Challenges and Solutions

Ross, Westerfield, and Jaffe
Corporate Finance
Fifth Edition

Ross, Westerfield, and Jordan
Essentials of Corporate Finance
Second Edition

Ross, Westerfield, and Jordan
Fundamentals of Corporate Finance
Fourth Edition

Schall and Haley
Introduction to Financial Management
Sixth Edition

Smith
The Modern Theory of Corporate Finance
Second Edition

White
Financial Analysis with an Electronic Calculator
Third Edition

INVESTMENTS

Ball and Kothari
Financial Statement Analysis

Bodie, Kane, and Marcus
Essentials of Investments
Third Edition

Bodie, Kane, and Marcus
Investments
Fourth Edition

Cohen, Zinbarg, and Zeikel
Investment Analysis and Portfolio Management
Fifth Edition

Farrell
Portfolio Management: Theory and Applications
Second Edition

Hirt and Block
Fundamentals of Investment Management
Sixth Edition

Jarrow
Modeling Fixed Income Securities and Interest Rate Options

Morningstar, Inc., and Remaley
U.S. Equities OnFloppy Educational Version
Annual Edition

Shimko
The Innovative Investor
Excel Version

FINANCIAL INSTITUTIONS AND MARKETS

Cornett and Saunders
Fundamentals of Financial Institutions Management

Flannery and Flood
Flannery and Flood's ProBanker: A Financial Services Simulation

Johnson
Financial Institutions and Markets: A Global Perspective

Rose
Commercial Bank Management
Fourth Edition

Rose
Money and Capital Markets: Financial Institutions and Instruments in a Global Marketplace
Sixth Edition

Rose and Kolari
Financial Institutions: Understanding and Managing Financial Services
Fifth Edition

Santomero and Babbel
Financial Markets, Instruments, and Institutions

COMMERCIAL BANK MANAGEMENT

Peter S. Rose

Texas A & M University

Irwin
McGraw-Hill

Boston   Burr Ridge, IL   Dubuque, IA   Madison, WI   New York   San Francisco   St. Louis
Bangkok   Bogotá   Caracas   Lisbon   London   Madrid
Mexico City   Milan   New Delhi   Seoul   Singapore   Sydney   Taipei   Toronto

Irwin/McGraw-Hill

A Division of The **McGraw·Hill** *Companies*

COMMERCIAL BANK MANAGEMENT

This book is printed on acid-free paper.

2 3 4 5 6 7 8 9 0 DOC/DOC 9 3 2 1 0 9

ISBN 0-256-15211-X

Vice president and editorial director: *Michael W. Junior*
Publisher: *Craig S. Beytien*
Senior sponsoring editor: *Randall Adams*
Senior marketing manager: *Katie Rose-Matthews*
Project manager: *Amy Hill*
Production supervisor: *Michael R. McCormick*
Cover design: *Gino Cieslik*
Supplement coordinator: *Rose M. Range*
Compositor: *Shepherd, Inc.*
Typeface: *10/12 Times Roman*
Printer: *R. R. Donnelley & Sons Company*

Library of Congress Cataloging-in-Publication Data
Rose, Peter S.
    Commercial bank management / Peter Rose. — 4th ed.
      p. cm. — (The Irwin series in finance)
    Includes bibliographical references and index.
    ISBN 0-256-15211-X (acid free paper)
    1. Bank management. 2. Financial services industry—Management.
  I. Title. II. Series.
  HG1615.R66 1999
  332. 1'2' 0685—dc21   98-16998

http://www.mhhe.com

To my family.

B R I E F   C O N T E N T S

ix

C O N T E N T S

Banking is an essential industry to most of us. It is where we often wind up when we're seeking a loan to purchase a new automobile, tuition for college or trade school, financial advice on how to invest our savings, credit to begin a new business, a safe deposit box to safeguard our valuable documents, or even more commonly, a checking account to keep track of when and where we spend our money. This is an industry, composed of thousands of firms worldwide, that literally affects the welfare of every other industry and the economy as a whole. As many countries in Asia have recently discovered, when banks stop lending and accepting the risks that go with it, the rest of the economy grinds nearly to a halt, land and security prices fall, unemployment lines lengthen, and businesses begin to fail. Healthy banks and healthy economies just seem to go together.

Today banking is an industry in *change*. Rather than being something in particular, it is continually becoming something *new*—offering new services, merging and consolidating into much larger and more complex businesses, adopting new technologies that seem to change faster than most of us can comprehend, and facing a new and changing set of rules as more and more nations cooperate to regulate and supervise the banks that serve their citizens.

Banking is one of the most heavily regulated businesses in the world. No one can start a bank without some government's permission to do so, and no one can close a bank without the government's approval. Yet, the extensive rules that constrain bankers' services, behavior, and performance are changing as well. Regulators looking over the industry are paying more attention to its risk and to signals from the private marketplace. We now seem to recognize today that government rules and regulations can only do so much, and that private decision-makers—businesses and consumers—can do as much or more to determine which banks are most accommodating and efficient and which should be allowed to fail (or, perhaps, be absorbed by other, better managed institutions).

Banking is also changing as a place to find a job. Traditionally, bankers hired one of the biggest shares of business, finance, and economics majors graduating from colleges and universities each year. Banks are still important sources of career opportunities for people of all ages, but overall employment in the industry is dropping. Fewer human tellers and fewer workers who sort checks and other paper items are needed;

machines are increasingly taking over these routine banking transactions After all, banking is nothing more nor less than an *information-gathering industry*. Writing a check, transferring money by wire, or spending the proceeds of a loan to buy a car involves simply moving bits of information from one computer file or account to another and, increasingly, automated equipment is carrying out these tasks faster, more accurately, and more conveniently than humans can do by hand. So rapid is the switch to computers and other electronic machines in the industry that banking's operating costs are becoming more like fixed costs (i.e., the cost of purchasing and maintaining equipment) and less like variable costs (i.e., labor time).

In short, modern banking is looking more and more like a fixed-cost industry, with dramatic effects on the optimal size banking firm that you need to achieve maximum operating efficiency (i.e., lowest-cost production of banking services). In an increasingly automated-service world, banks interested in competitive and sustained profits must increase their volume of operations, often by acquiring scores of smaller banks that are often less able to keep abreast of changing technology. Then, too, electronic banking is rapidly broadening the geographic extent of banking markets, leaping over state and national boundaries, and bringing continents closer together. This brings thousands of banks and nonbank financial-service firms in direct competition with each other, creating the need for fewer banks. The industry finds itself in a wave of *consolidation*—giant banks emerging through mega-mergers, and smaller banks disappearing through consolidations and acquisitions. There is much less room today for the small, locally owned bank, though many of these institutions still continue to survive and even prosper by finding niches for fulfilling service needs that the industry's giants ignore or overlook, such as personalized service for the aging consumer, small business financing, and personal financial advice from bankers willing to take the time to listen to their customers' special service needs.

Despite all of the epic changes sweeping through this vital industry, there are still some things in banking that never seem to change. It is and probably always will be a service industry, producing an intangible product that is hard (some say, impossible) to differentiate from the products offered by competitors. One bank's deposit or loan looks pretty much like another's deposit or loan. However, service accuracy, friendliness, and quality of service will vary from bank to bank in most market areas. Unlike many other jobs in private industry and government, banking requires both technical skills and people skills, rather than just one or the other. Bankers are often heard to say, "It's a relationship business." People come to trust in a bank and rely on its accuracy and stability when they need financial guidance, and they routinely expect courtesy from the bankers they deal with.

Despite banking's transition and turmoil, it requires special personal traits that not everyone possesses. Among the most important of these are honesty, reliability, thoroughness (attention to detail), and a willingness to always be open to new ideas and new ways of meeting customer needs Bankers can never stop learning because their industry is becoming something new every day, and their customers expect them to be "ahead of the curve," financially speaking, no matter how fast things happen to be changing.

New Elements in This Fourth Edition

As *Commercial Bank Management* enters its fourth edition, the changing world of banking has compelled the author to make important and significant changes in this new edition in a continuing race to stay up with (and sometimes look just a bit ahead of) this very dynamic and still highly important industry. Among the most important new additions are:

- A more in-depth discussion of *interstate banking* and the new Reigle-Neal Interstate Banking Act which now allows banking companies, both foreign and domestic, to reach across state lines and acquire banking firms (subject to regulatory approval) in any of the 50 states of the United States. The reader needs to know what the possibilities are for future bank expansion in the United States and also what the research evidence is on the effects of interstate, increasingly nationwide, banking in the United States. The new edition tackles this dynamic and challenging area, particularly in Chapters 2, 3, 21, and 22.

- A sharply expanded exploration of the rise of *Internet banking* through the World Wide Web which has opened up all kinds of service and information opportunities for bankers and for bank customers. The readers of *Commercial Bank Management* need to know what bankers have done on the "Net" thus far, what the problems and special challenges are that Net banking imposes on customers, and how bankers are dealing with these challenges. This new edition examines the available Internet services, looks at key Net banks, and explores ideas for promoting and selling Net services in Chapter 21 and the Appendix to Chapter 5.

- An examination of the growing penetration of *investment banking and security underwriting of* corporate stocks and bonds by banks in the United States as the Glass-Steagall Act is gradually modified by law and by regulatory decision—an issue currently of vital importance to the banking industry. The new edition of *Commercial Bank Management* reviews the history of this critical topic and then looks in detail at what the Federal Reserve Board has recently done to change the rules of the game for banks that are aggressively pursuing investment banking and underwriting services. Chapters 1, 2, 12, 22, and 23 look at this important subject.

- The new edition tackles the challenges banks face on all sides today from *nonbank competitors,* particularly mutual funds and pension funds, offering stocks, bonds, and mutual funds as an attractive alternative to traditional bank deposits. Banks have not achieved unblemished success in fighting this new trend, struggling hard to respond positively with attractive alternatives to maintain a healthy share of the growing public market for securities. The new text brings up this issue in several chapters, particularly Chapters 1, 2, and 12, and discusses how new regulations pose real challenges for banks trying to respond to the public's greater preference for financial assets, like mutual funds, that appear to offer superior long-range returns.

New Developments

A hot issue confronting many banks of all sizes today lies in the area of *selling* such *nontraditional banking products* as insurance sales and underwriting, and brokering commercial and residential real estate—services currently prohibited to most banks operating in the U.S. The proposed Financial Services Competitiveness Act and parallel proposals recently introduced into the U.S. House and Senate would lead to a wholesale redesign of the U.S. banking industry closer to European and Canadian models where these services can be offered either by banks themselves or through special banking affiliates and subsidiary firms. Indeed, recently proposed U.S. federal legislation goes even farther, proposing to allow banks to merge their activities with industrial and manufacturing companies, eroding the traditional distinction between banking and most other industries. The financial management and public policy issues inherent in these sweeping reform proposals are tackled in a number of places in the text, especially in Chapters 1, 2, 3, 12, and 23.

- *Asset-Liability Management*—the use of a collection of current risk management tools in banking—has now become a much larger subject for exploration and discussion than ever before The use of interest-sensitive GAP management and duration GAP analysis, financial futures, options, and swaps is receiving far greater attention and emphasis today than ever before, as is the rapidly expanding use of income-generating and risk-hedging mechanisms recorded off the balance sheet in banking. While interest rate derivatives have been in use for more than two decades now, a whole new market for *credit derivatives* has recently emerged, including credit swaps and options, granting bankers new ways to deal with the risk of default in their loans and other credit assets. These newest developments and instruments of bank risk management are discussed in several locations, particularly in Part II, Chapters 6 through 9, of this new edition.

- *New ways of managing a bank's liquidity needs* have emerged along with further changes in Federal Reserve rules for managing a bank's legal reserve (money) position. The development of special new contracts called *sweep accounts* have opened up ways for bankers to sharply reduce their volume of legal reserves, which currently earn no interest, by moving funds overnight from reservable transaction deposits to nonreservable deposit accounts. Fears for the damage these recent developments might do to the successful conduct of monetary policy have led to proposals in the U.S. Congress (recently endorsed by the Federal Reserve) that interest be paid on bank reserve balances held at the Fed in the future. As discussed in Chapter 11, it will be fascinating to watch this issue unfold in the period ahead.

- Changes in the federal *insurance coverage of deposits* have now become an important topic area in banking, especially with the strong consolidation trend now underway in the global banking system. As large numbers of banks are merged out of existence and converted into branch offices of their acquirers, depositors now have fewer independent banks to go to in order to maximize their deposit insurance protection. As a result, more attention is being paid around the world today to evaluating bank risk, and the largest bank customers more closely scrutinize bank performance, as is discussed in Chapters 5, 12, 13, and 22.

- *Trust services* have become more important in the industry and deserve more attention now than in the past in discussions of what bankers do. For example, retirement planning increasingly is being taken over by the private sector, with government playing a lesser role. Accordingly, bank trust departments have become one of the most important institutions in modern society for protection and managing the public's retirement assets as well as protecting and managing other forms of business and family property. Their role is discussed in more detail in Chapter 12.

- *New rules for managing bank capital*—the reservoir of long-term funds that keep banks open and operating for a time even when they're losing money—are emerging as the "age of risk management" in banking grows and intensifies. Increasingly around the globe the *owners* of banks are expected to carry more and more of the industry's risk exposure by pledging more capital to support the banks they own. Bankers are being forced to learn many new ways of handling the risks-to-asset values that shifting market prices and interest rates generate. Future bankers and their customers need to learn more about what these changes in bank capital management are and what they might mean for the future of the industry—a subject discussed more fully in Chapter 15.

- *The year 2000 dilemma* for bankers grows bigger by the month as more and more members of the industry discover what could happen to their ability to collect loan revenues, to the correct recognition and customers' use of credit cards, to bankers' relationships with their depositors, and to the security of bank funds (as, for example, when locks on bank vaults set to a 20th century computer clock schedule suddenly begin to open erratically as the new century dawns!). The accounting and management information systems problems that the arrival of a new century seems to pose for modern banking must be explored in greater detail as bankers around the globe work hard today to prepare for the new millennium. This issue is explored in Chapter 5.

- Finally, we must explore further *what is happening in the bank merger and acquisitions field* as banking companies reach out to purchase ever-expanding numbers of other banks, thrift institutions, insurance agencies and underwriters, security and credit-card companies, etc. We need greater understanding of the motivations behind these newly emerging financial-service combinations and what lessons they hold for bank managers and for the public they will serve in the years to come. We also need to see how bank mergers and acquisitions today have become much more than just matters of finance, but also matters of community development, of the continuing availability of financial services to all segments of the population in communities and neighborhoods, and of the growth and stability of well-paying jobs in an era when machines, rather than people, continue to loom larger in the daily routine of banking. These important modern-day issues are considered in Chapters 1, 2, 22, and 23.

As all of these new developments in banking unfold, we surely must come to the right conclusion: This *is* an exciting time to find out more about how banks function and how truly important they are in our daily lives.

Pedagogical Features

Several unique and important educational aids are included to assist the reader in understanding the material more thoroughly:

- Each chapter opens with *Learning and Management Decision Objectives,* which describe the principal goal of the material.
- *Key terms* are listed at the end of each chapter They are also identified in boldface within the body of the text to guide the reader toward a clear definition of each term.
- A *Glossary of Banking Terms* is listed at the end of the text.
- *Concept checks* are included after each major section to help determine whether the reader understands the material just presented
- A generous number of *end-of-chapter problems* is included, as well as extensive references. Many of the problems offer alternative scenarios to illustrate what happens if the facts involved shift or the assumptions suddenly change.
- Many *new boxed readings* introduce the reader to current trends in banking and bank management, including new service areas in banking, such as sales of mutual funds, insurance, security underwriting, brokerage services, and trust operations.
- Numerous *diagrams, exhibits, tables, and real-world examples* from the banking industry are integrated throughout the text to help clarify important points.
- Two new *cases* appear at the end of the text—one dealing with the key topic of asset-liability management, featuring the Banc One Corporation, and the other with the building of America's currently largest bank through the epic merger of Chase Manhattan Corporation and Chemical Banking Corporation. The cases from the previous edition plus several additional cases and their solutions appear in the *Instructor's Manual.*

Acknowledgments

The author has benefited in many ways from the criticisms and ideas of banking professors and experts in the banking field. Several well-qualified professionals have read and criticized the text as it has progressed through four editions. These committed and talented individuals include Oliver G. Wood, Jr., University of South Carolina; Edwin Cox, Boston University; James E. McNulty, Florida Atlantic University; Tony Cherin, San Diego State University; Edward C. Lawrence, the University of Missouri–St. Louis; James B. Kehr, Miami University; Emile J. Brinkmann, the University of Houston; David G. Martin, Bloomsburg University; David R. Durst, the University of

Akron; Nelson J. Lacey, the University of Massachusetts–Amherst; William Sackley, the University of Southern Mississippi; Iqbal Memon, Fort Lewis College; David Rand of Northwest Tech College in Ohio; and Jack Griggs of Abilene Christian University.

We greatly appreciate the efforts of the following individuals for their special assistance in the preparation of the fourth edition:

David Carter, University of North Carolina at Wilmington

James Kehr, Miami University of Ohio

Alan Gruenwald, Michigan State University

A special thank you also goes to Professor Anne Gleason of the University of Central Oklahoma, for her review work and in creating the Instructor's Manual and Power Point slides.

The author also wishes to extend his thanks to the President and Fellows of Harvard College and to the Harvard Business School for permission to reprint the two new cases: *Banc One Corporation: Asset and Liability Management;* and *Chase Manhattan Corporation.: The Making of America's Largest Bank.* He is particularly grateful for the fine work done by the cases' authors: Professors Ben Esty and Peter Tufano and Research Assistant Jonathan S. Headley for the Banc One case, and to Professor Stuart C. Gilson and Research Associate Cedric X. Escalle for the Chase Manhattan case.

A special note of gratitude must be extended to *The Canadian Banker* and the Canadian Bankers' Association for permission to use some of the author's earlier articles, published originally in *The Canadian Banker.* The author is also grateful to Shelley Kronzek, Holly Zemsta, Amy Hill, Gino Cieslik, and Jen Frazier as well as the other Irwin/McGraw-Hill staff for their editorial, design, and production efforts and their high degree of professionalism in seeing this new edition through to completion. Nonetheless, whatever failings and errors the book contains reflect only the author's shortcomings.

A Note to the Student

Banking is one of those indispensable industries about which few of us can afford to be ignorant. As recent problems in the global economy have demonstrated, our lifestyles and living standards often depend heavily on a bankers' willingness to extend credit, deposits, and other financial services to us as individuals and to the businesses and institutions we work for and trade with. But banking is changing so rapidly today that we cannot be content with merely a casual inquiry. This book is designed to help you dig deeply into this fascinating and frequently trouble-plagued industry in order to master established principles of bank management and to confront head-on the perplexing issues of risk, regulation, technology, and competition that bankers see as their greatest challenges for the future.

The text contains a number of pedagogical aids to help you accomplish this task. In particular:

1. Each chapter begins with *Learning and Management Decision Objectives* to provide you with a grasp of the chapter's goals. The management decision objectives attempt to convey what a bank manager should find of particular interest in each chapter.

2. A list of *Key Terms* appears at the end of each chapter so that you may review them before you proceed to the next chapter. Each term is presented in bold-face where it is defined to help you spot it immediately.

3. A *Glossary of Banking Terms* at the end of the book supplies definitions of all key terms, so that when you are assigned a specific chapter, you can double-check your understanding by turning to the portions of the glossary where that chapter's key terms are defined.

4. *Concept Checks* appear in each chapter at crucial points to allow you to determine whether you have grasped an understanding of the material before you proceed.

5. *Problems* at the end of the chapter assist you in reviewing key points and equations. Many alternative scenarios are presented so that you can explore what happens if the facts involved shift or the assumptions suddenly change.

While this book presents several devices to help you along the way, like every textbook, it is locked in time. It presents a snapshot of an industry that is rapidly changing—a service industry that may soon be very different from what we understand banking to be today. Therefore your journey toward understanding banks and the banking system cannot end here. A central mission of this book is to arouse your interest in banking practices and problems. If *Commercial Bank Management* makes you want to read and understand more about banking and financial services, it will have done its job.

This is a field where the amount of personal effort and your feeling of accomplishment are closely correlated, both in the near term and for a lifetime. Confidence, determination, and careful study usually pay off in banking, no matter what twists and turns the future may bring to this industry. Best wishes for success on your journey into the fascinating marketplace of modern banking.

Peter S. Rose

I   AN INTRODUCTION TO THE BUSINESS OF BANKING

1   AN OVERVIEW OF BANKS AND THEIR SERVICES

Learning and Management Decision Objectives

In this chapter you will learn about the many roles banks play in the economy today and see how recent trends in banking, including increased competition, technological change, consolidation into larger firms, and globalization, can affect a bank manager's decision making. The chapter explains why bank decision makers must take these trends into account if their banks are to survive and prosper.

Introduction

Banks are among the most important financial institutions in the economy. They are the principal source of credit (loanable funds) for millions of households (individuals and families) and for most local units of government (school districts, cities, counties, etc.). Moreover, for small local businesses ranging from grocery stores to automobile dealers, banks are often the major source of credit to stock the shelves with merchandise or to fill a dealer's showroom with new cars. When businesses and consumers must make payments for purchases of goods and services, more often than not they use bank-provided checks, credit or debit cards, or electronic accounts connected to a computer network. And when they need financial information and financial planning, it is the banker to whom they turn most frequently for advice and counsel.

Worldwide, banks grant more installment loans to consumers than any other financial institution. In most years, they are among the leading buyers of bonds and notes issued by governments to finance public facilities, ranging from auditoriums and football stadiums to airports and highways. Banks are among the most important sources of short-term working capital for businesses and have become increasingly active in recent years in making long-term business loans for new plant and equipment. The assets held by U.S. banks represent about one-third of the total assets and a

3

roughly equal proportion of the earnings of all U.S.-based financial institutions. In other countries, such as Japan, banks hold the majority of assets possessed by all financial institutions. Moreover, bank reserves are the principal channel for government economic policy to stabilize the economy. For all these reasons and more, banks are one of the most important of society's institutions for us to study and understand.

What Is a Bank?

As important as banks are to the economy as a whole and to local communities, there is much confusion about exactly what a **bank** is. Certainly banks can be identified by

Bankers' Insights and Issues

The Emergence of Modern Banking

When did the first banks appear? *Linguistics* (the science of language) and *etymology* (the study of the origin of words) suggest an interesting story about banking's origins. Both the Old French word *banque* and the Italian word *banca* were used centuries ago to mean a "bench" or "money changer's table." This describes quite well what historians have observed concerning the first bankers, who lived more than 2,000 years ago. They were money changers, situated usually at a table or in a small shop in the commercial district, aiding travelers who came to town by exchanging foreign coins for local money or discounting commercial notes for a fee in order to supply merchants with working capital.

The first bankers probably used their own capital to fund their activities, but it wasn't long before the idea of attracting deposits and securing temporary loans from wealthy customers became an important source of bank funding. Loans were then made to merchants, shippers, and landowners at rates of interest as low as 6 percent per annum to as high as 48 percent a month for the riskiest ventures! Most of the early banks of any size were Greek in origin.

The banking industry gradually spread outward from the classical civilizations of Greece and Rome into northern and western Europe. Banking encountered religious opposition during the Middle Ages, primarily because loans made to the poor often carried very high interest rates. However, as the Middle Ages drew to a close and the Renaissance began in Europe, the bulk of bank loans and deposits involved relatively wealthy customers, which helped to reduce religious opposition to banking practices.

The development of new overland trade routes and improvements in navigation in the 15th, 16th, and 17th centuries gradually shifted the center of world commerce from the Mediterranean region toward Europe and the British Isles, where banking became a leading industry. During this period were planted the seeds of the Industrial Revolution, which demanded a well-developed financial system. In particular, the adoption of mass

the *functions* (services or roles) they perform in the economy. The problem is that not only are the functions of banks changing, but the functions of their principal competitors are changing as well. Indeed, many financial institutions—including leading security dealers, brokerage firms, mutual funds, and insurance companies—are trying to be as similar as possible to banks in the services they offer. Bankers, in turn, are challenging these nonbank competitors by seeking expanded authority to offer real estate and security brokerage services, insurance coverage, investments in mutual funds, and many other new products.

A good example of the strenuous efforts on the part of many institutions to become banklike occurred in the 1980s when several large insurance and security firms, including Merrill Lynch, Dreyfus Corporation, and Prudential, moved aggressively to

production methods required a corresponding expansion in global trade to absorb industrial output, requiring new methods for making payments and credit available. Banks that could deliver on these needs grew rapidly, led by such institutions as the Medici Bank in Italy and the Hochstetter Bank in Germany.

The early banks in Europe were places for safekeeping of valuable items (such as gold and silver bullion) as people came to fear loss of their assets due to war, theft, or expropriation by government. Merchants shipping goods across the sea found it safer to place the gold and silver they were paid at the nearest bank rather than risking its loss to pirates or to storms at sea. In England during the reigns of King Henry VIII and Charles I, government efforts to seize private holdings of gold and silver resulted in people depositing their valuables in goldsmiths' shops, who, in turn, would issue tokens or certificates, indicating that the customer had made a deposit at these businesses. Soon, goldsmith tokens or certificates began to circulate as money because they were more convenient and less risky to carry around than gold or other valuables. The goldsmiths also offered *certification of value* services—what we today might call property appraisals. Customers would bring in gold, silver, jewels, or other valuables to have an expert certify that these items were, indeed, real and not fakes—a service many banks still provide their customers.

When colonies were established in North and South America, Old World banking practices were transferred to the New World. At first the colonists dealt primarily with established banks in the countries from which they had come. As the 19th century began, however, state governments in the United States began chartering banking companies. Many of these were simply extensions of other commercial enterprises in which banking services were largely secondary to merchants' sales—for example, the farm equipment business. The development of large, professionally managed banking firms was centered in a few leading commercial centers, especially New York. The federal government became a major force in U.S. banking during the Civil War. The Office of the Comptroller of the Currency (OCC) was established in 1864, created by Congress to charter national banks. This divided bank regulatory system, with both the federal government and the states playing key roles in the control and supervision of banking activity, has persisted in the United States to the present day.

enter the banking business by establishing what they called **nonbank banks.** They were aware that under law in the United States any institution *offering deposits subject to withdrawal on demand* (such as by writing a check or by making an electronic withdrawal) and *making loans of a commercial or business nature* is a bank. Merrill Lynch and other nonbank firms decided they could skirt around these laws, avoid regulation, and still sell banklike services to the public simply by stripping the banks they controlled of *either* their business loans or their checking accounts. However, the Federal Reserve Board, unhappy with the invasion of banking by these pseudobanks, decided to include the making of loans to individuals and families as one of the activities that differentiated banks from other financial institutions, thus bringing Merrill Lynch and similar businesses under the definition of a bank, subject to stringent government regulation.

Leading security and brokerage firms then sued in federal court, charging that the Federal Reserve Board had exceeded its authority. In 1984, the federal courts agreed and ordered the Fed to allow the formation of nonbank banks and grant them access to federal deposit insurance. Within a few weeks of their authorization, dozens of applications for nonbank banks were filed. Among the leading financial-service companies organizing nonbank banks were E. F. Hutton, J. C. Penney, and Sears Roebuck. Moreover, several leading bank holding companies, including Citicorp and Chase Manhattan, launched their own nonbank banks because they could establish these service units freely across state lines. In 1987, Congress put a halt to further nonbank bank expansion by subjecting the parent companies of nonbank banks to the same regulatory restrictions that traditional banking organizations face. Moreover, Congress took one last shot at pinning down the legal definition of a bank, defining it as a corporation that is *a member of the Federal Deposit Insurance Corporation.* A clever move— under current U.S. law a bank is not what a bank does; rather, its identity depends on which government agency insures its deposits!

The water was muddied even further in the 1990s when the administrations of Presidents George Bush and Bill Clinton proposed that banks with adequate capital be allowed to offer a wide range of services, affiliate with security broker/dealer firms and investment companies (mutual funds), and allow industrial firms to own financial-service holding companies that can control banks and insurance companies as well as allow banking companies to venture into nonfinancial industries on a limited basis. Thus, the historic legal barriers in the United States separating banking from other businesses, which have prevailed for generations, are under attack and may soon have little meaning in defining what banks are and what they do.

The result of all these legal maneuverings is a state of confusion in the public's mind today over what is or is not a *bank.* The safest approach is probably to view these institutions in terms of what types of services they offer the public. *Banks are those financial institutions that offer the widest range of financial services*—especially credit, savings, and payments services—and *perform the widest range of financial functions of any business firm in the economy.* This multiplicity of bank services and functions has led to banks being labeled "financial department stores" and to such familiar advertising slogans as Your Bank—a Full-Service Financial Institution (see Exhibit 1–1).

Exhibit 1–1
*Vital Functions
Performed by
Full-Service
Banking
Institutions
Today*

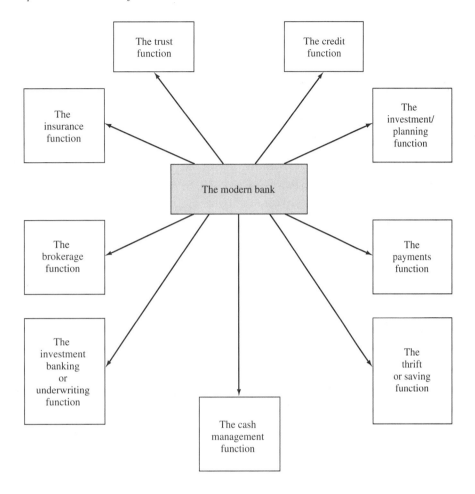

The trust
function

The credit
function

The
insurance
function

The
investment/
planning
function

The modern bank

The
brokerage
function

The
payments
function

The
investment
banking
or
underwriting
function

The
thrift
or saving
function

The cash
management
function

Concept Checks

1–1.   What is a *bank?*

1–2.   Under current U.S. federal law, what must a corporation do to qualify as
a *commercial bank?*

The Services Banks Offer the Public

Banks are financial-service firms, producing and selling professional management of the
public's funds as well as performing many other roles in the economy. (See Table 1–1.)
Their success hinges on their ability to identify the financial services the public demands,

---

Table 1–1   **The Many Different Roles Banks Play in the Economy**

While many people believe that banks play only a narrow role in the economy—taking deposits and making loans—the modern bank has had to adopt new roles in order to remain competitive and responsive to public needs. Banking's principal roles today are as follows:

The intermediation role	Transforming savings received primarily from households into credit (loans) for business firms and others in order to make investments in new buildings, equipment, and other goods.
The payments role	Carrying out payments for goods and services on behalf of their customers (such as by issuing and clearing checks, wiring funds, providing a conduit for electronic payments, and dispensing currency and coin).
The guarantor role	Standing behind their customers to pay off customer debts when those customers are unable to pay (such as by issuing letters of credit).
The agency role	Acting on behalf of customers to manage and protect their property or issue and redeem their securities (usually provided through the bank's trust department).
The policy role	Serving as a conduit for government policy in attempting to regulate the growth of the economy and pursue social goals.

---

produce those services efficiently, and sell them at a competitive price. And what services does the public demand from banks today? In this section, we present an overview of banking's *service menu.*

Services Banks Have Offered throughout History

Carrying Out Currency Exchanges.   History shows that one of the first services offered by banks was **currency exchange**—a bank stood ready to trade one form of currency, such as dollars, for another, such as francs or pesos, in return for a service fee. Such exchanges were very important to travelers in the ancient world (as they are today) because the travelers' survival and comfort depended on gaining access to the local currency of the country or city through which they were journeying. In today's financial marketplace, trading in foreign currency is usually carried out primarily by the largest banks due to the risks involved and the expertise required to carry out such transactions.

Discounting Commercial Notes and Making Business Loans.   Early in their history, bankers began **discounting commercial notes**—in effect, making loans to local merchants who sold the debts (accounts receivable) they held against their customers to a bank in order to raise cash quickly. It was a short step from discounting commercial notes to making direct loans to businesses for purchasing inventories of goods or for constructing new offices and production facilities.

Offering Savings Deposits.   Making loans proved so profitable that banks began searching for ways to raise additional loanable funds. One of the earliest sources of funds consisted of offering **savings deposits**—interest-bearing funds left with banks for a period of weeks, months, or years, sometimes bearing relatively high rates of interest. There are historical records of banks in ancient Greece, for example, paying as high as 16 percent in annual interest to attract savings deposits and then making loans to ship owners in the Mediterranean region at loan rates double or triple the interest rate on savings deposits.

Safekeeping of Valuables.   During the Middle Ages, banks began the practice of holding gold, securities, and other valuables owned by their customers in secure vaults. Interestingly enough, the receipts bankers gave their customers acknowledging the deposit of valuable property often circulated as money—the forerunners of modern checks and credit cards. Today the *safekeeping* of customer valuables is usually handled by a bank's *safety deposit* department, which keeps the customer's valuable property under lock and key until the customer demands access to that property.

Supporting Government Activities with Credit.   During the Middle Ages and the early years of the Industrial Revolution, the ability of bankers to mobilize large amounts of funds and make loans came to the attention of governments in Europe and America. Frequently, banks were chartered under the proviso that they would *purchase government bonds* with a portion of any deposits they received. This lesson was not lost on the fledgling American government during the Revolutionary War. The Bank of North America, chartered by the Continental Congress in Philadelphia in 1781, was set up to help fund the struggle to throw off British rule and make the United States a sovereign nation. Similarly, during the Civil War, Congress created a whole new federal banking system, agreeing to charter *national banks* in every state of the union provided these banks purchased government bonds, which were used to help fund that war.

Offering Checking Accounts (Demand Deposits).   The Industrial Revolution in Europe and the United States ushered in new banking practices and services. Probably the most important of the new services developed during this period was the **demand deposit**—a checking account that permitted the depositor to write drafts in payment for goods and services that the bank had to honor immediately. Offering demand deposits proved to be one of the industry's most important services because it significantly improved the efficiency of the payments process, making business transactions easier, faster, and safer. Now the checking account concept has been extended to the Internet and to so-called smart cards, where funds can be spent electronically to pay for purchases of goods and services.

Offering Trust Services.   For many years banks have managed the financial affairs and property of individuals and business firms in return for a fee that is often based on the value of properties or the amount of funds under management. This property management function is known as **trust services.** Most banks offer both *personal trust* services to individuals and families and *commercial trust* services to corporations and other businesses.

Through a personal trust department, customers can set aside funds for the education of their children, for example, with the bank managing and investing the money until it is needed. Even more commonly, banks act as trustees for wills, managing a deceased customer's estate by paying claims against the estate, keeping valuable assets

Bankers' Insights and Issues

The Role of Banks in Theory

Above all else, banks are *financial intermediaries,* similar to credit unions, insurance companies, and other institutions selling financial services. The term *financial intermediary* simply means a business that interacts with two types of *individuals and institutions* in the economy: (1) *deficit-spending individuals and institutions,* whose current expenditures for consumption and investment exceed their current receipts of income and who, therefore, need to raise funds externally through borrowing; and *(2) surplus-spending individuals and institutions,* whose current receipts of income exceed their current expenditures on goods and services so they have surplus funds to save and invest. Banks perform the indispensable task of intermediating between these two groups, offering convenient financial services to surplus-spending individuals and institutions in order to attract funds and then loaning those funds to deficit-spending individuals and institutions.

Banks' intermediation activities will take place (*a*) if there is a positive spread between the expected yields on the loans banks make to deficit-spending individuals and institutions and the expected interest rate (cost) on the funds banks borrow from surplus-spending individuals and institutions, and (*b*) if there is a positive correlation between the yields on bank loans and the interest rate banks pay for deposits and other funds provided by surplus-spending units. If a bank's loan rates and its borrowing costs are positively correlated, this will reduce the uncertainty around its expected profits, encouraging it to continue borrowing from and lending funds to its customers.

There is an ongoing debate in the theory of finance and economics about *why* banks exist. What essential services do banks provide that other businesses and individuals cannot provide for themselves?

This question has proven to be extremely difficult to answer. Research evidence has accumulated over many years showing that our financial system and financial markets are extremely *efficient.* Funds and information flow readily to both lenders and borrowers, and the prices of loans and securities seem to be determined in highly competitive markets. In a perfectly competitive and efficient financial system, in which all participants have open and equal access to the financial markets and can borrow and lend at the same interest rate, in which no one participant can exercise control over interest rates or prices, in which all pertinent information affecting the value of loans, securities, and other assets is readily available to all market participants at negligible cost, in which transactions costs are not significant impediments to trading assets, and all loans and securities are available in denominations anyone can afford, *why* would banks be needed at all?

Most current theories explain the existence of banks by pointing to *imperfections* in our financial system. For example, all loans and securities are *not* perfectly divisible into small denominations that everyone can afford. To take one well-known example, U.S. Treasury bills—probably the most popular short-term marketable security in the world—have a minimum denomination of $10,000, which is clearly beyond the reach of most small savers. Banks provide a valuable service in dividing up such instruments into smaller securities (in the form of deposits) that are readily affordable for millions of people. In this instance a less-than-perfect financial system creates a role for banks in serving small savers and depositors.

Another contribution banks make is their willingness to accept risky loans from borrowers, while issuing low-risk securities to their depositors. In effect, banks engage in risky *arbitrage* across the financial markets.

Banks also satisfy the strong need of many customers for *liquidity*. Financial instruments are liquid if they can be sold quickly in a ready market with little risk of loss to the seller. Many households and businesses, for example, demand large precautionary balances of liquid funds to cover expected future cash needs and to meet emergencies. Banks satisfy this need by offering high liquidity in the deposits they sell and in the loans they provide, giving borrowers access to liquid funds to spend precisely when those funds are needed.

Still another reason banks have prospered is their *superior ability to evaluate information*. Pertinent data on financial investments is both limited and costly. Some borrowers and lenders know more than others, and some individuals and institutions possess inside information that allows them to choose exceptionally profitable investments while avoiding the poorest ones. This uneven distribution of information and the talent to analyze information is known as *informational asymmetry*. Informational asymmetries reduce the efficiency of markets, but provide a profitable role for banks that have the expertise and experience to evaluate financial instruments and to choose those with the most desirable risk-return features.

Moreover, the ability of banks to gather and analyze financial information has given rise to another view of why banks exist in modern society—the *delegated monitoring theory*. Most borrowers and depositors prefer to keep their financial records confidential, shielded especially from competitors and neighbors. Banks are able to attract borrowing customers, this theory suggests, because they pledge confidentiality. Even a bank's own depositors are not privileged to review the financial reports of its borrowing customers. Bank depositors often have neither the time nor the skill to evaluate the credentials of a borrower and to choose good loans over bad loans. They turn the monitoring process over to a bank that has invested human and reputational capital in the monitoring process. Thus, a bank serves as an *agent* on behalf of its depositors, monitoring the financial condition of those customers who do receive loans in order to ensure that the depositors will recover their funds. In return for monitoring services, depositors pay a fee to the bank that is probably less than the cost they would incur if they monitored borrowers themselves.

By making a large volume of loans, banks as delegated monitors can diversify and reduce their risk exposure, resulting in increased safety for their depositors. Moreover, when a borrowing customer has received the bank's stamp of approval, it is easier and less costly for that customer to raise funds elsewhere. This *signals* the financial marketplace that the borrower is trustworthy and likely to repay his or her loans. This *signaling effect* of bank lending seems to be strongest, not when a bank makes the first loan to a new borrower, but when it grants renewal of a maturing loan.

safe and productively invested, and seeing to it that the legal heirs receive their rightful inheritance. In their commercial trust departments, banks manage security portfolios and pension plans for business firms and act as agents for corporations issuing stocks and bonds. This requires the trust department to pay interest or dividends on the corporation's securities and retire maturing corporate securities by paying off their holders.

Services Banks Have Developed More Recently

Granting Consumer Loans.   Historically, most banks did not actively pursue loan accounts from individuals and families, believing that the relatively small size of most consumer loans and their relatively high default rate would make such lending unprofitable. Early in this century, however, bankers began to rely more heavily on consumers for deposits to help fund their large corporate loans. Then, too, heavy competition for business deposits and loans caused bankers increasingly to turn to the *consumer* as a potentially more loyal customer. By the 1920s and 1930s several major banks, led by one of the forerunners of New York's Citicorp and by the Bank of America, had established strong consumer loan departments. Following World War II, consumer loans were among the fastest-growing forms of bank credit. Their rate of growth has slowed recently, though, as banks have run into stiff competition for consumer credit accounts and the economy has slowed. However, consumers continue to be the principal source of bank funds and one of the most important sources of bank revenue today.

Financial Advising.   Bankers have long been asked for financial advice by their customers, particularly when it comes to the use of credit and the saving or investing of funds. Many banks today offer a wide range of **financial advisory services,** from helping to prepare tax returns and financial plans for individuals to consulting about marketing opportunities at home and abroad for their business customers.

Cash Management.   Over the years, banks have found that some of the services they provide for themselves are also valuable for their customers. One of the most prominent examples is **cash management services,** in which a bank agrees to handle cash collections and disbursements for a business firm and to invest any temporary cash surpluses in short-term interest-bearing securities and loans until the cash is needed to pay bills.

While banks tend to specialize mainly in *business* cash management services, there is a growing trend today toward offering similar services for *consumers*. This trend arose largely because of competition from brokerage companies and other financial conglomerates that offer consumers special brokerage accounts with a wide array of associated financial services. A well-known example is Merrill Lynch's *Cash Management Account,* which allows its customers to buy and sell securities, move funds around among a variety of mutual funds, write checks, and use credit cards for instant loans.

Offering Equipment Leasing.   Many banks have moved aggressively to offer their business customers the option to purchase needed equipment through a lease arrangement in which the bank buys the equipment and rents it to the customer. Regulations originally required customers using **equipment leasing services** to make lease payments that would eventually cover the full cost of purchasing the rented equipment and to be responsible for any repairs and taxes incurred. In 1987, however, the U.S. Congress voted to allow national banks to keep possession of at least some assets leased by their customers after the leases expire. This arrangement benefits banks as well as customers because, as the real owner of the leased equipment, the bank can depreciate it for additional tax benefits.

Making Venture Capital Loans.   Increasingly, banks have become active in financing the start-up costs of new companies, particularly in high-tech industries. Because of the added risk involved in such loans, this is generally done through a venture capital firm that is a subsidiary of a bank holding company, and other investors are often brought in to share the risk. Prominent examples of bank-affiliated venture capital firms include Bankers Trust Venture Capital and Citicorp Venture, Inc.

Selling Insurance Services.   For many years, banks have sold credit life insurance to customers receiving loans, thus guaranteeing repayment of the loan if the customer dies or becomes disabled. While regulations in the United States prohibit commercial banks from direct selling and underwriting of many insurance services, many banks hope to be able to offer regular life insurance policies and property-casualty policies, such as auto or home owners' insurance, in the future. Banks that now make **insurance policies** available to their customers usually do so through joint ventures or franchise arrangements, where an insurance company agrees to set up a booth in the bank's lobby and the bank receives a share of the proceeds from any policies sold there. Some states, such as Delaware and South Dakota, already permit their banks to offer selected insurance services nationwide. Federally chartered banks in the United States, with regulatory approval, can offer insurance products through a separate subsidiary, but their investments must be limited to 10 percent of their capital. Recently Citicorp announced plans to merge with Travelers Insurance in an effort to offer an expanded range of insurance services.

Selling Retirement Plans.   Bank trust departments are active in managing the **retirement plans** that most businesses make available to their employees, investing incoming funds and dispensing payments to qualified recipients who have reached retirement or become disabled. Banks also sell deposit retirement plans (known as IRAs and Keoghs) to individuals holding these deposits until the funds are needed for income by the individual owning the plan.

Offering Security Brokerage Investment Services.   In today's financial marketplace, many banks are striving to become true "financial department stores"—offering a sufficiently wide array of financial services to permit customers to meet all of their financial needs at one location. This is one of the main reasons banks have begun to market **security brokerage** services, offering their customers the opportunity to buy individual stocks, bonds, and other securities without having to go to a security dealer. In some cases, banks have purchased an existing brokerage company (e.g., Bank of America's acquisition of Robertson Stephens Co.) or created a joint venture with an established brokerage firm.

Bankers' Insights and Issues

How and Why Banks Create Money and Credit When They Make Loans

All modern banks *create money* (instant spending power), and they *create credit* (the obligation to pay money in the future) as well. Exactly how does this occur?

First, remember that money is simply a medium of exchange—an object or data item that is readily accepted by sellers in payment for the goods and services they offer. In most industrialized economies, checks are still the principal means of paying for goods and services, though electronic media are capturing a growing share of all payments. In the United States, for example, checks account for about four-fifths of the dollar value of all payments made annually.

When and how do banks create money? It happens in two ways. First, when a customer is granted a loan (credit), he or she will sign a promissory note and receive, in turn, a bank's deposit (transaction account). The customer's promissory note is *not* money; it cannot be used to buy goods and services. But a bank's transaction deposit *is* money and can readily be spent almost anywhere. Thus, in granting loans (creating credit), banks create money as well by setting up a spendable deposit in the name of the borrower.

Second, the entire system of banks also creates money as the deposits generated by lending flow from bank to bank. By law, each bank must set aside only a fractional reserve behind each deposit it receives and the remaining excess reserves can be loaned out. As customers spend the proceeds of their loans, these funds flow out to other banks, giving them deposits from which to create loans (credit) as well. *While no single bank can lend out more than its excess reserves, the entire banking system can create a multiple volume of deposits* (money creation) *through bank lending* (credit creation). If there were no leakages from the banking system (such as customers withdrawing cash from

Offering Mutual Funds and Annuities.   Concerned that many banks have offered too-low interest rates on traditional deposit accounts, many customers have come to demand so-called *investment products* from their banker, especially mutual funds accounts and annuities that offer the prospect of higher yields than are currently available on conventional bank deposits, but also carry more risk. *Annuities* consist of long-term savings plans that promise the payment of a stream of income to the annuity holder beginning on a designated future date (such as at retirement). In contrast, *mutual funds* are professionally managed investment programs which acquire stocks, bonds, and other securities that appear to "fit" the funds' announced goals (e.g., to maximize income or to achieve long-term capital appreciation). While the growth of bank-offered annuity plans has been slowed somewhat recently by lawsuits brought by opponents of the industry's expansion into this new service area after an early period of rapid growth in bank annuity sales, offerings of shares in mutual funds by U.S. banks grew rapidly in the mid-1990s, with bank-managed funds accounting for about 15 percent of all mutual funds' assets. Some banking firms have organized special

their transaction accounts or unutilized reserves), an initial deposit of $1 of new reserves in the banking system would result in:

$$\text{Amount of new money creation} = \frac{1}{RR} \times \text{Amount of new reserves}$$

where RR is the reserve requirement ratio (or percentage of cash banks themselves must keep in reserve) imposed either by the central bank (e.g., the Federal Reserve System in the United States) or by bankers themselves. The term 1/RR is often called the *money multiplier.* If, for example, the reserve requirement ratio is 10%, then each dollar of new reserves placed in the banking system would result in new money creation in the amount of:

$$\frac{1}{0.10} \times \$1 = 10 \times \$1 = \$10$$

If leakages exist in the form of the public withdrawing cash (pocket money) from their transaction accounts and placing some portion of their incoming funds in nonspendable savings instruments, then these leakages (L) from the banking system would reduce the money multiplier to 1/(RR + L). If L has a value of 0.20 and RR is 0.10, then the amount of new money creation for each $1 of new reserves placed in the banking system would be:

$$\frac{1}{(0.10 + 0.20)} \times \$1 = 3.33 \times \$1 = \$3.33$$

Given all the leakages from money flows that occur in the real world, most authorities believe that the real-world deposit multiplier the banking system can generate is probably somewhat less than 2. The banking system's capacity to create money is one reason banks are so closely regulated by government.

subsidiary organizations to market these services (e.g., Citicorp's Investment Services) or entered into joint ventures with security brokers and dealers. Recently bank mutual fund sales have slowed due to lack of strong profitability, strict regulations, and changing public attitudes.

Offering Investment Banking and Merchant Banking Services.   Banks today are following in the footsteps of leading financial institutions all over the globe in offering *investment banking* and *merchant banking* services to larger corporations. These services include identifying possible merger targets, financing acquisitions of other companies, dealing in a customer's securities (i.e., new security underwriting), providing strategic marketing advice, and offering hedging services to protect their customers against risk from fluctuating world currency prices and changing interest rates. Banks have also plunged heavily into the guarantee market, backing up the debt issued by their business and governmental customers so that these customers can borrow money at lower cost from the open market or from other lending institutions.

In the United States investment banking (security underwriting) services involving the purchase and sale of new stocks and debt by banks on behalf of their corporate customers were outlawed with the passage of the Glass-Steagall Act in 1933. However, political pressure from the largest domestic banking companies and the success of foreign competitors led the Federal Reserve Board in the 1980s to begin loosening the legal barriers to U.S. banks trading the new securities issued by their corporate customers. By offering corporations security underwriting services U.S. banks were granting their corporate customers another way to raise cash besides the traditional route of granting bank loans. Many corporations saw security offerings as a better alternative than traditional bank loans, due in part to the availability of longer-term funds at lower cost. By the late 1990s the Federal Reserve Board had granted more than 40 banking companies security underwriting powers, in effect allowing security traders and bank loan officers to work together to help a business customer obtain financing. In 1996 the Comptroller of the Currency ruled that underwriting activities were permissible for national (federally chartered) U.S. banks if conducted through a separate subsidiary company with limited bank investment (no more than 10 percent of capital) in the project. These broader security-trading powers have allowed many commercial banking companies to acquire security dealer houses and, thereby, offer a more complete line of business financing and managerial advising services. Recent examples of such acquisitions include NationsBank's acquisition of Montgomery Securities, Inc., BankAmerica Corporation's purchase of Robertson Stephens Co., and Bankers Trust of New York's acquisition of Alex Brown, Inc.

Convenience: The Sum Total of All Bank Services.   It should be clear from the list of services we have described that not only are most banks offering a wide array of financial services today, but the banker's service menu is growing rapidly. New types of loans and deposits are being developed, new service delivery methods like the Internet and smart cards with digital cash are expanding, and whole new service lines (e.g., insurance, annuities, and security-trading activities) are being launched every year. Viewed as a whole, the impressive array of services offered and service delivery channels used by modern banks adds up to greater convenience for their customers. Customers can satisfy virtually all their financial service needs at one financial institution in one location. Truly, banks are the "financial department stores" of the modern era, working to unify banking, fiduciary, insurance, and security brokerage services under one roof—a trend often referred to as *universal banking* in the United States, Canada, and Great Britain, as *allfinanz* in Germany, and as *bancassurance* in France.

Concept Checks

1–3.   What different kinds of services do banks offer to the public?

1–4.   Why do banks exist in modern society, according to the theory of finance?

Trends Affecting All Banks

The foregoing survey of bank services suggests that banks are currently undergoing sweeping changes in function and form. In fact, the changes affecting the banking business today are so important that many industry analysts refer to these trends as a *banking revolution*—one that may well leave banks of the next generation almost unrecognizable from those of today. What are the key trends reshaping banking today?

Service Proliferation.   As the preceding section points out, banks have been rapidly expanding the menu of financial services they offer to their customers. This proliferation of new services has accelerated in recent years under the pressure of increasing competition from other financial firms, more knowledgeable and demanding customers, and shifting technology. It has also increased bank costs and posed greater risk of bank failure. The new services have had a positive effect in the industry, however, by opening up a major new source of bank revenue—noninterest service fees (what bankers call *fee income*), which are likely to continue to grow relative to the more traditional source of bank revenue, the interest earned on loans.

Rising Competition.   The level and intensity of competition in the financial services field have grown as banks and their competitors have expanded their service offerings. The local bank offering business and consumer credit, savings and retirement plans, and financial counseling faces direct competition for all of these services today from other banks, credit unions, securities firms like Merrill Lynch, finance companies like GE Capital, and insurance companies and agencies like Prudential. These competitive pressures have acted as a spur to develop still more services for the future.

Deregulation.   Rising competition and the proliferation of banking services have also been spurred on by deregulation—a loosening of government control—of the financial services industry, which began roughly two decades ago in the United States and has spread around the globe. As we will see more fully in the chapters ahead, deregulation began with the lifting of government-imposed interest rate ceilings on savings deposits in an effort to give the public a fairer return on their savings. At the same time, new types of checkable deposits were developed to permit the public to earn interest on transaction (payments) accounts. Almost simultaneously, the services that many of banking's key competitors, such as savings and loans and credit unions, could offer were sharply expanded by legislation so they too could remain competitive with banks. Such leading nations as Australia, Canada, Great Britain, and Japan have recently joined the deregulation movement, broadening the legal playing field for banks, security dealers, and other financial-service companies, driving bank costs higher and increasing the industry's exposure to risk.

Rising Funding Costs.   Deregulation, in combination with increased competition, dramatically increased the real average cost of selling *deposits*—the principal source of funds for most banks. With deregulation bankers have been forced to pay competitive

The World's Largest Banks
(with their total assets in billions of U.S. dollars, at mid-year 1995)

Deutsche Bank, Germany	$502.3	West LG, Germany	$290.6
Sumitomo Bank, Japan	498.9	Mitsubishi Trust and Banking, Japan	283.7
Dai-Ichi Kangyo Bank, Japan	497.6	Mitsui Trust & Banking, Japan	283.7
Fuji Bank, Japan	486.4	Compagnie Financiere de Paribas, France	270.8
Bank of Tokyo—Mitsubishi Bank, Ltd., Japan*	711.0	Asahi Bank, Japan	266.0
Sakura Bank, Japan	477.1	National Westminster Bank, United Kingdom	257.8
Norinchukin Bank, Japan	428.6	Citicorp, United States	255.3
Credit Agricole Mutuel, France	384.3	Barclays, United Kingdom	254.5
Industrial Bank, Japan	360.6	Daiwa Bank, Japan	248.3
ABN-AMRO Holdings, Netherlands	339.4	Dresdner Bank, Germany	232.1
Credit Lyonnais, France	337.6	BankAmerica, United States	230.2
Union Bank of Switzerland	335.3	Yasuda Trust & Banking, Japan	224.2
Chase Manhattan, United States†	333.8	Toyo Trust, Tokyo	189.7
Societe Generale, France	324.8	International Nederlanden, Netherlands	153.5
Banque Nationale de Paris, France	323.5		
Sumitomo Trust & Banking, Japan	299.2		
Tokai Bank, Japan	297.7		
Long-Term Credit Bank, Japan	297.4		

*Reflects subsequent merger of Bank of Tokyo and Mitsubishi Bank.
†Reflects subsequent merger with Chemical Bank of New York.
Sources: Board of Governors of the Federal Reserve System; Federal Deposit Insurance Corporation; and American Bankers Association.

market-determined interest rates for the bulk of their deposit funds. At the same time government regulators have demanded that banks use more of their owner's capital—a highly expensive source of funds—to support banks' assets. These more expensive sources of funds have encouraged banks to look for ways to cut other operating expenses, such as reducing the number of employees and replacing aging equipment with modern electronic processing systems. Bankers have also been forced to find *new* sources of funds, such as *securitization,* in which some bank loans are packaged together in pools and removed from the balance sheet; securities backed by the packaged loans are sold in the open market in order to raise new funds that may be cheaper and more reliable, and that may generate more fees for banks than traditional funding sources (such as selling deposits).

An Increasingly Interest-Sensitive Mix of Funds.   Government deregulation of the industry has made it possible for customers to earn higher rates of return on their bank deposits, but only the public could translate that opportunity into action. And act the public did! Billions of dollars formerly deposited in older, low-yielding savings accounts and non-interest-bearing checking accounts flowed into new higher-yielding accounts whose rates of return change with market conditions. Bankers have discovered that they are facing a better educated, more interest-sensitive customer today, whose "loyal" deposit can more easily be lured away by aggressive competitors. Thus,

The Largest United States Banks
(with their total assets in billions of U.S. dollars at mid-year 1996)

The Chase Manhattan Bank, New York City	$272.4	Fleet National Bank, Springfield, Massachusetts	$46.6
Citibank, N.A., New York City	241.0	The First National Bank of Boston	45.9
Bank of America National Trust and Savings Association, San Francisco	180.5	CoreStates Bank, Philadelphia	42.7
		First Union National Bank of Florida, Jacksonville	39.3
Morgan Guaranty Trust Company of New York, New York City	172.6	Barnett Banks, Jacksonville	39.2
		NationsBank of Texas, Dallas	39.1
Wells Fargo Bank, N.A., San Francisco	99.2	Mellon Bank, Greensberg, Pennsylvania	37.3
Bankers Trust Company, New York City	90.4	First Union National Bank of North Carolina, Charlotte	32.4
NationsBank, National Association, Charlotte	80.9	State Street Bank and Trust Co., Boston	31.4
		Union Bank of California, San Francisco	29.2
PNC Bank, Pittsburgh	57.3	KeyBank, N.A., Cleveland	27.8
The Bank of New York, New York City	52.1	First Union National Bank, Avondale, Pennsylvania	27.1
The First National Bank of Chicago	51.6	Comerica Bank, Detroit	27.1
Home Savings of America, FSB, Irwindale, California	49.6	Wachovia Bank of North Carolina, Winston-Salem	26.8
Republic National Bank of New York, New York City	47.0	Chase Manhattan Bank USA, Wilmington	25.3
		Marine Midland Bank, Buffalo	23.3
NationsBank, National Association (South), Atlanta	46.8	Fleet Bank, Jersey City	23.1

Sources: Board of Governors of the Federal Reserve System; Federal Deposit Insurance Corporation; and American Bankers Association.

bankers must now strive to be more competitive in the returns they offer on the public's money and more sensitive to changing public preferences with regard to how savings are allocated.

A Technological Revolution.   Banks faced with higher operating costs in recent years have increasingly turned toward automation and electronic networks to replace labor-based production systems—especially for taking deposits, dispensing payments, and making credit available. The most prominent examples include ATMs (automated teller machines; there are well over 100,000 ATMs in the United States today), which give individual customers 24-hour access to their deposit accounts; point-of-sale (POS) terminals in stores and shopping centers that replace paper-based means of paying for goods and services; and computer networks that rapidly process thousands of transactions around the globe.

Thus, banking is becoming more of a capital-intensive, fixed-cost industry and less of a labor-intensive, variable-cost industry. Many experts believe that traditional brick-and-mortar bank buildings and face-to-face meetings between bankers and their customers eventually will become relics of the past, replaced by electronic communication. Service production and service delivery will be fully automated. Such steps will significantly lower the per-unit costs associated with high-volume transactions, such as assisting customers with payments, but they will depersonalize banking and result in further loss of jobs as capital equipment is substituted for labor. Recent experience suggests, however, that fully automated banking for all customers may be a long time in coming. A substantial proportion of bank customers still prefer personalized service and the opportunity to consult personally with their bankers about a broad range of financial matters.

Consolidation and Geographic Expansion.   Making efficient use of automation and other technological innovations requires high-volume banking. So banks have had to expand their customer base by reaching into new and more distant markets and by increasing account volume. The result has been a dramatic increase in bank branching activity, the formation of holding companies that purchase smaller banks and enclose them in large multiple-office banking institutions, and mergers among some of the largest banks in the industry (such as Chemical Bank and Chase Manhattan in New York or BankAmerica and NationsBank). The number of independently owned banks is declining, and the average size of individual banking firms has risen significantly. At the same time the number of smaller U.S. banks (under $1 billion in assets) has fallen by at least a third since the mid-1980s, while the number of full-time workers employed by the industry fell by more than a hundred thousand over the same time period.

Moreover, the 1980s and 1990s have ushered in an era of rapid interstate expansion in the United States. More than 300 banking organizations have reached across state lines to gobble up smaller banking firms into regional and nationwide banking organizations. So service diversified are banks striving to become today that many bankers would prefer to drop the old word "bank" from their advertising programs and stress their role as far broader "financial service firms"—innovative, dynamic, and customer-oriented service companies.

With the spread of automation in the industry, more banks will branch into distant regions electronically with automated teller and telecommunications equipment—a much cheaper way to expand the size of their markets than building elaborate new facilities. In many cases, limited-service satellite facilities and computer networks are taking the place of full-service branch offices.

Globalization of Banking.   The geographic expansion and consolidation of banking units have reached well beyond the boundaries of a single nation to encompass the entire globe. Today the largest banks in the world compete with each other for business on every continent. In the 1980s Japanese banks, led by a Dai-Ichi Kangyo Bank and Fuji Bank, grew much faster than most of their competitors worldwide. Huge banks headquartered in France (led by Caisse Nationale de Credit Agricole), Germany (led by the Deutsche Bank), and Great Britain (led by Barclays PLC) have also become heavyweight competitors in the global market for corporate and government loans. Deregulation has helped all of these institutions compete more effectively against U.S. banks and capture growing shares of the global market for banking services. Today Canada, the United States, and Mexico have adopted a North American Free Trade Agreement (NAFTA) that will allow banks in these countries to own and operate banking subsidiaries in each other's countries with eventual service powers fully comparable to those possessed by domestic banks.

Increased Risk of Failure and the Weakening of Government Deposit Insurance Systems.   While consolidation and geographic expansion have helped to make many banks less vulnerable to local economic conditions, increasing competition between banks and nonbanks coupled with problem loans and a volatile economy have led to *bank failures* in nations all over the world. Deregulation of the financial sector has expanded the range of opportunity for bankers, but only at the cost of creating a more treacherous financial marketplace where bank failures, absorptions, and liquidations are more likely to occur.

Are Banks Dying?

Recently, with hundreds of banks and other depository institutions merging or failing in the United States, Europe, and Asia, there has been great concern over the future of the banking industry. Even for those banks that survive there is evidence (e.g., Gorton and Rosen [10]) that banking's share of the market for financial services appears to be declining, while security firms, some insurance companies, mutual funds, and finance companies have snared a growing share of available customers. Recently the Federal Reserve Bank of St. Louis calculated that the share of total assets held by banks and other depository institutions relative to all financial intermediaries combined fell from 56 percent in 1982 to less than 40 percent in the 1990s—a drop attributed to "natural shrinkage" following deregulation of the industry and greater financial market sophistication by banking customers. Some analysts (e.g., Beim [8]) have declared that banking as we know it today is "dying."

As markets have become increasingly efficient with recent advances in technology and with larger bank customers finding other ways to obtain credit (such as by selling securities in the open market), *traditional banks* do appear to be less and less necessary. At the very least there appear to be too many banks—the United States has about 9,000—and too many resources tied up in the banking sector. It may be argued that many of these banks are simply being "propped up" by government protection in the form of cheap deposit insurance and cheap government loans. Perhaps recent bank mergers and failures worldwide are simply a sign that the banking industry is overcrowded and facing declining demand for its traditional services.

Then, too, banks face a far heavier burden of government regulation than most of their competitors. In the 1990s the American Bankers Association conducted an industry survey which estimated that the cost of complying with federal and state banking regulations came to almost $11 billion (or about 60 percent of the industry's annual profits). The decline in banking's share of the total financial-services marketplace has

Bank Management in Action

The Changing Characteristics of Bank Customers

Banking faces many pressures today from changing regulations, intensifying competition from nonbank financial-service firms, the spreading internationalization of banking markets, and continuing innovations in technology and automation. Equally important for the future of banking, however, are powerful economic and social trends affecting banking's customer base.

For example, *scores of major corporations*—once a banker's biggest and best loan customers—*have deserted the banking system in recent years to raise the borrowed funds they need either directly from the open market or through nonbank businesses* (such as security dealers and finance companies). Not only has this structural shift reduced bank revenues from making loans, but it also has led to a dramatic shift in the makeup of bank loan portfolios with a smaller fraction of large, top-credit-quality loans on the books and a much greater proportion of small-business loans and lower-quality, more-risky credits on bank ledgers. In response, bankers have had to develop improved methods for evaluating and pricing smaller and more risky loans and new fee-generating services, such as helping their biggest customers protect themselves against interest rate and currency risk.

Another powerful trend in the customer base bankers must deal with is the *aging of the population*. The huge numbers of "baby boomers" born in the decade after World War II are approaching their retirement years. The result will be a momentous decline in the ratio of working adults to retired individuals. At the same time a growing number of people are choosing to change careers or start new businesses during their 40s and 50s. Bankers of the future must learn to see the implications of this demographic change for the design of banking facilities (e.g., the need for greater ease of access to both automated equipment and branch offices) and the design of marketing programs that direct the older customer's attention to service features he or she values most highly (such as safety, guaranteed income, and user-friendliness). In dealing with older customers, bankers must learn to emphasize relationship banking rather than transaction banking and customer specialization rather than product specialization.

One area of potentially great demand for banking services will be financial and retirement planning for older customers, many of whom will have greater discretionary income and more available savings as their home mortgages are paid off and their children finish college and leave home. Also, more employers are forcing their employees to become responsible for their own retirement planning. According to recent estimates there are more than 50 million U.S. workers without pension coverage, most of whom will need professional help in preparing for their retirement years.

Another aspect of banking's aging customer base not often recognized is its future impact on younger customers. *As the elderly population passes on, there will be huge transfers of wealth to younger individuals and families.* Bankers will have to work to develop new investment and financial-planning products to appeal to the special financial needs of their retired customers and for those younger customers who will inherit the assets of retired persons in the future.

Also, America's population, as well as that of many other nations, is becoming more *ethnically diverse.* Today about one in every four Americans has African, Asian, Hispanic, or Native American ethnic roots, and these important population groups are among the fastest growing segments of the population. Bankers are likely to face increased loan demand from businesses that provide the products and services of greatest interest to this more ethnically diverse population. There will be increased numbers of minority-owned businesses as well as many new businesses owned and operated by women. Inside banks themselves, management must find ways to smoothly incorporate a more ethnically diverse workforce and train bank personnel on how to respond with sensitivity to the special service needs of a more ethnically diverse customer base.

Bankers will also have to grapple with loan requests from customers who have *different lifestyles* from traditional household borrowers. For example, more individuals today either choose not to marry and start a family or plan to postpone marriage until much later in their lives. Individuals and families are also more mobile today than in the past and there are many more single-parent households and families without children. Many of these customers will have below-average incomes and less job and residential stability than in the past, forcing banks to consider making smaller and more risky loans. Many banks will have to reconsider their credit standards and improve their institution's operating efficiency in processing numerous small loan requests in order to keep bank costs under control.

Finally, banking and other financial firms today are being asked to play bigger roles in crafting *private-sector solutions to social problems.* These include community development programs in which bankers are providing financing and technical advice to help revitalize downtown areas and inner city neighborhoods. Banks, by virtue of their government charters and because of the government assistance they receive, are being pressured today to respond to communitywide financial needs and to keep community interests in mind when they decide to open or close branch offices, advertise services, and fund economic development. These new developments will place a premium on creativity and demand quality training for those men and women who work for tomorrow's banks.

Source: Much of the foregoing analysis is based on a speech by Dr. Susan M. Phillips, member of the Board of Governors of the Federal Reserve System, before the Stonier Graduate School of Banking, University of Delaware, June 23, 1993, entitled "Banking in a Changing World."

aroused concern among some government policymakers and bank customers. Among these concerns are fears that banks' declining importance could:

- Weaken the central bank's ability to control the growth of the money supply and achieve the nation's economic goals.
- Damage those customers (mainly small businesses and families) who rely most heavily on banks for loans and other financial services.
- Make banking services less conveniently available to customers as bank offices are consolidated and closed.

Many economists have argued that excessive regulation of banks and little or no regulation of many of their competitors is a primary cause of these recent developments and that greater deregulation of the industry is a *must* if banking is to remain strong and viable. Many banks, especially the largest, are trying to fight back and slow the loss of market share by (1) offering new services (such as selling shares in mutual funds, annuities, and insurance policies), (2) charging higher user fees for many former "free" services, (3) offering more services through subsidiary businesses that are not as closely regulated as banks, or (4) entering into joint ventures with independent companies and thereby avoid at least *some* burdensome regulations.

Then, too, there are experts in the field (e.g., Kaufman and Mote [9]) who argue that banking's decline may be more apparent than real. The nature of banking has changed so drastically in recent years with the development of new services, not all of which are revealed on bank balance sheets, that new measures of banking's size may be needed to determine if banks are really declining in importance relative to other financial institutions. At the same time government programs to support and subsidize banks will probably have to be reformed and curtailed. This seems to be especially true of government-supplied deposit insurance, which deludes many customers into thinking all banks are safe and may be giving some banks an unfair advantage in attracting the public's money. Unhealthy banks must be allowed to exit the industry in order to promote greater efficiency in utilizing scarce resources. While all banks won't survive, most banks should be able to live on if they are given broader service powers and deposit insurance is priced correctly to reflect the riskiness of each banking firm. In short, traditional banking may be dying, but if banks are given greater freedom to respond to the public's changing demands for new services, they need *not* pass away.

Concept Checks

1–5.   How has banking changed in recent years?

1–6.   Can you explain why many of these changes have led to significant problems for bank managers and stockholders?

The Plan of This Book

This book has a twofold purpose: (1) to provide the reader with a comprehensive picture of the importance of banking to the economy and financial system and (2) to assist in educating tomorrow's bank managers. Through its six major parts, these two key objectives are pursued both by presenting an overview of banking as a whole and then pointing the reader toward specific questions and issues that bankers must resolve every day.

Part I provides a basic introduction to banking and its functions in the global economy and financial system. The principal services offered by banks are defined and explained, and the reader is introduced to bank financial statements. We also explore the various ways banks are organized, both internally and industrywide, to bring together human skill, capital equipment, and natural resources to produce and sell their services. Part I also examines how and why banks are regulated and who the principal regulators are that influence the growth, profitability, and services banks are able to offer today.

Part II explores the dynamic area of bank asset-liability management and risk hedging. Chapters 6, 7, 8, and 9 describe how bankers have changed their views on managing assets, liabilities, and capital in recent years and on how to control their banks' risk exposure. These chapters take a detailed look at the most important techniques for *hedging* against changing interest rates (including financial futures, options, and swaps), recognizing that banks are one of the most sensitive of all business firms to movements in market interest rates. Part II also explores some of the newest tools to deal with bank credit risk and the use of off-balance-sheet financing techniques (including securitizations, loan sales, and standby credits).

Part III addresses two ages-old problem areas for banks—managing a bank's portfolio of investment securities and making sure that a bank has enough liquidity to meet its cash needs. The different types of investment securities acquired by modern banks are examined and the factors that each bank's investment officer must weigh in choosing what investment securities to buy or sell are reviewed. This part of the book also takes a critical look at why banks must constantly struggle to ensure that they have access to cash precisely when and where they need it.

Part IV directs our attention to the funding side of a bank's balance sheet—raising money to support the bank's acquisition of assets and meet its expenses. The principal types of bank deposits and nondeposit investment products are presented, and recent trends in the mix and pricing of bank deposits are reviewed for their implications for managing banks today and tomorrow. Next, we explore all the important nondeposit funding sources for banks—federal funds, security repurchase agreements, Eurodollars, etc.—and assess their impact on bank profitability and risk. The final source of bank funds reviewed is equity capital—the source of funding provided by a bank's owners.

Part V takes up what many bankers regard as the essence of the business—granting credit to customers through the making of *loans.* The types of loans banks make, the regulations applicable to the bank lending process, and the procedures for evaluating and granting loans are all discussed. The emphasis in this section is fourfold: (1) to review the key features of each type of loan, (2) to explore the factors the loan officer and credit analyst must consider in making lending decisions, (3) to see how loans can be structured to protect the bank and still serve the customer, and (4) to explain how regulations enter into the bank's credit decision process.

Part VI tackles an issue that other banking texts often ignore or pass over lightly—how the bank can *organize* its operations to achieve the goals most desired by management and the stockholders. Among the organizational issues addressed in Part VI are chartering and opening new banks, branch offices, automated facilities, and electronic networks, analyzing potential mergers and acquisitions, and engaging in international operations. We observe in this final segment of the book that the future of banking mirrors, in several important respects, our own future and the type of world we will all share as the 20th century closes and a challenging new century beckons us forward.

Summary

In this opening chapter, we have viewed the modern bank as a business firm performing a number of important roles in our economy. We have glimpsed banks from their earliest origins as they evolved from simple money changers to the highly diversified organizations of today, offering the widest range of financial services of any financial institution in the economy. The most important bank functions examined in this chapter were lending and investing money (the credit function), making payments on behalf of customers for their purchases of goods and services (the payments function), managing financial assets and real property for customers (the cash management and trust functions), and assisting customers in investing and raising funds (through the brokerage, investment banking, and savings functions).

This chapter has traced the most important trends reshaping the global banking industry in what many have called a *banking revolution.* Among the most important trends discussed were the proliferation of new services, rising competition between domestic and foreign financial firms, deregulation of banking and the financial markets, rising bank operating costs, the expanding use of automated equipment and electronic transfers of financial information, consolidation of the banking industry into fewer units, globalization of financial markets, and increased risk of bank failure, liquidation, or absorption. These trends have profoundly changed the business of banking, and in the years ahead they will continue to make banks a truly fascinating institution to study.

Key Terms in This Chapter

Bank
Nonbank banks
Currency exchange
Discounting commercial notes
Savings deposits
Demand deposit
Trust services

Financial advisory services
Cash management services
Equipment leasing services
Insurance policies
Retirement plans
Security brokerage

Problems and Projects

1. You have just been hired as the marketing officer for the new First National Bank of Vincent, a suburban banking institution that will soon be serving a local community of 120,000 people. The town is adjacent to a major metropolitan area with a total population of well over 1 million. Opening day for the newly chartered bank is just two months away, and the president and the board of directors are concerned that the new bank may not be able to attract enough depositors and good-quality loan customers to meet its growth and profit projections. Your task is to recommend the various services the bank should offer initially to build up an adequate customer base. You are asked to do the following:

   a. Make a list of all the services the new bank could offer, according to current regulations.

   b. List the types of information you will need about the local community to help you decide which of many possible services are likely to have sufficient demand to make them profitable.

   c. Divide the possible services into two groups—those that you think are essential to customers and that should be offered beginning with opening day, and those that can be offered later as the bank grows.

   d. Briefly describe the kind of advertising campaign you would like to run to help the public see how your bank is different from all the other financial-service providers in the local area.

2. Leading money center banks in the United States have accelerated their investment banking activities all over the globe in recent years, purchasing corporate debt securities and stock from their business customers and reselling those securities to investors in the open market. Is this a desirable move by banking organizations from a profit standpoint? From a risk standpoint? From the public interest point of view? If you were managing a corporation that had placed large deposits with a bank engaged in such activities, would you be concerned about the risk to your company's funds? What could you do to better safeguard those funds?

3. Many financial analysts have warned that the traditional bank—the maker of loans and acceptor of deposits—is doomed in the future due to the pirating of the best and largest bank customers by competing nonbank financial institutions, the growing tendency of even modest-size businesses to bypass banks for credit and borrow instead in the open market, and constraining regulations on the services banks are allowed to develop and offer. Do you agree with this assessment of traditional banking's future? See if you can develop good arguments on *both* sides of this issue—for and against the survival of the traditional banking organization.

4. Suppose that $5 million in new reserves is deposited in the banking system from some outside source (such as through the central bank supplying more reserves). If the current reserve requirement is 20 percent and the public wishes to place 35 percent of each new dollar received in their checking accounts into long-term savings and to place another 5 percent of incoming funds into currency for their wallets and purses, what is the size of the banking system's *deposit multiplier*? How much in new money creation by the banking system will occur as a result of the injection of $5 million in new reserves?

5. Suppose the banking system creates $116 million in new money as the result of $25 million in new reserves generated by the banking system. What is the banking system's deposit multiplier? If there are no leakages from the banking system except for a central-bank-imposed reserve requirement, what must the central bank's required reserve ratio be?

6. Western National Bank receives a new deposit of $124,000 from one of its commercial customers. The customer places $44,000 in a commercial checking account which carries a legal reserve requirement of 10 percent and the remainder of the deposit in an 18-month certificate of deposit which has a zero legal reserve requirement (however, as a precaution the bank's management automatically establishes a reserve of 2 percent against such deposits). How much of this new deposit can Western National Bank safely lend out to its borrowing customers?

Selected References

See the following for an overview and explanation of the services banks offer today:
1. Baughn, William H., and Charles E. Walker, eds. *The Banker's Handbook.* 4th ed. Homewood, Ill.: Business One Irwin, 1990.

For a review of banking's history, see the following:
2. Homer, Sidney. *A History of Interest Rates.* Englewood Cliffs, N.J.: Prentice Hall, 1963.
3. Kindleberger, Charles P. *A Financial History of Western Europe.* Boston: Allen and Unwin, 1984.

For a deeper exploration of the role of banks in modern financial theory, see the following:
4. Diamond, Douglas. "Financial Intermediation and Delegated Monitoring." *Review of Economic Studies* 51 (1984), pp. 393–414.

See the following for an analysis of key trends affecting banking and other financial institutions:
5. Jordan, Jerry L. "The Functions and Future of Retail Banking." *Economic Commentary,* Federal Reserve Bank of Cleveland, September 15, 1996.
6. Rose, Peter S. *Money and Capital Markets: The Financial System in the Economy.* 6th ed. Homewood, Ill.: Richard D. Irwin, 1996. See especially Chapters 4, 6, and 30.

7. Wright, Richard W., and Gunter A. Pauli. *The Second Wave: Japan's Global Assault on Financial Services.* New York: St. Martin's Press, 1987.

For a discussion of the future of traditional banking see:
8. Beim, David U. "Why Are Banks Dying?" *The Columbia Journal of World Business,* Spring 1992, pp. 4–12.
9. Kaufman, George G., and Larry R. Mote. "Is Banking a Declining Industry? A Historical Perspective." *Economic Perspectives,* Federal Reserve Bank of Chicago, May/June 1994, pp. 2–21.
10. Gorton, Gary, and Richard Rosen. "Corporate Control, Portfolio Choice, and the Decline of Banking." *Finance and Economics Discussion Series,* No. 215, Board of Governors of the Federal Reserve System, December 1992.
11. Samolyn, Katherine A. "Banking and the Flow of Funds: Are Banks Losing Market Share?" *Economic Commentary,* Federal Reserve Bank of Cleveland, September 1, 1994.
12. Levonian, Mark E. "Why Banking Isn't Declining." *FRBSF Weekly Letter,* No. 95-03 (January 20, 1995), pp. 1–3.

APPENDIX: CAREER OPPORTUNITIES IN BANKING

In this chapter, we have focused on the great importance of banks in the functioning of the economy and on their many services and roles in dealing with the public. But banks are more than just financial-service providers; they can also be a vehicle for a satisfying professional career. What opportunities are there for careers in banking? To answer this question, the principal employment options in banking today are described below.

Loan Officers. Most bank managers begin their careers accepting and analyzing loan applications submitted by business and household customers. Bank loan officers make initial contacts with potential new customers and assist them in filling out loan requests and in developing a service relationship with the bank.

Credit Analysts. The credit analyst backstops the work of the loan officer by preparing detailed written assessments of each loan applicant's financial position and advises the bank's management on the wisdom of granting any particular loan. Credit analysts and loan officers need professional training in accounting, financial statement analysis, and business finance.

Loan Workout Specialists. With the substantial numbers of business failures in recent years, many loans to businesses and consumers have gone bad, requiring the services of skilled professionals to identify the causes of each problem loan situation and to find solutions that maximize the chances for recovering the bank's funds. This is the job of the loan workout specialist, who must have a strong background in accounting, financial statement analysis, business law, and economics, as well as good negotiating skills.

Managers of Bank Operations. Managers in the operations division of a bank are responsible for processing checks and clearing other cash items on behalf of their customers, for maintaining and improving the bank's computer facilities and electronic networks, for supervising the activities of tellers, for handling customer problems with checking accounts and other bank services, for maintaining security systems to protect the bank's property, and for overseeing the operation of the bank's personnel (human resources) department. Managers in the operations division need sound training in the principles of business and financial management and in computers and management information systems, and they must have the ability to interact with large groups of people.

Branch Managers. When banks operate large branch systems, many of these functions are supervised by the manager of each branch office. Branch managers lead each branch's effort to attract new accounts, calling on business firms and households in their local area. They also approve loan requests and resolve customer complaints. Branch managers must know how to motivate employees and how to represent the bank well in the local community.

Systems Analysts. These highly trained computer specialists work with officers and staff in all departments of a bank, translating their production and information needs into programming language. The systems analyst provides a vital link between bankers and computer programmers in making the computer an effective problem-solving tool for management and an efficient, accurate, and safe channel for delivering customer services. Systems analysts need in-depth training in computer programming and mathematics as well as courses emphasizing business problem solving.

Auditing and Control Personnel. Keeping abreast of the inflow of revenues and the outflow of expenses from a bank and tracking changes in the bank's financial position are the responsibilities of auditors and accountants. These are some of the most important tasks within the bank because they help guard against losses from criminal activity and waste. Jobs as important as these require considerable training in accounting and auditing.

Financial Analysts. These quantitatively skilled professionals often work in a bank's auditing and planning departments. Financial analysts are "number crunchers" who analyze the performance of the bank and its employees. They look for activities that need improvement and identify areas of superior performance within the banking firm.

Trust Department Specialists. Specialists in a bank's trust department provide a wide variety of customer services. They aid companies in managing their employee retirement programs, issuing securities, maintaining business records, and investing funds. Consumers also receive help in managing their property and in building an estate for retirement. Men and women employed in bank trust departments usually possess a wide range of backgrounds in commercial and property law, real estate appraisal, securities investment strategies, financial statement analysis, and marketing.

Personal Banking Services Specialists. Personal bankers are responsible for helping individuals and families identify and use the bank's services. This often means taking loan applications, marketing consumer deposits, and advising household customers on which of the bank's services meet their particular needs. Personal bankers must have excellent interpersonal skills and an in-depth knowledge of the bank's menu of services.

Tellers. One bank employee that many customers see and talk with is the teller—the individual who occupies a fixed station or location within a bank office or drive-in window, receiving deposits and dispensing cash and information. Bank tellers must sort and file deposit receipts and withdrawal slips, verify customer signatures, check account balances, and balance their own cash position at least once each day. Because of their pivotal role in communicating with customers, bank tellers must be friendly with customers, accurate, and knowledgeable about the other departments of the bank and the services they sell.

Security Analysts and Traders. Security analysts and traders are usually found in a bank's bond department and in its trust department. All banks have a pressing need for individuals skilled in evaluating the businesses and governments issuing securities that the bank might buy and in assessing financial market conditions. Such courses as economics, money and banking, money and capital markets, and investment analysis are usually the best fields of study for a person interested in becoming a bank security analyst or security trader.

Long-Range Planning and Business Acquisitions Specialists. Banks must plan for the long term if they are to survive and effectively meet their competition. Bank planners usually prepare a variety of projected budgets and forecasts, showing what the bank's financial and market position will be under a variety of assumptions about the future. Acquisitions specialists search for desirable market areas and businesses that might be advantageous for a bank or bank holding company to acquire. College courses in economics, money and banking, accounting, and business finance are particularly good preparation for building a career in these fields.

Marketing Personnel. With greater competition today, banks have an urgent need to develop new services and to more aggressively sell existing services—tasks that usually fall primarily to a bank's marketing department. This important function requires an understanding of the problems involved in producing and selling services and familiarity with service advertising techniques and cost accounting. Course work in economics, services marketing, statistics, and business management is especially helpful in this field.

Human Resources Managers. A bank's performance in serving the public and its owners depends, more than anything else, on the talent, training, and dedication of its management and staff. The job of human resources (personnel) managers is to find and hire people with superior skills and to train them to fill the roles needed by the bank. Most major banks operate intensive management training programs, lasting from 6 months to as long as 18 months, which typically are directed by the human resources division. Human resources managers keep records on employee performance and counsel employees

on ways to improve their performance and opportunities for promotion.

International Finance and Business Development Specialists. The market for many banking services is global in scale. Business customers frequently need loans, credit guarantees, help with floating new security issues, and analyses of business conditions in foreign markets. Men and women interested in this exciting banking field will require training in business finance, marketing, accounting, international trade, and cultural diversity.

Foreign Exchange Traders. A handful of the largest banks buy and sell foreign currencies for their own account and for their customers who are traveling or trading abroad. Foreign exchange traders within a bank search the market for the best prices on currencies and try to profit from currency-trading operations. They must also be able to negotiate with other currency traders and with the bank's customers. They often travel extensively and must be able to make decisions rapidly while under great pressure.

Investment Banking Specialists. Banks are becoming increasingly involved in assisting their business customers with the issue of bonds, notes, and stock to raise new capital, and they frequently render advice on financial market opportunities and on business mergers and acquisitions. This is the dynamic, fast-paced field of investment banking—one of the highest-paid and most challenging areas in the financial marketplace. Investment banking personnel must have intensive training in accounting, economics, strategic planning, investments, and international finance.

Bank Examiners and Regulators. Because banks are among the most heavily regulated of all business firms, there is an ongoing need for men and women to examine the financial condition and operating procedures of banks and to prepare and enforce banking regulations. Bank regulatory agencies such as the FDIC hire bank examiners from time to time, often by visiting college campuses or as a result of phone calls and letters from applicants. Examiners and regulators must have knowledge of accounting, business management, economics, and banking laws and regulations.

Bank Training Programs. Bank employees hired into management positions typically go through training programs which vary considerably in length and content, though most seem to average a year to 18 months in length. While the great majority of money-center and regional banks have such programs, only about half of the smaller community banks appear to have formal training programs. Trainees are generally rotated through different departments of the bank and also are given classroom instruction. Most bank training programs also encourage their trainees to seek additional education, including computer classes, accounting and MBA programs, and foreign language instruction (reflecting the growing internationalization of banking). The majority of banks prefer that their new management personnel hold at least a bachelor's degree (with an apparent preference for business and economics degrees), while the demand for MBAs and other master's degrees is considerably smaller except at the very largest banks.

In summary, there are professional career opportunities in banking for those who have received the necessary education and training. Moreover, with recent changes in services offered, technology, and regulations, banking can be an exciting and challenging career. However, finding a good job in the industry today will *not* be easy because consolidation is underway; hundreds of smaller banks are being absorbed by larger ones, with subsequent reductions in staff. Nevertheless, if such a career sounds interesting to you, there is no substitute for further study of the industry—its history, services, and problems. It is also important to visit with current bank personnel to learn more about the daily work environment inside a bank. Only then can you be sure that professional banking is really a good career target for you.

2 THE IMPACT OF GOVERNMENT POLICY AND REGULATION ON BANKING

Learning and Management Decision Objectives

The purpose of this chapter is to discover how the range of bank management decisions is limited by government regulation and to see how laws and regulations shape the services that banks can offer the public.

Introduction

This chapter is devoted to the regulatory and government policy environment within which the modern bank must operate. Banks operating in the United States and in most other countries must contend with heavy *regulation*—rules enforced by federal and state agencies governing their operations, service offerings, credit quality and quantity, capital positions, and the manner in which they grow and expand their facilities to better serve the public. We will identify *all* the principal bank regulatory agencies, as well as those that regulate and supervise banklike financial institutions, and describe the principal roles of each agency. The latter half of this chapter examines how economic policy, carried out in the United States by the Federal Reserve System, the Congress, and the Treasury, affects the banking system and, through that system, the economy as a whole.

Banking Regulation

As bankers work within the financial system to supply loans, accept deposits, and provide other services to their customers, they must do so within a climate of extensive *regulation,* designed primarily to protect the public interest.

There is a popular saying among bankers that the letters FDIC (Federal Deposit Insurance Corporation) really mean Forever Demanding Increased Capital! To American bankers, at least, the FDIC and the other bank regulatory agencies seem to be forever demanding something—more capital, more reports, more public service, and so on. No new bank can enter the industry in the United States, and in most other countries as well, without government approval. The types of deposits and other financial instruments banks sell to the public to raise funds must be sanctioned by each bank's principal regulatory agency. The quality of a bank's loans and investments and the adequacy of its capital are carefully reviewed by bank examiners. When a bank seeks to expand by constructing a new building, merging with another bank, setting up a branch office, or acquiring or starting a nonbank business, regulatory approval must first be obtained. Finally, a bank's owners cannot even choose to close its doors and leave the industry unless they obtain explicit approval from the government agency that granted each bank's original charter of incorporation.

Why Banks Are So Heavily Regulated—Pros and Cons

Why are most banks so closely regulated? There are a number of reasons for this heavy burden of government supervision, some of them centuries old.

First, banks are among the leading repositories of the *public's savings*—especially the savings of individuals and families. While most of the public's savings are placed in relatively short-term, highly liquid deposits, banks also hold large amounts of *long-term* savings in retirement accounts (known as Individual Retirement Accounts, or IRAs, in the United States). The loss of these funds due to bank failure or bank crime would be catastrophic to many individuals and families. But, many savers lack the financial expertise and depth of information needed to correctly evaluate the riskiness of a bank. Therefore, regulatory agencies are charged with the responsibility of gathering and evaluating the information needed to assess the true financial condition of banks in order to protect the public against loss. Cameras and guards patrol bank lobbies to reduce the risk of loss due to theft. Periodic bank examinations and audits are aimed at limiting losses from embezzlement, fraud, or mismanagement. Government agencies stand ready to loan funds to banks faced with unexpected shortfalls of spendable reserves so that the public's savings are protected.

Banks are also closely watched because of their power to *create money* in the form of readily spendable deposits by making loans and investments (extending credit). Changes in the volume of money created by banks appear to be closely correlated with economic conditions, especially the growth of jobs and the presence or absence of inflation. However, the fact that banks create money, which impacts the vitality of the economy, is not necessarily a valid excuse for regulating them. As long as central banks as government policymakers can control a nation's money supply growth, the volume of money that individual banks create should be of no great concern to the regulatory authorities or to the public.

Banks are also regulated because *they provide individuals and businesses with loans that support consumption and investment spending.* Regulatory authorities argue that the public has a keen interest in an adequate supply of loans flowing from the banking system. Moreover, where discrimination in the granting of credit is present, those individuals

Bankers' Insights and Issues

The Principal Reasons Banks Are Subject to Government Regulation

- To protect the safety of the public's savings.
- To control the supply of money and credit in order to achieve a nation's broad economic goals (such as high employment and low inflation).
- To ensure equal opportunity and fairness in the public's access to credit and other vital financial services.
- To promote public confidence in the financial system, so that savings flow smoothly into productive investment, and payments for goods and services are made speedily and efficiently.
- To avoid concentrations of financial power in the hands of a few individuals and institutions.
- To provide the government with credit, tax revenues, and other services.
- To help sectors of the economy that have special credit needs (such as housing, small business, and agriculture).

However, regulation must be balanced and limited so that: (*a*) banks can develop new services that the public demands, (*b*) competition in financial services remains strong enough to ensure reasonable prices and an adequate quantity and quality of service to the public, and (*c*) private-sector decisions are not distorted in ways that misallocate and waste scarce resources (such as by governments propping up banks that should be allowed to fail).

who are discriminated against face a significant obstacle to their personal well-being and an improved standard of living. This is especially true if access to credit is denied because of age, sex, race, national origin, or other irrelevant factors. Perhaps, however, the government could eliminate discrimination in providing services to the public simply by promoting more competition among banks and other providers of financial services, such as by vigorous enforcement of the antitrust laws, rather than through regulation.

Finally, banks have a long history of *involvement with government*—federal, state, and local. Early in the history of the industry governments relied upon cheap bank credit and the taxation of banks to finance armies and to supply the funds they were unwilling to raise through direct taxation of their citizens. More recently, governments have relied upon banks to assist in conducting economic policy, in collecting taxes, and in dispensing government payments. This reason for banking regulation has come under attack recently, however, because banks probably would provide financial services to governments if it were profitable to do so, even in the absence of regulation.

In the United States, banks are regulated through a **dual banking system**—that is, *both* federal and state authorities have significant bank regulatory powers. This system was designed to give the states closer control over industries operating within their borders, but also, through federal regulation, to ensure that banks would be treated fairly by individual states and local communities as their activities expanded across state lines. The key regulatory agencies within the U.S. government are the Comptroller of the Currency, the Federal Reserve System, and the Federal Deposit Insurance Corporation.

TABLE 2–1   **Banking's Principal Regulatory Agencies and
Their Responsibilities**

Federal Reserve System
- Supervises and regularly examines all state-chartered member banks and bank holding companies operating in the United States
- Imposes reserve requirements on deposits (Regulation D).
- Must approve all applications of member banks to merge, establish branches, or exercise trust powers.
- Charters, supervises, and examines international banking corporations operating in the United States.

Comptroller of the Currency
- Issues charters for new national banks.
- Supervises and regularly examines all national banks.
- Must approve all national bank applications for new branch offices, trust powers, mergers, and acquisitions.

Federal Deposit Insurance Corporation
- Insures deposits of banks conforming to its regulations.
- Must approve all applications of insured banks to establish branches, merge, or exercise trust powers.
- Requires all insured banks to submit reports on their financial condition.

Department of Justice
- Must review and approve proposed bank mergers and holding company acquisitions for their effects on competition and file suit if competition would be significantly damaged by these proposed organizational changes.

Securities and Exchange Commission
- Must approve public offerings of debt and equity securities by banks or bank holding companies.

State Banking Boards or Commissions
- Issue charters for new banks.
- Supervise and regularly examine all state-chartered banks.
- Reserve the right to approve all applications of banks operating within state borders to form a holding company, acquire affiliates and subsidiaries, or establish branch offices.

The Department of Justice and the Securities and Exchange Commission have important, but smaller, federal regulatory roles in banking, while **state banking commissions** are the primary regulators of American banks at the state level, as shown in Table 2–1.

The Impact of Regulation on Banks

While the reasons for bank regulation are well-known, the possible impacts of regulation on the industry are in dispute. One of the earliest theories about regulation, by economist George Stigler [8], contends that firms in regulated industries actually seek out regulation because it brings benefits in the form of monopolistic rents due to the fact that regulations often block entry into the regulated industry. Thus, some banks may lose money if regulations are lifted because they will no longer enjoy protected monopoly rents which increase their earnings. Sam Peltzman [5], on the other hand, contends that regulation shelters a firm from changes in demand and cost, lowering its risk. If true, this implies that the lifting of regulations in banking would subject individual banks to greater risk and eventually result in more bank failures.

More recently, Edward Kane [3] has argued that regulations can increase customer confidence in banks, which, in turn, may create greater customer loyalty toward banks. Kane believes that regulators actually *compete* with each other in offering regulatory services in an attempt to broaden their influence among regulated firms and with the general public. Moreover, he argues that there is an ongoing struggle between regulated firms and the regulators, called the *regulatory dialectic*. This means that once regulations are drafted and set in place, bankers will inevitably search to find ways around the new rules through innovation in order to maximize the value of each banking firm. If bankers are successful in skirting around existing regulations, then *new* rules will be created, encouraging bankers to seek further innovations in services and methods and, thus, the struggle between regulated firms and the regulators goes on indefinitely. Kane also believes that regulations provide an incentive for less-regulated businesses to try to win customers away from more-regulated firms—something that appears to have happened in banking in recent years as mutual funds, pension programs, and other less-regulated businesses have stolen away many of banking's best customers.

Concept Checks

2–1. What key areas or functions of a bank are regulated today?

2–2. What are the *reasons* for regulating each of the key areas or functions named above?

Major Banking Laws

One useful way to see the potent influence exercised by regulatory authorities on the banking industry is to review some of the major laws from which U.S. federal and state regulatory agencies receive their authority and direction. (See Table 2–2 for a summary of these U.S. laws.)

National Currency and Bank Acts (1863–64).   The first major federal laws in U.S. banking were the National Currency and Bank Acts, passed during the Civil War. These laws set up a system for chartering *national banks* through a newly created division of the U.S. Treasury Department, the **Comptroller of the Currency** (or Administrator of National Banks). Any group of individuals could seek a federal bank charter provided they agreed to adhere to federal laws and regulations and pledged enough of their owners' equity capital to open for business.

The Comptroller of the Currency not only assesses the need for and charters new national banks, but also regularly examines all existing national banks. These examinations vary in frequency and intensity with the bank's overall financial condition. However, every national bank is examined by a team of federal examiners at least once every 12 to 18 months. In addition, as Table 2–1 indicates, the Comptroller's office must approve all applications for the establishment of new branch offices by national banks and any mergers where national banks are involved. The Comptroller can close a national bank that, in its judgment, is insolvent or in danger of imposing substantial losses on its depositors.

The Federal Reserve Act (1913).   A series of severe economic depressions and financial panics in the 19th and early 20th centuries led to the creation of a second federal bank regulatory agency—the **Federal Reserve System.** Its principal roles vis-à-vis the banking industry are to serve as a lender of last resort—providing temporary loans to banks facing financial emergencies—and to help stabilize the financial markets in

---

Bankers' Insights and Issues

Regulators of U.S. Insured Banks (showing numbers of U.S. banks covered by deposit insurance as of December 31, 1996)

Types of U.S. Insured Banks	Number of Insured Banks	Number of Branch Offices of Insured Banks
Banks chartered by the federal government:		
U.S. insured banks with national (federal) charters issued by the Comptroller of the Currency	2,726	30,833
Banks chartered by state governments:		
State-chartered member banks of the Federal Reserve System, insured by the Federal Deposit Insurance Corporation	1,016	8,981
State-chartered nonmember banks, insured by the Federal Deposit Insurance Corporation	5,786	17,974
Total of all U.S.-insured banks and branches	9,528	57,788

Primary Federal Regulators of U.S. Insured Banks:

Primary Federal Regulator	Number of Insured Banks*
Federal Deposit Insurance Corporation	5,728
Office of the Comptroller of the Currency	2,702
Board of Governors of the Federal Reserve System	1,011

*Notes: The number of insured banks subject to each of the three federal regulatory agencies listed below do not exactly match the numbers in the top portion of the exhibit due to shared jurisdictions and other special arrangements among the regulatory agencies.
Source: Federal Deposit Insurance Corporation.

TABLE 2–2   Summary of Major Banking Laws and Their Provisions

Laws limiting bank lending and loan risk:

National Bank Act (1863–64)

Federal Reserve Act (1913)

Banking Act of 1933 (Glass-Steagall)

Laws restricting the services banks and thrifts can offer:

National Bank Act (1863–64)

Banking Act of 1933 (Glass-Steagall)

Competitive Equality in Banking Act (1987)

FDIC Improvement Act (1991)

Laws expanding the services banks and thrifts can offer:

Depository Institutions Deregulation and Monetary Control Act (1980)

Garn–St Germain Depository Institutions Act (1982)

Laws prohibiting discrimination in offering banking services:

Equal Credit Opportunity Act (1974)

Community Reinvestment Act (1977)

Laws mandating increased information to the consumer of banking services:

Consumer Credit Protection Act (Truth in Lending, 1968)

Fair Credit Reporting Act (1974)

Competitive Equality in Banking Act (1987)

Truth in Savings Act (1991)

Laws regulating branch banking:

McFadden-Pepper Act (1927)

Banking Act of 1933 (Glass-Steagall)

Riegle-Neal Interstate Banking and Branching Efficiency Act (1994)

Laws regulating bank holding company activity:

Bank Holding Company Act of 1956

Bank Holding Company Act Amendments of 1966 and 1970

Riegle-Neal Interstate Banking and Branching Efficiency Act (1994)

Laws regulating bank mergers:

Bank Merger Act (1960)

Bank Merger Act Amendments (1966)

Riegle-Neal Interstate Banking and Branching Efficiency Act (1994)

Laws assisting federal agencies in dealing with failing banks and thrifts:

Garn–St Germain Depository Institutions Act (1982)

Competitive Equality in Banking Act (1987)

Financial Institutions Reform, Recovery, and Enforcement Act (1989)

Federal Deposit Insurance Corporation Improvement Act (1991)

order to preserve public confidence. The Fed was created also to provide important services to the banking industry, including the establishment of a nationwide network to clear and collect checks. The Federal Reserve's most important job today, however, is to control money and credit conditions in order to promote economic stability. This final task assigned to the Fed is known as *monetary policy*—a topic we will examine in detail later in this chapter.

The McFadden-Pepper Act (1927).   Earlier federal laws had been silent on the issue of whether national banks could establish branch offices and, if so, under what terms. There was also the question of whether federally chartered banks were bound by state laws or only by federal laws. The **McFadden-Pepper Act** endeavored to answer these questions by allowing national banks to branch within the city where they were headquartered if the laws of the state involved did not forbid such branches. However, branching across state lines was *not* permitted unless expressly approved by state governments. In effect, individual states were granted the reserve power of deciding when and where both national and state-chartered banks operating within their borders would be allowed to set up branch offices.

The Banking Act of 1933 (Glass-Steagall).   From the perspective of history perhaps the most important of all federal banking laws was the **Glass-Steagall Act,** named for its sponsors in the U.S. Senate and House and passed during the depths of the Great Depression. Glass-Steagall specified that national banks would be allowed to branch statewide, provided the state where they were headquartered granted similar powers to its own state-chartered banks. However, because of a political compromise, national banks (which include the largest banking institutions in the United States) lost the power to engage in *investment banking* on most privately issued securities, especially the underwriting of new issues of corporate stocks and bonds—a privilege they had previously won with passage of the McFadden-Pepper Act in 1927.

Section 16 of the Glass-Steagall Act prohibited national banks from investing in stocks, limited their ability to act as an agent in buying and selling securities, and prohibited national banks from security underwriting and dealing in so-called ineligible securities issued by corporations, while Section 20 prohibited commercial banks that are members of the Federal Reserve from becoming affiliated with a firm "engaged principally" in dealing in or underwriting securities. Section 21 erected a barrier for securities firms, forbidding them from taking deposits from the public, while Section 32 blocked officers, directors, or employees of banks from serving at the same time in the same capacity for businesses dealing in or underwriting securities. Glass-Steagall did exempt *some* types of securities from its prohibitions, allowing banks to underwrite certain so-called *eligible securities*—U.S. government securities, general-obligation municipal bonds, privately placed commercial notes, and real estate bonds. Moreover, securities underwriters were prohibited from offering depository services, thus walling off commercial banking from investment banking. One major New York banking organization, J. P. Morgan, soon split into two separate entities—J. P. Morgan, a commercial banking firm, and Morgan Stanley, an investment bank.

Glass-Steagall and Securities Underwriting.   The legally mandated separation of commercial and investment banking was motivated both by fears of excessive risk taking and by fears of customer coercion by the nation's largest banks. It was alleged, for example, that some banks, anxious to sell shares of corporate stock they had previously underwritten, had coerced their customers to buy the stock as a condition for getting a bank loan. Another questionable practice consisted of allowing customers to use stock the bank was underwriting as security for a loan.

Bankers representing some of the leading U.S. banking organizations, including Citicorp, Bankers Trust, and Morgan Stanley, repeatedly down through the years urged repeal of the investment banking prohibitions contained in the Glass-Steagall Act. They argued that adding banks to the picture would increase competition for the privilege of underwriting securities, give borrowers more service options, and lower borrowing costs. Moreover, repeal of Glass-Steagall allegedly would give smaller business firms greater access to the capital markets as a source of funds. At the same time, many of the largest and soundest bank loan customers in recent years have by-passed their banks as sources of borrowed funds and turned to selling securities in the open market. Proponents of repealing the Glass-Steagall Act argued that these customers might once again return to banks for their funding needs.

Several large U.S. banks managed to secure restricted underwriting powers from the Federal Reserve Board during the 1980s. For example, in December 1986, Bankers Trust Company of New York received permission to underwrite and sell (through an affiliated firm) commercial paper issued by its corporate customers. In 1987, Citicorp, Morgan, and Bankers Trust were granted authority to underwrite and deal in municipal revenue bonds, commercial paper, and securities backed by pools of mortgages and consumer loans. A further step was taken in January 1989, when authority to under-write corporate bonds was granted to Chase Manhattan, Morgan, Bankers Trust, Citi-corp, and Security Pacific (later merged with Bank of America) through their affiliated companies. Finally, in September 1990 J. P. Morgan became the first U.S. banking firm in over half a century to be permitted to underwrite corporate stock issues.

Nevertheless, the risk and conflict-of-interest issues in security underwriting remain to be fully dealt with. The prohibitions against stock and bond underwriting contained in the Glass-Steagall Act reflected the concerns of many financial analysts and legislators when that law was passed that commercial bank involvement in the underwriting of privately issued (as opposed to government-issued) securities would increase the risk of bank failure if stock and bond prices fell. Moreover, a change in interest rates could drastically alter the demand for underwriting services, creating great volatility in underwriting revenues. If investment banking is inherently more risky than commercial banking and if the former comes to represent a significant share of all commercial bank revenues, then the overall risk of banking firms will increase and some will undoubtedly fail. On the other hand, the proponents of full bank participation in security underwriting argue that U.S. banks could lose out in the race for large corporate contracts to foreign banks and domestic and foreign securities firms if they cannot offer to underwrite their customers' securities as well as make loans to those same customers. Moreover, recent research evidence by Gande, et al. [9] finds no evidence of conflict of interest damaging customers when banks serve as both lenders and security underwriters and that smaller business borrowers tend to benefit in terms of greater access to capital markets and lower borrowing costs when banks can under-write business debt securities.

Establishing the FDIC Under the Glass-Steagall Act.   One of the Glass-Steagall Act's most important legacies in quieting public fears over the soundness of the banking system was the creation of the **Federal Deposit Insurance Corporation** (FDIC) to guarantee the public's deposits up to a stipulated maximum amount (initially $2,500; today up to $100,000 per account holder). Without question, the FDIC, since its inception in 1934, has helped to reduce the number of potential bank runs significantly, though it has not prevented large numbers of bank failures in recent years. In fact, it may have contributed to individual bank risk taking and failure in some instances. Each

Bank Management in Action

U.S. Banks Struggle to Offer Investment Banking Services

American banks have been struggling for many years to expand their *investment banking services*—the underwriting of securities (especially the buying and selling of new corporate bonds and stock) issued by their largest corporate customers. Their foreign bank competitors, particularly the leading banks in Japan, Canada, and Western Europe, already offer investment banking services to their corporate customers with few restraints. However, U.S. banks are restricted in offering these fund-raising services by the terms of the Glass-Steagall Act passed in 1933 and by regulations imposed by the Federal Reserve Board.

In 1986 the Federal Reserve opted for a policy of allowing selected U.S. banking companies to offer limited investment banking services. Because Section 20 of the Glass-Steagall Act forbids U.S. banks from becoming "principally engaged" in investment banking activities involving the issue, floatation, underwriting, public sale, or syndication of "ineligible" securities (i.e., private bonds and stocks), the Fed voted to allow a small number of domestic and foreign bank holding companies to offer investment banking services to their U.S. corporate customers through special security underwriting subsidiaries, called *Section 20 firms* after the relevant section of the Glass-Steagall Act. However, the revenues from these activities could not represent more than 5 percent of the security subsidiary's gross revenues averaged over an eight-quarter period. By 1997 the Fed had included corporate debt securities, stocks, commercial paper, municipal revenue bonds, mortgage-backed securities, and asset-backed securities in the list of permissible "ineligible securities" that Section 20 subsidiaries could trade. Earlier, in 1989 the security trading revenue limit for banks' Section 20 security affiliates was increased from 5 to 10 percent and, in 1996, 25 percent of a Section 20 firm's security trading revenues could come from trading in "ineligible" securities, such as corporate stocks and corporate bonds. Moreover, the Section 20 firms were granted the option to index their percentage-of-revenue figure based on interest-rate changes so they could continue to receive substantial security trading revenues no matter which way interest rates went. By 1998, more than 40 bank holding companies operating in the United States had established Section 20 subsidiaries, offering what amounts to one-stop shopping for corporations needing funding. Among the most prominent of these security-underwriting banks are those listed below:

insured bank is required to pay to the federal insurance system an insurance premium each year based upon its volume of insurance-eligible deposits and its risk exposure. The hope was that, over time, the FDIC's pool of insurance funds would grow large enough to handle a considerable number of bank failures. However, the federal insurance plan was never designed to handle a rash of bank closings like the one that occurred in the United States during the 1980s. This is why the FDIC was forced to petition Congress

Selected American Banking Companies with Security Underwriting Powers Granted by the Federal Reserve Board in the Indicated Years

1987	Bankers Trust Company of New York	1990	BancOne Corporation
1987	Chase Manhattan Corp.	1992	BankAmerica Corp.
1987	Citicorp	1992	Huntington BancShares
1987	J. P. Morgan	1993	Bank South
1987	PNC Financial Group	1994	First of America
1988	First Chicago NBD	1994	National City Corp.
1988	Fleet Financial Corp.	1994	Republic New York
1989	Barnett Banks	1994	Sun Trust Banks
1989	First Union Corp.	1994	Synovus Financial Corp.
1989	NationsBank	1995	Mellon Bank Corp.
1989	Norwest Corp.	1996	Key Corp.
1989	SouthTrust Corp.	1997	U.S. BanCorp.

Source: Board of Governors of the Federal Reserve System.

In order to protect the banks affiliated with a holding company from the underwriting activities of the company's Section 20 subsidiary, the Federal Reserve Board set up several so-called firewalls separating investment banking from commercial banking activities. For example, affiliated banks were originally prohibited from making any loans to corporate security issuers that were having their securities underwritten by the affiliated Section 20 subsidiary. Moreover, an affiliated bank could not purchase the securities underwritten by its Section 20 securities company nor buy financial assets from or sell assets to its related securities firm. In addition, a Section 20 securities firm and its affiliated banks could not share officers, directors, or employees, nor cross-market their services, nor share information from customer files—all of these provisions designed to reduce possible conflicts of interest between commercial and investment banking activities and protect banks and their depositors from excessive risk.

While bank holding companies with Section 20 subsidiaries have been quite successful in underwriting corporate bonds, their share of the riskier stock underwriting market has been much smaller, though it is rising rapidly so that by 1997 bank-affiliated securities firms accounted for close to one-fifth of all new stock issues, helping to reduce underwriting fees. Moreover, several banking companies have recently moved up close to

for additional borrowing authority in 1991, when the U.S. deposit insurance fund had become nearly insolvent.

Criticisms of the FDIC and the Need for New Legislation. The FDIC became the object of strong criticism during the 1980s and early 1990s, not over the fundamental concept of deposit insurance but over the way the federal deposit insurance system had

the Fed's revenue percentage limits. By the fall of 1996 the Federal Reserve Board began to loosen the reins further to give bank security firms more latitude. Common officers and directors between affiliated banks and security subsidiaries were allowed, provided the directors of one firm represented less than half the directors of the other firm. However, an affiliated bank's chief executive officer cannot be a director, officer, or employee of a securities' affiliate and vice versa. The original prohibition against cross-selling services was reduced and transactions between affiliated banks and Section 20 securities companies would also be allowed provided the assets involved were readily identifiable and carried values commonly quoted in the public market.

Then in August of 1997 the Board announced a significant reduction in the firewalls separating commercial banks and their investment (Section 20) security subsidiaries, arguing that existing securities laws and other banking regulations adequately protected the public and promoted bank safety. Among other changes, banks are no longer prohibited from extending credit to or enhancing the credit quality of the customers of their Section 20 security affiliates provided these credit-related services are priced at market levels and bank customers are not pressured to purchase the services of a banking company's Section 20 affiliate as a condition for getting a loan or credit enhancement. Moreover, banking companies are no longer prohibited from loaning money to a customer for purposes of repaying principal, interest, or dividends on any securities underwritten by that company's securities affiliate, provided the loan is made on market terms. Security underwriting subsidiaries are no longer required to have separate offices from any affiliated bank, except that sales of nondeposit investment products by a securities affiliate cannot be in the same area of a bank where retail deposits are sold.

In addition, banks and other affiliate companies of a bank holding company are now permitted to purchase securities from their securities (Section 20) affiliate, even those being underwritten by the Section 20 affiliate, provided these purchases are made at market, any purchases by an affiliated bank are adequately backed by bank capital, and the securities bought meet the quality standards required in banking regulations. Regulatory restrictions on banks funding an affiliated securities company, including purchasing its assets, are substantially reduced and banks and their securities affiliates may share information about a customer without the customer's consent. In total, these more liberal rules surrounding bank holding companies and their security trading companies will permit U.S. banking organizations to offer their business customers a full range of financing options—marketing their bonds and stock as well as providing direct loans to those same customers.

been administered through most of its history. Prior to 1993, the FDIC levied *fixed* insurance premiums on all deposits eligible for insurance coverage, regardless of the riskiness of an individual bank's balance sheet.

This fixed-fee system led to a *moral hazard* problem: it encouraged banks to accept greater risk, because the government was pledged to pay off their depositors if they failed. Because all banks paid an identical insurance fee (quite unlike most private insurance systems), more-risk-oriented banks were being supported by more

Concept Checks

2–3. What is the principal role of the Comptroller of the Currency?

2–4. What is the principal job performed by the FDIC?

2–5. What key roles does the Federal Reserve System perform in the banking and financial system?

2–6. What is the Glass-Steagall Act and why is it important? Should banks face any restrictions in offering investment banking services to corporations and other borrowers?

conservative banks. The moral hazard problem created the need for bank regulation because it encouraged some banks to take on greater risk than they otherwise would if there was no low-cost federal insurance system available.[1]

Most depositors (except for the very largest) do *not* carefully monitor bank risk; instead, they rely on the FDIC for protection. Because this results in subsidizing the riskiest banks—encouraging them to gamble with their depositors' money—there was a definite need for a risk-scaled insurance system in which the riskiest banks paid the highest insurance premiums. As we will see shortly, the U.S. Congress in 1991 finally moved to order the FDIC to develop a risk-sensitive fee schedule (first put in place in 1993) under which the riskiest banks pay the highest insurance premiums and face the most restrictive regulations. Nevertheless, the federal government sells most U.S. banks relatively inexpensive deposit insurance that may still encourage bank risk taking.

One popular proposal for revamping or replacing the current federal deposit insurance system includes turning over deposit insurance to the private sector (privatization). Presumably, a private insurer would be more aggressive in assessing the riskiness of individual banks and would compel risky banks buying its insurance plan to pay much greater insurance fees. However, privatization of the deposit insurance system would not solve all of the problems of trying to protect the public's deposits. For example, an effective private insurance system would be difficult to devise because, unlike most other forms of insured risk, where the appearance of one claim does not necessarily lead to other claims, depositors' risks can be highly intercorrelated. The failure of a single bank can result in thousands of claims. Moreover, the failure of one bank may lead to still other bank failures. If a state's or region's economy turns downward, there may be hundreds of bank failures almost simultaneously. Could private insurers correctly price or even withstand that kind of risk?

Moreover, as we will see in Chapter 4, banks rely heavily upon *book value accounting,* where most loans and liabilities are recorded at face value or at whatever value applies the day an asset or liability is acquired. Subsequent results usually do not

---

[1]For an in-depth discussion of the moral hazard problem see, for example, Kareken [4].

Bank Management in Action

Banks Jump into the Mutual Fund Business

Mutual funds—open-ended pools of stocks, bonds, and other financial instruments against which investors hold shares of stock—have been the most rapidly growing financial intermediary of the past decade. Mutual funds, or *investment companies,* as they are often called, are a potentially high-volume product that is popular with the general public, especially the small investor who receives the benefit of professional portfolio management services at low cost. During the late 1980s and early 1990s a growing interest of the public in preparing for their retirement years supplemented by falling or low interest rates posted on bank deposits, a steeply sloped yield curve favoring investments in stocks, bonds, and other long-term instruments, and weak bank loan demand resulted in the movement of huge amounts of funds out of bank deposit accounts toward mutual fund shares. Thousands of investors appeared to be convinced that investments in stocks and bonds would bring significantly higher long-run returns. Mutual funds' shares outstanding increased fifteen-fold between 1980 and 1993, with most of their growth occurring in the 1990s.

Faced with a substantial loss of funds (disintermediation) and a declining share of the financial-services market, bankers fought back by offering *their* customers access to mutual funds as well. But, under federal statutes mutual funds' shares are considered to be securities, not deposits, and the Glass-Steagall Act of 1933 prohibits banks from underwriting and dealing in most shares of stock. Initially, many banks negotiated special arrangements with security brokers to direct customer purchases and sales through a broker's account, with the bank merely acting as a convenient pipeline to get customer funds placed in mutual fund shares. In 1972 U.S. bank holding companies were first granted permission by the Federal Reserve Board to act as mutual fund investment advisors and custodians and, in 1986, the Fed voted to allow holding company subsidiaries to provide investment advice and other brokerage services to individual customers. These liberalized regulations allowed banking companies to generate sales commissions and fee income from sales of mutual funds and other securities to partially offset their falling net interest margins as loan income declined and deposits became more difficult to sell to the public. In addition, security sales offered the possibility of reducing unsystematic risk in bank investment portfolios through diversification into new product lines and the lowering of average operating costs due to economies of scale and scope. Finally, offering this new service may keep customers coming back to the bank for their other financial-service needs.

cause a revaluation of many assets and liabilities on a bank's books. Many financial analysts have recommended *market value accounting* for banks, because measures of bank condition based on book values are unlikely to be timely predictors of bank risk. Then, too, a bank risk-rating system that is disclosed to the public may create unwarranted fears if depositors become aware that any given bank's risk index has been increased by examiners, setting in motion the very thing the FDIC was created to prevent—panicky withdrawals of bank deposits.

Indeed, something like this occurred not long ago when federal banking agencies leaked the information that a particular bank had been added to their "problem bank" list. What the public did not realize, however, is that being on a regulatory agency's problem-bank list does not mean that failure is inevitable. Many banks have been able to leave the problem list as a result of management changes or renewed vigor in the economy of their market area.

Moreover, there are several different levels of bank problems. For example, the FDIC maintains a problem-bank list containing three different categories of banks: (1) *potential payoff* (PPO), the gravest situation, where the FDIC believes there is a 50-50 chance of a bank needing government assistance to survive in the near term; (2) *serious problem* (SP), where the FDIC may eventually have to contribute some of its own resources to the troubled bank unless significant changes are made by its owners and managers; and (3) *other problem* (OP), where the listed bank has financial weaknesses that must be closely watched but is of less concern to the FDIC than the two preceding categories. Unfortunately, the public is usually unaware of these differences in the severity of problems faced by individual banks, which may result in sound and insolvent banks inappropriately being linked together. In its earlier history, the FDIC's principal task was to restore public confidence in banks and avoid panic on the part of the public. Today, the challenge is how to price deposit insurance fairly so that risk is managed and the government is not forced to use excessive amounts of taxpayer funds to support private bank risk taking—a problem that has not yet been fully resolved.[2]

The Bank Holding Company Act and Its Amendments (1956, 1966, and 1970). In 1956, following a wave of bank holding company formations, Congress passed the **Bank Holding Company Act.** This law brought bank holding companies—corporations set up to buy and hold bank stock—under comprehensive federal regulation for the first time. Congress and the public feared that holding companies threatened the independence of many banks and might reduce government influence over bank performance. Today, if bankers want to form a holding company to acquire other banks or to purchase nonbank businesses, they must seek approval from the Federal Reserve Board. Moreover, all bank holding companies with controlling interest in two or more banks were required to register with the Fed, file periodic financial reports, and submit to Federal Reserve examination of their books. This law was amended in 1966 to permit greater latitude for transactions within the same holding company among affiliated businesses and to mitigate the heavy taxation of these firms. In 1970, even holding

---

[2]The powers of the FDIC to correct abuse among federally insured banks and prevent drains on the federal insurance fund are awesome. It can remove management or directors if it decides they have deliberately and recklessly weakened the banks they control. It can even ban an individual from being involved in the operations of any FDIC-insured bank where there is "demonstrated disregard" for bank safety and soundness, and it can assess monetary penalties for violations of the Federal Deposit Insurance Act.

companies controlling just *one* U.S. bank were required to register with the Fed, and their acquisitions of nonbank business firms were limited to those business activities defined by the Federal Reserve Board to be "closely related" to banking.[3]

The Bank Merger Act and its Amendments (1960 and 1966).   Closer federal regulation of bank holding companies was a prophetic development in banking history, because it soon led to closer federal regulation of bank mergers as well. A merger, by definition, is a transaction in which two or more banks combine their assets and liabilities and become *one* corporation, usually bearing the name of the acquiring bank. Concerned about possible damage to competition and public service from bank mergers that reduce the number of competitors in any given market, Congress required in the **Bank Merger Act** of 1960 that all mergers must be approved by each U.S. bank's chief federal regulatory agency.

For example, national banks could not merge without prior approval of the Comptroller of the Currency, while state-chartered member banks of the Federal Reserve System must seek Federal Reserve Board approval for a proposed merger. The FDIC also reviews all mergers involving insured banks and is the principal agency for approving or denying merger applications involving insured banks that are *not* members of the Federal Reserve System.

In these required agency reviews of pending merger transactions, *the probable impact on competition* in serving the public is weighted most heavily. A proposed bank merger having a substantially adverse effect on competition is likely to be denied. A series of amendments to the Bank Merger Act in 1966, however, modified this top-heavy emphasis on competition in the federal evaluation of proposed bank mergers. Thereafter, other factors, such as the possibility that a merger would increase convenience for the public or would strengthen a troubled bank, were given somewhat stronger consideration. Many more mergers subsequently were approved because they appeared to enhance the public's access to financial services.

Social Responsibility Laws of the 1960s, 1970s, and 1980s.   The 1960s and 1970s also ushered in a concern with the impact banks were having on the *quality of life* in the communities they served. Congress feared that banks were not adequately informing their customers of the terms under which loans were made and especially about the true cost of borrowing money. In 1968 Congress moved to improve the *flow of information* to the consumer of financial services by passing the Consumer Credit Protection Act (known as Truth in Lending), which required that banks and other lenders clearly spell out all the customer's rights and responsibilities under a loan agreement.

In 1974, Congress targeted possible *discrimination* in providing bank services to the public with passage of the Equal Credit Opportunity Act. Individuals and families could *not* be denied a loan merely because of their age, sex, national origin, or religious

---

[3]See Chapter 3 for a more detailed description of the types of businesses a bank holding company can acquire and the rules of operation it must follow.

affiliation, or because they were recipients of public welfare. In 1977, Congress passed the Community Reinvestment Act, prohibiting U.S. banks from discriminating against customers residing within their trade territories merely on the basis of the neighborhood they happened to live in. A further step toward requiring fair and equitable treatment of customers and improving the flow of information from banks to consumers was taken in 1987 with passage of the Competitive Equality in Banking Act and in 1991 with the approval of the Truth in Savings Act. These federal laws required banks to more fully disclose their deposit service policies and the true rates of return offered on the public's savings accounts. These social responsibility laws all had laudable goals, but they also tended to increase bank operating costs.

Deregulation Laws of the 1970s and 1980s.   Early in the 1970s, a movement to *deregulate* banking services began in New England and gradually spread throughout the United States and to several nations in Western Europe and around the Pacific Rim. Initially, savings banks in Massachusetts and New Hampshire developed the NOW (negotiable order of withdrawal, or interest-bearing checking) account to get around federal regulations prohibiting the payment of interest on regular checking accounts. Earlier, in the 1930s the Glass-Steagall Act had empowered the FDIC and the Federal Reserve Board to enforce legal limits on both checking and savings deposit interest rates in the hope of protecting bank earnings, thereby reducing the number of bank failures. However, these deposit rate restrictions did little to prevent bank failures and often placed federally supervised banks at a competitive disadvantage in attracting and retaining deposits. The competition among depository institutions brought about by the New England NOW experiment led Congress in the 1970s and 1980s to allow banks to offer interest-bearing checking accounts and money market certificates of deposit (CDs) with flexible market-based interest rates, thereby helping banks to fight back against the growing competition from money market funds for the public's payments and savings accounts.

Concept Checks

2–7.   Which banking laws appear to have been the most significant in restricting the services banks can offer and the markets they can enter?

2–8.   Why has the federal insurance system run into serious problems in recent years?

2–9.   What restrictions do U.S. banks face in offering shares in mutual funds? What advantages and disadvantages do offerings of mutual funds pose for banks?

The Depository Institutions Deregulation and Monetary Control Act (1980).   The first sweeping federal deregulation law, the **Depository Institutions Deregulation**

and Monetary Control Act (DIDMCA), was passed in 1980. It contained the following key provisions applying to commercial banks:

1. Legally mandated federal interest rate ceilings on deposits sold to the public were to be phased out from 1981 to 1986 so that deposit interest rates would be more responsive to free competition and market conditions.
2. NOW accounts that pay an explicit interest return to the customer and have third-party payment (checking) powers could be offered nationwide to individuals and nonprofit institutions by all federally supervised depository institutions.

The fundamental purpose of DIDMCA, however, was to help make *nonbank* depository institutions, especially credit unions, savings and loan associations, and savings banks, more competitive and viable by expanding their range of permissible services. The result was to intensify competition for both loans and deposits between banks and nonbank depositories.

The Garn–St Germain Depository Institutions Act (1982).   Another deregulation bill was passed in 1982—the **Garn–St Germain Depository Institutions Act**—to fine-tune some of the provisions of DIDMCA. This law made the following changes applicable to U.S. commercial banks:

1. The Depository Institutions Deregulation Commission (set up in 1980 under terms of the Depository Institutions Deregulation Act) was permitted to authorize all federally supervised, deposit-taking intermediaries to sell a deposit account "directly equivalent to and competitive with money market mutual funds."
2. Banks and other depository institutions were allowed to sell NOW (interest-bearing checking) accounts to governments as well as to individuals and nonprofit associations.
3. Loan limits were liberalized for national banks, allowing them to lend up to 15 percent of their capital and surplus unsecured to a single borrower, or as much as 25 percent of their capital and surplus to one borrower if the loan was fully secured.
4. Banks in need of strengthening their capital to head off failure could issue net worth certificates to the FDIC and receive an infusion of new capital.
5. The FDIC could arrange mergers across state lines to absorb large failing banks, provided no suitable intrastate merger partners could be found.

The Garn–St Germain bill was an attempt by Congress to make nonbank thrift institutions more like banks in the services they could offer and to make all depository institutions more competitive with money market mutual funds, which had successfully attracted away billions of dollars from banks and other depository institutions.

Bank Failures and the Competitive Equality in Banking Act of 1987.   Many of the Garn bill's provisions were enacted into law to deal with a rising tide of bank and thrift institution failures. However, the failure problem continued to grow; by the late 1980s, the largest number of U.S. bank and thrift failures since the founding of the FDIC occurred. Congress took further steps to attack the bank failure problem with passage of the **Competitive Equality in Banking Act** in 1987. The Equality Act authorized emergency interstate bank acquisitions and okayed FDIC takeover and operation of banks failing or soon to fail. The 1987 law allowed the FDIC to create *bridge banks*—new national banks specifically created to take over the assets and liabilities of a failed bank and operated by the FDIC for a limited period before their stock must be sold to the highest private bidders. Bridge banks could be established only where the cost of creating and operating them appeared to be less than that of liquidating a troubled bank and continued banking service appeared to be essential to the local community involved.[4]

The Financial Institutions Reform, Recovery, and Enforcement Act (1989).   The failure of hundreds of depository institutions in the 1980s and declining public confidence in the banking system led President George Bush to recommend, and Congress ultimately to pass in August 1989, the **Financial Institutions Reform, Recovery, and Enforcement Act** (FIRREA). While most of FIRREA's provisions applied directly to the savings and loan industry, several important new rules affecting banks were also laid down. For example, bank holding companies were authorized for the first time to acquire healthy savings banks and savings and loans. (Previously, the Federal Reserve Board had allowed them to purchase only failing thrift institutions.) This proved to be a significant aid to banking organizations (such as Citicorp) seeking to expand geographically because they now have a new avenue through which to acquire distant deposits and branch offices.

FIRREA also granted the FDIC power to levy *cross-guarantee assessments*. These charges can be assessed against the surviving banks of holding companies for any losses to the FDIC's insurance fund due to the failure of other banks owned by the same holding company. Such assessments have been levied against such companies as the Bank of New England Corporation of Boston, Southeast Bancorp of Miami, and First City Bancorporation of Texas before the latter's acquisition by Texas Commerce Bancshares (now an affiliate of Chase Manhattan/Chemical Banking Corporation of New York), to name just a few.

FIRREA restructured the FDIC, dividing its insurance fund into a new Bank Insurance Fund (BIF) and a Savings Association Insurance Fund (SAIF), the latter to insure savings and loan deposits. The new law stipulated that both of these insurance units must gradually increase the fees assessed depository institutions that receive federal insurance coverage in order to increase the funds' reserves to at least 1.25 percent of all insured deposits. FIRREA allowed savings and loans to convert to commercial banks if they can meet bank regulatory standards.

By 1996 and 1997 public support appeared to be building for leveling out the differences in capitalization and fees assessed by the Savings Association Insurance Fund

---

[4]Still another device for dealing with problem banks recently applied for by owners of several large troubled banks is the splitting of a bank with a troubled loan portfolio into a "good bank" and a "bad bank." Nonperforming loans are sold by the good bank to the bad bank, which is given a separate charter. Money for purchasing these loans may be derived from sales of stocks or bonds. The bad bank then attempts to collect all or a portion of the troubled loans it has purchased. For further discussion of this innovative technique, see Crockett [2].

Bankers' Insights and Issues

How the FDIC Usually Resolves a Bank Failure

Most troubled bank situations are detected in a regular bank examination conducted by either federal or state banking agencies. If examiners find a serious problem, they ask the management and board of directors of the troubled bank to prepare a report on the most pressing problems and a follow-up examination normally is scheduled several weeks or months later. If failure seems likely, FDIC examiners are called in to see if they concur that the bank is about to fail.

The FDIC then must choose which of several possible methods will be used to resolve each failure. The two most widely used methods are a *deposit payoff* or a *purchase and assumption* transaction. A deposit payoff is used when the closed bank's offices are not to be reopened, often because there are no interested bidders to buy the troubled firm and the FDIC perceives that the public has other convenient banking alternatives. With a payoff, all insured depositors will receive checks from the FDIC for up to $100,000, while uninsured depositors and other creditors receive a *pro rata* share of any funds generated from the liquidation of the bank's assets. A purchase and assumption transaction, on the other hand, is employed if a healthy bank can be found to take over selected assets and the deposits of the failed institution. (If a deposit payoff is used, insured depositors receive interest on their funds only up to the day of the closing; on the other hand, if the failed bank is taken over by a healthy bank in a pur-

(SAIF), which insures the public's deposits held by nonbank thrifts, and the Bank Insurance Fund (BIF) and, perhaps, allowing them to merge along with eliminating the essential legal differences between bank and thrift charters. The Deposit Insurance Funds Act of 1996 imposed a special one-time assessment fee on the deposits held by thrift institutions to bring SAIF up to its required insurance reserve ratio of 1.25 percent of all insured deposits by the year 2000, just like the bank insurance fund (BIF). The Deposit Insurance Funds Act aims ultimately to merge the thrift and bank insurance funds by 1999, but not until the remaining differences between bank and thrift charters are eliminated.

Reform Legislation Proposed by the U.S. Treasury.   In February of 1991, a massive banking reform plan was proposed by the U.S. Treasury under President George Bush. One of the many elements of this package of proposed banking reforms called for repeal of the Douglas Amendment to the Bank Holding Company Act, thereby permitting bank holding companies to cross state lines and acquire control of banks in all 50 states. Moreover, the Treasury's proposals called for amending the McFadden and Glass-Steagall acts to allow U.S. banks to operate branch offices throughout the United States. Eventually, banks could expand across state lines using the lowest-cost organizational vehicle available, rather than having to organize separate holding companies in each state, unnecessarily duplicating personnel, equipment, and capital.

chase and assumption transaction, the depositors continue to accrue interest without interruption.)

When a purchase and assumption is employed, shortly before the bank's closing the FDIC will contact healthy banks that might be interested in an effort to solicit bids for the failing bank. Generally, the FDIC prefers to find a healthy bank at least twice the size of the failing institution. Interested buyers will negotiate with FDIC officials on the value of the failing bank's "good" and "bad" assets and on which assets and debts will be retained by the FDIC for collection and which will become the responsibility of the buyer.

On a predetermined date the state or federal agency that issued the bank's charter officially closes the troubled bank and its directors and officers meet with FDIC officials. After that meeting a press release is issued and local newspapers are contacted.

On the designated closing date the FDIC's liquidation team assembles at some agreed-upon location (often in a shopping center or other site near the troubled bank, but in a manner that avoids attracting public attention). When all team members are ready (and often just after the bank's offices are closed for the day), the liquidation team will enter the failed bank and place signs on the doors indicating that the bank has been seized by the FDIC. The team will move swiftly to take inventory of the failed bank's assets and determine what funds the depositors and other creditors are owed. Such closings often occur on a Friday to give the FDIC liquidators the weekend to fully inventory the failed bank's assets before the new week begins. In subsequent days the liquidators may move their operations to rented office space nearby so the closed bank's facilities can open for business as usual on Monday morning under the control of its new owners.

Security underwriting, insurance sales, the underwriting of mutual funds, and other innovative services then prohibited to most American banks could be offered under the Treasury's proposals through separately regulated firms part of the same bank holding company organization. Banks would continue to be regulated by the federal banking agencies, while bank holding company subsidiaries offering security broker/dealer services or selling shares in mutual funds would be regulated by the Securities and Exchange Commission. Those holding company subsidiaries selling insurance services would be regulated by state insurance commissions. The overall ("umbrella") supervisor of each holding company would be the primary regulator of the largest bank in the company, who would be responsible for deciding if the banks involved were being threatened with excessive risk due to the activities of their nonbank subsidiary firms. If so, the Treasury proposed allowing bank regulators to order divestiture of any troublesome nonbank subsidiaries. Moreover, financial transactions between bank and nonbank subsidiaries of the same holding company would be closely monitored to protect bank depositors and the interests of holding company stockholders. These proposals were based on the idea of *functional regulation,* linking government supervision to the particular types of activities banking organizations undertake with different regulators responsible for overseeing different activities (e.g., insurance commissions monitoring banks' insurance sales, while bank regulators monitor bank lending).

Bank Management in Action

The Battle to Allow U.S. Banks to Sell Insurance Services

For more than 60 years U.S. commercial banks have sought federal and state approval to be able to sell life and property/casualty insurance policies and to underwrite insurance risks. Prior to the 1930s many U.S. banks sold general insurance coverage to their customers along with traditional banking products. However, record numbers of bank failures during the Great Depression years led Congress and the states to confine banking's permissible activities largely to deposit taking, lending, and the discounting of commercial notes. Repeated attempts by bankers to obtain insurance powers during the era of banking deregulation in the 1980s were turned back by Congress out of fear of excessive risk and due to opposition from the insurance industry. The only widely agreed-upon exceptions to this prohibition in the United States are sales of life, accident, health, and unemployment insurance to guarantee repayment of a loan and operating an insurance agency in a small town (with population of 5,000 or less) not currently served by an insurance agency. Overseas, many banks already own insurance companies—examples include Germany's Deutsche Bank which owns insurance subsidiary dbLeben and Canada's Royal Bank which controls Voyageur Travel Insurance Ltd.

Bankers argue that selling insurance would offer multiple benefits for banks and their customers. Allegedly, this service would be offered through existing bank branch offices at relatively small additional cost and would generate cash flows *not* strongly correlated with traditional banking services, thereby reducing the variance of the bank's overall cash flow and making its earnings less risky. At the same time bank customers could purchase more services from a single location, increasing customer convenience and reducing customer transactions costs. Bankers and insurance companies could cross-sell each other's services, benefiting both types of financial institutions and offering customers a bigger service menu.

Opponents of selling insurance services from banks contend that adding these services would only increase bank risk, particularly if banks underwrote large-scale medical

---

In an effort to bring more capital into the banking industry, the U.S. Treasury urged Congress to dismantle the traditional walls between banking and commerce, allowing commercial firms to acquire bank holding companies if affiliated banks belonging to the acquired holding company are strongly capitalized. This infusion of outside capital into banking could decrease the risk of bank failures, especially if strong "fire walls" were erected (such as restrictions on intracompany loans) to protect banks from any losses suffered by the commercial company that happens to own them.

Debate over the sweeping Treasury banking reform proposals began in Congress in the late spring 1991, not only among various segments of the banking and financial community, but also among the regulatory agencies themselves. By November 1991, it became clear that Congress could not agree on giving banks broader service powers or simplifying the regulatory structure and that a much simpler, stripped-down banking

and property claims arising from hurricanes, tornadoes, earthquakes, and other natural disasters, leading eventually to more bank failures. The availability of insurance coverage at thousands of local bank branch offices would also tend to drive local independent insurance agents out of business.

In November 1996, the Comptroller of the Currency announced that U.S. federally chartered banks would be allowed to submit applications to underwrite the offering of new securities, sell some types of insurance, and offer other previously prohibited or restricted services and these service offerings would be permitted following a case-by-case review by that regulatory agency. However, these new services must be offered through separate subsidiaries, with an investment of no more than 10 percent of a national bank's capital committed to each of these new subsidiaries, and any new subsidiaries created must bear a different name and be located in a different facility than the bank itself. Moreover, any loans made by a bank to its subsidiaries must be "at arm's length" and fully collateralized.

Recently several states (e.g., Delaware and Indiana) have allowed the banks they supervise to offer insurance services, and recent court rulings have allowed banks with insurance operations in these states to sell insurance policies nationwide. The U.S. Treasury Department has recommended that well-capitalized banks sell and underwrite life and property/casualty insurance, but the U.S. Congress has, thus far, failed to grant these service powers directly to American banks, though the late 1990s ushered in new proposals from Congress and the Clinton administration to expand banks' insurance activities. Meanwhile, several leading insurance companies, such as Nationwide Mutual and Hartford Financial Services Group, Inc. have begun selling insurance policies through banks (with bank employees often taking customer orders) in an effort to take advantage of bankers' superior customer distribution networks.

U.S. banks have also sought federal and state permission to offer another insurance product—*annuities,* a type of savings instrument into which a customer pools his or her funds until some future date when he or she will receive a stream of income until death occurs. Recently the Comptroller of the Currency approved of national banks acting as agents for life insurance companies selling annuities to the public, though legal appeals of this decision are expected.

bill was the only one likely to pass. Faced with predictions from the General Accounting Office that expected claims against the FDIC would render the deposit insurance fund insolvent by the end of 1991, the Senate and House banking committees hastily drafted a plan to give the FDIC broader authority to raise new money.

The FDIC Improvement Act (1991).   On November 27, 1991, Congress passed a banking bill known as the **Federal Deposit Insurance Corporation Improvement Act,** which permitted the FDIC to borrow up to $30 billion from the U.S. Treasury, with the loans to be repaid by insurance premiums assessed against banks over the next 15 years. The FDIC was also authorized to borrow up to $45 billion more in working capital against its assets and to repay these borrowings by selling the assets of failed banks.

Congress ordered the bank regulatory agencies to develop a new measurement scale for describing how well capitalized each bank and thrift institution is and to take "prompt corrective action" when a depository institution's capital begins to weaken, using such steps as slowing bank growth, prohibiting the payment of stockholder dividends or employee bonuses, restricting the interest rates offered depositors, requiring the owners to raise additional capital, or replacing management. If steps such as these do not solve the problem, the government can seize a bank whose ratio of tangible capital to total risk-adjusted assets falls to 2 percent or below and sell it to a healthy bank, thus wiping out the investments of the troubled institution's stockholders.

Under the new law, regulators have to examine all banks over $100 million in assets on site at least once a year; for smaller banks, on-site examinations had to take place at least every 18 months. In a move toward "reregulating" the banking industry—bringing it under tighter control—federal banking agencies were required to develop new standards for the banks they regulate regarding loan documentation, internal management controls, management information systems, growth in real estate loans, interest-rate risk exposure, and salaries and benefits paid to bank employees and make sure that banks are not violating these new guidelines. At the same time, in reaction to the debacle of the huge Bank of Credit and Commerce International (BCCI) of Luxembourg in the early 1990s, which allegedly laundered drug money and illegally tried to secure control of U.S. banks without regulatory approval, Congress ordered foreign banks to seek approval from the Federal Reserve Board before opening or closing any U.S. offices. They must also apply for FDIC insurance coverage if they wish to accept domestic deposits under $100,000. Moreover, foreign bank offices in the U.S. can be closed if their home countries do not adequately supervise their activities.

After 1994, the FDIC was restricted from fully reimbursing uninsured and foreign depositors if their banks fail, and the Federal Reserve was restrained from propping up failing banks with long-term loans unless the Fed, the FDIC, and the current presidential administration agree that all the depositors of a particular bank should be protected in order to avoid damage to public confidence in the financial system. Congress's intent was to bring the force of "market discipline" to bear on banks that have taken on too much risk (i.e., customers choosing to avoid problem banks) and encourage problem banks to solve their own problems without government help.

In an interesting final twist, Congress ordered the FDIC to undertake a study of the feasibility of having private insurers backstop the federal insurance fund's losses. The FDIC was told to develop a demonstration project in which selected private insurance companies would cover a small percentage (no more than 10 percent) of the FDIC's losses when an insured depository institution fails or receives government assistance, with the FDIC paying premiums to the private companies that provide this coverage.[5]

---

[5]Several other significant provisions of the FDIC Improvement Act were passed to regulate the selling of bank deposits. Federal deposit insurance on personal retirement accounts will henceforth be limited to a combined *total* of $100,000 per customer per bank, instead of granting coverage up to a full $100,000 for every account that a depositor may own jointly with others as now applies to nonretirement deposits. Later, in August of 1993 the FDIC's hand in protecting its scarce insurance reserves was further strengthened when the U.S. Congress passed the National Depositor Preference Law, permitting the FDIC to place insured depositors and the FDIC itself ahead of other creditors in recovering funds from a failed bank.

Bank Management in Action

Banks Expand Their Security Brokerage Activities

Many banks, especially the largest money center institutions, have recently moved to provide *security brokerage* services—that is, offer to execute customer orders to buy or sell stocks, bonds, and other financial instruments. The customer usually can place an order for securities either by visiting the bank's branch offices, via computer, or by telephone. Today some banks offer *full-service security brokerage,* in which they not only execute a customer's order to buy or sell stocks and bonds but also give out investment advice to their customers. More common are *discount brokerage services* in which the bank or its affiliated firms agree to execute customer orders for a low transactions charge, but provide no investment advice to help the customer decide which securities to trade.

On the surface, at least, security brokerage services appear to have conferred several benefits upon those banks choosing to offer them: (*a*) raising fee income for banks who pass on or execute customer orders—income that formerly would have flowed to a security broker or dealer; (*b*) helping to retain customer deposits that otherwise might have gone to a nonbank financial institution offering the customer a broader range of services; and (*c*) attracting new customers who are seeking in one stop a financial-service firm offering a wide selection of services. On the negative side, however, many banks have discovered that these securities services are costly to provide and often generate more expense than revenue because they appeal to a relatively narrow group of customers.

According to Federal Reserve Board regulations, brokerage services may be offered through a securities affiliate of the bank with bank employees taking customer trading orders or via a joint venture with a securities firm who may place brokers in bank branch offices or lease space inside bank buildings. Moreover, in recent years banks and securities firms entering into joint ventures have been permitted by bank regulators to cross-sell each other's services to customers.

Legislation Aimed at Allowing Interstate Banking.   Unfortunately, the FDIC Improvement Act of 1991 left most of the proposals for reform of the bank regulatory system untouched. U.S. banks were granted *no* new service powers, such as permission to sell insurance policies or underwrite corporate stocks and bonds, and Congress simply ignored the issue of interstate banking. In order to cross state lines and take deposits, most U.S. banks had to form holding companies and purchase banks in other states as affiliates of holding companies. This forced an expansion-minded banking organization to form several different companies with costly duplication of capital and management.

The Riegle-Neal Interstate Banking Law (1994).   In an effort to reduce the cost of duplicating banking companies and personnel in order to cross state lines and to provide more convenient services to the estimated 60 million Americans who cross state lines every day, both houses of Congress voted in August 1994 to approve two new banking-related bills—the **Riegle-Neal Interstate Banking and Branching Efficiency Act** and the **Riegle Community Development and Regulatory Improvement Act**—which were both signed into law by President Bill Clinton in September 1994. These two new laws contain dozens of provisions in three areas: (1) interstate banking, (2) regulatory relief, and (3) community development. A few of their most notable provisions include:

• Bank holding companies could acquire banks anywhere in the United States beginning in September 1995. However, no banking firm can acquire another if the resulting institution would control at least 30 percent of the insured deposits in a single state or as much as 10 percent of nationwide insured deposits.

• Interstate bank holding companies could consolidate their affiliated banks acquired across state lines into branch offices as early as June 1, 1997, unless a state acted to outlaw this branching activity. Branch offices established across state lines to take deposits from the public must create an adequate volume of loans to support their local communities.

• Smaller, well-managed banks (up to $250 million in assets) need only be examined once every 18 months rather than every year and most banks will have to report fewer large currency transactions (originally set up to stop illegal money laundering) to the U.S. Treasury Department. Federal banking agencies must eliminate outmoded regulations within two years and set up an appeals system for bankers who feel that regulatory decisions are unfair.

• A Community Development Financial Institutions Fund is established in Washington, D.C., to provide funding and technical support to banks and other community organizations acting to promote local economic development in depressed communities and neighborhoods. The creation and growth of small businesses will be supported by the development of a resale market for small business loans; banks can invest in securities issued against pools of small business loans.

Thus, for the first time in U.S. history, these new banking laws gave a wide spectrum of American banks the power to take deposits and follow their customers across state lines.[6] While banking convenience will undoubtedly be enhanced for some customers, some industry analysts fear that these new laws will increase the consolidation of the industry into larger banks and threaten the survival of many smaller banks. We will return to these issues in Chapter 3.

---

[6]U.S. banks still face restrictions on their branching activity even in the wake of passage of the Riegle-Neal Interstate Banking Act. In contrast, banks in other industrialized countries generally do not face regulatory barriers to creating new branch offices, though some countries (such as Canada and the European Community) either restrict foreign banks' branching into their territory (in the case of Canada) or reserve the right to treat foreign banks differently if they choose. Within the European Community (EC) itself, however, EC-based banks may offer any services throughout the EC that are permitted by each bank's home country. Moreover, each home country must regulate and supervise its own banks no matter where they operate in Europe (a principle of regulation referred to as "mutual recognition"). Banks chartered by an EC member nation receive, in effect, a single banking license to operate wherever they wish inside the EC. However, because EC countries do differ slightly in the activities each country allows its banks to engage in, some "regulatory arbitrage" may exist in which banks and other financial-service firms migrate to those areas inside Europe that permit the greatest span of activities and the fewest restrictions on bank operations and expansion.

Impact of Deregulation on Bank Performance

Changes in banking law and regulation in recent years have had a variety of effects on banks and the customers they serve. While there is still considerable debate about the pros and cons of U.S. banking deregulation and about how much more deregulation the industry needs, a consensus is emerging among industry analysts on what changes deregulation has brought to banking and to financial service markets thus far. The following are considered the most important effects:

1. The composition of deposits held by most banks has definitely shifted toward more expensive customer accounts. That is, the average real cost over all deposits has probably been raised because more deposits bear explicit interest rates closely linked to current market conditions, rather than government-controlled interest rates.

2. Several forms of bank risk have probably increased, especially interest rate risk and the risk of bank failure. With deposit rates more closely linked to interest rates in the open market, fluctuations in market interest rates are affecting a greater proportion of incoming bank funds. Banks are more exposed to and more quickly affected by changes in economic and financial conditions and are less sheltered from the consequences of their managements' mistakes.

3. Rising operating costs, especially on deposits, land, and operating equipment, have encouraged banks to save money in other ways, such as by reducing personnel expenses and overhead costs and substituting automation for full-service, fully staffed branch offices.

4. Rising operating costs have encouraged banks to be more aggressive in increasing their revenues. Many formerly free services now carry explicit fees; there is greater emphasis on charging customers who use particular bank services for the full cost of those services, and most banks are searching for new services that can generate more fee income to offset their costs and build profits.

5. Finally, customers appear to have benefited from deregulation in the form of higher interest returns on their deposits that more closely reflect market conditions and more new service options.

Key Issues Unresolved by Recent U.S. Banking Legislation

As impressive as the deregulation movement has been over the past decade, recent legislation has left major areas of banking under a heavy burden of regulation or simply left many important issues unresolved. For example, *regulatory simplification,* proposed by the U.S. Treasury in 1991 and recommended again by the Clinton Administration in 1993, 1994, and 1996, remains an important and completely unsolved issue. The basic idea is that each banking firm and thrift institution would be supervised by *one* principal federal regulatory agency, rather than having to report to several different agencies, which drives up bank costs. Under the federal proposals of the early 1990s, the FDIC and the Federal Reserve would have their bank regulatory roles sharply reduced, while a new superagency within the U.S. Treasury Department would

Bankers' Insights and Issues

Interstate Banking Rules under the Riegle-Neal Interstate Banking and Branching Efficiency Act of 1994

After years of debate and delay the U.S. House of Representatives on August 4, 1994, and the U.S. Senate on September 13, 1994, passed a new law repealing provisions of the Glass-Steagall, McFadden-Pepper, and Bank Holding Company Acts. Designated the Riegle-Neal Interstate Banking and Branching Efficiency Act, the new law allowed bank holding companies operating in the United States to expand across state lines by acquiring full-service banking firms even if individual states objected and, eventually, to set up a national branching system unless individual states passed contrary laws. This new law—the Riegle-Neal Interstate Banking and Branching Efficiency Act—finally achieved passage after years of debate largely because bankers were not demanding broader new service powers (like insurance underwriting or real estate brokering) at the same time. Moreover, millions of bank customers were crossing state boundaries every day to work, school, and shopping, so that interstate banking privileges seemed to promise more customer convenience, greater competition, and lower bank organizational costs. President Bill Clinton added his signature to the Riegle-Neal bill on September 29, 1994, as the 193rd U.S. Congress drew to a close.

The Riegle-Neal interstate banking law is extremely complicated, including several key elements:

• Bank holding companies that have both adequate capital and are judged by regulators to be adequately managed can acquire control of a bank or bank holding company anywhere in U.S. territory one year after the Riegle-Neal bill was signed into law on September 29, 1994.

• Individual states cannot outlaw bank holding company acquisitions of their banks except they can protect any *new* banks chartered within their territory from out-of-state acquirers for up to five years. However, no banking company can control more than 10 percent of all insured deposits nationwide or more than 30 percent of insured deposits in a single state (though an individual state can erase the 30-percent limit if it wishes to do so or vote in another desired limit and the statewide deposit limit does *not* apply to the first acquisition in a given state or to mergers among banks already affiliated with each other).

• Any bank subsidiary of a holding company can act as *agent* for an interstate banking company, receiving and renewing deposits and closing and servicing loans, and cannot be declared to be a branch office subject to state and federal restrictions. Thus, customers can access their accounts across state lines through bank affiliates without needing regulatory approval. Therefore, bank holding companies can offer a number of key interstate

take over the supervision and examination of banks and thrift institutions, which eventually would have a common charter, common insurance fund, and comparable regulatory rules. Some of these proposals, which seem to promise greater regulatory efficiency, have been bitterly opposed by both the FDIC and the Federal Reserve. The Federal Reserve, in particular, fears that loss of a supervisory role over individual

services without setting up branch offices by simply using their current affiliated banks in distant states as "agents" for their banking affiliates located in other states.

• Bank holding companies can convert their banks acquired in different states into branch offices beginning no later than June 1, 1997, if the holding companies proposing to do so are adequately managed and adequately capitalized and the host state where the proposed branches are located did not act to prevent ("opt out" of) interstate branching on or before June 1997.

• Individual states could "opt in" (allow) interstate branching earlier than June 1997 (which states like Connecticut, Delaware, Maryland, Nevada, North Carolina, Oregon, Pennsylvania, Rhode Island, Utah, and Tennessee did, while Texas voted to "opt out" of interstate branching for a time). However, a state choosing to "opt out" of interstate branching would automatically deny its own banks the power to participate in interstate mergers.

• While most of the interstate branching activity expected in the first few years of the interstate movement was expected to be simple conversions of out-of-state affiliated banks into branch offices of a bank in a holding company's home state, the Riegle-Neal law also allows a federally insured bank to branch *de novo* into a state where it currently has no branch offices provided state law specifically approves the setting up of new branches owned by out-of-state banking firms. Moreover, the states entered by new branch offices of out-of-state banking companies can levy taxes against those offices. One offsetting advantage, however, is that national or state deposit share limits do not apply to *de novo* branches, and once a single *de novo* branch is allowed into a given state, additional branching or merger activity in that state becomes legal.

• No banking company can establish branch offices across state lines merely for the purpose of gathering up new deposits. Interstate-owned branch offices must adequately support their local communities with loans or they can be closed down (indeed, each branch's ratio of loans to deposits must be at least half the value of the average loan-deposit ratio inside the state entered). Moreover, no banking company can cross state lines with full-service offices if it has an unacceptable record (as determined by regulators) of service to all segments of its local communities or if the entry into another state would violate that state's antitrust laws.

• A bank holding company can buy selected branch offices of a banking firm located in another state (instead of having to purchase the whole banking firm) provided the state to be entered approves the proposed transaction.

• Foreign banks can branch in the United States under the same rules as domestic banks.

• While the Riegle-Neal Interstate Banking Act grants the federal government priority over state governments in reshaping the future structure of American banking, federal regulators must ask for public input before preempting any state laws. Moreover, state laws apply to the interstate activities of federally chartered depository institutions. Any bank branching into another state must follow the laws of that state applying to branching activity, customer service without discrimination, tax levies, and antitrust laws.

banks threatens its ability to control inflation. The opposition of these federal agencies is so strong that regulatory simplification may not take place for many years.

Under current federal law, banks cannot offer a full line of insurance services under their own name, broker real estate, or freely underwrite corporate securities without rigid controls unless the laws in a particular state extend these service powers

Bankers' Insights and Issues

The Proposed Financial Services Competitiveness Act

In 1997, Congressman Jim Leach (R-Iowa) introduced a bill that would repeal banking legislation from the 1930s (most notably, portions of the 1933 Glass-Steagall Act) separating banking from nonbank thrift institutions and from the securities and insurance industries. Instead, banks would be allowed to merge with insurance companies and securities firms. Moreover, banks and federally chartered nonbank thrifts would be forced to conform to the same operating rules, and thrift charters would be eliminated in favor of bank charters for all federally chartered depository institutions. The Bank Insurance Fund and Savings Association Insurance Fund would be merged into one insurance pool managed by the FDIC. Any securities firms affiliated with banks would be supervised by the Securities and Exchange Commission (SEC), while insurance affiliates would fall under the scrutiny of state insurance commissions.

Other members of the U.S. Congress have proposed expanding banking activities to include at least some nonfinancial activities—for example, aligning banks with manufacturing, communications, utilities, or transportation firms. However, even the proponents of these banking-commerce alliances would place limits on the cross ownership of banks and nonfinancial businesses. For example, one congresswoman would limit banks' nonfinancial revenues to no more than one-fourth of their total revenues from all activities. The administration of President Bill Clinton has proposed allowing banks to affiliate with any nonfinancial firms except for the biggest 1,000 U.S. nonfinancial companies. Another proposal calls for limiting banks' nonfinancial business activities to perhaps no more than 5 to 10 percent of all their revenues. New types of financial services such as real estate investments could be added if approved by the Federal Reserve Board. Congressman Leach's bill calls for the creation of so-called wholesale banks that could affiliate with nonfinancial businesses. However, these proposed wholesale banks would not have their deposits covered by federal insurance.

Proponents of these proposed new laws see benefits for consumers in more service options and increased efficiency in utilizing scarce resources, thus providing financial

to the banks chartered there. In 1997 and 1998, Congress debated the proposed Financial Services Competitiveness Act (H. R. 10) and related bills that would lift the barriers to U.S. banks, securities firms, and insurance companies acquiring each other and allow these financial-service firms to venture into nonfinancial industries and derive at least a limited portion of their revenues (perhaps 5 to 10 percent) from these nonfinancial activities. The proposed new law would set up new Financial Services Holding Companies (FSHCs), allowing affiliations among different kinds of businesses, one of which could be a depository institution. Provided suitable firewalls are erected to protect federally insured deposits, each FSHC could acquire control of a securities underwriter and broker and an insurance company affiliate. While banks that are part of these new holding companies would continue to be regulated and supervised by

services at lower cost. Opponents of the proposed new legislation fear greater concentration of power in the hands of a few companies that might come to dominate both financial-services and nonfinancial industries. Proponents counter that the financial marketplace worldwide is moving in this direction with all financial firms offering similar products and that U.S. banks will be hurt if they cannot compete on equal terms with better diversified foreign financial-service firms.

In contrast to the United States, most other industrialized nations place no restrictions on bank involvement in the securities markets (including banks engaging in underwriting, dealing, and brokering securities, and selling shares in mutual funds) and on banks underwriting and selling insurance (including acting as agent and as principal in underwriting and selling insurance services). The United States, Japan, Canada, Italy, and Sweden generally place tight restrictions on banks buying nonfinancial companies (whether the purchase of nonfinancial firms is to be made by banks themselves or by companies affiliated with banks). These countries also limit by law and regulation nonfinancial companies investing in banking corporations. However, most other industrialized countries have reduced or eliminated the walls separating banks from nonbank firms. The United States (along with Japan) is particularly strict about keeping high walls between bank and nonbank companies and, thus far, has resisted a worldwide trend toward "universal banks" (such as those in Germany), which offer securities underwriting and trading, insurance underwriting and sales, and real estate brokerage all under one roof. Indeed, the United States seems to be moving in a somewhat different direction than the European community, which has recently moved to liberalize its financial regulations and create still more universal banks. Indeed, in most industrialized countries other than the United States banks can offer security and insurance-based products and activities through banks themselves or through bank subsidiaries without having to create separate affiliated companies to carry on these activities. (Generally, bank subsidiaries in the United States are limited to those activities banks themselves can engage in.) Some economists would argue that the relatively stricter rules under which U.S. banks must operate lead to unfair competition for American banks and a less-than-efficient distribution of financial resources around the globe.

banking agencies, securities affiliates would be regulated by the Securities and Exchange Commission and insurance affiliates would fall under the supervision of state insurance commissions. However, this proposed new law is highly controversial and appears to have several powerful groups opposed to its passage. In effect, the fundamental questions—What is a bank? and What should banks be allowed to do?—remain partly unanswered in the United States and in many other countries as well.

One of the most pressing areas for regulatory reform is in international banking. Leading banks from Japan, the United States, Great Britain, France, Germany, Canada, Switzerland, and other industrialized nations have spread their offices and service activities around the globe. Nations must cooperate, however, in order for international banking regulation to be effective. Otherwise, banks will tend to gravitate toward those national

Bankers' Insights and Issues

The Notorious BCCI Case

One of the most notorious bank failures in history occurred in 1991 when the Bank of Credit and Commerce International, S.A. (hereafter, BCCI) collapsed as the result of a massive investigation by banking and legal authorities in the United States, Great Britain, and several other nations. BCCI was based in Luxembourg, where its controlling holding company was located. Because Luxembourg exercised little regulatory control over holding companies, BCCI was able to expand worldwide from its Luxembourg base with few limits and establish bank offices in numerous countries around the world. Investigators found evidence of massive fraud (including misappropriation of funds, unrecorded deposits, and the creation of fictitious accounts to conceal the bank's losses) among its banking affiliates in Europe and the United States.

BCCI's fraudulent and deceptive activities came to light when it financed several individuals to secretly acquire voting shares in selected U.S. banks (beginning in 1981) through its holding-company affiliate, Credit and Commerce American Holdings, N.V., which was created to acquire First American Banks (with offices in Virginia, Maryland, New York, Tennessee, and Washington, D.C.), the Independence Bank in California, and the National Bank of Georgia. These secret acquisitions violated American law which requires an application for approval to the Federal Reserve Board before a U.S. bank can be acquired.

As part of an agreement reached between BCCI, its principal owners, and the Federal Reserve Board, the U.S. Department of Justice, and New York City's District Attorney, BCCI agreed to forfeit its U.S. assets to the United States government, half of which were to be liquidated to compensate injured depositors. BCCI also agreed to divest itself of any ownership interests in U.S. banks. The Federal Reserve Board levied multimillion-dollar civil money penalties against BCCI itself and several of its officials. Recently Abu Dhabi, a major shareholder in BCCI, agreed to hand over crucial BCCI documents to U.S. authorities and to allow certain senior BCCI staff members to be transported to the United States for trial.

In November 1991 the U.S. Congress moved to head off future BCCI-type scandals by bringing foreign bank operations in the United States under closer domestic regulatory control, empowering the Federal Reserve to approve or deny the creation of new foreign bank offices in the United States, and authorizing the Fed to close the U.S. offices of any foreign banks not adequately supervised by regulators in their home country.

systems with the loosest rules, resulting in increased risk of bank crime and collapse (as illustrated, for example, by the criminal indictments surrounding the financial collapse of the Bank of Credit and Commerce International in 1991 [see the adjacent box]).

In Western Europe, as the consolidated European Economic Community comes closer to full reality, consideration is being given to requiring a bank's home country to be responsible for losses to its depositors, no matter where around the globe those losses occur. A major step toward cooperative international banking regulation was taken in 1987 with an agreement among leading industrialized nations to impose common capital requirements on their banks (discussed later in detail in Chapter 15). However, more cooperation and exchange of information across a broad front are needed if the international banking system is to achieve reasonable stability. Among the most pressing areas where international regulatory cooperation is a must are the control of criminal banking activities, insider access to bank resources, loan quality and risk exposure, the correct pricing of government guarantees behind bank deposits, and the private ownership of banks.

Are Any *Bank Regulations Really Necessary?*

A great debate is raging today about whether any of the remaining regulations affecting commercial banks are really necessary. Perhaps, as banking expert George Benston [1] suggests, "It is time we recognize that financial institutions are simply businesses with only a few special features that require regulation." He contends that depository institutions should be regulated no differently from any other corporation with no tax subsidies or other special privileges. Why? Benston argues that the historical reasons for banking regulation—taxation of banks as monopolies in supplying money, prevention of centralized power, preservation of bank solvency to mitigate the impact of bank failures on the economy, and the pursuit of social goals (such as ensuring an adequate supply of banking services, supporting housing for families, and preventing discrimination and unfair dealing)—are no longer relevant today. Moreover, these regulations are *not* free—they impose real costs in the form of taxes on money users, production inefficiencies, and reduced competition.

Concept Checks

2–10. How does the FDIC deal with bank failures?

2–11. What services and functions of U.S. banks have been deregulated in recent years?

2–12. What changes have occurred in U.S. banks' authority to cross state lines?

2–13. How has the increase in bank failures influenced recent banking legislation?

2–14. What are the most important elements in recent banking reform proposals?

Benston and others contend that restrictions on bank branching, chartering, and services offered make little sense in today's marketplace because modern communications technology allows buyers and sellers of financial services to trade over vast distances. Moreover, there is as yet little evidence of significant economies of scale in banking, so banking is *not* a natural monopoly. Small banks need not fear being driven out of business by large banks if they are willing to compete aggressively.

Moreover, bank failures and other threats to bank safety often arise from the very regulations that are designed to promote bank safety—for example, restrictions against offering certain services, which limit a bank's ability to diversify its operations and generate more revenue.

In addition, deposit insurance has made most bank runs a relic of history. And history suggests that, in most cases, losses to depositors due to bank failures are relatively small—often less than those associated with nonbank businesses that fail. To eliminate completely the possibility of bank failure also eliminates the benefits of discipline from the marketplace of bank behavior, especially risk taking, and unnecessarily restricts the appearance of new competitors to whom the customers of a failing bank can go to secure the services they need. In summary, there is a trend underway today all over the globe to free banking from the rigid boundaries of regulation; however, much still remains to be done if we wish to bring the benefits of free competition to banks and the public they serve.

The Central Banking System: Its Impact on the Decisions and Policies of Individual Banks

No discussion of banks and their regulators would be complete without a discussion of the policy decisions and activities of the *central banks* around the world, including the central bank of the United States—the Federal Reserve System (the Fed). Like all central banks around the globe, the Fed probably has more impact on the day-to-day activities of banks than any other government agency. A central bank's primary job is to carry out **monetary policy,** which involves making sure that the banking and financial system functions smoothly and that the supply of money and credit from that system contributes to the nation's economic goals. By controlling the growth of money and credit (including the loans and security investments made by banks), the Fed and other central banks around the globe try to ensure that the economy grows at an adequate rate, unemployment is kept as low as possible, inflation is held down, and the value of the dollar in international markets is protected.

In the United States the Fed is relatively free to pursue these goals because it does *not* depend on the government for its funding. Instead, the Fed raises its own funds from sales of its services and from securities trading, and it passes along most of its earnings (after making small additions to its capital and paying dividends to member banks holding Federal Reserve bank stock) to the U.S. Treasury. Switzerland and Germany also have relatively free and independent central banks that have been quite successful in holding inflation in check. In contrast, central banks in Japan, the United Kingdom, France, Italy, Spain, and other countries appear to be under closer government control, and these nations have experienced generally higher inflation rates and other economic problems in recent years. Though the matter is still hotly disputed, recent research studies (e.g., Pollard [12] and Walsh [13]) suggest that more independent central banks have been able to come closer to their nation's long-run economic goals (particularly inflation control) due to less political pressure.

Organizational Structure of the Federal Reserve System

To carry out these important objectives, the Fed has evolved into a large and complex quasi-governmental bureaucracy with many divisions and responsibilities. (See Exhibit 2–1.) The center of authority and decision making within the Federal Reserve System is the **Board of Governors** in Washington, D.C. By law, this governing body must contain no more than seven persons, each selected by the president of the United States and confirmed by the U.S. Senate for terms not exceeding 14 years. The board chairman and vice chairman are appointed by the president from among the seven board members, each for four-year terms. The board regulates and supervises the activities of the 12 district Reserve banks and their branch offices. It sets reserve requirements on deposits held by banks and other depository institutions, approves all changes in the discount rates posted by the 12 Reserve banks, and takes the lead within the system in determining open market policy to affect interest rates and the growth of money and bank credit.

The Federal Reserve Board members make up a majority of the voting members of the **Federal Open Market Committee (FOMC)**. The other voting members are

EXHIBIT 2–1

Organization Chart for the Federal Reserve System

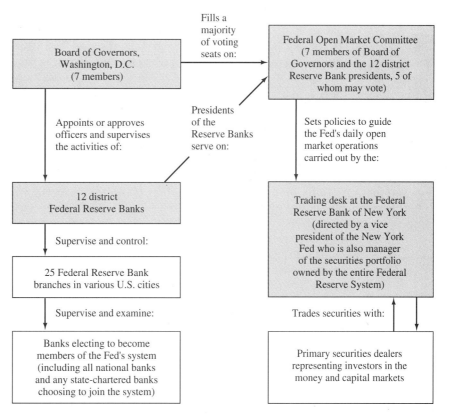

5 of the 12 Federal Reserve bank presidents, who each serve one year in filling the five official voting seats on the FOMC (except for the president of the New York Federal Reserve Bank, who is a permanent voting member). While the FOMC's specific task is to set policies that guide the conduct of **open market operations**—the buying and selling of securities by the Federal Reserve banks—this body actually looks at the whole range of Fed policies and actions to influence the economy and banking system.

The Federal Reserve System is divided into 12 districts, with a **Federal Reserve Bank** chartered in each district to supervise and serve member banks. Among the key services the Federal Reserve banks offer to depository institutions in their districts are (1) wire transfers of funds between banks and other depository institutions, (2) safekeeping of securities owned by banks and their customers, (3) issuing new securities from the U.S. Treasury and selected other federal agencies, (4) making short-term loans to banks and other depository institutions through the "Discount Window" in each Federal Reserve bank, (5) maintaining and dispensing supplies of currency and coin, (6) clearing and collecting checks and other cash items moving between cities, and (7) providing information to keep bankers and the public informed about regulatory changes and other developments affecting the welfare of their institutions.

All banks chartered by the Comptroller of the Currency (national banks) and those few state banks willing to conform to the Fed's supervision and regulation are designated **member banks.** Member institutions must purchase stock (up to 6 percent of their paid-in capital and surplus) in the district Reserve bank and submit to comprehensive examinations of their operations by Fed staff. There are few unique privileges stemming from being a member bank of the Federal Reserve System, because Fed services are also available on the same terms to other depository institutions keeping reserve deposits at the Fed. Many bankers believe, however, that belonging to the system carries prestige and the aura of added safety, which helps member banks attract and hold large deposits.

The Central Bank's Principal Task—Making and Implementing Monetary Policy

A central bank's principal function is to create and conduct money and credit policy in order to promote sustainable growth in the economy, avoid severe inflation, and achieve the nation's other economic goals. To pursue these important objectives, most central banks use a variety of tools to affect the *legal reserves of the banking system,* the *interest rates charged on loans* made in the financial system, and relative *currency values* in the global foreign exchange markets.

By definition, *legal reserves* consist of bank-held assets that qualify in meeting the reserve requirements imposed on an individual bank by central banking authorities. In the United States legal reserves consist of cash banks keep in their vaults and the deposits these institutions hold in their legal reserve accounts at the district Federal Reserve banks. Each of the Fed's policy tools also affects the level and rate of change of interest rates. The Fed drives interest rates higher when it wants to reduce lending and borrowing in the economy and slow down the pace of economic activity; on the other hand, it lowers interest rates when it wishes to stimulate business and consumer borrowing. Central banks also can influence the demand for their home nation's currency by varying the level of interest rates and by altering the pace of domestic economic activity.

To influence the behavior of legal reserves, interest rates, and currency values, the Fed employs three main tools—open market operations, the discount rate, and legal reserve requirements on various bank liabilities. The policy tools used by other central banks vary. For example, the Bank of England uses open market operations in the form of purchases of short-term government and commercial bills and makes discount loans. The Bank of Japan conducts open market purchases and sales primarily in commercial bills, notes, and deposits and sets its discount rate on the loans it grants to banks that need to borrow reserves. The Swiss National Bank conducts open market operations in the currency markets (employing U.S. dollar-Swiss franc swaps), while Germany's Bundesbank trades security repurchase agreements and sets its preferred interest (discount and Lombard) rates on short-term loans. In contrast, the Bank of Canada uses both open market operations and daily transfers of government deposits between private banks and the central bank in order to influence credit conditions. The fundamental point is that while different tools are used by different central banks, nearly all focus upon the reserves of the banking system, interest rates, and, to some extent, currency prices as key operating targets to help achieve each nation's most cherished economic goals.

The Open Market Policy Tool.   In the United States purchases and sales of securities—in most cases, direct obligations (bills, bonds, and notes) of the U.S. government—that are designed to move bank reserves and interest rates toward desired levels are called open market operations (OMO). OMO is considered the Fed's most flexible policy tool because (*a*) this tool can be used every day (and sometimes more than once on any given day), and (*b*) if the Fed makes a mistake, it can quickly reverse itself through an offsetting buy or sell transaction.

All purchases and sales of securities take place via the Trading Desk located inside the Federal Reserve Bank of New York in Manhattan's financial district. The Trading Desk manager and staff meet each morning to review conditions in the financial markets and recent developments in the economy and decide whether to buy or sell selected securities. These trades are made only with approved (primary) government securities dealers. The desk manager and staff select those securities offered by dealers that carry the best prices. Trading is concluded when payment is made in federal funds to the dealer's bank when the Fed is *buying* securities, or when the dealer's bank transfers funds to the Fed when the Fed is *selling* securities, as shown in Exhibit 2–2.

Central bank *sales* of securities tend to *decrease* the growth of bank deposits and loans. When the Fed sells U.S. government securities, the dealers purchasing those securities authorize the Fed to deduct the dollar amount of the purchase from the reserve accounts dealers' banks hold at a district Federal Reserve bank. Banks have less raw material for making loans and extending other types of credit. In contrast, central bank *purchases* of securities tend to *increase* the growth of bank deposits and loans. The Federal Reserve pays for its purchases of U.S. government securities simply by crediting the reserve deposits of the dealers' banks that are held at the district Federal Reserve banks. This means that the banks and dealers involved in the transaction have the proceeds of the securities' sale immediately available for their use.

Today the Federal Reserve targets the *federal funds interest rate* attached to overnight loans of reserves between banks. If the Fed wishes to nudge the federal funds rate higher to discourage some borrowing and spending, it will usually *sell* securities in the open market, reducing the reserves banks have available to generate new loans and forcing banks to borrow more reserves, which tends to drive up market interest rates and slow the economy. On the other hand, if the Fed wishes to push interest rates down in order to stimulate borrowing and spending in the economy, it will usually *buy* securities in the open market, expanding the reserves banks have available to generate new loans and relieving banks of some of the pressure to borrow more reserves in the federal funds market, which tends to lower prevailing interest rates and stimulate the economy.

The Discount Rate Policy Tool.   Most central banks are an important source of short-term funds for banks and other depository institutions, especially the largest banks, which tend to borrow frequently to replenish their legal reserves. Most U.S. banks place signed borrowing authorizations at the Federal Reserve bank in their district for this purpose. As Exhibit 2–3 shows, when the Fed loans reserves to borrowing banks the supply of legal reserves expands temporarily, which may cause bank loans and deposits to expand. Later, when the discount window loans are repaid, the borrowing banks lose reserves and may be forced to curtail the growth of their deposits and loans.

The loan rate charged by the Fed—the *discount rate*—is set by each Reserve bank's board of directors (though any changes in this basic rate must also be approved by the Federal Reserve Board). Most discount window loans are for short-term adjustment credit or for seasonal credit to meet temporary shortages of reserves and usually

EXHIBIT 2–2

Federal Reserve Open Market Operations

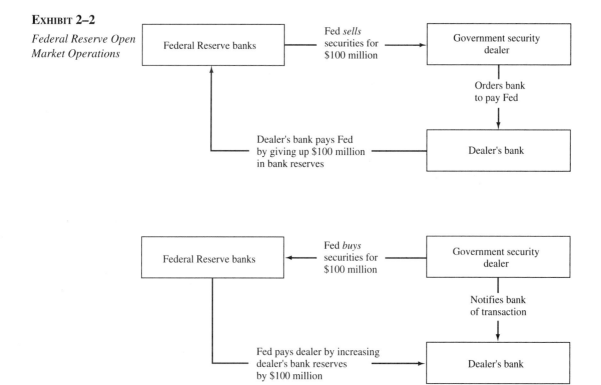

last only a few days. Longer-term credit, stretching over a month or more, is designed to aid banks facing longer-term liquidity shortages and carries a higher discount rate.

By *raising* the discount rate, the Fed makes new loans from the discount window more costly. This discourages some banks from borrowing reserves, which may lead to slower growth in bank credit. *Lowering* the discount rate, on the other hand, acts to stimulate bank borrowing from the Fed. Banks may become more liberal in making credit available to their customers. Changes in the discount rate seem to affect *other* interest rates in the financial system, generally pushing them in the same direction as the move in the discount rate. Finally, changing the discount rate seems to have a psychological "announcement effect," bringing on investor expectations of higher or lower interest rates.

Changing Reserve Requirements on Deposits and Other Bank Liabilities.   Banks and other depository institutions selling transaction deposits (such as checking accounts) must place a small percentage of each dollar of those deposits in reserve, either in the form of vault cash or in a deposit at the regional Federal Reserve bank. Selected other bank sources of funds, such as time deposits sold to businesses and institutions and Eurodollar deposits borrowed from abroad, are also subject to reserve requirements set by the Board of Governors of the Federal Reserve System, but at present only checkable (transaction) deposits carry reserve requirements.

Changes in the percentage of deposits and other bank funds sources that must be held in reserve can have a potent impact on bank credit expansion. Raising reserve requirements, for example, means that banks must set aside more of each incoming dollar of deposits into required reserves, and less money is available to support the making of new loans. Moreover, a higher required reserve tends to increase interest rates because banks have fewer reserves available that can be used to make loans. Lowering reserve requirements, on the other hand, releases reserves for additional bank lending. Interest rates also tend to decline because banks have more funds to loan.

Even though the Fed is empowered to do so, it rarely changes the percentage of deposits and other reservable liabilities that must be held in reserve form. Experience has shown that any such move can set in motion substantial changes in bank credit availability and interest rates. The Fed usually prefers to use open market operations and the discount rate to change credit policy and economic conditions. We should note that there is

EXHIBIT 2-3

Bank Borrowing from the Fed's Discount Window

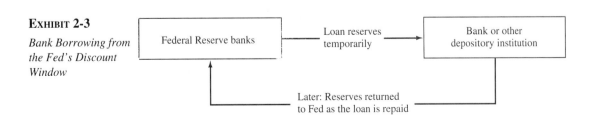

a trend around the globe to eliminate legally imposed bank reserve requirements (as exemplified, for example, by recent central bank action in Canada and Switzerland).

Other Fed Policy Tools.   Two other policy tools the Federal Reserve uses to influence the economy and bank behavior are *moral suasion* and *margin requirements*. Through moral suasion, the Fed tries to bring psychological pressure to bear on individuals and institutions to conform to the Fed's policies, using telephone calls or letters to bankers, making speeches explaining the Fed's policies, and testifying before Congress to explain what the Fed is doing and to clarify its objectives. Bankers tend to pay close attention to a letter or phone call from central bank officials out of concern that tougher regulations may be on the way.

A second and rarely used tool is control over margin requirements on the public's purchases of stocks and bonds. An investor buying certain listed securities must use his or her own funds to cover a specified percentage of the securities' purchase price; the rest of that price may be borrowed, using the purchased securities as collateral. Since 1974, margin requirements in the United States applying to selected convertible bonds and stocks and short sales of those securities have stood at 50 percent, which means that investors purchasing those securities must pay half the purchase price from their own funds and may borrow the remaining 50 percent against the securities' market value. The Federal Reserve Board does not change these cash-purchase requirements often, reflecting the general impression that margin requirements are ineffective as a monetary policy tool.

Congress and the Treasury: Two Other Key Factors Affecting Banks and Their Management Decisions

The Federal Reserve is *not* the only arm of government bankers need to watch carefully for its impact on the economy and financial system. The legislative branch of government and the Treasury make vital decisions every day regarding government revenues, government expenditures, and tax policy that affect bank profitability, risk, and growth.

In the United States, *Congress* decides how much will be spent on government programs and what taxes and other sources of funds will be drawn upon to support public spending programs. For many years, Congress relied heavily upon the U.S. Treasury's ability to borrow funds in the money and capital markets in order to fund programs when tax revenues come up short, resulting in a persistent federal government budget deficit and a substantial rise in the public debt of the United States relative to the U.S. gross national product (GNP). By the late 1990s, however, the U.S. federal budget appeared to be approaching a surplus for the first time since the 1960s, sharply reducing the federal government's borrowing needs. Moreover, commercial banks have purchased a growing proportion of these debt obligations to help offset risk in their lending programs and provide additional liquidity to meet future loan demand and deposit withdrawals.

What impact do changes in government spending, taxes, budget deficits, and borrowing—often called **fiscal policy**—have upon banks and other institutions operating in the financial markets? In general, the following effects usually result from government fiscal operations:

1. Increases in government spending usually lead to increases in business and household incomes, which increase both bank deposit and loan demand, eventually accelerating the pace of economic activity—and perhaps inflation as well.

2. When increases in government spending must be financed by added government borrowing, the tendency is to push interest rates higher as government credit demands are added to private credit demands, placing banks under increased pressure to meet all of their customers' funding needs. Moreover, additional government borrowing and spending tend to increase aggregate demand for goods and services in the economy, which also tends to increase bank deposits and loans. In the short run, they may generate increased inflation, reducing the real value of bank assets, revenues, and net earnings.

3. Decisions by Congress to raise taxes and reduce budget deficits normally lead to decreases in Treasury borrowing and eventually push interest rates lower. Private-sector incomes, bank deposits, and loan demand are also likely to fall. The economy usually grows more slowly and unemployment may rise. During such periods, there is usually less risk of inflation, which holds interest rates down and may lead to an interest rate decline, lowering the cost of bank funds but also reducing bank revenues from loans and other services affected by movements in interest rates.

Clearly, bankers must be aware of the likely impact of fiscal policy actions, of the Treasury's current funding operations and projected borrowing needs, and of the Federal Reserve's likely response to these and other developments in the economic system. No banker can ignore the effects of these background factors in making sound borrowing and lending decisions, for they directly affect the value of bank assets, liabilities, and equity capital and the magnitude of bank revenue flows and expenses.

Concept Checks

2–15. What is *monetary policy*?

2–16. What services does the Federal Reserve provide to banks?

2–17. How does the Federal Reserve affect the banking system through open market operations? Suppose the Fed purchases $500 million in government securities from a security dealer. What will happen to the level of bank reserves and by how much will they change? If the Federal Reserve imposes a 10 percent reserve requirement on deposits and there are no other leakages from the banking system, by how much will deposits and loans change as a result of the Fed's purchase of securities?

2–18. How may changes in reserve requirements and the discount rate affect a bank's operations? If the Fed loans banks $200 million in reserves from the discount windows of the Federal Reserve banks, by how much will the legal reserves of the banking system change? What happens when these loans are repaid by the borrowing banks?

2–19. What impact do government spending and budget deficits have on interest rates, bank loans, and deposits?

Summary

What banks and other financial institutions can do within the financial system is closely monitored by *regulation.* Moreover, banks are among the most heavily regulated of all financial institutions in an effort to protect the public's savings, control the growth of money and credit, promote public confidence in the banking and financial system, and provide the public adequate financial information and credit without discrimination. Important banking laws limit whether and where banks can branch, the formation of holding companies, and proposed mergers. The quality of bank loans and the adequacy of bank capital are subject to regulation and periodic examination by federal and state regulatory authorities. Banks cannot enter or leave the industry without regulatory approval.

Government deregulation of banking gained powerful momentum in the United States in the 1970s and 1980s and in Canada, Great Britain, Japan, and other countries during the 1980s and 1990s. Banks were permitted to offer deposits paying market interest rates, and nonbank thrift institutions were authorized to offer services fully competitive with bank services. However, more probably needs to be done in allowing banks to enter related service lines if they are to compete effectively in tomorrow's financial-services industry.

The policy decisions and activities of central banks have a powerful impact on banks and their ability to serve the public. The Fed's *monetary policy* activities affect the value of bank assets, liabilities, and net worth, and they shape the volume of bank revenues and expenses. The key decision-making body within the Fed is the Board of Governors, which has control over the Fed's key policy tools—open market operations, the discount rate, and reserve requirements. These tools are used by the Fed to push bank reserves, interest rates, and the growth of money and credit in the economy toward levels the central bank thinks will contribute the most toward society's primary economic goals: high employment, low inflation, and sustainable economic growth. Bankers have learned that they must pay close attention to monetary policy decisions and actions of the central bank, as well as to the spending, taxing, and borrowing decisions of the Treasury department. All have profound effects on the successful pursuit of individual bank goals and the continued viability of banking institutions.

Key Terms in This Chapter

Dual banking system
State banking commissions
Comptroller of the Currency
Federal Reserve System
McFadden-Pepper Act
Glass-Steagall Act
Federal Deposit Insurance Corporation
Bank Holding Company Act
Bank Merger Act
Depository Institutions
    Deregulation and Monetary Control Act
Garn–St Germain Depository Institutions Act
Competitive Equality in Banking Act
Financial Institutions Reform, Recovery, and
    Enforcement Act

Federal Deposit Insurance Corporation
    Improvement Act
Riegle-Neal Interstate Banking and Branching
    Efficiency Act
Riegle Community Development and Regulatory
    Improvement Act
Monetary policy
Board of Governors
Federal Open Market Committee (FOMC)
Open market operations (OMO)
Federal Reserve Bank
Member bank
Fiscal policy

Problems and Projects

1. For each of the actions described, explain which government agency or agencies a banker must deal with and what banking laws are involved:
   a. Chartering a new bank.
   b. Establishing new branch offices.
   c. Forming a bank holding company.
   d. Completing a merger.
   e. Making holding company acquisitions.

2. See if you can develop a good case for and against the regulation of banking in the following areas:
   a. Restrictions on the number of new banks allowed to enter the industry each year.
   b. Restrictions on which banks are eligible for government-sponsored deposit insurance.
   c. Restrictions on the ability of banking firms to underwrite debt and equity securities issued by their business customers.
   d. Restrictions on the geographic expansion of banks (e.g., limits on branching and holding company acquisitions across county, state, and international borders).
   e. Regulations on the bank failure process, defining when banks are to be allowed to fail and how their assets are to be liquidated.

3. Consider the issue of whether or not the government should provide a system of deposit insurance. Should it be wholly or partly subsidized by the taxpayers? What portion of the cost should be borne by banks? by the depositors? Should riskier banks pay higher deposit insurance premiums? Explain how you would determine exactly how big an insurance premium each bank should pay each year.

4. The Trading Desk at the Federal Reserve Bank of New York elects to sell $100 million in U.S. government securities to its list of primary dealers. If other factors are held constant, what will happen to the supply of legal reserves available to banks? to deposits and loans? to interest rates?

   Suppose the Fed made $100 million available to the banking system by lending banks that amount through the discount windows of the Federal Reserve banks. Would this decision affect the banking system differently from purchasing $100 million in securities from dealers? Please explain.

5. Suppose the Federal Reserve's discount rate is 7 percent. This afternoon the Federal Reserve Board announces that it is approving the request of several of its Reserve banks to raise their discount rates to 7.5 percent. What will happen to other interest rates (particularly money market interest rates) tomorrow morning? Carefully explain the reasoning behind your answer.

   Would the impact of the discount rate change described above be somewhat different if:
   a. Loan demand at banks was increasing or decreasing?
   b. There existed a large or a very small spread between prevailing money market rates (especially the Federal funds rate) and the Fed's discount rate?
   c. The Fed simultaneously *sold* $100 million in securities through its Trading Desk at the New York Fed? What if it *purchased* $100 million in securities instead?

6. Discuss the probable effects upon (*a*) bank deposit growth, (*b*) loan demand, and (*c*) bank net income if the federal government announces an increase in aggregate government spending. What if that additional spending is financed entirely by Treasury borrowing?

Selected References

See the following for a good discussion of the reasons for and against the regulation of banking:

1. Benston, George G. "Federal Regulation of Banks: Analysis and Policy Recommendations." *Journal of Bank Research,* Winter 1983, pp. 216–44.
2. Crockett, J. "The Good Bank/Bad Bank Restructuring of Financial Institutions." *The Bankers Magazine,* November/December 1988, pp. 32–36.
3. Kane, Edward J. "Metamorphosis in Financial-Services Delivery and Production." In *Strategic Planning of Economic and Technological Change in the Federal Savings and Loan,* Federal Home Loan Bank Board, San Francisco, 1983, pp. 49–64.
4. Kareken, John H. "Deposit Insurance Reform: Or Deregulation Is the Cart, Not the Horse." *Quarterly Review,* Federal Reserve Bank of Minneapolis, Winter 1990, pp. 3-11.
5. Peltzman, Samuel. "Toward a More General Theory of Regulation." *Journal of Law and Economics,* August 1976, pp. 211–40.
6. Rose, Peter S. *Banking Across State Lines: Public and Private Consequences.* Westport, Conn.: Quorum Books, 1997.
7. Spong, Kenneth. *Banking Regulation: Its Purposes, Implementation and Effects.* Federal Reserve Bank of Kansas City, 1994.
8. Stigler, George J. "The Theory of Economic Regulation." *The Bell Journal of Economics and Management Science* II (1971), pp. 3–21.

9. Gande, Amar, Manju Puvi, Anthony Saunders, and Ingo Walter. "Bank Underwriting of Debt Securities: Modern Evidence." *The Review of Financial Studies* 10, No. 4 (Winter 1997), pp. 1175–202.

For an overview of the consequences and controversy surrounding the Glass-Steagall Act, see the following:

10. Haberman, Gary. "Capital Requirements of Commercial and Investment Banks: Contrast in Regulation." *Quarterly Review,* Federal Reserve Bank of New York, Autumn 1987, pp. 1–10.

For a discussion of the methods and procedures of monetary policy, see the following:

11. Heller, H. Robert. "The Monetary Policymaking Process." Speech by a Member of the Board of Governors before the Money Marketeers, New York City, April 11, 1989.
12. Pollard, Patricia S. "Central Bank Independence and Economic Performance." *Review,* Federal Reserve Bank of St. Louis, July/August 1993, pp. 21–36.
13. Walsh, Carl E. "Is There a Cost to Having An Independent Central Bank?" *FRBSF Weekly Letter,* Federal Reserve Bank of San Francisco, February 4, 1994, pp. 1-3.
14. Rose, Peter S. *Money and Capital Markets: Financial Institutions and Instruments in a Global Marketplace,* 6th ed. Burr Ridge, IL: Irwin, 1997.

3   THE ORGANIZATION AND STRUCTURE OF BANKS AND THEIR INDUSTRY

Learning and Management Decision Objectives

The goals of this chapter are to explore the different types of organizations used in the banking industry, to see how each organizational type affects bank behavior and service to the public, and to determine how management's choice of a particular kind of banking organization can affect profits, risks, and operating efficiency.

Introduction

Chapter 1 explored the many roles performed and the services offered by the modern bank. In that chapter we viewed banks as providers of credit, channels for making payments, repositories of the public's savings, managers of business and household cash balances, trustees of customer property, providers of insurance coverage in some instances, and brokers charged with carrying out purchases and sales of securities and other assets on behalf of their customers. Over the years, bankers have evolved different **organizational forms** to perform these various roles and to supply the services their customers demand.

Truly, organizational form follows function, for banks usually are organized to carry out the roles assigned to them as efficiently as possible. Because larger banks generally play a wider range of roles and offer more services, bank size is also a significant factor in determining how banks are organized. However, a bank's roles and size are not the only determinants of how it is organized or how well it performs. Government regulation, too, has played a major role in shaping the performance and diversity of banking organizations that operate around the globe.

Organization Chart for a Typical Bank

Most banks in the United States are very small by world standards. As Exhibit 3–1 shows, just about 65 percent of all U.S. banking organizations (about, 6,200 banks) hold total assets of less than $100 million apiece. Yet the American banking industry also contains some of the largest banking organizations on the planet. For example, Citicorp of New York holds sufficient assets to place it among the 20 largest financial institutions in the world. And, by some measures at least, banking in the United States is becoming increasingly concentrated in the largest firms. For example, in 1996 the 100 largest U.S. banking organizations held about three-fifths of industrywide domestic deposits, compared to slightly less than half of all domestic deposits as recently as 1980. However, in local towns and cities the concentration of deposits seems to have changed little, on average, in recent years. The great differences in bank size across the United States have led to greater differences in the way banks are organized and in the types and variety of financial services each bank offers in the markets that it serves.

EXHIBIT 3–1 *Asset Size Categories for U.S. Commercial Banking Organizations (asset totals for all FDIC-insured U.S. banks as of December 31, 1996)*

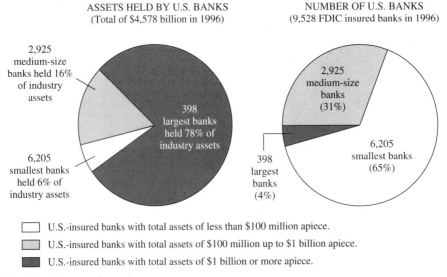

Source: Federal Deposit Insurance Corporation

Differences between Large and Small Banks' Organization Charts

The influence of bank *size* upon internal organization can be seen most directly by looking at the typical organization chart for large versus small banks. The first example is an organization chart supplied by the management of a small suburban bank of about $100 million in assets located in the Midwest (see Exhibit 3–2). Like hundreds of banks serving small and medium-size communities, this bank is heavily committed to attracting smaller, consumer-oriented deposits and making consumer installment and small business loans. A bank like this, with heavy involvement in consumer loans and deposits, is often called a *retail bank,* as opposed to a *wholesale institution* (like J. P. Morgan and Bankers Trust in New York) which concentrates mainly upon serving commercial customers and making large corporate loans.

The service operations of a small bank are usually monitored by a cashier and auditor working in the accounting division and by vice presidents heading up the bank's loan, fund-raising, marketing, and trust departments. These officers report to the senior executives of the firm, consisting of the board chairman, the president (who usually runs the bank from day to day), and senior vice presidents, who are responsible for long-range planning and for assisting heads of the various departments in solving their most pressing problems. Senior management, in turn, reports periodically (at least once each month) to members of the **board of directors**—the committee selected by the **stockholders** (owners) to set policy and oversee the bank's performance.

EXHIBIT 3–2
Organization Chart for a Small Community Bank

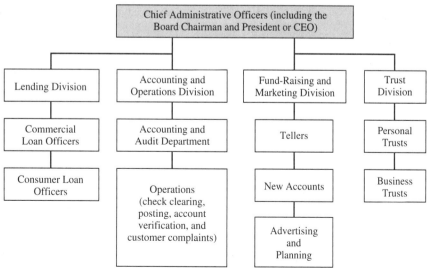

The organization chart in Exhibit 3–2 is not complicated. There is often close contact between top management and the management and staff of each division. If smaller banks have serious problems, they usually center on trying to find competent new managers to replace aging administrators and struggling to afford the cost of new electronic and automated equipment. Also, smaller banks are usually heavily affected by changes in the health of the local economy. For example, many are closely tied to agriculture or to the strength of other local businesses, so when local business sales are depressed, the bank experiences slower growth and its deposits, loans, and earnings may fall. Such banks often present a relatively low risk working environment, but one with limited opportunities for rapid advancement or for the development of new banking skills. Nevertheless, banks of this size and location often represent attractive employment opportunities because they place the banker close to his or her customers and give bank employees the opportunity to see how their activities, especially the granting of loans, can have a real impact on the quality of life in local communities.

The organization chart of a large money center bank is much more complex than that of a small bank. A fairly typical organization chart from an eastern U.S. bank with about $10 billion in assets is shown in Exhibit 3–3. This bank is owned and controlled by a holding company whose stockholders elect a board of directors to oversee the bank and nonbank firms allied with the same holding company. Selected members of the holding company's board of directors serve on the bank's board as well. The key problem in such an organization is *span of control:* top management is often knowledgeable about banking practices but less well informed about the products and services offered by subsidiary companies. Moreover, because the bank itself offers so many different services in both domestic and foreign markets, serious problems may not surface for weeks or months. In recent years, a number of the largest banks have moved toward the profit-center approach, in which each major department strives to maximize its contribution to the bank's profitability and closely monitors its own performance.

The largest banks possess some advantages over small and medium-size banks. Because the largest institutions serve many different markets with many different services, they are better diversified—both geographically and by product line—to withstand the risks of a fluctuating economy. These institutions are rarely dependent on the economic fortunes of a single industry or, in many cases, even a single nation. For example, such banks as Citicorp and Chase Manhattan often receive more than half of their net earnings from sources outside the United States. They also possess the important advantage of being able to raise financial capital at relatively low cost. As interstate banking spreads across the nation, these banks are well situated because of their greater capacity to accept the risks of entering new markets and greater access to capital and managerial talent.

Recent Trends in Bank Organization

The tendency in recent years has been for most banking institutions to become *more complex* organizations over time. When a bank begins to grow, it usually adds new services and new facilities. With them come new departments and divisions to help management more effectively focus and control the bank's resources.

EXHIBIT 3–3

Organization Chart for a Money Center Bank Serving International Business Markets

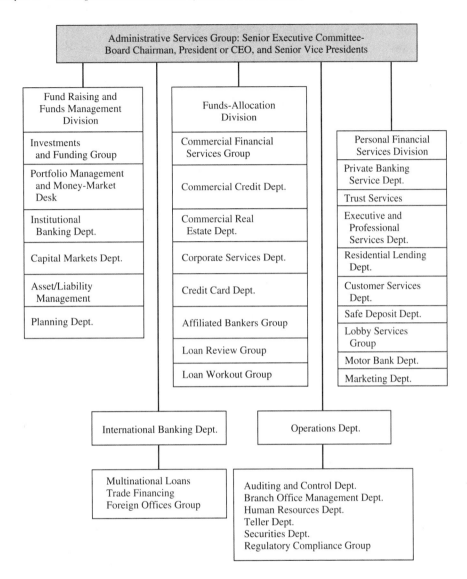

Another significant factor influencing banking organizations today is the *changing makeup of the skills bankers need to function effectively and efficiently as market conditions and technology change.* For example, with the global spread of government deregulation and the resultant increase in the number of competitors banks face in their major markets, more and more banking firms have become *market driven* and *sales oriented*—more alert to the changing service demands of their customers and also to the challenges posed by bank and nonbank competitors. This trend has forced bank managers to become more concerned with service marketing activities and the reactions of their stockholders.

These newer activities require the appointment of bank management and staff who can devote more time to surveying customer service needs, developing new services based upon those customer surveys and modifying old service offerings to reflect changing customer needs. Similarly, as the technology of financial-services production and delivery has shifted more and more in recent years toward computer-based systems and electronic service delivery, banks have needed growing numbers of people with computer skills and the electronic equipment they work with. At the same time, automated bookkeeping has reduced the time managers spend in routine operations, thus allowing greater opportunity for planning new services and new service-delivery facilities.

Concept Checks

3–1. Describe the typical organization of both a small bank and a large bank. What does each major division or administrative unit do?

3–2. What trends have affected the way banks are organized today?

The Array of Organizational Structures in Banking

Whatever financial services a banking organization offers to the public, it must make them available through one or more *office facilities*—physical locations from which bank personnel and equipment sell and make services available to the public. These offices may be placed under the control of either a single banking corporation or multiple corporations linked to each other through a common group of stockholders.

Getting a New Charter

However, before any services can be offered the bank must have a *charter of incorporation.* Where can a bank secure a charter to get its business off and running? In the United States, from one of two places—through a formal application submitted either (*a*) to the banking commission of the state where the bank is to be headquartered in order to form a *state-chartered bank* or (*b*) to the Administrator of National Banks (the Comptroller of the Currency), who is empowered to issue a certificate of association for a *national bank.* (See Chapter 21 for a more detailed discussion of the bank charter process.)

If a national bank is chartered, it must also join the Federal Reserve System and secure a certificate of approval for deposit insurance from the Federal Deposit Insurance Corporation. However, a state-chartered bank is not obligated to join the Federal Reserve System and apply for federal deposit insurance, though the overwhelming majority of banks do seek deposit insurance in order to win public confidence. In fact, most states today require insurance certification before they will grant a charter. Even so, the majority of U.S. banks have *not* joined the Federal Reserve System due to its tougher regulations. (See Exhibit 3–4 for a breakdown of the major types of U.S. banks and their relative importance within the U.S. banking system.)

Getting a federal or state bank charter is only the beginning. The organizers must select management for the bank and, jointly with management, decide such matters as the number of offices needed, types of physical and electronic facilities desired, and the preferred form of corporate organization. Moreover, these decisions must conform to the requirements of government legislation and regulation, as well as the demands of the market area each bank serves. We will see in the discussion that follows that banks around the world generally have moved toward larger organizations with many branch offices or automated service units, toward the formation of holding companies, and toward expansion across state and national boundaries to find greater opportunities for profit.

Unit Banking Organizations

Unit banks—one of the oldest kinds of banking—offer all of their services from *one office,* though a small number of services (such as taking deposits or cashing checks) may be offered from limited-service facilities, such as drive-in windows, automated teller machines, and retail store point-of-sale terminals that are linked to the bank's computer system (see Exhibit 3–5). These organizations are very common in U.S. banking today. For example, in 1996 just over 3,200 of the nation's banks—about one-third—operated out of just one full-service office, compared to about 6,200 banks with one or more branch offices.

One reason for the comparatively large number of unit banks is the rapid formation of *new banks,* even in an age of electronic banking and megamergers among industry leaders. Many customers still seem to prefer small banks, which get to know their customers well and often provide personalized service. Between 1980 and 1996 close to 4,000 new banks were chartered in the United States (about 250 per year, on average), substantially more than the average number of failing banks each year, as Table 3–1 shows.

Most new banks start out as unit organizations, in part because their capital, management, and staff are severely limited until the bank can grow and attract additional resources and professional staff. Moreover, until recently a handful of states completely outlawed full-service branches. Today the majority of states permit statewide establishment of branch offices. Despite the economic and legal barriers to establishing branch offices that still exist in some places, most banks desire to create multiple-office facilities to open up new market areas and diversify geographically in order to reduce the risk that comes from relying on a single office location for customers and income.

Concept Checks

3–3.   What are unit banks and unit banking states?

3–4.   What advantages might a unit bank have over banks of other types? What disadvantages?

EXHIBIT 3–4

U.S. Banks with Federal and State Charters, Membership in the Federal Reserve System, and Deposit Insurance from the Federal Government (as of December 31, 1996)

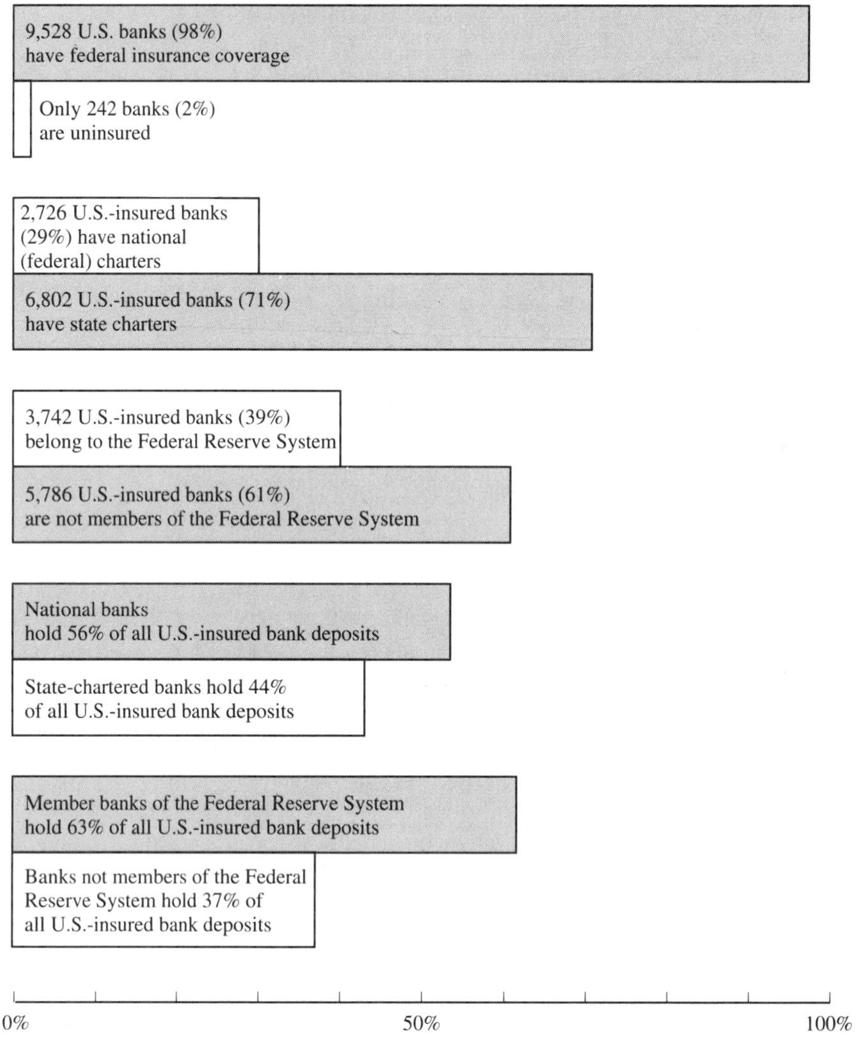

9,528 U.S. banks (98%) have federal insurance coverage

Only 242 banks (2%) are uninsured

2,726 U.S.-insured banks (29%) have national (federal) charters

6,802 U.S.-insured banks (71%) have state charters

3,742 U.S.-insured banks (39%) belong to the Federal Reserve System

5,786 U.S.-insured banks (61%) are not members of the Federal Reserve System

National banks hold 56% of all U.S.-insured bank deposits

State-chartered banks hold 44% of all U.S.-insured bank deposits

Member banks of the Federal Reserve System hold 63% of all U.S.-insured bank deposits

Banks not members of the Federal Reserve System hold 37% of all U.S.-insured bank deposits

0%   50%   100%

Note: Deposit percentages are as of December 21, 1996.

Source: Board of Governors of the Federal Reserve System and Federal Deposit Insurance Corporation.

EXHIBIT 3–5
The Unit Banking Organization

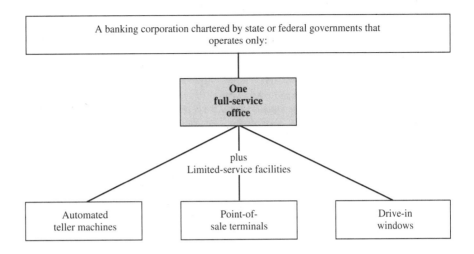

TABLE 3–1   Entry and Exit in U.S. Banking, 1980–1996

Year	Newly Chartered Banks	Failures of FDIC- Insured Banks	Number of Mergers and Acquisitions*	Large (billion-dollar-plus) Mergers and Acquisitions**	Bank Branches Opened and Closed	
					Opened	Closed
1980	267	10	188	0	2,397	287
1981	286	10	359	1	2,326	364
1982	378	42	422	2	1,666	443
1983	419	48	432	6	1,320	567
1984	489	79	553	14	1,405	889
1985	346	120	553	7	1,480	617
1986	283	145	625	20	1,387	763
1987	217	203	710	21	1,117	960
1988	234	221	569	18	1,676	1,082
1989	204	207	388	9	1,825	758
1990	165	169	442	20	2,987	926
1991	106	127	345	23	2,788	1,456
1992	94	122	401	25	1,677	1,313
1993	71	42	436	15	1,499	1,215
1994	66	13	446	15	2,461	1,146
1995	125	6	345	20	2,367	1,319
1996	146	5	312	26	2,487	1,870
Totals for entire period	3,896	1,569	7,526	242	32,865	15,975

*The number of mergers and acquisitions reflects the number of different transactions where some mergers and acquisitions encompass more than one bank.
**The term *large merger or acquisition* includes only those transactions in which both the acquirer and the acquired organization hold total deposits over $1 billion and do not include acquisitions of thrifts or failing banks.

Sources: John P. LaWare, member, Board of Governors of the Federal Reserve System, testimony before the Subcommittee on Financial Institutions Supervision, Regulation, and Deposit Insurance of the Committee on Banking, Finance, and Urban Affairs, U.S. House of Representatives, June 22, 1993; Federal Deposit Insurance Corporation, *Statistics on Banking,* various years; Dr. Stephen A. Rhoades, "Mergers and Acquisitions by Commercial Banks, 1960–83," Staff Economic Study No. 42, Federal Reserve Board, January 1985; and annual updates supplied by the author of this study.

Branch Banking Organizations

Where regulations permit, a bank may decide to establish a **branch banking** organization, particularly if it serves a rapidly growing region and finds itself under pressure either to follow its business and household customers as they move into new areas or lose them to more conveniently located competitors. The full range of banking services is offered from several locations, including a head office and one or more full-service branch offices. Such an organization is also likely to offer limited services through a supporting network of drive-in windows, automated teller machines, mini-branches, and point-of-sale terminals in stores and shopping centers (see Exhibit 3–6).

Senior management of a branch banking organization is usually located at the home office, though each full-service branch has its own management team with limited authority to make decisions on customer loan applications and other facets of daily operations. For example, a branch manager may be authorized to approve a customer loan of up to $25,000. Larger loan requests, however, must be referred to the home office for a final decision. Thus, some services and functions in a branch banking organization is highly centralized, while others are decentralized at the branch-office level.

Branching Laws

Most branch banks in the United States are small compared to other banks around the globe. For example, in 1996 there were about 6,200 branch banking organizations in the United States, operating approximately 58,000 full-service branch offices besides their main offices. As Table 3–2 reminds us, while the number of U.S. banks declined over this last half-century from around 14,000 to about 9,000, the number of branch offices has soared from only about 3,000 to almost 60,000. During the 1930s, only one in five banks, on average, had a full-service branch office, but by the 1990s the average U.S. bank operated about six full-service branches. But this is "small potatoes" compared to leading banks in Great Britain and Western Europe, which operate dozens or even hundreds of full-service branch outlets. This wide disparity in national banking structures arises from differences in public attitudes toward branch banking. Early in the history of the United States, there was great fear of the power of branch banks to eliminate competition and charge their customers excessive prices for banking services.

As a result, most states passed laws to limit branching activity to designated areas, such as the city or county of a bank's home office. Unfortunately, this antibranching device may have allowed some banks, freed from the danger of outside entry by other banking organizations, to act as monopolies, raising prices and restricting output. In recent years, however, bank branching has spread rapidly across the United States. Today all 50 states and the District of Columbia permit some form of bank branching.

How well do branch banks perform? Are they more profitable than single-office (unit) banks? Why has branching activity spread widely in recent years? These questions are addressed in the following sections.

Reasons for Branching's Growth.   The causes of the rapid growth in branch banking are many and varied. One factor has been the exodus of population over the past several decades from the cities to suburban communities, forcing many large downtown banks

EXHIBIT 3–6
The Branch Banking Organization

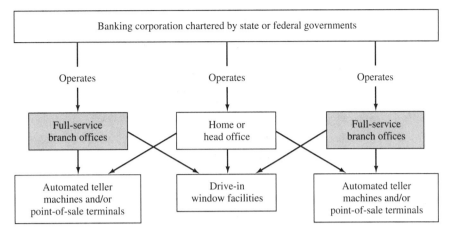

TABLE 3–2   Growth of Banking Offices in U.S. Banking

Year	Number of Bank Home (main) Offices	Number of Branch Offices	Total of All U.S. Bank Offices	Average Number of Branches per U.S. Bank
1934	14,146	2,985	17,131	0.21
1940	13,442	3,489	16,931	0.26
1952	13,439	5,486	18,925	0.41
1964	13,493	14,703	28,196	1.09
1970	13,511	21,810	35,321	1.61
1982*	14,451	39,784	54,235	2.75
1985	14,417	43,347	57,764	3.01
1988	13,137	46,619	59,756	3.55
1993	11,212	53,049	64,261	4.73
1996	9,528	57,788	67,316	6.07

*Beginning in 1982, remote service facilities (ATMs) were *not* included in the count of total branches. At year-end 1981, there were approximately 3,000 remote service facilities.

Source: Federal Deposit Insurance Corporation.

to either follow or lose their most mobile customers. The result has been the expansion of full-service branch offices and automated tellers, radiating out from downtown areas of major cities like the spokes of a wheel, with the leading money center banks at the hub of the branching wheel, along with growing telephone and computer networks to serve distant and more mobile customers. Bank failures have also spawned branching activity as larger, healthier banks have been allowed to take over sick ones and convert them into branch offices. Business growth, too, has fueled the spread of branch banking; the credit needs of rapidly growing corporations necessitate larger and more diversified banks that can reach into many local markets for small deposits and pool those funds into large-volume loans.

However, growth in new full-service branch offices has slowed somewhat in recent years. As Exhibit 3–6 shows, the number of *new* branch offices has averaged about 2,000 per year in recent years, but branch office closings have accelerated to average more than 1,000 per year recently. The sharply higher rate of full-service branch closings in recent years reflects multiple forces. One obvious cause is the skyrocketing costs of land and office facilities in leading cities like New York and Los Angeles. Then, too, automated teller machines (ATMs) and electronic networks have taken over many routine banking transactions, and their cost has declined significantly in recent years with continuing improvements in technology. By the 1990s, there were well over 100,000 ATMs in operation in the continental United States and thousands more in Europe and Asia, while the number of banks offering services via telephone, fax machine, and the Internet continues to expand at a rapid pace.

Advantages and Disadvantages of Branch Banking.   Whether or not banks should be allowed to branch and, if so, over what areas has been one of the most controversial issues in the history of banking. Opponents of full-service branching fear that it drives out smaller competitors (leaving the customer with fewer total sources of banking services), leads to higher service fees, and drains scarce capital away from local communities toward the largest cities, thus slowing local economic development.

Supporters of branch banking, on the other hand, argue that it results in greater operating efficiency, increases the availability and convenience of services to customers because branch banks are large enough to support a full menu of services in each branch office, and stimulates faster economic growth because branch banks tend to make more loans available. They also argue that branching leads to fewer bank failures because a branch bank is less dependent on the volume of business from a single industry or single local market area.

What does recent banking research have to say about these claims for and against branch banking? Branch banking areas do, in most cases, contain significantly smaller numbers of banking firms than states and nations that restrict branching activity, and the concentration of industry assets in a few large banks tends to be much greater in branching areas. For example, Arizona has had statewide branch banking for many years and its four largest banks hold better than 80 percent of statewide assets and deposits. In contrast, Texas, now a statewide branching state, was a unit banking state until 1987 and, as a result, the percentage of industrywide assets and deposits in the four largest Texas banks is only about half the Arizona total. However, this does not necessarily mean that competition is lessened. In fact, areas where branching is allowed greater freedom tend to have more banking offices per unit of population, which helps to reduce their customers' transactions cost. For example, Texas had fewer than 400 branch offices when it moved to allow statewide branching in 1987; today it has more than 2,600 branch offices.

There is no consistent evidence that either branch banks or unit banks charge higher fees for banking services. However, when a large branch banking organization absorbs a smaller bank in a merger, the loan and deposit interest rates and service charges levied by the acquired bank typically are *raised* to meet those of the acquiring institution.[1] Most research studies find little difference in loan rates or deposit interest rates between branch and unit banks, though there is some evidence that branch banks post higher checkbook fees. This may merely reflect a tendency for larger branch banks to be somewhat more knowledgeable concerning their costs and, therefore, less likely to underprice their services.

The argument that branch banks discriminate against local borrowers and drain funds away from local communities, limiting their growth, is difficult to evaluate objectively. In general, market-oriented economies seem to work best when scarce loanable funds flow toward those uses whose expected returns are the greatest for any given level of risk. A banking system that collects and directs capital to those regions and projects offering the highest returns would seem to promote the most efficient use of society's scarce resources. If branch banks facilitate this market allocation process, they perform a valuable service. Moreover, a study by Dunham [20] found that large regional and money center branch banks tended to be net importers, rather than exporters, of funds to their local communities.

Branch banks tend to offer a wider menu of services than unit banks, though part of this net service gain is due to bank size rather than to type of banking organization. But there is no convincing evidence of greater operating efficiency among branch banks as compared to unit banks. In fact, recent research suggests the reverse is often true: *Unit banks usually enjoy lower operating costs than branch banks of comparable size.* Setting up new full-service branches seems to be an especially costly way to grow. Some banking experts believe this conclusion may need to be revised in the future, however, with the continuing spread of computer technology and automation in banking. This development would seem to favor banks with greater resources and technical expertise.[2] Branch banks also have much lower failure rates than banks without full-service branch offices. However, branch banks do not seem to earn higher average profits than other banks.

Neither branch banks nor unit banks seem to have an edge in speeding up the economic development of the areas they serve. There are numerous examples of rapidly developing local communities served by both branch and unit banks.[3] The organizational form adopted by a bank is probably far less important to the economic well-being of communities than such forces as geographic accessibility and location (particularly access to seaports, rail lines, highways, and concentrations of population), the presence of recoverable resources (such as oil, coal, or timber), a favorable climate, and supportive public attitudes toward saving and spending money. However, recent evidence offered by Jayaratne and Strahan [35] suggests that removal of restrictions against branch banking has tended to improve overall bank efficiency, lower loan losses, and decrease loan rates, while local economies tended to grow faster.

---

[1]See, for example, Rose [3], and Kohn and Carlo [14].
[2]See, for example, Hunter and Timme [8] and [9].
[3]See especially Darnell [13].

Concept Checks

3–5.   What is a branch banking organization?

3–6.   What are limited and statewide branching states?

3–7.   What trend in branch banking has been prominent in the United States in recent years?

Bank Holding Company Organizations

In earlier decades when states and other governments prohibited or severely restricted branch banking, the bank holding company often became the most attractive organizational alternative inside the United States and in several other countries as well. A **bank holding company** is simply a corporation chartered for the purpose of holding the stock (equity shares) of at least one bank. Many holding companies hold only a small minority of the outstanding shares of one or more banks, thereby escaping government regulation. However, if a holding company operating in the United States seeks to *control* a bank whose shares it has acquired, it must seek approval from the Federal Reserve Board to become a registered bank holding company. Under the terms of the Bank Holding Company Act of 1956 (as amended in 1970), control is assumed to exist if the holding company acquires 25 percent or more of the outstanding equity shares of at least one bank or can elect at least two directors of at least one bank. Once registered, the company must submit to periodic examinations of its records by the Federal Reserve Board.

Why Holding Companies Have Grown.   The growth of bank holding companies has been very rapid in recent decades, especially during the 1970s and 1980s. As long ago as 1971 these organizations controlled banks holding more than half of U.S. bank deposits. By the 1990s, they controlled about 8,700 banks, accounting for well over 90 percent of the industry's total assets. (A list of the largest U.S. bank holding companies appears in Table 3–3.) The principal reasons for this rapid upsurge in bank holding company activity include their greater ease of access to capital markets in raising funds, their ability to use higher leverage (more debt capital relative to equity capital) than nonaffiliated banking firms, their tax advantages in being able to offset profits from one business with losses generated by other firms that are part of the same company, and their ability to expand across state lines and national boundaries.

One-Bank Holding Companies.   Most registered bank holding companies in the United States are one-bank holding companies. In 1992 there were about 6,400 bank holding companies, and about 5,500 of these owned stock in just *one* bank. However, these one-bank companies frequently owned and operated one or more nonbank businesses as well. Once a holding company registers with the Federal Reserve Board, any nonbank business activities it starts or acquires must first be approved by the Federal Reserve Board or the Federal Reserve banks. These nonbank businesses must offer services "closely related to banking" that also yield "public benefits," such as improved availability of financial services or lower service prices.

TABLE 3–3   The Largest Bank Holding Companies in the United States
(as of December 31, 1996)

	Assets in Billions of Dollars	Number of Affiliated Banks	Number of Branch Offices
The Chase Manhattan Corporation, New York City	$321.8	7	822
Citicorp, New York City	249.2	3	265
NationsBank Corporation, Charlotte	220.9	62	2,596
BankAmerica Corporation, San Francisco	196.5	4	1,888
J. P. Morgan & Company, Inc., New York City	172.6	1	5
First Union Corporation, Charlotte	141.0	11	2,168
Wells Fargo & Company, San Francisco	115.8	6	1,827
Bankers Trust New York Corp.	92.2	4	8
First Chicago NBD Corp.	92.1	6	480
Fleet Financial Group, Inc., Providence	84.2	5	1,427
KeyCorp., Cleveland	67.8	15	1,221
Bank of Boston Corporation	66.4	6	528
Norwest Corporation, Minneapolis	66.2	40	732
PNC Bank Corp., Pittsburgh	65.9	5	812
Wachovia Corporation, Winston-Salem	53.3	4	487
The Bank of New York Company, Inc.	52.3	3	389
National City Corporation, Cleveland	51.1	11	908
H. F. Ahmanson & Co., Irwindale, CA	49.6	1	408
Republic New York Corporation	47.6	3	114
Core States Financial Corp., Philadelphia	44.8	4	607

Sources: Board of Governors of the Federal Reserve System; Federal Deposit Insurance Corporation; and American Bankers Association.

Types of Nonbank Businesses Holding Companies Can Own.   Since 1971, the Federal Reserve Board has developed a list of nonbank businesses that registered bank holding companies are allowed to own and control (see Exhibit 3–4). The most important types have been finance companies, mortgage companies, and data processing firms. Additional nonbank businesses popular with bank holding companies in recent years include leasing companies, security brokerage firms, credit life insurance companies, credit card companies, and management consulting firms. In 1996 The Federal Reserve Board announced that well-capitalized and well-managed bank holding companies would no longer need Fed approval to begin new nonbank businesses in industries already declared permissible for bank holding companies to enter.

Today, the principal advantages for bank holding companies entering nonbank lines of business are (*a*) the ability of the nonbank firms to expand across national and state lines without many of the legal restrictions banks often face; and (*b*) the prospect of diversifying sources of revenue and profits (and, therefore, reducing risk exposure) from service lines that are not perfectly correlated with each other. In the United States few states have ever passed laws limiting holding company acquisitions of nonbank firms within their borders. Indeed, several states have passed laws allowing outside banking organizations to set up affiliated bank or nonbank firms that offer services not permitted to banks or bank holding companies under federal law.

One example is South Dakota, which in the early 1980s voted to allow out-of-state banking organizations to establish credit card and insurance companies as bases from

---

TABLE 3–4   **The Most Important Nonbank Financially-Related Businesses Bank Holding Companies Can Acquire under U.S. Regulations**

Finance Companies
Lend short- and long-term funds to businesses and households

Mortgage Companies
Provide short-term credit to improve real property for residential or commercial use

Data Processing Companies
Provide computer processing services and information transmission

Factoring Companies
Purchase short-term assets (mainly accounts receivable) from businesses in exchange for supplying temporary financing

Insurance Underwriters
Supply life, accident, or health insurance directly related to the granting of credit

Security Brokerage Firms
Execute customer buy and sell orders for marketable securities, foreign exchange, and exchange-traded financial futures and option contracts and provide other full-service brokerage functions

Financial Advising
Advise institutions and high-net-worth individual customers on investing funds, managing assets, mergers, reorganizations, raising capital, and feasibility studies

Security Underwriting Firms
Purchase new U.S. government and general-obligation municipal bonds and (with Federal Reserve Board permission) corporate stock, corporate debt obligations, mortgage-backed securities, consumer-receivable-backed securities, municipal revenue bonds, and selected money market instruments from their issuers and offer these securities for resale to investors

Trust Companies
Manage and protect the property of businesses, individuals, and nonprofit organizations and place customers' securities with private investors

Credit Card Companies
Provide short-term credit to individuals and businesses in order to support retail trade

Leasing Companies
Purchase and lease equipment and other assets to businesses and individuals needing those assets

Insurance Agencies
Sell credit-related or financial-service-related insurance or offer a full menu of insurance agency and brokerage services in communities of 5,000 or fewer people

Real Estate Services
Supply real estate appraisals and arrange for the financing of commercial real estate projects

Savings and Loan Associations
Offer savings deposit plans and housing-related credit, predominantly to individuals and families.

---

which these services could be marketed nationwide without any government-imposed interest-rate ceilings on credit card loans. Because the federal courts have held that the home state of a bank determines what rules it must adhere to in setting loan rates and other terms of trade, South Dakota soon proved to be an attractive target for entry by leading credit card companies (such as the credit card operations of New York's Citicorp). More recently, Alaska and California decided to permit out-of-state banks to engage in consulting and securities activities within their borders.

Multibank Companies.   A minority of bank holding company organizations are **multibank holding companies**. In the 1990s multibank companies numbered just under 900 but controlled about 70 percent of the total assets of all U.S. banking organizations. This form of banking organization appeals especially to bank stockholders and managers who wish to set up multiple bank offices in locations where branching is restricted or where they wish to create an interstate banking organization out of several formerly independent banking firms. (See Table 3–3.) Thus, a multibank holding company may permit greater *geographic diversification* for a banking organization, helping it to stabilize its earnings. One very dramatic effect of holding company expansion and acquisition has been a sharp decline in the number of independently owned banking organizations—a decline proceeding even faster than the recent decrease in the total number of insured U.S. banks.

A bank holding company that wishes to acquire 5 percent or more of the equity shares of an additional bank must seek approval from the Federal Reserve Board and demonstrate that such an acquisition will not significantly damage competition in the local market, will promote public convenience, and better serve the public's need for financial services. Banks acquired by holding companies are referred to as **affiliated banks.** (See Exhibit 3–7.) Banks that are not owned by holding companies are known as *independent banks.*

Advantages and Disadvantages of Holding Company Banking.   Many of the advantages and disadvantages of branch banking are often assumed to apply to holding company banking as well. Thus, holding company banking has been blamed for allegedly reducing or eliminating competition, overcharging the customer, being callously indifferent to local community needs, and taking excessive risks. In contrast, supporters of the holding company movement claim these organizations promote greater efficiency in banking by increasing a banking firm's size and by adding to competitive rivalry in the industry, strengthen individual banks against failure, and offer the public more services more conveniently than independent banks can do.[4]

Research on Holding Company Behavior.   What are we to make of these claims and counterclaims? As with the older branch banking controversy, the facts seem to speak in a far more modest voice than the loud claims of supporters and critics of bank holding companies. For example, if holding companies reduce competition in banking, we might expect this to result in higher profits for holding company banks relative to other

Exhibit 3–7
The Multibank Holding Company

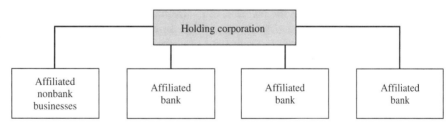

---

[4]The bank holding company form is widely used in the United States as a way around regulatory restrictions against offering certain services and expanding across state lines. The holding company form permits the *de jure* (legal) separation between banks and nonbank businesses having greater risk, yet it allows the same stockholders to control both bank and nonbank firms. Outside the United States, however, the holding company form is usually legal but is not often used (except in the Netherlands and Italy). This is because most industrialized countries other than the United States allow banks themselves to offer more services or permit a bank to set up a subsidiary company under direct bank ownership and sell services not allowed to the bank itself. In addition, most other countries do not place restrictions on banks branching into new territory as the United States often does. In general, the United States demands a more complicated and probably more costly organizational form—the bank holding company—to facilitate bank service and geographic expansion. However, recent court rulings, such as *NationsBank* v. *Variable Annuity Life Insurance Company* in 1995, appear to give regulators such as the Comptroller of the Currency greater authority to allow U.S. banks to expand their services through bank subsidiaries when a new service is sought that is not currently allowed to be sold through banks themselves.

banks. There is, however, little convincing evidence that this has happened. However, several studies suggest that while individual banks may not benefit from acquisition by holding companies, the holding company as a whole tends to be more profitable than banking organizations that do *not* form holding companies.[5] This occurs because of service fees holding companies collect from their affiliated banks and because of the companies' access to long-term capital at lower cost. Moreover, the failure rate for holding company banks is well below that of comparable-size independent banks.

Do holding companies drain scarce capital from some communities and impoverish smaller towns and rural areas? We have no solid evidence on this claim today, though a survey by Leonard M. Apcor and Buck Brown [4] of small towns in Texas suggests the issue may be worth further study. These reporters observed a tendency in some small southwestern cities for local funds to be siphoned away in an effort to shore up the troubled lead banks of major holding companies. The result was less credit available for local community projects and a rise in local business failures. Similarly, in a survey by John Helyon [7], some customers of holding company affiliates in Florida complained about the rapid turnover of bank personnel, the lack of personalized service, and long delays when local branch office managers were forced to refer questions to the home office.

As we saw earlier, bank holding companies have reached outside the banking business in recent years, acquiring or starting finance companies, leasing firms, insurance agencies, and other businesses. Have these nonbank acquisitions paid off? If added profitability was the goal, the results must be described as disappointing. Frequently, acquiring companies have lacked sufficient experience with nonbank products to manage their nonbank firms successfully. However, not all nonbank business ventures of holding companies have been unprofitable. In fact, a study by Nellie Liang and Donald Savage [10] of nearly 300 bank holding companies with nonbank subsidiaries found that the average profitability of the nonbank firms was higher than that of banking firms belonging to the same company, though the nonbank firms also tended to make riskier loans than banks did. Certainly, the attractiveness of nonbank firms as a vehicle for interstate expansion has declined with the spread of full-service interstate banking. Over the past two decades a growing number of bank holding companies have sold off the assets of one or more of their nonbank affiliates.[6]

Concept Checks

3–8. What is a bank holding company?

3–9. When must a holding company register with the Federal Reserve Board?

3–10. What nonbank businesses are bank holding companies permitted to acquire under the law?

3–11. Are there any significant advantages or disadvantages for holding companies from launching nonbank business ventures?

---

[5]See, for example, Rhoades and Savage [26], Varvel [11], and Frieder and Apilado [6].
[6]See especially Whalen [12].

Bank Management in Action

Advantages of the Bank Holding Company Form of Organization

- Greater *geographic diversification* by acquiring or establishing banks in distant markets, including bank acquisitions across state lines.
- Greater *product-line diversification,* allowing banking organizations to offer services that individual banks may be prohibited from offering through a bank itself (such as private security underwriting activities) or that a single bank cannot afford to offer due to the costs and risks involved.
- Greater *tax sheltering* of current income, where a holding company can consolidate the net earnings or losses of its various bank and nonbank affiliated businesses and pay taxes only on the net amount of any positive earnings across the whole organization provided it owns at least 80 percent of these firms.
- Use of *double leveraging,* in which a holding company organization can borrow against the assets of its affiliated businesses as well as against its own assets in order to raise cheap debt capital; this feature may also permit the owners of a bank to refinance their own personal indebtedness that may have been used to buy the bank by drawing upon the holding company's borrowing capacity as well as permit the majority ownership of a banking organization to more easily and more cheaply buy out the interests of its minority shareholders.
- Serve as a *source of strength,* in which the holding company can provide expert advice and supply lower-cost capital to any of its affiliated banks that might be in trouble, shifting funds within the organization to those businesses with the greatest prospects for success or experiencing the greatest problems.

Correspondent Banking

The existence of numerous small banks and so many different kinds of banking organizations has created the need for strong *interbank relationships* so that many financial services can be provided efficiently at the local level. This need for significant interbank relationships became evident early in banking's history, when checks became a popular means of making payments for goods and services. With depositors sending checks out of town to pay for goods produced outside their local area, an interbank check collection system had to be developed so that funds could be transferred from the depositor's bank to the bank receiving the check. Individual banks had to agree on a system for routing and collecting checks that was efficient and profitable for all the banks involved.

A related problem emerged in meeting customer loan requests. As business and industry expanded and large corporations appeared, the need for large loans—often far larger than the capital resources of a single bank—brought groups of banks together to work out *participation loans.* Participations generally involve large-denomination loans extended jointly by two or more banks to a single customer. This practice has been particularly important for smaller banks, because it enables them to continue to serve the credit needs of their largest customers and to spread the risks of large loans across several banks.

These various financial needs gave rise to an extensive system of **correspondent banking** in which banks set up both formal and informal relationships with each other. The banks involved agree to exchange deposits to provide for clearing checks and settling payments made by wire and to compensate each other for any other services rendered, usually by paying fees or by placing more deposits at those banks supplying correspondent services. The smallest banks often keep sizable deposits with larger correspondent banks in the principal cities around the globe, who in turn provide such services as collecting on checks, managing smaller banks' investment portfolios, providing loans to support equipment purchases and the construction of new facilities, and supplying data processing and other electronic recordkeeping and transfer services.

Today the traditional correspondent banking network is shrinking in size and importance. Many smaller banks have been absorbed into larger companies that provide many services internally that once flowed between independent banks linked through the old correspondent network. As interstate banking continues to expand in the United States, there will be less need for independently provided correspondent banking services.

Bankers' Banks

A potential competitor to the correspondent banking system came along in 1982 when the Garn–St Germain Depository Institutions Act was passed. This federal law permitted the development of federally chartered **bankers' banks,** in which groups of banks could set up joint special-service firms to facilitate the development and delivery of certain financial services that normally are too costly for one or a few banks (especially small banks) acting alone. As the 1990s began, there were about 16 bankers' banks in the United States whose stock was collectively owned by more than 155 banks, and about 3,700 banks were using the services offered by these institutions.

Bankers' banks function much like correspondent banks, making loans to banking firms short of cash, clearing checks, and investing in securities for member banks of the system. Recently some bankers' banks have assisted their affiliated banks with credit card operations and begun offering auditing and management consulting services to smaller banks at a cost below what many large correspondent banks charge. Bankers' banks can also invest in export trading companies to help banks expand their activities in foreign markets, create secondary (resale) markets for any loans bankers wish to sell, and operate automated teller networks.

The Garn–St Germain Depository Institutions Act of 1982 made it lawful for national banks to establish or buy the shares of bankers' banks, provided such an investment does not amount to more than 10 percent of a national bank's capital and surplus. Bankers' banks are *not* subject to deposit reserve requirements and generally face lower capital requirements than banks themselves.

Networking

Among the more recent institutions that permit banks to serve each other and communicate are so-called **networking** systems, in which facilities for the movement of funds and financial information are *shared* by groups of banks. The most familiar examples today are networks of automated teller machines (ATMs), such as CIRRUS, PLUS, and EXPRESS CASH, in which customers holding credit and debit cards issued by one bank in the network can carry out financial transactions through any ATM belonging to the same network, no matter which bank owns the particular machine being used. Some network vendors give banks access to several different ATM networks so the customer can interface with multiple systems. The number of ATMs worldwide is now well over half a million and most of these belong to one or more information-transfer networks for greater customer convenience.

A related development is the appearance of *point-of-sale* (POS) *networks,* in which a customer purchasing goods or services from a merchant that is part of such a network can use a *debit card* to pay for those purchases. Insertion of the card in the store's terminal sends electronic signals through the network to verify that the customer has an active account. Then the customer's account at one bank is debited, while the merchant's account at another bank sharing the same network is credited for the amount of the purchase. (See Exhibit 3–8.) Both ATM and POS networks lower payment costs by eliminating paper and generally operate with great speed and accuracy. Eventually electronic purchases and funds transfers through the Internet and the World Wide Web may slow the growth of both ATMs and conventional POS terminals in stores.[7]

EXHIBIT 3–8
A Typical Computer Network Involving POS Terminals and ATMs

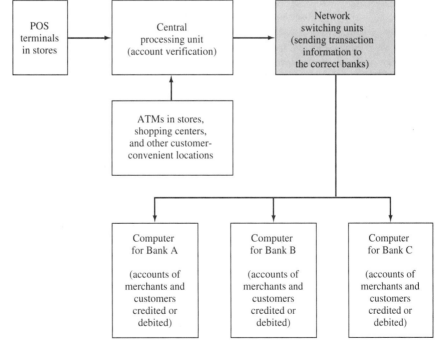

---

[7]See Chapter 21 for a detailed discussion of the services offered by and the growing use of ATMs, POS terminals, and Internet transactions.

Joint Ventures

Still another approach to cooperative service delivery between banks or between banks and nonbank firms is the **joint venture.** Some banks have formed joint subsidiaries with auto manufacturers to lease cars (e.g., Marine Midland Bank of New York and Subaru), with insurance agents to sell life insurance policies (e.g., John Hancock Mutual Life Insurance and Wilbur National Bank of New York), and with security firms to sell bank customers shares in mutual funds and stocks and bonds (e.g., Dreyfus Corporation and Mellon Bank).

Other popular joint ventures have included jointly owned automated teller machines, check printing companies, Internet sites and services, trust companies, and security insurance firms (such as Bond Investors Guarantee Insurance Company, which insures investors against default on municipal bonds). The company entering a joint venture with a bank may set up a shop or a booth in the bank's lobby and pay a rental fee. The bank may allow customers to pay for any services offered jointly with another firm through such devices as automatic deductions from the customers' deposits or by using the bank's credit card to pay. Most banks advertise their joint ventures by notices included with the customer's monthly bank statement through special mail-outs and media advertising as well as the World Wide Web.

Joint ventures are banking's response to such nonbank competitors as security firms, insurance companies, and mutual funds, and are usually launched through bank holding companies. This means the Federal Reserve Board usually must approve or reject the proposed joint undertaking. Banks have found such ventures helpful in sharing risks, particularly the risk of offering new services, and in raising their sales volume high enough to lower operating costs. The key disadvantage of joint ventures appears to be disputes between the partners concerning cost sharing, revenues, the need for new technology, and sales territories.

Concept Checks

3–12. What services do correspondent banks and bankers' banks provide?

3–13. Explain the meaning of *networking.* What are its advantages for the public?

3–14. What are *joint ventures?* What advantages and disadvantages do they offer for bankers?

Interstate Banking and the Riegle-Neal Interstate Banking and Branching Efficiency Act of 1994

Many banking authorities today confidently predict that **full-service interstate banking** will invade every corner of the United States. Indeed, the federal government took a giant step toward this goal when the U.S. Congress passed the Riegle-Neal Interstate Banking and Branching Efficiency Act as a companion to the Riegle Community Development and Regulatory Improvement Act of 1994. As we saw in Chapter 2, these new federal laws allow bank holding companies operating in the United States to acquire banks throughout the nation without needing the states' permission to do so. Beginning June 1, 1997, banking companies could also branch across state lines provided individual states did not vote to "opt out" of interstate branching before the June 1997 deadline, as the state of Texas did, for example. The states can protect new banks from being acquired across state lines for up to five years, and no single banking company can hold more than 10 percent of insured deposits nationwide or more than 30 percent of the insured deposits in a single state (unless a state waives this restriction).

Of course, in the earlier years when they faced tight restrictions against full-service banking across state lines, U.S. bankers had developed several routes around the interstate banking barrier even before the majority of states and the federal government recently voted to allow bank acquisitions across state lines. For example:

1. Acquisition of a failing commercial bank, savings bank, or savings and loan association, permitting the merger of a troubled financial institution with out-of-state banks or bank holding companies.

2. Permission from a state legislature to enter in order to provide selected banking services, such as credit card loans, insurance sales, or brokering real estate, in a given state (e.g., Alaska, Arizona, Delaware, and South Dakota in the 1980s).

3. Edge Act and Agreement corporations, which may be established irrespective of state boundaries provided the majority of their accounts come from international customers.

4. Grandfathered interstate acquisitions, which were made before restrictive laws were passed. For example, a total of 19 U.S. multistate banking organizations beat the passage of federal legislation prohibiting interstate banking decades ago.

5. Loan production offices (LPOs), which cannot take deposits directly but use marketing representatives to gather local loan and deposit business for the bank's headquarters.

6. Nonbank business affiliates, which offer financial services (such as credit and savings plans) that are closely related to banking services but face fewer restrictions.

While these channels of interstate expansion gave many leading banks such as Citicorp, BankAmerica, and Chase Manhattan a nationwide presence, they all faced one significant limitation—most of them did not allow banks to *take deposits* through offices established outside each bank's home state. This is a particularly significant barrier to developing a nationwide consumer banking business, because many households (and smaller businesses) prefer to have a *local* institution hold their checking and savings accounts. Accordingly, many of the nation's leading banks carried out an intense lobbying effort in the 1970s and 1980s within the various state legislatures to amend state laws restricting branching and holding company acquisitions. One by one, in domino fashion, the states fell into line, letting in outside banking firms but subjecting them to a variety of entry conditions.

Bankers' Insights and Issues

Trade Associations in Banking

In addition to formal links between banking organizations, individual banks have also banded together informally through various groups or **trade associations** in order (*a*) to promote the industry's viewpoint with the public and with various legislative and regulatory bodies (especially Congress and the state legislatures) and (*b*) to help educate bankers, especially new employees, on management fundamentals and on the latest economic and regulatory trends affecting the industry. The following are major bankers' associations:

- The American Bankers Association, headquartered in Washington, D.C., with most banks in the industry as members.
- The Association of Bank Holding Companies, also in Washington, D.C., representing more than 100 of the largest U.S. banking organizations.
- The Independent Bankers Association of America, with membership among hundreds of smaller banks not affiliated with holding companies and devoted to preserving the quality of services offered by community-oriented banks.
- Robert Morris Associates, the National Association of Credit Officers, in Philadelphia, aimed at promoting more ethical and better-informed lending practices.
- Bank Administration Institute, in Rolling Meadows, Illinois, organized to develop informational materials to aid banks in improving their performance and planning.
- Consumer Bankers Association, representing banks and thrift institutions with significant banking programs serving household customers.
- Association of Reserve City Bankers, consisting of large banking organizations in principal U.S. money centers.
- Bank Capital Markets Association, containing representatives from banks that have security dealer units.
- Professional Bankers Schools, located in all U.S. regions and designed primarily to train middle-level managers to rise to senior-level bank management positions. Examples include the Stonier Graduate School of Banking and the School of Banking of the South.

New Interstate Legislation.   The first state to pass an interstate banking law was Maine, which amended its state banking code in 1975 to permit out-of-state holding companies to acquire its banks beginning in 1978, provided other states granted Maine's banking organizations similar entry privileges. In 1981, Delaware allowed outside banking organizations to enter and establish new banks, subject to minimum capital and employment requirements, while Illinois moved to permit interstate holding companies already present in that state to acquire additional Illinois banks. In 1982 New York approved of out-of-state banking institutions entering *de novo* or by acquiring existing New York banks provided reciprocal entry privileges were extended to New York's banking organizations. The same year Alaska and Massachusetts passed similar legislation. The federal government made a gesture in the same direction when Congress passed the Garn–St Germain

Bankers' Insights and Issues

Electronic Wire Networks Linking Banks and Other Institutions

Most banking services involve the movement of financial information from one account to another and from one financial institution to another. Financial information can often be transferred most efficiently through electronic wire networks, which span the nation and even link institutions worldwide. The three most widely used electronic wire networks are FEDWIRE, CHIPS, and S.W.I.F.T.

FEDWIRE is an electronic network linking all 12 Federal Reserve Banks, their 25 branch Reserve banks, and those U.S. depository institutions eligible to join the system. This network accounts for most of the daily interbank transfers of reserves and deposits and for most government security purchases and sales between banks in the United States. Each Federal Reserve bank has a wire transfer manager, who provides information about prices charged for wire transfers and how the network may be used.

CHIPS stands for the Clearing House Interbank Payment System, centered in New York City. This privately owned wire network links major commercial banks in the New York City area and in selected other U.S. locations, as well as agency, branch, and Edge Act offices of foreign banks operating in New York. Operated by the New York Clearinghouse Association, CHIPS handles the majority of foreign currency transactions and Euro-dollar trades, as well as transfers of funds between New York banks and other U.S. banks on a same-day settlement basis.

S.W.I.F.T. is a global funds transfer system linking major banks in the United States, Canada, Western Europe, and a widely scattered group of other nations. It is a cooperative venture owned by the Society for Worldwide Interbank Financial Telecommunications, headquartered in Belgium.

Depository Institutions Act of 1982, amending the Bank Holding Company Act to permit interstate acquisition of large banks in danger of failing.

By 1993, 49 states and the District of Columbia had enacted interstate banking laws, most of them requiring reciprocal entry privileges for their banks from other states. Most states began their foray into interstate banking by permitting entry from a limited group of states, usually in the same region, known as **regional reciprocity**. Later, however, most states adopted a policy of **national reciprocity** so that banking companies from any other state in the nation could enter and purchase their banks provided banking organizations in the state entered were also granted the same entry privileges. Finally, a significant group of states (including Arizona, Colorado, New Hampshire, Oregon, and Texas) voted to allow outside entry *without* reciprocity required from any other state (often referred to as **national nonreciprocity**).

Why did so many states enact interstate banking laws in the 1980s and 1990s? Multiple factors were at work, including: (*a*) the need to bring in new capital in order to revive struggling local economies; (*b*) the expansion of financial services by nonbank financial institutions which face few restrictions on their ability to expand nationwide; (*c*) competition with neighboring states that may have already liberalized their interstate banking laws; (*d*) a strong desire on the part of the largest banks to geographically diversify their operations and open up new marketing opportunities; (*e*) the belief among regulators and many bankers that large banks may be more efficient and less prone to failure; (*f*) advances in the technology of financial-service delivery, permitting banks to serve customers in broader geographic areas; and (*g*) the opinion among the stockholders of many smaller banks that bank stock prices might rise if larger banks could cross state lines and buy out smaller competitors.[8]

Reflecting the widening possibilities for venturing across state lines, interstate banking companies have in the most recent decade begun to have a significant effect on restructuring the U.S. banking industry. For example, by 1993 the nearly 180 out-of-state holding companies held an average of nearly 23 percent of statewide deposits across the nation, up from only about 6 percent of average statewide deposits just six years before. By the late 1990s out-of-state banking companies controlled close to 30 percent of all domestic deposits per state, on average. In more than a dozen leading states (including Arizona, Colorado, Connecticut, Florida, Idaho, Indiana, Maine, Nevada, Oregon, South Carolina, South Dakota, Texas, Washington, and the District of Columbia) out-of-state holding companies accounted for half or more of statewide deposits. Several megacompanies, including BankAmerica, Wells Fargo, Norwest Corporation, Citicorp, and BancOne Corporation, soon controlled depository institutions in 10 or more states. One of the most outstanding examples was NationsBank, which, with its acquisition of Boatman's Bancshares in 1996 and Barnett Banks in 1998, controlled banks in 17 different states, and then NationsBank and BankAmerica proposed a merger that would create a chain of banks and branches coast to coast.

Proponents of interstate banking argue that it will bring new capital into a state (especially for those states in the South and West that are rapidly growing and short of investment capital), result in greater convenience for the customer (especially if the customer is traveling or changing residence to another state), and stimulate competitive rivalry that will promote greater efficiency in the use of scarce resources and lower prices for financial services. The interstate movement may also bring greater stability to the U.S. banking system by allowing individual banking organizations to further diversify their operations across different markets and regions, offsetting losses that may arise in one market with gains in other markets. In the long run interstate banking may improve the efficiency of the entire U.S. financial market system by facilitating the flow of credit toward areas offering the highest expected rates of

---

[8]Reflecting the unique political structure of each state, a variety of special entry conditions were imposed by numerous states. For example, 18 states placed a cap on the proportion of bank deposits that could be held by any one out-of-state banking organization, ranging from as low as a 10 percent cap in Iowa to as high as 30 percent in the state of Minnesota. Selected other states sought to protect their own banks from quick absorption by an out-of-state firm. Other states (e.g., Delaware and South Dakota) extended more generous terms of entry only for those banks offering specialized financial services, such as credit cards and insurance policies, which tends to limit competition between interstate and local banks. Several other states either prohibited or limited acquisitions of local banks by foreign-owned banking organizations.

return at acceptable levels of risk. The efficiency of individual banks may increase if interstate branching is allowed because branch offices are probably less costly to operate and administer than are separately owned, separately capitalized banks.

Opponents of interstate banking, on the other hand, contend that it will lead to increases in banking concentration as smaller banks are merged into larger interstate organizations, possibly leading to less competition and higher prices and to the draining of funds from local areas into the nation's financial centers. Indeed, there is some evidence that on a nationwide basis concentration of banking resources in the nation's banks has significantly increased since 1980 when the interstate banking movement took hold, though not all of the increase in nationwide concentration can be attributed to interstate banking alone. As Table 3–5 indicates, the top 100 U.S. banks held only about half of all U.S. domestic banking assets in 1980, but by 1995 their proportion of the nation's domestic banking assets had climbed to over 70 percent. At the same time the top 10 U.S. banking organizations rose sharply to capture more than a quarter of all domestic banking assets. However, small banks seem to have little to fear from large interstate banks if the former are willing to compete aggressively for their customers' business.

Doesn't this national concentration trend suggest possible damage to the consumer of banking services? Not necessarily. Many experts believe that those banking customers most likely to be hurt by a reduced number of competitors—the so-called potentially most damaged market—are households and small businesses who trade for financial services mainly in local cities and towns. Interestingly enough, there has apparently been very little change in the concentration of bank deposits at the *local* level—in urban or

TABLE 3–5   Concentration of Domestic Assets in the Largest U.S. Banks

	Percentage of All Domestic Assets Held by:			
Year	*Top 10 Banking Organizations*	*Top 25 Banking Organizations*	*Top 50 Banking Organizations*	*Top 100 Banking Organizations*
1980	21.6%	33.1%	41.6%	51.4%
1982	21.8	34.2	43.8	53.6
1984	20.4	33.3	43.7	55.4
1986	20.2	34.1	47.3	60.4
1988	20.4	35.7	51.1	64.0
1990	21.8	37.8	52.7	65.4
1992	25.6	41.8	55.6	67.1
1994	27.9	45.7	59.9	71.3
1995*	27.1	45.3	60.0	71.5

Note: *Figures are for June 1995.
Sources: Federal Deposit Insurance Corporation and Board of Governors of the Federal Reserve System.

metropolitan statistical areas (MSAs) and rural counties.[9] Therefore, it appears that in the interstate banking movement, thus far, most customers, particularly the smallest, have seen very little change in their alternatives for obtaining banking services.

Research on Interstate Banking.   Thanks to recent research we are beginning to get a good picture of *who* the major players in interstate banking are likely to be, as well as which banking organizations are unlikely to be significantly involved in the interstate banking movement. For example, a study by Dave Phillips and Christine Pavel [2] finds that *acquiring* banks tend to be among the very largest banking institutions, averaging about $4 billion in assets and well over 100 branch offices. They observed that the acquired banks in interstate transactions, while averaging much smaller than their acquirers, also tend to be well above average size (with about $1 billion in assets and close to 50 branch offices, on average).

Thus, there is little evidence that small community banks will be gobbled up in the interstate movement. Moreover, acquired banks tend to be more consumer oriented, with higher proportions of consumer deposits and consumer loans than other banks, while their acquirers tend to be banks that are primarily business oriented but also have significant consumer banking departments. Therefore, most interstate acquisitions to date appear to have focused largely on the *consumer market,* and it seems likely they will try to add further to their consumer base in the future.

Recent research suggests that the benefits the public and bank stockholders can expect from the coming of full-service interstate banking *may* be very limited. For example, an interesting study by Goldberg and Hanweck [22] of the few early interstate banking organizations protected by grandfather provisions of federal law found that banks previously acquired across state lines did *not* gain on their in-state competitors. In fact, these older interstate-controlled banks actually *lost* statewide market share over time and were, on average, no more profitable than were neighboring banks serving the same states.

Moreover, studies by Rose [27, 28] of interstate acquisitions during the 1980s found that many of the banks bought by interstate acquirers were in poor financial condition, with low or even negative earnings and high loan losses, which severely limited the growth and profitability of the interstate banking firms that acquired them. However, there is evidence that the stockholders of the banks *acquired* by interstate firms have often benefited from the high prices paid for their stock and the superior liquidity of the stock they received from interstate banking organizations, as noted by Trifts and Scanlon [33].

---

[9]Concentration in the U.S. banking industry (measured by the share of assets or deposits held by the largest banks in the system) is among the lowest in the world. For example, while the three largest banking organizations in the United States hold less than 15 percent of the U.S. banking industry's total assets, in most other industrialized countries (such as Canada, France, Germany, the Netherlands, Spain, Sweden, and Switzerland) half or more of all banking assets rest in the hands of the three largest banking companies. Germany posts the highest three-bank concentration ratio, with the three largest banks accounting for about 90 percent of all industry assets, followed closely by Sweden and Switzerland, where the three top banks account for 80 percent or more of industry assets.

Have the new and more liberal bank entry laws enacted in recent years resulted in any tangible benefits for the stockholders and employees of interstate banks? The evidence is mixed for both groups. Employees of interstate banking organizations often have more opportunity for job mobility and promotion in an expanding organization. However, many of the largest interstate firms (e.g., Chase Manhattan, Chemical Bank, and Wells Fargo) have laid off substantial numbers of personnel in an effort to cut expenses and increase efficiency. Some interstate banking firms apparently experienced an increase in the market value of their stock when several states passed laws permitting interstate banking. For example, Black, Fields, and Schweitzer [18] found that leading U.S. regional banks experienced higher returns on their stock when new interstate entry laws appeared, because these regional leaders now had more target banks and target markets to choose from. In contrast, economists Laderman and Pozdena [24] found that the stock returns of bank holding companies went *down* as the number of states allowing entry across state lines increased. These two researchers point out that interstate banking tends to increase competition, which erodes the economic rents (excess returns) many banks enjoyed in the past due to restrictive legislation that sheltered them from entry by new competitors. Nevertheless, the most recent studies find that interstate mergers usually generate positive abnormal returns on bank stock for the stockholders of *both* acquiring and acquired banking firms, though the biggest gains in stock returns generally go to the *acquired* bank's stockholders.

Research evidence is slowly beginning to emerge on whether interstate expansion can reduce the risk to a bank's earnings. In theory, if an interstate organization can acquire banks in states where bank earnings have a negative or low-positive correlation with bank earnings in those states where the interstate company is already represented, a "portfolio effect" could occur in which earnings losses at banks in one group of states offset profits earned at banks in other states, resulting in lower overall earnings risk for the interstate banking firm. However, as recent research by Mark Levonian [25] and Rose [30] suggests, reduction of bank earnings risk does not occur automatically simply because a banking organization crosses state lines. For example, Levonian studied earnings correlations for smaller banks in the western United States. He found that *only three pairs of states*—Arizona-California, Utah-Hawaii, and Hawaii-Oregon—displayed significant negatively correlated bank earnings for the 1985–93 period. The remaining states all had positively correlated bank earnings or displayed no significant correlations. Moreover, he found that some states (such as Arizona) generated high bank earnings variances, suggesting that bank earnings there are so volatile that adding banks from those particular states to an interstate organization might *increase* an interstate banking firm's overall risk. Rose's study covering all 50 states found similar patterns in earnings correlations and that to achieve at least some reduction in earnings risk, interstate banks must expand into a number of different states (at least four) and different regions (at least two economically distinct regions of the nation). The bottom line is that *interstate banking organizations must be selective about which states they enter if risk reduction is an important consideration.*

Interstate Banking and Bank Size.   Finally, are there any benefits from the *bank size* effects of interstate banking? That is, because interstate banks tend to be multibillion-dollar institutions—much larger than the average-size community bank—could the cost to the public of banking services be reduced because bigger banks may be more efficient than smaller banks?

This is not an easy question to answer. There are two possible sources of cost savings due to growth in the size of banks: (1) *economies of scale,* which, if they exist, mean that a doubling of bank output for any one service or package of services will result in *less* than a doubling of bank production costs because of greater efficiencies in using the bank's resources to produce multiple units of the same service package; and (2) *economies of scope*, which imply that a bank can save on operating costs when it expands the mix of its output because some resources, such as management skill and plant and equipment, are more efficiently utilized in jointly producing multiple services rather than just turning out one service from the same location because fixed costs can be spread over a greater number of different service outputs.

Banking Efficiency

Most recent research suggests that banking's average cost curve—the relationship between bank size (measured usually by total assets or total deposits) and the cost of production per unit of bank output—is roughly U-shaped (like that shown in Exhibit 3–9), but appears to have a fairly flat middle portion. This implies that a fairly wide range of banks lie close to being at maximally efficient size. However, recent studies also reveal that smaller banks tend to produce a somewhat different menu of services than do larger banks, with larger banks typically offering many *more* services. As a result, some bank cost studies have attempted to figure out the average costs for smaller banks separately from their cost calculations for larger banks. These newer studies suggest that smaller and middle-size banks tend to reach their lowest production costs somewhere between $100 million and $500 million in aggregate assets. Larger banks,

EXHIBIT 3–9
The Most Efficient Sizes of Banks

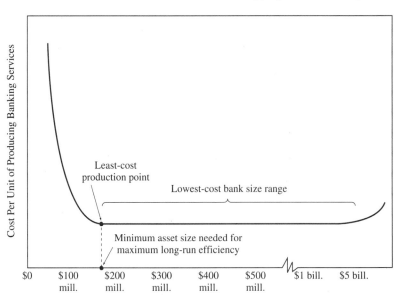

Size of the Banking Firm (in Total Assets)

on the other hand, tend to achieve an optimal (lowest-cost) size at somewhere between $2 and $10 billion in total assets.[10]

Of course, the problem with these findings is that they leave unresolved the question of why there are many banks around the world much larger than any of these so-called optimal size levels. For example, when Chase Manhattan and Chemical Banking Corporation, both of New York, merged in the 1990s, their combined assets were almost $300 billion and both banks claimed substantial "cost savings" flowing from their merger. Indeed, it may be true that the optimal-size operating point in banking is a moving target, increasing as new laws and new technologies come into existence favoring ever larger banks. For example, with banks increasingly producing and delivering services via computers, over the telephone, and through the Internet, bank operating costs may have fallen substantially. At the same time new laws and regulations in the United States have made it possible for banking companies to establish smaller branches inside malls and retail stores and in the form of limited-service machines and to branch more freely within the territories of individual states. More recently, U.S. banks have been permitted, as the result of passage of the Riegle-Neal Interstate Banking Act, to branch via merger across state lines rather than having to set up separate firms in each state. These lower-cost delivery vehicles suggest that recent bank cost studies must be regarded with some suspicion unless, of course, larger banks are currently gaining something other than lower operating costs from their mergers, such as higher operating revenues or bigger rewards for their managers at the expense of their shareholders.

One other important aspect of the more recent banking cost studies asks a slightly different question than earlier cost studies: Is a bank, regardless of its size, operating as efficiently as it possibly can? This question raises an issue known to economists as *x-efficiency*. Given the size of a bank, is it operating near to or far away from its lowest possible operating cost? Another way of posing the same question is to ask if the bank is currently situated along what economists would label its cost-efficient frontier, with little or no waste? Research evidence to date is not encouraging, suggesting that most banks do *not* operate at their minimum possible cost. Rather, their degree of x-efficiency tends to be 20 to 25 percent greater in aggregate production costs than it should be under conditions of maximum efficiency.

This latter finding implies that most banks could gain more from lowering operating costs at their current size than they could from changing their scale of output (i.e., by shrinking or growing bigger) in order to reach a lower cost point on their average cost curve. Thus, x-efficiencies seem to override economies of scale for most banks. To be sure, larger banks seem to operate closer to their low-cost point than do many smaller banks, probably because the larger institutions generally operate in more intensely competitive markets. Moreover, riskier banks and those in financial trouble tend to be less efficient than the average bank in the industry.

Either way, however, we must remain cautious about bank cost studies. Banking itself is changing rapidly in form and content. The statistical methodologies available today

---

[10]See especially the studies by Berger, Hanweck, and Humphrey [15], Berger and Humphrey [16], Berger, Hunter, and Timme [17], and Humphrey [23].

to carry out bank cost studies have serious limitations and tend to focus upon a single point in time rather than trying to capture the dynamics of this ever-changing industry.

Foreign Bank Penetration of Domestic Markets

All over the globe foreign banks have entered to add another dimension to domestic competition and alter significantly the structure of domestic banking markets. This is particularly evident in the United States and Western Europe where foreign-owned banks have captured a growing share of key markets, especially the markets for corporate loans, security underwriting, and credit guarantees. In order to penetrate both the United States and other nations abroad foreign banks use a wide variety of organizational forms, including representative offices, full-service branches, shell branches, subsidiary firms, joint ventures, and selected other organizational forms unique to certain nations.

Representative offices are service facilities that serve as points of contact for a bank's existing overseas customers, routing customer service needs back to the home office, and as a vehicle for surfacing new customers for the home office. These limited-service facilities cannot accept deposits or make loans, but can serve as marketing agencies to facilitate contact between a bank and its overseas customers. **Agency offices,** a related form, offer credit and nondeposit services, such as making, buying, and selling loans, trading foreign currencies, issuing and redeeming letters of credit, and transferring funds, but usually do not accept deposits.

Full-service branches offer the complete line of financial services similar to those available from a foreign bank's home office. In contrast, **shell branches** are merely booking facilities where deposits are recorded, but the funds represented by those recorded deposits are loaned and invested through the full-service offices of the bank. Shell branches are often used to circumvent domestic banking regulations, such as offices in the Caribbean basin operated by U.S. banks that take deposits without having to conform to all U.S. regulations, such as paying government-imposed insurance fees.

Foreign banks will also set up or acquire *subsidiaries,* which are corporations wholly or partly owned by a foreign banking company. Frequently domestic banks are purchased to become subsidiaries of a foreign bank so that the foreign banking firm has immediate access to a substantial group of domestic customers or avoids regulations that limit the setting up of new branches. Foreign-owned banks can also set up *joint ventures* with a domestic banking firm in the market it wishes to enter, often because of lack of knowledge about an overseas market or to escape confining regulations.

Several specialized banking forms are frequently used by U.S. banks to penetrate domestic and foreign markets and by foreign banks seeking entry into U.S. markets. These specialized organizational forms include *Edge Act Subsidiaries,* which are separate corporations, the majority of whose transactions must arise from foreign business activity, but are free of certain regulations (such as laws that prohibit branching across state lines). Edge Acts must be chartered by the Federal Reserve Board. Similar to shell branches, *international banking facilities* (IBFs) are accounts kept in a computer that must be listed separately from a U.S. bank's domestic customer accounts. IBFs are directed mainly toward the service needs of foreign customers and their deposits are not subject to federal deposit insurance fees or domestic reserve requirements. *Export trading companies* devote most of their resources to encouraging exports from domestic producers by providing trade financing and conducting market research on foreign business opportunities. Finally, *investment companies* engage in security trading and cash management on behalf of a foreign bank and its customers.

By 1996 foreign bank offices in the United States posted U.S. financial assets of more than $800 billion, or just over one-fifth of the nearly $4 trillion in assets held by U.S.-chartered banks. (See Table 3–6.) Foreign banks from more than 60 nations were operating over 500 state-licensed branch, agency, and other facilities inside U.S. territory. The principal types of foreign-bank units selling financial services inside the United States included full-service branch offices, agency offices, U.S.-chartered full-service bank subsidiaries, investment companies, and foreign-owned Edge Act or Agreement corporations.

The rapid growth of foreign banks inside U.S. borders has aroused a storm of controversy. Some U.S. business and government leaders have objected to the apparent loss of local control over banking and to what they regard as unfair competitive advantages for foreign banks over more tightly regulated U.S. domestic banking firms. On the other side of the coin, foreign banking institutions have ushered in intense competition for financial services and have expedited the flow of foreign capital into the United States to help fund federal and state government deficits and private spending needs.

Among the leading countries with banking units in the United States are Japan (whose banks control over half the assets held by all foreign banks inside U.S. territory), Canada, Great Britain, France, and Germany. These institutions are particularly important in several key U.S. metropolitan centers—Atlanta, Boston, Chicago, Dallas, Los Angeles, New York City, and San Francisco—where they provide a wide array of financial services to both domestic and foreign clients. A variety of forces appear to have propelled the recent rapid growth of foreign bank activities in the United States.

TABLE 3–6   Total Financial Assets of Foreign Banks Operating in the United States

Year	*U.S. Financial Assets Held by Foreign Banks (in billions of dollars)*	*Total Business Loans in the U.S. Held by Foreign Banks*	Percentage of All Assets and Business Loans Held by All U.S.-Chartered Commercial Banks	
			Percentage of U.S. Assets	*Percentage of U.S. Business Loans*
1980	$ 98.1	$ 75.3	7.7%	19.9%
1990	363.1	156.5	13.7	24.4
1992	491.5	194.2	17.7	34.5
1994	557.4	189.1	18.2	31.4
1996	820.8	221.5	21.5	38.9

Note: Figures are for the branches and agencies of foreign banks, Edge Act and Agreement Corporations, New York Investment Companies, and IBFS. 1994 figures are through the third quarter.
Source: Board of Governors of the Federal Reserve System, *Flow of Funds Accounts.*

They include the following:

1. The financing of exports from the home country into the United States.
2. Providing services to foreign nationals who have come to study or work in the United States.
3. Tapping the American money market for liquid funds.
4. Assisting with the flow of foreign capital into the most promising U.S. investments.
5. Avoiding regulatory restrictions on banking in their home countries by entering the more open U.S. markets.

Once established inside U.S. borders, however, these foreign banking firms have reached out to domestic business owners, state and local governments, and households to offer loans, credit cards, credit guarantees, financial planning, and other services and gained market share in the business loan field recently when U.S. banks were struggling with severe loan-quality problems.

While the foreign banking presence inside U.S. borders is not expected to shrink significantly over time, its growth may slow as the U.S. further deregulates its financial-service markets, giving its own banks greater latitude to defend their market shares. Moreover, as the deregulation movement proceeds overseas and governments abroad allow private firms and individuals to operate without so much government control, foreign banks may find conditions in their own markets more to their liking and divert more funds there instead of bringing them to the United States.

Conclusions Concerning the Impact of Organization Type and Size on Bank Performance

Can we draw any meaningful conclusions from research that has evaluated the different types and sizes of banking organizations? What does it all add up to?

A few conclusions seem safe at this point:

1. The profitability of a bank is *not* determined primarily by how it is organized; the quality of its management and the economic conditions in its market area appear to be far more important to its success.
2. Small banks of any organizational type can compete successfully with large banks, provided they aggressively seek to preserve their profits and market share. Economies of scale from bank growth appear to be limited to banks of relatively modest size.
3. Branch banks and banks affiliated with holding companies have greater protection against failure than small (single-office) unit banks. They also tend to offer more services than unit banks and operate more offices per unit of population, thus providing more convenient services.
4. The prices charged and deposit interest rates paid by banks do *not* appear to depend greatly on how each bank is organized but rather on the amount of

competition the bank faces, the strength of market demand for banking services, and the rate of inflation. The public receives about the same quality of banking services and pays about the same for them under branching, holding company, or independent unit banking systems.

5. The types of banking organizations serving the public do *not* appear to be a key factor in the growth and development of the economy, though greater branching activity seems to accelerate economic growth.

6. The American banking industry is definitely consolidating. In 1984 there were 14,500 U.S. banking firms—the highest number since the Great Depression of the 1930s—but by the late 1990s the industry's population had shrunk to about 9,000, a decrease of more than a third, due to numerous failures and mergers. Moreover, the number of independently owned banks is declining even faster. At the same time the average size of the banks remaining is growing rapidly, despite the fact that a substantial number (100 or more in the United States) of new banks are still being chartered each year.

One of the principal reasons why the way a bank is organized does *not* appear to affect its performance significantly is the wide variety of management styles and capabilities among banks of all sizes and organizational structures. Some bankers are strongly profit motivated and expense-control conscious; they can often push their banks toward earnings success regardless of what their institution's organization chart looks like. Other bank managers may prefer greater bank size or possibly greater bank safety as key objectives, and their bank's earnings performance may take a back seat as a result.

Expense-Preference Behavior.   In fact, there is evidence of considerable *expense-preference behavior* among some bank managers, who value fringe benefits, plush offices, and ample travel budgets over the pursuit of maximum returns for the bank's stockholders. Such expense-preference behavior may show up in the form of bank staffs larger than required to maximize profits or excessively rapid growth, which causes expenses to get out of control. Some economists believe that expense-preference behavior is more likely in those banking organizations where management is dominant and the stockholders are not well organized. There, managers have more opportunity to enjoy a lavish lifestyle at the shareholder's expense.

Agency Theory.   The concept of expense-preference behavior is part of a much larger view of how modern corporations operate, called *agency theory,* which analyzes relationships between a firm's owners (stockholders) and its managers, who are agents of the owners. Agency theory explores whether mechanisms exist in a given situation to compel managers to act in order to maximize the welfare of their firm's owners. If a bank's owners do not have access to all the information its managers possess, they cannot fully evaluate how good management has been at making decisions. In commercial banking, ownership is increasingly being spread out, and the dominance of individual stockholders in the industry appears to be decreasing. These two trends are likely to worsen any agency problems that may be present in the banking industry.

One way to reduce costs from agency problems is to develop better systems for monitoring management behavior and strong management incentives to follow the wishes of the stockholders. In the long run, many economists believe, agency problems can be reduced by efficient labor and capital markets. Labor markets can reduce management's tendency to feather its own nest at the expense of the stockholders by rewarding better-performing managers with higher salaries and more job opportunities. Capital markets can help eliminate bad managers and poor bank performance with the threat of corporate takeovers (which could lead new owners to fire existing management) and by lowering the stock price of poorly managed banks. Because recent changes in banking laws have tended to allow more takeovers, we can entertain the hope that agency problems in banking will diminish over time as the industry faces more intense competition.

Concept Checks

3–15. How have banks gotten around federal and state restrictions against interstate banking?

3–16. Can you foresee any potential problems with interstate banking?

3–17. Does the type of banking organization seem to affect how well banks perform in serving the public and in serving the interests of their owners?

Summary

This chapter has highlighted the different ways banks are organized, in terms of both personnel and the arrangement of offices, in order to serve the public. It also examined the relationships among bank organization, profitability, and efficient service delivery. A central theme of the chapter was that banks, on average, are becoming more complex and much larger, offering a growing menu of services through multiple departments and divisions. Moreover, the skills bankers need to function efficiently are changing rapidly with new technology and increasing competition both at home and abroad. There is growing emphasis on services marketing, corporate planning, electronic recordkeeping and service delivery, and improved management information systems that link the computer more closely with both management and customer service needs.

Regardless of how large a bank becomes, however, it must start its corporate life by obtaining a charter of incorporation from government authorities. Along the way banks face other crucial organizational decisions, such as whether or not to join the central banking system (e.g., in the United States to become a member bank of the Federal Reserve System), whether to remain a unit institution without branches or become a branching system, and whether to remain independent or agree to be bought out by a holding company. We noted that each of these decisions is fraught with benefits and costs related to the burden of regulation, the prospects for greater bank stability and reduced chances of failure, access to new markets, and the problems associated with trying to coordinate and control a much larger and more complex financial institution.

We explored the claims for and against branch banking and bank holding companies. We found that most of the alleged benefits and costs are generally far less significant than claimed by either side in the decades-old debate. We also noted the spread of interstate banking, something recently legalized at the federal level by the U.S. Congress through a new interstate banking law passed in 1994. Interstate banking has raised new concerns in the United States about the dominance of a few banks and whether consumers will benefit or lose in terms of the quality, quantity, and pricing of the financial services they demand.

Key Terms in This Chapter

Organizational forms
Board of directors
Stockholders
Unit banks
Branch banking
Bank holding company
Multibank holding companies
Affiliated banks
Correspondent banking
Bankers' banks
Networking

Joint venture
Full-service interstate banking
Trade associations
Regional reciprocity
National reciprocity
National nonreciprocity
Representative offices
Agency offices
Full-service branches
Shell branches

Problems and Projects

1. Suppose you owned a bank holding company headquartered in each of the following states:
   a. California
   b. Texas
   c. New York
   d. Wisconsin
   e. Florida.
   Into what other states could you enter and acquire banks through your bank holding company?

2. Inside what states can a bank holding company convert its affiliated banks into full-service branch offices under current federal law?

3. Of the business activities listed below, which activities can be conducted through U.S.-regulated bank holding companies and which are *not* authorized for all U.S.-regulated bank holding companies?
   a. Data processing companies.
   b. Office furniture sales.
   c. Auto and truck leasing companies.
   d. General life insurance and property-casualty insurance sales.
   e. Savings and loan associations.
   f. Mortgage companies.
   g. General insurance underwriting activities.
   h. Professional advertising services.
   i. Underwriting of new common stock issues by nonfinancial corporations.

4. You are currently serving as president and chief executive officer of a *unit bank* that has been operating out of its present location for five years. Due to the rapid growth of households and businesses in the market area served by the bank and the challenges posed to your share of this market by several aggressive competitors, you want to become a *branch bank* by establishing two satellite offices. Please answer the following questions:
   a. How would you go about deciding: (1) where to locate the new offices and (2) which services each office should make available?
   b. How are you going to evaluate each new office's performance in deciding whether to keep it open?
   c. Based on the content of this chapter, what advantages would your branch be likely to have over the old unit bank? What disadvantages are likely to come with adding branch offices? Any ideas on how you might minimize these disadvantages?
   d. Would it be a good idea to form a holding company at the same time or perhaps before or after setting up the new branches? Based on the material in this chapter, what advantages could a holding company bring to your bank? Disadvantages?

5. The organization chart of a bank usually gives us clues about the services the bank offers and which services it tends to emphasize in its selling efforts. Unfortunately, a bank's organization chart often tells us very little about the lines of authority and responsibility within a banking organization and who does the real work or makes the most crucial decisions. To quote an old joke: "An organization chart shows only how we line up before the ball is snapped." Contact some of the banks in your area and ask for a copy of each institution's organization chart. After carefully examining each one, can you explain the differences you see from bank to bank? Do the organizational differences seem to reflect (*a*) the size of each organization, (*b*) the services offered, (*c*) the philosophy of senior management, or (*d*) other factors? Is each bank well organized, in your opinion, for the services it offers? If you have the opportunity, interview selected members of each bank's management team and staff. Do they have differing perceptions of the bank's objectives, management philosophy, and lines of authority and responsibility? Do the individuals you interviewed appear to be thoroughly versed in the bank's long- and short-range goals, services offered, and decision-making processes?

6. The U.S. banking industry today is sharply divided in its attitude toward new service powers for banks. Money center banks, for example, tend to favor an expansion of services into private security underwriting, real estate ventures, and insurance sales and the right to branch nationwide without restrictions. Small, locally oriented banks generally fear such changes. This conflict places many trade associations, such as the American Bankers Association, in a dilemma concerning what position to take before Congress and the state legislatures. Suppose you were representing the industry as a lobbyist before Congress and were asked to take a position on legislation affecting new bank services and geographic expansion. What new legislation would you recommend that would answer the concerns of bankers representing both large and small banks? Is there a compromise position that would minimize the damage to both groups?

Selected References

See the following for good discussions of recent trends in banking structure and organization:

1. Horvitz, Paul M., and Bernard Shull. "The Impact of Branch Banking on Bank Performance." *National Banking Review* 2 (December 1964), pp. 143–88.
2. Phillips, Dave, and Christine Pavel. "Interstate Banking Game Plans: Implications for the Midwest." *Economic Perspectives,* Federal Reserve Bank of Chicago, 1986.
3. Rose, Peter S. *The Changing Structure of American Banking.* New York: Columbia University Press, 1987.

Information on the advantages and disadvantages of bank holding companies may be found in the following:

4. Apcor, Leonard M., and Buck Brown. "Branch Bullying: Small Texas Towns Are the Latest Victims of Big Banks' Crisis." *The Wall Street Journal,* May 25, 1988, pp. 1 and 8.
5. Barkley, David L.; Cindy Mellon; and Glenn T. Potts. "Effects of Banking Structure on the Allocation of Credit to Metropolitan Communities." *Western Journal of Agricultural Economics* 9, no. 2 (1984), pp. 283–92.
6. Frieder, Larry A., and Vincent P. Apilado. "Bank Holding Company Research: Classification, Synthesis, and New Directions." *Journal of Bank Research,* Summer 1982, pp. 80–95.
7. Helyon, John. "Multistate Banks Rile Many Customers." *The Wall Street Journal,* April 20, 1988, p. 22.
8. Hunter, William C., and Stephen G. Timme. "Concentration and Innovation: Striking a Balance in Deregulation." *Economic Review,* Federal Reserve Bank of Atlanta, January/February 1987, pp. 11–20.
9. ———. "Technical Change, Organizational Form and the Structure of Bank Production." *Journal of Money, Credit, and Banking* 43 (May 1986), pp. 152–66.
10. Liang, Nellie, and Donald Savage. *New Data on the Performance of Nonbank Subsidiaries of Bank Holding Companies.* Staff Study No. 159, Board of Governors of the Federal Reserve System, February 1990.

11. Varvel, Walter A. "A Valuation Approach to Bank Holding Company Acquisitions." *Economic Review,* Federal Reserve Bank of Richmond, July/August 1975, pp. 9–15.
12. Whalen, Gary. "Bank Holding Company Voluntary Nonbanking Asset Divestitures." *Economic Commentary,* Federal Reserve Bank of Cleveland, January 15, 1986.

A good review of the issues involved in branch banking may be found in the following:

13. Darnell, Jerome C. "Banking Structure and Economic Growth." In *Changing Pennsylvania's Branching Laws: An Economic Analysis,* Federal Reserve Bank of Philadelphia, 1973.
14. Kohn, Ernest, and Carmen J. Carlo. *The Competitive Impact of New Branches.* New York State Banking Department, 1969.

See the following for a discussion of the benefits, costs, and characteristics of interstate banking and economies of scale in banking:

15. Berger, Allen N.; Gerald A. Hanweck; and David B. Humphrey. "Competitive Viability in Banking: Scale, Scope, and Product Mix Economics." *Journal of Monetary Economics* 20, no. 4 (December 1987).
16. Berger, Allen N., and David B. Humphrey. "The Dominance of Inefficiencies Over Scale and Product Mix Economies in Banking." Finance and Economics Discussion Series No. 107, Board of Governors of the Federal Reserve System, January 1990.
17. Berger, Alan N.; W. C. Hunter; and S. G. Timme. "The Efficiency of Financial Institutions: A Review and Preview of Research Past, Present, and Future." *Journal of Banking and Finance* 17 (1993), pp. 221–49.
18. Black, Harold A.; M. Andrew Fields; and Robert L. Schweitzer. "Changes in Interstate Banking Laws: The Impact on Shareholder Wealth." *Journal of Finance* 45 (1990), pp. 1663–71.
19. Cushing, Woodrow W., and James E. McNulty. "Scale Economies at Large Commercial Banks, 1985–89: An Intertemporal Approach under Alternative Model Specifications." Paper presented at the Annual Meeting of the Financial Management Association, Chicago, October 1991.
20. Dunham, Constance. "Interstate Banking and Intermediation." *New England Economic Review,* Federal Reserve Bank of Boston, May/June 1987, pp. 3–21.
21. Evanoff, Douglas D., and Philip R. Israilevich. "Deregulation, Cost Economies and Allocative Efficiency of Large Commercial Banks." *Issues in Financial Regulation,* Federal Reserve Bank of Chicago, Working Paper No. 1990–19.
22. Goldberg, Lawrence G., and Gerald A. Hanweck. "What Can We Expect from Interstate Banking?" *Journal of Banking and Finance* 12 (1988), pp. 51–67.
23. Humphrey, David B. "Why Do Estimates of Bank Scale Economies Differ?" *Economic Review,* Federal Reserve Bank of Richmond 76 (September/October 1990), pp. 38–50.
24. Laderman, Elizabeth S., and Randall J. Pozdena. "Interstate Banking and Competition: Evidence from the Behavior of Stock Returns." *Economic Review,* Federal Reserve Bank of San Francisco, Spring 1991, pp. 32–47.
25. Levonian, Mark E. "Interstate Banking and Risk." *FRBSF Weekly Letter,* July 22, 1994, pp. 1–2.
26. Rhoades, Stephen A., and Donald T. Savage. "The Relative Performance of Bank Holding Companies and Branch Banking Systems." *Journal of Economics and Business,* Winter 1981, pp. 132–41.
27. Rose, Peter S. "The Firms Acquired by Interstate Banks: Testable Hypotheses and Consistent Evidence." *Journal of Business and Economic Perspectives* 15, no. 2 (1989), pp. 127–35.
28. ———. "The Banking Firms Making Interstate Acquisitions: Theory and Observable Motives." *Review of Business and Economic Research* 25, no. 1 (Fall 1989), pp. 1–18.
29. ———. *Banking across State Lines: Public and Private Consequences.* Westport, Conn.: Quorum Books, 1997.
30. ———. "Diversification and Cost Effects of Interstate Banking." *The Financial Review* 33, no. 2 (May 1996).
31. Savage, Donald T. "Interstate Banking: A Status Report." *Federal Reserve Bulletin,* December 1993, pp. 1075–89.
32. Shaffer, Sherrill. *Potential Synergies among Large Commercial Banks.* Working Paper No. 91-17, Federal Reserve Bank of Philadelphia, October 1991.
33. Trifts, Jack W., and Kevin P. Scanlon. "Interstate Bank Mergers: The Early Evidence." *Journal of Financial Research* 10 (Winter 1987), pp. 305–11.
34. LaWare, John P. *Testimony Before the Committee on Banking, Finance, and Urban Affairs.* U.S. House of Representatives, September 24, 1991. Mr. LaWare was a member of the Board of Governors of the Federal Reserve System.
35. Jayaratne, Jith, and Philip E. Strahan. "The Benefits of Branching Deregulation." *Economic Policy Review,* Federal Reserve Bank of New York, December 1997, pp. 13–29.

4   THE FINANCIAL STATEMENTS OF A BANK

Learning and Management Decision Objectives

The purpose of this chapter is to acquaint the reader with the content, structure, and purpose of bank financial statements and to help bank managers understand how information from bank financial statements can be used as tools to reveal how well their banks are performing.

Introduction

The particular services each bank chooses to offer and the overall size of a banking organization are reflected in its *financial statements*. The two main financial statements that bank managers, customers (particularly large depositors not fully protected by deposit insurance), and the regulatory authorities look at are the balance sheet (Report of Condition) and the income statement (Report of Income). We will examine these two very important bank financial reports in depth in this chapter. In addition, we will explore briefly the makeup of two other key financial statements often used by credit analysts and bank managers in assessing changes in the funds-using and funds-raising activities of a bank—the Sources and Uses of Funds Statement (also known as the Funds-Flow Statement) and the Statement of Stockholders' Equity.

An Overview of Bank Balance Sheets and Income Statements

The two most important bank financial statements—the balance sheet, or Report of Condition, and the income statement, or Report of Income—may be viewed as a list of bank financial inputs and outputs, as Table 4–1 shows. The Report of Condition shows the amount and composition of funds sources (financial inputs) the bank has drawn upon to finance its lending and investing activities and how much has been allocated to loans, securities, and other funds uses (financial outputs) at any given time.

117

In contrast, the financial inputs and outputs on the Report of Income show how much it has cost the bank to acquire its deposits and other funds sources and to generate revenues from the uses the bank has made of those funds. These costs include interest paid to depositors and other creditors of the bank, the expenses of hiring management and staff, overhead costs in acquiring and using office facilities, and taxes paid for government services. The Report of Income also shows the revenues (cash flow) generated by selling bank services to the public, including making loans and leases and servicing customer deposits. Finally, the bank's Report of Income shows the bank's net earnings after all costs are deducted from the sum of all revenues, some of which will be reinvested in the business for future growth and some of which will flow to the stockholders as dividends.

The Bank's Balance Sheet (Report of Condition)

The Principal Types of Accounts

A bank's balance sheet, or **Report of Condition,** lists the assets, liabilities, and equity capital (owners' funds) held by or invested in the bank on any given date. Because

TABLE 4–1   Financial Outputs and Inputs in the Two Key Bank Financial Statements

The Balance Sheet (Report of Condition)

Financial Outputs (uses of bank funds or assets)	*Financial Inputs (sources of bank funds or liabilities plus equity capital)*
Loans and leases	Deposits from the public
Investments in securities	Nondeposit borrowings
Cash and deposits in other institutions	Equity capital from stockholders

As with any firm's balance sheet, total sources of bank funds must equal total uses of bank funds (i.e., Total assets = Total liabilities + Equity capital).

The Income Statement (Report of Income)

Financial Outputs (revenues from making use of bank funds and other resources to produce and sell services)	*Financial Inputs (the cost of acquiring funds and other resources the bank needs to produce services)*
Loan income	Deposit costs
Security income	Costs of nondeposit borrowings
Income from deposits in other institutions	Employee costs
Income from miscellaneous services	Overhead expenses
	Taxes

As with any firm's income statement, total revenues minus total costs must equal net earnings (income) of the bank.

banks are simply business firms selling a particular kind of product, the basic balance sheet identity

$$\text{Assets} = \text{Liabilities} + \text{Equity capital} \qquad (1)$$

must be valid.

In banking, the *assets* on the balance sheet include four major kinds of assets—cash in the vault and deposits held at other depository institutions (C), government and private interest-bearing securities purchased in the open market (S), loans and lease financing made available to customers (L), and miscellaneous assets (MA). *Liabilities* fall into two principal categories—deposits made by and owed to various customers (D), and nondeposit borrowings of funds in the money and capital markets (NDB). Finally, *equity capital* represents long-term funds that the owners contribute to the bank (EC). (See Table 4–2.) Therefore, the bank's balance sheet identity can be written as follows:

$$C + S + L + MA = D + NDB + EC \qquad (2)$$

Cash assets (C) are designed to meet the bank's need for *liquidity* (i.e., immediately spendable cash) in order to meet deposit withdrawals, customer demands for loans, and other unexpected or immediate needs for cash. Security holdings (S) are a backup source of liquidity and provide another source of income. Loans (L) are made principally to supply income, while miscellaneous assets (MA) are usually dominated by the fixed assets owned by the bank (its plant and equipment) and investments in bank subsidiaries (if any). Deposits (D) are typically the main source of funding for banks, with nondeposit borrowings (NDB) carried out mainly to supplement deposits and provide the additional liquidity that cash assets and securities cannot provide. Finally, equity capital (EC) supplies the long-term, relatively stable base of financial support upon which the bank will rely to grow and to cover any extraordinary losses it incurs.

One useful way to view this balance sheet identity is to note that bank liabilities and equity capital represent *accumulated sources of funds,* which provide the needed spending power for the bank to acquire its assets. A bank's assets, on the other hand, are its *accumulated uses of funds,* which are made to generate income for its stockholders, pay interest to its depositors, and compensate the bank's employees for their labor and skill. Thus, the bank's balance sheet identity can be pictured simply as follows:

$$\begin{matrix} \text{Accumulated uses} & & \text{Accumulated sources} & (3) \\ \text{of bank funds} & = & \text{of bank funds} \\ \text{(assets)} & & \text{(liabilities and equity capital)} \end{matrix}$$

Clearly, each use of funds must be backed by a source of funds, so that accumulated uses of funds must equal accumulated sources of funds.

Of course, in the real world, bank balance sheets are more complicated than this simple accumulated sources and uses statement because each item on a bank's balance sheet usually contains several component accounts. A more inclusive balance sheet, or Report of Condition, contains many more accounts. This is illustrated by the balance sheet of a large midwestern banking organization shown in Table 4–3. Let's take a closer look at its principal components.

TABLE 4–2   **Key Items on Bank Financial Statements**

The Balance Sheet (Report of Condition)

Assets (accumulated uses of funds)	*Liabilities and Equity (accumulated sources of funds)*
Cash (primary reserves)	Deposits:
Liquid security holdings (secondary reserves)	Demand
Investment securities	NOWs
Loans:	Money market
Consumer	Savings
Real estate	Time
Commercial	Nondeposit borrowings
Agriculture	Equity capital:
Financial institutions	Stock
Miscellaneous assets (buildings, equipment, etc.)	Surplus
	Retained earnings
	Capital reserves

*Income Statement or Statement of Earnings
and Expenses (Report of Income)*

Revenues (revenues from the bank's service outputs)
Loan income
Investment income
Noninterest sources of income (such as deposit service fees)

Expenses (cost of the bank's inputs of resources needed to produce its services)
Interest paid on deposits
Interest paid on nondeposit borrowings
Salaries and wages (employee compensation)
Provision for loan losses (allocations to the reserve for possible losses on any loans made)
Other expenses
Income before taxes and securities transactions
Taxes
Gains or losses from trading in securities
Net income after taxes and securities gains or losses

Bank Assets

The Cash Account.   The first asset item normally listed on a bank's Report of Condition is *cash and deposits due from banks.* This item, which includes cash held in the bank's vault, any deposits the bank has placed with other banks (correspondent deposits), cash items in the process of collection (mainly uncollected checks), and the bank's reserve account held with the Federal Reserve bank in the region, is often labeled *primary reserves.* This means that these cash assets are the bank's first line of defense against deposit withdrawals and the first source of funds to look to when a customer comes in with an unexpected loan request that the bank feels compelled to meet. Normally, banks strive to keep the size of this account as low as possible, because cash balances earn little or no interest income for the bank. Note that the $1,643 million in cash and due from other banks listed in Table 4–3 for this large bank represents less than 8 percent of its total assets of $21.7 billion in a recent year.

TABLE 4–3   Balance Sheet (Report of Condition) for a Large Bank
(figures in millions of dollars)

	Year Just Concluded	Six Months Ago
Assets (accumulated uses of funds)		
Cash and deposits due from banks	**$ 1,643**	**$ 2,300**
Investment securities	**2,803**	**3,002**
Trading account securities	21	96
Federal funds sold and securities purchased under resale agreements	278	425
Loans, gross (including real estate, commercial, agricultural, financial institution, and consumer loans and leases)	**15,887**	**15,412**
Less: Allowance for possible loan losses	(349)	(195)
Unearned discount on loans	(117)	(137)
Loans, net	15,421	15,080
Lease financing receivables	201	150
Bank premises and equipment, net	365	363
Customers' liability on acceptances	70	111
Miscellaneous assets	903	1,059
Total assets	$21,705	$22,586
Liabilities and Stockholders' Equity (accumulated sources of funds)		
Deposits:		
Noninterest-bearing demand (checking) deposits	$ 3,427	$ 3,831
Savings deposits and NOW accounts	914	937
Money market deposit accounts	1,914	1,965
Time deposits	9,452	9,981
Deposits at foreign branches	787	869
Total deposits	**16,494**	**17,583**
Nondeposit borrowings:		
Federal funds purchased and securities sold under agreements to repurchase	2,132	1,836
Other short-term debt	897	714
Mortgage indebtedness	417	439
Subordinated notes and debentures	200	200
Other liabilities:		
Acceptances outstanding	70	111
Miscellaneous liabilities	348	423
Total liabilities	20,558	21,306
Stockholders' equity capital:		
Common stock	212	212
Preferred stock	1	1
Capital surplus	603	601
Retained earnings	332	466
Treasury stock	(1)	—
Total stockholders' equity capital	**1,147**	**1,280**
Total liabilities and stockholders' equity	$21,705	$22,586

Investment Securities: The Liquid Portion.   A second line of defense to meet demands for cash and serve as a quick source of funds is the bank's liquid security holdings, often called *secondary reserves.* These typically include holdings of shorter-term government securities—both U.S. government and municipal (state and local government) securities—and money market securities, including interest-bearing time deposits held with other banks and commercial paper. Secondary reserves occupy the middle ground between cash assets and loans, earning some income but held mainly for the ease with which they can be converted into cash on short notice. In Table 4–3, some portion of the $2,803 million shown as investment securities held by this bank will serve as a secondary reserve to help deal with liquidity needs.

Investment Securities: The Income-Generating Portion.   Bonds, notes, and other securities held by the bank primarily for their expected rate of return or yield are known simply as *investment securities.* Frequently these are divided into *taxable securities*—mainly U.S. government bonds and notes, securities issued by various federal agencies (such as the Federal National Mortgage Association, known as Fannie Mae), and corporate bonds and notes—and *tax-exempt securities,* which consist principally of state and local government (municipal) bonds. The latter generate interest income that is exempt from federal income taxes.

Investment securities may be recorded on a bank's books at their original cost, at market value, or at the lower of cost or market value. Most banks record their security purchases and their other assets and liabilities at their original cost. Of course, if interest rates rise after the securities are purchased, their market value will be less than their original cost (book value). Therefore, banks that record securities on their balance sheets at cost often include a parenthetical note giving the securities' current market value. However, as we will soon see, accounting rules for U.S. banks are currently under great pressure for change with a trend toward replacing original or historical cost figures with current market values.

This bank also holds a small amount of *trading account securities.* This means the bank serves as a security dealer for certain kinds of securities (mainly federal, state, and local government obligations). The amount recorded in the trading account represents those securities the bank intends to sell before they reach maturity, valued at market.

Loans.   By far the largest asset item is *loans,* which generally·account for half to almost three-quarters of the total value of all bank assets. As Table 4–3 shows, *two* loan figures appear on bank balance sheets. The larger, called *gross loans,* is the sum of all outstanding IOUs owed to the bank in the form of consumer, real estate, commercial, and agricultural loans plus any credit extended by the bank to security dealers and other financial institutions. In Table 4–3, gross loans amounted to $15,887 million in the most recent year, or about 73 percent of the bank's total assets.

However, loan losses, both current and projected, are deducted from the amount of this total (gross) loan figure. Under current U.S. tax law, banks are allowed to build up a reserve for future loan losses, called the *allowance for possible loan losses* (ALL), from their flow of income based on their recent loan-loss experience. The ALL, which is a contra-asset account, represents an accumulated reserve against which loans declared to be uncollectible can be charged off.[1] This means that bad loans normally do *not* affect a bank's current income (unless the loan default is unexpected and no reserves had been set aside). Rather, when a loan is considered uncollectible, the bank's accounting department will write (charge) it off the books by reducing the ALL account by the amount of the uncollectible loan while simultaneously decreasing the asset account for gross loans. For example, suppose a bank granted a $10 million loan to a property development company to build a shopping center and the company subsequently went out of business. If the bank could reasonably expect to collect only $1 million of the original $10 million owed, the unpaid $9 million would be subtracted from the bank's total (gross) loans and from the ALL account.

The allowance for possible loan losses is built up gradually over time by annual deductions from current income. These deductions appear on the bank's income statement as a noncash expense item called the *provision for loan losses* (PLL). If writing off a large loan reduces the balance in the ALL account too much, management will be called upon to increase the annual PLL deduction (which will lower its current net income) in order to restore the ALL to a safer level. Additions to ALL are usually made when a bank's loan portfolio grows in size, when any loan is judged to be completely or partially uncollectible, or when an unexpected loan default occurs that has not already been reserved. The required accounting entries simply increase the contra-asset ALL and the expense account PLL.[2] The total amount in the loan-loss reserve (ALL) as of the date of the bank's Report of Condition is then deducted from gross

---

[1]Many banks divide the ALL account into two parts: specific reserves and general reserves. *Specific reserves* are set aside to cover a particular loan or loans expected to be a problem or that present the bank with above-average risk. Management may simply designate a portion of the reserves already in the ALL account as specific reserves or add more reserves to cover specific loan problems. The remaining reserves in the loan-loss account are called *general reserves*. This division of loan-loss reserves helps bank managers better understand their bank's needs for protection against current or future loan defaults. (See especially Walter [10].)

[2]Recently U.S. banks have been allowing their ALL loan-loss reserve to fall relative to the amount of their total loans. One reason is a provision in the Tax Reform Act of 1986 that, for the largest banking companies (assets over $500 million), mandates that only loans actually declared to be worthless can be expensed through the loan-loss provision (PLL) expense item. Unfortunately, this prevents banks from using the loan-loss reserve as a forward-looking reserve to deal with future losses and forces bank managers to look backward at past loan-loss experience. One reason the Tax Reform law was passed, changing the loan-loss reserve from forward looking (dealing with expected losses) to backward-looking (focusing on past loan problems), was that many bankers were using their loan-loss reserve to smooth out bank income, increasing loan-loss provisioning when bank income was high and reducing additions to loan-loss reserves when bank income was low. Thus, bank loan-loss reserves used to play a bigger role in stabilizing bank earnings over the business cycle than they do at many large banks today.

As we will see later on in Chapter 15, loan-loss reserves (the ALL account) are counted as part of bank capital up to 1.25 percent of a bank's total risk-weighted assets. However, these reserves are not considered permanent capital (known as Tier I capital), whereas a bank's retained earnings are considered permanent capital. This fact has encouraged many banks to reduce their loan-loss provisioning expense so they will have more net income left over after expenses in order to build up their permanent capital. This is another reason U.S. banks' ratios of loan-loss reserves to their total loans have generally been falling or have remained at relatively low levels in recent years. (See especially O'Toole [6].)

loans to help derive the account entry called *net loans* on the bank's balance sheet—a measure of the net realizable value of all loans outstanding.[3]

Another item that is deducted from gross loans to derive net loans is called *unearned discounts.* These discounts consist of interest income from loans that has been received from customers but not yet earned under the accrual method of accounting used by banks today. For example, if a customer receives a loan and pays all or some portion of the interest up front, the bank cannot record that interest payment as earned income because the customer involved has not yet had use of the loan for any length of time. Over the life of the loan, the interest income will gradually be earned by the bank and the necessary amounts will be transferred from unearned discount to the bank's interest income account.

Banks have another loan category on their books called *nonperforming loans,* which are credits that no longer accrue interest income for the bank or have had to be restructured to accommodate a borrower's changed circumstances. Under current regulations, a loan is placed in the nonperforming category when any scheduled loan repayment is past due for more than 90 days. Once a loan is classified as nonperforming, any accrued interest recorded on the bank's books, but not actually received, must be deducted from loan revenues. The bank is then forbidden to record any interest income from the loan until a cash payment actually comes in.

Federal Funds Sold and Securities Purchased under Resale Agreements.   Another type of loan listed as a separate item on the Report of Condition is *federal funds sold and securities purchased under agreements to resell.* This item includes mainly temporary loans (usually extended overnight, with the funds returned the next day) made to other banks, securities dealers, or even major corporations. The funds for these temporary loans often come from the reserves a bank has on deposit with the Federal Reserve Bank in its district—hence the name *federal funds.* Some of these temporary credits are extended in the form of repurchase (resale) agreements (RPs) in which the bank acquires temporary title to securities owned by the borrower and holds those securities as collateral until the loan is paid off.

Customers' Liability on Acceptances.   Larger banks often provide a form of credit for their customers known as *acceptance financing.* The amount of funds involved will appear in an asset account labeled *customers' liability on acceptances outstanding.* The reader will note that this term coincides exactly with an item listed under bank liabilities, *acceptances outstanding.* This dual pair of accounts increases each time a bank agrees to stand behind a customer's credit, usually to help that customer pay for goods imported from overseas. In this instance, the bank agrees to issue an acceptance (i.e, a signed letter of credit), which authorizes a third party (such as a foreign exporter of goods) to draw a draft against the issuing bank for a specified amount on a designated future date. On or before the date specified, the customer that requested the acceptance must pay the bank

---

[3]The largest U.S. banks that make international loans to less-developed countries are required to set aside *allocated transfer-risk reserves,* which are also deducted from their gross loans in determining net loans, to deal with potential losses on loans to these countries. These reserve requirements are established by the Intercountry Exposure Review Committee (ICERC), consisting of representatives from the FDIC, the Federal Reserve System, and the Comptroller of the Currency.

in full. The issuing bank, in turn, will honor the acceptance on its due date, paying the full amount printed on the draft's face to the current holder of the instrument.

Thus, the creation of bankers' acceptances gives rise simultaneously to both an asset item (the customer's liability to the bank) and a liability item (the bank's promise to honor the acceptance draft on the date specified). Bankers' acceptances are widely used today for financing international trade, for purchasing foreign currencies, and even to support the shipment and storage of goods and agricultural commodities in the domestic economy.

Miscellaneous Assets.   Bank assets also include the net (adjusted for depreciation) value of bank buildings and equipment, investments in subsidiary firms, prepaid insurance, and other relatively insignificant asset items. A bank usually devotes only a small percentage (between 1 and 2 percent) of its assets to the institution's physical plant—that is, the fixed assets represented by buildings and equipment needed to carry on daily operations. Indeed, as we have seen, the great majority of a bank's assets are financial claims (loans and securities) rather than fixed assets. However, fixed assets typically generate fixed operating costs in the form of depreciation expenses, property taxes, and so on, which provide *operating leverage,* enabling the bank to boost its operating earnings if it can increase its sales volume to a high enough level and earn more from using its fixed assets than those assets cost. But with so few fixed assets relative to other assets, banks cannot rely heavily on operating leverage to increase their earnings; they must instead rely mainly upon *financial leverage*—the use of borrowed funds—to boost their earnings performance and remain competitive with other industries in attracting capital.

Bank Liabilities

Deposits.   The principal liability of any bank is its deposits, representing the financial claims held by businesses, households, and governments against the bank. In the event a bank is liquidated, the proceeds from the sale of its assets must first be used to pay off the claims of its depositors (along with the IRS!). Other creditors and bank stockholders receive whatever funds remain. There are five major types of deposits:

1. *Noninterest-bearing demand deposits,* or regular checking accounts, generally permit unlimited check writing. But, under a federal law passed in 1933, they cannot pay any explicit interest rate (though many banks offer to pay postage costs and offer other "free" services that yield the demand deposit customer an implicit rate of return on these deposits).

2. *Savings deposits* generally bear the lowest rate of interest offered to depositors by a bank but may be of any denomination (though most banks impose a minimum size requirement) and permit the customer to withdraw at will.

3. *NOW accounts,* which can be held only by individuals and nonprofit institutions, bear interest and permit drafts (checks) to be written against each account in order to pay third parties.

4. *Money market deposit accounts* (MMDAs) can pay whatever interest rate the offering bank feels is competitive and have limited check-writing privileges

attached. No minimum denomination or maturity is required by law, though depository institutions must reserve the right to require seven days' notice before any withdrawals are made.

5. *Time deposits* (mainly certificates of deposit, or CDs), usually carry a fixed maturity (term) and a stipulated interest rate but may be of any denomination, maturity, and yield agreed upon by the bank and its depositor. Included are large ($100,000-plus) *negotiable CDs*—interest-bearing deposits that banks use to raise money from their most well-to-do customers.

The bulk of bank deposits are held by individuals and business firms. However, governments (federal, state, and local) also hold substantial deposit accounts—known as *public fund deposits.* Any time a school district sells bonds to construct a new school building, for example, the proceeds of the bond issue will flow into its deposit in a local bank. Similarly, when the U.S. Treasury collects taxes or sells securities to raise funds, the proceeds normally flow initially into public deposits that the Treasury has established in thousands of banks across the United States. Major banks also draw upon their foreign branch offices for deposits and record the amounts received from abroad simply as *deposits at foreign branches.*

Clearly, as Table 4–3 suggests, banks are heavily dependent upon their deposits, which today usually support between 70 and 80 percent of their total assets. In the case of the bank we have been analyzing, total deposits of $16,494 million funded 76 percent of its assets in the most recent year. Because these financial claims of the public are often volatile, and because they are so large relative to the owners' capital investment in the bank, the average banking institution has considerable exposure to failure risk. It must continually stand ready (be liquid) to meet deposit withdrawals. These twin pressures of risk and liquidity force bankers to exercise great caution in their choices of loans and other assets. Failure to do so threatens the bank with collapse under the weight of depositors' claims.

Borrowings from Nondeposit Sources.   While deposits, typically, represent the largest portion of bank sources of funds, sizable amounts of funds also stem from miscellaneous liability accounts. All other factors held equal, the larger the bank, the greater use it tends to make of nondeposit sources of funds. One reason bank borrowings from nondeposit funds sources have grown rapidly in recent years is that there are no reserve requirements on most of these funds, which lowers the cost of nondeposit funding. Also, borrowings in the money market usually can be arranged in a few minutes and the funds wired immediately to the bank that needs them. One drawback, however, is that interest rates on nondeposit funds are highly volatile. If there is even a hint of financial problems at a bank trying to borrow from these sources, that bank's borrowing cost can rise rapidly, or money market lenders may simply refuse to extend it any more credit.

The most important nondeposit funding source for most U.S. banks, typically, is represented by *federal funds purchased and securities sold under agreements to repurchase.* This account tracks the bank's temporary borrowings in the money market, mainly from reserves loaned to it by other banks (federal funds purchased) or from repurchase agreements where the bank has borrowed funds collateralized by some of its own securities from another bank or a large corporate customer. Other short-term borrowings the bank may draw upon include *borrowing reserves from the discount windows of the Federal Reserve banks* and *Eurodollar borrowings from multinational banks abroad or from the borrowing bank's own overseas branches.* In the worldwide banking system *Eurocurrency borrowings* (i.e., transferable time deposits denominated in a variety of currencies) represent the principal source of short-term borrowings by banks. Many banks also issue *long-term debt,* often in the form of real estate mortgages for the purpose of constructing new office facilities or modernizing plant and equipment. Finally, an *other liabilities* account serves as a catch-all for miscellaneous amounts owned by the bank, such as a deferred tax liability and obligations to pay off investors who hold *bankers' acceptances* (explained earlier).

Capital Accounts.   The capital accounts on a bank's Report of Condition represent the owners' (stockholders') share of the business. Every new bank begins with a minimum amount of owners' capital (normally at least $1 million) and then borrows funds from the public to "lever up" its operations. In fact, banks are among the most heavily leveraged (debt-financed) of all businesses. Their capital accounts normally represent less than 10 percent of the value of their total assets. In the case of the bank whose balance sheet appears in Table 4–3, the *stockholders' equity capital* of $1,147 million in the most recent year accounted for just 5.3 percent of its total assets.

Though a relatively small amount, bank capital accounts typically include many of the same items that other business corporations display on their balance sheets. The total par (face) value of *common stock outstanding* is listed, and where that stock is sold for more than its par value, the excess market value of the stock flows into a *capital surplus* account. Few banks issue *preferred stock,* which guarantees its holders an annual dividend before common stockholders receive any dividend payments. Preferred stock is generally viewed in the banking community as expensive to issue (principally because the annual dividend is not tax deductible) and a drain on the earnings that normally would flow to the bank's common stockholders, though the largest bank holding companies have issued substantial amounts of preferred shares in recent years in order to open up a new source of capital. Usually, the largest item in the capital account is *retained earnings* (undivided profits), which represent accumulated net income left over each year after payment of stockholder dividends. There may also be a *contingency reserve* held as protection against unforeseen losses and *treasury stock* that has been retired.

One unusual item that shows up in some bank capital accounts, particularly among medium-size and large banks, is *subordinated notes and debentures*—debt securities that are long-term and carry a claim on the bank's assets and income that comes after (is subordinated to) the claims of its depositors. Many bank analysts view subordinated notes as part of a bank's capital base, like common stockholders' equity, because the claim of subordinated note holders on bank resources has such a low priority and their claims can be used to reinforce the claims of depositors.

Comparative Balance Sheet Ratios for Different Size Banks.   The items we discussed above generally appear on *all* bank balance sheets, regardless of the bank's size. But the relative importance of each balance sheet item varies greatly with *bank size.* A good illustration of how bank size affects the mix of balance sheet items is shown in Table 4–4. For example, the largest banks hold more total (gross) loans relative to their assets than smaller banks. Smaller banks hold more investment securities and make fewer loans relative to their assets than larger firms. Smaller banking organizations rely more heavily on deposits to support their assets than do larger banks, while the larger institutions make heavier use of money market borrowings (such as the purchase of Eurocurrencies or federal funds). Clearly, the analyst examining a bank's financial condition must consider the *size* of the bank and compare it to other institutions of the same size (and, preferably, serving a similar market area as well).

TABLE 4–4   The Composition of Bank Balance Statements
(Percentage Mix of Bank Sources and Uses of Funds for Year-End 1996)

Assets, Liabilities, and Capital Items	All U.S. Insured Banks	U.S. Banks with Less Than $100 Million in Total Assets	U.S. Banks with $100 Million to $1 Billion in Total Assets	U.S. Banks with $1 Billion or More in Total Assets
			Percentage of Total Assets for:	
Cash and deposits due from depository institutions	7.34%	5.32%	5.25%	7.92%
Investment securities	17.49	29.66	26.90	14.67
Federal funds sold and securities purchased under agreements to resell	3.58	4.79	3.56	3.49
Total loans and leases:	61.40	57.16	61.09	61.79
Commercial and industrial	25.25	16.39	17.60	27.40
Consumer	19.95	15.45	17.64	20.73
Real estate	40.56	56.08	59.79	35.65
To depository institutions	4.06	0.11	0.54	5.04
To foreign governments	0.38	*	0.02	0.48
Agricultural production	1.47	11.00	2.60	0.56
Other loans	5.54	0.60	1.24	6.74
Leases	2.79	0.37	0.57	3.40
Assets held in trading accounts	5.26	0.03	0.04	6.71
Bank premises and fixed assets	1.41	1.77	1.75	1.32
Other assets	3.52	1.27	1.41	4.11
Total assets	100.0%	100.0%	100.0%	100.0%
Interest-bearing deposits	55.32	73.29	69.21	51.16
Noninterest-bearing (demand) deposits	14.51	13.34	14.00	14.70
Federal funds purchased and securities sold under agreements to repurchase	6.94	0.97	3.57	8.08
Other liabilities	15.03	1.84	3.78	19.29
Total equity capital	8.20	10.56	9.44	7.77
Total liabilities and equity capital	100.0%	100.0%	100.0%	100.0%

*Less than 0.005 percent.

Source: Federal Deposit Insurance Corporation.

The Expansion of Off-Balance-Sheet Items in Banking

As we will see in much greater detail in Chapters 8 and 9, banks have converted many of their customer services in recent years into fee-generating transactions that are *not* recorded on their balance sheets. Prominent examples of these *off-balance-sheet items* include:

1. *Standby credit agreements,* in which a bank pledges to guarantee repayment of a customer's loan received from a third party.
2. *Interest rate swaps,* in which a bank promises to exchange interest payments on debt securities with another party.
3. *Financial futures and option interest-rate contracts,* in which a bank agrees to deliver or to take delivery of securities from another party at a guaranteed price.
4. *Loan commitments,* in which a bank pledges to lend up to a certain amount of funds until the commitment matures.
5. *Foreign exchange rate contracts,* in which a bank agrees to deliver or accept delivery of foreign currencies.

The problem with these off-balance-sheet transactions is that they often expose a bank to added risk even though they may not show up in conventional bank condition reports. This is particularly true of standby credit agreements issued to back a loan that a customer has received from another lender. If the customer defaults on the loan, the bank is pledged to pay off the customer's IOU. Moreover, as Table 4–5 illustrates,

TABLE 4–5   Examples of Off-Balance-Sheet Items Reported by U.S. Banks

Off-Balance-Sheet Items	Total Reported for All Insured U.S. Banks in Billions of Dollars on December 31, 1996:			
	All U.S. Insured Banks	*U.S. Insured Banks Under $100 Million in Total Assets*	*U.S. Insured Banks $100 Million to $1 Billion in Total Assets*	*U.S. Insured Banks $1 Billion or More in Total Assets*
Standby credit agreements	$ 211.0	$ 0.8	$ 5.7	$ 204.5
Interest-rate swaps (notional value)	7,069.4	0.1	7.1	7,062.2
Financial futures and forward contracts	3,201.2	0.3	0.8	3,200.1
Loan commitments (unused)	2,528.7	52.9	246.8	2,229.0
Foreign exchange contracts	6,503.8	*	2.5	6,501.3
Other off-balance-sheet items	3,839.4	1.0	8.4	3,830.0
Total off-balance-sheet items	$23,353.5	$55.1	$271.3	$23,027.1
Total assets reported on the balance sheet ($)	$4,578.3	$280.2	$713.3	$3,584.8
Off-balance-sheet items as a percent of total assets reported on the balance sheet (%)	510.1%	19.7%	38.0%	642.4%

Source: Federal Deposit Insurance Corporation.

off-balance-sheet items have grown so rapidly they now exceed total bank assets by more than 500 percent! These contingent contracts are heavily concentrated in the largest banks—over $1 billion in total assets—where they are more than six times larger than the total of all reported bank assets.

Reflecting concerns about bank risk exposure from off-balance-sheet items, the Financial Accounting Standards Board (FASB) ruled in 1996 that banks and other corporations must report the fair market value of their derivative contracts (such as futures, options, and swaps) on their financial reports and also report any gains or losses from using derivatives to hedge their earnings. A derivative's gain or loss could be reported during the same time period that the earnings from a hedged asset or liability item on the balance sheet is reported. However, strong opposition to this proposal from Citicorp and other leading companies caused FASB to reconsider and delay implementation of its derivatives rule. Critics have argued that many derivative contracts have no readily determinable fair market value and the implementation of the proposed FASB rule would make corporate earnings unnecessarily volatile. The outcome of this FASB rule controversy remains highly uncertain at this time. In later chapters, we will explore how bank regulators have acted in recent years to deal with these new forms of off-balance-sheet risk exposure.

The Problem of Book-Value Accounting in Banking

Another problem affecting the meaning and interpretation of bank balance sheets today centers around the industry's unique accounting methods. For decades the banking industry has followed the practice of recording assets and liabilities on bank balance sheets at their original cost on the day they were received. This accounting practice, known as book-value, historical, or original cost accounting, has come under attack in recent years. The book-value accounting method assumes that all loans and other balance-sheet items will be held to maturity. It does not reflect the impact on a bank's balance sheet of changing interest rates and changing default risk, which affect both the value and the cash flows associated with bank loans, securities, and debt.[4]

For example, if market interest rates on government bonds maturing in one year are currently at 10 percent, a $1,000 par-value bond held by a bank and promising an annual interest (coupon) rate of 10 percent would likely sell at a current market price of $1,000. However, if market interest rates rise to 12 percent, the value of the bank's bond must fall to about $980 so that the institution's return from this asset at the end of the bond's life is also about 12 percent.

Similarly, changes in the default risk exposure of borrowers will affect the current market value of a bank's loans and securities. Clearly, if some bank loans are less

---

[4]While we usually say that most bank assets are valued at historical or original cost, the traditional bank accounting procedure should really be called *amortized cost*. For example, if a loan's principal is gradually paid off over time, a bank will deduct from the original face value of the loan (its historical recorded value) the amount of any repayments of the loan's principal, thus reflecting the fact that the amount owed by the bank's borrowing customer is being amortized over time. Similarly, if a security is acquired at a discounted price below its par value, the spread between the security's original discounted value and its value at maturity will be amortized over time as bank income until the security reaches maturity.

likely to be repaid than was true when they were granted, their market value *must* be lower. For example, a $1,000 loan for a year granted to a borrower at a loan rate of 10 percent clearly must fall in market value if the borrower's financial situation deteriorates and he or she becomes more risky. If interest rates applicable to other borrowers in the same higher risk class stand at 12 percent, the $1,000 loan will decline to only about $833 in market value. Recording a bank's assets at their original (or historical) cost and never changing that number to reflect current market conditions does not give bank depositors, stockholders, and other investors interested in buying bank-issued stock or debt a true picture of a banking firm's real financial condition. Investors could easily be deceived.[5]

As the decade of the 1990s began the Financial Accounting Standards Board ruled initially that businesses with less than $150 million in total assets (which would include at least two-thirds of all U.S. banks) could wait until 1995 to disclose updated asset and liability values in their annual reports. In the summer of 1992, however, FASB issued a compromise plan that focused only upon bank security investments—probably the easiest balance sheet item for a banker to value at market. FASB asked banks to divide their security holdings into two broad groups—those they planned to hold to maturity and those that may be traded before they reach maturity. Securities that a bank plans to hold to maturity could be valued at their original cost while tradable securities would be valued at their current market price. At the same time the Securities and Exchange Commission (SEC) asked leading banks that were actively trading securities to put any securities they expected to sell into a special balance sheet account labeled *assets held for sale*. These reclassified assets must be valued at cost or market, whichever is lower at the time. FASB and the SEC seemed determined to eradicate "gains trading"— a practice in which bank managers sell any securities that have appreciated in order to reap a capital gain, but hold onto those securities whose prices have declined and continue to value these lower priced instruments at their historical cost.[6]

---

[5]Under the historical or book-value accounting system used in banking, interest rate changes do *not* affect the value of bank capital because they do not affect the values of bank assets and liabilities recorded at cost. Moreover, only *realized* capital gains and losses affect the book values on a bank's balance sheet under traditional bank accounting practices. Banks can increase their current income and their capital, for example, by selling assets which have risen in value while ignoring any losses in value experienced by other bank-held assets.

[6]In addition to requiring greater disclosure of the market value of bank assets, federal regulatory agencies began in 1994 to require the largest U.S. banks (with $500 million or more in assets) to file financial statements audited by an independent public accountant with their principal federal regulator, the FDIC, and any appropriate state agency within 90 days of the end of their fiscal year. Along with audited financial statements each bank must also submit a statement by its management concerning the effectiveness of the bank's internal controls over financial reporting in preserving the bank's safety and soundness. An independent accountant must also evaluate and give an opinion on the quality of the bank's internal controls and its compliance with safety and soundness laws. Moreover, an audit committee consisting entirely of outside directors must review and evaluate a bank's annual audit with its management and an independent public accountant. Larger U.S. banks, with $3 billion or more in total assets, must meet even more stringent requirements for setting up outside audit committees, including requiring at least two audit committee members to have prior banking experience, prohibiting large bank customers from serving on such a committee, and mandating that audit committees must have access to legal counsel that is independent of the management of a bank. These tough new reporting rules are a consequence of the FDIC Improvement Act, passed by the U.S. Congress in 1991.

Bankers' Insights and Issues

The Bank Accounting Controversy:
Where It Came From and Where It Is Headed

As we have seen in this chapter, various government agencies regulating banks have begun to eat away at banking's traditional practice of recording assets and liabilities on the day these items are added to the bank's books and not changing that value during the life of the account regardless of fluctuations in market prices or interest rates. In the 1980s the Securities and Exchange Commission along with the Financial Accounting Standards Board began questioning that traditional practice out of fear it was giving buyers of bank-issued securities misleading information concerning the true value of their investments. Indeed, historical cost accounting can effectively conceal that a troubled bank has actually become insolvent in market-value terms. Many banks and near-bank thrifts (like savings and loans) failed during this period and the public was becoming wary of buying bank-issued stock and debt securities.

One of the most serious controversies regarding bankers' valuation of their assets centered around the investment security portfolio, consisting mainly of government bonds and notes. For many years bankers were required to set aside in a separate "trading account" any investment securities that they did not intend to hold to maturity and to value those securities at their current market values. Nearly all other securities, however, were carried on the books at historical (original) cost. Yet, the investment portfolio seemed to be the easiest of all bank balance sheet items to value at market because most of the securities held in that portfolio have active resale markets and readily available daily price quotations.

In 1991 the U.S. Congress passed the Federal Deposit Insurance Corporation Improvement Act (FDICIA) which, in Section 121, required federal banking agencies to develop a method of assigning supplemental "fair value" to a depository institution's assets and liabilities. To most authorities this means reporting the value of bank assets and liabilities in terms of both their original or historical cost and their market values—that is, "marking to market" all bank assets and liabilities according to the price at which each asset and liability would sell on the day a financial statement is prepared. In February 1992 the Federal Financial Institutions Examination Council voted to require U.S. banks to value any loans and securities "held for trading" at market value, while loans and securities "held for possible sale" must be valued at the lower of their cost or market value.

In 1992 and 1993 the Financial Accounting Standards Board put the finishing touches on a new accounting rule labeled FASB 115. In its final form FASB 115 requires banks and other financial institutions to divide their holdings of debt and equity securities into three groups:

A. Investment securities purchased with "the positive intent and ability to hold to maturity," which may be valued at their original or historical cost.

B. Investment securities "held for future sale," which are to be valued at market so that changes in their market price will be reflected in both a bank's net earnings and its capital.

C. Investment securities that do not fit in the above categories, which should be recorded in an account labeled "available for sale" and should be valued at their market price with any changes in value reflected in bank capital (stockholders' equity) but not in bank earnings.

This decision by the FASB has made few people happy, inside or outside the SEC, the bank regulatory agencies, or the banking industry. For one thing it deals only with securities and not the biggest portion of a bank's assets—its loans—and completely ignores deposits and other bank liabilities. This means that only selected bank assets will be periodically "marked to market" and, therefore, a bank's net worth is likely to be more volatile than it would be if *both* sides of its balance sheet were similarly treated.

Bankers have complained because FASB 115 will require more personnel time and paperwork to determine market values and because the new ruling may distort bank portfolio choices. Moreover, interest rate hedging will be more difficult due to the unbalanced treatment of assets and liabilities.

Not long after FASB 115 appeared, a new ruling, Statement 114, surfaced to deal with another long-standing, but questionable bank accounting practice. FASB 114 requires banks and other financial institutions to account for the *expected loss of interest income on nonperforming loans* when calculating their loan-loss provisions. Many banks still base their loan-loss reserves only upon their projected loss of *principal* from a troubled loan, not including the expected loss or delay in receiving interest payments. A similar problem arises when the terms of a loan must be renegotiated to a longer payout schedule or the bank agrees to reduce or delay interest payments because the borrower cannot successfully handle the originally negotiated terms of the loan. Currently, many banks do not report lost interest if they expect eventual repayment of all of the principal of a troubled loan. Statement 114 requires banks to reduce the value of a loan on their books in order to reflect any reduction in expected interest payments as well as any loss of principal. While both secured and unsecured loans are covered, certain loans (such as credit cards and home mortgages) are exempt.

When the adjustment for loss of interest is made, the result is likely to be an increase in loan-loss provisions at those banks not already recognizing interest losses on their nonperforming loans. In figuring the value of impaired loans, banks are required by the new FASB rule to measure the value of bank loans by the present value of their expected future cash flows discounted at the loan's effective interest (which is the contractual loan rate adjusted for any deferred loan fees, costs, premiums, or discounts that prevailed when the loan was extended or acquired). Each quarter bankers must estimate when their troubled loans are likely to be repaid, if ever.

Note: See especially Sherrill Shaffer, "Marking Banks to Market," *Business Review,* Federal Reserve Bank of Philadelphia, July/August 1992, pp. 13–22; and Charles S. Morris and Gordon H. Sellon, Jr., "Market Value Accounting for Banks Pros and Cons," *Economic Review,* Federal Reserve Bank of Kansas City, March/April 1991, pp. 5–19.

Bankers have argued that these moves toward market-value accounting will increase the volatility of reported earnings, force their institutions to pay higher returns to stockholders and debtholders, and require their banks to hold more capital. They point out that many banks, forced to value assets at market, will hesitate to buy long-term bonds (including bonds issued by local city and county governments) due to their greater volatility in market price, thus reducing the supply of credit to corporations and governments issuing long-term debt. Moreover, market valuation may encourage banks to sell off lower-valued loans too quickly or push troubled borrowers into bankruptcy rather than continuing to work with a customer in the hope of turning a bad situation around. A massive bank sell-off of troubled loans could seriously depress property values and the entire economy—a possibility that has given rise to considerable concern about the potential effects of the FASB rulings. Debate over these bank accounting issues is likely to continue for some time.

Concept Checks

4–1. What are the principal accounts that appear on a bank's balance sheet (Report of Condition)?

4–2. Which accounts are most important and which are least important on the asset side of a bank's balance sheet?

4–3. What accounts are most important on the liability side of a bank's balance sheet?

4–4. What are the essential differences among demand deposits, savings deposits, and time deposits?

4–5. What are primary reserves and secondary reserves and what are they supposed to do?

4–6. Suppose that a bank holds cash in its vault of $1.4 million, short-term government securities of $12.4 million, privately issued money market instruments of $5.2 million, deposits at the Federal Reserve banks of $20.1 million, cash items in the process of collection of $0.6 million, and deposits placed with other banks of $16.4 million. How much in primary reserves does this bank hold? in secondary reserves?

4–7. What are off-balance-sheet items and why are they important to some banks?

4–8. Why are bank accounting practices under attack right now? In what ways could banks improve their accounting methods?

Components of the Income Statement (Report of Income)

A bank's income statement, or **Report of Income,** indicates the amount of revenue received and expenses incurred over a specific period of time, such as the current year. There is usually a close correlation between the size of the principal items on a bank's balance sheet (Report of Condition) and its income statement. After all, assets on the balance sheet account for the majority of operating revenues, while liabilities generate most of a bank's operating expenses.

The principal source of bank revenue is the interest income generated by the bank's earning assets, mainly its loans (L), securities (S), any interest-bearing deposits that are part of cash assets (C) held with other banks, and any miscellaneous assets (M) generating revenue (including any income earned by subsidiaries of the bank or rental income from property that it owns). The major expenses incurred in generating this revenue include interest paid out to depositors (D), interest owed on nondeposit borrowings (NDB), the cost of equity capital (EC), salaries, wages, and benefits paid to bank employees (SWB), overhead expenses associated with the bank's physical plant (O), funds set aside for possible loan losses (PLL), taxes owed (T), and miscellaneous expenses (ME). The difference between all revenues and expenses is *net income.* Thus:

$$\text{Net income = Total revenue items – Total expense items} \qquad (4)$$

where:

Revenue items

↓

(cash assets × average yield on cash assets + security investments × average yield on security investments + loans outstanding × average yield on loans + miscellaneous assets × average yield on miscellaneous assets)

Minus (–) Expense items

↓

(total deposits × average interest cost on deposits + nondeposit borrowings × average interest cost on nondeposit borrowings + owners' capital × average cost of owners' capital + employee salaries, wages, and benefits expense + overhead expense + provision for possible loan losses + miscellaneous expenses + taxes owed)

Using r to represent average yields on assets and i to represent the interest cost on deposits, nondeposit borrowings, and owners' capital, the bank's *net income* as reported at the bottom of its Report of Income (income statement) must be the following:

$$\text{Net income} = (C \times r_{cash} + S \times r_{sec} + L \times r_{loans} + M \times r_M) \qquad (5)$$
$$- (D \times i_d + NDB \times i_{ndb} + EC \times i_{ec} + SWB$$
$$+ O + PLL + ME + T).$$

This equation reminds us that banks interested in increasing their net income have a number of possible options: (1) increase the average yield on each asset held; (2) redistribute their earning assets toward those assets with higher average yields; (3) reduce their interest or noninterest expenses on deposits, nondeposit borrowings, and owners' capital; (4) shift their funding sources toward less-costly deposits and other borrowings; (5) find ways to reduce their employee (SWB), overhead (O), loan-loss

(PLL), and miscellaneous operating expenses (ME); or (6) reduce their taxes owed (T) through improved tax management practices.[7]

Of course, management does not have full control of all of these items that affect the bank's net income. The yields earned on various bank assets, the revenues generated by sales of services, and the interest rates that must be paid to attract deposits and nondeposit borrowings are determined by demand and supply forces in the *market* the bank serves. Over the long run, the *public* will be the principal factor shaping what types of loans the bank will be able to make and what types of deposit services it will be able to sell in its market area. Within the broad boundaries allowed by competition in the marketplace, by regulation, and the pressures exerted by public demand, however, management decisions are still a major factor in determining the particular mix of loans, securities, cash, and deposits each bank holds and the size and composition of its revenues and expenses.

Financial Flows and Stocks

The bank's income statement is a record of *financial flows* over time (in contrast to the balance sheet, which is a statement of *stocks* of assets, liabilities, and equity held at any given point in time). Therefore, we can represent the bank's income statement as a report of *financial outflows* (expenses) and *financial inflows* (revenues):

The Income Statement (Report of Income)

Financial Inflows	*Financial Outflows*
Loan income	Deposit costs
Security income	Nondeposit borrowing costs
Income from cash assets	Salaries and wages expense
Miscellaneous income	Miscellaneous expenses
	Tax expense

Total financial inflows – Total financial outflows = Net income
 (all revenues)   (all expenses)

Actual bank income reports are usually more complicated than the simple statements shown above because each item may have several component accounts. Most bank income statements will closely resemble the income statement shown in Table 4–6 for a large midwestern banking organization—the same institution whose balance sheet we looked at earlier. Table 4–6 is divided into four main sections: (1) interest income, (2) interest expenses, (3) noninterest income, and (4) noninterest expenses.

---

[7]Because the bulk of taxes owed (T) by a U.S. bank consists of federal and state income taxes, which depend directly upon the size of a bank's net income, most authorities would write the equation for net income as follows:

$$\text{Net income} = (1-t)\,(C \times r_{cash} + S \times r_{sec} + L \times r_{loans} + M \times r_M - D \times i_d - NDB$$
$$\times i_{ndb} - EC \times i_{ec} - SWB - O - PLL - ME)$$

where t is the bank's income tax bracket or marginal income tax rate. It should be noted, however, that many states levy nonincome forms of taxes on banks, the most popular being the franchise tax. Over half of U.S. state governments tax banks the same way that they tax any business corporation. Since 1969 national banks have been liable for the same tax treatment as state-chartered banks within their headquarter's state.

TABLE 4–6   Income Statement (Report of Income) for a Large Midwestern Bank

(all figures in millions of dollars)

Revenue and Expense Items	Most Recent Six-Month Period
Interest income:	
Interest and fees on loans	**$780**
Interest on investment securities:	
Taxable securities' revenue	76
Tax-exempt securities' revenue	40
Other interest income	37
Total interest income	933
Interest expenses:	
Deposit interest costs	513
Interest on short-term debt	101
Interest on long-term debt	30
Total interest expenses	644
Net interest income, or interest margin (equals total interest income less total interest expenses)	**289**
Provision for possible loan losses	255
Net interest income after provision for possible loan losses	34
Noninterest income:	
Service charges on customer deposits	29
Trust department income	26
Other operating income	119
Total noninterest income	**174**
Noninterest expenses:	
Wages and salaries and other personnel expenses	130
Net occupancy and equipment expenses	44
Other operating expenses	135
Total noninterest expenses	309
Net noninterest income, or noninterest margin (equals noninterest income less noninterest expenses)	(135)
Income (or loss) before income taxes	(101)
Provision for income taxes	(3)
Net income (or loss) after taxes	**(98)**
Average number of common shares of stock outstanding (actual)	42,384,000
Income (loss) per share of common stock (actual)	$(2.45)

Interest income.   Not surprisingly, interest and fees generated from loans account for most bank revenues (normally two-thirds or more of the total). In the case of the bank we have been following, the $780 million in loan revenues represents about 70 percent of total interest and noninterest income of this bank. Loan revenues are usually followed in importance by investment earnings from taxable and tax-exempt securities, interest

Bankers' Insights and Issues

Banks and the Year 2000

Like thousands of other businesses that adopted computers over the years to handle their recordkeeping, most bank computer systems set up in the 1900s cannot distinguish between the year 1900 and the year 2000. This problem arose because most computer operating systems and software programs use six-digit data fields with a space of only two digits wide to record the year a loan or other transaction is started or completed. Such a system would not be able to record and recognize unambiguously a date after 1999. For example, consider the date 000101, which most computer systems put together in the 20th century would recognize as January 1, 1900. However, in a conventional six-digit data field this could also be January 1, 2000. On many bank computer systems the program called up to record the transaction and the date would read the date given above as an illogical error and not complete the transaction. Equally damaging, some customers scheduled to be billed could get refunds and vice versa. Some credit card accounts would be wrongly declared as "closed," while bank security systems might, in some cases, suddenly shut down.

The bank regulatory agencies worldwide have been pressuring the banks under their supervision to work quickly to remedy these computer problems out of fear that bank loan departments and payments systems might be severely disrupted if their computer systems cannot function as more and more transactions carry 21st-century dates. Worse, some customers could lose access to their bank funds and credit risk could increase. Most banks appear to have hired third-party computer vendors and software providers to help deal with this problem. Bank examiners in many countries have been asked to review the plans that banks they oversee have set in motion to prepare for the turn of the century so that customer services will not be interrupted. Bankers must be able to show they are making adequate progress toward becoming "Year 2000 Compliant."

Some banks will expand the size of their date fields, while others will change the logic of their date accounting systems to read years beyond 1999 as greater than 99. All institutions will have to create planning committees from all major areas of the bank and review all existing internal and external computer systems each bank accesses and then test thoroughly any changes that are made to bring the bank into Year 2000 compliance. Not an easy or cheap exercise!

earned on federal funds loans and repurchase (resale) agreements, and interest received on time deposits placed with other banks. The relative importance of these various income items fluctuates from year to year with shifts in interest rates and loan demand, though loan income is nearly always the dominant revenue source. It must be noted, however, that the relative importance of loan revenue versus noninterest revenue sources (so-called *fee income*) is changing rapidly, with fee income today growing much faster than interest income on loans as bankers work to develop fee-based services.

Interest Expenses.   The number 1 expense item for a bank is *interest on its deposits.* As Table 4–6 shows, interest on deposits totaled almost 54 percent of this bank's total expenses. An important and rapidly growing interest expense item in recent years is the interest owed on short-term borrowings in the money market—mainly borrowings of federal funds (reserves) from other banks and borrowings back-stopped by security repurchase agreements. Interest on short-term debt was just over 15 percent of this bank's total expenses in the most recent year.

Net Interest Income.   Many banks subtract total interest expenses from total interest income to yield *net interest income.* This important item is often referred to as the *interest margin*—the gap between the interest income the bank receives on loans and securities and the interest cost of its borrowed funds. It is usually a key determinant of bank profitability. When the interest margin falls, bank stockholders will usually experience a weakening in the bank's bottom line—its net after-tax earnings—and, perhaps, in the dividends they receive on each share of stock held.

Loan-Loss Expense.   Another expense item that banks can deduct from current income is known as the *provision for possible loan losses.* This provision account is really a *noncash* expense, created by a simple bookkeeping entry. Its purpose is to shelter a portion of the bank's current earnings from taxes in order to help prepare for bad loans. The annual loan-loss provision is deducted from current revenues before taxes are applied to earnings.

Because this expense item is tax deductible, banks have had a strong incentive in the past to inflate the provision for loan losses in order to shelter more of their current earnings from taxes. Congress decided to severely restrict use of this unique tax shelter by large banking organizations (defined as banks or bank holding companies with more than $500 million in assets) through the passage of the Tax Reform Act of 1986. Prior to the Reform Act's passage, all U.S. banks could figure their loan-loss deductions using either the *experience method* (in which the amount of deductible loan-loss expense would be the product of the average ratio of net loan charge-offs to total loans in the most recent six years times the current total of outstanding loans) or the *reserve method* (which allowed banks to automatically deduct, without being taxed, up to 0.6 percent of their eligible loans at year-end). U.S. banks could choose the particular loan-loss expensing method that resulted in the greatest tax savings.

The Tax Reform Act, however, required large U.S. banks and bank holding companies to use the *specific charge-off method,* which allows them to add to loan-loss reserves out of pre-tax income each year no more than the amount of those loans actually written off as uncollectible. The expensing of a worthless loan usually must occur in the year that loan becomes worthless. Small banks and banking companies (under $500 million in assets) could continue to use the experience method or switch to the specific charge-off method.

Once a bank calculates its provision for loan losses for the year, it adds the calculated amount to its allowance for loan losses on the balance sheet. It must also add to its allowance for loan losses any funds recovered (through litigation or liquidation of borrower assets) on loans previously charged off as losses. For example, suppose First National Bank of Irwin had an allowance for loan losses at the end of the previous year of $2,500,000, and it recorded $400,000 as loan-loss expenses (provision) for the current year. However, the bank recovered $150,000 from loans previously written off against the allowance for loan-loss account. This $150,000 in recoveries should be added back to the loan-loss account to restore a portion of what was deducted from the loan-loss allowance when the original troubled loans were written off. Finally, suppose the bank's management decided to declare $300,000 in current loans as uncollectible and worthless this year. Its allowance for loan-loss account at the end of the current year would appear as follows:

Reconciliation of Loan-Loss Reserve	
Balance in allowance for loan losses, end of previous year	$2,500,000
Add: Recoveries on loans previously charged off	$ 150,000
Subtract: Charge-offs of loans declared uncollectible this year	$ 300,000
Add: Current provision for loan losses	$ 400,000
Balance in allowance for loan losses, end of current year	$2,750,000

When loans are deemed worthless, the amount of loss is deducted from total gross loans on the balance sheet and also from the loan-loss reserve. For example, suppose a bank's total (gross) loans are $10 million and it expects worthless loans this year to amount to $250,000. Its current loan-loss reserve (allowance) is $2,750,000. Before the $250,000 in worthless loans is removed its balance sheet would appear as follows:

Assets	
Gross loans	$10,000,000
– Allowance for	
loan–loss reserves	– 2,750,000
Net loans	$ 7,250,000

Now suppose management determines that $250,000 in current loans are indeed worthless and should be written off. The bank's balance sheet would appear as follows:

Assets	
Gross loans	$9,750,000
– Allowance for	
loan–loss reserves	–2,500,000
Net loans	$7,250,000

Current interest income accrued, but not received from a worthless nonpaying loan is deducted from a bank's current income.

As Walter [10] notes, if a bank is careful in its evaluation of its possible future needs for loan-loss reserves, the difference between total (gross) loans and the allowance for loan losses should yield us the best estimate of the net realizable value of the bank's total loan portfolio.

Noninterest Income.   Sources of income other than earnings from loans and securities are called simply *noninterest income* and usually include fees earned from offering trust services, service charges on deposit accounts, and miscellaneous fees and charges for other bank services. Recently, bankers have targeted noninterest income—known as *fee* *income*—as a key source of future revenues. By more aggressively selling services other than loans (such as security brokerage, insurance, and trust services), bankers have found a promising channel for boosting the bottom line on their income statements, for diversifying their income sources, and for insulating their banks more adequately from fluctuations in interest rates. The $174 million of noninterest income reported by the bank in Table 4–6 was almost 16 percent of its total revenue for the six-month reporting period.

Noninterest Expenses.   The key noninterest expense item for most banks is *wages, salaries, and other personnel expenses*—which has been a rapidly rising expense item in recent years, as banking firms have pursued top-quality college graduates to head their management teams and lured experienced senior management away from their competitors. The costs of maintaining bank properties and rental fees on office space show up in *net occupancy and equipment expense.* The cost of bank furniture and equipment also appears under the noninterest expense category, along with numerous small expense items including legal fees, paper and office supplies, and repair costs.

Net Income.   Bank accounting practices call for the deduction of both noninterest expenses (including the annual provision for loan losses) and interest expenses from the sum of interest and noninterest income to yield income (or loss) before taxes. Applicable federal and state income tax rates are applied to this income figure to derive the bank's net after-tax income (or loss).

One usually small item that can be substantial for some banks is *securities gains or losses.* Most banks purchase, sell, or redeem securities during the year, and this trading activity often results in gains or losses above or below the original cost (book value) of the securities. In 1983 the Securities and Exchange Commission required U.S. banks to record their gains or losses on investment securities as ordinary operating income or operating losses. This means that security gains, like bank earnings on loans, are subject to the full corporate income tax rate. Most banks today now report securities gains or losses as a component of noninterest income, either as a separate line item in the noninterest income section of the bank's income statement or as a part of "other" (miscellaneous) noninterest income. A bank can use these gains or losses on securities to smooth out its net income from year to year. If earnings from loans decline, securities gains may offset all or part of the decline. In contrast, when loan revenues (which are fully taxable) are high, securities losses can be used to reduce the bank's taxable income.

Another method for stabilizing bank earnings consists of *nonrecurring sales of assets.* These one-time-only (*extraordinary income or loss*) transactions often involve financial assets (such as common stock) or real property pledged as collateral behind a loan upon which the bank has foreclosed. A bank may also sell real estate or subsidiary firms that it owns. Such transactions frequently have a substantial effect on current earnings, particularly if the bank sells property it acquired in a loan foreclosure. Such property is usually carried on its books at minimal market value, but its sale price may turn out to be substantially higher.

The key bottom-line item on bank income statements is *net income after taxes,* which is usually divided into two categories by the board of directors. Some funds may flow to the stockholders in the form of *cash dividends.* Another portion (usually the larger part) will go into *retained earnings* (also called *undivided profits*) in the bank's capital accounts in order to provide a larger capital base to support the institution's future growth.

We note that this bank reported an income *loss* for the six-month period just ended. The bank had been facing substantial losses from its energy loans and from its foreclosures on delinquent real estate loans. As a result, it significantly increased its provision for loan losses, which eroded its net interest earnings. Because operating expenses could not be reduced to match the decline in loan income, a net loss resulted for the current income reporting period. Since passage of the Tax Reform Act of 1986, banks have been allowed to carry net operating losses backward for only three years, but these losses may be carried forward for up to 15 years.

Comparative Income Statement Ratios for Banks of Different Sizes

Like bank balance sheets, income statements usually contain much the same items for both large and small banks, but the relative importance of individual income and expense items varies substantially with the size of a bank. For example, as shown in Table 4–7, larger banks receive more of their total income from noninterest fees (e.g., service charges and commissions) than do small banks, while smaller banks rely more heavily on deposits than on money market borrowings for their funding and, thus, pay out relatively more deposit interest than many larger banks. Any meaningful analysis of an individual bank's income statement requires comparisons with other banks of comparable size and location.

Concept Checks

4–9. What accounts make up the Report of Income (income statement) of a bank?

4–10. In rank order, what are the most important revenue and expense items on a bank's Report of Income?

4–11. What is the relationship between the provision for loan losses on a bank's Report of Income and the allowance for loan losses on its Report of Condition?

4–12. Suppose a bank has an allowance for loan losses of $1.25 million at the beginning of the year, charges current income for a $250,000 provision for loan losses, charges off worthless loans of $150,000, and recovers $50,000 on loans previously charged off. What will be the balance in the bank's allowance for loan losses at year-end?

Other Useful Bank Financial Statements

Many bankers and bank analysts like to supplement the information provided on the balance sheet and the income statement by looking at two other financial statements that display balance sheet and income statement items in a different and frequently revealing format. These are (*a*) the Funds-Flow, or Sources and Uses of Funds, Statement

TABLE 4–7   **The Composition of Bank Income Statements**
(Percentage of Total Assets as of Year-End 1996)

Revenue and Expense Items	Percentage of Total Assets for:			
	All U.S. Insured Banks	*U.S. Banks with Less Than $100 Million in Total Assets*	*U.S. Banks with $100 Million to $1 Billion in Total Assets*	*U.S. Banks with $1 Billion or More in Total Assets*
Total interest income:	6.83%	7.33%	7.30%	6.70%
Loan income	5.12	5.23	5.43	5.04
Security income	1.11	1.78	1.62	0.95
Federal funds sold and repurchase agreements	0.20	0.25	0.18	0.20
Other interest income	0.41	0.06	0.06	1.22
Total interest expense:	3.28	3.23	3.18	3.31
Deposit interest	2.35	3.13	2.88	3.30
Federal funds purchased and repurchase agreements	0.37	0.04	0.17	0.43
Other interest expenses	0.56	0.05	0.13	0.69
Net interest income	3.55	4.10	4.12	3.39
Provision for loan losses	0.35	0.20	0.28	0.38
Noninterest income:	2.04	1.04	1.37	2.26
Service charges on deposits	0.37	0.44	0.39	0.36
Other noninterest income	1.67	0.60	0.98	1.90
Noninterest expense:	3.51	3.32	3.41	3.55
Salaries and employee benefits	1.46	1.67	1.58	1.43
Occupancy expenses	0.45	0.44	0.46	0.45
Other noninterest expenses	1.60	1.21	1.37	1.67
Net noninterest income	−1.47	−2.28	−2.04	−1.29
Pre-tax net operating income	1.73	1.63	1.80	1.73
Securities gains or losses	0.02	0.01	0.01	0.03
Income before taxes	1.75	1.64	1.81	1.76
Taxes	0.62	0.51	0.59	0.63
Income before extraordinary items	1.13	1.13	1.22	1.13
Extraordinary items, net	*	*	*	*
Net Income	1.14	1.13	1.23	1.13

Source: Federal Deposit Insurance Corporation.
*Less than 0.005 percent.

and (*b*) the Capital-Account Statement, or Statement of Stockholders' Equity. Let's look briefly at these two useful sources of financial information.

The Funds-Flow Statement (Sources and Uses of Funds Statement)

The **Funds-Flow Statement,** also called the **Sources and Uses of Funds Statement,** answers two questions: Where did the funds a bank used over a certain period of time come from? How were those funds utilized? It is based upon the following relationships:

$$\begin{array}{rcl} \text{Funds provided to the bank over a} & & \text{Funds provided from operations} \quad (6) \\ \text{specific period of time} & = & + \text{ Decreases in bank assets} \\ & & + \text{ Increases in bank liabilities} \end{array}$$

$$\begin{array}{rcl} \text{Funds used by the bank during} & & \text{Dividends paid out to stockholders} \ (7) \\ \text{a specific period of time} & = & + \text{ Increases in bank assets} \\ & & + \text{ Decreases in bank liabilities} \end{array}$$

And, of course:

$$\begin{array}{rcl} \text{Funds provided to the bank over a} & & \text{Funds used by the bank during} \quad (8) \\ \text{specific time period} & = & \text{the same time period.} \end{array}$$

It is useful to review briefly how the U.S. bank we have been following raised its funds in the most recent six-month period and what happened to the funds it raised. (See Table 4–8.) We note that deductions on the income statement for noncash expenses—allocations to depreciation reserves ($16 million) and to the loan-loss reserve account ($255 million)—more than offset a loss in net income (–$98 million). When the noncash expense items were added back in to derive the amount of cash (funds-flow) actually generated from the bank's sales of its services, total funds provided by operations reached + $68 million.

However, service revenues were dwarfed in importance by four other sources of bank funds: (1) heavy draw-downs of the cash account ($657 million), (2) sales of investment and trading-account securities (totaling $274 million), (3) borrowing through short-term debt (in the amount of $479 million), and (4) recapturing funds previously loaned to other banks and securities dealers ($147 million). Where did most of these funds go? Clearly, as the bottom section of the Funds-Flow Statement (Table 4–8) shows, the funds raised went principally to make loans ($475 million) and to cover deposit withdrawals ($1,089 million), which for the majority of banks are the two most important uses of any funds raised.

The Capital-Account Statement (Statement of Stockholders' Equity)

A second useful supplemental financial report is the Capital-Account Statement, or **Statement of Stockholders' Equity.** This financial report reveals changes in the all-important capital account, showing how the owners' investment of funds in the bank (i.e., their claim on the bank's assets) has changed over time. Because stockholders' equity represents a cushion of financial strength for the bank that can be used to absorb losses and protect the depositors and other creditors, changes in the bank's capital account are closely followed by regulators and large depositors.

A Capital-Account Statement for the bank we have been tracking is shown in Table 4–9. We note that it indicates the balance in the bank's capital account at the beginning of the period of time under study and ends with the balance in the capital account at the end of the study period. All the factors that cause the beginning and ending capital-account balances to differ are listed in the statement. The principal factors

TABLE 4–8   Bank Funds-Flow Statement: Sources and Uses of Funds (for the 6-month period just concluded)

Funds were provided from (sources of funds):

Bank operations:

Net income (or loss)	$ (98)
Items charged against, but not using up, income:	
Depreciation and amortization expenses	16
Provision for possible loan losses	255
Other items, net	(105)
Funds provided from bank operations	**68**
Decreases in assets on the balance sheet:	
Cash and deposits due from banks	**657**
Investment securities	199
Trading-account securities	75
Federal funds sold and securities purchased from agreements to resell	147
Other assets	195
Increases in liabilities on the balance sheet:	
Short-term debt	**479**
Long-term debt (subordinated notes)	0
Other funds sources	2
Total sources of funds	$1,822

Funds were used for (uses of funds):

Dividends paid to stockholders	$ 36
Increases in assets on the balance sheet:	
Investment securities	—
Gross loans	**475**
Gross other assets	—
Decreases in liability items on the balance sheet	
Deposits	**1,089**
Long-term debt (mortgage)	22
Other liabilities	116
Other funds uses	84
Total uses of funds	$1,822

TABLE 4–9   Statement of Stockholders' Equity (capital account)

	Most Recent 6-Month Period *(in millions of dollars)*
Balance in capital account at beginning of period	$1,280
Net income(or loss) for the period	(98)
Dividends paid out to stockholders:	
Preferred stock dividends	(6)
Common stock dividends	(30)
New shares of stock issued	2
Purchases of treasury stock	(1)
Balance in capital account at end of period	$1,147

for most banks are net income (or loss) for the period and the amount of any dividends paid out to bank stockholders.

For this bank, the sizable net loss over the most recent six months resulted in a decline in the bank's overall equity capitalization. Interestingly enough, despite the income loss, management still elected to pay stockholder dividends (in the total amount of $36 million), presumably to head off a decline in the bank's stock price. Bank analysts look closely at these statements to make sure that the bank's capital account is still growing fast enough to keep up with the growth of its assets (especially loans). If the capital account is declining, analysts try to determine if the amount of owners' capital remaining is sufficient to absorb all expected losses with an added cushion to deal with unexpected losses.

An Overview

We have explored a substantial number of details regarding bank financial statements in this chapter. Table 4–10 provides a useful summary and overview of the key features of bank financial statements and their consequences for bank managers.

Concept Checks

4–13. What types of information are provided in a Funds-Flow or Sources and Uses of Funds Statement?

4–14. What does the Statement of Stockholders' Equity reveal about how well a bank is being managed and what stresses it is under?

4–15. Suppose a bank has an initial balance in its capital account of $26 million, receives net income during the year of $3 million, pays out stockholder dividends of $2 million, and issues $1 million in new stock during the year. What balance remained in the bank's capital account at the end of the year?

Summary

This chapter presented an overview of bank financial statements that captures both how and how well banks use the resources—people, capital, and raw materials—given to them by the marketplace to produce their services and sell them to the public. The bank's balance sheet (Report of Condition) was broken down into its major components—cash assets,

investment security holdings, loans, deposits, nondeposit borrowings, and capital—and the function of each of these components was examined. Similarly, the bank's statement of earnings and expenses (Report of Income) was decomposed into its key elements—source of revenues (loan income, investment income, and income from the sale of other

---

TABLE 4–10   Features and Consequences of Bank Financial Statements

Key Features of Bank Financial Statements	*Consequences for Bank Managers*
• Heavy dependence on borrowed funds supplied by others (including deposits and nondeposit borrowings in the money market); thus, banks make heavy use of financial leverage (debt) in an effort to boost their stockholders' earnings.	• The bank's earnings and its very existence are exposed to significant risk if those borrowings cannot be repaid when due.
• Growing use of nondeposit borrowings as a supplement to depositors' funds; little owners' capital is invested in most banks.	• The bank must hold a significant proportion of high-quality and readily marketable assets to meet its most pressing debt obligations.
• Most revenues stem from interest on loans and securities. The largest expense item is the interest cost of borrowed funds.	• Bank management must choose loans and investments carefully to avoid a high proportion of earning assets that fail to pay out as planned, damaging expected revenue flows. Since the bank's revenues and expenses are sensitive to changing interest rates, management must be competent either at interest-rate forecasting or, more practically, at protecting the bank against losses due to interest rate movements by using interest-rate hedging techniques.
• The greatest proportion of a bank's assets are financial assets (principally loans and securities). A relatively small proportion of assets is devoted to plant and equipment (fixed assets); thus, banks make very limited use of operating leverage in most cases.	• With only limited resources devoted to fixed assets and, therefore, few fixed costs stemming from plant and equipment, bank earnings are less sensitive to fluctuations in sales volume (operating revenues) than those of many other businesses, but this also limits a bank's potential earnings (i.e., banking tends to be a moderately profitable industry).

---

fee-generating services) and sources of expense (interest on deposits and other borrowed funds, employee compensation, taxes, and other expenses).

The reader was also introduced to two important supplementary bank financial statements known as the Funds-Flow, or Sources and Uses of Funds, Statement and the Capital-Account Statement, or Statement of Stockholders' Equity. The latter shows what has happened recently to the owners' stake in the business, while the former shows where funds were obtained and how they were used during the reporting period. Through these basic financial statements we can grasp more fully what services banks provide, how those service offerings shape the financial position and condition of banks, and why banks represent a critically important area for future study and understanding. In the next chapter, we look closely at how the information provided by the foregoing financial statements can be used to assess a bank's financial health—its soundness and success (or lack thereof) in pursuing the goals set forth by its management and stockholders.

Key Terms in This Chapter

Report of Condition
Report of Income
Funds-Flow Statement

Sources and Uses of Funds Statement
Statement of Stockholders' Equity

Problems and Projects

1. Evergreen National Bank has just submitted its Report of Condition and Report of Income to its principal government regulator, the Comptroller of the Currency. Please fill in the missing items from its statement shown below (all figures in millions of dollars):

Report of Condition

Assets		Liabilities and Equity Capital	
Cash and deposits due from banks	?	Noninterest-bearing demand deposits	$107
Investment securities	$ 87	Savings deposits and NOW accounts	?
Trading account securities	6	Money market deposit accounts	49
Federal funds sold	11	Time deposits	227
Loans, gross	?	Deposits at foreign branches	21
Allowance for loan loss	(19)	Total deposits	440
Unearned discount on loans	(6)	Nondeposit borrowings	41
Loans, net	348	Other liabilities	19
Bank premises and equipment	10	Stockholders' equity capital	?
Customers' liability on acceptances	18		
Miscellaneous assets	43	Total liabilities and	
Total assets	$550	equity capital	$550

Report of Income

Interest and fees on loans	?	Service charges on customer deposits	?
Interest on investment securities	$ 7	Trust department income	$ 8
Other interest income	5	Other operating income	20
Total interest income	$180	Total noninterest income	39
		Wages, salaries, and employee benefits	?
Total interest expense	$159	Net occupancy and equipment expense	7
Net interest income	?	Other expenses	5
Provision for possible loan losses	4	Total noninterest expenses	54
		Net noninterest income	?

Provision for income taxes   2
Net income (or loss) after taxes ?

Alternative scenarios:
(1) Suppose total revenues for Evergreen National Bank rise to $225, while total interest expenses climb to $185. Total noninterest income increases to $51, while total noninterest expenses rocket to $72. What would happen to the bank's net after-tax income?
(2) Many bank analysts believe that commercial banks experience modest economies of scale (cost savings) as they grow. For example, when revenues and assets increase by 100 percent, expenses may grow by only about 92 percent. Suppose all of Evergreen National Bank's revenue items increase by 100 percent and all the expense items on its Report of Income increase by 92 percent. What happens to the bank's net income after taxes?

2. If you know the following figures:

Total interest income	$271	Provision for loan losses	$13
Total interest expenses	205	Income taxes	5
Total noninterest income	23	Dividends to common	
Total noninterest expenses	40	stockholders	11

Please calculate these items:

Net interest income	____	Total operating revenues	____
Net noninterest income	____	Total operating expenses	____
Net income before income		Increases in bank's	
taxes	____	undivided profits	____
Net income after taxes	____		

Alternative scenarios:
(1) Many banking experts expect continuing deregulation of banks to sharply narrow the spread between banks' interest income and interest expenses. Suppose the gap between the total interest income and total interest expense figures given above decreases by 10 percent. What happens to the bank's after-tax net income?
(2) As a result of recent problems with loan quality in the banking industry, suppose the provision for loan losses shown above triples. How does the value of net after-tax income change?

3. If you know the following figures:

Gross loans	$294	Trading-account securities	$ 2
Allowance for loan losses	13	Federal funds sold	26
Unearned discount on loans	5	Savings deposits	12
Common stock	12	Total liabilities	380
Surplus	11	Preferred stock	3
Capital reserves	8	Nondeposit borrowings	10
Total equity capital	49	Time deposits	160
Cash and due from banks	9	Money market deposits	88
Miscellaneous assets	38	Bank premises and	
		equipment, net	29
Bank premises and		Customers' liability on	
equipment, gross	34	acceptances	7

Please calculate these items:

Total assets	_____	Investment securities	_____
Net loans	_____	Depreciation	_____
Undivided profits	_____	Total deposits	_____

Alternative scenarios:

(1) Suppose all items on the asset side of the above balance sheet double in value and all liabilities also double. What happens to the bank's total equity capital and undivided profits? Can you explain why?

(2) If total deposits increase by 10 percent and gross loans go up by only 5 percent, what asset item on the bank's balance sheet is likely to increase to fill in the difference in growth rates? Why?

4. To test your understanding of the basic bank financial statements presented in this chapter, consider the account entries listed below, which are arranged in random order. See if you can reconstruct in correct order the balance sheet and income statement of the bank whose figures for the latest year are given below. (Balance sheet items are in thousands of dollars, while income statement items are in the hundreds of dollars.) Consider using EXCEL or a similar software program to assist you in constructing the required balance sheet and income statement.

Agricultural production loans	$ 246
All other assets	1,087
All other liabilities	756
All other loans	2,258
Applicable income taxes	399,806
Cash and due from depository institutions	3,992
Commercial and industrial loans	6,372
Common stock	414
Credit cards and related plans	790
Demand notes issued to U.S. Treasury and other borrowings	439
Domestic office loan revenues	2,368,736
Expense of federal funds purchased and reverse repurchase agreements	175,624
Expense of premises and fixed assets, net of rental income	187,676
Federal funds purchased and reverse repurchase agreements	2,757
Federal funds sold and repurchase agreements	1,359
Foreign office loan revenues	5,290
Income before extraordinary items	44,411
Income from interest earned on balances due from depository institutions	70,073
Income from lease financing receivables	15,269
Intangible assets	86
Interest and dividend income on securities	755,715
Interest income from trading-account securities	8,696
Interest income from federal funds sold and repurchase agreements	91,362
Interest on domestic office deposits	1,585,024

Interest on foreign office deposits	15,710
Interest-bearing deposits	27,486
Interest on demand notes issued to the U.S. Treasury and other borrowings	23,613
Interest on mortgage indebtedness and other obligations	3,811
Interest on subordinated notes and debentures	6,694
Lease financing receivables	147
Loans and leases, gross	24,795
Loans and leases, net	24,066
Plus: Allowance for loan losses	361
Plus: Unearned income	368
Loans to financial institutions	406
Mortgage indebtedness	45
Net income after taxes	49,256
Noninterest-bearing deposits	6,569
Other loans to individuals	5,032
Other noninterest expense	538,125
Other noninterest income	326,847
Other real estate owned	89
Perpetual preferred stock	12
Premises and fixed assets (including capitalized leases)	648
Provisions for loan and lease losses and allocated transfer risk	221,967
Real estate loans, total	9,544
Salaries and employee benefits	619,207
Securities	9,837
Securities gains (or losses), net of taxes	4,845
Service charges on deposit accounts	179,680
Subordinated notes and debentures	116
Surplus	758
Undivided profits	1,812

5. First National Bank of Irwin reports loan losses and eligible (reservable) total loans over the past five years as shown below. First National currently holds total assets of $465 million. Which method of figuring this bank's deductible loan-loss expense should management use? Why?

	Loan Losses	Total Eligible Loans
Current year	$1.34 million	$279 million
One year ago	$1.19 million	$258 million
Two years ago	$1.08 million	$249 million
Three years ago	$0.85 million	$240 million
Four years ago	$0.71 million	$235 million
Five years ago	$0.59 million	$228 million

Suppose that next year First National of Irwin holds total assets of $507 million. Would this development require a change in its method of expressing loan losses? Please explain. On what basis would management then have to determine the bank's annual loan-loss expense?

6. For each of the following transactions which items on a bank's statement of income and expenses would be affected?

   a. Office supplies are purchased so the bank will have enough deposit slips and other necessary forms for customer and employee use next week.

   b. The bank sets aside funds to be contributed through its monthly payroll to the employee pension plan in the name of all its eligible employees.

   c. The bank posts the amount of interest earned on the savings account of one of its customers.

   d. Management expects that among a series of real estate loans recently granted the default rate will probably be close to 3 percent.

   e. Mr. and Mrs. Harold Jones just purchased a safety deposit box to hold their stock certificates and wills.

   f. The bank collects $1 million in interest payments from loans it made earlier this year to Intel Composition Corp.

   g. Hal Jones's checking account is charged $30 for two of Hal's checks that were returned for insufficient funds.

   h. The bank earns $5 million in interest on the government securities it has held since the middle of last year.

   i. The bank has to pay its $5,000 monthly utility bill today to the local electric company.

   j. A sale of government securities has just netted the bank a $290,000 capital gain (net of taxes).

7. For each of the transactions described below which of at least two accounts on a bank's balance sheet would be affected by each transaction.

   a. Sally Mayfield has just opened a time deposit in the amount of $6,000 and these funds are immediately loaned to Robert Jones to purchase a used car.

   b. Arthur Blode deposits his payroll check for $1,000 in the bank and the bank invests the funds in a government security.

   c. The bank sells a new issue of common stock for $100,000 to investors living in its community and the proceeds of that sale are spent on the installation of new ATMs.

   d. Jane Gavel withdraws her checking account balance of $2,500 from the bank and moves her deposit to a credit union; the bank employs the funds received from Mr. Alan James, who has just paid off his home equity loan, to provide Ms. Gavel with the funds she withdrew.

   e. The bank purchases a bulldozer from Ace Manufacturing Company for $750,000 and leases it to Cespan Construction Company.

   f. Signet National Bank makes a loan of reserves in the amount of $5 million to Quesan State Bank and the funds are returned the next day.

   g. The bank declares its outstanding loan of $1 million to Deprina Corp. to be uncollectible.

8. See if you can construct a simple balance sheet for River's Edge National Bank from the following information (all figures in millions of dollars) for the year-end date just concluded. What item is clearly missing from the above accounts that you need to add in so that the bank's balance sheet will be fully in balance?

Municipal bonds	$12	Credit card loans	$22
Time deposits	25	Deposits due from other banks	25
Federal funds sold and securities purchased under repurchase agreements	5	Savings deposits	15
		Bank building and equipment	7
Subordinated notes and debentures	20	Money market deposits	31
		Federal funds purchased	34
Leases of assets to business customers	3	Mortgage against the bank's building	26

Automobile loans	21	Real estate loans	42
Loans to commercial and industrial firms	64	Deposits due to other banks	5
Demand deposits	55	Securities sold under repurchase agreements	4
U.S. Treasury bills	10		
Cash	13		

9. See if you can determine the amount of Rosebush State Bank's current net income after taxes from the figures (stated in millions of dollars) given below and the amount of its retained earnings from current income that it will be able to reinvest in the bank. (Be sure to arrange all the figures given in correct sequence to derive the bank's report of income.)

Depreciation on the bank's plant and equipment	$ 8	Capital gains on securities sold, net of taxes	$1
Effective tax rate of 25%		Interest paid on federal funds purchased	6
Interest and fees on loans	62	Common stockholders will be paid $2 per share on 1 million outstanding shares	
Employee wages, salaries, and benefits	13	Interest paid to customers holding time and savings deposits	32
Interest and dividends earned on government bonds and notes	9	Trust department fees	1
Provision for loan losses	2		
Overhead expenses	3		
Service charges paid by depositors	4		

10. Which account items or entries shown below would normally occur on a bank's balance sheet and which on a bank's income and expense statement?

Federal funds sold
Retained earnings
Credit card loans
Utility expense
Vault cash
Allowance for loan losses
Depreciation on bank plant and equipment
Commercial and industrial loans
Repayments of credit card loans
Common stock
Interest paid on money market deposits

Securities gains or losses
Deposits due to banks
Leases of business equipment to customers
Interest received on credit card loans
Employee benefits
Savings deposits
Provision for loan losses
Service charges on deposits
Undivided profits
Mortgage owed on the bank's buildings
Customer liability on acceptances

Selected References

See the following for an overview of bank financial statements and their components:

1. Baughn, William H., and Charles E. Walker, ed. *The Bankers' Handbook.* 3rd ed. Homewood, Ill.: Business One Irwin, 1989.
2. Cocheo, Steve. "If You Liked FASB 115, You'll Love FASB 114." *ABA Banking Journal,* January 1994, pp. 44–45.
3. Board of Governors of the Federal Reserve System. *Century Date Change News.* Washington, D.C., Spring 1997.
4. Giroux, Gary A., and Peter S. Rose. *Financial Forecasting in Banking: Methods and Applications.* Ann Arbor, Mich.: UMI Research Press, 1981.
5. Morris, Charles S., and G. H. Sellon, Jr. "Market Value Accounting for Banks: Pros and Cons." *Economic Review,* Federal Reserve Bank of Kansas City 76, March/April 1991, pp. 5–19.
6. O'Toole, Randy. "Recent Developments in Loan Loss Provisioning at U.S. Commercial Banks." *FRBSF Economic Letter,* Federal Reserve Bank of San Francisco, No. 97–21, July 25, 1997.
7. Rose, Peter S. *Money and Capital Markets.* 6th ed. Homewood, Ill.: Richard D. Irwin, 1997, chap. 4.
8. ———. *Bank Mergers in a Deregulated Environment.* Rolling Meadows, Ill.: Bank Administration Institute, 1988.
9. Shaffer, Sherrill. "Marking Banks to Market." *Business Review,* Federal Reserve Bank of Philadelphia, July/August 1992, pp. 13–22.
10. Walter, John R. "Loan Loss Reserves." *Economic Review,* Federal Reserve Bank of Richmond, July/August 1991, pp. 20–30.
11. Klemme, Kelly. "The Clock is Ticking: Are Financial Institutions Prepared for the Turn of the Century." *Financial Industry Issues,* Federal Reserve Bank of Dallas, Fourth Quarter 1997.

5   MEASURING AND EVALUATING BANK PERFORMANCE

Learning and Management Decision Objectives

The purpose of this chapter is to discover what analytical tools can be applied to a bank's financial statements so that management and the public can identify the most critical problems inside each bank and develop ways to deal with those problems.

Introduction

Banks today are under great pressure to *perform*—to meet the objectives of their stockholders, employees, depositors, and borrowing customers, while somehow keeping government regulators satisfied that the bank's policies, loans, and investments are sound. As banking organizations have grown in recent years, more and more of them have been forced to turn to the money and capital markets to raise funds by selling stocks, bonds, and short-term IOUs. In many cases, the growth of local deposits has simply been inadequate to fund the growing needs of customers for loans and new services. But banks' entry into the open market to raise funds means that their financial statements are increasingly being scrutinized by investors and by the general public. This development has placed management under great pressure to set and meet bank performance goals.

At the same time, competition for banks' traditional loan and deposit customers has increased dramatically. Credit unions, money market mutual funds, insurance companies, brokerage firms, and even chain stores like Sears Roebuck and J.C. Penney are fighting for a slice of nearly every credit and deposit market traditionally served by banks. Bankers have been called upon to continually reevaluate their loan and deposit policies, review their plans for expansion and growth, and assess their returns and risk in light of this new competitive environment. In addition, there is the added problem of bank failures. Many of these failures have been associated with managerial mistakes, outright fraud, and a more volatile and uncertain economy that demands new standards for bank management.

In this chapter, we take a detailed look at the most widely used indicators of the quality and quantity of bank performance. The chapter centers on the most important performance dimensions for any bank—*profitability* and *risk*. After all, a commercial bank is simply a business corporation organized for the purpose of maximizing the value of the shareholders' wealth invested in the firm at an acceptable level of risk. The objective of maximum (or at least satisfactory) profitability with a level of risk acceptable to the bank's stockholders (owners) is not easy to achieve, as the recent upsurge in bank failures around the globe clearly suggests. Aggressive pursuit of such an objective requires an institution to be continually on the lookout for new opportunities for further revenue growth, greater efficiency, and more effective planning and control. The pages that follow examine the most important measures of a bank's rate of return and risk.

Evaluating a Bank's Performance

How can we use a bank's financial statements—particularly its Report of Condition (balance sheet) and Report of Income (income statement)—to evaluate how well the bank is performing? What do we look at to help decide if a bank is facing serious problems that its management should deal with?

Determining the Bank's Long-Range Objectives

The first step in analyzing any bank's financial statements is to decide what objectives the bank is or should be seeking. Bank performance must be directed toward *specific objectives*. A fair evaluation of any bank's performance should start by evaluating whether it has been able to achieve the objectives its management and stockholders have chosen.

Certainly many banks have their own unique objectives. Some wish to grow faster and achieve some long-range growth objective. Others seem to prefer the quiet life—*minimizing risk,* conveying the image of a sound bank but with modest rewards for their shareholders.

Maximizing the Value of the Firm: A Key Objective for Any Bank

While all of the foregoing goals have something to recommend them, increasingly banks are finding that they must pay close attention to the *value of their stock*. Indeed, the basic principles of financial management, as that science is practiced today, suggest strongly that attempting to maximize a bank's stock value is the key objective that should have priority over all others. All banks are corporations, with stockholders interested in what happens to the value and yield of their stock. If the stock fails to rise in value commensurate with stockholder expectations, current investors may seek to unload their shares and the bank will have difficulty in raising new capital to support its future growth. Clearly, then, bank management should pursue the objective of maximizing the value of the bank's stock.

What will cause a bank's stock to rise in value? Each institution's stock price is a function of:

$$\begin{array}{c}\text{Value of the} \\ \text{bank's stock} \\ (P_o)\end{array} = \frac{\begin{array}{c}\text{Expected stream of future} \\ \text{stockholder dividends}\end{array}}{\begin{array}{c}\text{Discount factor (based on} \\ \text{the minimum required market} \\ \text{rate of return on equity capital} \\ \text{given each bank's} \\ \text{perceived level of risk)}\end{array}} = \sum_{t=0}^{\infty} \frac{E(D_t)}{(1+r)^t} \tag{1}$$

where $E(D_t)$ represents stockholder dividends expected to be paid in future periods, discounted by a minimum acceptable rate of return (r) tied to the bank's perceived level of risk. The value of the bank's stock will tend to *rise* in any of the following situations:

1. The value of the stream of future stockholder dividends is expected to increase, due perhaps to recent growth in some of the markets served by the bank or perhaps because of profitable acquisitions the banking organization has made.
2. The banking organization's perceived level of risk has fallen, due perhaps to an increase in capital or a decrease in loan losses.
3. Expected dividend increases combined with declining risk, as perceived by investors in the bank's stock.

Research evidence over the years has found bank stock values to be especially sensitive to changes in interest rates, currency rates, and the strength or weakness of the economy or economies that each bank serves. Clearly, management can work to

---

Concept Checks

5–1. Why should banks be concerned about their level of profitability and exposure to risk?

5–2. What individuals or groups are likely to be interested in these dimensions of bank performance?

5–3. What factors influence a bank's stock price?

5–4. Suppose that a bank is expected to pay an annual dividend of $4 per share on its stock in the current period and dividends are expected to grow 5 percent a year every year, and the minimum required return to equity capital based on the bank's perceived level of risk is 10 percent. Can you estimate the current value of the bank's stock?

achieve policies that increase future bank earnings, reduce risk, or pursue a combination of *both* actions in order to raise the bank's stock price.[1]

Profitability Ratios: A Surrogate for Stock Values

While the behavior of a stock price is, in theory, the best indicator of a business firm's performance because it reflects the *market's evaluation* of the firm's performance, this indicator is often *not* reliable in banking. The reason is that most bank stock, especially stock issued by smaller banks, is *not* actively traded in international or national markets. This fact forces the financial analyst to fall back on surrogates for market-value indicators in the form of various *profitability ratios.*

Key Profitability Ratios in Banking.   Among the most important ratio measures of **bank profitability** used today are the following:

$$\frac{\text{Return on equity capital}}{(\text{ROE})} = \frac{\text{Net income after taxes}}{\text{Total equity capital}} \tag{2}$$

$$\frac{\text{Return on assets}}{(\text{ROA})} = \frac{\text{Net income after taxes}}{\text{Total assets}} \tag{3}$$

---

[1]The formula for a bank's stock price shown above assumes that bank stock may pay dividends of varying amount. However, if the dividends a bank pays its stockholders are expected to grow at a constant rate over time (perhaps reflecting steady growth in earnings), the bank stock price equation can be greatly simplified into the form:

$$P_0 = D_1 / (r-g)$$

where D_1 is the expected dividend on bank stock in period 1, r is the rate of discount reflecting the preceived level of risk attached to investing in the bank's stock, g is the expected constant growth rate at which bank stock dividends will grow each year, and r must be greater than g. For example, suppose that a bank is expected to pay a dividend of $5 per share in period 1, dividends are expected to grow by 6 percent a year, and the discount rate is 10 percent. Then the bank's stock price must be:

$$P_0 = \$5/(0.10 - 0.06) = \$125 \text{ per share.}$$

The two bank stock-price formulas discussed above assume the bank will possibly pay dividends indefinitely into the future. Most capital-market investors have a limited time horizon, however, and plan to sell the bank's stock at the end of their planned investment horizon. In this case the current value of the bank's stock is determined from:

$$P_0 = \frac{D_1}{(1+r)^1} + \frac{D_2}{(1+r)^2} + \cdots + \frac{D_n}{(1+r)^n} + \frac{P_n}{(1+r)^n}$$

where we assume the investor will hold the bank's stock for n periods, receiving the stream of dividends D_1, D_2, . . . , D_n, and sell the stock for price P_n at the end of the planned investment horizon. For example, suppose investors expect the bank to pay a $5 dividend at the end of period 1, $10 at the end of period 2, and then plan to sell the stock for a price of $150. If the relevant discount rate is 10 percent, the current value of the bank's stock should approach:

$$P_0 = \frac{\$5}{(1+0.10)^1} + \frac{\$10}{(1+0.10)^2} + \frac{\$150}{(1+10)^2} = \$136.78$$

The present value and annuity tables on the inside cover of the text can be used to help solve the above equation for the bank's stock price.

$$\text{Net interest margin} = \frac{\begin{pmatrix} \text{Interest income from loans and} \\ \text{security investments} - \text{Interest} \\ \text{expense on deposits and on other} \\ \text{debt issued} \end{pmatrix}}{\text{Total assets}^2} \quad (4)$$

$$\text{Net noninterest margin} = \frac{\begin{pmatrix} \text{Noninterest revenues} \\ -\text{Noninterest expenses} \end{pmatrix}}{\text{Total assets}^2} \quad (5)$$

$$\text{Net bank operating margin} = \frac{\begin{pmatrix} \text{Total operating revenues} \\ -\text{Total operating expenses} \end{pmatrix}}{\text{Total assets}} \quad (6)$$

$$\text{Net returns prior to special transactions (NRST)} = \frac{\begin{bmatrix} \text{Net income after taxes and prior} \\ \text{to security gains (or losses) and} \\ \text{other extraordinary items} \end{bmatrix}}{\text{Total assets}} \quad (7)$$

$$\text{Earnings per share of stock (EPS)} = \frac{\text{Net income after taxes}}{\text{Common equity shares outstanding}} \quad (8)$$

Like all financial ratios, each of these profitability measures varies substantially over time and from banking market to banking market.

Interpreting Profitability Ratios.   Each of the foregoing ratios looks at a slightly different aspect of bank profitability. Thus, **ROA** is primarily an indicator of *managerial efficiency;* it indicates how capably the management of the bank has been converting the institution's assets into net earnings. **ROE,** on the other hand, is a measure of the *rate of return flowing to the bank's shareholders.* It approximates the net benefit that the stockholders have received from investing their capital in the bank (i.e., placing their funds at risk in the hope of earning a suitable profit).

The net operating margin, net interest margin, and noninterest margin are **efficiency** measures as well as profitability measures, indicating how well management and staff have been able to keep the growth of revenues (which come primarily from the bank's loans, investments, and service fees) ahead of rising costs (principally the interest on deposits and money market borrowings and employee salaries and benefits). The **net interest margin** measures how large a spread between interest revenues

---

[2]Many banking authorities prefer to use total *earning assets* in the denominator of the net interest margin and the noninterest margin. Earning assets are those generating interest or fee income, principally the loans and security investments the bank has made. The reasoning is that net interest income as well as net noninterest income should be compared, not to all bank assets, but rather to those assets—principally loans and security holdings—that account for the majority of all bank income.

and interest costs management has been able to achieve by close control over the bank's earning assets and the pursuit of the cheapest sources of funding. The **noninterest margin,** in contrast, measures the amount of noninterest revenues stemming from deposit service charges and other service fees the bank has been able to collect (called fee income) relative to the amount of noninterest costs incurred (including salaries and wages, repair and maintenance costs on bank facilities, and loan-loss expenses). For most banks, the noninterest margin is negative—noninterest costs generally outstrip fee income, though bank fee income has been rising rapidly in recent years as a percentage of all bank revenues.

Net returns before special transactions measure the bank's income from routine, recurring sources of revenue, including revenues generated by loans, investments, and fees from selling other financial services (such as checking accounts), relative to the bank's total resources (assets). Unusual or nonrecurring items, such as gains from the sale of bank property and equipment or profits and losses from selling securities, are often excluded from bank profitability measures by financial analysts. Finally, EPS provides a direct measure of the returns flowing to the bank's owners—its stockholders—measured relative to the number of shares sold to the public.

Another traditional measure of the earnings efficiency with which a bank is managed is called the *earnings spread* (or simply the spread), calculated from:

$$\text{Earnings spread} = \frac{\text{Total interest income}}{\text{Total earning assets}} - \frac{\text{Total interest expense}}{\text{Total interest-bearing bank liabilities}} \tag{9}$$

The spread measures the effectiveness of the bank's intermediation function in borrowing and lending money and also the intensity of competition in the bank's market area. Greater competition tends to squeeze the difference between average asset yields and average liability costs. If other factors are held constant, the bank's spread will decline as competition increases, forcing management to try to find other ways (such as generating fee income from new services) to make up for an eroding earnings spread.

Another useful measure of profitability is the operating-income (or asset utilization) ratio, which is total operating revenue (income) divided by total assets. This earnings measure can be broken down into two important components, the average interest return on assets and the average noninterest return on assets, the latter arising from fees charged for various services (such as checking accounts or trust services). That is:

$$\frac{\text{Total operating income}}{\text{Total assets}} = \frac{\text{Interest income}}{\text{Total assets}} + \frac{\text{Total noninterest income}}{\text{Total assets}} \tag{10}$$

As competition for loans and other income-generating assets has grown and many loans have turned sour, more and more banks have shifted their attention to increasing noninterest income from fees. These fees boost total revenue and help to raise net income flowing to bank stockholders. Bank managers today also strive to reduce the proportion of total resources devoted to *nonearning* assets (including cash, fixed assets, and intangibles). One widely used measure of the relative importance of nonearning assets versus those assets, such as loans and securities, that directly contribute to a bank's earnings is the *earnings base* ratio:

$$\text{Earnings base in assets} = \frac{\text{Total interest assets}}{\text{Total assets}} = \frac{\text{Loans + Leases + Security investments}}{\text{Total assets}} \qquad (11)$$

$$= \frac{\text{Total assets} - \text{Nonearning assets}}{\text{Total assets}}$$

In a bank whose earnings base is falling, management and staff must generally work harder just to sustain the current level of earnings.

Concept Checks

5–5. What is return on equity capital and what aspect of bank performance is it supposed to measure?

5–6. Suppose a bank reports that its net after-tax income for the current year is $51 million, its assets total $1,444 million, and its liabilities amount to $926 million. What is its return on equity capital? Is the ROE you have calculated good or bad? What information do you need to answer this last question?

5–7. What is the return on assets and why is it important in banking?

5–8. A bank estimates that its total revenues from all sources will amount to $155 million and its total expenses (including taxes) will equal $107 million this year. Its liabilities total $4,960 million while its equity capital amounts to $52 million. What is the bank's return on assets? Is this ROA high or low? How could you find out?

5–9. Why do bankers pay close attention today to the net interest margin and noninterest margin? To the earnings base and spread?

5–10. Suppose a banker tells you that his bank in the year just completed had total interest expenses on all borrowings of $12 million and noninterest expenses of $5 million, while interest income from earning assets totaled $16 million and noninterest revenues added to a total of $2 million. Suppose further that assets amounted to $480 million of which earning assets represented 85 percent of total assets, while total interest-bearing liabilities amounted to 75 percent of the bank's total assets. See if you can determine this bank's net interest and noninterest margins and its earnings base and earnings spread for the most recent year.

Useful Profitability Formulas

In analyzing how well any given bank is performing, it is often useful to break down some of these profitability ratios into their key components. For example, it is easy to see that ROE and ROA—two of the most popular bank profitability measures in use today—are closely related. Both use the same numerator: *net income after taxes.* Therefore, these two profit indicators can be linked directly:

$$\text{ROE} = \text{ROA} \times \frac{\text{Total assets}}{\text{Total equity capital accounts}} \qquad (12)$$

Or, in other words:

$$\frac{\text{Net income after taxes}}{\text{Total equity capital accounts}} = \frac{\text{Net income after taxes}}{\text{Total assets}} \qquad (13)$$

$$\times \frac{\text{Total assets}}{\text{Total equity capital accounts}}$$

But we note that the bank's net income is equal to its total revenues minus its operating expenses (including interest expenses) and taxes. Therefore:

$$\text{ROE} = \frac{\text{Total revenues} - \text{Total operating expenses} - \text{Taxes}}{\text{Total assets}} \times \frac{\text{Total assets}}{\text{Total equity capital}} \qquad (14)$$

The relationships in Equations (13) and (14) remind us that a bank's return to its shareholders is highly sensitive to how the bank's assets are financed—whether more debt (including deposits) or more owners' capital is used. Even a bank with a low ROA can achieve a relatively high ROE through heavy use of debt (leverage) and minimal use of owners' capital.

In fact, the ROE-ROA relationship illustrates quite clearly the fundamental trade-off bank managers face between risk and return. For example, a bank whose ROA is projected to be about 1 percent this year will need $10 in assets for each $1 in capital in order to achieve a 10 percent ROE. That is, following Equation (12):

$$\text{ROE} = \text{ROA} \times \frac{\text{Total assets}}{\text{Total equity capital accounts}}$$

$$= \frac{0.01 \times \$10 \times 100}{\$1} = 10 \text{ percent}$$

If, however, the bank's ROA is expected to fall to 0.5 percent, a 10 percent ROE is attainable only if each $1 of capital supports $20 in assets. In other words:

$$\text{ROE} = \frac{0.005 \times \$20 \times 100}{\$1} = 10 \text{ percent}$$

Indeed, we could construct a risk-return trade-off table like the one shown below that would tell us how much leverage (debt relative to equity) must be used to achieve a bank's desired rate of return to its stockholders. The trade-off table indicates that a bank with a 5-to-1 assets-to-capital ratio can expect (*a*) a 2.5 percent ROE if ROA is

Risk-Return Trade-Offs for a Bank

Ratio of Total Assets to Total Equity Capital Accounts	ROE with an ROA of:			
	0.5%	*1.0%*	*1.5%*	*2.0%*
5:1	2.5%	5.0%	7.5%	10.0%
10:1	5.0%	10.0%	15.0%	20.0%
15:1	7.5%	15.0%	22.5%	30.0%
20:1	10.0%	20.0%	30.0%	40.0%

0.5 percent and (*b*) a 10 percent ROE if ROA is 2 percent. In contrast, with a 20 to 1 assets-to-capital ratio, a bank can achieve a 10 percent ROE simply by earning a modest 0.5 percent ROA.

Clearly, as earning efficiency represented by ROA declines, the bank must take on more risk in the form of higher leverage to have any chance of achieving its desired rate of return to its shareholders.

Breaking Down Equity Returns for Closer Analysis

Another highly useful profitability formula focusing upon ROE is:

$$\text{ROE} = \frac{\text{Net income after taxes}}{\text{Total operating revenue}} \times \frac{\text{Total operating revenue}}{\text{Total assets}} \quad (15)$$

$$\times \frac{\text{Total assets}}{\text{Total equity capital accounts}}$$

or

ROE = Net profit margin × Asset utilization ratio × Equity multiplier

where:

$$\text{The bank's } \textbf{net profit margin} \text{ (NPM)} = \frac{\text{Net income after taxes}}{\text{Total operating revenues}} \quad (16)$$

$$\text{The bank's degree of } \textbf{asset utilization} \text{ (AU)} = \frac{\text{Total operating revenues}}{\text{Total assets}} \quad (17)$$

$$\text{The bank's } \textbf{equity multiplier} \text{ (EM)} = \frac{\text{Total assets}}{\text{Total equity capital accounts}} \quad (18)$$

Each component of this simple equation is a telltale indicator of a different aspect of the bank's operations. (See Exhibit 5–1.)

EXHIBIT 5–1 *Elements that Determine a Bank's Rate of Return Earned
on the Stockholders' Investment in the Bank (ROE)*

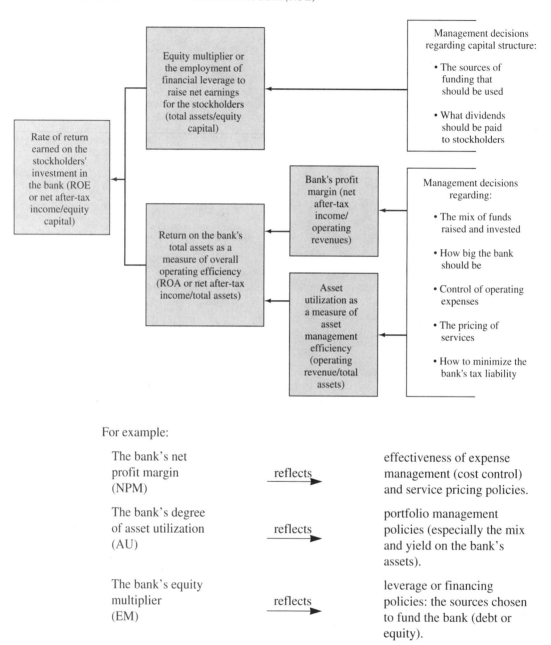

For example:

The bank's net profit margin (NPM)	reflects⟶	effectiveness of expense management (cost control) and service pricing policies.
The bank's degree of asset utilization (AU)	reflects⟶	portfolio management policies (especially the mix and yield on the bank's assets).
The bank's equity multiplier (EM)	reflects⟶	leverage or financing policies: the sources chosen to fund the bank (debt or equity).

   If any of these ratios begins to decline, management needs to pay close attention to this development and assess the *reasons* behind the change. Of these three financial ratios, the equity multiplier (EM), or assets-to-equity-capital ratio, is normally the largest, averaging about 15 × or larger for most banks. The biggest banks in the industry often operate with multipliers of 20 × or more. The multiplier is a direct measure of the bank's degree of financial leverage—how many dollars of assets must be supported by each dollar of equity (owners') capital and how much of the bank's resources therefore must rest on debt. Because equity must absorb losses on the bank's assets, the larger the multiplier, the more exposed to failure risk the bank is. However, the larger the multiplier, the greater the bank's potential for high returns for its stockholders.

The profit margin (PM), or the ratio of net income to total revenues, is also subject to some degree of management control and direction. It reminds us that banks can increase their earnings and their returns to their stockholders by successfully controlling expenses and maximizing revenues. Similarly, by carefully allocating the bank's assets to the highest-yielding loans and investments while avoiding excessive risk, management can raise the bank's average yield on its assets (AU, or asset utilization).

An interesting case in point is the recent track record of the average ROE for all U.S. banks between 1986 and 1996, shown in Table 5–1. Careful perusal of the figures shows that the ROE for all U.S.-insured banks began the period with one of the lowest equity returns in U.S. banking history when ROE dropped below 2 percent in 1987, due almost entirely to an unusually low profit margin. U.S. banks were finding their earnings squeezed by rising expenses and exacerbated by heavy deductions from current revenues to cover record loan losses, particularly on real estate loans. However, industry earnings as measured by ROE roared back in 1988 to one of the highest returns to bank shareholders in American history, averaging nearly 13 percent and then beat that record in 1993, climbing to more than 15 percent—a post–World War II high. While earnings fell slightly in 1994, 1995, and 1996, the industry's ROE still averaged an exceptional 14 percent in these most recent years.

TABLE 5–1   Components of Return on Equity (ROE) for All Insured U.S. Banks (1986–1996)

Year	Return on Equity Capital (ROE)	=	Net Profit Margin (Net After-Tax Income/ Total Revenues)	×	Asset Utilization (Total Revenues/ Total Assets)	×	Equity Multiplier (Total Assets/ Equity Capital)
1996*	13.96%	=	12.89%	×	8.88%	×	12.20×
1995	13.95	=	12.68	×	8.93	×	12.33
1994	14.31	=	13.37	×	8.33	×	12.85
1993	15.68	=	13.47	×	8.87	×	12.66
1992	12.18	=	10.01	×	9.15	×	13.30
1991	8.00	=	5.32	×	10.17	×	14.77
1990	7.48	=	4.36	×	11.08	×	15.48
1989	7.63	=	4.24	×	11.17	×	16.11
1988	12.73	=	7.90	×	10.13	×	15.91
1987	1.52	=	0.96	×	9.54	×	16.55
1986	9.76	=	6.51	×	9.31	×	16.10

Note: *Based on three quarters in 1996.

Source: Federal Deposit Insurance Corporation, Quarterly Releases and Annual Reports.

What caused such a dramatic turnaround? Table 5–1 shows clearly the primary cause—the industry's profit margin surged upward as revenues (particularly noninterest, or fee, revenues) grew substantially faster than operating expenses, which caused U.S. banking's asset utilization ratio to rise as well. Partially offsetting these positive influences the industry's equity multiplier has fallen in recent years as banking's equity capital also increased faster than its assets. One reason was pressure from regulators to use more equity capital and less debt to finance the acquisition of bank assets in hopes of protecting depositors and government insurance reserves. This regulatory pressure reduced banking's equity multiplier, but not nearly enough to damage significantly the gains in profit margin.

A slight variation on this simple ROE model produces an efficiency equation useful for diagnosing problems in *four* different areas of bank management:

$$\text{ROE} = \frac{\text{Net income after taxes}}{\text{Net income before taxes and securities gains (or losses)}} \times \frac{\text{Net income before taxes and securities gains (or losses)}}{\text{Total operating revenue}} \tag{19}$$

$$\times \frac{\text{Total operating revenue}}{\text{Total assets}} \times \frac{\text{Total assets}}{\text{Total equity capital accounts}}$$

Or:

$$\text{ROE} = \begin{array}{c}\text{Tax} \\ \text{management} \\ \text{efficiency}\end{array} \times \begin{array}{c}\text{Expense} \\ \text{control} \\ \text{efficiency}\end{array} \times \begin{array}{c}\text{Asset} \\ \text{management} \\ \text{efficiency}\end{array} \times \begin{array}{c}\text{Funds} \\ \text{management} \\ \text{efficiency.}\end{array} \tag{20}$$

In this case we have merely split the bank's profit margin (net after-tax income to revenue) into two parts: (1) a tax-management efficiency ratio, reflecting the bank's use of security gains or losses and other tax-management tools (such as buying tax-exempt municipal bonds) to minimize its tax exposure, and (2) the ratio of before-tax income to total revenue as an indicator of how many dollars of revenue survive after operating expenses are removed—a measure of operating efficiency and expense control. For example, suppose a bank's most recent Report of Condition and Report of Income show the following figures:

Net income after taxes = $1.0 million.
Net income before taxes and securities gains (or losses) = $1.3 million.
Total operating revenue = $39.3 million.
Total assets = $122.0 million.
Total equity capital accounts = $7.3 million.

Its ROE must be

$$\text{ROE} = \frac{\$1.0 \text{ mil}}{\$1.3 \text{ mil}} \times \frac{\$1.3 \text{ mil}}{\$39.3 \text{ mil}} \times \frac{\$39.3 \text{ mil}}{\$122.0 \text{ mil}} \times \frac{\$122.0 \text{ mil}}{\$7.3 \text{ mil}}$$

$$\text{ROE} = 0.769 \times 0.033 \times 0.322 \times 16.71 = 0.137, \text{ or } 13.7 \text{ percent}$$

Clearly, when any one of these four ratios begins to drop, management needs to reevaluate the banking organization's efficiency in that area. For example, if the ratio of after-tax net income to income before securities gains or losses falls from 0.769 to 0.610 next year, management will want to look closely at how well the bank's tax exposure is being monitored and controlled. If after-tax net income before special transactions to operating revenue drops from 0.033 to 0.025 in the coming year, the bank's effectiveness in controlling operating expenses needs to be reviewed. And if the ratio of operating revenues to assets plummets from 0.322 to 0.270, a careful reexamination of asset portfolio policies is warranted to see if the decline in asset yields is due to factors within management's control.

Breakdown Analysis of a Bank's Return on Assets

We can also divide the bank's return on assets (ROA) into its component parts, as shown in Table 5–2. Actually, ROA is based on three simple component ratios:

Components of a Bank's ROA

$$\text{Net interest margin} = \frac{(\text{Interest income} - \text{Interest expense})}{\text{Total assets}}$$

PLUS

$$\text{Noninterest margin} = \frac{(\text{Noninterest income} - \text{Noninterest expense})}{\text{Total assets}}$$

LESS

$$\text{Special transactions affecting its net income}^3 = \frac{\text{Special income and expense items}}{\text{Total assets}}$$

EQUALS

$$\text{Return on assets (ROA, or the ability of the bank to generate income from assets)} = \frac{\text{Net income after taxes}}{\text{Total assets}}$$

Such a breakdown can be very useful in explaining some of the recent changes banks have experienced in their financial position. For example, as shown in Table 5–3, the average ROA for all insured U.S. banks declined to a modern record low in 1987 of 0.09 percent. Why did this happen? As Table 5–3 reveals, part of the problem was due to a slight decline in U.S. banks' net interest margin, or spread between interest income and interest expenses, which declined modestly from 3.47 percent to 3.44 percent. However, this adverse change was more than offset by a small improvement in the industry's noninterest margin of noninterest income less noninterest expenses, and neither change was sufficient to really explain why the industry's ROA took such an incredible beating in

---

[3]The special income and expense items include provision for loan losses, taxes, securities gains or losses, and extraordinary income or losses.

TABLE 5–2   Calculating a Bank's Return on Assets (ROA)

	Gross interest income ÷ Average assets	← Income from holding assets
–	*Interest expense ÷ Average assets*	← Supply cost of funds for holding assets
=	Net interest margin ÷ Average assets	← Return the bank earns because its credit quality is better than its customers' credit quality
+	Noninterest income ÷ Average assets	← Income from handling customer transactions
–	Noninterest expenses ÷ Average assets	← Costs of operating the bank
–	Provision for loan losses ÷ Average assets	← *Accrual expense*
=	Pre-tax income ÷ Average assets	← Return on assets before taxes
–	*Income taxes ÷ Average assets**	← Bank's share of the cost of government services
=	Income before special transactions ÷ Average assets	← Net income from recurring sources of revenue
+	Securities gains or losses and other special transactions ÷ Average assets	← Nonrecurring sources of income or loss to the bank
=	Net income after taxes ÷ Average assets (or ROA)	← Earnings left over for the stockholders after all costs are met

*Both income and taxes applicable to income need to be adjusted for any tax-exempt earnings the bank has received. One can restate such income on a fully tax-equivalent basis by multiplying the amount of tax-exempt income by the expression $1 \div (1 - t)$ where t is the bank's tax bracket rate.

TABLE 5–3   Components of Return on Assets (ROA) for All Insured U.S. Banks (1986–96)

	1996*	1995	1994	1993	1992	1991	1990	1989	1988	1987	1986
Interest Income/ Total Assets	6.83%	7.02%	6.29%	6.62%	7.47%	8.59%	9.60%	9.99%	8.98%	8.45%	8.70%
– Interest Expense/ Total Assets	–3.28	–3.44	–2.67	–2.85	–3.57	–4.98	–6.14	–6.46	–5.44	–4.99	–5.23
= Net Interest Income/ Total Assets	3.56	3.58	3.62	3.77	3.90	3.61	3.46	3.53	3.54	3.44	3.47
+ Noninterest Income/ Total Assets	2.04	1.91	1.88	2.02	1.95	1.81	1.67	1.63	1.51	1.44	1.32
– Noninterest Expense/ Total Assets	–3.51	–3.47	–3.52	–3.77	–3.87	–3.74	–3.49	–3.43	–3.37	–3.36	–3.32
= Net Noninterest Income/Total Assets	–1.47	–1.56	–1.64	–1.75	–1.92	–1.93	–1.82	–1.80	–1.86	–1.92	–2.00
– Prov. for Loan Losses/ Total Assets	–0.35	–0.29	–0.27	–0.45	–0.77	–1.02	–0.96	–0.98	–0.58	–1.30	–0.81
= Pretax Oper. Income/ Total Assets	1.73	1.73	1.71	1.57	1.21	0.66	0.68	0.75	1.10	0.22	0.66
– Taxes Paid/ Total Assets	–0.62	–0.61	–0.59	–0.54	–0.42	–0.25	–0.24	–0.30	–0.33	–0.19	–0.19
± Security Gains or Losses/Total Assets	+0.02	+0.01	+0.01	+0.14	+0.13	+0.11	+0.03	+0.04	+0.04	+0.06	+0.15
= Net After-Tax Income/ Total Assets	1.14%	1.13%	1.13%	1.17%	0.92%	0.52%	0.47%	0.49%	0.81%	0.09%	0.62%

Note: Figures may not add exactly to totals due to rounding.

*Based on three quarters for 1996.

Source: FDIC, Quarterly Releases and Annual Reports.

1987. The primary cause of that record low in bank earnings was the nearly unprecedented increase in the provision for loan losses, which rose more than 50 percent between 1986 and 1987. Clearly, the huge loan losses incurred, including record losses on real estate loans and on international loans held at the biggest American banks, dictated the industry's abysmal ROA record in 1987.

Yet, remarkably, this measure of bank profitability recovered dramatically in 1988, as Table 5–3 also shows. Again, why? Clearly, U.S. banking's spread of interest income over interest expense improved as loan demand and loan revenues rose. Noninterest (fee) income also increased as U.S. bankers pursued sales of more fee-based services (especially mortgage servicing and refinancing fees). Most importantly, however, U.S. banking's return on assets improved significantly in 1988 because the industry's provision for loan losses was returning to more normal levels. Unfortunately, in 1989, 1990, and 1991, loan losses increased sharply again, as did the noninterest expenses associated with employee salaries and overhead costs. So the industry's ROA was forced to retreat once again in the 1989–91 period from the high it reached in 1988. However, U.S. bank asset returns increased significantly again in 1992 as loan losses eased, noninterest fees from services sold rose substantially, and gains from sales of investment securities continued to rise. Finally, in 1993 U.S. banks posted their strongest earnings performance in more than half a century. In fact, 1993's ROA was the largest rate of return on assets since the Federal Deposit Insurance Corporation began operations in 1934. During the subsequent 1994–96 period U.S. banking's ROA remained near record high levels due to lower borrowing costs (interest expense) and reduced loan losses. By the third quarter of 1997 U.S. banking's ROA was at record levels again, averaging about 1.24 percent industrywide.

What a Breakdown of Bank Profitability Measures Can Tell Us

Clearly, breaking down bank profitability measures into their respective components tells us much about the causes of bank earnings difficulties and suggests where management needs to look for possible cures for any earnings problems that do surface. The foregoing analysis reminds us that achieving superior profitability for a bank depends upon several crucial factors:

1. Careful use of financial leverage (or the proportion of bank assets financed by debt as opposed to shareholders' equity capital).
2. Careful use of operating leverage from fixed assets (or the proportion of fixed-cost inputs the bank uses to boost its operating earnings before taxes as bank output grows).
3. Careful control of operating expenses so that more dollars of sales revenue become net income.
4. Careful management of the asset portfolio to meet liquidity needs while seeking the highest returns from any assets acquired.
5. Careful control of the bank's exposure to risk so that losses don't overwhelm its income and equity capital.

Concept Checks

5–11. What are the principal components of ROE and what does each of these components measure?

5–12. If a bank has an ROA of 0.80 percent and an equity multiplier of 12×, what is its ROE? Suppose this bank's ROA falls to 0.60 percent. What size equity multiplier must it have to hold its ROE unchanged?

5–13. Suppose a bank reports net income after taxes of $12, before-tax net income of $15, operating revenues of $100, assets of $600, and $50 in equity capital. What is the bank's ROE? Tax-management efficiency indicator? Expense control efficiency indicator? Asset management efficiency indicator? Funds management efficiency indicator?

5–14. What are the most important components of ROA and what aspects of bank performance do they reflect?

5–15. If a bank has a net interest margin of 2.50%, a noninterest margin of –1.85%, and a ratio of provision for loan losses, taxes, security gains, and extraordinary items of –0.47%, what is its ROA?

Measuring Risk in Banking[4]

Risk to a banker means the perceived uncertainty connected with some event. For example, will the customer renew his or her loan? Will deposits grow next month? Will the bank's stock price rise and its earnings increase? Are interest rates going to rise or fall next week and will the bank lose income or value if they do?

Bankers may be most interested in achieving high stock values and high profitability, but none can fail to pay attention to the risks they are accepting as well. A more volatile economy and recent problems with energy, real estate, and foreign loans have led bankers in recent years to focus increased attention and concern on how banking risk can be measured and kept under control. Bankers are concerned with six main types of risk:

1. Credit risk.
2. Liquidity risk.
3. Market risk.
4. Interest rate risk.
5. Earnings risk.
6. Solvency risk.

Credit Risk.   The probability that some of a bank's assets, especially its loans, will decline in value and perhaps become worthless is known as **credit risk.** Because

---

[4]This section is based on the author's 1987 article in the *Canadian Banker* [5] and is used with permission.

banks hold little owners' capital relative to the aggregate value of their assets, only a relatively small percentage of total loans needs to turn bad in order to push any bank to the brink of failure.The following are four of the most widely used indicators of bank credit risk:

- The ratio of nonperforming assets to total loans and leases.
- The ratio of net charge-offs of loans to total loans and leases.
- The ratio of the annual provision for loan losses to total loans and leases or to total equity capital.
- The ratio of allowance for loan losses to total loans and leases or to total equity capital.

Nonperforming assets are income-generating assets, including loans, that are past due for 90 days or more. *Charge-offs,* on the other hand, are loans that have been declared worthless by the bank and written off its books. If some of these loans ultimately generate income for the bank, the amounts recovered are deducted from gross charge-offs to yield net charge-offs. As both of the above ratios rise, the bank's exposure to credit risk grows, and bank failure may be just around the corner. The final two credit-risk indicator ratios reveal the extent to which a bank is preparing for loan losses by building up its loan-loss reserves (the allowance for loan losses) through annual charges against current income (the provision for loan losses).

Liquidity Risk.   Bankers are also very concerned about the danger of not having sufficient cash and borrowing capacity to meet deposit withdrawals, net loan demand, and other cash needs. Faced with **liquidity risk,** a bank may be forced to borrow emergency funds at excessive cost to cover its immediate cash needs, reducing its earnings. Very few banks ever actually run out of cash because of the ease with which liquid funds can be borrowed from other banks. In fact, so rare is such an event that when a small Montana bank in the early 1980s had to refuse to cash checks for a few hours due to a temporary "cash-out," there was a federal investigation of the incident!

Somewhat more common is a shortage of liquidity due to unexpectedly heavy deposit withdrawals, which forces a bank to borrow funds at an elevated interest rate—higher than the interest rates other banks are paying for similar borrowings. A significant decline in a bank's liquidity position often forces it to pay higher interest rates to attract negotiable money market CDs (which are sold in million-dollar units and therefore are largely unprotected by deposit insurance). One useful measure of liquidity risk exposure is the ratio of:

- Purchased funds (including Eurodollars, federal funds, security RPs, large CDs, and commercial paper) to total assets.

Heavier use of purchased funds increases the chances of a liquidity crunch in the event deposit withdrawals rise or loan quality declines. Other indicators of a bank's exposure to liquidity risk include the ratios of:

- Net loans to total assets.
- Cash and due-from deposit balances held at other banks to total assets.
- Cash assets and government securities to total assets.

Bank Management in Action

How High-Earning Banks Get That Way

A large number of research studies over the years have examined the top-earning banks in the industry in an effort to answer a simple question: *what distinguishes a bank with above-average profitability from banks that are only average performers?* How did top-earning banks get that way?

Bank size is clearly one factor. The top-earning banks in the industry, at least as measured by their return on assets (ROA), are usually small to medium-size institutions (ranging from $100 million to perhaps a few billion dollars of assets), who seem to benefit from lower overall operating costs. On the other hand, when profitability is measured by the returns to the bank's owners (ROE), the largest banks in the industry often lead the pack, fueled by their greater use of financial leverage (i.e., using less equity capital and more debt to fund their assets).

Expense control stands out as the most important discriminator between top performers and the also-rans. High-profit banks manage their operating expenses better, generally posting lower average interest costs, and especially lower noninterest costs—personnel expenses, overhead, and loan losses. Their ratios of operating expenses to operating revenues tend to be significantly below the expense-to-revenue ratios of low-profit banks.

The *deposit structure* of banks also appears to influence their profit performance. Top-earning banks often hold more demand deposits than other banks; these checkable deposits pay little or no interest and carry customer service fees which help to bring in more revenues. Relatedly, many highly profitable banks attract and hold a large volume of *core deposits*—smaller denomination deposits from individuals and

Cash assets include vault cash held on bank premises, deposits the bank holds at the Federal Reserve bank in its district, deposits held with other banks to compensate them for clearing checks and other interbank services, and cash items in the process of collection (mainly uncollected checks). Standard remedies for reducing a bank's exposure to liquidity risk include increasing the proportion of bank funds committed to cash and readily marketable assets, such as government securities, or using longer-term liabilities to fund the bank's operations.

Market Risk.   Volatile changes in interest rates have created havoc for managers of bank asset portfolios, particularly for those responsible for bank investments in government bonds and other marketable securities. When interest rates catapulted to record levels a few years ago, the market value of bank-held bonds plummeted, forcing many banking firms to accept substantial losses on any securities that had to be sold—a potent example of what financial analysts call **market risk.** If interest rates increase, the market value of fixed-income securities (such as bonds) and fixed-rate loans will fall. A bank faced with the need to sell these assets in a rising-rate market

small businesses—that pay low interest rates and are more loyal to the bank than larger deposit accounts.

Employee productivity tends to be higher among the top earners. Banks with the best profits seem to generate and manage more assets and income per employee and often pay their more productive employees higher wages and salaries.

Leverage (lower equity-capital-to-asset ratios and greater use of debt) also emerges as a profit motivator. Top-earning banks generally economize on utilizing high-cost owners' capital and rely on the earnings-leveraging effects of cheaper short- and long-term debt.

The *expansion of fee income* has become a key element in bank strategies to increase profits in recent years. Deregulation of the industry has put added pressure on banks to charge fees for many formerly "free" services and to develop new, fee-generating services, such as selling shares in mutual funds and offering security management, processing, and underwriting services.

Growth in assets, deposits, and loans seems to play a role because top-earning banks seem to grow faster than the average bank, possibly reflecting the presence of more aggressive management or greater customer acceptance of their services. However, growth should *not* become a substitute for profits. Top-earning banks seem to recognize that growth can be overdone, resulting in uncontrolled expansion which tends to increase operating expenses faster than revenues. Moderate growth is a better route to high profits for most banks.

For further information on the characteristics and features of high-profit banks see especially U.S. General Accounting Office, *Commercial Banking: Trends in Performance from December 1976 through June 1987*, Washington, D.C., July 1988; and Robert E. Goudreau, "FYI-Commercial Bank Profitability Rises as Interest Margins and Securities Sales Increase," *Economic Review*, Federal Reserve Bank of Atlanta, May–June 1992, pp. 33–52.

will take losses. Falling interest rates, in contrast, will increase the value of fixed-income securities and fixed-rate loans, resulting in capital gains when they are sold. Among the most important indicators of market risk in banking are:

- The ratio of a bank's book-value assets to the estimated market value of those same assets.
- The ratios of fixed-rate loans and securities to floating-rate loans and securities and of fixed-rate liabilities to floating-rate liabilities.
- The ratio of book-value equity capital to the market value of a bank's equity capital.

Interest Rate Risk.   Movements in market interest rates can also have potent effects on a bank's margin of revenues over operating costs. For example, rising interest rates can lower a bank's margin of profit if the structure of the institution's assets and liabilities is such that interest expenses on borrowed money increase more rapidly than interest revenues on loans and security investments. However, if the bank has an excess of flexible-rate assets (especially loans) over flexible-rate liabilities (especially rate-sensitive CDs and money market borrowings), falling interest rates will erode the bank's profit margin. In this case, asset revenues will drop faster than borrowing costs.

The impact of changing interest rates on a bank's margin of profit is usually called **interest rate risk.** Among the most widely used measures of bank interest-rate risk exposure are:

- The ratio of interest-sensitive assets to interest-sensitive liabilities: when interest-sensitive assets exceed interest-sensitive liabilities in a particular maturity range, a bank is vulnerable to losses from falling interest rates. In contrast, when rate-sensitive liabilities exceed rate-sensitive assets in volume, losses are likely to be incurred if market interest rates rise.
- The ratio of uninsured deposits to total deposits, where uninsured deposits are usually government and corporate deposits that exceed the amount covered by insurance and are usually so highly sensitive to changing interest rates that they will be withdrawn if yields offered by competitors rise even slightly higher.

With more volatile market interest rates in recent years, banks have developed several new ways to defend their earnings margins against interest-rate changes, including interest-rate swaps and financial futures contracts. We will examine these risk management tools closely in Chapters 6, 7, 8, and 9.

Earnings Risk.   The risk to the bank's bottom line—its net income after all expenses, including taxes, are covered—is known as **earnings risk.** Earnings may decline unexpectedly due to factors inside the bank or due to external factors, such as changes in economic conditions or changes in laws and regulations. Recent increases in banking competition have tended to narrow the spread between earnings on bank assets and the cost of raising bank funds. Thus, a bank's stockholders always face the possibility of a decline in their earnings per share of stock, which would cause the value of the bank's stock to fall, eroding its resources for future growth. Among the more popular measures of bank earnings risk are the following:

- Standard deviation (σ) or variance (σ^2) of after-tax net income.
- Standard deviation or variance of the bank's return on equity (ROE) and return on assets (ROA).

The higher the standard deviation or variance of bank income, the more risky the bank's earnings picture is. If investors in the bank's securities expect higher earnings risk to persist into the future, they will seek compensation for that added risk in the form of higher yields from the bank or go elsewhere with their money.

Solvency (or Default) Risk.   Bankers must be directly concerned about risks to their institutions' long-run survival, usually called **solvency risk.** If the bank takes on an excessive number of bad loans or if a large portion of its security portfolio declines in market value, generating serious capital losses when sold, then its capital account, which is designed to absorb such losses, may be overwhelmed. If investors and depositors become aware of the problem and begin to withdraw their funds, the regulators may have no choice but to declare the bank insolvent and close its doors.

A bank's failure may leave its stockholders with none of the funds they committed to the institution. Depositors not covered by insurance also risk losing all or a substantial portion of their funds. For this reason, the prices and yields on bank stock and on large, uninsured deposits can serve as an early warning sign of bank solvency problems. When investors believe that a bank has an increased chance of failing, the market value of its stock usually begins to fall and it must post higher interest rates on its CDs and other borrowings in order to attract needed funds. Economists call this phenomenon *market discipline*—interest rates and security prices in the financial marketplace move against a troubled firm, forcing it to make crucial adjustments in policies and performance in order to calm investors' worst fears about the firm.[5] This suggests that a bank's default or failure risk can be measured approximately by such factors as:

- The interest rate spread between market yields on bank debt issues (such as capital notes and CDs) and the market yields on government securities of the same maturity. A widening in that spread indicates that investors in the market expect increased risk of loss from purchasing the bank's debt securities.
- The ratio of a bank's stock price to its annual earnings per share. This ratio often falls if investors come to believe that a bank is undercapitalized relative to the risks it has taken on.
- The ratio of equity capital (net worth) to total assets held by the bank, where a decline in equity funding relative to assets may indicate increased risk exposure for the bank's shareholders and debtholders.
- The ratio of purchased funds to total liabilities. Purchased funds usually include uninsured deposits and borrowings in the money market from other banks, corporations, and governmental units that fall due within one year.

Other popular measures of a bank's degree of solvency risk include the ratios of (*a*) equity capital to risk assets and (*b*) primary capital to total assets. *Risk assets* consist mainly of loans and securities and exclude cash, plant and equipment, and miscellaneous bank assets. Some authorities also exclude holdings of short-term U.S. government securities from risk assets because the market values of these securities tend to be stable and there is always a ready resale market for them. *Primary capital* includes all bank reserves that can be used to absorb losses, including equity capital, the allowance for loan losses, minority investments in subsidiaries of the bank, and long-term bank debt that is subordinated to the claims of the depositors minus any intangible assets (goodwill) recorded on the bank's books. Concern in the regulatory community over bank solvency risk has resulted in heavy pressure on management to increase these two capital ratios. In general, both ratios have moved higher in recent years.

---

[5]For further discussion of market discipline and its possible effectiveness in getting banks to reduce their risk exposure see Baer and Brewer [1] and Brewer and Cheng [2].

Other Forms of Risk in Banking

Certainly credit, liquidity, market, interest rate, earnings, and solvency risk are not the only forms of risk affecting banking today. Banks of all sizes and shapes also face several other important types of risk:

Inflation risk—the probability that an increasing price level for goods and services (inflation) will unexpectedly erode the purchasing power of bank earnings and the return to its shareholders.

Currency or exchange rate risk—the probability that fluctuations in the market value of foreign currencies (the dollar, pound, franc, yen, etc.) will create losses for the bank by altering the market values of its assets and liabilities.

Political risk—the probability that changes in government laws or regulations, at home or abroad, will adversely affect the bank's earnings, operations, and future prospects.

Crime risk—the possibility that bank owners, employees, or customers may choose to violate the law and subject the bank to loss from fraud, embezzlement, theft, or other illegal acts.

We will look more closely at these other forms of banking risk later in this book, examining the threat they pose to bank well-being and how management can respond to each of these risk factors.

Other Goals in Banking

In an effort to maximize profitability and the value of the shareholders' investment in the bank, many banking organizations recognize the need for greater *efficiency* in their operations. This usually means reducing operating expenses and increasing the productivity of their employees through the use of automated equipment and improved employee training. The deregulation movement has forced banks to pay higher interest costs for their funds and encouraged management to reduce noninterest costs, especially employee salaries, wages, and benefits and overhead costs. Among the most revealing measures of a bank's operating efficiency and employee productivity are its:

$$\text{Operating efficiency ratio} = \frac{\text{Total operating expenses}}{\text{Total operating revenues}}$$

$$\text{Employee productivity ratio} = \frac{\text{Net operating income}}{\text{Number of full-time-equivalent employees}}$$

Not all banks pursue high profitability, maximum stock values, increased growth, or greater efficiency as key goals, however. There is considerable evidence that some institutions prefer greater *market power* in the markets they serve, not only because it gives them increased control over prices and customer relationships, but also because a bank with greater market influence can enjoy a more "quiet life" (i.e., face less risk of losing earnings or market share). Several recent studies have found that some banks in this situation display expense-preference behavior—they spend more on salaries and wages of management and staff, enjoy more fringe benefits, or build larger and more sumptuous

---

Concept Checks

5–16. To what different kinds of risk are banks subjected today?

5–17. What items on a bank's balance sheet and income statement can be used to measure its risk exposure?

5–18. A bank reports that the total amount of its net loans and leases outstanding is $936 million, its assets total $1,324 million, its equity capital amounts to $110 million, and it holds $1,150 million in deposits, all expressed in book value. The estimated market values of the bank's total assets and equity capital are $1,443 million and $130 million, respectively. The bank's stock is currently valued at $60 per share with annual per-share earnings of $2.50. Uninsured deposits amount to $243 million and money-market borrowings total $132 million, while nonperforming loans currently amount to $43 million and the bank just charged off $21 million in loans. Calculate as many of the bank's risk measures as you can from the foregoing data.

---

offices. Unfortunately for the stockholders of these banks, a preference for expenses sacrifices profits and limits potential gains in bank stock prices, as we noted in Chapter 3.

The Impact of Bank Size on Performance

When the performance of one bank is compared to another, *bank size*—usually measured by total assets or total deposits—becomes a critical factor. Most of the bank performance ratios presented in this chapter are highly sensitive to the size group in which a bank falls. As Table 5–4 shows, key earnings and risk measures change dramatically as we move from the smallest banks (those in the exhibit with total assets of less than $100 million) to the largest banking firms (with assets exceeding $10 billion). For example, the most profitable banks in terms of ROA tend to be in the medium-size ranges, while the largest banks often report the lowest average ROA. However, ROE usually reaches the highest level among billion-dollar-plus-size banks.

On the other hand, middle-size banks with assets ranging from $100 million up to $10 billion in total assets display the most favorable net interest and net operating margins, the best earnings spread, and the best operating efficiency ratios (with the lowest operating-expense-to-revenue ratio). In contrast, the largest banks generally report the highest (least negative) noninterest margins because they charge fees for so many of their services. Smaller and medium-size banks frequently display larger net interest margins and, therefore, greater spreads between interest revenue and interest costs because most of their deposits are small-denomination accounts with lower average interest costs. Moreover, a larger proportion of small and medium-size banks' loans tend to be high-interest consumer loans.

In terms of balance-sheet ratios, many of which reflect the various kinds of risk exposure banks face, the smallest banks usually report higher ratios of equity capital to assets, while the largest, billion-dollar-plus institutions have much thinner

TABLE 5-4 Important Bank Performance Indicators Related to Bank Size and Location
(First 3 Quarters of 1996, Annualized)

Performance Indicators	Average for All Institutions	Banks Arranged by Total Assets Size Range:				Banks in Selected Regions of the United States:		
		Under $100 Million	$100 Million to $1 Billion	$1 Billion to $10 Billion	Greater Than $10 Billion	Southwest Region	Northeast Region	Midwest Region
ROA (Return on Assets)	1.19%	1.23%	1.29%	1.31%	1.10%	1.23%	1.08%	1.44%
ROE (Return on Equity Capital)	14.40	11.69	13.63	14.82	14.93	14.15	14.41	16.31
Net Operating Margin to Total Assets (total operating revenue less total operating expenses ÷ total assets)	1.17	1.23	1.28	1.30	1.07	1.24	1.05	1.44
Net Interest Margin (net interest income ÷ total earning assets)	4.27	4.65	4.70	4.79	3.84	4.41	3.78	4.53
Noninterest Income Margin (net noninterest margin/ earning assets)	-1.78	-2.51	-2.33	-1.66	-1.56	-2.12	-1.42	-1.80
Operating Efficiency Ratio (operating expenses/operating revenues)	0.7646	0.7818	0.7597	0.7643	*	*	*	*
Annual Loan-Loss Provision/Net Charge-Offs of Bad Loans	103.99	125.25	126.92	113.59	84.88	104.88	89.62	111.03
Net Charge-Offs of Bad Loans/Total Loans and Leases	0.56	0.22	0.37	0.99	0.44	0.31	0.62	0.66
Allowance for Loan Losses/Total Loans and Leases	1.96	1.52	1.58	2.09	2.06	1.53	2.30	1.79
Noncurrent Assets + Other Real Estate Owned/Total Assets	0.80	0.82	0.81	0.89	0.76	0.65	0.92	0.68
Net Loans and Leases/Total Assets	86.70	65.81	72.61	96.81	90.62	67.54	87.95	80.43
Cash Assets/Total Assets	6.41	5.32	5.25	7.91	*	*	*	*
Equity Capital/Total Assets	8.31	10.57	9.45	8.96	7.44	8.90	7.39	8.86
Cost of Funding Earning Assets	3.93	3.66	3.63	3.87	4.09	3.43	4.27	3.86
Annual Growth Rate (percent) in:								
Total Assets	5.41	--	--	--	--	3.94	4.57	5.56
Total Equity Capital	7.65	--	--	--	--	6.14	1.99	5.93

*Data available only for U.S.-insured banks under $10 billion and not available by region.

Source: Federal Deposit Insurance Corporation, *The FDIC Quarterly Banking Profile*, Third Quarter 1996. Figures are for all FDIC-insured commercial banks.

capital-to-asset ratios. Some bank analysts argue that larger banks can get by with lower capital-to-asset cushions because they are more diversified across many different markets and have more risk-hedging tools at their disposal. Smaller banks appear to be more liquid, as reflected in their lower ratios of total (net) loans to total deposits, because loans are often among a bank's least liquid assets. However, the biggest banks hold larger proportions of cash assets relative to total assets because they hold the deposits of many smaller banks. The biggest banks also appear to carry greater credit risk as revealed by their higher loan-loss ratios.

Watching Out for Size, Location, and Regulatory Bias in Analyzing Bank Performance

As we saw in the preceding section, the *size* of a bank (often measured by its total assets, deposits, or equity capital) can have a highly significant impact on its profitability and other performance measures. Thus, when we compare the performance of one bank with another, it is best to compare banks of *similar size*. One reason is that similar-size banks tend to offer the same or similar services, so you can be a little more confident that your performance comparisons have some validity.

But, to conduct even more valid performance comparisons we should also compare banks serving the same or *similar market areas.* The performance of a bank is usually greatly influenced by whether it operates in a major financial center, smaller town or city, or rural area. The best performance comparison of all is to choose banks of similar size serving the same market area. Unfortunately, in some smaller communities it may be difficult or impossible to find another banking firm comparable in size. The financial analyst will then usually look for another community with a similar-size bank—preferably a community housing similar-type businesses and industries because the character of a bank's customer base significantly affects how well it performs.

Finally, where possible, it's a good idea to compare banks subject to *similar regulations* and regulatory agencies. Each bank regulator has a somewhat different set of rules banks must follow, and these government-imposed rules can have a profound impact on bank performance. This is why comparisons of banks in different countries is often so difficult and must be done with great caution.

Even in the United States with so many different bank regulatory agencies, analysts often stress the importance of comparing member banks of the Federal Reserve System against other member banks or nonmember banks against other nonmember banks. Similarly, the performance of national banks, where possible, should be compared against that of other national banks, and state-chartered institutions should be compared against other state banks. If a bank is an affiliate of a bank holding company, it can be revealing to compare its performance with other holding company affiliates rather than with independently owned banks. There is an old saying about avoiding comparing apples and oranges because of their obvious differences; the same is true in banking—no two banks are ever exactly alike in size, location, service menu, or customer base. The bank performance analyst must make his or her "best effort" to find the most comparable institutions and then proceed with caution.

Bankers' Insights and Issues

Why Banks Fail

Bank failures have been relatively high in recent years, averaging well over a hundred bank closings a year in the United States during the 1980s before slowing in the 1990s as the economy improved and bank capital strengthened. While each bank failure is a somewhat unique experience, recent studies have identified a few factors that most failing banks seem to have in common.

Most banks that fail seem to do so because of *problems in their loan portfolio.* Nonperforming loans grow to such an extent that revenues fall off and loan-loss expenses, as well as operating costs, absorb all the earnings that remain. The bad loan situation usually arises from a combination of factors. Failing banks often have inadequate systems for spotting problem loans early. Management may be too aggressive in expanding the bank's loans, such as by "overlending" in which borrowers receive larger loans than they can comfortably carry, by heavy use of "collateral loans" in which credit is extended, not on the basis of cash-flow or borrower income, but primarily relying on the assets pledged as collateral (which is very dangerous because asset values can change drastically in a short period of time), and by concentrating loans in one industry or in a single group of businesses. Moreover, banks that fail often don't follow their own loan policies and have numerous credit exceptions in their loan portfolios (such as missing borrower financial statements).

The *economy* certainly plays a role. When a bank's market area experiences economic decline, with rising unemployment, sluggish business sales, and increasing business failures, banks can suffer along with their beleaguered customers. However, it is easy to overstress the role of the economy in bank failures. Many banks survive and some gener-

Using Financial Ratios and Other Analytical Tools to Track Bank Performance—The UBPR

During the 1980s, bankers and other financial analysts received an important new tool to aid them in analyzing a bank's financial condition. This new tool, the cooperative effort of the three federal banking agencies—the Federal Reserve System, the Federal Deposit Insurance Corporation, and the Office of the Comptroller of the Currency—is called the Uniform Bank Performance Report (UBPR). The **UBPR,** which is sent quarterly to all federally supervised banks, reports each bank's assets, liabilities, capital, revenues, and expenses for the current quarter and for three prior years. Supplementary items include breakdowns of loan and lease commitments, analysis of problem loans and loan losses, and a profile of each bank's exposure to risk and sources of capital. Banks can also purchase *peer group reports,* which allow them to compare their bank with other banks of comparable size, and *state reports,* which allow comparisons with the combined financial statements of all banks in each state. An important added feature is that a banker can purchase the UBPR report for

ate exceptional profits even in a depressed economy. These are banks that control their expenses well and find ways to reach into other market areas *not* experiencing economic decline, such as by purchasing loans from banks operating in stronger market areas or reaching directly into *new* market areas through branching.

Many banks that fail seem to encounter *leadership problems.* Their boards of directors may lack knowledge of banking and play only a passive role in overseeing the bank, instead of carefully monitoring management decisions, earnings, and expenses and helping a bank shape its strategic plan. Moreover, many bank failures seem to arise from mistakes and lack of scruples among senior management who may not be capable or honest. Relatedly, *audit and control procedures* are often neglected in failing banks, and *insider transactions* lead many banks to failure as stockholders, directors, officers, or staff engage in self-dealing, granting excessive loans to themselves or to their businesses at preferential interest rates.

Finally, failing banks frequently have *expense control problems.* Management may invest the bank's money in lavish offices and enjoy handsome fringe benefits that the bank's earnings simply cannot support. When the bank's troubles become evident to depositors, it must then pay higher interest rates to secure funding, further increasing its operating costs. Eventually, expenses may erode what limited earnings are available and bank capital begins to fall.

Fur further information on bank failures see especially Gary Whalen, "A Proportional Hazards Model of Bank Failure: An Examination of Its Usefulness as an Early Warning Tool," *Economic Review,* Federal Reserve Bank of Cleveland, First Quarter 1991, pp. 21–31; and Colleen C. Pantalone and Marjorie B. Platt, "Predicting Commercial Bank Failure Since Deregulation," *New England Economic Review,* Federal Reserve Bank of Boston, July/August 1987, pp. 37–47.

any other federally supervised bank, thus enabling comparison of banks in the same market area subject to the same environmental conditions.[6]

To get a better picture of the type of information in the UBPR, we present below an example based upon the UBPR of a bank that we will call Security National Bank (not its real name). Security National is a large bank located in a moderate-size U.S. metropolitan area and has total assets approaching $7 billion. How well or how poorly has Security National performed in recent years?

Tables 5–5 through 5–9, taken from one of the bank's UBPR reports, help us answer that question. Tables 5–5 and 5–6 indicate the principal assets, liabilities, and capital held by the bank and show how those items and their components have increased or decreased in volume since the same time one year ago.

In terms of *growth,* Security National has not done badly. Its total assets increased by nearly $600 million during the year, for a 9.3 percent annual rate of growth

---

[6]The UBPR is available for purchase from the Federal Financial Institutions Examination Council, 490 L'Enfant Plaza, SW, Washington, D.C., 20219.

Bankers' Insights and Issues

Bank Credit Ratings by Thomson's BankWatch, Inc.

One of the most widely respected private institutions that rates the credit quality of banks and selected other financial institutions is Thomson's BankWatch, Inc. Thomson's is a bank credit-rating agency, evaluating more than a thousand banks in over 80 different countries. Thomson's rates both short-term debt having original maturities of a year or less and long-term obligations (debt and preferred stock), assessing the likelihood that the banks and securities firms issuing these obligations may not be able to pay in timely fashion or may require government aid to avoid failure. BankWatch's credit ratings are among the most widely followed banking risk indicators anywhere, particularly by large depositors and those who purchase bank stock and bank capital notes and debentures.

Examples of Thomson's BankWatch ratings of credit worthiness include:

Short-Term Ratings	*Long-Term Ratings*
TBW-1: very high likelihood of timely repayment of principal and interest.	AAA: extremely high capacity to repay principal and interest.
TBW-2: strong likelihood of timely repayment of principal and interest.	AA: strong ability to repay principal and interest.
TBW-3: adequate capacity to service principal and interest in a timely way.	A: relatively strong ability to timely repay principal and interest.
TBW-4: noninvestment grade and speculative in nature.	BBB: lowest investment grade rating with an acceptable capacity to repay principal and interest.
	BB: likelihood of default just above investment grade with some significant uncertainties affecting the capacity to repay.
	B: higher degree of uncertainty and greater likelihood of default than for higher-rated issues.
	CCC: high likelihood of default.
	CC: subordinated to CCC obligations with less bankruptcy or reorganization risk protection.
	D: defaulted obligation.

The long-term bank credit ratings may be marked with a + or a − depending upon whether the rated institution appears to lie nearer the top or nearer the bottom of each rating category.

(Table 5–5, line 23). Nearly all categories of deposits increased, especially checkable accounts (regular demand deposits, money market accounts, and super NOWs), with only foreign deposits and regular savings deposits declining (Table 5–6, lines 1 through 9).

Similarly, all types of loans rose at Security National, except for agricultural loans, foreign loans, and miscellaneous (other) loans (Table 5–5, lines 1 to 11)—sectors that were hit hard by adverse economic developments during the year. The bank

**TABLE 5–5   The Assets Section from the Balance Sheet
for Security National Bank**

Items	Dollar Amounts (millions)		Percentage Change
	Most Recent Year	One Year Ago	
Assets:			
1. Real estate loans	$1,030	$ 835	23.4%
2. Financial institutions' loans	229	179	27.9
3. Agricultural loans	122	126	–3.2
4. Commercial and industrial loans	1,023	916	11.7
5. Loans to individuals	525	481	9.1
6. Municipal loans	404	354	14.1
7. Acceptances from other banks	10	9	11.1
8. Other loans from domestic offices	154	164	–6.1
9. Foreign office loans and leases	114	118	–3.4
10. Lease financing receivables	222	190	16.8
11. Gross loans and leases	3,833	3,372	13.7
12. Less: Unearned income	17	15	13.3
Loan-loss reserve	57	51	11.8
13. Net loans and leases	3,759	3,306	13.7
14. Securities over one year	**1,291**	**574**	**124.9**
15. Interest-bearing bank balances	304	665	–54.3
16. Federal funds sold and resale agreements	363	378	–4.0
17. Trading-account assets	150	111	35.1
18. Debt securities one year and less in maturity	**179**	**409**	**–56.2**
19. Noninterest-bearing cash and deposits due from banks	311	299	4.0
20. Acceptances	223	275	–18.9
21. Premises, fixed assets, and capital leases	170	165	3.0
22. Other assets	183	179	2.2
23. Total assets	$6,951	$6,361	9.3%
Memo items:			
24. U.S. Treasury and federal agency securities	**1,105**	**730**	**51.4**
25. Municipal securities	348	240	45.0
26. Foreign securities	3	2	50.0
27. All other securities	14	21	–33.3

also increased the credit it provides to customers by purchasing more securities from various borrowers, especially federal, state, and local governments. Security National increased its holdings of longer-term notes and bonds, while decreasing its holdings of shorter-term securities (under one year to maturity), probably because management was seeking higher yields. (See Table 5–5, lines 14 through 18 and 24 through 27.)

Security's loans and securities rose faster than its deposits, creating a funding gap between the bank's uses of funds (mainly loans and securities) and its sources of funds

**TABLE 5–6   Liabilities and Capital Section from the Balance Sheet
for Security National Bank**

Items	Dollar Amounts (millions)		Percentage Change
	Most Recent Year	*One Year Ago*	
1. Demand deposits	$ 748	$ 660	13.3%
2. NOW and ATS accounts	313	295	6.1
3. Regular savings deposits	301	308	–2.3
4. Money market deposit accounts	639	567	12.7
5. Super NOWs	10	7	42.9
6. Small time deposits			
(under $100,000)	865	762	13.5
7. Core deposits	2,876	2,599	10.7
8. Large time deposits			
(over $100,000)	357	258	38.4
9. Deposits held in foreign offices	277	948	–70.8
10. Federal funds purchased and			
security resale agreements	**1,780**	**913**	**95.0**
11. Volatile liabilities	2,624	2,271	15.5
12. Acceptances and other liabilities	1,152	1,228	–6.2
13. Total liabilities	6,442	5,946	8.3
14. Mortgages and capitalized leases	15	14	7.1
15. Subordinated notes and debentures	12	20	–40.0
16. Total liabilities and debt	6,469	5,980	8.2
17. Common equity	467	368	26.9
18. Preferred stock	15	13	15.4
19. Total equity capital	**482**	**381**	**26.5**
20. Total liabilities and equity capital	6,951	6,361	9.3
Alternative deposit presentation			
21. Noninterest-bearing deposits	809	713	13.5
22. Interest-bearing deposits	2,698	3,135	–13.9
23. Total deposits	**3,507**	**3,848**	**–8.9**
24. Transaction accounts	1,071	962	11.3
25. Money market deposit accounts	639	567	12.7
26. Other nontransaction deposits	1,797	2,319	–22.5

Source: Format supplied by the Federal Financial Institutions Examination Council; figures inserted by the author.

(principally deposits). As a result, the bank was forced to draw heavily upon nonde-posit borrowings, particularly in the form of federal funds purchases (i.e., reserves borrowed from other banks overnight) and security sales under repurchase agreements (Table 5–6, line 10). Because these sources of funds tend to be both more expensive and less reliable than most deposit accounts, this nondeposit funding strategy, along with other factors, served to reduce the bank's profitability, as we will see shortly.

Table 5–7, which shows the composition of assets and liabilities held by Security National, indicates that the bank made some significant changes in the makeup of its portfolio during the past year. Loans rose relative to other assets (line 1), though the bank still lagged behind other banks in its peer group in the percentage of assets accounted for by

TABLE 5–7   Percentage Composition of Assets and Liabilities for Security National Bank and Its Peer Group (all figures are percentages of total assets)

	Security National Bank		Peer Group	
Items	*Most Recent Year*	*One Year Ago*	*Most Recent Year*	*One Year Ago*
Assets:				
1. Total (gross) loans	**55.14%**	53.01%	59.58%	55.05%
2. Lease financing receivables	3.19	2.99	0.93	0.74
3. Less: Loss reserves	0.82	0.80	0.79	0.69
4. Net loans and leases	54.08	51.97	60.43	55.28
5. Securities over one year	**18.57**	**9.02**	**8.95**	**10.14**
6. Subtotals	72.65	60.99	69.92	66.30
7. Interest-bearing bank balances	4.37	10.45	5.60	9.03
8. Federal funds sold and resale agreements	5.22	5.94	4.03	3.52
9. Trading-account assets	2.16	1.75	0.66	0.45
10. Debt securities one year and less	**2.58**	**6.43**	**3.41**	**3.45**
11. Temporary investments	14.33	24.57	15.00	18.14
12. Total earning assets	86.98	85.56	85.07	84.61
13. Noninterest-bearing cash and deposits due from other banks	**4.47**	**4.70**	**8.64**	**8.35**
14. Premises, fixed assets, and capital leases	2.45	2.59	1.55	1.57
15. Other real estate owned	0.06	0.03	0.16	0.12
16. Acceptances and other assets	5.78	7.11	4.46	5.14
17. Subtotals	12.76	14.43	14.93	15.39
18. Total assets	100.00	100.00	100.00	100.00
Liabilities:				
19. Demand deposits	10.76	10.38	18.52	18.25
20. Regular savings, NOW, and ATS accounts	8.83	9.48	7.37	7.70
21. Small time deposits (under $100,000)	12.44	11.98	14.11	7.95
22. Super NOW and money market deposit accounts	9.34	9.02	13.18	10.61
23. Core deposits	**41.38**	**40.86**	**53.18**	**49.35**
24. Large time deposits (over $100,000)	5.14	4.06	12.52	13.94
25. Deposits held in foreign offices	3.99	14.90	7.84	9.94
26. Federal funds purchased and security resale agreements	25.61	14.35	12.63	13.35
27. Other borrowings	3.02	2.39	2.44	2.04
28. Volatile liabilities	**37.75**	**35.70**	**36.32**	**39.45**
29. Acceptances and other liabilities	13.55	16.92	4.38	5.22
30. Total liabilities	92.89	93.70	93.88	94.10
31. Subordinated notes and debentures	0.17	0.31	0.35	0.31
32. All common and preferred stock (equity)	**6.93**	**5.99**	**5.72**	**5.49**
33. Total liabilities and capital	100.00	100.00	100.00	100.00
34. Noninterest-bearing deposits	**11.64**	**11.21**	**19.04**	**18.59**
35. Interest-bearing deposits	**38.81**	**49.28**	**54.78**	**54.08**

Source: Format supplied by the Federal Financial Institutions Examination Council; figures inserted by the author.

loans. Because loans usually represent the highest-yielding assets a bank can hold, Security's relatively low loan-asset ratio would tend to reduce its potential earnings, though it may help to hold the bank's credit and liquidity risk down. Security National held more long-term securities over one year than its peer group, but fewer short-term securities (lines 5 and 10). Longer-term securities tend to carry greater market risk due to changes in interest rates, and those not government guaranteed usually face greater credit risk than short-term securities. Both of these forms of risk could threaten the bank's future earnings.

Security National Bank holds significantly lower portions of liquid assets—short-term securities (under one year) and cash assets (noninterest-bearing cash and deposit balances due from banks)—than other banks of comparable size. For example, the volume of cash and deposits due from other banks was only about half the proportion of total assets that peer banks hold (line 13). Could management be accepting greater liquidity risk (i.e., the possibility of a cash-out) than is warranted? Is this possible shortage of liquid assets one reason the bank has been forced to borrow such a relatively large proportion of nondeposit funds to meet its funding needs? These are questions management needs to explore right away.

On the sources of funds side, we note from Table 5–7 that the bank holds a significantly smaller proportion of checkable deposits, especially regular demand deposits, than its peers (line 19). Because demand deposits tend to be among the least expensive and most profitable sources of funds for a bank, could the low proportion of checkable deposits suggest excessive funding costs and low profitability for the bank? Adding fuel to the fire, perhaps, Security National holds a low ratio of core deposits to its total sources of funds (line 23). *Core deposits,* as reported in the UBPR, include demand deposits, NOWs, regular savings deposits, money market deposits, and time deposits of less than $100,000. These categories are assumed to be more stable and more loyal to the bank than the other types of deposit accounts, thereby presenting lower risk of illiquidity at times when the bank really needs immediately spendable funds. Core deposits also tend to be among the least expensive sources of bank funding.

Could Security's management be accepting greater liquidity risk with its relatively low proportion of core deposits as the bank strives to increase its profitability? One good sign is that the bank's proportion of volatile liabilities—large ($100,000+) time deposits, foreign-office deposits, federal funds purchased and security resale agreements, and other nondeposit obligations—is within normal ranges for the peer group of banks, helping to hold down Security's funding costs and exposure to liquidity risk (Table 5–7, line 28). Moreover, the bank's overall ratio of interest-bearing (more expensive) deposits to noninterest-bearing deposits is favorable relative to its peer group (lines 34 and 35).

When we turn to the bank's statement of earnings and expenses (Table 5–8), the questions that concerned us on the balance sheet come home to roost in the form of poor earnings and weak expense control. We note, for example, that the bank's earnings from loans and its overall interest income from loans, leases, and security holdings have been growing slowly—in fact, much more slowly than its expenses and assets. For example, Table 5–8 reveals that total interest income grew only 1.2 percent between the most recent year and one year ago (line 15). In contrast, total interest expenses on deposits and nondeposit borrowings increased more than three times as fast (4.5 percent) for the latest year (line 23). Leading the list were sharp increases in interest paid on large ($100,000+) CDs, on deposits in foreign offices, and on other borrowings, such as mortgages and lease contracts against the bank's property and equipment (lines 16, 17, and 20).

TABLE 5–8 Security National Bank Income Statement (revenues and expenses)

Items	Dollar Amounts (millions)		
	Most Recent Year	One Year Ago	Percentage Change
1. Interest and fees on loans	$401	$373	7.5%
2. Income from lease financing	8	7	14.3
3. Fully taxable income	393	367	7.1
4. Tax-exempt income	34	40	−15.0
5. Estimated tax benefits	28	33	−15.2
6. Income on loans and leases (tax-equivalent basis)	455	440	3.4
7. Income from U.S. Treasury and agency securities	75	73	2.7
8. Municipal security income	12	15	−20.0
9. Tax benefit on municipals	9	10	−10.0
10. Income from other securities	1	1	0.0
11. Investment income (tax-equivalent basis)	97	99	−2.0
12. Interest on deposits due from other banks	15	20	−25.0
13. Interest on federal funds sold and RPs	13	15	−13.3
14. Trading-account income	2	1	100.0
15. Total interest income (tax-equivalent basis)	582	575	1.2
16. Interest paid on large CDs (over $100,000)	47	41	14.6
17. Interest paid on deposits in foreign offices	30	28	7.1
18. Interest on all other deposits	175	169	3.6
19. Interest on federal funds purchased and RPs	152	149	2.0
20. Interest on borrowed money (notes)	11	10	10.0
21. Interest on mortgages and leases for property and equipment			
22. Interest on subordinated notes and debentures	___	___	___
23. Total interest expense	415	397	4.5
24. Net interest income (tax-equivalent basis)	165	176	−6.3
25. Noninterest income	22	18	22.2
26. Adjusted operating income (tax-equivalent basis)	187	194	−3.6
27. Overhead expense	72	70	2.9
28. Provision for loan and lease losses	11	6	83.3
29. Pre-tax operating income (tax-equivalent basis)	104	118	−11.9
30. Securities gains (or losses)	−4	−5	20.0
31. Pre-tax net operating income (tax-equivalent basis)	100	113	−11.5
32. Applicable income taxes	25	22	13.6
33. Current tax-equivalent adjustment	37	48	−22.9
34. Applicable income taxes (tax-equivalent basis)	62	70	−11.4
35. Net operating income	38	43	−11.6
36. Net extraordinary items	−5	+3	−266.7
37. Net income	33	46	−28.3
38. Cash dividends declared	18	18	0.0
39. Retained earnings	15	28	−46.4

Source: Format supplied by the Federal Financial Institutions Examination Council; figures inserted by the author.

As a result of these adverse trends, Security National's net interest margin has fallen by more than 6 percent during the past year (line 24). Its net interest margin measured relative to total assets has changed as follows:

$$\frac{\begin{array}{c}\text{Interest income}\\\text{from loans and}\\\text{security investments}\end{array} - \begin{array}{c}\text{Interest expense on}\\\text{borrowed funds}\end{array}}{\text{Total assets}} = \text{Net interest margin.}$$

Most Recent Year[7]   *One Year Ago*

$$\frac{\$165}{\$6,951} = 2.37 \text{ percent.} \qquad\qquad \frac{\$176}{\$6,361} = 2.77 \text{ percent}$$

As Table 5–9 illustrates, this is well below the average for peer group banks, which reported net interest margins of 3.91 percent in the most recent year and 3.66 percent one year ago (line 3). Security National's *net operating margin*—the gap between its total operating revenues and total operating expenses—has changed as follows (based on lines 15, 23, 25, 27, and 28 in Table 5–8 and line 23 in Table 5–5):

$$\frac{\begin{array}{c}(\text{Total operating revenue}\\- \text{Total operating expenses})\end{array}}{\text{Total assets}} = \text{Net operating margin.}$$

Most Recent Year   *One Year Ago*

$$\frac{(\$604 - \$498)}{\$6,951} = 1.52 \text{ percent.} \qquad \frac{(\$593 - \$473)}{\$6,361} = 1.89 \text{ percent.}$$

Clearly, the bank's growth in expenses outstripped its overall revenue growth. Further indication of this problem is provided by the figures on net returns prior to special transactions (NRST) (Table 5–8, lines 29 and 34), which performed as follows:

$$\begin{array}{c}\text{Net returns prior to}\\\text{special transactions}\end{array} = \frac{\begin{array}{c}\text{Net income after taxes and prior to}\\\text{security gains or losses and other}\\\text{extraordinary items}\end{array}}{\text{Total assets}}$$

Most Recent Year[7]   *One Year Ago*[7]

$$\frac{\$165}{\$6,951} = 2.37 \text{ percent.} \qquad\qquad \frac{(\$118 - \$70)}{\$6,361} = 0.75 \text{ percent.}$$

This ratio removes much of the possible distortion from a bank's net earnings figures that may be caused by tax-motivated or other unusual, nonrecurring events and shows more clearly the bank's recent changes in income once all regularly occurring expenses are taken into account.

---

[7]The figures needed to calculate this ratio are in Table 5–8, lines 29 and 34, and in Table 5–5, line 23.

TABLE 5-9   **Relative Income Statement and Margin Analysis for Security National Bank and Its Peer Group (all figures are percentages of total assets)**

	Security National Bank		Peer Group	
Items	Most Recent Year	One Year Ago	Most Recent Year	One Year Ago
1. Interest Income (tax-equivalent basis)	8.37%	8.27%	9.86%	10.26%
2. Less: Interest expense	6.00	6.27	5.98	6.63
3. Equals: Net interest income (tax-equivalent basis)	**2.37**	**2.77**	**3.91**	**3.66**
4. Plus: noninterest income	**0.32**	**0.28**	**1.23**	**1.21**
5. Equals: Adjusted operating income (tax-equivalent basis)	2.69	3.05	5.21	4.89
6. Less: Overhead expense	**1.04**	**1.10**	**3.30**	**3.21**
7. Less: Provision for loan and lease losses	**0.16**	**0.08**	**0.41**	**0.34**
8. Plus: Securities gains (losses)	−0.06	−0.07	0.02	0.00
9. Equals: Pre-tax net operating income (tax-equivalent basis)	1.43	1.78	1.53	1.37
10. Less: applicable income taxes (tax-equivalent basis)	0.89	1.10	0.71	0.61
11. Equals: Net operating income	0.55	0.68	0.82	0.75
12. Plus: Extraordinary income (loss)	−0.07	0.05	____	____
13. Equals: Net Income	**0.48**	**0.72**	**0.83**	**0.76**

Source: Format supplied by the Federal Financial Institutions Examination Council; figures inserted by the author.

Security National Bank's stockholders will, of course, be most concerned about their earnings per share of stock held. The bank has 300,000 shares of stock outstanding. Therefore, its EPS over the last two years (based on Table 5–8, line 37) has changed as follows:

$$EPS = \frac{\text{Net income after taxes}}{\text{Common equity shares outstanding}}$$

Most Recent Year   *One Year Ago*

$$\frac{\$33 \text{ million}}{300,000 \text{ shares}} = \frac{\$110.00}{\text{per share.}} \qquad \frac{\$46 \text{ million}}{300,000 \text{ shares}} = \frac{\$153.33}{\text{per share}}$$

The bank has clearly suffered a significant decline in stockholder earnings per share. Management needs to begin work immediately on expanding the bank's revenues from assets and services sold, while moving toward a less-expensive mix of deposits and nondeposit sources of funds.

As we move further down the income and expense statement in Table 5–8, there are some favorable developments in the bank's financial position. For example, noninterest income (line 25), which stems from fees earned from deposits, trust management, and other services, is growing rapidly (by 22 percent during the past year). Banks have made strenuous efforts in recent years to expand noninterest (fee) income—a source of earnings that is not directly dependent on changing interest rates and therefore has relatively low interest rate risk. Apparently, Security National has been quite successful during the past year in marketing its fee-paying services. Nevertheless, the bank still lags behind its peers in the proportion of noninterest income relative to other sources of income and relative to its assets (Table 5–9, line 4).

Another favorable omen is management's apparent success in controlling overhead costs associated with the bank's buildings and equipment. Overhead expenses are increasing slowly (2.9 percent in the most recent year, as shown in Table 5–8, line 27) and the bank has a significantly lower overhead-to-assets ratio than its peers (just 1.04 percent compared to 3.30 percent, as indicated in Table 5–9, line 6). The overhead expense burden posed by large numbers of branch offices has become a major concern, particularly among the biggest banks, in recent years. With more and more banking services available through home, office, or shopping center computer terminals, there is less need for elaborate physical facilities. Banks that can keep their overhead costs low possess a key advantage for the future.

These favorable signs are more than offset by two other developing problems, however. For one thing, the bank's provision for loan and lease losses (Table 5–8, line 28) increased sharply this past year (by more than 80 percent). In part, Security may be playing catch-up; as shown in Table 5–9, the bank is well below the loan-loss ratio reported by its peers (line 7). However, if the sharp increase in additions to loan-loss reserves reflects a sudden increase in bad loans, management needs to take a thorough look at the bank's lending program and loan policies.

The second problem area is also potentially troublesome—the bank's tax liability is increasing even as its earnings picture weakens. Applicable income taxes jumped almost 14 percent over the most recent year, while the bank's total tax benefit from investing in tax-exempt assets declined (Table 5–8, lines 32 and 33). The increase in taxes threatens to erode the net income left over for the bank's stockholders. As Table 5–5 shows, the bank experienced a sizable jump in tax-exempt municipal securities this past year (line 25); however, its investments in fully taxable U.S. government and federal agency securities rose even faster (line 24). Security National seems to have a tax-management problem, calling for a complete review of its asset management policies.

With these adverse trends under way, it should not surprise us to learn that the bank's net income after taxes and all other expenses declined (by 28.3 percent) in the most recently completed year (Table 5–8, line 37). The bank's ratio of net income to assets (ROA), 0.48 percent, was well below the peer group ROA of 0.83 percent (Table 5–9, line 13). This is all the more alarming to management because last year the bank did reasonably well, with a 0.72 percent ROA. Mirroring what happened to ROA, the bank's return on equity (ROE) declined from 12.08 percent one year ago to 6.84 percent in the most recent year (line 37 in Table 5–8 divided by line 19 in Table 5–6).

We can determine the factors that contributed the most to Security Bank's decline in earnings using Equations 12, 13, and 17, discussed earlier in this chapter. For example, Equation 12 shows us that:

$$\begin{matrix} \text{Security National's} \\ \text{ROE in the most} \\ \text{recent year}[8] \end{matrix} = \text{ROA} \times \frac{\text{Total assets}}{\text{Total equity capital}}$$

$$= 0.4748 \text{ percent} \times 14.4212$$

$$= 6.48 \text{ percent.}$$

$$\begin{matrix} \text{Security National's} \\ \text{ROE in the} \\ \text{previous year}[8] \end{matrix} = \text{ROA} \times \frac{\text{Total assets}}{\text{Total equity capital}}$$

$$= 0.72316 \text{ percent} \times 16.6955$$

$$= 12.08 \text{ percent.}$$

Clearly, Security's ROE declined partly because its ROA moved lower and its use of leverage (i.e., the proportion of assets supported by debt capital instead of owners' equity) declined. If the bank can get by with less equity capital and not significantly increase its borrowing costs, it can increase its ratio of assets to equity capital and boost its ROE.

We can expand this analysis a bit further using formula 13 for ROE:

$$\begin{matrix} \text{Security National's} \\ \text{ROE in the most} \\ \text{recent year}[9] \end{matrix} = \frac{\text{Net income after taxes}}{\text{Total operating revenues}} \times \frac{\text{Total operating revenues}}{\text{Total assets}} \times \frac{\text{Total assets}}{\text{Total equity capital}}$$

$$= \frac{\$33}{\$604} \times \frac{\$604}{\$6,951} \times \frac{\$6,951}{\$482}$$

$$= 0.0546 \times 0.0869 \times 14.42$$

$$= 0.0684, \text{ or } 6.84 \text{ percent.}$$

$$\begin{matrix} \text{Security National's} \\ \text{ROE in the} \\ \text{previous year}[9] \end{matrix} = \frac{\text{Net income after taxes}}{\text{Total operating revenues}} \times \frac{\text{Total operating revenues}}{\text{Total assets}} \times \frac{\text{Total assets}}{\text{Total equity capital}}$$

$$= \frac{\$46}{\$593} \times \frac{\$593}{\$6,361} \times \frac{\$6,361}{\$381}$$

$$= 0.0776 \times 0.0932 \times 16.70$$

$$= 0.1208, \text{ or } 12.08 \text{ percent.}$$

---

[8]The figures presented here are taken from Table 5–5, line 23; Table 5–6, line 19; and Table 5–8, line 37.

[9]The figures presented here are taken from Table 5–8 (lines 15, 25, and 37); Table 5–5 (line 23); and Table 5–6 (line 19).

What factors in these earnings relationships caused Security's return to its stockholders (ROE) to fall? All three factors deteriorated, some faster than others. For example, the bank's *net profit margin* (net income after taxes to operating revenue) declined about 30 percent, reflecting both higher expenses and lower revenues from sales (probably due, in part, to poor pricing policies). Security's *asset utilization ratio* (operating revenues to total assets) dropped nearly 7 percent, due to a decline in average asset yields. Finally, the bank's *equity multiplier* (assets to equity capital) fell almost 14 percent. From the point of view of this ROE model, the bank's management needs first to review the reasons behind the declines in the equity multiplier and net profit margin, which contributed the most to its decreasing ROE.

Analysis of ROE using Equation 17 highlights the bank's problems with tax efficiency and expense control:

$$
\begin{aligned}
\text{Security National's ROE in the most recent year}[10] &= \frac{\text{Net income after taxes}}{\text{Net income before taxes and security gains (or losses)}} \times \frac{\text{Net income before taxes and security gains (or losses)}}{\text{Total operating revenues}} \\
&\quad \times \frac{\text{Total operating revenues}}{\text{Total assets}} \times \frac{\text{Total assets}}{\text{Total equity capital}} \\
&= \frac{\$33}{\$104} \times \frac{\$104}{\$604} \times \frac{\$604}{\$6,951} \times \frac{\$6,951}{\$482} \\
&= 0.3173 \times 0.1722 \times 0.0869 \times 14.42 \\
&= 0.0684, \text{ or } 6.84 \text{ percent.}
\end{aligned}
$$

$$
\begin{aligned}
\text{Security National's ROE in the previous year}[10] &= \frac{\text{Net income after taxes}}{\text{Net income before taxes and security gains (or losses)}} \times \frac{\text{Net income before taxes and security gains (or losses)}}{\text{Total operating revenues}} \\
&\quad \times \frac{\text{Total operating revenues}}{\text{Total assets}} \times \frac{\text{Total assets}}{\text{Total equity capital}} \\
&= \frac{\$46}{\$118} \times \frac{\$118}{\$593} \times \frac{\$593}{\$6,361} \times \frac{\$6,361}{\$381} \\
&= 0.3898 \times 0.1990 \times 0.0932 \times 16.70. \\
&= 0.1208, \text{ or } 12.08 \text{ percent.}
\end{aligned}
$$

[10]The figures used in these calculations are drawn from Table 5–8, line 29, for net income before taxes and securities gains (or losses) and also from Table 5–8, lines 15, 25, and 37; Table 5–6, line 19; and Table 5–5, line 23.

In this instance, the measure of tax-management efficiency (net after-tax income to net income before taxes and securities gains or losses) dropped almost 19 percent. The bank paid higher taxes in its most recent year, which clearly resulted in less net income available after taxes for its shareholders. Similarly, its measure of expense-control efficiency (net income before taxes and securities gains or losses to total operating revenues) fell more than 13 percent. The increase in Security's tax liability was therefore somewhat more destructive to its net income than the bank's expense-control problems, though both trends require bank management to take action quickly.

Banks experiencing declining earnings usually find that their capital-adequacy position (or ratio of owners' equity capital to assets) is weakened because less earnings are available to retain in the business. In this instance, the bank refused to cut its dividends to shareholders (Table 5–8, line 38), so retained earnings grew only $15 million, after a $28 million increase the preceding year (line 39). Fortunately, the bank has a relatively high ratio of equity capital to total assets (6.93 percent) compared to peer group banks (Table 5–7, line 32). Equity capital gives the bank protection against declining income and grants management time to correct the bank's earnings problems. However, these problems must be addressed quickly before continuing earnings losses erode the bank's remaining capital and threaten its survival.

Summary

This chapter focused on measuring how well banks perform in serving their customers and in providing acceptable returns to their stockholders. Increasingly, bankers are being forced by both competition and regulatory pressure to assess their bank's performance over time and relative to other banks, analyze the reasons behind any performance problems that appear, and find ways to strengthen the bank's performance in the future.

The chapter discussed two key dimensions of bank performance—profitability and exposure to risk. Profitability is clearly the more important, because satisfactory profits preserve the bank's capital, providing it with a base for future survival and growth. For larger banks, the value of their stock in the market is the best overall indicator of whether they are achieving adequate profitability relative to the risks they have assumed. However, the stock of many medium-size and small banks is often *not* actively traded, so that stock price provides no reliable guide for management. These banks must focus instead on certain key profitability ratios, such as return on assets, return on equity capital, and the net interest margin of interest revenues minus interest costs. Each of these ratios can be divided into several key components to help the management of a bank find out where its earnings problems really lie.

Pursuit of bank profits must be tempered with concern for risk. Management must pay particular attention to (1) *credit risk* (the probability of substantial losses on loans and other assets due to borrower default), (2) *liquidity risk* (the danger of running short of immediately spendable funds when they are needed), (3) *market risk* (adverse changes in the value of a bank's assets and liabilities), (4) *interest rate risk* (potential damage to the bank's spread between interest revenues and interest expenses due to changing interest rates), (5) *earnings risk* (the possibility of fluctuations in net income), and (6) *solvency risk* (the possibility of bank failure). Each of these forms of risk must be carefully monitored by a bank's management and shareholders.

Key Terms in This Chapter

Bank profitability
ROA
ROE
Efficiency
Net interest margin
Noninterest margin
Net profit margin
Asset utilization

Equity multiplier
Credit risk
Liquidity risk
Market risk
Interest rate risk
Earnings risk
Solvency risk
UBPR

Problems and Projects

1. An investor holds the stock of First National Bank of Inseco and expects to receive a dividend of $12 per share at the end of the year. Stock analysts have recently predicted that the bank's dividends will grow at approximately 8 percent a year indefinitely into the future. If this is true, and if the appropriate risk-adjusted cost of capital (discount rate) for the bank is 15 percent, what should be the current price per share of Inseco's stock?

2. Suppose that stock brokers have projected that Price State Bank and Trust Company will pay a dividend of $3 per share on its common stock at the end of the year; a dividend of $4.50 per share is expected for the next year, and $6 per share in the following year. The risk-adjusted cost of capital for banks in Price State's risk class is 12 percent. If an investor holding Price State's stock plans to hold that stock for only three years and hopes to sell it at a price of $60 per share, what should the value of the bank's stock be in today's market?

3. Depositors and Merchants Bank has a ratio of equity capital to total assets of 7.5 percent. In contrast, Newton National Bank reports an equity-capital-to-asset ratio of 6 percent. What is the value of the equity multiplier for each of these banks? Suppose that both banks have an ROA of 0.85 percent. What must each bank's return on equity capital be? What do your calculations tell you about the benefits of a bank having as little equity capital as regulations or the marketplace will allow?

4. The latest balance and income statements for Gilcrest Merchants National Bank are as shown below. Utilizing these statements, please calculate for Gilcrest Merchants National Bank all the performance measures discussed in this chapter that you can. What strengths and weaknesses are you able to detect in this bank's performance?

GILCREST MERCHANTS NATIONAL BANK
Report of Income
(in millions of dollars)

Interest and fees on loans	$61	Noninterest income and fees	$ 7
Interest and dividends on		Salaries and employee benefits*	10
securities	12	Overhead expenses	5
Interest paid on deposits	49	Other noninterest expenses	3
Interest paid on nondeposit		Securities gains (or losses),	
borrowings	6	net of taxes	1
Provision for loan losses	2	Taxes	1

*The bank has 40 full-time-equivalent employees.

GILCREST MERCHANTS NATIONAL BANK
Report of Condition (in millions of dollars)

Assets		Liabilities	
Cash and deposits due		Demand deposits*	$210
from banks	$ 120	Savings deposits*	180
Investment securities	150	Time deposits*	470
Federal funds sold	10	Federal funds purchased	60
Net loans	670	Total liabilities	$920
(Allowance for loan losses 25)		*Equity Capital*	
(Unearned income on loans 5)		Common stock	20
Plant and equipment	50	Surplus	25
Total assets	$1,000	Retained earnings	35
		Total capital	$ 80

*Interest-bearing deposits totaled $650, while noninterest-bearing deposits amounted to $210.

5. The following information is for Shadowwood
    National Bank:

Interest income	$1,875 million	Shares of common stock	
Interest expenses	$1,210 million	outstanding	145,000
Total assets	$15,765 million	Noninterest income	$501 million
Securities gains		Noninterest expenses	$685 million
(or losses)	$21 million	Provision for loan	
Earning assets	$12,612 million	losses	$381 million
Total liabilities	$15,440 million		
Taxes	$16 million		

Please calculate:

a. ROE.

b. ROA.

c. Net interest margin.

Alternative scenarios:

(1) Suppose interest income, interest expenses, noninterest income, and noninterest expenses each increase by 5 percent while all other revenue and expense items shown above remain unchanged. What will happen to Shadowwood's ROE, ROA, and earnings per share?

6. Farmers and Merchants National Bank holds total assets of $1.69 billion and equity capital of $139 million, and has just posted an ROA of 0.0076. What is the bank's ROE?

Alternative scenarios:

(1) Suppose Farmers and Merchants Bank finds its ROA climbing by 50 percent, with assets and equity capital unchanged. What will happen to its ROE? Why?

7. Granite Dells State Bank reports total operating revenues of $135 million, with total operating expenses of $121 million, and owes taxes of $2 million. It has total assets of $1.17 billion and total liabilities of $989 million. What is the bank's ROE?

Alternative scenarios:

(1) How will the ROE for Granite Dells State Bank change if total operating expenses, taxes, and total operating revenues each grow by 10 percent while assets and liabilities remain fixed?

8. Suppose a bank is projected to achieve a 1.25 percent ROA during the coming year. What must its ratio of total assets to equity capital be if it is to achieve its target ROE of

d. Earnings per share.

e. Net noninterest margin.

f. Net operating margin.

g. Net returns before special transactions.

(2) On the other hand, suppose Shadowwood's interest income and expenses as well as its noninterest income and expenses decline by 5 percent, again with all other factors held constant. How would the bank's ROE, ROA, and per-share earnings change?

(2) On the other hand, suppose the bank's ROA drops by 50 percent. If total assets and equity capital hold their present positions, what change will there be in ROE?

(3) If ROA at Farmers and Merchants National remains fixed at 0.0076 but both total assets and equity double, how does ROE change? Why?

(4) How would a decline in total assets and equity by half (with ROA still at 0.0076) affect the bank's ROE?

(2) Suppose Granite Dells' total assets and total liabilities increase by 10 percent, but its revenues and expenses (including taxes) are unchanged. How will the bank's ROE change?

(3) Can you determine what will happen to ROE if both operating revenues and expenses (including taxes) decline by 10 percent, with the bank's total assets and liabilities held constant?

(4) What does ROE become if Granite Dells' assets and liabilities decrease by 10 percent, while its operating revenues, taxes, and operating expenses do not change?

12 percent? If the bank's ROA unexpectedly falls to 0.75 percent, what asset-to-capital ratio must it then have to reach a 12 percent ROE?

Alternative scenarios:

(1) If ROA next year reaches 1.50 percent, achieving a 12 percent ROE will require what total-assets-to-equity-capital ratio for a bank?

(2) If the bank's ROA unexpectedly declines to 0.75 percent, what asset-to-capital ratio must it then have to reach a 12 percent ROE?

9. Blythe County National Bank presents us with the figures below for the year just concluded.

Please determine the net profit margin, equity multiplier, asset utilization, and ROE.

Net income after taxes	$16 million
Total operating revenues	$215 million
Total assets	$1,250 million
Total equity capital accounts	$111 million

Alternative scenario:

Suppose you found that Blythe County National Bank had total liabilities of $1,475 million, equity capital of $140 million, total noninterest income of $88 million, total interest income of $155 million, and after-tax net income of $24 million. What would its net profit margin, asset utilization ratio, equity multiplier, and ROE be?

10. Lochiel Commonwealth Bank and Trust Company has experienced the following trends over the past five years (all figures in millions of dollars):

Year	Net Income after Taxes	Total Operating Revenues	Total Assets	Total Equity Capital
1	$2.7	$26.5	$293	$18
2	3.5	30.1	382	20
3	4.1	39.8	474	22
4	4.8	47.5	508	25
5	5.7	55.9	599	28

Determine the figures for ROE, profit margin, asset utilization, and equity multiplier for this bank. Are any adverse trends evident? Where would you recommend that management look to deal with the bank's emerging problem(s)?

Alternative scenarios:

(1) Would you be more content with recent trends at Lochiel Commonwealth Bank if its total equity capital increased by 30 percent between year 1 and year 5? Why?

(2) Suppose the bank's asset utilization ratio increased by 25 percent between year 1 and year 5. How would its ROE be affected?

(3) What change would take place in ROE if Lochiel's profit margin rose by 15 percent between years 1 and 5?

11. Wilmington Hills State Bank has just submitted its Report of Condition and Report of Income to its principal supervisory agency. The bank reported net income before taxes and securities transactions of $27 million and taxes of $6 million. If its total operating revenues were $780 million, its total assets $2.1 billion, and its equity capital $125 million, determine the following for Wilmington:

    a. Tax management efficiency ratio.

    b. Expense control efficiency ratio.

    c. Asset management efficiency ratio.

    d. Funds management efficiency ratio.

    e. ROE.

12. Using the information below for Laredo International Bank and Trust Company, calculate the bank's net interest margin, noninterest margin, and ROA.

Alternative scenarios:

(1) Suppose Wilmington Hills State Bank experienced a 20 percent rise in net before-tax income, with its tax obligation, operating revenues, assets, and equity unchanged. What would happen to ROE and its components?

(2) If total assets climb by 20 percent, what will happen to Wilmington's efficiency ratios and ROE?

(3) What effect would a 20 percent higher level of equity capital have upon ROE and its components?

Interest income	$55	Noninterest expense	$8
Interest expense	$38	Noninterest income	$5
Provision for loan losses	$3	Special income and expense	$1
Security gains (or losses)	$2	(including taxes)	
		Total assets	$986

Alternative scenario:

Suppose that Laredo International Bank experiences a rise in interest income to $61 and a rise in noninterest income to $58, while interest expenses and noninterest expenses climb to $45 and $11, respectively. Meanwhile, total assets grow to $1,042, while special income and expense items double to $2. What will Laredo's net interest margin, noninterest margin, and ROA become?

13. Valley State Bank reported the figures below on its income statement for the past five years. Calculate the bank's ROA in each year. Are there any adverse trends? Any favorable trends? What seems to be happening to this bank?

	Current Year	One Year Ago	Two Years Ago	Three Years Ago	Four Years Ago
Gross interest income	$ 40	$ 41	$ 38	$ 35	$ 33
Interest expenses	24	23	20	18	15
Noninterest income	4	4	3	2	1
Noninterest expenses	8	7	7	6	5
Provision for loan losses	2	1	1	0*	0*
Income taxes owed	1	1	0	1	0
Net securities gains (or losses)	(2)	(1)	0	1	2
Total assets	385	360	331	319	293

*Less than 0.5.

14. An analysis of the UBPR reports on Security National Bank was presented in this chapter. We examined a wide variety of profitability measures for that bank, including ROA, ROE, net profit margin, net interest and operating margins, and asset utilization. However, the various measures of earnings risk, credit risk, solvency risk, liquidity risk, market risk, and interest-rate risk were not discussed in detail and most were not calculated. Using the data in Tables 5–5 through 5–9, calculate each of these dimensions of risk for Security National Bank for the most recent two years and discuss how the bank's risk exposure appears to be changing over time. What steps would you recommend to management in order to deal with any risk exposure problems you observe?

Selected References

For an explanation of measuring and evaluating bank risk see the following:

1. Baer, Herbert, and Elijah Brewer. "Uninsured Deposits as a Source of Market Discipline: Some New Evidence." *Economic Perspectives,* Federal Reserve Bank of Chicago, September/October 1986, pp. 23–31.

2. Brewer, Elijah, III, and Cheng Few Lee. "How the Market Judges Bank Risk." *Economic Perspectives,* Federal Reserve Bank of Chicago, November/December 1986, pp. 25–31.

3. Nelson, William R., and Ann L. Owen. "Profits and Balance Sheet Developments at U.S. Commercial Banks in 1996." *Federal Reserve Bulletin,* June 1997, pp. 475–89.

4. Rose, Peter S. *Bank Mergers in a Deregulated Environment.* Rolling Meadows, Ill.: Bank Administration Institute, 1987.

5. ———. "Risk—Taking the Temperature and Finding a Cure." *The Canadian Banker,* November/December 1987, pp. 54–63.

6. Short, Eugenia D. "Bank Problems and Financial Safety Nets." *Economic Review,* Federal Reserve Bank of Dallas, March 1987, pp. 17–28.

7. Williams, Edward J. "Pools of Risk, Article No. 4: The Risk Matrix—A Tool for Bank Analysis." *Journal of Commercial Bank Lending,* January 1986, pp. 2–6.

8. Siems, Thomas F., and Kelly Klemme. "Banking in a Changing World." *Financial Industry Issues,* Federal Reserve Bank of Dallas, Second Quarter 1997, pp. 1–6.

9. Wright, David M., and James V. Houpt. "An Analysis of Commercial Bank Exposure to Interest Rate Risk." *Federal Reserve Bulletin,* February 1996, pp. 116–28.

For information on how to read bank financial statements and make comparisons among banks, see the following:

10. Federal Financial Institutions Examination Council. *A User's Guide for the Uniform Bank Performance Report,* Washington, D.C., July 1984.

11. Rose, Peter S. *Money and Capital Markets.* New York: McGraw-Hill/Irwin, 1997, Chapters 4–6.

12. Wetmore, Jill L., and John R. Brick. "The Basis Risk Component of Commercial Bank Stock Returns." *Journal of Economics and Business* 50 (1998), pp. 67–76.

APPENDIX: IMPROVING BANK PERFORMANCE THROUGH KNOWLEDGE: SOURCES OF INFORMATION FOR BANKERS, THEIR CUSTOMERS, AND BANK REGULATORS

The chapter just concluded focused on how to measure the performance of banks—their profitability, efficiency, growth, risk exposure, and so forth. However, mere measurement of bank performance is not enough. Bankers must have the tools and the knowledge necessary to improve bank performance and to keep top-performing banks on target. The chapters that follow will provide many of the tools needed for successful bank management, but bankers will always need more information than textbooks can provide. Their problems may be highly technical and specific and will change over time, often faster than textbooks are rewritten. The same difficulty confronts bank regulators and bank customers—they must often reach far afield to gather vital information in order to evaluate their banks and get the most service from them.

Where do bankers find the information they need? One good source is the professional bankers' schools that are offered in all regions of the nation. Among the most popular of these are the following: Stonier Graduate School of Banking, sponsored by the American Bankers Association, or the Banking School of the South, which meets each summer at Louisiana State University in Baton Rouge. There are other bankers' schools as well, many devoted to specific problem areas within banking, such as bank marketing and consumer lending. Each offers classroom instruction during the summer and project assignments covering other periods of the year.

Beyond the professional bankers' schools, there are selected industry trade associations that annually publish a prodigious volume of written studies and management guidelines for wrestling with important bank problems, such as developing and promoting new services, working out problem loans, creating a planning system, and so on. Among the most popular trade associations publishing problem-solving information are the following:

1. The American Bankers Association, 1120 Connecticut Avenue, N.W., Washington, D.C. 20036.
2. Bank Administration Institute, One North Franklin, Chicago, Illinois 60606.
3. The Robert Morris Associates (RMA), The National Association of Bank Loan and Credit Officers, One Liberty Place, Suite 2300, 1650 Market Street, Philadelphia, PA 19103–7398.

In addition to the material provided by these trade associations, dozens of journals, news releases, and books are turned out each year by these same trade associations, by magazine publishers, and by government agencies. The most important of these recurring news releases and data sources are the following:

General Banking Information

ABA Banking Journal
(published by the American
Bankers Association)
The Bankers' Magazine
Banking Strategies
Journal of Commercial Bank Lending
(published by Robert Morris
Associates monthly)
The Bank Loan Officer's Report
The Canadian Banker
Bank Marketing
Journal of Retail Banking

Sources of Data on Individual Banks

Uniform Bank Performance Reports
(published quarterly by the Federal
Financial Institutions Examination
Council)
Call Report and Report of Income
Computer Tapes (available on an annual
or quarterly basis from the National
Technical Information Service)
Moody's Bank and Finance Manual
(published by Moody's Investor Service)
The American Banker
(five-day-a-week newspaper published
by the American Bankers Association)
The Wall Street Journal
(published by Dow Jones & Co., Inc.)
SNL Bank Quarterly Digest

Economic and Financial Trends
Affecting the Banking Industry
Survey of Current Business
(published by the U.S. Department of Commerce)
Federal Reserve Bulletin
(published by the Board of Governors of the Federal
Reserve System)
U.S. Financial Data, National
Economic Trends, and Monetary Trends
(all published by the Federal Reserve Bank of St. Louis)

Journals Focusing on Banking Laws
and Regulations
Banking Law Journal

International Banking Trends
International Economic Conditions
(published by the Federal Reserve Bank of St. Louis)
Journal of International Business
The Banker (London)
The Economist (London)

There are also *directories* that list the name, city, and state of location of all banks, routing numbers for sending checks and other cash items and, often, the names of key officers within each banking firm. Included in many bankers' directories are abbreviated financial statements of each bank, whether or not the bank belongs to a holding company or is a member of the Federal Reserve System, and the names of the principal correspondent banks that handle each bank's check clearings and provide it with other services. Both bankers and students use these directories to contact banking organizations about possible future employment. Among the most important bankers' directories today are the *Thompson/Polk Directory,* the *Financial Institutions Directory, Moody's Bank and Finance Manual,* and the *Banker's Almanac.*

Many items of information about banking are now available on the Internet via the World Wide Web from bank regulatory agencies in the United States and around the world. For example, in the United States the Federal Deposit Insurance Corporation (FDIC) makes

several of its releases available at its web site or by fax (at 1-804-642-0003), or, of course, by mail or telephone through the FDIC's Public Information Center in Washington, D.C. One of the best-known of the FDIC's releases on bank performance is the *Quarterly Banking Profile,* which tracks industry profits, growth, risk, and efficiency measures every quarter of the year.

Central banks around the world are also prominently represented on the World Wide Web. Each issues an annual report and a wide variety of data releases with information on the economy and financial markets of their home countries. The U.S. central bank, the Federal Reserve System, issues a tremendous volume of information by mail and over the Internet, including numerous studies of the banking industry—its performance, trends, and problems. In order to find out what is available from the Federal Reserve System, you may contact the Board of Governors of the Federal Reserve System by mail in Washington, D.C.; or by fax at 202-728-5886. Order forms for Federal Reserve publications are available via the Internet.

Addresses of U.S. Bank Regulatory Agencies

Federal Deposit Insurance Corporation
Public Information Center
801 17th Street, NW
Washington, D.C. 20434-0001
1-800-276-6003

Office of the Comptroller of the Currency
250 E Street, SW
Washington, D.C. 20219
202-874-5043

Board of Governors of the Federal Reserve System
Publications Services, Mail Stop 127
20th Street and Constitution Ave., NW
Washington, D.C. 20551-0001
202-452-3244

Federal Reserve Bank of New York
New York City, New York 10045

Federal Reserve Bank of Boston
P.O. Box 2076
Boston, Massachusetts 02106-2076

Federal Reserve Bank of Philadelphia
Ten Independence Mall
Philadelphia, Pennsylvania 19106-1574

Federal Reserve Bank of Cleveland
P.O. Box 6387
Cleveland, Ohio 44101

Federal Reserve Bank of Richmond
Richmond, Virginia 23219

Federal Reserve Bank of Atlanta
104 Marietta Street, N.W.
Atlanta, Georgia 30303-2713

Federal Reserve Bank of Chicago
P.O. Box 834
Chicago, Illinois 60690-0834

Federal Reserve Bank of St. Louis
P.O. Box 442
St. Louis, Missouri 63166-0442

Federal Reserve Bank of Minneapolis
P.O. Box 291
Minneapolis, Minnesota 55480-0291

Federal Reserve Bank of Kansas City
Kansas City, Missouri 64198

Federal Reserve Bank of Dallas
P.O. Box 655906
Dallas, Texas 75265-5906

Federal Reserve Bank of San Francisco
P.O. Box 7702
San Francisco, California 94120

Addresses of Key Foreign Central Banks

Director, Research and Publications
Bank of Canada
Ottawa
Ontario, Canada KIA 0G9

Publications Group
Bank of England
Threadneedle Street
London, EC2R 8AH
Great Britain

Public Relations Dept.
Bank of Japan
C.P.O. Box 203
Tokyo, 100-91 Japan

Research and Public Information
Deutsche Bundesbank
Wilhelm-Epstein-Strasse 14
60431 Frankfurt am Main,
P.O.B. 10 06 02
Federal Republic of Germany

Directeur General de la Communication
Service Relation savec le public
Banque de France
48, rue Croix-des-Petits-Champs
75001 Paris, France

Oficina de Servicios de Informacion
Banco de Mexico
AU. 5 de Mayo No. 20 Col Entro,
Delegacion Cuauhtemoc
6059 Mexico, D.F.

European Monetary Institute
Postfach 10 20 31
D-60020 Frankfurt am Main
Federal Republic of Germany

Key Internet Addresses for the Banking Industry

Bank Regulatory Agencies

Federal Deposit Insurance Corporation
Institution Directory System
www.fdic.gov

Office of the Comptroller of the Currency
www.occ.treas.gov

Board of Governors of the Federal Reserve System
www.bog.frb.fed.us

Federal Reserve Bank of New York
www.ny.frb.org

Federal Reserve Bank of Boston
www.bos.frb.org

Federal Reserve Bank of Philadelphia
www.PHIL.frb.org

Federal Reserve Bank of Cleveland
www.clev.frb.org

Federal Reserve Bank of Minneapolis
http://woodrow.mpls.frb.fed.us

Federal Reserve Bank of Atlanta
www.frbatlanta.org

Federal Reserve Bank of Dallas
www.dallasfed.org

Federal Reserve Bank of Chicago
www.frbchi.org

Federal Reserve Bank of St. Louis
www.stls.frb.org

Federal Reserve Bank of San Francisco
www.sf.frb.org

Selected Banks' Addresses on the Internet

Advance Bank
www.advance.com.au/default.htm

Deutsche Bank
www.deutsche.bank.de/inder-e.htm

AM South
www.amsouth.com

NationsBank
www.nationsbank.com

Atlanta Internet Bank
www.atlantabank.com

First Union National Bank
www.firstunion.com

Bank of America
www.bofa.com

Security First Network Bank
www.sfnb.com

Bank United
www.bankunited.com

Signet Bank
www.signet.com

Compass Bank
www.compassweb.com

Wells Fargo Bank
www.wellsfargo.com

Internet Addresses or Information on Groups of Banks Represented on the Internet:

www.netbanker.com/news
www.onlinebankingreport.com/top100bank.htm
www.qualisteam.com/eng/conf.html

Other Important Internet Addresses for the Banking Industry:

The Wall Street Journal (Dow Jones & Company)
http://wsj.com
Robert Morris Associates (National Association of Loan Officers):
www.RMAHQ.org

II ASSET-LIABILITY MANAGEMENT TECHNIQUES AND HEDGING AGAINST INTEREST RATE AND CREDIT RISK

6 ASSET-LIABILITY MANAGEMENT: DETERMINING AND MEASURING INTEREST RATES AND CONTROLLING A BANK'S INTEREST-SENSITIVE GAP

Learning and Management Decision Objectives

The purpose of this chapter is to explore the options bankers have today for dealing with risk—especially the risk of loss due to changing interest rates—and to see how a bank's management can coordinate the management of its assets with the management of its liabilities in order to achieve the institution's goals.

Introduction

Banks today are highly complex organizations—offering multiple services through multiple departments, each staffed by specialists in making different kinds of financial decisions.[1] Thus, different groups of individuals inside the bank usually make the decisions on what customers are to receive loans, what securities the bank should add to its investment portfolio, what terms should be quoted to the public on deposits and other services the bank offers, and what sources of capital the bank should draw upon. However, bankers today realize that all of these management decisions are intimately *linked* to each other. For example, decisions on which customer loan requests should be fulfilled are closely related to the bank's ability to raise deposit and nondeposit funds to support those new loans. Similarly, the amount of risk that a bank accepts in its loan portfolio is related to the adequacy of the bank's capital, which protects its shareholders and depositors against loss from bad loans.

---

[1]Portions of this chapter are based upon the author's article in *The Canadian Banker* [5] and are used with the permission of the publisher.

207

In a well-managed bank all of these management decisions must be *coordinated* across the whole bank to ensure that they do not clash with each other, leading to inconsistent actions that damage the bank's earnings and value. Today bankers have learned to look at their asset and liability portfolios as an *integrated whole,* considering how the bank's *total portfolio* contributes to its broad goals of adequate profitability and acceptable risk. This type of coordinated and integrated bank decision making is known as **asset-liability management.** The techniques of asset-liability management provide the bank with the defensive weapons to handle business cycles and seasonal pressures on its deposits and loans and with the offensive weapons to construct portfolios of assets that promote the bank's goals.

The purpose of asset-liability management is to formulate strategies and take actions that shape a bank's balance sheet as a whole in a way that contributes to its desired goals. Usually, the principal goals of asset-liability management are: (*a*) to maximize, or at least stabilize, the bank's *margin,* or *spread* between interest revenues and interest expenses, and (*b*) to maximize, or at least protect, the *value* (stock price) of the bank, at an acceptable level of risk. The purpose of this chapter is to give the reader a sense of this integrated approach to managing bank assets, liabilities, and equity.

Asset-Liability Management Strategies

Asset Management Strategy

Banks have not always possessed a completely integrated view of their assets and liabilities. Indeed, for much of banking's history, bankers tended to take their sources of funds—liabilities and equity—largely for granted. This so-called **asset management** view held that the amount and kinds of deposits a bank held and the volume of other borrowed funds it was able to attract were largely determined by its customers. Under this view, the *public* determined the relative amounts of checkable deposits, savings accounts, and other sources of funds available to banks. The key decision area for bank management was not deposits and other borrowings but assets. The banker could exercise control only over the *allocation* of incoming funds by deciding who was to receive the scarce quantity of loans available and what the terms on those loans would be. Indeed, there was some logic behind this asset management approach because, prior to deregulation of the industry, the types of deposits, the rates offered on deposits, and the nondeposit sources of funds banks could draw upon were closely regulated. Bank managers had only limited discretion in reshaping their sources of funds.

Liability Management Strategy

The 1960s and 1970s ushered in dramatic changes in bank asset-liability management strategies. Confronted with soaring interest rates and intense competition for funds, bankers began to devote greater attention to opening up new sources of funding and monitoring the mix and cost of their deposit and nondeposit liabilities. The new strategy was called **liability management.** Its goal was simply to *gain control over the bank's* *funds sources* comparable to the control bankers had long exercised over their assets. The key control lever was *price*—the interest rate and other terms banks could offer on their deposits and borrowings to achieve the volume, mix, and cost desired. A bank faced with heavy loan demand that exceeded its available funds could simply raise the *offer rate* on its deposits and money market borrowings relative to its competitors, and funds would flow in. On the other hand, a bank flush with funds but with few profitable outlets for those funds could leave its offer rate unchanged or even lower that price, letting competitors outbid it for whatever funds were available in the marketplace.

Funds Management Strategy

The maturing of liability management techniques, coupled with more volatile interest rates and greater banking risk, eventually gave birth to the **funds management** approach, which dominates banking today. This view is a much more *balanced* approach to asset and liability management that stresses several key objectives:

1. Bank management should exercise as much control as possible over the volume, mix, and return or cost of *both* assets and liabilities in order to achieve the bank's short-run and long-run goals.

2. Management's control over assets must be *coordinated* with its control over liabilities so that asset and liability management are internally consistent and do not pull against each other; effective coordination in managing assets and liabilities will help to maximize the *spread* between bank revenues from earning assets and the costs of issuing liabilities and control risk exposure.

3. Revenues and costs arise from *both* sides of the bank's balance sheet (i.e., from both assets and liabilities). Bank policies need to be developed that maximize returns and minimize costs from bank services that result in assets (e.g., the making of loans) or in liabilities (e.g., the sale of deposits).

Thus, the traditional view that all bank income must come from loans and investments has given way to the notion that banks sell a *bundle of financial services*—credit, payments, savings, financial advice, etc.—which should each be priced to cover their cost of production. *Fee income* from managing the liability side of the balance sheet can help achieve a bank's profitability goals as much as revenues earned from managing bank loans and other assets.

Concept Checks

6–1. What do the following terms mean: *Asset management? Liability management? Funds management?*

6–2. What factors have motivated banks to develop funds management techniques in recent years?

Interest Rate Risk: One of the Banker's Greatest Challenges in Asset-Liability Management

Regardless of what asset-liability or funds management strategy a bank decides to follow, no banker can completely avoid one of the toughest and potentially most damaging forms of risk that a bank must face—**interest rate risk.** When interest rates change in the financial marketplace, bankers find that the change affects their most important source of revenue—interest income on loans and securities—and their most important source of expenses—interest cost on deposits and other bank borrowings. Moreover, changing interest rates also change the market value of a bank's assets and liabilities, thereby changing the bank's net worth—that is, the value of the owners' investment in the bank. Thus, changing interest rates impact *both* a bank's balance sheet and its statement of income and expenses.

Forces Determining Interest Rates.   The problem with interest rates is that although interest rates are critical to every bank, bankers simply cannot control either the level of or the trend in market rates of interest. The rate of interest on any particular loan or security is ultimately determined by the financial marketplace where suppliers of loanable funds (credit) interact with demanders of loanable funds (credit) and the interest rate (price of credit) tends to settle at the point where the quantities of loanable funds (credit) demanded and supplied are equal, as shown in Exhibit 6–1 below.

In granting loans, bankers are on the *supply* side of the loanable funds (credit) market, but each bank is only *one* supplier of credit in an international market for loanable funds that includes many thousands of lenders. Similarly, bankers come into the financial marketplace as demanders of loanable funds (credit) when they offer deposit services to the public or issue nondeposit IOUs to raise funds for lending and investing.

EXHIBIT 6–1
*Determination
of the Rate
of Interest*

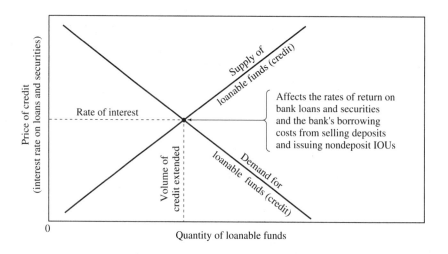

But, again, each bank, no matter how large it is, is only *one* demander of loanable funds in a market containing thousands of borrowers.

Thus, whether a banker is on the supply side or the demand side of the loanable funds (credit) market at any given moment (and banks are usually on *both* sides of the credit market simultaneously), he or she cannot determine the level, or be sure about the trend, of market interest rates. Rather, the individual bank can only *react* to the level of and trend in interest rates in a way that best allows each bank to achieve its goals. In other words, most individual banks must be *price takers,* not price makers, and must accept the level and trend of interest rates as a given and plan accordingly.

As market interest rates move, bankers face at least two major kinds of interest rate risk—price risk and reinvestment risk. *Price risk* arises when market interest rates rise, causing the market values of most bonds and fixed-rate loans that a bank may hold to fall. If the bank wishes to sell these financial instruments in a rising rate period, it must be prepared to accept capital losses. *Reinvestment risk* rears its head when market interest rates fall, forcing a bank to invest incoming funds in lower yielding loans, bonds, and other earning assets, lowering its expected future income. A big part of managing a bank's assets and liabilities consists of finding ways to deal effectively with these two forms of risk from changing interest rates.

The Measurement of Interest Rates.   When we use the term *interest rates* exactly what do we mean? How are interest rates measured?

Most of us understand what interest rates are because we have borrowed money at one time or another and know that interest rates are the *price of credit*—what is demanded by lenders as compensation for the use of borrowed funds. In simplest terms the interest rate is a ratio of the fees we must pay to obtain the use of credit divided by the amount of credit obtained. However, over the years a bewildering array of interest rate measures have been developed as we will see in future chapters of this book.

One of the most popular rate measures (particularly in the bond market) is the **yield to maturity, (YTM)** which is the discount rate that equalizes the current market value of a loan or security with the expected stream of future income payments that the loan or security will generate. In terms of a formula, the yield to maturity may be found from:

$$\begin{aligned} \text{Current market price} \atop \text{of a loan or security} = \frac{\text{Expected cash flow in Period 1}}{(1+\text{YTM})^1} + \frac{\text{Expected cash flow in Period 2}}{(1+\text{YTM})^2} \tag{1} \\[2em] + \cdots + \frac{\text{Expected cash flow in Period n}}{(1+\text{YTM})^n} + \frac{\text{Sale or redemption price of security or loan in Period n}}{(1+\text{YTM})^n} \end{aligned}$$

For example, a bond purchased today at a price of \$950 and promising an interest payment of \$100 each over the next three years, when it will be redeemed by the bond's issuer for $1,000, will have a promised interest rate, measured by the yield to maturity, determined by solving:

$$\$950 = \frac{\$100}{(1+\text{YTM})^1} + \frac{\$100}{(1+\text{YTM})^2} + \frac{\$100}{(1+\text{YTM})^3} + \frac{\$1000}{(1+\text{YTM})^3}$$

In this instance the present value and annuity tables in Appendix B help us to determine that this bond's yield to maturity must be 12.10 percent.[2]

Another popular interest rate measure is the **bank discount rate,** which is often quoted on short-term loans and money market securities (such as U.S. Treasury bills). The formula for calculating the discount rate (DR) is as follows:

$$DR = \left(\frac{100 - \text{Purchase price of loan or security}}{100} \right) \quad (2)$$

$$\times \frac{360}{\text{Number of days to maturity}}$$

For example, suppose a money market loan or security can be purchased for a price of $96 and has a face value of $100 to be paid at maturity. If the loan or security matures in 90 days, its interest rate measured by the bank discount rate (DR) must be:

$$DR = \frac{(100-96)}{100} \times \frac{360}{90} = 0.16, \text{ or 16 percent}$$

We note that this interest rate measure ignores the effect of compounding of interest and is based on a 360-day year, unlike the yield to maturity measure which assumes a 365-day year and assumes as well that interest income is compounded at the calculated yield to maturity (YTM). To convert a bank discount rate to the equivalent yield to maturity we can use the formula:

$$\begin{array}{c} \text{YTM} \\ \text{equivalent} \\ \text{yield} \end{array} = \frac{(100 - \text{Purchase price})}{\text{Purchase price}} \times \frac{365}{\text{Days to maturity}} \quad (3)$$

---

[2]Many programmable calculators will give this yield to maturity directly after entering the bond's purchase price, promised interest payments, sales or redemption price, and number of periods covered. A good approximation to the correct YTM can be obtained by linear interpolation from the present-value and annuity tables inside the front cover. If we insert 12 percent as a trial interest rate in the YTM equation above, the bond's price turns out to be $952.20, slightly higher than the actual price of $950. If we insert 14 percent as the trial discount rate (YTM), the calculated price of the bond is $907.20, which is too low. This tells us the true YTM must be *between* 12 and 14 percent. To determine the bond's YTM more closely we use the interpolation formula:

Price at lower rate (12%)	$952.20
Price at higher rate (14%)	907.20
Price difference	$ 45.00

Difference between actual price ($950) and price at lower rate (12%) is $952.20 – $950 = $2.20.

Then the approximate YTM for this bond must be:

12 percent + ($2.20/$45.00) × 2 percent ≈ 12.10 percent

For the money market security discussed previously, its equivalent yield to maturity would be:

$$\text{YTM equivalent} = \frac{(100 - 96)}{96} \times \frac{365}{90} = 0.1690, \text{ or } 16.90 \text{ percent}$$

While the two interest rate measures listed above are very popular, we should keep in mind that there are literally dozens of other measures of "the interest rate," many of which we will encounter in later chapters of this book.

The Components of Interest Rates.   Over the years many banks have tried to *forecast* future movements in market interest rates as an aid to combating interest rate risk. However, the fact that interest rates are determined by the interactions of thousands of credit suppliers and demanders makes consistently accurate rate forecasting virtually impossible. Adding to the forecasting problem is the fact that any particular interest rate attached to a loan or security is composed of *multiple* elements or building blocks, including:

| Market interest rate on a risky loan or security | = | Risk-free real interest rate (such as the inflation-adjusted return on government bonds) | + | Risk premia to compensate lenders who accept risky IOUs for their default (credit) risk, inflation risk, term or maturity risk, marketability risk, call risk, and so on | (4) |

Not only does the *risk-free real* (inflation-adjusted) *interest rate* change over time with shifts in the demand and supply for loanable funds, but the perceptions of lenders and borrowers in the financial marketplace concerning each of the *risk premia* that make up any particular market interest rate on a risky loan or security also change over time, causing interest rates to move up or down, often erratically.

To cite some examples, when the economy goes into a recession with declining business sales and rising unemployment, many lenders will conclude that some businesses will fail and some individuals will lose their jobs, increasing the risk of borrower default. The *default-risk premium* component of the interest rate charged a risky borrower will increase, raising the borrower's loan rate (all other factors held constant). Similarly, an announcement of rising prices on goods and services may trigger lenders to expect a trend toward higher inflation, reducing the purchasing power of their loan income unless they demand from borrowers a higher *inflation-risk premium* to compensate for their projected loss in purchasing power. Many loan and security interest rates also contain a premium for *marketability risk,* because some of these financial instruments are more difficult to sell at a favorable price to another lender, and for *call risk,* which arises when a borrower has the right to pay off a loan early, reducing the lender's expected rate of return.

Another key component of each interest rate is the *maturity,* or *term, premium.* Longer-term loans and securities often carry higher market interest rates than shorter-term loans and securities due to term, or maturity, risk because of greater opportunities for loss over the life of a longer-term loan. The graphic picture of how interest rates vary with different maturities of loans viewed at a single point in time (and assuming that all other factors, such as credit risk, are held constant) is called a *yield curve.*

Exhibit 6–2 contains a U.S. Treasury security yield curve plotted at the end of December 1990. The maturities of Treasury securities (in months and years) are plotted along the horizontal axis, and the yields to maturity (YTM) of all securities represented along the curve are plotted along the vertical axis. Yield curves are constantly changing, since the yields on securities included in each curve change every day. Moreover, yields to maturity change at different speeds, with *short-term interest rates tending to rise faster than long-term interest rates and to fall faster when all interest rates in the market are headed lower.*

EXHIBIT 6–2

Yield Curve for U.S. Treasury Securities (based on closing bid quotations as of December 31, 1990)

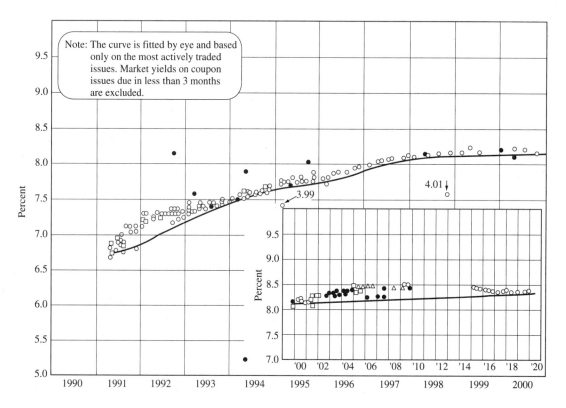

○ Fixed maturity coupon issues under 12%
□ Fixed maturity coupon issues of 12% or more
● Callable coupon issues under 12%

△ Callable coupon issues of 12% or more
Note: Callable issues are plotted to the earliest
    call date when prices are above par and to
    maturity when prices are at par or below
▲ Bills. Coupon equivalent yield of the latest
    13-week, 26-week, and 52-week bills

Source: U.S. Treasury Department, *Treasury Bulletin*, First Quarter 1991, p. 63.

TABLE 6–1   **Annual Interest Rates Attached to U.S. Government Securities and to Bonds of Varying Maturity and Default Risk Issued by Private Corporations**

	Annual Rate of Interest in:			
	1994	*1995*	*1996*	*1997**
Three-month U.S. government bills	4.25%	5.49%	5.01%	5.05%
30-year U.S. government bonds	7.37	6.88	6.71	6.94
Highest-rated (Aaa) corporate bonds	7.97	7.59	7.37	7.58
Low-rated (Baa) corporate bonds	8.63	8.20	8.05	8.34

*Rates for 1997 are as of May.
Source: Board of Governors of the Federal Reserve System, *Federal Reserve Bulletin,* selected issues.

Yield curves will display an *upward slope* (i.e., a rising yield curve) when long-term interest rates exceed short-term interest rates. This often happens when all interest rates are rising but short-term rates have started from a lower level than long-term rates. Yield curves can also slope downward (i.e., a negative yield curve), with short-term interest rates higher than long-term interest rates. Negatively sloped yield curves are often seen at or near a cyclical peak in the economy and during the early stages of a recession, when all interest rates are declining, but short-term rates have declined much faster than long-term rates. Finally, *horizontal* yield curves prevail when long-term interest rates and short-term rates are at approximately the same level so that the investor receives the same yield to maturity no matter what maturity of security he or she buys.

An illustration of some of these rate-determining forces is provided by Table 6–1, which shows the market interest rates attached to four different types of debt securities— short-term (3-month) U.S. government bills and long-term (30-year) U.S. government bonds, which are considered free of default risk (i.e., have a zero default-risk premium), and high-quality (Aaa-rated) long-term bonds issued by private corporations as well as lower quality (Baa) corporate bonds. We observe considerable differences among these four representative interest rates. For example, the term risk premium accounts for much of the substantial difference between the interest rates attached to short-term (3-month) government bills versus long-term (30-year) government bonds. Differences in default risk help us explain the differences in interest rates between the long-term (30-year) government bonds and both Aaa and Baa corporate bonds, which range from about half a percentage point to more than a full percentage point, with the lowest-quality (Baa) corporate bonds carrying the highest rates to compensate lenders for the added default risk they take on from acquiring these bonds.

We notice that not only are the interest rate differences shown in Table 6–1 substantial, but they vary significantly over time. Unfortunately, consistently correct interest rate forecasting would require bankers to have the ability to anticipate changes in market perceptions of *all* of the above interest-rate determining factors—the real risk-free interest rate, the default risk premium, the inflation risk premium, the term risk premium, and the like. The imposing nature of such a task has led bankers in recent years to accept the fact that interest rates cannot be controlled or predicted accurately and to find new ways to protect themselves against loss from interest rate risk.

Bankers' Response to Interest Rate Risk.   As we noted at the outset, changes in market interest rates can damage a bank's profitability by increasing its cost of funds, lowering its returns from earning assets, and reducing the value of the owners' investment (net worth or equity capital) in the bank. Moreover, recent decades have ushered in a period of volatile interest rates, confronting bankers with an entirely new and more unpredictable environment to work in. A dramatic example of the huge losses that interest rate risk exposure can bring to a bank occurred in Minnesota when First Bank System, Inc., of Minneapolis, bought unusually large quantities of government bonds. First Bank's management had forecast a decline in interest rates during the late 1980s. Unfortunately, bond prices fell as interest rates rose, and First Bank reported a loss of about $500 million, resulting in the sale of its headquarters building (see Bailey [1]).

Over the last two decades bankers have aggressively sought ways to insulate their asset and liability portfolios and their profits from the ravages of changing interest rates. Many banks now conduct their asset-liability management strategies under the guidance of an *asset-liability committee,* which usually meets daily. Such a committee not only chooses strategies to deal with interest rate risk but also participates in both short- and long-range planning, in preparing strategies to handle the bank's liquidity needs, and in dealing with other management issues.

One of the Goals of Interest Rate Hedging

In dealing with interest rate risk, one important goal is to insulate the bank's *profits*— net income after taxes and all other expenses—from the damaging effects of fluctuating interest rates. No matter which way interest rates go, the banker wants profits that achieve the level desired and are stable.

To accomplish this particular goal, management must concentrate on those elements of the bank's portfolio of assets and liabilities that are most sensitive to interest rate movements. Normally this includes the bank's loans and investments on the asset side of the balance sheet—its earning assets—and its interest-bearing deposits and money market borrowings on the liability side. In order to protect bank profits against adverse interest rate changes, then, management seeks to hold *fixed* the bank's **net interest margin** (NIM), expressed as follows:

$$\text{NIM} = \frac{\left(\begin{array}{ccc}\text{Interest income} & & \text{Interest expenses on} \\ \text{from bank loans} & - & \text{deposits and other} \\ \text{and investments} & & \text{borrowed funds}\end{array}\right)}{\text{Total earning assets}} \qquad (5)$$

$$= \frac{\text{Net interest income after expenses}}{\text{Total earning assets}}$$

For example, suppose a large international bank records $4 billion in interest revenues from its loans and security investments and $2.6 billion in interest expenses paid out to attract deposits and other borrowed funds. If the bank holds $40 billion in earning assets, its net interest margin is

$$\text{NIM} = \frac{(\$4 \text{ billion} - \$2.6 \text{ billion})}{\$40 \text{ billion}} \times 100 = 3.50 \text{ percent}$$

Note how narrow this net interest margin (which is fairly close to the average for the banking industry) is at just 3.5 percent. Remember that this is not yet the bank's profit from borrowing and lending funds because we have not considered noninterest expenses (such as employee wages and salaries and overhead expenses). Once these expenses are also deducted, the banker generally has very little margin for error in protecting against interest rate risk. If the bank's management does find this 3.5 percent net interest margin acceptable, it will probably use a variety of interest-rate risk hedging methods to protect this NIM ratio, thereby helping to stabilize the bank's net earnings.

If the interest cost of borrowed funds rises faster than bank income from loans and securities, the bank's NIM will be squeezed, with adverse effects on bank profits.[3] If interest rates fall and cause income from loans and securities to decline faster than interest costs on borrowings, the bank's NIM will again be squeezed. In other words, yield curves do not usually move in parallel fashion over time, so that the yield spread between bank borrowing costs and interest revenues is never perfectly constant. Management must struggle continuously to find ways to ensure that borrowing costs do not rise significantly relative to interest income and threaten the bank's margin.

Concept Checks

6–3. What forces cause interest rates to change? What kinds of risk do bankers face when interest rates change?

6–4. What makes it so difficult for bankers to correctly forecast interest rate changes?

6–5. What is the yield curve and why is it important for bankers to know about its shape or slope?

6–6. What is it that a bank wishes to protect from adverse movements in interest rates?

6–7. What is the goal of hedging in banking?

6–8. First National Bank of Bannerville has posted interest revenues of $63 million and interest costs from all of its borrowings of $42 million. If the bank possesses $700 million in total earning assets, what is First National's net interest margin? Suppose the bank's interest revenues and interest costs double, while its earning assets increase by 50 percent. What will happen to its net interest margin?

---

[3]In recent years, as noted by Alden Toevs [6], the net interest income of U.S. banks has accounted for about 60 to 80 percent of their net earnings. Toevs also found evidence of a substantial increase in the volatility of net interest income over time, encouraging bank managers to find better methods for managing interest rate risk.

Bankers' Insights and Issues

Market Interest Rates and Bank Profits

There is an old myth that bankers benefit the most (in terms of the profitability of their institutions) when market interest rates are high and rising. Conversely, many members of the public believe that banks are less profitable in periods when interest rates are relatively low. As the annual figures for U.S. insured banks' return on assets (ROA) and the market interest rates on 6-month U.S. Treasury bills in the table below suggest, these widely held generalizations aren't necessarily so. We notice, for example, that some of the highest industry average ROAs occurred during some of the lowest interest-rate periods in recent history. Examples include 1993 when U.S. banking's average ROA reached a record high of 1.17 percent, while the U.S. Treasury bill interest rate dropped below 3 percent—one of the lowest annual average T-bill rates in modern history. We also notice that in 1989 when T-bill rates averaged among the highest in recent years, climbing above 8 percent, the U.S. banking industry's mean ROA for the year was one of the lowest historically at 0.49 percent.

Year	U.S. Insured Banks' Average Return on Assets	Market Yield on 6-Month U.S. Treasury Bills
1985	0.71%	7.48%
1986	0.62	5.98
1987	0.09	5.78
1988	0.81	6.67
1989	0.49	8.11
1990	0.47	7.50
1991	0.52	5.38
1992	0.92	3.43
1993	1.17	2.95
1994	1.13	4.64
1995	1.13	5.56
1996	1.14*	5.08

*Based on the first three quarters of 1996.

It is important, therefore, to be particularly careful when we attempt to generalize about the relationship between interest rates and bank profits. As we will see in this portion of the book, the relationship between bank profits and market interest rates depends crucially upon the makeup of a particular bank's balance sheet, its sources of revenue and expense as reflected on its income statement, and other factors. Well-managed banks that carefully control their exposure to interest rate risk can be profitable whether interest rates are rising or falling and whether they are high or low by historical standards.

Interest-Sensitive Gap Management

The most popular interest-rate hedging strategy in use by banks today is often called **interest-sensitive gap management.** Gap management techniques require management to perform an analysis of the maturities and repricing opportunities associated with the bank's interest-bearing assets, deposits, and money market borrowings. If management feels its institution is excessively exposed to interest rate risk, it will try to match as closely as possible the volume of bank assets that can be repriced as interest rates change with the volume of deposits and other liabilities whose rates can also be adjusted with market conditions during the same time period.

Thus, a bank can hedge itself against interest rate changes—no matter which way rates move—by making sure for each time period that the

$$\begin{array}{ccc} \text{Dollar amount of repriceable} & \text{Dollar amount of repriceable} & \quad(6) \\ \text{(interest-sensitive) bank} \quad = & \text{(interest-sensitive) bank} \\ \text{assets} & \text{liabilities} \end{array}$$

In this case, the revenue from earning assets will change in the same direction and by approximately the same proportion as the interest cost of liabilities.

What is a repriceable asset? A repriceable liability? The most familiar examples of repriceable assets are loans that are about to mature or are coming up for renewal. If interest rates have risen since these loans were first made, the bank will renew them only if it can get an expected yield that approximates the higher yields currently expected on

Examples of Repriceable Bank Assets and Liabilities and Nonrepriceable Assets and Liabilities

Repriceable Assets	*Repriceable Liabilities*	*Nonrepriceable Assets*	*Nonrepriceable Liabilities*
Short-term securities issued by governments and private borrowers (about to mature)	Borrowings from the money market (such as federal funds or RP borrowings)	Cash held in the bank's vault and deposits at the Central Bank (legal reserves)	Demand deposit accounts (which pay no rate of return or a fixed interest rate)
Short-term loans made by the bank to borrowing customers (about to mature)	Short-term savings accounts	Long-term loans made at a fixed interest rate to borrowing customers	Long-term savings and retirement accounts
Variable-rate (floating or adjustable rate) loans and securities	Money-market deposits (whose interest rates often are adjustable every few days)	Long-term securities carrying fixed (coupon) rates	Equity capital provided by the bank's owners
	Variable rate (floating or adjustable rate) deposits	Bank buildings and equipment and other nonearning assets	

other financial instruments of comparable quality. Similarly, loans that are maturing will provide the bank with funds to reinvest in new loans at today's interest rates, so they represent repriceable assets as well. Repriceable liabilities include CDs about to mature or be renewed, where the bank and its customers must negotiate a new deposit interest rate to capture current market conditions; floating-rate deposits whose yields move automatically with market interest rates; and money-market borrowings whose rates are often adjusted daily to reflect the latest market developments.

What happens when the amount of repriceable assets does *not* equal the amount of repriceable liabilities? Clearly, a *gap* exists between these interest-sensitive assets and interest-sensitive liabilities:

$$\text{Interest-sensitive gap} = \text{Interest-sensitive assets} \atop - \text{Interest-sensitive liabilities} \tag{7}$$

If interest-sensitive assets in each planning period (day, week, month, etc.) *exceed* the volume of interest-sensitive liabilities subject to repricing, the bank is said to have a *positive gap* and to be *asset sensitive.* Thus:

$$\begin{matrix} \text{Asset-sensitive} \\ \text{(positive) gap} \end{matrix} = \begin{matrix} \text{Interest-sensitive assets} - \\ \text{Interest-sensitive liabilities} > 0 \end{matrix} \tag{8}$$

For example, a bank with interest-sensitive assets of $500 million and interest-sensitive liabilities of $400 million is asset sensitive with a positive gap of $100 million. If interest rates *rise,* the bank's net interest margin will *increase* because the interest revenue generated by bank assets will increase more than the cost of borrowed funds. Other things being equal, the bank will experience an *increase* in its net interest income. On the other hand, if interest rates *fall* when the bank is asset sensitive, the bank's NIM will *decline* as interest revenues from assets drop by more than interest expenses associated with liabilities. The bank with a positive gap will lose net interest income if interest rates fall.

In the opposite situation, suppose interest-sensitive bank liabilities are larger than interest-sensitive assets. The bank then has a *negative gap* and is said to be *liability sensitive.* Thus:

$$\begin{matrix} \text{Liability-sensitive} \\ \text{(negative) gap} \end{matrix} = \begin{matrix} \text{Interest-sensitive assets} - \\ \text{Interest-sensitive liabilities} < 0 \end{matrix} \tag{9}$$

A bank holding interest-sensitive assets of $150 million and interest-sensitive liabilities of $200 million is liability sensitive, with a negative gap of $50 million. Rising interest rates will *lower* the bank's net interest margin, because the rising cost associated with interest-sensitive liabilities will exceed increases in interest revenue from the bank's interest-sensitive assets. Falling interest rates will generate a higher interest margin and probably greater earnings as well, because borrowing costs will decline by more than interest revenues.

Actually, there are several ways to measure a bank's interest-sensitive gap (IS GAP). One method is called simply the Dollar IS GAP. For example, as we saw above, if interest-sensitive assets (ISA) are $150 million and interest-sensitive liabilities (ISL) are $200 million, then Dollar IS GAP = ISA − ISL = $150 million − $200 million = −$50 million. Clearly, a bank whose Dollar IS GAP is *positive* is *asset sensitive,* while a *negative* Dollar IS GAP describes a *liability-sensitive* condition.

We can also form a bank's Relative IS GAP ratio:

$$\text{Relative IS GAP} = \frac{\text{IS GAP}}{\text{Bank size}} = \frac{-\$50 \text{ million}}{\$150 \text{ million}} = -0.33 \qquad (10)$$
$$\text{(measured for example,}$$
$$\text{by total assets)}$$

A Relative IS GAP greater than zero means the bank is asset sensitive, while a negative Relative IS GAP describes a liability-sensitive bank. Finally, we can simply compare the ratio of ISA to ISL, sometimes called the Interest Sensitivity Ratio (ISR). In our example above,

$$\text{Interest Sensitivity Ratio} = \frac{\text{ISA}}{\text{ISL}} = \frac{\$150 \text{ million}}{\$200 \text{ million}} = 0.75 \qquad (11)$$

In this instance an Interest Sensitivity Ratio (ISR) of less than one tells us we are looking at a liability-sensitive bank, while an ISR greater than unity points to an asset-sensitive bank.

An Asset-Sensitive Bank Has:	*A Liability-Sensitive Bank Has:*
Positive Dollars IS GAP	Negative Dollar IS GAP
Positive Relative IS GAP	Negative Relative IS GAP
Interest Sensitivity Ratio greater than one	Interest Sensitivity Ratio less than one

Only if interest-sensitive assets and liabilities are *equal* is a bank relatively insulated from interest rate risk. In this case, interest revenues from assets and funding costs will change at the *same* rate. The bank's gap is *zero,* and its net interest margin is protected regardless of which way interest rates go. As a practical matter, however, a zero gap does *not* eliminate *all* interest rate risk, because the interest rates attached to bank assets and liabilities are not perfectly correlated in the real world. Loan interest rates, for example, tend to lag behind interest rates on money market borrowings. So bank interest revenues tend to grow more slowly than expenses during economic expansions, while interest expenses tend to fall more rapidly than revenues during economic downturns.

Gapping methods used by banks today vary greatly in complexity and form. All methods, however, require bank management to make some important decisions:

1. Management must choose the time period during which the bank's net interest margin (NIM) is to be managed (e.g., six months, one year), in order to achieve some desired value and the length of subperiods ("maturity buckets") into which the planning period is to be divided.

2. Management must choose a target level for the net interest margin—that is, whether to freeze the margin roughly where it is or perhaps increase the NIM.

3. If management wishes to increase the NIM, it must either develop a correct interest rate forecast or find ways to reallocate earning assets and liabilities in order to increase the spread between interest revenues and interest expenses.

4. Management must determine the dollar volume of interest-sensitive assets and interest-sensitive liabilities it wants the bank to hold.

Computer-Based Techniques.   Many banks use computer-based techniques in which their assets and liabilities are classified as due or repriceable today, during the coming week, in the next 30 days, and so on. Management tries to match interest-sensitive assets with interest-sensitive liabilities in each of these maturity buckets in order to improve the chances of achieving the bank's earnings goals. For example, the bank's latest computer run might reveal the following:

Maturity Buckets	Interest-Sensitive Assets	Interest-Sensitive Liabilities	(dollars in millions)	
			Size of Gap	Cumulative Gap
Next 24 hours	$ 40	$ 30	+10	+10
Next 7 days	120	160	−40	−30
Next 30 days	85	65	+20	−10
Next 90 days	280	250	+30	+20
Next 120 days	455	395	+60	+80
.	.	.	.	.
.	.	.	.	.
.	.	.	.	.

It is obvious from this table that the *time period* over which the gap is measured is crucial to understanding the bank's true interest-sensitive position. For example, within the next 24 hours, the bank shown above has a *positive gap;* its earnings will benefit if interest rates rise between today and tomorrow. However, a forecast of rising money market interest rates over the next week would be bad news because there is a negative gap for the next seven days, which will result in interest expenses rising by more than interest revenues. If the interest rate increase is expected to be substantial, management should consider taking countermeasures to protect the bank's earnings. These might include selling longer-term CDs right away or using futures contracts to earn a profit that will help offset the margin losses that rising interest rates will almost surely bring in the coming week. Looking over the remainder of the table, it is clear the bank will fare much better over the next several months if rates rise, because its gap eventually turns positive again.

The foregoing example reminds us that the net interest margin of a bank is influenced by multiple factors:

1. Changes in the level of interest rates, up or down.
2. Changes in the spread between asset yields and liability costs (often reflected in the changing shape of the *yield curve* between long-term rates and short-term rates, because many bank liabilities are short-term while a significant portion of bank assets bear longer maturities).
3. Changes in the volume of interest-bearing (earning) assets a bank holds as the institution expands or shrinks the overall scale of its activities.
4. Changes in the volume of interest-bearing liabilities the bank uses to fund its earning assets as the institution grows or shrinks in size.

5. Changes in the mix of assets and liabilities that the management of each bank draws upon as it shifts between floating and fixed-rate assets and liabilities, between shorter and longer maturity assets and liabilities, and between assets bearing higher versus lower expected yields (e.g., a shift from less cash to more loans or from higher-yielding consumer and real estate loans to lower-yielding commercial loans).

Table 6–2 provides a more detailed example of gap management applied to the asset and liability figures of an individual bank. In it, management has arrayed (with the help of a computer) the amount of all the bank's assets and liabilities, grouped by the future time period when those assets and liabilities will reach maturity or their interest rates will be subject to repricing. Note that this bank is liability sensitive during the coming week and over the next 90 days and then becomes asset sensitive in later periods. This is typical of many banks, which tend to have short-term liabilities and longer-term assets. Consciously or unconsciously, management has positioned this bank for falling interest rates over the next three months and for rising interest rates over the longer horizon.

At the bottom of Table 6–2, we calculate the bank's net interest income and net interest margin to see how they will change if interest rates *rise*. The bank's net interest income can be derived from the following formula:

$$\text{Net interest income} = \text{Total interest income} - \text{Total interest cost} = \qquad (12)$$

Interest yield on rate-sensitive assets × Volume of rate-sensitive assets + Interest yield on fixed (non-rate-sensitive) assets × Volume of fixed assets – Interest cost on rate-sensitive liabilities × Volume of interest-sensitive liabilities – Interest cost on fixed (non-rate-sensitive) liabilities × Volume of fixed (non-rate-sensitive) liabilities.

For example, suppose the yields on rate-sensitive and fixed assets are 10 percent and 11 percent, respectively, while rate-sensitive and non-rate-sensitive liabilities cost 8 percent and 9 percent, respectively, and during the coming week the bank holds $1,700 million in rate-sensitive assets (out of an asset total of $4,100 million) and $1,800 million in rate-sensitive liabilities. Suppose, too, that these interest rates remain steady. Then the bank's net interest income will be:

$$0.10 \times \$1,700 + 0.11 \times [4,100 - 1,700] - 0.08 \times \$1,800 - 0.09$$
$$\times [4,100 - 1,800] = \$83 \text{ million}$$

However, if the interest rate on rate-sensitive assets rises to 12 percent and the rate on rate-sensitive liabilities rises to 10 percent during the first week, this liability-sensitive bank will have a net interest income of only:

$$0.12 \times \$1,700 + 0.11 \times [4,100 - 1,700] - 0.10 \times \$1,800 - 0.09$$
$$\times [4,100 - 1,800] = \$81 \text{ million}$$

Therefore, the bank will lose $2 million in net interest income if interest rates rise in the coming week. Management must decide whether to accept that risk or to counter it with hedging strategies or tools.

TABLE 6–2   **Sample Interest-Sensitivity Analysis (GAP management) for an Individual Bank**

Asset and Liability Items	Volume of Bank Asset and Liability Items Maturing or Subject to Repricing within the Following Maturity Buckets (in millions of dollars)					
	One Week	*Next 30 Days*	*Next 31–90 Days*	*Next 91–360 Days*	*More Than One Year*	*Totals*
Assets						
Cash and deposits owned	$ 100	—	—	—	—	$ 100
Marketable securities	200	$ 50	$ 80	$110	$ 460	900
Business loans	750	150	220	170	210	1,500
Real estate loans	500	80	80	70	170	900
Consumer loans	100	20	20	70	90	300
Farm loans	50	10	40	60	40	200
Bank buildings and equipment	—	—	—	—	200	200
Total repriceable (interest-sensitive) assets	**$1,700**	**$310**	**$440**	**$480**	**$1,170**	**$4,100**
Liabilities and Net Worth						
Checkable deposits	$ 800	$100	—	—	—	$ 900
Savings accounts	50	50	—	—	—	100
Money market deposits	550	150	—	—	—	700
Long-term time deposits	100	200	450	150	300	1,200
Short-term borrowings	300	100	—	—	—	400
Other liabilities	—	—	—	—	100	100
Net worth	—	—	—	—	700	700
Total repriceable (interest-sensitive) liabilities and net worth	**$1,800**	**$600**	**$450**	**$150**	**$1,100**	**$4,100**
Interest-sensitive gap (repriceable assets – repriceable liabilities)	–$100	–$290	–$10	+$330	+$70	
Cumulative gap	–$100	–$390	–$400	–$ 70	–0	
Ratio of interest-sensitive assets to interest-sensitive liabilities	94.4%	51.7%	97.8%	320%	106.4%	
The bank is	liability sensitive	liability sensitive	liability sensitive	asset sensitive	asset sensitive	
Bank's net interest margin will be squeezed if	Interest rates rise	Interest rates rise	Interest rates rise	Interest rates fall	Interest rates fall	

A useful overall measure of interest-rate risk exposure is the *cumulative gap,* which is the total difference in dollars between those bank assets and liabilities that can be repriced over a designated period of time. For example, if a bank has $100 million in earning assets and $200 million in liabilities subject to an interest rate change each month over the next six months, its *cumulative gap* must be –$600 million. That is, ($100 million in earning assets per month × 6) – ($200 million in liabilities per month × 6) = –$600 million. The cumulative gap concept is useful because, given any specific change in market interest rates, we can calculate *approximately* how

---

TABLE 6–2 *Continued*

Suppose that interest yields on interest-sensitive assets currently are 10%, while interest-sensitive liabilities cost 8%. In contrast, fixed assets yield 11% and fixed liabilities cost 9%. If rates stay at these levels, the bank's net interest income and net interest margin in each time period will be:

	One Week	Next 30 Days	Next 31–90 Days	Next 91–360 Days	More Than One Year
Total interest income	$0.10 \times \$1,700 +$ $0.11 \times [4,100 -$ $1,700]$	$0.10 \times \$310$ $+ 0.11$ $[4,100 - 310]$	$0.10 \times \$440$ $+ 0.11 \times$ $[4,100 - 440]$	$0.10 \times \$480$ $+ 0.11 \times$ $[4,100 - 480]$	$0.10 \times \$1,170$ $+ 0.11 \times$ $[4,100 - 1,170]$
Total interest costs	$-0.08 \times \$1,800$ $-0.09 \times [4,100 -$ $1,800]$	$-0.08 \times$ $\$600 - 0.09 \times$ $[4,100 - 600]$	$-0.08 \times$ $\$450 - 0.09 \times$ $[4,100 - 45]$	$-0.08 \times$ $\$150 - 0.09$ $\times [4,100 - 150]$	$-0.08 \times$ $\$1,100 - 0.09$ $\times [4,100 -$ $1,100]$
Net interest income	$= \$83$	$= \$84.9$	$= \$82.10$	$= \$80.20$	$= \$81.30$
Net interest margin	$83 \div 4,100$ $= 2.02\%$	$84.9 \div 4,100$ $= 2.07\%$	$\$82.10 \div 4,100$ $= 2.00\%$	$\$78.7 \div 4,100$ $= 1.92\%$	$81.3 \div 4,100$ $= 1.98\%$

Suppose the interest rates attached to rate-sensitive assets and liabilities *rise* two full percentage points, to 12% and 10%, respectively.

	One Week	Next 30 Days	Next 31–90 Days	Next 91–360 Days	More Than One Year
	$0.12 \times \$1,700 +$ $0.11 \times [4,100 -$ $[1,700] - 0.10 \times$ $\$1,800 - 0.09 \times$ $[4,100 - 1,800]$	$0.12 \times \$310$ $+ 0.11 [4,100$ $- 310]$ $- 0.10 \times 600$ $- 0.09 \times$ $[4,100 - 600]$	0.12×440 $+ 0.11 \times [4,100 -$ $440]$ $- 0.10 \times 450$ $- 0.09 \times$ $[4,100 - 450]$	$0.12 \times \$480$ $+ 0.11 \times$ $[4,100 - 480]$ $- 0.10 \times 150$ $- 0.09 [4,100$ $- 150]$	$0.12 \times \$1,170$ $+ 0.11 \times$ $[4,100 -$ $1,170] - 0.10$ $\times 1,100$ $- 0.09 [4,100$ $- 1,100]$
Net interest income	$= \$81$	$= \$79.10$	$= \$81.90$	$= \$85.30$	$= \$82.70$
Net interest margin	$\$81 \div 4,100$ $= 1.98\%$	$\$79.1 \div 4,100$ $= 1.93\%$	$\$81.9 \div 4,100$ $= 2.00\%$	$\$85.3 \div 4,100$ $= 2.08\%$	$\$82.7 \div 4,100$ $= 2.02\%$

We note by comparing interest income and margins for each time period (maturity bucket) that the bank's net interest income and margin fall if it is liability sensitive when interest rates go up. When the bank is asset sensitive and rates rise, the bank's net interest income and margin increase.

---

the bank's net interest income will be affected by the interest rate change. The key relationship is:

$$\begin{array}{llll} \text{Change in the} & \text{Overall change in} & \text{Size of the} & (13) \\ \text{bank's net} & = \text{interest rates (in} & \times \text{ cumulative gap} \\ \text{interest income} & \text{percentage points)} & \text{(in dollars)} \end{array}$$

For example, if interest rates suddenly rise by one full percentage point, this bank will suffer a net interest income loss of approximately:

$$(+0.01) \times (-\$600 \text{ million}) = -\$6 \text{ million}.$$

If management anticipates an increase in interest rates, it may be able to head off this pending loss of income by shifting some of the bank's assets and liabilities to reduce the size of the cumulative gap or by using hedging instruments (such as financial futures contracts, to be discussed in the next chapter). In general, banks with a negative cumulative gap will benefit from falling interest rates but lose net interest income when interest rates rise. Banks with a positive cumulative gap will benefit if interest rates rise, but lose net interest income if interest rates decline.

Some banks shade their interest-sensitive gaps toward either asset sensitivity or liability sensitivity, depending on their degree of confidence in their own interest rate forecasts. This is often referred to as *aggressive GAP management*. For example, if manage-

Aggressive Interest-Sensitive GAP Management

Expected Changes in Interest Rates (Management's Forecast)	Best Interest-Sensitive GAP Position to Be in:	Aggressive Management's Most Likely Action
Rising market interest rates	Positive IS GAP	Increase interest-sensitive assets Decrease interest-sensitive liabilities
Falling market interest rates	Negative IS GAP	Decrease interest-sensitive assets Increase interest-sensitive liabilities

ment firmly believes interest rates are going to fall over the current planning horizon, it will probably allow interest-sensitive liabilities to climb above interest-sensitive assets. If interest rates do fall as predicted, liability costs will drop by more than revenues and the bank's NIM will grow. Similarly, a confident forecast of higher interest rates will trigger many banks to become asset sensitive, knowing that if rates do rise, bank revenues will rise by more than interest expenses. Of course, such an aggressive strategy creates greater risk for the bank. Consistently correct interest rate forecasting is impossible; most bank managers have learned to rely on hedging against, not forecasting, changes in interest rates. Interest rates that move in the wrong direction can magnify the bank's losses. (See Table 6–3.)

Many bankers have chosen, instead, to adopt a purely defensive GAP management strategy:

Defensive Interest-Sensitive GAP Management

Set Interest-Sensitive GAP as Close to Zero as
Possible to Reduce the Expected Volatility of
the Bank's Net Interest Income

While gap management works beautifully in theory, practical problems in its implementation always leave the bank with at least *some* interest-rate risk exposure. For example, interest rates paid on liabilities (which are usually short term) tend to move

TABLE 6-3   Eliminating a Bank's Interest-Sensitive Gap

With Positive Gap	*The Risk*	*Possible Management Responses*
Interest-sensitive assets > interest-sensitive liabilities (asset sensitive)	Losses if interest rates fall because the bank's net interest margin will be reduced.	1. Do nothing (perhaps interest rates will rise or be stable). 2. Extend asset maturities or shorten liability maturities. 3. Increase interest-sensitive liabilities or reduce interest-sensitive assets.

With Negative Gap	*The Risk*	*Possible Management Responses*
Interest-sensitive assets < interest-sensitive liabilities (liability sensitive)	Losses if interest rates rise because the bank's net interest margin will be reduced.	1. Do nothing (perhaps interest rates will fall or be stable). 2. Shorten asset maturities or lengthen liability maturities 3. Decrease interest-sensitive liabilities or increase interest-sensitive assets.

faster than interest rates earned on assets (many of which are long term). Then too, changes in interest rates attached to bank assets and liabilities do not necessarily move at the same speed as interest rates in the open market, and deposit interest rates typically lag loan interest rates.

Some banks have developed a *weighted* interest-sensitive gap approach that takes into account the tendency of bank interest rates to vary in speed and magnitude relative to each other and the up and down cycle of business activity. The interest rates attached to bank assets of various kinds often change by different amounts and by different speeds than many of the interest rates attached to bank liabilities—a phenomenon called *basis risk.* For example, suppose that a bank has the current amount and distribution of interest-sensitive assets and liabilities shown below with rate-sensitive assets totaling $200 million and rate-sensitive liabilities amounting to $223 million, yielding an interest-sensitive GAP of –$23 on its present balance sheet. Its Federal funds loans generally carry interest rates set in the open market, so these loans have an interest rate sensitivity weight of 1.0—that is, the bank's Fed funds rate tracks market rates one for one. In the bank's investment security portfolio, however, the bank has some riskier, somewhat more rate-volatile investments than most of the security interest rates reported daily in the financial press. Therefore, its average security yield moves up and down by somewhat more than the interest rate on Federal funds loans—here the interest-rate sensitivity weight is 1.3. Loans and leases are the most rate-volatile of all with an interest-rate sensitivity weight half again as volatile as Federal funds rates at 1.5. On the liability side deposit interest rates and some money-market borrowings (such as borrowing from the central bank) may change more slowly than market interest rates. In this example, we assume deposits have a rate-sensitive weight of 0.86 and money-market borrowings are slightly more volatile at 0.91, close to but still less than the volatility of Federal funds interest rates.

The Weighted Interest-Sensitive Gap for a Bank: Dealing with Basis Risk

	Original Balance Sheet Entries		Interest-Rate Sensitivity Weight		Balance Sheet Refigured to Reflect Interest Rate Sensitivities
Asset items sensitive to interest rate movements:					
Federal funds loans	$ 50	×	1.0	=	$ 50.00
Government securities and other investments	25	×	1.3	=	32.50
Loans and leases	125	×	1.5	=	187.50
Total rate-sensitive assets	$200				$270.00
Liability items sensitive to interest rate movements:					
Interest-bearing deposits	$159	×	0.86	=	$137.00
Other borrowings in the money market	64	×	0.91	=	58.00
Total rate-sensitive liabilities	$223				$195.00
The bank's interest-sensitive GAP	−$23				+$75

How Net Interest Income of the Bank Would Move if the Federal Funds Rate in the Money Market Increases by 2 Percentage Points:

	Original Balance Sheet	*Refigured Balance Sheet*
Predicted movement in net interest income	−$0.46 (= −$23 × .02)	+$1.50 (= +$75 × .02)

We can simply multiply each of the rate-sensitive balance-sheet items by its appropriate interest-rate sensitivity indicator, which acts as a weight. More rate-volatile assets and liabilities will weigh more heavily in the refigured (weighted) balance sheet we are constructing in the table above. Notice that after multiplying by the interest rate weights we have created, the new weighted balance sheet has rate-sensitive assets of $270 and rate-sensitive liabilities of $195. Now, instead of a negative (liability-sensitive) interest rate gap of −$23 we have a positive (asset-sensitive) rate gap of +$75.

Thus, the bank's interest-sensitive gap has changed direction and, instead of being hurt by rising market interest rates, for example, this bank would actually *benefit* from higher market interest rates. Suppose the Federal funds interest rate rose by two percentage points (+.02). Now instead of declining by −$0.46, the bank's net interest income increases by $1.50. Clearly, management would have an entirely different reaction to a forecast of rising interest rates with the new weighted balance sheet than it would have with its original, conventionally constructed balance sheet. Indeed, when it comes to assessing interest rate risk, things are not always as they appear!

Moreover, the point at which certain bank assets and liabilities can be repriced is not always easy to identify. And the choice of planning periods over which to balance interest-sensitive assets and liabilities is highly arbitrary. Some items always fall between the cracks in setting planning periods, and they could cause trouble if interest rates move against the bank. Wise asset-liability managers use several different lengths of planning periods ("maturity buckets") in measuring their banks' exposure to changing interest rates.

Finally, interest-sensitive gap management does *not* consider the impact of changing interest rates on the owners' (stockholders') position in the bank as represented by the institution's *net worth.* Management choosing to pursue an aggressive interest-rate sensitive gap policy may be able to expand their bank's net interest margin, but at the cost of increasing the volatility of the bank's net earnings and reducing the value of the stockholders' investment in the bank. Effective asset-liability management demands that bank managers must work to achieve desirable levels of *both* a bank's net interest income and its net worth.

Concept Checks

6–9. Can you explain the concept of gap management?

6–10. When is a bank asset sensitive? Liability sensitive?

6–11. Commerce National Bank reports interest-sensitive assets of $870 million and interest-sensitive liabilities of $625 million during the coming month. Is the bank asset sensitive or liability sensitive? What is likely to happen to the bank's net interest margin if interest rates rise? If they fall?

6–12. First National Bank has a cumulative gap for the coming year of +$135 million and interest rates are expected to fall by two and a half percentage points. Can you calculate the expected change in net interest income that the bank could experience? What change will occur in net interest income if interest rates rise by one and a quarter percentage points?

6–13. How do you measure a bank's dollar interest-sensitive gap? Its relative interest-sensitive gap? What is the interest-sensitivity ratio?

6–14. Suppose Carroll Bank and Trust reports interest-sensitive assets of $570 million and interest-sensitive liabilities of $685 million. What is the bank's dollar interest-sensitive gap? Its relative interest-sensitive gap and interest-sensitivity ratio?

6–15. Explain the concept of weighted interest-sensitive gap. How can this concept aid bank management in measuring a bank's real interest-sensitive gap risk exposure?

Summary

Bankers today focus heavily on *managing risk*— attempting to control their exposure to loss due to changes in interest rates, the inability or unwillingness of borrowers to repay their loans, changing currency prices, and other risk-laden factors. But effective management of risk requires careful coordination of decisions made on the asset side of a bank with the decisions made on its liability side. Thus, the technique of *asset-liability management* was born to give bankers risk management tools that can be marshaled in a coordinated fashion to handle many of the risks banks face.

Early in the history of banking many experts believed that banks could only effectively manage their assets, making decisions about which loans, securities, and other investments to acquire (known as *asset management*) because bank liabilities (especially deposits) were subject to heavy government regulation. Then, beginning in the 1960s and 1970s, *liability management*—control over the composition and cost of borrowed funds raised by the bank—became popular as bankers discovered that manipulation of interest rates offered and fees charged could alter the volume and types of funds banks were able to attract. Most recently, bankers have learned that modern managers must practice *funds management*—using tools to control the volume, mix, return, and cost of the whole bank portfolio (assets and liabilities) with consistent coordination of both asset and liability management to maximize return, minimize cost, and manage risk exposure.

One of the strongest risk factors bankers have always faced is *interest rate risk.* Individual banks cannot control market interest rates; forces outside the bank's control, especially the demand for and supply of loanable funds (credit), shape the level of market interest rates and the changes those rates go through. A banker must learn how to *react* to changes in market interest rates in order to control and protect the institution's interest revenues, interest expenses, net interest margin, the value of a bank's assets, and its net worth—the owners' investment in the bank.

One of the most popular tools today for managing interest rate risk is known as *interest-sensitive GAP management.* This technique focuses upon protecting (if a *defensive* approach is used) or maximizing (where an *aggressive* approach is employed)

the net interest margin of a bank—its ratio of interest revenues less interest expenses divided by total assets or total earning assets. Assets and liabilities are divided into those that are interest rate sensitive (i.e., whose interest revenue flow or interest cost changes as market interest rates change) and those that are *not* rate sensitive. Bankers calculate the gap between the volume of their interest-sensitive assets and their interest-sensitive liabilities. A bank with an excess of interest-sensitive assets is considered to be *asset sensitive,* while banks with greater interest-sensitive liabilities than assets are said to be *liability sensitive.*

Banks that are asset sensitive tend to benefit in terms of greater net interest margins if interest rates rise, while falling interest rates cause asset-sensitive banks to suffer a decline in their interest margins. A bank that is liability sensitive generally experiences a rise in its net interest margin if market interest rates fall.

Major banks today use computers to determine their asset sensitivity or liability sensitivity across varying lengths of time (maturity buckets) and manage their interest-sensitivity depending upon management's risk-taking philosophy and sensitivity to risk. The interest-sensitive gap management technique has serious limitations, however. The choice of time intervals to analyze is highly arbitrary. Then, too, market interest rates and bank rates may change at different speeds. Finally, interest-sensitive gap management does *not* protect a bank's asset values and especially its net worth. To accomplish that, we must turn to another technique—duration gap analysis—which we look at in the next chapter.

Key Terms in This Chapter

Asset-liability management	Yield to maturity (YTM)
Asset management	Bank discount rate
Liability management	Net interest margin
Funds management	Interest-sensitive gap management
Interest rate risk	

Problems and Projects

1. A government bond is currently selling for $900 and pays $80 per year in interest for five years when it matures. If the redemption value of this bond is $1,000, what is its yield to maturity if purchased today for $900?

2. Suppose the government bond described in problem 1 above is held for three years and then the bank acquiring the bond decides to sell it at a price of $950. Can you figure out the average annual yield the bank will have earned for its three-year investment in the bond?

3. U.S. Treasury bills are available for purchase this week at the following prices (based upon $100 par value) and with the indicated maturities:
   a. $97.25, 182 days.
   b. $96.50, 270 days.
   c. $98.75, 91 days.

   Please calculate the bank discount rate (DR) on each bill if it is held to maturity. What is the equivalent yield to maturity (sometimes called the bond-equivalent or coupon-equivalent yield) on each of these Treasury bills?

4. The First State Bank of Ashfork reports a net interest margin of 3.25 percent in its most recent financial report, with total interest revenues of $88 million and total interest costs of $72 million. What volume of earning assets must the bank hold? Suppose the bank's interest revenues rise by 8 percent and its interest costs and earning assets increase 10 percent. What will happen to Ashfork's net interest margin?

5. If a bank's net interest margin, which was 2.85 percent, doubles and its total assets, which stood originally at $545 million, rise by 40 percent, what change will occur in the bank's net interest income?

6. The cumulative interest rate gap of Snidal State Bank and Trust Company doubles from an initial figure of –$35 million. If market interest rates fall by 25 percent from an initial level of 6 percent, what changes will occur in Snidal Bank's net interest income?

7. Merchants State Bank has recorded the following financial data for the past three years (dollars in millions):

	Current Year	Previous Year	Two Years Ago
Interest revenues	$ 57	$ 56	$ 55
Interest expenses	49	42	34
Loans (excluding nonperforming loans)	411	408	406
Investment securities and interest-bearing deposits in other banks	239	197	174
Total deposits	487	472	467
Money market borrowings	143	118	96

What has been happening to the bank's net interest margin? What do you think caused the changes you have observed? Do you have any recommendations for Merchants' management team?

8. The First National Bank of Wedora, California, finds that its asset and liability portfolio contains the following distribution of maturities and repricing opportunities:

	Dollar Volume of Assets and Liabilities Maturing or Subject to Repricing within:			
	Coming Week	Next 30 days	Next 31–90 Days	More Than 90 Days
Loans	$144	$110	$164	$184
Securities	29	19	29	8
Transaction deposits	232	—	—	—
Time accounts	98	84	196	35
Money market borrowings	36	6	—	—

When and by how much is the bank exposed to interest rate risk? For each maturity or repricing interval, what changes in interest rates will be beneficial to the bank and which will be damaging, given its current portfolio position?

9. First National Bank of Barnett currently has the following interest-sensitive assets and liabilities on its balance sheet:

Interest-Sensitive Assets		Interest-Sensitive Liabilities	
Federal funds loans	$65	Interest-bearing deposits	$185
Security holdings	42	Money-market borrowings	78
Loans and leases	230		

What is the bank's current interest-sensitive gap? Suppose its Federal funds loans carry an interest-rate sensitivity index of 1.0 while its investments have a rate-sensitivity index of 1.15 and its loans and leases display a rate-sensitivity index of 1.35. On the liability side First National's rate-sensitivity index is 0.79 for interest-bearing deposits and 0.98 for its money-market borrowings. Adjusted for these various interest-rate sensitivity weights, what is the bank's weighted interest-sensitive gap? Suppose the Federal funds interest rate increases or decreases one percentage point. How will the bank's net interest income be affected (a) given its current balance sheet makeup and (b) reflecting its weighted balance sheet adjusted for the foregoing rate-sensitivity indices?

10. McGraw Bank and Trust has interest-sensitive assets of $225 million and interest-sensitive liabilities of $168 million. What is the bank's dollar interest-sensitive gap? What is McGraw's relative interest-sensitive gap? What is the value of its interest-sensitivity ratio? Is the bank asset sensitive or liability sensitive? Under what scenario for market interest rates will the bank experience a gain in net interest income? A loss in net interest income?

Selected References

The following studies provide an overview of the effectiveness of bank risk-hedging techniques:

1. Bailey, Jess. "Minnesota Bank Begins to Shed Its U.S. Bonds." *The Wall Street Journal,* December 20, 1988, p. 3.
2. Glavin, William M. *Asset/Liability Management: A Handbook for Commercial Banks.* Rolling Meadows, Ill.: Bank Administration Institute, 1982.
3. Stigum, Marcia L., and Rene O. Branch. *Managing Bank Assets and Liabilities.* Homewood, Ill.: Dow Jones-Irwin, 1983.
4. Edwards, Gerald A., and Gregory E. Eller. "Derivative Disclosures by Major U.S. Banks, 1995." *Federal Reserve Bulletin,* September 1996, pp. 791–801.

For additional information about the technique of gap management, see these studies:

5. Rose, Peter S. "Defensive Banking in a Volatile Economy—Hedging Loan and Deposit Interest Rates." *The Canadian Banker* 93, no. 2 (April 1986), pp. 52–59.
6. Toevs, Alden L. "Gap Management: Managing Interest Rate Risk in Banks and Thrifts." *Economic Review,* Federal Reserve Bank of San Francisco, No. 2 (Spring 1983), pp. 20–35.
7. Wright, David M., and James V. Houpt. "An Analysis of Commercial Bank Exposure to Interest-Rate Risk." *Federal Reserve Bulletin,* February 1996, pp. 115–28.

7   Asset-Liability Management: The Concept of Duration and Managing a Bank's Duration Gap

Learning and Management Decision Objectives

This chapter introduces us to yet another way to measure a bank's exposure to loss from changing interest rates—the concept of duration. We also see how bankers use duration analysis as a management weapon, offsetting the potentially damaging effects of rising or falling market interest rates.

Introduction

In the preceding chapter we examined the factors that determine interest rates and saw that bankers cannot control market rates of interest, only react to their changes. We also explored a bank management tool that enables bankers to combat the possibility of losses due to interest rate movements—the technique of *interest-sensitive gap management*. While interest-sensitive gap management can be a useful tool in protecting against interest rate changes, it does not fully take into account the impact of changing interest rates on the market value of the bank's capital—the stockholders' investment in the bank. Moreover, the interest-sensitive gap approach provides no single number to tell bankers what their institutions' overall exposure to interest rate risk is. To add these valuable features, we need to calculate the **duration** of bank assets and liabilities.

The Concept of Duration

Duration is a value- and time-weighted measure of maturity that considers the timing of *all* cash inflows from earning assets and all cash outflows associated with liabilities. It measures the average maturity of a promised stream of future cash payments (such as the payment streams the bank expects to receive from its loans and securities or the stream of interest payments the bank must pay out to its depositors). In effect, duration measures the average time needed to recover the funds committed to an investment.

The standard formula for calculating the duration (D) of an individual financial instrument—such as a loan, security, deposit, or nondeposit borrowing—is:

$$D = \frac{\sum_{t=1}^{n} \text{Expected CF in Period t} \times \text{Period t} / (1 + \text{YTM})^t}{\sum_{t=1}^{n} \frac{\text{Expected CF in Period t}}{(1 + \text{YTM})^t}} \tag{1}$$

D stands for the instrument's duration in years and fractions of a year; t represents the period of time in which each flow of cash off the instrument (such as interest or dividend income) is to be received; the volume of each expected flow of cash in each time period (t) is indicated by CF; and YTM is the instrument's current yield to maturity. We note that the denominator of the above formula is equivalent to the instrument's current market value (price). So, the duration formula can be slightly abbreviated to:

$$D = \frac{\sum_{t=1}^{n} \text{Expected CF} / (1 + \text{YTM})^t}{\text{Current Market Value or Price}} \tag{2}$$

For example, suppose a bank loan is extended for five years. It promises the bank an annual interest payment of 10 percent (that is, $100 per year). The face (par) value of the loan is $1,000, which is also its current market value (price) because the loan's current yield to maturity is 10 percent. What is this loan's duration? The formula with the proper figures entered would be:

$$D_{\text{Loan}} = \frac{\sum_{t=1}^{5} \$100 \times t / (1 + .10)^t + \frac{\$1,000 \times 5}{(1 + .10)^5}}{\sum_{t=1}^{5} \frac{\$100}{(1 + .10)^t} + \frac{\$1,000}{(1 + .10)^5}} = \frac{\$4,169.87}{\$1,000}$$

$$D_{\text{Loan}} = 4.17 \text{ years}$$

We can calculate duration of the above loan a little more simply by setting up the table on page 235 to figure the components of the formula. As before, the duration of loan is $4,169.87/$1,000.00, or 4.17 years.

Now, we recognize from Chapter 4 that the net worth (NW) of any bank is equal to the value of its assets less the value of its liabilities:

$$NW = A - L \tag{3}$$

As interest rates change, the value of *both* a bank's assets and liabilities will change, resulting in a change in net worth (the owner's investment in the bank):

$$\Delta NW = \Delta A - \Delta L \tag{4}$$

	Period of Expected Cash Flow	Expected Cash Flow from Loan	Present Value of Expected Cash Flows (at 10% YTM in this case)	Time Period Cash Is to Be Received (t)	Present Value of Expected Cash Flows × t
Expected	1	$ 100	$90.91	1	$ 90.91
Interest	2	100	82.64	2	165.29
Income	3	100	75.13	3	225.39
From Loan	4	100	68.30	4	273.21
	5	100	62.09	5	310.46
Repayment of	5	1,000	620.92	5	3,104.61
Loan Principal				PV of	
		Price or Denominator =	$1,000.00	Cash Flows =	$4,169.87
		of Formula		× t	

Portfolio theory in finance teaches us that:

A. A rise in market rates of interest will cause the market value (price) of *both* bank fixed-rate assets and liabilities to decline.

B. The longer the maturity of a bank's assets and liabilities, the more they will decline in market value (price) when market interest rates rise.

Thus, a bank's change in net worth due to changing interest rates will vary depending upon the relative maturities of its assets and liabilities. Because duration is a measure of maturity, a bank with longer-duration assets than liabilities will suffer a greater decline in net worth when interest rates rise than a bank whose asset duration is relatively short term or a bank that matches the duration of its liabilities with the duration of its assets. By equating asset and liability durations, management can balance the average maturity of the bank's expected cash inflows from its assets with the average maturity of its expected cash outflows associated with its liabilities. Thus, duration analysis can be used to stabilize (*immunize*) the market value of a bank's net worth (NW).

The important feature of duration from a risk management point of view is that it measures the sensitivity of the market value of financial instruments to changes in interest rates. The percentage change in the market price of an asset or a liability is roughly equal to its duration times the relative change in interest rates attached to that particular asset or liability. That is,

$$\frac{\Delta P}{P} \approx -D \times \frac{\Delta i}{(1+i)} \tag{5}$$

where $\Delta P \div P$ represents the percentage change in market price and $\Delta i \div (1 + i)$ is the relative change in interest rates associated with the asset or liability. D represents duration, and the negative sign attached to it reminds us that market prices and interest rates on financial instruments move in opposite directions. For example, consider a bond held by a bank that carries a duration of four years and a current market value (price) of $1,000. Market interest rates attached to comparable bonds are about 10 percent currently, but recent forecasts suggest that market rates may rise to 11 percent. If this forecast turns out to be correct, what percentage change will occur in the bond's market value? The answer is:

$$\frac{\Delta P}{P} = -4 \text{ years } \times \left(0.01 / (1 + 0.10)\right) = -0.0364, \text{ or } -3.64 \text{ percent}$$

Equation 5 tells us that *the interest rate risk of financial instruments is directly proportional to their durations*. A financial instrument whose duration is 2 will be twice as risky (in terms of price volatility) as one with a duration of 1.

Using Duration to Hedge against Interest Rate Risk

A bank interested in fully hedging against interest rate fluctuations wants to choose assets and liabilities such that:

$$\begin{matrix} \text{The dollar-weighted duration} \\ \text{of the bank's asset portfolio} \end{matrix} \approx \begin{matrix} \text{The dollar-weighted duration} \\ \text{of the bank's liabilities} \end{matrix} \qquad (6)$$

so that the bank's **duration gap** is as close to zero as possible (see Table 7–1):

$$\text{Duration gap} = \begin{matrix} \text{Dollar-weighted} \\ \text{duration} \\ \text{of asset} \\ \text{portfolio} \end{matrix} - \begin{matrix} \text{Dollar-weighted} \\ \text{duration} \\ \text{of bank} \\ \text{liabilities} \end{matrix} \qquad (7)$$

Because the dollar volume of bank assets usually exceeds the dollar volume of bank liabilities (otherwise the bank would be insolvent!), a bank seeking a duration gap of zero would need to make sure that the:

$$\begin{matrix} \text{Dollar-weighted} \\ \text{duration of the} \\ \text{bank's asset} \\ \text{portfolio} \end{matrix} = \begin{matrix} \text{Dollar-weighted} \\ \text{duration of the} \\ \text{bank's liability} \\ \text{portfolio} \end{matrix} \times \frac{\text{Total liabilities}}{\text{Total assets}} \qquad (8)$$

Because a larger duration implies greater sensitivity to interest rate changes, Equation 8 tells us that the value of bank liabilities must change by slightly more than the value of bank assets to eliminate the bank's overall interest-rate risk exposure. If the duration of the bank's assets is not balanced with the dollar-weighted duration of its liabilities, that bank is exposed to interest rate risk. The larger the duration gap, the more sensitive will be the bank's net worth (equity capital) to a change in market interest rates.

For example, suppose asset duration exceeds liability duration. We then have a positive duration gap:

$$\begin{matrix} \text{Positive} \\ \text{duration gap} \end{matrix} = \begin{matrix} \text{Dollar-weighted} \\ \text{asset duration} \end{matrix} - \begin{matrix} \text{Dollar-weighted} \\ \text{liability duration} \end{matrix} > 0 \qquad (9)$$

A parallel change in all interest rates will result in the value of bank liabilities changing by less, up or down, than the value of bank assets. In this case, a rise in interest rates will

---

TABLE 7–1   Use of Duration Analysis to Hedge Interest Rate Movements

---

A. Calculate the dollar-weighted average duration of the bank's earning assets and liabilities from the following:

$$\begin{matrix} \text{Dollar-weighted} \\ \text{asset duration} \\ \text{in years} \end{matrix} = \frac{\begin{matrix} \text{Time-weighted distribution of expected cash} \\ \text{inflows from loans and securities} \end{matrix}}{\text{Present value of loans and securities held}}$$

$$D_A = \frac{\sum_{t=1}^{n} \dfrac{(\text{Expected cash inflows} \times \text{Time period received})}{(1 + \text{Discount rate})^t}}{\sum_{t=1}^{n} \dfrac{\text{Expected cash inflows}}{(1 + \text{Discount rate})^t}}$$

$$\begin{matrix} \text{Dollar-weighted} \\ \text{liability} \\ \text{duration in} \\ \text{years} \end{matrix} = \frac{\begin{matrix} \text{Time-weighted distribution of expected cash} \\ \text{outflows due to interest expenses} \end{matrix}}{\text{Present value of liabilities}}$$

$$D_A = \frac{\sum_{t=1}^{n} \dfrac{(\text{Expected cash outflows} \times \text{Time period paid out})}{(1 + \text{Discount rate})^t}}{\sum_{t=1}^{n} \dfrac{\text{Expected cash outflows}}{(1 + \text{Discount rate})^t}}$$

B. Plan the bank's acquisitions of earning assets and liabilities so that, as closely as possible,

$$\begin{matrix} \text{Dollar-weighted} \\ \text{asset duration} \end{matrix} \approx \begin{matrix} \text{Dollar-weighted} \\ \text{liability duration} \end{matrix} \times \frac{\text{Total liabilities}}{\text{Total assets}}$$

in order to protect the value of the bank's net worth (equity capital).

---

tend to lower the market value of the bank's net worth as asset values fall farther than the value of liabilities. The owner's equity in the bank will decline in market value terms.

On the other hand, a bank has a negative duration gap if:

$$\begin{matrix} \text{Negative} \\ \text{duration gap} \end{matrix} = \begin{matrix} \text{Dollar-weighted} \\ \text{asset duration} \end{matrix} - \begin{matrix} \text{Dollar-weighted} \\ \text{liability duration} \end{matrix} < 0 \qquad (10)$$

With liabilities having a longer duration than the bank's assets, a parallel change in all interest rates will generate a larger change in liability values than asset values. If interest rates fall, the bank's liabilities will increase more in value than its assets and net worth (owners' equity) will decline. Should interest rates rise, however, liability values will decrease faster than asset values and the bank's net worth position will increase in value.

We can calculate the change in the market value of a bank's equity (net worth) if we know the bank's dollar-weighted average asset duration, its dollar-weighted average liability duration, the original rate of discount applied to the institution's cash flows, and how interest rates have changed during the period we are concerned about. The relevant formula is based upon the balance-sheet relationship we discussed earlier in Equation 4:

$$\Delta NW = \Delta A - \Delta L$$

Bankers' Insights and Issues

The Behavior of Market Interest Rates When the Economy Changes

One of the most powerful influences upon the interest rates that banks receive from their loans and investments and the interest rates they must pay on their borrowings is the *business cycle*—the periodic fluctuations in the scale of economic activity, with production and incomes rising in periods of economic expansion and falling in recessions. The most marked association between market interest rates and the economy occurs in short-term interest rates displayed in the money market. Long-term interest rates appear to change very little with the cycle of economic activity (unless the economy experiences extremely deep recessions or rapid, inflationary booms).

The greater volatility of short-term interest rates creates special problems for banks with more long-duration loans and investments in their asset portfolios than short-duration liabilities. These institutions rely heavily upon short-term deposits and money-market borrowings for the majority of their funding and therefore experience volatile funding costs that are highly sensitive to the economy's ups and downs. Their longer-duration loans and securities, however, vary considerably less in rate of return. When market interest rates are climbing, then, these bankers often find their interest rate spread being squeezed, putting downward pressure on bank net earnings, while the greater economic volatility of short-term interest rates increases the volatility (risk) of bank net earnings. Thus, bankers with significantly longer duration assets than liabilities can face a double whammy—lower average net interest income and greater net interest income risk at the same time.

A recent study by Sill (1996) of the Federal Reserve Bank of Philadelphia (see below) finds that short-term interest rates (especially those under one year) tend to be positively correlated with real output in the economy (measured by U.S. Gross Domestic Product, or GDP) at a fairly high level (about +0.30 or higher). However, longer-term interest rates (particularly those on financial instruments 10 years or longer to maturity) have little or no correlation with real economic activity or are negatively related to the economy. This pattern suggests that yield curves tend to flatten out as the economy expands and tend to get steeper as the economy slows or falls into a recession. Sill concludes that income growth in the economy and inflation affect both the level and volatility of interest rates, but in the real world tend to impact short-term rates more than long-term rates. Moreover, current increases in economic output appear to be related to a rise in future interest rates, while increased longer-term interest rates seem to be able to forecast economic output that will be lower in the future.

Source: See especially Keith Sill, "The Cyclical Volatility of Interest Rates," *Business Review*, Federal Reserve Bank of Philadelphia, January/February 1996, p. 29.

Because $\Delta A/A$ is approximately equal to the product of asset duration times the change in interest rates $(-D_A \times \dfrac{\Delta i}{(1+i)})$ and $\Delta L/L$ is approximately equal to liability duration times the change in interest rates $(-D_L \times \dfrac{\Delta i}{(1+i)})$ it follows that:

$$\Delta NW = \left[-D_A \times \frac{\Delta i}{(1+i)} \times A\right] - \left[-D_L \times \frac{\Delta i}{(1+i)} \times L\right] \tag{11}$$

In words,

$$
\begin{array}{c}
\text{Change in value} \\
\text{of bank's net} \\
\text{worth}
\end{array}
=
\left[
\begin{array}{c}
-\text{Average} \\
\text{duration} \\
\text{of assets}
\end{array}
\times
\begin{array}{c}
\text{Change in} \\
\text{interest rate} \\
\overline{(1+ \text{Original}} \\
\text{discount rate)}
\end{array}
\times
\begin{array}{c}
\text{Total} \\
\text{assets}
\end{array}
\right] \tag{12}
$$

$$
-
\left[
\begin{array}{c}
-\text{Average} \\
\text{duration} \\
\text{of liabilities}
\end{array}
\times
\begin{array}{c}
\text{Change in} \\
\text{interest rates} \\
\overline{(1+ \text{Original}} \\
\text{discount rate)}
\end{array}
\times
\begin{array}{c}
\text{Total} \\
\text{liabilities}
\end{array}
\right]
$$

For example, suppose that a bank has an average duration in its assets of three years, an average liability duration of two years, total liabilities of $100 million, and total assets of $120 million. Interest rates were originally 10 percent, but suddenly they rise to 12 percent.

In this example:

$$
\begin{array}{c}
\text{Change in} \\
\text{value of bank's} \\
\text{net worth}
\end{array}
=
\left[-3 \times \frac{+0.02}{(1+0.10)} \times \$120 \text{ million}\right]
$$

$$
-\left[-2 \times \frac{+0.02}{(1+0.10)} \times \$100 \text{ million}\right] = -\$2.91 \text{ million}
$$

Clearly, this bank faces a substantial decline in the value of its net worth unless it can hedge itself against the projected loss due to rising interest rates.

Let's consider an example of how duration can be calculated and used to hedge a bank's asset and liability portfolio. We take advantage of the fact that *the duration of a portfolio of bank assets and of a portfolio of deposits and other borrowings equals the value-weighted average of the duration of each instrument in the portfolio.* We can start by (1) calculating the duration of each loan, deposit, and the like; (2) weighting each of these durations by the market values of the instruments involved; and (3) adding all the value-weighted durations together to derive the duration of the entire bank portfolio.

For example, suppose the bank's management finds that it holds a U.S. Treasury $1,000 par bond with 10 years to final maturity, bearing a 10 percent coupon rate with a current price of $900. Based on the formula shown in Equation 2, this bond's duration is 7.49 years.

Suppose this bank holds $90 million of these Treasury bonds, each with a duration of 7.49 years. The bank also holds other assets with durations and market values as follows:

Bank Assets	Actual or Estimated Market Values	Durations
Commercial loans	$100 million	0.60 years
Consumer loans	50 million	1.20 years
Real estate loans	40 million	2.25 years
Municipal bonds	20 million	1.50 years

Weighting each asset duration by its associated dollar volume, we calculate the duration of the bank's asset portfolio as follows:

$$
\begin{aligned}
\text{Dollar-weighted asset portfolio duration} &= \frac{\sum_{i=1}^{n} \begin{array}{c}\text{Duration of} \\ \text{each asset in} \\ \text{the portfolio}\end{array} \times \begin{array}{c}\text{Market value} \\ \text{of each asset} \\ \text{in the portfolio}\end{array}}{\begin{array}{c}\text{Total market value} \\ \text{of all assets}\end{array}}
\end{aligned}
$$

$$
= \frac{\begin{pmatrix} 7.49 \text{ years} \times \$90 \text{ million in Treasury bonds} + \\ 0.60 \text{ years} \times \$100 \text{ million in commercial loans} + \\ 1.20 \text{ years} \times \$50 \text{ million in consumer loans} + \\ 2.25 \text{ years} \times \$40 \text{ million in real estate loans} + \\ 1.50 \text{ years} \times \$20 \text{ million in municipal bonds} \end{pmatrix}}{\begin{pmatrix}\$90 \text{ million} + \$100 \text{ million} + \$50 \text{ million} + \\ \$40 \text{ million} + \$20 \text{ million}\end{pmatrix}}
$$

$$
= \frac{\$914.10 \text{ million}}{\$300 \text{ million}}
$$

$$
= 3.047 \text{ years}
$$

Because duration is a measure of *average maturity,* the average maturity of this bank's portfolio of assets is about three years. The bank can hedge against the damaging effects of rising deposit interest rates by making sure the dollar-weighted average duration of its deposits and other liabilities is also approximately three years.[1] In this

---

[1]As noted earlier, we must adjust the duration of the bank's liability portfolio by the value of the ratio of total liabilities to total assets, because asset volume usually exceeds the volume of bank liabilities. For example, if this bank has an asset duration of three years and its total assets are $100 million while total liabilities are $92 million, management will want to achieve an approximate average duration for liabilities of 3.261 years (or asset duration × total assets ÷ total liabilities = 3 years × $100 million ÷ $92 million = 3.261 years).

way the present value of bank assets will balance the present value of liabilities, approximately insulating the bank from losses due to fluctuating interest rates.

The calculation of duration for the bank's liabilities proceeds in the same way as asset durations are calculated. For example, suppose the bank has $100 million in negotiable CDs outstanding on which it must pay its customers a 6 percent annual yield over the next two calendar years. The duration of these CDs will be determined by the distribution of cash payments made by the bank over the next two years in present-value terms. Thus:

$$\text{Duration of negotiable CDs} = \frac{\dfrac{\$6 \times 1}{(1.06)^1} + \dfrac{\$6 \times 2}{(1.06)^2} + \dfrac{\$100 \times 2}{(1.06)^2}}{\$100} = 1.943 \text{ years}$$

We would go through the same calculation for the remaining liabilities of the bank, as illustrated in Table 7–2. This bank has an average liability duration of 2.669 years—substantially *less* than the average duration of its asset portfolio, which is 3.047 years. Because the average maturity of its liabilities is shorter than the average maturity of its assets, the bank's net worth will decrease if interest rates rise and increase if interest rates fall. Clearly, management has positioned this bank in the hope that interest rates will fall in the period ahead. If there is a substantial probability interest rates will rise, management may want to hedge against damage from rising interest rates by lengthening the average maturity of its liabilities, shortening the average maturity of its assets, or employing hedging tools (such as financial futures or swaps, as discussed in the next chapter) to cover this duration gap.

In summary, the impact of changing market interest rates on a bank's net worth is indicated by entries in the following table:

If the Bank's Duration GAP Is:	And If Interest Rates:	The Bank's Net Worth Will:
Positive $\left(D_A > D_L \times \dfrac{\text{Liabilities}}{\text{Assets}} \right)$	Rise	Decrease
	Fall	Increase
Negative $\left(D_L \times \dfrac{\text{Liabilities}}{\text{Assets}} > D_A \right)$	Rise	Increase
	Fall	Decrease
Zero $\left(D_A = D_L \times \dfrac{\text{Liabilities}}{\text{Assets}} \right)$	Rise	No Change
	Fall	No Change

In the latter case, with a duration gap of zero, the bank is *immunized* against changes in the value of its net worth. Changes in the market values of assets and liabilities will simply offset each other and the net worth will remain where it is.

Of course, more aggressive managers may not like the seemingly "wimpy" strategy of **portfolio immunization** (Duration Gap = 0). They may be willing to take some chances to maximize the shareholders' position. For example,

Expected Change in Interest Rates	Management Action	Possible Outcome
Rates will rise	Reduce D_A and increase D_L (moving closer to a negative duration gap).	Net worth increases (if management's rate forecast is correct).
Rates will fall	Increase D_A and reduce D_L (moving closer to a positive duration gap).	Net worth increases (if management's rate forecast is correct).

TABLE 7–2   Calculating the Duration of a Bank's Assets and Liabilities (dollars in millions)

Composition of Assets (uses of funds)	Market Value of Assets	Interest Rate Attached to Each Category of Assets	Average Duration of Each Category of Assets (in years)	Composition of Liabilities and Equity Capital (sources of funds)	Market Value of Liabilities	Interest Rate Attached to Each Liability Category	Average Duration of Each Liability Category (in years)
U.S. Treasury Securities	$ 90	10.00%	7.490	Negotiable CDs	$100	6.00%	1.943
Municipal bonds	20	6.00	1.500	Other time deposits	125	7.20	2.750
Commercial loans	100	12.00	0.600	Subordinated notes	50	9.00	3.918
Consumer loans	50	15.00	1.200	Total liabilities	275		
				Stockholders'			
Real estate				equity capital			
loans	40	13.00	2.250		25		
			Average in Years				Average in Years
Total	$300		3.047	Total	$300		2.669

$$\text{Duration of bank assets} = \frac{\$90}{\$300} \times 7.49 + \frac{\$20}{\$300} \times 1.50 + \frac{\$100}{\$300} \times 0.60 + \frac{\$50}{\$300} \times 1.20 + \frac{\$40}{\$300} \times 2.25$$

$$= 3.047 \text{ years}$$

$$\text{Duration of bank liabilities} = \frac{\$100}{\$275} \times 1.943 + \frac{\$125}{\$275} \times 2.750 + \frac{\$50}{\$275} \times 3.918 = 2.669 \text{ years}$$

$$\frac{\text{Current duration gap}}{\text{the bank faces}} = \frac{\text{Average asset}}{\text{duration}} - \frac{\text{Average liability}}{\text{duration}} \times \frac{\text{Total liabilities}}{\text{Total assets}}$$

$$= 3.047 \text{ years} - 2.669 \text{ years} \times \frac{\$275}{\$300} = +0.60 \text{ years}$$

Management Interpretation

The positive duration gap of .60 years means that the bank's net worth will decline if interest rates rise and increase if interest rates fall. Management may be anticipating a decrease in the level of interest rates. If there is significant risk of rising market interest rates, however, the asset-liability management committee will want to use hedging tools to reduce the exposure of the bank's net worth to interest rate risk.

How much will the value of the bank's net worth change for any given change in interest rates? The appropriate formula is:

$$\frac{\text{Change in value}}{\text{of bank's net worth}} = -D_A \cdot \frac{\Delta r}{(1+r)} \cdot A - \left[-D_L \cdot \frac{\Delta r}{(1+r)} \cdot L \right]$$

where A is total assets, D_A the average duration of assets, r the initial interest rate, Δr the change in interest rates, L is total liabilities, and D_L equals the average duration of liabilities. Let's illustrate the use of this formula with an example.

Example: Suppose interest rates on both assets and liabilities *rise* from 8 percent to 10 percent. Then filling in the asset and liability figures from the table above gives:

$$\frac{\text{Change in value of}}{\text{bank's net worth}} = -3.047 \text{ years} \times \frac{(+0.02)}{(1+0.08)} \times \$300 \text{ million} - \left[-2.669 \text{ years} \times \frac{(+0.02)}{(1+0.08)} \times \$275 \text{ million} \right]$$

$$= -\$16.93 \text{ million} + \$13.59 \text{ million}$$

$$= -\$3.34 \text{ million}$$

This bank's net worth would fall by approximately $3.34 million if all interest rates—both those attached to the bank's assets and its liabilities—increase by 2 percentage points.

TABLE 7–2   Continued

Suppose interest rates *fall* by two percentage points—from 8 percent to 6 percent. What would happen to the value of the above bank's net worth? Again, substituting in the same formula:

$$\begin{array}{c}\text{Change in value} \\ \text{of bank's net worth}\end{array} = -3.047 \text{ years} \times \frac{(-0.02)}{(1+0.08)} \times \$300 \text{ million}$$

$$- \left[-2.669 \text{ years} \times \frac{(-0.02)}{(1.08)} \times \$275 \text{ million} \right]$$

$$= \$16.93 \text{ million} - \$13.59 \text{ million} = +\$3.34 \text{ million}.$$

In this instance, the value of the bank's net worth would *rise* by about \$3.34 million if all asset and liability interest rates fell by 2 percentage points.

The above formula reminds us that the impact of interest rate changes on the market value of a bank's net worth (or owners' equity) depends upon three crucial size factors:

A. The size of the duration gap $(D_A - D_L)$, with a larger duration gap indicating greater exposure of a bank to interest rate risk.
B. The size of a bank (A and L), with a larger-size bank experiencing a greater change in net worth (in dollar terms) for any given change in interest rates.
C. The size of the change in interest rates, with larger rate changes generating greater interest-rate risk exposure.

Management can *reduce* a banking firm's exposure to interest rate risk by closing up the firm's duration gap (changing D_A, D_L, or both) or by changing the relative amounts of assets and liabilities (A and L) outstanding.

The Limitations of Duration Gap Management

While duration is simple to interpret, it has several limitations. For one thing, finding assets and liabilities of the same duration that fit into a bank's portfolio is often a frustrating task. It would be much easier if the maturity of a loan or security equaled its duration; however, for financial instruments paying out gradually over time, duration is always less than calendar maturity. Only in the case of instruments like zero coupon securities, single-payment loans, and Treasury bills does the duration of a financial instrument equal its calendar maturity. The more frequently a financial instrument pays interest or pays off principal, the shorter is its duration. One useful fact is that the shorter the maturity of an instrument, the closer the match between its maturity and its duration is likely to be.

Some accounts held by a bank—for example, checkable deposits and passbook savings accounts—may have a pattern of cash flows that is not well defined, making the calculation of duration very difficult. Moreover, customer prepayments distort the expected cash flows from loans and so do customer defaults (credit risk) when expected cash flows do not happen. Moreover, duration gap models assume that a linear relationship exists between the market values (prices) of assets and liabilities and interest rates, which is not quite true. Fortunately, recent research suggests that duration balancing can still be effective, even with moderate violations of the technique's underlying assumptions.

Concept Checks

7–1. What is *duration?*

7–2. How is a bank's *duration gap* determined?

7–3. Suppose that a bank has an average asset duration of 2.5 years and an average liability duration of 3.0 years. If the bank holds total assets of $560 million and total liabilities of $467 million, does it have a significant duration gap? If interest rates rise, what will happen to the value of the bank's net worth?

7–4. Stilwater Bank and Trust Company has an average asset duration of 3.25 years and an average liability duration of 1.75 years. Its liabilities amount to $485 million, while its assets total $512 million. Suppose that interest rates were 7 percent and then rise to 8 percent. What will happen to the value of the Stilwater bank's net worth as a result of a decline in interest rates?

Summary

The hedging techniques reviewed in this and the previous chapter represent only a few examples of the many creative methods bankers have devised to deal with a volatile economy. They reflect one of the oldest principles of human behavior in a free market system: *Whenever there is a problem and a significant economic incentive to solve it, creative businessmen and women will find ways to solve that problem or to minimize its effects.*

No problem has been more consequential for banking in recent years than the volatility of interest rates. Fueled by inflation and record government deficits, interest rates have repeatedly soared to record highs, only to tumble in recessions and then once again challenge heights previously attained. Both deposit growth and loan demand have experienced much the same roller-coaster ride, exposing bankers to the continued threat of eroding profit margins.

Indeed, bankers in recent years have faced earnings pressures from *two* directions at once—volatile and unpredictable interest rates and new,

more intense competition from both old and new types of financial-service firms. Competition cannot be eliminated, but the powerful ebb and flow of interest rates can be managed more successfully. As we have seen and will see in these chapters, a wide variety of interest rate hedging techniques have been pressed into service. Among them are interest-sensitive gap management and duration, which aid bank portfolio managers in balancing the interest sensitivity and maturity of bank assets with the rate sensitivity and maturity of bank liabilities.

Of course, interest rate risk is not the only form of risk that banks will face in the future. They must also grapple with the risks of changing currency values, shifts in political regimes and regulations, and criminal activity. In fact, more than at any other time in the past half century, bankers are focusing on the pursuit of *risk management,* identifying sources of risk exposure and finding ways to control that exposure in order to survive in an ever-changing and volatile marketplace.

Key Terms in This Chapter

Duration
Duration gap

Portfolio immunization

Problems and Projects

1. Casio Merchants and Trust Bank, N.A., has a portfolio of loans and securities expected to generate cash inflows for the bank as follows:

Expected Cash Inflows of Principal and Interest Payments	Annual Period in Which Cash Receipts Are Expected
$1,385,421	Current year
746,872	Two years from today
341,555	Three years from today
62,482	Four years from today
9,871	Five years from today

Deposits and money market borrowings are expected to require the following cash outflows:

Expected Cash Outflows of Principal and Interest Payments	Annual Period during Which Cash Payments Must Be Made
$1,427,886	Current year
831,454	Two years from today
123,897	Three years from today
1,005	Four years from today
—	Five years from today

If the discount rate applicable to the above cash flows is 8 percent, what is the duration of the bank's portfolio of earning assets and of its deposits and money market borrowings? What will happen to the bank's total returns, assuming all other factors are held constant, if interest rates rise? If interest rates fall? Given the size of the duration gap you have calculated, what type of hedging should the bank engage in? Please be specific about the hedging transactions that are needed and their expected effects.

Alternative scenarios:

(1) If the discount rate applicable to Casio's cash inflows and outflows falls to 6 percent, how does the duration of its earning assets and liabilities change? How does this change affect the bank's sensitivity to interest rate movements?

(2) Suppose the appropriate discount rate climbs, instead, to 10 percent. What happens to the durations of Casio's earning assets and liabilities? How does the interest rate sensitivity of Casio's total return change as a result of this upward movement in the discount rate?

2. Given the cash inflow and outflow figures in Problem 1 for Casio Merchants and Trust Bank, N.A., suppose that interest rates began at a level of 8 percent and then suddenly rise to 9 percent. If the bank has total assets of $125 million, and total liabilities of $110 million, by how much would the value of Casio's net worth change as a result of this movement in interest rates? Suppose, on the other hand, that interest rates decline from 8 percent to 7 percent. What happens to the value of Casio's net worth in this case and by how much in dollars does it change? What is the size of the bank's duration gap?

3. Leland National Bank reports an average asset duration of 4.5 years and an average liability duration of 3.25 years. In its latest financial report, the bank recorded total assets of $1.8 billion and total liabilities of $1.5 billion. If interest rates

began at 7 percent and then suddenly climbed to 9 percent, what change will occur in the value of Leland's net worth? By how much would Leland's net worth change if, instead of rising, interest rates fell from 7 percent to 5 percent?

4. A bank holds a bond in its investment portfolio whose duration is 5.5 years. Its current market price is $950. While market interest rates are currently at 8 percent for comparable quality securities, an increase in interest rates to 10 percent is expected in the coming weeks. What change (in percentage terms) will this bond's price experience if market interest rates change as anticipated?

5. A bank's dollar-weighted asset duration is six years. Its total liabilities amount to $750 million, while its assets total $900 million. What is the dollar-weighted duration of the bank's liability portfolio if the bank has a zero-duration gap?

6. Commerce National Bank holds assets and liabilities whose average duration and dollar amount are as shown below:

Asset and Liability Items	Average Duration	Dollar Amount
Investment-grade bonds	8.0 years	$ 60 million
Commercial loans	3.6	320
Consumer loans	4.5	140
Deposits	1.1	490
Nondeposit borrowings	0.1	20

What is the dollar-weighted duration of the bank's asset portfolio and liability portfolio? What is the duration gap?

7. A government bond currently carries a yield to maturity of 12 percent and a market price of $940. If the bond promises to pay $100 in interest annually for five years, can you calculate its current duration?

8. Dewey National Bank holds $15 million in government bonds having a duration of six years. If interest rates suddenly rise from 6 percent to 7 percent, what percentage change should occur in the bonds' market price?

Selected References

For useful descriptions of measuring and interpreting duration in banking, see these studies:

1. Bierwag, G. O., and George G. Kaufman. "Duration Gap for Financial Institutions." *Financial Analysts Journal,* March/April 1985, pp. 68–71.
2. Shaffer, Sherrill. "Interest Rate Risk: What's a Bank to Do?" *Business Review,* Federal Reserve Bank of Philadelphia, May/June 1991, pp. 17–27.
3. Wright, David M., and James V. Houpt. "An Analysis of Commercial Bank Exposure to Interest-Rate Risk." *Federal Reserve Bulletin,* February 1996, pp. 115–28.
4. Cherin, Antony C., and Robert C. Hanson. "Consistent Treatment of Interest Payments in Immunization Examples." *Financial Practice and Education,* Spring/Summer, 1997, pp. 122–26.

8 FINANCIAL FUTURES, OPTIONS, SWAPS, AND OTHER ASSET-LIABILITY MANAGEMENT TECHNIQUES

Learning and Management Decision Objectives

The purpose of this chapter is to explore the ways that financial futures contracts, options, swaps, and other asset-liability management techniques can be used to reduce a bank's potential exposure to loss due to changing interest rates and to examine the factors that bank managers should consider in deciding which of these tools to use.

Introduction

The preceding two chapters introduced one of the most important topics in bank management today, *asset-liability management.* As we saw there, the techniques and tools of asset-liability management are designed to control a bank's risk exposure, particularly the threat of significant losses due to changes in interest rates. Bank asset-liability managers are especially concerned about stabilizing their *margin*—the *spread* between their institution's interest revenues and interest expenses—and about protecting a bank's *net worth*—the value of the stockholders' investment in the bank. This chapter explores several of the most widely used tools for dealing with bank exposure to interest rate risk, including financial futures and option contracts, interest rate swaps, loan options, and interest rate insurance.[1]

---

[1]Portions of this chapter are based on the author's article in *The Canadian Banker* [10] and are used with the permission of the publisher.

Financial Futures Contracts: Promises of Future Security Trades at a Set Price

In Chapters 6 and 7, we explored the nature of *gaps* between a bank's assets and liabilities that are exposed to interest rate risk. For example, we developed the concept of an interest-sensitive gap:

$$\begin{matrix} \text{Interest-sensitive} \\ \text{gap} \end{matrix} = \begin{matrix} \text{Interest-sensitive} \\ \text{assets} \end{matrix} - \begin{matrix} \text{Interest-sensitive} \\ \text{liabilities} \end{matrix} \qquad (1)$$

where interest-sensitive assets and liabilities are those items on a bank's balance sheet that mature or whose interest rates can be changed, up or down, during a given interval of time. As we saw earlier, a bank that is *asset sensitive* (whose interest-sensitive assets exceed its interest-sensitive liabilities) will suffer a decline in its net interest margin if market interest rates fall. A bank that is *liability sensitive* (whose interest-sensitive liabilities are greater than its interest-sensitive assets) will experience a decrease in its net interest margin when interest rates rise.

The preceding chapter developed one other measure of the difference between a bank's risk-exposed assets and liabilities—the *duration gap,* which measures the difference in weighted-average maturity between a bank's assets and its liabilities. Specifically:

$$\begin{matrix} \text{Duration gap} = \begin{matrix} \text{Average} \\ \text{(dollar-weighted)} \\ \text{duration of} \\ \text{assets} \end{matrix} - \begin{matrix} \text{Average} \\ \text{(dollar-weighted)} \\ \text{duration of} \\ \text{liabilities} \end{matrix} \\ \\ \times \dfrac{\text{Total liabilities}}{\text{Total assets}} \end{matrix} \qquad (2)$$

A bank whose asset portfolio has an average duration longer than the average duration of its liabilities (multiplied by the ratio of its total liabilities to its total assets) has a positive duration gap. A rise in market interest rates will cause the value of the bank's assets to decline faster than its liabilities, reducing the institution's net worth. On the other hand, if a bank has a negative duration gap, falling interest rates will cause the value of its liabilities to rise faster than the value of its asset portfolio; its net worth will decline, lowering the value of the stockholders' investment. One of the most popular methods of neutralizing these gap risks is to buy and sell **financial futures** contracts.

Nature of Financial Futures.   A financial futures contract is an agreement between a buyer and a seller reached today that calls for the delivery of a particular security in exchange for cash at some future date. The market value of a futures contract changes daily as the market price of the security to be exchanged moves over time. As a result, futures contracts are "marked to market" each day to reflect the current value of the assets subject to eventual delivery under each futures contract, and a cash payment may have to be made (usually to a broker) by one or the other party to the contract in order to protect against possible loss.

Purpose of Financial Futures Trading.   The financial futures markets are designed to shift the risk of interest rate fluctuations from risk-averse investors, such as commercial banks, to speculators willing to accept and possibly profit from such risks. Futures contracts are traded on organized exchanges (such as the Chicago Board of Trade, the Chicago Mercantile Exchange, or the London Futures Exchange), where floor brokers execute orders received from the public to buy or sell these contracts at the best prices available. When a bank contacts an exchange broker and offers to *sell* futures contracts (i.e., the bank wishes to "go short" in futures), this means it is *promising to deliver securities* of a certain kind and quality to the buyer of those contracts on a stipulated date at a predetermined price. Conversely, a bank may enter the futures market as a *buyer* of futures contracts (i.e., the bank chooses to "go long" in futures), *agreeing to accept delivery* of the particular securities named in each contract or to pay cash to the exchange clearinghouse the day the contracts mature, based on their price at that time.

Futures contracts are also traded over the counter, without the involvement of an exchange, which is often less costly for traders. However, over-the-counter futures trades generally are more risky because the exchange guarantees the settlement of each contract even if one or the other party to the contract defaults. Moreover, liquidity risk is usually less for exchange-traded futures, options, and other financial instruments because of the presence of substantial numbers of speculators and specialists on the exchanges always ready to make a market for the instruments traded there.

The most popular financial futures contracts traded by banks today include the following:

1. The U.S. *Treasury bond futures contract,* which calls for the delivery of a $100,000-denomination bond (measured at its par value) carrying a minimum maturity of 15 years and a promised (coupon) rate of return of 8 percent. Bonds whose coupon rates lie above or below the 8 percent standard are deliverable to the buyer at a premium or discount from their par value. Actually the deliverer of these contracts can deliver any U.S. Treasury bonds from 15-year maturities upward based on a prespecified conversion factor. T-bond futures contracts have maturities extending out to almost two years and are deliverable in March, June, September, and December.

2. The most popular U.S. *Treasury bill futures contract* calls for the future delivery of 90-day T-bills in denominations of $1 million each. Ninety-day T-bill contracts mature in March, June, September, and December of each year.

3. Futures contracts on *three-month Eurodollar time deposits* are traded in million-dollar units at exchanges in Chicago, London, Tokyo, Singapore, and elsewhere around the globe, offering banks and other investors the opportunity to hedge against interest rate changes in bank deposits, money market borrowings, and commercial loans. Prices of these contracts are quoted as an index equal to 100 minus the current London Interbank Offer Rate (LIBOR) on short-term deposits set daily based on a survey of leading international banks.

4. The 30-day *Federal funds futures contracts* are traded at the Chicago Board of Trade in units of $5 million with an index price equal to 100 less the prevailing Federal funds interest rate. These contracts are settled in cash based on the monthly average of the daily interest rate quoted by Federal funds brokers.

5. The *one-month LIBOR futures contract* traded in $3 million units and quoted as an index price of 100 less the one-month Eurodollar time deposit interest rate. These contracts are settled in cash rather than through the actual delivery of Eurodeposits.

Other regularly traded interest rate futures contracts include a $100,000 denomination Treasury notes contract and two-year and five-year T-note contracts (with $100,000 and $500,000 denominations respectively), and a Municipal Bond Index contract—all currently traded on the Chicago Board of Trade (CBT). Added to these are several foreign-related contracts on non-U.S. financial instruments, including Euroyen deposits, British sterling accounts, the long-gilt British bond, Euromark, EuroSwiss, and EuroLira deposits, Canadian, German, French, and Italian government bonds, and Canadian bankers' acceptances.

Today's selling price on a futures contract presumably reflects what investors in the market expect cash prices to be on the day delivery of the securities called for by the contract must be made. A futures hedge against interest rate changes generally requires a bank to take an *opposite* position in the futures market from its current position in the cash (immediate delivery) market. Thus, a bank planning to buy bonds ("go long") in the cash market today may try to protect the bonds' value by selling bond contracts ("go short") in the futures market. Then if bond prices fall in the cash market there will be an offsetting profit in the futures market, minimizing the loss due to changing interest rates. While banks make heavy use today of financial futures in their security dealer operations and in bond portfolio management, futures contracts can also be used to protect returns and costs on loans, deposits, and money market borrowings.

The Short Hedge in Futures

For example, suppose interest rates are expected to *rise,* boosting the cost of selling deposits or the cost of a bank's borrowings in the money market and lowering the value of any bonds or fixed-rate loans that the bank holds or expects to buy. In this instance a *short hedge* in financial futures can be used. The bank's asset-liability manager will *sell* contracts calling for the future delivery of securities on a futures exchange around the time new deposit borrowings will occur, when a fixed-rate loan is made, or when bonds are added to the bank's portfolio. Later, as borrowings and loans approach maturity or securities are sold and before the first futures contract matures, a like amount of futures contracts will be *purchased* on a futures exchange. If market interest rates have risen significantly, the interest cost of bank borrowings will increase and the value of any fixed-rate loans and securities held by the bank will decline. However, those losses will be approximately offset by a price gain on the futures contracts. Moreover, if the bank makes an offsetting sale and purchase of the *same* futures contracts on a futures exchange, it then has no obligation either to deliver or to take delivery of the securities named in the contracts. The clearinghouse that keeps records for each futures exchange will simply cancel out the two offsetting transactions. (See the box called "Bank Management in Action—Hedging a Bank's Deposit Costs with Financial Futures" for an example of how banks can protect themselves from rising deposit rates using futures contracts.)

The Long Hedge in Futures

While banks are generally more concerned about the potentially damaging effects of *rising* interest rates, there are times when a bank wishes to hedge itself against *falling* interest rates. Usually this occurs when the bank is expecting a *cash inflow* in the near future. For example, suppose management expects to receive a sizable inflow of deposits a few weeks or months from today but forecasts lower interest rates by that time. This sounds favorable from a cost-of-funds point of view, but it is *not* favorable for the future growth of bank revenues and net income. If management takes no action and the forecast turns out to be true, the bank will suffer an *opportunity loss* (i.e., reduced potential earnings) because those expected deposits will have to be invested in loans and securities bearing lower yields. To offset this opportunity loss, management can use a *long hedge:* Futures contracts can be purchased today and then sold in like amount at approximately the same time deposits come flowing in. The result will be a profit on the futures contracts if interest rates do decline, because those contracts will rise in value.

Using Long and Short Hedges to Protect Bank Income and Value.   Table 8–1 provides examples of other short and long hedges using financial futures. In general, the three most typical interest rate hedging problems faced by banks are (1) protecting the value of their securities and fixed-rate loans from losses due to rising interest rates; (2) avoiding a rise in bank borrowing costs; (3) avoiding a fall in the interest rates expected from bank loans and security holdings. In most cases, the appropriate hedging strategy using financial futures is as follows:

Avoiding higher borrowing costs and declining asset values.	→	Use a short (or selling) hedge: sell futures and then cancel with a subsequent purchase of similar futures contracts.
Avoiding lower than expected yields from loans and security investments.	→	Use a long (or buying) hedge: buy futures and then cancel with a subsequent sale of similar contracts.

Where the bank faces a *positive interest-sensitive gap* (interest-sensitive assets > interest-sensitive liabilities), it can protect against loss due to falling interest rates by covering the gap with a *long hedge* (buy and then sell futures) of approximately the same dollar amount as the gap. On the other hand, if the bank is confronted with a *negative interest-sensitive gap* (interest-sensitive liabilities > interest-sensitive assets), it can avoid unacceptable losses from rising interest rates by covering with a *short hedge* (sell and then buy futures) approximately matching the amount of the gap.

TABLE 8–1   Examples of Popular Financial Futures Transactions

The Short, or Selling, Hedge to Protect a Bank against Rising Interest Rates

Fearing *rising* interest rates over the next several months, which will lower the value of its bonds, the management of a bank takes the following steps:

Today—contracts are *sold* through a futures exchange to another investor, with the bank promising to deliver a specific dollar amount of securities (such as Treasury bills) at a set price six months from today.

Six Months in the Future—contracts in the same denominations are *purchased* through the same futures exchange, according to which the bank promises to take delivery of the same or similar securities at a future date at a set price.

Results—the two contracts are canceled out by the futures exchange clearinghouse ("zero out"), so the bank no longer has a commitment to sell or take delivery of securities.

However, if interest rates rise over the life of the first futures contracts that are sold, security prices will fall. When the bank then purchases future contracts at the end of the six-month period, they will be obtainable for a lower price than when it sold the same futures contracts six months earlier. Therefore, a *profit* will be made on futures trading, which will offset some or all of the *loss* in the value of any bonds still held by the bank.

The Long, or Buying, Hedge to Protect a Bank against Falling Interest Rates

The bank's economist has just predicted *lower* interest rates over the next six months, and management fears a decline in bank profits as interest rates on loans fall relative to deposit rates and other operating costs. Moreover, incoming funds must be invested in lower-yielding assets, thus incurring an opportunity loss for the bank. Management elects to do the following:

Today—contracts are *purchased* through a futures exchange, committing the bank to take delivery of a specific amount of securities (such as Treasury bills) at a set price six months from today.

Six Months in the Future—contracts are *sold* on the same futures exchange, committing the bank to deliver the same amount of securities at a set price on the same future date.

Results—the two contracts are canceled by the clearinghouse, so the bank is not obligated to either make or take delivery of the securities involved.

However, if interest rates do fall while the futures contracts are in force, security prices must rise. Therefore, the bank will be able to sell futures contracts for a higher price than it paid for them six months earlier. The resulting *profit* from trading in financial futures will offset some or all of the *loss* in revenue due to lower interest rates on loans.

Active trading in futures contracts for a wide variety of securities—ranging from U.S. government bills to long-term government and municipal bonds, corporate stock, and bank CDs—now takes place on several exchanges worldwide. One distinct advantage of this method of hedging interest rates is that only a *fraction* of the value of a futures contract must be pledged as collateral. Moreover, brokers' commissions for trading futures are relatively low (e.g., a "round-trip" consisting of a buy and a sell transaction using T-bill futures of $1 million may result in commissions as low as $60). Thus, traders of financial futures can hedge large amounts of deposits, money market borrowings, loans, and securities with only a small outlay of cash.

Basis Risk.   However, there are some significant limitations to financial futures as interest rate hedging devices, among them a special form of risk known as *basis risk.*

Bank Management in Action

Hedging a Bank's Deposit Costs with Financial Futures

The Problem

Bank management is expecting a *rise* in interest rates over the next three months. Currently deposits can be sold to customers at a promised interest rate of 10 percent. However, management is fearful that deposit interest rates may rise at least one-half of a percentage point (50 basis points) in the next three months, eroding the bank's profit margin of loan revenues over deposit costs.

For example, if the bank needed to raise $100 million from sales of deposits over the next 90 days, its marginal cost of issuing the new deposits at a 10 percent annual rate would be as follows:

$$\begin{array}{c} \text{Amount of new} \\ \text{deposits to be} \\ \text{issued} \end{array} \times \begin{array}{c} \text{Annual} \\ \text{interest rate} \end{array} \times \frac{\text{Maturity of deposit in days}}{360} = \begin{array}{c} \text{Marginal} \\ \text{deposit interest} \\ \text{cost} \end{array}$$

$$\$100 \text{ million} \times 0.10 \times 90 \div 360 = \$2{,}500{,}000$$

However, if deposit interest rates climb to 10.50 percent, the marginal deposit cost becomes:

$$\$100 \text{ million} \times 0.1050 \times 90 \div 360 = \$2{,}625{,}000$$

$$\begin{array}{c} \text{Amount of added fund-raising} \\ \text{costs for the bank (and potential} \\ \text{loss in profit)} \end{array} = \$2{,}625{,}000 - \$2{,}500{,}000 = \$125{,}000$$

An Offsetting Financial Futures Transaction

To counteract the potential profit loss of $125,000, bank management might select the following financial futures transaction:

Today: Sell 100 90-day T-bill futures contracts priced today at 8.88 percent for a total market value of $91,125,000

Within next 90 days: Buy 100 90-day T-bill futures contracts priced on day of purchase at 9 percent for a total value of $91,000,000

Profit on the completion of sale and purchase of futures $125,000

Result: Higher deposit cost has been offset by a gain in futures.

Basis is the difference in interest rates or prices between the cash (immediate-delivery) market and the futures (postponed-delivery) market. Thus

$$\text{Basis} = \text{Cash-market price (or interest rate)} \tag{3}$$
$$- \text{Futures market price (or interest rate)}$$

when both are measured at the same moment in time. For example, suppose 10-year U.S. government bonds are selling today in the cash market for \$95 per \$100 bond while futures contracts on the same bonds calling for delivery in six months are trading today at a price of \$87. Then the current basis must be:

$$\$95 - \$87 = \$8 \text{ per contract}$$

If the basis changes between the opening and closing of a futures position, the result can be a significant loss, which subtracts from any gains a trader might make in the cash market. Fortunately, basis risk is usually less than interest rate risk in the cash market, so hedging reduces (but usually does not completely eliminate) overall risk exposure. Another way to express this point is with the following equation:

$$
\begin{array}{l}
\text{Realized return to a} \\
\text{bank from a combined} \\
\text{cash and futures market} \\
\text{trading operation}
\end{array}
=
\begin{array}{l}
\text{Return} \\
\text{earned in} \\
\text{the cash} \\
\text{market}
\end{array}
\begin{array}{l}
\text{Profit or loss} \\
\pm \text{ from futures} \\
\text{trading}
\end{array}
\tag{4}
$$

$$
-
\begin{array}{l}
\text{Closing basis} \\
\text{between the} \\
\text{cash and} \\
\text{futures markets}
\end{array}
-
\begin{array}{l}
\text{Opening basis} \\
\text{between the} \\
\text{cash and} \\
\text{futures markets}
\end{array}
$$

With an effective hedge, the positive or negative returns earned in the cash market will be approximately offset by the profit or loss from futures trading. The real risk the bank faces from hedging with futures stems from the last two terms in Equation 4—the movement in basis that may occur over the life of a futures contract because cash and futures prices are not perfectly synchronized with each other. Futures market prices and interest rates may change more or less than cash-market prices or rates, resulting in gains or losses for the trader.

The sensitivity of the market price of a financial futures contract depends, in part, upon the duration of the security to be delivered under the futures contract. (See Chapters 7 and 10 for a discussion of calculating duration for individual securities.) That is,

$$
\frac{\text{Change in futures price}}{\text{Initial futures price}} = -
\begin{bmatrix}
\text{Duration of the} \\
\text{underlying security} \\
\text{named in the} \\
\text{futures contract}
\end{bmatrix}
\tag{5}
$$

$$
\times
\begin{bmatrix}
\dfrac{\text{Change expected in}}{\text{interest rates}} \\[4pt]
\dfrac{}{1+ \text{Original}} \\
\text{interest rate}
\end{bmatrix}
$$

If we rewrite this equation slightly we get an expression for the gain or loss to a bank from the use of a financial futures contract:

$$
\begin{bmatrix} \text{Positive or negative} \\ \text{change in futures} \\ \text{contract value} \end{bmatrix} = - \begin{bmatrix} \text{Duration of the} \\ \text{underlying security} \\ \text{named in the} \\ \text{futures contract(s)} \end{bmatrix} \times \begin{bmatrix} \text{Initial} \\ \text{futures} \\ \text{price} \end{bmatrix} \quad (6)
$$

$$
\times \begin{bmatrix} \dfrac{\text{Change expected in}}{\text{interest rates}} \\ \dfrac{}{1 + \text{Original}} \\ \text{interest rate} \end{bmatrix}
$$

The negative sign in the above equation clearly shows that when interest rates rise, the market value (price) of futures contracts must fall. For example, suppose a $100,000 par value Treasury bond futures contract is traded at a price of $99,700 initially but then interest rates on T-bonds increase a full percentage point from 7 to 8 percent. If the T-bond has a duration of nine years, then the change in the value of the T-bond futures contracts would be:

$$
\begin{matrix} \text{Change in} \\ \text{market value of} \\ \text{futures contracts} \end{matrix} = -9 \text{ years} \times \$99,700 \times \frac{+0.01}{1 + 0.07} = -\$8,385.98
$$

In this case the one percentage point rise in interest rates lowered the price of a $100,000 futures contract for Treasury bonds by almost $8,386.

Exhibit 8–1 summarizes how trading in financial futures contracts can help protect a bank against loss due to interest rate risk. The *long hedge* in financial futures consists of first *buying* futures contracts (at price F_0) and, then, if interest rates fall, *selling* comparable futures contracts (in which case the futures price moves toward F_t). The decline in interest rates will generate a gross profit of $F_t - F_0 > 0$, less, of course, any taxes or broker commissions that have to be paid to carry out the long-hedge transaction. In contrast, the *short hedge* in futures consists of first *selling* futures contracts (at price F_0) and, then, if interest rates rise, *buying* comparable futures contracts (whose price may move to F_n). The rise in interest rates will generate a profit of $F_0 - F_n > 0$, net of any tax obligations created or traders' commissions. These profitable trades can be used to help offset any losses resulting from a decline in the market value of bank assets or a decline in a bank's net worth or in its net interest income due to adverse changes in market interest rates.

Number of Contracts Needed.   How many futures contracts does a bank need to cover a given size risk exposure? Let's suppose the number of futures contracts needed is designated by N and the price of each futures contract is P. Suppose that the bank has an average asset duration represented by D_{assets} and the average duration of the bank's liabilities is labeled $D_{liabilities}$. (See Chapter 7 for a description of how to calculate the average duration of a bank's assets and liabilities.) Then the number of futures contracts needed to fully hedge the bank's overall interest rate risk exposure and protect the bank's net worth (owners' equity) depends upon:

EXHIBIT 8–1

Payoff Diagrams for Financial Futures Contracts

The Long Hedge in Financial Futures
(Initial transaction: Buy futures in
expectation of falling interest rates;
then sell comparable contracts)

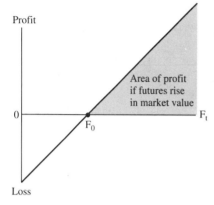

Purpose: Protect against falling yields on bank
assets (such as current loans and future loans and
investments in securities).

The Short Hedge in Financial Futures
(Initial transaction: Sell futures in
expectation of rising interest rates;
then buy comparable contracts)

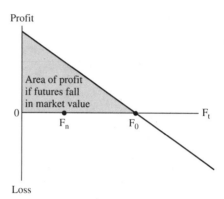

Purpose: Protect against rising deposit and
other borrowing costs and falling market
values of bank assets (such as bank investments).

$$\text{Number of futures contracts needed} = \frac{(D_{assets} - \dfrac{\text{Total liabilitiy}}{\text{Total assets}} \times D_{liabilities}) \times \text{Total assets}}{\text{Duration of the underlying security named in the futures contract} \times \text{Price of the futures contract}} \quad (7)$$

For example, suppose a bank has an average asset duration of four years, an average liability duration of two years, total assets of $500 million, and total liabilities of $460 million. Suppose, too, that the bank plans to trade in Treasury bond futures contracts. The T-bonds named in the futures contracts have a duration of nine years and the T-bonds' current price is $99,700 per $100,000 contract. Then the bank would need about

$$\text{Number of futures contracts needed} = \frac{(\text{four years} - \dfrac{\$460 \text{ million}}{\$500 \text{ million}} \times \text{two years}) \times \$500 \text{ Million}}{\text{nine years} \times \$99,700}$$

$$\approx 1,200 \text{ contracts.}$$

We note that this bank has a positive duration gap of +2.16 years (or 4 years − $460/$500 million × 2 years), indicating its assets have a longer average maturity than its liabilities. Then if interest rates rise, its assets will decline in value by more than its liabilities, reducing the stockholder's investment in the bank (net worth). To protect against an interest rate *rise,* the bank would probably want to adopt a *short hedge* in T-bond futures contracts, *selling* about 1,200 of these contracts initially. An interest rate *decline,* on the other hand, usually would call for a *long hedge, purchasing* contracts on T-bonds or other securities.

Regulations and Accounting Rules for Bank Futures Trading.   All three federal banking agencies in the United States require that American banks put in writing their guidelines for hedging using financial futures, set up limits as to the type and volume of futures trading, and fully disclose any large positions in financial futures that could significantly affect each bank's risk exposure to its stockholders. Under U.S. regulations any gains or losses from futures trading must be "coincidental" to the main purpose of this trading, which is to hedge against interest rate risk rather than to speculate in futures or security prices.

If the bank's hedging in futures can be linked to a particular asset or liability position, then it can defer recognition of gains or losses from futures trading until that asset or liability position is closed out. However, if the bank's futures hedge cannot be directly linked to any particular asset or liability position, then the bank must take immediate recognition of any losses or gains it experiences from futures trading.

More recently, the Financial Accounting Standards Board (FASB) has brought forward a proposed new rule requiring banks and other companies to report the fair market value of any futures contracts and other derivative instruments on their books. The proposed FASB rule asks all publicly traded corporations to adjust their earnings in order to capture changes in the market values of their derivative positions. Scheduled to take effect for fiscal years starting after December 15, 1998, the new derivatives regulation could have a significant impact on the earnings of banks by compelling them to reveal the potential profit or loss from their current derivatives holdings. The gain or loss of a derivative instrument can be recorded in the same period as the asset or liability being hedged. Opponents of this proposed rule (including the Federal Reserve) are concerned about possible increases in the volatility of bank earnings and about the potential for discouraging banks' hedging operations to reduce their risk exposure. Thus far, however, FASB seems determined to stick by its new derivatives ruling.

Interest Rate Options

The 1970s and 1980s ushered in still another hedging device that gives "one-sided" insurance against interest rate risk. The **interest rate option** grants a holder of securities the right to either (1) place (put) those instruments with another investor at a prespecified exercise price before the option expires or (2) take delivery of securities (call) from another investor at a prespecified price before the option's expiration date. In the put option, the option writer must stand ready to accept delivery of securities from the option buyer if the latter requests. In the call option, the option writer must stand ready

Concept Checks

8–1. What are *financial futures* contracts?

8–2. How can financial futures help banks deal with interest rate risk?

8–3. What is a long hedge in financial futures? A short hedge?

8–4. What financial futures transactions would most likely be used in a period of rising interest rates? Falling interest rates?

8–5. A futures contract calling for delivery of Treasury bills in 90 days is currently selling at an interest yield of 4 percent, while yields on Treasury bills available for immediate delivery currently stand at 4.60 percent. What is the *basis* for the T-bill futures contracts?

8–6. Suppose a bank wishes to sell $150 million in new deposits next month. Interest rates today on comparable deposits stand at 8 percent, but are expected to rise to 8.25 percent next month. Concerned about the possible rise in borrowing costs, management wishes to use a futures contract. What type of contract would you recommend? If the bank does not cover the interest rate risk involved, how much in lost potential profits could the bank experience?

8–7. What kind of futures hedge would be appropriate in each of the following situations:

a. A bank fears that rising deposit interest rates will result in losses on fixed-rate loans?

b. A bank holds a large block of floating-rate loans and market interest rates are falling?

c. A projected rise in market rates of interest threatens the value of the bank's bond portfolio?

to deliver securities to the option buyer upon request. The fee that the buyer must pay for the privilege of being able to put securities to, or call securities away from, the option writer is known as the *option premium.*

How do options differ from financial futures contracts? Unlike futures contracts, options do *not* obligate any party to deliver securities. They grant the *right* to deliver or take delivery, not the obligation to do so. The option buyer can (1) exercise the option, (2) sell the option to another buyer, or (3) simply allow the option to expire. Most options written today are traded on an *options exchange* (such as the Chicago Board of Trade or the Chicago Mercantile Exchange). Exchange-traded options are standardized to make it easier to offset an existing position in options by establishing a counter-position (such as by balancing a put option with a call option for the same securities). Exchange trading of stock options began in the United States in 1973, while options trading for U.S. government securities was launched in 1982 with the introduction of put and call options on selected long-term Treasury bonds and T-bond futures.

TABLE 8–2   Put Options to Offset Rising Interest Rates

Put Option

Buyer receives from an option writer the right to sell and deliver securities, loans, or futures contracts to the writer at an agreed-upon *strike price* up to a specified date in return for paying a fee (*premium*) to the option writer. If interest rates *rise,* the market value of the optioned securities, loans, or futures contracts will fall. Exercise of the put results in a gain for the buyer, because he or she can now purchase the optioned securities, loans, or contracts at a lower market price and deliver them to the option writer at the higher strike price. Commissions and any resulting tax liability will reduce the size of the buyer's gain.

Example of a Put Option Transaction: A bank plans to issue $150 million in new 180-day interest-bearing deposits (CDs) at the end of the week but is concerned that CD rates in the market, which now stand at 6.5 percent (annual yield), will rise to 7 percent. An increase in deposit interest rates of this magnitude will result in an additional $375,000 in interest costs on the $150 million in new CDs, possibly eroding any potential bank profits from lending and investing the funds provided by issuing the CDs. In order to reduce the potential loss from these higher borrowing costs the bank's asset-liability manager contacts a dealer willing to write a put option on Eurodollar deposit futures contracts at a strike price of $960,000 (on a $1 million contract) for a fee (premium) of $5,000. If interest rates rise as predicted, the market value of the Eurodollar futures will fall below 96, perhaps to 94 (or $940,000 on a $1 million contract). If the market price of the futures contracts drops far enough, the put option will be exercised because it is now "in the money" since the security named in the put option has fallen in value below its strike price. The bank's asset-liability manager can buy the now cheaper Eurodollar contracts in the market and deliver them at the option's higher strike price.

The bank's before-tax profit on this put option transaction could be found from:

$$\begin{array}{ccccccc} \text{Before-tax} & & \text{Option's} & & \text{Security} & & \\ \text{profit on put} & = & \text{strike} & - & \text{market} & - & \text{Option premium} \\ \text{option} & & \text{price} & & \text{price} & & \end{array} \qquad (8)$$

The before-tax profit on each million-dollar Eurodollar futures contracts would be:

$$\begin{array}{l} \text{Before-tax} \\ \text{profit on put} \end{array} = \$960,000 - \$940,000 - \$5,000 = \$15,000 \text{ per contract.}$$

The $15,000 option profit per futures contract will at least partially offset the higher borrowing costs should interest rates rise. If interest rates don't rise, the option will likely remain "out of the money" and the bank will lose money equal to the option premium. However, if interest rates do not rise, the bank will not face higher borrowing costs, and therefore has no need of the option. Put options can also be used to protect the value of bank-held bonds and loans against rising interest rates.

As initiated by the Chicago Board Options Exchange, for example, the buyer of an exchange-traded T-bond option is granted the right to purchase or sell designated Treasury bonds or bond futures at the exercise (strike) price until the option expires. If interest rates rise, *put* (sell) options are most likely to be exercised. If interest rates fall, holders of *call* (buy) options will be more inclined to exercise their option right and demand delivery of bonds or bond futures at the agreed-upon *strike price*. The reason is that falling interest rates can push bond prices higher than the strike price specified in the option contract. (See Tables 8–2 and 8–3.)

Exchange-traded options are generally set to expire in March, June, September, or December to conform with most futures contracts. The exchange's clearinghouse normally

---

TABLE 8–3   Call Options to Offset Falling Interest Rates

Call Option

Buyer receives the right from an option writer to buy and take delivery of securities, loans, or futures contracts from the writer at a mutually agreeable *strike price* on or before a specific expiration date in return for paying a *premium* to the writer. If interest rates *fall,* the market value of the optioned securities, loans, or contracts must rise. Exercising the call option gives the buyer a gain, because he or she will acquire securities, loans, or contracts whose value exceeds the strike price that the buyer must pay. Of course, commissions and taxes will reduce the size of the buyer's gain.

Example of a Call Option Transaction: A bank plans to purchase $50 million in Treasury bonds in a few days and hopes to earn an interest return of 8 percent. The bank's investment officer fears a drop in market interest rates before she is ready to buy, so she asks a security dealer to write a call option on Treasury bonds at a strike price of $95,000 for each $100,000 bond. The investment officer had to pay the dealer a premium of $500 to write this call option. If market interest rates fall as predicted, the T-bonds' market price may climb up to $97,000 per $100,000 bond, permitting the investment officer to demand delivery of the bonds at the cheaper price of $95,000. The call option would then be "in the money" because the securities' market price is above the option's strike price of $95,000.

What profit could the bank earn from this call option transaction? On a before-tax basis the profit formula for a call option is:

$$\text{Before-tax profit on call option} = \text{Security market price} - \text{Strike price} - \text{option premium} \tag{9}$$

The before-tax profit on each $100,000 bond would be:

$$\text{Before-tax profit on call} = \$97,000 - \$95,000 - \$500 = \$1,500 \text{ per bond.}$$

The projected profit per bond will at least partially offset any loss in interest return experienced on the bonds traded in the cash market if interest rates fall. If interest rates rise instead of fall, the option would likely have dropped "out of the money" as Treasury bond prices fell below the strike price. In this case the T-bond option would likely expire unused and the bank would suffer a loss equal to the option premium. However, the rise in interest rates would permit the bank to come closer to achieving its desired interest return on any newly purchased T-bonds. A call option could also be used to help combat falling interest returns on loans.

---

guarantees fulfillment of any option agreements traded on that exchange just as the exchange also stands behind any exchange-traded futures contracts. Interest rate options offer the buyer added leverage—control of large amounts of financial capital with a limited investment and limited risk. The maximum loss to the option buyer is the *premium* paid to acquire the option.

The most popular options contracts used by banks today are:

1. *U.S. Treasury bill futures options,* which call for the delivery of three-month T-bill futures contracts on or before a specific expiration date at a prespecified price. The delivery or strike price is expressed in terms of a price index equal to 100 less the T-bill futures' discount rate.

2. *Eurodollar futures options* give their buyer the right to receive Eurodollar deposit futures contracts denominated in million-dollar units, expiring on the last day for trading the Eurodollar deposit futures contract named in the option. These options are settled in cash, not by the actual delivery of Eurodollar futures or Eurodeposits, and may stretch out as long as 18 months.

3. U.S. *Treasury bond options* grant the option buyer the right to deliver or accept delivery of T-bond futures contracts in units of $100,000, which are based on U.S. Treasury bonds with maturities of at least 15 years.

4. *LIBOR futures options,* which are settled in cash the day the underlying one-month futures contract on Eurodeposits reaches its maturity.

Other regularly traded options include the Municipal Bond Index option contract (traded on the Chicago Board of Trade [CBT] exchange), one-year and two-year mid-curve Eurodollar options (both traded on the Chicago Mercantile Exchange [CME]), and options on Euromarks, the British long-gilt bond, and German government bond options (all three of the latter contracts currently traded on the London International Financial Futures Exchange [LIFFE]).

Most options in banking are used by money center banks. They appear to be directed at two principal uses:

1. *Protection of the bond portfolio* through the use of *put* options to insulate the bank against falling bond prices (rising interest rates); however, there is no delivery obligation under an option contract, so the bank can benefit from keeping its bonds if interest rates fall and bond prices rise.

2. *Hedging against positive or negative gaps between interest-sensitive assets and interest-sensitive liabilities;* for example, put options can be used to offset losses from a negative gap (interest-sensitive liabilities > interest-sensitive assets) when interest rates rise, while call options can be used to offset a positive gap (interest-sensitive assets > interest-sensitive liabilities) when interest rates fall.

Banks can both buy and sell (write) options, but are usually *buyers* of puts and calls rather than sellers (writers) of these instruments. The reason is the much greater risk faced by option writers compared to that faced by option buyers; an option seller's potential profit is limited to the premium charged the buyer, but the potential loss if interest rates move against the seller is much greater. Regulations in the United States prohibit banks from writing put and call options in some high-risk areas and generally require any options purchased to be directly linked to specific risk exposures faced by a bank.

Exhibits 8–2 and 8–3 provide us with a convenient summary of how banks can profit or at least protect their current position through the careful use of options. A bank concerned about possible losses in net earnings due to *falling* interest rates, for example, may elect to purchase a *call* option from an option writer (such as a securities dealer). The call option grants the bank the right to demand delivery of securities or futures contracts at price S (as shown in the left panel of Exhibit 8–2). If interest rates do fall, the securities or futures contracts will rise in price toward F_t, opening up the opportunity for profit equal to $F_t - S$ (less the premium the bank must pay to buy the call option and any taxes that may be owed). Conversely, as the right panel in Exhibit 8–2 suggests, an expectation of *rising* interest rates may lead bank management to purchase a *put* option on securities or futures contracts. The upward movement in interest rates will perhaps be large enough to send market prices down to F_n, below strike price S. The bank will purchase the securities or futures contracts mentioned in the put option at current price F_n and deliver them to the writer of the option at price S, pocketing the difference $S - F_n$ (less the premium charged by the option writer and any tax payments due).

Banks can also be option writers, offering to sell calls or puts to option buyers. For example, as illustrated in Exhibit 8–3, suppose a bank sells a *call* option to another institution and the option carries a strike price of S. As shown in the left panel of Exhibit 8–3, if interest rates *rise,* the call option's market value may fall to F_n and the option will have no value to the buyer. It will go unused and the bank will pocket the option's premium as a profit to help offset any damaging losses due to a trend of rising market interest rates. On the other hand, a banker fearful of losses on account of

EXHIBIT 8–2
Payoff Diagrams for Put and Call Options Purchased by a Bank

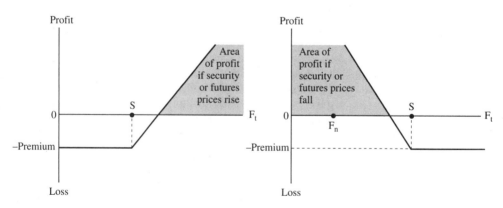

Bank Purchase of a Call Option
(right to call away from option writer
securities or futures contracts at a
specific price (S) if interest rates fall)

Bank Purchase of a Put Option
(right to deliver to option writer
securities or futures contracts at a
specific price (S) if interest rates rise)

Purpose: Protect against falling yields on bank assets (such as current loans and future loans and investments in securities).

Purpose: Protect against rising deposit and other borrowing costs and falling market values of bank assets (such as bank investments).

falling interest rates may find another institution interested in purchasing a *put* option at strike price S. If market interest rates do, in fact, decline, the market price of the securities or futures contracts mentioned in the option will rise, and the put will be of no value to its buyer. The banker will simply pocket the option's premium, helping to offset any losses the bank may be anticipating due to falling interest rates.

Interest Rate Swaps

Early in the 1980s, an interest rate hedging device was developed in the Eurobond market that enables two borrowers of funds (including banks) to aid each other by exchanging some of the most favorable features of their loans. For example, one borrower may be so small or have such a low credit rating that it cannot go into the open market and sell bonds at low fixed rates of interest. This borrower may be forced to use short-term

EXHIBIT 8–3

Payoff Diagrams for Put and Call Options Written by a Bank

Bank Sells a Call Option to a Buyer
(giving the buyer the right to call
away securities or futures contracts
from the bank at the price (S) specified
in the option if interest rates rise)

Bank Sells a Put Option to a Buyer
(giving the buyer the right to deliver
securities or futures contracts to the
bank at the price specified (S) in the
option if interest rates fall)

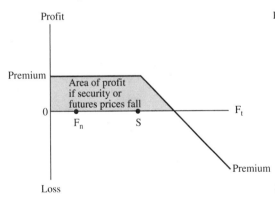

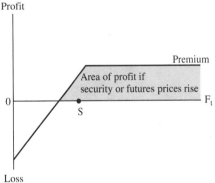

Purpose: Protect against rising deposit and
other borrowing costs and falling market
values of bank assets (such as bank investments).

Purpose: Protect against falling yields on bank
assets (such as current loans and future loans and
investments in securities).

Concept Checks

8–8. Explain what is involved in a *put option.*

8–9. What is a *call option?*

8–10. Suppose market interest rates were expected to *rise.* What type of option would normally be used?

8–11. If market interest rates were expected to *fall,* what type of option would a bank manager be likely to employ?

---

credit and accept relatively high cost variable-rate loans. The other borrower, in contrast, may have a high credit rating and be able to borrow long term in the open market at a relatively low fixed interest rate. However, the highly rated company (which is often a large bank) may desire a more flexible short-term loan if the interest rate can be made low enough. These two borrowers, often with the help of a bank or other intermediary, can simply agree to *swap interest payments,* tapping the best features of each other's borrowings. (See Exhibit 8–4.)

An **interest rate swap,** then, is a way to change an institution's exposure to interest rate fluctuations and achieve lower borrowing costs. Swap participants can convert from fixed to floating rates or from floating to fixed rates and more closely match the maturities of their assets and liabilities. Swaps can transform cash flows through a bank to more closely match the pattern of cash flows desired by management. In addition, a bank arranging a swap for its customers earns fee income (usually amounting to 0.25 to 0.50 percent of the amount involved) for serving as an intermediary and may earn additional fees if it agrees to guarantee a swap agreement against default. So successful has been the swap as a financial instrument that by the mid-1990s the dollar volume of outstanding swaps exceeded $4 trillion.

Under the terms of an agreement called a *quality swap,* a borrower with a lower credit rating (perhaps with a rating of BBB—the lowest investment grade) enters into an agreement to exchange interest payments with a borrower having a higher credit rating (perhaps with a top-quality rating of AAA). In this case the low-credit-rated borrower agrees to pay the high-credit-rated borrower's fixed long-term borrowing cost. In effect, the low-credit-rated borrower receives a long-term loan at a much lower interest cost than the low-rated borrower could obtain alone. At the same time, the borrower with the higher credit rating covers all or a portion of the lower-rated borrower's short-term floating loan rate, thus converting a fixed long-term interest rate into a more flexible and possibly cheaper short-term interest rate. In summary, the high-credit-rated borrower gets a long-term fixed-rate loan, but pays a floating interest rate to the low-credit-rated borrower; in turn, the low-credit-rated borrower

EXHIBIT 8–4

The Interest Rate Swap

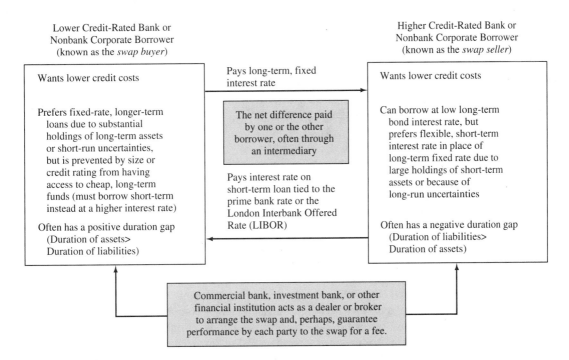

gets a short-term, floating-rate loan, but pays a fixed interest rate to the high-credit-rated borrower. Often the lower-rated borrower (such as a savings and loan or insurance company) has longer duration assets than liabilities, while the higher-rated borrower may have longer duration liabilities than assets (such as a commercial bank). Through the swap agreement just described, each party achieves cash outflows in the form of interest costs on liabilities that more closely match the interest revenues generated by its assets.

The most popular short-term, floating rates used in interest rate swaps today include the London Interbank Offered Rate (LIBOR) on Eurodollar deposits, the Treasury bill rate, the prime bank rate, the Federal funds rate, and interest rates on bank and thrift CDs and commercial paper. Each swap partner simply borrows in that market in which it has the greatest comparative cost advantage, and then the two parties exchange interest payments owed on the funds they have each borrowed. In total, the cost of borrowing is lower after a swap is arranged, even though one of the parties (the borrower with the highest credit rating) can usually borrow more cheaply in *both* short-term and long-term markets than the borrower with the lower credit rating.

Notice that neither firm lends money to the other. The principal amount of the loans—usually called the *notional* amount—is *not* exchanged.[2] Each party to the swap must still pay off its own debt. In fact, only the *net* amount of interest due usually flows to one or the other party to the swap, depending on how high short-term interest rates in the market rise relative to long-term interest rates on each interest-due date. The swap itself normally will not show up on a swap participant's balance sheet, though it can reduce interest rate risk associated with the assets and liabilities on that balance sheet.[3]

As noted earlier, swaps are often employed to deal with asset-liability maturity mismatches. For example, as shown in Exhibit 8–4, one firm may have short-term assets with flexible yields and long-term liabilities carrying fixed interest rates. Such a firm fears that a decline in market interest rates will reduce its earnings. In contrast, a company having long-term assets with fixed rates of return, but facing shorter-term liabilities, fears rising interest rates. These two firms are likely candidates for a swap. The one with long-term fixed-rate assets can agree to take over the interest payments of the one with long-term fixed-rate liabilities, and vice versa.

A bank can also use swaps to alter the effective duration of its assets and liabilities. It can shorten asset duration by swapping out a fixed interest rate income stream in favor of a variable interest rate income stream. If the duration of a bank's liabilities is too short, it can swap out a variable interest rate expense in favor of a fixed interest rate expense. Thus, interest rate swaps can help a bank immunize its portfolio by moving closer to a balance between asset and liability durations.

Why use swaps for these problem situations? Wouldn't refinancing a bank's outstanding debt obligations, or perhaps using financial futures, accomplish the same thing? In principle, yes, but there are practical problems that frequently favor swaps. For example, retiring old debt and issuing new securities with more favorable characteristics can be expensive and risky. New borrowing may have to take place in an environment of higher interest rates. Underwriting costs, registration fees, time delays, and regulations often severely limit how far any business firm can go in attempting to restructure its balance sheet. Financial futures also present problems for hedgers because of their rigid maturity dates (they usually fall due within a few weeks or months) and the limited number of financial instruments they cover.

In contrast, swaps can be negotiated to cover virtually any period of time or borrowing instrument desired, though most fall into the 3-year to 10-year range. They are also easy to carry out, usually negotiated and agreed to over the telephone through a broker or dealer. During the 1980s, several large American and British banks devel-

---

[2]Swaps in which the notional amount is constant are often called "bullet" swaps. There are also *amortizing* swaps, whose notional amount declines over time, and *accruing* swaps, whose notional principal accumulates during their term. *Seasonal* swaps have notional principals that vary according to the seasonal cash flow patterns experienced by the swap parties.

[3]If a bank agrees to guarantee a swap agreement negotiated between two of its customers or if it participates in a swap with another firm, it usually merely marks the transaction down as a contingent liability. Because such arrangements may become real liabilities for a bank, many financial analysts seek out information on any outstanding swaps in evaluating individual banks' desirability as investments.

oped a communications network to make swap trading relatively easy even for small-denomination, short-maturity swaps.

Reverse swaps can also be arranged, in which a new swap agreement offsets the effects of an existing swap contract. Many swap agreements today contain termination options, allowing either party to end the agreement for a fee. Other swaps carry interest rate ceilings (caps), interest rate minimums (floors), or both ceilings and floors (collars), which limit the risk of large changes in interest rate payments. There may also be escape clauses and "swaptions," which are options for one or both parties to make certain changes in the agreement, take out a new option, or cancel an existing swap agreement.

On the negative side, swaps may carry substantial brokerage fees, credit risk, basis risk, and interest rate risk. With *credit risk* either or both parties to a swap may go bankrupt or fail to honor their half of the swap agreement, though the loss would be limited to promised interest payments, not repayment of loan principal. Moreover, a third party with a top credit rating, such as a commercial bank or investment bank, may be willing to *guarantee* the agreed-upon interest payments through a letter of credit if the swap partner seeking the guarantee pays a suitable fee (usually 10 to 50 basis points). The most heavily used intermediaries in arranging and guaranteeing swap contracts include the largest U.S., Canadian, Japanese, and European commercial banks and investment banks (such as J.P. Morgan, Merrill Lynch, and Salomon Brothers). Sometimes the lower-rated swap partner may be asked to post *collateral* to help strengthen the swap contract.

In fairness to swaps, we should note that actual defaults are rare.[4] One element that significantly reduces the potential damage if a swap partner does default on its obligation to pay is called *netting*. As we noted earlier, on each payment due date the swap parties exchange only the *net difference* between the interest payments each owes the other. This amount is much smaller than either the fixed or floating interest payment by itself and would be the actual amount subject to default. Moreover, when a bank is involved in several swap contracts with another party, it will often calculate only the *net amount owed across all swap contracts* with that other party, which further reduces the actual amount of credit risk.

Basis risk arises because the particular interest rates that define the terms of a swap (such as a long-term bond rate and a floating short-term rate like LIBOR or the prime rate) are not exactly the same interest rates as those attached to all the assets and liabilities that either or both swap partners hold. This means that as a swap's reference interest rate changes, it may not change in exactly the same proportion as the interest rates attached to the swap buyer's and seller's various assets and liabilities. Thus, an

---

[4]Besides conventional interest rate swaps, banks today engage in several other types of swaps, including commodity swaps, equity swaps, and currency swaps. *Commodity* swaps are designed to hedge against price fluctuations in oil, natural gas, coal, copper, and selected other commodities where one party fears rising prices and the other fears falling prices for a commodity that it sells. *Equity* swaps are designed to convert the interest flows on debt into cash flows related to the behavior of a stock index, which allows swap partners to benefit from favorable movements in stock prices. *Currency* swaps are discussed in Chapter 23.

Bank Management in Action

An Example of a Swap Transaction

This example shows how two firms (bank or nonbank) can each save on borrowing costs by agreeing to swap interest payments with each other. The savings arise principally because interest rate spreads (often called *quality spreads*) are normally much wider in the long-term credit market than in the short-term market.

Parties to the Swap	Fixed Interest Rates Parties Must Pay If They Issue Long-Term Bonds	Floating Interest Rates Parties Must Pay If They Receive a Short-Term Loan	Potential Interest Rate Savings of Each Borrower
A lower credit-rated bank or nonbank corporate borrower	11.50%	Prime + 1.75%	0.50%
A higher credit-rated bank or nonbank corporate borrower	9.00	Prime interest rate	0.25%
Difference in interest rates due to differences in borrowers' credit ratings (*quality spread*)	2.50%	1.75%	0.75%

Financing Methods Used

The higher-rated borrower issues long-term bonds at 9 percent, while the lower-rated borrower gets a bank loan at prime plus 1.75 percent. They then swap interest payments as described below.

A swap transaction might be arranged in which the lower-rated borrower agrees to pay the higher-rated borrower's 9 percent interest cost, thus saving 2.5 percent in long-term borrowing

interest rate swap cannot hedge away all interest rate risk for both parties to the agreement; some interest-rate risk exposure must remain in any real-world situation.[5]

Swaps can also carry substantial *interest rate risk.* For example, if the yield curve slopes upward, the swap buyer (who pays the fixed interest rate) normally would

---

[5]The special risk exposures faced by banks and other swap parties that conventional swaps cannot deal with completely may be met by specially tailored *off-market swaps* that use interest rate indicators more relevant to each swap party and may also allow the notional value of a swap to vary over time (e.g., to handle the gradual amortization of loans that either or both swap partners may hold as assets).

costs because it would have had to pay 11.5 percent for long-term credit. The higher-rated borrower pays the lower-rated borrower's prime interest rate minus 0.25 percent, thus saving the higher-rated borrower, who normally would borrow at prime, a quarter of a percentage point (–0.25 percent) on a short-term loan. Notice that the lower-credit-rated borrower saves a *net* interest rate of 0.50 percent (that is, 2.50 percentage points saved on the long-term rate minus the 2 percent additional it must pay above the amount of the prime rate less 0.25 percent contributed by the higher-rated borrower).

Thus:

Low-credit-rated borrower pays	. . . . .	9 percent (fixed rate)
High-credit-rated borrower pays	. . . .	Prime rate less 0.25 percent (floating rate)
Low-credit-rated borrower saves	. . . .	[(11.5 percent − 9 percent) − (1.75 percent more than the prime rate + 0.25 percent less than the prime rate)] = 0.50 percent
High-credit-rated borrower saves	. . . .	0.25 percent (below the prime rate)

The lower-rated borrower may also agree to pay the underwriting costs associated with the higher-rated borrower's issue of long-term bonds so that both ultimately wind up with roughly equal savings of about 0.5 percent.

Clearly, *both* parties save as a result of this interest rate swap. They also benefit from a closer matching of cash inflows and outflows from their respective portfolios of assets and liabilities.

Some authorities argue, however, that the savings described above are really illusory— that an efficient financial marketplace will rapidly eliminate such arbitrage opportunities between long-term and short-term markets except for possible market imperfections (such as those introduced by government restrictions and regulations). Others contend that the supposed savings from a swap are counterbalanced by the surrender of valuable options by the swap parties, who, were it not for the swap agreement, could refinance their loans if interest rates move in a favorable direction. However, they must honor the terms of a swap contract regardless of how interest rates subsequently behave.

expect to pay a greater amount of interest cost during the early years of a swap contract and to receive greater amounts of interest income from the swap seller (who pays the floating interest rate) toward the end of the swap contract. This could encourage the seller to default on the swap agreement near the end of the contract, possibly forcing the swap buyer to negotiate a new agreement with a new partner under less-favorable market conditions.

Concept Checks

8–12. What is the purpose of an *interest rate swap*?

8–13. What are the principal advantages and disadvantages of rate swaps?

8–14. How can a bank get itself out of a swap agreement?

Caps, Floors, and Collars

Finally, among the most familiar interest rate hedging devices developed by banks for themselves and their customers are caps, floors, and collars.

Interest Rate Caps

An **interest rate cap** protects its holder against rising market interest rates. In return for paying an up-front premium, borrowers are assured that institutions lending them money cannot increase their loan rate above the level of the cap. Alternatively, the borrower may purchase an interest rate cap from a third party, with that party promising to reimburse borrowers for any additional interest they owe their creditors beyond the cap. For example, if a bank purchases a cap of 11 percent on $100 million that it borrowed in the Eurodollar market, the bank has a guarantee that its effective borrowing cost cannot climb above 11 percent. If a bank sells a rate cap to one of its borrowing customers, it takes on interest rate risk from that customer, but earns a fee (premium) as compensation for added risk taking. If a bank takes on a large volume of cap agreements it can reduce its overall risk exposure by using another hedging device, such as an interest rate swap.

Interest rate caps are administered very simply. Consider the example in the preceding paragraph—a bank purchases a cap of 11 percent from another financial institution on its borrowings of $100 million in the Eurodollar market for one year. Suppose interest rates in this market rise to 12 percent for the year. Then the institution selling the cap will reimburse the bank purchasing the cap the additional 1 percent in interest costs due to the recent rise in market interest rates. In terms of dollars, the bank will receive a rebate of

$$\left(\begin{array}{c} \text{Market} \\ \text{interest rate} \end{array} - \begin{array}{c} \text{Cap} \\ \text{rate} \end{array} \right) \times \begin{array}{c} \text{Amount} \\ \text{borrowed} \end{array} = (12 \text{ percent} \tag{10}$$

$$- 11 \text{ percent}) \times \$100 \text{ million} = \$1 \text{ million}$$

for one year. Thus, the bank's effective borrowing rate can float over time but it will never exceed 11 percent. Banks buy interest rate caps when conditions arise that could generate losses, such as when a bank finds itself funding fixed-rate assets with floating-rate liabilities, possesses longer-term assets than liabilities, or perhaps holds a large portfolio of bonds that will drop in value when interest rates rise.

Interest Rate Floors

As we saw earlier, banks can also lose earnings in periods of falling interest rates, especially when rates on floating-rate loans decline. A bank can insist on establishing an **interest rate floor** under its loans so that, no matter how far loan rates tumble, it is guaranteed some minimum rate of return.

Another popular use of interest rate floors arises when a bank sells an interest rate floor to its customers who hold securities but are concerned that the yields on those securities might fall to unacceptable levels. For example, a bank customer may hold a 90-day negotiable CD promising 6.75 percent but anticipates selling the CD in a few days. Suppose the customer does not want to see the CD's yield drop below 6.25 percent. In this instance, the customer's bank may sell its client a rate floor of 6.25 percent, agreeing to pay the customer the difference between the floor rate and the actual CD rate if interest rates fall too far at the end of the 90 days.

How can the bank itself benefit from an interest rate floor? To cite one example, suppose a bank extending a $10 million floating-rate loan to one of its corporate customers for a year at prime insists on a minimum (floor) interest rate on this loan of 7 percent. If the prime rate drops below the floor to 6 percent for one year, the customer will pay not only the 6 percent loan rate (or $10 million $\times$ 0.06 = $600,000 in interest) but also pay out an interest rebate to the bank of:

$$\left(\begin{matrix} \text{Floor} \\ \text{rate} \end{matrix} - \begin{matrix} \text{Current loan} \\ \text{interest rate} \end{matrix} \right) \times \begin{matrix} \text{Amount} \\ \text{borrowed} \end{matrix} = (7\% - 6\%) \tag{11}$$

$$\times \ \$10 \text{ million} \ = \ \$100,000$$

Through this hedging device the bank is guaranteed (assuming the borrower doesn't default) a minimum return of 7 percent on its loan. Banks use interest rate floors most often when their liabilities have longer maturities than their assets or when they are funding floating-rate assets with fixed-rate debt.

Interest Rate Collars

Both banks and their borrowing customers also make heavy use of the **interest rate collar,** which combines in one agreement a rate floor and a rate cap. Many banks sell collars as a separate fee-based service for the loans they make to their customers. For example, a customer who has just received a $100 million loan may ask the bank for a collar on the loan's prime rate between 11 percent and 7 percent. In this instance, the bank will pay its customer's added interest cost if prime rises above 11 percent, while the customer reimburses the bank if prime drops below 7 percent. In effect, the collar's purchaser pays a premium for a rate cap while receiving a premium for accepting a rate floor. The *net* premium paid for the collar can be positive or negative, depending upon the outlook for interest rates and the risk aversion of borrower and lender at the time of the agreement.

Normally, caps, collars, and floors range in maturity from a few weeks out to as long as 10 years. Most such agreements are tied to interest rates on government securities, commercial paper, prime-rated loans, or Eurodollar deposits (LIBOR). Banks themselves often make heavy use of collars to protect their earnings when interest rates appear to be unusually volatile and there is considerable uncertainty about the direction in which market interest rates may move.

Caps, collars, and floors are simply special types of options designed to deal with interest-rate risk exposure from assets and liabilities held by banks and their customers. Sales of caps, collars, and floors to customers have generated a large volume of fee income (up-front revenues) for banks in recent years, but these special options carry both credit risk (when the party obligated to pay defaults) and interest rate risk that must be carefully weighed by bank managers when making the decision to sell or use these rate-hedging tools.

Concept Checks

8–15. How can banks make use of interest rate *caps, floors,* and *collars* to generate revenue and help manage interest rate risk?

8–16. Suppose a bank enters into an agreement to make a $10 million, three-year floating-rate loan to one of its best corporate customers at an initial rate of 8 percent. The bank and its customer agree to a cap and a floor arrangement in which the customer reimburses the bank if the floating loan rate drops below 6 percent and the bank reimburses the customer if the floating loan rate rises above 10 percent. Suppose that at the beginning of the loan's second year, the floating loan rate drops to 5 percent for a year and then, at the beginning of the third year, the loan rate increases to 10 percent for the year. What rebates must be paid by each party to the agreement?

Summary

In this third chapter dealing with asset-liability management techniques, we have examined several of the most popular methods—including financial futures, options, interest rate swaps, rate caps, collars, and floors—for dealing with the interest rate risk exposure of banks. *Financial futures contracts* are agreements to deliver or take delivery of securities at a stipulated price on a specific future date. These contracts have grown rapidly in popularity, because they are a relatively low cost hedging tool and are readily available in a variety of types and maturities through hundreds of dealer/broker firms. Futures contracts are traded on exchanges in standardized forms that closely match many bank assets and deposits, thus permitting more effective hedges for bank interest costs and revenues. *Option contracts* give their holders the right to deliver (put) or take delivery of (call) specified securities at a prespecified (strike) price on or before a stipulated future date. Options are also widely traded on organized exchanges and are particularly effective when bank management wants to achieve downside risk protection but does not want to restrict potential gains if interest rates move in a favorable direction. Options tend to be more expensive than financial futures contracts, but they still carry relatively low costs compared to the amount of risk protection they provide.

Interest rate swaps represent one of the fastest-growing markets for hedging instruments. Under a conventional swap contract, the parties agree to exchange interest payments so that each participating institution can achieve a better match of cash inflows with cash outflows. Swaps also help to lower interest costs, because each party to the agreement borrows in that credit market in which it enjoys the greatest comparative advantage.

Interest rate *caps* place an upper limit on a borrower's loan rate, while interest rate *floors* protect a lender from declining loan yields if market interest rates fall. *Collars* combine caps and floors in one contract, freezing loan rates within the limits spelled out by a loan's cap rate and its floor rate.

Key Terms in This Chapter

Financial futures
Interest rate option
Interest rate swap

Interest rate cap
Interest rate floor
Interest rate collar

Problems and Projects

1. What kind of futures or options hedges usually would be called for in the following situations?

   a. Interest rates are expected to decline, and First National Bank of Scanton expects a sharp seasonal rise in loan demand in the coming spring quarter.

   b. Silsabee State Bank has interest-sensitive assets of $79 million and interest-sensitive liabilities of $68 million over the next 30-day period, and market interest rates appear likely to decline over that same time period.

   c. A survey of Tuskee Bank's corporate loan customers this month (October) indicates that, on balance, this group of firms will need to draw $155 million from their credit lines in November and December, which is $80 million more than the banks' management has forecast and prepared for. The bank's economist has predicted a significant increase in money market interest rates over the next 60 days.

   d. Settlement Hills National Bank reports that its interest-sensitive liabilities for the next week will be approximately $42 million, while interest-sensitive assets will approach $31 million. Data provided by the Federal Reserve Board suggest a near-term rise in money market interest rates.

   e. Caufield Bank and Trust Company finds that its portfolio of earning assets has an average duration of 1.35 years and its liabilities have an average duration of 0.95 years. Interest rates are expected to rise by 50 basis points between now and year-end.

2. A savings and loan whose credit rating has just slipped and half of whose assets are long-term mortgages offers to swap interest payments with a money center bank in a $100 million deal. The bank can borrow short term at LIBOR (8.05 percent) and long term at 8.95 percent. The S&L must pay LIBOR plus 1.5 percent on short-term debt and 10.75 percent on long-term debt. Show how these parties

could put together a swap deal that benefits both of them about equally.

Alternative scenarios:

(1) Will an interest rate swap still be beneficial for both the S&L and the bank if the bank, following release of the news that its credit rating had just been lowered, is forced to borrow short term at LIBOR plus one-half percent and long term at 10 percent, while the S&L must still pay LIBOR plus 1.5 percent for short-term funds and 10.75 percent on long-term debt?

(2) Suppose the S&L has just released a new, highly favorable earnings report and it now finds it can borrow at LIBOR plus 0.75 percent for short-term money, while its long-term debt is now accessible with a 10 percent coupon rate. If the bank's situation remains unchanged, do these changes make the swap more or less attractive to either party?

(3) Does the swap described above still look as favorable to both parties if all interest rates rise by 2 percentage points? What if all rates decline by 2 percentage points?

3. A bank plans to borrow $55 million in the money market at a current interest rate of 8.5 percent. However, the borrowing rate will float with market conditions. To protect itself the bank has purchased an interest rate cap of 10 percent to cover this borrowing. If money market interest rates on these funds sources suddenly rise to 11.5 percent as the borrowing begins, how much interest in total will the bank owe and how much of an interest rebate will it receive (assuming the borrowing is for only one month)?

4. Suppose that Exeter National Bank has recently granted a loan of $3.6 million to Fairhills Farms at prime plus 0.5 percent for six months. In return for granting Fairhills an interest rate cap of 12 percent on its loan, the bank has received from this customer a floor rate on the loan of 7.5 percent. Suppose that, as the loan is about to start, the prime rate declines to 6.25 percent and remains there for the

duration of the loan. How much (in dollars) will Fairhills Farms have to pay in total interest on this six-month loan? How much in interest rebates will Fairhills have to pay due to the fall in the prime rate?

5. Starshine Bank and Trust Company reports the following data derived from its latest financial report:

Total assets	$88 million	Other liabilities	$32 million
Average asset duration	2.61 years	Average duration of liabilities	1.85 years
Total deposits	$49 million		

Is Starshine fully hedged or does it have a duration gap? If so, what is the size of its duration gap?

6. A bank needs to borrow $250 million by selling time deposits bearing 180-day maturities. If interest rates on comparable deposits are currently at 6 percent, what is the marginal cost of issuing these deposits? Suppose deposit interest rates rise to 7 percent. What then will be the marginal cost of these deposits? What kind of futures contract could be used to deal with this cost problem?

7. With reference to the facts stated in problem 6 above, suppose the bank sells 250 90-day Euro dollar time deposit *futures contracts* priced today at a market value of $920,000 and plans to subsequently purchase 90-day Eurodollar deposit contracts at a hoped-for price of $915,000. What before-tax profit or loss would the bank likely experience from this transaction? What type of hedge is this?

8. A bank is considering the use of *options* to deal with a serious cost problem. Deposit interest rates have been rising for six months, currently average 5 percent, and are expected to climb as high as 6.75 percent over the next 90 days. The bank plans to issue $60 million in new money market deposits in about 90 days and has determined that it can obtain an option on $1 million, 90-day Eurodollar time deposit futures contracts from a security dealer for a $780 premium. The option is currently priced at $950,000 for each

million-dollar-denomination contract and is forecast to fall to a market value of $932,500 per contract within 90 days. What kind of option should the bank use? What before-tax profit could be earned by the bank from the option under the terms described?

9. Silver Beach National Bank wants to purchase a portfolio of million-dollar-denomination commercial loans with an expected average rate of return of 11 percent. However, when funds become available to purchase the loans in six months, market interest rates are expected to be in the 10 percent range. If the total size of the portfolio is $100 million and Treasury bill options are available today at a price in the market of $890,000 (per million-dollar contract) upon payment of a $12,000 premium and are forecast to rise to a market value of $900,000 per contract, what before-tax profit could the bank earn from this transaction?

10. Treasury bill futures contracts carry denominations of $1 million but have a current market value of $960,000. Suppose the duration of these bills is 0.33 years and market interest rates fall from 4 percent to 3 percent. What change in the index value of these futures contracts will occur?

11. Suppose a bank wishes to hedge its overall asset-liability position using financial futures contracts for U.S. Treasury bonds ($100,000 in denomination). Using the information given below, can you calculate the approximate number of futures contracts the bank will need to fully cover the interest rate risk it faces?

Total assets	$835 million	Duration of	
Total liabilities	$790 million	bank assets	3.5 years
Price of futures	$95,000	Duration of bank	
Duration of T-bonds	9.5 years	liabilities	1.7 years

12. By what amount will the market value of Treasury bond futures contracts change if they have a duration of 8.80 years, and a current market price of $98,500, and if interest rates rise from 8.50 to 9.50 percent?

13. Cleberg National Bank reports that its assets have a duration of 1.90 years and its liabilities average 1.12 years in duration. In order to hedge this duration gap, management plans to employ Treasury bond futures ($100,000 denominations) which have a current price of $99,250 and a duration of 9 years. Cleberg's latest financial report shows total assets of $144 million and total liabilities of $132 million. Approximately how many futures contracts for T-bonds will the bank need to cover its overall interest-rate risk exposure?

Selected References

For excellent readings on the use of financial futures in bank risk management, see the following studies:

1. Brewer, Elijah. "Bank Gap Management and the Use of Financial Futures." *Economic Perspectives,* Federal Reserve Bank of Chicago, March/April 1985, pp. 12–22.

2. Rolls, Robert W.; Stephen G. Timme; and Gerald D. Gray. "Macro versus Micro Futures Hedges at Commercial Banks." *Journal of the Futures Markets,* Spring 1984, pp. 47–54.

3. Cook, Timothy Q., and Robert K. LaRoche. *Instruments of the Money Market.* Federal Reserve Bank of Richmond, 1993, Chapters 14–16.

4. Ardalan, Kavous. "Textbook Treatment of Volatility in Valuing Options and Corporate Liabilities." *Financial Practice and Education,* Spring/Summer 1997, pp. 103–12.

5. Gilster, John E., Jr. "Option Pricing Theory: Is "Risk-Free" Hedging Feasible?" *Financial Management* 26, no. 1 (Spring 1997), pp. 91–105.

6. Koppenhaver, G. D. "Futures Options and Their Use by Financial Intermediaries." *Economic Perspectives,* Federal Reserve Bank of Chicago, January/February 1986, pp. 18–31.

These studies give a more detailed view of interest rate swaps:

7. Abken, Peter A. "Beyond Plain Vanilla: A Taxonomy of SWAPs." *Economic Review,* Federal Reserve Bank of Richmond, March/April 1991.

8. Goeys, Jan C. "Interest Rate SWAPs: A New Tool for Managing Risks." *Business Review,* Federal Reserve Bank of Philadelphia, May/June 1985, pp. 17–25.

For reviews of interest rate caps and related interest rate risk hedging tools, see:

9. Abken, Peter A. "Interest Rate Caps, Collars, and Floors." *Economic Review,* Federal Reserve Bank of Atlanta, November/December 1989, pp. 2–24.

10. Rose, Peter S. "Defensive Banking in a Volatile Economy—Hedging Loan and Deposit Interest Rates." *The Canadian Banker* 93, no. 2 (April 1986), pp. 52–59.

9   OFF-BALANCE-SHEET FINANCING IN BANKING AND CREDIT DERIVATIVES

Learning and Management Decision Objectives

The purpose of this chapter is to learn about some of the newer financial instruments that bankers have used in recent years to help reduce the risk exposure of their banks and, in some cases, to aid in generating new sources of fee income and in raising new funds to make loans and investments. We will view these newer risk-management and income-generating instruments from the point of view of the bank manager, exploring their key advantages and possible disadvantages.

Introduction

As we have seen in the preceding chapters, banks face many kinds of risk exposure.[1] Interest rates change and both bank interest revenues and interest costs are affected as is the value of many bank assets (especially the securities portfolio). Borrowing customers default on their loans, confronting the bank with serious credit risks and diminishing the bank's expected earnings. Added to these problems are the demands of the regulatory community to strengthen bank capital—the most expensive source of funds for most banks—in order to protect the institution against these and other forms of risk. Bankers have actively sought new ways to reduce their need for raising expensive capital by removing risky assets from their asset portfolio or by contracting away some of their risk exposure.

Confronted with these conflicting pressures of risk exposure and the demands of the regulatory community for stronger defenses against risk, bankers in recent years have responded by developing and making use of a wide variety of risk-management

---

[1]Portions of this chapter are taken from the author's articles focusing on off-balance-sheet financing in *The Canadian Banker* [11,12,16] and are used with permission.

tools. These risk-management weapons have included such devices as securitization of loans, loan sales, standby credit letters, and credit derivatives of various kinds. Not only have these newer tools helped bankers manage risk more effectively, but they have also opened up new sources of fee income for banks and helped them serve their customers even in times when available funding has been scarce and costly to obtain. We take a close look at each of these risk-management and fee-income generating tools in the sections that follow.

Securitizing Bank Loans and Other Assets

Securitization of a bank's loans and other assets is a simple idea for raising new funds and for reducing a bank's risk exposure—so simple, in fact, that one wonders why it was not fully developed until the 1970s and 1980s. Securitizing assets requires a bank to set aside a group of income-earning assets—such as mortgages or consumer loans—and to sell securities (financial claims) against those assets in the open market. (See Exhibit 9–1.) As the assets pay out—for example, as borrowing customers repay

EXHIBIT 9–1
Securitization: Turning Loans and Other Assets into Sources of Bank Funds

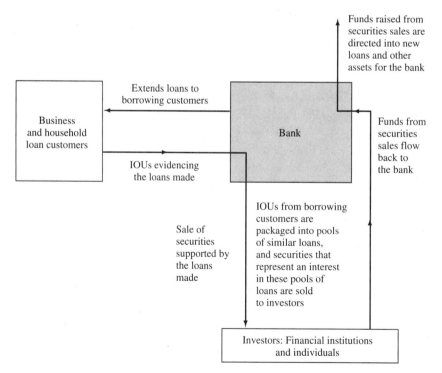

Source: Peter S. Rose, "The Quest for Funds: New Directions in a New Market." *The Canadian Banker,* September/October 1987.

the principal and interest owed on their loans—that income stream flows to the holders of the securities. In effect, bank loans are transformed into publicly traded securities. For its part, the bank receives back the money it expended to acquire the assets and uses those funds to acquire new assets or to cover operating expenses.

The bank or other lender whose loans are pooled is called the *originator* and the loans are then passed on to (acquired by) an *issuer,* who is usually a *special purpose entity* (SPE). The SPE is completely separate from the originator so that if the originating lender goes bankrupt, this event will not affect the credit status of the loans in the pool. A *trustee* is appointed to ensure that the issuer fulfills all the requirements of the transfer of loans to the pool and provides all the services promised (including, where stipulated, fulfilling any guarantees or collateral requirements in case a significant proportion of the pooled loans are defaulted). The trustee collects and disburses to investors any cash flows generated by the pooled loans and temporarily invests any cash generated by the loans between required investor payment dates.

Pooling loans through securitization helps to diversify a bank's credit risk exposure and reduces the need to monitor each individual loan's payment stream. It creates liquid assets out of relatively illiquid, expensive-to-sell assets and transforms these assets into new sources of capital.

Securitizations permit banks subject to economic downturns in their local areas to, in effect, hold a more geographically diversified loan portfolio, perhaps countering local losses with higher returns available from geographic areas experiencing more buoyant economic conditions.

Securitization is also a tool for managing interest rate risk, making it easier for any individual bank to adjust its asset portfolio so that the maturity (duration) of its assets more closely approximates the maturity (duration) of its liabilities.

Moreover, the bank can earn added *fee income* by agreeing to *service* the packaged assets. Usually this means monitoring the borrowers' performance in repaying their loans, collecting payments due, and making sure adequate collateral is posted to protect holders of any securities issued against those loans. While the bank may continue to service any assets pledged, it can remove those assets from its balance sheet, eliminating the risk of loss if the loans are not repaid or if interest rate movements lower their value.[2] (Securitization tends to shorten the maturity of a bank's assets, reducing their overall sensitivity to interest rate movements.) A bank may also secure additional earnings based on the spread between the interest rate being earned on the securitized assets and the interest rate paid to security holders, which usually is lower. Moreover, taxes may be reduced because of the deductibility of the interest expense incurred when assets are securitized and there is no regulatory tax in the form of deposit reserve requirements. However, the assets packaged to back any securities issued must be uniform in quality and purpose and carry investment features (such as high yields or ready marketability) that are attractive to investors.

---

[2]This step—removing loans in the securitized pool from the bank's balance sheet—can be a real plus from a regulatory point of view. Regulations generally limit the proportion of bank assets committed to loans in order to control risk exposure. A bank with a relatively high loan-asset ratio can bundle a group of loans and move them off its books to make the bank look financially stronger. Total assets will decline while capital remains the same, so the bank's capital-to-assets ratio improves.

While some bankers believe that securitization helps a bank get along with less capital (because risky assets are removed from the balance sheet), securitizing loans may not always reduce a bank's capital requirements as specified by regulators. Securitizations of commercial loans, for example, may carry the same regulatory capital requirements for a bank as the original loans themselves. According to the international capital standards (Basel) agreement between the United States, Canada, Japan, and leading European countries (discussed in Chapter 15), both commercial loans and securitized commercial loans can carry a capital requirement as high as 8 percent of their amount. For example, when loans are sold or securitized and the buyer is given recourse to the selling bank if those loans are defaulted, the full value of the loans must be included in the bank's capital requirements.

As the foregoing paragraphs suggest, securitization of loans creates numerous opportunities for revenue for the bank choosing this fund-raising alternative. A bank can benefit from the normal positive spread between the average yield on the packaged loans and the coupon (promised) rate on the securities issued, capturing at least a portion of the difference in interest rates between the loans themselves and the securities issued against the loans as *residual income*. The securitizing bank or another institution may be able to gain additional income by *servicing* the loans pledged behind the securities, collecting interest from the loans and monitoring their performance. Many banks have also gained added income by selling guarantees to protect investors who hold loan-backed securities, by advising institutions securitizing their loans on the correct procedures, and by providing backup liquidity in case a securitizing institution runs short of cash to meet its obligations to investors. Below is an illustration of a typical securitization transaction and the fees it might generate:

> Average expected yield on the pooled loans
> (as a percent of the total value of the securitized loans). 15%

Promised fees and payments on these securitized loans might include the following (expressed as a percent of the total value of the securitized loans):

- Coupon rate promised to investors who buy
  the securities issued against the pool of loans 9%
- Default rate on the pooled loans (often covered
  by a government or private guarantee or the
  placement of some revenues generated by the
  pooled loans in a special reserve to ensure
  security holders against default) 5%
- Fees to compensate a servicing institution
  for collecting payments from the loans
  in the pool and for monitoring the
  performance of the pooled loans. 0.25%
- Fees paid for advising on how to set
  up the securitized pool of loans 0.25%
- Fees paid for providing a liquidity facility
  to cover any temporary shortfalls in cash
  needed to pay security investors 0.25%

- Residual interest income for the securitizing
  institution (left over after payment of all fees
  and payment of the coupon rate promised to investors) 0.25%
- Sum of all fees, promised payments,
  and residual interest income 15%

Beginnings of Securitization—The Home Mortgage Market

The concept of securitization began in the residential mortgage market of the United States where three federal agencies—the Government National Mortgage Association (GNMA), the Federal National Mortgage Association (FNMA), and the Federal Home Loan Mortgage Corporation (FHLMC)—have worked to improve the salability of home mortgage loans. For example, GNMA sponsors a mortgage loan-backed securities program under which banks and other lenders can pool their home mortgages that are insured against default by the Federal Housing Administration (FHA), Veterans Administration (VA), and the Farmers Home Administration (FMHA), and issue so-called *pass-through securities* against the pooled loans. GNMA insures the interest and principal payments owed to holders of those pass-through securities it has agreed to sponsor. While GNMA sponsors and guarantees the issuance of pass-through securities by private lenders, FNMA creates its own mortgage-backed securities which it sells to individual investors and to major institutional investors like life insurance companies and retirement plans, using the proceeds of these sales to purchase packages of both conventional and government-insured home mortgage loans from banks and other lending institutions.

For its part, FHLMC purchases pools of both conventional and government-insured home mortgage loans from private lending institutions and pays for these by issuing FHLMC-guaranteed mortgage-backed securities. Beginning in the 1980s with the cooperation of First Boston Corporation, a major security dealer, FHLMC developed a new variety of mortgage loan-backed instrument—the CMO, or collateralized mortgage obligation—in which investors are offered different classes of mortgage-backed securities with different expected cash flow patterns. CMOs typically are created from a multistep process in which home mortgage loans are first pooled together, and then GNMA-guaranteed pass-through securities are issued against the mortgage pool and may be purchased by a bank or other investor. These pass-through securities are placed in a trust account off the bank's balance sheet and several different classes of CMOs are issued as claims against the pool of pass-throughs in order to raise new funds. The bank as issuer of CMOs hopes to make a profit by packaging the pass-through securities in a form that appeals to many different types of investors. Each class (tranche) of CMOs promises a different coupon rate of return to investors and carries a different maturity and risk that some of the mortgage loans in the underlying pool will be paid off early, reducing the investor's expected yield.[3]

With a CMO the different tiers ("tranches") in which bonds are issued receive the interest payments to which they are entitled, but all loan principal payments flow first

---

[3]See Chapter 10 for a discussion of *prepayment risk* and its implications for investors in loan-backed securities, such as CMOs and pass-throughs.

to bonds issued in the top tier until these top-tier instruments are fully retired. Subsequently received principal payments then go to investors who purchased bonds belonging to the next tier until the securities in that tier are paid out, and so on until the point is reached where all CMO tiers are finally paid off. The upper tiers of a CMO carry shorter and somewhat more predictable maturities, which reduces their reinvestment risk exposure. In contrast, the lower tiers carry lengthier maturities and more prepayment risk, but promise higher expected returns.

Certain CMO instruments today include a special Z tranche with the highest degree of risk exposure because this particular tranche generates no principal or interest payments until all other CMO tiers are paid off. Among the more exotic CMOs developed recently are floaters (whose rate of return is related to a particular interest rate index), superfloaters (which yield a multiple change in return based upon a particular interest rate index), and so-called "jump Z Tranches" that may suddenly catapult to first place among the tiers of a CMO depending upon events in the market. These and other complex loan-backed security instruments in recent years have become so complicated that even sophisticated traders have stumbled at times with sizable losses (for example, Goldman Sachs and Bear Stearns).

During the 1990s a new market for home equity loan-backed securities appeared and grew rapidly. *Home equity loans* permit a home owner to borrow against the residual value of their residence—that is, the difference between the current market value of their home and the amount of the mortgage loan against that property. Home equity loans have become very popular because their interest rates are often lower than on more conventional bank loans, they open up a new source of credit for households that gives them access to larger amounts of funds, may result in a tax deduction for the interest income the borrower pays, and are flexible in use (often employed to finance a child's education or to start a new business). Bonds backed by pools of home-equity loans often carry higher yields than other loan-backed securities because of their substantial prepayment risk when interest rates fall and homeowners pay off their home-equity loans early, though many home-equity borrowers do not appear to have the strong credit ratings often needed to refinance their loans. Competition in this market has become intense among banks and other lending institutions, trying to attract as many home-equity borrowers as possible, increasing the risk of home-equity-backed securities for investors buying them.

Yet another securitization device to help banks raise funds has appeared in recent years in the form of *loan-backed bonds.* Bankers can set aside a group of loans on their balance sheet, issue bonds, and pledge the loans as collateral to backstop the bonds. Unlike pass-throughs and CMOs which allow banks and other lending institutions to remove loans from their balance sheets, loan-backed bonds usually stay on the banker's balance sheet as liabilities. Moreover, while the loans backing these bonds provide the collateral for borrowing (so that if the bond-issuing bank fails, the bondholders will have a priority claim against the pledged loans), the cash flow from the pooled loans is not the sole source of cash to pay the bonds' interest and principal. Rather, monies owed on loan-backed bonds can come from any revenues generated by the issuing bank. Because the market value of the loans pledged as collateral is normally greater in amount than the volume of bonds issued, loan-backed bonds may actually carry higher credit ratings than the issuing bank itself.

What does a bank gain from issuing loan-backed bonds? First, the cost of the bank's funding may go down because the bonds are considered by investors to have low default risk due to the greater dollar value of the loans that back the bonds. In fact, it is often cheaper to issue such bonds than it is to sell large-denomination deposits that are not fully covered by government deposit insurance, suggesting that some banks can replace uninsured deposits with bonds backed by selected bank assets. Moreover, the bonds generally have longer maturities than deposits, so a bank can extend the maturity of the liability side of its balance sheet by issuing loan-backed bonds, perhaps to better match the longer maturities (durations) of its assets. Unfortunately, a portion of this double benefit from loan-backed bonds—lower funding costs and better matching of asset and liability maturities—stems from a bank's ability to sell insured deposits at very low interest rates because of government-supplied deposit insurance.

Of course, there are some offsetting disadvantages from issuing these loan-backed bonds, which help explain why loan-backed bonds are generally the least used of all bank securitization vehicles available today. For example, any loans pledged behind these bonds must be held on a bank's balance sheet until the bonds reach maturity, which decreases the overall liquidity of a bank's loan portfolio. Moreover, with these loans remaining on its balance sheet the bank must meet regulatory-imposed capital requirements to back the loans. At the same time, since a bank must hold more loans as collateral than the amount of bonds it issues, more deposits and other borrowings must be used to make up the difference, increasing the amount of liabilities taken on and possibly increasing a bank's legal reserve requirements if it is forced to issue more deposits.

Examples of Other Assets That Have Been Securitized

In addition to securitized home mortgages there are many other examples of securitized bank assets. For example, in October 1986, First Boston Corp., one of the world's leading investment banking firms, announced plans to sell $3.2 billion of securities backed by low-interest automobile loans made originally by General Motors Acceptance Corporation (GMAC). One unusual twist was the tiered structure of this security offering, which consisted of a combination of short-term, medium-term, and long-term bonds, each with a different priority of claim to the income from the packaged auto loans (labeled *CARs,* or certificates of automobile receivables). A subsidiary of First Boston actually owned the loans after purchasing them from GMAC; therefore, investors acquiring the associated bonds were not given recourse to either First Boston or GMAC in the event some of the loans defaulted. However, GMAC did promise to repurchase up to 5 percent of the loans securitized in order to cover any loans that turned sour.

Another prominent example of securitized loans is the market for participations in discounted debt issued by less-developed countries (LDCs) and syndicated Euroloans. These international loans, extended mainly to governments and multinational companies, frequently have not paid out as planned. In addition, many domestic securitizations have arisen out of adverse loan-loss situations faced by banks that have been battered by losses on energy, farm, and real estate loans and see securitization as a way to clean up their portfolios. With fewer risky and nonperforming loans on the books, a bank looks financially stronger and may be able to lower its borrowing costs. Even more importantly, securitization increases the liquidity and diversification of a loan portfolio and can be used to reduce a bank's interest rate risk by better matching the maturities of bank assets to the maturities of bank liabilities.

In the United States, loan-backed securities have been issued against an ever-widening range of loans, including commercial mortgages, Small Business Administration loans, mobile home loans, credit card receivables, truck leases, and computer leases. In March 1990, for example, Citicorp sold a $1.4 billion issue of securities backed by credit card loans into a market that has been one of the fastest-growing of all securities markets. Other leading banks that actively issue credit card–based securities today include Chase Manhattan/Chemical Bank, First National Bank of Chicago, and the Bank of America. A new dimension was added to the market in the late 1980s when banks began to help their corporate customers securitize credit and lease receivables and issue asset-backed commercial paper in order to provide these customers with low-cost, stable funding sources.

Securitization is *not* a funds source available to all banks. Recent estimates suggest that the minimum-size loan-backed securities offering likely to be successful is at least $50 million. However, smaller banks are often active investors in these securities, and it is possible for several small banks to pool their loans and jointly issue securities.

Loan-backed securities closely resemble traditional bonds, promising a fixed interest rate payable monthly, quarterly, or semiannually. These securities often carry various forms of **credit enhancement** to give buyers the impression that they are low-risk investments. These credit enhancers may include a credit letter from another financial institution willing to guarantee repayment of the securities. Another popular credit enhancement is for the issuer to set aside a cash reserve, created from the excess returns earned by the securitized loans over the amount of interest paid to security holders, in order to cover losses from any defaulted loans.

The Impact of Securitization on Banks

Securitization is likely to affect banks and bank management in several different ways. Certainly it raises the level of competition for the best-quality loans between banks and other lending institutions. Top-quality loans possess *two* advantages—they generally pay out as planned (with fewer account management problems for bank personnel) and they are most amenable to securitization, opening up a new source of bank funding that complements more traditional sources.

Securitization may also raise the level of competition among banks trying to attract deposits (particularly large-denomination CDs), because knowledgeable depositors may find that they can get a better yield by purchasing loan-backed securities from security dealers than by buying bank deposits. Securitization has made it possible for many corporations to bypass their banks for loans and seek credit in the open market through securities sales, thereby diminishing the growth rate of loans—the prime revenue source for most banks.

A good example of banks being bypassed by their best corporate customers is occurring today in the *commercial paper market;* many companies are now pooling their accounts receivable from credit sales and issuing commercial paper—short-term corporate notes—against those receivables. The issuance of this "asset-backed commercial paper," like most securitizations, takes place through an SPE (special purpose entity) which buys the company's receivables by using the cash raised from selling the securities that are backed by the receivables. Unlike other securitizations, asset-backed commercial paper is of short maturity (less than nine months) but the deal doesn't necessarily end when the receivables mature or the securities are paid off. Rather, new receivables may be sold to the same SPE to replace those paid off and new commercial notes can be issued to replace the commercial paper that is maturing.

Banks have been able to benefit indirectly from securitizations conducted by their corporate customers by providing, for a fee, credit letters to enhance the credit rating of corporations selling their securities in the public market. Moreover, banks can generate added fee income by providing a backup liquidity facility in case the securitizing company runs short of cash and by acting as underwriters for new asset-backed security issues. Banks also find they can use securitization to assist a good corporate customer in finding financing without the bank's having to make any direct loans, which would inflate the bank's risky assets and require it to raise more capital. The net result of all these changes is probably to decrease bank revenues somewhat and possibly to increase bank funding costs. Faced with intense competition on *both* sides of their balance sheets, recently many banks have more aggressively pursued service areas where securitization is less of a factor, such as loans to small and medium-size business firms and households.

Concept Checks

9–1.   What does *securitization* of assets mean?

9–2.   What kinds of assets are most amenable to the securitization process?

9–3.   What advantages does securitization offer for banks?

9–4.   What risks of securitization should bank managers be aware of?

9–5.   Suppose that a bank securitizes a package of its loans that bear a gross annual interest yield of 13 percent. The securities issued against the loan package promise interested investors an annualized yield of 8.25 percent. The expected default rate on the packaged loans is 3.5 percent. The bank agrees to pay an annual fee of 0.35 percent to a security dealer in order to cover the cost of underwriting and advisory services and a fee of 0.25 percent to Arunson Mortgage Servicing Corporation to process the expected payments generated by the packaged loans. If the above items represent all the costs associated with this securitization transaction, can you calculate the percentage amount of *residual income* the bank expects to earn from this particular transaction?

Sales of Loans to Raise Funds

Not only can bank loans be used as collateral for issuing securities to raise new funds, but the loans themselves can be sold in their entirety to a new owner. Indeed, **loan sales**—often done in the past by the largest banks in the industry—have now spread out to involve banks of widely varying sizes. Included among the principal buyers in bank loan sales are other banks (including foreign banking firms seeking a solid foothold in the domestic market), insurance companies, pension funds, large European and American nonfinancial corporations, mutual funds (including vulture funds that concentrate on buying troubled loans), and large investment banks (such as Goldman Sachs and Merrill Lynch). Among the leading sellers of these loans are money center banks (such as Bankers Trust Corporation of New York and BankAmerica) and such foreign banks as ING Bank of the Netherlands. (See Exhibit 9–2.)

The loans sold by banks usually fall within 90 days to maturity (though loans covering several months or years are also sold with some regularity) and may be either new loans or loans that have been on the selling bank's books for some time. The loan sale market received a strong boost during the 1980s when a wave of mergers and corporate buyouts led to the creation of thousands of loans to fund *highly leveraged transactions* (HLTs). The market for such loans in the United States expanded more than 10-fold during the 1980s, but then fell dramatically in the 1990s as mergers and corporate buyouts cooled off and federal banking agencies tightened their regulations regarding the acceptability of such loans. Generally, HLT-related loans are secured by the assets of the borrowing company and, typically, are long-term, covering in some

EXHIBIT 9–2

The Impact of Bank Loan Sales

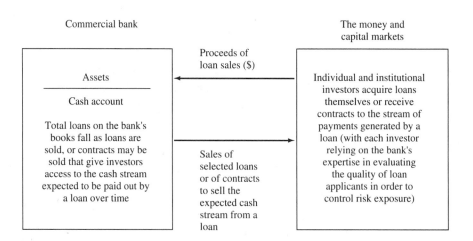

Source: Peter S. Rose, "New Benefits, New Pitfalls," *The Canadian Banker*, September/October 1988.

cases up to eight years, and carrying floating loan rates tied to prime, LIBOR, or some other widely publicized interest rate. In contrast, most other loans that banks sell carry maturities of only a few weeks or months, have minimum denominations of at least a million dollars, are generally extended to borrowers with investment-grade credit ratings, and carry interest rates that usually are connected to short-term corporate loan rates (such as the prevailing market interest rate on commercial paper IOUs issued by the largest and best-known companies).

Typically, the selling bank retains **servicing rights** on the sold loans. These rights enable the selling bank to generate fee income (often one-quarter or three-eighths of a percentage point of the amount of the loans sold) by collecting interest and principal payments from borrowers and passing the proceeds along to loan buyers. Servicing banks also monitor the performance of borrowers and act on behalf of loan buyers to make sure that borrowers are adhering to the terms of their loans.

One of the hottest loan resale markets in recent years has been trading in Third World debt. Old loans to Argentina, Brazil, Mexico, Peru, the Philippines, and other Third World nations often sell at deep discounts from their face value (in some cases as low as 5 cents on the dollar). Most of these loans are purchased in million-dollar units by banks and corporations that already operate in and have special knowledge of the debtor country. A few Third World credits have scored large capital gains for their buyers when conditions improved at home or when the government involved simply repurchased its own debt. Moreover, in the 1990s a multibillion-dollar market for floating-rate corporate loans arose with many insurance companies and mutual funds, who had purchased ordinary bonds in the past, switching some of their money into bank-originated corporate loans. These salable loans appear to have several advantages over bonds for many investors due to their strict loan covenants, floating interest rates, and the availability of both short-term and long-term financial instruments.

Loan sales occur in several different forms. For example, two of the most popular types are: (*a*) **participation loans** and (*b*) **assignments.** In a participation loan the purchaser is an outsider (i.e., not a partner) to the loan contract between the bank selling the loan and the borrower. Only if there are significant alterations in the terms of the original loan contract can the buyer of a participation in a bank loan exercise any influence over the terms of the loan contract. Thus, the buyer of a participation in an existing loan faces substantial risks—the selling bank may fail or the borrower may fail, presenting the participation purchaser with substantial losses. This means that the buyer of a loan participation must watch *both* the borrower and the seller bank closely. As a result of these and other limitations of participations, most loan sales today are by *assignment.* Under an assignment, ownership of a loan is transferred to the buyer, who thereby acquires a direct claim against the borrower. This means that, in some cases, the borrower has to agree to the sale of his or her loan before an assignment can be made.

A third type of loan sale, closely related to loan participations, is the **loan strip.** Loan strips are short-dated pieces of a longer-term loan and often mature quickly—a few days or weeks. The buyer of a strip is entitled to a fraction of the expected income from a loan. With strips, the selling bank retains the risk of borrower default and usually has to put up some of its own funds to support the loan until it reaches maturity.

Reasons behind Loan Sales

There are many reasons why leading banks in many countries have turned to loan sales as an important new method of funding bank operations. One reason is the opportunity loan sales provide for getting rid of lower-yielding assets in order to make room for higher-yielding assets when market interest rates rise. Selling loans and replacing them with more marketable assets, such as government securities, can increase a bank's liquidity, better preparing the institution for deposit withdrawals or other cash needs. Moreover, disposing of loans removes both credit risk and interest rate risk from a bank's balance sheet and may generate fee income up front rather than having to wait until the loans the bank is thinking of selling accrue some interest. Then, too, loan sales slow the growth of bank assets, which helps management maintain a better balance between the growth of bank capital and the acceptance of risk in the lending function. In this way loan sales help bankers please regulators, who have put considerable pressure on banks to get rid of their riskiest assets and strengthen their capital in recent years. A few recent studies, such as Benveniste and Berger [13] and Hassan [4], suggest that loan sales are generally viewed by investors in the capital markets as risk-reducing for the selling bank, helping to lower its cost of capital and diversify its asset portfolio by selling old loans and replacing them with new ones. Banks purchasing these loans receive help in diversifying their loan portfolio, acquiring loans from new regions and new industries outside their traditional trade areas. Diversification of this sort can lower risk exposure and result in lower borrowing costs for the bank buying the loans.

Recently, Haubrich and Thomson [7] have argued that the development of the loan sales market has profound implications for the future of banking. The growth of this market means that banks can make loans without taking in deposits and cover deposit withdrawals merely by selling loans. Moreover, if this market grows rapidly in the future, banks may have less need for deposit insurance or for borrowing from the discount windows of the Federal Reserve banks. Because loan sales are so similar to issuing securities, this bank financing device blurs the distinction between banks and other financial institutions that trade securities, suggesting the need for a complete review of government regulatory policy toward banks and nonbank financial institutions to ensure balance and fairness in the burden of regulation for different types of financial-service institutions.

The Risks in Loan Sales

Loan sales are just another form of investment banking, in which the banker trades on his or her superior ability to evaluate the creditworthiness of a borrower and sells that expertise (represented by the content of the loan contract itself) to another investor. Investors are willing to purchase loans that a bank originates because they have confidence in that bank's ability to identify good-quality borrowers and write an advantageous loan contract. Nevertheless, loan sales as a source of bank funds are not without their problems. For example, it is the best-quality loans that are most likely to find a ready resale market. But if a bank's management isn't careful, it will find itself selling off its soundest loans, leaving its portfolio heavily stocked with poor-quality loans, which may result in more volatile bank earnings. This development is likely to trigger the attention of bank regulators, and the bank may find itself facing demands from regulatory agencies to acquire more capital.

Moreover, a loan sold by one bank to another bank can turn sour just as easily as a direct loan from the originating bank to its own customers. Indeed, the selling bank may have done a poor job of evaluating the borrower's financial condition. Buying an existing loan, therefore, obligates the purchasing bank to review the financial condition not only of the selling bank but also of the borrower.

In some instances, the selling bank will agree to give the loan purchaser *recourse* to the seller for all or a portion of those sold loans that become delinquent. In effect, the purchaser gets a *put option,* allowing him or her to sell a troubled loan back to the bank that originated it. This arrangement forces buyer and seller to *share* the risk of loan default. Recourse agreements are not common in today's loan market because federal regulations require a bank selling loans with recourse to hold reserves behind those loans and to count them as part of its assets when determining the bank's required level of capital. However, many banks seem to feel obligated to reacquire the troubled loans they sold to a customer, even if there is no legal requirement to do so, simply to protect an established bank-customer relationship.

Often loans themselves are *not* sold. Instead, the originating bank sells claims to the expected stream of cash from a loan, and the purchaser of rights to that cash stream has no recourse to either the bank or its borrowing customer if the loan fails to pay out as planned.

Finally, banks must recognize that raising funds by selling loans is likely to be affected by a strong *cyclical* factor. In some years, particularly when the economy is expanding rapidly, there may be an abundance of salable loans, while in other years the volume of salable loans may decline significantly, particularly in recessions when bank loan demand is at a low ebb and there are fewer originations of *new* bank loans.

Indeed, the bank loan sales market declined sharply in the 1990s. A number of factors appear to have accounted for the decline: more businesses are bypassing banks for the loans they need, which has led to a decrease in the availability of quality loans that are the easiest for banks to sell; corporate merger and acquisition activity has slowed somewhat; there is tougher regulation of some of the types of loans (such as highly leveraged transactions or HLTs) that banks used to sell in high volume; and other sources of bank funds have opened up through deregulation (such as fewer restrictions on deposit terms and broader powers for U.S. banks to underwrite commercial paper issues). However, some banking authorities expect a future rebound in bank loan sales due to the trend toward market-value accounting in banking, which may cause better-informed buyers to view bank loans more favorably as investment vehicles; due to tougher capital-adequacy requirements (particularly on commercial loans), which may encourage banks to continue to sell off selected loans and lower their capital requirements; and also due to the continued swing of many large banks (such as Bankers Trust Company of New York and the Netherlands' ING) toward more market trading activities in place of traditional lending activities.

Bank Management in Action

Off-Balance-Sheet Activities and Bank Performance

The rise of off-balance-sheet transactions in banking appears to have affected the performance of banks and their success (or lack of success) in achieving their goals in recent years. Recent research by a variety of analysts (see below) suggests that banking's off-balance-sheet activities may have helped to reduce the variance of banker's net interest margins. Thus, the variability of the spread between banks' interest revenues and their interest expenses on borrowed funds appears to have been reduced in recent years even as off-balance-sheet activity in the industry has risen. Some experts argue, however, that this reduced interest-rate spread or margin variance may not be due just to greater off-balance-sheet trading activity. For example, interest margins may be more stable because of a more stable monetary policy on the part of central banks (such as the Federal Reserve System) and because of more attention in general paid by bankers and regulators to their institutions' credit and interest rate risk exposure.

Moreover, there is little convincing evidence today that the lower apparent variability in bank net interest margins has resulted in less variability in banks' bottom line—that is, their returns on assets (ROA) and on equity capital (ROE). Indeed, there is some research evidence that banks which make heavy use of off-balance-sheet interest rate and currency derivatives may actually tend to achieve lower average rates of return on their assets. Not surprisingly, banks that display greater gaps between the maturities of their assets and their liabilities tend to make heavier use of off-balance-sheet positions in swaps and other derivative-type instruments. Moreover, banks with greater off-balance-sheet activity seem to experience more rapid growth in their business loans and investment securities than do other banks.

For a good sampling of recent studies of the impact of banks' off-balance-sheet activity on bank behavior and performance see the studies by Elijah Brewer III, Bernadette A. Minton, and James T. Moser, "The Effect of Bank-Held Derivatives on Credit Accessibility," *Federal Reserve Bank of Chicago Working Paper,* November 1994; Sung-Hwa Kim and G. D. Koppenhaver, "An Empirical Analysis of Bank Interest-Rate Swaps," *Journal of Financial Services Research* 7 (January 1993), pp. 57–72; Joseph Sinkey and David Carter, "The Derivative Activities of U.S. Commercial Banks," in *Proceedings of the 30th Annual Conference on Bank Structure and Competition,* Federal Reserve Bank of Chicago, May 1994, pp. 175–88; and Arun Soni and Peter S. Rose, "The Impact of Derivatives' Usage on Commercial Bank Performance: Evidence from the Recent Portfolio Behavior of U.S. Banks," *Working Paper,* Finance Department, Texas A&M University, Summer 1997.

Concept Checks

9–6.   What advantages do *sales of loans* have for banks trying to raise funds?

9–7.   Are there any disadvantages to using loan sales as a significant source of bank funding?

9–8.   What is *loan servicing?*

9–9.   How can servicing be used to increase bank income?

Standby Credit Letters

One of the most rapidly growing of all markets in recent years has been the market for **financial guarantees**—instruments used to enhance the credit standing of a borrower to help ensure lenders against default on the borrower's loans and to reduce the borrower's financing costs. In short, financial guarantees are designed to ensure the timely repayment of the principal and interest from a loan even if the borrower goes bankrupt or cannot perform a contractual obligation. One of the most popular in the banking community is the **standby letter of credit (SLC).**

Standby letters of credit may include (1) *performance bond guarantees,* in which a bank guarantees that a building or other project will be completed on time, or (2) *default guarantees,* under which a bank pledges the repayment of defaulted corporate notes and state and local government bonds when the borrowers cannot pay. These standby letters enable borrowing customers to get the credit they require at lower cost and on more flexible terms. In order to sell these guarantees successfully, however, the bank must have a higher credit rating than its customer. Because many U.S. banks have experienced declines in their credit ratings in recent years, their competitors (including foreign banks and insurance companies) have recently moved in to capture a larger share of the credit guarantee market.

A standby credit letter is a **contingent obligation** of the letter's issuer. The issuing bank or nonbank firm, in return for a fee, agrees to *guarantee* the credit of its customer or to guarantee the fulfillment of a contract made by its customer with a third party. The key advantages to a bank issuing standbys are the following:

1. Letters of credit earn the bank a fee for providing the service (usually around 0.5 percent to 1 percent of the amount of credit involved).
2. They aid a customer, who can usually borrow more cheaply when armed with the bank's guarantee, without using up the bank's scarce reserves.
3. Such guarantees usually can be issued at relatively low cost because the issuing bank may already know the financial condition of its standby credit customer (e.g., when that customer applied for his or her last loan).

4. The probability is low that the issuer of the credit guarantee will ever be called upon to pay.

Standby credit letters have grown rapidly in recent years for several reasons:

1. The rapid growth of *direct finance* worldwide, with borrowers selling their securities directly to investors rather than going to a bank to borrow money; direct financings have increased investor concerns about borrower defaults and resulted in increased demand for credit guarantees.

2. The perception among bankers and their customers that the risk of economic fluctuations (recessions, inflation, etc.) has increased, which has led to increased demand for risk-reducing devices.

3. The opportunity standbys offer banks to use their credit evaluation skills to earn additional fee income by underwriting credit risk without the immediate commitment of bank funds.

4. The relatively low cost of issuing standbys—unlike deposits, they carry zero reserve requirements and no insurance fees.

Structure of Standby Letters of Credit

SLCs contain three essential elements: (1) a commitment from the **issuer** (usually a bank or insurance company today), (2) an **account party** (for whom the letter is issued), and (3) a **beneficiary** (usually a bank or other investor concerned about the safety of funds committed to the account party). The key feature of SLCs is that they are usually *not* listed on the issuer's or beneficiary's balance sheet. This is because a standby agreement is only a *contingent liability*. In most cases, it will expire unexercised. Delivery of funds to the beneficiary can occur only if something unexpected happens to the account party (such as bankruptcy or technical nonperformance). Moreover, the beneficiary can claim funds from the issuer only if the beneficiary meets *all* the conditions laid down in the credit letter. If any of those conditions are *not* met, the issuer is *not* obligated to pay. (See Exhibit 9–3.)

Exhibit 9–3

The Nature of a Standby Credit Agreement

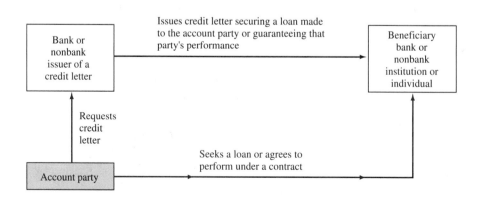

The Value and Pricing of Standby Letters

Under the terms of an SLC, the bank issuing the letter will pay any interest or principal to the beneficiary that is owed and left unpaid by its customer, the account party. In effect, the bank agrees for a fee to take on a risk that, in the absence of the SLC, would be carried fully by the beneficiary. Therefore, the beneficiary may be willing to lend the account party more money or provide the same amount of funds but at a lower interest rate than if there were no standby credit.

In general, an account party will seek a bank's standby guarantee if the bank's fee for issuing the guarantee is less than the value assigned to the bank's guarantee by the beneficiary. Thus, if P is the price of the standby guarantee, NL is the cost of a nonguaranteed loan, and GL is the cost of a loan backed by a standby guarantee, then a borrower is likely to seek a standby guarantee if:

$$P < NL - GL$$

For example, if a borrower can get a nonguaranteed loan at an interest cost of 7.50 percent, but is told that a quality standby credit guarantee would reduce the loan's interest cost to 6.75 percent and a bank offers the borrower a standby guarantee for 0.50 percent of the loan's face value, clearly it will pay the borrower to get the guarantee because the savings on the loan of (7.50% − 6.75%) or 0.75% exceeds the 0.50% guarantee fee.

In turn, the value to the beneficiary of an SLC is a function of the credit ratings of the issuer and the account party and the information cost of assessing their credit standing. Clearly, the guarantee of a bank with a superior credit rating will be valued highly by beneficiaries. Account parties will be less likely to seek out a weak bank to issue a credit letter, because such a guarantee gives them little bargaining power in obtaining better terms from the beneficiary. If the cost of obtaining relevant information about the condition of the guaranteeing bank or about the account party is high, the beneficiary also may find little or no value in a standby credit agreement.

Sources of Risk with Standby Credits

What kinds of risk do banks and other investors who become the beneficiaries of standby credit letters have to bear? Standby credits carry several forms of risk exposure for the bank or other lending institution relying upon them. For example, the issuing institution may not be able to cover its commitment, resulting in default. Because credit letters do not qualify as insured deposits, a bank holding the credit letter as beneficiary will probably receive little or nothing if the letter's issuer fails. Also, some jurisdictions have held that a bank cannot be forced to pay off on a credit letter if doing so would force it to violate banking regulations (e.g., if the amount to be paid exceeds the bank's legal lending limit).

Banks relying on standby credit assurances received from other institutions must take considerable care that such agreements are fully documented so they know how to file a valid claim for payment. Banks with beneficiary rights cannot legally obtain reimbursement from the issuer unless *all* of the conditions required for successful presentation of a credit letter are met. In addition, bankruptcy laws present a potential hazard for banks as beneficiaries trying to collect on letter of credits. In some court jurisdictions, it has been held that any payments made upon presentation of a valid credit letter are "preference items" under the federal bankruptcy code and therefore must be returned to the account party if bankruptcy is declared.

Do the banks issuing standby credits face any risk exposure? Yes, there may be substantial interest rate and liquidity risks. If the issuing bank is compelled to pay under a credit letter without prior notice, it may be forced to raise substantial amounts of funds at unfavorable interest rates. Indeed, if the letter is for a substantial sum of money relative to the bank's credit capacity, the institution may find itself in a very adverse borrowing position. Bankers can use various devices to reduce risk exposure from the standby credit letters they have issued, such as:

1. Frequently renegotiating the terms of any loans extended to customers who have standby credit guarantees so that loan terms are continually adjusted to the customer's changing circumstances and there is less need for the beneficiaries of those guarantees to press for collection.

2. Diversifying standby letters issued by region and by industry to avoid concentration of risk exposure.

3. Selling participations in standbys in order to share risk with a variety of other lending institutions.

Regulatory Concerns about Standby Credit Arrangements

The rapid growth of contingent obligations among major banks has raised the specter of more bank failures if more standby credits than expected are presented for collection. Many regulators fear that investors in bank securities (including holders of uninsured deposits) may be lulled to sleep (i.e., will tend to underprice bank risk) if a bank books fewer loans but at the same time takes on a large volume of standby credits. Unfortunately, there is ample incentive for banks to take on more standbys due to their relatively low production costs and the added leverage they generate because no bank reserves are required, at least at the beginning of the agreement.

Bank examiners and regulatory agencies are working to keep bank risk exposure from credit standbys under control. Several new regulatory rules are in use today:

1. Banks must apply the same credit standards for approving credit letters as they do for approving direct loans.

2. Banks must count standbys as loans when assessing how risk-exposed the bank is to a single credit customer.

3. Since the adoption of the 1987–88 international bank capital agreement between the United States and other leading nations (discussed in Chapter 15), banks have been required to post capital behind most standbys as though these contingent agreements were actual loans.

Research Studies on Standbys, Loan Sales, and Securitizations

Several studies have addressed the issue of the relative riskiness of direct loans versus standby credits, loan sales, and securitizations entered into by banks. For example, Bennett [1] observed that direct loans carry substantially higher market risk premiums than do credit letters; this supports the idea that investors as a whole believe standby credits carry significantly less risk than loans themselves. One reason may be that such credit letters are usually requested by prime-quality borrowers. Another factor may be the market's expectation that most credit letters will never be presented for collection. These suppositions were supported by an earlier study conducted by Goldberg and Lloyd-Davies [3], who found that issuing SLCs had essentially *no* impact on bank deposit costs.

More recently, Hassan [6] finds evidence from option-pricing models that both bank stockholders and bank creditors view off-balance-sheet standby credit letters as reducing bank risk by increasing the overall diversification of a bank's assets. Hassan argues that imposing capital requirements on standby letters of credit, therefore, may not be appropriate because standbys, if properly used, can reduce bank risk. Moreover, Pennacchi [9], Pavel and Phillis [8], and Pyle [10] have argued that standby credits, loan sales, and securitizations are principally *defensive* reactions by bankers to regulation. These off-balance-sheet activities can be viewed simply as attempts by banks to increase their financial leverage, thereby augmenting returns to their shareholders. Contingent obligations will be substituted for bank assets and deposits whenever regulation increases the cost of more traditional activities.

But according to James [5], regulation is not the only motivation for loan sales, standby credits, and other nontraditional bank fund-raising devices. James believes that these transactions are better viewed as substitutes for collateralized debt because banks are prohibited from selling collateralized deposits (with the exception of government deposits where specific assets are pledged to protect them). He argues that both regulations and government deposit insurance can be incentives for banks to pursue off-balance-sheet activities. However, if these new services and instruments increase the value of banks (i.e., raise their stock prices), it might be a mistake to severely restrict them by government regulation.

Concept Checks

9–10. What are *standby credit letters*? Why have they grown so rapidly in recent years?

9–11. Who are the principal parties to a standby credit agreement?

9–12. What risks accompany a standby credit letter for (*a*) the issuing bank and (*b*) the beneficiary?

9–13. How can a bank mitigate the risks inherent in issuing standby credit letters?

Credit Derivatives: A Rapidly Developing Alternative to Securitizations and Loan Sales

Securitizing assets, loan sales, and standby credit letters can help a bank reduce the credit risk associated with its loan portfolio as well as help with interest rate risk exposure. For example, removing a pool of loans from the bank's balance sheet reduces or disposes of the bank's credit risk exposure from those loans. Similarly, a bank that has just made loans to some of its customers can sell those loans to other investors, who now may take on the credit risks inherent in those loans.

However, securitizations and loan sales are usually not feasible for groups of loans that do not have some common features—that is, loans (such as many business loans) that do not have the same cash-flow schedules or comparable risk exposures. For these common types of loans **credit derivatives**—financial contracts offering protection to the beneficiary in case of loan default—can be helpful in reducing a bank's exposure to credit risk and, in some cases, interest rate risk as well.

Credit Swaps

One prominent example of a credit derivative is the **credit swap,** where two lenders simply agree to exchange a portion of their customers' loan repayments. For example, Banks A and B may find a swap dealer, such as a large insurance company, that agrees to draw up a credit swap contract between the two banks. Bank A then transmits an amount (perhaps $100 million) in interest and principal payments that it collects from its credit customers to the dealer. Bank B also sends $100 million worth of the loan payments its customers make to the same dealer. The swap dealer will ultimately pass these payments along to the other bank that signed the swap contract.

Example of a Credit Swap

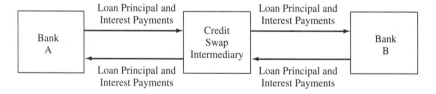

Usually the dealer levies a slight fee (perhaps 15 basis points) for the service of bringing these two swap partners together. The swap dealer may also guarantee each swap partner's performance under the agreement in return for an additional charge.

What is the advantage for each swap partner in participating in such an agreement? Clearly, each bank is granted the opportunity to further spread out the risk in its loan portfolio, especially if the banks involved are located in different market areas. Because each bank's loan portfolio may come from a different market, a credit swap permits each institution to broaden the number of markets from which it collects loan revenues and loan principal, thus reducing each bank's dependence on one or a narrow set of market areas.

A popular variation on the credit swap just described—a *total return swap*—may involve a financial institution (dealer) that guarantees the swap parties a specific rate of return on their credit assets. For example, a swap dealer may guarantee Bank A a return on its small business loans that is 3 percentage points higher than the long-term government bond rate. In this instance Bank A would have exchanged the risky return from a portion of its loans for a much more stable rate of reward based upon a government security (unless, of course, the swap dealer promising that more predictable source of income goes out of business).

Another example of a total return swap might rest upon a loan that Bank A has recently made to one of its commercial customers. Bank A then agrees to pay Bank B the total return earned on the loan (including interest and principal payments plus any increase [appreciation] in the loan's market value that occurs). Bank B, for its part, agrees to pay A the London InterBank Offer Rate (LIBOR) plus a small interest rate spread and to compensate A for any depreciation that occurs in the loan's market value. In essence, Bank B bears the credit risk (and also the interest rate risk if the loan involved is a floating-rate loan or its market value is highly sensitive to market interest rate movements) associated with Bank A's loan just as though it actually owned Bank A's loan, even though it is *not* the owner. This swap may terminate early if the loan involved is defaulted on by the borrower.

Example of a Total Return Swap

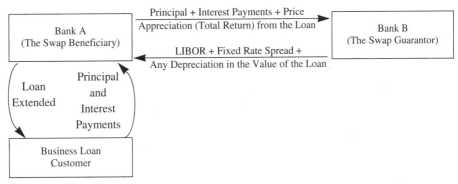

Credit Options

Another popular credit-risk derivative today is the **credit option,** which guards against losses in the value of a credit asset or helps to offset higher borrowing costs that may occur due to changes in credit ratings. For example, a bank worried about default on a large $100 million loan it has just made might approach an options dealer about an option contract that pays off if the loan declines significantly in value or completely turns bad. If the bank's borrowing customer pays off as promised, the bank collects the loan revenue it expected to gather in and the option issued by the dealer (option-writer) will go unused. The bank involved will, of course, lose the premium it paid to the dealer writing the option. Many banks will take out similar credit options to protect the value of securities held in their investment portfolios should the securities' issuer fail to pay or should the securities decline significantly in value due to a change in credit standing.

Example of a Credit Option

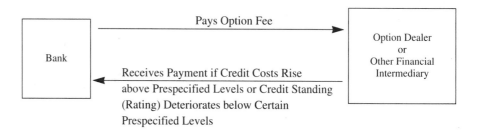

Another type of credit option can be used to hedge against a rise in borrowing costs due to a change in the borrower's default-risk or credit rating. For example, a bank or bank holding company may fear that its credit rating will be lowered just before it plans to issue some long-term notes or bonds to raise new capital. This would force the banking firm to pay a higher interest rate for its borrowed funds. One possible solution is for the banking company to purchase a call option on the default-risk interest rate spread prevailing in the market for debt securities similar in quality to its own securities at the time it needs to borrow money. Like other types of options, the credit risk option would have a *base rate spread* and would pay off if the market's default-risk rate spread over riskless securities climbs upward beyond the base rate spread specified in the option.

For example, suppose the banking company expected to pay a borrowing cost that was one percentage point over the five-year government bond rate. In this instance, the base rate spread is one percentage point. A lowering of the banking firm's credit rating or a recession in the economy might result in the default-risk rate spread the bank must pay ballooning upward from one percentage point to perhaps two percentage points above the government bond rate. The call option becomes profitable if this happens and helps cover the borrower's higher borrowing costs, in effect lowering the default risk interest-rate spread back to the neighborhood of one percentage point over the five-year government security rate. On the other hand, if default-risk rate spreads fall (perhaps due to a rise in the bank's credit rating or a strengthening in the economy), this option will not be profitable and the bank will lose the option premium that it paid.

Credit Default Swaps

A related form of credit option is the **credit default swap,** usually aimed at banks and other creditors able to handle comparatively limited declines in value, but wanting insurance against truly serious losses. In this case a bank may seek out a dealer willing to write a put option on a portfolio of loans or other assets. Suppose, for example, the bank has recently made a total of 100 million-dollar commercial real estate loans to support the building of several investment projects in various cities. Fearing that several of these 100 loans might turn sour because of weakening local economic conditions, it purchases a put option that pays off if more than two of these commercial real estate loans are defaulted. Thus, for each commercial real estate loan that fails to pay out, the bank may receive $1 million less the resale value of the building used to secure the loan.

In another example of a credit default swap, a bank may seek out a guarantor institution in order to unload the risk on one of its loans in case of default. For example, suppose Bank A swaps the credit risk from a five-year, $100 million construction loan to Bank B. Typically, A will pay B a fee based upon the loan's par or face value (for example, 1/2 percent of $100 million, or $500,000). For its part, B agrees to pay A a stipulated amount of money or a fixed percentage of the value of the loan *only if default occurs.* There may be a so-called *materiality threshold*—a minimum amount of loss required—before any payment occurs. If the swap ends in an actual default, the amount owed is normally the face value of the loan less the current market value of the defaulted asset.

Example of a Credit Default Swap

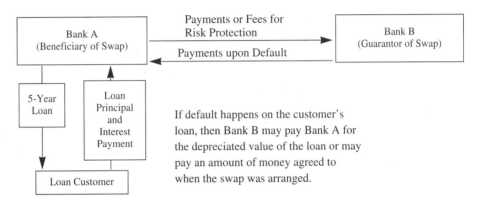

If default happens on the customer's loan, then Bank B may pay Bank A for the depreciated value of the loan or may pay an amount of money agreed to when the swap was arranged.

Credit-Linked Notes

Finally, *credit-linked notes* have recently appeared that fuse together a normal debt instrument (such as a note or bond) plus a credit option contract to give a borrower of funds greater payment flexibility. A credit-linked note grants its issuer the privilege of lowering the amount of loan repayments it must pay if some significant factor changes. For example, suppose a bank borrows through a bond issue in order to support a group of real estate loans it intends to make and agrees to pay the investors buying these bonds a 10 percent annual coupon payment (e.g., $100 a year for each $1,000 par-value bond). However, the credit-linked note agreement carries the stipulation that if defaults on the loans made with the borrowed funds rise significantly (perhaps above 7 percent of all the loans outstanding), then the note-issuing lender will only have to pay a 7 percent coupon rate (e.g., $70 a year per $1,000 bond). Therefore, the lender has taken on credit-related insurance from the investors who bought into its bond issue.

Risks Associated with Credit Derivatives

Credit derivatives are not without risk, though they can do much to protect a bank's loan, investment, and borrowing risk exposure. The partner to each swap or option may fail to perform, and now the bank has to find a *new* swap partner to hedge its credit risk exposure. Courts may rule that credit risk agreements are not legal or are improperly drawn and the bank will lose all or a portion of its risk protection. Finally, such agreements are still relatively small in volume compared to such popular hedging devices as financial futures contracts, interest rate and currency options, and interest rate and currency swaps, meaning that resale markets for these agreements are thinner and more volatile. In fact, the still relatively small credit derivatives market may, at times, leave a bank seeking risk protection with few attractive options.

Major regulatory issues also remain for banks that employ credit derivatives today. They are largely unregulated right now, but could become so at any time. Capital regulations for these instruments are currently being closely studied by the bank regulatory agencies, and no one knows for sure how regulators' and legislators' attitudes toward these instruments might change with time.

Recently the FDIC announced that "only those arrangements that provide virtually complete credit protection to the underlying asset will be considered effective guarantees for purposes of asset classification and risk-based capital calculations. On the other hand, if the amount of credit risk transferred by the beneficiary is severely limited or uncertain, then the limited credit protection the derivative provides the beneficiary should not be taken into account for these purposes" (FDIC, 1996, p. 3).

Should the regulatory community decide to lower the amount of capital needed by banks using these derivatives, this step would certainly cause the market to grow rapidly. If credit derivatives come to be regarded as inherently destabilizing and risky, however, forcing banks using them to pledge even more capital, the market could flounder and become less efficient. Many unknowns currently plague this relatively new risk-management arena in banking.

Concept Checks

9–14. Why were *credit derivatives* developed? What advantages do they have over loan sales and securitizations, if any?

9–15. What is a *credit swap?* For what kinds of situations was it developed?

9–16. What is a *total return swap?* What advantages does it offer the swap's beneficiary institution?

9–17. How do *credit options* work? What circumstances result in the option contract paying off?

9–18. When is a *credit default swap* useful? Why?

9–19. Of what use are *credit-linked notes?*

9–20. What risks do credit derivatives pose for banks using them? What is the attitude of the regulatory community, thus far, toward banks using these credit-related instruments? In your opinion what should regulators do about the recent rapid growth of this market, if anything?

Summary

This chapter has examined some of the newest sources of funding and income drawn upon by banks—securitization of assets, sales of loans, and issuing standby letters of credit (contingent obligations). Banks have turned to these newer sources of revenue and reserves increasingly because of regulation and changing investor behavior in the global financial marketplace. Security markets appear to have become more volatile, and business failure rates remain relatively high, creating more risk of loss for institutional and individual investors and encouraging them to seek safer assets to purchase and hold. In addition, new regulations have ordered bank managers to strengthen the long-term capital positions of their institutions. Many bankers have found it cost effective to improve their institutions' capital-to-assets ratio either by selling loans off the balance sheet or by packaging assets, issuing securities against them, and setting those assets aside.

The development of standby letters of credit has allowed banks to avoid using up their scarce reserves but still help their customers with needed financing. With a standby credit letter, a bank guarantees the loan made by another institution to its customer. SLCs make it possible for a customer to borrow at a lower interest cost, while still generating fee income for the bank issuing the standby letter. Nevertheless, standbys are not without potential pitfalls. For one thing, credit letters are not always collectible, especially where bankruptcy laws are invoked or careful documentation does not exist. Moreover, some banks have been frustrated by banking regulations or by securities laws in trying to collect monies owed them under standby credits issued by other institutions.

During the 1990s another group of off-balance-sheet instruments began to grow rapidly—so-called *credit derivatives.* These risk-reducing contracts are usually negotiated between two banks or between a bank and a nonbank financial institution (such as an insurance company) and are designed to: (1) reduce the risk of default in a bank's loan portfolio; (2) stabilize bank loan and investment income; or (3) reduce a bank's borrowing costs in the financial marketplace. Credit derivatives also can provide some protection against interest rate risk by helping a bank substitute a relatively safe and predictable flow of income for a volatile flow of loan or investment income.

Among the most prominent of credit derivatives today are *credit swaps* (in which two banks exchange cash flows from their loan portfolios to help diversify their sources of loan income); *total return swaps* (in which a bank pays a guarantor institution a stream of income from its loans and investments, which may be quite volatile, in exchange for a more certain income stream based upon a widely recognized market interest rate such as the return on government bonds); *credit options* (in which a bank pays a fee to a guarantor to "insure" a loan or security investment against default or to offset a possible rise in bank borrowing cost due to a decline in the bank's credit rating); and *credit default swaps* (where a bank protects itself against excessive numbers of borrower defaults from a group of large loans it has made). Recently another form of credit derivative has appeared in the guise of *credit-linked notes* in which banking companies selling bonds or notes to raise money also sell an option to investors to reduce the bank's borrowing costs in case too many of its loans turn into bad loans that will not pay out.

Credit derivatives carry their own special forms of risk exposure for a bank. For example, a bank's partner in a credit swap or option may go bankrupt and fail to hold up its end of the contract, forcing the bank to find another partner and a new credit derivative contract, possibly on unfavorable terms. Moreover, the contract that evidences a credit risk agreement may be invalidated by a court of law, once again forcing the parties to the contract to find credit-risk protection from some other source. Then, too, regulatory uncertainty has entered the picture as bank examiners and regulators try to adapt to this emerging derivatives market with new rules. Thus far, regulators seem determined to take a conservative approach, giving banks credit for lowering their risk exposure from these new contracts only if their language is clear and these instruments provide virtually complete risk protection for the bank's assets, income stream, or borrowing costs. As in some other areas of banking, careful attention to detail and a thorough understanding of banking regulations is the key to the successful use of off-balance-sheet instruments to reduce bank risk and better serve bank customers.

Key Terms in This Chapter

Securitization
Credit enhancement
Loan sales
Servicing rights
Participation loans
Assignments
Loan strip
Financial guarantees
Standby letter of credit (SLC)

Contingent obligation
Issuer
Account party
Beneficiary
Credit derivatives
Credit swap
Credit option
Credit default swaps

Problems and Projects

1. Deltone National Bank has placed a group of 10,000 consumer loans bearing an average expected gross annual yield of 14.5 percent in a package to be securitized. The investment bank advising Deltone estimates that the securities will sell at a slight discount from par that results in a net interest cost to the issuer of 10.08 percent. Based on recent experience with similar types of loans, the bank expects 2.67 percent of the packaged loans to default without any recovery for the lender and has agreed to set aside a cash reserve to cover this amount of anticipated loss. Underwriting and advisory services provided by the investment banking firm will cost 0.65 percent. Deltone will also seek a liquidity facility, costing 0.45 percent, and a credit guarantee if actual loan defaults should exceed the expected loan-default rate, costing 0.55 percent. Please calculate the estimated *residual income* for Deltone from this loan securitization.

2. Ryfield Corporation is requesting a loan for repair of some assembly line equipment in the amount of $5 million. The nine-month loan is priced by First National Bank at a 9.25 percent rate of interest. However, the bank tells Ryfield that if it obtains a suitable credit guarantee the loan will be priced at 9 percent. Quinmark Bank agrees to sell Ryfield a standby credit guarantee for $10,000. Is Ryfield likely to buy the standby credit guarantee Quinmark has offered? Please explain.

3. First Security National Bank has been approached by a long-standing corporate customer, United Safeco Industries, concerning a $30 million *term loan* for five years to purchase new stamping machines that would further automate the company's assembly line operations in the manufacture of metal toys and metal containers. The company also plans to use at least half the loan proceeds to facilitate its buyout of Calem Corp., which imports and partially assembles video recorders and cameras. Additional funds for the buyout will come from a corporate note issue that will be underwritten

by an investment banking firm not affiliated with First Security National Bank.

The problem faced by the bank's commercial credit division in assessing this customer loan request is a management decision reached several weeks ago that the bank should gradually work down its leveraged buyout loan portfolio due to recent quality problems, including a significant rise in nonperforming credits. Moreover, the prospect of sharply higher interest rates has caused the bank to revamp its loan policy toward more shorter-term loans (under one year) and fewer term loans. Senior management has indicated it will no longer approve *loans* that require a commitment of the bank's resources beyond a term of three years, except in special cases.

Does the bank have any service option in the form of off-balance-sheet instruments that could help this customer meet its credit needs while avoiding committing $30 million in reserves for a five-year loan? What would you recommend that management do to keep United Safeco happy with its current banking relationship? Could the bank earn any fee income if it pursued your idea?

Suppose the current interest rate on Eurodollar deposits (three-month maturities) in London is 8.40 percent, while federal funds and six-month CDs are trading in the United States at 8.55 percent and 8.21 percent, respectively. Term loans to comparable-quality corporate borrowers are trading at one-eighth to one-quarter percentage point above the three-month Eurodollar rate or one-quarter to one-half point over the secondary-market CD rate. Is there a way First Security National could earn at least as much fee income by providing Safeco with support services as it could from making the loan Safeco has asked for (after all loan costs are taken into account)? Please explain how the customer could also benefit even if the bank does not make the loan requested.

4. What type of credit derivative contract would you recommend for each of the situations described below?

a. A bank plans to issue a group of bonds backed by a pool of credit card loans but fears that the default rate on these credit card loans will rise well above 6 percent of the portfolio—the default rate it has projected. The bank wants to lower the interest cost on the bonds in case the loan default rate rises too high.

b. A bank is about to make a $50 million project loan to develop a new gas field and is concerned about the risks involved if petroleum geologists' estimates of the field's potential yield turn out to be much too high and the borrowing developer cannot repay.

c. A bank holding company plans to offer new capital notes in the open market next month, but knows that the company's credit rating is being reevaluated by two credit-rating agencies. The holding company wants to avoid paying sharply higher credit costs if its rating is lowered by the investigating credit-rating agencies.

d. A bank is concerned about possible excess volatility in its cash flow off a recently made group of commercial real estate loans supporting the building of several apartment complexes. Moreover, many of these loans were made at fixed interest rates, and the bank's economics department has forecast a substantial rise in capital market interest rates. The bank's management would prefer a more stable cash flow emerging from this group of loans if it could find a way to achieve it.

e. First National Bank of Ashton serves a relatively limited geographic area centered upon a moderate-size metropolitan area. It would like to diversify its loan income based upon loans from other market areas it does not presently serve, but does not wish to make loans itself in these other market areas due to its lack of familiarity with loan markets outside the region it has served for many years. Is there a credit derivative contract that could help the bank achieve the loan portfolio diversification it seeks?

Selected References

For a discussion of the characteristics of standby credit letters, see the following studies:

1. Bennett, Barbara. "Off Balance Sheet Risk in Banking: The Case of Standby Letters of Credit." *Economic Review,* Federal Reserve Bank of San Francisco, no. 1 (1986), pp. 19–29.

2. Boemio, Thomas R., and Gerald A. Edwards, Jr. "Asset Securitization: A Supervisory Perspective." *Federal Reserve Bulletin,* October 1989, pp. 659–69.

3. Goldberg, Michael, and Peter Lloyd-Davies. "Standby Letters of Credit: Are Banks Overextending Themselves?" *Journal of Bank Research,* Spring 1985, pp. 28–39.

4. Hassan, M. Kabir. "The Off-Balance-Sheet Banking Risk of Large U.S. Commercial Banks." *The Quarterly Review of Economics and Finance* 33, no. 1 (Spring 1993), pp. 51–69.

5. James, Christopher. "Off-Balance-Sheet Banking." *Economic Review,* Federal Reserve Bank of San Francisco, no. 4 (Fall 1987), pp. 21–36.

The following studies review the developing market for selling commercial loans:

6. Hassan, M. Kabir. "Capital Market Tests of Risk Exposure of Loan Sales Activities of Large U.S. Commercial Banks." *Quarterly Journal of Business and Economics* 32, no. 1 (Winter 1993), pp. 27–49.

7. Haubrich, Joseph G., and James B. Thomson. "The Evolving Loan Sales Market." *Economic Commentary,* Federal Reserve Bank of Cleveland, July 14, 1993, pp. 1–6.

8. Pavel, Christine, and David Phillis. "Why Commercial Banks Sell Loans: An Empirical Analysis." *Economic Perspectives,* Federal Reserve Bank of Chicago, no. 11 (1987), pp. 3–14.

9. Pennacchi, George. "Loan Sales and the Cost of Bank Capital." Working paper, University of Pennsylvania, 1987.

10. Pyle, David. "Discussion of Off-Balance-Sheet Banking." In *The Search for Financial Stability: The Past Fifty Years.* Federal Reserve Bank of San Francisco, 1985.

11. Rose, Peter S. "New Benefits, New Pitfalls." *The Canadian Banker* 95, no. 5 (September/October 1988), pp. 52–57.

12. ———. "The Search for Safety in an Uncertain Market." *The Canadian Banker* 97, no. 1 (January/February 1990).

For a discussion of securitization, see these studies:

13. Benveniste, Lawrence M., and Allen N. Berger. "Securitization with Recourse: An Investment That Offers Uninsured Bank Depositors Sequential Claims." *Journal of Banking Research,* September 1987, pp. 190–201.

14. Katz, Jane. "Securitization," *Regional Review,"* Federal Reserve Bank of Boston, Summer 1997, pp. 13–17.

15. Kavanagh, Barbara; Thomas R. Boemio; and Gerald A. Edwards, Jr. "Asset-Backed Commercial Paper Programs." *Federal Reserve Bulletin,* February 1992, pp. 107–16.

16. Rose, Peter S. "The Quest for Funds: New Directions in a New Market." *The Canadian Banker* 94, no. 5 (September/October 1987), pp. 46–55.

For a review of different types of credit derivatives see especially:

17. Das, Sanjiv. "Credit Risk Derivatives." *Journal of Derivatives,* Spring 1995, pp. 7–230.

18. Longstaff, Francis, and Edward Schwartz. "Valuing Credit Derivatives." *Journal of Fixed Income,* June 1995, pp. 6–14.

19. Neal, Robert S. "Credit Derivatives: New Financial Instruments for Controlling Credit Risk." *Economic Review,* Federal Reserve Bank of Kansas City, Second Quarter 1996, pp. 15–27.

20. Federal Deposit Insurance Corporation. "Credit Derivatives," FIL-62-96, Supervisory Guidance for Credit Derivatives, Office of the Director, Division of Supervision, August 19, 1996.

III MANAGING THE BANK'S INVESTMENT PORTFOLIO AND LIQUIDITY POSITION

10 THE INVESTMENT FUNCTION IN BANKING

Learning and Management Decision Objectives

The purpose of this chapter is to discover the types of securities that banks acquire for their investment portfolios and to explore the factors that a bank manager should consider in determining what securities a bank should buy or sell.

Introduction

The primary function of banks today is to produce and sell financial services demanded by the public. One of the most vital of those services is granting *loans,* particularly loans used to support business investment and consumer spending in the local community. Such loans ultimately provide jobs and income to thousands of community residents, many of whom are not borrowers from banks but are certainly indirect beneficiaries of a bank's willingness to lend in the local community.

Yet not all bank funds can be allocated to loans. For one thing, most loans are illiquid—they cannot easily be sold prior to maturity if the bank needs cash in a hurry. Another problem is that loans are among the riskiest bank assets, carrying the highest borrower default rate of any form of bank credit. Moreover, for small and medium-size banks at least, the majority of loans, typically, come from the local area. Therefore, any significant drop in local economic activity weakens the quality of a major portion of the average bank's loan portfolio. Then, too, all loan income is taxable, and banks in the United States and in many other nations as well, are subject to the full corporate income tax, necessitating the search for significant tax shelters in years when earnings from loans are high.

For all these reasons, banks have learned to devote a significant portion of their asset portfolios—usually a fifth to a third of all assets—to another major category of earning asset: *investments in securities*. These typically include government bonds and notes, corporate bonds and notes, other forms of debt securities, and certain limited kinds of stock permitted by law. As we will see in this chapter, these holdings perform a number of vital functions in bank asset portfolios, providing income, liquidity, diversification to reduce risk, and the sheltering of at least some portion of bank earnings from taxation. Investments also tend to stabilize bank earnings, providing supplemental income when other sources of revenue (especially interest on loans) decline. (See Exhibit 10–1 and Table 10–1 for a summary of the principal roles played by a bank's investment portfolio.)

Investment Instruments Available to Banks

The number of financial instruments available for banks to add to their securities portfolios is both large and growing. Moreover, each financial instrument has different characteristics with regard to risk, sensitivity to inflation, and sensitivity to shifting government policies and economic conditions. To examine the different investment vehicles open to banks, it is useful to divide them into two broad groups: (1) **money market instruments,** which reach maturity within one year and are noted for their low risk and ready marketability, and (2) **capital market instruments,** which have remaining maturities beyond one year and are generally noted for their higher expected rate of return and capital gains potential. (See Table 10–2 for a summary of the advantages and disadvantages of the various investment securities available to banks.)

Money Market Instruments

Treasury Bills

One of the most popular of all short-term investments is the **U.S. Treasury bill**—a debt obligation of the United States government that, by law, must mature within one year from date of issue. Three maturities of bills are routinely issued in weekly and monthly auctions: three- and six-month bills each week and one-year bills once each month. Bills are particularly attractive to banks because of their high degree of *safety*. Bills are supported by the taxing power of the federal government, their market prices are relatively stable, and they are readily marketable. Moreover, T-bills can serve as collateral for attracting loans from other institutions through repurchase agreements and other borrowing instruments. Bills are issued and traded at a discount from their par (face) value without a promised interest rate. Thus, the investor's return consists purely of price appreciation as the bill approaches maturity. The rate of return (yield) on T-bills is figured by the bank discount method, which uses the bill's par value at maturity as the basis for calculating its return, ignores the compounding of interest, and is based on a 360-day year, as we discussed in Chapter 6.

TABLE 10–1   Functions of a Bank's Security Portfolio

---

a. Stabilize the bank's income, so that bank revenues level out over the business cycle—when loan revenues fall, income from securities may rise.

b. Offset credit risk exposure in the bank's loan portfolio. High-quality securities can be purchased and held to balance out the risk from bank loans.

c. Provide geographic diversification. Securities often come from different regions than the sources of a bank's loans, helping a bank diversify its earnings.

d. Provide a backup source of liquidity, because securities can be sold to raise needed cash or used as collateral for bank borrowings of additional funds.

e. Reduce the bank's tax exposure, especially in offsetting taxable loan revenues.

f. Serve as collateral (pledged assets) to secure federal, state, and local government deposits held by the bank.

g. Help hedge the bank against losses due to changing interest rates.

h. Provide flexibility in a bank's asset portfolio because investment securities, unlike most loans, can be bought or sold quickly to restructure bank assets.

i. Dress up the bank's balance sheet and make it look financially stronger due to the high quality of most bank-held securities.

Federal regulations stress the need for every bank to develop a *written* investment policy giving specific guidelines on the following:

a. The quality or degree of default risk exposure the bank is willing to accept.

b. The desired maturity range and degree of marketability sought for all securities purchased.

c. The goals sought by the bank from its investment portfolio.

d. The degree of portfolio diversification to reduce risk the bank wishes to achieve with its investment portfolio.

Examiners review a bank's investment portfolio and its written investment policy to be sure speculation has not replaced more acceptable bank investment goals.

EXHIBIT 10–1

Investments: The Crossroads Account on a Bank's Balance Sheet

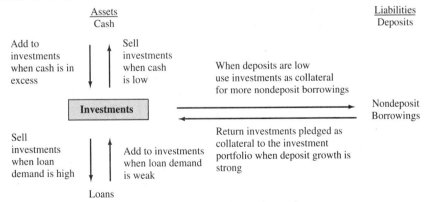

Some authorities refer to bank investments as the "crossroads account." Investments literally stand between cash, loans, and deposits. When cash is low, some investments will be sold to raise more cash. On the other hand, if cash is too high, some cash will be placed in investment securities. If loan demand is weak, investments will rise in order to provide the bank with more earning assets. But, if loan demand is strong, some investments will be sold to accommodate the heavy loan demand. Finally, when deposits—the main source of funds for most banks—are not growing fast enough, some investment securities will be used as collateral to borrow nondeposit funds in order to supplement the funds that deposits provide to the bank. No other account on a bank's balance sheet occupies such a critical intersection position as do investments, fulfilling so many important roles.

TABLE 10–2 Key Advantages and Disadvantages of Popular Investment Securities Purchased by Banks

| | Treasury Bills | Short-Term Treasury Notes and Bonds | Federal Agency Securities | Money Market Instruments | | | | |
				Certificates of Deposit	International Eurocurrency Deposits	Bankers' Acceptances	Commercial Paper	Short-Term Municipal Obligations
Key advantages:	Safety and high liquidity Ready marketability Good collateral for borrowing Can pledge behind government deposits	Safety Good resale market Good collateral for borrowing Offer yields usually higher than bill yields	Safety Good to average resale market Good collateral for borrowing Higher yields than on U.S. government securities	Safety (insured to $100,000) Yields higher than on T-bills Over $100,000 denominations are often marketable through dealers.	Low risk Higher yields than on many domestic CDs	Low risk due to multiple credit guarantees	Low risk due to high quality of borrowers	Tax-exempt interest income
Key disadvantages:	Low yields relative to other financial instruments	More price risk than T-bills	Less marketable than Treasury securities	Limited resale market on longer-term CDs	Volatile interest rates	Limited availability at specific maturities	Volatile market Poor to nonexistent resale market	Limited to nonexistent resale market

TABLE 10-2 *(concluded)*

	Capital Market Instruments			
	Treasury Notes and Bonds	*Municipal (state and local government) Bonds*	*Corporate Notes and Bonds*	*Mortgage-Backed Securities (including CMOs)*
Key advantages:	Safety Good resale market Good collateral for borrowing May be pledged behind government deposits	Tax-exempt interest income High credit quality Liquidity and marketability of selected securities	Higher pre-tax yields than on government securities Aid in locking in long-term rates of return	Higher pre-tax yields than on Treasury securities Safety Adequate resale market Good collateral for borrowing
Key disadvantages:	Low yields relative to long-term private securities	Volatile market Some issues have limited resale possibilities.	Limited resale market Inflexible terms	Less marketable and more unstable in price than Treasury securities Maturity uncertain and realized yield subject to reinvestment risk.

Short-Term Treasury Notes and Bonds

At the time they are issued, **Treasury notes** and **Treasury bonds** have relatively long maturities: 1 to 10 years for notes and over 10 years for bonds. However, when these securities come within one year of maturity, they are considered money market instruments. While Treasury notes and bonds are more sensitive to interest rate risk and less marketable than Treasury bills, their expected returns (yields) are usually higher than for bills with greater potential for capital gains. Treasury notes and bonds are *coupon instruments,* which means they promise investors a *fixed* rate of return, though the expected return may fall below or climb above the promised coupon rate due to fluctuations in the security's market price.

Beginning in July of 1986, *all* negotiable Treasury Department securities were converted to electronic book entry, with no registered or engraved certificates issued. This system, known as Treasury Direct, supplies each bank and nonbank owner of U.S. Treasury securities a statement showing the bills, notes, and bonds he or she holds. Any interest and principal payments earned are deposited directly into the owners' checking or savings account. This approach means not only greater convenience for banks and other investors purchasing and selling Treasury securities, but also provides increased protection against theft.

Federal Agency Securities

Marketable notes and bonds sold by agencies owned by or started by the federal government are known as **federal agency securities**. Familiar examples include securities issued by the Federal National Mortgage Association (FNMA, or Fannie Mae), the Farm Credit System (FCS), the Federal Land Banks (FLBs), the Federal Home Loan Mortgage Corporation (FHLMC, or Freddie Mac), and the Student Loan Marketing Association (SLMA, or Sallie Mae). Most of these securities are not formally guaranteed by the federal government, though most financial analysts believe Congress would move quickly to rescue any agency in trouble. This implied government support keeps agency yields close to those on Treasury securities (normally within one percentage point) and contributes to the high liquidity of most agency securities.

Among the most popular of all federal agency securities are *discount notes.* These short-term agency borrowings are sold at prices below their face value and usually have a maturity range of overnight to one year. Most discount notes are issued in book entry form, though a few are still available as bearer certificates, with yields figured (as with Treasury bills) on a 360-day basis. Interest income on agency-issued discount notes is federally taxable and, in most cases, subject to state and local taxation as well.

Certificates of Deposit

A **certificate of deposit (CD)** is simply an interest-bearing receipt for the deposit of funds in a bank or nonbank thrift institution. Thus, the primary role of CDs is to provide banks with an additional source of funds. However, banks often buy the CDs issued by other depository institutions, regarding them as an attractive, lower-risk investment. CDs carry a fixed term, and there is a federally imposed penalty for early withdrawal. Banks and thrifts issue both small *consumer-oriented CDs,* ranging in denomination from $500 to $100,000, and large *business-oriented* or *institution-oriented CDs* (often called jumbos), with denominations over $100,000 (though only the first $100,000 is federally insured) and negotiated interest rates that, while normally fixed, may be allowed to fluctuate with market conditions. Securities dealers make an active secondary market for $100,000-plus CDs maturing within six months.

International Eurocurrency Deposits

The 1950s in Western Europe ushered in the development of high-quality international bank deposits, sold in million-dollar units and denominated in a currency other than the home currency of the country in which they are deposited. *Eurocurrency deposits* are not checking accounts, but time deposits of fixed maturity issued by the world's largest banks headquartered in financial centers around the globe, though the heart of the Eurocurrency deposit market is in London. Most of these international deposits are of short maturity—30, 60, or 90 days—to correspond with the funding requirements of international trade. They are *not* insured, and due to their perceived higher credit risk, lower liquidity, and greater sensitivity to foreign economic and political developments, they normally carry slightly higher market yields than domestic time deposits issued by comparable-size U.S. banks. (For a detailed discussion of the role and creation of Eurocurrency deposits, see Chapter 14.)

Bankers' Acceptances

Because they represent a bank's promise to pay the holder a designated amount of money (indicated on the face of the acceptance) on a designated future date (also shown on the acceptance), **bankers' acceptances** are considered to be among the safest of all money market instruments. Most acceptances arise from a bank's decision to guarantee the credit of one of its customers who is exporting, importing, or storing goods or purchasing currency. In legal language, the bank agrees to be the "primary obligor," committed to paying off the customer's debt regardless of what happens subsequently, in return for a fee. Through the acceptance vehicle, the bank supplies its name and credit standing so that its customer will be able to obtain credit from someone else more easily and at lower cost.

The holder of the acceptance on its maturity date may be a foreign exporter, another bank, or a money market investor attracted by its safety and active resale market. Because acceptances have a ready resale market, they may be traded from one investor to another before reaching maturity. If a bank sells the acceptances it holds, this does not erase the issuing bank's obligation to pay off its outstanding acceptances at maturity. However, by selling an acceptance, a bank adds to its reserves and transfers interest rate risk to another investor. The acceptance is a discount instrument and, therefore, is always sold at a price below par before it reaches maturity. As with Treasury bills, the investor's expected return comes solely from the prospect that the acceptance will rise in price as it gets closer to maturity. Rates of return on acceptances generally lie between the yield on Eurocurrency deposits and the yield on Treasury bills.

One other important advantage of acceptances is that they may qualify for discounting (borrowing) at the Federal Reserve Banks, provided they qualify as *eligible* acceptances. To be eligible as collateral for borrowing from the Fed, the acceptance must be denominated in dollars, normally cannot exceed six months to maturity, and must arise from the export or import of goods or from the storage of marketable staples. Ineligible acceptances do not meet all of these requirements and are not extensively traded in the money market. Acceptances classified as "ineligible" carry Federal Reserve legal reserve requirements, making them more costly to issue than eligible acceptances. The total of all a U.S. bank's acceptances outstanding cannot exceed 150 percent of its paid-in capital and surplus, though with Federal Reserve Board permission, additional acceptances may be issued up to 200 percent of a bank's capital and surplus account.

Commercial Paper

Many smaller banks find **commercial paper**—short-term, unsecured IOUs offered by major corporations—an attractive investment that is safer than most types of bank loans. Commercial paper sold in the United States is of relatively short maturity—the bulk of it matures in 90 days or less—and generally is issued by borrowers with the highest credit ratings. A rapidly developing market in western Europe and in Japan for Europaper has attracted participation by major international banks. Europaper generally carries longer maturities and higher interest rates than U.S. commercial paper due to its greater perceived credit risk; however, there is a more active resale market for Europaper than for most U.S. commercial paper issues.

Substantial quantities of commercial paper have been issued in recent years by smaller, lower-rated companies in the form of *documented notes* with a bank's irrevocable guarantee of payment behind them. When a bank irrevocably guarantees a commercial paper issue, the bank's credit rating substitutes for the borrower's credit rating, allowing the paper to be sold to a larger group of investors at lower interest cost. Most commercial paper is issued at a discount from par, like T-bills and acceptances, though some paper bearing a promised rate of return (coupon) is also issued today.

Short-Term Municipal Obligations

State and local governments (including counties, cities, and special districts) issue a wide variety of short-term debt instruments to cover temporary cash shortages. Two of the most common are tax-anticipation notes (TANs), issued in lieu of expected future tax revenues, and revenue-anticipation notes (RANs), issued to cover expenses from special projects, such as the construction of a toll bridge, highway, or airport, in lieu of expected future revenues from those projects. All interest earned on such municipal notes is exempt from federal income taxation, so they are attractive to banks. However, as we will see later in this chapter, the tax deductibility of interest income from municipal obligations has been sharply limited for U.S. banks in recent years, reducing their attractiveness relative to federal securities. At the same time, many state and local governments have encountered serious financial problems that have weakened the credit quality of their notes, forcing bankers to take a closer look at the quality of the municipals they choose to buy.

Capital Market Instruments

Treasury Notes and Bonds Over One Year to Maturity

Among the safest and most liquid long-term investments that banks can make are U.S. Treasury notes and bonds. U.S. Treasury notes are available in a wide variety of maturities (ranging from 1 year to 10 years when issued) and in large volume. In 1994, about $1.8 trillion were outstanding, and banks were among the leading investors in these instruments. Treasury bonds (with original maturities of more than 10 years) totaled about $500 billion and were, therefore, traded in a more limited market with wider price fluctuations than is usually the case with Treasury notes. Treasury bonds and notes carry higher expected returns than bills, but present a bank with greater price risk and liquidity risk. They are issued normally in dominations of $1,000, $5,000, $10,000, $100,000, and $1 million.

Municipal Notes and Bonds

Long-term debt obligations issued by states, cities, and other governmental units are known collectively as **municipal bonds**. As with short-term municipal notes, interest on the majority of these bonds is exempt from federal income tax provided they are issued to fund public, rather than private, projects. Capital gains on municipals are fully taxable, however, except for bonds sold at a discounted price, where the gain from purchase price to par value is considered a portion of the investor's tax-exempt interest earnings. Banks often submit competitive bids for, or purchase after private negotiation, the debt issued by local cities, counties, and school districts as a way of demonstrating support for their local communities and to attract other business. They also purchase municipal securities from brokers and dealers in the national market for reasons strictly related to after-tax return and risk, because many municipal bonds have high credit ratings and an active resale market.

Many different types of municipal bonds are issued today, but the majority fall into one of two categories: (1) *general obligation* (GO) *bonds,* backed by the full faith and credit of the issuing unit of government, which means they may be paid from any available source of revenue (including the levying of additional taxes); and (2) *revenue bonds,* which can be used to fund long-term revenue-raising projects and are payable only from certain stipulated sources of funds. U.S. banks are allowed to trade in and underwrite GOs, but may not underwrite most new issues of revenue bonds due to their greater credit risk. Such underwriting activity may, however, be legally conducted through a subsidiary firm that is part of the same bank holding company (with the approval of the Federal Reserve Board).

Corporate Notes and Bonds

Long-term debt securities issued by corporations are usually called **corporate notes** when they mature within five years or **corporate bonds** when they carry longer maturities. There are many different varieties, depending on the types of security pledged (e.g., mortgages versus debentures), purposes of issue, and terms of issue. In the past, most corporate bonds carried 10- to 30-year maturities, but there has been a trend toward shorter maturities in recent years. Corporate notes and bonds generally are more attractive to insurance companies and pension funds than to banks because of their higher credit risk relative to government securities and their more limited resale market. However, they do offer significantly higher average yields than government securities of comparable maturity.

Other Investment Instruments Developed More Recently

The range of investment opportunities for banks has expanded tremendously in recent years. Many new securities have been developed; some of these are variations on traditional notes and bonds, while others represent entirely new investment vehicles. Examples include structured notes, securitized assets, and stripped securities.

Structured Notes.   In their search to protect themselves against shifting interest rates many banks have added *structured notes* to their investment portfolios. Most of these notes arise from security brokers and dealers who assemble pools of federal agency securities (issued by such well-known agencies as the Federal Home Loan Banks) and offer a bank's investment officer a package investment whose interest yield may be periodically reset (perhaps every quarter, semiannually, or after a certain number of years) based on what happens to a stated reference rate (such as the U.S. Treasury bill or bond rate). A guaranteed floor rate and cap rate may be added in which the bank's promised investment return may not drop below a stated (floor) level or rise above some maximum (cap) level. Some structured notes carry multiple coupon (promised) rates that periodically are given a boost ("step-up") to give investors a higher yield; others have adjustable coupon (promised) rates determined by a specific formula. The complexity of these notes have resulted in substantial losses for some banks, not from credit risk (because few of these notes are actually defaulted upon), but from substantial interest rate risk. The net yields on many structured-note deals have been even lower than on U.S. Treasury securities. In July 1994 the Comptroller of the Currency, the principal regulator for U.S. national banks, warned that "investment in a significant amount of structured notes is an unsafe and unsound practice if the bank lacks a full understanding of the risks involved."

Securitized Assets.   In recent years hybrid securities based upon pools of loans have been one of the most rapidly growing bank investments. These **securitized assets** are backed by selected loans of uniform type and quality, such as FHA- and VA-insured home mortgages, automobile loans, and credit card loans.[1] The most popular securitized assets that banks buy as investments today are based upon mortgage loans.

There are three main types of mortgage-backed securitized assets: (1) pass-through securities, (2) collateralized mortgage obligations (CMOs), and (3) mortgage-backed bonds. *Pass-through securities* arise when a bank or other lender pools a group of similar home mortgage loans appearing on its balance sheet, removes them from the balance sheet into an account controlled by a legal trustee, and issues securities to interested investors using the mortgage loans as collateral. As the mortgage loan pool generates principal and interest payments these are "passed through" to investors holding the mortgage-backed securities. Repayment of principal and interest on the calendar dates promised is guaranteed by the Government National Mortgage Association (GNMA, or Ginnie Mae), an agency of the U.S. government, in return for a small fee (currently 6 basis points or 0.06 percent of the total amount of loans placed in the pool).

The Federal National Mortgage Corporation (FNMA, or Fannie Mae), which was chartered by Congress but is legally separate from the U.S. government, also helps create pass-through securities by purchasing packages of mortgage loans from banks and thrift institutions. While GNMA aids in the creation of mortgage-loan-backed securities for government-insured home loans, FNMA securitizes both conventional (noninsured) and government-insured home mortgages. Banks and other investors who acquire pass-through securities issued against pools of government-insured home mortgages are protected against default on those securities because the Federal Housing and Veterans Administrations ensure that the pooled loans will be repaid even if the homeowner abandons his or her home. Moreover, GNMA and FNMA may add their own guarantees of timely repayment of principal and interest.

In 1983 another government-sponsored agency, the Federal Home Loan Mortgage Corporation (FHLMC, or Freddie Mac), now legally separate from the U.S. government, developed the *Collateralized Mortgage Obligation* (CMO). A CMO is a pass-through security divided into multiple classes (tranches), each with a different promised (coupon) rate and level of risk exposure. CMOs arise either from the securitizing of mortgage loans themselves or from the securitizing of pass-through securities, taking these instruments off the balance sheet of the firm holding them. As we will see later on in this chapter, the principal risk to a bank or other investor buying these securities is *prepayment risk* because some borrowers will pay off their home mortgages early or default on their loans, meaning that the holder of these securities may receive diminished income and declining value in the future.

CMOs are usually divided into three or more maturity and risk classes. Generally, those classes composed of shorter-term maturities of CMOs have the greatest risk of early prepayment. As some borrowers prepay their loans, holders of the shortest-term CMOs receive these prepayments first until all short-term CMOs are paid off. Investors in longer-term classes of CMOs have the least chance of having their rates of return reduced through prepayment risk because they only receive any loan prepayments after investors

---

[1]See Chapter 9 for a discussion of how banks use securitized assets to raise new funds and to restructure their sources and uses of funds.

holding shorter-term CMOs are fully paid. Banks often buy a substantial proportion of the shortest-term CMOs as investment assets in order to match the short-term liabilities they carry. The longest-term CMOs have an average life that can approach 20 years and appeal to such long-term investors as insurance companies and pension funds.

The final type of mortgage-loan-related security is the **mortgage-backed bond**. Unlike pass-throughs and CMOs where mortgage loans are removed from the balance sheet, mortgage-backed bonds (MBBs) and the mortgage loans backing them stay on the issuer's balance sheet, and there is no direct connection between the principal and interest payments coming from the mortgage loans themselves and the interest and principal payments owed on the MBBs. The financial institution issuing these bonds will separate the mortgage loans held on its balance sheet from its other assets and pledge those loans as collateral to support the MBBs. A trustee acting on behalf of the mortgage bondholders keeps track of the dedicated loans and checks periodically to be sure that the market value of the loans is greater than what is owed on the bonds.

Pass-throughs, CMOs, and other securitized assets have been among the most rapidly growing financial instruments of the 1980s and 1990s. Several factors appear to account for the popularity of these loan-backed investment securities:

1. Guarantees from federal agencies (in the case of home-mortgage-related securities) or from private institutions (such as banks or insurance companies pledging to back credit card loans).
2. The higher average yields available on securitized assets than on U.S. Treasury securities.
3. The lack of good-quality loans and securities of other kinds in a more slowly growing economy.
4. The superior liquidity and marketability of securities backed by loans compared to the loans themselves.

Stripped Securities.   In the early 1980s, security dealers developed and marketed a hybrid instrument known as the **stripped security**—a claim against either the principal or interest payments associated with a debt security, such as a U.S. Treasury bond. Dealers create stripped securities by separating the principal and interest payments from an underlying debt security and selling separate claims to these two promised income streams. Claims against only the *principal* payments from a security are called PO (principal-only) securities, while claims against only the stream of *interest* payments promised by a security are referred to as IO (interest-only) securities.

Stripped securities often display markedly different behavior from the underlying securities from which they come. In particular, some stripped securities offer interest rate hedging possibilities to help protect a portfolio of bonds and other traditional security holdings against loss from interest rate changes. The two securities whose interest and principal payments are most likely to be stripped today are longer-term (10 years and longer) U.S. Treasury bonds and mortgage-backed securities. While Treasury bonds were first offered in stripped form by security dealers early in the 1980s, the U.S. Treasury itself agreed to strip long-term bonds on its books beginning in 1985. Both PO and IO Treasury bond strips are really *zero coupon bonds* with no periodic interest payments;

they therefore carry zero reinvestment risk when used correctly. Each stripped Treasury security is sold at a discount from its par value, so the investor's rate of return is based solely on the security's price appreciation. Because Treasury bonds normally pay interest twice a year, an investor can lock in a fixed rate of return for a holding period as short as six months out to several years up to the time to maturity of the original bond. POs tend to be *more* price sensitive to interest rate changes than regular Treasury bonds, while IO strips tend to be *less* price sensitive than the original bonds.

Mortgage-backed securities are also being stripped in growing numbers but have different characteristics from stripped Treasury bonds. For example, mortgage-backed securities carry significant *prepayment risk,* as described earlier in this chapter. These securities normally are divided into a PO strip, with all expected principal payments included, and an IO strip, containing just the interest payments from the underlying pool of mortgage loans. However, due to the risk that some mortgage loans will be paid off early, stripping mortgage instruments does not fully protect investors from having to reinvest their income at lower and lower interest rates. Stripped mortgage-backed securities make maturity matching of bank assets and liabilities difficult because their final maturity date is uncertain.

Investment Securities Actually Held by Banks

We have now examined the principal investment opportunities available to banks, but which of these investments do banks actually prefer? Table 10–3 provides an overview of investment securities held by all U.S.-insured banks as of year-end 1996. Clearly two types of securities dominate U.S. bank portfolios—U.S. Treasury securities and other federal government (federal agency) or government-sponsored IOUs. Treasury and federal agency or federally sponsored investment securities now account for about three-quarters of the dollar volume of all investments held by U.S. banks. Federal agency instruments outnumber direct obligations of the U.S. Treasury by better than two to one in dollar volume, due principally to the higher average returns on agency and government-sponsored securities relative to U.S. Treasuries. A distant third, but still important in bank investment portfolios, are state and local government (municipal) bonds and notes.

Banks hold relatively few private-sector securities, such as corporate bonds and notes. They would prefer to make direct loans to customers rather than buy their securities because the yield is normally lower on securities than on loans, and because purchasing securities may generate no new deposits for the bank.

As might be expected, the largest and smallest banks differ in the makeup of their investment portfolios. Table 10–3 shows that the smallest banks tend to invest more heavily in government securities than do the largest. The smaller institutions tend to be more heavily exposed to risk of loss from economic problems in their local areas and therefore tend to use the lowest-risk securities to offset the high risk inherent in their loans. In contrast, the largest banks tend to be more heavily invested in foreign securities and private debt and equity obligations (especially corporate bonds and commercial paper)—all of which tend to carry greater risk exposure than government and federal agency securities.

TABLE 10–3   **Investments That U.S. Banks Hold**
(Year-end 1996, Billions of Dollars at All U.S. Insured Banks)

| Types of Securities Held | All Insured U.S. Banks: | | Percent Held at U.S. Banks with Assets of: | | |
	Totals	Percent	Less than $100 Mill.	$100 Mill. to $1 Bill.	$1 Bill. or More
U.S. Treasury and federal agency securities:	$610.9	76.2%	80.1%	79.4%	74.5%
U.S. Treasuries	169.0	21.1	26.1	24.5	19.1
Agency securities	441.9	55.2	54.0	54.9	55.4
State and local government obligations	74.9	9.4	16.1	14.8	6.3
Domestic debt securities	50.2	6.3	2.3	3.3	8.0
Foreign debt securities	43.0	5.4	*	0.2	8.1
Equities	21.9	2.7	1.4	2.2	3.1
Total security investments and percent of total bank assets	$800.8	17.5%	29.7%	26.9%	14.7%
Memo Items:					
Securities held to maturity (at cost)	$174.2	21.8	31.6	30.3	17.1
Securities available for sale (at fair value)	626.6	78.2	68.4	69.6	82.9
Pledged securities	356.0	44.5	30.3	37.3	49.3
Securities with maturities of:					
Under 1 Year	216.9	27.1	28.3	27.3	26.4
1 to 5 Years	254.1	31.7	46.1	40.1	26.4
Over 5 Years	306.9	38.3	24.1	29.8	43.7

Source: Federal Deposit Insurance Corporation, *Bank Operating Statistics, 1996.*

In total, investment securities represent just under a fifth of all U.S. bank assets nationwide. But this proportion of total bank assets varies with bank size and location. Banks operating in areas with weak loan demand usually hold significantly greater percentages of investment securities relative to their total assets. Moreover, as Table 10–3 suggests, bank size also plays a key role. The smallest size group of banks holds nearly 30 percent of its assets in the form of investments, while the largest multibillion-dollar banks hold just under 15 percent of their assets in investment securities, reflecting the relatively heavy loan demand most large banks face. In contrast, loans represent over half of all bank assets and a majority of bank revenues come from loans; therefore, bank loans generally carry significantly higher average yields than bank investments. But as we have already seen, the investment portfolio is expected to do several jobs in addition to generating income for the bank, such as tax sheltering, reducing overall risk exposure, and serving as sources of additional cash and as collateral for bank borrowing.

Concept Checks

10–1. Why do banks choose to devote a significant proportion of their assets to investments in securities? What roles do investments play in the management of a bank?

10–2. What are the principal money market and capital market instruments available to banks today?

10–3. What types of investment securities do banks prefer the most?

10–4. What are securitized assets? Why have they grown so rapidly over the past two decades? What special risks do securitized assets present to banks investing in them?

10–5. What are structured notes and stripped securities? What unusual features do they have?

Factors Affecting the Banker's Choice among Investment Securities

As we look at the investment securities actually held by banks, it becomes evident that a bank's investment officer must consider several factors in deciding which securities to buy or sell. The principal factors bearing on a bank's investment choices are:

1. Expected rate of return.
2. Tax exposure.
3. Interest rate risk.
4. Credit risk.
5. Business risk.
6. Liquidity risk.
7. Call risk.
8. Prepayment risk.
9. Inflation risk.
10. Pledging and collateral requirements.

We will briefly review each of these factors.

Expected Rate of Return

The investment officer must determine the total rate of return that can reasonably be expected from each security, including the interest payments promised by the issuer of that security and possible capital gains or losses. For most investments, this requires the investment manager to calculate the **yield to maturity (YTM)** if a security is to be held to maturity or the planned **holding period yield (HPY)** between point of purchase and point of sale.

As we saw in Chapter 6, the yield to maturity formula determines the rate of discount (or yield) on a loan or security which equalizes the market price of the loan or security with the expected stream of cash flows (interest and principal) the loan or security will generate. To illustrate how the YTM formula can be useful to a bank's investment officer, suppose the investment officer is considering purchasing a $1,000 par-value U.S. Treasury note that promises an 8-percent coupon rate and is slated to mature in five years. If the T-note's current price is $900, we have:

$$\$900 = \frac{\$80}{(1+YTM)^1} + \frac{\$80}{(1+YTM)^2} + \cdots \qquad (1)$$
$$+ \frac{\$80}{(1+YTM)^5} + \frac{\$1,000}{(1+YTM)^{5}}$$

Solving for the yield to maturity using the present value and annuity tables inside this book's front cover reveals that the yield is 10.74 percent. The calculated YTM then should be *compared* with the expected yields on other loans and investments the bank might acquire to determine where the best possible rate of return lies.

However, banks frequently do not hold all their securities to maturity. Some securities must be sold off early to accommodate new loan demand or to cover deposit withdrawals. To deal with this situation, the bank's investment officer needs to know how to calculate the holding period yield (HPY) earned by the bank. The HPY is simply the rate of return (discount factor) that equates a security's purchase price with the stream of income expected from that security until it is sold by the bank to another investor. For example, suppose the 8-percent Treasury note described above was sold at the end of two years for $950. Its holding period yield could be found from

$$\$900 = \frac{\$80}{(1+HPY)^1} + \frac{\$80}{(1+HPY)^2} + \frac{\$950}{(1+HPY)^2} \qquad (2)$$

In this case, the note's HPY would be 11.51 percent, based upon the present value and annuity tables inside the cover of this text.[2]

Tax Exposure

Interest and capital gains income from most U.S. bank investments are taxed as *ordinary income* for tax purposes, just as are the wages and salaries earned by most U.S. citizens. Because of their relatively high tax exposure, banks are more interested in the *after-tax* rate of return on loans and securities than in their before-tax return.

The Tax Status of State and Local Government Bonds.   For banks in the upper tax brackets, tax-exempt state and local government (municipal) bonds and notes have been attractive from time to time, depending upon the status of current tax laws.

---

[2]Please see Chapter 6 for a brief explanation on how to use linear interpolation and the present value and annuity tables inside the front cover to closely approximate the true yield to maturity or holding period yield on an investment security.

For example, suppose that Aaa-rated corporate bonds are carrying an average gross yield to maturity of about 7 percent, the prime rate on top-quality corporate loans is about 6 percent, and Aaa-rated municipal bonds have a 5.5 percent gross yield to maturity. The bank's investment officer could compare each of these potential yields using the formula:

$$\text{Before-tax gross yield to the bank} \times (1 - \text{Bank's marginal income tax rate}) \tag{3}$$

$$= \text{After-tax gross yield}$$

This comparison yields the following expected after-tax gross returns for a bank in the top 35 percent federal income tax bracket:

$$\underline{\text{Aaa - rated corporate bonds}}$$
$$7.00 \text{ percent} \times (1 - 0.35) = 4.55 \text{ percent}$$

$$\underline{\text{Prime - rated loans}}$$
$$6 \text{ percent} \times (1 - 0.35) = 3.90 \text{ percent}$$

$$\underline{\text{Aaa - rated municipal bonds}}$$
$$5.50 \text{ percent } (1 - 0) = 5.50 \text{ percent before and after taxes}$$

Under the assumptions given, the municipal bond is the most attractive investment in gross yield. However, other considerations do enter into this decision, such as the need to attract and hold deposits, management's desire to keep good loan customers, and recent changes in tax laws.

For example, tax reform in the United States has had a major impact on the relative attractiveness of state and local government bonds as bank investments. Prior to federal tax reform legislation during the 1980s, commercial banks held close to 30 percent of all state and local government debt outstanding. But their share of the municipal market has been falling steadily since that time, due to the impact of tax reform and to occasional periods of depressed industry earnings. The first blow came in 1982 with passage of the Tax Equity and Fiscal Responsibility Act (TEFRA), which altered the federal tax code that had formerly allowed banks to take a full (100 percent) tax deduction for any interest expense incurred in borrowing money to buy municipal bonds. After December 31, 1982, banks could deduct only 85 percent of any interest paid to fund the acquisition of tax-exempt notes and bonds, which in 1985 was lowered to only 80 percent. In 1986, the Tax Reform Act was passed, denying *any* tax deduction in most instances for the interest cost involved in purchasing or carrying tax-exempt securities after August 7, 1986. The Tax Reform Act also lowered the top-bracket corporate tax rate from 46 percent to 34 percent, which made tax-exempt municipals less attractive as tax shelters for top-earning banks. However, the Revenue Reconciliation Act passed in 1993 made municipal securities slightly more attractive because it raised the top corporate tax rate to 35 percent for those banks and other corporations earning more than $10 million in annual taxable income.[3]

---

[3] Under current federal law U.S. banks must calculate their income taxes in two different ways—using a normal tax rate schedule (maximum 35 percent tax rate) and using an alternative minimum tax rate of 20 percent, paying the greater of the two different amounts. Interest income from municipals has to be added in to determine each bank's alternative minimum tax, making municipal income subject to at least some taxation.

When tax reform was passed in the United States, a special exemption was granted to smaller local governments that issue only small amounts of municipal bonds in any one year. Banks buying securities from these smaller governmental borrowers are allowed to deduct 80 percent of any interest costs involved in such a purchase. Tax reform legislation also reduced the potential supply of municipals by declaring some state and local bonds *private activity* issues if 10 percent or more of their proceeds were to be used to benefit a private individual or business firm. In these instances, the state or local government bond would be considered a fully taxable security, and the bank buying that security would have to pay income tax on its earnings at the full corporate income tax rate (except for local government bonds supporting charitable or hospital projects). Moreover, Congress placed ceilings on the amount of industrial development bonds (IDBs) local governments could issue to provide facilities or tax breaks in order to attract new industry.

Recent federal tax reform legislation has, therefore, altered the way a bank figures the net after-tax return on its municipal notes and bonds after deducting all interest costs and taxes. Specifically:

$$
\begin{gathered}
\begin{bmatrix} \text{Net after-tax} \\ \text{return on} \\ \text{municipals} \\ \text{(in percent)} \end{bmatrix}
=
\begin{bmatrix} \text{Nominal return} & \text{Interest expense incurred} \\ \text{on municipals} & \text{in acquiring the} \\ \text{after taxes} & - & \text{municipals} \\ \text{(in percent)} & \text{(in percent)} \end{bmatrix} \qquad (4) \\[2em]
+
\begin{bmatrix} \text{The bank's} & \text{Percentage of} & \text{Interest expense} \\ \text{marginal} & \text{interest expense} & \text{incurred in} \\ \text{income} & \times & \text{that is still} & \times & \text{acquiring the} \\ \text{tax rate} & \text{tax deductible} & \text{municipals} \\ \text{(in percent)} & \text{(if any)} & \text{(in percent)} \end{bmatrix}
\end{gathered}
$$

As we have seen, for banks holding state and local government securities purchased before August 7, 1986, and for banks holding municipals issued by smaller cities and other modest-size local governments, 80 percent of the interest expense incurred in buying these securities *is* tax deductible. This special exemption applies to local governments that issue no more than $10 million of public, rather than private-purpose, securities (often called *bank-qualified* securities) in one year. For example, suppose a bank purchases a public-purpose ("bank-qualified") bond from a small city, county, or school district issuing no more than $10 million in securities annually and the bond carries a nominal (published) gross rate of return of 7 percent. Assume also that the bank had to borrow the funds needed to make this purchase at an interest rate of 6.5 percent and is in the top (35 percent) income tax bracket. Because this bond comes from a small local government that qualifies for special tax treatment under the 1986 Tax Reform Act, the bond's *net* annual after-tax return to the bank (after all funding costs and taxes) must be as follows:

$$
\begin{aligned}
\begin{matrix} \text{Net after-tax return} \\ \text{on a qualified} \\ \text{municipal security} \end{matrix}
&= (7.00 - 6.50) + (0.35 \times 0.80 \times 6.50) \\
&= 0.50 \text{ percent} + 1.82 \text{ percent} \\
&= 2.32 \text{ percent}
\end{aligned}
$$

The investment officer would want to compare this calculated *net* after-tax rate of return to the net returns after taxes available from other securities and loans, both taxable and tax-exempt.

Notice, however, that if the municipal bond described above had come from a *larger* state or local government *not* eligible for special treatment under the Tax Reform Act, *none* of the interest expense would have been tax deductible. In this case, the bank's *net* after-tax return from the municipal bond could be determined from Equation 5:

$$
\begin{array}{l}
\text{Net after-tax return} \\
\text{on municipals}
\end{array}
=
\begin{array}{l}
\text{Nominal after-} \\
\text{tax return}
\end{array}
-
\begin{array}{l}
\text{Nondeductible} \\
\text{interest expense}
\end{array}
\qquad (5)
$$

In this particular example:

$$
\begin{array}{l}
\text{Net after-tax} \\
\text{return on} \\
\text{municipals}
\end{array}
= 7.00 - 6.50 = 0.50 \text{ percent, or 50 basis points}
$$

As we saw earlier, it is often useful to translate a tax-exempt bond's expected return into the tax-equivalent yield, assuming the bond is fully taxable. If the bank is interested in *taxable securities,* their *net* after-tax yield may be found from this formula:

$$
\begin{array}{l}
\text{Net after-tax} \\
\text{yield on a} \\
\text{taxable security}
\end{array}
=
\left[
\begin{array}{l}
\text{Nominal} \\
\text{yield}
\end{array}
-
\begin{array}{l}
\text{Interest expense} \\
\text{of acquiring} \\
\text{the security}
\end{array}
\right]
\qquad (6)
$$

$$
+
\left[
\begin{array}{l}
\text{The bank's} \\
\text{marginal} \\
\text{income tax} \\
\text{bracket}
\end{array}
\times
\begin{array}{l}
\text{Percentage of} \\
\text{interest expense} \\
\text{that is} \\
\text{deductible}
\end{array}
\times
\begin{array}{l}
\text{Interest} \\
\text{expense of} \\
\text{acquiring} \\
\text{the security}
\end{array}
\right]
$$

We can bring together Equations 5 and 6 to solve for the rate of return that would equalize tax-exempt security yields with taxable security yields and derive the tax-equivalent yield (TEY) on a tax-exempt security. This TEY must be as follows:

$$
\begin{array}{l}
\text{Tax-equivalent} \\
\text{yield from a tax-} \\
\text{exempt security}
\end{array}
=
\dfrac{
\begin{array}{l}
\text{Tax exempt} \\
\text{yield}
\end{array}
-
\begin{array}{l}
\text{Percentage of} \\
\text{interest expense} \\
\text{that is} \\
\text{taxable}
\end{array}
\times
\begin{array}{l}
\text{The bank's} \\
\text{marginal} \\
\text{income tax} \\
\text{bracket}
\end{array}
\times
\begin{array}{l}
\text{Interest} \\
\text{expense of} \\
\text{acquiring} \\
\text{the security}
\end{array}
}{
(1 - \text{Bank's marginal income tax bracket})
}
\qquad (7)
$$

Using the example of bonds issued by small cities and other small local units of government, we find the TEY on the 7 percent municipal bond discussed above to be

$$
\text{TEY} = \frac{(7.00 - 0.20 \times 0.35 \times 6.50)}{(1 - 0.35)}
$$

$$
= \frac{7.00 - 0.445}{0.65}
$$

$$
= 10.08 \text{ percent}
$$

If other factors are held constant, a taxable security (such as a corporate bond or U.S. government bond) would have to carry a yield of at least 10.08 percent to have the same after-tax return to a bank as the tax-exempt municipal bond described above.

The Tax Swapping Tool.   The size of a bank's revenue from *loans* in any given year also plays a key role in how its security investments are handled. In years when loan revenues are high, it is often beneficial to engage in tax swapping. In a **tax swap,** the bank usually sells lower-yielding securities at a loss to reduce its current taxable income, while simultaneously purchasing new higher-yielding securities to boost future expected returns on its investment portfolio.

Tax considerations in choosing securities to buy and sell tend to be more important for larger banks than for smaller banks. Usually the larger banks are in the top income tax bracket and have the most to gain from security portfolio trades that minimize their tax exposure. The security portfolio manager tries to estimate the bank's projected net taxable income under alternative portfolio choices. This involves, among other things, estimating how much tax-exempt income the bank could use.

No bank can use unlimited amounts of tax-exempt income. At least some taxable income will be necessary to offset a bank's allowable annual deduction for possible loan losses and to cover any other losses the bank suffers. However, once these conditions are met, the basic decision between purchasing tax-exempt securities or purchasing taxable securities and loans comes down to the relative after-tax returns of the two.

The Portfolio Shifting Tool.   Banks also do a great deal of **portfolio shifting** in their holdings of investment securities with both taxes and higher returns in mind. Banks often sell off selected securities at a loss in order to offset large amounts of loan income, thereby reducing their tax liability. They may also shift their portfolio simply to substitute new, higher-yielding securities for old security holdings whose yields are well below current market levels. The result may be to take substantial short-run losses in return for the prospect of higher long-run profits.

For example, the investment officer of First National Bank may be considering the following *shift* in its municipal bond portfolio:

Find a buyer for $10 million →	Current market price	=	$9.5 million
in 10-year New York City	Value recorded on the		
bonds bearing a 7 percent	bank's balance sheet	=	$10 million
coupon rate that the bank	Annual interest income	=	$0.7 million
currently holds.			
Then acquire $10 million in →	Current market price	=	$10 million
10-year Orange County			
(City of Los Angeles) bonds			
bearing a 9 percent coupon			
rate to add to the bank's			
investment portfolio.	Annual interest income	=	$0.9 million

Clearly, the bank takes an immediate $500,000 loss before taxes ($10 million – $9.5 million) on selling the 7 percent New York City bonds. But if First National is in the 35 percent tax bracket, its immediate loss after taxes becomes only $500,000 × (1 − 0.35), or $325,000. Moreover, it has swapped this loss for an additional $200,000 annually in tax-exempt income for 10 years. This portfolio shift is probably worth the immediate loss the bank must absorb from its current earnings. Moreover, if the bank has high taxable income from its loans, that near-term loss can be used to lower current taxable income and perhaps even increase this year's after-tax profits.

Interest Rate Risk

Changing interest rates create real risk for the bank's investment officer. Rising interest rates lower the market value of previously issued bonds and notes, with the longest-term security issues generally suffering the greatest losses. Moreover, periods of rising interest rates are often marked by surging loan demand. Because a banker's first priority is to make loans, many security investments must be sold off to generate cash for lending. Such sales frequently result in substantial capital losses, which the banker hopes to counteract by a combination of tax benefits and the relatively higher yields available on loans. A growing number of tools to hedge (counteract) **interest rate risk** have appeared in recent years, including financial futures contracts, option contracts, interest rate swaps, gap management, and duration, as we saw earlier in Chapters 6–8.

Credit or Default Risk

Bank security investments are closely regulated due to the **credit risk** displayed by many securities, especially those issued by private corporations and some local governments. The risk that the security issuer may default on the principal or interest owed on a bond or note has led to regulatory controls that prohibit the acquisition of speculative securities—those rated below Baa by Moody's or BBB on Standard & Poor's bond-rating schedule. (See Table 10–4 for definitions of the various credit rating symbols used today on debt securities.) U.S. banks generally are allowed to buy only *investment-grade securities,* rated at least Baa or BBB, in order to protect the bank's depositors against excessive risk. Moreover, banks are permitted to underwrite (i.e., purchase for resale) only U.S. government and general-obligation municipal bonds, though some bank holding companies have been allowed to underwrite privately issued securities if approved by the Federal Reserve Board. (See Chapters 1, 2, and 3 for a review of regulatory and court decisions that have significantly expanded the security underwriting powers of banking organizations in recent years.)

In January 1997 Moody's Investors Service announced some significant modification in its credit rating system for bonds issued by state and local (municipal) governments. Specifically, securities in selected categories (such as Aa, A, and Baa) will have a 2 or 3 numerical modifier added to their rating to differentiate securities slightly different in quality that carry similar letter credit grades. (Please see below.) In 1981 Moody's added the number 1 to the letter grades attached to some A- and B-rated municipals. Now, with the numbers 2 and 3 added to some letter grades, a bank investment officer is alerted that a "1" means the municipal security in question ranks at the upper end of its letter rating category, while 2 implies the issue lies in the middle range

TABLE 10–4   Default Risk Ratings on Marketable Securities

Investment securities sold by corporations and state and local governments must be assigned credit ratings, assessing their probability of default, before they can be successfully marketed. The two most popular private security rating companies are Standard & Poor's Corporation and Moody's Investor Service. They use the following credit rating symbols:

	Rating Symbols		
Credit Quality of Securities	*Moody's Rating Category*	*Standard & Poor's Rating Category*	
Best quality/smallest investment risk	Aaa	AAA	Investment quality or investment
High grade or high quality	Aa	AA	grade/considered
Upper medium grade	A	A	acceptable for most
Medium grade	Baa	BBB	banks
Medium grade with some speculative elements	Ba	BB	Speculative quality and junk bonds/ not
Lower medium grade	B	B	considered suitable
Poor standing/may be in default	Caa	CCC	for most banks
Speculative/often in default	Ca	CC	
Lowest-grade speculative securities/poor pro– spects	C	C	
Defaulted securities and securities issued by firms that have declared		DDD	
		DD	
bankruptcy	Not rated	D	

Most banks are limited to investment-grade securities—that is, they must purchase securities rated AAA to BBB (by Standard & Poor's) or Aaa to Baa (by Moody's). Unrated securities may also be acquired, but the bank must be able to demonstrate that they are of investment-grade quality.

of its letter rating group and 3 suggests the security in question lies at the low end of its letter grade category. These 1, 2, and 3 numerical modifiers were also added to corporate bond ratings from Aa to B a number of years ago.

New Credit Rating Symbols Used by Moody's Investor Service for State and Local Government Securities

Aaa	
Aa1	Ba1
Aa2	Ba2
Aa3	Ba3
A1	B1
A2	B2
A3	B3
Baa1	Caa
Baa2	Ca
Baa3	C

The new rating modifiers reflect growing concern about recent trends in the municipal market, especially increased credit risk and volatility.

There has been an uptrend of municipal default since the mid-1970s. In 1991 a record 258 municipal bond defaults occurred, involving about $5 billion in total defaulted IOUs. While the number of defaulted issues annually has since fallen, many state and local governments are under great stress today due to declining federal monies to support local welfare and other programs, rising needs for street, sewer, bridge, and other infrastructure repairs, and local taxpayer resistance to higher taxes. Moreover, with many local areas opposing new taxes and spending programs, more state and local governments have turned to more risky revenue bonds to supplement their financing options.

As we saw in the preceding chapter, bankers have helped to develop new methods for dealing with credit risk in both their investments and their loans in recent years. Credit options and swaps can be used to protect the expected yield on investment securities. For example, the bank's investment officer may be able to find another institution (often an insurance company) willing to swap an uncertain return on securities the bank holds for a lower but more certain return based upon a standard reference interest rate (such as the market yield on Treasury bills or notes). Credit options are now available in today's markets that help to hedge the value of a corporate bond, for example. If the bond issuer defaults, the bank receives a payoff from the credit option that at least partially offsets the bond's loss. Bank investment officers can also use credit options to protect the price (market value) of a bond in case its credit rating is lowered, dropping its value. In this instance the bank receives a payoff from the option writer if the bond's credit rating falls.

Business Risk

Banks of all sizes face significant risk that the economy of the market area they serve may turn down, with falling business sales and rising bankruptcies and unemployment. These adverse developments, often called **business risk,** would be reflected quickly in the bank's loan portfolio, where delinquent loans would rise as borrowers struggled to generate enough cash flow to pay the bank. Because business risk is always present, many banks rely heavily on their security portfolios to offset the impact of economic risk on their loan portfolios. This usually means that many of the securities purchased by the bank will come from borrowers located *outside* the bank's market for loans. Thus, a bank located in Dallas or Kansas City will probably purchase a substantial quantity of municipal bonds from cities and other local governments outside the Midwest (e.g., Los Angeles or New York debt securities). Bank examiners encourage out-of-market security purchases to balance risk exposure in the loan portfolio.

Liquidity Risk

Banks must be ever mindful of the possibility they will be required to sell investment securities in advance of their maturity due to **liquidity risk**. Thus, a key issue that a portfolio manager must face in selecting a security for investment purposes is *the breadth and depth of its resale market. Liquid* securities are, by definition, those investments that have a ready market, relatively stable price over time, and high probability of recovering the bank's original invested capital (i.e., the risk to principal is low). U.S. government securities are generally the most liquid and have the most active resale markets, followed by federal agency securities, municipal bonds, and mortgage securities. Unfortunately, the purchase of a large volume of liquid, readily marketable securities tends to lower a bank's average yield from its earning assets and, other factors held constant, tends to reduce its profitability. Thus, bank management faces a trade-off between profitability and liquidity that must be reevaluated daily as market interest rates and the bank's exposure to liquidity risk change.

Call Risk

Many corporations and some governments that issue investment securities reserve the right to call in those instruments in advance of their maturity and pay them off. Because such calls usually take place when market interest rates have declined (and the borrower can issue new securities bearing lower interest costs), the bank investing in callable bonds and notes runs the risk of an earnings loss because it must reinvest its recovered funds at today's lower interest rates. Banks generally try to minimize this **call risk** by purchasing bonds bearing longer call deferments (so that a call cannot occur for several years) or simply by avoiding the purchase of callable securities. Fortunately for bank investment officers and other active investors call privileges attached to bonds have been declining significantly in recent years due to the availability of other tools to manage interest rate risk.

Prepayment Risk

A form of risk specific to certain kinds of investment securities that banks buy for their investment portfolios is known as **prepayment risk**. This form of risk arises because the realized interest and principal payments (cash flow) from a pool of securitized loans (such as GNMA or FNMA pass-throughs, collateralized mortgage obligations (CMOs), or securitized packages of auto or credit card loans) may be quite different from the payments (cash flow) expected. Indeed, having to price the prepayment option associated with loan-backed securities distinguishes these investments from any other investment securities a bank might buy. For example, consider what can happen to the planned interest and principal payments from a pool of home mortgage loans that serve as collateral for the issuance of mortgage-backed securities. Variations in cash flow to holders of the securities backed by these loans can arise from:

A. *Loan refinancings,* which tend to accelerate when market interest rates fall significantly and yield curves achieve a substantial positive slope (in this case, borrowers may come to believe that they will save on loan payments if they replace their existing loan with a new lower-rate loan).

B. *Turnover of the assets behind the loan* (in this case borrowers may sell out and move away or some borrowers may not be able to meet their required loan payments and default on their loans).

In either or both of the above cases some loans will be terminated or paid off ahead of schedule, generating smaller or larger cash flows sooner than expected that can lower the expected rate of return to a bank that has invested in loan-backed securities.

The pace at which loans that underlie loan-backed investment securities are terminated or paid off depends heavily upon the interest rate spread between current interest rates on similar type loans and the interest rates attached to loans in the securitized pool. When market interest rates drop below the interest rates attached to loans in the pool far enough to cover refinancing costs, more and more borrowers will call in their loans and pay them off early. This means that the market value of a loan-backed security depends, not only upon the promised cash flows (interest and principal payments) it will generate, but also on the projected prepayments and loan defaults that occur—that is:

$$\begin{matrix} \text{Market value} \\ \text{(price) of a} \\ \text{loan-backed} \\ \text{security} \end{matrix} = \frac{\begin{matrix}\text{Expected cash flows} \\ \text{adjusted for any} \\ \text{prepayments or} \\ \text{defaults of} \\ \text{existing loans in} \\ \text{the pool in Period 1}\end{matrix}}{(1 + y/m)^1} + \cdots + \frac{\begin{matrix}\text{Expected cash flows} \\ \text{adjusted for any} \\ \text{prepayments or} \\ \text{defaults of} \\ \text{existing loans in} \\ \text{the pool in Period nxm}\end{matrix}}{(1 + y/m)^{nxm}} \qquad (8)$$

where n is the number of years required for the last of the loans in the pool to be paid off or retired, m represents the number of times during the year interest and principal must be paid to holders of the loan-backed securities, and y is the expected yield to maturity of these securities.

In order to properly value a loan-backed security, a bank's investment officer needs to make some reasonable assumptions about what volume of loans might be prepaid or terminated while the bank is holding the security. In making estimates of loan prepayment behavior, the investment officer must consider such factors as expected market interest rates, future changes in the shape of the yield curve, the impact of seasonal factors (e.g., in the case of home-mortgage-backed securities, most homes are bought and sold in the spring of each year), the condition of the economy and the availability of jobs, and how old the loans in the pool are (because new loans are less likely to be repaid than older loans).

One commonly employed way of making loan prepayment estimates is to use the prepayment model developed by the Public Securities Association (PSA), which calculates an average loan prepayment rate based upon past experience. The so-called PSA model assumes, for example, that insured home mortgages will prepay at an annual rate of 0.2 percent the first month and the prepayment rate will grow by 0.2 percent each month for the first 30 months. Loan prepayments are then assumed to level off at a 6 percent annual rate for the remainder of the loan pool's life. When an investment officer adopts the PSA model without any modifications, he or she is said to be assuming a 100 percent PSA repayment rate. However, the bank's investment officer may decide to alter the PSA model to 75 percent PSA, 110 percent PSA, or some other percentage multiplier based upon his or her special knowledge of the nature of loans in the pool (such as their geographic location, distribution of maturities, or average age of borrowers).

It must be noted that while prepayments of securitized loans tend to accelerate in periods of falling interest rates, this is not always an adverse development for banks and other holders of loan-backed securities. For example, as prepayments accelerate, a bank investing in these assets recovers its invested cash at a faster rate, which can be a favorable development if it has other profitable uses for those funds (such as making direct loans to customers). Moreover, lower interest rates increase the present value of all projected cash flows from a loan-backed security so that its market value could rise. These potential benefits must be compared by the bank's investment officer to the potential losses from falling interest payments in the form of lower reinvestment rates and lost future income from loans that are prepaid. In general, loan-backed securities will fall in value when interest rates decline if the expected loss of interest income from prepaid loans and reduced reinvestment earnings exceed the benefits that arise from recovering cash more quickly from prepaid loans and from the higher present values attached to expected cash flows.

As a result of the FDIC Improvement Act of 1991, U.S. banks that are not well capitalized cannot place so-called high-risk mortgage-backed securities acquired after February 10, 1992, into their investment portfolios. Instead, high-risk mortgage-backed instruments must be placed in security trading accounts or listed as "assets held for sale." The definition of *high risk* includes those mortgage-backed securities whose average life exceeds 10 years and whose price and weighted average life change markedly when the overall level of interest rates moves up or down.[4]

Inflation Risk

While there is less of a problem today than in the 1970s, banks must be alert to the possibility that the purchasing power of both the interest income and repaid principal from a security or loan will be eroded by rising prices for goods and services. Inflation can also erode the value of the stockholders' investment in a bank—its *net worth*. Some protection against **inflation risk** is provided by short-term securities and those with variable interest rates, which usually grant the bank's investment officer greater flexibility in responding to any flare-up in inflationary pressures.

Pledging Requirements

Banks in the United States cannot accept deposits from federal, state, and local governments unless they post collateral acceptable to these governmental units in order to safeguard the deposit of public funds. The first $100,000 of these public deposits is covered by federal deposit insurance; the rest must be backed up by the bank's holdings of U.S. Treasury and federal agency securities valued at their par values. Some municipal bonds (provided they are at least A-rated) can also be used to secure the federal government's deposits in banks, but these securities must be valued at a discount from par (usually only 80 to 90 percent of their face value) in order to give governmental depositors an added cushion of safety. State and local government deposit **pledging** requirements differ widely from state to state, though most allow banks to use a combination of federal and municipal securities to meet government deposit pledging

---

[4]Under the FDIC's rules, a mortgage-backed security is considered "high-risk if: (*a*) the weighted average life of the security increases by more than four years when the yield curve experiences a parallel shift upward by three percentage points (or less) or shortens in maturity by more than six years when the yield curve shifts downward by three percentage points (or less) and (*b*) the security's price changes by more than 17 percent when the yield curve shifts upward or downward by as much as three percentage points. Certain floating-rate, mortgage-backed securities (particularly those whose interest rates are below their contractual cap rates or whose floating rate is tied to some widely used market reference rate like prime or LIBOR) are exempt from some of these sensitivity tests. However, if a mortgage-backed security of any kind is found to have excessive price sensitivity, it will be placed in the high-risk category by regulators and the bank may have to remove it from its investment portfolio.

requirements. Sometimes the government owning the deposit requires that the pledged securities be placed with a trustee not affiliated with the bank receiving the deposit.

Pledging requirements also exist for selected other bank liabilities. For example, when a bank borrows from the discount window of the Federal Reserve bank in its district, it must pledge either federal government securities or other collateral acceptable to the Fed. If a bank uses repurchase agreements (RPs) to raise money, it must pledge some of its securities (usually U.S. Treasury and federal agency issues) as collateral in order to receive funds at the low RP interest rate.

Concept Checks

10–6. How is the expected yield on most bonds held by banks determined?

10–7. If a government bond is expected to mature in two years and has a current price of $950, what is the bond's YTM if it has a par value of $1,000 and a promised coupon rate of 10 percent. Suppose this bond is sold one year after purchase for a price of $970. What would this investor's holding period yield be?

10–8. What forms of risk affect bank security investments?

10–9. How has the tax exposure of various U.S. bank security investments changed in recent years?

10–10. Suppose a corporate bond that a bank's investment officer would like to purchase for her bank has a before-tax yield of 8.98 percent and the bank is in the 35 percent federal income tax bracket. What is the bond's after-tax gross yield? What after-tax rate of return must a prospective loan generate to be competitive with the corporate bond? Does a loan have some advantages for a bank that a corporate bond would not have?

10–11. What is the net after-tax return on a qualified municipal security whose nominal gross return is 6 percent, the cost of borrowed funds is 5 percent, and the bank is in the 35 percent tax bracket? What is the tax-equivalent yield (TEY) on this tax-exempt security?

10–12. Spiro National Bank currently holds a government bond valued on the day of its purchase at $5 million, with a promised interest yield of 6 percent, whose current market value is $3.9 million. Comparable quality bonds are available today for a promised yield of 8 percent. What are the advantages to this bank from selling the government bond bearing a 6 percent promised yield and buying some 8 percent bonds?

10–13. What is tax swapping? What is portfolio shifting? Give an example of each.

10–14. Why do banks face pledging requirements when they accept government deposits?

10–15. What types of securities are used to meet bank collateralization requirements?

Investment Maturity Strategies

Once the investment officer chooses the type of securities he or she believes the bank should hold, based on their expected return and risk, pledging requirements, tax exposure, and other factors, there remains the question of *how to distribute those security holdings over time.* That is, what *maturities* of securities should the bank hold? Should it purchase mainly short-term bills and notes, or only long-term bonds, or perhaps some combination of the two? Several alternative maturity distribution strategies have been developed over the years, each with its own unique set of advantages and disadvantages. (See Exhibits 10–2 and 10–3.)

The Ladder, or Spaced-Maturity, Policy.   One popular approach to the maturity problem, particularly among smaller financial institutions, is to choose some maximum acceptable maturity and then invest in an *equal* proportion of securities in each of several maturity intervals until the maximum acceptable maturity is reached.

For example, suppose bank management decided that it did not want to purchase any bonds or notes with maturities longer than five years. This bank might then decide to invest 20 percent of its investment portfolio in securities one year or less from maturity, another 20 percent in securities maturing within two years but no less than one year, another 20 percent in the interval of two to three years, and so forth, until the five-year point is reached. This strategy certainly does *not* maximize investment income, but it has the advantage of reducing income fluctuations and requires little management expertise to carry out. Moreover, this "ladder" approach tends to build in investment flexibility. Because some securities are always rolling over into cash, the bank can take advantage of any promising opportunities that may appear.

The Front-End Load Maturity Policy.   Another popular strategy, especially among commercial banks, is to purchase only short-term securities and place all investments within a certain brief interval of time. For example, the bank's investment officer may decide to invest 100 percent of the bank's funds not needed for loans or cash reserves in securities two years or less from maturity. This approach stresses using the investment portfolio primarily as a source of *liquidity* rather than as a source of income.

The Back-End Load Maturity Policy.   An opposite approach would stress the investment portfolio as a source of *income.* A bank following the so-called *back-end load* approach might decide to invest only in bonds in the 5- to 10-year maturity range. This bank would probably rely heavily on borrowing in the money market to help meet its liquidity requirements.

The Barbell Strategy.   A combination of the front-end and back-end load approaches is the *barbell strategy,* in which a bank places most of its funds in a short-term portfolio of highly liquid securities at one extreme and in a long-term portfolio of bonds at the other extreme, with minimal or no investment holdings in intermediate maturities. The short-term portfolio provides liquidity, while the long-term portfolio is designed to generate income.

Exhibit 10–2

Alternative Maturity Strategies for Managing Bank Investment Portfolios

THE LADDER OR SPACED-MATURITY POLICY

STRATEGY: Divide investment portfolio equally among all maturities acceptable to the bank.
ADVANTAGES: Reduces investment income fluctuations/requires little management expertise.

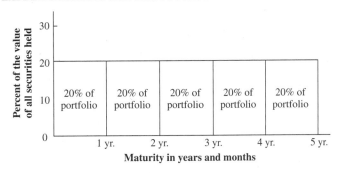

THE FRONT-END-LOADED MATURITY POLICY

STRATEGY: All security investments are short-term.
ADVANTAGES: Strengthens the bank's liquidity position and avoids large capital losses if interest rates rise.

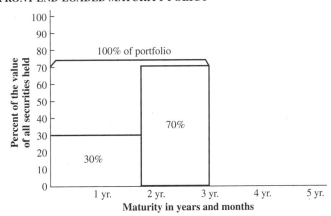

THE BACK-END-LOADED MATURITY POLICY

STRATEGY: All security investments are long-term.
ADVANTAGES: Maximizes the bank's income potential from security investments if interest rates fall.

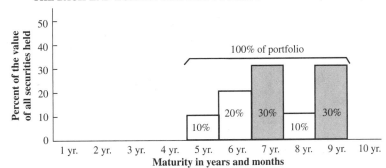

The Rate Expectations Approach.   The most aggressive of all maturity strategies is one that continually shifts maturities of securities held, in line with current forecasts of interest rates and the economy. This *total performance,* or *rate expectation,* approach calls for shifting bank investments toward the short end of the maturity spectrum when interest rates are expected to rise and toward the long end when falling interest rates are expected. Such an approach offers the potential for large capital gains, but also raises the specter of substantial capital losses. It requires in-depth knowledge of market forces, presents greater risk if expectations turn out to be wrong, and carries greater transactions costs because it may require frequent security trading and switching.

Banks do not hesitate to trade their unpledged security holdings whenever there is the prospect of significant gains in expected returns or the opportunity to reduce asset risk without a significant loss in expected yield. They are particularly aggressive when loan revenues are down and the sale of securities whose market value has risen will boost net income and shareholder returns. However, because losses on security trades

Exhibit 10–3
Additional Maturity Strategies for Managing Bank Investment Portfolios

THE BARBELL INVESTMENT PORTFOLIO STRATEGY

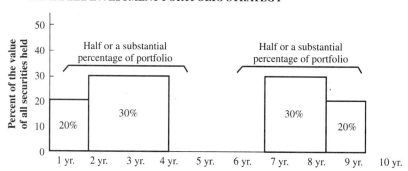

STRATEGY:
Security holdings are divided between short-term and long-term.
ADVANTAGES:
Helps to meet bank's liquidity needs with short-term securities and to achieve earnings goals due to higher potential earnings from long-term portfolio.

THE RATE-EXPECTATIONS APPROACH

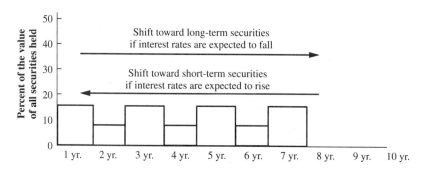

STRATEGY:
Change the mix of investment maturities as the interest-rate outlook changes.
ADVANTAGES:
Maximizes the potential for earnings (and also for losses).

reduce before-tax net income, portfolio managers do not like to take such losses unless they can demonstrate to the bank's board of directors that the loss will be more than made up by higher expected returns on any new assets acquired from the proceeds of the security sale. In general, banks are inclined to trade securities if: (*a*) their expected after-tax returns can be raised through effective tax management strategies, (*b*) higher yields can be locked in at the long-term end of the yield curve when the forecast is for falling interest rates, (*c*) the trade would contribute to an overall improvement in asset quality that would enable the bank to better weather an economic downturn, or (*d*) the investment portfolio can be moved toward higher-grade securities without an appreciable loss in expected return, especially if problems are developing in the loan portfolio.

Maturity Management Tools

In choosing among various maturities of short-term and long-term securities to acquire, the bank's investment officer needs to consider carefully the use of two key maturity management tools—the *yield curve* and *duration*. These two tools help the investment officer understand more fully the consequences and potential impact on bank earnings and risk of any particular maturity mix of securities he or she chooses.

The Yield Curve

As we saw in Chapter 6, the **yield curve** is simply a picture of how market interest rates differ across loans and securities of varying term or time to maturity. Each yield curve, such as the one drawn in Exhibit 10–4, assumes that all interest rates (or yields) included along the curve are measured at the same time and that all other rate-determining forces are held constant. While the curve in Exhibit 10–4 slopes upward as we move to

EXHIBIT 10–4
The Yield Curve

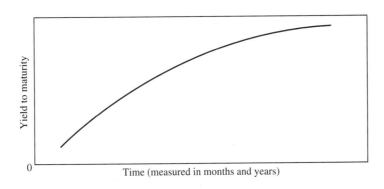

the right, yield curves may also slope downward or be horizontal, indicating that short- and long-term interest rates at that particular moment are about the same.

Yield curve shapes have several critical implications for the decisions a bank's investment officer must make. For example, the yield curve contains an implicit *forecast of future interest rate changes*. Positively sloped yield curves reflect the average expectation in the market that future short-term interest rates will be higher than they are today. In this case, investors expect to see an upward rate movement, and they translate this expectation into action by shifting their investment holdings away from longer-term securities (which will incur the greatest capital losses when interest rates do rise) toward shorter-term securities. Thus, banks following the interest rate expectations approach to security management will tend to avoid purchasing long-term securities because their market prices are expected to fall, generating future losses, and will place more emphasis on shorter-term securities. Conversely, a downward-sloping yield curve points to investor expectations of declining short-term interest rates in the period ahead. The investment officer will probably consider lengthening the maturities of at least some of the bank's securities, because falling interest rates offer the prospect of substantial capital gains income from longer-term securities.

In the short run, yield curves provide the bank's investment officer with a clue about overpriced and underpriced securities. Because the yield curve indicates what the yield to maturity should be for each maturity of security, a security whose yield lies *above* the curve at a particular maturity represents a tempting buy situation; its yield is temporarily too high (and, therefore, its price is too low). On the other hand, a security whose yield lies *below* the curve represents a possible sell or "don't buy" situation because its yield, momentarily, is too low for its maturity (and, thus, its price is too high). In the long run, yield curves send signals about what stage of the business cycle the economy presently occupies; they generally rise in economic expansions and fall in recessions.

The yield curve is also useful because it tells the investment officer something important about the *current trade-offs between seeking greater returns and accepting greater risks*. The yield curve's shape determines how much additional yield the investment officer can earn for the bank by replacing shorter-term securities with longer-term issues, or vice versa. For example, a steeply sloped positive yield curve that rises 150 basis points between 5-year and 10-year maturity bonds indicates the investment officer can pick up 1.5 percentage points in extra yield (less broker or dealer commissions and any tax liability incurred) by switching from 5-year bonds to 10-year bonds. However, 10-year bonds are generally more volatile in price than 5-year bonds, so the investment officer must be willing to accept greater risk of a capital loss on the 10-year bonds if interest rates rise. Longer-term bonds are also generally less liquid, with a thinner market in case the bank must raise cash quickly by selling them. The investment officer can measure along the curve what gain in yield will result from maturity extension and compare that gain against the likelihood the bank will face a liquidity crisis ("cash out") or suffer capital losses if interest rates go in an unexpected direction.

If the yield curve has a sufficiently strong positive slope, the bank may be able to score significant portfolio gains with a maneuver known as *riding the yield curve*.

The investment officer looks for a situation in which some of the bank's securities are approaching maturity and their prices have risen significantly while their yields to maturity have fallen. If the yield curve's slope is steep enough to more than cover transactions costs, the bank can sell those securities, scoring a capital gain due to the rise in their prices, and reinvest the proceeds of that sale in longer-term securities carrying higher rates of return. If the riding maneuver works (i.e., the slope of the yield curve does not change significantly against the bank), the bank will reap *both* higher current income and greater future returns on the portfolio.

Duration

While the yield curve presents the bank's investment officer with valuable information and occasionally the opportunity for substantial gains in income, it has several limitations, such as uncertainty over exactly how and why the curve appears the way it does at any particular moment and the possibility of a change in the curve's shape at any time. Moreover, the yield curve concept is based on a crude, but traditional, measure of the maturity of a security—the amount of calendar time in days, weeks, months, or years remaining until any particular security will be paid off and retired. This traditional maturity measure counts only clock time, not the income or cash flow expected from a security. The most critical information for the bank's investment officer is usually not how long any particular security will be around but, rather, *when* it will generate cash flow or income for the bank and *how much* cash will be generated each month, quarter, or year that the bank holds the security.

The need for this kind of information gave rise to the concept of **duration**—a present value-weighted measure of maturity of an individual security or portfolio of securities. As we saw earlier in Chapter 7, duration measures the average amount of time it takes for all of the cash flows from a security to reach the bank that holds it. In effect, it gives the investment officer a measure of how long it will take for a security to pay back to the bank its purchase price in present value terms.

To illustrate how to calculate the duration of an investment security that a bank might wish to buy, we use the equation illustrated in Chapter 7, Equation 2 and the example of the Treasury note presented earlier in this chapter. Recall that this was a $1,000 par value T-note scheduled to mature in five years and paying $80 per year in interest. Earlier we found that this note's yield to maturity was 10.73 percent and its current market price was $900. If interest is paid just once each year at year-end, what is this note's duration?

$$D = \frac{\left[\dfrac{\$80 \times 1}{(1+0.1073)^1} + \dfrac{\$80 \times 2}{(1+0.1073)^2} + \dfrac{\$80 \times 3}{(1+0.1073)^3} + \dfrac{\$80 \times 4}{(1+0.1073)^4} + \dfrac{\$1,080 \times 5}{(1+0.1073)^5} \right]}{\$900}$$

$$= \frac{\$72.75 + \$130.50 + \$176.77 + \$212.85 + \$3,243.83}{\$900} = \frac{\$3,836.20}{\$900}$$

$$D = 4.26 \text{ years}$$

Thus, this Treasury note will pay itself out in present value terms in 4.26 years (or about 4 years and 3 months), which is its *average* maturity considering the amount and timing of all of its expected cash flows of principal and interest.[5]

We recall from Equation 5 in Chapter 7 that there is an important linear relationship between the duration of an investment security that a bank might be interested in and its price sensitivity to interest rate changes. Specifically, *the percentage change in the price of an investment security is equal to the negative of its duration times the change in interest rates divided by one plus the initial interest rate or yield.*[6] To illustrate how this relationship can provide the bank's investment officer with valuable information, consider the Treasury note whose duration we calculated above to be 4.26 years. Suppose market interest rates rose from the note's current yield of 10.73 percent to 12 percent—a change in rate of 1.27 percentage points. The approximate change in the T-note's price then would be:

$$\text{Percentage change in security's price} = -4.26 \times \left(\frac{0.0127}{1 + 0.1073}\right) \times 100\% = -4.89\%$$

In this instance, a rise in interest rates of just over one percentage point produces almost a 5 percent decline in the security's price. The bank's investment officer must now decide how much chance there is that interest rates will rise, whether this kind of price sensitivity is acceptable to the bank, and whether other investment securities would better suit the bank's current needs.

Duration also suggests a way to minimize the damage to the bank's earnings that changes in interest rates may cause. That is, *duration gives the investment officer a tool to reduce the bank's exposure to interest rate risk.* It suggests a formula for minimizing and possibly eliminating rate risk:

---

[5]A relatively easy method for calculating the *duration* of the Treasury note discussed above is to construct the table shown below:

Year (A)	Cash Flow (B)	Present Value Factor* (C)	Present Value of Cash Flow (B × C)	Present Value ÷ Price (B × C/ Price)	Duration Components $\left[A \times \frac{B \times C}{\text{Price}}\right]$
1	$ 80	0.9031	$ 72.25	0.0803	0.0803
2	80	0.8156	65.25	0.0725	0.1450
3	80	0.7365	58.92	0.0655	0.1965
4	80	0.6652	53.22	0.0591	0.2364
5	1080	0.6007	648.76	0.7208	3.6040
					Duration = 4.2622 yrs.

*Based on a YTM of 0.1073.

[6]The formula described in this sentence (and presented in Chapter 7) applies if a security pays interest once each year. If interest is paid more than once each year the appropriate formula is:

$$\text{Percentage change in price} = -\text{Duration} \times \left[\frac{\text{Change in interest rate}}{1 + (1/m)(\text{Initial interest rate})}\right]$$

where m is the number of times during a year that the security pays interest. For example, most bonds pay interest semiannually, in which case m = 2.

$$
\begin{array}{c}
\text{Duration of} \\
\text{an individual} \\
\text{security or a} \\
\text{security portfolio}
\end{array}
=
\begin{array}{c}
\text{Length of the bank's} \\
\text{planned holding period} \\
\text{for a security or a} \\
\text{security portfolio}
\end{array}
\qquad (9)
$$

For example, a bank interested in buying U.S. Treasury notes and bonds today, perhaps because loan demand currently is weak, fears that it may be required to sell those securities at this time next year in order to accommodate its best customers when loan demand recovers. Faced with this prospect and determined to minimize interest rate risk, the investment officer could choose those government notes and bonds with a *duration of one year.* The effect of this step is to immunize the securities purchased from loss of return, no matter which way interest rates go.

Duration works to immunize a security or portfolio of securities against interest rate changes because the two key forms of risk—*interest rate risk,* or the danger of falling security prices, and *reinvestment risk,* or the possibility that cash flows received from securities must be invested at lower and lower interest rates—*offset* each other when duration is set equal to the bank's planned holding period. If interest rates *rise* after the securities are purchased, their market price will decline, but the bank can reinvest the cash flow those securities are generating at higher market interest rates. Similarly, if interest rates *fall,* the bank will be forced to reinvest the cash flow from its securities at lower interest rates but, correspondingly, the prices of those securities will have risen. The net result is to *freeze the total return from the bank's securities holdings.* Capital gains or losses are counterbalanced by falling or rising reinvestment yields when duration equals the bank's planned holding period.

As we saw in Chapter 7, the duration concept can be applied to the bank's entire portfolio of assets and liabilities in order to hedge against interest rates changes. However, as we also noted in Chapter 7, the duration concept has a few limitations that must be seriously considered. For example, it assumes that the slope of the yield curve remains essentially constant over time which is rarely true. However, recent research suggests that duration can still be effective in protecting a bank's security holdings against interest rate risk even with moderate violations of the duration model's basic assumptions.

Summary

Bank investments in marketable securities play several important roles inside the bank. These securities provide a supplemental source of income after loans—a source that is particularly significant for the bank's management and stockholders when loan income is depressed. Bank security investments also represent a source of liquidity to back-stop cash and borrowings from the money market when funds are needed in a hurry to cover deposit withdrawals or to meet other pressing cash needs.

Finally, security investments help to reduce the bank's tax liability through tax-exempt investments and to offset, through acquisition of low-risk securities, the high credit risk centered in the bank's loan portfolio.

Banks purchase a wide range of investment securities. The most popular in recent years have included such money market instruments as Treasury bills, federal agency securities, certificates of deposit (CDs) issued by other depository institutions,

Concept Checks

10–16. What factors affect a bank's decision regarding the different maturities of securities it should hold?

10–17. What maturity strategies do banks employ in managing their investment portfolios?

10–18. Bacone National Bank has structured its investment portfolio, which extends out to four-year maturities, so that it holds about $11 million each in one-year, two-year, three-year, and four-year securities. In contrast, Dunham National Bank and Trust holds $36 million in one- and two-year securities and about $30 million in 8- to 10-year maturities. What investment maturity strategy is each bank following? Why do you believe that each of these banks has adopted the particular strategy it has as reflected in the maturity structure of its portfolio?

10–19. How can the yield curve and duration help a bank's investment officer choose which securities to acquire or sell?

10–20. A bond currently sells for $950 based on a par value of $1,000 and promises $100 in interest for three years before being retired. Yields to maturity on comparable-quality securities are currently at 12 percent. What is the bond's duration? Suppose interest rates in the market fall to 10 percent. What will be the approximate percent change in the bond's price.

Eurodollar deposits, bankers' acceptances, commercial paper, short-term municipal obligations, and long-term capital market instruments, including Treasury notes and bonds, state and local government notes and bonds, mortgage-backed securities, and corporate notes and bonds. In considering what securities to acquire and hold, bank management must consider a number of important factors: expected rates of return (yields), the bank's tax exposure, interest rate risk, credit risk, liquidity risk, inflation risk, and pledging requirements.

Knowledge of the concepts of duration and the yield curve can aid the bank's portfolio manager in making security investments that contribute to the bank's goals. The yield curve, showing the distribution of long- and short-term interest rates, helps the bank's investment officer assess the outlook for interest rates and evaluate the trade-offs between risk and return. Duration, which is a present value-weighted measure of the maturity of a security or portfolio of securities, enables the investment officer to help reduce the bank's exposure to interest rate risk. He or she can accomplish this by equalizing the duration of securities purchased to the bank's planned holding period for those securities.

Key Terms in This Chapter

Money market instruments

Capital market instruments

U.S. Treasury bill

Treasury notes

Treasury bonds

Federal agency securities

Certificate of deposit (CD)

Bankers' acceptances

Commercial paper

Municipal bonds

Corporate notes

Corporate bonds

Securitized assets

Mortgage-backed bond

Stripped security

Yield to maturity (YTM)

Holding period yield (HPY)

Tax swap

Portfolio shifting

Interest rate risk

Credit risk

Business risk

Liquidity risk

Call risk

Prepayment risk

Inflation risk

Pledging

Yield curve

Duration

Problems and Projects

1. A 10-year U.S. Treasury bond with a par value of $1,000 is currently selling for $775 from various security dealers. The bond carries a 9 percent coupon rate. If purchased today and held to maturity, what is its expected yield to maturity?

   Alternative scenarios:

   (1) Suppose the bank purchases the Treasury bond described above today at $775 and is forced to sell the bond at the end of three years for $880. What is its holding period yield?

   (2) Suppose the bank later repurchases the same Treasury bond on the open market. This time it pays $940 for the 9 percent coupon instrument, which has a remaining term of only four years. What is the bond's yield to maturity?

2. A state government bond is selling today for $962.77 and has a $1,000 face (par) value. Its yield to maturity is 6 percent, and the bond promises its holders $55 per year in interest for the next 10 years before it matures. What is the bond's duration?

   Alternative scenarios:

   (1) Suppose the bond's market price climbs to $950 before the bank can get in its purchase order. What is the change in duration as a result of this price increase?

   (2) If the bank buys the state government bond described above for $950 and holds it for the full term, what *after-tax* yield to maturity will the bank receive?

3. Calculate the yield to maturity of a 10-year U.S. government bond that is currently selling for $800 in today's market and carries a 10 percent coupon rate with interest paid semiannually.

   Alternative scenarios:

   (1) Suppose a bank decides to purchase the above 10-year government bond for $800 and five years hence is compelled to sell it for $900. What holding period yield can the bank expect after five years?

   (2) Suppose this bond purchased at $800 suddenly rises to a premium of $1,100 after two years and the bank alters its plan, selling the bond immediately to capture the premium. What will its holding period return be?

(3) Finally, suppose First National Bank of Richland elected to purchase the 10-year Treasury bond described above and hold it until its maturity date. If First National carries a 35 percent income tax rate, what expected after-tax yield to maturity would result?

4. A corporate bond being seriously considered for purchase by First Bank and Trust will mature 20 years from today and promises a 12 percent interest payment once a year. Recent inflation in the economy has driven the yield to maturity on this bond to 15 percent, and it carries a face value of $1,000. Calculate this bond's duration.

Alternative scenarios:

Suppose the bank plans to hold the corporate bond described above for 12 years. Will the bond carry market risk for the bank? How could the bank reduce the risk of loss from this bond if interest rates move in an unfavorable direction? Please explain carefully.

5. City National Bank regularly purchases municipal bonds issued by small rural school districts in its region of the state. At the moment, the bank is considering purchasing an $8 million general obligation issue from the Youngstown school district, the only bond issue that district plans this year. The bonds, which mature in 15 years, carry a nominal annual rate of return of 7.75 percent. City National, which is in the top corporate tax bracket of 35 percent, must pay an average interest rate of 7.38 percent to borrow the funds needed to purchase the municipals. Would you recommend purchasing these bonds?

Alternative scenario:

What if the bank has to choose between the $8 million in municipals and a package of loans of an equivalent amount that promise a before-tax return of 9.20 percent? Which use of the bank's funds would you recommend? Please explain.

6. Lakeway State Bank and Trust Company is interested in doing some investment portfolio shifting. The bank has had a good year thus far,

with strong loan demand; its loan revenue has increased by 16 percent over last year's level. Lakeway is subject to the 35 percent corporate income tax rate. The bank's investment officer has several options in the form of bonds that have been held for some time in its portfolio:

a. Selling $4 million in 12-year City of Dallas bonds with a coupon rate of 7.5 percent and purchasing $4 million in bonds from Bexar County (also with 12-year maturities) with a coupon of 8 percent and issued at par. The Dallas bonds have a current market value of $3,750,000 but are listed at par on the bank's books.

b. Selling $4 million in 12-year U.S. Treasury bonds that carry a coupon rate of 12 percent and are recorded at par, which was the price when the bank purchased them. The market value of these bonds has risen to $4,330,000.

Which of these two portfolio shifts would you recommend? Is there a good reason for *not* selling these Treasury bonds? What other information is needed to make the best decision? Please explain.

7. Current market yields on U.S. government securities are distributed by maturity as follows:

3-month Treasury bills	= 7.69 percent
6-month Treasury bills	= 7.49 percent
1-year Treasury notes	= 7.77 percent
2-year Treasury notes	= 7.80 percent
3-year Treasury notes	= 7.80 percent
5-year Treasury notes	= 7.81 percent
7-year Treasury notes	= 7.86 percent
10-year Treasury bonds	= 7.87 percent
30-year Treasury bonds	= 7.90 percent

Draw a *yield curve* for the above securities. What shape does the curve have? What significance might this yield curve have for a bank with 75 percent of its investment portfolio in 7-year to 30-year U.S. Treasury bonds and 25 percent in U.S. government bills and notes with maturities under one year? What would you recommend to the bank's management?

8. A bond possesses a duration of 5.82 years. Suppose that market interest rates on comparable bonds were 7 percent this morning, but have now shifted upward to 7.5 percent. What percentage change in the bond's value occurred when interest rates moved 0.5 percent higher?

9. The investment officer for Sillistine State Bank is concerned about interest rate risk lowering the value of the bank's bonds. A check of the bank's bond portfolio reveals an average duration of 4.5 years. How could this bond portfolio be altered in order to minimize interest rate risk should interest rates change significantly within the next year?

10. A bank's economics department has just forecast accelerated growth in the economy with GDP expected to grow at a 4.5 percent annual growth rate for at least the next two years. What are the implications of this economic forecast for a bank's investment officer? What types of securities should the investment officer think most seriously about adding to the bank's investment portfolio? Why? Suppose the bank holds a security portfolio similar to that described in Table 10–3 for all insured U.S. banks. Which types of securities might the bank's investment officer want to think seriously about selling if the projected economic expansion takes place? What losses might occur and how could these losses be minimized?

11. Contrary to the exuberant economic forecast described in problem 10 above, suppose a bank's economics department is forecasting a significant recession in economic activity. Output and employment are projected to decline significantly over the next 18 months. What are the implications of this forecast for a bank's investment portfolio manager? What is the outlook for interest rates and inflation under the foregoing assumptions? What types of securities would you recommend as good additions to the bank's portfolio during the period covered by the recession forecast and why? What other kinds of information would you like to have about the bank's current balance sheet and earnings report in order to help you make the best quality decisions regarding the bank's security portfolio?

12. Arrington Hills National Bank, a $3.5 billion asset institution, holds the security portfolio outlined below. The bank serves a rapidly growing money center into which substantial numbers of businesses are relocating their corporate headquarters. Suburban areas around the city are also growing rapidly as large numbers of business owners and managers along with retired professionals are purchasing new homes and condominiums. Would you recommend any changes in the makeup of the security portfolio outlined below? Please explain why.

Types of Securities Held	Percent of Total Portfolio	Types of Securities Held	Percent of Total Portfolio
U.S. Treasury securities	38.7%	Securities available for sale	45.6%
Federal agency securities	35.2	Securities with maturities:	
State and local government obligations	15.5	Under one year	11.3
Domestic debt securities	5.1	One to five years	37.9
Foreign debt securities	4.9	Over five years	50.8
Equities	0.6		

Selected References

See below for a discussion of securitized assets and security stripping.

1. Becketti, Sean. "The Role of Stripped Securities in Portfolio Management." *Economic Review,* Federal Reserve Bank of Kansas City, May 1988, pp. 20–31.
2. ———. "The Prepayment Risk of Mortgage-Backed Securities." *Economic Review,* Federal Reserve Bank of Kansas City, February 1989, pp. 32–43.
3. Smith, Stephen D. "Analyzing Risk and Return for Mortgage-Backed Securities." *Economic Review,* Federal Reserve Bank of Richmond, January/February 1991, pp. 2–10.

For a review of tax management issues in banking, see the following:

4. French, George E. "Tax Reform and Its Effects on the Banking Industry." *Issues in Bank Regulation,* Summer 1987, pp. 3–10.

The following review yield to maturity and other yield measures:

5. Rose, Peter S. *Money and Capital Markets.* 6th ed. Burr Ridge, Ill.: Richard D. Irwin, 1997, chap. 8 ("Relationships between Interest Rates and Security Prices").
6. Kalotay, Andrew. J. "The After-Tax Duration of Original Issue Discount Bonds." *Journal of Portfolio Management,* Winter 1985, pp. 70–72.

For a thorough discussion of investment strategies involving many securities purchased by banks, see:

7. Sundaresan, Suresh M. *Fixed Income Markets and Their Derivatives.* Cincinnati, Ohio: South-Western Publishing Company, 1997.

11 LIQUIDITY AND RESERVE MANAGEMENT STRATEGIES AND POLICIES

Learning and Management Decision Objectives

The purpose of this chapter is to explore the reasons why banks often face heavy demands for immediately spendable funds (liquidity) and learn about the methods banks can use to prepare for meeting their cash needs.

Introduction

One of the most important tasks faced by the management of any bank is ensuring adequate **liquidity.** A bank is considered to be *liquid* if it has ready access to immediately spendable funds at reasonable cost at precisely the time those funds are needed. This suggests that a liquid bank either has the right amount of immediately spendable funds on hand when they are required or can quickly raise liquid funds by borrowing or by selling assets.

Lack of adequate liquidity is often one of the first signs that a bank is in serious financial trouble. The troubled bank usually begins to lose deposits, which erodes its supply of cash and forces the institution to dispose of its more liquid assets. Other banks become increasingly reluctant to lend the troubled bank any funds without additional security or a higher rate of interest, which further reduces the earnings of the problem institution and threatens it with failure.

Many banks assume that liquid funds can be borrowed virtually without limit any time they are needed. Therefore, they see little need to store liquidity in the form of easily marketed, stable-price assets. The enormous cash shortages experienced in recent years by banks in trouble (such as Continental Illinois National Bank of Chicago) make clear that liquidity needs cannot be ignored. Liquidity management is far more important than ever before, because a bank can be closed if it cannot raise enough liquidity even though, technically, it may still be solvent. For example, in 1991 the Federal Reserve forced the closure of the $10 billion Southeast Bank of Miami because it couldn't come up with enough liquidity to repay the loans it had received from the Fed. Moreover, the competence of a bank's liquidity managers is an important barometer of management's overall effectiveness in achieving the bank's long-term goals.

The Demand for and Supply of Bank Liquidity

A bank's need for liquidity—immediately spendable funds—can be viewed within a demand-supply framework. What activities give rise to the *demand* for liquidity inside a bank? And what sources can the bank rely upon to *supply* liquidity when spendable funds are needed?

For most banks, the most pressing *demands* for spendable funds come from two sources: (1) customers withdrawing money from their deposits, and (2) credit requests from customers the bank wishes to keep, either in the form of new loan requests, renewals of expiring loan agreements, or drawings upon existing credit lines. Other sources of liquidity demand include paying off obligations arising from bank borrowings, such as loans the bank may have received from other banks or from the central bank (i.e., the Federal Reserve, the Bank of England, or the Bank of Japan). Similarly, payment of income taxes or cash dividends to the bank's stockholders periodically gives rise to a demand for immediately spendable cash. (See Table 11–1.)

To meet the foregoing demands for liquidity, banks can draw upon several potential sources of *supply*. The most important source normally is receipt of new customer deposits, both from newly opened accounts and from new deposits placed in existing accounts. These deposit inflows are heavy the first of each month as business payrolls are dispensed, and they may reach a secondary peak toward the middle of each month as bills are paid and other payrolls are met. Another important element in the supply of bank liquidity comes from customers repaying their loans, which provides fresh funds for meeting new liquidity needs, as do sales of bank assets—especially marketable securities—from the bank's investment portfolio. Liquidity also flows in from revenues generated by selling nondeposit services and from borrowings in the money market.

TABLE 11–1   Sources of Demand and Supply for Liquidity within the Bank

Supplies of Liquid Funds Come From:	Demands for Bank Liquidity Typically Arise From:
Incoming customer deposits	Customer deposit withdrawals
Revenues from the sale of non-deposit services	Credit requests from quality loan customers
Customer loan repayments	Repayment of nondeposit borrowings
Sales of bank assets	Operating expenses and taxes incurred in producing and selling services
Borrowings from the money market	Payment of stockholder cash dividends

These various sources of liquidity demand and supply come together to determine each bank's **net liquidity position** at any moment in time. That net liquidity position at time t is as follows:

Supplies of Liquidity Flowing into the Bank

$$
\begin{array}{l}
\text{A bank's} \\
\text{net liquidity} = \\
\text{position} \\
(L_t)
\end{array}
\begin{array}{l}
\text{Incoming} \\
\text{deposits} \ + \\
\text{(inflows)}
\end{array}
\begin{array}{l}
\text{Revenues from} \\
\text{the sale of} \\
\text{nondeposit} \ + \\
\text{services}
\end{array}
\begin{array}{l}
\text{Customer} \\
\text{loan} \ + \\
\text{repayments}
\end{array}
\begin{array}{l}
\text{Sales of} \\
\text{bank} \ + \\
\text{assets}
\end{array}
\begin{array}{l}
\text{Borrowings} \\
\text{from the} \\
\text{money} \\
\text{market}
\end{array}
$$

– Demands on the Bank for Liquidity

$$
\begin{array}{l}
\text{Deposit} \\
- \text{withdrawals} \ - \\
\text{(outflows)}
\end{array}
\begin{array}{l}
\text{Volume of} \\
\text{acceptable} \ - \\
\text{loan requests}
\end{array}
\begin{array}{l}
\text{Repayments} \\
\text{of bank} \ - \\
\text{borrowings}
\end{array}
\begin{array}{l}
\text{Other} \\
\text{operating} \ - \\
\text{expenses}
\end{array}
\begin{array}{l}
\text{Dividend} \\
\text{payments} \\
\text{to bank} \\
\text{stockholders.}
\end{array}
$$

When the bank's total demand for liquidity exceeds its total supply of liquidity (i.e., $L_t < 0$), management must prepare for a *liquidity deficit,* deciding when and where to raise additional liquid funds. On the other hand, if at any point in time the total supply of liquidity to the bank exceeds all of its liquidity demands (i.e., $L_t > 0$), management must prepare for a *liquidity surplus,* deciding when and where to profitably invest surplus liquid funds until they are needed to cover future liquidity demands.

Liquidity has a critical *time dimension.* Some bank liquidity needs are *immediate* or nearly so. For example, several large CDs may be due to mature tomorrow, and the customers may have indicated that they plan to withdraw these deposits rather than simply rolling them over into new deposits. Sources of funds that can be accessed immediately, such as borrowing reserves from another bank, must be used to meet these near-term liquidity pressures.

Longer-term liquidity demands arise from seasonal, cyclical, and trend factors. For example, liquid funds are generally in greater demand during the fall and summer coincident with school, holidays, and customer travel plans. Anticipating these longer-term liquidity needs, bankers can draw upon a wider array of alternative sources of funds than is true for immediate liquidity needs—such as selling off accumulated liquid assets, aggressively advertising the bank's current menu of deposits and other services, or negotiating long-term borrowings of reserves from other banks. Of course, a bank need not meet all demands for liquidity by selling assets or borrowing new money. For example, just the right amount of new deposits may flow in, or loan repayments from borrowing customers may occur very close to the date that new funds are needed. But *timing* is critical to liquidity management—bankers must plan carefully how, when, and where needed liquid funds can be raised.

Most liquidity problems in banking arise from *outside* the bank as a result of the financial activities of its customers. In effect, customers' liquidity problems gravitate toward their banks. If a business is short on liquid reserves, for example, it will ask for a loan or draw down its deposit balances, either of which will require the firm's bank to come up with additional funds. A dramatic example of this phenomenon occurred in the wake of the worldwide stock market crash in October 1987. Investors who had borrowed heavily to buy stock on margin were forced to come up with additional funds to secure their stock loans. They went to their banks in huge numbers, turning a liquidity crisis in the capital market into a liquidity crisis for banks.

The essence of the liquidity management problem for a bank may be described in two succinct statements:

1. Rarely are the demands for bank liquidity equal to the supply of liquidity at any particular moment in time. The bank must continually deal with either a liquidity deficit or a liquidity surplus.
2. There is a trade-off between bank liquidity and profitability. The more bank resources are tied up in readiness to meet demands for liquidity, the lower is that bank's expected profitability (other factors held constant).

Thus, ensuring adequate liquidity is a never-ending problem for bank management that will always have significant implications for the bank's profitability. Liquidity management decisions cannot be made in isolation from all the other service areas and departments of the bank.

Moreover, resolving liquidity problems subjects a bank to *costs,* including the interest cost on borrowed funds, the transactions cost of time and money in finding adequate liquid funds, and an *opportunity cost* in the form of future earnings that must be forgone when earning assets are sold in order to help meet a bank's liquidity needs. Clearly, management must weigh these costs against the immediacy of the institution's liquidity needs. If a bank winds up with excess liquidity at any time, its management must be prepared to invest those excess funds immediately in order to avoid incurring an opportunity cost from idle funds that are not generating earnings for the bank.

From a slightly different vantage point, we could say that management of bank liquidity is subject to the risk that interest rates will change (*interest rate risk*) and the risk that liquid funds will not be available in the volume needed by the bank (*availability risk*). If interest rates rise, financial assets that the bank plans to sell to raise liquid funds (such as government bonds) will decline in value, and some must be sold at a loss. Not only will the bank raise fewer liquid funds from the sale of those assets, but the losses incurred will reduce bank earnings as well. Then, too, raising liquid funds by borrowing will cost more as interest rates rise, and some forms of borrowed liquidity may no longer be available to the bank. If the lenders of liquidity perceive a bank to be more risky than before, that bank will be forced to pay higher interest rates in order to borrow liquidity, and some lenders will simply refuse to make liquid funds available at all.

Why Banks Face Significant Liquidity Problems

It should be clear from the foregoing discussion that banks face major liquidity problems. The significant exposure of banks to liquidity pressures arises from several sources.

First, banks borrow large amounts of short-term deposits and reserves from individuals and businesses and from other lending institutions and then turn around and make long-term credit available to their borrowing customers. Thus, most banks face some *imbalances between the maturity dates on their assets and the maturity dates attached to their liabilities.* Rarely will incoming cash flows from assets exactly balance the cash flowing out to cover liabilities.

A problem related to the maturity mismatch situation is that banks hold an unusually *high proportion of liabilities subject to immediate payment,* such as demand deposits, NOW accounts, and money market borrowings. Thus, banks must always stand ready to meet immediate cash demands that can be substantial at times, especially near the end of a week, the first of each month, and during certain seasons of the year.

Another source of liquidity problems is the *bank's sensitivity to changes in interest rates.* When interest rates rise, some depositors will withdraw their funds in search of higher returns elsewhere. Many loan customers may postpone new loan requests or speed up their drawings on those credit lines that carry lower interest rates. Thus, changing interest rates affect *both* customer demand for deposits and customer demand for loans, each of which has a potent impact on a bank's liquidity position. Moreover, movements in interest rates affect the market values of assets the bank may need to sell in order to raise additional liquid funds, and they directly affect the cost of borrowing in the money market.

Beyond these factors, a bank must give high priority to meeting demands for liquidity. To fail in this area may severely damage public confidence in the institution. We can imagine the reaction of bank customers if the teller windows and teller machines had to be closed one morning because the bank was temporarily out of cash and could not cash checks or meet deposit withdrawals (as happened to a bank in Montana several years ago, prompting a federal investigation). One of the most important tasks of a bank's liquidity manager is to keep close contact with the bank's largest depositors and holders of large unused credit lines to determine if and when withdrawals of funds will be made and to make sure adequate funds are available.

Concept Checks

11–1. What are the principal sources of *liquidity demand* for a bank?

11–2. What are the principal sources from which a bank's *supply of liquidity* comes?

11–3. Suppose that a bank faces the following cash inflows and outflows during the coming week: (*a*) deposit withdrawals are expected to total $33 million, (*b*) customer loan repayments are expected to amount to $108 million, (*c*) operating expenses demanding cash payment will probably approach $51 million, (*d*) acceptable new loan requests should reach $294 million, (*e*) sales of bank assets are projected to be $18 million, (*f*) new deposits should total $670 million, (*g*) borrowings from the money market are expected to be about $43 million, (*h*) nondeposit service fees should amount to $27 million, (*i*) previous bank borrowings totaling $23 million are scheduled to be repaid, and (*j*) a dividend payment to bank stockholders of $140 million is scheduled. What is this bank's projected net liquidity position for the coming week?

11–4. When is a bank *adequately liquid?*

11–5. Why do banks face significant liquidity management problems?

Strategies for Liquidity Managers

Over the years, experienced liquidity managers have developed several broad strategies for dealing with bank liquidity problems: (1) providing liquidity from assets (asset liquidity management), (2) relying on borrowed liquidity to meet cash demands (liability management), and (3) balanced (asset and liability) liquidity management.

Asset Liquidity Management (or Asset Conversion) Strategies

The oldest approach to meeting bank liquidity needs is known as **asset liquidity management.** In its purest form, this strategy calls for *storing* liquidity in the form of holdings of *liquid assets*—predominantly in cash and marketable securities. When liquidity is needed, selected assets are sold for cash until all the bank's demands for cash are met. This liquidity management strategy is often called *asset conversion* because liquid funds are raised by converting noncash assets into cash.

What is a **liquid asset?** It must have three characteristics:

1. A liquid asset must have a *ready market* so that it can be converted into cash without delay.
2. It must have a reasonably *stable price* so that, no matter how quickly the asset must be sold or how large the sale is, the market is deep enough to absorb the sale without a significant decline in price.
3. It must be *reversible* so that the seller can recover his or her original investment (principal) with little risk of loss.

Among the most popular liquid assets for banks are Treasury bills, federal funds loans, deposits held with other banks, municipal bonds, federal agency securities, bankers' acceptances, and Eurocurrency loans. (See the box entitled "Storing Liquidity in Bank Assets—The Principal Options" for brief descriptions of these assets.) Although a bank can strengthen its liquidity position by holding more liquid assets, it will not necessarily be a liquid institution if it does so, because a bank's liquidity position is also influenced by the demands for liquidity made against it. *Remember: a bank is liquid only if it has access, at reasonable cost, to liquid funds in exactly the amounts required at the time they are needed.*

Asset liquidity management strategy is used mainly by smaller banks that find it a less risky approach to liquidity management than relying on borrowings. But asset conversion is *not* a cost-less approach to liquidity management. First, selling assets means the bank loses the future earnings those assets would have generated had they not been sold off. Thus, there is an **opportunity cost** to storing liquidity in assets when those assets must be sold. Most asset sales also involve transactions costs (commissions) paid to security brokers. Moreover, the assets in question may need to be sold in a market experiencing declining prices, subjecting the bank to the risk of substantial capital losses. Management must take care that those assets with the least profit potential are

Storing Liquidity in Bank Assets—
The Principal Options

The principal options open to bank managers for holdings of liquid assets that can be sold when additional cash is needed are:

1. *Treasury bills*—direct obligations of the United States government or of foreign governments issued at a discount and redeemed at par (face value) when they reach maturity; T-bills have original maturities of 3, 6, and 12 months, with an active resale market through security dealers.

2. *Federal funds loans to other institutions*—loans of bank reserves with short (often overnight) maturities.

3. *Purchase of liquid securities under a repurchase agreement (RP)*—using high-quality securities as collateral to secure loans from dealers and other lending institutions.

4. *Placing of correspondent deposits with other banks*—these interbank deposits can be borrowed or loaned in minutes by telephone or by wire.

5. *Municipal bonds and notes*—debt securities issued by state and local governments that range in maturity from a few days to several years.

6. *Federal agency securities*—short- and long-term debt instruments sold by federally sponsored agencies such as FNMA (Fannie Mae).

7. *Bankers' acceptances*—liquid claims against a bank arising from credit extended to customers, normally coming due within six months.

8. *Commercial paper*—short-term debt issued by large corporations with excellent credit ratings.

9. *Eurocurrency loans*—the lending of deposits accepted by banks and bank branches located outside a particular currency's home country for periods stretching from a few days to a few months.

sold *first* in order to minimize the opportunity cost of future earnings forgone. Selling assets to raise liquidity also tends to weaken the appearance of the bank's balance sheet, because the assets sold are often low-risk government securities that give the impression the bank is financially strong. Finally, liquid assets generally carry the lowest rates of return of all financial assets. Bankers investing heavily in liquid assets must forgo higher returns on other assets they would prefer to acquire if they did not have to be so well prepared for liquidity demands.

Borrowed Liquidity (Liability) Management Strategies

In the 1960s and 1970s, many banks, led by the largest in the industry, began to raise more of their liquid funds through borrowings in the money market. This borrowed liquidity strategy—often called *purchased liquidity* or **liability management**—in its purest form calls for borrowing enough immediately spendable funds to cover *all* anticipated demands for liquidity.

Borrowing liquid funds has a number of advantages. A bank can choose to borrow only when it actually needs funds, unlike storing liquidity in assets where a storehouse of at least some liquid assets must be held at all times, lowering the bank's potential return because liquid assets usually have such low yields. Then, too, using borrowed funds permits a bank to leave the volume and composition of its asset portfolio unchanged if it is satisfied with the assets it currently holds. In contrast, selling assets to provide liquidity shrinks the size of a bank as its total asset holdings decline. Finally, as we saw in Chapter 6, liability management comes with its own *control lever*—the interest rate offered to borrow funds. If the borrowing bank needs more funds, it merely raises its *offer rate* until the requisite amount of funds flow in. If fewer funds are required, the bank's offer rate may be lowered.

Borrowing Liquidity—The Principal Options

When a liquidity deficit arises, the bank can usually borrow funds from any of the following sources:

1. *Federal funds borrowings*—reserves from banks and other money market lenders that can be accessed immediately.

2. *Selling liquid, low-risk securities under a repurchase agreement (RP)* to banks and other institutions having temporary surpluses of funds. RPs generally carry a fixed rate of interest and maturity, though continuing-contract RPs remain in force until either the borrower or the lender terminates the loan.

3. *Issuing large ($100,000+) negotiable CDs* to major corporations, governmental units, and wealthy individuals for periods ranging from a few days to several months at an interest rate negotiated between the issuing bank and its customer.

4. *Issuing Eurocurrency deposits* to multinational banks and other corporations at interest rates determined by the demand and supply for these short-term international deposits.

5. *Borrowing reserves from the discount window of the central bank* (such as the Federal Reserve or the Bank of Japan)—usually available within a matter of minutes provided the bank has collateral on hand (typically government securities) and a signed borrowing authorization on file with the central bank. Most of these borrowings cover only a few days.

The principal sources of borrowed liquidity for a bank include large ($100,000+) negotiable CDs, federal funds borrowings, repurchase agreements (in which securities are sold temporarily with an agreement to buy them back), Eurocurrency borrowings, and borrowings at the discount window of the central bank in each nation or region. (See the box entitled "Borrowing Liquidity—The Principal Options" for a description of these instruments.) Liability management techniques are used most extensively by the largest banks, which often borrow close to 100 percent of their liquidity needs.

Borrowing liquidity is the most *risky* approach to solving bank liquidity problems (but also has the highest expected return) because of the volatility of money market interest rates and the rapidity with which the availability of credit can change. Often banks must purchase liquidity when it is most difficult to do so—both in cost and in availability. The bank's borrowing cost is always uncertain, which adds greater uncertainty to the bank's net earnings. Moreover, a bank that gets into financial trouble is usually most in need of borrowed liquidity, particularly because knowledge of the bank's difficulties spreads and depositors begin to withdraw their funds. At the same time, other financial institutions become less willing to lend to the troubled bank due to the risk involved.

Balanced (Asset and Liability) Liquidity Management Strategies

Due to the risks inherent in relying on borrowed liquidity and the costs of storing liquidity in assets, most banks compromise in choosing their liquidity management strategy and use *both* asset management and liability management. Under a **balanced liquidity management** strategy some of the expected demands for liquidity are stored in assets (principally holdings of marketable securities and deposits at other banks), while other anticipated liquidity needs are backstopped by advance arrangements for lines of credit from correspondent banks or other suppliers of funds. Unexpected cash needs are typically met from near-term borrowings. Longer-term liquidity needs can be planned for and funds to meet them parked in short-term and medium-term loans and securities that will roll over into cash as those liquidity needs arise.

Guidelines for Liquidity Managers

Over the years, bank liquidity managers have developed several rules of thumb that guide their activities. First, the liquidity manager must *keep track of the activities of all funds-using and funds-raising departments within the bank* and coordinate his or her department's activities with theirs. Whenever the commercial loan department grants a new credit line to a customer, for example, the liquidity manager must prepare for possible drawings against that line. If the time and savings account division expects to receive several large CDs in the next few days, this information should be passed on to the liquidity manager.

Second, the liquidity manager should know *in advance,* wherever possible, when the bank's biggest credit or deposit customers plan to withdraw their funds or add to their deposits. This allows the manager to *plan ahead* to deal more effectively with emerging liquidity surpluses and deficits.

Third, the liquidity manager, in cooperation with senior management and the board of directors, must make sure the bank's *priorities and objectives for liquidity management are clear.* In the recent past, a bank's liquidity position was often assigned top priority when it came to allocating funds. A typical assumption was that the bank had little or no control over its sources of funds (mainly deposits)—those were determined by the public—but the bank could control its uses of funds. In addition, because the law usually requires each bank to set aside liquid funds at the central bank to cover deposit reserve requirements and because the bank must be ready at all times to handle deposit withdrawals, liquidity management and the diverting of sufficient funds into liquid assets were given the highest priority. Today, liquidity management has generally been relegated to a supporting role compared to a bank's number one priority—making loans and supplying other fee-generating services to all qualified customers. The bank should grant all profitable loans, leaving to the liquidity manager the task of finding sufficient cash to fund them.

Fourth, *the bank's liquidity needs and liquidity decisions must be analyzed on a continuing basis to avoid both excess and deficit liquidity positions.* Excess liquidity that is not reinvested the same day it occurs results in lost income for the bank, while liquidity deficits must be dealt with quickly to avoid dire emergencies with hurried borrowings or sales of assets, resulting in excessive losses for the bank.

Concept Checks

11–6. What are the principal differences among *asset management, liability management,* and *balanced liquidity management?*

11–7. What guidelines should management keep in mind when it manages a bank's liquidity position?

Estimating a Bank's Liquidity Needs

Several methods have been developed in recent years for estimating each bank's liquidity requirements: the *sources and uses of funds approach,* the *structure of funds approach,* and the *liquidity indicator approach.* Each method rests on specific assumptions and yields only an *approximation* of actual liquidity requirements at any given time. This is why a liquidity manager must always be ready to fine-tune estimates of the bank's liquidity requirements as new information becomes available. In fact, most banks make sure their liquidity reserves include both a *planned* component, consisting of the reserves called for by the latest liquidity forecast, and a *protective* component, consisting of an extra margin of liquid reserves over those dictated by the most recent forecast. The protective liquidity component may be large or small, depending on management's philosophy and attitude toward risk—that is, how much chance of running a cash-out management wishes to accept.

The Sources and Uses of Funds Approach

The **sources and uses of funds method** begins with two simple facts:

1. Bank liquidity rises as deposits increase and loans decrease.
2. Bank liquidity declines when deposits decrease and loans increase.

Whenever sources and uses of liquidity do *not* match, the bank has a **liquidity gap,** measured by the size of the total difference between its sources and uses of funds. When sources of liquidity (i.e., increasing deposits or decreasing loans) exceed uses of liquidity (i.e., decreasing deposits or increasing loans), the bank will have a *positive liquidity gap.* Its *surplus* liquid funds must be quickly invested in earning assets until they are needed to cover future cash needs. On the other hand, when uses of liquidity exceed sources of liquidity, the bank faces a liquidity *deficit,* or *negative liquidity gap.* It now must raise funds from the cheapest and most timely sources available.

The key steps in the sources and uses of funds approach are as follows:

1. Loans and deposits must be *forecast* for a given liquidity planning period.
2. The estimated *change* in loans and deposits must be calculated for that same planning period.
3. The liquidity manager must estimate the bank's net liquid funds, surplus or deficit, for the planning period by comparing the estimated change in loans to the estimated change in deposits.

Banks use a wide variety of statistical techniques, supplemented by management's judgment and experience, to prepare forecasts of deposits and loans. For example, the bank's economics department or its liquidity managers might develop the following forecasting models:

$$
\begin{array}{l}
\text{Estimated} \\
\text{change in total} \\
\text{loans for the} \\
\text{coming period}
\end{array}
\begin{array}{l}
\text{is a} \\
\text{function} \\
\text{of}
\end{array}
\left[
\begin{array}{l}
\text{projected growth in the} \\
\text{economy that the bank} \\
\text{serves (for example, the} \\
\text{growth of gross domestic} \\
\text{product (GDP) or} \\
\text{business sales),}
\end{array}
\begin{array}{l}
\text{projected} \\
\text{quarterly} \\
\text{corporate} \\
\text{earnings,}
\end{array}
\right.
$$

$$
\left.
\begin{array}{l}
\text{current rate of} \\
\text{growth in the} \\
\text{nation's money} \\
\text{supply,}
\end{array}
\begin{array}{l}
\text{projected prime} \\
\text{bank loan rate} \\
\text{minus the} \\
\text{commercial} \\
\text{paper rate,}
\end{array}
\begin{array}{l}
\text{and}
\end{array}
\begin{array}{l}
\text{estimated} \\
\text{rate of} \\
\text{inflation}
\end{array}
\right]
$$

$$
\begin{bmatrix}
\text{Estimated} \\
\text{change in total} \\
\text{deposits for} \\
\text{the coming} \\
\text{period}
\end{bmatrix}
\begin{array}{c}
\text{is a} \\
\text{function} \\
\text{of}
\end{array}
\begin{bmatrix}
\text{projected} \\
\text{growth in} \quad \text{estimated} \\
\text{personal income} \quad \text{increase in} \\
\text{in the economy} \quad \text{retail sales,} \\
\text{the bank serves,}
\end{bmatrix}
$$

$$
\begin{bmatrix}
\text{current rate of} \quad \text{projected yield on} \\
\text{growth of the} \quad\quad \text{money market} \quad\quad \text{and} \quad \text{estimated rate} \\
\text{nation's money supply,} \quad\quad \text{deposits,} \quad\quad\quad\quad \text{of inflation}
\end{bmatrix}
$$

Using the forecasts of loans and deposits generated by the foregoing models, management could then estimate the bank's need for liquidity by calculating:

$$
\begin{array}{c}
\text{Estimated liquidity} \\
\text{deficit } (-) \text{ or surplus } (+) \\
\text{for the coming period}
\end{array}
=
\begin{array}{c}
\text{Estimated change in} \\
\text{total deposits}
\end{array}
-
\begin{array}{c}
\text{Estimated} \\
\text{change in} \\
\text{total loans}
\end{array}
$$

A somewhat simpler approach for estimating future deposits and loans is to divide the forecast of future deposit and loan growth into three key components:

1. A *trend component,* which the bank can estimate by constructing a trend (constant-growth) line using as reference points year-end, quarterly, or monthly deposit and loan totals established over at least the last 10 years (or some other base period sufficiently long to define a trend or long-run average growth rate).

2. A *seasonal component,* which measures how deposits and loans are expected to behave in any given week or month due to seasonal factors, as compared to the most recent year-end deposit or loan level.

3. A *cyclical component,* which represents positive or negative deviations from total expected deposits and loans (measured by the sum of trend and seasonal components), depending upon the strength or weakness of the economy in the current year.

For example, suppose we are managing a bank whose trend growth rate in total deposits over the past decade has averaged about 10 percent a year. Loan growth has been slightly less rapid, averaging 8 percent a year for the past 10 years. Our bank's total deposits stood at $1,200 million and total loans outstanding reached $800 million at year-end. Table 11–2 presents a forecast of weekly deposit and loan totals for our bank for the first six weeks of the new year. Each weekly loan and deposit *trend* figure shown in column 1 accounts for a one-week portion of the projected 10 percent annual increase in deposits and the expected 8 percent annual increase in total loans. To derive the appropriate *seasonal* element shown in column 2, we compare the ratio for the average (trend) deposit and loan figure for each week of the year to the average deposit and loan level during the final week of the year for each of the past 10 years. We assume the seasonal ratio of the current week's level to the preceding year-end level applies in the current year in the same way as it did for all past years, so we simply add or subtract the calculated seasonal element to the trend element.

TABLE 11–2 **Forecasting Deposits and Loans with the Sources and Uses of Funds Approach**
(figures in millions of dollars)

Deposit Forecast For	Trend Estimate for Deposits	Seasonal Element*	Cyclical Element**	Estimated Total Deposits
January, Week 1	$1,210	−4	−6	$1,200
January, Week 2	1,212	−54	−58	1,100
January, Week 3	1,214	−121	−93	1,000
January, Week 4	1,216	−165	−101	950
February, Week 1	1,218	+70	−38	1,250
February, Week 2	1,220	−32	−52	1,200

Loan Forecast For	Trend Estimate for Loans	Seasonal Element*	Cyclical Element**	Estimated Total Loans
January, Week 1	$799	+6	−5	$ 800
January, Week 2	800	+59	−9	850
January, Week 3	801	+174	−25	950
January, Week 4	802	+166	+32	1,000
February, Week 1	803	+27	−80	750
February, Week 2	804	+98	−2	900

*The seasonal element compares the average level of deposits and loans for each week over the past 10 years to the average level of deposits and loans for the final week of December over the preceding 10 years.

**The cyclical element reflects the difference between the expected deposit and loan levels in each week during the preceding year (measured by the trend and seasonal elements) and the actual volume of total deposits and total loans the bank posted that week.

The *cyclical* element, given in column 3, compares the sum of the estimated trend and seasonal elements with the actual level of deposits and loans the previous year. The dollar gap between these two numbers is presumed to result from cyclical forces, and we assume that roughly the same cyclical pressures that prevailed last year apply to the current year. Finally, column 4 reports the estimated *total* deposits and loans, consisting of the sum of trend (column 1), seasonal (column 2), and cyclical components (column 3).

Table 11–3 shows how we can take estimated deposit and loan figures, such as those given in column 4 of Table 11–2, and use them to estimate a bank's expected liquidity deficits and surpluses in the period ahead. In this instance, the liquidity manager has estimated expected liquidity needs for the next six weeks. Columns 1 and 2 in Table 11–3 merely repeat the estimated total deposit and total loan figures from column 4 in Table 11–2. Columns 3 and 4 in Table 11–3 calculate the *change* in total deposits and total loans from one week to the next. Column 5 shows the differences between the change in loans and the change in deposits each week. When deposits fall and loans rise, a liquidity deficit usually occurs. When deposits grow and loans decline, a bank usually moves toward a liquidity surplus position.

As Table 11–3 reveals, our bank has a projected liquidity *deficit* over the next three weeks—$150 million next week, $200 million the third week, and $100 million in the fourth week—because its loans are growing while its deposit levels are declining. Due to a forecast of rising deposits and falling loans in the fifth week, a liquidity surplus of $550 million is expected then, followed by a $200 million liquidity deficit in week 6. What liquidity management decisions must be made over the six-week period shown in

TABLE 11–3   **Forecasting Liquidity Deficits and Surpluses with the Sources and Uses of Funds Approach**
(figures in millions of dollars)

Time Period	Estimated Total Deposits	Estimated Total Loans	Estimated Deposit Change	Estimated Loan Change	Estimated Liquidity Deficit (−) or Surplus (+)
January, Week 1	$1,200	$ 800	$____	$____	$____
January, Week 2	1,100	850	−100	+50	−150
January, Week 3	1,000	950	−100	+100	−200
January, Week 4	950	1,000	−50	+50	−100
February, Week 1	1,250	750	+300	−250	+550
February, Week 2	1,200	900	−50	+150	−200

Table 11–3? The liquidity manager must prepare to raise new funds in weeks 2, 3, 4, and 6 from the cheapest and most reliable funds sources available and to profitably invest the expected funds surplus in week 5.

Management can now begin planning which sources of liquid funds to draw upon, first evaluating the bank's stock of liquid assets to see which assets are likely to be available for use and then determining if adequate sources of borrowed funds are also likely to be available. For example, the bank probably has already set up lines of credit for borrowing from its principal correspondent banks. The liquidity manager wants to be sure these credit lines are still in place and adequate to meet the projected amount of borrowing that will be needed.

The Structure of Funds Approach

Another approach to estimating a bank's liquidity requirements is the **structure of funds method.** In the first step, the bank's deposits and other funds sources are divided into categories based on their estimated probability of being withdrawn and therefore lost to the bank. As an illustration, we might divide the bank's deposit and nondeposit liabilities into three categories:

1. *"Hot money" liabilities*—deposits and other borrowed funds (such as federal funds) that are very interest sensitive or that management is sure will be withdrawn during the current period.

2. *Vulnerable funds*—customer deposits of which a substantial portion (perhaps 25 or 30 percent) will probably be removed from the bank sometime during the current time period.

3. *Stable funds* (often called core deposits or core liabilities)—funds that management considers most unlikely to be removed from the bank (except for a minor percentage of the total).

Second, the liquidity manager must set aside liquid funds according to some desired *operating rule* for each of the three kinds of funds sources listed above. For example, the manager may decide to set up a 95 percent liquid reserve behind all hot money funds (less any required reserves the bank holds behind hot money deposits). This liquidity reserve might consist of holdings of immediately spendable deposits in correspondent banks plus investments in Treasury bills and repurchase agreements where the committed funds can be recovered in a matter of minutes or hours.

A common rule of thumb for vulnerable deposit and nondeposit liabilities is to hold a fixed percentage of their total amount—say, 30 percent—in liquidity reserves. For stable (core) funds sources, the bank may decide to place a small proportion—perhaps 15 percent or less—of their total in liquidity reserves. Thus, the liquidity reserve behind the bank's deposit and nondeposit liabilities would be as follows:

Liability liquidity reserve = 0.95 × (Hot money deposits and non-deposit funds − Legal reserves held) + 0.30 × (Vulnerable deposit and nondeposit funds − Legal reserves held) + 0.15 × (Stable deposits and nondeposit funds − Legal reserves held)

In the case of *loans,* the bank must be ready at all times to make good loans—that is, meet the legitimate credit needs of those customers who satisfy the bank's loan quality standards. The bank must have sufficient liquid reserves on hand because, once a loan is made, the borrowing customer will spend the proceeds, usually within hours or days, and those funds will flow out to other banks. However, the bank does not want to turn down any good loan, because loan customers bring in new deposits and normally are the principal source of bank earnings from interest and fees.

Indeed, a substantial body of current thinking in banking suggests that a bank should make *all* good loans, counting on its ability to borrow liquid funds, if necessary, to cover any pressing cash needs. This is known as the *customer relationship doctrine*—management should strive to meet all good loans that walk in the door in order to build lasting customer relationships that will continue to generate deposits and loans into the future. Under today's concept of *relationship banking,* once the customer is sold a loan, the bank can then proceed to sell that customer other bank services, establishing a multidimensional relationship that will bring in additional fee income and increase the customer's dependence on (and, therefore, loyalty to) the institution. This reasoning suggests that management must try to estimate the maximum possible figure for total loans and hold in liquid reserves or borrowing capacity the full amount of the difference (100 percent) between the actual amount of loans outstanding and the maximum potential for *total loans.*

Combining both loan and deposit liquidity requirements, the bank's *total liquidity requirement* would be:

Total liquidity requirement for a bank = Deposit and nondeposit liability liquidity requirement and loan liquidity requirement = 0.95 × (Hot money funds − Required legal reserves held behind hot money deposits) + 0.30 × (Vulnerable deposits and nondeposit funds − Required legal reserves) + 0.15 × (Stable deposits and nondeposit funds − Required legal reserves) + 1.00 × (Potential loans outstanding − Actual loans outstanding).

Admittedly, the deposit and loan liquidity requirements that make up the above equation are subjective estimates that rely heavily on management's judgment, experience, and attitude toward risk.

An example of this liquidity management method is shown in Table 11–4. First National Bank has broken down its deposit and nondeposit liabilities into hot money, vulnerable funds, and stable (core) funds, amounting to $25 million, $24 million, and $100 million, respectively. The bank's loans total $135 million currently, but recently have been as high as $140 million, and loans are projected to grow at a 10 percent annual rate. Thus, within the coming year, the bank's total loans might reach as high as $154 million, or $140 million + (0.10 × $140 million), which would be $19 million higher than they are now. Applying the percentages of deposits that management wishes to hold in liquid reserves, we find that the bank needs more than $63 million in total liquidity, consisting of both liquid assets and borrowing capacity.

Many banks like to use *probabilities* in deciding how much liquidity to hold behind their deposits and loans. Under this refinement of the structure of funds approach, the liquidity manager will want to define the *best* and the *worst* possible liquidity positions the bank might find itself in and assign probabilities to as many of these situations as possible. For example:

1. *The worst possible liquidity position for the bank.* Suppose deposit growth falls significantly *below* management's expectations, so that actual deposit totals

---

TABLE 11–4   Estimating Bank Liquidity Needs with the Structure of Funds Method

A. First National Bank estimates that its current deposits and nondeposit liabilities break down as follows:

Hot money	$ 25 million
Vulnerable funds (including the largest deposit and nondeposit liability accounts)	$ 24 million
Stable (core) funds	$100 million

First National's management wants to keep a 95% reserve behind its hot money deposits (less the 3% legal reserve requirement behind many of these deposits) and nondeposit liabilities, a 30% liquidity reserve in back of its vulnerable deposits and borrowings (less required reserves), and a 15% liquidity reserve behind its core deposit and nondeposit funds (less required reserves).

B. First National Bank's *loans* total $135 million but recently have been as high as $140 million, with a trend growth rate of about 10 percent a year. The bank wishes to be ready at all times to honor customer demands for *all* those loans that meet its quality standards.

C. The bank's total liquidity requirement is as follows:

Deposit/Nondeposit Funds plus Loans

$$0.95 (\$25 \text{ million} - 0.03 \times \$25 \text{ million})$$
$$+0.30 (\$24 \text{ million} - 0.03 \times \$24 \text{ million})$$
$$+0.15 (\$100 \text{ million} - 0.03 \times \$100 \text{ million})$$
$$\$140 \text{ million} \times 0.10 + (\$140 - \$135 \text{ million})$$
$$= \$23.04 \text{ million} + \$6.98 \text{ million} + \$14.55 \text{ million} + \$19 \text{ million}$$
$$= \$63.57 \text{ million (held in liquid assets and additional borrowing capacity)}$$

sometimes go below the lowest points on the bank's historical minimum deposit growth track. Moreover, suppose loan demand from qualified credit customers rises significantly *above* management's expectations, so that loan demand sometimes goes beyond the high points of the bank's loan growth track. In this instance, the bank would face maximum pressure on its available liquid reserves because deposit growth would not likely be able to fund all the loans customers were demanding. In this worst situation the liquidity manager would have to prepare for a sizable *liquidity deficit* and develop a plan for raising substantial amounts of liquid funds.

2. *The best possible liquidity position for the bank.* Suppose deposit growth turns out to be significantly *above* management's expectations, so that it touches the highest points in the bank's deposit growth track record. Moreover, suppose loan demand turns out to be significantly *below* management's expectations, so that loan demand grows along a minimum path that touches the low points in the bank's loan growth track. In this case, the bank would face minimum pressure on its liquid reserves because deposit growth probably could fund nearly all the quality loans that walk in the door. In this best situation, it is highly likely that a *liquidity surplus* will develop. The liquidity manager must have a plan for investing these surplus funds in order to maximize the bank's return.

Of course, neither the worst nor the best possible outcome is likely for both deposit and loan growth. The most likely outcome lies somewhere between these extremes. Many banks like to calculate their *expected liquidity requirement,* based on the probabilities they assign to different possible outcomes. For example, suppose the liquidity manager considers the bank's liquidity situation next week as likely to fall into one of three possible situations:

Possible Liquidity Outcomes for Next Week	Estimated Average Volume of Deposits Next Week (millions)	Estimated Average Volume of Acceptable Loans Next Week (millions)	Estimated Liquidity Surplus or Deficit Position Next Week (millions)	Probability Assigned by Management to Each Possible Outcome
Best possible liquidity position (maximum deposits, minimum loans)	$170	$110	+$60	15%
Liquidity position with the highest probability of occurrence	$150	$140	+$10	60%
Worst possible liquidity position (minimum deposits, maximum loans)	$130	$150	−$20	25%

Thus, management sees the worst possible situation next week as one characterized by a $20 million liquidity deficit, but this least desirable outcome is assigned a probability of only 25 percent. Similarly, the best possible outcome would be a $60 million liquidity surplus, which the bank could invest in profitable loans and security investments; however, this is judged to have only a 15 percent probability of occurring. Much more likely is the middle ground—a $10 million liquidity surplus—with a management-estimated probability of 60 percent.

What, then, is the bank's expected liquidity requirement? We can find the answer from the formula:

$$
\begin{aligned}
\text{Bank's expected liquidity requirement} = {} & \text{Probability of Outcome A} \times \left(\begin{array}{c}\text{Estimated liquidity} \\ \text{surplus or} \\ \text{deficit in} \\ \text{Outcome A}\end{array}\right) \\
{} + {} & \text{Probability of Outcome B} \times \left(\begin{array}{c}\text{Estimated liquidity} \\ \text{surplus or} \\ \text{deficit in} \\ \text{Outcome B}\end{array}\right) \\
{} + {} & \ldots + \ldots
\end{aligned}
$$

for all possible outcomes, subject to the restriction that the sum of all probabilities assigned by management must be 1.

Using this formula, this bank's *expected liquidity requirement* must be as follows:

$$
\begin{aligned}
\text{Bank's expected liquidity requirement} &= 0.15 \times (+\$60 \text{ million}) + 0.60 \times (+\$10 \text{ million}) \\
&\quad + 0.25 \times (-\$20 \text{ million}) \\
&= +\$10 \text{ million.}
\end{aligned}
$$

On average, management should plan for a $10 million liquidity surplus next week and begin now to review the options for investing this expected surplus. Of course, bank management would also do well to have a contingency plan ready in case the worst possible outcome does occur.

Liquidity Indicator Approach

Many banks estimate their liquidity needs based on experience and industry averages. This often means using certain bellwether financial ratios or **liquidity indicators.** For example:

1. *Cash position indicator:* Cash and deposits due from depository institutions ÷ total assets, where a greater proportion of cash implies the bank is in a stronger position to handle immediate cash needs.

2. *Liquid securities indicator:* U.S. government securities ÷ total assets, which compares the most marketable securities a bank can hold with the overall size of its asset portfolio; the greater the proportion of government securities, the more liquid the bank's position tends to be.

3. *Net Federal funds position:* (Federal funds sold − Federal funds purchased) ÷ total assets, which measures the comparative importance of overnight loans (Federal funds sold) to overnight borrowings of reserves (Federal funds purchased); liquidity tends to increase when this ratio rises.

4. *Capacity ratio:* Net loans and leases ÷ total assets, which is really a negative liquidity indicator because loans and leases are often among the most illiquid assets a bank can hold.

5. *Pledged securities ratio:* Pledged securities ÷ total security holdings, also a negative liquidity indicator because the greater the proportion of securities pledged to back government deposits, the fewer securities are available to sell when liquidity needs arise.[1]

6. *Hot money ratio:* Money market assets ÷ money market liabilities = [cash + short-term U.S. government securities + Federal funds loans + reverse RPs (where the bank loans funds by temporarily buying securities)] ÷ [large CDs + Eurocurrency deposits + Federal funds borrowings + RPs (where the bank borrows by temporarily selling securities]—a ratio that reflects whether the bank has balanced its borrowings in the money market with increases in its money market assets that could be sold quickly to cover those money market liabilities.

7. *Short-term investments to sensitive liabilities ratio:* Short-term investments ÷ sensitive liabilities, where short-term investments include short-term deposits held with other banks, Federal funds sold, and short-term securities held, while sensitive liabilities consist of the sum of all time deposits of $100,000 or more, foreign-office deposits, purchases of Federal funds and securities sold under RP agreements, demand notes held by the U.S. Treasury, and miscellaneous liabilities—all of which are sources of bank funds that are so highly interest sensitive they may easily be lost to other banks. A rise in this ratio indicates that a stronger bank liquidity position is emerging.

8. *Deposit brokerage index:* Brokered deposits ÷ total deposits, where brokered deposits consist of packages of funds (usually $100,000 or less to gain the advantage of deposit insurance) placed by securities brokers for their customers with banks paying the highest yields. Brokered deposits are highly interest sensitive and may be quickly withdrawn; the more the bank holds, the greater the chance of a liquidity crisis.

9. *Core deposit ratio:* Core deposits ÷ total assets, where core deposits are defined as total deposits less all deposits over $100,000. Core deposits are primarily small-denomination accounts from local customers that are considered unlikely to be withdrawn on short notice and so carry lower liquidity requirements.

---

[1]See Chapter 10 for a discussion of the nature and use of pledged securities.

TABLE 11–5   **Recent Trends in Liquidity Indicators for U.S.-Insured Banks**

Selected Liquidity Indicators	1985	1987	1989	1991	1993	1996
Cash position indicator: Cash and deposits due from depository institutions ÷ total assets	12.5%	11.9%	10.6%	8.9%	6.3%	7.3%
Net Federal funds position: (Federal funds sold − Federal funds purchased) ÷ total assets	−3.3	−3.7	−3.9	−2.4	−3.4	−3.4
Capacity ratio: Net loans and leases ÷ total assets	58.9	59.3	60.7	57.0	56.6	60.2
Deposit composition ratio: Demand deposits ÷ time deposits	68.4	55.8	44.8	44.7	52.4	58.2

Source: Federal Deposit Insurance Corporation and Board of Governors of the Federal Reserve System.

10. *Deposit composition ratio:* Demand deposits ÷ time deposits, where demand deposits are subject to immediate withdrawal via check writing, while time deposits have fixed maturities with penalties for early withdrawal. This ratio measures how stable a funding base each bank possesses; a decline in the ratio suggests greater deposit stability and, therefore, a lessened need for liquidity.

Table 11–5 indicates recent trends in a few of these liquidity indicators among U.S.-insured banks. In general, most indicators seem to show a gradual *decline* in bank liquidity, particularly in liquid assets. One reason is a gradual shift in bank deposits toward longer-maturity instruments that are more stable and have fewer unexpected withdrawals. Another important factor is a recent decline in deposit reserve requirements levied by the Federal Reserve, which has reduced the cash reserves U.S. banks need to hold. There are also more ways to raise liquidity today, and advancing technology has made it easier to anticipate bank liquidity needs and to prepare for them.

The first five liquidity indicators discussed above focus principally upon *assets,* or *stored liquidity.* The last five focus mainly on a bank's *liabilities,* or *purchased liquidity.* Each liquidity indicator needs to be compared with the average value of that indicator for banks of comparable size in a similar location. These indicators are highly sensitive to the season of the year and the stage of the business cycle. Liquidity indicators often decline in a boom period under pressure from heavy loan demand, only to rise again during the ensuing business recession. Therefore, industrywide averages are often misleading. Each bank's liquidity position must be judged relative to peer institutions of similar size operating in similar market environments. Moreover, bank managers usually focus on *changes* in their institution's liquidity indicators rather than on the level of each indicator. They want to know whether liquidity is rising or falling and *why.*

The Ultimate Standard for Assessing Liquidity Management: Signals from the Marketplace

Many financial analysts believe there is one ultimate method for assessing a bank's liquidity needs and how well it is fulfilling them. This method centers on *the discipline of the financial marketplace.* For example, consider this question: Does a bank really hold adequate liquidity reserves? The answer depends upon the bank's standing in the market. No bank can tell for sure if it has sufficient liquidity until it has passed the market's test. Specifically, management should look at these signals:

1. *Public confidence.* Is there evidence the bank is losing deposits because individuals and institutions believe there is some danger it will run out of cash and be unable to pay its obligations?

2. *Stock price behavior.* Is the bank's stock price falling because investors perceive the bank has an actual or pending liquidity crisis?

3. *Risk premiums on CDs and other borrowings.* Is there evidence that the bank is paying significantly higher interest rates on its offerings of time and savings deposits (especially on large negotiable CDs) and money market borrowings than other banks of similar size and location? In other words, is the market imposing a *risk premium* in the form of higher borrowing costs because it believes the bank is headed for a liquidity crisis?

4. *Loss sales of assets.* Has the bank recently been forced to sell assets in a hurry, with significant losses, in order to meet demands for liquidity? Is this a rare event or has it become a frequent occurrence?

5. *Meeting commitments to credit customers.* Has the bank been able to honor all reasonable and potentially profitable requests for loans from its valued customers? Or have liquidity pressures compelled management to turn down some otherwise acceptable loan applications?

6. *Borrowings from the central bank.* Has the bank been forced to borrow in larger volume and more frequently from the central bank in its home territory (such as the Federal Reserve, Bank of England, or Bank of Japan) lately? Have central bank officials begun to question the bank's borrowings?

If the answer to any of these questions is *yes,* management needs to take a close look at its liquidity management policies and practices to determine whether changes are in order.

Concept Checks

11–8.   How does the sources and uses of funds approach help a manager estimate a bank's need for liquidity?

11–9.   Suppose that a bank estimates its total deposits for the next six months will be, respectively, $112, $132, $121, $147, $151, and $139, while its loans will total an estimated $87, $95, $102, $113, $101, and $124, respectively, over the same six months. (All figures are in millions of dollars.) Under the sources and uses of funds approach when does this bank face liquidity deficits, if any?

11–10.   What steps are needed to carry out the structure of funds approach to bank liquidity management?

11–11.   Suppose a bank's liquidity division estimates that it holds $19 million in hot money deposits and other IOUs against which it will hold an 80 percent liquidity reserve, $54 million in vulnerable funds against which it plans to hold a 25 percent liquidity reserve, and $112 million in stable or core funds against which it will hold a 5 percent liquidity reserve. The bank expects its loans to grow 8 percent annually; its loans currently total $117 million but have recently reached $132 million. If reserve requirements on liabilities currently stand at 3 percent, what is this bank's total liquidity requirement?

11–12.   What is the liquidity indicator approach to bank liquidity management?

11–13.   First National Bank posts the following balance sheet entries on today's date: Net loans and leases, $3,502 million; cash and deposits held at other banks, $633 million; federal funds sold of $48 million; U.S. government securities, $185 million; Federal funds purchased of $62 million; demand deposits of $988 million; time deposits of $2,627 million; and total assets of $4,446 million. How many liquidity indicators can you calculate from these figures?

11–14.   How can the discipline of the marketplace be used as a guide for bank liquidity management decisions?

Legal Reserves and Money Position Management

Management of a bank's liquidity position can be a harrowing job, requiring quick decisions that have major long-run consequences for the bank's profitability. Nowhere within the bank is this more evident than in the job of the **money position manager.** The manager of a bank's money position is responsible for ensuring that the institution maintains an adequate level of **legal reserves**—assets the law says must be held behind the institution's deposits. In the United States, only two kinds of assets can be used for this purpose—cash in the bank's vault and deposits held with the Federal Reserve bank in the region or with a Fed-approved depository institution that passes its reserves through to the Fed.[2]

How much money must be held in legal reserves? That depends on the volume and mix of each bank's deposits. For transaction deposits—checking accounts, NOWs, and other deposits that can be used to make payments—the reserve requirement is 3 percent of the end-of-the-day daily average amount held over a two-week period, up to $47.8 million. Transaction deposits over $47.8 million carry a 10 percent reserve requirement.[3] Thus, the largest banks must hold the largest amount of legal reserves, reflecting their great importance as funds managers within the banking system. Eurodollar liabilities and nonpersonal time deposits (mainly short-term business CDs) can also carry reserve requirements, but these funds sources currently have zero reserve requirements in the United States as do consumer-type CDs and savings deposits. Each reservable liability item is multiplied by the stipulated reserve requirement percentage set by the central bank (in the United States, the Federal Reserve Board) to derive the bank's total legal reserve requirement. Thus:

| Total required legal reserves | = | Reserve requirement on transaction deposits $\times$ Daily average amount of net transaction deposits over a designated period + Reserve requirement on nontransaction reservable liabilities $\times$ Daily average amount of nontransaction reservable liabilities |

A sample calculation of a U.S. bank's total required legal reserves is shown in Table 11–6.

Once a bank determines its required reserve, it compares this figure against its daily average holdings of legal reserve assets—vault cash and the size of its reserve deposit at the central bank. If total legal reserves held are greater than the calculated required reserves, the bank has *excess reserves.* Management will move quickly to invest the excess, because excess reserves pay no interest. Excess reserves carry an opportunity cost in the form of interest income that is not earned because management failed to invest them, even overnight.

If, on the other hand, the calculated required reserve figure exceeds the amount of legal reserves actually held on a daily average basis, the bank has a *reserve deficit.* The law requires that the bank cover this deficit by acquiring additional legal reserves. Actually, current regulations allow the bank to run up to a 4 percent deficit from its required

---

[2]Not all central banks impose reserve requirements on the banks they regulate. For example, the Bank of England has not established official reserve requirements for its banks. Nevertheless, banks will hold some cash reserves even in the absence of official reserve requirements because they need reserves to handle customer deposit withdrawals, meet new loan demand, and for other purposes.

[3]The $47.8 million figure was specified by the Federal Reserve Board as of December 1997. This figure, by law, is to increase as deposit volume grows each year. The Depository Institutions Deregulation and Monetary Control Act of 1980 requires the Federal Reserve Board to calculate the June-to-June growth rate of reservable deposits. The dollar cutoff point above which reserve requirements on transaction deposits become 10 percent instead of 3 percent is then adjusted by 80 percent of the calculated annual deposit growth rate. This annual adjustment is designed to eliminate some of the effects of inflation in pushing banks into higher reserve requirement categories. The first $4.7 million of reservable deposits currently is exempt from reserve requirements.

TABLE 11–6   **Sample Calculation of a Bank's Legal Reserve Requirement**

First National Bank reported the following deposit and cash account figures for the most recent legal reserve computation period:

Net transaction deposits*	=	100 million daily average for two-week reserve computation period.
Nonpersonal time deposits and other reservable nontransaction liabilities	=	$200 million daily average for two-week reserve computation period.
Daily average vault cash held	=	$5 million daily average over the same two-week computation period that is used for net transaction deposits

The applicable percentage reserve requirements imposed by the Federal Reserve Board are as follows:**

First $47.8 million of net transaction deposits: 3% reserve requirement. Amount over $47.8 million of net transaction deposits: 10% reserve requirement. Nontransaction reservable liabilities (including nonpersonal time deposits and Eurocurrency liabilities): 0% reserve requirement.***

Then First National's daily average required legal reserve level $= 0.03 \times \$47.8$ million $+ 0.10 \times (\$100$ million $- \$47.8$ million$) + 0.0 \times \$200$ million $= \$1.434$ million $+ \$5.22$ million $+ \$0.00$ million $= \$6.554$ million.

First National held a daily average of $5 million in vault cash over the required two-week computation period. Therefore, it must hold at the Federal Reserve Bank in its district the following amount, on average, over its two-week reserve maintenance period:

Daily average level of required legal reserves to hold on deposit at the Fed		Total required legal reserves		Daily average vault cash holdings		
	=		−		=	$6.554 million – $5.00 million
					=	$1.554 million

*Net transaction deposits are gross demand deposits less cash items in process of collection and deposits due from other banks.

**As of January 1, 1998.

***The percentage reserve requirements on nonpersonal time deposits with an original maturity of less than 18 months and on Eurocurrency liabilities were reduced to zero in the United States in 1991. Nonpersonal time deposits 18 months or longer to maturity were assigned a zero reserve requirement in 1983.

daily average reserve position, provided this shortfall is balanced out by a corresponding excess during the next reserve period.[4] Any deficit above 4 percent is assessed an interest penalty equal to the Federal Reserve's discount rate plus 2 percent applied to the amount of the deficiency. Thus, reserve deficits incur a possible penalty cost imposed by the regulatory authorities (in the case of U.S. banks, by the Federal Reserve bank in the district). There may also be increased surveillance costs if repeated reserve deficits lead regulators to examine and monitor the bank's operations more closely, interfering with its daily routine and perhaps damaging its efficiency.

In addition to holding a legal reserve account at the central bank, many bankers also hold a so-called **clearing balance** there to cover any checks drawn against their banks. In the United States any bank using the Federal Reserve's check-clearing facilities must maintain a minimum-size clearing balance—an amount that is set by agreement between each bank and its district Federal Reserve bank, based on its estimated check-clearing needs and the bank's recent record of overdrafts. Banks posting such clearing balances at the Fed earn credits, which they can use to help pay for Federal Reserve services (such as the use of FEDWIRE—the Federal Reserve's electronic funds-transfer wire service or to help offset the fees the Fed will charge for clearing checks and drafts each day).

Clearing balances work just like legal required reserve balances with bankers required to maintain a minimum daily average amount in their clearing account over the same two-week maintenance period that applies to legal reserve balances. The amount of credit a bank earns from holding a Fed clearing balance depends on the size of the average account balance and the level of the Federal funds interest rate over the period. For example, if a bank had a clearing balance average of $1 million over the two-week reserve maintenance period, it would earn Federal Reserve credit of:

$$\text{Average clearing balance} \times \text{Annualized Fed funds rate} \times 14 \text{ days}/360 \text{ days}$$

$$= \$1,000,000 \times .055 \times .0389 = \$2,138.89.$$

Assuming a Federal funds rate of 5.5 percent and a 360-day year, this bank could apply up to $2,138.89 to offset any fees the Fed charged the bank for the use of Federal Reserve services.

Factors Influencing a Bank's Money Position

A bank's money position, especially the size of its legal reserve account at the central bank in its nation or district, is influenced by a long list of factors, some of which are listed below. Among the most important of these factors are the volume of checks cleared each day, the amount of currency and coin shipments back and forth between each bank and the central bank's vault, purchases and sales of government securities,

---

[4]The current Federal Reserve rule allows a bank to carry over from one reserve maintenance period to another the larger of $50,000 or 4 percent of the sum of a bank's required level of reserves plus the net amount of its clearing balance at the Federal Reserve bank in its district.

and borrowing and lending in the Federal funds (interbank) market. Some of these factors are largely *controllable* by bank management, while others are essentially *noncontrollable*, and management needs to anticipate and to react quickly to them.

Controllable Factors Increasing a Bank's Legal Reserves	*Controllable Factors Decreasing a Bank's Legal Reserves*
• Selling securities.	• Purchasing securities.
• Receiving interest payments on securities.	• Making interest payments to investors holding the bank's securities.
• Borrowing reserves from the Federal Reserve bank.	• Repaying a loan from the Federal Reserve bank.
• Purchasing Federal funds from other banks.	• Selling Federal funds to other institutions in need of reserves.
• Selling securities under a repurchase agreement (RP).	• Security purchases under a repurchase agreement (RP).
• Selling new CDs, Eurocurrency deposits, or other deposits to customers (with the new funds coming into the bank's reserve account by check or by wire).	• Receiving into the bank's vault currency and coin shipments from the Federal Reserve bank.

Noncontrollable Factors Increasing a Bank's Legal Reserves	*Noncontrollable Factors Decreasing a Bank's Legal Reserves*
• Surplus position at the local clearinghouse due to receiving more deposited checks in its favor than checks drawn against it.	• Deficit position at the local clearinghouse due to more checks drawn against the bank than in its favor.
• Credit from cash letters sent to the Fed, listing drafts received by the bank.	• Calls of funds from the bank's tax and loan account by the U.S. Treasury.
• Deposits made by the U.S. Treasury into a tax and loan account held at the bank.	• Debits received from the Federal Reserve bank for checks drawn against the bank's reserve account.
• Credit received from the Federal Reserve bank for checks previously sent for collection (deferred availability items, which the Fed credits to the bank's reserve accounts each day according to a fixed schedule).	• Withdrawal of large deposit accounts (such as CDs and Eurodollar deposits), often immediately by wire.

The basic task of a bank's money position manager is to *use the controllable factors to offset or supplement the noncontrollable factors affecting legal reserves,* so the bank achieves its preferred legal reserve position over the reserve maintenance period set by the central bank.

In recent years the volume of legal reserves held at the Federal Reserve banks by depository institutions operating in the United States has declined sharply. Today, for example, bank reserves held at the Federal Reserve are less than half of their volume in 1994. This significant decline in bank reserves is largely due to the development of **sweep accounts**—a banking service that results in bankers shifting their customers' deposited funds out of accounts that carry reserve requirements (currently demand deposits and other checkable accounts), usually on an overnight basis, into savings accounts (not currently bearing reserve requirements). Such sweeps yield an advantage to a bank because they lower the bank's overall cost of funds, while still preserving for the depositor the ability to access his or her checking account and make payments or execute withdrawals. These sweep arrangements have ballooned in size today to cover nearly $200 billion in deposit balances, substantially lowering bankers' total required reserves. Bankers have been aided in their sweep activities by computer screens made available by the Federal Reserve that track on a real-time basis any large dollar payments flowing into or out of their reserve balances at the Fed each day, allowing bank money managers to better plan what happens to their banks' legal reserve positions on a daily basis. Recently, proposed legislation in the U.S. Congress would call for allowing the Federal Reserve to pay interest on legal reserve balances, thereby reducing the pressure on banks to seek ways to avoid holding legal reserves.

Regulations on Calculating Legal Reserve Requirements

Exhibit 11–1 summarizes the specific rules the Federal Reserve has created for all U.S. depository institutions holding reservable liabilities. As the exhibit shows, under the current system of accounting for legal reserves, called **lagged reserve accounting (LRA),** the daily average amount of transaction deposits is computed over a two-week

EXHIBIT 11–1
Federal Reserve Rules for Calculating a Bank's Required Legal Reserves

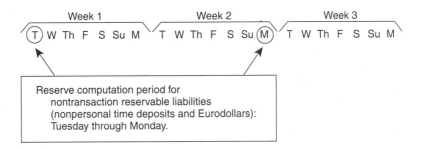

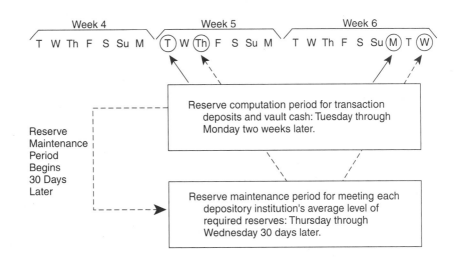

period stretching from a Tuesday to a Monday, 13 days later. This period is known as the **reserve computation period** for transaction deposits. The daily average amount of nontransaction reservable liabilities is figured during a two-week period ending 14 days before the reserve computation period for transaction deposits begins. The daily average amount of *vault cash* held by each bank is figured over the same two-week computation period used to determine the average amount of transaction deposits.

After the money position manager calculates daily average deposits and the bank's required legal reserve, he or she must maintain that required legal reserve on deposit with the Federal Reserve bank in the region (less the amount of daily average vault cash held), on average, over a 14-day period stretching from a Thursday to a Wednesday. This is known as the **reserve maintenance period.** Notice from Exhibit 11–1 that this period begins 30 days after the beginning of the reserve computation period for transaction deposits. Thus, the money position manager has several extra days (about two more weeks) in which to hit the target level of required reserves after all daily average deposit levels have been determined.[5]

The key goal of money position management is to keep legal reserves at the required level, with no excess reserves and no reserve deficit large enough to incur a penalty. If the bank has an *excess* reserve position, it will sell Federal funds to other banks short of legal reserves, or if the excess appears to be longer lasting, purchase securities or perhaps make new loans. If the bank has a legal reserve *deficit,* it will usually purchase Federal funds or borrow from the Federal Reserve bank in the district. If the deficit appears to be especially large or long lasting, the bank may sell some of its marketable securities and cut back on its lending.

Table 11–7 illustrates how a bank can keep track of its reserve position on a daily basis. The exhibit also illustrates the money desk manager's principal problem—trying to keep track of the many transactions each day during the reserve maintenance period that will affect the bank's legal reserves held at the district Federal Reserve bank. In this exhibit, the money desk manager had estimated that the bank needed to average $500 million per day in its reserve account at the district Federal Reserve bank. However, at the end of the first day (Thursday) of the new reserve maintenance period, it had a $550 million reserve position. The bank's money manager tried to take advantage of this excess reserve position the next day (Friday) by purchasing $100 million in U.S. Treasury securities. The result was a reserve deficit of $130 million, much deeper than expected, due in part to a $80 million adverse clearing balance (that is, the bank had more checks presented for deduction from its customers' deposits than it received from other banks for crediting to its own customers' accounts).

---

[5]In the Fall of 1997 the Federal Reserve Board proposed doing away with the so-called contemporaneous reserve accounting system (CRA) and moving to a new lagged requirement system (LRA). Larger, weekly reporting banks would begin holding their required reserves 30 days after the beginning of the reserve computation period, instead of beginning to hold their legal reserves only two days after the reserve computation period under the old CRA system. The Fed argued that the new LRA system would make it easier for depository institutions to calculate their reserve requirements and improve the quality of the information needed by the Fed's open-market trading desk to carry out monetary policy. Smaller banks that report their legal reserves quarterly or annually (mainly those holding less than $75 million in deposits) must still conform to the old CRA reporting system under the Fed's new proposal, however. The new LRA system became effective July 30, 1998.

TABLE 11-7 **Daily Schedule for Evaluating a Bank's Money Position**
(all figures in millions of dollars)

Day in the Reserve Maintenance Period	Required Daily Average Balance at the Fed	Daily Adjustments to the Bank's Balance Held at the Federal Reserve Bank								Closing Daily Average Balance at the Federal Reserve Bank	Excess or Deficit in Legal Reserve Position	Cumulative Excess or Deficit in Legal Reserves	Cumulative Closing Balance at the Fed
		Federal Funds Transactions		Fed's Discount Window		Treasury Securities		Check Clearing					
		Purchases (+)	Sales (−)	Borrow (+)	Repay (−)	Redeem (+)	Purchase (−)	Credit (+)	Debit (−)				
Carryover excess (+) or deficit (−) in legal reserves from previous period:												0	
Thursday	$500	+50	−25		−25			+50		$550	+50	+50	$ 550
Friday	500			+50			−100		−80	370	−130	−80	920
Saturday	500			+50			−100		−80	370	−130	−210	1,290
Sunday	500			+50			−100		−80	370	−130	−340	1,660
Monday	500				−50			+40		465	−35	−375	2,125
Tuesday	500	+50	−25						−25	525	+25	−350	2,650
Wednesday	500					+50			−60	490	−10	−360	3,140
Thursday	500							+10		510	+10	−350	3,650
Friday	500	+100	−50						−70	480	−20	−370	4,130
Saturday	500	+100	−50						−70	480	−20	−390	4,610
Sunday	500	+100	−50						−70	480	−20	−410	5,090
Monday	500	+250					−25	+15		740	+240	−170	5,830
Tuesday	500	+100								600	+100	−70	6,430
Wednesday	500	+70								570	+70	0	7,000
Cumulative	$7,000												
Daily average	$ 500												

To help offset this steep decline in its reserve account, the money manager borrowed $50 million from the Federal Reserve bank's discount window on Friday afternoon. This helped a little because Friday's reserve position counts for Saturday and Sunday as well, when most banks are closed, so the $130 million reserve deficit on Friday resulted in a $390 million (3 × $130 million) cumulative reserve deficit for the whole weekend. If the money desk manager had not borrowed the $50 million from the Fed, the deficit would have been $180 million for Friday, and, thus $540 million (3 × $180 million) for the entire weekend.

The bank depicted in Exhibit 11–1 continued to operate below its required daily average legal reserve of $500 million through the next Friday of the reserve maintenance period, when a fateful decision was made. The money manager decided to borrow $100 million in Federal funds, but at the same time to sell $50 million in Federal funds to other banks. Unfortunately, the manager did not realize until day's end on Friday that the bank had suffered a $70 million adverse clearing balance due to numerous checks written by its depositors that came back for collection. On balance, the bank's reserve deficit increased another $10 million, for a closing balance on Friday of $480 million. Once again, because Friday's balance carried over for Saturday and Sunday, the money desk manager faced a cumulative reserve deficit of $410 million on Monday morning, with only that day plus Tuesday and Wednesday to offset the deficit before the reserve maintenance period ended. As we noted earlier, Federal Reserve regulations require a bank to be within 4 percent of its required daily average reserve level or pay a penalty on the amount of the deficit. Trying to avoid the penalty, the money manager swung into high gear, borrowing $250 million in Federal funds on Monday and $100 million on Tuesday. Over two days this injected $350 million in new reserves. With an additional borrowing of $70 million in the Federal funds market on Wednesday, the last day of the reserve maintenance period, the bank ended the period with a zero cumulative reserve deficit.

In the foregoing example, the money position manager had a large reserve deficit to cover in a hurry. This manager elected to borrow heavily in the Federal funds market. While the Federal funds market is the most popular route for solving immediate shortages of legal reserves, the money position manager usually has a number of options to draw on from both the asset (stored liquidity) and liability (purchased liquidity) sides of the bank's balance sheet, including selling Treasury bills the bank holds, drawing upon any excess correspondent balances held with other banks, entering into repurchase agreements, issuing new time deposits, and borrowing in the Eurocurrency market.

Factors in Choosing among the Different Sources of Reserves

In choosing which source of reserves to draw upon in order to cover a legal reserve deficit, bankers must carefully consider several aspects of their need for liquid funds:

1. *Immediacy of the bank's need.* If a reserve deficit comes due within minutes or a few hours, the liquidity manager will normally tap the Federal funds market for an overnight loan or contact the central bank for a loan from its discount window. In contrast, the bank can meet its nonimmediate reserve needs

by selling deposits or assets, which may require more time to arrange than immediately available borrowings normally do.

2. *Duration of the bank's need.* If the liquidity deficit is expected to last for only a few hours, the Federal funds market or the central bank's discount window is normally the preferred source of funds. Liquidity shortages lasting days, weeks, or months, on the other hand, are often covered with sales of assets or long-term borrowings.

3. *The bank's access to the market for liquid funds.* Not all banks have equal access to all markets for funds. For example, smaller banks cannot, as a practical matter, draw upon the Eurocurrency market or sell commercial paper. Liquidity managers must restrict their range of choices to those their bank can access quickly.

4. *Relative costs and risks of alternative sources of funds.* The cost of each source of reserves changes daily, and the availability of surplus liquidity is also highly uncertain. Other things being equal, the liquidity manager will draw on the cheapest source of reliable funds and, therefore, must maintain constant contact with the money and capital markets to be aware of how interest rates and credit conditions are changing.

5. *Interest rate outlook and the shape of the yield curve.* When planning to deal with a future liquidity deficit, the liquidity manager wants to draw on those funds sources whose interest rates are expected to be the lowest. Often, with an upward-sloping yield curve, this means borrowing liquidity cheaply in the short-term market and loaning out any funds raised at a higher long-term interest rate. Management must be cautious here, however, because this strategy opens a bank up to additional interest rate risk.

6. *Outlook for central bank monetary policy and for government borrowing.* Central bank and government borrowing operations should be studied carefully to determine which way credit conditions and interest rates in the financial markets are moving. A heavy government borrowing schedule or restrictive money and credit policy implies higher interest rates and reduced credit availability, making the raising of liquid funds more costly and more difficult for a bank's liquidity manager.

7. *Hedging capability.* Banks that make heavy use of borrowed sources of liquidity must wrestle with the problem of interest cost uncertainty. They do not know what their future borrowing costs will be. If management has sufficient skill, it can use hedging techniques (such as trading in options or financial futures) to reduce that uncertainty.

8. *Regulations applicable to a liquidity source.* Sources of liquidity cannot be used indiscriminately. For example, reserve requirements on deposits and restrictions on borrowing from the discount windows of the central bank (which may prohibit frequent borrowing and borrowing simply to loan to a customer) limit bank drawings from these sources and force liquidity managers to look elsewhere.

The liquidity manager must carefully weigh each of these factors in order to make a rational choice among alternative sources of reserves.

Concept Checks

11–15. What is *money position* management?

11–16. What is the principal *goal* of bank money position management?

11–17. Exactly how is a U.S. bank's legal reserve requirement determined?

11–18. First National Bank finds that its net transaction deposits average $140 million over the latest reserve computation period. Using the reserve requirement ratios imposed by the Federal Reserve as given in the textbook, what is the bank's total required legal reserve?

11–19. A U.S. bank has a daily average reserve balance at the Federal Reserve bank in its district of $25 million during the latest reserve maintenance period. Its vault cash holdings averaged $1 million and the bank's total transaction deposits (net of interbank deposits and cash items in collection) averaged $200 million daily over the latest reserve maintenance period. Does this bank currently have a legal reserve deficiency? How would you recommend that its management respond to the current situation?

11–20. What factors should a money position manager consider in meeting a deficit in a bank's legal reserve account?

11–21. What are clearing balances? Of what benefit can clearing balances be to a bank that uses the Federal Reserve System's check-clearing network?

11–22. Suppose a bank maintains an average clearing balance of $5 million during a period in which the Federal funds rate averages 6 percent. How much would this bank have available in credits at the Federal Reserve Bank in its district to help offset the charges assessed against the bank for using Federal Reserve services?

11–23. What are *sweep accounts?* Why have they led to a significant decline in the total legal reserves held at the Federal Reserve banks by depository institutions operating in the United States?

Summary

Managing liquidity for a bank involves having enough cash on hand and being able to borrow cash at reasonable cost in order to meet cash needs exactly when they arise. The two most common uses of the bank's liquid funds are to cover deposit withdrawals and to meet requests for loans. Banks can meet those funds needs by selling assets (i.e., disposing of *stored* liquidity) or borrowing in the money market (i.e., using *purchased* liquidity).

Banks have developed a number of methods to assess what their true liquidity needs are. The *sources and uses of funds method* estimates total uses and sources of funds over the bank's desired planning horizon and attempts to forecast any resulting liquidity deficits and surpluses. In contrast, the *structure of funds method* requires each bank to classify its funds uses and sources according to whether they are stable or vulnerable (especially to movements in interest rates). Still another approach to estimating liquidity needs is the *liquidity indicator method,* in which selected financial ratios measuring bank liquidity are *compared* with those same ratios for other banks of comparable size and location.

Banks today can draw on multiple sources of asset liquidity and borrowed liquidity. Key sources of liquidity from selling assets include drawings from deposits held with other banks (correspondent balances) and sales of nonpledged ("free") government securities and private money market securities. Important borrowed liquidity sources include borrowing from central bank discount windows, purchasing Federal funds, using repurchase agreements (RPs), issuing money market CDs, borrowing Eurocurrency deposits, and, for bank holding companies, issuing commercial paper. Bank managers choose one or another of these sources according to (1) the immediacy of the bank's liquidity need, (2) the duration of that need, (3) market access, (4) relative costs and risk, (5) the interest rate outlook, (6) the outlook for monetary policy and government borrowing, (7) hedging capability, and (8) banking regulations.

Key Terms in This Chapter

Liquidity	Structure of funds method
Net liquidity position	Liquidity indicators
Asset liquidity management	Money position manager
Liquid asset	Legal reserves
Opportunity cost	Clearing balances
Liability management	Sweep accounts
Balanced liquidity management	Lagged reserve accounting (LRA)
Sources and uses of funds method	Reserve computation period
Liquidity gap	Reserve maintenance period

Problems and Projects

1. Caesar Hills State Bank estimates that over the next 24 hours the following cash inflows and outflows will occur (all figures in millions of dollars):

Deposit withdrawals	$ 47	Stockholder dividend payments	$178
Deposit inflows	87	Revenues from sale of non-	33
Scheduled loan repayments	55	deposit services	
Acceptable loan requests	102	Repayments of bank borrowings	67
Borrowings from the money			
market	61	Operating expenses	45
Sales of bank assets	16		

What is the bank's projected net liquidity position in the next 24 hours? From what sources can the bank cover its liquidity needs?

2. See if you can determine from the following information the volume of deposit withdrawals that Hillpeak State Bank is expecting to occur next week? Hillpeak is projecting a net liquidity surplus of $2 million next week partially as a result of expected quality loan demand of $24 million, necessary repayments of previous bank borrowings of $15 million, disbursements to cover operating expenses of $18 million, planned stockholder dividend payments of $5 million, expected deposit inflows of $26 million, revenues from nondeposit service sales of $18 million, scheduled repayments of previously made customer loans of $23 million, bank asset sales of $10 million, and money market borrowings of $11 million. How much must the bank's expected deposit withdrawals be for the coming week?

3. First National Bank of Los Alamos has forecast its checkable deposits, time and savings deposits, and commercial and household loans over the next eight months. The resulting estimates (in millions) are as shown below. Use the sources and uses of funds approach to indicate which months are likely to result in liquidity deficits and which in liquidity surpluses if these forecasts turn out to be true. Explain carefully what you would do to deal with each month's projected liquidity position.

	Checkable Deposits	Time and Savings Deposits	Commercial Loans	Consumer Loans
January	$111	$543	$682	$137
February	102	527	657	148
March	98	508	688	. 153
April	91	491	699	161
May	101	475	708	165
June	87	489	691	170
July	84	516	699	172
August	99	510	672	156

Alternative scenarios:

(1) How would the liquidity situation of First National Bank of Los Alamos change if its checkable deposits and time and savings deposits behaved as shown below (with loans unchanged) over the January through August period? What months would display the largest liquidity surpluses? The largest deficits?

	January	February	March	April	May	June	July	August
Checkable deposits	$120	$125	$132	$137	$141	$147	$150	$153
Time and savings deposits	$545	$552	$559	$558	$565	$587	$585	$592

(2) Suppose, on the other hand, that First National's commercial and consumer loans changed as shown below (with deposits remaining as they are). How would you deal with any projected liquidity deficits or surpluses that you detect?

	January	February	March	April	May	June	July	August
Commercial loans	$680	$705	$706	$698	$703	$711	$718	$75
Consumer loans	$135	$129	$131	$125	$107	$114	$104	$99

4. Hamilton Security Bank of Houston is attempting to determine its liquidity requirements today (the last day in August) for the month of September. This is usually a month of heavy business and consumer loan demand due to the beginning of the school term and the buildup of business inventories of goods and services for the fall season and the winter. The bank has analyzed its deposit accounts thoroughly and classified them as follows (in millions).

   Management has elected to hold a 75 percent reserve in liquid assets or borrowing capacity (0.75) for each dollar of hot money deposits, a 20 percent reserve behind the vulnerable deposits, and a 5 percent reserve for its holdings of core funds. The estimated reserve requirements on most deposits are 3 percent, except that savings deposits carry a zero percent reserve requirement and all checkable deposits above $42.2 million carry a 12 percent reserve requirement. Hamilton currently has total loans outstanding of $2,389 million, which two weeks ago were as high as $2,567 million. Its loans' mean annual growth rate over the past three years has been about 8 percent. Carefully estimate Hamilton's total liquidity requirement for September.

	Checkable Deposits	Savings Deposits	Nonpersonal Time Deposits
Hot money funds	$132	$___	$782
Vulnerable funds	207	52	540
Stable (core) funds	821	285	72

5. Using the financial information shown below for Wilson National Bank, calculate as many of the *liquidity indicators* discussed in this chapter for Wilson as you are able to. Do you detect any significant liquidity trends at this bank? Which trends should management investigate?

	Most Recent Year	Previous Year
Assets:		
Cash and due from depository institutions	$ 358,000	$ 379,000
U.S. Treasury securities	178,000	127,000
Other securities	343,000	358,000
Pledged securities	223,000	202,000
Federal funds sold	131,000	139,000
Loans and leases net	1,948,000	1,728,000
Total assets	3,001,000	2,941,000
Liabilities:		
Demand deposits	$ 456,000	$ 511,000
Savings deposits	721,000	715,000
Time deposits	853,000	744,000
Transaction accounts	644,000	630,000
Nontransaction accounts	1,349.000	1,328,000
Brokered deposits	37,000	12,000
Federal funds purchased	237,000	248,000
Other money market borrowings	16,000	84,000

6. Suppose a bank's liquidity manager estimates that the bank will experience a $550 million liquidity deficit next month with a probability of 10 percent, a $700 million liquidity deficit with a probability of 40 percent, a $230 million liquidity surplus with a probability of 30 percent, and a $425 million liquidity surplus bearing a probability of 20 percent. What is this bank's *expected liquidity requirement?* What should management do?

7. Merchants State Bank of Pierce, Iowa, reported transaction deposits of $75 million (the daily average for the latest two-week reserve computation period). Its nonpersonal time deposits over the most recent reserve computation period averaged $37 million daily, while vault cash averaged $0.978 million over the vault-cash computation period. Assuming that reserve requirements on transactions deposits are 3 percent of the total amount outstanding up to $46.8 million and 12 percent for all transaction deposits over $46.8 million while time deposits carry a 3 percent required reserve, calculate this bank's required daily average legal reserve at the Federal Reserve Bank in the district.

8. Elton Harbor National Bank has a cumulative legal reserve deficit of $44 million at the Federal Reserve bank in the district as of the close of business this Tuesday. The bank must cover this deficit by the close of business tomorrow (Wednesday). Charles Tilby, the bank's money desk supervisor, examines the current distribution of money market and long-term interest rates and discovers the following:

Money Market Instruments	Current Market Yield
Federal funds	8.46%
Borrowing from the central bank's discount window	7.00
Commercial paper (one-month maturity)	8.40
Banker's acceptances (three-month maturity)	8.12
Certificates of deposit (one-month maturity)	8.35
Eurodollar deposits (three-month maturity)	8.38
U.S. Treasury bills (three-month maturity)	7.60
U.S. Treasury notes and bonds (one-year maturity)	7.64
U.S. Treasury notes and bonds (five-year maturity)	7.75
U.S. Treasury notes and bonds (10-year maturity)	7.83

One week ago, the bank borrowed $20 million from the Federal Reserve's discount window, which it paid back yesterday. The bank had a $5 million legal reserve deficit during the previous reserve maintenance period. From the bank's standpoint, which sources of reserves appear to be the most promising? Which source would you recommend to cover the bank's legal reserve deficit? Why?

9. Eckhardt County National Bank estimates the following information regarding the bank's legal reserve position at the Federal Reserve for the reserve maintenance period that begins today (Thursday):

Calculated required daily average balance at the Federal Reserve bank	=	$750 million
A loan received by the bank from the Fed's discount window a week ago that comes due next Friday	=	$70 million

Planned purchases of U.S. Treasury securities
  on behalf of the bank and its customers:

Tomorrow (Friday)	=	$80 million
Next Wednesday	=	$35 million
Next Friday	=	$18 million

The bank also had a $750 million required daily average reserve requirement during the preceding reserve maintenance period. What problems are likely to emerge as the bank tries to manage its legal reserve position over the next two weeks? Relying on the Federal funds market and loans from the Federal Reserve's discount window as tools to manage the bank's reserve position, carefully construct a pro forma daily worksheet for the bank's money position over the next two weeks. Insert your planned adjustments in discount window borrowings and Federal funds purchases and sales over the period to show how you plan to manage the bank's legal reserve position and hit your desired reserve target.

Check-clearing estimates over the next 14 days:

Day	Credit Balance in Millions (+)	Debit Balance in Millions (−)
1	+10	
2		−60
3	Closed	
4	Closed	
5		−40
6		−25
7	+30	
8		−45
9		−5
10	Closed	
11	Closed	
12	+20	
13		−70
14	+10	

Closing reserve position in the previous reserve maintenance period
= $–5 million.

10. NCA Bank and Trust Co. has calculated its daily average deposits and vault cash holdings for the most recent two-week computation period as follows:

Net transaction deposits:	=	$81,655,474
Nonpersonal time deposits under 18 months to maturity	=	$147,643,589
Eurocurrency liabilities	=	$5,840,210
Daily average balance in vault cash	=	$1,002,031

Suppose the reserve requirements posted by the Board of Governors of the Federal Reserve System are:

Net transaction accounts:	
$0 to 42.2 million	3%
More than $42.2 million	12%
Nonpersonal time deposits:	
Less than 18 months	3%
18 months or more	0%
Eurocurrency liabilities—all types	3%

What is the bank's total required level of legal reserves? How much must the bank hold on a daily average basis with the Federal Reserve bank in its district?

11. Frost Street National Bank currently holds $750 million in transaction deposits subject to legal reserve requirements but has managed to enter into sweep account arrangements with its transaction deposit customers affecting $150 million of their deposits. Given the current legal reserve requirements applying to transaction deposits (as mentioned in this chapter), by how much would Frost Street's total legal reserves decrease as a result of these new sweep account arrangements (which stipulate that transaction deposit balances covered by the sweep agreements will be moved overnight into savings deposits)?

12. Lindberg State Bank maintains a clearing account at the Federal Reserve Bank in its district and agrees to keep a minimum balance of $22 million in its clearing account. Over the two-week reserve maintenance period ending today Lindberg managed to keep an average clearing account balance of $24 million. If the Federal funds interest rate has averaged 5.25 percent over this particular maintenance period, what maximum amount would Lindberg State Bank have available in the form of Federal Reserve credit to help offset any fees the Federal Reserve bank might charge the bank for using Federal Reserve services?

Selected References

The following studies discuss the instruments used to manage bank liquidity positions:

1. Bennett, Paul, and Spence Hilton. "Falling Reserve Balances and the Federal Funds Rate." *Current Issues in Economics and Finance,* Federal Reserve Bank of New York, 3, no. 5 (April 1997), pp. 1–6.
2. First Boston Corporation. *Handbook of Securities of the United States Government and Federal Agencies.* 33rd edition. New York, 1988.
3. Lumpkin, Stephen A. "Repurchase and Reverse Repurchase Agreements." *Economic Review,* Federal Reserve Bank of Richmond, January/February 1987, pp. 15–23.

4. Stevens, E. J. "Is There Any Rationale for Reserve Requirements?" *Economic Review,* Federal Reserve Bank of Cleveland, Third Quarter 1991.

For a review of the rules for meeting Federal Reserve deposit reserve requirements, see the following:

5. Tarban, Vefa. "Individual Bank Reserve Management." *Business Conditions,* Federal Reserve Bank of Chicago, 1988.
6. Board of Governors of the Federal Reserve System. Press Release, March 26, 1998, No. R-0988.

IV   MANAGING BANK SOURCES OF FUNDS

12 MANAGING DEPOSIT SERVICES AND NONDEPOSIT INVESTMENT PRODUCTS

Learning and Management Decision Objectives

The purpose of this chapter is to learn about the different types of deposits banks offer and, from the perspective of the bank manager, to discover which kinds of deposits are among the most profitable for banks to offer their customers.

Introduction

Deposits are the foundation upon which banks thrive and grow. They are a unique item on a bank's balance sheet that distinguishes it from other types of business firms. The ability of a bank's management and staff to attract checking and savings accounts from businesses and consumers is an important measure of the bank's acceptance by the public. Deposits provide most of the raw material for bank loans and, thus, represent the ultimate source of bank profits and growth. Deposits generate cash reserves, and it is out of the excess cash reserves a bank holds that new loans are created. Important indicators of management effectiveness in any bank are whether or not deposited funds have been raised at the lowest possible cost and whether enough deposits are available to fund those loans the bank wishes to make.[1]

This last point highlights the two key *issues* that *every bank* must deal with in managing its deposits: (1) Where can the bank raise funds at the lowest possible cost? and (2) How can management ensure that the bank always has enough deposits to support the desired volume of loans and other financial services demanded by the public? Neither question is easy to answer, especially in today's intensely competitive, increasingly deregulated financial marketplace. Both the cost and amount of deposits banks can sell to

---

[1]Portions of this chapter are based upon the author's recent articles in *The Canadian Banker* [4, 5] and are used with permission of the publisher.

the public are heavily influenced by the pricing schedules and competitive maneuverings of scores of bank and nonbank institutions offering similar services, such as share accounts in money market mutual funds, cash management accounts offered by brokerage and insurance companies, and interest-bearing checkable accounts offered by credit unions and savings and loans. *Innovation,* in the form of new deposit plans, service delivery methods, and pricing schemes, is rampant in banking today. Bankers who fail to stay abreast of changes in their competitors' deposit pricing and marketing programs stand to lose *both* customers and profits.

Types of Deposits Offered by Banks

The number and range of deposit services offered by banks is impressive indeed, and often confusing for bank customers. Like a Baskin-Robbins ice cream store, deposit plans designed to attract customer funds today come in 31 flavors and more, each plan having features intended to closely match business and household needs for saving money and making payments for goods and services.

Transaction (Payments) Deposits

One of the oldest deposit services offered by banks has centered on making *payments* on behalf of the bank's customers. This **transaction,** or *demand,* **deposit** service requires the bank to honor *immediately* any withdrawals made either in person by the customer or by a third party designated by the customer to be the recipient of the funds withdrawn. Transaction deposits include *regular noninterest-bearing demand deposits,* which do *not* earn an explicit interest payment but provide the customer with payment services, safekeeping of funds, and recordkeeping for any transactions carried out by check, and *interest-bearing demand deposits* that provide all of the foregoing services and pay interest to the depositor as well.

Noninterest-Bearing Demand Deposits.   Interest payments have been prohibited on regular checking accounts in the United States since passage of the Glass-Steagall Act of 1933. Congress feared at the time that paying interest on immediately withdrawable deposits endangered bank safety—a proposition that researchers have subsequently found to have little support. However, demand deposits are among the most volatile and least predictable of a bank's sources of funds, with the shortest potential maturity, because they can be withdrawn without prior notice. Most noninterest-bearing demand deposits are held by business firms; however, many consumers today have moved their funds into other types of checkable deposits that bear interest. In 1998 proposals were introduced in the U.S. Congress to allow American banks to pay interest on all demand deposits, including business demand accounts.

Interest-Bearing Demand Deposits.   Beginning in New England during the 1970s, hybrid checking-savings deposits began to appear in the form of *negotiable order of withdrawal* (**NOW**) **accounts.** NOWs are interest-bearing savings deposits that give the bank the right to insist on prior notice before the customer withdraws funds. Because this notice requirement is rarely exercised, the NOW can be used just like a checking account to pay for purchases of goods and services. NOWs were permitted nationwide beginning in 1981 as a result of passage of the Depository Institutions Deregulation Act of 1980. However, they can be held only by individuals and nonprofit institutions. When NOWs became legal nationwide, Congress also sanctioned the offering of automatic transfers (ATS), which permit the customer to preauthorize a bank to move funds from a savings account to a checking account in order to cover overdrafts. The net effect was to pay interest on transaction balances equal to the interest earned on a savings account.

Two other important interest-bearing transaction accounts were created in the United States in 1982 with passage of the Garn–St Germain Depository Institutions Act. Banks and nonbank thrift institutions could offer deposits competitive with the share accounts offered by money market funds that carried higher, unregulated interest rates and were backed by a pool of high-quality securities. The result was the appearance of **money market deposit accounts** (MMDAs) and **Super NOWs** (SNOWs), offering flexible money market interest rates but accessible via check or preauthorized draft to pay for goods and services.

MMDAs are short-maturity deposits that may have a term of only a few days, weeks, or months, and the bank can pay any interest rate that is competitive enough to attract and hold the customer's deposit. Up to six preauthorized drafts per month are allowed, but only three withdrawals may be made by writing checks. There is no limit to the personal withdrawals the customer may make (though banks reserve the right to set maximum amounts and frequencies for personal withdrawals). Unlike NOWs, MMDAs can be held by businesses as well as individuals.

Super NOWs were authorized at about the same time as MMDAs, but may be held only by individuals and nonprofit institutions. The number of checks the depositor may write is not limited by regulation. However, banks post lower yields on SNOWs than on MMDAs because the former can be drafted more frequently by customers. Incidentally, federal regulatory authorities classify MMDAs today, not as transaction (payments) deposits, but as savings deposits. We included them in this section on transaction accounts because they carry check-writing privileges.

Nontransaction (Savings, or Thrift) Deposits

Savings deposits, or **thrift deposits,** are designed to attract funds from customers who wish to set aside money in anticipation of future expenditures or financial emergencies. These deposits generally pay significantly higher interest rates than transaction deposits do. While their interest cost is higher, thrift deposits are generally less costly for a bank to process and to manage.

Just as banks for decades offered only one basic transaction deposit—the regular checking account—so it was with savings plans. **Passbook savings deposits** were sold to household customers in small denominations (frequently a passbook deposit could be opened for as little as $5), and withdrawal privileges were unlimited. While legally a banker could insist on receiving prior notice of a planned withdrawal from a passbook savings deposit, few banks have insisted on this technicality because of the low interest rate paid on these accounts and because passbook deposits tend to be stable anyway, with little sensitivity to changes in interest rates. Individuals, nonprofit organizations, and governments can hold savings deposits, as can business firms, but in the United States businesses cannot place more than $150,000 in such a deposit.

Some banks offer *statement savings deposits,* evidenced only by computer entry. The customer can get monthly printouts showing deposits, withdrawals, interest earned, and the balance in the account. Many banks, however, still offer the more traditional passbook savings deposit, where the customer is given a booklet showing the account's balance, interest earnings, deposits, and withdrawals, as well as the rules that bind both bank and depositor. Usually the depositor must present the passbook to a teller in order to make deposits or withdrawals.

For many years, wealthier individuals and businesses have been offered **time deposits,** which carry fixed maturity dates (usually covering 30, 60, 90, or 180 days) with fixed interest rates. More recently, time deposits have been issued with interest rates that are adjusted periodically (such as every 90 days, known as a *leg* or *roll period*). Time deposits must carry a minimum maturity of seven days and cannot be withdrawn before that. They come in a wide variety of types, ranging from negotiable CDs (to be discussed later) to Christmas and vacation club deposits. CDs are issued in *negotiable* form—the $100,000-plus instruments bought principally by corporations and wealthy individuals—and in *non-negotiable* form (i.e., cannot be traded prior to maturity), usually purchased by individuals.

In 1981, with passage of the Economic Recovery Tax Act, Congress opened the door to yet another deposit instrument—retirement savings accounts. Wage earners and salaried individuals were granted the right to make limited contributions each year, tax free, to an *individual retirement account* (IRA), offered by banks, savings institutions, brokerage firms, insurance companies, and mutual funds, or by employers with qualified pension or profit-sharing plans. There was ample precedent for the creation of IRAs; in 1962, Congress had authorized financial institutions to sell *Keogh plan* retirement deposits, which are available to self-employed persons. Unfortunately for banks and their customers interested in IRAs, the Tax Reform Act of 1986 restricted the tax deductibility of additions to an IRA account, which sharply reduced their growth, though Keogh deposits retained full tax benefits.

Then, in August 1997 the U.S. Congress, in an effort to encourage saving for retirement, purchases of new homes, and for childrens' future education, modified the rules for IRA accounts, allowing individuals and couples with higher incomes (up to $50,000 in annual income for individuals) to make annual tax-deductible contributions to their retirement accounts and allowed individuals and families to set up new education savings accounts that could grow tax free until needed to cover college tuition, room and board, and other qualified educational expenses. Finally, the Tax Relief Act of 1997 also created a so-called Roth IRA, which allows individuals and couples to accumulate investment earnings tax free and also pay no tax on their investment earnings when withdrawn provided the taxpayer follows the new account's rules for qualified withdrawals and annual contributions.

Today the banking industry in the United States holds about one-fifth of all IRA and Keogh retirement accounts outstanding, ranking second only to mutual funds. Their great appeal for bankers is the high degree of stability possessed by IRA and Keogh deposits—banks can rely on having these funds around for several years. Moreover, many IRAs and Keoghs carry fixed interest rates—an advantage if market interest rates are rising—allowing banks to earn higher returns on their loans and investments that more than cover the interest costs associated with IRAs and Keoghs.

Interest Rates Offered on Different Types of Deposits

Each of the different types of deposits we have discussed, typically, carries a different rate of interest. In general, the longer the *maturity* of a deposit, the greater the yield that must be offered to depositors, because of the time value of money and the frequent upward slope of the yield curve. For example, NOW accounts and savings deposits are subject to immediate withdrawal by the customer; accordingly, their offer rate to bank customers is among the lowest of all deposits. In contrast, negotiable CDs and deposits of a year or longer to maturity often carry the highest deposit interest rates that banks can offer.

The size and perceived risk exposure of the offering banks also play an important role in shaping deposit interest rates. For example, banks in New York and London, due to their greater size and strength, are able to offer deposits at the lowest average interest rates, while deposit rates posted by other banks are generally scaled upward from that level. Other key factors are the marketing philosophy and goals of the offering bank. Banks that choose to compete for deposits aggressively usually will post higher offer rates to bid deposits away from their competitors. In contrast, when a bank wants to discourage or deemphasize a type of deposit, it will allow its posted rate to fall relative to interest rates offered by competing institutions.

Composition of Bank Deposits

The particular types of deposits held by a bank at any moment in time depend, most importantly, on *the public's demand for deposit services.* A second key factor is *bank fundraising policies,* including the service fees charged and the interest rates offered on various deposit plans, the aggressiveness with which different deposit plans are advertised, and the time and resources devoted to attracting and retaining deposit customers.

In recent years, the most readily salable deposits banks have offered to the public have been time and savings deposits. As Table 12–1 shows, time and savings deposits represented about four-fifths of the total domestic deposits held by all U.S.-insured commercial banks at year-end 1996. Not surprisingly, then, interest-bearing deposits and nontransactions deposits—both of which include time and savings deposits— have captured the majority share of all U.S. bank deposit accounts. In contrast, regular

TABLE 12–1   **Changing Mix of Bank Deposits in the United States**
(Percentages are for all U.S.-insured banks at years' end)

Deposit Type or Category	1983	1985	1987	1989	1991	1993	1996
Noninterest-bearing deposits	37.9%	22.3%	20.5%	19.0%	17.9%	20.8%	19.8%
Interest-bearing deposits	62.1	77.7	79.5	81.0	82.1	79.2	80.2
Total deposits	100.0%	100.0%	100.0%	100.0%	100.0%	100.0%	100.0%
Transaction deposits	31.9%	32.5%	32.3%	29.9%	29.7%	33.4%	29.3%
Nontransaction deposits	68.1	67.5	67.7	70.1	70.3	66.6	70.7
Total domestic office deposits	100.0%	100.0%	100.0%	100.0%	100.0%	100.0%	100.0%
Demand deposits	25.4%	25.1%	22.9%	20.6%	19.1%	20.2%	22.1%
Savings deposits*	30.2	32.8	36.2	33.5	38.3	41.2	39.8
Time deposits	44.4	42.1	40.9	45.9	42.6	38.6	38.1
Total domestic office deposits	100.0%	100.0%	100.0%	100.0%	100.0%	100.0%	100.0%

*The savings deposit figures shown include money market deposit accounts (MMDAs).

Source: Federal Deposit Insurance Corporation, *Statistics on Banking,* selected years.

demand deposits, which generally pay no interest and make up the majority of transaction and noninterest-bearing deposits, have declined significantly to represent only about one-fifth of total bank deposits inside the United States.

Bankers, if left to decide for themselves about the best mix of deposits, would generally prefer a high proportion of demand deposits and low-yielding time and savings deposits. These accounts are among the least expensive of all bank sources of funds and often include a substantial percentage of **core deposits**—a stable base of deposited funds that is not highly sensitive to movements in market interest rates (i.e., bears a low interest rate elasticity) and tends to remain with the bank. While many core deposits (such as small savings accounts) could be withdrawn immediately, they have an effective maturity often spanning several years. Thus, the availability of a large block of core deposits increases the duration of a bank's liabilities and makes the institution less vulnerable to swings in interest rates. The presence of substantial amounts of core deposits in smaller banks helps explain why large banks and bank holding companies in recent years have acquired so many smaller banking firms—to gain access to a more stable and less-expensive deposit base. However, the combination of inflation, deregulation, stiff competition, and better-educated bank customers has resulted in a dramatic shift in the mix of deposits banks are able to sell.

Bank operating costs in offering deposit services have soared in recent years. For example, interest payments on deposits for all insured U.S. commercial banks amounted to $10.5 billion in 1970, or 38 percent of total operating expenses, but had jumped to over $100 billion, or more than half of total bank operating expenses, by the 1990s. At the same time the new, higher-yielding deposits proved to be more interest sensitive than the older, less-expensive deposits, thus putting pressure on bank managers to pay competitive rates on their deposit offerings. Banks that didn't keep up

---

**TABLE 12–2   Changing Ownership Composition of Bank Deposits
in the United States**

Deposit Owner Group	*1983*	*1985*	*1987*	*1989*	*1991*	*1993*	*1996*
Individuals, partnerships, and corporations	73.5%	75.2%	77.0%	80.3%	82.2%	89.2%	88.5%
U.S. government	0.2	0.2	0.3	0.2	0.3	0.3	0.3
States and political subdivisions in the United States	4.5	4.8	4.5	4.3	3.7	3.5	3.7
Foreign office deposits	16.7	15.2	14.6	12.2	11.3	4.1	4.5
All other deposits (including correspondent deposits)	5.1	4.6	3.6	3.0	2.5	2.9	3.0
Total deposits	100.0%	100.0%	100.0%	100.0%	100.0%	100.0%	100.0%

Note: Columns may not add to totals shown due to rounding error.

Source: Federal Deposit Insurance Corporation, *Statistics on Banking,* selected years.

with market interest rates had to be prepared for extra liquidity demands—substantial deposit withdrawals and fluctuating deposit levels. Faced with substantial interest cost pressures, many bankers have pushed hard to reduce their noninterest expenses (e.g., by automating their operations and reducing the number of employees on the payroll) and to increase operating efficiency.

As Table 12–2 shows, the dominant holder of bank deposits inside the United States is the private sector—individuals, partnerships, and corporations (IPC), accounting for more than four-fifths of all U.S. bank deposits. The next largest type of domestic deposit is state and local government deposits (under 4 percent of the total), representing the funds accumulated by counties, cities, and other local units of government. These deposits are often highly volatile, rising sharply when tax collections roll in or bonds are sold, and falling precipitously when local government payrolls must be met or construction begins on a new public building. Many bankers accept state and local deposits as a service to their communities even though these deposits frequently are not highly profitable.

Commercial banks also hold small amounts of U.S. government deposits. In fact, the U.S. Treasury keeps most of its operating funds at domestic banks in *Treasury Tax and Loan (TT&L) Accounts.* When taxes are collected from the public or Treasury securities are sold to investors, the federal government usually directs these funds into TT&L deposits first, in order to minimize the impact of government operations on the banking system. The Treasury then makes periodic withdrawals of these funds (directing the money into its accounts at the Federal Reserve banks) when it needs to make expenditures. Today the Treasury pays fees to depository institutions to help lower the cost of handling government deposits and the Treasury receives interest income on many of the balances held with depository institutions.

Another deposit category of substantial size held by U.S. banks is the deposits held by *foreign* governments, businesses, and individuals, most of which are received in offshore offices. Foreign-owned deposits rose rapidly during the 1960s and 1970s, climbing to nearly one-fifth of total U.S. bank deposits in 1980, reflecting the rapid growth in world trade and investments by U.S. businesses abroad. However, foreign-owned deposits then declined as a proportion of U.S. bank funds as U.S. domestic interest rates proved to be significantly cheaper for banks. Moreover, an international debt crisis and a stronger economy at home encouraged American banks to scale down their overseas expansion plans.

The final major deposit category is *deposits of other banks,* which include *correspondent deposits,* representing funds that banks hold with each other to pay for correspondent services. For example, large metropolitan banks provide data processing and computerized recordkeeping, investment and tax counseling, participation in loans, and the clearing and collection of checks for smaller urban and outlying depository institutions. A bank that holds deposits received from other banks will record them as a liability on its balance sheet under the label *deposits due to banks.* The bank that owns such deposits will record them as assets under the label *deposits due from banks.*

The Functional Cost Analysis of Different Deposit Accounts

Other factors held constant, bankers would prefer to raise funds by selling those types of deposits that cost the bank the *least* amount of money or, when revenues generated by the use of deposited funds are considered, generate the greatest net revenue after all expenses. If a bank can raise all of its capital from sales of the cheapest deposits and then turn around and purchase the highest-yielding assets, it will maximize its spread and, possibly, maximize the bank's net income flowing to its stockholders. But, what are the cheapest deposits for a bank? And which deposits generate the highest net revenues?

The Federal Reserve banks provide important clues about the costs and revenues from bank deposits via their cost accounting system, known as Functional Cost Analysis (FCA). The FCA program generates information about the earnings and costs associated with many banking services, based upon data that selected banks voluntarily supply to the Fed each year. As shown in Tables 12–3, 12–4, and 12–5, FCA data reveal that *checkable* (demand) *deposits*—including regular checking accounts and special checkbook deposits (which usually pay no interest to the depositor) and interest-bearing checking accounts—are typically among the *cheapest* deposits that banks sell to the public. While check processing and account maintenance costs are major expense items, the absence of an interest payment on regular and special checking accounts and the low interest rate usually paid on interest-bearing checking (demand) accounts help keep the cost of these deposits down relative to the cost of time and savings deposits and other bank sources of funds.

Moreover, check processing costs should move substantially lower in the late 1990s and early into the next century as *check imaging* services become more readily available from the Federal Reserve banks and other service providers. Paper checks will gradually be supplanted with electronic images stored on CDs, permitting more storage and much faster retrieval, cutting bank costs and improving customer services.

Thrift deposits—particularly money market accounts, time deposits, and savings accounts—generally rank second to demand deposits as the least costly deposits for a

**TABLE 12–3   Effective Interest Rates Paid by Banks
on Different Kinds of Deposits**

	Effective Annual Interest Rates Paid by:		
Deposit Type	*Small Banks (deposits up to $50 million)*	*Medium Banks (deposits of $50 to $200 million)*	*Large Banks (deposits over $200 million)*
Regular and special checking accounts	0.00%	0.00%	0.00%
Interest-bearing checking accounts	2.77	2.23	2.06
Regular (passbook) savings deposits	2.70	2.94	2.70
Money market deposit accounts	3.89	3.47	3.64
Retirement deposits	5.65	5.59	5.60
Certificates of deposit (CDs) under $100,000	5.63	5.51	5.55
Certificates of deposit (CDs) $100,000 and over	5.39	5.57	5.38
Other time deposits	5.42	5.35	5.16

Source: Federal Reserve Banks, Functional Cost and Profit Analysis Program, *National Average Report 1996,* Washington, D.C., 1997.

bank. Savings deposits are relatively cheap for banks because of the low interest rate they carry—one of the lowest most banks offer—and, in many cases, the absence of monthly statements for depositors. However, many passbook savings accounts have substantial deposit and withdrawal activity; some savers attempt to use them as checking accounts. Many banks have moved to discourage rapid turnover in their savings deposits by limiting withdrawals and charging activity fees.

Table 12–4 shows that while demand (checking) deposits have about the same gross expenses (including interest and operating expenses) per dollar of deposit as time deposits do, the higher service fees levied against checking account customers help to lower the *net* cost of checkable deposits (after service revenues are netted out) below the *net* cost of time (thrift) accounts. When we give each type of deposit credit for the earnings it generates for a bank through loans and investments, checkable (demand) deposits appear to be roughly 40 percent more profitable than thrift (time) deposits for the average bank. On average, checking-account service fees offset about one-third of a checking account's cost to a bank. In contrast, service fees on time (thrift) deposits make only a negligible contribution to offsetting their cost. Moreover, the interest expense per dollar of time deposits averages about triple the interest expense associated with each dollar of demand (checking) deposits.

To be sure, demand deposits incur much greater operating expenses for a bank due to the high employee and equipment costs associated with processing checks and recording deposits, while these "activity expenses" are far less for thrift (time) deposits. The critical difference in terms of bank profitability, as we observed above, is the service fees most checkable accounts generate for a bank. This fact helps explain why, faced with rising operating costs in recent years, banks have more aggressively

TABLE 12–4   **Cost and Profitability of Demand (Checking) and Time (Thrift) Deposits for U.S. Banks**

Type of Deposit	Expenses, Fees, and Profits Measured as a Percent of Total Funds Raised by Each Type of Deposit for:		
	Small Banks (deposits up to $50 million)	*Medium Banks (deposits of $50 to $100 million)*	*Large Banks (deposits over $200 million)*
Demand (checking) deposits:			
Interest expense	1.69%	1.15%	1.01%
Operating expenses	<u>3.53</u>	<u>3.95</u>	<u>4.67</u>
Gross expenses	5.22	5.10	5.68
Less: Service fees charged the customer	<u>−1.74</u>	<u>−1.80</u>	<u>−1.99</u>
Net cost of demand deposits	3.48%	3.30%	3.69%
Add: Credit given to demand deposits for the income they generate when invested in a bank's earning assets	<u>6.08</u>%	<u>6.05</u>%	<u>5.67</u>%
Equals: Net profits earned for a bank by selling demand deposits expressed as a percent of all funds raised	2.60%	2.75%	1.98%
Time (thrift) deposits:			
Interest expense	5.00%	4.74%	4.70%
Operating expenses	<u>0.56</u>	<u>0.68</u>	<u>0.66</u>
Gross expenses	5.56	5.42	5.36
Less: Service fees charged the customer	<u>−0.04</u>	<u>−0.05</u>	<u>−0.04</u>
Net cost of time deposits	5.52%	5.37%	5.32%
Add: Credit given to time deposits for the income they generate when invested in a bank's earning assets	<u>6.81</u>	<u>6.93</u>	<u>6.83</u>
Equals: Net profits earned for a bank by selling time deposits expressed as a percent of all funds raised	1.29%	1.56%	1.51%

Note: Columns may not add correctly due to rounding error.

Source: Federal Reserve Banks, Functional Cost and Profit Analysis Program, *National Average Report 1996*, Washington, D.C., 1997.

priced their checkable deposits, asking depositors to pay a bigger share of the activity costs they create for a bank when their customers write checks.

If checkable (demand) deposits tend to be more profitable for banks in general, what particular types of checking accounts yield the greatest profits? Table 12–5 suggests that interest-bearing checking accounts generate about twice the volume of net returns (after earnings from bank loan and investment portfolios are added in) that regular (noninterest-bearing) checking accounts generate. For banks of all sizes, special checking accounts, which charge the customer a fee for each check written but generally require low or no minimum balances, tend to be the least profitable of

TABLE 12–5   **Bank Earnings per Account per Month on Different Types of Checking (Demand) Accounts**

Type of Checking Account	Average Account Generated the Following Income, Expenses, and Net Earnings For:		
	Small Banks (deposits up to $50 million)	Medium Banks (deposits of $50 to $200 million)	Large Banks (deposits over $200 million)
Regular Checking Accounts			
Total income earned per account per month	$ 8.09	$ 8.45	$ 8.73
Less activity expenses:			
On-us debits	$ 5.22	$ 5.53	$ 6.28
Deposits	1.87	2.21	2.67
Transit checks	2.27	2.53	3.28
Account maintenance	6.28	6.82	7.57
Total activity expenses	15.64	17.08	19.80
Net earnings	–7.55	–8.63	–11.07
Net earnings after portfolio credit	$ 6.55	$ 9.84	$ 8.71
Special Checking Accounts			
Total income earned per account per month	$ 8.43	$ 6.98	$ 6.03
Less activity expenses:			
On-us debits	$ 3.58	$ 4.43	$ 6.48
Deposits	1.49	1.36	2.12
Transit checks	0.18	0.27	0.48
Account maintenance	5.29	5.20	7.76
Total activity expenses	10.54	11.27	16.84
Net earnings	–2.11	–4.28	–10.81
Net earnings after portfolio credit	$ 0.93	$ 4.64	–$ 6.31
Interest-Bearing Checking Accounts			
Total income earned per account per month	$ 4.34	$ 3.41	$ 3.92
Less activity expenses:			
On-us debits	$ 4.15	$ 4.58	$ 4.46
Deposits	2.28	1.78	2.17
Transit checks	1.66	1.23	1.82
Account maintenance	6.17	6.86	7.81
Total activity expenses	14.26	14.46	16.26
Interest expense	29.00	17.16	13.07
Net earnings	–38.92	–28.21	–25.40
Net earnings after portfolio credit	$25.52	$19.79	$11.78

(concluded on next page)

all demand deposits principally because the average special checking account generates a very small volume of investable funds for a bank.

According to the data presented in Table 12–5, commercial checking accounts are considerably more profitable than personal checking accounts for banks of all sizes that reported their deposit revenues and expenses to the Federal Reserve's FCA program. One reason is the lack of a significant interest expense with

TABLE 12–5   *(concluded)*

Type of Checking Account	Average Account Generated the Following Income, Expenses, and Net Earnings For:		
	Small Banks (deposits up to $50 million)*	*Medium Banks (deposits of $50 to $200 million)*	*Large Banks (deposits over $200 million)*
Commercial Checking Accounts			
Total income per account per month	—	$15.43	$12.47
Less activity expenses:			
On-us debits	—	$15.47	$11.49
Deposits	—	6.07	9.20
Transit checks	—	7.54	14.49
Account maintenance	—	7.82	9.90
Total activity expenses	—	$38.39	$45.08
Net earnings	—	–23.47	–32.61
Net earnings after portfolio credit	—	$48.31	$63.67
Personal Checking Accounts			
Total income per account per month	—	$ 8.11	$ 5.92
Less activity expenses:			
On-us debits	—	3.96	6.10
Deposits	—	1.58	2.44
Transit checks	—	1.43	0.05
Account maintenance	—	7.61	9.10
Total activity expenses	—	$14.58	$17.70
Interest expense	—	5.35	6.74
Net earnings	—	–11.82	–18.52
Net earnings after portfolio credit	—	$ 6.31	$ 0.07

Note*: Data not available for the smallest banks.

Source: Federal Reserve Banks, Functional Cost and Profit Analysis Program, *National Average Report 1996,* Washington, D.C., 1997.

commercial deposits, while personal checking accounts carry an average interest expense that often exceeds the amount of fee income these deposits generate. Thus, even though the cost per dollar of funds raised is almost the same for both commercial and personal checking accounts, the added interest costs attached to many personal demand deposits often drive their return for a typical bank below the net return from commercial demand deposits. Indeed, even after adjustment for the earnings from a bank's loan and investment portfolio, the net return from personal checking accounts in 1996 was slightly negative for the smallest and largest U.S. banks. Moreover, the average size of a personal checking account normally is less than one-third the average size of a commercial account, so a bank receives substantially more investable funds from commercial demand deposits. However, competition posed by foreign financial-service firms for commercial checking accounts has become so intense that many banks find the profit margins on these accounts are razor thin in today's market.

Time deposits, retirement accounts, CDs, and money market accounts generally display low account activity in terms of deposits and withdrawals compared to savings accounts. However, the higher interest costs on most time and money market accounts come close to erasing their slight cost advantage over savings deposits. Smaller banks often incur higher costs on savings and money market deposits than do larger banks, but they offset this by issuing time deposits and retirement accounts at a lower average cost than the average cost of time and retirement deposits issued by larger banks. Nevertheless, larger banks generate more revenue from checkable and thrift deposits because of the greater average size of these deposits at the biggest banks.

While bankers would prefer to sell only the cheapest deposits to the public, it is predominantly *public preference* that determines which types of deposits will be created. Banks that do not wish to conform to customer preferences will simply be outbid for deposits by those who do. In recent years, the public has demanded both higher-yielding (more costly) thrift accounts and checkable deposits that pay interest rates comparable to returns available in the open market. At the same time, deregulation of the financial markets has made it possible for more kinds of financial-service firms to respond to the public's deposit preferences. This combination of greater competition and higher costs helps to explain why bank profits have become more volatile and uncertain in recent years.

Concept Checks

12–1. What are the major types of deposit plans banks offer today?

12–2. What are *core deposits* and why are they so important in banking today?

12–3. How has the composition of bank deposits changed in recent years?

12–4. What are the consequences for bank management and bank performance of recent changes in deposit composition?

12–5. Which deposits are the least costly for banks? The most costly?

12–6. First State Bank of Pine is considering a change of marketing strategy in an effort to lower its cost of funding and to maximize the bank's profitability. The new strategy calls for aggressive advertising of new commercial checking accounts and interest-bearing household checking accounts and for deemphasizing regular and special checking accounts. What are the possible advantages and possible weaknesses of this new marketing strategy?

Trust Department Services:
An Important Source of Bank Deposits

A major source of bank deposits that the public often knows very little about is a bank's trust department. Not all banks have trust powers, which must be applied for from the bank's chartering agency or principal regulator, but most medium and large banks do operate trust departments. Trust personnel are *not* permitted to share client information on those customers they serve with bank personnel in other parts of the bank.

Trust departments often generate very large deposits for a bank because they manage property (including deposits as well as other assets) for their customers, which usually include business firms, units of government, individuals and families, and charities and foundations. A bank trust officer may be instructed by a customer or the trust officer may decide himself or herself to place certain monies in a checking or time deposit account for future use (such as to pay bills or to seek out a more favorable rate of return) on behalf of a client served by the trust department. Deposits placed in a bank by that bank's trust department must be *fully secured.* They are covered by deposit insurance, like any other deposit up to the legal insurance limit, and any amount over the insurance limit must be protected by investment-grade securities the bank holds while the deposit is present in the bank.

The trust business is very old, stretching back to the Middle Ages when landowners and other wealthy individuals (trustors) often chose to turn their property over to a manager (trustee), who would protect and control the use of that property for the benefit of its owner or owners. State-chartered U.S. banks have provided **trust services** for many years, while national banks were granted the right to seek trust powers with passage of the Federal Reserve Act in 1913. For most of banking's history trust departments were regarded as a needed service area for the benefit of a bank's customers, but trust operations were usually regarded as an unprofitable activity due to the large space and the highly skilled personnel required—usually a combination of portfolio managers, lawyers (particularly specialists in trust and tax law), and professional accountants—needed to serve trust customers. However, with the advent of government deregulation of the banking system and the increasing tendency of banks to levy fees for their services, bank trust departments became increasingly popular as a source of *fee income.* For example, trust departments typically levy asset management (trustee) fees based upon the value of a customer's assets that they are called upon to manage and for filing tax reports. These fees are popular with bankers today because they are often less sensitive to fluctuations in market interest rates than are other bank revenues (such as interest on loans).

Trust departments function in a tremendous variety of roles. They routinely serve as executors or administrators of wills, identifying, inventorying, and protecting the property (estate) of a deceased person, ensuring that any unpaid bills are met and that the heirs of the deceased receive the income or assets to which they are entitled. Trust departments act as *agents* for companies that need to service security issues (such as by issuing new stock, paying stockholder dividends, and issuing or retiring bonds for client firms) and often manage the pension or retirement plans of both businesses and individuals. They also serve as guardians of assets held for the benefit of minors or act on behalf of adult persons judged to be legally incompetent to manage their own affairs.

In fulfilling these many roles trust departments promulgate basic trust agreements—contracts that grant a bank officer legal authority on behalf of a customer to invest funds, pay bills, and dispense income to persons or institutions with valid claims against the trust's assets. Many different types of trusts are permitted under the laws of different states (though the types and procedures often vary from state to state so that state trust codes always need to be consulted by anyone desiring to enter into a trust agreement). More complex trust arrangements often require the services of an outside attorney as well.

Among the more popular kinds of trusts are *living trusts* or grantor revocable trusts (which allow bank trust officers to act on behalf of a living customer without a court order, generally help to avoid expensive probate proceedings if the property owner dies or becomes legally incompetent, and may be revoked or amended by the customer as desired). There are also *testamentary trusts* (which arise under a probated will and are often used to help save on estate taxes). If properly drawn, a testamentary trust can sometimes be used to protect a customer's property from the claims of creditors or beneficiaries who may make unreasonable demands that might prematurely exhaust the trust's assets. Other common types of trust agreements include *irrevocable trusts* (that allow wealth to be passed free of gift and estate taxes or may be used to allocate funds arising from court settlements or private contracts); *charitable trusts* (which support worthwhile causes, such as medical research, the arts, care of the needy, student scholarships, and orphanages); and *indenture trusts* (which usually collect, hold, and manage assets used to back an issue of securities by a corporation raising funds in the financial markets and then are employed to retire the securities on behalf of the issuing company when their term ends).

Clearly, trust departments perform a remarkable collection of roles and functions that are often unseen or unknown, even by many bank employees. However, their activities usually center upon establishing a *fiduciary relationship* with a customer, protecting that customer's property, making asset management and asset allocation decisions, planning a customer's estate and ensuring that estate property is passed in timely fashion to those entitled to its benefits under law, and assisting businesses in raising and managing funds and in providing retirement benefits to their employees. Trust departments must follow the terms of a trust or agency agreement and any court orders that have been issued. They are expected to be highly competent and diligent in their fiduciary and agency activities and are legally liable for losses due to negligence or for failure to act as a prudent decision maker, intelligently pursuing the best interests of their customers. Trust departments have come to play vital and often highly profitable roles for modern banks, including the attraction of a considerable volume of deposits. Moreover, many banks have used their trust departments to create mutual funds that grow rapidly in size and provide their trust customers with multiple advantages as well as permit a bank to achieve an efficient size mutual fund more quickly.

Source: The author acknowledges the very helpful comments and suggestions of Mark S. Browning, portfolio manager for Chase Bank of Texas in McAllen, in preparing this foregoing summary of bank trust activities.

Basic (Lifeline) Banking

Our overview of bank deposit services in this chapter would not be complete without a brief look at a controversial consumer issue likely to grow in importance in future years—the issue of **basic (lifeline) banking.** Should every adult citizen be guaranteed access to certain basic financial services, such as a checking account or personal loan? Is there a basic minimum level of financial service to which everyone is entitled? Can an individual today really function—secure adequate shelter, food, education, and health care—without access to certain key financial services?

Some authorities refer to this issue as *lifeline banking* because it originated in the controversy surrounding electric, gas, and telephone services. Many people believe that these services are so essential for health and comfort that they should be provided at reduced prices to those who could not otherwise afford them. The basic, or lifeline, banking issue catapulted to nationwide attention in the early 1980s when several consumer groups, such as the Consumers Union and the American Association of Retired Persons, first studied the problem and then campaigned actively for a resolution of the issue. Some banks have been picketed and formal complaints have been lodged with federal and state banking agencies.

The dimensions of the problem have been hinted at in several recent consumer surveys conducted by researchers at the Federal Reserve Board [10]. For example, Fed studies indicate that about 20 percent of all U.S. households have no checking account and 12 percent hold neither a checking nor a savings account. Most of these families appear to be in the lowest income groups, with limited formal education, and often headed by single parents.

The lack of a deposit account usually leads to another problem. Without checking or savings accounts, few people can get approval for credit, because banks prefer to make loans to those customers who keep deposits with them. Yet access to credit is essential for most families to secure adequate housing, medical care, and other important services. Several banks have responded to this social problem with basic deposits that allow some checks to be cashed (such as Social Security checks) and permit a limited number of personal withdrawals or checks (such as 10 free checks per month) or offer interest earnings on even the smallest balances. As yet, few laws compel the offering of basic banking services, except in selected states—for example, Illinois, Massachusetts, Minnesota, Pennsylvania, and Rhode Island—though many states have recently debated such legislation. Illinois makes it mandatory to offer inexpensive checkable deposits to people at least 65 years old, while Massachusetts prohibits service charges on checking or savings deposits held by older (65 years old or more) or younger (18 years old or less) citizens.

What, if anything, should the federal government do? Even if new legislation is not forthcoming, do banks and other financial institutions have a responsibility to serve *all* customers within their local communities? These are not easy questions to answer. Banks are privately owned corporations responsible to their stockholders to earn competitive returns on invested capital. Providing financial services at prices so low they do not cover production costs interferes with that important goal.

However, the issue of lifeline banking may not be that simple, because banks are not treated in public policy like other private firms. Entry into the banking industry is

The Expedited Funds Availability Act

Responding to thousands of complaints from depositors across the United States that many banks were delaying too long in giving their customers credit in their accounts after checks were deposited, Congress passed the Expedited Funds Availability Act in 1987. Congress mandated a time schedule that set maximum delays for receipt of deposit credit that banks could use, and it required banks to *inform* their customers about their policies for making funds available for customer use. Specifically:

1. All depository institutions must let customers use funds deposited in checking, share draft, or NOW accounts within a fixed number of days. The number of days must be spelled out in writing and displayed in the bank lobby.

2. The longest permissible time delays under federal law and regulation before customers can use deposited funds are as follows:
    a. The next business day after deposits are made—applies to deposits of cash; the first $100 of deposited checks; government, certified, or cashier's checks; checks drawn on another account at the same institution; deposits made electronically or otherwise made directly into the customer's account (unless deposited after a specific closing time, in which case the deposit is considered as being made the next day).
    b. The second business day after the deposit is made—applies to checks drawn on local institutions.
    c. The fifth business day after the deposit is made—applies to checks drawn on nonlocal institutions.
    d. Deposits made at an ATM not belonging to the customer's depository institution must be available on the same time schedule as other deposits.

regulated, with federal and state regulatory agencies compelled by law to consider "public convenience and needs" in permitting new banks to be established. Moreover, the Community Reinvestment Act of 1977 requires regulatory agencies to consider whether a banking organization applying to set up new branch offices or merge with another bank has really made an "affirmative effort" to serve *all* segments of the communities in which it operates.

This most recent legal requirement to fully serve the local community *may* include the responsibility to offer lifeline banking services. Moreover, banks receive important aid from the government that grants them a competitive advantage over other financial institutions. One of the most important of these aids is *deposit insurance,* in which the government guarantees most of the deposits banks sell. If banks benefit from deposit insurance backed ultimately by the public's taxes, do banks have a public responsibility to offer some services that are accessible to all? If yes, how should banks decide which customers should have access to low-price services? Should they insist on imposing a means test on their customers? The cost of producing services has to be borne by someone—Who should bear the cost of lifeline banking services? Answers to these questions are not readily apparent, but one thing is certain: These issues are not likely to go away. They will probably become even more important in the future.

Nondeposit Investment Products in Banking

As the 1990s unfolded many of banking's largest business and household depositors began moving their funds out of deposits at banks and thrift institutions into so-called **nondeposit investment products**—stocks, bonds, mutual funds, annuities, and similar financial instruments that seemed to promise better returns than are available on many conventional bank deposits. In addition, the 1990s ushered in a growing public concern over preparing for their retirement years with what might be inadequate savings to cover today's longer average lifespans. Then, too, yield curves became more steeply sloped, suggesting that longer-term financial assets (such as stocks and bonds) might ultimately deliver higher returns than most bank deposits, which last only a few weeks or months.

For example, between 1991 and 1997 (second quarter) checkable deposits held by U.S. households, farms, and noncorporate businesses rose by only $298 billion or just under 10 percent, as Table 12–6 shows. In contrast, direct corporate stockholdings by these groups rose nearly $2.8 trillion over the same time span (or about 109 percent), holdings of mutual funds shares jumped more than $1.2 trillion (or about 212 percent), and pension reserves climbed almost $1.9 trillion (approximately 73 percent). The willingness of traditional bank customers to convert many of their conservative investments in bank deposits (most of which are normally covered by federal insurance) into

TABLE 12–6   Growth of Deposits and Nondeposit Investment Products
(Sales to Households and Businesses in the U.S. Economy)

Financial Instrument Held	Billions of Dollars Acquired In:							Percentage Change 1991–1997*
	1991	*1992*	*1993*	*1994*	*1995*	*1996*	*1997**	
Checkable and time savings deposits at banks and other depository institutions	$3002.2	$3,029.4	$2,981.4	$2,959.3	$3,081.9	$3,212.2	$3,299.8	9.9%
Corporate stock **	2,577.9	2,923.2	3,216.6	3,059.9	4,086.1	4,651.3	5,377.7	108.6%
Mutual funds shares	586.6	727.9	990.9	1,047.4	1,247.8	1,582.9	1,827.4	211.5%
Private life insurance reserves	393.8	421.5	457.2	491.5	536.3	580.1	607.4	79.6%
Private pension fund reserves	2,548.1	2,726.1	3,055.3	3,186.5	3,755.8	4,079.9	4,410.0	73.1%
Investments in bank personal trusts	639.3	660.6	691.3	699.4	767.4	872.0	969.7	51.7%

Notes:*Through second quarter 1997.

**Includes only directly held stocks and those in closed-end mutual funds. Other equities are included in mutual funds, life insurance and pension reserves, and bank personal trusts.

Source: Board of Governors of the Federal Reserve System, *Flow of Funds Accounts of the United States,* Washington, D.C., second quarter, 1997.

uninsured stocks, mutual funds, annuities, and other investment products has caused banks to scramble to win back some of these deposits or, at least, to get their customers to let the bank carry out their purchases and sales of nondeposit investment products in return for fee income for the bank.

The most popular of the nondeposit investment products sold by banks recently have been shares in **mutual funds.** First set up in Great Britain in the 19th century, mutual funds came to the United States in the 1920s. Each share in a mutual fund permits an investor to receive a *pro rata* share of any dividends, interest payments, or other forms of income generated by a pool of stocks, bonds, or other securities that the fund holds. If a mutual fund is liquidated, each investor receives a portion of the total NAV (net asset value) of the fund after its liabilities are paid off, based on the number of shares each investor holds. Each fund has an announced investment purpose or objective (such as capital growth or the maximization of current income) and in the United States must register with the Securities and Exchange Commission (SEC) and provide investors with a prospectus describing its purpose, recent performance, and makeup.

Mutual funds have been very attractive to both individuals and institutional investors in the 1990s because their long-run yields appear to be relatively high and most funds are well diversified, spreading the investor's risk exposure across many different types of stocks, bonds, and other financial instruments. Mutual funds offer the advantage of having a professional money manager who monitors daily the performance of each security held by the fund and constantly looks for profitable trading opportunities. For many small investors, who have neither the expertise nor the time to constantly watch the market, access to professional money management services can be a significant advantage (though some authorities argue that mutual funds and other security brokers and dealers often engage in too much daily manipulation of security portfolios, running up their costs and reducing an investor's net return).

Most banks are involved in the mutual fund business in two different ways. First, larger banks may offer *proprietary funds* through one of their affiliated companies. In this case the banking firm's staff will advise the fund about trading opportunities and will buy and sell shares at the request of its customers, working through a securities firm affiliated with the bank. However, an unaffiliated company must organize the fund and underwrite (distribute) its shares to investors. Current U.S. regulations prohibit a bank from acting as an underwriter for mutual funds. However, banks are allowed to offer investment advice (normally the greatest source of fee income) and serve as transfer agent and custodian for mutual fund shares, keeping records of who owns shares and who is entitled to receive fund reports and earnings and executing the transactions dictated by the fund's investment adviser. Alternatively, banks may offer *nonproprietary funds,* in which the bank acts as a broker for an unaffiliated mutual fund or group of mutual funds but does *not* act as an investment advisor. Nonproprietary funds are organized, distributed, and managed by an unaffiliated nonbank company that may, however, rent lobby space inside a bank's branches or sell its shares through a broker who is related to the bank in some way. Usually the bank receives a fee or commission from nonproprietary funds sold from bank offices.

Some experts argue that proprietary funds have the advantage of providing a relatively continuous stream of income to a bank, while fee income generated by sales of nonproprietary funds may fluctuate and is often quite small. Some banks merely advertise access to nonproprietary funds without earning substantial fees from their sales. Nevertheless, advertising the availability of nonproprietary funds may serve to bring customers into the bank and hopefully lead to selling them other bank services.

Certainly banks offering their customers access to mutual funds and other security investments promises some real advantages for those banks able to offer these products. As we noted earlier, there is the possibility of earning substantial fee income for brokerage and other related services, and some of that fee income may be less sensitive to interest rate movements than are bank deposits and loans. (Most banks charge sales fees or "loads," either up front or when funds are withdrawn or remain with the bank over time.) In addition, many banks appear to gain added prestige from offering their own (proprietary) funds. Some bank CEOs argue that offering this service positions a bank well for the future, particularly with respect to those customers planning for their retirement and accumulating large amounts of savings.

A somewhat different bank investment product, **annuities,** come in either fixed or variable form. *Fixed annuities* promise a customer who contributes a lump sum of savings a fixed rate of return over the life of the annuity contract. The fixed-rate annuity generates a continuous level income stream to the customer or to his or her beneficiaries after a number of years have elapsed. Usually the customer pays no taxes on the annuity until he or she actually begins to receive the promised stream of income. *Variable annuities,* on the other hand, allow investors to invest a lump sum of money (perhaps $10,000 or more) in a basket of stocks, mutual funds, or other investments under a tax-deferred agreement, but there is no promise of a guaranteed or level rate of return. The customer can usually add more funds to the variable annuity contract as time goes by and then at some designated future point receive a stream of income payments whose amount is based upon the accumulated market value in the contract. If the prices of assets placed in the annuity's fund have declined in value, the customer (annuitant) may receive less income than expected. On the other hand, the annuitant may receive a larger income stream if the value of accumulated assets has risen. Most of these contracts also promise death benefits, so that if the customer dies, his or her heirs receive money based on the value of assets held in the contract. Some variable annuity contracts promise a *minimum* rate of return (often based on the amount of your initial investment) even if the market value of the contract's assets has fallen over time. One advantage for selling banks: variable annuities often carry substantial annual fees. An annuity is the reverse of life insurance; instead of hedging against dying too soon, annuities are a hedge against living too long and outlasting one's savings. Recently insurance companies have been working with banks to create proprietary variable annuities carrying the bank's label.

By 1997, nearly 1,500 U.S. banking organizations—about one-fifth of the banking industry—were selling third-party or proprietary mutual funds and/or annuity plans. Most of these sales (better than 90 percent) were made by multibillion-dollar banks—the industry's largest institutions. Unfortunately, not all of these bank product-line innovations have been particularly successful. For example, bank mutual fund and annuity sales have accounted recently for less than 5 percent of total bank fee (noninterest) income. Banks have been more successful at selling shares in low-risk money market (short-term) mutual funds than at selling shares in longer-term stock and bond mutual funds, due, in part, to the close affinity between money market fund shares and bank money market deposits. U.S. banks' share of equity and bond funds sales reached a high of about 8 percent of all mutual fund sales in 1994 and has fallen somewhat since that time.

In part, these disappointing sales of many bank investment products may be due to the appearance of record bank profits during much of the 1990s. With their earnings at record levels many banks felt less pressure to push hard on their investment products' sales. Bank sales fees also tend to be on the high side. At the same time regulators have placed bank sales of mutual funds and other investment products under intense scrutiny, while regulations applying to deposits (particularly deposit insurance fees and reserve requirements) have recently been lowered, making it more attractive and less costly to sell traditional deposits rather than the newer and more exotic savings instruments. Early in 1998 the Internal Revenue ruled against banks offering annuity-like deposits covered by federal insurance. Then, too, the start-up costs of mutual funds are high (especially the legal fees) and the minimum size fund needed to be really competitive may be $100 million or much more in total assets, larger than many bank funds.

Some banks have found other ways to profit from the public's strong interest in securities today, however, by serving as recordkeepers for and processors for security purchases and sales. Among the most famous of these institutions are the Bank of New York and the State Street Bank of Boston, which do such things as transferring the ownership of securities bought and sold, managing the foreign stocks purchased by U.S. investors, and accounting for mutual fund sales of new shares and the redemption of already issued shares.

There are several potential problems and risks associated with bank sales of nondeposit investment products. For one thing, their value is market determined and their performance can turn out to be highly disappointing, angering customers who may hold the bank to a higher standard of performance than it would a securities broker or dealer. Moreover, some banks have become embroiled in costly lawsuits filed by disappointed customers who allege that they were misled about the risks associated with nondeposit investment products. Banks may also run into *compliance* problems if they fail to properly register their nondeposit products' activities with the Securities and Exchange Commission or comply with all the rules laid down by bank regulatory agencies, state commissions, and other legal bodies that monitor this market.

Current U.S. regulations require that customers must be told orally (and sign a document indicating that they were informed) that nondeposit investment products are:

1. Not insured by the Federal Deposit Insurance Corporation (FDIC).
2. Not a deposit or other obligation of a bank and are not guaranteed by the bank.
3. Subject to investment risks, including possible loss of the principal value of the customer's investment.

These and other regulatory rules must be conspicuously displayed inside bank offices where nondeposit investment products are sold. Moreover, investment products must be sold in an office area that is separate from the area where deposits are taken from the public. Bankers must demonstrate to government examiners that they are closely monitoring their investment products' sales practices, literally policing themselves in order to avoid serious problems that may adversely affect the public's confidence in banks. Bankers must also have blanket bond insurance coverage for their retail nondeposit sales and make only those sales recommendations to customers that are "suitable" for each customer's situation and needs. Finally, bankers cannot adopt names for bank-related mutual funds that are similar to the bank or banking company's name, which might lead to confusion on the part of the public about the safety of investments in nondeposit products compared to the safety of deposits.

Concept Checks

12–7. What is *lifeline banking*? What pressures does it impose on bank managers?

12–8. What does the Expedited Funds Availability Act require U.S. banks to do?

12–9. How does the offering of trust services help a bank attract deposits? What special precautions must a bank take in receiving and managing customer deposits received through the trust department?

12–10. What are nondeposit investment products? What advantages do they give to a bank choosing to offer these products? What risks do these products pose for banks associated with them?

12–11. How has *regulation* impacted the sale of nondeposit investment products in banking? Do you believe the regulatory rules that currently guide banks' offering these products are really necessary?

Summary

Deposits are the vital input in banking—the principal source of financial capital to fund bank loans and security purchases and help generate profits to support long-term growth. In managing their deposits, bank managers must grapple with two key questions centered upon *cost* and *volume*. Which types of deposits will help minimize the bank's cost of fund-raising? How can the bank raise a volume of deposits adequate to meet its fund-raising needs?

The principal types of deposits offered by banks include: (1) *transaction,* or *payments,* accounts, which customers can use for drafting in order to pay for purchases of goods and services, and (2) *nontransaction (savings,* or *thrift*) deposits, which are held primarily as savings to prepare for future emergencies and for the expected yield they promise to the depositor. Transaction deposits include regular checking accounts, which typically bear no interest, and interest-bearing transaction deposits (such as NOWs), which pay at least a low interest yield and, in some cases, limit the number of checks that can be written against the account. Transaction deposits often are among the most profitable deposit services a bank can sell because of their nonexistent or low interest rate and the service fees these accounts usually carry. In contrast, nontransaction, or thrift, deposits generally have the advantage of a more stable funding base for the bank that allows it to reach for longer-term and higher-yielding assets. However, many nontransaction deposits carry higher interest costs for the bank which threaten to reduce bank profits. Unfortunately for many banks today, bank deposit composition is shifting toward more costly nontransaction and interest-bearing transaction deposits, forcing bankers to be more aware of what various funds sources are costing their institutions.

One of the most important sources of deposit business for many banks is the *trust department.* Banks offering trust services agree to manage the property of their trust customers, protecting those assets and earning a competitive rate of return on the assets entrusted to them by a customer. Many of the assets managed through the trust department are interest-bearing deposits, which must be fully protected by the bank through a combination of deposit insurance and the pledging of high-quality securities to back these deposits.

Bankers have discovered in recent years that there is a "social" dimension to their offering of deposit services. In recent years the issue of *lifeline banking* has become an important area of controversy between banks and various consumer groups. Lifeline banking refers to the offering of low-cost bank services (such as low-cost checking and savings plans) to members of local communities who cannot afford conventional banking services. While many banks contend that such services are often unprofitable, advocates of the lifeline banking concept frequently argue that banks "owe" their communities the offering of low-cost deposit and credit services because banks receive subsidized support from the government in the form of low-cost deposit insurance, reduced-rate loans from the central bank, and

other valuable services. This controversy is likely to go on for many years to come, and many banks are already responding by designing new products for lower-income customers.

Finally, in the 1990s banks in great numbers began to offer *nondeposit investment products* to their customers, responding to a great shift in the public's preferences away from traditional deposits into stocks, bonds, mutual funds, and annuities, to name the most popular. Many bank customers anticipated receiving higher returns on these uninsured assets and were willing to take on the added risk in the expectation of greater long-run returns. While banks generally gain few new funds from offering mutual funds, annuities, and other nondeposit products, these services may generate additional fee income in order to boost net earnings and help retain customers who might otherwise leave a bank and conduct their financial transactions through a nonbank financial institution (such as a securities broker or dealer).

Bankers have found that offering shares of stock in a mutual fund, long-term savings plans through an annuity program, and similar investment products can be a risky and high-cost venture. When these market-driven products lag in performance or even decline in value, their customers may hold the bank responsible. Moreover, a whole new set of regulations has emerged to make sure bankers are warning their customers of the risks inherent in these products, that none of these products are debt obligations of a bank, and that they are not insured by the government. Many banks have found their nondeposit investment sales have been well below expectations and that the costs and regulations involved have made many of these products unprofitable. However, some bank customers do appear to enjoy the convenience of being able to buy nondeposit investment products from their local bank rather than having to deal with separate financial institutions for each service they wish to buy.

Key Terms in This Chapter

Transaction deposit

NOW accounts

Money market deposit accounts

Super NOWs

Thrift deposits

Passbook savings deposits

Time deposits

Core deposits

Trust services

Basic (lifeline) banking

Nondeposit investment products

Mutual funds

Annuities

Problems and Projects

1. Exeter National Bank reports the following figures in its current Report of Condition:

Assets (millions)		*Liabilities (millions)*	
Cash and inter-		Core deposits	$ 50
bank deposits	$ 50	Large nego-	
Short-term		tiable CDs	150
security		Deposits placed	
investments	15	by brokers	65
Total loans, gross	375	Other deposits	140
Long-term		Money market	
securities	150	liabilities	95
Other assets	10	Other liabilities	70
Total assets	$600	Equity capital	30
		Total liabilities and	
		equity capital	$600

a. Evaluate the funding mix of deposits and nondeposit sources of funds employed by Exeter. Given the mix of its assets, do you see any potential problems? What changes would you like to see the management of this bank make? Why?

b. Suppose market interest rates are projected to rise significantly. Does Exeter appear to face significant losses due to liquidity risk? Due to interest rate risk? Please be as specific as possible.

2. Kalewood National Bank has experienced recent changes in the composition of its deposits (see the table below; all figures in millions of dollars). What changes have recently occurred in Kalewood's deposit mix? Do these recent changes suggest possible problems for management in trying to increase the bank's profitability and stabilize its earnings?

Types of Deposits Held by the Bank	This Year	One Year Ago	Two Years Ago	Three Years Ago
Regular and special checking accounts	$235	$294	$337	$378
Interest-bearing checking accounts	392	358	329	287
Regular (passbook) savings deposits	501	596	646	709
Money market deposit accounts	863	812	749	725
Retirement deposits	650	603	542	498
CDs under $100,000	327	298	261	244
CDs $100,000 and over	606	587	522	495

3. Cotter National Bank has recently subscribed through a New York money center bank to an investment products service for its customers. Cotter will offer nonproprietary mutual funds to its customers as well as a variable annuity program for those interested in accumulating savings for retirement and to help with the costs of a college education for their children. The bank's marketing officer is struggling with several important issues, however, and needs your input and advice. For example:

   a. As the bank likely to be better off offering a nonproprietary fund or should it attempt to help create a proprietary mutual fund service?

   b. What should Cotter do about setting up an investment products division within the bank to offer these two services? Are there any special requirements the bank needs to be aware of in designing the location of that new division, and how it will offer these services?

   c. What risks will the bank be confronted with when it actually begins offering these services? What kind of action plan might be designed to help minimize those risks and make Cotter National's program successful?

Selected References

For a discussion of recent trends in deposit services and customer use of those services see:

1. Avery, Robert B. "Survey of Consumer Finances, 1983." *Federal Reserve Bulletin 70* (September 1984), pp. 679–92.

2. Durkin, Thomas A., and Gregory E. Elliehausen. *1977 Consumer Credit Survey.* Washington, DC: Board of Governors of the Federal Reserve System, 1977.

3. Federal Reserve Banks. *Functional Cost and Profit Analysis: National Average Report, 1996.* Federal Reserve Bank of San Francisco, 1997.

4. Rose, Peter S. "Pricing Deposits in an Era of Competition and Change." *The Canadian Banker* 93, no. 1 (February 1986), pp. 44–51.

5. ———. "Defensive Banking in a Volatile Economy." *The Canadian Banker* 92, no. 5 (April 1986), pp. 44–49.

For a detailed discussion of bank trust services, see:

6. Reed, Edward W., Richard V. Cotter, Edward K. Gill, and Richard K. Smith. *Commercial Banking,* 2nd ed. Englewood Cliffs, NJ: Prentice Hall, 1980.

For a discussion of the advantages and disadvantages for banks offering nondeposit investment products see:

7. Federal Reserve System. *Retail Sales of Nondeposit Investment Products: Compliance Checklists.* Washington, D.C., July 1995.

8. Golter, Jay W. "Banks and Mutual Funds." *FDIC Banking Review,* August 1995, pp. 10–20.

9. Neely, Michelle Clark. "Banks and Mutual Funds: Hype or Hope?" *Monetary Trends.* Federal Reserve Bank of St. Louis, March 1997.

10. Collins, Sean, and Phillip Mack. *Will Bank Proprietary Mutual Funds Survive? Assessing Their Viability Via Scope and Scale Estimates,* Finance and Discussion Series 95-52, Board of Governors of the Federal Reserve System, December 1995.

For a discussion of the issues surrounding lifeline banking services, see:

11. Canner, Glenn B., and Ellen Maland. "Basic Banking." *Federal Reserve Bulletin,* April 1987, pp. 255–69.

13 PRICING DEPOSIT-RELATED SERVICES

Learning and Management Decision Objectives

The purpose of this chapter is to see how a bank's cost of funding can be determined and the different methods open to banks to price the deposit and deposit-related services they sell to the public.

Introduction

In pricing deposit-related services—the most important source of funding for most banks today—management is caught between the horns of an old dilemma. It needs to pay a high enough interest return to customers to attract and hold their funds, but must avoid paying an interest rate that is so costly it erodes any potential profit margin from using customer funds. Intense competition in today's markets compounds this dilemma, because competition tends to raise deposit interest costs while lowering expected returns to a bank from putting its deposits and other funds to work.[1]

In fact, in a financial marketplace that closely approaches perfect competition, the individual bank has little control over its prices in the long run. It is the marketplace, *not* the individual bank, that ultimately sets all prices. In such a market, bank management must decide if it wishes to attract more deposits and hold all those it currently has by offering depositors at least the market-determined price, or whether it is willing to lose funds by offering customers terms different from what the market requires. Often bank managers must choose between growth and profitability. Aggressive competition for costly deposits and other sources of funds will help the bank grow faster, but often at the price of severe profit erosion.

---

[1]Portions of this chapter are based upon the author's recent articles [9, 10] in the *Canadian Banker* and are used with the permission of the publisher.

Pricing Deposits at Cost Plus Profit Margin

The idea of charging the customer for the *total cost* of deposit-related services has not been universally accepted in banking. In fact, until a few years ago the notion that customers should receive most deposit-related services *free* of charge was hailed as a wise innovation—one that responded to the growing challenge posed by other financial intermediaries that were invading traditional banking markets. Many banks soon found reason to question the wisdom of this new marketing strategy, however, because they were flooded with numerous low-balance, high-activity accounts that ballooned their operating costs.

The development of interest-bearing checkable deposits, particularly NOWs, offered bankers the opportunity to reconsider the pricing of their deposit services. Unfortunately, many of the early entrants into this new market moved aggressively to capture a major share of the customers through *below-cost pricing.* Customer charges were set below the true level of operating and overhead costs associated with providing checkable deposits and other deposit plans. The result was a substantially increased rate of return to the customer, known as the *implicit interest rate*—the difference between the true cost of supplying fund-raising services and the service charges actually assessed the customer.

In the United States, variations in the implicit interest rate paid to the customer were the principal way most banks competed for deposits over a period of 50 years stretching from the Great Depression to the beginning of the 1980s. This was due to the presence of regulatory ceilings on deposit interest rates, beginning in 1933 with passage of the Glass-Steagall Act. These legal interest rate ceilings were designed to protect banks from excessive interest rate competition for deposits, which could allegedly cause them to fail. Prevented from offering higher explicit interest rates, U.S. banks competed instead by offering higher implicit returns with bank-by-mail services in which the bank promised to pay the postage both ways, by tempting depositors with gifts ranging from teddy bears to toasters, and by building convenient neighborhood branch office systems.

Unfortunately, such forms of *nonprice competition* tended to distort the allocation of scarce resources in the banking sector. Congress finally responded to these problems with passage of the Depository Institutions Deregulation Act of 1980, a federal law that called for a gradual phaseout of deposit rate ceilings. Today, the responsibility for setting deposit prices in the United States (and in other leading industrialized nations as well) has been transferred from public regulators to private decision makers—that is, to banks and their customers.

Deregulation has brought more frequent use of *unbundled* service pricing as greater competition, along with rising insurance fees, has raised the average cost of a deposit for bankers. This means, for example, that deposits are usually priced *separately* from loans and other bank services. And each deposit service is often priced high enough to recover all or most of the cost of providing that service. Thus, the price of deposit services would conform to the following **cost-plus-profit deposit pricing** formula:

$$
\begin{array}{c}
\text{Unit price} \\
\text{charged the} \\
\text{customer for each} \\
\text{deposit service}
\end{array}
=
\begin{array}{c}
\text{Operating} \\
\text{expense} \\
\text{per unit of} \\
\text{deposit service}
\end{array}
+
\begin{array}{c}
\text{Estimated overhead} \\
\text{expense allocated} \\
\text{to the bank's} \\
\text{deposit function}
\end{array}
+
\begin{array}{c}
\text{Planned profit} \\
\text{from each deposit} \\
\text{service unit sold}
\end{array}
$$

Tying deposit pricing to bank costs, as the above formula does, has encouraged bankers everywhere to *match* prices and costs more closely and to eliminate many formerly free services. In the United States, for example, more and more banks are now levying fees for excessive withdrawals from savings deposits, charging for customer balance inquiries, increasing fees on bounced checks and stop-payment orders, assessing charges on cash withdrawals and balance inquires made through ATMs, charging monthly maintenance fees even on small savings deposits, and raising required minimum deposit balances. In most cases, these fees appear to have climbed faster than the rate of inflation. The results of these trends have generally been favorable to banks, with increases in service fee income outstripping losses from angry customers closing their accounts.

Estimating Average Deposit Service Costs

Cost-plus pricing demands an accurate calculation of the cost of each deposit service. How can this be done? One popular approach, discussed by Simonson and Marks [12, 13] and by Edmister [5], is to base deposit prices on the bank's estimated cost of funds. This requires the banker (1) to calculate the *cost rate* of each source of bank funds (adjusted for reserves required by the central bank, deposit insurance fees, and float); (2) to multiply each cost rate by the relative proportion of bank funds coming from that particular source; and (3) to sum all resulting products to derive the weighted average cost of bank funds. This so-called *pooled-funds approach* is based on the assumption that it is not the cost of each type of deposit that matters, but rather the weighted average cost of *all* bank funding sources.

An Example of Pooled-Funds Costing

Let's consider an example of the pooled-funds cost approach. Suppose a bank has raised a total of $400 million, including $100 million in checkable deposits, $200 million in time and savings deposits, $500 million borrowed from the money market, and $50 million from its owners in the form of equity capital. Suppose that interest and noninterest costs spent to attract the checkable deposits total 10 percent of the amount of these deposits, while thrift deposits and money market borrowings each cost the bank 11 percent of funds raised in interest and noninterest expenses. Owners' equity is the most expensive funding source for most banks; assume that equity capital costs the bank an estimated 22 percent of any new equity raised. Suppose reserve requirements, deposit insurance fees, and uncollected balances (float) reduce the amount of money actually available to the bank for investing in interest-bearing assets by 15 percent for checkbook deposits, 5 percent for thrift deposits, and 2 percent

Summary of Deposit Insurance Coverage Provided in the U.S. by the FDIC

A major reason banks are able to sell deposits at relatively low rates of interest compared to interest rates offered on other financial instruments is because of the existence of government-supplied deposit insurance. The **Federal Deposit Insurance Corporation (FDIC)** was established by the U.S. Congress in 1933 to insure bank deposits and protect the nation's money supply in those cases where banks and other depository institutions having FDIC membership failed. Today this federal corporation insures the deposits of banks through its Bank Insurance Fund (BIF) and insures the deposits of savings associations through its Savings Association Insurance Fund (SAIF), both of which are backed by the full faith and credit of the U.S. government. Insured depository institutions must display an official sign at each teller window or teller station, indicating that they hold an FDIC membership certificate.

FDIC insurance covers only those deposits payable in the United States, though the depositor does *not* have to be a U.S. citizen or resident to receive FDIC protection. All types of deposits normally are covered up to $100,000 for each single account holder. Savings deposits, checking accounts, NOW accounts, Christmas Club accounts, time deposits, cashiers' checks, money orders, officers' checks, and any outstanding bank drafts normally are protected by federal insurance. Certified checks, letters of credit, and travelers' checks for which an insured depository institution is primarily liable also are insured if these are issued in exchange for money or in return for a charge against a deposit. On the other hand, U.S. government securities, shares in mutual funds, safe deposit boxes, and funds stolen from an insured depository are *not* covered by FDIC insurance. Banks generally carry private insurance against losses due to fire, storm damage, and theft, fraud, or other crimes.

Deposits placed in separate financial institutions (including different banks that belong to the same holding company) are insured separately, each eligible for insurance coverage up to $100,000 per depositor. However, deposits held in more than one branch office of the *same* depository institution are added together to determine the total amount of insurance protection available. In this case the depositor can receive no more than $100,000 in insurance protection. If two formerly independent banks merge, for example, and a depositor holds $100,000 in each of these two banks, the total protection afforded this depositor would then be a maximum of $100,000, not $200,000, as it was before the merger. However, the FDIC normally allows a grace period (e.g., six months) so that, for a short time, a depositor with large deposits in two banks that merge can receive expanded coverage up to $200,000 until arrangements can be made to transfer some of the depositor's funds to other banks in order to gain more insurance protection.

Insurance coverage can also be increased at a single banking institution by placing funds under different categories of legal ownership. For example, a single depositor with

$100,000 in a savings deposit and another $100,000 in a time deposit might achieve $200,000 in insurance coverage by making one of these two accounts a *joint ownership account* with his or her spouse. Also, if a family is composed of husband and wife plus one child, for example, each family member could own an account and each pair of family members (e.g., husband and wife, husband and child, and wife and child) could also hold joint accounts, resulting in FDIC insurance coverage up to $600,000 in total. Only natural persons, not corporations or partnerships, can set up FDIC insurance-eligible joint accounts, however.

Each co-owner of a joint account is assumed to have *equal* right of withdrawal and is also assumed to own an equal share of a joint account unless otherwise stated in the account record. No one person's total insured interest in all joint accounts at the same insured depository institution can exceed $100,000. For example, suppose Mr. Jones has a joint account with Mrs. Jones amounting to $120,000. Then each is presumed to have a $60,000 share and each would have FDIC insurance coverage of $60,000 unless the deposit record at the bank specifically shows that, for example, Mrs. Jones owns $100,000 of the $120,000 balance and Mr. Jones owns just $20,000. In this instance Mrs. Jones would receive the full $100,000 in insurance protection and Mr. Jones would be covered for a maximum of $20,000.

In addition, a husband or wife could set up a testamentary trust account (sometimes called a revocable trust or payable-on-death account). Testamentary deposits are insured separately from single owner and joint ownership accounts provided they meet certain requirements:

1. The designated beneficiary in case of the owner's death must be the owner's spouse, child, or grandchild (including any adopted children or stepchildren).

2. The owner's intention to transfer control of the funds in the trust to the beneficiary must be reflected in the account's title, which must say "in trust for" or "as trustee for" or "payable-on-death."

3. All beneficiaries must be specifically identified *by name* on the record books of the depository (instead of being listed as a general class of beneficiaries—e.g., "all the children"). Each owner of a trust account fulfilling the above requirements has FDIC protection up to $100,000 per beneficiary. Additional insurance coverage can be obtained by setting up testamentary trust accounts with co-owners (e.g., husband and wife in trust for each of their children). If a co-owner of such an account dies, however, insurance coverage decreases. Irrevocable trust accounts can also be set up and are insured up to $100,000 separately from the other deposits held by the grantor, trustee, or beneficiary provided the account is properly labeled, the interest of each beneficiary can be determined, and the trust is valid under state law.

Summary of Deposit Insurance Coverage Provided in the U.S. by the FDIC—*continued*

After December 19, 1993, IRA and Keogh retirement deposits become separately insured from nonretirement deposits. All retirement accounts are added together for a maximum amount of insurance protection of $100,000. Deposits belonging to pension and profit-sharing plans receive "pass-through insurance" up to $100,000 per beneficiary, provided the participants' beneficial interests are ascertainable and the depository institution involved is at least "adequately capitalized" and is eligible to take deposits placed by brokers on behalf of their customers. Otherwise, "pass-through insurance" is not available on pension and profit-sharing plans, which then would receive no more than $100,000 in total FDIC insurance protection for all participants.

Funds deposited by a corporation, partnership, or unincorporated business or association (including all of its departments or divisions) are insured up to $100,000 and are insured separately from the personal accounts of the company's stockholders, partners, or members. Funds deposited by a sole proprietor of a business are considered to be personal funds, however, and are added to any other single-owner accounts the individual business owner has, and are protected only up to $100,000 in total.

The amount of insurance premiums that each FDIC-insured depository must pay is determined by the volume of deposits it receives from the public and by the insurance rate category in which each institution falls. Under the new risk-based deposit insurance system begun in the United States in 1993 (as mandated by the FDIC Improvement Act of 1991) more risky banks (that is, those that present greater risk of loss to the FDIC) must pay higher insurance premiums. The degree of risk exposure is determined by the interplay of two factors: (1) the adequacy of capital maintained by each depository institution; and (2) the risk class in which the institution is judged to be by its regulatory supervisors. There are three classes of capitalization—well capitalized, adequately capitalized, and undercapitalized—and three supervisory risk categories—A, B, and C. The well-capitalized, A-rated depositories pay the lowest deposit insurance fee per each $100 of deposit they hold, while the undercapitalized, C-rated institutions pay the greatest insurance fees.

for borrowings in the money market. Therefore, this bank's weighted average before-tax cost of funds would be:

$$(\text{Checkbook deposits} \div \text{Total funds raised}) \times$$

$$\left(\frac{\text{Interest and noninterest fund-raising costs}}{100 \text{ percent} - \text{Percentage reserve requirements and float}} \right)$$

$$+$$

$$(\text{Time and savings deposits} \div \text{Total funds raised}) \times$$

$$\left(\frac{\text{Interest and noninterest fund-raising costs}}{100 \text{ percent} - \text{Percentage reserve requirements and float}} \right)$$

$$+$$

Twice each year the board of directors of the FDIC must decide what deposit insurance rates to assess each insured bank and thrift institution. An example of a recent fee schedule posted by the FDIC for BIF-insured institutions is shown below:

**Deposit Insurance Rate Schedule Assessed
by the FDIC for the First Six Months of 1998**
(All Insurance Rates are Quoted in Cents per $100)

	Supervisory Risk Subgroups		
Capital Groups	*Group A*	*Group B*	*Group C*
Well capitalized	0¢	3¢	17¢
Adequate capitalization	3	10	24
Undercapitalized	10	24	27

According to the above schedule the least risky depositories (risk group A, and well capitalized) paid a zero deposit insurance rate during the second six months of 1996, while the most risky institutions (risk group C, and undercapitalized) paid a rate of 27 cents per each $100 of deposits held for half a year's insurance coverage. How were these insurance rates determined? The FDIC uses its judgment and must take into account legally imposed insurance reserve requirements spelled out by Congress (in this case, by the FDIC Improvement Act of 1991). These insurance reserve requirements stipulate that the FDIC must hold a reserve of $1.25 per each $100 of insured deposits. If the federal insurance fund falls below $1.25 in reserves per $100 in covered deposits (known as the Designated Reserve Ratio [DRR]), the FDIC will raise its insurance assessment fees. When the amount of reserves exceeds the $1.25 per $100 standard, fees will be lowered or eliminated. For example, at year-end 1995 the Bank Insurance Fund (BIF) had a DRR of $1.30 per $100, so most banks (about 9,600) were assessed a zero insurance fee, while close to 700 riskier banks paid fees ranging from 3 cents to 27 cents per $100, as shown in the table above.

Source: Federal Deposit Insurance Corporation.

(Owners' capital ÷ Total funds raised) ×

(Interest and noninterest costs ÷ 100 percent)

= $100 million ÷ $400 million × 10 percent ÷ (100 percent − 15 percent) +

$200 million ÷ $400 million × 11 percent ÷ (100 percent − 5 percent)

+ $50 million ÷ $400 million × 11 percent ÷ (100 percent − 2 percent)

+ $50 million ÷ $400 million × 22 percent ÷ 100 percent

= 0.1288, or 12.88 percent of funds raised

In this example, the bank's management will want to make sure it earns at least a before-tax of rate of return of 12.88 percent on its portfolio of loans and other earning assets. If the bank can earn more from its loans and investments than 12.88 percent before taxes, the extra return (less taxes) will flow to the stockholders in the form of increased dividends and into retained earnings to strengthen the bank's capital.

The pooled-funds cost approach provides bank managers with a way to calculate the effects of any change in bank funding costs or deposit prices. For example, management can experiment with alternative deposit terms (interest rates, fees, and minimum balance requirements) for any deposit plan the bank offers and estimate their impact on funding costs. Of course, bank managers cannot safely price deposits without knowing how low customer balances can go and still be profitable for the bank. Overly generous pricing terms can set in motion substantial account shifting by customers, leading to a sharp increase in the cost of funds without significantly increasing total funds available to the bank.

Using Marginal Cost to Set Interest Rates on Deposits

Many financial analysts would argue that, whenever possible, *marginal cost*—the added cost of bringing in *new* funds—and not weighted average cost, should be used to help price deposits and other bank funds sources. The reason is that frequent changes in interest rates will make average cost a treacherous and unrealistic standard for pricing. For example, if interest rates are declining, the added (marginal) cost of raising new money may fall well below the average cost over all funds raised by the bank. Some loans and investments that looked unprofitable when compared to average cost will now look quite profitable when measured against the lower marginal interest cost we must pay today to make those new loans and investments. Conversely, if interest rates are on the rise, the marginal cost of today's new money may substantially exceed the bank's average cost of funds. If management books new loans based on average cost, they may turn out to be highly unprofitable when measured against the higher marginal cost of raising new funds in today's market.

Indeed, as Sanford Rose [11] reports, one of the most highly publicized failures in banking history—the 1974 collapse of Franklin National Bank of New York—was caused in part by a management strategy that compared the expected yield on new loan requests to the bank's average cost of funds. If the new loan's yield appeared to exceed Franklin's average cost by one percentage point or more, loan officers were instructed to grant the loan. Unfortunately, when interest rates on new borrowings (marginal cost) rose sharply, Franklin's 0.5 percent profit margin over average cost was just too thin. Huge quantities of its loans and investments were generating yields well below their current funding costs. These losses eventually eroded Franklin's capital base.

Economist James E. McNulty [14] has suggested a way to use the *marginal,* or *new money,* cost idea to help a bank set the interest rates it will offer on new deposit accounts.[2] To understand McNulty's recommended marginal cost pricing method,

---

[2]See also Watson [15] for a further discussion of marginal cost pricing for banks.

suppose a bank expects to raise $25 million in new deposits by offering its depositors an interest rate of 7 percent. Management estimates that if the bank offers a 7.50 percent interest rate, it can raise $50 million in new deposit money. At 8 percent, $75 million is expected to flow in, while a posted deposit rate of 8.5 percent will bring in a projected $100 million. Finally, if the bank promises an estimated 9 percent yield, management projects that $125 million in new funds will appear in the form of both new deposits and existing deposits that customers will keep in the bank to take advantage of the higher rates offered. Let's assume as well that management believes it can invest the new deposit money at a yield of 10 percent. This new loan yield represents *marginal revenue*—the added operating revenue the bank will generate by making new loans from the new deposits. Given these facts, what deposit interest rate should the bank offer its customers?

As Table 13–1 shows, based on McNulty's [14] method, we need to know at least two crucial items to answer this deposit rate question: the *marginal cost* of moving the deposit rate from one level to another and the *marginal cost rate,* expressed as a percentage of the volume of additional funds coming into the bank. Once we know the marginal cost rate, we can compare it to the expected additional revenue (marginal revenue) the bank expects to earn from investing its new deposits. The two items we need to know are the following:

$$\text{Marginal cost} = \text{Change in total cost} = \text{New interest rate} \times \text{Total funds}$$

raised at new rate − Old interest rate × Total funds raised at old rate

and

$$\text{Marginal cost rate} = \frac{\text{Change in total cost}}{\text{Additional funds raised}}$$

For example, if the bank raises its offer rate on new deposits from 7 percent to 7.5 percent, Table 13–1 shows the marginal cost of this change: Change in total

---

TABLE 13–1 Using Marginal Cost to Choose the Interest Rate to Offer Customers on Deposits

Expected Amounts of Deposits that Will Flow In	*Average Interest the Bank Will Pay on New Funds*	*Total Interest Cost of New Funds Raised*	*Marginal Cost of New Deposit Money*	*Marginal Cost as a Percentage of New Funds Attracted (marginal cost rate)*	*Expected Marginal Revenue (return) from Investing the New Funds*	*Difference between Marginal Revenue and Marginal Cost Rate*	*Total Profits Earned (after interest cost)*
$ 25	7.0%	$ 1.75	$1.75	7.0%	10.0%	+3%	$0.75
50	7.5	3.75	2.00	8.0	10.0	+2%	1.25
75	8.0	6.00	2.25	9.0	10.0	+1%	1.50
100	8.5	8.50	2.50	10.0	10.0	+0	1.50
125	9.0	11.25	2.75	11.0	10.0	−1%	1.25

Note: Figures in millions except percentages.

Figuring the Cost of Bank Deposits and Other Borrowed Funds

The Historical Average Cost Approach   This approach for determining how much bank funds cost looks at the *past*. It asks: what funds has the bank raised to date and what did they cost?

Sources of Funds Drawn Upon	Average Amount of Funds Raised by the Bank (millions)	Average Rate of Interest Incurred	Total Interest Paid by Banks for Each Funds Source (millions)
Noninterest-bearing demand deposits	$100	0%	$ 0
Interest-bearing transaction deposits	200	7%	14
Savings accounts	100	5%	5
Time deposits	500	8%	40
Money market borrowings	100	6%	6
Total funds raised = $1,000		All interest costs = $65	

Then the average interest cost of deposits and money market borrowings is:

$$\frac{\text{Weighted average}}{\text{interest expense}} = \frac{\text{All interest paid}}{\text{Total funds raised}} = \frac{65}{1,000} = 6.5 \text{ percent}$$

But other operating costs, such as salaries and overhead, are incurred to attract deposits. If these are an estimated $10 million, we have:

$$\begin{array}{l}\text{Break-even cost} \\ \text{rate on borrowed} \\ \text{funds invested} \\ \text{in earning assets}\end{array} = \frac{\text{Interest} + \text{Other operating costs}}{\text{All earning assets}} = \frac{\$65 + \$10}{\$750} = 10 \text{ percent}$$

This cost rate is called *break even* because the bank must earn at least this rate on its earning assets (primarily loans and securities) just to meet the total operating costs of raising borrowed funds. But what about the bank's stockholders and their required rate of return (assumed here to be 12 percent after taxes)?

$$\begin{array}{l}\text{Weighted} \\ \text{average} \\ \text{overall} \\ \text{cost of} \\ \text{capital}\end{array} = \begin{array}{l}\text{Break-even} \\ \text{cost on} \\ \text{borrowed} \\ \text{funds}\end{array} + \begin{array}{l}\text{Before-tax cost of} \\ \text{stockholders'} \\ \text{investment} \\ \text{in the bank}\end{array}$$

$$= \begin{array}{l}\text{Break-even} \\ \text{cost}\end{array} + \frac{\begin{array}{l}\text{After-tax cost of} \\ \text{stockholders'} \\ \text{investment}\end{array}}{(1 - \text{Tax rate})} \times \frac{\text{Stockholders'}}{\text{investment}}{\text{Earning assets}}$$

$$= 10 \text{ percent} + \frac{12 \text{ percent}}{(1-0.35)} \times \frac{\$100}{\$750} = 10 \text{ percent} + 2.5 \text{ percent}$$

$$= 12.5 \text{ percent}$$

Thus, 12.5 percent is the lowest rate of return over *all* fund-raising costs that the bank can afford to earn on its assets if its shareholders invest $100 million in the bank.

The Pooled-Funds Approach

This method of costing bank funds looks at the *future:* What minimum rate of return are we going to have to earn on any future loans and security investments just to cover the cost of all *new* funds raised? Suppose our estimate for future funding sources and funding costs is as follows:

Profitable New Deposits and Nondeposit Borrowings	Dollars of New Deposit and Nondeposit Borrowings (millions)	Fraction of New Borrowings that Will Be Placed in New Earning Assets	Dollar Amount that Can Be Placed in Earning Assets (millions)	Interest Expense and Other Operating Expenses of Borrowing Relative to Amounts Raised	All Operating Expenses Incurred (millions)
Interest-bearing transaction deposits	$100	50%	$ 50	8%	$ 8
Time deposits	100	60%	60	9%	9
New stockholders' investment in the bank	100	90%	90	13%	13
Total	$300		$200		$30

The overall cost of new deposits and other borrowing sources must be

$$\begin{array}{c}\text{Pooled} \\ \text{deposit and} \\ \text{nondeposit} \\ \text{funds expense}\end{array} = \frac{\begin{array}{c}\text{All expected} \\ \text{operating expenses}\end{array}}{\begin{array}{c}\text{All new} \\ \text{funds expected}\end{array}} = \frac{\$30 \text{ million}}{\$300 \text{ million}} = 10 \text{ percent}$$

But because only two-thirds of these expected new funds ($200 million out of $300 million raised) will actually be available to acquire earning assets,

$$\begin{array}{c}\text{Hurdle} \\ \text{rate over} \\ \text{the bank's total} \\ \text{earning assets}\end{array} = \frac{\begin{array}{c}\text{All expected} \\ \text{operating costs}\end{array}}{\begin{array}{c}\text{Dollars available} \\ \text{to place in} \\ \text{earning assets}\end{array}} = \frac{\$30 \text{ million}}{\$200 \text{ million}} = 15 \text{ percent}$$

Thus, the bank must earn *at least* 15 percent (before taxes), on average, on all the *new* funds it invests to fully meet its expected fund-raising costs.

cost = $50 million × 7.5 percent – $25 million × 7 percent = $3.75 million – $1.75 million = $2.00 million. The marginal cost rate, then, is the change in total cost divided by the additional funds raised, or:

$$\frac{\$2 \text{ million}}{\$25 \text{ million}} = 8 \text{ percent}$$

Notice that the marginal cost rate at 8 percent is substantially above the average deposit cost of 7.5 percent. This happens, not only because the bank must pay a rate of 7.5 percent to attract the second $25 million, but it must also pay out the same 7.5 percent rate to those depositors who were willing to contribute the first $25 million at only 7 percent.

Because the bank expects to earn 10 percent on these new deposit funds, marginal revenue exceeds marginal cost by 2 percent at a deposit interest cost of 8 percent. Clearly, the new deposits will add more to revenue than they will add to cost. The bank is clearly justified (assuming its projections are right) in offering a deposit rate at least as high as 7.5 percent. Its total profit will equal the difference between total revenue ($50 million × 10 percent = $5 million) and total cost ($50 million × 7.5 percent = $3.75 million), for a profit of $1.25 million.

Scanning down Table 13–1, we note that the bank continues to improve its total profits, with marginal revenue exceeding marginal cost, up to a deposit interest rate of 8.5 percent. At that rate the bank raises $100 million in new deposit money at a marginal cost rate of 10 percent, matching its expected marginal revenue of 10 percent. There, total profit tops out at $1.5 million. It would *not* pay the bank to go beyond this point, however. For example, if a deposit rate of 9 percent is offered, the marginal cost rate balloons upward to 11 percent, which exceeds marginal revenue by a full percentage point. Attracting new deposits at a 9 percent offer rate adds more to bank cost than to its revenue. Note, too, that total profits at a 9 percent deposit rate fall back to $1.25 million. The 8.5 percent deposit rate is clearly the *best* choice for the bank, given all the assumptions and forecasts it has made.

The marginal cost approach provides valuable information to bank managers, not only about setting deposit interest rates, but also about deciding just how far the bank should go in expanding its deposit base before the added cost of deposit growth catches up with additional revenues, and total profits begin to decline. When profits start to fall, management needs either to find new sources of funding with lower marginal costs, or to identify new loans and investments promising greater marginal revenues, or both.

Market-Penetration Deposit Pricing

A pricing method that does not emphasize profits and cost recovery, at least in the short run, is **market-penetration deposit pricing.** The idea here is to offer high interest rates—usually well above market levels—or charge customer fees well below market standards in order to bring in as many new customers as possible. Management hopes that the resulting larger deposit volume and the associated loan business brought in will offset a thinner profit margin. Market-penetration pricing is a strategy aimed primarily at rapidly growing markets in which a bank is determined to capture the largest possible market share.

Implicit here is a concept, suggested by Flannery [6], that identifying a bank to hold one's deposit account is an expensive process for most customers. After all, the customer usually buys more than one banking service. A deposit account represents an ongoing relationship between customer and bank that usually grows to encompass loans, trust services, and so on. Tearing up this relationship can be costly for the customer, a fact that tends to make many customers loyal to the bank they have already chosen. Thus, deposits tend to be *quasi-fixed factors of production* for banks. They are usually less sensitive than other funds sources to changes in fees or interest rates or to deposit plans offered by competing banks. If the bank can offer an above-market rate of return to the depositor long enough to capture his or her deposit, the high cost of moving that deposit will tend to keep the customer loyal to the bank even after less-generous deposit pricing occurs.

Incidentally, the fixed-factor aspect of deposits is one reason bankers often get a disappointing response from the public when they start reducing fees or raising interest rates to attract *new* deposits. Customers do not change banks on the spur of the moment—the costs and risks associated with that change are *not* trivial. Both households and businesses consider multiple factors, not just price, in deciding where to place their deposits, as two recent studies prepared at the Federal Reserve Board and another by Greenwich Associates suggest. As shown in Table 13–2, these studies suggest that households generally rank convenience, service availability, and safety above price in choosing which bank will hold their *checking account.* Moreover, familiarity (which may represent not only name recognition but also safety) ranks above the interest rate

---

TABLE 13–2   Factors in Household and Business Customers' Choice of a Bank for Deposit Accounts

(ranked from most important to least important)

In Choosing a Bank to Hold Their Checking Accounts, Households Consider	*In Choosing a Bank to Hold Their Savings Deposits, Households Consider*	*In Choosing a Bank to Supply Their Deposits and Other Services, Business Firms Consider*
1. Convenient location.	1. Familiarity.	1. Financial health of lending institution.
2. Availability of many other services.	2. Interest rate paid.	2. Whether bank will be a reliable source of credit in the future.
3. Safety.	3. Transactional convenience (not location).	3. Quality of bank officers.
4. Low fees and low minimum balance.	4. Location.	4. Whether loans are competitively priced.
5. High deposit interest rates.	5. Availability of payroll deduction.	5. Quality of financial advice given.
	6. Fees charged.	6. Whether cash management and operations services are provided.

Source: Based on studies by the Federal Reserve Board, *Survey of Consumer Finances,* 1983; Glenn B. Canner and Robert D. Kuntz, *Service Charges as a Source of Bank Income and Their Impact on Consumers,* Board of Governors of the Federal Reserve System, 1986; and Greenwich Associates, *Commercial Banking,* 1987, Greenwich, Connecticut.

The National Depositor Preference Law

On August 10, 1993, the U.S. Congress passed the Omnibus Budget Reconciliation Act, a portion of which amended the Federal Deposit Insurance Corporation Act to give greater priority to the claims of depositors if a bank fails. Under the 1993 law depositors (and, therefore, the FDIC) have a claim against a failed bank's assets superior to the claims of general creditors. The idea is to decrease the FDIC's expected losses (i.e., payouts to depositors) when a bank fails. In effect, the new law improves the priority (and, therefore, the safety) of larger deposits (above $100,000) not fully protected by deposit insurance and may cause nondeposit general creditors to demand more collateral before lending money to a bank, helping to force a banking firm to be more cautious about accepting additional risk. Unfortunately, there is very little evidence that earlier depositor preference laws passed by some states generated the benefits expected, such as reducing the costs of resolving bank failures or generating greater market discipline to keep banks from taking on additional risk.

paid as an important factor in how individuals and families choose a bank to hold their savings account. Business firms, on the other hand, prefer to leave their deposits with banks that will be reliable sources of credit and, relatedly, are in good financial shape. They also rate highly the quality of a bank's officers and the quality of advice they receive from the banker. Recent research suggests that bankers need to do a better job of letting their customers know about the cost pressures they face today and why they need to charge fully and fairly for any services that customers use.

Establishing Price Schedules to Segment Deposit Customers

The appearance of interest-bearing checking accounts in the New England states during the 1970s led to fierce competition for customer transaction deposits among banks and nonbank thrift institutions across the United States. Out of that boiling competitive cauldron came widespread use of **deposit fee schedules.** Some economists call this approach *conditional pricing* because the bank sets up a schedule of fees in which the customer pays a low fee or even no fee if the deposit balance remains *above* some minimum level, but a higher fee is assessed if the average balance falls *below* that minimum. Thus, the customer pays a price conditioned on how he or she uses the deposit.

Deposit fee schedules vary deposit prices according to one or more of these factors:

1. The number of transactions passing through the account (e.g., number of checks written, deposits made, wire transfers, stop-payment orders, or notices of insufficient funds issued).
2. The average balance held in the account over a designated period (usually per month).
3. The maturity of the deposit in days, weeks, or months.

The customer selects that bank and deposit plan that results in the lowest fees possible and/or the maximum yields, given the number of checks he or she plans to write, the number of deposits and withdrawals expected, and the planned average balance.

Of course, the bank must also be acceptable to the customer from the standpoint of safety, convenience, and service availability.

Economist Constance Dunham [4] classified checking account price schedules observed in the New England area into three categories: (1) flat-rate pricing, (2) free pricing, and (3) conditionally free pricing. In *flat-rate pricing,* the depositor's cost is a fixed charge per check, per time period, or both. Thus, there may be a monthly account maintenance fee of $2, and each check written against that account may cost the customer 10 cents, regardless of the level of account activity.

Free pricing, on the other hand, refers to the absence of a monthly account maintenance fee or per-transaction charge. Of course, the word *free* can be misleading. Even if a bank does not charge an explicit fee for deposit services, the customer may incur an implicit fee in the form of lost income (opportunity cost), because the effective interest rate paid on the deposit may be less than the going rate on investments of comparable risk. Many banks have found free pricing decidedly unprofitable because it tends to attract many small, highly active deposits that earn positive returns for the bank only when market interest rates are very high.

Conditionally free deposits have come to replace both flat-rate and free deposit pricing systems in many banking markets. Conditionally free pricing favors large-denomination deposits, because services are free if the account balance stays above some minimum figure. One of the advantages of this pricing method is that the customer, not the bank, chooses which deposit plan is preferable. This self-selection process is a form of *market signaling* that can give the bank valuable data on the behavior and cost of its deposits. Conditionally free pricing also allows a bank to divide its deposit market into high-balance, low-activity deposits and low-balance, high-activity accounts.

As an example of the use of *conditional pricing* techniques for deposits, the fees posted for regular checking accounts and savings accounts posted by two banks in the United States are given below:

Bank A		Bank B	
Regular checking account:		*Regular checking account:*	
Minimum opening balance	$100	Minimum opening balance	$100
If minimum daily balance is:		If minimum daily balance is:	
$600 or more	No fee	$500 or more	No fee
$300 to $599	$5.00 per mo.	Less than $500	$3.50 per mo.
Less than $300	$10.00 per mo.		
If the depositor's collected monthly balance		If checks written or ATM	
averages $1,500, there is no fee		transactions (debits)	
No limit on number of checks written		exceed 10 per month and	
		balance is below $500	$0.15 per debit
Regular savings account:		*Regular savings account:*	
Minimum opening balance	$100	Minimum opening balance	$100
Service fees:		Service fees:	
If balance falls below $200	$3.00 per mo.	If balance falls below $100	$2.00 per mo.
Balance of $200 or more	No fee	Balance above $100	No fee
Fee for more than two		Fee for more than three	
withdrawals per month	$2.00	withdrawals per month	$2.00

The Truth in Savings Act (1991)

In November 1991, the U.S. Congress passed the **Truth in Savings Act,** which requires depository institutions to make greater disclosure of the fees, interest rates, and other terms attached to the deposits they sell to the public. On September 14, 1992, the Federal Reserve Board issued Regulation DD to spell out the rules that banks and other depositories must follow to conform with this new law.

The Fed's regulation stipulates that consumers must be fully informed of the terms on deposit plans before they open a new account. If the consumer is not physically present when the account is opened, disclosure of the terms of the deposit account must be sent to him or her within 10 business days of the initial deposit. A depository institution must disclose the amount of the minimum balance that is required to open the account, how much must be kept on deposit to avoid paying fees or to obtain the promised yield, how the balance in each account is figured, when interest actually begins to accrue, any penalty provisions for early withdrawal, options available at maturity, reinvestment and disbursement options, any grace periods, advance notice of the approaching end of the deposit's term if it has a fixed maturity, and any bonuses available.

When a consumer asks for the current interest rate the bank is promising to pay, the bank must provide that customer with the interest rate that was offered within the most recent seven calendar days and also provide a telephone number so consumers can call and get the latest offered rate if interest rates have changed. On fixed-rate accounts the offering institution must disclose to its customers for what period of time the fixed rate will be in effect. And, on variable-rate deposits banks must warn consumers that interest rates can change, inform them how frequently rates can change, explain how a variable rate is determined, and if there are limits on how far deposit rates can move over time. For all interest-bearing accounts the bank must disclose the frequency with which interest is compounded and credited, both in writing and in advertising.

If a customer decides to renew a deposit that would not be automatically renewed on its own, the renewed deposit is considered a *new* account, requiring full bank disclosure of fees and other terms. Customers must also be told if their account is automatically renewed and, if not, what will happen to their funds (e.g., will they be placed in a noninterest-bearing account?) if the customer does not remember to renew his or her deposit. (Generally, customers must receive at least 10 days' advance notice of the approaching maturity

---

We note that Bank A appears to favor high-balance, low-activity checking deposits, while Bank B is more lenient toward smaller checking accounts. For example, Bank A begins assessing a checking-account service fee when the customer's balance falls below $600, while Bank B charges no fees for checking-account services until the customer's account balance drops below $500. Moreover, Bank A assesses significantly higher service fees on low-balance checking accounts than does Bank B—$5 to $10 per month versus $3.50 per month. On the other hand, Bank A allows unlimited check writing from its regular accounts, while B assesses a fee if more than 10 checks or withdrawals occur in any month. Similarly, Bank A assesses a $3 per month service fee if a customer's savings account dips below $200, while Bank B charges only a $2 fee if the customer's savings balance drops below $100.

date for deposits over 1 year to maturity that are not automatically renewed.) If a change is made in fees or other terms of a deposit that could reduce a depositor's yield, a 30-day advance notice must be sent to the depositor.

Depository institutions must also include information in each statement sent to their customers on the amount of interest earnings the depositor has received, along with a statement of the annual percentage yield the deposit has earned. The *annual percentage yield* (or *APY*) must be calculated using the following formula:

$$\text{APY earned} = 100[(1 + \text{Interest earned/Average account balance})^{(365/\text{Days in period})} - 1]$$

where the account balance in the formula is the average daily balance kept in the deposit for the period covered by the account statement sent to the customer. Customers must be informed of the impact of early withdrawals on their account's expected APY.

For example, suppose a depositor had $1,500 on deposit in an interest-bearing account for the first 15 days and $500 in the account for the remaining 15 days of a 30-day period. The average daily balance in this case is clearly $1,000, or [($1,500 × 15 days + $500 × 15 days)/30 days] Suppose the bank has just credited the account with $5.25 in interest for the latest 30-day period. Then the APY earned by this depositor would be:

$$\text{APY} = 100[(1 + 5.25/1000)^{365/30} - 1] = 6.58 \text{ percent}$$

In determining the balance on which interest earnings are figured, the bank must use the *full* amount of the principal in the deposit for each day, rather than, for example, counting only the minimum balance that was in the account on one day during the statement period. (Depository institutions may use either the exact daily balance or the average daily balance in calculating interest owed the customer.) Methods that do not pay interest on the full principal balance are prohibited. The daily rate earned by the depositor must be at least 1/365 of the normal interest rate quoted on the deposit.

In 1994 the U.S. Congress passed the Riegle Community Development and Regulatory Improvement Act of 1994, which narrowed the scope of deposit plans covered by the Truth in Savings Act to those accounts held by individuals for a personal, family, or household purpose. Deposits held by unincorporated nonbusiness associations of individuals are no longer subject to the disclosure requirements of the Truth in Savings Act.

These price differences reflect differences in the philosophy of the management and owners of these two banks and the types of customers each bank is seeking to attract. Bank A is located in an affluent neighborhood of homes and offices and is patronized primarily by high-income individuals and businesses who usually keep high deposit balances, but also write many checks. Bank B, on the other hand, is located across the street from a large university and actively solicits student deposits, which tend to have relatively low balances. Bank B's pricing schedules are set up to accept low-balance deposits, but the bank also recognizes that it needs to discourage excessive check writing by numerous small depositors, which would run up its costs; it does so by charging higher per-check fees than Bank A. In these two instances we can see that bank deposit pricing policy is generally sensitive to:

How U.S. Banks Should Disclose the Terms on Their Deposits to Customers

In order to help banks selling deposit services in the United States conform to the Truth in Savings Act, passed in 1991, the Federal Reserve Board now provides banks with examples of proper disclosure forms to use in order to inform customers of the terms the bank is quoting on their deposits. For example, the Fed has provided banks with an example of a proper disclosure form for certificates of deposit accounts as shown below.

**Sample Disclosure Form for XYZ Savings Bank
One-Year Certificate of Deposit**

Rate Information.   The interest rate for your account is *5.20%* with an annual percentage yield of *5.34%*. You will be paid this rate until the maturity date of the certificate. Your certificate will mature on September 30, 1996. The annual percentage yield assumes interest remains on deposit until maturity. A withdrawal will reduce earnings.

Interest for your account will be compounded daily and credited to your account on the last day of each month. Interest begins to accrue on the business day you deposit any noncash item (for example, checks).

Minimum Balance Requirements.   You must deposit $1,000 to open this account. You must maintain a minimum balance of $1,000 in your account every day to obtain the annual percentage yield listed above.

Balance Computation Method.   We use the daily balance method to calculate the interest on your account. This method applies a daily periodic rate to the principal in the account each day.

Transaction Limitations.   After the account is opened, you may not make deposits into or withdrawals from the account until the maturity date.

Early Withdrawal Penalty.   If you withdraw any principal before the maturity date, a penalty equal to three months' interest will be charged to your account.

Renewal Policy.   This account will be automatically renewed at maturity. You have a grace period of ten (10) calendar days after the maturity date to withdraw the funds without being charged a penalty.

1. *The types of customers each bank plans to serve,* with each institution establishing price schedules that appeal to the needs of individuals and businesses representing a significant portion of its market area.

2. *The cost that serving different types of depositors will present to the bank,* with most banks today pricing deposit plans in such a way as to cover all or at least a portion of anticipated service costs.

Both the Truth in Savings Act and the Federal Reserve's Regulation DD stipulate that advertising of deposit terms not be misleading. If interest rates are quoted in an advertisement, the bank must also tell the public what the other relevant terms of the deposit are, such as the minimum balance needed to earn the advertised yield and whether any fees charged could reduce the depositor's overall yield.

The Federal Reserve has recently developed sample advertisements to guide management in making sure that bank advertising contains all the essential information needed by the consumer. For example, the following sample advertisement form for CDs was developed recently by the Federal Reserve Board:

Bank XYZ
Always Offers You Competitive CD Rates!!

CERTIFICATE OF DEPOSIT	ANNUAL PERCENTAGE YIELD (APY)
5-year	6.31%
4-year	6.07%
3-year	5.72%
2-year	5.52%
1-year	4.54%
6-month	4.34%
90-day	4.21%
	APYs are offered on accounts from 5/9/93 through 5/18/93
The minimum balance to open an account and obtain the APY is $1,000. A penalty may be imposed for early withdrawal.	
For more information call: (202) 123-1234	

The foregoing sample advertisement illustrates the basic requirements for legitimate advertising of deposits under the Truth in Savings Act: (*a*) deposit rates must be quoted as annual percentage yields (APY), (*b*) the dates and minimum balance required must be stated explicitly, and (*c*) the depositor must be warned of penalties or fees that could reduce his or her yield.

Using Upscale Target Pricing

Some banks, particularly in large urban communities, have aggressively gone after high-balance, low-activity deposits with **upscale target pricing.** They use carefully designed advertising programs to target established professionals (e.g., doctors and lawyers), business owners and managers, and other high-income households with services and service fees that build in high profit margins. Other deposit accounts, especially the low-balance, high-activity ones, may be priced to break even, or they may be discouraged altogether through higher prices. Often the upscale strategy is blended with a *personal banker* program in which each upscale customer is assigned a particular bank officer who handles *all* that customer's banking needs.

Research in New England by Crane and Reilly [3] and by Murphy and Mandell [8] suggests that some bank customers today—especially upscale customers—respond very quickly to deposit price differentials. These customers know that deregulation is under way and expect falling service prices as time passes. Increasingly, local deposit markets are characterized by widespread use of conditional and upscale target pricing, intense competition, and a growing cadre of informed, price-sensitive customers shopping around for the best terms available.

Pricing Deposits Based on the Total Customer Relationship

Related to the idea of courting the bank's best customers is the notion of pricing deposits according to the *number of services the customer uses.* Customers who purchase two or more bank services may be granted lower deposit fees or have some fees waived compared to the fees charged customers having only a limited relationship to the bank. The idea is that selling a customer multiple services increases the customer's *dependence* on the bank and makes it harder for that customer to go elsewhere because of the strong *relationship* between customer and bank. Thus, in theory at least, **relationship pricing** promotes greater customer loyalty and makes the customer less sensitive to the interest rates offered on deposits or the prices posted on other banking services by competing financial-service firms.

Using Deposit Pricing to Achieve Bank Goals

Bankers have learned in recent years that deposit pricing can be used to shape the kind of *customer base* each bank serves. As Edmister [5] points out, changing deposit prices affects not only the spread between bank loan rates and deposit rates but also customer balances and deposit mix decisions, which in turn influence bank growth and profit margins. That is:

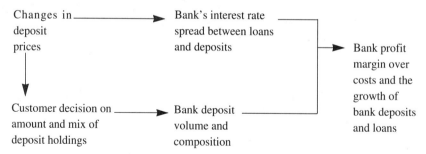

Moreover, the smaller the difference between loan and deposit interest rates, the greater the sensitivity of bank profit margins to changes in deposit prices.

Deposit pricing is best used to protect and increase bank profitability, rather than to simply add more customers and take market share away from competitors. Indeed, when new deposit plans are introduced, their biggest appeal and greatest chance for success lies with those customers who already hold deposits with the bank. And even those customers the bank already has will not automatically pay higher prices for deposit services. They will pay no more for a deposit than the sum total of its benefits to them and will go elsewhere when the value of those benefits falls below each service's price.

Concept Checks

13–1. Describe the essential differences between the following deposit pricing methods in use today: cost-plus pricing, market-penetration pricing, conditional pricing, upscale target pricing, and relationship pricing.

13–2. A bank determines from an analysis of its cost-accounting figures that for each $500 minimum-balance checking account that it sells, account processing and other operating costs will average $4.87 per month and overhead expenses will run an average of $1.21 per month. The bank hopes to achieve a profit margin on these particular costs of 10 percent of total monthly costs. What monthly fee should it charge a customer who opens one of these checking accounts?

13–3. To price deposits successfully, banks must know their costs. How are these costs determined using the historical average cost approach? The marginal cost of funds approach? What are the advantages and disadvantages of each approach?

13–4. How can the historical average cost and marginal cost of funds approaches be used to help select assets (such as loans) that a bank might wish to acquire?

13–5. What is meant by the statement, "Deposits are quasi-fixed factors of production for banks."? Does this statement have any bearing on how banks market their deposit services?

13–6. What factors do household depositors rank most highly in choosing a bank for their checking account? Their savings account? What about business firms?

13–7. What does the 1991 Truth in Savings Act require bankers selling deposits inside the United States to tell their customers?

13–8. Use the APY formula required by the Truth in Savings Act for the following calculation. Suppose that a customer holds a savings deposit for a year. The balance in the account stood at $2,000 for 180 days and $100 for the remaining days in the year. If the bank paid this depositor $8.50 in interest earnings for the year, what APY did this customer receive?

Summary

Recent deregulation of the banking industry has encouraged bankers to think creatively about their pricing policies. The key deposit pricing models banks use today fall into five broad categories: (1) cost-plus-profit pricing; (2) market-penetration pricing; (3) scheduled, or conditional, pricing; (4) upscale target pricing; and (5) relationship pricing.

The most popular of these deposit pricing approaches is the setting of *price schedules* where the fee the customer is assessed is conditional on the degree to which he or she uses a particular deposit service. This approach gives customers more options in choosing the particular deposit plan they find the least expensive and signals to a banker information about the customer's money-using habits. In cost-plus-profit pricing, on the other hand, a bank estimates all the operating and overhead costs incurred in providing each deposit service unit and adds in a margin for profit to compensate the bank's shareholders for placing their funds at the bank's disposal. In market-penetration pricing a bank will set its prices below market in an effort to attract new depositors, build up its market, and, hopefully, sell the new depositors added services that generate more revenues for the bank.

Upscale target pricing, in contrast, aims to attract individual depositors and businesses through favorable deposit terms in the hope of bringing in larger-volume deposit accounts, giving the bank more funds to work with. Finally, relationship pricing calls for assessing lower fees or more generous yields on the deposits of customers who have a strong relationship with the bank—that is, who buy more bank services. Most bankers argue that customers who purchase more services from a bank are likely to be more loyal to the institution and in the long run generate more revenue for the bank.

Recently, new rules and regulations have entered the deposit services market in the United States. The Truth in Savings Act of 1991 requires U.S. banks and foreign-owned banks selling deposits to U.S. customers to make full and timely disclosure of the terms under which each deposit service is offered. This includes information on minimum-balance requirements, how deposits balances are calculated, what yield is promised, what is required of the depositor to achieve the promised yield or rate of return, any penalties or extra fees, and when interest earnings begin to accrue. A 30-day advance notice of any planned changes in deposit fees must be sent to each depositor affected.

Key Terms in This Chapter

Cost-plus-profit deposit pricing
Federal Deposit Insurance Corporation (FDIC)
Market-penetration deposit pricing
Deposit fee schedules

Truth in Savings Act
Upscale target pricing
Relationship pricing

Problems and Projects

1. Merchants National Bank has received $800 million in total funding, consisting of $200 million in checkable deposit accounts, $400 million in time and savings deposits, $100 million in money market borrowings, and $100 million in stockholders' equity. Interest costs on time and savings deposits are 9 percent, on average, while noninterest costs of raising the

particular deposits equal approximately 2 percent of their dollar volume. Interest costs on checkable deposits average only 3 percent since many of these deposits pay no interest, but noninterest costs of raising checkable accounts are about 7 percent of their dollar total. Money market borrowings cost the bank an average of 10 percent in interest costs and 1 percent in noninterest costs. Bank management estimates the cost of stockholders' equity capital at 22 percent before taxes. (The bank is currently in the 35 percent tax bracket.) When reserve requirements are added in, along with uncollected dollar balances, these factors are estimated to contribute another 15 percent to the cost of securing checkable deposits and 5 percent to the cost of acquiring time and savings deposits. Reserve requirements (on Eurodeposits only) and collection delays add an estimated 2 percent to the cost of the money market borrowings.

a. Calculate Merchants National Bank's weighted average interest cost on total funds raised, figured on a before-tax basis.

b. If the bank's earning assets total $700 million, what is its break-even cost rate?

c. What is Merchants' overall historical weighted average cost of capital?

2. State Security Bank is considering funding a package of new loans in the amount of $400 million. Security has projected that it must raise $450 million in order to have $400 million available to make new loans. It expects to raise $325 million of the total by selling time deposits at an average interest rate of 8.75 percent. Noninterest costs from selling time deposits will add an estimated 0.45 percent in operating expenses. The bank expects another $125 million to come from noninterest-bearing transaction deposits, whose noninterest costs are expected to be 7.25 percent of the total amount of these deposits. What is the bank's projected pooled-funds marginal cost? What hurdle rate must the bank achieve on its earning assets?

3. First Metrocentre Bank posts the following schedule of fees for its household and small business checking accounts:

- For average monthly account balances over $1,500, there is no monthly maintenance fee and no charge per check.

- For average monthly account balances of $1,000 to $1,500, a $2 monthly maintenance fee is assessed and there is a 10¢ charge per check cleared.

- For average monthly account balances of less than $1,000, a $4 monthly maintenance fee is assessed and there is a 15¢ per check fee.

What form of deposit pricing is this? What is First Metrocentre trying to accomplish with its pricing schedule? Can you foresee any problems with this pricing plan?

4. Emerald Isle National Bank finds that it can attract the following amounts of deposits if it offers new depositors and those rolling over their maturing CDs the interest rates indicated below:

Expected Volume of New Deposits	Rate of Interest Offered Depositors
$ 5 million	5.0%
15 million	5.5
19 million	6.0
22 million	6.5
23 million	7.0

Management anticipates being able to invest any new deposits raised in loans yielding 8 percent. How far should the bank go in raising its deposit rate in order to maximize total profits (excluding interest costs)?

5. Silverton Bank plans to launch a new deposit campaign next week in hopes of bringing in from $100 million to $600 million in new deposit money, which it expects to invest at an 8.75 percent yield. Management believes that an offer rate on new deposits of 5.75 percent would attract $100 million in new deposits and rollover funds. To attract $200 million the bank would probably be forced to offer 6.25 percent.

The bank's forecast suggests that $300 million might be available at 6.8 percent, $400 million at 7.4 percent, $500 million at 8.2 percent, and $600 million at 9 percent. What volume of deposits should the bank try to attract to ensure that marginal cost does not exceed marginal revenue?

6. Needles State Bank finds that its basic checking account, which requires a $400 minimum balance, costs the bank an average of $3.13 per month in servicing costs (including labor and computer time) and $1.18 per month in overhead expenses. The bank also tries to build in a $0.50 per month profit margin on these accounts. What monthly fee should the bank charge each customer?

Further analysis of customer accounts reveals that for each $100 in average balance maintained in its checking accounts, the bank saves about 5 percent in operating expenses associated with each account. For a customer who consistently maintains an average balance of $1,000 per month, how much should the bank charge this customer and still protect its profit margin?

7. Clyde Appleton maintains a savings deposit with Santa Paribe National Bank. This past year Clyde received $12.24 in interest earnings from his savings account. His savings deposit had the following average balance each month:

January	$400	July	$350
February	250	August	425
March	300	September	550
April	150	October	600
May	225	November	625
June	300	December	300

What was the annual percentage yield (APY) earned on Clyde Appleton's account?

8. First and Merchants National Bank of Leetown quotes an APY of 7 percent on a one-year money market CD sold to one of the small businesses in town. The firm posted a balance of $2,500 for the first 90 days of the year, $3,000 over the next 180 days, and $2,750 for the remainder of the year. How much in total interest earnings did this small business customer receive for the year?

Selected References

For a discussion of deposit pricing techniques and issues, see these studies:

1. Board of Governors of the Federal Reserve System. *Bank Service Charges and Fees: Their Impact on Consumers.* A Study Prepared at the Request of the Consumer Advisory Council, 1985.
2. Canner, Glenn B., and Robert D. Kuntz. *Service Charges as a Source of Bank Income and Their Impact on Consumers.* Staff Economic Study No. 145, Board of Governors of the Federal Reserve System, 1984.
3. Crane, Dwight B., and Michael J. Reilly. *NOW Deposits.* Lexington, Mass.: Lexington Books, 1978.
4. Dunham, Constance. "Unravelling the Complexity of NOW Account Pricing." *New England Economic Review,* Federal Reserve Bank of Boston, May/June 1983, pp. 30–45.
5. Edmister, Robert O. "Margin Analysis for Consumer Deposit Interest Rate Policy." *Journal of Bank Research,* Autumn 1982, pp. 179–84.
6. Flannery, Mark. "Retail Bank Deposits as Quasi-Fixed Factors of Production." *American Economic Review* 72, no. 3, pp. 527–36.
7. Logue, James A. "Pricing Strategies for the 1980s." *The Magazine of Bank Administration,* September 1983, pp. 21–26.
8. Murphy, Neil B., and Lewis Mandell. *The NOW Account Decision: Profitability and Pricing Strategy.* Rolling Meadows, Ill.: Bank Administration Institute, 1981.
9. Rose, Peter S. "Pricing Deposits in an Era of Competition and Change." *The Canadian Banker* 93, no. 1 (February 1986), pp. 44–51.

10. ———. "Defensive Banking in a Volatile Economy." *The Canadian Banker* 92, no. 5 (April 1986), pp. 44–49.

11. Rose, Sanford. "What Really Went Wrong at Franklin National." *Fortune,* October 1974, p. 118.

12. Simonson, Donald G., and Peter C. Marks. "Pricing NOW Deposits and the Cost of Bank Funds—Part One: Break-Even Analysis of NOW Deposits." *The Magazine of Bank Administration,* November 1980, pp. 28–31.

13. ———. "Pricing NOW Deposits and the Costs of Bank Funds—Part Two." *The Magazine of Bank Administration,* December 1980, pp. 21–24.

14. McNulty, James E. "Do You Know the True Cost of Your Deposits?" *Review,* Federal Home Loan Bank of Atlanta, October 1986, pp. 1–6.

15. Watson, Ronald D. "Estimating the Cost of Your Bank's Funds." *Business Review,* Federal Reserve Bank of Philadelphia, May/June 1978.

For a discussion of recent trends in service availability and service fees levied by banks and thrift institutions see:

16. Phillips, Susan M. *Testimony Before the Subcommittee on Consumer Credit and Insurance of the Committee on Banking, Finance, and Urban Affairs,* U.S. House of Representatives, June 22, 1994.

17. Hannan, Timothy H. "Recent Trends in Retail Fees and Services of Depository Institutions." *Federal Reserve Bulletin,* September 1994, pp. 771–81.

For a discussion of factors influencing deposit growth in recent years, see especially:

18. Laderman, Elizabeth. "Deposits and Demographics?" *FRBSF Economic Letter,* Federal Reserve Bank of San Francisco, No. 97-19 (June 27, 1997).

19. Morgan, Donald M. "Will the Shift to Stocks and Bonds by Households be Destabilizing?" *Economic Review,* Federal Reserve Bank of Kansas City, Second Quarter, 1994, pp. 31–44.

For a discussion of the impact of the Truth in Savings Act on the cost of bank compliance see:

20. Elliehausen, Gregory, and Barbara R. Lowrey. *The Cost of Implementing Consumer Financial Regulations: An Analysis of the Experience with the Truth in Savings Act.* Staff Study No. 170, Board of Governors of the Federal Reserve System, December 1997.

14   MANAGING NONDEPOSIT LIABILITIES AND OTHER SOURCES OF BANK FUNDS

Learning and Management Decision Objectives

The purpose of this chapter is to learn about the principal nondeposit sources of funds that bankers can borrow to help finance their activities and to see how bank managers choose among the various nondeposit funds sources currently available to them.

Introduction

The traditional source of bank funds is *deposits*. It is the public's demand for bank checking and savings deposits that supplies most of the raw material for bank lending and investing and, ultimately, bank profits.[1] But what does management do when deposit volume and growth are inadequate to fund all the loans and investments the bank would like to make?

Liability Management

Bankers have learned over the years that turning down a profitable loan request by saying "We do not have enough deposits to support the loan" is not well received by their customers. Denial of a loan request often means the immediate loss of a deposit and perhaps the loss of any *future* business from the disappointed customer as well. On the other hand, granting a loan request—even when deposit flows are inadequate— usually brings in both new deposits and the demand for other banking services as well. And the benefits may reach far beyond the borrowing customer alone. For example, a loan made to a business firm often brings in personal accounts from the firm's owners and employees.

---

[1]Portions of this chapter are based on the author's article published in *The Canadian Banker* [5] and are used with permission.

Bankers learned long ago the importance of the **customer relationship doctrine,** which says that the *first* priority of a bank is to make loans to all those customers from whom the bank expects to receive positive net earnings. Thus, the lending decision of bank managers often *precedes* their funding decision; all loans and investments whose returns exceed their costs and whose quality meets the bank's credit standards should be made. If deposits are not immediately available to cover these loans, management should seek out the lowest-cost source of borrowed funds available to meet its customers' credit needs.

During the 1960s and 1970s, the customer relationship doctrine spawned an even broader view of bank management strategy, known as **liability management.** Liability management banking consists of *buying funds,* mainly from other financial institutions, in order to cover good-quality loan requests and satisfy deposit reserve requirements. As we saw in Chapter 11, a bank may acquire the needed funds by borrowing in the domestic Federal funds market, borrowing abroad through the Eurocurrency market, selling money market ($100,000+) negotiable CDs to customers, securing a loan from the central bank, negotiating security repurchase agreements with individuals and institutions having temporary surpluses of funds, or issuing commercial paper through a subsidiary that is part of the same bank holding company.

Table 14–1 illustrates the basic idea behind liability management. A bank's business and household customers have requested new loans and renewals of old loans for today amounting to $100 million. However, the bank's deposit division reports that only $50 million in new deposits and renewals of maturing deposits are expected today. If management wishes to make all of the $100 million in new loans, it must find another $50 million, mainly from nondeposit sources. Some quick work by the bank's money market division, which called correspondent banks inside the United States and in London and negotiated with nonbank institutions carrying temporary cash surpluses, resulted in raising the entire $50 million through domestic Federal funds borrowings, borrowing funds from a subsidiary part of the same holding company that sold notes (commercial paper) in the open market, sales of bank securities under a security repurchase agreement, and borrowing Eurodollars from bank branches abroad.

Unfortunately, the money market and deposit divisions of the bank cannot rest on their laurels. They know that most of the $50 million just raised will be available only until tomorrow morning, when the majority of borrowed funds must be returned to the owners. These departing borrowed funds will need to be replaced quickly to continue to support the new loans. Customers who receive loans spend their funds quickly (otherwise, why get a loan?) by writing checks and wiring funds to other banks. This bank, therefore, must find sufficient new funds to honor all those checks and wire transfers of funds away from the bank made by its borrowing customers.

Clearly, liability management banking is an essential tool banks need to sustain the growth of their lending programs. However, liability management also poses real challenges for bankers, who must keep abreast of the market every day to make sure their bank is fully funded. Moreover, liability management is an *interest-sensitive* approach to raising bank funds. If interest rates rise and our bank is unwilling to pay those higher rates, funds borrowed from the money market will be gone in minutes. Money market lenders of funds typically have a highly elastic response to changes in market interest rates.

TABLE 14–1   **Sample Use of Nondeposit Funds Sources to Supplement Deposits and Make Loans**

FIRST NATIONAL BANK AND TRUST COMPANY
Balance Sheet
(Report of Condition)

Assets	*Liabilities and Equity*	
Loans	Funding sources found	
New loans to be made $100,000,000	to support the new loans:	
	Newly deposited funds	
	expected today	$50,000,000
	Nondeposit funds sources:	
	Federal funds purchased	19,000,000
	Borrowings of Eurodollars	
	abroad	20,000,000
	Securities sold under	
	agreements to repurchase	
	(RPs)	3,000,000
	Borrowings from a nonbank	
	subsidiary of the bank's	
	holding company that sold	
	commercial paper in the	
	money market	+8,000,000
	Total new deposit and	
	nondeposit funds	
	raised to cover	
	the new loans	$100,000,000

Yet, viewed from another perspective, funds raised by the use of liability management techniques are *flexible*—the banker can decide exactly how much it needs and for how long and usually find a source of funds that meets those requirements. In contrast, when a bank sells deposits to raise funds, it is the depositor who decides how much and how long funds will be left with the individual banking firm. With liability management, banks in need of more funds to cover expanding loan commitments or deficiencies in required reserves can simply raise their *offer rate* until enough funds are offered to them by money market lenders. Banks confronted with declining loan demand and excess reserves can simply *lower* their offer rate in order to reduce their volume of money market borrowing. Thus, the hallmarks of liability management banking are (1) *buying funds* by selling liabilities in the money market and (2) *using price* (the interest rate offered) *as the control lever to regulate incoming funds* and, thereby, shape the bank's response to customer loan demand.

Alternative Nondeposit Sources of Bank Funds

As Table 14–2 suggests, nondeposit sources of bank funds and a unique type of deposit—the large-denomination CD—have fluctuated in recent years among banks, reaching record highs in the late 1980s and then declining in dollar volume due to a

TABLE 14–2   **Growth in Selected Nondeposit Sources of Bank Funds and Negotiable CDs**

Sources of Bank Funds (billions of dollars in daily averages)	1988	1990	1992	1994	1996	1997**
Money Market ($100,000+) negotiable CDs	$429.2	$431.8	$366.5	$344.9	$412.3	$468.5
Eurodollar borrowings from the bank's own foreign offices	160.8	168.0	160.4	185.9	228.2	207.6
Federal funds borrowings and security RPs	159.3	180.1	149.9	221.1	199.8	166.5
Bank-related commercial paper issues*	43.2	—	—	—	—	—
Borrowings from the Federal Reserve banks	1.7	0.3	0.1	0.5	0.1	1.7
Total nondeposit funds raised (in billions of dollars)	$794.2	$790.9	$676.9	$752.4	$840.4	$844.3
Ratio of nondeposit funds to total bank deposits for all U.S. banks	10.00%	15.19%	24.2%	29.8%	29.1%	28.2%

*Data series has been discontinued.
**Figures for 1997 as of July.
Source: Board of Governors of the Federal Reserve System, Federal Reserve Bulletin, selected issues.

slowdown in the global economy's rate of growth and subdued growth in loan demand. However, relative to banks' total deposits, especially at the largest banks—which make substantially greater use of nondeposit funds than do small and medium-size banks—nondeposit funds appear to have captured a growing share of all bank sources of funding. In the sections that follow we examine the most popular nondeposit funds sources used by banks today.

Federal Funds Market

The most popular domestic source of borrowed reserves is the **Federal funds market.** Originally, Federal funds consisted exclusively of deposits held by U.S. banks at the Federal Reserve banks. These deposits are owned by banks and are held at the Fed primarily to satisfy legal reserve requirements, clear checks, and pay for purchases of government securities. These Federal Reserve balances can be transferred from one bank to another in seconds through the Fed's wire transfer network (FED WIRE), linking all Federal Reserve banks across the United States. Today, however, interbank (correspondent) deposits that banks hold with each other also can be moved around the banking system the same day a request is made. The same is true of large collected demand deposit balances that securities dealers and governments own, which also can be transferred by wire. All three of these types of deposits make up the raw material that is traded in the market for Federal funds. In technical terms, *Federal funds are simply short-term borrowings of immediately available money.*

It did not take bankers long to realize the potential source of profit inherent in these *same-day monies.* Because reserves deposited with the Federal Reserve banks and most demand deposits held by business firms pay no interest, banks and nonbank firms have a strong economic incentive to lend excess reserves or any demand deposit balances not needed to cover immediate cash needs. Moreover, there are no reserve requirements on Federal funds borrowings currently and few regulatory controls, features that have stimulated the growth of the market and helped keep the cost of borrowing down. Banks, thrifts, securities houses, and other firms in need of immediate funds can negotiate a loan with a holder of surplus interbank deposits or reserves at the Fed, promising to return the borrowed funds the next day if need be.

The main use of the Federal funds market today is still the traditional one: *a mechanism that allows banks short of reserves to meet their legal reserve requirements or to satisfy customer loan demand by tapping immediately usable funds from other institutions possessing temporarily idle funds.* Fed funds are also used to supplement deposit growth and give lenders a relatively safe outlet for temporary cash surpluses on which interest can be earned (even for a loan lasting only a few hours). Moreover, the Federal funds market serves as a conduit for the policy initiatives of the Federal Reserve System designed to control the growth of money and credit in order to stabilize the economy.

By performing all of these functions, the Federal funds market efficiently distributes reserves throughout the banking system to areas of greatest need. To help suppliers and demanders of Federal funds find each other, *funds brokers* soon appeared to trade Federal funds in return for commissions. Large correspondent banks, known as *accommodating banks,* play a role similar to that of funds brokers for smaller banks in their region. An accommodating bank buys and sells Federal funds simultaneously in order to make a market for the reserves of its customer banks, even though the accommodating bank itself may have no need for extra funds.

The procedure for borrowing and lending Federal funds is a simple one. Borrowing and lending institutions communicate either directly with each other or indirectly through a correspondent bank or funds broker. Once borrowing and lending institutions agree on the terms of a Federal funds loan—especially its interest rate and maturity—the lending institution arranges to transfer reserves from a deposit it holds, either at the Federal Reserve bank in its district or with a correspondent bank, into a deposit controlled by the borrowing bank. This may be accomplished by wiring Federal funds if the banks are in different regions of the country. If both lending and borrowing banks hold reserve deposits with the same Federal Reserve bank or with the same correspondent bank, the lending institution simply asks that bank to transfer funds from its reserve account to the borrower's reserve account—a series of bookkeeping entries accomplished in seconds via computer. When the loan comes due, the funds are automatically transferred back to the lending institution's reserve account. (See Table 14–3 for a description of the bookkeeping entries involved.) The interest owed may also be transferred at this time, or the borrower may simply send a check to the lender to cover any interest owed.

The interest rate on a Federal funds loan is subject to negotiation between borrowing and lending institutions. While the interest rate attached to each Federal funds loan

---

TABLE 14–3   **The Mechanics of Borrowing and Lending Federal Funds**
(in millions of dollars)

Step 1. Lending Reserve Balances Held at the Federal Reserve Banks

Lending Bank's Balance Sheet		**Borrowing Bank's Balance Sheet**	
Assets	*Liabilities and Net Worth*	*Assets*	*Liabilities and Net Worth*
Federal funds sold (loaned) +100		Reserves on deposit at the Fed +100	Federal funds purchased (borrowed) +100
Reserves on deposit at the Fed −100			

Step 2. Borrowing Bank Uses the Federal Funds It Obtains to Make Loans

Borrowing Bank's Balance Sheet	
Assets	*Liabilities and Net Worth*
Reserves on deposit at the Fed −100	
Loans +100	

Step 3. Repaying the Loan of Federal Funds

Lending Bank's Balance Sheet		**Borrowing Bank's Balance Sheet**	
Assets	*Liabilities and Net Worth*	*Assets*	*Liabilities and Net Worth*
Reserves on deposit at the Fed +100		Reserves on deposit at the Fed −100	Federal funds purchased −100
Federal funds sold (loaned) −100			

---

may differ from the rate on any other loan, most of these loans use the effective interest rate prevailing each day in the national market—a rate of interest posted by Federal funds brokers and major accommodating banks. In recent years, tiered Federal funds rates (i.e., interest rate schedules) have appeared at various times, with banks in trouble paying higher interest rates or simply being shut out of the market completely.

Three types of loan agreements are used in the Federal funds market: (1) overnight loans, (2) term loans, and (3) continuing contracts. *Overnight loans* are

TABLE 14–3   (concluded)

Step 1. Lending Federal Funds by a Respondent (usually smaller) Bank to a Correspondent (usually larger) Bank

Lending (respondent) **Bank's Balance Sheet**		**Borrowing (correspondent)** **Bank's Balance Sheet**	
Assets	*Liabilities and Net Worth*	*Assets*	*Liabilities and Net worth*
Deposits held with correspondent −100 Federal funds loaned +100			Federal funds purchased +100 Respondent bank's deposit −100

Step 2. The Correspondent Bank May Use the Federal Funds Borrowed to Meet Its Own Reserve Needs or Loan Those Funds to Another Bank (usually located in a major money center where credit demands are heavy)

Correspondent (lending) **Bank's Balance Sheet**		**Money Center (borrowing)** **Bank's Balance Sheet**	
Assets	*Liabilities and Net Worth*	*Assets*	*Liabilities and Net Worth*
Reserves −100 Federal funds loaned +100		Reserves +100	Federal funds purchased +100

Step 3. Repaying the Loan to the Respondent Bank

Respondent Bank		**Correspondent Bank**	
Assets	*Liabilities and Net Worth*	*Assets*	*Liabilities and Net Worth*
Deposits held with correspondent +100 Federal funds loaned −100			Federal funds purchased −100 Respondent bank's deposit +100

unwritten agreements, negotiated via wire or telephone, with the borrowed funds returned the next day. Normally these loans are not secured by specific collateral, though where borrower and lender do not know each other well or there is doubt about the borrower's credit standing, the borrower may be required to place selected government securities in a custody account in the name of the lender until the loan is repaid. *Term loans* are longer-term Federal funds contracts lasting several days, weeks, or months, often accompanied by a written contract. *Continuing contracts* are automatically renewed each day unless either the borrower or the lender decides to end this agreement. Most continuing contracts are made between smaller respondent banks and their larger correspondents, with the correspondent bank automatically investing the smaller bank's deposits held with it in Federal funds loans until told to do otherwise.

Concept Checks

14–1. What is *liability management?*

14–2. What advantages and risks does the pursuit of liability management bring to a bank?

14–3. What is the *customer relationship doctrine* and what are its implications for bank fund-raising?

14–4. For what kinds of bank funding situations are Federal funds best suited?

14–5. Chequers State Bank loans $50 million from its reserve account at the Federal Reserve Bank of Philadelphia to First National Bank of Smithville, located in the New York Federal Reserve Bank's district, for 24 hours, with the funds returned the next day. Can you show the correct accounting entries for the making of this loan and for the return of the loaned funds?

14–6. Hillside Security Bank has an excess balance of $35 million in a deposit at its principal correspondent, Sterling City Bank, and instructs the latter institution to loan the funds today to another bank, returning them to its correspondent deposit the next business day. Sterling loans the $35 million to Imperial Security National Bank for 24 hours. Can you show the proper accounting entries for the extension of this loan and for the recovery of the loaned funds by Hillside Security Bank?

Borrowing from the Federal Reserve Bank in the District

For a bank with immediate reserve needs, a viable alternative to the Federal funds market is negotiating a loan from a Federal Reserve bank for a short period of time (in most cases, no more than two weeks). The Fed will make the loan through its **discount window** by crediting the borrowing bank's reserve account held at the Federal Reserve bank in its district. Each loan made by the 12 Federal Reserve banks must be backed by collateral. Most banks keep U.S. government securities in the vaults of the Federal Reserve banks for this purpose. The Fed will also accept certain federal agency securities or high-grade commercial paper to secure these borrowings. (See Table 14–4.)

The types of Federal Reserve loans available include:

TABLE 14–4   Borrowing Reserves from the Federal Reserve Bank in the District
(in millions of dollars)

Securing a Loan from the District Reserve Bank

Borrowing Bank

Assets	Liabilities and Net Worth
Reserves on deposit at the Federal Reserve Bank +100	Notes Payable +100

Federal Reserve Bank

Assets	Liabilities and Net Worth
Loan and advances +100	Bank reserve accounts +100

Repaying a Loan from the District Reserve Bank

Borrowing Bank

Assets	Liabilities and Net Worth
Reserves on deposit at the Federal Reserve bank −100	Notes Payable −100

Federal Reserve Bank

Assets	Liabilities and Net Worth
Loan and advances −100	Bank reserve accounts −100

1. *Adjustment credit,* normally lasting only a few days and designed to provide immediate aid in meeting a bank's reserve requirements.
2. *Seasonal credit,* extended for longer periods than adjustment credit for banks with seasonal swings in deposits and loans (such as those experienced by farm banks during planting or harvesting time).
3. *Extended credit,* for banks experiencing longer-term funding problems (perhaps due to a downturn in the local economy).

Each type of loan carries a different interest rate, with longer-term extended credit generally carrying the highest interest rate of all.

While few banks are denied Federal Reserve credit, the central bank does frown upon borrowing to support *new* loans, repetitive borrowing, or borrowing predicated on *rate arbitrage* (i.e., raising funds at the Fed's discount window because the Fed is the cheapest source of credit and reinvesting those funds in loans bearing higher rates of interest). There is evidence that rate arbitraging does occur, however. As Goodfriend [4] observes, borrowing from the Federal Reserve tends to accelerate when the Federal funds rate moves higher against the Fed's discount rate.

The Federal Reserve's rules for banks borrowing from the discount window are spelled out in its Regulation A. In the case of banks applying for the most common discount window loan, *adjustment credit,* Regulation A states:

> Federal Reserve Credit is available on a short-term basis to a depository institution under such rules as may be prescribed to assist the institution, to the extent appropriate, in meeting temporary requirements for funds, or to cushion more persistent out flows of funds pending an orderly adjustment of the institution's assets and liabilities (Reg. A[1980], Sec. 210.3).

Borrowing from the Fed is a *privilege* extended to banks, not a right. It is expected that such borrowing will be temporary. To ensure that this is so, the Fed has set numerical guidelines (a recent example appears in Table 14–5) to control the frequency and amount of borrowing by individual banks. Borrowing guidelines are more liberal for smaller banks. But regardless of a bank's size, rarely are its borrowings permitted to exceed 2 percent of its total domestic deposits. Borrowing for consecutive weeks covering more than one month for the smallest banks or one to two weeks for the largest banks is discouraged by the Fed.

In 1991 the U.S. Congress passed the FDIC Improvement Act, which places strict limits on how far the Federal Reserve banks can go in supporting a troubled bank with loans. Generally speaking, undercapitalized banks cannot be granted discount window loans for more than 60 days in each 120-day period. Long-term Fed support of a bank is only permissible if the bank is a "viable entity." If the Federal Reserve exceeds these limitations, it could be held liable to the FDIC for any losses incurred by the insurance fund should the troubled bank ultimately fail.[2]

U.S. banks beginning in 1989 became eligible for the first time to borrow from the Federal Home Loan Banks, created by the U.S. Congress during the 1930s. FHLB advances can range from overnight to as long as 20 years (the latter loans often used to fund home mortgages). These loans are available at both fixed and variable rates and are usually among the cheapest of wholesale interest rates.

Development and Sale of Large Negotiable CDs

The concept of liability management and short-term borrowing to supplement bank deposit growth was given a significant boost early in the 1960s with the development of a new kind of deposit, the **negotiable CD.** This bank funding source is really a *hybrid* account—legally, it is a deposit, but, in practical terms, the negotiable CD is just

---

[2]Section 142 of the 1991 FDIC Improvement Act makes the Federal Reserve financially liable to the FDIC if the Fed makes continuing loans to a critically undercapitalized insured depository institution for more than 60 days in any 120-day period unless the principal federal supervisory agency of the institution or the Federal Reserve Board, following an examination, certifies that the borrowing institution is "viable." In most cases an undercapitalized depository institution will be judged viable if it has submitted a plan to restore its capital, its primary federal supervisor has accepted the plan, and the institution is complying with the plan. The Fed may also be liable to the FDIC for insurance fund losses if it loans funds to a critically undercapitalized insured depository after a five-day period beginning on the day the depository becomes critically undercapitalized. If the Fed does incur any liability for losses of the FDIC, it must report this information to the U.S. Congress.

TABLE 14–5   **Federal Reserve Guidelines for Frequency and Volume of Borrowing from the Discount Window**

Bank Size Measured by Total Domestic Deposits	Maximum Consecutive Weeks of Borrowing from the Discount Window	Total Number of Weeks Discount Window Borrowing May Occur within the Following Periods of Time		Permissible Amount of Borrowing as a Percentage of a Bank's Total Domestic Deposits
		13 Weeks	*26 Weeks*	
Under $200 million	4–5 weeks	6–7 weeks	7–8 weeks	2.0%
$200 million to under $1 billion	3–4	5–6	7–8	2.0
$1 billion to under $3 billion	2–3	4–5	6–7	1.5
More than $3 billion	1–2	3–4	4–5	1.0

Source: Board of Governors of the Federal Reserve System and Richard L. Mugel, "Reserve Borrowings and the Money Market," *Economic Commentary*, Federal Reserve Bank of Cleveland, November 1, 1985, p. 1.

another form of IOU issued to tap temporary surplus funds held by large corporations, wealthy individuals, and governments. A CD is an interest-bearing receipt evidencing the deposit of funds in the accepting bank for a specified time period at a specified interest rate or specified formula for calculating the contract interest rate.

There are four main types of negotiable CDs today. *Domestic* CDs are issued by U.S. banks inside the territory of the United States. Dollar-denominated CDs issued by banks outside the United States are known as *EuroCD*s. The largest foreign banks active in the United States sell CDs through their U.S. branches, called *Yankee* CDs. Finally, large savings and loan associations and other nonbank savings institutions sell *thrift* CDs.

During the 1960s, faced with slow or nonexistent growth in checkbook deposits held by their largest customers because these customers had found higher-yielding outlets for their cash surpluses elsewhere, U.S. money center banks began to search the market for *new* sources of funds. First National City Bank of New York (later Citicorp), one of the most innovative banks in the world, was the first to develop the large ($100,000+) negotiable CD in 1961. Citicorp designed this marketable deposit to compete for funds with government bills and other well-known money market instruments. It was made large enough—generally sold in multiples of $1 million—to appeal to major corporations holding large quantities of liquid funds. Negotiable CDs would be confined to short maturities—ranging from seven days to one or two years in most cases, but concentrated mainly in the one- to six-month maturity range for the convenience of the majority of CD buyers. And the new instrument would be *negotiable*—able to be sold in the secondary market any number of times before reaching maturity—in order to provide corporate customers with *liquidity* in case their cash surpluses proved to be smaller or less stable than originally forecast. To make the sale of negotiable CDs in advance of their maturity easier, they were issued in *bearer* form.

Moreover, several securities dealers agreed to make a market in negotiable CDs carrying maturities of six months or less.

The negotiable CD was an almost instant success. Large-denomination CDs grew from zero in the early 1960s to nearly $100 billion by the end of the 1960s and then surged upward in the high interest rate period of the 1970s and early 1980s. By 1997, time accounts of $100,000+ at U.S. banks totaled more than $450 billion. Their growth was aided by suspension of federal interest rate ceilings beginning in the 1970s. As with all liability management instruments, bank management could control the quantity of CDs outstanding simply by varying the yield offered to CD customers.

Interest rates on *fixed-rate* CDs, which represent about four-fifths of all large negotiable CDs issued, are quoted on an interest-bearing basis, and the rate is computed assuming a 360-day year. For example, if a bank promises an 8 percent annual interest rate to the buyer of a $100,000 six-month (180-day) CD, the depositor will have the following at the end of six months:

$$\begin{matrix} \text{Amount} \\ \text{due} \\ \text{customer} \end{matrix} = \text{Principal} + \text{Principal} \times \frac{\text{Days to maturity}}{360 \text{ days}} \times \begin{matrix} \text{Annual rate} \\ \text{of interest} \end{matrix}$$

$$= \$100{,}000 + \$100{,}000 \times \frac{180}{360} \times 0.08$$

$$= \$100{,}000 + \$4{,}000$$

$$= \$104{,}000$$

CDs that have maturities over one year normally pay interest to the depositor every six months. *Variable-rate* CDs, which make up about 20 percent of the market, have their interest rates reset after a designated period of time (called a *leg* or *roll* period). The new rate is based on a mutually accepted reference interest rate, such as the London Interbank Offer Rate (LIBOR) attached to borrowings of Eurodollar deposits or the average interest rate prevailing on prime-quality CDs traded in the secondary market.

The net result of CD sales to a bank's major customers is often a simple transfer of funds from one deposit to another in the same bank, particularly from checkable deposits into CDs. The selling bank gains loanable funds even from this simple transfer because, in the United States at least, legal reserve requirements are currently zero for CDs, while checking accounts at the largest banks carry a reserve requirement of 10 percent. Also, deposit stability is likely to be greater for the bank because the CD has a set maturity and normally will not be withdrawn until maturity. In contrast, checkable (demand) deposits can be withdrawn at any time. However, the sensitive interest rates attached to the largest negotiable CDs mean that banks making heavy use of negotiable CDs and other liability management techniques must work harder to combat volatile net earnings (including aggressive use of rate-hedging techniques, discussed in Chapters 6–9).

Given the history of how CDs developed, it should not surprise us to learn that a close correlation exists between changes in business loan demand and negotiable CDs.

An increase in business credit demands is usually associated with an upsurge in sales of negotiable CDs and other large time deposits held by money center banks. In offering large negotiable CDs, most banks are borrowing from some corporations in order to fund their loans to other corporations, hoping to profit from the spread between corporate deposit rates and corporate loan rates.

Eurocurrency Deposit Market

The development of the U.S. negotiable CD market came on the heels of another deposit market that began in Europe in the 1950s—the **Eurocurrency deposit** market. Eurocurrency deposits were developed originally in western Europe to provide liquid funds that could be swapped among multinational banks or loaned to the banks' largest customers. The bulk of such international borrowing and lending has occurred in the Eurodollar market.

Eurodollars are dollar-denominated deposits placed in bank offices outside the United States. Because Eurodollar deposits are denominated on the receiving banks' books in dollars rather than in the currency of the home country, they consist merely of bookkeeping entries in the form of *time deposits*.[3] They are *not* spendable on the street like currency.

The banks accepting these deposits may be foreign banks, branches of U.S. banks overseas, or international banking facilities (IBFs) set up on U.S. soil but devoted to foreign transactions on behalf of a parent U.S. bank. The heart of the worldwide Eurodollar market is in London, where British banks compete with scores of American and other foreign banks for Eurodollar deposits. The Eurocurrency market is the largest unregulated financial marketplace in the world, which is one reason it has also been one of the fastest-growing of all financial markets.[4]

A domestic bank can tap the Euromarket for funds by contacting one of the major international banks that borrow and lend Eurocurrencies every day. The largest U.S. banks also use their own overseas branches to tap this market. When one of these branches lends a Eurodeposit to its home office in the United States, the home office records the deposit in an account labeled *liabilities to foreign branches*. When a U.S. bank borrows Eurodeposits from a bank operating overseas, the transaction takes place through the correspondent banking system. The lending bank will instruct a U.S. correspondent bank where it has a deposit to transfer funds in the amount of the Eurocurrency loan to the correspondent account of the borrowing bank. These borrowed funds

---

[3]In general, whenever a deposit is accepted by a bank denominated in the units of a currency other than the home currency, that deposit is known as a *Eurocurrency deposit*. While the Eurocurrency market began in Europe (hence the prefix *Euro*), it reaches worldwide today, including such diverse locations as the Bahamas, Singapore, and Japan.

[4]Most banks located outside the United States do not have to hold legal reserves against dollar-denominated deposits, and there is no assessment for government deposit insurance because Eurodollar deposits are *not* insured by the U.S. government. Similarly, deposits booked at U.S. IBFs, which are computerized bookkeeping facilities of American banks located inside U.S. borders, carry no reserve requirements. *However,* only non-U.S. residents can hold deposits at the IBFs operated by U.S. banks.

Bankers' Insights and Issues

The Safety Net for Banks

Banks in most countries, including the United States, have access to a group of government-provided and, often, government-subsidized services known as the "safety net." For example, banks are usually allowed to borrow from their nation's central bank, and the interest rate on such loans is often among the lowest rates charged for money market loans. Central banks like the Federal Reserve System also may provide banks in their system with intraday loans (known as "daylight overdrafts") to make it easier and faster for bankers to clear payments for their customers. In effect, the central bank guarantees that these intraday transfers are "good funds" for those institutions receiving them through the payments system.

Also a part of the "safety net," most governments in industrialized economies provide deposit insurance at low or no insurance fees, enabling bankers to sell deposits to the public at relatively low interest cost. Deposit insurance also benefits nondeposit borrowing by banks because it enables banks to more easily raise additional liquidity via deposit sales in order to cover repayments of nondeposit borrowings if normal nondeposit sources dry up or become too expensive. Moreover, deposit insurance allows banks to get by with less capital and hold riskier assets than they otherwise would be forced to hold.

The government "safety net" for banking becomes a true government subsidy when it allows individual banks to secure monies at lower interest rates than the private financial marketplace normally would assess if the bank receiving safety-net support had to borrow from private, unsubsidized sources. In general, the riskier a bank is, the greater is the size of the subsidy provided by the safety net if a bank's home government provides such a net.

However, the safety net is *not* without its costs for banks. For example, to qualify for safety-net support a bank usually must hold a recognized charter of incorporation (i.e., a valid license to do business as a bank) from a government agency and conform to the rules and regulations that go with that charter. These rules often prohibit banks from freely selling certain nonbank goods and services (such as providing unlimited stock underwriting for corporations, selling life insurance, or manufacturing widgets). Otherwise, a bank must surrender its charter and cease to be a banking firm. No bank in the United States, for example, is allowed to borrow money from the Federal Reserve unless it has a valid federal or state bank charter and fully conforms to the Federal Reserve's rules. It also must post collateral for its

will be quickly loaned to qualified borrowers or, perhaps, used to meet a reserve deficit. Later, when the loan falls due, the entries on the books of correspondent banks are reversed. This process of borrowing and lending Eurodollars is traced out in Tables 14–6 and 14–7.

Most Eurodollar deposits are *fixed-rate time deposits*. Beginning in the 1970s, however, floating-rate CDs (FRCDs) and floating-rate notes (FRNs) were introduced in an effort to protect banks and their Eurodepositors from the risk of fluctuating interest

borrowings with the Federal Reserve bank in its district. Moreover, a bank borrowing from the Fed cannot turn around and make loans to its customers using those borrowings. Finally, banks drawing upon Federal Reserve services must maintain legal reserves at the Fed, which pay no interest earnings.

One indication that government safety nets are not without their cost to banks is the fact that, in many countries including the United States, bankings' share of the financial-services marketplace is declining. This trend suggests that the government's support does not necessarily provide banks with an unmixed competitive blessing that allows them to outbid their competitors for resources. On the other hand, there must be *some* competitive advantages to the safety net because few banks in recent years have elected to give up their banking charters.

The presence of the safety net and the subsidies it provides many, if not most, banks creates a tricky situation for financial reformers. By voting, for example, to allow banks to offer more innovative services to their customers (such as selling insurance or trading corporate stock) this step tends to increase the market value of bank charters. The value of the safety net tends to rise also as that net is extended to protect a wider range of banking products and services. In effect, the amount of the subsidy government provides the industry will tend to increase if reforms allow bankers to do more things.

The ultimate result is a greater financial burden on the public should banks get into trouble with their new service powers and begin to fail, requiring the safety net to supply resources to save some banks and resolve the failure of others. The government's taxpayers become the ultimate losers in this situation. This is why many banking reform proposals and regulatory actions in the United States, Europe, and Asia in recent years have focused upon keeping banks, securities firms, insurance companies, and other financial-service companies as distinct and separate as possible (such as by creating separate affiliated corporations within the same holding company or by forbidding marriages between firms in different industries) and forcing banks to conform to the toughest regulatory rules of all.

Source: For an excellent discussion of the concept of a government safety net and its possible impact on the public and the banking system, see Frederick Furlong, "Federal Subsidies in Banking: The Link to Financial Modernization," *FRBSRF Economic Letter*, Federal Reserve Bank of San Francisco, No. 97-31, October 24, 1997.

rates. FRCDs and FRNs tend to be medium-term to long-term, stretching from 1 year to as long as 20 years. The offer rates on these longer-term negotiable deposits are adjusted, usually every three to six months, based upon interest rate movements in the interbank Eurodollar market. The majority of Eurodollar deposits mature within six months; however, some are as short as overnight. Most are interbank liabilities whose interest yield is tied closely to LIBOR, which is the interest rate money center banks quote each other for the loan of short-term Eurodollar deposits. Large-denomination

TABLE 14–6   U.S. Bank Borrowing Eurodollars from Foreign Banks
(in millions of dollars)

Step 1. The Loan Is Made to a U.S. Bank from the Eurodollar Market

U.S. Bank Borrowing Eurodollars		U.S. Bank Serving as Correspondent to Foreign Bank		Foreign Bank Lending Eurodollars	
Assets	*Liabilities*	*Assets*	*Liabilities*	*Assets*	*Liabilities*
Deposits held at other banks +100	Deposits due to foreign bank +100 (Eurodollars borrowed)		Deposits due to foreign bank −100 Deposits of U.S. correspondent bank doing the bor- rowing +100 (Eurodollars borrowed)	Deposit at U.S. correspondent bank −100 Eurodollar loan to U.S. bank +100	

Step 2. The Loan Is Repaid by the Borrowing U.S. Bank

U.S. Bank Borrowing Eurodollars		U.S. Bank Serving as Correspondent to Foreign Bank		Foreign Bank Lending Eurodollars	
Assets	*Liabilities*	*Assets*	*Liabilities*	*Assets*	*Liabilities*
Deposits held at other banks −100	Deposits due to foreign bank −100 (Eurodollars borrowed)		Deposits due to foreign bank +100 Deposits of U.S. corespondent bank doing the bor- rowing −100 (Eurodollars borrowed)	Deposit at U.S. correspondent bank +100 Eurodollar loan to U.S. Bank −100	

EuroCDs issued in the interbank market are called *tap CDs,* while smaller-denomination EuroCDs sold to a wide range of investors are called *tranche CDs.* As with domestic CDs, there is an active resale market for these deposits.

Considerable evidence exists today (e.g., see Kreichen [3]) that both major banks and their large corporate customers practice *arbitrage* between the Eurodollar and

TABLE 14–7   U.S. Bank Borrowing Eurodollars from Its Own Foreign Branch Office
(in millions of dollars)

Step 1. U.S. Bank Home Office Credits Its Foreign Branch for a Deposit

Home Office of U.S. Bank		**Foreign Branch Office of U.S. Bank**	
Assets	Liabilities and Net Worth	Assets	Liabilities and Net Worth
Reserves +100	Liabilities to foreign branches +100	Deposit at home office +100	Deposit from branch office customers +100

Step 2. U.S. Bank Home Office Makes a Loan with the Newly Borrowed Reserves

Home Office of U.S. Bank	
Assets	Liabilities and Net Worth
Reserves −100	
Loans +100	

Step 3. The Loan Is Repaid, Funds Are Returned to the Branch Office, and the Deposits of Branch Office Customers Are Withdrawn

Home Office of U.S. Bank		**Foreign Branch Office of U.S. Bank**	
Assets	Liabilities and Net Worth	Assets	Liabilities and Net Worth
Reserves −100	Liabilities to foreign branches −100	Deposit at home office −100	Deposit from branch office customers −100

American CD markets. For example, if domestic CD rates were to drop significantly below Eurodollar interest rates on deposits of comparable maturity, a bank or its corporate customers could borrow in the domestic CD market and lend those funds off-shore in the Euromarket. Similarly, an interest rate spread in the opposite direction might well lead to increased Eurodollar borrowings, with the proceeds flowing into CD markets inside the United States.

Concept Checks

14–7.   What are the advantages of borrowing from the Federal Reserve banks?

14–8.   How is a discount window loan from the Federal Reserve secured?

14–9.   Posner State Bank borrows $10 million in adjustment credit from the Federal Reserve Bank of Cleveland. Can you show the correct entries for the granting and repayment of this loan?

14–10. Why were negotiable CDs developed?

14–11. What are the advantages and disadvantages of CDs as a bank funding source?

14–12. Suppose a bank customer purchases a $1 million 90-day CD, carrying a promised 6 percent annualized yield. How much in interest income will the customer earn when this 90-day instrument matures? What total volume of funds will be available to the depositor at the end of 90 days?

14–13. Where do Eurodollars come from?

14–14. How does a bank gain access to funds from the Eurocurrency markets?

14–15. Suppose that Chase Manhattan Bank in New York elects to borrow $250 million from one of its London branches, loans the borrowed funds for a week to a security dealer, and then returns the borrowed funds to its branch office in London. Can you trace through what accounting entries must be made? What if Chase had decided to borrow the $250 million from a foreign bank not related to Chase? How do the accounting entries differ in these two cases?

Commercial Paper Market

Late in the 1960s, large banks faced with intense demand for loans found a *new* source of loanable funds—the **commercial paper market.** Commercial paper consists of short-term notes, with maturities ranging from three or four days to nine months, issued by well-known companies to raise working capital. Most such paper is designed to finance the purchase of inventories of goods or raw materials, cover taxes, or meet other immediate corporate cash needs. The notes are sold at a discount from their face value through dealers or through direct contact between the issuing company and interested investors.

Under current federal law, commercial banks cannot issue commercial paper directly but their affiliated companies can do so. In the years before deregulation of deposit interest rates in the United States, many banks formed one-bank holding companies to issue commercial paper that was *not* regulated in preference to selling deposits that are regulated. Most bank-related paper today is issued by bank holding companies or by nonbank firms that they control. Once it is sold, the proceeds can be used to purchase loans off the books of banks in the same organization, giving these institutions additional funds to make new loans. Table 14–8 summarizes this process of indirect bank borrowing through commercial paper issued by affiliated firms.

TABLE 14–8 Commercial Paper Borrowing by a Holding Company That Channels the Borrowed Funds to One of Its Banks

(in millions of dollars)

Step 1. Commercial Paper Is Sold by an Affiliated Nonbank Corporation in the Money Market

Commercial Bank		**Affiliated Corporation**	
Assets	*Liabilities and Net Worth*	*Assets*	*Liabilities and Net Worth*
		Cash account +100	Commercial paper +100

Step 2. The Affiliated Corporation Purchases Loans from the Bank or Banks That Are Part of the Same Organization

Commercial Bank		**Affiliated Corporation**	
Assets	*Liabilities and Net Worth*	*Assets*	*Liabilities and Net Worth*
Loans −100 Reserves +100		Cash account −100 Loans purchased from bank +100	

Repurchase Agreements as a Source of Bank Funds

Still another nondeposit source of bank funds that emerged many years ago was the use of low-risk bank assets as collateral for short-term borrowings. This was done through a **repurchase agreement** (RP, or repo). RPs involve the temporary sale of high-quality, easily liquidated assets, such as U.S. Treasury bills, accompanied by an agreement to buy back those assets on a specific future date at a predetermined price. (See Table 14–9.) An RP transaction may be as short as overnight or as long as several months. Most agreements cover a few days, though there has been a trend in recent years toward *continuing contracts,* in which the funds raised by the seller of securities under an RP may be used indefinitely until either the seller or the buyer cancels the deal.

RPs have several advantages as a nondeposit source of bank reserves. If the RP agreement is made with a customer who keeps a checkable deposit with the borrowing bank, the customer normally purchases the securities involved by issuing a check against his or her deposit account, thus reducing both the bank's deposit and its reserve requirements. Simultaneously, the bank gains excess reserves that can be used to make new loans. RPs make use of high-quality (but low-yielding) bank assets without having to dispose of those assets permanently. The interest rate the bank must pay for such a loan is low (usually close to the U.S. Treasury bill rate) because RPs generally are backed by high-quality collateral. Moreover, the length or term of the RP agreement can be tailored exactly to the liquidity needs of both borrower and lender, though most RP agreements expire within one or a few days.

TABLE 14–9   **Raising Loanable Funds through a Repurchase Agreement Involving Bank Securities**

(in millions of dollars)

Step 1. Bank Sells Some of Its Securities under an RP Agreement

Commercial Bank			**Temporary Buyer of the Bank's Securities**		
Assets		*Liabilities and Net Worth*	*Assets*		*Liabilities and Net Worth*
Securities	−100				
Reserves	+100		Securities	+100	
			Cash account	−100	

Step 2. The RP Agreement Ends and the Securities Are Returned

Commercial Bank			**Temporary Buyer of the Bank's Securities**		
Assets		*Liabilities and Net Worth*	*Assets*		*Liabilities and Net Worth*
Securities	+100				
Reserves	−100		Securities	−100	
			Cash account	+100	

The bank's interest cost can be figured from the following formula:

$$\text{Interest cost of RP} = \text{Amount borrowed} \times \text{Current RP rate} \times \frac{\text{Number of days in RP borrowing}}{360 \text{ days}}$$

For example, suppose that a bank borrows $50 million through an RP transaction collateralized by government bonds for three days and the current RP rate in the market is 6 percent. Then the bank's total interest cost would be:

$$\text{Interest cost of RP} = \$50,000,000 \times 0.06 \times \frac{3}{360} = \$24,995$$

Because of the low interest cost on the RP, the bank can earn a highly favorable margin between its interest earnings on RP-funded loans and the cost of the RP itself.

We must add a word of caution here about RPs. They are not always free of default. In 1985, for example, two dealers in government securities—Bevill, Bresler, & Schulman and E.S.M. Government Securities, Inc.—collapsed, presenting a number of banks, savings and loan associations, and state and local governments with losses on funds they had loaned to these dealers through repurchase agreements. As a result, Congress and the Federal Reserve System acted to more closely regulate the government securities market in an effort to restore safety to RP trading. In 1986, Congress passed the Government Securities Act, which requires dealers in U.S. government securities to report their activities and requires borrowers and lenders to put their RP contracts in writing, specifying the location of any collateral involved.

The new regulations increased the cost to banks that desire to use repurchase agreements as a source of funds. Today, experts in the field caution bankers lending to other institutions through RPs *(a)* to check out the borrower's equity capital to be sure it is adequate to cover possible losses, *(b)* to make sure that the securities posted as collateral are actually set aside to secure the RP and have not been pledged behind other borrowings as well, and *(c)* where there is any question about the borrower's viability, avoid making the loan or use a repurchase agreement with a very short term (such as an overnight loan or continuing contract that can be canceled on short notice).

Long-Term Nondeposit Funds Sources

The nondeposit sources of funds discussed to this point are, in the main, *short-term* borrowings. The loans involved range from hours to days, occasionally stretching into weeks or months with term Federal funds contracts, commercial paper, and similar funding instruments. However, banks also tap longer-term nondeposit funds stretching well beyond one year. Examples include *mortgages* issued to fund the construction of bank buildings and *capital notes and debentures* (which usually range from 7 to 12 years in maturity and are used to supplement bank equity capital). Capital notes and debentures are discussed in greater detail in Chapter 15.

These longer-term nondeposit funds sources have remained relatively modest over the years due to regulatory restrictions and the augmented risks associated with long-term borrowing. Also, since most bank assets and liabilities are short- to medium-term, issuing long-term indebtedness creates a significant maturity mismatch for most banks. Nevertheless, the favorable leveraging effects of such debt have made it attractive to large banking organizations in recent years.

In the case of long-term capital notes and debentures issued by the largest U.S. banks, there is evidence of tacit government support for these securities, which makes them more attractive to capital market investors. For example, when First Republic Bank of Dallas, then the Southwest's largest banking organization, was taken over by the FDIC and sold to NCNB Corp. (later known as NationsBank) of Charlotte, North Carolina, the capital investments of that banking firm's noteholders were generally protected. However, because of the long-term nature of these bank funding sources, they are a sensitive barometer of the perceived risk exposure (particularly the risk of default) of their issuing banks. In 1990, for example, when there were fears of major bank defaults, the capital notes of troubled Southeast Banking Corp. and the Bank of Boston carried annual yields of close to 20 percent, while notes issued by the Bank of New England were trading at a discount equal to only about one-fifth of their face value.

By year-end 1996, a total of $1.9 billion in mortgage indebtedness and $51.2 billion in capital notes and debentures had been issued by all U.S. banks. These two long-term borrowing totals represented just over 1 percent of the industry's total liabilities, yet were costing U.S. insured banks more than $3.6 billion in annual interest payments.

Concept Checks

14–16. What is *commercial paper?* What types of banking organizations issue such paper?

14–17. Suppose that the finance company affiliate of Citicorp issues $325 million in 90-day commercial paper to interested investors and uses the proceeds to purchase loans from Citibank. What accounting entries should be made on the balance sheets of Citibank and Citicorp's finance company affiliate?

14–18. How do RPs arise?

14–19. What are the principal advantages to the borrower of funds under an RP agreement?

14–20. What long-term nondeposit funds sources do banks draw upon today? How do these interest costs differ from most money market borrowings?

Choosing among Alternative Nondeposit Sources

With so many different nondeposit funds sources to draw on, bank managers must make choices among them. In using nondeposit funds, funds managers must answer the following key questions:

1. How much in total must be borrowed from these sources to meet the bank's needs?
2. Which nondeposit sources are best, given the bank's goals, at any given moment in time?

Measuring a Bank's Total Need for Nondeposit Funds: The Funds Gap

Each bank's demand for nondeposit funds is determined basically by the size of the *gap* between its total credit demands and its deposits. Bank managers responsible for the asset side of the institution's balance sheet must choose which of a wide variety of customer credit requests they will meet by adding direct loans and investment securities to the bank's asset portfolio. Management must be prepared to meet, not only today's credit requests, but also all those it can reasonably anticipate in the future. This means that *projections* of current and anticipated credit demands must be based on knowledge of the current and probable future funding needs of the bank's customers, especially its largest borrowers. Such projections should not be wild guesses; they should be based on information gathered from frequent contacts between the bank's officers and both existing and potential customers.

The second decision that must be made is *how much in deposits* the bank is likely to be able to attract in order to finance the desired volume of loans and security investments it would like to make. Again, projections must be made of customer deposits and withdrawals, with special attention to the bank's largest depositors. Deposit projections must take into account current and future economic conditions, interest rates, and the cash flow requirements of the bank's largest depositors.

The difference between current and projected credit and deposit flows yields an estimate of the individual bank's **funds gap.** Thus:

$$
\begin{aligned}
\text{The funds gap} \;=\; & \text{Current and projected loans} \\
& \text{and investments the bank} \\
& \text{desires to make} \;-\; \text{Current and} \\
& \text{expected deposit inflows}
\end{aligned}
$$

For example, suppose a bank has new loan requests that meet its quality standards of $150 million; it wishes to purchase $75 million in new Treasury securities being issued this week and expects drawings on credit lines from its best corporate customers of $135 million. Deposits received today total $185 million, and those expected in the coming week will bring in another $100 million. This bank's estimated funds gap (FG) for the coming week will be as follows (in millions of dollars):

$$
\begin{aligned}
FG \;&=\; \big(\$150 \;+\; \$75 \;+\; \$135\big) \;-\; \big(\$185 \;+\; \$100\big) \\
&=\; \$360 \;-\; \$285 \\
&=\; \$75
\end{aligned}
$$

Most banks will add a small amount to this funds gap estimate to cover unexpected credit demands or unanticipated shortfalls in deposit inflows. Various *nondeposit* funds sources then may be tapped to cover the estimated funds gap.

Nondeposit Funding Sources: Factors to Consider

Which nondeposit sources will bank management use to cover its projected funding gap? The answer to that question depends largely upon five factors:

1. The *relative costs* of raising funds from each nondeposit source.
2. The *risk* (volatility and dependability) of each funding source.
3. The *length of time* (maturity or term) for which funds are needed.
4. The *size of the bank* that requires nondeposit funds.
5. *Regulations* limiting the use of alternative funds sources.

Relative Costs.   Bankers practicing liability management must constantly be aware of the going market interest rates attached to different sources of borrowed funds. Major lenders post daily interest rates at which they are willing to commit funds to banks in need of additional reserves. In general, bank managers would prefer to borrow from the *cheapest* sources of funds, though they also consider factors other than cost.

A sample of these interest rates on money market borrowings, averaged over selected years, is shown in Table 14–10. Note that the various funds sources vary significantly in price—the interest rate the bank must pay. Usually, the cheapest short-term funds source is a loan from the Federal Reserve bank in the district. Because this rate is set administratively by the board of directors of each Federal Reserve bank, the discount

TABLE 14–10   Money Market Interest Rates for Nondeposit Borrowings and Large CDs

Sources of Funds	Interest Rates Quoted for the Years				
	1990	*1992*	*1994*	*1996*	*1998***
Federal funds loans	8.10%	3.52%	4.47%	5.30%	5.50%
Borrowing from the Federal Reserve banks*	6.98	3.25	3.76	5.00	5.00
Selling commercial paper (one-month maturities, directly placed)	8.15	3.71	4.65	5.43	5.49
Large negotiable CDs, secondary market yield (one-month maturities)	8.15	3.64	4.60	5.35	5.25
Eurodollar deposits (three-month maturities)	8.16	3.70	4.80	5.38	5.63

*Average rate posted by the Federal Reserve Bank of New York.
**1998 figures as of February.

Source: Board of Governors of the Federal Reserve System, *Federal Reserve Bulletin,* selected monthly issues.

rate normally is stable and predictable over several weeks or months. As we have seen, however, the key disadvantage of borrowing from the Fed is the rules and regulations that surround these loans.

The going interest rate on Federal funds normally hovers slightly above the Fed's discount rate. Banks with immediate reserve deficiencies can gain the reserves they need by either borrowing from the Fed or buying Federal funds. The spread between the Fed's discount rate and the Federal funds rate measures the *opportunity cost* of going to the open market for reserves rather than to the Federal Reserve. The narrower that rate spread, the smaller the opportunity cost and the more likely banks will choose Federal funds over loans from the Federal Reserve.

The Federal funds rate is highly volatile, however, changing several times during the course of the normal business day. Thus, bankers active as either borrowers or lenders in this market must stay in frequent touch with major banks trading in Federal funds and with Federal funds brokers. The key advantage of Federal funds is their ready availability through a simple phone call or an online computer request. Moreover, their maturities are flexible and may be as short as 24 hours or as long as several months. The key disadvantage of Federal funds is their volatile market interest rate; its wide fluctuations make advance planning difficult.

As Table 14–10 indicates, the interest rates on large negotiable CDs and commercial paper can be highly competitive with other short-term interest rates. However, the sale of commercial paper incurs marketing costs in seeking out buyers for these notes, and the loan normally must cover at least three or four days and often stretches over several weeks. Thus, a bank needing funds for only a few hours might not be inclined to tap negotiable CDs or commercial paper.

The final interest rate shown in Table 14–10 applies to Eurodollar deposits. The posted rate on shorter-term Eurodeposits, LIBOR, is the key reference rate for lenders and borrowers of short-term funds in the global market. There is a time lag factor in these borrowings, which makes them difficult to use for immediate funding needs.

Bank managers must stay abreast, minute by minute, of changing interest rates in the money market, because the rate of interest is the principal cost of borrowing nondeposit funds for a bank. However, *noninterest* costs cannot be ignored in calculating the true cost of borrowing nondeposit funds, including the time spent by bank personnel and the telephone and wire transfer charges that may be involved in negotiating and completing a loan transaction. As we saw in Chapter 13, a good formula for doing cost comparisons among alternative sources of funds is:

$$
\begin{array}{l}
\text{Effective cost rate on} \\
\text{deposit and nondeposit} \\
\text{sources of bank funds}
\end{array}
=
\frac{
\begin{array}{l}
\text{Current interest} \\
\text{cost on amounts} \\
\text{borrowed}
\end{array}
+
\begin{array}{l}
\text{Noninterest costs} \\
\text{the bank will incur} \\
\text{to access these funds}
\end{array}
}{
\begin{array}{c}
\text{Net investable funds raised} \\
\text{from this source}
\end{array}
}
$$

where

$$
\begin{array}{l}
\text{Current interest cost} \\
\text{on amounts borrowed}
\end{array}
=
\begin{array}{l}
\text{Prevailing interest} \\
\text{rate in the money} \\
\text{market}
\end{array}
\times
\begin{array}{l}
\text{Amount of funds} \\
\text{borrowed}
\end{array}
$$

$$
\begin{array}{l}
\text{Noninterest costs to} \\
\text{access funds}
\end{array}
=
\begin{array}{l}
\text{Estimated cost} \\
\text{rate representing} \\
\text{staff time, facilities,} \\
\text{and transaction costs}
\end{array}
\times
\begin{array}{l}
\text{Amount of funds} \\
\text{borrowed}
\end{array}
$$

$$
\begin{array}{l}
\text{Net investable funds} \\
\text{raised}
\end{array}
=
\begin{array}{l}
\text{Total amount borrowed less legal reserve} \\
\text{requirements (if any), deposit insurance} \\
\text{assessments (if any), and funds placed} \\
\text{in nonearning assets}
\end{array}
$$

Note that the cost associated with attracting each funds source is compared to the *net* amount of funds raised after deductions are made (where necessary) for reserve requirements, federal deposit insurance fees, and that portion of borrowed funds diverted into such nonearning assets as excess cash reserves or the bank's fixed assets. We use *net investable funds* as the borrowing base because we wish to compare the dollar cost the bank must pay out to attract borrowed funds relative to the dollar amount of those funds that can actually be used to acquire earning assets and cover the costs of bank fund-raising.

For example, Table 14–10 shows that in the winter of 1998 Federal funds were trading at an average market interest rate of about 5.50 percent. Suppose management estimates that the marginal noninterest cost, in terms of personnel expenses and transactions fees, from raising additional monies in the Federal funds market is 0.25 percent. The bank will need $25 million to fund the loans it plans to make today, of which only $24 million can be fully invested due to other immediate cash demands. Then the effective cost rate for Federal funds today would be calculated as follows:

$$\begin{array}{l} \text{Current interest cost} \\ \text{on Federal funds} \end{array} = .055 \times \$25 \text{ million} = \$1.375 \text{ million}$$

$$\begin{array}{l} \text{Noninterest cost to} \\ \text{access Federal funds} \end{array} = 0.0025 \times \$25 \text{ million} = \$0.063 \text{ million}$$

$$\begin{array}{l} \text{Net investable funds} \\ \text{raised} \end{array} = \$25 \text{ million} - \$1 \text{ million} = \$24 \text{ million}$$

Therefore, the effective Federal funds cost rate is:

$$\frac{\$1.375 \text{ million} + \$0.063 \text{ million}}{\$24 \text{ million}} = 0.0599, \text{ or } 5.99 \text{ percent}$$

The bank would have to earn a net return of at least 5.99 percent on the loans and investments it plans to make with these borrowed funds just to break even.

A further look at Table 14–10 reveals some potentially cheaper sources of loanable funds than the Federal funds market. For example, the Federal Reserve's discount rate was only 5 percent in 1998; however, Fed regulations prohibit the use of borrowings from a Federal Reserve bank for the purpose of making new loans. The market rate on CDs (as quoted by major banks in New York) was marginally higher, at 5.25 percent, but lower than the Federal funds rate. However, raising money through CDs may result in somewhat higher noninterest costs than borrowing in the Federal funds market due to greater advertising and recordkeeping costs as well as the heavier use of employee time. Let's suppose that raising CD money costs the bank 0.75 percent in noninterest costs. Then the cost rate incurred by the bank from selling CDs would be:

$$\begin{array}{l} \text{Effective CD} \\ \text{cost rate} \end{array} = \frac{(0.0525 \times \$25 \text{ million} + \$0.0075 \times \$25 \text{ million})}{\$24 \text{ million}}$$

$$= \frac{\$1.3125 \text{ million} + \$0.1875 \text{ million}}{\$24 \text{ million}}$$

$$= \$1.50 \text{ million} / \$24 \text{ million} = 0.0625, \text{ or } 6.25 \text{ percent}$$

There is an additional expense associated with selling CDs to raise the funds a bank needs, however. CDs and all other deposits received from the public carry a deposit insurance fee. In 1998, for example, this fee, which must be paid in installments each year to the Federal Deposit Insurance Corporation (FDIC), was $0.0027 per dollar for the riskiest U.S. banks. (Most U.S. banks paid a zero insurance fee in 1998 because the FDIC's insurance reserves were then large enough to meet the minimum amount of total insurance reserves required by law—$1.25 in reserves for every $100 in insured deposits held by depository institutions that have FDIC insurance coverage.) Moreover, FDIC rules require a bank to pay this fee not just on the first $100,000 actually covered by insurance but on the full face amount of every deposit received from the public. Thus, the total insurance cost for the riskiest banks on the $25 million to be raised through selling CDs is:

$$\begin{array}{c} \text{Total deposits} \\ \text{received from} \\ \text{the public} \end{array} \times \begin{array}{c} \text{Insurance} \\ \text{fee per} \\ \text{dollar} \end{array} = \$25 \text{ million} \times 0.0027$$

$$= \$67,500, \text{ or } \$0.0675 \text{ million}$$

If we deduct this fee from the net amount of CDs available for the bank's use we get:

$$\begin{array}{c} \text{Effective CD} \\ \text{cost rate} \end{array} = \frac{\$1.50 \text{ million}}{\$24 \text{ million} - \$0.0675 \text{ million}}$$

$$= \frac{\$1.50 \text{ million}}{\$23.925 \text{ million}} = 6.27 \text{ percent}$$

Clearly, in this example issuing CDs would be *more* expensive for the bank than borrowing Federal funds. However, the CDs have the advantage of being available for several days or weeks, whereas Federal funds loans must usually be repaid in 24 hours.

Functional cost analysis data assembled each year by the Federal Reserve banks indicates that nondeposit sources of funds generally are moderate in cost compared to other bank funding sources. Generally nondeposit sources of bank funds are more expensive than demand deposits but less expensive than time deposits. We must add a note of caution here, however, because the costs and the profits associated with nondeposit sources of funds tend to be more volatile from year to year than the cost and profitability of deposits. Nondeposit funds do have the advantage of *quick availability* compared to most types of deposits, but are clearly not as stable a funding source for banks as are time and savings deposits.

The Risk Factor.   Bank managers must consider at least two types of *risk* when selecting among different nondeposit sources. There is **interest rate risk**—the volatility of credit costs. All the interest rates shown in Table 14–10, except the Federal Reserve's discount rate, are determined by demand and supply forces in the open market and therefore are subject to erratic fluctuations. The shorter the term of the loan, the more volatile the prevailing market interest rate tends to be. Thus, most Federal funds loans are overnight and, not surprisingly, this market interest rate tends to be the most volatile of all.

There is also **credit availability risk.** There is no guarantee in any credit market that lenders will be willing and able to accommodate every borrower. When general credit conditions are tight, lenders may have limited funds to loan and may ration credit, confining loans only to their soundest and most loyal customers. Sometimes a borrowing bank may appear so risky to money market lenders that they will deny it credit or make the price so high that the bank's earnings will suffer. Experience has shown that the negotiable CD, Eurodollar, and commercial paper markets are especially sensitive to credit availability risks. Bank funds managers must be prepared to switch to alternative sources of credit and, if necessary, pay more for any funds they receive.

The Length of Time Funds Are Needed.   As we have seen, some funds sources cannot be relied on for immediate credit (such as commercial paper and Eurodollars). A bank manager in need of loanable funds this afternoon would be inclined to borrow in the Federal funds market. However, if funds are not needed for a few days, selling

CDs or commercial paper becomes a more viable option. Thus, the *term,* or *maturity,* of the funds need plays a key role as well.

The Size of the Borrowing Bank.   The standard trading unit for most money market loans is $1 million, a denomination that often exceeds the borrowing requirements of the smallest banks. For example, Eurodollar borrowings are in multiples of $1 million and go only to banks with the highest credit ratings. Large negotiable CDs of the largest banks are preferred by most investors because there is an active secondary market for prime-rated CDs. Smaller banks do not have the credit standing to be able to sell most large negotiable CDs. The same is true of commercial paper. Only the Federal Reserve's discount window and the Federal funds market make the relatively small denomination loans that are suitable for smaller banks.

Regulations.   Federal or state banking regulations may limit the amount, frequency, and use of borrowings by banks. For example, CDs must be issued with maturities of at least seven days. As we have seen, the Federal Reserve banks restrict continuous borrowing from the discount window and the use of borrowed reserves to make loans to customers. Other forms of borrowing may be subjected to reserve requirements by action of the Federal Reserve Board. For example, during the late 1960s and early 1970s, when the Federal Reserve was attempting to fight inflation with tight-money policies, it imposed reserve requirements for a time on Federal funds borrowings from nonbank sources, on repurchase agreements, and on commercial paper issued to purchase assets from affiliated banks. While these particular requirements are not currently in force, it seems clear that in times of national emergency government policymakers would move swiftly to impose new controls, affecting both the costs and the risks associated with nondeposit borrowings.

Concept Checks

14–21.   What is the *funds gap* for a bank?

14–22.   Suppose that Bankers Trust Company of New York discovers that projected new loan demand next week should total $325 million and customers holding confirmed credit lines plan to draw down $510 million in funds to cover their cash needs next week, while new deposits next week are projected to equal $680 million. The bank also plans to acquire $420 million in corporate and government bonds next week. What is the bank's projected *funds gap?*

14–23.   What factors must a bank manager weigh in choosing among the various nondeposit sources of bank funding available today?

Summary

While the principal funding source for banks is still deposits, nearly all banks today supplement their deposits with nondeposit borrowings in the money market. The principal sources of these nondeposit IOUs include the market for Federal funds, loans from the discount windows of the Federal Reserve banks, the sale of negotiable CDs, borrowings of Eurodollars offshore, the commercial paper market, and repurchase agreements.

In tapping these nondeposit funding sources, bankers first must estimate their total funding requirements. One commonly used approach is to measure their *funds gap*—the spread between current and expected loans and investments and current and expected deposit inflows. Then they select the particular nondeposit sources of funds most appropriate at the time, based on five key factors: (1) the relative costs of each nondeposit funding source under consideration, (2) the risk or dependability of each source, (3) the length of time each funds source will be needed, (4) the size of the borrowing bank and its funding need, and (5) the content of government regulations. Among the most important regulations bearing on bank use of nondeposit borrowings are the reserve requirements imposed by the Federal Reserve Board in the United States and other central banks around the world and the rules laid down by the Federal Reserve banks.

Key Terms in This Chapter

Customer relationship doctrine
Liability management
Federal funds market
Discount window
Negotiable CD
Eurocurrency deposit

Commercial paper market
Repurchase agreement (RP)
Funds gap
Interest rate risk
Credit availability risk

Problems and Projects

1. Robertson State Bank of Clayton decides to loan a portion of its reserves in the amount of $70 million held at the Federal Reserve Bank to Tenison National Security Bank for 24 hours. For its part, Tenison plans to make a 24-hour loan to a security dealer before it must return the funds to Robertson State Bank. Please show all the proper accounting entries for these transactions.

2. Masoner National Bank, headquartered in a small community, holds most of its correspondent deposits with Flagg Metrocenter Bank, a money center institution. When Masoner has a cash surplus in its correspondent deposit, Flagg automatically invests the surplus in Federal funds loans to other money center banks. A check of Masoner's records this morning reveals a temporary surplus of $11 million for 48 hours. Flagg will loan this surplus for two business days to Secoro Central City Bank, which is in need of additional reserves. Please show the correct balance sheet entries to carry out this loan and to pay off the loan when its term ends.

3. Relgade National Bank secures adjustment credit from the Federal Reserve Bank of San Francisco in the amount of $32 million for a term of seven days. Please show the proper

entries for granting this loan and then paying off the loan.

4. Itec Corporation purchases a 45-day negotiable CD with a $5 million denomination from Payson Guaranty Bank and Trust, bearing a 6.75 percent annual yield. How much in interest will the bank have to pay when this CD matures? What amount in total will the bank have to pay back to Itec at the end of 45 days?

5. International Commerce Bank borrows $125 million overnight through a repurchase agreement (RP) collateralized by Treasury bills. The current RP rate is 4.5 percent. How much will the bank pay in interest cost due to this borrowing?

6. National Commerce Bank of New York expects new deposit inflows next month of $330 million and deposit withdrawals of $275 million. The bank's economics department has projected that new loan demand will reach $621 million and customers with approved credit lines will need $266 million in cash. The bank will sell $480 million in securities, but plans to add $155 million in new securities to its portfolio. What is the bank's projected funds gap?

7. Manufacturers Hanover Bank borrowed $150 million in Federal funds from Chemical Bank, also headquartered in New York City, for 24 hours in order to fund a 30-day loan. The prevailing Federal funds rate on loans of this maturity stood at 7.85 percent when the loan was agreed to. The funds loaned by Chemical were in the reserve deposit that the bank keeps at the Federal Reserve Bank of New York. When the loan to Manufacturers was repaid the next day, Chemical used $50 million of the returned funds to cover its own reserve needs and loaned $100 million in Federal funds to Texas Commerce Bank, Houston, for a two-day period at the prevailing Federal funds rate of 7.92 percent. With respect to these transactions, *(a)* construct T-account entries similar to those you encountered in this chapter, showing the original Federal funds loan and its repayment on the books of Chemical, Manufacturers Hanover, and Texas Commerce banks, and *(b)* calculate the total interest income earned by Chemical on both Federal funds loans.

8. BancOne of Ohio issues a three-month (90-day) negotiable CD in the amount of $14 million to Travelers Insurance Company at a negotiated annual interest rate of 8.47 percent (360-day basis). Calculate the value of this CD account on the day it matures and the amount of interest income Travelers will earn. What interest return will Travelers Insurance earn in a 365-day year?

9. Banks within the holding company of Interstate National Bank are reporting heavy loan demand this week from companies in the southeastern United States that are planning a significant expansion of inventories and facilities before the beginning of the fall season. The holding company and its lead bank plan to raise $850 million in short-term funds this week, of which about $835 million will be used to meet these new loan requests. Federal funds are currently trading at 8.73 percent, negotiable ($100,000+) CDs are trading in New York at 8.69 percent, and Eurodollar borrowings are available in London at all maturities under one year at 9.11 percent. One-month maturities of directly placed commercial paper carry market rates of 8.65 percent, while the discount rate of the Federal Reserve Bank of Richmond is currently set at 7.25 percent—a source that Interstate has used in each of the past two weeks. Noninterest costs are estimated at 0.25 percent for Fed funds, discount window borrowings, and CDs; 0.35 percent for Eurodollar borrowings; and 0.50 percent for commercial paper. Calculate the effective cost rate of each of these sources of funds for Interstate and make a management decision on what sources to use. Be prepared to defend your decision.

10. Hamilton Security Bank is considering the problem of trying to raise $80 million in money market funds to cover a loan request from one of its largest corporate customers, who needs a six-

week loan. Money market interest rates are currently at the levels indicated below:

Federal funds, average	
for week just concluded	8.72%
Discount window of the	
Federal Reserve bank	7.00
CDs (prime rated,	
secondary market):	
One month	8.45
Three months	8.49
Six months	8.58
Eurodollar deposits	
(three months)	8.58
Commercial paper	
(directly placed):	
One month	8.55
Three months	8.42

Unfortunately, the bank's economics department is forecasting a substantial rise in money market interest rates over the next six weeks. What would you recommend to the bank's funds management department regarding how and where to raise the funds needed? Be sure to consider such cost factors as reserve requirements, regulations, and what happens to the relative attractiveness of each funding source if interest rates rise continually over the period of the proposed loan.

Alternative scenario:

What if Hamilton's economists are wrong and money market rates *decline* significantly over the next six weeks? How would your recommendation to the bank's funds management department change on how and where to raise the funds needed?

Selected References

For a discussion of borrowing reserves from the discount windows of the Federal Reserve banks, see the following study:

1. Goodfriend, Marvin. "Discount Window Borrowing, Monetary Policy, and the Post-October 6, 1979, Federal Reserve Operating Procedures." *Journal of Monetary Economics* 12 (1983), pp. 343–56.

For an analysis of recent developments in the Federal funds market, see especially:

2. Bennett, Paul, and Spence Hilton. "Falling Reserve Balances and the Federal Funds Rate." *Current Issues in Economics and Finance,* Federal Reserve Bank of New York, 3, no. 5 (April 1997), pp. 1–6.

For an analysis of the causes and effects of Eurodollar borrowing, see:

3. Kreichen, Lawrence L. "Eurodollar Arbitrage." *Quarterly Review,* Federal Reserve Bank of New York, Summer 1982, pp. 10–22.

4. Goodfriend, Marvin. "Eurodollars." *Instruments of the Money Market,* Federal Reserve Bank of Richmond, 1986, pp. 53–64.

For an analysis of commercial paper as a borrowing instrument for banks, see the following:

5. Rose, Peter S. "The Quest for Funds: New Directions in a New Market." *The Canadian Banker* 94, no. 5 (September/October 1987), pp. 46–55.

6. McCauley, Robert N., and Lauren A. Hargraves. "Eurocommercial Paper and U.S. Commercial Paper: Converging Money Markets?" *Quarterly Review,* Federal Reserve Bank of New York, Autumn 1987, pp. 24–35.

This study contains an excellent discussion of the development and uses of the negotiable CD:

7. Willernse, Rob J. "Large Certificates of Deposit." *Instruments of the Money Market,* Federal Reserve Bank of Richmond, 1986, pp. 36–52.

15   MANAGEMENT OF A BANK'S EQUITY CAPITAL POSITION

Learning and Management Decision Objectives

The purpose of this chapter is to discover why capital—particularly equity capital—is so important in banking, to learn how bankers and regulators assess the adequacy of a bank's capital position, and to explore the ways that bank management can raise new capital.

Introduction

One of the most critical of all banking problems in recent years centers upon raising and maintaining sufficient **capital.** The word has special meaning to a banker—*capital* refers principally to funds contributed by the bank's *owners,* consisting mainly of stock, reserves, and those earnings that are retained in the bank. As we shall see in this chapter, capital performs several indispensable jobs in the operation of a bank, such as supplying resources to get a new bank started, providing a base for growth and expansion, defending the bank against risk, and maintaining public confidence in the bank's management and stockholders.

The Many Tasks Performed by Bank Capital

The capital accounts of a commercial bank play several vital roles in supporting its daily operations and ensuring its long-run viability. In the first place, *capital provides a cushion against the risk of failure* by absorbing financial and operating losses until management can address the bank's problems and restore the institution's profitability.

Second, *capital provides the funds needed to get the bank chartered, organized, and operating* before deposits come flowing in. A new bank needs start-up funding to acquire land, build a new structure or lease space, equip its facilities, and hire officers and staff even before opening day.

Third, *capital promotes public confidence* in a bank and reassures its creditors (including the depositors) of the bank's financial strength. Capital also must be strong enough to reassure borrowers that the bank will be able to meet their credit needs even if the economy turns down.

Fourth, *capital provides funds for the organization's growth and the development of new services, programs, and facilities.* When a bank grows, it needs additional capital to support that growth and to accept the risks that come with offering new services and building new facilities. Most banks eventually outgrow the facilities they start with. An infusion of additional capital will permit a bank to expand into larger quarters or build additional branch offices in order to keep pace with its expanding market area and follow its customers with convenient service offerings.

Fifth, capital serves as a *regulator of bank growth,* helping to ensure that the individual bank's growth is held to a pace that is sustainable in the long run. Both the regulatory authorities and the financial markets require that bank capital increases roughly in line with the growth of loans and other risky bank assets. Thus, the cushion to absorb losses is supposed to increase along with a banking institution's growing risk exposure. A bank that expands its loans and deposits too fast will start receiving signals from the market and the regulatory community that its growth must be slowed or additional capital must be acquired.

Relatedly, there is recent research evidence that capital has played a key role in the rapid growth of bank mergers. For example, Peek and Rosengren [7] of the Federal Reserve Bank of Boston find evidence that hundreds of smaller banks have disappeared via merger because of burgeoning growth in large business loans (over $1 million each), which can only be made by bigger banks with stronger capital positions. Both banks' internal loan policies and federal bank regulations limit the maximum size of not-fully secured loans made to a single borrower to no more than 15 percent of a bank's unimpaired capital and surplus while fully collateralized loans are limited to no more than 25 percent of a federally chartered bank's unimpaired capital and surplus. Banks whose capital fails to grow fast enough find themselves losing market share in the competition for the largest borrowing customers.

Finally, capital regulation by the bank regulatory agencies has become an increasingly important tool to limit how much risk exposure banks can accept. In this role capital not only tends to promote public confidence in banks and the banking system but also serves to *protect the government's deposit insurance system from serious losses.*

Bank Capital and Risk

Bank *capital* and *risk* are intimately related to each other. Capital itself is mainly the funds contributed by the owners of a bank that have been placed there at the *owners' risk*—the risk that the bank will earn a less-than-satisfactory return on the owners' funds or may even fail, with the stockholders recovering little or nothing. And the risks facing the owners of a bank are substantial. They include credit risk, liquidity risk, interest rate risk, operating risk, exchange risk, and crime risk.

Key Risks in Banking

Credit Risk.   There is, first of all, *credit risk*. Banks make loans and take on securities that are nothing more than *promises* to pay. When borrowing customers fail to make some or all of their promised interest and principal payments, these defaulted loans and securities result in losses that can eventually erode the bank's capital. Because owners' capital is usually no more than 10 percent of the volume of bank loans and risky securities (and often much less than that), it doesn't take too many defaults on loans and securities before bank capital simply becomes inadequate to absorb further losses. At this point, the bank fails and will close unless the regulatory authorities elect to keep it afloat until a buyer can be found.

Liquidity Risk.   There is also substantial *liquidity risk* in banking—the danger of running out of cash when cash is needed to cover deposit withdrawals and to meet the credit requests of good customers. If a bank cannot raise cash in timely fashion, it is likely to lose many of its customers and suffer a loss in earnings for its owners. If the cash shortage persists, this may lead to runs on the bank and ultimate collapse. The inability of a bank to meet its liquidity needs at reasonable cost is often a prime signal that it is in serious trouble.

Interest Rate Risk.   Banks also encounter risk to their *spread*—that is, the danger that revenues from earning assets will decline or that interest expenses will rise significantly, squeezing the spread between revenues and expenses, thereby reducing net income. Changes in the spread between bank revenues and expenses are usually related to either *portfolio management decisions* (i.e., changes in the composition of bank assets and liabilities) or *interest rate risk*—the probability that fluctuating interest rates will result in significant appreciation or depreciation of the value of and the return from the bank's assets. In recent years, banks have found ways to reduce their interest rate risk exposure, but such risks have not been completely eliminated—nor can they be.

Operating Risk.   Banks also face significant **operating risk** due to possible breakdowns in quality control, inefficiencies in producing and delivering services, or simple errors in judgment by management, fluctuations in the economy that impact the demand for each individual bank's services, and shifts in competition as new suppliers of financial services enter or leave a particular bank's market area. These changes can adversely affect a bank's revenue flows, its operating costs, and the value of the owner's investment in the bank (e.g., its stock price).

Exchange Risk.   Larger banks face **exchange risk** from their dealings in foreign currency. The world's most tradable currencies float with changing market conditions today. Banks trading in these currencies for themselves and their customers continually run the risk of adverse price movements on both the buying and selling sides of this market.

Crime Risk.   Finally, banks encounter significant **crime risk.** Fraud or embezzlement by bank employees or directors can weaken a bank severely and, in some instances, lead to its failure. In fact, the Federal Deposit Insurance Corporation lists fraud and embezzlement from insiders as one of the prime causes of recent bank closings. Moreover, the large amounts of money that banks keep in their vaults often proves to be an irresistible attraction to outsiders. As the famous outlaw Jesse James was reputed to have said when he was asked why he robbed banks, "because that's where the money is."

Bank robberies approached record levels during the 1970s and 1980s. These thefts were frequently a by-product of bankers' efforts to make their lobbies, drive-in windows, and teller machines more accessible to the public. While the 1990s brought a decline in the daily rate at which bank robberies were occurring, the extent and intensity of bank crime still remain high by historical standards. The focus of bank robberies has shifted somewhat with changes in banking technology; theft from ATMs and from patrons using those money machines has become one of the most problematic aspects of bank crime risk today.

Bank Defenses against Risk

Of course, banks are not devoid of protection against these many risks. In fact, there are several rings of defense that the bank's owners can rely upon to protect their institution's financial position. Among them are quality management, diversification, deposit insurance, and, ultimately, owners' capital.

Quality Management.   One of these defenses is *quality management*—the ability of top-notch managers to move swiftly to deal with a bank's problems before they overwhelm the institution.

Diversification.   Diversification of a bank's sources and uses of funds also has risk-reducing benefits. Banks generally strive to achieve two types of risk-reducing diversification: portfolio and geographic. **Portfolio diversification** means spreading out a bank's credit accounts and deposits among a wide variety of customers, including large and small business accounts, different industries, and households with a variety of sources of income and collateral. **Geographic diversification** refers to seeking out customers located in different communities or countries, which presumably will experience different economic conditions. These forms of diversification are most effective in reducing the bank's risk of loss when cash flows from different groups of customers move in different patterns over time. Thus, declines in cash flow from one customer segment may be at least partially offset by increases in cash flow from other customer segments.

Deposit Insurance.   Still another line of defense against the risks inherent in banking is *deposit insurance.* The Federal Deposit Insurance Corporation, established in the United States in 1934 and today protecting depositors holding up to $100,000 in any federally insured bank, was designed to promote public confidence in the banking system. While it has not stopped banks from failing, the FDIC appears to have stopped runs on neighboring banks when any particular bank fails. Moreover, its power to examine banks, issue cease and desist orders, levy civil money penalties, and seek criminal prosecution of violators of federal banking laws inhibits much risk taking by bank management and shareholders. This is why most industrialized countries today have some form of deposit insurance system.

Owners' Capital.   When all else fails, it is *owners' capital* (net worth) that forms the ultimate defense against risk in banking. Owners' capital absorbs losses from bad loans, poor securities' investments, crime, and management misjudgment so that the bank can keep operating until its problems are corrected and its losses are recovered. Only when the bank's losses are so large that they overwhelm not only all the other defenses but also the owners' capital will the institution be forced to close its doors. Owners' capital is the bank's *last line of defense* against failure. Thus, the greater the risk of failure, from whatever source, the more capital a bank should hold.

Concept Checks

15–1. What does the term *capital* as it applies to banking really mean?

15–2. What crucial roles does capital play in the management and viability of a bank?

15–3. What are the links between capital and risk exposure in banking?

Types of Bank Capital

There are several different types of bank capital:

1. **Common stock,** measured by the par (face) value of common equity shares outstanding, which pay a variable return depending on whether the bank's board of directors votes to pay a dividend.

2. **Preferred stock,** measured by the par value of any shares outstanding that promise to pay a fixed rate of return (dividend rate); preferred stock may be perpetual or have only limited life.

3. **Surplus,** representing the excess amount above each share of stock's par value paid in by the bank's shareholders.

4. **Undivided profits,** representing the net earnings of the bank that have been retained in the business rather than being paid out as dividends.

5. **Equity reserves,** representing funds set aside for contingencies such as legal action against the bank, as well as providing a reserve for dividends expected to be paid but not yet declared and a sinking fund to retire stock or debt in the future.

6. **Subordinated debentures,** representing long-term debt capital contributed by outside investors, whose claims against the bank legally follow (i.e., are subordinated to) the claims of depositors; these debt securities may carry a convertibility feature, permitting their future exchange for shares of bank stock.

7. The bank's **minority interest in consolidated subsidiaries,** where the bank holds ownership shares in other businesses.

8. **Equity commitment notes,** which are debt securities repayable only from the sale of stock.

Relative Importance of the Sources of Bank Capital

Table 15–1 shows that these various sources of bank capital are by no means equal in importance. *Undivided profits* (or *retained earnings*) and *capital reserves* represent the largest category of U.S. bank capital by dollar volume, accounting for about 40 percent of total long-term debt and equity capital. Close behind is the *surplus* market value of all common and preferred stock above the stock's par value, accounting for about 39 percent of U.S. banks' capital funds. Most of the remaining sources of bank capital come from long-term debt issues (subordinated notes and debentures) and the par value of common stock.

Preferred stock is relatively insignificant—less than 1 percent of the U.S. banking industry's capital—though preferred has increased in importance in recent years at larger banks and bank holding companies around the world. Bank preferred stock often carries floating dividend rates and a callability or redeemability feature that allows management to call in outstanding preferred shares and pay off the shareholders when it is financially advantageous to do so. However, bank preferred stock has been slow to win the confidence of many investors, in part because of bad experiences during the Great Depression of the 1930s when many troubled banks sold preferred shares just to stay afloat. Thus, preferred stock became associated in the minds of many investors with financial distress in banking.

TABLE 15–1   Capital Accounts of U.S.-Insured Commercial Banks, December 31, 1996

Forms of Bank Capital	*Amounts in Billions of Dollars*	*Percentage of Total Debt and Equity Capital*
Long-term debt capital:		
Subordinated notes and debentures	$ 51.2	12.0%
Equity capital:		
Common stock, par value	35.1	8.2
Perpetual preferred stock, par value	2.0	0.5
Surplus	167.7	39.3
Undivided profits and capital reserves	171.6	40.2
Foreign currency translation adjustment	(1.1)	(0.3)
Total equity capital	$375.3	87.9
Total long-term debt and equity capital	$426.5	100.0%

Source: Federal Deposit Insurance Corporation, *Statistics on Banking, 1996,* Washington, D.C., 1997.

Subordinated notes and *debentures* are a relatively small component of bank capital but a growing source of long-term funding for banks. Regulations require that these capital notes be subordinated to the claims of general creditors of the bank, including the depositors. Thus, if a bank closes and its assets are liquidated, the depositors have first claim on the proceeds and investors in debentures have a secondary claim. However, subordinated debtholders have a prior claim over common and preferred stockholders against the bank's earnings and assets.

Bank holding companies have issued substantial quantities of subordinated debt in recent years (especially to large institutional buyers such as pension funds and insurance companies). Frequently, such notes are callable shortly after issue and carry either fixed or floating interest rates (often tied to interest rates on government securities or short-term Eurodollar deposits). In a few instances, these capital notes have been issued as *zeros*—notes without a promised interest rate but sold instead at a discount from their face value, with the investors' yield determined solely by future price appreciation.

One distinct advantage of subordinated debt from a regulatory viewpoint is that it provides a form of *market discipline* for banks. Because bank debt subordinated to deposits is not covered by federal insurance, investors in subordinated notes will demand higher yields on their securities due to the bank's acceptance of more risk. Holders of subordinated debt tend to be more risk sensitive than depositors and will therefore monitor bank behavior more closely, reducing the incidence of bank failure. Subordinated notes and debentures generally can be issued successfully only by medium-size and larger banks and bank holding companies whose credit standing is trusted by securities investors. Many securities dealers simply refuse to handle small-bank debt issues because of the cost and risk involved.

Table 15–2 shows us how markedly different the composition of bank capital is for the largest versus the smallest banks. The smallest banks, for example, rely most heavily upon retained earnings (undivided profits) to build their capital positions and issue minuscule amounts of long-term debt (subordinated notes and debentures). In contrast, the biggest banks rely principally upon the surplus value of their stock sold in the financial marketplace, as well as retained earnings, and also issue significant amounts of long-term debt capital. These differences reflect, in part, the greater ability of the biggest banks to sell their capital securities in the open market and attract thousands of investors, while the smallest institutions, having only limited access to the financial markets, must depend principally upon their ability to generate adequate income and retain a significant portion of those earnings in order to build an acceptable capital cushion. Nevertheless, it is generally the smallest banks that maintain the thickest cushion of capital relative to their asset size. For example, at year-end 1996 the smallest U.S. banks (less than $100 million in assets apiece) posted an overall capital-to-assets ratio of 10.4 percent compared to a capital-to-asset ratio of only 9.3 percent for the largest U.S. banks (each with assets exceeding a billion dollars). Many authorities in the field argue that smaller banks need to hold higher ratios of capital relative to their assets because smaller banks tend to be less well diversified and face greater failure risk.

TABLE 15–2   **Amount and Composition of Bank Capital by Size of U.S.-Insured Bank, December 31, 1996**

	Amounts in Billions of Dollars and Percentages of Total Capital For					
	The Smallest Banks (less than $100 million in assets)		Medium-Size Banks ($100 million to $1 billion in assets)		The Largest Banks ($1 billion and over in assets)	
	Amount	*Percent*	*Amount*	*Percent*	*Amount*	*Percent*
Long-term debt capital:						
Subordinated notes and debentures	*	0.1%	$ 0.3	0.4%	$ 47.5	15.0%
Equity capital:						
Common stock, par value	$ 4.3	14.1	7.4	11.5	24.0	7.5
Perpetual preferred stock, par value	0.1	0.3	0.4	0.5	1.5	0.5
Surplus	11.1	36.8	24.2	37.6	127.8	40.2
Undivided profits and capital reserves	14.8	48.8	32.1	49.9	118.3	37.2
Foreign currency translation adjustment	0	(0.0)	0	(0.00)	(1.1)	(–0.1)
Total equity capital	30.2	99.7	64.1	99.5	270.5	85.1
Total long-term debt and equity capital	$30.2	100.0%	$64.4	100.0%	$318.0	100.0%

*Less than $50 million.

Source: Federal Deposit Insurance Corporation, *Statistics on Banking, 1996,* Washington, D.C., 1997.

Measuring the Size of Bank Capital

Before deciding *how much* capital a bank should have, we must know how a bank's capital is *measured.* There are, unfortunately, several different capital measures in use today, and the messages they send to the public and the regulatory community frequently conflict.

Book or GAAP Capital.   For example, bank capital may be measured by *book value* (in accounting terminology, by GAAP—generally accepted accounting principles). Most bank assets and liabilities are recorded at the value they contained on the day they were acquired or issued and posted on the bank's books. Over time, as interest rates change and some loans and securities are defaulted, the market value of both bank assets and liabilities will diverge from their original book values. Nevertheless, to many bank managers book value, not market value, is the proper measuring rod to use. In this case:

$$\begin{array}{c} \text{Book value} \\ \text{of bank} \\ \text{capital (GAAP)} \end{array} = \begin{array}{c} \text{Book value} \\ \text{of bank} \\ \text{assets} \end{array} - \begin{array}{c} \text{Book value} \\ \text{of bank} \\ \text{liabilities} \end{array}$$

$$= \begin{array}{c} \text{Par value} \\ \text{of equity} \\ \text{capital} \end{array} + \text{Surplus} + \begin{array}{c} \text{Undivided} \\ \text{profits (or} \\ \text{retained} \\ \text{earnings)} \end{array} + \begin{array}{c} \text{Reserves for} \\ \text{losses on loans} \\ \text{and leases} \end{array}$$

However, as we saw in Chapter 4, in periods when banks' loans and securities are plummeting in value, book value capital is a poor indicator of whether a bank has enough capital to deal with its current exposure to risk.

RAP Capital.   An alternative measure of bank capital, no better than book value, is *regulatory capital* as spelled out by RAP (regulatory accounting principles). For many years, in an effort to make banks appear to be safe—indeed, safer than they really were—some bank regulatory agencies came to define bank capital as:

$$
\begin{array}{c}
\text{RAP} \\
\text{bank} \\
\text{capital}
\end{array}
=
\begin{array}{c}
\text{Stockholders'} \\
\text{equity (i.e.,} \\
\text{common stock,} \\
\text{retained earnings,} \\
\text{and equity} \\
\text{reserves)}
\end{array}
+
\begin{array}{c}
\text{Perpetual} \\
\text{referred} \\
\text{stock}
\end{array}
+
\begin{array}{c}
\text{Bad-debt} \\
\text{reserves} \\
\text{for losses} \\
\text{on loans} \\
\text{and leases}
\end{array}
$$

$$
+
\begin{array}{c}
\text{Subordinated} \\
\text{debentures} \\
\text{that are} \\
\text{mandatorily} \\
\text{convertible} \\
\text{into common} \\
\text{stock}
\end{array}
+
\begin{array}{c}
\text{Miscellaneous} \\
\text{items (such} \\
\text{as minority} \\
\text{interest in subsidiaries} \\
\text{and net} \\
\text{worth} \\
\text{certificates)}
\end{array}
$$

Many readers will find it more than a little strange that regulators interested in bank safety would toss debt securities, stock holdings in subsidiary companies, and bad-debt reserves into the definition of capital and then declare that banks are really financially stronger than the public first believed. We are dangerously close here to public deception on a grand scale.

Market-Value Capital.   Of far greater relevance for both students of the banking system and investors (including depositors) who buy bank IOUs today is *market-value capital* (MVC):

$$
\begin{array}{c}
\text{Market value} \\
\text{of bank} \\
\text{capital} \\
\text{(MVC)}
\end{array}
=
\begin{array}{c}
\text{Market value} \\
\text{of bank} \\
\text{assets} \\
\text{(MVA)}
\end{array}
-
\begin{array}{c}
\text{Market value} \\
\text{of bank} \\
\text{liabilities} \\
\text{(MVL)}
\end{array}
$$

A banker can obtain a quick approximation of a bank's market-value capital each day by calculating:

$$
\text{MVC} =
\begin{array}{c}
\text{Current} \\
\text{market price} \\
\text{per share of} \\
\text{stock outstanding}
\end{array}
\times
\begin{array}{c}
\text{Number of} \\
\text{equity shares} \\
\text{issued and} \\
\text{outstanding}
\end{array}
$$

Obviously, the MVC approach to measuring the amount of bank capital results in a highly volatile capital figure, one that changes daily for large banks whose stock is actively traded. MVC is difficult to measure for small banks because their stock usually is not actively traded enough to establish a market value. This limits the usefulness of MVC for the smallest banks in the industry. Yet the market value of capital is a reflection of the amount of real protection each bank has against the risk of failure. If a bank's assets and liabilities were valued at their true market value, depositors would be better able to gauge whether their bank held enough salable collateral to back their deposits and, therefore, could make a more rational decision on which banking institution should receive their deposit business. As we saw in Chapter 4, accountants and the regulatory agencies have made at least a start toward market valuing key bank assets, particularly bank investments. We turn now to a closer look at the reasons usually given for regulating bank capital and at what telltale indicators of bank capital adequacy regulators examine today to assess the safety and soundness of banks.

Concept Checks

15–4. What forms of bank capital are in use today?

15–5. How is the size of a bank's capital measured?

15–6. What is the difference between GAAP and RAP capital?

How Much Capital Does a Bank Need?

How much capital a bank should have has been one of the most controversial issues in the history of the industry. Much of the controversy has evolved around two questions: *Who should set capital standards for banks,* the market or the regulatory agencies? *What is a reasonable standard for bank capital?*

Regulatory Approach to Evaluating Capital Needs

Reasons behind Capital Regulation.   The capital position of banks has been closely regulated for decades. Banks must meet minimum capital requirements before they can be chartered, and they must hold at least the minimum required level of capital throughout their corporate life. Regulatory agencies also indicate the forms of capital that are acceptable. As Wall [9] notes, the fundamental purposes of regulating bank capital are threefold:

1. To limit the risk of bank failures.
2. To preserve public confidence in banks.
3. To limit losses to the federal government arising from deposit insurance claims.

There is an underlying assumption that the private marketplace cannot accomplish all three of these objectives simultaneously, because the market does not correctly price the impact of bank failures on the banking system's stability nor is the market likely to accurately price the cost of bank failure to the deposit insurance fund.

Banks are unique in that they hold short-term liabilities (especially demand deposits) that can be withdrawn immediately when public confidence falls. Few banks are in a position to liquidate their loan portfolios immediately when threatened with massive deposit withdrawals. Moreover, the managers of individual banks do not consider the possible external effects of their risk taking on other banks, which may be dragged down by the collapse of neighboring institutions.

Large bank failures are a special problem, as Wall [9] observes. The failure of a big bank attracts significant media attention, causing depositors to raise questions about the soundness of their banks. Moreover, the largest banking organizations generally have a high proportion of nondeposit liabilities and large-denomination deposits that are not adequately covered by insurance. The failure of a large bank can have a greater impact on the government's deposit insurance fund than the failures of a considerable number of small banks.

One of the damaging side effects of government-funded deposit insurance is that it lowers the normal level of vigilance among depositors over bank safety and risk taking. Feeling fully protected, most depositors do not monitor the risk of the banks they use, nor do they penalize those banks that take on excessive risk by moving their funds to lower-risk banks. This "moral hazard" feature of government-sponsored insurance plans encourages banks to drive their capital-to-deposit ratios lower, thus exposing government insurance funds to even greater risk of loss.

Research Evidence.   Considerable research has been conducted in recent years on the issue of whether the private marketplace or government regulatory agencies exert a bigger effect on bank risk taking and on bank capital decisions. The results of these studies are varied, but most find that the private marketplace is probably more important than government regulation in the long run in determining the amount and type of capital banks must hold. However, government regulation appears to have become at least as important as the private marketplace in the 1980s and 1990s, with the tightening of capital regulations and the imposition of minimum capital requirements.

The financial markets do seem to react to the differential risk positions of banks by downgrading the debt and equity securities offered by riskier banking companies. However, as Eisenbeis and Gilbert [4] note, we are not at all sure market disciplining works as well for small and medium-size banks, whose securities are not as actively traded in the open market. Nor is it clear that the risk premiums imposed by the market on lower-quality bank securities (in the form of lower prices and higher interest rates) are really large enough to discipline bank risk taking. Also, while the market may make efficient use of all the information it possesses, some of the most pertinent information needed to assess a bank's true level of risk exposure is hidden from the market and is known only to bank examiners.

Is a bank's capital-to-assets ratio significantly related to its probability of failure? Most research studies find little connection between capital ratios and the incidence of bank failure. For example, Santomero and Vinso [1] found that increased capital does not materially lower a bank's failure risk. Many banks would still fail even if their capital were doubled or tripled—a conclusion backed up by a recent study in New

England by Peek and Rosengren [8], which found that four-fifths of bank's failing there in the 1980s and early 1990s were classified by examiners as "well capitalized" before they failed. It is by no means certain that imposing higher capital requirements will reduce banking risk. As Wall [9] observes, banks faced with tougher capital standards may take on more risk in other aspects of their operations in order to keep from earning lower returns.

Alternative Policy Strategies for Regulating Capital.   Regulation of bank capital today is in a state of transition as regulators move further into a new system that covers all banks in the world's leading industrialized nations and stipulates a minimum level below which bank capital, as a percentage of a bank's assets, is not supposed to fall.

The idea of imposing minimum levels of capital on all banks actually began in the United States in December 1981. Prior to that date, federal and state regulatory authorities used a subjective approach that relied on *peer group comparisons* to decide if a bank had enough capital. Selected *capital ratios* were used to measure capital adequacy:

$$\text{total capital : total deposits}$$

$$\text{total capital : total assets}$$

$$\text{total capital : total risk assets}$$

where risk assets include all the bank's assets except cash and U.S. government securities (viewed as essentially riskless in quality). Each regulatory agency used both *cross-section analysis,* comparing each bank's capital ratios with the same ratios for comparable banks at a given moment in time, and *time series analysis,* tracking changes in a bank's capital ratios over time to determine if capital adequacy appeared to be rising or falling. The problem with comparing the capital ratios of one bank against those of its peers is that if the peers' capital ratios are also deteriorating, the result can be growing capital inadequacy for the whole industry. In fact, the capital ratios of U.S. banks fell almost continuously from the 1930s to the 1980s, in part due to the federal government's providing deposit insurance, weakening the willingness of private investors to monitor and control bank risk taking.

Certainly the latest strategy, imposing *one minimum capital standard on all banks,* is easier for regulators to enforce and avoids the pitfall of peer group comparisons in not letting all capital ratios drift too low over time—provided, of course, that regulators stick to the capital minimums established. However, there are some potential problems with this simple approach to capital adequacy. For one thing, a system of capital minimums may precipitate bank runs by the public, even though the banks losing their deposits may, in fact, be sound. How could this happen? When the public sees a bank's capital ratio dropping below the minimum required, the bank's largest uninsured depositors may start a run on the bank even if it still has adequate capitalization from a market perspective.

Another problem is the difficulty faced by the public in trying to determine what a particular capital ratio for a particular bank really means. For example, if all banks hold at least the minimum required amount of capital, this may suggest that all banks are equally safe—which is obviously untrue. Moreover, how are we to fit into a minimum capital standard the fact that a bank's ratio of capital to total assets seems to depend heavily upon the *size* of the bank, with smaller banks generally reporting larger capital-asset ratios than larger banks report. Does this mean that the largest banks are not adequately capitalized, or that smaller banks are overcapitalized? Are small banks a lot safer than large banks? Obviously, we cannot say for sure without considering other facts pertaining to conditions inside each bank—such as its earnings record and quality of management—and conditions in each bank's market area, whether strong and robust or weak and declining.

The Judgment Approach.   Because the imposition of minimum capital ratios on all banks *can* be misleading, the regulatory agencies have also applied the yardstick of *regulatory judgment* in assessing the adequacy of a bank's capital position. This requires viewing each bank within the context of its own market environment and looking at several different dimensions of internal and external conditions surrounding the bank. The *judgment method* for assessing the adequacy of a bank's capital looks at the following:

1. Management quality.
2. Asset liquidity.
3. Earnings history.
4. Quality of ownership.
5. Occupancy costs.
6. Quality of operating procedures.
7. Deposit volatility.
8. Local market conditions.

Even those banks that meet minimum capital requirements may be judged capital deficient if they operate within a market environment that appears to require more capital or if they have internal weaknesses. Such banks would be asked to develop a plan for strengthening their capital positions above the minimums required for other banks.

Concept Checks

15–7. What is the rationale for having the government set capital standards for banks, as opposed to letting the private marketplace set those standards?

15–8. What evidence does recent research provide on the role of the private marketplace in determining bank capital standards?

15–9. According to recent research, does capital prevent a bank from failing?

The Imposition of Minimum Capital Requirements.   While each bank's capital position must be evaluated relative to its own internal and external situation, concern over recent bank failures led U.S. bank regulatory agencies in the early 1980s to set up *minimum capital requirements* for all banks, regardless of their own internal or market situation. These minimums were mandated by congressional passage of the **International Lending and Supervision Act of 1983.**

The centerpiece of this minimum capital program was the concept of *primary capital.* The Comptroller of the Currency and the Federal Reserve, which set capital requirements for national and state-chartered U.S. member banks, defined primary capital as common stock; perpetual preferred stock; surplus and undivided profits; capital reserves; mandatory convertible debt; loan and lease loss reserves; and minority interest in consolidated subsidiaries less equity commitment notes and intangible assets. These components are relatively permanent sources of bank capital. Less-permanent forms of capital were grouped under *secondary capital,* defined to include limited-life preferred stock, subordinated notes and debentures, and mandatory convertible debt instruments not eligible to be counted as primary capital. The total capital of a bank could then be derived from the sum of its primary capital and secondary capital.

The federal banking agencies called for a minimum ratio of primary capital to total assets of 5.5 percent and of total capital to total assets of 6 percent. These agencies insisted that if a bank fell below the minimum capital requirement, it must submit a plan describing how it would remedy the shortfall as quickly as possible.

Subsequently, in 1987 U.S. banks were required to meet a so-called *leverage standard* based on the following ratio:

$$\frac{\text{Leverage}}{\text{ratio}} = \frac{\text{Core capital}}{\text{Total assets}}$$

$$= \frac{\left[\begin{array}{ccccc} \text{Book value} & & \text{Cumulative} & & \text{Minority interest in} \\ \text{of common} & + & \text{perpetual} & + & \text{the equity accounts} \\ \text{equity capital} & & \text{preferred stock} & & \text{of consolidated subsidiaries} \end{array}\right]}{\text{Total assets}}$$

As a result of passage of the FDIC Improvement Act of 1991, a bank possessing a leverage ratio greater than 5 percent would be considered *well capitalized.* A leverage ratio of 4 percent or more would be considered *adequate* capitalization. Below a 4 percent leverage ratio a bank would be labeled *undercapitalized.* If the leverage ratio falls below 3 percent, a banking firm would be considered *significantly undercapitalized.* Finally, should the leverage ratio fall to 2 percent or less, the bank involved would be designated *critically undercapitalized.* Once a U.S. bank becomes undercapitalized, increasing pressure will be applied by federal regulators in order to force its ownership and management to strengthen its capital position.

The Basle Agreement on International Capital Standards.   In 1987 the Federal Reserve Board, representing the United States, and representatives from 11 other leading industrialized countries (Belgium, Canada, France, Germany, Italy, Japan, the Netherlands,

Sweden, Switzerland, the United Kingdom, and Luxembourg) announced preliminary agreement on new capital standards—often referred to as the **Basle Agreement**—that would be uniformly applied to all banking institutions in their respective jurisdictions. Formally approved in July 1988, those new requirements are designed to encourage leading banks to strengthen their capital positions, reduce inequality in the regulatory rules of different nations, and consider the risk to banks of the off-balance-sheet commitments they have made in recent years. The new capital requirements were phased in gradually over time and became fully enforceable beginning January 1, 1993, though adjustments and modifications continue to be made, particularly in allowing or denying new instruments to be added, in changing the relative weights attached to various bank assets and types of capital, and in adjusting for different types of risk exposure. The Federal Reserve Board announced that the new capital guidelines would also apply, with small modifications, to the state-chartered member banks it examines regularly and to bank holding companies on a consolidated basis.

Under the terms of the new international agreement, sources of bank capital are divided into two tiers:

Tier 1 capital (core capital) includes common stock and surplus, undivided profits (retained earnings), qualifying noncumulative perpetual preferred stock, minority interest in the equity accounts of consolidated subsidiaries, and selected identifiable intangible assets less goodwill and other intangible assets.[1]

---

[1]Banks are allowed to record an intangible asset known as *goodwill* on their balance sheets, which is an asset that arises when the stock of a bank or nonbank business is purchased for cash at a price that exceeds the firm's book value. The goodwill that an established banking firm has attracted by providing good service to its customers helps explain the extra market value the bank has as a going concern over its book value. Most regulatory agencies do *not* allow goodwill to count as bank capital. However, another intangible asset found in most banks is called *identifiable intangible assets*—intangibles other than goodwill; some portion of these intangibles *is* allowed to be counted as part of a bank's capital. One important identifiable intangible asset today is *mortgage servicing rights* (MSRs), in which a bank can earn income by collecting and distributing loan payments and monitoring borrower compliance with the terms of loans it may have originated or that were granted by another lender. The future fees expected to be earned by a servicing bank are usually based on the remaining principal due on the mortgage loans the bank is servicing.

Still another prominent identifiable intangible today is *purchased credit card relationships* (PCCRs). A bank buying into a credit card program acquires access to a new group of potential customers who may need future cash advances and other services that will generate expected profits for the bank in the future. Thus, PCCRs hold the promise of future income for a bank acquiring this intangible asset.

Many bankers argue that a portion of their core deposits—a bank liability—should be considered to be intangible assets, calling them *core deposit intangibles* (CDIs). Core deposits, as we saw in Chapter 12, are usually the most loyal and low-cost deposits a bank holds (consisting principally of small-denomination checking and savings deposits). When a bank is acquired by another organization, the CDIs are believed to give extra value to the bank's assets because it is assumed the core deposits will remain with the bank for some indefinite period into the future.

In February 1993 the Federal Reserve Board announced that purchased mortgage servicing rights (PMSRs) and PCCRs would be counted as qualifying intangible assets and would not have to be deducted from a bank's capital, provided they do not exceed 50 percent of Tier 1 capital with all intangibles included. Later in 1997 the limitation on the amount of mortgage servicing rights (both those purchased and those originated by a bank) when combined with purchased credit card relationships (PCCRs) was proposed by federal regulators to be increased from 50 percent to 100 percent of Tier 1 capital. However, there is an added requirement that PCCRs

Tier 2 capital (supplemental capital) includes the allowance (reserves) for loan and lease losses, subordinated debt capital instruments, mandatory convertible debt, intermediate-term preferred stock, cumulative perpetual preferred stock with unpaid dividends, and equity notes and other long-term capital instruments that combine both debt and equity features.

To determine each bank's *total capital,* regulators must deduct from the sum of Tier 1 and Tier 2 capital several additional items, including investments in unconsolidated subsidiaries, capital securities held by the bank that were issued by other depository institutions and are held under a reciprocity agreement, activities pursued by savings and loan associations that may have been acquired by a banking organization but are not permissible for national banks, and any other deductions that the bank's principal regulatory supervisor may demand.

The newly agreed-on capital requirements include:

1. Ratio of core capital (Tier 1) to risk-weighted assets must be at least 4 percent.

2. Ratio of total capital (the sum of Tier 1 and Tier 2 capital) to total risk-weighted assets must be at least 8 percent, with the amount of Tier 2 capital limited to 100 percent of Tier 1 capital.[2]

Calculating Risk-Weighted Assets.   If a bank must compare its Tier 1 and Tier 2 capital to its risk-weighted assets in order to determine if it is adequately capitalized, what exactly are risk-weighted assets?

Each asset item on a bank's balance sheet and any off-balance-sheet commitments it has made are each multiplied by a *risk-weighting factor* designed to reflect its credit risk exposure. Among the most closely watched off-balance-sheet items are the standby

---

not exceed 25 percent of Tier 1 capital. Any amounts of PMSRs or PCCRs above the maximum allowable amount must be deducted from core capital. Moreover, PMSRs and PCCRs must be included in the calculation of a bank's total risk-weighted assets with a risk weight of 100 percent. However, those PMSRs and PCCRs not allowed in as part of Tier 1 capital do not need to be included in a bank's total risk-weighted assets.

Banks having PMSRs and PCCRs must determine their fair market value at least quarterly. Those purchased rights that are included in capital cannot exceed the lesser of 90 percent of their fair market value or 100 percent of their book value (which must be based upon discounted expected cash flows from these intangibles and net of any valuation allowances). Thus, PMSRs and PCCRs are now considered to be a component of a U.S. bank's capital resources subject to well-defined limits. However, core deposit intangibles (CDIs) and other identifiable intangibles must be deducted from Tier 1 capital and are not to be included in a bank's risk-weighted assets for purposes of determining its capital requirements (except for intangibles acquired prior to February 19, 1992, which were grandfathered in and may be counted as capital).

[2]The new international capital standard will permit subordinated debt with an original average maturity of at least five years to count toward required supplemental capital (Tier 2). The combined maximum amount of subordinated debt and intermediate-term preferred stock that qualifies as Tier 2 capital is limited to 50 percent of Tier 1 capital (net of goodwill and any other intangibles required to be deducted). Allowance for loan and lease losses also counts as supplemental capital, provided the loan-loss reserves are *general* (not specific) reserves and do not exceed 1.25 percent of a bank's risk-weighted assets. The components of Tier 2 capital are subject to the discretion of bank regulatory agencies in each nation covered by the Basle Agreement. Tier 2 capital as a whole, however, must be limited to 100 percent of the Tier 1 capital.

letters of credit banks issue to back the general-obligation notes and bonds of state and local governments and the loans and security issues of business firms, and the long-term, legally binding credit commitments banks make to private corporate customers.

Here is an example of how bankers calculate their minimum required level of capital under the new international standards. Suppose a state-chartered member bank of the Federal Reserve System has $6,000 in total capital, $100,000 in total assets, and the following balance sheet and off-balance-sheet (OBS) items:

Balance Sheet Items (Assets)	
Cash	$ 5,000
U.S. Treasury securities	20,000
Deposit balances held at domestic banks	5,000
Loans secured by first liens on 1–4 family residential properties	5,000
Loans to private corporations	65,000
Total balance sheet assets	$100,000
Off-Balance-Sheet (OBS) Items	
Standby letters of credit backing general obligation debt issues of U.S. municipal governments	$10,000
Long-term, legally binding credit commitments to private corporations	20,000
Total off-balance-sheet items	$30,000

This bank's total capital to total balance sheet assets ratio would be:

$$\$6{,}000 \div \$100{,}000 = 6.00 \text{ percent}$$

However, the new international capital standards are based upon risk-weighted assets, *not* total assets. To compute this bank's risk-weighted assets, we proceed as follows:

1. Compute the *credit-equivalent amount* of each off-balance-sheet (OBS) item. This figure is supposed to translate each OBS item into the equivalent amount of a direct loan considered to be of equal risk to the bank.

Off-Balance-Sheet (OBS) Items	*Face Value*		*Conversion Factor*		*Credit Equivalent Amount*
Standby letters of credit issued by bank to back municipal bonds and other direct credit substitutes, asset sales with recourse and repurchase agreements, and forward asset purchases	$10,000	×	1.00	=	$10,000
Long-term credit commitments made to private corporations	$20,000	×	0.50	=	$10,000

2. Then multiply each balance sheet item and the credit-equivalent amount of each OBS item by its *risk weight,* as determined by the regulatory authorities. The weights given to each item in the bank's portfolio are 0 percent (for cash, U.S. Government securities, including GNMA mortgage-backed securities, and unconditionally cancelable credit commitments), 20 percent (for deposits held at other banks and short-term self-liquidating trade-related contingencies), 50 percent (for home mortgage loans and note-issuance facilities and credit commitments over one year), and 100 percent (applying to corporate loans and credit commitments and all other claims on the private sector as well as bank premises and other fixed assets and investments in real estate).

In the case of the bank we are using as an example, it would have the following risk-weighted assets:

---

0 Percent
Risk Weighting Category

Cash	$ 5,000
U.S. Treasury securities	20,000
	$25,000 × 0 = $ 0

---

20 Percent
Risk Weighting Category

Balances at domestic banks	$ 5,000
Credit-equivalent amounts of	10,000
SLCs backing bonds of U.S. municipalities	$15,000 × 0.20 = $ 3,000

---

50 Percent
Risk Weighting Category

Loans secured by first liens on 1–4 family residential properties	$ 5,000 × 0.50 = $ 2,500

---

100 Percent
Risk Weighting Category

Loans to private corporations	$65,000
Credit-equivalent amounts of	10,000
long-term commitments to private corporations	$75,000 × 1.00 = $75,000
Total risk-weighted assets held by this bank	$80,500

Calculating the Capital-to-Risk-Weighted Assets Ratio.   Once we know a bank's total risk-weighted assets and the total amount of its capital (Tier 1 + Tier 2) we can determine its capital adequacy ratio as required under the Basle Agreement on International Capital Standards. The key formula is:

$$\begin{matrix} \text{Capital adequacy} \\ \text{ratio under the} \\ \text{Basle Agreement} \\ \text{on International} \\ \text{Bank Capital Standards} \end{matrix} = \frac{\text{Total capital (or Tier 1 + Tier 2 Capital)}}{\text{Total risk-weighted bank assets}}$$

For the bank whose risk-weighted assets we just calculated above at $80,500 that currently has $6,000 in total capital, its capital adequacy ratio would be:

$$\begin{matrix} \text{Total capital /} \\ \text{Total risk-weighted} \\ \text{assets} \end{matrix} = \frac{\$6,000}{\$80,500} = 0.0745, \text{ or } 7.45 \text{ percent}.$$

Note that this bank's total-capital-to-risk-weighted assets ratio of 7.45 percent is more than the required minimum for Tier 1 capital of 4 percent but lies below the combined Tier 1 plus Tier 2 capital requirements of 8 percent. Therefore, this bank will have to raise new capital to comply with the new international capital standards.[3]

Capital Requirements Attached to Derivatives

Recently, the new Basle International Capital Standards have been adjusted to take account of the risk exposure that banks face today from *derivatives*—futures, options, forward contracts, interest rate and currency swaps, interest rate cap and floor contracts, and other instruments designed to hedge against changing currency prices, interest rates and positions in commodities. Many of these instruments expose a bank to *counterparty risk*—the danger that a customer the bank has entered into a contract with will fail to pay or to perform, forcing the bank to find a replacement contract with another party who may be less satisfactory.

One significant factor that limits bank risk exposure in many of these cases is that most futures and option contracts are traded on organized exchanges, such as the London International Financial Futures Exchange or the Chicago Mercantile Exchange, that guarantees the performance of each party to these contracts. Thus, if a bank's customer fails to deliver under an exchange-traded futures or options contract, the exchange involved will make delivery in full to the bank. In these instances banks would not normally be expected to post capital behind such exchange-traded contracts.

For other types of contracts, however, the revised Basle Agreement requires bankers, first, to convert each risk-exposed contract into its credit-equivalent amount as though it were a risky asset listed on a bank's balance sheet. Then, for example, the credit-equivalent amount of each interest rate or currency contract is multiplied by a prespecified risk weight. Recent research suggests that interest rate

---

[3]The source of the above example was the Board of Governors of the Federal Reserve System, *Press Release,* January 19, 1989, pp. 67–68.

contracts display considerably less risk exposure than do foreign-currency contracts. Accordingly, the Basle Agreement's credit-conversion factors for interest rate derivatives are set far lower than for contracts tied to the value of foreign currencies. For example, interest rate contracts with a maturity of one year or less have been assigned a 0 credit-conversion factor, while rate contracts over one year carry a credit conversion factor of only 0.005 or 0.5 percent. In contrast, currency-based contracts one year or less to maturity carry a credit-conversion factor of 0.01 or 1 percent and those with maturities over one year have been assigned a credit-conversion factor of 0.05 or 5 percent.

In determining the credit-equivalent amounts of these off-balance-sheet contracts, the Basle Agreement requires a banker to divide each contract's risk exposure to the bank into two categories: (1) potential market risk exposure and (2) current market risk exposure. *Potential market risk exposure* refers to the danger of bank loss *at some future time* if the customer who entered into a market-based contract with the bank fails to perform. In contrast, the *current market risk exposure* is designed to measure the risk of loss to the bank should a customer default *today* on its contract, which would compel the bank to replace the failed contract with a new one. The Basle Agreement requires bankers to determine the current market value for a contract that is similar to the contract they have made with a customer in order to figure out the latter's replacement cost. Future cash flows expected under current contracts must be discounted back to their present values using today's interest rates, currency, or commodity prices in order to determine the value of such a contract in today's market.

Once the replacement cost of a contract is determined, the estimated potential market risk exposure amount is added to the estimated current market risk exposure amount to derive the total credit-equivalent amount of each contract. This total is multiplied by the correct risk weight, which in most cases is 50 percent or 0.50, to find the equivalent amount of risk-weighted bank assets represented by each contract. We then add this risk-weighted amount to all of a bank's other risk-weighted assets to derive its total on-balance-sheet and off-balance-sheet risk-weighted assets. As we saw in the preceding section, the total of all risk-weighted assets is then divided into each bank's total capital (Tier 1 plus Tier 2) to determine if a bank is adequately capitalized.

For example, consider again the bank whose risk-weighted assets we previously calculated in the last section to be $80,500. Suppose this bank has also entered into a $100,000 five-year interest rate swap agreement with one of its customers and a $50,000 three-year currency swap agreement with another customer. First, we multiply the face amount (notional value) of these two contracts by the appropriate credit conversion factor for each instrument—in this case, by 0.005 for the interest rate swap contract and by 0.05 for the currency swap contract—in order to find the bank's potential market risk exposure from each instrument. Second, we add the estimated replacement cost if suddenly the bank had to substitute *new* swap contracts at today's prices and interest rates for the original contracts. Let's assume these replacement costs amount to $2,500 for the interest rate contract and $1,500 for the currency contract. Then:

Interest Rate and Currency Contracts	Face Amount of Contract		Conversion Factor for Potential Market Risk Exposure		Potential Market Risk Exposure		Current Market Risk Exposure (replacement cost)		Credit-Equivalent Volume of Interest Rate and Currency Contracts
Five-year interest rate swap contract	$100,000	×	0.005	=	$500	+	$2,500	=	$3,000
Three-year currency swap contract	$ 50,000	×	0.05	=	$2,500	+	$1,500	=	$4,000

The total credit-equivalent amount of both of these contracts combined is $7,000.

The final step is to multiply this total by the correct risk weight, which is 50 percent, or 0.50. This step gives:

$$\begin{matrix} \text{Volume of risk-weighted assets} \\ \text{represented by the bank's off-} \\ \text{balance-sheet interest rate and} \\ \text{currency contracts} \end{matrix} = \begin{matrix} \text{Credit-equivalent} \\ \text{volume of} \\ \text{interest rate} \\ \text{and currency contracts} \end{matrix} \times \begin{matrix} \text{Credit} \\ \text{risk} \\ \text{weight} \end{matrix}$$

$$= \$7,000 \times 0.50 = \$3,500$$

To make use of this result let's return to our previous example. Recall that the bank we examined earlier held total capital of $6,000, and total risk-weighted assets of $80,500. Its total risk-weighted assets included total on-balance-sheet assets of $68,500 and off-balance-sheet standby credit letters and corporate loan commitments of $12,000. We now must add to these other assets the $3,500 in risk-weighted currency and interest rate contracts that we just determined above. In this case the bank's ratio of total capital to risk-weighted assets would be:

$$\begin{matrix} \text{Total capital} \div \\ \text{Total risk-} \\ \text{weighted assets} \end{matrix} = \cfrac{\text{Total (Tier 1 + Tier 2) capital}}{\begin{matrix} \text{Risk-weighted} \\ \text{on-balance-sheet} \\ \text{assets} \end{matrix} + \begin{matrix} \text{Risk-weighted} \\ \text{off-balance-sheet} \\ \text{items} \end{matrix}}$$

$$= \cfrac{\$6,000}{(\$68,500 + \$12,000 + \$3,500)}$$

$$= \cfrac{\$6,000}{\$84,000} = 0.0714, \text{ or } 7.14 \text{ percent}$$

Bankers' Insights and Issues

Risk Weights Applied to Bank Assets and Off-Balance-Sheet Items under the Basle Agreement

A. Credit Risk Categories for Bank Assets on the Balance Sheet

Credit Risk Weights Used in the Calculation of a Bank's Risk-Weighted Assets (percent of amount of each bank's asset)	*Assumed Amount of Credit Risk Exposure from Each Category of Bank Assets*	*Categories or Types of Bank Assets*
0%	Zero credit risk	Cash; deposits at the Federal Reserve Banks; U.S. Treasury bills, notes, and bonds of all maturities; Government National Mortgage Association (GNMA) mortgage-backed securities; debt securities issued by governments of the world's leading industrial countries belonging to the Organization for Economic Cooperation and Development (OECD); and well-secured claims backed by cash on deposit or by OECD central governments (including the U.S. federal government)
20	Low credit risk	Checkbook float (cash items in process of collection), interbank (correspondent) deposits, general obligation bonds and notes issued by states and local governments, securities issued or backed by U.S. government agencies, and mortgage-backed securities issued or guaranteed by the Federal National Mortgage Association (FNMA) or by the Federal Home Loan Mortgage Corporation (FHLMC)
50	Moderate credit risk	Residential (home) mortgage loans on one-to-four family dwellings, selected multifamily housing loans that are well secured and adequately performing, and revenue bonds issued by state and local government units or agencies
100	Highest credit risk	Commercial and industrial (business) loans, credit card loans, real property assets, investments in bank subsidiary companies, and all other bank assets not listed above

B. Credit Risk Categories for Off-Balance-Sheet Items

Conversion Factor for Converting Off-Balance-Sheet Items into Equivalent Amounts of On-Balance-Sheet Assets	Credit Risk Weights (percent)	Assumed Amount of Credit Risk	Categories or Types of Off-Balance-Sheet Items
0	0%	Zero or lowest credit risk	Loan commitments with less than one year to go, guarantees of federal or central government borrowings
0.20	20	Low credit risk	Standby credit letters backing the issue of state and local government general obligation bonds
0.20	100	Modest credit risk	Trade-based commercial letters of credit and bankers' acceptances
0.50	100	Moderate credit risk	Standby credit letters guaranteeing a customer's future performance and unused bank loan commitments covering periods longer than a year
1.00	100	Highest credit risk	Standby credit letters issued to back the repayment of commercial paper (short-term unsecured corporate IOUs)

C. Credit Risk Categories for Derivatives and Other Market-Based Contracts Not Shown on a Bank's Balance Sheet

Conversion Factor for Converting Derivatives and Other Market-Based Interest Rate and Currency Contracts into Equivalent Amounts of On-Balance-Sheet Assets	Credit Risk Weights (percent)	Assumed Amount of Credit Risk	Categories or Types of Off-Balance-Sheet Currency and Interest Rate Contracts
0	50%	Lowest credit risk	Interest rate contracts one year or less to maturity
0.005	50	Modest credit risk	Interest rate contracts over one year to maturity
0.01	50	Moderate credit risk	Currency contracts one year or less to maturity
0.05	50	Highest credit risk	Currency contracts over one year to maturity

Source: Board of Governors of the Federal Reserve System, *Press Release*, January 19, 1989.

We note that this bank is now substantially *below* the minimum total capital requirement of 8 percent of total risk-weighted assets as required by the Basle Agreement. This capital-deficient bank will probably be compelled to dispose of some of its risky assets and to raise new capital through retained earnings or, perhaps, through sales of bank stock to bring its capital position up to the levels stipulated in the Basle Agreement. Notice, too, that we have only taken *credit risk* into account in the calculation of capital adequacy. We have not even considered the possibility of declines in the market value of assets on bank balance sheets due to increasing interest rates or falling currency or commodity prices. If regulators detected an excessive amount of risk exposure from these market forces, the bank would be asked to post even more capital than the $6,000 it already holds. In this instance the bank would face an even deeper capital deficiency than we calculated above and would be placed under considerable regulatory pressure to improve its capital position.

Bank Capital Standards and Market Risk. One of the most glaring holes left by the original Basle Agreement on bank capital was its failure to deal with *market risk.* The risk weights on bank assets mentioned above were designed primarily to take account of *credit risk*—the danger that a borrowing customer might default on his or her loan. But banks also face significant *market risk*—the losses a bank may suffer due to adverse changes in interest rates, security prices, currency and commodity prices. For example, banks are leading traders in government bonds and, particularly among banks headquartered outside the United States, substantial dealers in corporate stock, which can plunge in value due to a sharp upward movement in market interest rates. Banks are also among the world's leading traders in foreign securities and overseas business property and can be severely damaged financially when foreign currency prices change (usually referred to as *exchange rate* or *currency risk*).

In an effort to deal with these and other forms of market risk, the Basle Committee on Banking Supervision released new proposals in April 1993 that would require banks facing significant exposure to market risk due to the impact of changing interest rates, currency prices, and commodity prices to hold larger amounts of capital relative to the size of their assets than would banks not subject to significant risk due to security trading or the positions they may hold in foreign currencies or commodities. One approach to this market risk problem followed by some regulators outside the United States is called the *standard approach* because it is so similar to the way the Basle Agreement deals with credit risk—something we saw earlier in this chapter. Specifically, different market-risk-exposed assets held by banks would be divided into different risk classes, and a fixed capital charge would then be applied to each risk class of assets.

In December 1995 the member nations of the Basle Capital Accord announced their consent to new *market risk* capital requirements for their banks, rules that would become mandatory for all member-country banks beginning January 1, 1998. The ultimate objective of the new market-risk rules was to add a protective layer of capital to combat the price risks that banks are exposed to due primarily to their trading activities in securities, interest rate and credit derivatives, currencies, and/or commodities. In an innovative stroke the United States has developed new market risk capital standards that allow bankers to develop their own *in-house models* to measure their own degree of market risk exposure independent of general industry standards. However, banks using their own privately developed market risk models (primarily the largest banks in the industry) must pledge to set up an independent risk control group, get senior management actively involved in the risk control process, and conduct frequent stress tests to determine how well the bank's risk defenses will work under different market performance scenarios. The bank using its own risk assessment model must determine the maximum loss it might sustain over a 10-day period (under a 99 percent statistical confidence standard)—known as the *value at risk* (VAR) approach, where VAR is the maximum amount a bank's portfolio can lose with a given probability in a given period of time. Regulators will then determine the amount of capital the bank needs to cover its market risk exposure based upon a specific multiple of the bank's estimated VAR. Banks developing market risk assessment models that generate repeatedly poor estimates would be asked to hold more capital, thereby providing some incentive for bankers to do a better job in assessing their institution's market risk exposure as accurately as possible. In the U.S., banks and bank holding companies whose trading activities in securities, currencies, and/or commodities equal or exceed 10 percent of their total assets or amount to at least $1 billion must hold some capital specifically aimed at protecting their market risk exposure.

Consequences of the Basle Agreement for Banks and the Economy

The new international capital requirements are expected to set in motion significant changes in the financial system and especially in the market values of loans and securities. This situation may arise because of the differing risk weights the new capital requirements apply to different kinds of bank assets. Each dollar of high-risk assets, such as corporate loans and home mortgages, requires a greater proportion of bank capital pledged behind it than a dollar of low-risk assets, such as government securities. Banks desiring to keep their capital costs as low as possible may therefore switch many of their assets toward government securities and away from corporate loans and home mortgage loans. Many foreign banks, especially those in Japan and Germany, hold large quantities of corporate stocks and bonds, and there is fear within the international financial system that in tough economic times these more risky securities may be dumped on the security markets, driving stock and bond prices downward.

Another consequence of the new international capital rules is the possibility of a substantial rise in bank loan rates charged businesses and home buyers as banks seek to be compensated for the stiffer capital requirements associated with these particular types of loans. In contrast, the securities of government agencies may experience lower interest rates and higher prices because they carry a zero or minimal capital requirement. Higher business loan rates may well encourage more corporations to turn to the open market for funds and to bypass their banks, thus helping to broaden the market for corporate securities and bring in many new investors, such as pension funds and mutual funds, as active business lenders. The new capital rules could also stimulate more loan sales and securitizations of loans (discussed in Chapter 9) as important sources of bank funds.

Concept Checks

15–10. What are the most popular financial ratios regulators use to assess the adequacy of bank capital today?

15–11. What is the difference between core (or Tier 1) capital and supplemental (or Tier 2) capital?

15–12. A bank reports the following items on its latest balance sheet: allowance for loan and lease losses, $42 million; undivided profits, $81 million; subordinated debt capital, $3 million; common stock and surplus, $27 million; equity notes, $2 million; minority interest in subsidiaries, $4 million; mandatory convertible debt, $5 million; identifiable intangible assets, $3 million; and noncumulative perpetual preferred stock, $5 million. How much does the bank hold in Tier 1 capital? In Tier 2 capital? Does the bank have too much Tier 2 capital?

15–13. What changes in the regulation of bank capital were brought into being by the Basle Agreement?

15–14. First National Bank reports the following items on its balance sheet: cash, $200 million; U.S. government securities, $150 million; residential real estate loans, $300 million; and corporate loans, $350 million. Its off-balance-sheet items include: standby credit letters, $20 million, and long-term credit commitments to corporations, $160 million. What are First National's total risk-weighted assets? If the bank reports Tier 1 capital of $30 million and Tier 2 capital of $20 million, does it have a capital deficiency?

15–15. How is the Basle Agreement likely to affect a bank's choices among assets it would like to acquire?

Current Pressure to Raise More Capital

Banks around the world have been under intense pressure in recent years to raise more capital to support their growth and reduce risk to their depositors. A number of factors have contributed to this pressure, which has come from both the regulatory community and the financial marketplace. *Inflation* has been an important factor spurring on the pressure for more capital, because inflation increases a bank's assets and liabilities but tends to squeeze its net worth. The *more volatile economy* of recent years also calls for more capital, because it leads to a more risky bank earnings stream. *State and federal lending limits* require a bank's capital to grow in order to be able to accommodate the need for loans on the part of its largest and fastest growing customers. *Rising operating costs,* especially the cost of land, equipment, and skilled bank personnel, have tended to squeeze the earnings of many banks—the prime source of year-to-year capital growth. Finally, many capital market investors today see banks as *more risky* due to the effects of deregulation, intense competition between bank and nonbank financial institutions, and volatile economic conditions. Capital market investors appear to be demanding that banks pay more attention to the strength of their capital and seem reluctant to buy the securities or deposits of weakly capitalized banks.

Inside the United States, bank regulatory agencies have recently stressed the need for stronger bank capital positions before they will approve the offering of new services or the establishment or acquisition of new offices or subsidiary firms. Strongly capitalized banks will be allowed to venture into new fields and expand across state lines. Banks with weak capital will face more regulatory pressure and will be severely restricted in their activities until they improve their capital positions. The underlying rationale for "capital-based supervision" is that banks will be less likely to fail or take on excessive risk if their owners are forced to place more of their own money at risk. In effect, the more capital backing a bank's activities, the more its stockholders will likely exercise quality control over the bank's operations. However, there are limits on how much capital regulators can demand from banks. Demanding too much capital throttles back a bank's ability to lend funds profitably in order to support economic growth and, other factors held equal, tends to lower the bank's overall return on equity (ROE), making it less attractive to capital market investors and making it also more difficult for the bank to raise new capital in the future.

Several new capital rules created recently by U.S. regulatory agencies were mandated by the FDIC Improvement Act passed by the United States' Congress in November 1991. The new law requires federal regulators to take "prompt corrective action" when an insured institution's capital falls below acceptable levels. Section 131 of the act allows regulators to impose tougher restrictions on an insured bank or thrift institution as its capital level declines, such as prohibiting the payment of management fees or stockholder dividends. (See Table 15–3 for a summary.) If an institution's ratio of tangible equity capital to total assets drops to 2 percent or less, a bank is considered "critically undercapitalized" and it can be placed in conservatorship or receivership within 90 days unless the bank's principal regulator and the Federal Deposit Insurance Corporation determine that it would be in the interest of the public and the deposit insurance fund to allow the bank to continue under present ownership and management.

**TABLE 15–3   A Brief Look at the "Prompt Corrective Action" Provisions of the
FDIC Improvement Act of 1991**

Capital Condition of a Bank	Capital Ratios Used to Assess a Bank's Capital Condition	What the Regulatory Authorities Can Do	
		Mandatory Steps	*Discretionary Steps*
Well capitalized	Total capital/risk-weighted assets = 10 percent or more; Tier 1 capital to risk-weighted assets = at least 6 percent; leverage ratio (Tier 1 capital/total average assets) = 5 percent or more.	No regulatory restrictions.	
Adequately capitalized	Total capital/risk-weighted assets = 8 percent or more; Tier 1 capital to risk-weighted assets = at least 4 percent; leverage ratio = 4 percent or more.	Broker-placed deposits cannot be accepted unless approved by the FDIC.	
Undercapitalized	Bank fails to meet one or more of the minimum capital ratios defined above.	Brokered deposits cannot be accepted; dividends and management fees are suspended; asset growth is restricted; new activities, branches, and business acquisitions must be approved; capital-raising plan must be submitted.	Deposit interest rates may be restricted along with transactions with affiliated firms; the bank may have to be recapitalized; service offerings may be restricted.
Significantly undercapitalized	Total capital/risk-weighted assets = less than 6 percent; Tier 1 capital to risk-weighted assets = less than 3 percent; leverage ratio = less than 3 percent; Tangible equity capital less than 2 percent of assets.	Bank is subject to all restrictions listed above for undercapitalized banks plus management salaries are restricted; deposit interest rates must be restricted along with transactions with affiliated firms; and recapitalization of bank may be ordered unless primary supervisor finds these actions would not be helpful to the purposes of the law.	Bank is subject to all discretionary steps listed above, plus it could be placed in conservatorship or receivership if it fails to submit or implement capital plan or recapitalize if ordered to do so.
Critically undercapitalized	Tangible equity capital to total assets equal to or less than 2 percent.	Bank is subject to all restrictions listed above, plus payments on subordinated debt will be suspended; bank may be placed in receivership or conservatorship within 90 days if purposes of the law are fulfilled; bank will be placed in receivership if it is still critically undercapitalized 4 quarters later.	None

Notes: Total capital consists of Tier 1 plus Tier 2 capital. Tier 1 capital includes common stockholders' equity, noncumulative perpetual preferred stock, and minority interests in the equity accounts of consolidated subsidiaries excluding goodwill and most other intangible assets. Tier 2 capital includes allowance for loan and lease losses up to a maximum of 1.25 percent of risk-weighted assets, cumulative perpetual preferred stock, subordinated debt, and other selected capital instruments. Tangible equity capital includes Tier 1 capital plus cumulative perpetual preferred stock.

Source: Board of Governors of the Federal Reserve System.

To avoid seizure the bank must have a positive net worth and demonstrate that it is actually improving its condition.

In the fall of 1992 the FDIC and the other federal bank regulators created five capital-adequacy categories of banks for purposes of implementing "prompt corrective action" when a bank becomes inadequately capitalized. These five categories describing how well capitalized each bank is include:

A. *Well capitalized*—for a U.S. bank to be in this category it must have a ratio of total capital to risk-weighted assets of at least 10 percent, a ratio of Tier 1 (or core) capital to risk-weighted assets of at least 6 percent, and a leverage ratio (Tier 1 capital to average total assets) of at least 5 percent.

B. *Adequately capitalized*—a U.S. bank in this group must have a minimum ratio of total capital to risk-weighted assets of at least 8 percent, a ratio of Tier 1 (core) capital to risk-weighted assets of at least 4 percent, and a leverage ratio of at least 4 percent.

C. *Undercapitalized*—a U.S. bank that fails to meet one or more of the capital minimums for an adequately capitalized bank as defined above is considered "undercapitalized" and is subject to a variety of mandatory or discretionary regulatory restrictions, including limits on the dividends and management fees it is allowed to pay, on its maximum asset growth rate, on the expansion of its facilities or services, or on any proposed merger unless approval is obtained in advance from federal regulators.

D. *Significantly undercapitalized*—a U.S. bank belonging to this group possesses a ratio of total capital to risk-weighted assets of less than 6 percent, a core (Tier 1) capital to risk-weighted assets ratio of under 3 percent, and a leverage ratio average of less than 3 percent. A bank in this category is subject to all the restrictions faced by undercapitalized banks (as described above) plus other restrictions such as mandatory prohibitions on paying bonuses and raises to senior officers without regulator approval.

E. *Critically undercapitalized*—this category applies to those U.S. banks whose ratio of tangible equity capital to total assets is 2 percent or less (where tangible equity includes common equity capital and cumulative perpetual preferred stock minus most forms of intangible assets). Banks in this lowest capital group face all the restrictions applying to undercapitalized banks as described above plus having to get regulator approval for such transactions as granting loans to highly leveraged borrowers, making changes in their charter or bylaws, paying above-market interest rates on deposits, changing their accounting methods, or paying excessive compensation or bonuses to consultants or staff. A critically undercapitalized bank may be prevented from paying principal and interest on its subordinated debt and will be placed in conservatorship or receivership if its capital level is not increased within a prescribed time limit.

In recent years the FDIC has analyzed the financial reports of federally insured banks and found that well over 90 percent of U.S. banks fall in either the *well-capitalized* or *adequately capitalized* groups. Regulators have repeatedly concluded that the

American banking system must be in reasonably good shape. Unfortunately, this conclusion usually is based upon the book values of assets reported by the nation's banks and on the book value of their capital, not on market values, and could turn out to be a gross exaggeration of the industry's true condition. Only time will tell.

Planning to Meet a Bank's Capital Needs

Facing growing pressures to strengthen their capital positions and maintain adequate capital, commercial banks are increasingly recognizing the need to plan for their long-range capital needs. While a variety of different planning systems are in use, the majority seem to focus on four key components or phases.

Phase 1: Develop an Overall Financial Plan for the Bank.   Management and the board of directors must decide what kind of bank they want to have. This involves such key questions as: How large should the bank be? What mix of services should the bank offer? How profitable will the bank need to be in the long run?

Increasingly, banks are having to tie capital planning to the question of what kinds of services they must offer in the future. Deregulation of banking in the United States and in many foreign nations as well has ushered in new service possibilities in security trading, insurance, and other fields. Management must decide which of these new services would increase the bank's risk exposure, especially exposure to the risk of earnings fluctuations and the risk of failure. Some new services could actually reduce those risks, thus calling for less bank capital, while others could increase risk, leading to the need for more capital. Of course, the quality of bank management is crucial to determining whether banks really can reduce their risk exposure by offering new services and therefore get by with less capital.

Phase one of planning for bank capital needs also involves developing *pro forma* financial statements, performing a sensitivity analysis of possible outcomes, and developing baseline projections of capital needs, assuming that no changes are made in the bank's procedures or policies. It is essential that management be prepared for a wide range of future outcomes, because long-term capital is the most costly of all bank sources of funds. Moreover, no bank enjoys being pressured by its principal regulatory supervisor to strengthen its capital position.

Phase 2: Determine the Amount of Capital That Is Appropriate for the Bank Given Its Goals, Planned Service Offerings, Acceptable Risk Exposure, and State and Federal Regulations.   Management must recognize that it faces *two* capital requirements, one set by bank regulatory authorities and a second standard set by investors in the capital market. Too much equity capital, as viewed by the financial marketplace, reduces the leveraging effect of borrowing and profitably investing borrowed funds, giving the bank less earnings potential and lowering the price of its stock as investors come to expect lower bank earnings in the future. Too little equity capital relative to a bank's risk exposure may create an impression among capital market investors that the bank's earnings will become more volatile and that its largest depositors (who benefit very little from deposit insurance) are in danger of losing their funds. The bank's stock price will tend to fall, and depositors and other creditors will demand higher yields for the loan of their funds to a bank.

Phase 3: Determine How Much Capital Can Be Generated Internally through Profits Retained in the Business.   Management must decide what proportion of current earnings it will pay out as stockholder dividends and how much must be retained inside the bank to support future growth in loans and meet regulatory capital requirements. It must forecast the growth of the bank's earnings to see if earnings growth is likely to provide all or at least a significant portion of total capital needs.

Phase 4: Evaluate and Choose That Source of Capital Best Suited to the Bank's Needs and Goals.   The choice of a "best" source of capital includes several factors: market conditions if stock or debt must be issued, the rights and interests of current shareholders, and the confidence bank management has in its earnings forecasts. Most banks today have available a number of ways to raise long-term capital, such as selling stock, offering capital notes, selling assets, leasing their headquarters, or accelerating the growth of earnings. We may divide the various capital sources available into two groups: (1) internal funding sources and (2) external funding sources. We now examine these two broad capital-raising alternatives in detail.

Raising Capital Internally

In most years, the principal source of capital is from earnings kept in the bank rather than paid out to the stockholders. Internally generated capital has the advantage of not having to depend on the open market for funds, thus avoiding flotation costs. Not only is internal capital generally less expensive to raise, but it also does not threaten existing stockholders with loss of control—that is, it avoids dilution of their share of bank ownership and dilution of their earnings per share of stock held. For example, if the bank chooses to sell stock, some shares may be sold to new stockholders, who will then be entitled to share in any future earnings and to vote on the bank's policies. However, internal capital has the disadvantage of being fully taxable by the federal government and being significantly affected by changing interest rates and economic conditions not controllable by management.

Dividend Policy.   Relying on the growth of net earnings to fill the bank's capital needs means that a decision must be made concerning how much of current earnings must be retained in the business and how much must go to the stockholders in the form of dividends. That is, the board of directors and management must agree on the appropriate *retention ratio*—current retained earnings divided by current after-tax net income—which then determines the *dividend payout ratio*—current dividends to stockholders divided by current after-tax net income.

The retention ratio is of great importance to bank management. A retention ratio set too low (and, therefore, a dividend payout ratio set too high) results in slower growth of internal capital, which may increase the bank's failure risk and retard the expansion of its earning assets. A retention ratio set too high (and, therefore, a dividend payout ratio set too low) can result in a cut in the stockholders' dividend income. Other factors held constant, such a cut would reduce the market value of the bank's stock. The optimal dividend policy for a bank is one that maximizes the value of the stockholders' investment. New stockholders will be attracted to the bank and existing stockholders retained if the rate of return on owners' equity capital at least equals returns generated by other investments of comparable risk.

It is particularly important for bank management to try to achieve a *stable* dividend track record. If the bank's dividend payout ratio is kept relatively constant, interested investors will perceive less risk in their dividend payments and the bank will look more attractive to investors. As a recent study by Keen [5] suggests, bank stock prices typically drop quickly (usually within a week) after a dividend cut is announced. This not only disappoints current stockholders but also discourages potential buyers of the bank's equity shares, making it more difficult to raise new capital in the future.

How Fast Must Internally Generated Funds Grow?   A key factor affecting bank management's decision about an appropriate retention ratio and dividend payout ratio is how fast the bank can allow its assets (especially loans) to grow so that its existing ratio of capital to assets is protected from erosion. In other words, how fast must the bank's earnings grow to keep its capital-to-assets ratio protected if the bank continues paying the same dividend rate to its stockholders?

The following formula helps management and the board of directors answer such questions:

$$\text{\textbf{Internal capital growth rate,} or Retained earnings} \tag{1}$$

$$\div \text{ Equity capital } = \text{ROE} \times \text{Retention ratio}$$

$$= \frac{\text{Net income after taxes}}{\text{Equity capital}} \times \frac{\text{Retained earnings}}{\text{Net income after taxes}}$$

The reader will recall the ROE relationship discussed in Chapter 5 on bank performance:

$$\text{ROE} = \text{Profit margin} \times \text{Asset utilization} \times \text{Equity multiplier} \tag{2}$$

Then it must be true that

$$\begin{array}{c}\text{Internal}\\ \text{capital}\\ \text{growth rate}\end{array} = \begin{array}{c}\text{Profit}\\ \text{margin}\end{array} \times \begin{array}{c}\text{Asset}\\ \text{utilization}\end{array} \times \begin{array}{c}\text{Equity}\\ \text{multiplier}\end{array} \times \begin{array}{c}\text{Retention}\\ \text{ratio}\end{array} \tag{3}$$

or

$$\frac{\text{Retained earnings}}{\text{Equity capital}} = \frac{\text{Net income}\ \text{after taxes}}{\text{Operating revenue}} \times \frac{\text{Operating revenue}}{\text{Total assets}} \tag{4}$$

$$\times \frac{\text{Total assets}}{\text{Equity capital}} \times \frac{\text{Retained earnings}}{\begin{array}{c}\text{Net income}\\ \text{after taxes}\end{array}}$$

This formula shows that if we want to increase internally generated capital, we must increase our net earnings (through a higher profit margin, asset utilization ratio, and/or equity multiplier) or increase the earnings retention ratio, or both.

To illustrate the use of this formula, imagine that management has forecast a return on equity (ROE) of 10 percent for this year and plans to pay the bank's stockholders 50 percent of any net earnings the bank will earn. How fast can the bank's assets grow without reducing its current ratio of total capital to total assets? Equation 1 above yields

$$\text{ICGR} = \text{ROE} \times \text{Retention ratio} = 0.10 \times 0.50 = 5 \text{ percent.}$$

Thus, the bank's assets cannot grow more than 5 percent under the assumptions made. Otherwise, the bank's capital-to-assets ratio will fall, and if it falls far enough, the regulatory authorities will insist that the bank increase its capital position.

To take one more example, suppose a bank's assets are forecast to grow 10 percent this year. What options are open to management in terms of an earnings rate, measured by ROE, and an earnings retention ratio if the current ratio of capital to total assets is to be preserved? There are, of course, numerous possibilities that the formula will generate, as revealed in the table below. For example, if management can boost the bank's return on equity to 20 percent, it can pay out 50 percent of the bank's net after-tax income, retain the other 50 percent, and still protect its current capital-to-assets ratio. With an ROE of 10 percent, however, the bank must retain *all* of its current earnings. It should also be clear that if ROE falls *below* 10 percent, the bank's capital-to-assets ratio must decline as well, even if it retains all of its current income. In this instance, management may find the regulators insisting on raising more capital from outside the bank to offset a poor earnings record.

Example: If bank assets are expected to grow at a 10 percent rate this year, what combinations of return on equity and retention rate for earnings will preserve the bank's current capital-to-assets ratio?

Forecasted asset growth rate of 10 percent	= ROE × retention ratio.	
0.10	= 0.20 ×	0.50
0.10	= 0.50 ×	0.67
0.10	= 0.10 ×	1.00

Raising Capital Externally

If a bank does need to raise capital from outside, it has several options: (1) selling common stock, (2) selling preferred stock, (3) issuing capital notes, (4) selling assets, (5) leasing certain fixed assets, especially the bank's building and (6) swapping stock for debt securities. Which alternative the bank chooses will depend primarily on the impact each source would have on returns to the stockholders, usually measured by earnings per share (EPS). Other key factors to consider are the bank's risk exposure, the impact on control of the institution by its existing stockholders, the state of the market for the assets or securities being sold, and regulations. (See Table 15–4.)

Issuing Common Stock.   The sale of equity shares is generally the most expensive way to raise external capital, considering flotation costs and the greater risk

---

TABLE 15–4   **Determining the Best Sources of Capital**

- Relative cost of each source of capital funds (including interest cost, if any; underwriting fees and commissions, if any; and regulatory surveillance).
- Impact on stockholder returns, measured by earnings per share (EPS).
- Impact on ownership and control of the bank by current and possible future bank shareholders.
- Relative risk of each capital source.
- Overall risk exposure of the bank (as indicated by such measures as the total amount of loans outstanding relative to bank assets, deposits, or capital).
- Strength or weakness of the capital markets where new capital can be raised.
- Regulations affecting both the amount and mix of capital funds.

---

to earnings that stockholders face compared to debtholders. Unless the existing stockholders can absorb all the new shares, a new stock issue may dilute control of the bank and its EPS unless more can be earned on the funds raised than their cost of issue. Issuing stock also reduces the degree of leverage the bank can employ. The offsetting advantage, however, is that increasing the amount of ownership shares increases the bank's future borrowing capacity.

Issuing Preferred Stock.   The sale of preferred stock is, like the sale of common stock, generally among the most expensive sources of bank capital. Because preferred shareholders have a prior claim on the bank's earnings over holders of common equity, dividends to the common stockholder may be lower after preferred shares are issued. However, preferred stock has an advantage over debt in the form of greater flexibility (because dividends need not be paid) and newly issued preferred shares add future borrowing capacity for the bank.

Issuing Subordinated Notes and Debentures.   The advantage of subordinated debt is the generation of increased financial leverage to boost EPS if more can be earned on borrowed funds than their interest cost. Moreover, interest payments on debt securities are tax deductible. However, debt adds to failure risk and earnings risk and may make it more difficult to sell stock in the future.

Selling Assets and Leasing Facilities.   Occasionally, banks sell all or a portion of their office facilities and lease back from the new owner space to carry on their operations. Such a transaction usually creates a substantial inflow of cash (which is reinvested at current interest rates) and a sizable addition to net worth as well, strengthening the bank's capital position. The most successful sale-and-leaseback transactions have occurred where inflation and economic growth have significantly increased current property values over the book value of the property recorded on the bank's balance sheet. When faster write-offs of commercial real estate are possible—such as following passage of the 1981 Economic Recovery Act, which allowed commercial buildings to be fully depreciated in 15 years versus 30 years or more in early periods—the economic incentive from selling and leasing back bank property can be most attractive. However, this attractive feature was dimmed significantly in 1986 with passage of the Tax Reform Bill. The new law lengthened real estate depreciation requirements from 15 to 27 years for most structures, thus requiring bankers to evaluate their real estate transactions more in terms of their economic benefits rather than their tax benefits.

Many banks in recent years have *sold assets* to improve their capital-to-assets ratios. They have also frequently slowed the growth of more risky assets and redistributed some of their assets toward government securities and other low-risk investments so that their risk-weighted assets decline. A related strategy is to avoid booking loans, thereby avoiding an increase in assets and capital requirements, by referring loan customers to alternative sources of funds outside the bank, such as securitizations or standby credit agreements (as described, for example, in Chapter 9).

One recent innovation, called a *script issue,* recognizes that while some bank assets (particularly buildings) have appreciated in market value well beyond their book value, management has no desire to sell those assets. With a script issue, property revaluation reserves are created to capture the difference between the market value and book value of selected bank assets, and these reserves are capitalized to give bank shareholders bonus shares of stock. The new shares increase equity capital but do not dilute ownership or reduce the value of stock already issued.

Swapping Stock for Debt Securities.   In recent years many banking organizations (especially bank holding companies) have undertaken stock-for-debt swaps. For example, a bank may have $2 million in subordinated debentures on its balance sheet, issued at an interest cost of 8 percent. Following conventional practice, these bonds are recorded at their issue price (book value). If interest rates have risen recently, say to 10 percent, these notes may now have a *market value* of just $1 million. By selling new stock in the amount of $1 million and buying back the notes at their current market price, the bank is able to remove a $2 million debt from its balance sheet. From the regulators' perspective, the bank has strengthened its capital and saved the cost of future interest payments on the notes. Moreover, most debt issues have a sinking fund requirement, which requires annual payments into the fund to retire the bonds. These future cash outlays are no longer needed after a stock-for-debt swap is completed.

Choosing the Best Alternative for Raising Outside Capital.   The choice of which method to use in raising outside capital should be made on the basis of a careful financial analysis of the alternatives and their effects on bank earnings per share. Table 15–5 gives an example of a bank that needs to raise $20 million in external capital. The institution currently has 8 million shares of common stock outstanding at a $4-per-share par value and has total assets of close to $1 billion, with $60 million in

TABLE 15–5   Methods of Raising External Capital for a Bank

Income or Expense Item	Sell Common Stock at $10 per Share	Sell Preferred Stock Promising an 8 Percent Dividend at $20 per Share	Sell Capital Notes with a 10 Percent Coupon Rate
Estimated revenues	$100 million	$100 million	$100 million
Estimated operating expenses	80	80	80
Net revenues	20	20	20
Interest expense on capital notes	—	—	2
Estimated before-tax net income	20	20	18
Estimated income taxes (35%)	7	7	6.3
Estimated after-tax net income	13	13	11.7
Preferred stock dividends	—	1.6	—
Net income available to common stockholders	$13 million	$11.4 million	$11.7 million
Earnings per share of common stock	$1.30	$1.43	$1.46
	(10 million shares)	(8 million shares)	(8 million shares)

Note: Initially the bank has 8 million shares of common stock outstanding, with a $4-per-share par value.

equity capital. If the bank can generate total revenue of about $100 million and hold operating expenses to no more than $80 million, it should have about $10.8 million in earnings left after taxes. If management elects to raise the needed $20 million in new capital by issuing 2 million new equity shares, each at a net price of $10, the common stockholders will receive $1.30 in earnings per share.

Is the issue of common stock the *best* alternative for the bank? Not if its goal is to maximize earnings per share. For example, management finds that it could issue preferred stock, bearing an 8 percent dividend, at $20 per share. If the board of directors elects to declare an annual dividend on these preferred shares, this will drain $1.6 million ($20 million × 0.08) each year from earnings that would normally flow to the common stockholders. But it will still leave $11.6 million for holders of the 8 million in common shares, or a dividend rate of $1.43 per share. Thus, the preferred stock route would yield the bank's common stockholders $0.13 more in dividends per share than would the issue of additional common stock.

Management also discovers that it could sell $20 million in subordinated capital notes bearing a 10 percent coupon rate. While the bank must pay $2 million in interest annually on these notes, this still leaves almost $12 million left over after all expenses (including taxes). When distributed among the 8 million common shares, this will yield $1.46 per share. Clearly, the best of the three capital-raising options in this instance is *issuing capital notes*. Moreover, the capital notes carry no voting power, so the current stockholders retain control.

Concept Checks

15–16. What four phases should be part of any plan for meeting a bank's long-range need for capital?

15–17. How does dividend policy affect a bank's need for capital?

15–18. What is the ICGR and why is it important to bank management?

15–19. Suppose that a bank has a return on equity capital of 12 percent and that its retention ratio is 35 percent. How fast can this bank's assets grow without reducing its current ratio of capital to assets? Suppose that the bank's earnings (measured by ROE) drop unexpectedly to only two-thirds of the expected 12 percent figure. What would happen to the bank's ICGR?

15–20. What are the principal sources of external capital for a bank?

15–21. What factors should bank management consider in choosing among the various sources of external capital?

Summary

In the history of banking, there are few more controversial issues than those surrounding bank capital. There is a long-standing controversy between bankers and bank regulators, representing the public, over how much and what types of capital banks should hold. Not only the definition and concept of bank capital but also our views on the proper role for capital in controlling bank behavior are changing.

In banking, the term *capital* usually refers to those funds contributed by the bank's owners, consisting principally of stock, surplus, reserves for contingencies, and retained earnings. The capital account represents each bank's ultimate line of defense against failure, protecting the bank against risk in its various forms. Capital also supplies long-term funds that build a base for continued future growth in bank lending and physical facilities. The principal forms of bank capital in use today include common stock, preferred stock, surplus, undivided profits, equity reserves, subordinated debentures (or capital notes), minority interest in consolidated subsidiaries, and equity commitment notes.

The amount of capital a bank holds and the makeup of its capital account are determined by both regulation and the marketplace. Regulation entered the picture early in banking history due to fears that the private marketplace was not completely reliable as a regulator for bank capital. It is usually argued that free markets are not effective controllers of all the risks to the public from loss of deposits and cannot prevent erosion of deposit insurance reserves (such as the FDIC's insurance fund).

Minimum required capital ratios (relative to total assets) are now imposed on all banks. These required minimums stemmed from public fears over bank failures, passage in the United States of the International Lending and Supervision Act of 1983, and the adoption of the Basle Agreement on International Capital Standards in 1988. Faced with increased regulatory pressure to raise capital, banks can turn to either internal sources or external sources of capital funds. The principal internal source is retained earnings. The principal external sources of bank capital are (1) selling common stock, (2) selling preferred stock, (3) issuing capital notes, (4) selling bank assets, (5) leasing fixed assets, and (6) swapping stock for debt securities. In choosing among these various capital sources, banks must consider the relative cost and risk of each source of capital funding, the bank's overall risk exposure, the impact on returns to the institution's stockholders, and government regulations.

Key Terms in This Chapter

Capital
Operating risk
Exchange risk
Crime risk
Portfolio diversification
Geographic diversification
Common stock
Preferred stock
Surplus
Undivided profits
Equity reserves

Subordinated debentures
Minority interest in consolidated subsidiaries
Equity commitment notes
International Lending and Supervision Act of 1983
Basle Agreement
Tier 1 capital
Tier 2 capital
Internal capital growth rate

Problems and Projects

1. Several different measures of bank capital were discussed in this chapter, including GAAP, RAP, primary capital, secondary capital, core capital (Tier 1), and supplemental capital (Tier 2). Using the figures below calculate as many of these capital measures as you can:

Perpetual preferred stock	$ 1,644,000,000	Minority interest in subsidiaries	$ 3,075
Common stock	31,428,000,000	Subordinated notes and debentures	20,998
Surplus	71,412	Intangible assets	5,070
Undivided profits and reserves	44,060	Limited-life preferred stock	102
Foreign currency translation adjustment	(298)	Allowance for loan losses	54,077
Mandatory convertible debentures	3,001	Total assets (book value)	3,355,666
		Total liabilities	3,120,501
		Equity notes	815

2. First National Bank of Harrison has forecast the following performance ratios for the year ahead (see the next page).

   How fast can First National allow its assets to grow without reducing its ratio of equity capital to total assets, assuming the above figures hold reasonably steady over its planning period?

| Profit margin of net income over operating revenue | 0.0875 | Equity multiplier | 15.22X |
| Asset utilization (operating revenue ÷ assets) | 0.0963 | Net earnings retention ratio | 0.4000 |

Alternative scenarios:

(1) Suppose recent negative economic developments, including a prolonged recession, have caused First National to revise its estimates of the bank's profit margin downward to 0.0755 and its asset utilization ratio to 0.0904. What rate of asset growth will leave its ratio of equity capital to assets unchanged in the year ahead?

(2) Suppose that as a result of a recent examination by national bank examiners, First National has been told it must lower its equity multiplier (by a combination of selling off assets and raising new equity capital) in the coming year by 12 percent. What asset growth rate would help keep its equity-to-assets ratio at the new required level?

3. Using the formulas developed in this chapter and in Chapter 5, and the information presented below, calculate the ratios of total capital to total assets for the banks listed below. What relationship among these banks' return on assets, return on equity capital, and capital-to-assets ratios did you observe? What implications or recommendations would you draw for the management of each of these banks?

Name of Bank	Net After-Tax Income ÷ Total Assets (or ROA)	Net After-Tax Income ÷ Total Equity Capital (or ROE)
First National Bank of Domen	0.0149	0.125
Security National Bank	0.0070	0.125
Ilsher State Bank	0.0082	0.1005
Mercantile Bank and Trust Company	0.0037	0.1005
Westlake National Trust	–0.0045	–0.0500

4. Using the information presented below for Premier Western National Bank, calculate that bank's required level of capital based on the new international capital standards discussed in this chapter. Does the bank have sufficient capital under the new international capital standards?

On-Balance-Sheet Items (Assets)		Off-Balance-Sheet Items	
Cash	$ 2.5 million	Standby credit letters backing municipal bonds	$18.1 million
U.S. Treasury securities	25.6		
Deposit balances due from other banks	4.0	Long-term binding commitments to corporate customers	40.2 million
Loans secured by first lines on residential property (1–4 family dwellings)	8.7	Total of all off-balance-sheet items	$58.3 million
Loans to corporations	108.4		
Total assets	$149.2 million	Total capital	$10.5 million

Alternative scenarios:

(1) What would happen to Premier's capital adequacy position under the new international capital standards if its loans to corporations increased by 10 percent while its standby credit letters fell by 5 percent and its long-term credit commitments to corporations also declined by 5 percent?

(2) Suppose Premier's U.S. government security holdings expanded by 20 percent due to a temporary falloff in loan demand. Assuming no other changes, how would this development affect the bank's capital position under the Basle Agreement's capital standards?

(3) If loans secured by primary mortgages on residential property rose by 15 percent, how would this change (assuming all else held constant) affect Premier's ratio of capital to risk-adjusted assets?

5. Silsbee National Bank and Trust Co. reported its capital position to examiners earlier this month. The bank currently has $825 million in total assets, $779 million in total liabilities, and $46 million in total capital, broken down in the table below:

Components of Total Capital	Dollar Amount of Each Capital Component (millions)
Common stock	$ 3.1
Surplus on common	4.7
Perpetual preferred stock	0.8
Surplus on preferred	0.6
Limited-life preferred stock	0.2
Retained earnings	26.3
Mandatorily convertible capital notes and debentures	5.9
Reserve for loan losses	4.4
	$46.0

Silsbee's current price on its common stock is $3.50 per share, with 10 million common equity shares outstanding. It has 50,000 shares of preferred stock outstanding at $10 per share. What is the market value of the bank's capital? What size capital deficiency does the bank have, if any, according to the international capital standards in this chapter? What is the bank's capital position according to the GAAP measure? The RAP measure? What is the market value of the bank's capital in dollar terms and relative to its book value?

Alternative scenarios:

(1) If Silsbee's current common stock price rises to $4.25 a share, while its preferred stock increases to $10.50 per share, how will these changes affect the market value of the bank's capital? Are the GAAP and RAP measures affected?

(2) Suppose Silsbee's common stock falls to $3.15 a share, while its preferred stock sells now for $9.44 per share. How will the market value of the bank's capital and the GAAP and RAP capital measures change?

6. Crossroads National Bank has been told by examiners that it needs to raise an additional $8 million in long-term capital. Its outstanding common equity shares total 7.5 million, each bearing a par value of $1. The bank currently holds total assets of nearly $2 billion, with $105 million in total equity. During the coming year, the bank's economists have forecast operating revenues of $175 million, of which operating expenses will absorb 96 percent.

Among the options for raising capital considered by management are (*a*) selling $8 million in common stock, or 320,000 shares at $25 per share; (*b*) selling $8 million in preferred stock bearing a 9 percent annual dividend yield at $12 per share; or (*c*) selling $8 million in 10-year capital notes with a 10 percent coupon rate. Which option would be of most benefit to the bank's stockholders? What happens if operating revenues increase more than the forecast? Cite examples of the consequences. What happens if there is a slower-than-expected volume of revenues (only $125 million instead of $175 million)? Please explain.

Alternative scenarios:

(1) Suppose Crossroads National Bank finds that due to favorable developments in the capital market, its common stock can now

be sold at $27.50 per share while preferred will sell for $14 per share and it can issue 10-year capital notes with a 9.75 percent coupon rate. Under these conditions, which capital-raising option will be of most benefit to the bank's current shareholders?

(2) Suppose Crossroads common stock dips in price to $22.50 per share, while its preferred stock falls to $10.75 per share and Crossroads capital notes must carry an 11 percent coupon rate. Which long-term funding option seems best for current stockholders?

(3) What happens to shareholders' returns and to the bank if operating revenues rise to $200 million (all else held constant) instead of $175 million?

7. Please calculate Willow River National Bank's total risk-weighted assets, based on the items that the bank reported on its latest balance sheet, shown below. Does the bank appear to have a capital deficiency?

Cash	$ 120 million
Domestic interbank deposits	240 million
U.S. government securities	450 million
Residential real estate loans	370 million
Commercial loans	520 million
Total assets	$1,700 million
Total liabilities	$1,569 million
Total capital	$ 136 million

Off-balance-sheet items include:

Standby credit letters	$ 75 million
Long-term loan commitments to private companies	180 million

8. Suppose that Willow River National Bank, whose balance sheet is given in problem 7, reports the forms of capital shown in the table below as of the date of its latest financial statement. What is the total dollar volume of the bank's Tier 1 capital? Tier 2 capital? According to the data given in problems 7 and 8, does Willow River National Bank have a capital deficiency?

Common stock (par value)	$18 million
Surplus 22 million	
Undivided profits	84 million
Allowance for loan losses	75 million
Subordinated debt capital40 million	
Intermediate-term preferred stock	12 million

9. Please indicate which items below appearing on bank financial statements would be classified under the terms of the Basle Agreement as (*a*) Tier 1 capital and (*b*) Tier 2 capital.

Allowance for loan
  and lease losses
Subordinated debt under
  two years to maturity
Intermediate-term
  preferred stock
Qualifying noncumulative
  perpetual preferred stock
Cumulative perpetual preferred
  stock with unpaid dividends
Subordinated debt capital
  instruments with an original
  average maturity of at
  least five years

Common stock
Equity notes
Undivided profits
Mandatory convertible
  debt
Minority interest in the
  equity accounts of
  consolidated
  subsidiaries

10. Under the terms of the Basle Agreement, what *risk weights* apply to the following on-balance- sheet and off-balance-sheet items for a bank?

Residential real
  estate loans
Cash
Commercial loans
U.S. Treasury
  securities
Deposits held at
  other domestic banks
GNMA mortgage-
  backed securities
Standby credit letters
  for commercial paper
Federal agency securities
Municipal general
  obligation bonds
Investments in subsidiaries
FNMA or FHLMC
  issued or guaranteed securities

Credit card loans
Standby letters of credit
  for municipal bonds
Long-term commitments
  to make corporate loans
Currency derivative
  contracts
Interest-rate derivative
  contracts
Short-term (under one
  year) loan commitments
Bank real estate
Bankers' acceptances
Municipal revenue bonds
Reserves on deposit at the
  Federal Reserve banks

Selected References

The following studies discuss the factors contributing to bank failure:

1. Santomero, Anthony M., and Joseph D. Vinso. "Estimating the Probability of Failure for Commercial Banks and the Banking System." *Journal of Banking and Finance* 1 (1977), pp. 185–205.
2. Short, Eugene D.; Gerald P. O'Driscoll, Jr.; and Franklin D. Berger. "Recent Bank Failures: Determinants and Consequences." *Proceedings of a Conference on Bank Structure and Competition,* Federal Reserve Bank of Chicago, 1985.

These studies present an overview of the market's role in influencing bank capital positions:

3. Berkovec, James A., and J. Nellie Liang. *Changes in the Cost of Equity Capital for Bank Holding Companies and the Effects on Raising Capital.* Study No. 160, Board of Governors of the Federal Reserve System, June 1991.
4. Eisenbeis, Robert A., and Gary G. Gilbert. "Market Discipline and the Prevention of Bank Problems and Failure." *Issues in Bank Regulation* 3 (Winter 1985), pp. 16–23.
5. Keen, Howard, Jr. "The Impact of a Dividend-Cut Announcement on Bank Share Prices." *Journal of Bank Research,* Winter 1983, pp. 274–81.

For a discussion of capital adequacy standards, their effects, and recent changes, see the following:

6. Eubanks, Walter W. "Risk-Based Bank Capital and Regulatory Enforcement." *CRS Review,* May/June 1991, pp. 16–18.
7. Peek, Joe, and Eric S. Rosengren. "Have Borrower Concentration Limits Encouraged Bank Consolidation?" *New England Economic Review,* Federal Reserve Bank of Boston, January/February 1997, pp. 37–47.
8. _____. "How Well Capitalized are 'Well-Capitalized Banks?" *New England Economic Review,* September/October 1997, pp. 41–50.

9. Wall, Larry D. "Regulation of Banks' Equity Capital." *Economic Review,* Federal Reserve Bank of Atlanta, November 1985, pp. 4–18.

These studies discuss methods banks use to raise capital:

10. Miller, Richard B. "Raising Bank Capital." *Bankers Monthly Magazine,* January 15, 1986, pp. 17–21.
11. Nagle, Reid, and Bruce Petersen. "Capitalization Problems in Perspective." In *Handbook for Banking Strategy,* ed. Richard C. Aspinwall and Robert A. Eisenbeis. New York: Wiley, 1985.

For a discussion of recent steps to broaden the Basle Agreement on international bank capital standards to take account of market risk and interest rate risk, see especially:

12. Levonian, Mark E. "Market Risk and Bank Capital: Part I." *FRBSF Weekly Letter,* Federal Reserve Bank of San Francisco, January 7, 1994, pp. 1–3.
13. ———. "Market Risk and Bank Capital: Part 2." *FRBSF Weekly Letter,* Federal Reserve Bank of San Francisco, January 14, 1994, pp. 1–3.
14. Marshall, David, and Subu Venkatarainan. "Bank Capital for Market Risk: A Study in Incentive-Compatible Regulation," *Chicago Fed Letter,* No. 104 (April 1996), pp. 1–3.
15. Federal Deposit Insurance Corporation. *Final Rule Amending Risk-Based Capital Requirements to Incorporate Market Risk,* October 10, 1996.
16. Hendricks, Darryll, and Beverly Hirtle. "Bank Capital Requirements for a Market Risk: The Internal Models Approach." *Economic Policy Review,* Federal Reserve Bank of New York, December 1997, pp. 1–12.

V Providing Loans to Businesses and Consumers

16 BANK LENDING: POLICIES AND PROCEDURES

Learning and Management Decision Objectives

The purpose of this chapter is to learn why sound bank lending policies are important to banks and the public they serve and how to spot and deal with problem loans when they appear in a bank's portfolio.

Introduction

The principal reason banks are chartered by state and federal authorities is to make *loans* to their customers.[1] Banks are expected to support their local communities with an adequate supply of credit for all legitimate business and consumer financial needs and to price that credit reasonably in line with competitively determined interest rates. Indeed, making loans is the principal economic function of banks—to fund consumption and investment spending by businesses, individuals, and units of government. How well a bank performs its lending function has a great deal to do with the economic health of its region, because bank loans support the growth of new businesses and jobs within the bank's trade territory and promote economic vitality. Moreover, bank loans often seem to convey positive information to the marketplace about a borrower's credit quality, enabling a borrower to obtain more and perhaps somewhat cheaper funds from other sources.

For most banks, loans account for half or more of their total assets and about half to two-thirds of their revenues. Moreover, *risk* in banking tends to be concentrated in the loan portfolio. When a bank gets into serious financial trouble, its problems usually spring from loans that have become uncollectible due to mismanagement, illegal manipulation of loans, misguided lending policies, or an unexpected economic downturn. No wonder, then, when examiners appear at a bank they make a thorough review of the bank's loan portfolio. Usually this involves a detailed analysis of the documentation and collateral for

---

[1]Portions of this chapter are based upon the author's article in the *Canadian Banker* [6] and are used with permission of the publisher.

517

the largest loans, a review of a sample of small loans, and an evaluation of the bank's loan policy to ensure that it is sound and prudent in order to protect the public's funds.

Types of Loans Made by Banks

What *types* of loans do banks make? The answer, of course, is that banks make a wide variety of loans to a wide variety of customers for many different purposes—from purchasing automobiles and buying new furniture, taking dream vacations, or pursuing college educations to constructing homes and office buildings. Fortunately, we can bring some order to the diversity of bank lending by grouping bank loans according to their *purpose*—what the customer plans to do with the proceeds of his or her bank loan. At least once a year, the Federal Reserve System, the FDIC, and Comptroller of the Currency require each U.S. bank to report the composition of its loan portfolio by purpose of loan on a report form known as Schedule A, attached to its balance sheet. Table 16–1 summarizes the major items reported on Schedule A for all U.S. commercial banks as of December 31, 1996.

We note from Table 16–1 that bank loans may be divided into seven broad categories of loans, delineated by their purposes:

1. **Real estate loans,** which are secured by real property—land, buildings, and other structures—and include short-term loans for construction and land development and longer-term loans to finance the purchase of farmland, homes, apartments, commercial structures, and foreign properties.

2. **Financial institution loans,** including credit to banks, insurance companies, finance companies, and other financial institutions.

3. **Agricultural loans,** extended to farm and ranch operations to assist in planting and harvesting crops and to support the feeding and care of livestock.

4. **Commercial and industrial loans,** granted to businesses to cover such expenses as purchasing inventories, paying taxes, and meeting payrolls.

5. **Loans to individuals,** including credit to finance the purchase of automobiles, mobile homes, appliances, and other retail goods to repair and modernize homes, cover the cost of medical care and other personal expenses, either extended directly to individuals or indirectly through retail dealers.

6. *Miscellaneous loans,* which include all those loans not classified above, including securities' loans.

7. *Lease financing receivables,* where the bank buys equipment or vehicles and leases them to its customers.

Of the loan categories shown, the largest in dollar volume is real estate loans, accounting for about two-fifths of total bank loans. The next largest category is commercial and industrial (C&I) loans, representing about one quarter of the total, followed by loans to individuals and families, accounting for about one-fifth of all loans made by federally insured U.S. commercial banks.

TABLE 16–1   Loans Outstanding for All U.S. Insured Commercial Banks as of December 31, 1996 (consolidated domestic and foreign offices)

Bank Loans Classified by Purpose	Amount ($ billions)	Percentage of Total Loans	Percentage of Loan Portfolio	
			Smallest U.S. Banks (less than $100 million in total assets)	Largest U.S. Banks (over $1 billion in total assets)
1. Total real estate loans[a]	$1,140.0	40.5%	55.8%	35.6%
2. Loans to financial institutions[b]	114.2	4.1	0.1	5.0
3. Loans to finance agricultural production and other loans to farmers	41.3	1.5	10.9	0.6
4. Commercial and industrial loans[c]	709.9	25.2	16.3	27.4
5. Loans to individuals[d]	560.9	19.9	15.4	20.7
6. Miscellaneous loans[e]	171.7	6.1	1.0	7.4
7. Lease finance receivables	78.4	2.8	0.4	3.4
Total (gross) loans shown on U.S. banks' balance sheet	$2,816.3	100.0%	100.0%	100.0%

[a]Construction and land development loans; loans to finance one-to-four family homes; multifamily residential property loans; nonfarm, nonresidential property loans; foreign real estate loans.

[b]Loans to commercial banks; loans to other financial institutions.

[c]Credit to construct business plant and equipment; loans for business operating expenses; loans for other business uses, including international loans and acceptances.

[d]Loans to purchase automobiles; credit cards; mobile home loans; loans to purchase consumer goods; loans to repair and modernize residences; all other personal installment loans; single-payment loans; other personal loans.

[e]Includes loans to foreign governments and state and local governments as well as acceptances of other banks.

Note: columns may not add exactly to totals due to rounding error.

Source: Federal Deposit Insurance Corporation, *Statistics on Banking,* 1996.

Factors Determining the Growth and Mix of Bank Loans

While Table 16–1 indicates the relative amounts of different kinds of loans for the whole banking industry, the mix usually differs quite markedly from institution to institution. One of the key factors in shaping an individual bank's loan portfolio is the profile of *characteristics of the market area* it serves. Each bank must respond to the particular demands for credit arising from customers in its own market. A bank serving a suburban community with large numbers of single-family homes and small retail stores will normally have mainly residential real estate loans, automobile loans, and credit for the purchase of home appliances and for meeting household expenses. In contrast, a bank situated in a central city surrounded by office buildings, department stores, and manufacturing establishments will typically devote the bulk of its loan portfolio to business loans designed to stock shelves with inventory, purchase equipment, and meet payrolls.

Of course, banks are not totally dependent on the local areas they serve for *all* the loans they acquire. They can purchase whole loans or pieces of loans from other banks, share in loans with other banks (known as *participations*), or even use credit derivatives to offset the economic volatility inherent in loans from their trade territory (as we saw in Chapter 9, for example). These steps can help to reduce the risk of loss if the local areas served by the bank incur severe economic problems. However, most banks are chartered by government authorities primarily to service selected markets and, as a practical matter, most of their loan applications will come from these areas.

Bank size is also a key factor shaping the composition of the bank's loan portfolio mix, especially the size of the bank's capital, which determines its legal lending limit to a single borrowing customer. Larger banks typically are **wholesale lenders,** devoting the bulk of their credit portfolios to large-denomination loans to corporations and other business firms. Smaller banks, on the other hand, tend to emphasize **retail credit,** in the form of smaller-denomination personal cash and installment loans and home mortgage loans extended to individuals and families, as well as smaller business loans to farms and ranches. Table 16–1 reveals some of the differences between the largest and smallest U.S. banks in loan portfolio mix. The smallest banks (under $100 million in total assets) are more heavily committed to real estate and agricultural loans compared to the largest banking firms (over $1 billion in assets), which are more heavily committed to commercial loans. The *experience and expertise of management* in making different types of loans also shape a bank's loan portfolio mix, as does the bank's official *loan policy,* which prohibits its loan officers from making certain kinds of loans.

Loan mix at any particular bank depends heavily as well upon the *expected yield* to the bank that each loan offers compared to the yields on all other assets the bank could acquire. Other factors held equal, a bank would generally prefer to make loans bearing the highest expected returns after all expenses and the risk of loan losses are taken into account. One way bankers can assess this yield versus cost factor is to set up a cost accounting system that considers all expected revenues along with the direct and indirect costs of making each type of loan. For banks that don't possess their own sophisticated cost accounting systems, the Federal Reserve banks have created a program called *Functional Cost Analysis* (FCA), which collects data on bank assets, income, expenses, and service volume and calculates an estimated yield and cost for loans and other bank service functions. An example of recent loan yield and loan cost calculations generated by the Fed's FCA program for different size groups of banks is given in Table 16–2.

Let's examine the figures in Table 16–2 closely. The first column of data is called the *gross yield* for each loan type, or the ratio of the total revenue received from each category of loan to the total dollar amount of loans outstanding in that category. The expenses incurred in making each loan (including the salaries of loan officers, but not the cost of borrowed funds) is then deducted, along with the percentage of loans that turned out to be losses, in order to determine the *net yield* to the bank from each loan category. We can easily see why some categories—for example, real estate loans, and commercial loans—are very popular with bankers. Their net yields are quite high compared to the yields of other assets banks could acquire.

Notice, however, that the track record of expenses and loan losses can play a significant role in a banker's decision about which loans to make. For example, the gross

TABLE 16–2   Net Yields on Loans Earned by U.S. Banks, 1996

Types of Loans	Gross Yields on Each Loan Category	Deductions For		Net Yield on Each Loan Category
		Expenses	Losses	
Real estate loans:				
Smallest banks*	9.37%	1.46%	0.02%	7.88%
Medium-size banks*	9.27	1.30	0.08	7.89
Largest banks*	8.94	1.09	0.19	7.66
Installment loans:**				
Smallest banks	10.32	4.43	0.23	5.66
Medium-size banks	10.37	4.11	0.44	5.82
Largest banks	9.75	3.56	0.74	5.45
Credit card loans:				
Smallest banks	17.51	22.55	0.71	–5.74
Medium-size banks	24.33	19.13	2.39	2.82
Largest banks	24.52	20.53	1.88	2.12
Commercial and other loans:***				
Smallest banks	10.04	2.42	0.44	7.17
Medium-size banks	9.98	2.69	0.34	6.96
Largest banks	9.35	2.43	0.33	6.60

NA = not available.

*The smallest U.S. banks hold total deposits up to $50 million, medium-size banks hold deposits of between $50 and $200 million, and the largest banks hold total deposits of over $200 million.

**Installment loans are mainly loans to households but also include loans to dealers in consumer goods and other commercial loans normally amortized through installments.

***Commercial and other loans also include leased equipment, agricultural loans, and construction loans made to proprietorships, partnerships, and corporations not serviced by the installment loan department.

Source: Federal Reserve System, *National Average Report 1996,* Functional Cost and Profit Analysis Program of the Federal Reserve Banks, Washington, D.C., 1997.

yield on credit card loans shown in Table 16–2 is exceptionally high, 17.5 to almost 25 percent. But the expenses associated with making these loans are also very high, as is their loss rate due to failure and fraud. Indeed, for the smallest banks the estimated *net* yield on credit card loans was negative in the year shown.

Bank size appears to have a significant influence on the net yield from different kinds of loans. Smaller banks, for example, seem to average higher net returns from granting real estate and commercial loans, while larger banks appear to have a net yield advantage in making credit card loans to households. Of course, *customer size* as well as bank size can affect relative loan yields. For example, the largest banks make loans to the largest corporations where loan rates are relatively low due to generally lower risk and the force of competition; in contrast, small banks loan money primarily to the smallest-size businesses, whose loan rates tend to be much higher than those for large corporate loans. Thus, it is not too surprising that the net yields on commercial loans tend to be higher among the smallest banks.

As a general rule, a bank should make those types of loans for which it is the most efficient producer. In 1996, as Table 16–2 indicates, the largest banks in the industry had a cost advantage in making nearly all types of real estate and consumer installment loans. Medium-size banks were the lowest-cost producers of credit card loans. The smallest banks had no cost advantage for any of these loan categories except for a marginal advantage in making commercial loans. The smallest banks were clearly more effective at controlling losses in most categories of loans (except commercial loans) than larger banks, perhaps because they often have better knowledge of their customers.

Concept Checks

16–1. In what ways does a bank's lending function affect the economy of its community or region?

16–2. What are the principal types of loans made by banks?

16–3. What factors appear to influence the growth and mix of bank loans?

16–4. A bank's cost accounting system reveals that its losses on real estate loans average 0.45 percent of loan volume and its operating expenses from making these loans average 1.85 percent of loan volume. If the gross yield on real estate loans is currently 8.80 percent, what is the bank's net yield on these loans?

Regulation of Lending

The loan portfolio of any bank is heavily influenced by *regulation,* because the quality of a bank's loan portfolio has more to do with risk and safety than any other aspect of the banking business. Some loans are restricted or prohibited by law.

For example, banks are frequently prohibited from making loans collateralized by their own stock. Real estate loans granted by a national bank cannot exceed the bank's capital and surplus or 70 percent of its total time and savings deposits, whichever is greater. A loan to a single customer normally cannot exceed 15 percent of a national bank's capital and surplus account. Loans to a bank's officers extended for purposes other than funding education, the purchase of a home, or that are not fully backed by U.S. government securities or deposits are limited to the greater of 2.5 percent of the bank's capital and unimpaired surplus or $25,000, but cannot be more than $100,000. State-chartered banks face similar restrictions in their home states and from the Federal Deposit Insurance Corporation.

The Community Reinvestment Act (1977) requires all banks to make "an affirmative effort" to meet the credit needs of individuals and businesses in their trade territories so that no areas of the local community are discriminated against in seeking access to bank credit. Moreover, under the Equal Credit Opportunity Act (1974), no individual can be denied credit because of race, sex, religious affiliation, age, or receipt of public assistance. Disclosure laws, such as the federal Truth-in-Lending Act (1968), require that the household borrower be quoted the "true cost" of a loan, as reflected in the annual percentage interest rate (APR) and all required charges and fees for obtaining credit, *before* the loan agreement is signed.[2]

In the field of international lending special regulations have appeared in recent years in an effort to reduce the risk exposure associated with granting loans overseas. In this field banks often face significant political risk, when foreign governments pass restrictive laws or seize foreign-owned property, as well as substantial business risk due to lack of information and knowledge concerning foreign markets. U.S. law in the form of the International Lending and Supervision Act requires U.S. banks to report to bank regulatory agencies and make public any credit exposures to a single country that exceed 15 percent of their primary capital or 0.75 percent of their total capital, whichever is the smaller of the two. This law also imposes restrictions on the fees banks may charge a troubled international borrower to restructure a loan.

The quality of a bank's loan portfolio and the soundness of its lending policies are the areas federal and state bank examiners look at most closely when examining a bank. Under the Uniform Financial Institutions Rating System used by federal bank examiners, each bank is assigned a numerical rating based on the quality of its asset portfolio, including its loans. The possible examiner ratings are:

1 = strong performance.

2 = satisfactory performance.

3 = fair performance.

4 = marginal performance.

5 = unsatisfactory performance.

The higher a bank's asset-quality rating, the less frequently it will be subject to review and examination by federal banking agencies.

Examiners generally look at all of a bank's loans above a designated minimum size and at a random sample of small loans. Loans that are performing well but have minor weaknesses because the bank has not followed its own loan policy or has failed to get full documentation from the borrower are called *criticized loans.* Loans that appear to contain significant weaknesses or that represent what the examiner regards as a dangerous concentration of credit in one borrower or in one industry are called *scheduled loans.* A scheduled loan is a warning to a bank's management to monitor that credit carefully and to work toward reducing the bank's concentrated risk exposure from it.

When an examiner finds some loans that carry an immediate risk of not paying out as planned, these credits are *adversely classified.* Typically, examiners will place adversely classified loans into one of three groupings: (1) *substandard loans,* where the bank's margin of protection is inadequate due to weaknesses in collateral or in the borrower's repayment abilities; (2) *doubtful loans,* which carry a strong probability of loss to the bank; and (3) *loss loans,* which are regarded as uncollectible. A common procedure for examiners is to multiply the total of all substandard loans by 0.20, the total of

---

[2]See Chapter 19 for a more detailed discussion of antidiscrimination and disclosure laws applying to bank loans to individuals.

all doubtful loans by 0.50, and the total of all loss loans by 1.00, then sum these weighted amounts together and compare their grand total with the bank's sum of loan-loss reserves and equity capital. If the weighted sum of all adversely classified loans appears too large relative to loan-loss reserves and bank equity, examiners will demand changes in the bank's policies and procedures or, possibly, require additions to the bank's loan-loss reserves and capital. Beginning in 1995 financial institutions that disagree with examiner classifications of their loans can appeal these examiner rulings.

Of course, the quality of loans and other bank assets is only *one* dimension of a bank's performance that is rated under the Uniform Financial Institutions Rating System. Numerical ratings are also assigned based on examiner judgment of the bank's capital adequacy, management quality, earnings record, liquidity position, and sensitivity to market risk exposure. All five dimensions of bank performance are combined into one overall numerical rating, popularly referred to as the **CAMELS rating.** The letters are derived from

*C*apital adequacy.

*A*sset quality.

*M*anagement quality.

*E*arnings record.

*L*iquidity position.

*S*ensitivity to market risk

Banks whose overall CAMELS rating is toward the low, riskier end of the numerical scale—an overall rating of 4 or 5—are examined more frequently than the highest-rated banks, those with ratings of 1, 2, or 3.

Establishing a Written Loan Policy

One of the most important ways a bank can make sure its loans meet regulatory standards and are profitable is to establish a *written loan policy.* Such a policy gives loan officers and the bank's management specific guidelines in making individual loan decisions and in shaping the bank's overall loan portfolio. The actual makeup of a bank's loan portfolio should reflect what its loan policy says. Otherwise, the loan policy is not functioning effectively and should be either revised or more strongly enforced by senior management.

What should a bank's written loan policy contain? The examinations manual, which the Federal Deposit Insurance Corporation gives to new bank examiners, suggests the most important elements of a good bank loan policy. These elements include:

1. A goal statement for the bank's loan portfolio (i.e., statement of the characteristics of a good loan portfolio for the bank in terms of types, maturities, sizes, and quality of loans).
2. Specification of the lending authority given to each loan officer and loan committee (measuring the maximum amount and types of loan that each person and committee can approve and what signatures are required).

3. Lines of responsibility in making assignments and reporting information within the loan department.

4. Operating procedures for soliciting, reviewing, evaluating, and making decisions on customer loan applications.

5. The required documentation that is to accompany each loan application and what must be kept in the bank's credit files (required financial statements, security agreements, etc.).

6. Lines of authority within the bank, detailing who is responsible for maintaining and reviewing the bank's credit files.

7. Guidelines for taking, evaluating, and perfecting loan collateral.

8. A presentation of policies and procedures for setting loan interest rates and fees and the terms for repayment of loans.

9. A statement of quality standards applicable to all loans.

10. A statement of the preferred upper limit for total loans outstanding (i.e., the maximum ratio of total loans to total assets allowed).

11. A description of the bank's principal trade area, from which most loans should come.

12. A discussion of the preferred procedures for detecting, analyzing, and working out problem loan situations.

Other authorities would add to this list such items as specifying what loans the bank would prefer *not* to make, such as loans to support the construction of speculative housing or loans to support leveraged buyouts (LBOs) of companies by a small group of insiders who typically make heavy use of debt to finance the purchase, as well as a list of preferred loans (such as short-term business inventory loans that are self-liquidating).

A *written* loan policy statement carries a number of advantages for the bank adopting it. It communicates to employees working in the loan department what procedures they must follow and what their responsibilities are. It helps the bank move toward a loan portfolio that can successfully blend *multiple objectives,* such as promoting the bank's profitability, controlling its risk exposure, and satisfying regulatory requirements. Any exceptions to the bank's written loan policy should be fully documented, and the reasons why a variance from the loan policy was permitted should be listed. While any written loan policy must be flexible due to continuing changes in economic conditions and regulations, violations of a bank's loan policy should be *infrequent* events.

Concept Checks

16–5. Why is bank lending so closely regulated by state and federal authorities?

16–6. What is the CAMELS rating and what is it used for?

16–7. What should a good written bank loan policy contain?

Steps in the Lending Process

Most bank loans to individuals arise from a direct request from a customer who approaches a member of the bank's staff and asks to fill out a loan application. Business loan requests, on the other hand, often arise from contacts the bank's loan officers and sales representatives make as they solicit new accounts from firms operating in the bank's market area. Sometimes loan officers will call on the same company for months before the customer finally agrees to give the bank a try by filling out a loan application. Most bank loan personnel fill out a customer contact report similar to the one shown in Table 16–3 when they visit a potential new customer's place of business. This report is updated after each subsequent visit, giving the next loan officer crucial information about a prospective client before any other personal contracts are made.

Once a customer decides to request a loan, an interview with a loan officer usually follows right away, giving the customer the opportunity to explain his or her credit needs. That interview is particularly important because it provides an opportunity for the bank's loan officer to assess the customer's *character* and *sincerity of purpose*. If the customer appears to lack sincerity in acknowledging the need to adhere to the terms of a loan, this must be recorded as a strong factor weighing against approval of the loan request.

If a business or mortgage loan is applied for, a *site visit* is usually made by an officer of the bank to assess the customer's location and the condition of the property and to ask clarifying questions. The loan officer may contact other creditors who have previously loaned money to this customer to see what their experience has been. Did the customer fully adhere to previous loan agreements and keep satisfactory deposit balances? A previous payment record often reveals much about the customer's character, sincerity of purpose, and sense of responsibility in making use of bank credit.

If all is favorable to this point, the customer is asked to submit several crucial documents the bank needs in order to fully evaluate the loan request, including complete financial statements and, in the case of a corporation, board of directors' resolutions authorizing the negotiation of a loan with the bank. Once all documents are on file, the credit analysis division of the bank conducts a thorough financial analysis of them aimed at determining whether the customer has sufficient cash flows and backup assets to repay the loan. The credit analysis division then prepares a brief summary and recommendation, which goes to the loan committee for approval. On larger loans, members of the credit analysis division give an oral presentation, and discussion will ensue between staff analysts and the loan committee over the strong and weak points of a loan request.

If the loan committee approves the customer's request, the loan officer or the credit committee will usually check on the property or other assets to be pledged as collateral in order to ensure that the bank has immediate access to the collateral or can acquire title to the property involved if the loan agreement is defaulted. This is often referred to as *perfecting* the bank's claim to collateral. Once the loan officer and the bank's loan committee are satisfied that both the loan and the proposed collateral are sound, the note and other documents that make up a loan agreement are prepared and are signed by all parties to the agreement.

TABLE 16–3   Sample Customer Contact Report
(results of previous calls on this customer)

Name of customer: _____

Address: _____ Telephone: (___)_____

Bank personnel making the most recent contact: _____

Names of bank employees making previous contacts with this customer: _____

_____

Does this customer currently use any services of our bank? ____Yes ____No

Which ones?   _____

If no, has the customer used any of our bank's services in the past? _____

If a business firm, what officials or principals with the customer's firm have been contacted by our

bank? _____

_____

If an individual, what is the customer's occupation? _____

If a business firm, what line of business is the customer in? _____

Approximate annual sales: $_____ Size of labor force: _____

With whom does the customer bank at present? _____

What problems (if any) does the customer report having with his/her current banking relationship?

_____

What banking services does this customer use at present? (Please Check)

_____ Line of credit   _____ Letters of credit

_____ Term loan   _____ Funds transfers

_____ Checkable deposits   _____ Cash management services

_____ CDs and other time accounts   _____ Trust services

What banking services does this customer *not* use currently that might be useful to him or her? ____

_____

Describe the results of the most recent contact with this customer: _____

_____

Recommended steps to prepare for the next call (e.g., special information needed, additional bank

personnel needed): _____

_____

Is this the end of the process? Can the loan officer put the signed loan agreement on the shelf and forget about it? Hardly! The new agreement must be monitored continuously to ensure that the terms of the loan are being followed and that all required payments of principal and/or interest are being made as promised. For larger commercial credits, the loan officer will visit the customer's business periodically to check on the firm's progress and to see what other services the customer may need. Usually a loan officer or other staff member places information about a new loan customer in a computer file known as a *bank customer profile*. This file shows what bank services the customer is currently using and contains other information required by bank management to monitor a customer's progress and financial-service needs.

Credit Analysis: What Makes a Good Loan?

The division of the bank responsible for analyzing and making recommendations on the fate of most loan applications is the *credit department*. Experience has shown that this department must satisfactorily answer three major questions regarding each loan application:

1. Is the borrower *creditworthy?* How do you know?
2. Can the loan agreement be properly structured and documented so that the bank and its depositors are adequately protected and the customer has a high probability of being able to service the loan without excessive strain?
3. Can the bank *perfect* its claim against the assets or earnings of the customer so that, in the event of default, bank funds can be recovered rapidly at low cost and with low risk?

Let's look in turn at each of these three key issues in the "yes" or "no" decision a bank must make on every loan request.

Is the Borrower Creditworthy?

The question that must be dealt with before any other is whether or not the customer can *service the loan*—that is, pay out the credit when due, with a comfortable margin for error. This usually involves a detailed study of six aspects of the loan application—character, capacity, cash, collateral, conditions, and control. *All* must be satisfactory for the loan to be a good one from the lender's point of view. (See Table 16–4.)

Character. The loan officer must be convinced that the customer has a well-defined *purpose* for requesting bank credit and a serious intention to repay. If the officer is not sure exactly why the customer is requesting a loan, this purpose must be clarified to the bank's satisfaction. Once the purpose is known, the loan officer must determine if it is consistent with the bank's current loan policy. Even with a good purpose, however, the loan officer must determine that the borrower has a responsible attitude toward using borrowed funds, is truthful in answering the bank's questions, and will make every effort to repay what is owed. Responsibility, truthfulness, serious purpose,

TABLE 16–4 The Six Basic Cs of Lending

Character	Capacity	Cash	Collateral	Conditions	Control
Customer's past payment record	Identity of customer and guarantors	Take-home pay for an individual, the past earnings, dividends, and sales record for a business firm	Ownership of assets	Customer's current position in industry and expected market share	Applicable banking laws and regulations regarding the character and quality of acceptable loans
Experience of other lenders with this customer	Copies of Social Security cards, driver's licenses, corporate charters, resolutions, partnership agreements, and other legal documents	Adequacy of past and projected cash flow	Vulnerability of assets to obsolescence	Customer's performance vis-á-vis comparable firms in the same industry	Adequate documentation for examiners who may review the loan
Purpose of loan	Description of history, legal structure, owners, nature of operations, products, and principal customers and suppliers for a business borrower	Availability of liquid reserves	Liquidation value of assets	Competitive climate for customer's product	Signed acknowledgments and correctly prepared loan documents
Customer's track record in forecasting business or personal income		Turnover of payables, accounts receivable, and inventory	Degree of specialization in assets	Sensitivity of customer and industry to business cycles and changes in technology	Consistency of loan request with bank's written loan policy
Credit rating		Capital structure and leverage	Liens, encumbrances, and restrictions against property held	Labor market conditions in customer's industry or market area	Inputs from noncredit personnel (such as economists or political experts) on the external factors affecting loan repayment
Presence of cosigners or guarantors of the proposed loan		Expense controls	Leases and mortgages issued against property and equipment	Impact of inflation on customer's balance sheet and cash flow	
		Coverage ratios	Insurance coverage	Long-run industry or job outlook	
		Recent performance of borrower's stock and price-earnings (P/E) ratio	Guarantees and warranties issued to others	Regulations, political, and environmental factors affecting the customer and/or his or her job, business, and industry	
		Management quality	Bank's relative position as creditor in placing a claim against borrower's assets		
		Recent accounting changes	Probable future financing needs		

Source: Peter S. Rose, "Loans in a Troubled Economy," *Canadian Banker, ICB Review* 90, no. 3 (June 1983), p. 55.

and serious intention to repay all monies owed make up what a loan officer calls *character*. If the bank's loan officer feels the customer is insincere in promising to use borrowed funds as planned and in repaying as agreed, the loan should *not* be made, for it will almost certainly become a problem credit for the bank.

Capacity.   The loan officer must be sure that the customer requesting credit has the authority to request a loan and the legal standing to sign a binding loan agreement. This customer characteristic is known as the *capacity* to borrow money. For example, in most states a *minor* (e.g., under age 18 or 21) cannot legally be held responsible for a credit agreement; thus, the bank would have great difficulty collecting on such a loan. Similarly, the loan officer must be sure that the representative from a corporation asking for credit has proper authority from the company's board of directors to negotiate a loan and sign a credit agreement binding the corporation. Usually this can be determined by obtaining a copy of the resolution passed by a corporate customer's board of directors, authorizing the company to borrow money. Where a business partnership is involved, the loan officer must ask to see the firm's partnership agreement to determine which individuals are authorized to borrow for the firm. A loan agreement signed by unauthorized persons could prove to be uncollectible and, therefore, result in substantial losses for the bank.

Cash.   This key feature of any loan application centers on the question: Does the borrower have the ability to generate enough **cash**, in the form of cash flow, to repay the loan? In general, borrowing customers have only three sources to draw upon to repay their loans: (*a*) cash flows generated from sales or income, (*b*) the sale or liquidation of assets, or (*c*) funds raised by issuing debt or equity securities. Any of these sources may provide sufficient cash to repay a bank loan. However, bankers have a strong preference for *cash flow* as the principal source of loan repayment because asset sales can weaken a borrowing customer and make the bank's position as creditor less secure. Moreover, shortfalls in cash flow are common indicators of failing businesses and troubled loan relationships.

What is **cash flow?** In an accounting sense, it is usually defined as:

$$\text{Cash flow} = \begin{array}{c} \text{Net profits} \\ \text{(or total} \\ \text{revenues less} \\ \text{all expenses)} \end{array} + \begin{array}{c} \text{Noncash expenses} \\ \text{(especially} \\ \text{depreciation)} \end{array}$$

Another definition used by some accountants and financial analysts is:

$$\begin{array}{rl} \text{Cash flows} = & \text{Net profits} + \text{Noncash expenses} \\ & + \text{Additions to accounts payable} \\ & - \text{Additions to inventories and accounts receivable.} \end{array}$$

One of the benefits of this latter definition of cash flow is that it helps to focus a bank loan officer's attention on those facets of a customer's business that reflect the quality and experience of its management and the strength of the market the customer serves. A borrowing customer that stays afloat through heavy use of trade credit (accounts payable), is piling up large inventories of unsold goods, or is having difficulty collecting from its own credit customers (accounts receivable) is likely to be a problem credit for a bank. Most banks would hesitate to commit their scarce reserves to such a customer without the good prospect of a turnaround in the customer's circumstances.

The loan officer's evaluation of a borrower's cash flow involves asking and answering such questions as these: Is there a history of steady growth in earnings or sales? Is there a high probability that such growth will continue to support the loan? Current borrower income and the borrower's income history are important pieces of evidence in answering such questions.

Collateral. In assessing the *collateral* aspect of a loan request, the loan officer must ask, Does the borrower possess adequate net worth or own enough quality assets to provide adequate support for the loan? The loan officer is particularly sensitive to such features as the age, condition, and degree of specialization of the borrower's assets. Technology plays an important role here as well. If the borrower's assets are technologically obsolete, they will have limited value as collateral because of the difficulty of finding a buyer for those assets should the borrower's income falter.

Conditions. The loan officer and credit analyst must be aware of recent trends in the borrower's line of work or industry and how changing economic *conditions* might affect the loan. A loan can look very good on paper, only to have its value eroded by declining sales or income in a recession or by the high interest rates occasioned by inflation. To assess industry and economic conditions, most banks maintain files of information—newspaper clippings, magazine articles, and research reports—on the industries represented by their major borrowing customers.

Control. The last factor in assessing a borrower's creditworthy status is *control,* which centers on such questions as whether changes in law and regulation could adversely affect the borrower and whether the loan request meets the bank's and the regulatory authorities' standards for loan quality. For example, a few years ago passage of the windfall profits tax in the United States made a number of energy companies somewhat less desirable as borrowing customers because that tax absorbed a substantial proportion of their current cash flow.

Can the Loan Agreement Be Properly Structured and Documented?

The six Cs of credit aid the loan officer and bank credit analyst in answering the broad question: Is the borrower creditworthy? Once that question is answered, however, a second issue must be faced: Can the proposed loan agreement be structured and documented to satisfy the needs of both borrower and bank?

The loan officer is responsible to both the customer and the bank's depositors and stockholders and must seek to satisfy the demands of *all.* This requires, first, the drafting of a loan agreement that meets the borrower's need for funds with a comfortable repayment schedule. The borrower must be able to comfortably handle any required loan payments, because the bank's success depends fundamentally on the success of its customers. If a major borrower gets into trouble because it is unable to service a loan, the bank may find itself in serious trouble as well. Proper accommodation of a customer may involve lending more or less money than asked for (because many customers do not know their own financial needs), over a longer or shorter period than requested. Thus, the bank's loan officer must be a financial counselor to customers as well as a conduit for their loan applications.

A properly structured loan agreement must also protect the bank and those it represents—principally its depositors and stockholders—by imposing certain restrictions (covenants) on the borrower's activities when these activities could threaten the recovery of bank funds. The process of recovering the bank's funds—when and where the bank can take action to get its funds returned—also must be carefully spelled out in a loan agreement.

Can the Bank Perfect Its Claim against the Borrower's Earnings and Any Assets That May Be Pledged as Collateral?

Reasons for Taking Collateral.   While large corporations and other borrowers with impeccable credit ratings often borrow unsecured, with *no* specific collateral pledged behind their loans except their reputation and ability to generate earnings, most borrowers at one time or another will be asked to pledge some of their assets or to personally guarantee the repayment of their loans. Getting a pledge of certain borrower assets as *collateral* behind a loan really serves *two* purposes for a lender. If the borrower cannot pay, the pledge of collateral gives the lender the right to seize and sell those assets designated as loan collateral, using the proceeds of the sale to cover what the borrower did not pay back. Secondly, collateralization of a loan gives the lender a psychological advantage over the borrower. Because specific assets may be at stake (such as the customer's automobile or home), a borrower feels more obligated to work hard to repay his or her loan and avoid losing valuable assets. Thus, the third key question faced with many loan applications is, Can the bank *perfect* its claim against the assets or earnings of a borrowing customer?

The goal of a bank taking collateral is to precisely *define* which borrower assets are subject to seizure and sale and to *document* for all other creditors to see that the bank has a legal claim to those assets in the event of nonperformance on a loan. When a bank holds a claim against a borrower's assets that stands superior to the claims of other lenders and to the borrower's own claim, we say the bank's claim to collateral has been *perfected.* Bankers have learned that the procedures necessary for establishing a perfected claim on someone else's property differ depending on the nature of the assets pledged by the borrower and depending on the laws of the state or nation where the assets reside. For example, a different set of steps is necessary to perfect a claim if the bank has actual possession of the assets pledged (e.g., if the borrower pledges a deposit already held in the bank or lets the bank hold some of the customer's stocks and bonds) as opposed to the case where the borrower retains possession of the pledged assets (e.g., an automobile). Yet another procedure must be followed if the property pledged is real estate—land and buildings.

Common Types of Loan Collateral.   Examples of the most popular assets pledged as collateral for bank loans and what is usually done to legally attach those assets in order to collaterize a loan are listed below:

Accounts Receivable.   The bank takes a security interest in the form of a stated percentage (usually somewhere between 40 and 90 percent) of the face amount of accounts receivable (sales on credit) shown on a business borrower's balance sheet. When the borrower's credit customers send in cash to retire their debts, these cash payments are applied to the balance of the borrower's loan. The bank may agree to lend still more money as new receivables arise from the borrower's sales to its customers, thus allowing the loan to continue as long as the borrower has need for credit and continues to generate an adequate volume of sales and credit repayments.

Factoring.   A bank can purchase a borrower's accounts receivable based upon some percentage of their book value. The percentage figure used depends on the quality and age of the receivables. Moreover, because the bank takes over ownership of the receivables, it will inform the borrower's customers that they should send their payments to the purchasing bank. Usually the borrower promises to set aside funds in order to cover some or all of the losses that the bank may suffer from any unpaid receivables.

Inventory.   In return for a loan, a bank may take a security interest against the current amount of inventory of goods or raw materials owned by a business borrower. Usually a bank will lend only a percentage (30 to 80 percent is common) of the estimated market value of a borrower's inventory in order to leave a substantial cushion in case the inventory's value begins to decline. The inventory pledged may be controlled completely by the borrower, using a so-called *floating lien* approach. Another option, often used for auto and truck dealers or sellers of home appliances, is called *floor planning,* in which the lender takes temporary ownership of any goods placed in inventory and the borrower sends payments or sales contracts to the lender as the goods are sold.[3]

Real Property.   Following a title search, appraisal, and land survey, a bank may take a security interest in land and/or improvements on land owned by the borrower and record its claim—a *mortgage*—with a government agency in order to warn other lenders that the property has already been pledged (i.e., has a lien against it) and to help

---

[3]Banks seeking closer control over a borrower's inventory will often employ a technique called *warehousing* in which the goods are stored and monitored by the bank or by an independent agent working to protect the bank's interest. (The warehouse site may be in a location away from the borrower's place of business–a *field warehouse.*) As the inventory grows, warehouse receipts are issued to the bank, giving it a legal claim against the warehoused goods or materials. The bank will make the borrower a loan equal to some agreed-upon percentage of the expected market value of the inventory covered by the warehouse receipts. When the public buys goods from the borrowing firms, the lender surrenders its claim so the company's product can be delivered to its customers. However, the customers' cash payments go straight to the bank to be applied to the loan's balance. Because of the potential for fraud or theft, bank loan officers may inspect a business borrower's inventory periodically to ensure that the bank's loan is well secured and that proper procedures for protecting and valuing inventory are being followed.

defend the original lender's position against claims by others. Usually public notice of a mortgage against real estate is filed with the county courthouse or tax assessor/collector in the county where the property resides. The bank may also take out title insurance and insist that the borrower purchase insurance to cover damage from floods and other hazards, with the bank receiving first claim on any insurance settlement that is made.

Personal Property.   Banks take a security interest in automobiles, furniture, jewelry, securities, and other forms of personal property owned by a borrower. A *financing statement* will be filed publicly (e.g., with the secretary of state, county clerk, or other public official in the state or local area where the borrower's property resides) in those cases where the borrower keeps possession of any personal property pledged as collateral during the term of a loan. To be effective, the financing statement must be signed by both the borrower and an officer of the bank. On the other hand, a *pledge agreement* may be prepared (but will usually not be publicly filed) if the bank or its agent holds the pledged property, giving the bank the right to control that property until the loan is repaid in full.

Personal Guarantees.   A pledge of the stock, deposits, or other personal assets held by the major stockholders or owners of a company may be required as collateral to secure a business loan. Guarantees are often sought by banks in lending to smaller businesses or to firms that have fallen on difficult times. Then, too, getting pledges of

Exhibit 16–1

Safety Zones Surrounding the Funds Loaned by a Bank

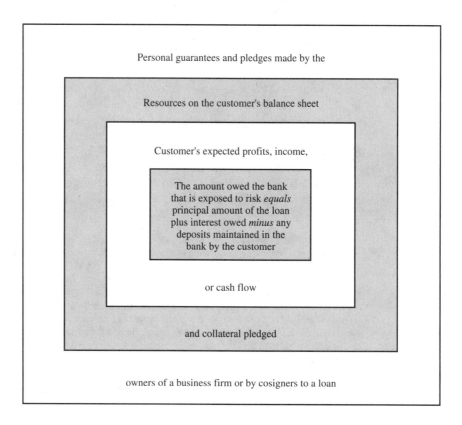

Personal guarantees and pledges made by the

Resources on the customer's balance sheet

Customer's expected profits, income,

The amount owed the bank that is exposed to risk *equals* principal amount of the loan plus interest owed *minus* any deposits maintained in the bank by the customer

or cash flow

and collateral pledged

owners of a business firm or by cosigners to a loan

personal assets from the owners of a business firm gives the owners an additional reason to want their firm to prosper and to repay their loan.

Other Safety Devices to Protect a Loan.   Many bank loan officers argue that the collateral a customer pledges behind a loan is just *one* of the safety zones a bank must wrap around the funds it has loaned for adequate protection. As Exhibit 16–1 indicates, most bank loan officers prefer to have at least *two* safety zones—ideally, three—around the funds they have placed at risk with the customer. The primary safety zone is income or cash flow—the preferred source from which the customer will repay the loan. The second consists of strength on the customer's balance sheet, in the form of assets that can be pledged as collateral or liquid assets that can be sold for cash in order to fill any gaps in the customer's cash flow. Finally, the outer safety zone consists of guarantees from a business firm's owners to support a loan to their firm or from third-party cosigners who pledge their personal assets to back another person's loan.

Concept Checks

16–8. What are the typical steps in a loan request from a customer?

16–9. What three major questions or issues must a bank consider in evaluating nearly all loan requests?

16–10. Explain the following terms: character, capacity, cash, collateral, conditions, and control.

16–11. Suppose a business borrower projects that it will experience net profits of $2.1 million, compared to $2.7 million the previous year, and will record depreciation and other noncash expenses of $0.7 million this year versus $0.6 million last year. The firm expects its accounts payable to decrease from $24.2 million at the beginning of the year to $20.9 million at year's end, while inventories and accounts receivable will rise from $7.8 million at the end of last year to $8.4 million and from $16.8 million last year to $20.1 million, respectively, by the end of the current year. What is this firm's project cash flow figure for this year? Is the firm's cash flow rising or falling? What are the implications for a bank thinking of loaning money to this firm?

Sources of Information about Loan Customers

The bank relies principally on outside information to assess the character, financial position, and collateral of a loan customer (see Table 16–5). Such an analysis begins with a review of information supplied by the borrower in the loan application. How much money is being requested? For what purpose? What other obligations does the customer have? What assets might be used as collateral to back up the loan?

The bank may contact other lenders to determine their experience with this customer. Were all scheduled payments in previous loan agreements made on time? Were

---

TABLE 16–5   **Sources of Information about Businesses, Consumers, and Governments Borrowing Money**

Consumer Information
Local or regional credit bureaus
Customer financial statements
Experience of other lenders with this customer
Business Information
Customer financial statements
Customer annual reports
Experience of other lenders
Securities and Exchange Commission *10-K Reports*
Moody's *Industrial Manual* or *Banking and Finance Manual*
Robert Morris Associates, *Annual Statement Studies* and *Compare2* computer analysis
Standard and Poor's *Industry Surveys*
Standard and Poor's *Stock Market Encyclopedia*
Troy's Almanac of Business and Industrial Ratios
Dun & Bradstreet's *Business Ratings, Key Business Ratios,* and *Industry Norm Book*
The Wall Street Journal and *WSJ Index*
Business Periodicals Index
Barron's Magazine and *Barron's Index*
New York Times and *New York Times Index*
Government Information
Moody's *Government Manual*
Government budget reports
Credit rating agencies
General Economic Information
Board of Governors of the Federal Reserve System, *Federal Reserve Bulletin*
U.S. Department of Commerce, *Survey of Current Business*
Federal Reserve Bank of St. Louis, *U.S. Financial Data, National Economic Trends,*
International Economic Conditions, and *Monetary Trends*
The Wall Street Journal
Newsletters published by money center banks
Local newspapers
Local chamber of commerce

---

deposit balances kept at high enough levels? In the case of a household borrower, the local or regional *credit bureau* will be contacted to ascertain the customer's credit history. How much was borrowed previously and how well were those earlier loans handled? Is there any evidence of slow or delinquent payments? Has the customer ever declared bankruptcy?

Most business borrowers of any size carry credit ratings on their bonds and other debt securities and on the firm's overall credit record. Moody's and Standard & Poor's assign ratings reflecting the probability of default on bonds and shorter-term notes. Dun & Bradstreet provides overall credit ratings for several thousand corporations. It and other firms and organizations, such as Robert Morris Associates and Leo Troy, provide benchmark operating and financial ratios for whole industries so that the borrower's particular operating and financial ratios in any given year can *be compared to industry standards.*

One of the most widely consulted sources of data on business firm performance is Robert Morris Associates, founded in Philadelphia in 1914, to exchange credit information among business lending institutions as well as organize conferences and publish educational materials to help train loan officers and credit analysts. While RMA began in the United States, its members have now spread over much of the globe with especially active groups in Canada, Great Britain, Hong Kong, and Mexico. RMA publishes a popular monthly journal, called *The Journal of Lending and Credit Risk Management,* to help inform and train credit decision makers.

Another very popular RMA publication is its *Annual Statement Studies,* which provides financial performance data on businesses grouped by industry type and by size category. Loan officers who are members of RMA submit financial performance information based on data supplied by their borrowing customers. RMA then groups this data and calculates average values for selected firm performance ratios. Among the ratios published by RMA and grouped by industry and firm size are:

Current assets to current liabilities (the current ratio).

Current assets minus inventories to current liabilities (the quick ratio).

Sales to accounts receivable.

Cost of sales to inventory (the inventory turnover ratio).

Earnings before interest and taxes to total interest payments (the interest coverage ratio).

Fixed assets to net worth.

Total debt to net worth (the leverage ratio).

Profits before taxes to total assets and tangible net worth.

Total sales to net fixed assets and to total assets.

RMA also calculates common-size balance sheets (with all major asset and liability items expressed as a percentage of total assets) and common-size income statements (with profits and operating expense items expressed as a percentage of total sales) for different size groups of firms within an industry.

RMA has recently developed a Windows-based version of its *Annual Statement Studies,* called COMPARE2, which permits a bank's credit analyst and loan officer to do a *spread sheet analysis*—arraying the loan customer's financial statements and key financial and operating ratios over time relative to industry averages based upon data from more than 130,000 different businesses. The new COMPARE2 system enables a loan officer to counsel with his or her borrowing customer, pointing out any apparent weaknesses in the customer's financial or operating situation compared to industry standards. It also reports on recent developments in each of about 450 different industries. This new credit analysis routine is also available to business firms planning to submit a loan request to a bank or other lending institution so the customer can personally evaluate his or her firm's financial condition from a lender's perspective.

Standard & Poor's Industry Surveys are a particularly useful information source for analyzing loan applications from business borrowers because they provide a detailed analysis of recent trends in the borrower's industry and that industry's future outlook. Analysts working for Standard & Poor's examine the prospects for each industry's future sales growth and profitability, the expected impact of technological changes, trends in industry organizational structure and competition, what's happening to the prices of industry goods and services, and new product developments within each major industrial group where banks make loans.

Standard and Poor's also publishes at least three other information sources of considerable interest to bank managers evaluating loan requests from business corporations and governments. S&P's *Ratings Handbook* publishes credit ratings and the ratings outlook on more than 21,000 security issues sold by over 5,000 domestic and foreign companies and units of government. This S&P service also provides a Phone Look Up Service to provide updated information on credit quality in the event a borrower's credit rating has changed. Standard & Poor's *NYSE Stock Reports* contain two-page reports on each of more than 1,800 corporations whose stocks are listed on the New York Stock Exchange, showing each firm's near-term sales, earnings, dividend prospects, key income statement and balance sheet items for 10 years, changes in top management, the recent performance of a firm's stock price and price-earnings ratios, and the track record of a firm's major product lines, as well as a commentary on each business's overall long-term outlook. Finally, S&P's *Analyst's Handbook* provides figures on total sales, profit margins, taxes, and stock dividends and prices, all on a per-share basis, covering a wide variety of industries for up to 30 years in order to yield industry benchmarks that loan officers can use to compare against their borrowing customers' financial positions.

The *Almanac of Business and Industrial Financial Ratios,* prepared annually by Dr. Leo Troy, uses Internal Revenue Service data to assemble average operating and financial ratios for firms in different industries and asset-size groups. Twenty-two different ratios are presented for firms grouped by asset size within each industry, including the current ratio, the quick ratio, the ratio of net sales to net working capital, the interest coverage ratio, asset turnover, and the ratios of total liabilities to net worth, return on assets, and return on equity capital.

A similar array of industry data is provided by Dun & Bradstreet Credit Services. This credit-rating agency collects information on approximately 3 million firms in 800 different business lines (captured by Standard Industrial Classifications, or SIC, codes). D&B prepares detailed financial reports on individual borrowing companies for its subscribers. For each firm reviewed, the D&B *Business Information Reports* provide a credit rating, a brief financial and management history of the firm, a summary of recent balance sheet and income and expense statement trends, a listing of any major loans known to be still outstanding against the firm, its terms of trade, the names of its key managers, and the location and condition of the firm's facilities. Dun & Bradstreet also prepares an *Industry Norm Book,* containing annual financial and operating data for firms grouped by industry for the most recent year and the past three years. D&B calculates 14 key ratios measuring efficiency, profitability, and solvency, as well as common-size balance sheets and income statements (with each entry expressed as a percent of total assets or total net sales) for the medium-size, or typical, firm and for the uppermost and lowest quartiles of firms in each industry.

In evaluating a credit application, the loan officer must look beyond the customer to the economy of the local area for smaller loan requests and to the national or international economy for larger credit requests. Many loan customers are especially sensitive to the fluctuations in economic activity known as the *business cycle.* For example, auto dealers, producers of farm and other commodities, home builders, and security dealers and brokers face cyclically sensitive markets for their goods and services. This does not mean that banks should not lend to such firms. Rather, they must be aware of the vulnerability of some of their borrowers to cyclical changes and structure loan terms to take care of such fluctuations in economic conditions. Moreover, for all business borrowers it is important to develop a forecast of future industry conditions. The loan officer must determine if the customer's projections for the future conform to the outlook for the industry as a whole. Any differences in outlook need to be explained before a final decision is made about approving or denying a loan request.

Parts of a Typical Loan Agreement

The Note.   When a bank grants a loan to one of its customers, such an extension of credit is always accompanied by a *written contract* with several different parts. First, there is a **note,** signed by the borrower, which specifies the principal amount of the loan. The face of the note will also indicate the interest rate attached to the principal amount and the terms under which repayment must take place (including the dates on which any installment payments are due).

Loan Commitment Agreement.   In addition, larger business loans and home mortgage loans often are accompanied by **loan commitment agreements,** in which the bank promises to make credit available to the borrower over a designated future period up to a maximum amount in return for a commitment fee (usually expressed as a percentage—such as 0.5 percent—of the maximum amount of credit available) This practice is very common in the extension of short-term business credit lines, where, for example, a business customer may draw against a maximum $1 million credit line as needed over a given period (such as six months).

Collateral.   Bank loans may be either secured or unsecured. Secured loans have a pledge of some of the borrower's property behind them (such as a home or an automobile) as **collateral** that may have to be sold if the borrower has no other way to repay the bank. Unsecured loans have no specific borrower assets pledged behind them; these loans rest largely on the reputation and estimated earning power of the borrower. Secured loan agreements include a section describing any assets that are pledged as collateral to protect the bank's interest, along with an explanation of how and when the bank can take possession of the collateral in order to recover its funds. For example, an individual seeking an auto loan usually must sign a *chattel mortgage* agreement, which means that the borrower temporarily assigns the vehicle's title to the bank until the loan is paid off.

Covenants.   Most formal loan agreements also contain **restrictive covenants,** which are usually one of two types: *affirmative* or *negative.*

1. *Affirmative covenants* require the borrower to take certain actions, such as periodically filing financial statements with the bank, maintaining insurance coverage on the loan and on any collateral pledged, and maintaining specified levels of liquidity and equity.

2. *Negative covenants* restrict the borrower from doing certain things without the bank's approval, such as taking on new debt, acquiring additional fixed assets, participating in mergers, selling assets, or paying excessive dividends to stockholders.

Borrower Guaranties or Warranties.   In most loan agreements, the borrower specifically *guarantees* or **warranties** that the information supplied in the loan application is true and correct. The borrower may also be required to pledge personal assets—a house, land, automobiles, and so on—behind a business loan or against a loan that is cosigned by a third party. Whether collateral is posted or not, the loan agreement must identify who or what institution is responsible for the loan and obligated to make payment.

Events of Default.   Finally, most loans contain a section listing **events of default,** specifying what actions or inactions by the borrower would represent a significant violation of the terms of the loan agreement and what actions the bank is legally authorized to take in order to secure the recovery of its funds. The events-of-default section also clarifies who is responsible for collection costs, court costs, and attorney's fees that may arise from litigation of the loan agreement.

Loan Review

What happens to a loan agreement after it has been endorsed by the borrower and the bank? Should it be filed away and forgotten until the loan falls due and the borrower makes the final payment? Obviously that would be a foolish thing for a bank to do because the conditions under which each loan is made are constantly changing, affecting the borrower's financial condition and his or her ability to repay a loan. Fluctuations in the economy weaken some businesses and increase the credit needs of others, while individuals may lose their jobs or contract serious health problems, imperiling their ability to repay any outstanding loans. The bank's loan department must be sensitive to these developments and periodically review *all* loans until they reach maturity.

While banks today use a variety of different **loan review** procedures, a few general principles are followed by nearly all banks. These include:

1. Carrying out reviews of all types of loans on a periodic basis—for example, every 30, 60, or 90 days the largest loans outstanding may be routinely examined, along with a random sample of smaller loans.

2. Structuring the loan review process carefully to make sure the most important features of each loan are checked, including:

    a. The record of borrower payments, to ensure that the customer is not falling behind the planned repayment schedule.

    b. The quality and condition of any collateral pledged behind the loan.

    c. The completeness of loan documentation, to make sure the bank has access to any collateral pledged and possesses the full legal authority to take action against the borrower in the courts if necessary.

    d. An evaluation of whether the borrower's financial condition and forecasts have changed, which may have increased or decreased the borrower's need for bank credit.

    e. An assessment of whether the loan conforms to the bank's lending policies and to the standards applied to its loan portfolio by examiners from the regulatory agencies.

3. Reviewing most frequently the largest loans, because default on these credit agreements could seriously affect the bank's own financial condition.

4. Conducting more frequent reviews of troubled loans, with the frequency of review increasing as the problems surrounding any particular loan increase.

5. Accelerating the loan review schedule if the economy slows down or if the industries in which the bank has made a substantial portion of its loans develop significant problems (e.g., the appearance of new competitors or shifts in technology that will demand new products and new delivery methods).

Loan review is *not* a luxury but a *necessity* for a sound bank lending program. It not only helps management spot problem loans more quickly but also acts as a continuing check on whether loan officers are adhering to the bank's loan policy. For this reason, as well as to promote objectivity in the loan review process, many of the largest banks separate their loan review personnel from the loan department itself. Loan reviews also aid senior management and the bank's board of directors in assessing the bank's overall exposure to risk and its possible need for more capital in the future.

Handling Problem Loan Situations

Inevitably, despite the safeguards most banks build into their lending programs, some loans on a bank's books will become *problem loans.* Usually this means the borrower has missed one or more promised payments or the collateral pledged behind a loan has declined significantly in value. While each problem loan situation is somewhat different, several features common to most such situations should warn a banker that troubles have set in (see Table 16–6):

1. Unusual or unexplained delays in receiving promised financial reports and payments or in communicating with bank personnel.

2. For business loans, any sudden change in methods used by the borrowing firm to account for depreciation, make pension plan contributions, value inventories, account for taxes, or recognize income.

3. For business loans, restructuring outstanding debt or eliminating dividends, or experiencing a change in the customer's credit rating.

4. Adverse changes in the price of a borrowing customer's stock.

TABLE 16–6   Warning Signs of Weak Loans and Poor Bank Lending Policies

The manual given to bank examiners by the FDIC discusses several telltale indicators of problem loans and poor bank lending policies:

Indicators of a Weak or Troubled Loan	*Indicators of Inadequate or Poor Bank Lending Policies*
Irregular or delinquent loan payments.	Poor selection of risks among borrowing customers.
Frequent alterations in loan terms.	
Poor loan renewal record (with little reduction of principal each time the loan is renewed).	Lending money contingent on possible future events (such as a merger).
Unusually high loan rate (perhaps an attempt to compensate the bank for a high-risk loan).	Lending money because a customer promises a large deposit.
Unusual or unexpected buildup of the borrowing customer's accounts receivable and/or inventories.	Failure to specify a plan for the liquidation of each loan.
Rising debt-to-net-worth (leverage) ratio.	High proportion of loans made to borrowers outside the bank's trade territory.
Missing documentation (especially missing customer financial statements).	Incomplete credit files.
Poor quality collateral.	Substantial self-dealing credits (loans to insiders— employees, directors, or stockholders).
Reliance on reappraisals of assets to increase the borrowing customers' net worth.	Tendency to overreact to competition (making poor loans to keep customers from going to other banks).
Absence of cash flow statements or projections.	
Customer reliance on nonrecurring sources of funds to meet loan payments (e.g., selling buildings or equipment).	Lending money to support speculative purchases.
	Lack of sensitivity to changing economic conditions.

Source: Federal Deposit Insurance Corporation, *Bank Examination Policies,* Washington, D.C., selected years.

---

5. Net earnings losses in one or more years, especially as measured by returns on the borrower's assets (ROA), or equity capital (ROE), or earnings before interest and taxes (EBIT).

6. Adverse changes in the borrower's capital structure (equity/debt ratio), liquidity (current ratio), or activity levels (e.g., the ratio of sales to inventory).

7. Deviations of actual sales or cash flow from those projected when the loan was requested.

8. Sudden, unexpected, and unexplained changes in deposit balances maintained by the customer.

What should a banker do when a loan is in trouble? Experts in **loan workouts**— the process of recovering the bank's funds from a problem loan situation—suggest the following key steps:

1. Always keep the goal of loan workouts firmly in mind: to maximize the bank's chances for the full recovery of its funds.

2. The rapid detection and reporting of any problems with a loan are essential; delay often worsens a problem loan situation.

Bankers' Insights and Issues

Bank Lending and Economic Growth

In the late 1990s governments and investors around the world became very concerned about economic developments in Asia, particularly in such leading Asian nations as Korea, Indonesia, Japan, Thailand, Malaysia, and Hong Kong. As several economies in the region weakened and the international value of several Asian currencies sagged, many economists and financial analysts began to point to the crucial role of *bank lending* in determining the health of *any* economy. When bank loan quality declines, bankers typically respond by cutting back on the new loans they plan to make and also refuse a higher portion of customer requests for loan renewals. As the supply of bank credit declines, business investment spending and spending by consumers begins to fall, causing rising unemployment and eventual economic stagnation if bank loan volume continues to fall. (The problem of declining bank credit volume has been especially severe in parts of Asia recently as land and stock market prices have fallen sharply, reducing the value of the collateral posted behind many bank loans. Then, too, many banks with little or no remaining equity capital have frequently been allowed to stay open and grant still more troubled loans.)

The foregoing chain of events is particularly likely to happen in those countries where banks account for the majority of assets and loans in the financial system. Moreover, several countries around the world recently have made the mistake of directing their banks to lend to government-favored projects or to support troubled firms in struggling industries rather than letting the private marketplace direct the flow of bank credit toward those borrowers and investment projects offering the highest expected returns. At the same time banks with troubled loans were frequently permitted to keep those loans on their books at full face value and to delay recognition of declining values of land, stock prices, and other assets (called "regulatory forbearance"). Recent banking developments in portions of Asia and in other corners of the world remind us that bank credit can be a powerful force for good in a nation's economy, stimulating economic activity and creating new jobs, but if poorly managed, fluctuations in the supply and quality of bank credit can lead to serious economic distress.

3. Keep the loan workout responsibility separate from the lending function to avoid possible conflicts of interest for the loan officer.
4. Bank workout specialists should confer with the troubled customer *quickly* on possible options, especially for cutting expenses, increasing cash flow, and improving management control. Precede this meeting with a preliminary analysis of the problem and its possible causes, noting any special workout problems (including the presence of competing creditors). Develop a preliminary plan of action after determining the bank's risk exposure and the sufficiency of loan documents (especially any claims against the customer's collateral other than that held by the bank.)

5. Estimate what resources are available to collect the troubled loan (including the estimated liquidation values of assets and deposits).

6. Loan workout personnel should conduct a tax and litigation search to see if the borrower has other unpaid obligations.

7. For business borrowers, bank loan personnel must evaluate the quality, competence, and integrity of current management and visit the site to assess the borrower's property and operations.

8. Bank workout professionals must consider all reasonable alternatives for cleaning up the troubled loan, including making a new, temporary agreement if loan problems appear to be short-term in nature or finding a way to help the customer strengthen cash flow (such as reducing expenses or entering new markets) or to infuse new capital into the business. Other possibilities include finding additional collateral, securing endorsements or guarantees, reorganizing, merging or liquidating the firm, or filing a bankruptcy petition.

Of course, *the preferred option nearly always is to seek a revised loan agreement that gives both the bank and its customer the chance to restore normal operations.* Indeed, loan experts often argue that even when a loan agreement is in serious trouble, the customer may not be. This means that a properly structured loan agreement rarely runs into irreparable problems. However, an improperly structured loan agreement can contribute to a borrower's financial problems and be a cause of loan default.

Concept Checks

16–12. What sources of information are available today for bank loan officers and credit analysts to use in evaluating a customer loan application?

16–13. What are the principal parts of a loan agreement? What is each part designed to do?

16–14. What is *loan review*? How should a loan review be conducted?

16–15. What are some warning signs to bank management that a problem loan may be developing?

16–16. What steps should a banker go through in trying to resolve a problem loan situation?

Summary

Banks are expected to make loans to all qualified customers and thereby aid the communities they serve to grow and to improve their living standards. Indeed, making loans is the principal *economic function* of banks. But it is also a risky function because both external factors (principally economic conditions) and internal factors (including management errors and illegal manipulation) can result in substantial losses for the bank. In order to keep this risk factor under control, the bank lending function is closely regulated to ensure prudent policies and practices.

Banks also control risk in the lending function by setting up written policies and procedures for processing each loan request. Each bank should have a written loan policy that describes what types of loans and loan terms best protect the bank's soundness and also help to meet the needs of the communities the bank serves. The loan policy statement indicates the lines of authority and decision making within the loan department and the documentation that must accompany each loan application. Other features in a typical written bank loan policy include guidelines on taking, evaluating, and perfecting loan collateral; procedures for setting loan rates; and a description of those types of loans the bank prefers *not* to make.

Banks consider many factors in deciding whether or not to grant a loan to a borrower. Generally, however, the evaluation of a loan application will focus on six key factors: (1) *character,* which goes to the honesty and sincerity of the borrower and whether the loan is for a good purpose; (2) *capacity,* or whether the borrower has the legal standing necessary to sign a valid loan contract; (3) *cash,* which focuses on the borrower's estimated capacity to generate sufficient income or cash flow to repay the loan; (4) *collateral,* or whether the borrower has assets or other items of value that can be pledged to help secure the loan;

(5) *conditions,* or the broader environment of the industry and the economy in which the borrower operates that could adversely affect loan repayment; and (6) *control,* which refers to whether or not the borrower's application meets the bank's loan quality standards and the standards imposed by the regulatory authorities.

These facets of each loan application help bank officers and credit analysts deal with the three major questions that must be answered before any loan is approved: (1) Is the borrower creditworthy? (2) Can the loan agreement be properly structured to protect the bank and its depositors? and (3) Can the bank perfect its claim against the borrower's assets or earnings in the event of loan default? For most banks this involves a careful review of the borrower's payment record, the supporting documentation, and the loan's conformity to the bank's quality standards and government regulations.

Finally, a sound bank lending program must make provision for the periodic review of *all* loans until they are retired. When this *loan review* process turns up problem loans, they are generally turned over to a *loan workout* specialist, who must investigate the causes of the problem and work with the borrower to find a solution that maximizes the bank's chances of recovering its funds.

Key Terms in This Chapter

Real estate loans
Financial institution loans
Agricultural loans
Commercial and industrial loans
Loans to individuals
Wholesale lenders
Retail credit
CAMELS rating
Cash

Cash flow
Note
Loan commitment agreements
Collateral
Restrictive covenants
Warranties
Events of default
Loan review
Loan workouts

Problems and Projects

1. Karakee V. Corporation, seeking renewal of its $12 million credit line, reports the data in the table below (in millions of dollars) to Whelington National Bank's loan department. Please calculate the two measures of the firm's cash flow as defined earlier in this chapter. What trends do you observe and what are their implications for the decision to renew or not renew the firm's line of credit?

	19X1	19X2	19X3	19X4	Projections for Next Year
Accounts receivable	$ 5.1	$ 5.5	$ 5.7	$ 6.0	$ 6.4
Inventories	8.0	8.2	8.3	8.6	8.9
Accounts payable	7.9	8.4	8.8	9.5	9.9
Depreciation and other noncash expenses	11.2	11.2	11.1	11.0	10.9
Net profits	4.4	4.6	4.9	4.1	3.6

2. Silsbee Manufacturing and Service Company holds a sizable inventory of dishwashers and dryers which it hopes to sell to retail dealers over the next six months. These appliances have a total estimated market value currently of $16,357,422. The firm also reports accounts receivable currently amounting to $8,452,876. Under the guidelines for taking collateral discussed in this chapter, what is the *minimum* size loan or credit line Silsbee is likely to receive from the bank? What is the *maximum* size loan or credit line Silsbee is likely to receive?

3. Under which of the six Cs of credit discussed in this chapter does each of the following pieces of information belong?

   a. First National Bank discovers there is already a lien against the fixed assets of one of its customers asking for a loan.

   b. Xron Corporation has asked for a type of loan the bank normally refuses to make.

   c. John Selman has an excellent credit rating.

   d. Smithe Manufacturing Company has achieved higher earnings each year for the past six years.

   e. Commerce National Bank's auto loan officer asks a prospective customer, Harold Ikels, for his driver's license.

   f. Merchants Center National Bank is concerned about extending a loan for another year to Corrin Motors because a recession is predicted in the economy starting within the next quarter of the year.

   g. Wes Velman needs an immediate cash loan and has gotten his brother, Charles, to volunteer to cosign the note should the loan be approved.

   h. The bank checks out Mary Earl's estimate of her monthly take-home pay with Mary's employer, Bryan Sims Doors and Windows.

   i. Hillsoro Bank and Trust would like to make a loan to Pen-Tab Oil and Gas Company but fears a long-term decline in oil and gas prices.

   j. First State Bank of Jackson seeks the opinion of an expert on the outlook for sales growth and production in Mexico before granting a loan to a Mexican manufacturer of auto parts.

   k. The history of Membres Manufacture and Distributing Company indicates the firm has been through several recent changes of ownership and there has been a substantial shift in its principal suppliers and customers in recent years.

   l. Frank Evans, loan officer of Home and Office Bank, has decided to review the insurance coverages maintained by its borrowing customer, Plainsman Wholesale Distributors.

4. Butell Manufacturing has an outstanding $11 million loan with Citicenter Bank for the current year. As required in the loan agreement, Butell reports selected data items to the bank each month. Based on the information presented below, is there any indication of a developing *problem loan*? In what dimensions of the firm's performance should Citicenter Bank be concerned?

	Current Month	One Month Ago	Two Months Ago	Three Months Ago	Four Months Ago
Cash account (millions of dollars)	$33	$57	$51	$44	$43
Projected sales (millions of dollars)	$298	$295	$294	$291	$288
Stock price per share (monthly average)	$6.60	$6.50	$6.40	$6.25	$6.50
Capital structure (equity/debt ratio in percent)	32.8%	33.9%	34.6%	34.9%	35.7%
Liquidity ratio (current assets/current liabilities)	1.10x	1.23x	1.35x	1.39x	1.25x
Earnings before interest and taxes (EBIT; in millions of dollars)	$15	$14	$13	$11	$13
Return on assets (ROA; percent)	3.32%	3.25%	2.98%	3.13%	3.11%
Sales revenue (millions of dollars)	$290	$289	$290	$289	$287

Butell has announced within the past 30 days that it is switching to new methods for calculating the depreciation of its fixed assets and for valuing its inventories. The firm's board of directors is planning to discuss at its next meeting early next month a proposal to reduce stock dividends in the coming year.

5. Identify which of the following restrictive loan covenants are *affirmative* or *negative* covenants:
   a. Nige Trading Corporation must pay no dividends to its shareholders above $3 per share without express bank approval.
   b. HoneySmith Company pledges to fully insure its production line equipment against loss due to fire, theft, or adverse weather.
   c. Soft-Tech Industries cannot take on new debt without notifying its principal bank first.
   d. PennCost Manufacturing must file comprehensive financial statements each month with its principal bank.
   e. Dolbe King Company must secure bank approval prior to increasing its stock of fixed assets.
   f. Crestwin Service Industries must keep a minimum current (liquidity) ratio of 1.5x under the terms of its loan agreement.
   g. Dew Dairy Products is considering approaching Selwin Farm Transport Company about a possible merger but must first receive bank approval.

6. Please identify which of the six basic Cs of lending—character, capacity, cash, collateral, conditions, and control—applies to each of the loan factors listed below:

Insurance coverage	Asset liquidation
Competitive climate for customer's product	Inflation outlook
Credit rating	Adequate documentation
Corporate resolution	Changes in accounting standards
Liquid reserves	Written loan policy
Asset specialization	Coverage ratios
Driver's license	Purpose of loan
Expected market share	Banking laws and regulations
Economists' forecasts	Wages in the labor market
Business cycle	Changes in technology
Performance of comparable firms	Obsolescence
Guarantees/warranties	Liens
Expense controls	Management quality
Inventory turnover	Leverage
Projected cash flow	History of firm
Experience of other lenders	Customer identity
Social Security card	Payment record
Price-earnings ratio	Partnership agreement
Industry outlook	Accounts receivable turnover
Future financing needs	Accounts payable turnover

Selected References

See the following sources for additional information on the content and contributions of a written loan policy:

1. Malone, Robert B. "Written Loan Policies." *Journal of Commercial Bank Lending,* June 1976, pp. 18–24.
2. Mott, Hubert C. "Establishing Criteria and Concepts for a Written Credit Policy." *Journal of Commercial Bank Lending,* April 1977, pp. 2–16.

For a review of procedures for identifying and working out problem loan situations, see the following:

3. Rome, Donald Lee. "The Business Workout—A Primer for Participation Creditors." *Uniform Commercial Code Law Journal* 11, no. 3 (Winter 1979), pp. 183–206.
4. Eyring, Joseph R. "Five Key Steps for a Successful Workout Program." *Journal of Commercial Bank Lending,* December 1984, pp. 28–35.
5. NeMer, Gary. "Analysis of Problem Loan Alternatives for Secured Lenders." *Journal of Commercial Bank Lending,* October 1982, pp. 38–52.

6. Rose, Peter S. "Loans in Trouble in a Troubled Economy." *Canadian Banker and ICB Review* 90, no. 3 (June 1983), pp. 52–57.
7. ———. "Serving Loan Customers in Mexico: How U.S. Banks Manage Credit Risk." *The Journal of Lending and Credit Risk Management,* October 1996, pp. 27–35.
8. Taylor, Jeremy D. "Understanding Industry Risk: Parts 1, 2, and 3." *The Journal of Lending and Credit Risk Management,* August, September, and October 1996.

For a discussion of the impact of changing technology on lending, see:

9. McGinnis, Patricia. "The Place of Technology in Generating Credit Opportunities." *The Journal of Lending and Credit Risk Management,* June 1997, pp. 15–29.
10. Rose, Peter S. "Lenders and the Internet." *Journal of Lending and Credit Risk Management,* June 1997, pp. 31–40.

17   LENDING TO BUSINESS FIRMS

Learning and Management Decision Objectives

To explore how bankers can respond to a business customer seeking a loan and to reveal the factors bankers must consider in evaluating a business loan request. For most banks, business loans—often called commercial and industrial, or C&I, loans—rank among the most important loans made. Indeed, nationwide for all U.S.-insured banks, loans to business firms represent 25 percent or more of their entire loan portfolio and at least a fifth of their total assets. Therefore, any discussion of the methods and procedures used in granting different kinds of bank loans must begin with a discussion of commercial lending.

Types of Business Loans

Banks grant many different types of commercial loans. Among the most widely used forms of business credit are the following:

Short-Term Business Loans	*Long-Term Business Loans*
• Self-liquidating inventory loans.	• Term loans to support the purchase of equipment, rolling stock, and structures.
• Working capital loans.	• Revolving credit lines.
• Interim construction financing.	• Project loans.
• Security dealer financing.	• Loans to support acquisitions of other business firms.
• Retailer financing.	
• Asset-based loans (accounts receivable financing, factoring, and inventory financing).	

Short-Term Loans to Business Firms

Self-Liquidating Inventory Loans

Historically, banks have preferred to make short-term loans to businesses for nonpermanent additions to their working capital. In fact, until after World War II, banks granted mainly **self-liquidating loans** to business firms. These loans usually were used to finance the purchase of inventory—raw materials or finished goods to sell. Such loans take advantage of the normal *cash cycle* in a business firm:

1. Cash (including borrowed cash from the bank) is spent to acquire inventories of raw materials and semifinished or finished goods.
2. Goods are produced or shelved and listed for sale.
3. Sales are made (often on credit).
4. The cash received (immediately or later from credit sales) is then used to repay the bank's loan.

In this case, the term of the loan begins when cash is needed to purchase inventory and ends (perhaps in 60 to 90 days) when cash is available in the firm's account to write the bank a check for the balance of its loan.

While banks today make a far wider array of business loans than just simple self-liquidating credits, the short-term loan—frequently displaying many of the features of self-liquidation—continues to account for over half of all bank loans to business firms. In fact, most business loans cover only a few weeks or months and are usually related closely to the borrower's need for short-term cash to finance purchases of inventory or to cover production costs, the payment of taxes, interest payments on bonds and other debt, and dividend payments to stockholders.

Working Capital Loans

Working capital loans provide businesses with short-run credit, lasting from a few days to about one year. Working capital loans are most often used to fund the purchase of inventories in order to put goods on shelves or to purchase raw materials; thus, they come closest to the traditional self-liquidating loan described above.

Frequently the working capital loan is designed to cover seasonal peaks in the business customer's production levels and credit needs. For example, a clothing manufacturer anticipating heavy demand in the fall for back-to-school clothes and winter wear will need short-term credit in the late spring and summer to purchase inventories of cloth and hire additional workers so that output can be geared up in order to have clothes ready for shipment to retailers during the August-to-December period. The clothing manufacturer's bank can set up a line of credit stretching from six to nine months, permitting that manufacturer to draw upon the credit line as needed over this period. The amount of the line is determined from the manufacturer's estimate of the maximum amount of funds that will be needed at any point during the six-to-nine-month term of the bank's loan. Such loans are frequently renewed under the provision that the borrower pay off all or a significant portion of the loan before renewal is granted.

Normally, working capital loans are secured by accounts receivable or by pledges of inventory and carry a floating interest rate on the amounts actually *borrowed* against the approved credit line. A commitment fee is charged on the unused portion of the credit line and sometimes on the entire amount of funds made available. **Compensating deposit balances** are usually required from the customer. These include required deposits whose minimum size is based on the size of the credit line (e.g., 1 to 5 percent of the credit line) and required deposits equal to a stipulated percentage of the total amount of credit actually used by the customer (e.g., 15–20 percent of actual drawings against the line).

Interim Construction Financing

A popular form of secured short-term lending for most commercial banks is the **interim construction loan,** used to support the construction of homes, apartments, office buildings, shopping centers, and other permanent structures. While the structures involved are permanent, the loans themselves are temporary. They provide builders with the funds needed to hire workers, rent or lease construction equipment, purchase building materials, and develop land. But once the construction phase is over, the bank's loan usually is paid off with a longer-term mortgage loan issued by another lender (such as an insurance company or pension fund). In fact, banks usually will not lend money to a builder or land developer until that customer has secured a mortgage loan commitment to take over the long-term financing of a project once its construction is completed. Recently, some banks have issued "minipermanent" loans, providing funding for construction and the early operation of a project for as long as five to seven years.

Security Dealer Financing

Dealers in government and private securities need short-term financing to purchase new securities and carry their existing portfolios of securities until they are sold to customers or reach maturity. Such loans are readily granted by many of the largest banks because of their high quality—often backed by pledging the dealer's holdings of government securities as collateral. Moreover, many loans to securities dealers are so short—overnight to a few days—that the bank can quickly recover its funds or make a new loan at a higher interest rate if the credit markets have tightened up.

A closely related type of bank credit is extended to *investment banking firms* to support their underwriting of *new* corporate bonds, stocks, and government debt securities. Such issues of securities occur when investment bankers help their business clients finance a merger or the acquisition of another firm, assist in taking a company public (that is, issuing new stock to broaden an existing business's capital base and open its ownership shares to purchase by any interested investor), or aid in the launching of a completely new business venture. Once the investment banker is able to sell these new securities to investors in the capital market, the loan plus any interest owed is repaid.

Banks also lend directly to businesses and individuals buying stocks, bonds, options, and other financial instruments. Margin requirements enforced in the United

States by the Federal Reserve Board usually limit such loans to no more than *half* the purchase of the security or securities being acquired (under Regulation U). However, in an effort to aid the market for small business capital the Fed ruled in December 1997 that banks could lend up to 100 percent of the purchase price of "small cap" stocks that are listed by NASDAQ, effective beginning April 1st, 1998.

Retailer Financing

Banks support consumer installment purchases of automobiles, home appliances, furniture, and other durable goods by financing the receivables that dealers selling these goods take on when they write installment contracts to cover customer purchases. In turn, these contracts are reviewed by banks with whom the dealers have established credit relationships. If they meet acceptable credit standards, the contracts are purchased by banks at an interest rate that varies with the risk level of each borrower, the quality of collateral pledged, and the term of each loan.

In the case of dealers selling automobiles, TVs, furniture, or other durable goods, banks may agree to finance the dealer's whole inventory through what is called *floor-planning*. The bank will agree to extend credit to the dealer so he or she can place an order with a manufacturer to ship goods for resale. Most such loans are for 90-day terms initially and may be renewed for one or more 30-day periods. In return for the loan the bank gets the dealer to sign a security agreement, giving the bank a lien against the goods in the event of nonpayment. At the same time the manufacturer is authorized to ship goods to the dealer and to bill the bank for their value. Periodically, the bank will send an agent to check the goods on the dealer's floor to determine what is selling ("moving") and what remains unsold. As goods are sold, the dealer will send a check to the bank for the manufacturer's invoice amount for each item bought from the dealer (known as a "pay-as-sold" management agreement).

If the bank's agent visits the dealer and finds any items sold off for which the bank has not received payment (known as "sold out of trust") a check will be requested immediately for those particular items. If the dealer fails to pay, the bank may be forced to repossess the goods and return some or all of them to the manufacturer for credit. Floorplanning agreements typically include a loan-loss reserve, which is built up from the interest earned as borrowers repay their installment loans and is reduced if any loans are defaulted. Once the loan-loss reserve reaches a predetermined level, the dealer receives rebates for a portion of the interest earned on the installment contracts.

Asset-Based Financing

An increasing portion of short-term lending by banks in recent years has consisted of **asset-based loans**—credit secured by the shorter-term assets of a firm that are expected to roll over into cash in the future. The key business assets used for the majority of these loans are accounts receivable and inventories of raw materials or finished goods. The bank will lend funds against a specific percentage of the book value of outstanding credit accounts or against inventory. For example, it may be willing to loan an amount equal to 70 percent of a firm's *current* accounts receivable (i.e., all those credit accounts that are not past due). Alternatively, it may make a loan for 40 percent of the business customer's current inventory of goods on the shelf or sitting in a warehouse. As accounts receivable are collected or inventory is sold, a portion of the cash proceeds flow to the bank in order to retire the loan.

In most loans collateralized by accounts receivable and inventory the borrowing firm retains title to the assets pledged, but sometimes title is passed to the bank, which then assumes the risk that some of those assets will not pay out as expected. The most common example of this arrangement is **factoring,** where the bank actually takes on the responsibility of collecting the accounts receivable of one of its business customers. Because the bank incurs both additional expense and additional risk with a factored loan, it typically assesses a higher discount rate and lends a smaller fraction of the book value of the customer's accounts receivable.

Long-Term Loans to Business Firms

Term Business Loans

Term loans are designed to fund long- and medium-term business investments, such as the purchase of equipment or the construction of physical facilities, covering a period longer than one year. Usually the borrowing firm applies for a lump-sum loan based on the budgeted cost of its proposed project and then pledges to repay the loan in a series of installments. (Often payments are made every quarter or even monthly.)

Thus, term loans look to the flow of future earnings of the business firm to amortize and retire the credit. The schedule of installment payments is usually structured with the borrower's normal cycle of cash inflows and outflows firmly in mind. For example, there may be "blind spots" built into the repayment schedule, so no installment payments will be due at those times of the year when the customer is normally short of cash. Some term loan agreements do not call for repayments of principal until the end of the loan period. For example, in a "bullet loan" only interest is paid periodically, with the principal due only when the loan matures.

Term loans normally are secured by *fixed assets* (e.g., plant or equipment) owned by the borrower and may carry either a fixed or a floating interest rate. That rate is normally higher than on shorter-term business loans due to the bank's greater risk exposure from such loans. The probability of default or other adverse changes in the borrower's position is certain to be greater over the course of a long-term loan. For this reason, bank loan officers and credit analysts pay attention to several different dimensions of a customer's term loan application. As a survey of large U.S. banks by Ghee, Petty, and Griggs [2] suggests, in evaluating applications for long-term business loans, banks often carefully review: (1) the qualifications of management, (2) the quality of accounting and auditing systems used by the customer, (3) whether or not the customer in the past has conscientiously filed periodic financial statements with the bank, (4) whether the customer is willing to agree not to pledge assets to other creditors, (5) whether adequate insurance will be secured on business property, (6) whether the customer is excessively exposed to the risk of changing technology that might make plant and equipment soon outdated, (7) the length of time before a proposed long-term project will generate any positive cash flow, (8) trends in market demand, and (9) the strength of the customer's net worth position.

Revolving Credit Financing

A **revolving credit line** allows a business customer to borrow up to a prespecified limit, repay all or a portion of the borrowing, and reborrow as necessary until the credit line matures. One of the most flexible of all forms of business loans, revolving credit is often granted without specific collateral to secure the loan and may be short-term or cover as long as three, four, or five years. This form of business financing is particularly popular when the customer is highly uncertain about the timing of future cash flows or about the exact magnitude of his or her future borrowing needs. Revolving credit helps even out fluctuations in the business cycle for a firm, allowing it to borrow extra cash in recessions when sales are down, and to repay during boom periods when internally generated cash is more abundant. Where the bank is legally obligated to honor every customer request for funds up to the limit of the line, the banker normally will charge a *loan commitment fee* either on the unused portion of the credit line or, sometimes, on the entire amount of revolving credit available for customer use.

Loan commitments are usually of two types. The most common is a *formal loan commitment,* which is a contractual promise by a bank to lend to a customer up to a maximum amount of money at a set interest rate or rate markup over the prevailing prime or LIBOR rate. In this case, the bank can renege on its promise to lend only if there has been a "material adverse change" in the borrower's financial condition or if the borrower has not fulfilled some provision of the bank's commitment contract. A second, looser form of loan commitment is a *confirmed credit line,* where a bank indicates its approval of a customer's request for credit in an emergency, though the price of such a credit line may not be set in advance and the customer may have little intention to draw upon the credit line, using it instead as a guarantee to back up a loan obtained elsewhere. These looser commitments typically go only to top-credit-rated firms and are usually priced much lower than formal loan commitments. They help borrowers get advance approval for loans so they can access credit quickly and send favorable signals to other lenders who may be considering lending to the bank's commitment customer.

One form of business revolving credit that has grown rapidly in recent years is the use of *credit cards.* A third or more of small businesses today have come to depend upon credit cards as a source of operating capital, thus avoiding having to get approval for every loan request. Unfortunately, the interest rates charged usually wind up being very high and if a personal card is used, the business borrower winds up being personally liable for the business's debt.

Long-Term Project Loans

The most risky of all business loans are **project loans**—credit to finance the construction of fixed assets designed to generate a flow of revenue in future periods. Prominent examples include oil refineries, pipelines, mines, power plants, and harbor facilities.

The risks surrounding such projects are both large and numerous: (1) large amounts of funds, often several billion dollars' worth, are involved; (2) the project being funded may be delayed by weather or the shortage of building materials; (3) laws and regulations in the region or country where the project is under construction may change in a way that adversely affects the completion or cost of the project; and (4) interest rates may change, adversely affecting either the lender's return on the loan (many of which are made with fixed rates of interest) or the ability of the project's sponsors to repay (if the loan carries a floating rate). Project loans are usually granted to several companies jointly sponsoring a large project. Due to their size and risk, they are often shared by several lenders.

Project loans may be granted on a *recourse basis,* in which the lender can recover funds from the sponsoring companies if the project does not pay out as planned. At the other extreme, the loan may be extended on a nonrecourse basis, in which there are no sponsor guarantees; the project stands or falls on its own merits. In this case, the lender faces significant risks and, typically, demands a high contract loan rate to compensate for them. Many such loans require that the project's sponsors pledge enough of their own capital to see the project through to completion.

Loans to Support Acquisitions of Other Business Firms

The 1980s and 1990s ushered in an explosion of loans to finance mergers and acquisitions of businesses. Among the most noteworthy of these acquisition credits are **LBOs**—*leveraged buyouts* of firms by small groups of investors, often led by managers inside the firm who believe their firm is undervalued in the marketplace. A targeted company's stock price could be driven higher, it is usually argued, if its new owners could bring more aggressive management techniques to bear, including selling off some of its assets in order to generate more revenue. These insider purchases have often been carried out by highly optimistic groups of investors, who are willing to borrow heavily (often 80 to 90 percent or more of the LBOs are financed by debt) in the belief that revenues can be raised higher than debt-service costs through superior management practices. So rapid was the growth of LBO transactions from 1980 to 1990 that their dollar volume expanded nearly a hundredfold during this decade, to more than $100 billion.[1] LBO growth slowed substantially in the 1990s, though LBOs have remained a significant feature of the financial market landscape.

The Federal Reserve Board has recently become concerned about the risks inherent in leveraged buyouts and other forms of high-leveraged debt. The Fed's concern is that firms whose acquisition is financed with heavy use of debt may not be able to repay that debt if the economy enters a recession or if interest rates rise. In a recession, firms purchased via LBOs might not be able to attract enough product demand to repay their borrowings and cover other operating costs. Similarly, if market interest rates rose significantly, the higher interest costs facing LBOs might make it impossible for them to service their debt and avoid bankruptcy. During the late 1980s and early

---

[1]See especially Osterberg [8].

1990s numerous LBO defaults took place, apparently fueled by a combination of factors: (*a*) rising buyout prices relative to the target companies' cash flow, (*b*) an acceleration of required payout schedules by banks and other lenders, and (*c*) earlier withdrawals of cash by management and stockholders before the acquired firms' earnings were sufficiently strong to withstand those cash withdrawals.

In November 1989 the Federal Reserve Board gave its bank examiners guidelines for evaluating the cash flows required to pay off any debt associated with a business acquisition. If, in the judgment of examiners a bank has loaned excessive amounts of funds to finance LBOs and other highly leveraged transactions (HLTs), the loans in question will be placed on a special classified list and the bank could be asked to add to its capital as a reserve against potential loan losses.[2] In defense of bank loan programs, however, it should be noted that most banks take only senior credit positions in financing leveraged buyouts, securing a higher priority claim than, for example, holders of junk bonds (which have been heavily employed to finance LBOs).[3] In July 1991, the three federal bank regulatory agencies began to loosen restrictions on HLTs (including the use of cash flow rather than merely balance sheet numbers to define an HLT transaction) out of concern that the curtailment of bank credit growth that followed earlier LBO restrictions was hurting the U.S. economy. In 1992 it was announced that many of the special reporting requirements imposed on banks active in LBOs and other HLT transactions would be eliminated.

Concept Checks

17–1. What special problems does business lending present to the management of a bank?

17–2. What are the essential differences among working capital loans, open credit lines, asset-based loans, term loans, revolving credit lines, interim financing, project loans, and acquisition loans?

---

[2]To facilitate the job of bank examiners in identifying such loans, the three U.S. federal banking agencies announced a definition of HLTs to be used in examining each U.S. bank's loan portfolio. An HLT was defined to include the buyout, acquisition, or recapitalization of an existing business in which any one of three conditions is met: (1) the transaction at least doubles the firm's liabilities and generates a leverage ratio of total liabilities to total assets over 50 percent; (2) the transaction itself has a leverage ratio above 75 percent; or (3) a syndication agent labels the transaction an HLT.

[3]A sobering note was introduced into bank LBO lending in 1991, however, when a U.S. bankruptcy judge in Boston granted the unsecured lenders involved in a bankrupt HLT the privilege of collecting their funds ahead of the banks involved. This decision was based on *fraudulent conveyance* statutes, which stipulate that even a secured lender's position will be weakened if it can be shown that the secured lender should have known when it made the loan that the transaction it helped finance would probably fail. A related doctrine called *equitable subordination* permits courts to place unsecured creditors ahead of a secured creditor who has misused his or her preferred position (such as by engaging in fraud, misrepresentation, or excessive control over the borrower) to influence the debtor to the detriment of the unsecured creditors. Frequently, lawsuits are filed by unsecured creditors to force banks and other secured lenders to help protect their interests in the settlement that is finally worked out. See, for example, Pollock [9].

Analyzing Business Loan Applications

In making business loans, the bank's margin for error is relatively narrow. Many business loans are of such large denomination that the bank itself may be at risk if the loan goes bad. Moreover, competition for the best business customers reduces the spread between the bank's yield on such loans and its cost of funds, labor, taxes, and overhead, which the bank must pay in order to make these loans. For most business credits, the bank must commit roughly $100 in loanable funds for each $1 earned after all costs (including taxes). This is a modest *reward-to-risk* ratio, which means that banks need to take special care, particularly with business loans that often carry large denominations and, therefore, large risk exposure. With such a small reward-to-risk ratio, it doesn't take many business loan defaults to seriously erode bank profits.

As we noted in Chapter 16, most loan officers like to build several layers of protection around a business loan agreement to ensure return of loan principal and expected interest earnings to the bank. Typically, this requires finding two or three sources of funds the business borrower could draw upon to support the loan. The most common sources of repayment for business loans are the following:

1. The business borrower's profits or cash flow.
2. Business assets pledged as collateral behind the loan.
3. A strong balance sheet with ample amounts of marketable assets and net worth.
4. Guarantees given by the business, such as drawing on the owners' personal property to backstop a business loan.

Notice that each of these potential sources of repayment for a loan involves an analysis of customer financial statements—balance sheets and income statements. Let's turn to these two business financial statements now and look at them as a loan officer would.

Analysis of a Business Borrower's Financial Statements

Analysis of the financial statements of a business borrower, typically, begins when the bank's credit analysis department prepares an analysis over time of how the key figures on the borrower's financial statement have changed (usually during the last three, four, or five years). An example of such a historical analysis for an oil and gas company, Black Gold, Inc., is shown in Table 17–1. It presents balance sheets for the last four years and income statements for the same time period.

Note that these financial statements include both dollar figures and percentages of total assets (in the case of the balance sheet) and total sales (in the case of the income statement). These percentage figures (often called *common-size ratios*) show even more clearly than the dollar figures on each financial statement the most important financial trends experienced by this or any other business loan customer. These percentage-composition ratios control for differences in size of firm, permitting the loan officer to compare a particular business customer with other firms and with the industry as a whole. The common-size ratios most often used to help analyze a business borrower's financial statements include the following:

Important Balance Sheet Percentage-Composition Ratios

Percentage Composition of Assets	*Percentage Composition of Liabilities and Total Net Worth*
Cash/Total assets	Accounts payable/Total liabilities and net worth (= total assets)
Marketable securities/Total assets	Notes payable/Total liabilities and net worth
Accounts receivable/Total assets	Taxes payable/Total liabilities and net worth
Inventories/Total assets	Total current liabilities/Total liabilities and net worth
Fixed assets, net of depreciation/Total assets	Long-term debt obligations (including long-term bank loans)/Total liabilities and net worth
Other (miscellaneous) assets/Total assets	Other liabilities/Total liabilities and net worth
	Total net worth/Total liabilities and net worth

Important Income Statement Percentage-Composition Ratios

Percentage Composition of Total Income (gross revenues or sales)

Cost of sales/Sales
Gross profit/Sales
Labor costs (wages, salaries, and fringe benefits)/Sales
Selling, administrative, and other expenses/Sales
Depreciation expenses/Sales
Other operating expenses/Sales
Net operating profit/Sales
Interest expense on borrowed funds/Sales
Net income before taxes/Sales
Income taxes/Sales
Net income after taxes/Sales

Comparative analysis of *changes* in these ratios for the recent past helps the loan officer determine any developing weaknesses in protection for the bank's loan, such as decreases in assets that might be pledged as collateral or a reduction in the earning power of the borrowing firm. For example, we can analyze the percentage-composition statements showing assets, liabilities, and equity capital for Black Gold, Inc., as reported in Table 17–1. Based on these percentage-composition statements, would Black Gold represent a good risk for the bank?

In this case Black Gold is asking our bank for a $5 million working capital line of credit tied to a borrowing base of assets, in the guise of accounts receivable and inventory, in anticipation of a sharp upturn in oil and gas prices. Black Gold currently owes $3.9 million to another bank with whom it has had a relationship for several years, but now the company has expressed considerable unhappiness with its current banking relationship and wants to establish a *new* relationship. Sometimes a business customer's unhappiness springs from poor or inadequate service provided by its current bank; on other occasions, however, unhappiness with a banking relationship arises because the business customer is in trouble and its current bank is simply trying to work its way out of a troubled situation, either by demanding payment on current loans or by refusing to accommodate new credit requests. One of a bank loan officer's tasks is to find

TABLE 17–1   Historical Analysis of the Financial Statements of Black Gold, Inc.

(dollar figures in millions)

Black Gold's Balance Sheets Arrayed in a Spread Sheet

Balance Sheet Items	Most Recent Year Dollar Value	Most Recent Year Percentage of Total	One Year Ago Dollar Value	One Year Ago Percentage of Total	Two Years Ago Dollar Value	Two Years Ago Percentage of Total	Three Years Ago Dollar Value	Three Years Ago Percentage of Total
Assets								
Cash	$ 1.0	3.6%	$ 1.3	4.5%	$ 1.7	5.7%	$ 2.2	6.9%
Marketable securities	0.5	1.8	0.8	2.8	1.0	3.3	____	0.0
Accounts receivable	8.3	29.6	7.4	25.5	6.2	20.7	4.1	12.8
Inventories	5.2	18.6	4.5	15.5	3.4	11.3	2.3	7.2
Total current assets	$15.0	53.6	$14.0	48.3	$12.3	41.0	$ 8.6	26.9
Fixed assets, gross	19.4	69.3	20.2	69.7	21.5	71.7	22.4	70.0
Less: Accumulated depreciation	10.3	36.8	9.2	31.7	8.0	26.7	5.1	15.9
Fixed assets, net	9.3	33.2	11.0	37.9	13.5	45.0	17.3	54.1
Other assets	3.7	13.2	4.0	13.8	4.2	14.0	6.1	19.1
Total assets	$28.0	100.0%	$29.0	100.0%	$30.0	100.0%	$32.0	100.0%
Liabilities and Equity								
Accounts payable	$ 1.3	4.6%	$ 1.2	4.1%	$ 0.8	2.7%	$ 1.0	3.1%
Notes payable	3.9	13.9	3.4	11.7	3.2	10.7	1.7	8.4
Taxes payable	0.1	0.4	0.2	0.7	0.1	0.3	0.8	2.3
Total current liabilities	$ 5.3	18.9	$ 4.8	16.6	$ 4.1	13.7	$ 4.5	14.1
Long-term debt	12.2	43.6	13.2	45.5	12.5	41.6	11.4	35.6
Other liabilities	0.0	0.0	0.4	1.4	3.5	11.7	6.1	19.1
Total liabilities	$17.5	62.5%	$18.4	63.4%	$20.1	67.0%	$22.0	68.8%
Common stock	1.0	3.6	1.0	3.4	1.0	3.3	1.0	3.1
Paid-in surplus	3.0	10.7	3.0	10.3	3.0	10.0	3.0	9.4
Retained earnings	6.5	23.2	6.6	22.8	5.9	19.7	6.0	18.8
Total net worth	10.5	37.5	10.6	36.6	9.9	33.0	10.0	31.3

Black Gold's Income Statement

Income Statement Items	Most Recent Year Dollar Value	Most Recent Year Percentage of Total	One Year Ago Dollar Value	One Year Ago Percentage of Total	Two Years Ago Dollar Value	Two Years Ago Percentage of Total	Three Years Ago Dollar Value	Three Years Ago Percentage of Total
Net Sales	$32.0	100.0%	$30.0	100.0%	$28.0	100.0%	$31.0	100.0%
Less: Cost of goods sold	18.0	56.3	16.0	53.3	15.0	53.6	14.0	45.2
Gross profits	$14.0	43.8	$14.0	46.7	$13.0	46.4	$17.0	54.8
Less: Selling, administrative, and other expenses	9.0	28.1	9.0	30.0	8.0	28.6	11.0	35.5
Less: Depreciation expenses	3.0	9.4	3.0	10.0	3.0	10.7	2.0	6.5
Net operating income	$ 2.0	6.3	$ 2.0	6.7	$ 2.0	7.1	$ 4.0	12.9
Less: Interest expense on borrowed funds	2.0	6.3	1.0	3.3	2.0	7.1	2.0	6.5
Net income before taxes	0.0	0.0	1.0	3.3	0.0	0.0	2.0	6.5
Less: Income taxes	0.1	0.3	0.3	1.0	0.1	0.4	0.2	0.6
Net income after taxes	($ 0.1)	(0.3)%	$ 0.7	2.3%	($ 0.1)	(3.6)%	$ 1.8	5.8%

out as much as possible about a business customer's current banking relationships and why they are or are not working out.

Careful examination of Table 17–1 suggests that the loan officer involved in this case would have several important questions to ask this customer. For example, Black Gold's net income after taxes and net income as a percentage of total net sales has been negative in two of the last four years. Its sales revenues have been essentially flat over the past four years, while the cost of goods sold, both in dollar terms and relative to net sales, has risen significantly over the past four years. Moreover, if this loan is to be secured by accounts receivable and inventory, the loan officer, clearly, has reason to be concerned, because the dollar amount and percentage of total assets of both of these balance sheet items have risen sharply over the period covered by the spread-sheets. And the firm's short-term (current) liabilities have risen as well.

Financial Ratio Analysis of a Customer's Financial Statements

Information from balance sheets and income statements is typically supplemented by financial ratio analysis. By careful selection of items from a borrower's balance sheets and income statements, the loan officer can shed light on such critical areas in business lending as (1) a borrowing customer's ability to control expenses; (2) a borrower's operating efficiency in utilizing resources to generate sales and cash flow: (3) the marketability of the borrower's product line; (4) the coverage that earnings provide over a business firm's financing cost; (5) the borrower's liquidity position, indicating the availability of ready cash; (6) the borrower's track record of profitability or net income; (7) the amount of financial leverage (or debt relative to equity capital) a business borrower has taken on; and (8) whether a borrower faces significant contingent liabilities that may give rise to substantial claims in the future.

The Business Customer's Control over Expenses

A barometer of the quality of a business firm's management is how carefully it monitors and controls its expenses and how well its earnings—the primary source of cash to repay the bank's loan in most cases—are likely to be protected and grow. Selected financial ratios, usually computed by credit analysts to monitor a firm's expense control program, include the following:

Wages and salaries/Net sales	Cost of goods sold/Net sales
Overhead expenses/Net sales	Selling, administrative, and other
Depreciation expenses/Net sales	expenses/Net sales
Interest expense on borrowed funds/Net sales	Taxes/Net sales

A loan officer confronted with several of these expense-control measures for Black Gold, Inc., would probably have serious doubts about the firm's management quality and its earnings prospects for the future, as shown in Table 17–2. Some of Black Gold's expense ratios—selling, administrative, and other expenses and taxes

TABLE 17–2   **Expense-Control Ratios for Black Gold, Inc.**

	Most Recent Year	One Year Ago	Two Years Ago	Three Years Ago
Cost of goods sold ÷ net sales	**56.3%**	**53.5%**	**53.6%**	**45.2%**
Selling, administrative, and other expenses ÷ net sales	28.1	30.0	28.6	35.5
Depreciation expenses ÷ net sales	9.4	10.0	10.7	6.5
Interest expense on borrowed funds ÷ net sales	6.3	3.3	7.1	6.5
Taxes ÷ net sales	0.3	1.0	0.4	0.6

relative to net sales—have declined; however, the rest have either held steady or risen as a percentage of the firm's net sales. In fact, it is Black Gold's inability to reduce its expenses in the face of a relatively stagnant sales record that has caused its net earnings to decline over the past four years. The loan officer working on this case will need some highly convincing arguments from the customer to demonstrate that the firm's future expense and net earnings picture will improve.

Operating Efficiency: Measure of a Business Firm's Performance Effectiveness

It is also useful to look at a business customer's operating efficiency. How effectively are assets being utilized to generate sales and cash flow for the firm and how efficiently are sales converted into cash? Important financial ratios here are

Annual cost of goods sold/Average inventory (or inventory turnover ratio)

Net sales/Total assets

Net sales/Net fixed assets

Net sales/Accounts and notes receivable

Average collection period =

Accounts receivable ÷ Annual credit sales ÷ 360

In the case of Black Gold, what do these efficiency ratios show? Clearly, as Table 17–3 reveals, some measures of Black Gold's efficiency show nothing really conclusive, while others tell a story of deteriorating efficiency in the management of key assets, particularly in accounts receivable. Moreover, *inventory turnover*—an indicator of management's effectiveness in controlling the size of the firm's inventory position—has shown a declining trend.[4]

The *average collection period* (accounts receivable turnover ratio) for Black Gold reveals a disturbing trend. The collection period ratio reflects the firm's effectiveness in

---

[4]In general, the higher a firm's inventory ratio, the better it is for banks and other creditors, because this ratio shows the number of times during a year that the firm turns over its investment in inventories by converting those inventories into goods sold. When the inventory turnover ratio is too low, it may indicate poor customer acceptance of the firm's products or ineffective production and inventory control policies. Too high an inventory turnover ratio could reflect underpricing of the firm's product or inadequate stocks of goods available for sale, with frequent stockouts, which drives customers away.

TABLE 17–3   Efficiency Ratios for Black Gold, Inc.

	Most Recent Year	One Year Ago	Two Years Ago	Three Years Ago
Inventory turnover ratio: Annual cost of goods sold ÷ average inventory	**3.46X**	**3.56X**	**4.41X**	**6.09X**
Average collection period: Accounts receivable ÷ annual sales ÷ 360*	**93.4 days**	**88.8 days**	**79.7 days**	**47.6 days**
Turnover of fixed assets: Net sales ÷ net fixed assets	3.44X	2.73X	2.07X	1.79X
Turnover of total assets: Net sales ÷ total assets	1.14X	1.03X	0.93X	0.97X

*Note: 360 days is used for ease of computation in calculating this ratio.

collecting cash from its credit sales and provides evidence on the overall quality of the firm's credit accounts. A lengthening of the average collection period suggests a rise in past-due credit accounts and poor collection policies. Clearly, this has happened to Black Gold—its average collection period has almost doubled in the past four years, rising from 47.6 days to 93.4 days. The loan officer would certainly ask why this has occurred and what steps the firm was taking to bring the turnover of its receivables back into line.

The ratio measuring *turnover of fixed assets* indicates how rapidly sales revenues are being generated as a result of using up the firm's plant and equipment (net fixed assets) to produce goods or services.[5] In this instance, Black Gold's fixed-asset turnover is rising, but there is little cause for comfort because a quick check of the balance sheet in Table 17–1 shows that the primary reason for rising fixed-asset turnover is a declining base of plant and equipment. Black Gold is either selling some of its fixed assets to raise cash or simply not replacing depreciated worn-out plant and equipment. Black Gold's management has asked for a $5 million line of credit in anticipation of increasing sales, but it is doubtful that the firm could handle these sales increases even if they occurred, given its declining base of productive fixed assets. A similar trend is reflected in the turnover ratio of total assets, which is rising for the same reasons.

Marketability of the Customer's Product or Service

In order to generate adequate cash flow to repay a loan, the business customer must be able to market goods, services, or skills successfully. A bank can often assess public acceptance of what the business customer has to sell by analyzing such factors as the growth rate of sales revenues, changes in the business customer's share of the available market, and the *gross profit margin* (GPM), defined as:

---

[5]If the *fixed-asset turnover ratio* falls, this may indicate the firm has invested too heavily in plant and equipment, given the strength of current market demand for its product, and thus has substantial productive capacity that isn't being used. Alternatively, a fixed-asset ratio that is too high would lead the analyst to believe the firm has not devoted enough of its resources to increasing or upgrading its physical plant in order to achieve greater efficiency and productivity.

TABLE 17–4   Gross and Net Profit Margins of Black Gold, Inc.

	Most Recent Year	One Year Ago	Two Years Ago	Three Years Ago
Gross profit margin (GPM)	43.8%	46.7%	46.4%	54.8%
Net profit margin (NPM)	–0.3	2.3	–3.6	5.8

$$\text{GPM} = \frac{\text{Net sales} - \text{Cost of goods sold}}{\text{Net sales}}$$

A closely related and somewhat more refined ratio is the *net profit margin* (NPM):[6]

$$\text{NPM} = \frac{\text{Net income after taxes}}{\text{Net sales}}$$

What has happened to the GPM and NPM of Black Gold, Inc.? Clearly, as revealed in Table 17–4, both GPM and NPM are on a downward trend. This trend tips off the bank's loan officer to several actual or potential problems, including potentially inappropriate pricing policies, expense control problems, and market deterioration.

Coverage Ratios: Measuring the Adequacy of Earnings

Coverage refers to the protection afforded creditors of a firm (including its bank) based on the amount of the firm's earnings. The best-known coverage ratios include the following:

$$\text{Interest coverage:} \quad \frac{\text{Income before interest and taxes}}{\text{Interest payments}}$$

$$\text{Coverage of interest and principal payments:} \quad \frac{\text{Income before interest and taxes}}{\left[\text{Interest payments} + \dfrac{\text{Principal repayments}}{1 - \text{Firm's marginal tax rate)}}\right]}$$

$$\text{Coverage of all fixed payments:} \quad \frac{\text{Income before interest, taxes, and lease payments}}{\text{Interest payments} + \text{Lease payments}}$$

---

[6]The *gross profit margin* (GPM) measures both market conditions—that is, demand for the business customer's product or service and how competitive a marketplace the customer faces—and the strength of the business customer in its own market, as indicated by how much the market price of the firm's product or service exceeds the customer's unit cost of production and delivery. The *net profit margin* (NPM), on the other hand, indicates how much of the business customer's profit from each dollar of sales survives after all expenses (including taxes) are deducted, reflecting both the effectiveness of the firm's expense-control policies and the competitiveness of its pricing policies.

TABLE 17–5   **Coverage Ratios for Black Gold, Inc.**

	Most Recent Year	One Year Ago	Two Years Ago	Three Years Ago
Interest coverage	1.0X	2.0X	1.0X	2.0X
Coverage of interest and principal payments	**0.29X**	**0.22X**	**0.32X**	**0.43X**

Note that the second of these coverage ratios adjusts for the fact that repayments of the principal of a loan are *not* tax deductible, while interest and lease payments are generally tax-deductible expenses in the United States.

What has happened to Black Gold's coverage ratios? During the current year, Black Gold must pay back $930,000 of its long-term debt; it also owes $3.9 million in short-term notes payable. One year ago it paid back $1 million in long-term debt, while two and three years ago it paid back $1.1 million and $1.3 million in long-term obligations, respectively. As Table 17–5 shows, Black Gold's interest coverage is very weak. Its earnings are barely adequate to cover its interest payments, and once repayments of principal are thrown in, Black Gold's earnings are simply inadequate to cover both its interest and principal payments. The firm must content itself with less debt (and use more owners' equity) to finance itself, find ways to boost its earnings, or lengthen out its debt through restructuring so that current debt service payments are reduced. Perhaps all three steps need to be taken. The loan officer should offer counsel to this customer concerning these alternatives and suggest how the firm might strengthen its coverage ratios to increase its chances of securing a loan.

Liquidity Indicators for Business Customers

The borrower's liquidity position reflects his or her ability to raise cash in timely fashion at reasonable cost, including the ability to meet loan payments when they come due.[7] Popular measures of liquidity include the following:

$$\text{Current ratio} = \frac{\text{Current assets}}{\text{Current liabilities}}$$

$$\text{Acid-test ratio} = \frac{\text{Current assets} - \text{Inventory}}{\text{Current liabilities}}$$

$$\text{Net liquid assets} = \frac{\text{Current}}{\text{assets}} - \frac{\text{Inventories of}}{\text{raw materials}} - \frac{\text{Current}}{\text{liabilities}}$$
$$\text{or goods}$$

$$\text{Net working capital} = \text{Current assets} - \text{Current liabilities}$$

---

[7]An individual, business firm, or government is considered *liquid* if it can convert assets into cash or borrow immediately spendable funds precisely when cash is needed. Liquidity is therefore a short-run concept in which *time* plays a key role. For that reason, most measures of liquidity focus on the amount of *current assets* (cash, marketable securities, accounts receivable, inventory, prepaid expenses, and any other assets that normally roll over into cash within a year's time) and *current liabilities* (accounts payable, notes payable, taxes payable, and other short-term claims against the firm, including any interest and principal payments owed on long-term debt that must be paid during the current year).

TABLE 17–6   Changes in Liquidity at Black Gold, Inc.

	Most Recent Year	*One Year Ago*	*Two Years Ago*	*Three Years Ago*
Current ratio: Current assets ÷ current liabilities	2.83X	2.92X	3.00X	1.91X
Acid-test ratio: Current assets − inventories ÷ current liabilities	1.85X	1.98X	2.17X	1.40X
Working capital (= current assets − current liabilities)	$9.7 mil.	$9.2 mil.	$8.2 mil.	$4.1 mil.
Net liquid assets (= current assets − inventories − current liabilities)	$4.5 mil.	$4.7 mil.	$4.8 mil.	$1.8 mil.

The concept of **working capital** is important because it provides a measure of a firm's ability to meet its short-term debt obligations from its holdings of current assets.

What has happened to Black Gold's liquidity position? The firm made substantial progress in building up its liquidity two years ago, when current assets covered current liabilities three times over. Since that time, however, Black Gold's current and acid-test ratios have dipped significantly (see Table 17–6). The only bright spots in the firm's liquidity picture are the recent expansion in its working capital of $9.7 million and its relatively stable net liquid asset position. However, when we carefully examine the causes of this working capital gain, we discover that it has been brought about largely by selling off a portion of the firm's fixed assets (plant and equipment) and through increased long-term borrowing. Neither of these events is likely to be well received by the bank's loan officers or credit analysts.

Banks are especially sensitive to changes in a business customer's liquidity position, because it is through the conversion of liquid assets (including the cash account) that loan repayments usually come. Erosion in a firm's liquidity position increases the risk that the bank will have to attach the customer's other assets to recover its funds. Such a step is usually time-consuming, costly, and uncertain in its outcome. If the bank ultimately decides to make a loan to Black Gold, it will almost certainly insist on covenants in the loan agreement requiring the firm to strengthen its liquid reserves.

However, we must note, as Haubrich and Cabral dos Sontos [6] observe, that liquidity can also have a "dark side." A business borrower with too many assets tied up in liquid form, rather than in income-producing assets, loses opportunities to boost returns and invites dishonest managers and employees to "take the money and run"—a danger sign to many lenders.

Profitability Indicators

The ultimate standard of performance in a market-oriented economy is how much net income remains for the owners of a business firm after all expenses (except stockholder dividends) are charged against revenue. Most loan officers will look at both pretax net income and after-tax net income to measure the overall financial success or failure of a prospective borrower relative to comparable firms in the same industry. Popular bottom-line indicators of the financial success of business borrowers include the following:

TABLE 17–7   Profitability Trends at Black Gold, Inc.

	Most Recent Year	One Year Ago	Two Years Ago	Three Years Ago
Before-tax net income ÷ total assets	0.0%	3.4%	0.0%	6.3%
After-tax net income ÷ total assets	–0.4	2.4	–0.3	5.6
Before-tax net income ÷ net worth	0.0	9.4	0.0	20.0
After-tax net income ÷ net worth	–1.0	6.6	–1.0	18.0

Before-tax net income ÷ total assets, net worth, or total sales.
After-tax net income ÷ total assets, net worth, or total sales.

How profitable has Black Gold been? Table 17–7 summarizes key profitability trends for this oil and gas firm. Clearly, there is little cause for comfort for the loan officer handling this credit application. Black Gold's earnings began a long-term decline two to three years ago, and there is little evidence to suggest that a turnaround is in sight. The firm's management has predicted an upturn in sales, which may result also in an earnings upturn. However, the loan officer must be satisfied that the prospects for such a recovery are bright. Of course, the loan might be granted if sufficient collateral were available that could be sold to recover the bank's funds. But most loan officers would find this a poor substitute for earnings and cash flow in repaying a loan.

The Financial Leverage Factor as a Barometer of a Business Firm's Capital Structure

Any lender of funds is concerned about how much debt a borrower has taken on in addition to the loan being applied for. The term *financial leverage* refers to the use of debt in the hope that the borrower can generate earnings that exceed the cost of debt, thereby increasing the potential return to a business firm's owners (stockholders). Key financial ratios used to analyze any borrowing business's credit standing and use of financial leverage are as follows:[8]

$$\text{Leverage ratio} = \frac{\text{Total liabilities}}{\text{Total assets}}$$

$$\text{Capitalization ratio} = \frac{\text{Long-term debt}}{\text{Total long-term liabilities and net worth}}$$

$$\text{Debt-to-sales ratio} = \frac{\text{Total liabilities}}{\text{Net sales}}$$

[8]The greater the amount of indebtedness a borrowing customer has already taken on, other factors held equal, the less well secured is any particular lender's position. The higher the *leverage ratio* becomes, the less likely it is that additional loans will be granted to a customer until he or she pays down some of the outstanding indebtedness. Moreover, if a loan is granted to a highly leveraged borrower, it is likely to carry a higher interest rate plus a requirement that more collateral be pledged.

The capitalization ratio focuses upon the business customer's use of permanent financing, essentially comparing the degree to which the firm is supported by long-term creditors as opposed to its owners' equity capital (net worth). Business debt can also be linked to business sales, because those sales ultimately provide the funds needed to retire the debt. If a firm's liabilities increase relative to its sales, management will have to compensate for the heavier debt burden by either finding less-expensive sources of credit or lowering expenses so that more sales revenue reaches the firm's bottom line of net income.

TABLE 17–8   Leverage Trends at Black Gold, Inc.

	Most Recent Year	*One Year Ago*	*Two Years Ago*	*Three Years Ago*
Leverage ratio: Total liabilities ÷ total assets	62.5%	63.4%	67.0%	68.8%
Total liabilities ÷ net worth	1.67X	1.74X	2.03X	2.20X
Capitalization ratio: Long-term debt ÷ long-term debt plus net worth	53.7%	55.5%	55.8%	53.3%
Debt-to-sales ratio: Total liabilities ÷ net sales	54.7%	61.3%	71.8%	71.0%

What has happened to Black Gold's leverage, or debt position? As shown in Table 17–8, Black Gold's leverage ratio has improved in the most recent period, with assets and net worth generally growing faster than the firm's debt. Moreover, its mix of long-term funding sources—debt and equity capital—has been relatively constant, while total liabilities have declined relative to sales. Much of the firm's funding has come from sources other than debt, such as sales of fixed assets and a buildup in such current assets as accounts receivable and inventory.[9]

Contingent Liabilities

Types of Contingent Liabilities.   Usually not shown on customer balance sheets are other potential claims against the borrower that the loan officer must be aware of, such as:

1. Guaranties and warranties behind the business firm's products.
2. Litigation or pending lawsuits against the firm.

---

[9]The financial ratios discussed in this chapter have been used in several studies designed to predict which borrowing companies might be prone to default on their loans and ultimately fail. Studies by Altman [11], Altman, Haldeman, and Nurajanan [12], and others have found that selected financial ratios are good discriminators between successful and troubled firms. The most important of these indicators of impending firm failure, identified in earlier research studies, are the following:

Profitability (Return) Indicators	*Liquidity Indicators*
Net income after taxes/total assets.	Cash flow (or net income + depreciation expenses)/ total assets or total sales.
Earnings before interest and taxes/ total assets.	Current assets/current liabilities.
Net income after taxes/common equity.	Working capital/net sales.
Leverage of Capital Structure Indicators	*Activity or Turnover Indicators*
Market value of equity/total debt.	Total sales/inventory.
Total liabilities/total assets.	Total sales/total assets.
Fixed assets/net worth.	

Market Indicators
Percentage change in stock price.
Stock price/current earnings (or P/E ratio).

3. Unfunded pension liabilities the firm will likely owe to its employees in the future.

4. Taxes owed but unpaid.

5. Limiting regulations.

These so-called **contingent liabilities** can turn into actual claims against the firm's assets at a future date, reducing the funds available to repay the loan. The loan officer's best move in this circumstance is, first to ask the customer about pending or potential claims against the firm and then to follow up with his or her own investigation, checking courthouse records, public notices, and newspapers. In this instance, it is far better to be safe and well informed than to repose in blissful ignorance.

Environmental Liabilities.   A new contingent liability that has increasingly captured bankers' concern is the issue of possible lender liability for *environmental damage* under the terms of the Comprehensive Environmental Response, Compensation, and Liability Act of 1980, amended in 1986 with passage of the Super Fund Amendments and Reauthorization Act. These federal laws make current and past owners of contaminated property, current and prior operators of businesses located on contaminated property, and those who dispose of or transport hazardous substances potentially liable for any cleanup costs associated with environmental damage. (Most states have enacted similar environmental damage and cleanup laws.) Other federal government laws that establish liability for the creation, transportation, storage, and disposal of environmentally dangerous substances include the Resource Conservation and Recovery Act, the Clean Water Act, the Clean Air Act, and the Toxic Substance Control Act.

In 1990 a federal appeals court in the Fleet Factors case ruled that a lender *could* be held liable for the cleanup of hazardous wastes spilled by a firm to whom it had loaned money if the lender was "significantly involved" in the borrower's decision making on how to dispose of hazardous wastes.[10] Later, in the Mirable case a lender was found to be liable for cleanup costs because the lender had actively involved itself in the management of a borrowing firm's operations as well as in the borrower's decisions about how to get rid of hazardous substances.[11] Finally, in the Maryland Bank & Trust court case, a bank that was foreclosing on the property of a family-owned garbage business because of nonpayment of a loan was found to be responsible for the customer's environmental damages because, said the court, a bank should *not* be able to foreclose on property, let the government dispose of any environmental pollution, and, thereby, benefit from the government's cleanup without incurring any liability at all.[12]

Faced with court decisions such as these, many banks have felt compelled to closely scrutinize the pollution hazards of any property pledged as loan collateral upon which they might have the right to foreclose. These court cases imply an "I can't win no matter what happens" situation for banks. If a bank forces a borrower to remove hazardous waste from the borrower's property as a condition for extending credit and actively monitors the cleanup, then the bank could be liable to the government for environmental

---

[10]See especially *United States* v. *Fleet Factor Corp.*, 901F2d 1550.

[11]See *United States* v. *Mirable*, 15 Envil. L. Kep 20, 994.

[12]See especially *United States* v. *Maryland Bank & Trust Co.*, 632 F.Supp. 573.

Bank Management in Action

Expert Systems in Business Lending

Business lending is changing in form and practice as technology and competition continue to change how banks deal with their business credit customers. One of the most important business loan trends today focuses on the increasing use of so-called expert systems—predictive equations that use selected data on a customer's business and financial history to classify a loan request as likely or unlikely to meet the bank's quality standards. Advanced statistical techniques, such as multiple discriminant analysis and logistic regression analysis, are used to sample from a bank's past business loan records a limited set of variables such as the business customer's credit rating, recent profitability (e.g., ROE or ROA), degree of liquidity (e.g., current or acid-test ratio) and leverage (e.g., ratio of debt to equity capital), and coverage ratios (e.g., the customer's earnings before interest and taxes relative to interest and principal payments on debt and leases) as well as other variables that reflect economic or industry conditions. Statistical tests are conducted until a set of variables is found that appears to separate at a statistically significant level "good" from "bad" business loans that the bank has made in the past. It is assumed that these same variables will be able to distinguish (at a statistically valid level) between "good" and "bad" future loan requests.

Often called "credit scoring systems" in the consumer lending field, these predictive equations are sometimes used as the principal tool to evaluate certain business clients' loan requests. However, most bankers appear to use them as only one of several business credit evaluation tools, including the judgments of loan officers, past experience with each type of loan, and other factors to help reach a decision on each new business loan application.

cleanup simply because it had become involved in the management of environmental pollutants. On the other hand, if the bank doesn't act to ensure that the environment is cleaned up, it might be held liable for damage and cleanup costs once it forecloses on polluted property. Because environmental risks appear to be so great, many banks have simply walked away from property they could seize for nonpayment of a loan, staying as far away as possible to avoid liability.

In an effort to give banks and other lenders some general guidelines on how to evaluate their environmental risks, particularly if they must foreclose on polluted property, the U.S. Environmental Protection Agency (EPA) issued a new lender liability rule in April 1992, defining a "security interest exemption" that banks as creditors could take advantage of when taking possession of polluted property. The new EPA guidelines state that a bank or other lender holding "indicia of ownership" against property (such as a deed of trust, lien, or mortgage) can be exempted from any environmental liability associated with the owner's property provided that the lender takes certain steps. For one thing lenders must not participate in the management of the borrower's property and must take action primarily to protect the credit they have extended to the borrower rather than treating their interest in the borrower's property as a long-term investment. If the lender forecloses on environmentally damaged property, it must post that property for sale within 12 months after securing marketable title. After six months have elapsed from the foreclosure date, the lender must accept any *bona fide* offer (within 90 days of receiving the offer) if that offer would fully repay the remaining amounts owed the lender.

Before a loan is made, a lender is *not* required to make an environmental site assessment of the borrower's property in order to avoid environmental liability, but the lender must make sure that it does not become involved in "arranging for treatment, disposal, or transportation" of hazardous substances. However, a lender can: (*a*) require that a borrower perform an environmental assessment of his or her own property; (*b*) require that polluted property be cleaned up; (*c*) inspect and monitor the borrower's property; and (*d*) demand in writing that a borrower comply with all environmental laws and regulations.

Unfortunately, the new EPA rules still leave several loopholes that could be dangerous for banks. For example, compliance with federal rules does not guarantee that a lender will not violate environmental laws of the states where a borrower resides, which may differ markedly from federal legislation. Moreover, once a lender has foreclosed on polluted property, it will probably try to sell that property. The new owner may insist that the lender clean up any hazardous substances before the deal is closed, once again subjecting the lender to a possible claim from government environmental agencies.

While several bills have been introduced in Congress in an effort to protect banks and other lenders from environmental liability, recent court rulings have put bankers on notice of the need to investigate whether a prospective business borrower works with toxic wastes or is involved in polluting the environment. Moreover, in February 1993 the Federal Deposit Insurance Corporation issued guidelines to help federally supervised depository institutions develop an *environmental risk assessment program,* which government examiners will review each time a bank is examined. A senior officer inside each institution must be appointed to implement and administer procedures for protecting the bank against loss from environmental damage. Each bank is supposed to establish a training program for its staff, develop procedures for evaluating the environmental risks present in loans collaterized by a customer's property, and put in place safeguards to shield the bank from environmental liability. Increasingly in the future we can expect to see loan agreements with business customers that include covenants requiring that the borrower (*a*) comply with all federal and state environmental laws; (*b*) disclose to the bank all environmental risks associated with any property pledged as loan collateral; (*c*) grant the lender the right to call a loan for immediate repayment if environmental damage is subsequently discovered; and (*d*) indemnify the lending institution against all costs arising from any environmental liability that the borrower creates.

Preparing Sources and Uses of Funds Statements from Business Financial Statements

Besides balance sheets and income statements, bank loan officers frequently like to see a third accounting statement from a business borrower—the **Sources and Uses of Funds Statement.** Such a statement can provide vital information on how the business firm's financial position is changing over time, telling the loan officer how the firm is financing itself and allocating the funds it raises. This kind of statement usually has the following components:

Changes in Assets	*Changes in Liabilities and Equity*
Change in cash account.	Change in accounts payable.
Change in accounts receivable.	Change in other current liabilities (including short-term bank loans).
Change in inventory position.	Change in long-term debt (including term loans from banks).
Change in fixed assets (net).	Change in net worth.

Increases in assets = Uses of the firm's available funds

Decreases in assets = Sources of the firm's available funds

Increases in liabilities and net worth = Sources of the firm's available funds

Decreases in liabilities and net worth = Uses of the firm's available funds

Let's examine the Sources and Uses of Funds Statement in Table 17–9, compiled by the credit analyst who assisted the loan officer in the Black Gold case. This statement shows clearly how Black Gold supported its production and delivery of oil and gas over the past year. Its sources of funds totaled $3.2 million during the year, and more than half (53 percent, or $1.7 million) came from selling fixed assets. Nearly one-fifth of total funding (18.7 percent, or $0.6 million) came from drawing down liquid assets (cash and marketable securities) and another fifth was derived from short-term borrowings (accounts and notes payable). Clearly, Black Gold cannot continue to sell off its assets indefinitely. The firm needs to develop new sources of funding (preferably through expanded sales and net income) to remain viable in the long run. Black Gold's management must present a convincing argument to the loan officer on how the firm will improve its sales and net earnings.

How did Black Gold *use* the $3.2 million in total funds raised? Most of those funds (50 percent, or $1.6 million) went to build up accounts receivable and inventories—two asset items the loan officer will examine closely for quality and marketability because these assets can be very hard to liquidate in a down market. Most of the remaining funds (31.3 percent, or $1 million) went to pay off long-term debt; this, on its face, was a positive development, because it increased Black Gold's future borrowing capacity.

Pro Forma Sources and Uses Statements and Balance Sheets

Not only is it useful to look at historical data in a Sources and Uses of Funds Statement, but it is also extremely important to estimate the business borrower's *future* sources and uses of funds and its statement of financial condition. The bank often has the customer prepare *pro forma* statements, and then credit analysts within the bank will prepare their own version of these forecasts for comparison purposes.

TABLE 17-9   **Sources and Uses of Funds Statement for Black Gold, Inc.**
(figures in millions of dollars)

Items from the Balance Sheet	Year-End of the Most Recent Year	Year-End for One Year Ago	Sources and Uses of Funds over the Past Year	
			All Sources	All Uses
Asset items:				
Cash account	$ 1.0	$ 1.3	$0.3	—
Marketable securities	0.5	0.8	0.3	—
Accounts receivable	8.3	7.4	—	$0.9
Inventories	5.2	4.5		0.7
Current assets	15.0	14.0	0.6	1.6
Fixed assets, net of depreciation	9.3	11.0	1.7	—
Other assets	3.7	4.0	0.3	—
Total assets	$28.0	$29.0	$2.6	$1.6
Liabilities and net worth items:				
Accounts payable	$ 1.3	$ 1.2	$0.1	—
Notes payable	3.9	3.4	0.5	—
Taxes payable	0.1	0.2		$0.1
Current liabilities	5.3	4.8	0.6	0.1
Long-term debt obligations	12.2	13.2	—	1.0
Other liabilities	0.0	0.4	—	0.4
Common stock	1.0	1.0	—	—
Paid-in surplus	3.0	3.0	—	—
Retained earnings	6.5	6.6		0.1
Total liabilities and net worth	$28.0	$29.0		
Total sources and uses of funds			$3.2	$3.2

Note: An increase in any asset item is a *use of funds;* a decrease in any asset item is a *source of funds.* An increase in any liability or net worth item is a *source of funds;* a decrease in any liability or net worth item is a *use of funds.*

Table 17-10 shows a pro forma balance sheet and Sources and Uses of Funds Statement for Black Gold, Inc. To no one's surprise, Black Gold has predicted a rosy future for its oil and gas operations. Net sales are forecast to rebound by an estimated 10 percent, while Black Gold's total assets are predicted to climb from $28 to $31.8 million within the coming year. Predicted positive earnings would help to boost the firm's retained earnings account and thereby strengthen its equity capital. At the same time the cash account is forecasted to return to its level of two or three years ago at $2 million by the end of the current year. For added liquidity, the firm forecasts adding $1 million to its holdings of marketable securities—a readily available liquidity reserve—and the less-liquid receivables and inventory accounts allegedly will be worked down (each by $0.4 million) through improved credit collection methods and better pricing and restocking policies.

Not only will the decline in plant and equipment be halted, Black Gold's management estimates, but new fixed assets will be added to replace obsolete or worn-out

TABLE 17–10   Pro Forma Balance Sheet and Sources and Uses of Funds Statement Forecast for Black Gold, Inc. (figures in millions of dollars)

Items from the Balance Sheet	*Actual Balance Sheet at End of Most Recent Year*	*Pro Forma Balance Sheet One Year from Now*	Items from the Balance Sheet	*Actual Balance Sheet at End of Most Recent Year*	*Pro Forma Balance Sheet One Year from Now*
Asset items:			**Liabilities and net worth items:**		
Cash account	$ 1.0	$ 2.0	Accounts payable	$ 1.3	$ 1.4
Marketable securities	0.5	1.5	Notes payable	3.9	5.0
Accounts receivable	8.3	7.9	Taxes payable	_0.1_	_0.5_
Inventories held	_5.2_	_4.8_	Current liabilities	5.3	6.9
Current assets	15.0	16.2			
			Long-term debt obligations	12.2	12.0
Net fixed assets	9.3	10.3	Other liabilities	0.0	2.3
Other assets	_3.7_	_5.3_	Common stock outstanding	1.0	1.0
Total assets	$28.0	$31.8	Paid-in surplus	3.0	3.0
			Undivided profits	_6.5_	_6.6_
			Total liabilities and net worth	$28.0	$31.8

Source and Use Items	Sources and Uses of Funds for Coming Year		Source and Use Items	Sources and Uses of Funds for Coming Year	
	All Sources	*All Uses*		*All Sources*	*All Uses*
Asset items:			**Liabilities and net worth items:**		
Cash account	—	$1.0	Accounts payable	$0.1	—
Marketable securities	—	1.0	Notes payable	1.1	—
Accounts receivable	$0.4	—	Taxes payable	0.4	—
Inventories held	_0.4_	_=_	Current liabilities	1.6	—
Current assets	0.8	2.0			
			Long-term debt obligations	—	$0.2
Net fixed assets	—	1.0	Other liabilities	2.3	—
Other assets	_=_	_1.6_	Common stock understanding	—	—
Total assets	$0.8	$4.6	Paid-in surplus	—	—
			Undivided profits	_0.1_	_=_
			Total liabilities and net worth	$4.0	$0.2
			Total sources and uses of funds	$4.8	$4.8

Effect of the proposed bank loan: Black Gold proposes to pay off the $3.9 million note owed to its former bank with the $5 million it is requesting in new bank credit. If the loan is approved as requested, its cash account would rise by $1 million to $2 million and its notes payable account would increase by $1.1 million to $5 million, reflecting the amount owed the firm's new bank.

facilities. According to Table 17–10, the firm is planning to expand its fixed assets (plant and equipment) by $1 million and acquire other (miscellaneous) assets of $1.6 million as well as pay off $0.2 million of its outstanding long-term debt. These cash outflows reportedly are to be covered, in the main, by an increase in "other" (unspecified) liabilities. Because that additional debt could weaken the bank's claim against this customer, should it make a loan and that loan ultimately becomes a problem credit, the bank's loan officer will want to find out exactly why and how this proposed additional debt capital would be raised and assess its possible adverse consequences for the bank.

What will make possible all these adventurous plans for restructuring and rebuilding Black Gold's assets and capital? As Table 17–10 shows in the notes payable account, the firm is relying heavily on its $5 million credit request from the bank to pay off its outstanding $3.9 million in short-term notes and to provide an additional $1 million in new cash to strengthen its assets and help fuel the projected gains in its net earnings. Are these forecasts reasonable? That, of course, is the decision the loan officer and, ultimately, the bank's loan committee must make. Experienced loan officers know that, in most cases, the customer is more optimistic and far less objective about the future than a banker usually can afford to be.

A key factor shaping this customer's future performance will be what happens to energy prices in the global market. The bank would be well advised to carry out a *simulation analysis* of this customer's future financial condition, assuming an array of different possible oil and gas prices (and, therefore, net sales figures) and seeing what the consequences are for the firm's pro forma balance sheet, income statement, and Sources and Uses of Funds Statement. Armed with this information, the loan committee can move toward a more satisfactory credit decision based on its assessment of the most likely future conditions in the global energy market.

The Loan Officer's Responsibility to Bank and Customer

There is an understandable tendency on the part of many readers to look at the foregoing figures for Black Gold and simply say *no*. This proposed loan as requested does not appear to have reasonable prospects for being repaid to the bank. Indeed, many readers skilled in the methods of credit analysis would move very quickly to that opinion, given the firm's recent trends in sales revenue, expenses, and net earnings. But it is at this point that the credit analyst and the loan officer often part company. For a loan officer must look beyond the immediate facts to the broader, longer-term aspects of the bank-customer relationship. Denial of this loan request will almost certainly lose this customer's business (including any deposits the company may have placed with the bank) and probably lose the personal accounts of many stockholders and employees of Black Gold as well. Other firms in the same or related industries may also be discouraged from applying to this bank for coverage of their credit needs.

Banks cannot stay in business for long by making bad loans of this size, but they also cannot be successful by flatly turning away large corporate accounts without any recourse for the customer. That sort of policy soon leads to loss of market share and may ultimately damage bottom-line earnings. Experienced loan officers know that a better business loan policy is to *find a way to help the customer under terms that the bank feels adequately protect its funds and yield an acceptable long-run rate of return to the bank's stockholders.* If at all possible, within the limits of the bank's and the regulatory authorities' quality standards, find a way, in the vernacular of the industry, to "do the deal."

Clearly, many loan requests will be of such poor quality that there is, indeed, no way to do the deal. But other marginal requests may be acceptable with proper structuring of the loan to build in ample protection for the bank. For example, in the case of Black Gold, Inc., the bank is confronted with a request for a $5 million credit line—an amount that is considerably more than the bank loan officer is likely to be willing to grant, given this customer's apparent financial and operating weaknesses. Suppose, however, that the loan officer, with the approval of the bank's loan committee, proposes the following alternative plan to this customer:

> The bank will extend a $3 million line of credit for nine months, with the line to be cleaned up at the end of that period. If all payments on this credit are satisfactorily made and there is no further deterioration in the customer's financial position, the bank will renew the credit line on a quarterly basis. Any drawings against the line will be secured by a lien against all unencumbered fixed assets of the firm, 60 percent of all accounts receivable that are current, and 30 percent of the value of all inventories held. The bank will be granted a first lien against any new fixed assets acquired by the firm. Interest payments will be assessed monthly. The customer agrees to hold a deposit with the bank equal to 20 percent of the amount of any actual drawings against the line and 5 percent of the amount of any unused portion of the line.
>
> In addition, the customer agrees to file monthly reports on the status of sales, expenses, net income, accounts receivable, and inventory and to file quarterly audited balance sheet and income statements. Any changes in the management of the firm or any sales of plant and equipment, merger agreements, or liquidations must be approved in advance by the bank. The customer will maintain at least the current levels of the firm's leverage and liquidity ratios, and any significant deviations from the firm's projection or any significant changes in the firm's financial and operating position will be reported to the bank immediately. Any failure to conform to the terms of this agreement by the customer will make the loan immediately due and payable.

An agreement of this sort protects the bank in a number of important ways. For example, Black Gold has an estimated $2 million in unmortgaged fixed assets and plans to acquire an additional $1 million in new equipment. Added protection is provided by the conservative percentages of accounts receivable and inventory the bank is willing to take as collateral and by the required compensating balances (deposits) the customer must retain with the bank. In the event of a default on this loan, the bank could exercise its *right of offset* and take control of these deposits in order to repay the balance due on the loan. Interest must be paid monthly, which means the bank will recover a substantial portion of its expected interest income early in the loan's term, further reducing the bank's income risk associated with this credit. Any action by the customer or adverse change in the customer's position that leads to a violation of the loan agreement gives the bank legal grounds to take possession of the firm's assets pledged behind the loan and sell those assets to recover the loan's proceeds and any unpaid interest.

Black Gold may well decline this agreement, particularly because (*a*) it gives the customer much less money than requested ($3 million instead of $5 million), (*b*) the loan funds are offered for a shorter term than requested (nine months instead of one year), and (*c*) the agreement places many restrictions on the freedom of Black Gold's management decision making and flexibility. But the key point is this: *If the customer says "no" to this proposal by the bank, it is the customer, not the bank, who is declining to establish a banking relationship.* The bank has demonstrated a willingness to help meet at least a portion of this customer's financing needs. Moreover, good lending policy calls for the loan officer to assure the customer that even if he or she turns down the bank's offer, the bank still stands ready at any future time to try to work with Black Gold to find a suitable service package that will satisfy both parties.

The alert reader will note that we said nothing in the foregoing draft loan agreement about what rate of interest the loan should bear. The loan rate, too, can be shaped in such a way that it further protects or compensates the bank for any risks incurred. We turn our attention to this very important subject of how to price business loans in the next chapter.

Concept Checks

17–3. What aspects of a business firm's financial statements do bank loan officers and credit analysts examine carefully?

17–4. What aspect of a business firm's operations is reflected in its ratio of cost of goods sold to net sales? In its ratio of net sales to total assets? In its GPM ratio? In its ratio of income before interest and taxes to total interest payments? In its acid-test ratio? In its ratio of before-tax net income to net worth? In its ratio of total inabilities to net sales? What are the principal limitations of these ratios?

17–5. What are contingent liabilities and why might they be important in deciding whether to approve or disapprove a business loan request?

17–6. How can a Sources and Uses of Funds Statement aid a bank in making the decision to grant or deny a business loan request?

17–7. Should a bank loan officer ever say "no" to a business firm requesting a loan? Please explain.

Summary

In this chapter, we have examined the many types of loans that banks grant to business firms today. We have divided these into (1) *working capital loans,* which are short-term in nature and usually aimed at funding purchases of business inventories, meeting payrolls, paying taxes, and other short-term (temporary) expenses, and (2) *term loans,* typically employed to fund permanent additions to working capital or additions to plant and equipment. We have looked at several varieties of each of these two main types of bank business loans, including seasonal open credit lines, dealer financing, asset-based loans, revolving credit, and project loans.

The analysis and evaluation of each business loan application can be a complicated, time-consuming process involving the loan officer who contacts and negotiates with the customer, one or more credit analysts who evaluate the customer's financial strengths and weaknesses, and the bank's loan committee, which must ultimately approve or deny the loan. Deregulation of the banking industry and the advent of substantial competition from foreign banks have sharply narrowed bank profit margins, requiring bankers to evaluate each business loan request closely and carefully price those business loans that are made.

The chapter considered several major techniques for analyzing business loan requests. Among the most important credit evaluation techniques discussed are the following:

1. Composition analysis of borrower financial statements.
2. Financial ratio analysis (including ratio measures of expense control, efficiency, coverage, profitability, liquidity, and leverage).
3. Actual and pro forma Sources and Uses of Funds Statements, which trace the flow of funds through the business firm and show how the firm has financed itself from internal and external sources.

In the chapter that follows we carefully review the options for pricing business loans that are used by many bankers today.

Key Terms in This Chapter

Self-liquidating loans
Working capital loans
Compensating deposit balances
Interim construction loan
Asset-based loans
Factoring
Term loans

Revolving credit line
Project loans
LBOs
Working capital
Contingent liabilities
Sources and Uses of Funds Statement

Problems and Projects

1. From the descriptions given below please identify what *type* of business loan is being discussed.
   a. A temporary credit to support the construction of homes, apartments, office buildings, and other permanent structures.
   b. A loan is made to an automobile dealer to support the shipment of new cars to the dealer's showroom floor.
   c. Credit extended on the basis of a business's accounts receivable.
   d. The term of an inventory loan is being set to match the exact length of time needed to generate sufficient cash to repay the loan.
   e. Credit is extended for up to one year to purchase raw materials and cover a seasonal peak need for cash.
   f. A government security dealer requires credit to add new government bonds to his security portfolio.
   g. Credit is granted for a term longer than a year to support the purchase of plant and equipment.
   h. A group of investors wish to take over a firm using debt financing and improve its management and its earnings.
   i. A business firm receives a three-year line of credit against which it can borrow, repay, and borrow again if necessary during the loan's three-year term.
   j. Credit is extended to support the construction of a toll road.

2. As a new credit trainee for Evergreen National Bank, you have been asked to evaluate the financial position of a medium-size manufacturing corporation, Hamilton Steel Castings, which has asked for renewal of and an increase in its six-month credit line. Hamilton now requests a $7 million credit line, and you must draft your first credit opinion for a senior credit analyst.

Unfortunately, Hamilton just changed management, and its financial report for the last six months was not only late but also garbled. As best as you can tell, its sales, assets, operating expenses, and liabilities for the six-month period just concluded display the following patterns (figures in millions in dollars):

	January	February	March	April	May	June
Net sales	$48.1	$47.3	$45.2	$43.0	$43.9	$39.7
Cost of goods sold	27.8	28.1	27.4	26.9	27.3	26.6
Selling, administrative, and other expenses	19.2	18.9	17.6	16.5	16.7	15.3
Depreciation	3.1	3.0	3.0	2.9	3.0	2.8
Interest cost on borrowed funds	2.0	2.2	2.3	2.3	2.5	2.7
Expected tax obligation	1.3	1.0	0.7	0.9	0.7	0.4
Total assets	24.5	24.3	23.8	23.7	23.2	22.9
Current assets	6.4	6.1	5.5	5.4	5.0	4.8
Net fixed assets	17.2	17.4	17.5	17.6	18.0	18.0
Current liabilities	4.7	5.2	5.6	5.9	5.8	6.4
Total liabilities	15.9	16.1	16.4	16.5	17.1	17.2

You have been reassured by several analysts in the department that this is an easy account with which to start your career. Hamilton has a 16-year relationship with the bank and has routinely received and paid off a credit line of $4 to $5 million. Actually, the credit department has already decided to approve the request, which goes to the bank's loan committee this afternoon. The department's senior analyst tells you to prepare because you will be asked for your opinion on this loan request (though you have been led to believe the loan will be approved anyway, because Hamilton's president serves on Evergreen's board of directors).

What will you recommend if asked? Is there any reason to question the latest data supplied by this customer? Could other factors be at work that you do not yet understand about this customer's business? How could you find out in the short time available? If this loan request is granted, what do you think the customer will do with the funds?

Alternative scenarios:

(1) Would your evaluation of the Hamilton loan request change if its net sales, cost of goods sold, and selling and administrative expenses grew an average of 1 percent a month over the past six months? Please explain.

(2) Suppose Hamilton's current ratio was 1.0 in January with current assets of $7 million and rose gradually to 1.5 by June with current assets of $9 million. Would you change your opinion of this loan request?

(3) What if a senior credit analyst tells you not to be alarmed about any declining trends you observe on Hamilton's financial statements because they operate a *seasonal* business with a strong rebound in sales during the summer and fall months? Does this help you in reaching a decision? What other information would you like to have in order to assess this borrower's financial situation?

3. From the data given below, please construct as many of the financial ratios discussed in this chapter as you can and then indicate what dimension of a business firm's performance each ratio represents.

Business Assets		Annual Revenue and Expense Items	
Cash account	$ 10	Net sales	$680
Accounts receivable	95	Cost of goods sold	520
Inventories	108	Wages and salaries	61
Fixed assets	301	Interest expense	18
Miscellaneous assets	96	Overhead expenses	29
	610	Depreciation expenses	15
		Selling, administrative, and	
Liabilities and Equity		other expenses	30
Short-term debt:		Before-tax net income	7
Accounts payable	83	Taxes owed	2
Notes payable	107*	After-tax net income	5
Long-term debt (bonds)	325*		
Miscellaneous liabilities	15		
Equity capital	80		

*Annual principal payments on bonds and notes payable total $55. The firm's marginal tax rate is 35 percent.

4. Chamrod Corporation has placed a term loan request with its bank and submitted the balance sheets below for the year just concluded and the pro forma balance sheet expected by the end of the current year. Construct a pro forma Sources and Uses of Funds Statement for the current year. As you examine the Sources and Uses of Funds Statement projected by Chamrod, do you detect any changes in their projected financial position that might be of concern either to the bank's credit analyst, or loan officer, or both?

Chamrod Corporation
(all amounts in millions of dollars)

	Assets at the End of the Most Recent Year	Assets Projected for the End of the Current Year		Liabilities and Equity at the End of the Most Recent Year	Liabilities and Equity Projected for the End of the Most Current Year
Cash	$ 532	$ 417	Accounts payable	$ 970	$1,030
Accounts receivable	1,018	1,225	Notes payable	2,733	2,950
Inventories	894	973	Taxes payable	327	216
Net fixed assets	2,740	2,898	Long-term debt obligations	872	931
Other assets	66	87	Common stock	85	85
			Undivided profits	263	388
			Total liabilities and		
Total assets	$5,250	$5,600	equity capital	$5,250	$5,600

5. Which of the dimensions of a business firm's financial and operating performance do each of the following ratios measure?

Average collection period	Cost of goods sold/Net sales
Gross profit margin	Interest coverage
Current ratio	Before-tax net income/Total assets
Total liabilities/Total assets	Net sales/Total assets
Overhead expenses/Net sales	Net income after taxes/Net sales
Income before interest, taxes, and lease payments/(Interest plus lease payments)	Current assets less current liabilities
	Acid-test ratio
After-tax net income/Net worth	Long-term debt/(Total long-term liabilities and net worth)
Unfunded pension liabilities	
Annual cost of goods sold/Average inventory	Interest expense on borrowed funds/Net sales
Net sales/Net fixed assets	After-tax net income/Total sales
Depreciation expenses/Net sales	Net sales/Accounts and notes receivable
Total liabilities/Net sales	Percentage change in stock price

Selected References

Techniques for evaluating business loan requests are discussed in the following:

1. Goldberg, Michael A. "The Impact of Regulatory and Monetary Factors on Bank Loan Shares." *Journal of Financial and Quantitative Analysis* 16, no. 2 (June 1981), pp. 227–46.
2. Ghee, William K.; J. William Petty; and Jack A. Griggs. "The Banker's Perspective on Financing Capital Investment: An Update." Paper presented at the Southern Finance Association Meetings, Atlanta, Georgia, November 12, 1982.

The following studies discuss risks inherent in business lending:

3. Erdivig, Eleanor H. "Lender Liability under Environmental Law." *Chicago Fed Letter*, Federal Reserve Bank of Chicago, September 1991, pp. 1–3.
4. Former, John B. "What the New CERCLA Rule Means for Lenders." *The Bankers Magazine*, May/June 1993, pp. 51–58.
5. Graber, Ned W. "The EPA's New CERCLA Rule: An Aid, Not a Remedy." *The Bankers Magazine*, January/February 1993, pp. 43–58.
6. Haubrich, Joseph G., and Joãn Cabral dos Santos. "The Dark Side of Liquidity." *Economic Commentary*, Federal Reserve Bank of Cleveland, September 15, 1997.
7. Ireland, Oliver, Associate General Counsel, Federal Reserve Board. Testimony before the Subcommittee on Policy Research and Insurance, U.S. House of Representatives, July 10, 1991.
8. Osterberg, William P. "LBOs and Conflicts of Interest." *Economic Commentary,* Federal Reserve Bank of Cleveland, August 15, 1989, pp. 1–4.
9. Pollock, Ellen Joan. "Second Lenders Can Lose Place in Line." *The Wall Street Journal,* June 20, 1991, p. 38.
10. McElroy, John M. "Issues in Lending—How to Document Equipment Lease Financings." *The Journal of Lending and Credit Risk Management,* October 1996, pp. 50–56.

The following are studies of factors that may predict business failures or troubled loans:

11. Altman, Edward I. "Financial Ratios, Discriminant Analysis, and the Prediction of Corporate Bankruptcy." *Journal of Finance,* September 1968, pp. 589–609.
12. Altman, Edward I.; G. Haldeman; and P. Nurajanan. "Zeta Analysis: A New Model to Identify the Bankruptcy Risk of Corporations." *Journal of Banking and Finance* 1 (1977), pp. 29–54.
13. Stein, Jeremy C. "What Went Wrong with the LBO Boom." *The Wall Street Journal,* June 11, 1991, p. A10.
14. Taylor, Jeremy D. "Understanding Industry Risk: Part 3." *The Journal of Lending and Credit Risk Management,* October 1996, pp. 14–26.

18 PRICING BUSINESS LOANS

Learning and Management Decision Objectives

The purpose of this chapter is to explore the different methods used by bankers today to price business loans and to evaluate the strengths and weaknesses of these pricing methods for achieving a bank's goals.

Introduction

One of the most difficult tasks in lending to business firms and other borrowing customers is deciding how to *price* the loan.[1] The lender wants to charge a high enough rate to ensure that each loan will be profitable and compensate the bank fully for the risks involved. However, the loan rate must also be low enough to accommodate the business customer in such a way that he or she can successfully repay the loan and not be driven away to another lender or into the open market for credit. The more competition the bank faces for a customer's loan business, the more it will have to keep the price of that loan at a reasonable level consistent with competition in the financial marketplace. Indeed, in a loan market characterized by intense competition, the lender is a price *taker,* not a price setter. With deregulation of banking under way in many nations, deregulated competition has significantly narrowed the profit margins banks earn from selling deposits and making loans. This makes correct pricing of loans even more imperative for bankers today than in the past.

---

[1]This chapter is based upon the author's article [5], which appeared in *The Canadian Banker* and is used by permission of the publisher.

The Cost-Plus Loan-Pricing Method

In pricing a business loan, bank management must consider the cost of raising loanable funds and the operating costs of running the bank. This means that *banks must know what their costs are in order to consistently make profitable, correctly priced loans* of any type. There is no substitute for a well-designed *management information system* when it comes to pricing loans.

The simplest loan-pricing model assumes that the rate of interest charged on any loan includes four components: (1) the cost to the bank of raising adequate funds to lend, (2) the bank's nonfunds operating costs (including wages and salaries of loan personnel and the cost of materials and physical facilities used in granting and administering a loan), (3) necessary compensation paid to the bank for the degree of default risk inherent in a loan request, and (4) the desired profit margin on each loan that provides the bank's stockholders with an adequate return on their capital. A loan pricing scheme of this sort is often called **cost-plus loan pricing.** Thus:

$$
\begin{array}{c}
\text{Loan} \\ \text{interest} \\ \text{rate}
\end{array} =
\begin{array}{c}
\text{Marginal} \\ \text{cost of raising} \\ \text{loanable funds} \\ \text{to lend to} \\ \text{the borrower}
\end{array} +
\begin{array}{c}
\text{Nonfunds} \\ \text{bank} \\ \text{operating} \\ \text{costs}
\end{array} +
\begin{array}{c}
\text{Estimated} \\ \text{margin to} \\ \text{compensate} \\ \text{the bank for} \\ \text{default risk}
\end{array} +
\begin{array}{c}
\text{Bank's} \\ \text{desired} \\ \text{profit} \\ \text{margin}
\end{array}
$$

Each of these components can be expressed in annualized percentage terms relative to the amount of the loan.

For example, suppose the bank has a loan request from one of its corporate customers for $5 million (as in the Black Gold case discussed in the preceding chapter). If the bank must sell negotiable CDs in the money market at an interest rate of 5 percent to fund this loan, the marginal cost of loanable funds for this particular loan will be 5 percent. Nonfunds operating costs to analyze, grant, and monitor this loan are estimated at 2 percent of the $5 million request. The bank's credit department may recommend adding 2 percent of the amount requested to compensate the bank for the risk that the loan will not be repaid in full and on time. Finally, the bank may desire a 1 percent profit margin over and above the financial, operating, and risk-related costs of this loan. Thus, this loan will be offered to the borrower at a rate of 10 percent (= 5 percent + 2 percent + 2 percent + 1 percent).[2]

---

[2]The rate of return the borrower promises to pay on a loan often differs from the quoted loan interest rate itself and from a loan's expected return as well. The promised rate of return on a loan is a function of (*a*) the cost of bank funds committed to the borrower, (*b*) the default risk and other risk premiums attached to a loan, (*c*) any noninterest service fees (such as loan origination or appraisal fees) required of a borrowing customer, (*d*) the market value of collateral pledged behind a loan, and (*e*) any nonprice terms (such as required deposit balances the customer must keep in the bank) included as part of the loan agreement.

Thus, the promised overall return on a loan can be expressed as a ratio:

$$
\begin{array}{c}
\text{Promised} \\ \text{overall} \\ \text{return} \\ \text{from a loan}
\end{array} =
\frac{
\begin{array}{c}
\text{Cost of bank funds + Loan risk premiums +} \\ \text{Loan-related fees + Profit margin}
\end{array}
}{
\begin{array}{c}
\text{Net amount of funds committed to borrowing customer} \\ \text{after adjustments for required customer deposits,} \\ \text{reserve requirements, and nonprice terms of a loan}
\end{array}
}
$$

In contrast, the expected return on a loan depends not only on the rate of return the borrower promises to pay the bank, but also on the probability the borrower will default on some or all of the payments required in the loan contract.

The Price Leadership Model

One of the drawbacks of the cost-plus loan-pricing model is its assumption that a bank accurately knows what its costs are. This is often *not* the case. Banking is a multiproduct industry and, like most multiproduct businesses, often faces great difficulty in trying to properly allocate operating costs among the many different services each bank offers. Moreover, the cost-plus pricing method implies that a banker can price a loan with little regard for the competition posed by other lenders. For the vast majority of loans today, this is simply *not* true. Competition will impact the bank's desired profit margin on a loan; in general, the more intense the competition, the thinner the profit margin becomes.

These limitations of the cost-plus approach have led to a form of **price leadership** in banking, which began among leading money center banks half a century ago. During the Great Depression of the 1930s, major banks established a uniform base lending fee known as the **prime rate** (sometimes called the *base* or reference rate)—supposedly at that time the lowest rate charged a bank's most creditworthy customers on short-term, working capital loans. The actual loan rate charged any particular customer would be determined by the following formula:

$$
\begin{array}{ccc}
\text{Loan} & \text{Base or prime} & \overbrace{\hspace{8cm}}^{\text{Markup}} \\
\text{interest} = \text{rate (including the bank's desired profit margin over all operating and administrative costs)} & + \text{Default-risk premium paid by non-prime-rated borrowers} & + \text{Term-risk premium paid by borrowers seeking long-term credit} \\
\text{rate} & &
\end{array}
$$

For example, a medium-sized business customer asking for a three-year loan to purchase new equipment might be assessed a loan rate of 12 percent, consisting of a prime (or base) rate of 8 percent plus 2 percent for default risk and another 2 percent for term risk because of the long-term character of the loan. Longer-term loans are assigned a term-risk premium because lending over a longer period of time exposes the bank to more opportunities for loss than does an otherwise comparable short-term loan. Assignment of risk premiums is one of the most difficult aspects of loan pricing, with a wide variety of different risk-adjustment methods in use. Copeland [3] suggests assigning loan-quality *grades* according to the following schedule:

Risk Category	Risk Premium	Risk Category	Risk Premium
No risk	0.00%	Special-mention	1.50%
Minimal risk	0.25	Substandard	2.50
Standard risk	0.50	Doubtful	5.00

Many observers would argue, however, that a loan classified as *doubtful* or even *substandard* simply doesn't belong in a bank's portfolio.

The risk premiums attached to loans are often referred to collectively as the *markup*. Banks can expand or contract their loan portfolios simply by contracting or expanding their loan-rate markups. Many banks prefer, however, simply to vary their loan rejection rates rather than changing either their base rate or their markups.[3]

In the United States today, the *prevailing prime rate* is considered to be the most common base rate figure announced by the 30 money center banks that publish their loan rates regularly. Prime rates used by other, generally smaller U.S. banks often differ from the prevailing prime. For many years, the prime rate was changed only infrequently, requiring a resolution voted upon by each bank's board of directors. However, the growth of the commercial paper and certificate of deposit (CD) markets, as well as the advent of inflation and more volatile interest rates, gave rise to a *floating* prime rate, tied to changes in such important money market interest rates as the 90-day commercial paper rate and the 90-day CD rate. With floating primes, major corporate borrowers with impeccable credit ratings might be permitted to borrow, for example, at a prime rate one-half a percentage point above the most recent commercial paper rate or at a spread of one percentage point above the most recent four-week average CD rate.

Two different floating prime rate formulas were soon developed by leading money center banks: (1) the prime-plus method and (2) the times-prime method. For example, a borrowing corporate customer might be quoted a short-term *prime-plus-2* loan rate of 12 percent when the prime rate stands at 10 percent. Alternatively, this customer might be quoted a *1.2 times-prime rate,* that is:

Loan interest rate = 1.2 (prime rate) = 1.2 (10 percent) = 12 percent.

While these two formulas may lead to the same initial loan rate, as in the example above, they lead to very different loan rates when interest rates change and the borrower has a floating-rate loan.

For example, in a period of *rising* interest rates, the times-prime method causes the customer's loan rate to rise faster than the prime-plus method. If interest rates *fall,* the customer's loan rate declines more rapidly under the times-prime method. For example, if the prime rate rises from 10 percent to 15 percent, the above customer's loan rate increases from 12 percent to 17 percent with the prime-plus method and from 12 percent to 18 percent with the times-prime method. However, if prime drops from 10 percent to 8 percent, the prime-plus method yields a 10 percent loan rate, while the times-prime approach yields only 9.6 percent.

During the 1970s, the supremacy of the prime rate as a base for business loans was challenged by **LIBOR**—the London Interbank Offered Rate—on short-term Eurodollar deposits, which range in maturity from a few days to a few months. As time passed, more and more leading banks have switched to LIBOR-based loan pricing due

---

[3]Charging high-risk borrowers the full risk premium that their perceived risk to the bank seems to warrant is not always wise. Indeed, such a policy may increase the chances that a borrower will default on a loan agreement, resulting in the bank's earning a return on such a loan that is even less than earned on prime-quality loans. For example, if an A-rated borrower is charged a prime interest rate of 6 percent and a high-risk borrower is assessed a loan rate of 12 percent, the second borrower may feel compelled to adopt high-risk business strategies with small chance of success in an attempt to meet such high required loan payments. These high-risk business strategies may lead to default, sharply lowering the bank's actual return. This is why most banks use *both* price (loan rate) and credit rationing (i.e., denying some loans regardless of the price) to regulate the size and composition of their loan portfolios.

to the growing use of Eurodollars as a source of loanable funds. A second cause was the spreading internationalization of the banking system, with foreign banks entering many domestic loan markets, including Canada and the United States. LIBOR offered a common pricing standard for all banks, both foreign and domestic, and gave customers a common basis for comparing the terms on loans offered by different banks.

As an example of LIBOR-based pricing we note that late in 1997 prevailing interest rates on Eurodollar deposits in London fluctuated in a range of about 5.5 to 6 percent (annual rate). For example, on Tuesday, December 16, 1997, 16 major banks in London were quoting the following average annualized London Interbank Offered Rates:

Maturity Class	LIBOR
One month	5.96%
Three months	5.91
Six months	5.91
One year	6.00

Therefore, a large corporation borrowing short-term money for, say, 90 days from a domestic or foreign bank might be quoted an interest rate on a multimillion dollar loan of:

$$\begin{aligned} \text{LIBOR-based loan rate} &= \text{LIBOR} + \text{Default-risk premium} \\ &\quad + \text{Profit margin} \\[4pt] &= 5.91\% + 0.125\% + 0.125\% = 6.16\% \end{aligned}$$

For longer-term loans stretching over several months or years the banker might add a term-risk premium to the above formula to compensate the bank for the added risk of a longer-term commitment to its business customer. For example, a one-year loan based on a one-year LIBOR rate of 6.00% would be:

$$\begin{aligned} \text{LIBOR-based loan rate} &= \text{LIBOR} + \text{Default-risk premium} \\ &\quad + \text{Term-risk premium} + \text{Profit margin} \\[4pt] 6.00\% &+ 0.125\% + 0.25\% + 0.125\% = 6.50\% \end{aligned}$$

Below-Prime Market Pricing (The Markup Model)

Further modifications to the prime or LIBOR-based loan pricing systems were made in the 1980s and 1990s. One change was the appearance of **below-prime pricing** as major banks endeavored to compete more aggressively with the growing commercial paper market—an open and unregulated market for large corporate short-term securities—and with aggressive foreign banks that loaned money at interest rates close to their fund-raising costs. In the United States, for example, many banks announced that some large corporate loans covering only a few days or weeks would be made at low money market interest rates (such as the Federal funds rate used on domestic interbank loans of reserves) plus a small margin (perhaps

Bank Management in Action

Loan Rates Charged Business Borrowers—What Recent Federal Reserve Surveys Tell Us

The Federal Reserve System in the United States collects information on business loans extended to customers by 348 domestically chartered U.S. commercial banks and 50 U.S. branches and agencies of foreign banks during the mid-month of each quarter of the year. The Fed's recent loan surveys suggest that most business loans granted by the surveyed banks tend to be (or have):

1. Short-term loans (under one year) rather than long-term loans to the business sector by a wide margin.
2. The more numerous short-term loans to businesses average about 40 days to maturity, while long-term (over-one-year) bank business loans approach an average of just over 50 months (i.e., about 4 1/2 years) to maturity.
3. Fixed interest rates when granted for shorter maturities and floating interest rates for longer-maturity business loans due to the increased interest rate risk associated with longer-term credit.
4. Base loan rates tied most often to the Federal funds interest rate, foreign money market rates (such as LIBOR), the prime rate, or to other base rate negotiated between the lender and the business borrower.
5. Higher loan rates when loan maturity is longer (particularly over one year) in order to compensate the lender for added term risk associated with a longer-term loan.
6. Higher loan rates on smaller denomination business loans (especially for business credits under $1 million in size).
7. Secured by collateral more often if the loans carry longer maturities (especially longer than one year) or have smaller denominations (particularly if under $1 million and, for the biggest loans, if under $10 million).
8. Subject to a prepayment penalty should the borrower attempt to pay off the loan early if the loan is either short-term (under one year) or larger in size (particularly over $1 million in denomination).

Recent research cited by Samolyk [8] suggests that older firms, the longer the borrower–lender relationship, and the purchase of additional services from the same lender tend either to result in a lower loan rate or tend to reduce the chances of a loan denial. Also there is at least some evidence that audited firms pay somewhat lower loan rates than unaudited firms and business borrowers that successfully complete loan transactions ultimately get lower loan rates on subsequent borrowings and usually get monitored less frequently (as noted, for example, by Blackwell and Winters [9]).

For a more detailed analysis of the Federal Reserve's quarterly business loan survey please contact the Board of Governors of the Federal Reserve System, Washington, D.C., 20551-0001, concerning their Statistical Release E.2.

one-eighth to one-quarter of a percentage point) to cover risk exposure, other operating costs, and the profit margin. That is:

$$\begin{matrix}\text{Loan interest} \\ \text{rate}\end{matrix} = \begin{matrix}\text{Interest cost of} \\ \text{borrowing in the} \\ \text{money market}\end{matrix} + \begin{matrix}\text{Markup for risk} \\ \text{and profit}\end{matrix}$$

Thus, if we can borrow Federal funds in today's market for 5.50 percent and a top-quality business customer requests a 30-day $10 million credit line, we may choose to make the loan at 5.75 percent (or 5.50 percent to cover the money market cost of borrowing + 0.25 percent markup for risk, noninterest costs, and profitability).

The result is a short-term loan rate one or more percentage points *below* the posted prime rate, diminishing the importance of the prime rate as a reference point for business loans. Indeed, a survey by Brady [2] at the Federal Reserve Board indicated that approximately 90 percent of the business loan portfolios (including overnight loans) at 48 of the largest U.S. banks were made at interest rates *below* prime. Brady also found that million-dollar-plus loans with maturities of less than a month normally employ Federal funds interest rates as the proxy for estimated funding costs, with this rate calculated as an average of interest rates prevailing each day of the survey week, weighted according to the dollar volume of Federal funds loans occurring at each rate. Longer-term (out to one year) fixed-rate loans generally base their funding cost on the three-month CD rate, measured once a day.

Not surprisingly, as the prime rate became less important and market interest rates became more volatile, many major banks dropped the use of formulas linking prime to open-market interest rates. However, the prime rate continues to be important as a pricing method for smaller business loans, consumer credit, construction loans, and some Eurocurrency credits. Thus, a two-tiered business loan market has emerged. Loans to small and medium-size businesses are usually based on prime or some other base rate (such as LIBOR), while large-denomination business loans increasingly are based on money market interest costs at the time the loan is made. The narrow margins (markups) on such loans have spurred wider use of loan participations, with larger banks more actively sharing their biggest loans with smaller banks, generating fee income and moving at least a portion of these credits to banks with lower funding costs.

Loans Bearing Maximum Interest Rates (Caps)

Another recent variation on the old price leadership model has been the use of **cap rates**—an agreed-upon upper limit on the loan contract rate, regardless of the future course of market interest rates. Thus, a borrowing customer such as Black Gold, Inc., discussed in the previous chapter, might be offered a prime-plus-2 floating-rate loan with a cap of five percentage points above the initial loan rate. This means that if the loan were made when prime was 10 percent, the initial loan rate would be 10 percent + 2 percent, or 12 percent. But the rate could rise no higher than 17 percent (12 percent + 5 percent) regardless of how high market rates climbed during the life of the loan agreement.

Caps are simply another service option that a bank may offer its customers for a specific fee. Loan-rate caps grant the borrowing customer some reassurance about the maximum credit cost he or she could be facing, because any interest paid in excess of the cap rate will be refunded to the borrower, usually once a year or when the loan matures. However, bankers must be cautious in attaching cap rates to their loans; a prolonged period of high interest rates will effectively transfer the risk of fluctuating interest rates from borrower to lender.

Cost-Benefit Loan Pricing

While most loans are quoted to customers on the basis of prime, LIBOR, or some other money market base rate, many bankers have developed sophisticated loan-pricing systems that indicate whether the bank is charging enough for a loan to fully compensate it for all the costs and risks involved. One such system is called **cost-benefit loan pricing,** which consists of three simple steps: (1) estimate the total *revenue* the loan will generate under a variety of loan interest rates and other fees, (2) estimate the *net amount of loanable funds* the bank must turn over to the borrower (after deducting any deposits the borrower has pledged to hold at the bank and adding the Federal Reserve's deposit reserve requirements), and (3) estimate the *before-tax yield* from the loan by dividing the estimated loan revenue by the net amount of loanable funds the borrower will actually use.

For example, suppose a customer requests a $5 million line of credit, as in the Black Gold case discussed in Chapter 17, but actually uses only $4 million at a contract loan rate of 20 percent. The customer is asked to pay a commitment fee of 1 percent of the unused portion of the credit line. Moreover, the bank insists that the customer maintain a deposit (compensating balance) equal to 20 percent of the amount of the credit line actually used and 5 percent of any unused portion of the line. Deposit reserve requirements imposed by the central bank are assumed to be 10 percent. From this information, we have the following:

$$\underset{\substack{(Used\ portion \\ of\ credit\ line)}}{} \qquad \underset{\substack{(Unused\ portion \\ of\ credit\ line)}}{}$$

Estimated
loan revenue $= \$4,000,000 \times 0.10 + \$1,000,000 \times 0.01 = \$810,000$

Estimated
bank funds
drawn
upon by the
borrower $= \$4,000,000 - \overset{(Compensating\ balance\ requirement)}{(\$4,000,000 \times 0.20 + \$1,000,000 \times 0.05)}$

$$\overset{(Deposit\ reserve\ requirement)}{+ 0.10\,(\$4,000,000 \times 0.20 + \$1,000,000 \times 0.05)}$$
$$= \$3,235,000$$

Estimated before-
tax yield to
the bank from
the loan $= \$810,000 \div \$3,235,000 = 25.0\ \text{percent}$

The bank's management must decide if this 25 percent before-tax yield is adequate to cover the bank's cost of funds, the risks inherent in the customer's loan request, and the bank's desired profit margin once all costs (including taxes) are considered.

Customer Profitability Analysis

The cost-benefit loan pricing approach is really a narrow version of a much broader concept known as **customer profitability analysis** (CPA). This loan-pricing method begins with the assumption that the bank should take the *whole customer relationship into account when pricing each loan request.* CPA focuses on the rate of return from the entire customer relationship, calculated from the following formula:

$$\begin{matrix} \text{Net before-tax rate} \\ \text{of return to the} \\ \text{bank from the whole} \\ \text{customer relationship} \end{matrix} = \frac{\begin{matrix}\text{Revenue from} \\ \text{loans and other} \\ \text{services provided} \\ \text{to this customer}\end{matrix} - \begin{matrix}\text{Expenses from} \\ \text{providing loans} \\ \text{and other services} \\ \text{to this customer}\end{matrix}}{\begin{matrix}\text{Net loanable funds used in excess of this} \\ \text{customer's deposits}\end{matrix}}$$

Revenues paid in to the bank by a customer may include loan interest, commitment fees, fees for cash management services, and data processing charges. *Expenses* incurred on behalf of the customer may include wages and salaries of bank employees, credit investigation costs, interest accrued on deposits, account reconciliation and processing costs (including checks paid, loan and deposit recordkeeping and collection, and lockbox services), as well as loanable funds' acquisition costs. *Net loanable funds* are the amount of credit used by the customer minus his or her average collected deposits (adjusted for required reserves).

In effect, then, the amount of bank funds each customer uses over and above those funds he or she supplies to the bank is evaluated. If the calculated net rate of return from the entire relationship with the customer is *positive,* the loan request will probably be approved, because the bank will be earning a premium over *all* expenses incurred (including a competitive rate of return to the bank's shareholders). If the calculated net return is *negative,* the loan request may be denied or the bank may seek to raise the loan rate or increase the prices of other services requested by the customer in order to continue the relationship on a profitable basis. Customers who are perceived to be more risky are expected to return to the bank a higher calculated net rate of return. An example of customer profitability analysis (CPA) applied to the loan request of Black Gold, Inc., considered in the previous chapter, can be illustrated below:

An Example of Annualized Customer Profitability Analysis

Problem: The bank is considering granting a $3 million line of credit for nine months to Black Gold, Inc. Assuming Black Gold uses the full line and keeps a 20 percent compensating deposit with the bank, the following bank revenues and expenses should result from dealing with this customer:

Sources of Revenue Expected to Be Supplied by This Customer

Interest income from loan (12%, nine months)	$270,000
Loan commitment fees (1%)	30,000
Fee for managing customer's deposits	6,000
Funds transfer charges	2,000
Fees for trust services and recordkeeping	13,000
Total annualized revenues expected	$321,000

Costs Expected to Be Incurred in Serving This Customer

Deposit interest owed to the customer (10%)	$ 45,000
Cost of funds raised to lend this customer	160,000
Activity costs for this customer's accounts	25,000
Cost of funds transfers for this customer	1,000
Cost of processing the loan	3,000
Recordkeeping costs	1,000
Total annualized expenses	$235,000

Net Amount of the Bank's Reserves Expected to be Drawn
upon by This Customer This Year

Average amount of credit committed to customer	$3,000,000
Less: Average customer deposit balances (net of required reserves)	−540,000
Net amount of loanable reserves committed to customer	$2,460,000

$$\begin{array}{c}\text{Annual before-tax rate}\\ \text{of return over costs}\\ \text{from the entire}\\ \text{bank customer relationship}\end{array} = \frac{\text{Revenue expected} - \text{Cost expected}}{\text{Net amount of loanable funds supplied}}$$

$$= \frac{(\$321,000 - 235,000)}{\$2,460,000} = 0.035, \text{ or } 3.5\%$$

Interpretation: If the net rate of return from the entire bank–customer relationship is *positive,* the proposed loan is *acceptable* because all expenses have been met. If the calculated net rate of return is negative, however, the proposed loan and other services provided to the customer are *not* correctly priced as far as the bank is concerned. The greater the perceived *risk* of the loan request, the higher the net rate of return the bank should require.

Earnings Credit for Customer Deposits.   In calculating how much in revenues a customer generates for the bank, many banks give the customer credit for any earnings the bank has received from investing the balance in the customer's deposit account in earning assets. Of course, it would be unwise to include the full amount of the customer's deposit in calculating any earnings from investing deposit money because the bank has to post reserve requirements, and a substantial portion of the customer's deposit balance may consist of *float* arising from checks written by the customer against his or her account but not yet charged against the account. Most banks calculate the actual amount of *net investable funds* provided by a customer's deposit and the earnings credit for a customer using some version of the following formulas:

Net investable (usable) funds for the bank	=	Customer's average deposit balance	−	Average amount of float in the account	−	Required legal reserves behind the deposit	×	Net amount of collected funds in the account

$$\begin{array}{c}\text{Amount of}\\ \text{earnings credited}\\ \text{to the customer}\end{array} = \begin{array}{c}\text{Annual}\\ \text{earnings}\\ \text{rate}\end{array} \times \begin{array}{c}\text{Fraction of the year}\\ \text{funds are available}\\ \text{from the deposit}\end{array} \times \begin{array}{c}\text{Net investable}\\ \text{(usable) funds}\end{array}$$

For example, suppose a commercial customer posts an average deposit balance this month of $1,125,000. Float from uncollected checks accounts for $125,000 of this balance, yielding net collected funds of $1 million. If this is a checking account at a large bank, the applicable legal reserve requirement will be 10 percent. After negotiation with the customer, the bank has decided to give this customer credit for an annual interest return from use of the customer's deposit equal to the average 91-day Treasury bill rate, which is currently 6.60 percent. In this instance, the customer's net usable (investable) funds and earnings credit will be:

$$\begin{array}{c}\text{Net investable}\\ \text{(usable) funds}\\ \text{for the bank}\end{array} = \$1,125,000 - \$125,000 - \frac{10}{100} \times \$1,000,000 = \$900,000$$

$$\begin{array}{c}\text{Amount of earnings}\\ \text{credit to this customer}\end{array} = 6.60 \text{ percent} \times \frac{1}{12} \times \$900,000 = \$4,950$$

Therefore, in constructing a summary of revenues and expenses from all the bank's dealings with this customer, the bank would give the customer credit on the revenue side for $4,950 that the bank earned last month from investing the customer's deposits in earning assets.

The Future of Customer Profitability Analysis. Customer profitability analysis has become increasingly sophisticated and more encompassing in recent years. Detailed accounting statements showing sources of revenue and expenses from servicing each major customer have been developed. Often the borrowing company itself, its subsidiary firms, major stockholders, and top management are all consolidated into one profitability analysis statement so that the bank's management receives a comprehensive picture of the *total* bank–customer relationship. The consolidation approach can determine if losses suffered from servicing one account are, in fact, made up by another account that is part of the same overall customer relationship. Automated CPA systems permit lenders to plug in alternative loan and deposit pricing schedules to see which pricing schedule works best for both the customer and the bank. As Robert Knight [4] observes, CPA can also be used to identify the most profitable types of customers and loans and the most successful loan officers.

Concept Checks

18–1. What methods are in use today to price business loans?

18–2. Suppose a bank estimates that the marginal cost of raising loanable funds to make a $10 million loan to one of its corporate customers is 4 percent, its nonfunds operating costs to evaluate and offer this loan are 0.5 percent, the default-risk premium on the loan is 0.375 percent, a term-risk premium of 0.625 percent is to be added, and the bank's desired profit margin is 0.25 percent. What loan rate should be quoted this borrower? How much interest will the borrower pay in a year?

18–3. What are the principal strengths and weaknesses of the different loan-pricing methods in use today?

18–4. What is *customer profitability analysis*?

Bank Management in Action

Lease Financing as an Alternative to Lending by Banks

An alternative form of extending credit to a customer is to provide *lease financing,* with the bank serving as the lessor of an asset (such as business equipment) and the customer as lessee, obligated to make periodic lease payments. Indeed, for many businesses leased assets and lease payments substantially exceed borrowings and interest payments.

Under a lease financing arrangement title to the leased asset remains with the bank or other lessor; however, the customer lessee has physical control of the leased asset and is often responsible for its maintenance and repairs. Just as with ordinary loans, a number of risks confront banks that provide leases to their customers. For example, the bank's credit officer must ask himself or herself whether the lessee will be willing and able to conform to all the terms of the lease and also maintain the asset being leased in good condition for possible future sale when the lease term ends. Also, can the lease payments and other terms of the agreement be properly structured to fit with the customer's expected income or cash flow and still result in a competitive rate of return to the bank? Moreover, can the leased asset be recovered at minimal cost in the event the lessee defaults on the terms of the lease contract?

Leases present a number of problems for banks that are somewhat different from straight loans. For example, tax benefits (such as the tax deductibility of lease payments and the tax-deductible depreciation of leased equipment) are more uncertain under a lease agreement, which often covers a longer term than an ordinary loan. Moreover, the resale value of the asset at the end of the lease term (clearly, a portion of the expected cash flows associated with many lease agreements) can be exceedingly difficult to forecast due to the length of time involved, the possibility of disposal expenses, and the danger of obsolescence (e.g., of computer equipment) when the leased asset must finally be disposed of. These problem areas make it more difficult for a banker to estimate the correct discount rate (yield to maturity) that equalizes the stream of lease payments the bank expects to receive to the net cost (i.e., purchase price less residual or salvage value) of the leased asset. It is essential that the bank's discount rate or expected yield to maturity from the

Summary

This chapter has focused upon the different methods used by bankers to price business loans. Among the different pricing methods reviewed were cost-plus loan pricing, price leadership pricing, markup-market pricing, cap loan rates, cost-benefit pricing, and customer profitability analysis. We observed that many large corporate loans today are priced off current money market interest rates with narrow profit margins, reflecting intense competition among banks for the best and largest corporate customers. The chapter stressed the importance of setting loan prices that are competitive with other lenders but fully cover the bank's cost of raising loanable funds. Also emphasized was the trend toward pricing business loans based on the *total* relationship between a bank and its customer, taking into account all the fees the customer pays for various services and all the costs of providing those banking services the customer elects to use. Thus, bankers today are learning to package

lease transaction must be set high enough to cover the cost of funding the asset's purchase, the bank's risk exposure from the lease transaction, and still leave a competitive margin for profit.

In order to make leasing a profitable alternative to straight lending bankers must be able to do several things well:

1. Purchase leased assets at the lowest possible price from the manufacturer or dealer.

2. Have sufficient knowledge of tax laws and regulations to be able to obtain the maximum available tax benefits for the bank from each lease transaction and be able to understand the leasing customer's tax situation well.

3. Raise funds to carry out a purchase and lease transaction at the lowest possible bank debt and equity capital cost.

4. Accurately assess the degree of default risk exposure each leasing customer presents to the bank so that the rate (yield to maturity) used to discount all future lease payments is large enough to fully compensate the bank for the risk of nonpayment and the risk associated with disposal of the leased asset (in most cases the appropriate lease discount rate must be at least equal to the customer's current cost of obtaining funds in the credit markets, such as from a bank loan or from issuing bonds).

5. Possess the knowledge and market contacts to be able to sell or dispose of leased assets at the highest possible salvage value (or lowest possible disposal expense) when the lease agreement ends (including offering the lessee a discounted purchase price at the end of the lease term, which will free the bank from the cost of asset disposal).

Clearly, lease financing services present several challenges for bankers that conventional loans do not, requiring bank lenders to have adequate technical knowledge of both areas and be able to know which—loan or lease—to recommend to a valued customer. For most bank credit customers the key factors to weigh center upon the need for tax benefits, the length of time (term) for which an asset is needed, and the comparative net cost of leasing versus borrowing.

their service offerings into bundles of services unique to each customer and to view the profitability of their *total* relationship with a business borrower, not just the expected earnings on the loan currently being requested.

Key Terms in This Chapter

Cost-plus loan pricing
Price leadership
Prime rate
LIBOR

Below-prime pricing
Cap rates
Cost-benefit loan pricing
Customer profitability analysis

Problems and Projects

1. As a loan officer for Enterprise National Bank, you have been responsible for the bank's relationship with USF Corporation, a major producer of remote-control devices for activating television sets, VCRs, and other audio-video equipment. USF has just filed a request for renewal of its $10 million line of credit, which will cover approximately 10 1/2 months. USF also regularly uses several other services sold by the bank. Using the most recent year as a guide, you estimate that the expected revenues from this commercial loan customer and the expected costs to the bank of serving this customer will consist of the following:

Expected Revenues		*Expected Costs*	
Annual interest income from the requested loan (assuming a loan rate of prime + 1 percent, or 11% this month)	$1,100,000	Interest paid on customer deposits (9%)	$ 25,000
		Cost of funds raised	975,000
Loan commitment fee (1%)	100,000	Account activity costs	19,000
Deposit management fees	4,500	Wire transfer costs	1,300
Wire transfer fees	3,500	Loan processing costs	12,400
Fees for agency services	8,800	Recordkeeping costs	4,500

The bank's credit analysts have estimated the customer will keep an average deposit balance of $2,125,000 for the year in which the line is active. What is the expected net rate of return from this proposed loan renewal if the customer actually draws down the full amount of the requested line? What decision should the bank make under the foregoing assumptions? If you decide to turn down this request, under what assumptions regarding revenues, expenses, and customer-maintained deposit balances would you be willing to make this loan?

Alternative scenarios:

(1) How would your evaluation of this customer relationship change if the prime rate dropped from 10 percent to 8 percent and the interest costs to the bank did not fall?

(2) Would you come to a different conclusion regarding this loan request if the customer insisted on opening a time deposit account bearing a 9.25 percent interest rate (instead of 9 percent) and the cost of other funds raised to make this loan rose from $975,000 to $1,065,000, while the prime rate fell to 9.50 percent? Why or why not?

(3) At what prime rate does the bank merely break even on this customer relationship, assuming all other revenues and costs remain unchanged?

(4) At what interest cost level does the bank break even on this customer relationship, assuming the prime rate and all other revenues and costs are held constant?

2. In order to help fund a loan request of $10 million for one year from one of its best customers, Chilton Westover Bank sold negotiable CDs to its business customers in the amount of $6 million at a promised annual yield of 8.75 percent and borrowed $4 million in the Federal funds market from other banks at today's prevailing interest rate of 8.40 percent. Credit investigation and recordkeeping costs to process this loan application were an estimated $25,000. The Credit Analysis Division recommends a minimal 1 percent risk premium on this loan and a minimal profit margin of one-fourth of a percentage point. The bank prefers using cost-plus loan pricing in these cases. What loan rate should it charge?

Alternative scenarios:

(1) Suppose Chilton Westover is able to raise the entire amount needed to make the $10 million loan in the Federal funds market at 8.40 percent. What loan rate should be charged on a cost-plus basis? What risk does the bank face if it funds the whole loan in the Federal funds market?

(2) If the noninterest costs involved in making this loan rise unexpectedly to $38,000 and the customer insists on a maximum 10 percent loan rate, what happens to the bank's desired profit margin?

3. Many loans to larger domestic and foreign corporations are quoted today at small risk premiums and profit margins over the London Interbank Offered Rate (LIBOR) on short-term Eurodollar deposits. Englewood Bank has a $15 million loan request for working capital to fund accounts receivable and inventory from one of its largest corporate customers, APEX Exports. The bank offers its customer a floating-rate loan for 90 days with an interest rate equal to LIBOR on 30-day Eurodeposits (currently trading at a rate of 9.25) plus a one-quarter percentage point markup over LIBOR. APEX, however, wants the loan at a rate of 1.014 times LIBOR. If the bank agrees to this loan rate request, what interest rate will attach to the loan if it is made today? How does this compare with the loan rate the bank wanted to charge? What does this customer's request reveal about the borrowing firm's interest rate forecast for the next 90 days?

Alternative scenario:

Suppose the bank makes a counterproposal to APEX as follows: it will lend the money at LIBOR plus one-eighth of a percentage point in return for the customer keeping a minimal noninterest-bearing checking deposit of $250,000 at the bank during the loan's term. Is the customer likely to agree to this request? Please explain.

4. Five weeks ago, RJK Corporation borrowed from the bank that employs you as a loan officer. At that time, the decision was made (at your personal urging) to base the loan rate on the markup pricing model, using the average weekly Federal funds interest rate as the bank's money market borrowing cost. The loan was quoted to RJK at the Federal funds rate plus a three-eighths percentage point markup for risk and profit.

Today, this five-week loan is due, and RJK is asking for renewal of the loan at money market borrowing cost plus one-fourth of a percentage point. You must assess whether the bank did as well on this account using the Federal funds rate as the index of borrowing cost as it would have done by quoting RJK a markup over the CD rate, the commercial paper rate, the Eurodollar deposit rate, or possibly the prevailing rate on U.S. Treasury bills. To assess what would have happened (and might happen over the next five weeks if the loan is renewed at a markup over any of the money market rates listed above), you have assembled these data from a recent issue of the *Federal Reserve Bulletin*:

Money Market Interest Rates	Week 1	Week 2	Week 3	Week 4	Week 5
Federal funds	8.72%	8.80%	8.69%	8.46%	8.46%
Commercial paper (one-month maturity)	8.55	8.63	8.53	8.43	8.40
CDs (one-month maturity)	8.54	8.58	8.50	8.40	8.35
Eurodollar deposits (three-month maturity)	8.58	8.56	8.60	8.43	8.38
U.S. Treasury bills (three-month, secondary market)	7.60	7.77	7.74	7.67	7.60

Weekly Averages of Money Market Rates over the Most Recent 5 Weeks

What conclusion do you draw from studying the behavior of these common money market base rates for business loans? Should the RJK loan be renewed as requested, or should the bank press for a different loan pricing agreement? Please explain your reasoning. If you conclude that a change is needed, how would you explain the necessity for this change to the bank's customer?

Alternative scenario:

Suppose the bank decided to protect itself against further declines in money market interest rates by inserting a floor loan rate of 8 percent in the RJK loan contract. RJK agrees to this proposal, provided the bank is willing to make the loan at a markup for risk and profit of only 0.125 percent. What risks do you see here for the bank under this proposal? Would you recommend a change of base money market interest rate to which the markup should apply? Please explain.

5. RCB Corporation has posted an average total deposit balance this past month of $270,500. Float included in this one-month average balance has been estimated at $73,250. Required legal reserves are 3 percent of net collected funds. What is the amount of net investable (usable) funds available to the bank?

Suppose RCB's bank agrees to give RCB credit for an annual interest return of 5.75 percent on the net investable funds provided to the bank by the company. Measured in total dollars, how much of an earnings credit from the bank will RCB earn?

Selected References

See the following for good discussions of bank loan pricing techniques

1. Avery, Robert B., and Allen N. Berger. "Loan Commitments and Bank Risk Exposure." *Journal of Banking and Finance* 15 (1991), pp. 173–79.
2. Brady, Thomas F. "Changes in Loan Pricing and Business Lending at Commercial Banks." *Federal Reserve Bulletin,* January 1985, pp. 1–13.
3. Copeland, Timothy S. "Aspects to Consider in Developing a Loan-Pricing Microcomputer Model." *The Magazine of Bank Administration,* August 1983, pp. 32–34.
4. Knight, Robert E. "Customer Profitability Analysis—Part 1: Alternative Approaches Toward Customer Profitability." *Monthly Review,* Federal Reserve Bank of Kansas City, April 1975, pp. 11–20.
5. Rose, Peter S. "Loan Pricing in a Volatile Economy." *The Canadian Banker* 92, no. 5 (October 1985), pp. 44–49.
6. McElroy, John M. "Issues in Lending—How to Document Equipment Lease Financings." *The Journal of Lending and Credit Risk Management,* October 1996, pp. 50–56.
7. Van Horne, James C. *Financial Management and Policy,* 10th ed. Englewood Cliffs, NJ: Prentice-Hall, 1995.
8. Samolyk, H. "Small Business Credit Markets: Why Do We Know So Little About Them?" *FDIC Banking Review* X, no. 2 (1997), pp. 14–32.
9. Blackwell, David W., and Drew B. Winters. "Banking Relationships and the Effect of Monitoring on Loan Pricing." *The Journal of Financial Research* XX, no. 2 (Summer 1997), pp. 275–289.

19   CONSUMER AND REAL ESTATE LENDING

Learning and Management Decision Objectives

To learn about the many types of loans banks make to consumers (individuals and families) and to real estate borrowers and to understand the factors that influence the profitability and risk of consumer and real estate loans.

Introduction

In the period since World War II, banks have grown to be *the* dominant lenders in the consumer field. In part, the dominant position of banks stems from their growing reliance on individuals and families as a key source of bank funds (deposits). Many households would be hesitant to deposit their funds with a bank if they did not feel there was a good prospect of being able to borrow from that same bank when a loan was needed.

Then, too, recent research suggests that consumer credit is often among the most profitable loans a bank can make. Indeed, one of the best-known banks in the world, Citicorp of New York, has been directing a growing share of its resources toward consumer banking (especially the marketing of credit cards, residential real estate loans, and electronic consumer-service facilities) via its thousands of branch offices worldwide. However, banking services directed at consumers can also be among the most costly and risky products that a bank sells because the financial situations of individuals and families can change quickly due to illness or loss of employment. Consumer loans must therefore be managed with care and with sensitivity to the special problems they present.

Types of Loans Granted to Individuals and Families

There are several different types of consumer loans, and the number of credit plans to accommodate consumers' financial needs is growing in the wake of deregulation of depository institutions in the United States and in many other industrialized countries as well. We can classify consumer loans by *purpose*—what the borrowed funds will be used for—or by *type of loan*—for example, whether the borrower must repay in installments or repay in one lump sum when the loan comes due. One popular classification scheme for consumer loans combines *both* loan types and loan purposes.

For example, loans to individuals and families may be divided into two groups, depending upon whether they finance the purchase of new homes with *a residential mortgage loan* or whether they finance other, nonhousing consumer activities (vacations, purchases of automobiles, etc.) through *nonresidential loans.* Second, within the nonresidential category, consumer loans are often divided into two subcategories based on type of loan—*installment* versus *noninstallment* loans. We will look at the nature of these consumer loan types more closely in the paragraphs that follow.

Residential Mortgage Loans

Credit to finance the purchase of a home or to fund improvements on a private residence comes under the general label of **residential mortgage loans.** The purchase of residential property in the form of houses and multifamily dwellings (including duplexes, triplexes, and apartment buildings) usually gives rise to a long-term loan—usually bearing a term of 15 to 30 years—and is secured by the property itself. Such loans may carry either a fixed interest rate or, more commonly in recent years, a variable, or floating, interest rate that changes periodically with a specified base rate (such as the market yield on U.S. government bonds) or a national mortgage interest rate (for example, the Federal Home Loan Bank Board's average home mortgage yield). A commitment fee (typically 1 to 2 percent of the face amount of the loan) is routinely charged up front to assure the borrower that a residential loan will be available for a stipulated period. While banks themselves make a significant portion of home mortgage loans, increasingly in recent years such loans have been made through the mortgage banking subsidiary of a bank holding company.

Nonresidential Loans

In contrast to residential mortgage loans, nonresidential (or nonmortgage) loans to individuals and families include installment loans and noninstallment (or single-payment) loans.

Installment Loans.   Short-term to medium-term loans, repayable in two or more consecutive payments (usually monthly or quarterly), are known as **installment loans.** Such loans are frequently employed to buy big-ticket household items (e.g., automobiles, boats, recreational vehicles, furniture, and home appliances) or to consolidate existing household debts. While the installment loan normally carries a fixed interest rate, floating loan rates are becoming more common. Nevertheless, only about one-fourth of all consumer nonmortgage loans have variable interest rates today.

Many banks in recent years have handled a significant portion of their consumer installment loans through finance company subsidiaries that are part of a bank holding company. This is advantageous because there are no geographic restrictions on setting up finance company offices, whereas bank branching activity may be hampered by law or regulation. Moreover, finance companies can accept riskier loans with higher expected yields than banks are often allowed to make.

Noninstallment Loans.   Short-term loans drawn upon by individuals and families for immediate cash needs and repayable in a lump sum when the borrower's note matures are known as *noninstallment loans*. Such loans may be for relatively small amounts—for example, $500 or $1,000—and include charge accounts that often require payment in 30 days or some other relatively short time period. Noninstallment loans are made for a short period (usually six months or less) to wealthier individuals and may be quite large—often ranging from $5,000 to $10,000. Noninstallment loans are frequently used to cover the costs of vacations, medical and hospital care, the purchase of home appliances, and auto and home repairs.

Credit Card Loans

One popular form of consumer credit today is accessed via credit cards issued by Visa, MasterCard, and several smaller bank and nonbank credit card companies. Credit cards offer their holders access to *either* installment or noninstallment credit because the customer can charge a purchase on the account represented by the card and pay off the charge in one billing period, often escaping any finance charge, or choose to pay off the purchase price gradually, incurring a monthly finance charge that is based on an annual rate usually ranging from 12 percent to about 18 percent. Bank card companies find that *installment users* of credit cards are far more profitable due to the interest income they generate for the bank than are noninstallment users, who quickly pay off their card charges before interest can be assessed. Banks also earn discount fees (usually 1 to 6 percent of credit card sales) from the merchants who accept their cards. So rapid has been the acceptance of bank-issued and other charge cards that more than one trillion are estimated to be in use today around the globe.

Bank credit cards offer *convenience* and a *revolving line of credit* that the customer can assess whenever the need arises. Bankers have found, however, that careful management and control of their credit card programs is vital due to the growing proportion of delinquent borrowers and the large number of cards that have been stolen and used fraudulently. There is evidence that significant economies of scale pervade the credit card field for, in general, only the largest bank card operations are consistently profitable. Nevertheless, the future of the credit card appears bright because of advancing technology that will eventually give most cardholders access to a full range of financial services, including savings and payment accounts and revolving credit lines.

Characteristics of Consumer Loans

By and large, consumer loans are regarded by bankers as profitable credits with "sticky" interest rates. That is, they are typically priced well above the cost of funding them, but their contract interest rates usually don't change with market conditions during the life of the loan as do interest rates on most business loans today. This means that consumer loans are exposed to interest rate risk if the bank's funding cost rises high enough. However, consumer loans are usually priced so high (i.e., with a sufficiently large risk premium built into the loan rate) that market interest rates on bank borrowings and default rates on the loans themselves would have to rise substantially before most consumer credits would become unprofitable.

Why are interest rates so high on most consumer loans? One key reason is revealed by the Functional Cost Analysis (FCA) program conducted annually by the Federal Reserve banks. This cost accounting system suggests that consumer loans are among the most costly and most risky to make per dollar of loanable funds of any of the loans that banks grant to their customers. Consumer loans also tend to be *cyclically sensitive*. They rise in periods of economic expansion when consumers are generally more optimistic about the future. On the other hand, when the economy turns down into a recession, many individuals and families become more pessimistic about the future, particularly when they see growing unemployment, and reduce their bank borrowings accordingly.

Moreover, consumers seem to be relatively unresponsive to changes in interest rates when they go out to borrow money. Household borrowings appear to be relatively *interest inelastic*—consumers are more concerned about the size of monthly payments required by a loan agreement than the interest rate charged (though, obviously, the contract interest rate on a loan influences the size of required loan payments). While the level of the interest rate is often not a significant conscious factor among household borrowers, both education and income levels *do* materially influence consumers' use of credit. Individuals with higher incomes tend to borrow more in total and relative to the size of their annual incomes. Those households in which the head of the household or the principal breadwinner has more years of formal education also tend to borrow more heavily relative to their level of income. For these individuals and families, borrowing is viewed more as a *tool* to achieve a desired standard of living rather than as a safety net to be used only in serious emergencies.

Concept Checks

19–1. What are the principal differences among residential loans, nonresidential installment loans, noninstallment loans, and credit card loans?

19–2. Why do interest rates on consumer loans typically average higher than on most other kinds of bank loans?

Evaluating a Consumer Loan Application

Character and Purpose.   The key factors in analyzing any consumer loan application are the *character* of the borrower and the borrower's *ability to pay.* The loan officer must be assured that the borrowing customer feels a keen sense of moral responsibility to repay a loan fully and on time. Moreover, the borrower's income level and valuable assets (such as holdings of securities or savings deposits) must be sufficient to reassure the loan officer that the customer has the ability to repay the loan with a comfortable margin for safety. For this reason, a consumer loan officer nearly always checks with the local or regional **credit bureau** concerning the customer's credit history. More than 2,000 credit bureaus exist across the United States; these institutions hold files on most individuals who at one time or another have borrowed money, indicating their record of repayment and credit rating.

Often the fundamental character of the borrower is revealed in the *purpose* of the loan request. The loan officer must ask: Has the customer clearly stated what he or she plans to do with the money? Is the stated purpose of the loan consistent with the bank's written loan policy? Is there evidence of a sincere intention to repay any funds borrowed? Some senior loan officers often counsel new loan officers to take the extra time to visit with each customer, because such conversations often reveal flaws in character and sincerity that have a direct bearing on the likelihood of loan repayment. Frequently, experienced loan officers fill out the loan application rather than letting the borrowing customer do it alone. By asking the customer pertinent financial questions as the application is being filled out, a skilled lender often can make a better call on whether the customer's loan request meets the bank's quality standards. The customer's spoken answers may be far more revealing about character and sincerity of purpose than anything written on a piece of paper or typed in a computer file. Unfortunately, economic pressures encouraging automation in the consumer lending process have led many banks, particularly larger institutions, to spend less time with the customer. Information gathering and loan evaluation increasingly are being turned over to computer programs. The result is that many consumer loan officers today know very little about the personality and character traits of their customers beyond the information called for on a credit application, which may be faxed or telephoned in or sent via computer to the bank.

In the case of a borrower without a credit record or with a poor track record of repaying loans, a **cosigner** may be requested to support repayment. Technically, if the borrower defaults on a cosigned loan agreement, the cosigner is obligated to make good on the loan. However, many bankers regard a cosigner mainly as a psychological device to encourage repayment of the loan, rather than as a real alternative source of security. The borrower may feel a stronger moral obligation to repay the loan knowing the cosigner's credit rating also is on the line. But bankers often hesitate to pursue a cosigner vigorously, because this can mean the loss of all the cosigner's banking business and perhaps the accounts of other sympathetic customers as well.

Income Levels.   Both the *size* and *stability* of an individual's income are considered important by consumer loan officers. They generally prefer the customer to report *net salary,* or *take-home pay,* as opposed to gross salary, and will often check with the customer's employer to verify the accuracy of customer-supplied income figures, length of employment, residence address, and social security number.

Deposit Balances.   An indirect measure of income size and stability is the *daily average deposit balance* maintained by the customer, which the loan officer normally will verify with the bank involved. In most states, a bank is granted the **right of offset** against the customer's deposit as additional protection against the risks of consumer lending. This right permits the bank to call a loan that is in default and seize any checking or savings deposits the customer may hold with the bank in order to recover its funds. However, the customer normally must be notified at least 10 days in advance before this right is exercised, which can result in the funds disappearing before the bank can recover any portion of its loan.

Employment and Residential Stability.   Among the many factors considered by experienced consumer loan officers is *duration of employment.* Most lenders are not likely to grant a sizable loan to someone who has held his or her present job for only a few months. *Length of residence* is also frequently analyzed because the longer a person stays at one address, the more stable his or her personal situation is presumed to be. Frequent changes of address are a strong negative factor in deciding whether to grant a bank loan.

Pyramiding of Debt.   Consumer loan officers are especially sensitive to evidence that debt is piling up relative to a consumer's monthly or annual income. *Pyramiding of debt*—where the individual draws credit at one lending institution to pay another—is frowned upon by most bank loan officers, as are high or growing credit card balances and frequent returned checks drawn against the customer's deposit account. These items are viewed as indicators of the customer's money management skills. Customers lacking these basic skills may be unable to avoid taking on too much debt and thereby get themselves in serious trouble with the bank.

How to Qualify for a Consumer Loan.   Are there ways to improve one's chances of getting a bank loan? One positive factor is *home ownership* or, for that matter, ownership of any form of real property, such as land or buildings. Even if such property is not posted as collateral behind a loan, it conveys the impression of stability and good money management skills. Having a telephone is also important as a sign of stability and a low-cost way for the bank's collections department to contact the borrower in case of trouble. Another positive factor is maintaining *strong deposit balances* with the bank. Not only do above-average deposit levels suggest a financially disciplined individual determined to meet his or her obligations, but also the bank can profitably use those deposits to fund other loans.

The most important thing to do, however, is to answer all the loan officer's questions truthfully. Consumer loan officers look for *inconsistencies* on a loan application as a sign the borrower is untruthful or, at best, forgetful. For example, a Social Security or personal ID number often reveals what geographic area a person comes from. Does the borrower's Social Security number match his or her personal history as indicated on the loan application? Are the borrower and his or her employer located at the addresses indicated? Is the amount reported as take-home pay or annual income the same as what the employer reports? Has the customer reported all debts outstanding, or does a credit check reveal many unreported obligations the customer has forgotten or simply walked away from?

The Challenge of Consumer Lending.   Consumer loans are not easy to evaluate. For one thing, it is often easier for individuals to conceal pertinent information bearing on the payout of a loan (such as their health or future employment prospects) than for most businesses (whose loan applications are frequently accompanied by audited financial statements). Moreover, a business firm can more easily adjust to ill health, injury, or financial setbacks than can individuals and families. Indeed, the default rate on consumer loans usually is several times higher than that for many types of commercial loans. The key features of consumer loans that help the loan officer hold down potential losses are that most are small in denomination and are often secured by marketable collateral (such as an automobile). The loan officer can experience a substantially greater number of loan defaults in the consumer credit field than in virtually any other type of lending.

Example of a Consumer Loan Application

We can illustrate some of the most important types of information a consumer loan officer gathers and what these bits of information are designed to reveal by examining the sample loan application shown in Table 19–1. This is a credit application to finance the purchase of a new automobile—one of the most common and normally one of the more profitable and secure types of loans made by a bank. The customer, J. B. Skylark, is trading in an older used car in order to purchase a new Oldsmobile sedan. The trade-in value and down payment will cover nearly 20 percent of the purchase price, and the bank is asked to cover the remainder (80 percent) of the automobile's price. The bank will take a *chattel mortgage* against the vehicle in order to gain the legal right to repossess it if the loan is defaulted. As long as car prices remain fairly stable or increase, the bank's funds should be reasonably well secured.

However, character, stability, and adequate disposable income (not heavily burdened with fixed debt obligations and taxes) are important components of any consumer loan request, and these elements raise serious questions about this particular loan request. Skylark has been at his present address for only 10 months and stayed at his previous address in another city for just one year. He has worked only eight months for his present employer. Many banks prefer to lend only to consumers who have resided or worked in their market area for at least one year, which is often considered a sign of reliability. The loan officer must decide if Skylark's residential and employment situation comes close enough to the bank's standards in this regard.

The Skylarks' annual family income is slightly above average and, for both husband and wife, amounts to almost $39,000. Of course, this figure needs to be verified with the two employers involved. The family has debt obligations amounting to $102,469, which appears to be high but is only 2.6 times their annual income and includes their home

TABLE 19–1   **A Typical Consumer Loan Application**

Credit application submitted by J. P. L. Skylark V on December 1, this year to the First National Bank of Collridge.

Applicant's street address: 3701 Elm Street

City of residence: Orangeburg   State and Zip Code: CA 77804

Purpose of the requested loan: To purchase a new car for personal and family use

Desired term of loan: 4 years

For auto loan requests, please fill in the following information:

Auto is X New ____ Used.   Year: Current

Make: Oldsmobile Delta 88

Model: 4-Door Sedan   Vehicle identification no. 8073617

Optional equipment on the vehicle: Air conditioning, automatic transmission, power steering, power brakes, AM/FM stereo, automatic door locks.

Vehicle to be traded in: 1990 Ford LTD   Model: 4-door Sedan

Vehicle identification no. 6384061

Optional equipment on trade-in vehicle: Air conditioning, automatic transmission, power brakes, power steering, AM radio

Details of the proposed purchase:

Purchase price quoted by seller:	$ 15,750
Cash down payment to be made:	$ 1,575
Allowance on trade-in:	$ 0
Net value of trade-in:	$ 1,500
Total value put down:	$ 3,075
Unpaid portion of purchase price:	$ 12,675
Other items covered in the loan:	$ 650
Total amount of credit requested:	**$ 13,325**

Customer information:

Social Security no. 671-66-8324 _____

Birthdate 2/21/63 _____

Time at present address: 10 months _____   Phone no. 965-1321 _____

Previous home address: 302 W. Solar St., Casio City, California _____

How long at previous address: 1 year _____

Driver's license no. and state: A672435 California _____

Number of dependents: 3 __

Current employer: Hometown Warehouse Co. _____

Length of employment with current employer: 8 months _____

Nature of work: Drive truck, load merchandise, keep books _____

Annual salary: $26,000 _____   Employer's phone no. 963-8417 _____

Other income sources: Investments, Trust Fund _____

Annual income from other sources: $5,000 _____

Nearest living relative (not spouse): Elsa Lyone _____   Phone: 604-682-7899 _____

   Address: 6832 Willow Ave., Amera, OK. 73282 _____

Does the applicant want the bank to consider spouse's income in evaluating this loan?

X Yes ____ No

Spouse's current annual income: $7,800 ___

Name of spouse's employer: Dimmitt Savings and Security Association _____

Occupation: Secretary _____   Length of employment: 8 months _____

The information I have given in this credit application is true and correct to the best of my knowledge. I am aware that the bank will keep this credit application regardless of whether or not the loan is approved. The bank is hereby granted permission to investigate my credit and employment history for purpose of verifying the information submitted with this credit application and for evaluating my credit status.

Customer's signature: J. P. Skylark _____

Date signed: 12/1/current year _____

mortgage loan. Most home mortgage lenders would find a total debt to total annual income ratio of two and one-half to three times income not unusual by today's standards.

The monthly payments on this debt *are* on the high side, however, at $1,078 (including the home mortgage payment). Monthly installment payments account for one-third of monthly gross income, not counting the payments of $315 per month that the requested car loan will require. Most lenders prefer to see a required-monthly-payment-to-income ratio in the range of 25 to 30 percent. However, the bulk of the family's debt and debt service payments are on their home and, in a reasonably strong local real estate market, the value of that home would provide adequate security for the bank. Moreover, the Skylarks seem to have adequate insurance coverage and above-average holdings of liquid financial investments in the form of stocks, bonds, and other securities. The loan officer's check with both Mr. and Mrs. Skylark's employers revealed that they both have good prospects for continued employment.

The Skylarks' loan application is for a reasonable purpose, consistent with the bank's loan policy, and the family's reported income high enough to suggest a reasonably strong probability that the loan would be repaid. Accordingly, the loan officer accepted their application and proceeded to check out the Skylark's credit record. When the report from the regional credit bureau arrived on screen, however, the loan officer saw very quickly that there was a serious problem with this loan application. Unfortunately, as shown in Table 19–2, the Skylarks had a mixed credit record, with at least five instances of delinquent or unpaid bills: (*a*) from Windcrest Apartments (probably unpaid rent), (*b*) a bank loan that was both unreported and unpaid, (*c*) past-due credit card obligations, and (*d*) a billing dispute with Saint Barrio Hospital that the hospital has charged off as a loss. The other debts were essentially as reported on the loan application with only minor discrepancies. At best, the loan officer would ask the Sky-

---

TABLE 19–2   Sample Credit Bureau Report

E-Z Credit Bureau Report on J. P. L. Skylark, SSN 671-66-8324
Credit bureau address: 8750 Cafe Street, San Miguel, CA 87513
                        607-453-8862
Credit items as of: *6/15/Current Year*

Name of Creditor	Term Credit	Maximum Amount Owed	Outstanding Balance	Amount Past Due	Monthly Payments	Status
Windcrest Deluxe Apts.	Six months	$ 610	$ 610	$610	$305	Past due
Visa	Open	$1,680	$1,540	$250	$125	Past due
MasterCard	Open	$1,435	$1,250	$176	$ 88	Past due
First State Bank of Slyvon	Six months	$ 750	$ 150	$150	$ 75	Past due
Kinney's Furniture Mart and Emporium	One year	$ 847	$ 675	—	$ 34	Current
First National Bank of Orangeburg	One year	$2,500	$ 675	—	$120	Current
Saint Barrio Hospital and Medical Clinic	Open	$ 160	$ 160	—	—	Charged off

larks about these unreported credits, but more likely this loan request will simply be turned down due to an unacceptable credit record. The loan officer clearly would be justified in having doubts about this borrower's sense of judgment and responsibility in borrowing and repaying the bank's funds.

Federal law (specifically, the Equal Credit Opportunity Act) requires U.S. banks to notify their credit customers *in writing* when they *deny* a loan request. They must give *reasons* for the denial, and where a credit bureau report is used, the customer must be told where that credit bureau is located. This way the customer can verify his or her credit record and demand that any errors found in the report be corrected.[1] Table 19–3 shows the credit denial report form given to the Skylarks and the reasons they were given on why their loan was turned down. In this case, the loan officer cited the unpaid debts and the relatively short period of time the Skylarks had held their current jobs. A good feature of this particular denial form is that the customer is cordially invited to use other services at the bank and to reapply if his or her financial situation improves.

This section on evaluating consumer credit applications concludes by summarizing the key points that consumer loan officers must remember in evaluating requests for household credit. These barometers of credit quality in consumer lending are as follows:

1. Evidence of stability in employment and residence.
2. Consistency of information so that all information items and figures on the application fit with each other.
3. Legitimacy of purpose for obtaining credit.
4. Evidence of competent money management skills, as reflected in the conservative assumption of debt and a timely repayment record.
5. Good prospects for continuing employment.

A bankable consumer loan request will *not* display a significant weakness in *any* of the foregoing items. It is when a household loan application is weak in one or two of these features that bank loan officers face tough decisions and often must rely on either some sort of objective credit-scoring system (to be discussed in the next section of this chapter) or some measure of intuition to decide if the bank should risk its owners' and depositors' funds. The ultimate decision to deny or accept a particular loan request depends upon the expected return and risk of that loan request relative to the expected returns and risks of other possible loans and investments the bank might make or has already made, bank management's attitude toward risk, and the bank's standing in the eyes of the regulatory community.

---

[1]The Federal Reserve Board has followed a policy in recent years of exempting business borrowers from many of the disclosure and antidiscrimination rules that apply to consumers as borrowers. In 1988, however, Congress passed the Women's Business Ownership Act of 1988, which extends the same credit rights to small-business owners (whose firms have gross annual revenues of $1 million or less) who apply for credit, including the right to receive written notice of credit denials.

TABLE 19–3   **Statement of Denial, Termination, or Change on a Customer Credit Application**

First National Bank of Collridge

Statement to: __Mr. J. P. L. Skylark__
Customer's Name

__3701 Elm Street__   __Orangeburg, CA 77804__
Customer's residence address   City   State

Statement date: __6/18/current year__

Credit requested by customer: __$13,325, 4-year auto installment loan__

Action taken by the bank on the request: __Loan denied__

Unfortunately, the bank cannot approve the amount and terms of credit you have asked for as of the date indicated above. The reason(s) for our denial of your requested loan are: __Past-due loans and inadequate__ __length of employment__

Our investigation of your credit request included a credit report from: E-Z Credit Bureau, 8750 Cafe Street, San Miguel, CA 87513. Federal law allows you to obtain, upon submission of a written request, a copy of the information that led to a denial of this credit request.

If you believe you have been discriminated against in obtaining credit because of your race, color, religion, sex, national origin, marital status, legal age, receipt of public assistance, or exercise of rights under the Consumer Credit Protection Act, you may apply to the principal federal regulatory agency for this bank, which is the Comptroller of the Currency, U.S. Treasury Department, Washington, D.C. 20219

Please let me or the other employees of our bank know at any time in the future if we can assist you with other services this bank offers. We value your friendship and your business and would like to be of assistance to you in meeting your personal banking needs. Please consider submitting another loan request in the future if the situation that led to the denial of this credit request improves.

Sincerely,

_____W. A. Numone_____
William A. H. Numone III
Senior Vice President
Personal Banking Division

Credit Scoring Consumer Loan Applications

Many banks today use **credit scoring** to evaluate the loan applications they receive from consumers. In fact, major credit card systems, such as those run by J. C. Penney, MasterCard, Montgomery Ward, Sears, and VISA, use these systems routinely to evaluate their credit card applicants and growing numbers of banks and other lenders are using credit-scoring models to evaluate auto, home equity, first mortgage and small business loans.

Credit-scoring systems have the advantage of being able to handle a large volume of credit applications quickly with minimal labor, thus reducing operating costs, and they may be an effective substitute for the use of judgment among inexperienced loan officers, thus helping to control bad-debt losses. Many customers like the convenience and speed with which their credit applications can be handled by automated credit-scoring systems. Often the customer can phone in a loan request and in a matter of minutes the bank can dial up that customer's credit bureau report through its online computer network and reach a quick decision on the customer's request.

Credit-scoring systems are usually based on discriminant models or related techniques such as logit or probit models or neural networks, in which several variables are used jointly to establish a numerical score or ranking for each credit applicant. If the applicant's score exceeds a critical cutoff level, he or she is likely to be approved for credit in the absence of other damaging information. If the applicant's score falls below the cutoff level, credit is likely to be denied in the absence of mitigating factors. Among the most important variables used in evaluating consumer loans are credit bureau ratings, age, marital status, number of dependents, home ownership, income bracket, having a telephone at home, number and type of bank accounts owned, type of occupation, and time in current job.

The basic theory of credit scoring is that the bank can identify the financial, economic, and motivational factors that separate good loans from bad loans by observing large groups of people or businesses who have borrowed in the past. Moreover, it assumes that the same financial and other factors that separated good from bad loans in the past will, with a small acceptable risk of error, separate good from bad loans in the future. Obviously, this underlying assumption can be wrong if the economy or other factors change abruptly, which is one reason good credit scoring systems are frequently retested and revised as more sensitive predictors are identified.

Credit-scoring systems usually select between 7 and 12 items from a customer's credit application and assign each a point value from 1 to 10. For example, examination of the bank's consumer credit accounts might show that the factors in the table on page 610 were important in separating good loans (i.e., those that paid out in timely fashion) from bad loans (i.e., where repayment was seriously delayed or not made at all).

The highest score a customer could have in the eight-factor credit-scoring system shown below is 43 points. The lowest possible score is 9 points. Suppose the bank finds that, of those past-approved loan customers scoring 28 points or less, 40 percent (or 1,200) became *bad* loans that had to be written off as a loss. These losses averaged $600 per credit account, for a total loss of $720,000. Of all the *good* loans made, however, only 10 percent (300) scored 28 points or less under this scoring system. At $600 per loan, these low-scoring good loans amounted to $180,000. Therefore, if the bank's loan officer uses 28 points as the *criterion score,* or *break point,* the bank will save an estimated $720,000 minus $180,000, or $540,000, by following the decision rule of making only those loans where the credit applicant scores higher than 28 points. If the bank's future loan-loss experience is the same, denying all loan applications scoring 28 points or less will reduce loss accounts by about 40 percent and reject just 10 percent

Factors for Predicting Credit Quality	Point Value
1. Customer's occupation or line of work:	
Professional or business executive	10
Skilled worker	8
Clerical worker	7
Student	5
Unskilled worker	4
Part-time employee	2
2. Housing status:	
Owns home	6
Rents home or apartment	4
Lives with friend or relative	2
3. Credit rating:	
Excellent	10
Average	5
No record	2
Poor	0
4. Length of time in current job:	
More than one year	5
One year or less	2
5. Length of time at current address:	
More than one year	2
One year or less	1
6. Telephone in home or apartment:	
Yes	2
No	0
7. Number of dependents reported by customer:	
None	3
One	3
Two	4
Three	4
More than three	2
8. Bank accounts held:	
Both checking and savings	4
Savings account only	3
Checking account only	2
None	0

of the good loan customers. The bank's management can experiment with other criterion scores to determine *which cutoff point yields the greatest net savings in loan losses for the bank's consumer loan program.*

Let's suppose the bank finds that 28 points is, indeed, the optimal break point for maximum savings from loan losses. The bank's consumer credit history could be further analyzed to find out what influence the *amount of credit* extended to a customer has upon the bank's loan-loss experience. The bank might find that the point-scoring schedule on page 611 results in the largest net savings from consumer credit losses.

Clearly, such a system removes personal judgment from the lending process and reduces the bank's decision time from hours to minutes or from weeks to one or a few days. It does run the risk, however, of alienating those customers who feel the bank has

Point Score Value or Range	*Credit Decision*
28 points or less	Reject application
29–30 points	Extend credit up to $500
31–33 points	Extend credit up to $1,000
34–36 points	Extend credit up to $2,500
37–38 points	Extend credit up to $3,500
39–40 points	Extend credit up to $5,000
41–43 points	Extend credit up to $8,000

not fully considered their financial situation and the special circumstances that may have given rise to their loan request. There is also the danger of being sued by a customer under federal antidiscrimination laws (such as the Equal Credit Opportunity Act or the Federal Reserve Board's Regulation B) if race, gender, marital status, or other discriminating factors prohibited by statute or court rulings are used in the bank's credit scoring system. Federal regulations allow the use of age or certain other personal characteristics as discriminating factors if the bank can show that these factors *do* separate, at a statistically significant level, good from bad loans and that the credit-scoring system is frequently statistically tested and revised to take into account recent changes in actual credit experience.[2] The burden of proof is on the bank to demonstrate that its credit scoring system successfully identifies quality loan applications at a statistically significant level.

Frequent verification and revision of a credit-scoring system is not only wise from a legal and regulatory point of view, but it also mitigates the biggest potential weakness of such systems—their inability to adjust quickly to changes in the economy and in family lifestyles. An inflexible credit evaluation system can be a deadly menace to a bank's consumer loan program, driving away sound consumer credit requests, ruining the bank's reputation in the communities it serves, and adding unacceptably high credit risks to the loan portfolio.

Concept Checks

19–3. What features of a consumer loan application should a loan officer examine most carefully?

19–4. How do credit-scoring systems work?

19–5. What are the principal advantages to a bank of using a credit-scoring system to evaluate consumer loan applications?

19–6. Are there any significant disadvantages to a credit-scoring system?

19–7. In the credit-scoring system presented in this chapter would a loan applicant who is a skilled worker, lives with a relative, has an average credit rating, has been in his or her present job and at his or her current address for exactly one year, has four dependents and a telephone, and holds a checking account be likely to receive a loan? Please explain why.

---

[2]Age can be used in an empirically derived, statistically sound credit-scoring system if the weight assigned to a loan applicant 62 years old or older is not lower than that assigned to any other age category.

Laws and Regulations Applying to Consumer Loans

Numerous laws and regulations limiting the activities of consumer lending institutions have been enacted during the past four decades. The principal federal laws fall into two broad groups: (1) **disclosure rules,** which mandate telling the consumer about the cost and essential requirements of a loan or lease agreement; and (2) **antidiscrimination laws,** which prevent categorizing loan customers according to their age, sex, race, national origin, religious affiliation, location of residence, or receipt of public assistance and denying credit to anyone solely because of membership in one or more of these groups. Many bankers view such rules as burdensome and out-of-step with technological and service innovations. They are also a constant challenge to the enforcement powers of the regulatory community, which is burdened with numerous complaints and questions of interpretation. Yet, the flow of adequate financial information to consumers is becoming more and more vital in the wake of deregulation of the financial sector, which has been accompanied by greater risk for both financial institutions and their customers.

Customer Disclosure Requirements

One of the most prominent pieces of federal legislation in the consumer services field is the Consumer Credit Protection (or **Truth-in-Lending**) Act, passed in 1968 by the U.S. Congress and simplified in 1981 through passage of the Truth-in-Lending Simplification and Reform Act. The Federal Reserve Board has prepared Regulation Z to implement these two truth-in-lending laws. The express purpose of truth in lending is to promote the informed use of credit among consumers by requiring full disclosure of credit terms and costs. Lenders must tell customers the annual percentage rate (APR, or actuarial, rate) on the loan requested, the total dollar amount of all finance charges, and, in the case of home mortgage loans, the required fees for approvals, closing costs, and other loan-related expenses.

Subsequent amendments in 1970 and 1974 gave rise to the Fair Credit Reporting Act and the Fair Credit Billing Act. The former expressly grants consumers access to their credit files, usually kept by local or regional credit bureaus. The **Fair Credit Reporting Act** authorizes individuals and families to review their credit files for accuracy and to demand an investigation and correction of any apparent inaccuracies. The law requires a credit agency to correct these inaccuracies promptly and to allow the consumer to insert a brief statement of explanation for any damaging items displayed in the file. Moreover, the law severely restricts access to consumer credit files, requiring an individual's written consent to access his or her file.

Recently, controversy has swirled around the credit-reporting industry in the United States. Some credit bureaus have been accused of creating excessive errors in consumers' credit files (which often result in unwarranted denials of loans), of not fully investigating consumer complaints concerning inaccuracies, and of selling information about consumers to mail-order firms. Several bills have been introduced in Congress over the years to impose tighter regulations on credit bureau operations and tougher penalties for credit bureau errors.

The **Fair Credit Billing Act** of 1974 permits consumers to dispute billing errors with a merchant or credit card company and receive a prompt investigation of any billing

Bank Management in Action

Loan-Evaluation Centers in Consumer Banking

The lending process has become increasingly *automated* around the world as bankers have developed new technologies to speed up the credit-evaluation and credit-granting process. One new approach that has helped some banks make more efficient use of their most experienced loan officers is to create on-line *loan-evaluation centers* staffed by experienced loan officers. When a customer enters the loan department at one of the bank's branch offices, he or she is interviewed by an account representative who typically asks the customer a series of pertinent questions, entering the customer's answers into a computer file on the spot. Among the more common questions asked are the customer's Social Security number, driver's license number, annual or monthly income, outstanding debts, length of time in his or her present job, and length of time at his or her present residence. This same information is flashed electronically at the same instant to an experienced loan officer at the bank's loan-evaluation center.

When the account representative has received and entered sufficient information from the customer to make a decision, he or she flashes a suggested decision to the officer at the loan-evaluation center. If the loan officer concurs with the account representative's decision, this decision regarding the loan will be quickly communicated to the customer.

The loan-evaluation center approach has multiple advantages, particularly for large banks that receive hundreds of small loan requests each day. It makes intensive use of scarce senior loan-evaluation talent and speeds up the credit decision process. The customer can often get an answer regarding his or her loan request within a matter of minutes. It also saves significantly on space and equipment because the bank's senior loan staff can operate out of one centralized location rather than requiring duplicate staffs housed in multiple branch offices. The loan-evaluation center approach is a reflection of growing competition among financial-service providers and the rapidly changing technology of information. Intense competition between bank and nonbank lenders (such as finance companies and credit unions) has forced bankers to develop more economical and more rapid loan production processes while recent developments in electronic technology have made faster credit evaluation and quicker credit decisions possible.

disputes. The consumer may withhold payment on the disputed portions of a bill and cannot be reported as delinquent or forced to pay interest penalties until the dispute is settled. Any creditor that does not respond to a consumer's inquiry about a bill or, having responded, does not investigate and attempt to resolve the matter must ultimately forfeit the disputed charge, up to a maximum of $50. A 30-day notice to customers is required before a lending institution or merchant can alter credit charges or service fees.

The *Fair Credit and Charge-Card Disclosure Act* requires that customers applying for credit cards be given early written notice (usually before a credit card is used for the first time) about required fees to open or to renew a credit account. Also, if an existing credit card account is about to be renewed and a fee for renewal is charged, the customer must receive written notice in advance. The customer must also be told if there is any change in credit card insurance coverage or fees. These rules are designed especially for credit cards granted to customers following solicitations made by direct mail, by telephone, or through advertisements that reach the general public.

Finally, if a credit customer gets behind in his or her loan payments, the **Fair Debt Collection Practices Act** limits how far a creditor or credit collection agency can go in pressing that customer to pay up. For example, a bill collector is not allowed to "harass" a debtor or use misrepresentation to obtain information about or gain access to a debtor. Calls placed at unusual times or to a debtor's place of work are illegal if made without the debtor's permission, nor can a bill collector legally disclose the purpose of the call to someone other than the debtor. These debt collection rules are enforced in the United States by the Federal Trade Commission.

Outlawing Credit Discrimination

Access to credit is an essential ingredient of the good life for the average family today. Recognition of this fact led Congress during the 1970s to outlaw discrimination in the granting of credit based on age, sex, race, national origin, religion, location of residence, or receipt of public assistance. The **Equal Credit Opportunity Act** of 1974 prohibits lenders from asking certain questions of a customer, such as the borrower's age or race. (An exception is made for home mortgage loans so that the federal government can collect information on who is or is not receiving mortgage credit to determine if discrimination is being practiced in this vital loan area.) Also, the loan officer cannot ask about other income sources beyond wage and salary income unless the customer voluntarily supplies this information.

Another law, the **Community Reinvestment Act** (CRA), is designed to prevent a lender of funds from arbitrarily marking out certain neighborhoods deemed undesirable and refusing to lend to people whose addresses place them in the excluded area. The CRA requires each lending institution to delineate the *trade territory* it plans to serve and to offer all of its services without discrimination to all residents in that particular trade territory. The bank's board of directors must review annually the definition of trade territory that management has chosen to see if it is still valid. Moreover, each lending institution's performance in making an affirmative effort to serve the credit and other financial service needs of its trade territory is evaluated by bank examiners (known as a CRA rating). The regulatory authorities take a bank's CRA rating into account when it applies to establish a new branch office, requests approval of a merger or acquisition, or requests permission to offer new services.

In August of 1989, Title XII of the Financial Institutions Reform, Recovery, and Enforcement Act required the federal banking agencies to *publish* the CRA ratings of banks so their customers would be aware of which banks are providing broad-based support to their local communities. Each bank must place its CRA performance evaluation in a public file at its head office and in at least one office in each community that the bank serves within 30 days of receiving the examiner's report. This public file must be open for bank customers to inspect during regular business hours and the bank must provide copies (for a reasonable fee) to anyone requesting materials in the file.

CRA ratings are based on 12 "assessment factors" that examiners review when they visit a bank, including the bank's effort to communicate with members of the local community concerning their credit needs, its participation in government-related housing programs, the geographic distribution of loans the bank has made, and any evidence of illegal credit discrimination.

There are four different CRA ratings assigned by bank examiners: Outstanding (O), Satisfactory (S), Needs to Improve (N), or Substantial Noncompliance (SN). A banking firm with a low CRA rating (e.g., a rating of N or SN) may run into trouble in securing regulatory approval if it seeks permission to expand its service offerings or to acquire another bank.

A recent study by the author [5] finds that banks receiving a grade of "O"—the highest CRA rating—have done so by first carefully *documenting* their community-oriented activities. They periodically survey their employees who are active in the local community to be able to document their strong community involvement when bank regulators ask for evidence on their community activities. Top-rated banks also frequently survey their customers to determine customer perceptions about the quality of the bank's services and to keep up with changing customer service needs. Banks with the highest community ratings often get involved with local programs to provide affordable housing, hold seminars to counsel small businesses and new home buyers on how to apply for loans, and monitor the geographic distribution of their loans to make sure certain areas of the community are not systematically being shut out in their access to the bank's services. Banks awarded top CRA marks usually get a strong commitment from their boards of directors and senior management to promote greater community involvement, which seems to send a message about the importance of CRA-related activities to bank employees at all levels.

Laws that supplement the provisions of the Community Reinvestment Act are the Home Mortgage Disclosure Act and the Fair Housing Act. The former requires that banks and other institutional mortgage lenders publicly disclose at least once a year the areas of urban communities in which they have granted residential mortgage loans and home improvement loans. The Fair Housing Act prohibits discrimination in the sale, leasing, or financing of housing because of color, national origin, race, religion, or sex. The Financial Institutions Reform, Recovery, and Enforcement Act requires lending institutions to report the race, sex, and income of all those individuals *applying* for mortgage loans so that federal regulatory agencies can more easily detect possible discrimination in home mortgage lending.

These laws do not tell banks and other financial institutions *who* should receive credit. Rather, they require each lending institution to focus on the facts pertinent to each individual loan application, case by case, and prevent lenders from lumping their customers into categories (such as by age, sex, or race) and making credit decisions solely on the basis of group membership.

Concept Checks

19–8. What laws exist today to give consumers who are borrowing money fuller disclosure about the terms and risks of taking on credit?

19–9. What legal protections are available today to protect borrowers against discrimination?

19–10. In your opinion, are any additional laws needed in these areas?

Real Estate Loans

Banks make *real estate loans* to fund the acquisition of real property—homes, apartment complexes, shopping centers, office buildings, warehouses, and other physical structures, as well as land in some cases. Real estate lending is a field unto itself, possessing important differences from other types of bank loans. In banking, real estate loans typically are either short-term **construction loans,** paid out within months or weeks as a building project is completed, or long-term mortgages that may stretch out 25 to 30 years in order to provide permanent financing for the acquisition or improvement of real property. Whatever their maturity, real estate loans have been one of the most rapidly growing areas of bank lending over the past decade, climbing at a double-digit growth rate to reach nearly a third of all bank assets as the 1990s drew to a close. Unfortunately, such loans are also among the riskiest forms of bank credit. In the early 1990s, for example, nonperforming real estate loans represented close to half of all troubled assets held by U.S. banks.

Differences between Real Estate Loans and Other Loans

Real estate loans differ from most other kinds of loans in several key respects. First, the average size of a real-estate loan is usually much larger than the average size of other loans, especially consumer loans and small business loans. Moreover, certain mortgage loans, mainly on single-family homes, tend to have the longest maturities (from about 15 years to 25 or 30 years) of any loan a bank makes. Long-term lending of this sort carries considerable risk for the lending institution because many things can happen—including adverse changes in economic conditions, interest rates, and the financial health of the borrower—over the term of such a loan.

With most other types of loans, it is the projected cash flow or income of the borrower that is most important in the decision to approve or deny a loan application. With real estate lending, however, the condition and value of the property that is the object of the loan are nearly as important as the borrower's income. In real estate lending, competent property appraisal is vitally important to the decision on a loan request. Such appraisals must conform to industry and government standards, particularly if it is likely that the mortgage will be sold in the secondary market, enabling the lender to raise additional funds in order to make new loans.

One such regulation is the Federal National Mortgage Association's (FNMA, or Fannie Mae) requirement that any home mortgage loans acquired must come from borrowers whose monthly house payment (including loan principal and interest, taxes, and insurance) does not exceed 28 percent of their monthly gross income and the sum of whose regular monthly payments (including housing costs) does not exceed 36 percent of their monthly gross income. The maturity of the home mortgage loan cannot be less than 10 years or more than 30 years, and the property must be appraised by a Fannie Mae-approved appraiser. FNMA regulations also stipulate that the borrower's credit report cannot be more than 90 days old.

While rules such as these represent a burden to the home mortgage lender, they bring an offsetting benefit, because loans conforming to these regulatory standards usually can be sold quite readily in the secondary market to other financial institutions, particularly life insurance companies, savings banks, and pension funds, or to government agencies such as Fannie Mae or Ginnie Mae (i.e., the Government National Mortgage Association, or GNMA). Frequently a bank or other lending institution will package its mortgage loans into GNMA-sponsored loan pools and sell securities as claims against those pools to investors, thereby raising funds to make still more loans.

Changes in regulations and the shifting fortunes of different financial institutions have resulted in major changes in bank and nonbank firms making mortgage loans. While commercial banks often prefer to make shorter-term property loans (especially construction loans), the mortgage banking subsidiaries of bank holding companies now account for a major portion of all home mortgage loans. These subsidiary firms have strong market contacts and can usually resell any home mortgage loans they make in short order to long-distance lenders, such as life insurers, savings banks, or foreign investors. Mortgage subsidiaries usually establish short-term "warehouse lines" at banks in order to provide them with adequate funding to carry the mortgages they originate or buy until they sell those same loans to other investors. Moreover, the mortgage banking subsidiaries of a bank holding company can branch at will into distant cities and states where bank branching may be limited by law or regulation.

Factors in Evaluating Applications for Real Estate Loans

In evaluating real estate loan applications, loan officers must consider the following points:

1. The amount of the down payment planned by the borrower relative to the purchase price of mortgaged property is a critical factor in determining how safe a mortgage loan is from the lender's point of view. In general, the higher the ratio of loan amount to purchase price, the less incentive the borrower has to honor all the terms of the loan, because the borrower has less equity in the property. When mortgages reach 90 percent or more of the property's purchase price, mortgage insurance becomes very important and the lender must place added emphasis on assessing the borrower's character and sense of responsibility.

2. Real property loans often bring in other business (such as deposits and future property-improvement loans) from the borrowing customer. Therefore, they should be viewed in the context of a *total relationship* between borrower and lender. For example, the bank might be willing to give a mortgage loan customer a somewhat lower loan rate in return for a pledge that the customer will use other bank services and keep substantial deposits at the bank.

3. Deposit stability is a key factor for a bank in deciding what volume and type of real estate loans it should make. Banks with more stable deposits usually can be more aggressive with their real estate lending programs and reach for longer-term, higher-yielding mortgage loans.

4. Home mortgage loans require the bank's real estate loan officer to consider carefully the following aspects of the credit application:

Bank Management in Action

Community Development Lending by Banks

One of the most dynamic areas of bank lending today centers around community development programs. In the United States there are more than 2,500 nonprofit community development corporations (CDCs) that provide financial and technical assistance to those in need of affordable housing and, more recently, to local residents who wish to start new businesses or purchase existing small business firms and thereby develop another source of income.

Banks and bank holding companies (including some multibank consortia) have helped to organize and often become active partners in many CDCs, particularly to help revitalize neighborhoods that have been struggling economically and deteriorating. Participating lenders have developed low-down-payment/low-closing-cost loans that have made home and business ownership possible for thousands of individuals and families who previously thought such a goal was well out of reach. The impact on the U.S. housing market has been especially dramatic; for example, by 1997 home ownership had been attained by about two-thirds of American households—a record proportion—with minority groups representing nearly a third of recent new homeowners.

Many of the new homeowners created by CDCs and other housing programs have now turned toward a second goal—finding financial support and training to begin new business ventures. As a result, banks working through CDCs and other community groups have become more interested in supplying capital for business start-ups and acquisitions. Indeed, bankers' participation in the small business market is critical, as shown in a recent Federal Reserve National Survey of Small Business Finances that found that 84 percent of small and medium-sized businesses identified commercial banks as their primary source of financial services. However, supporting the development of small businesses, particularly in low- and middle-income neighborhoods, is a real challenge for bank managers and stockholders because small business borrowers, on the whole, present some serious credit problems. Often they have little or no credit history to base a loan decision upon, have spotty and generally inadequate financial records that are rarely audited, present little collateral of value, carry high loan production costs for the banker (usually because they require so much help in getting their loan application in bankable

a. Amount and stability of the borrower's income, especially relative to the size of the mortgage loan and to the size of the payments required.

b. The borrower's available savings and where the borrower will obtain the required down payment. If the down payment is made by drawing down savings significantly, the customer has fewer liquid assets available for future emergencies, such as paying off the mortgage if someone in the family gets ill or loses a job.

c. The borrower's track record in caring for and managing property. If the mortgaged property is not properly maintained, the bank may not fully recover the loaned funds in a foreclosure and sale.

d. The outlook for real estate sales in the local market area in case the property must be repossessed. In a depressed local economy with

shape with a reasonably complete business plan, market analysis, complete financial statements, and backup support in case the business grows more slowly than expected or runs into serious problems), present the banker with a loan that is difficult to sell in the secondary loan market (i.e., illiquidity), and experience exceptionally high failure rates.

Nevertheless, bankers all across the United States and in many other foreign countries as well have begun to accelerate their small-business-development activities. Some have developed new services that appeal to new business owners, including smaller-size revolving credit and term loans, cash management programs to help small businesses collect and invest their cash more quickly, and business credit card programs to facilitate purchases of supplies and equipment. Several banks have set up special small-business credit units, offering longer-term loans supported by guarantee programs run by the Small Business Administration (SBA), state and local economic development agencies, and other governmental institutions whose guarantees can make it possible to sell these small business loans in the secondary market, generating still more cash to support new lending programs. Increasing numbers of banks have also formed *community reinvestment corporations,* which bring in both bank and nonbank organizations to provide loans as small as a few hundred dollars or as large as several thousand dollars to finance construction or purchase heavy equipment.

Some banks and bank holding companies have sought and received permission from bank regulators to make *equity investments* in small firms, provided the majority of jobs and services flow to individuals with relatively low incomes. Bankers have also provided backup funds (loans or contributions) and technical advice to other lenders, including Small Business Administration Development Companies, revolving loan pools, and microenterprise loan funds. Frequently these institutions provide start-up funding and training for the smallest ("backyard") businesses started by individuals and families. Increasingly, bankers are getting actively involved in combined public and private partnerships to help rebuild and strengthen economically the neighborhoods and communities in which they operate.

Source: For an excellent discussion of these community development activities in the banking industry, see Lawrence H. Meyer, "New Approaches to Small Business Development Partnerships," Speech by a Member of the Board of Governors of the Federal Reserve System to the Urban Studies Program, University of Wisconsin, Milwaukee, Wisconsin, December 1, 1997.

substantial unemployment, many houses, apartments, and business structures are put up for sale, with few active buyers. The bank could wait a long time for the return of its funds.

e. The outlook for interest rates if the home mortgage loan carries a floating interest rate. While the secondary market for floating-rate mortgage loans has improved in recent years, fixed-rate home mortgages are still easier to sell.

During the past two decades severe problems have frequently appeared in the real estate loan portfolios of many U.S. banks. Several of the largest banks in the United States, such as Citicorp, Chase Manhattan, Security Pacific, Chemical, Fleet-Norstar, and Wells Fargo, from time to time have foreclosed on and sold substantial commercial and residential properties at deeply discounted prices. In response to these growing problems, Congress enacted Title XI of the Financial Institutions Reform, Recovery, and Enforcement Act of 1989. Title XI requires the use of state-certified or licensed appraisers for real estate loans that come under the regulatory authority of the federal banking and thrift supervisory agencies. The four chief federal regulators of banks and thrifts have recently ruled that certified or licensed appraisals are required for most real estate loans that exceed $250,000 in amount. (Renewals of existing loans are generally exempt from specific appraisal requirements.) For smaller denomination real estate loans a bank must follow "prudent" evaluation standards and document in writing its valuation of any property that is the basis for a real estate loan, including the assumptions upon which the bank's estimate of property values are based.

Further tightening of standards and regulations surrounding real estate loans occurred when Congress passed the National Affordable Housing Act in November 1990. This law and its supporting regulations require that applicants for mortgage loans must be given a disclosure statement indicating whether their loan could have its servicing rights (i.e., the right to collect payments from the borrower) transferred to another institution that borrowers will have to deal with during the life of their loan. In an effort to reduce the loss of homes through foreclosure, Congress stipulated that lenders must tell home mortgage borrowers who are delinquent in repaying their loans if the lender counsels home owners or knows of any nonprofit organizations that provide such counseling.

Concept Checks

19–11. In what ways is a real estate loan unique compared to other kinds of bank loans?

19–12. What factors should a banker consider in evaluating real estate loan applications?

Trends in Consumer and Real Estate Credit

Consumer loan and credit programs will continue to play a major role in bank management and services in the years ahead. Not only are consumer loans among the most profitable of all types of bank credit, but as consumers become better educated they are making more aggressive use of credit to upgrade their standard of living and to match their spending plans with expected future income.

Consumer lending in the future will have to be more *convenience* oriented, giving individuals and families fast access to credit while still maintaining enough control over customer borrowing to avoid a significant deterioration in loan quality. This will be a serious problem in the future, because aggressive, high-volume consumer lenders will undoubtedly push the concept of "instant credit" to its prudent and practical limits. For example, Citicorp recently launched a program of preapproved home mortgage loans, and many credit unions offer preapproved auto loans. Moreover, several other credit opportunities to better serve the consumer are unfolding, and to these we now turn.

Home Equity Lending

In the United States, the 1986 Tax Reform Act opened up even wider the rapidly growing field of **home equity loans.** Under these programs, home owners whose residence has appreciated in value can use the *equity* in their homes—the difference between a home's estimated market value and the amount of the mortgage loans against it—as a borrowing base. Thus, if a home was purchased for $100,000 and has a $70,000 mortgage loan against it today and, due to inflation and growing demand for housing, its market value is now $120,000, the home owner will have a *borrowing base* of about $50,000 (i.e., $120,000–$70,000). This base might be drawn upon as collateral for a $50,000 loan to remodel the home, to purchase a second home, or for some other legitimate purpose.

Two main types of home equity loans are in use today. The first is the so-called traditional home equity loan, which is a closed-end credit covering a specific period of months and years and is used mainly for home improvements. Traditional equity credits are normally repaid in equal installments, quarterly or monthly, and are most frequently secured by a second mortgage against the borrower's home.

Many banks have recently seized upon the home equity loan opportunity by offering consumers a second and newer type of home equity loan—lines of credit against their home's borrowing base. They usually determine the credit limit on these home equity lines by taking a percentage of the appraised value of the borrowing customer's home (say, 75 percent) and subtracting the amount the customer still owes on the existing home mortgage loan. That is:

Appraised value of home	$150,000
Times percentage allowed	× 75%
Equals percentage of home's appraised value	$112,500
Minus balance still owed on home mortgage	–60,500
Equals maximum credit line available to customer	$ 52,000

The maximum loan amount allowed may be adjusted based on the customer's income and other debts incurred plus his or her past repayment record with other loans.

These credit lines can be used for *any* legitimate purpose, not just housing-related expenditures—for example, to purchase an automobile or finance a college education. Moreover, many of these credit lines are revolving credits, which means the customer can borrow up to the maximum amount of the loan, repay all or a portion of the amount borrowed, and borrow again up to the stipulated maximum amount any number of times until the credit line matures, which usually occurs at some point within 10 years. Because home equity-based credit tends to be longer-term and more secure, it often carries a lower loan rate and longer payout period, thus reducing the borrower's installment payments below the required payments on more conventional consumer loans. Traditional home equity loans normally are priced using longer-term interest rates, while home equity credit lines usually have interest rates tied closely to short-term rates (such as the yield on U.S. Treasury bills or the prime lending rate).

In recent years, surveys conducted by the Federal Reserve Board ([1], [9]) and other institutions (such as the University of Michigan's Institute for Social Research) have revealed some useful information for both home equity loan customers and banks that make such loans. For example, the home equity market remains quite small relative to the number of homeowners—less than a fifth of all U.S. homeowners have accessed home equity credit, and this group is about equally split between traditional home equity loans and the newer home equity lines of credit. Thus, the home equity loan market could grow substantially larger with sufficient advertising and economic incentives.

In 1986, the Tax Reform Act made interest on home equity loans up to $100,000 tax deductible, and this feature accounts for much of their recent growth. With the coming of federal tax reform, interest costs on other loans gradually became fully taxable, giving a distinct advantage to home equity credit in the eyes of consumers. Mean loan sizes in recent years have averaged about $18,000 for traditional loans and $20,000 for home equity credit lines.

Demographically speaking, home equity borrowers tend to be more affluent than the average homeowner. They report higher levels of personal income and more equity in their homes. Home equity borrowers also tend to be older customers with a longer period of home ownership and a longer record of employment. Most home equity customers are in their late 40s or older; many are in retirement or near retirement and have substantially paid off their first home mortgage. Most equity loans are used to pay for home improvements, to repay old installment loans, to finance an education, to fund vacations, or to cover medical costs.

Bank loan officers need to exercise great care with home equity loan requests. For one thing, they rest on the assumption that housing prices will not decline significantly. Yet there is ample historical evidence that economic downturns and rising unemployment can flood local housing markets with homes for sale, with foreclosures on existing homes rapidly depressing market prices. While in most states a bank can repossess a home pledged as collateral for a loan, often the bank has difficulty selling the home for a price that recoups all its funds plus all the costs incurred in making and servicing the loan and in taking possession of the collateral. There is also room to question the wisdom of using an appreciating asset, such as a house, to purchase an asset not likely to appreciate, such as most automobiles, furniture, and appliances. Loan officers must exercise care in granting such credit requests, lending only a portion (perhaps no more than 60 or 70 percent) of the home's estimated equity value in order to allow an adequate cushion should real estate markets turn down.

Moreover, strict regulations at the federal level, stemming from the Competitive Equality in Banking Act of 1987 and the Home Equity Loan Consumer Protection Act of 1988, require the lender to put an interest rate cap on how high loan rates can go on floating-rate home equity loans. Lenders must also provide their customers with information on all loan charges and significant risks under a required Truth in Lending Act disclosure statement. The consumer's overriding risk is that the bank would be forced to repossess his or her home. Not only does such an event destroy customer relationships and result in adverse publicity for the bank, but it may saddle the bank with an asset that could be difficult to sell.

The Consumer Protection Act of 1988 prohibits a home equity lender from arbitrarily canceling a loan and demanding immediate payment. However, if the lender can show that the customer has committed fraud or misrepresentation, has failed to pay out the loan as promised, or has not kept up the value of the property involved, collection of the loan can be accelerated. The home equity loan customer then has little choice but to pay up or surrender the home that was pledged as collateral, unless protected in some way by federal, state, or local laws.

Consumer Cash Management Programs

Other promising consumer loan opportunities have recently appeared as well, especially those related to the use of consumer cash management programs. Developed successfully by Merrill Lynch in the 1970s, these financial packages offer household customers security brokerage and investment services so they can readily invest idle cash in stocks, bonds, and other investment outlets to earn income until those funds are needed to meet current obligations. Recently these cash management packages have been expanded to include checking accounts, savings plans, credit cards, and insurance. The result is one-stop convenience for the customer, who is typically sent combined monthly statements showing the status of his or her savings, loan balances, and investments.

Cash management programs can make consumer financial transactions easier and make the use of credit more convenient. While most successful cash management programs are aimed mainly at high-income households, the future is likely to bring larger-volume programs that reach middle-income households. The key to the success of these newer programs will be whether or not they can keep their costs low enough to be able to price their services competitively.

Changing Demographics and Consumer Borrowing

We should not leave the reader with the impression that bank consumer credit programs have no serious problems. In truth, they appear to face significant hurdles in the period ahead. For one thing, the population is *aging* rapidly in the United States, Japan, and other industrialized nations. As people grow older, especially beyond the age of 40 or 45, they tend to make *less* use of credit and to pay down their outstanding debt obligations. This suggests that the total demand for consumer credit per capita may fall, forcing banks and other consumer lenders to fight hard for profitable consumer loan accounts. Moreover, deregulation has brought more lenders into the consumer credit field. Financial institutions hoping to protect their revenues in this field will need to choose their fee schedules carefully.

A related trend in consumer lending—*point-of-sale loans*— also reflects changes going on in the population to whom banks market their consumer credit services. More loan customers today demand speed and convenience in the lending process. Many consumers want credit available instantly when they are making purchases rather than having to drive to a bank to request a loan. Many banks today are offering indirect loans through dealers in autos, home appliances, and other big-ticket items, so that the dealer prepares a credit agreement and phones or faxes the borrowing customer's information to the bank, seeking quick approval. Other institutions are offering "pre-approval" credit programs where the customer phones in or mails credit information to the bank and gets approval for a loan before a purchase is made. In this instance the store or dealer where the customer makes a purchase can simply verify with the bank that a loan has already been approved. These newer approaches sharply reduce the need to enter a bank and result in more indirect lending at the point at which a sale is being made, rather than direct lending to the customer at a bank office. The result is lower transactions cost and greater convenience for the customer, but bank managers must be alert to the added risks involved in making quick credit decisions and the possible loss of closer direct relationships with their customers.

Legal and Regulatory Changes Affecting Consumer Lending

During the 1990s, personal bankruptcies soared, with court filings averaging a million a year in the United States under a widening array of options granted by federal and state bankruptcy laws (including Chapters 7, 11, and 13). In order to keep pace with this upsurge in individual and family bankruptcies, consumer lenders have had to become intimately acquainted with the provisions of federal and state bankruptcy codes. Unfortunately, recent changes in bankruptcy laws present serious challenges to consumer lending institutions. Congress passed the Bankruptcy Reform Act in 1978, amending a federal bankruptcy code that had stood since the turn of the century. While subsequent amendments tightened up some of the loopholes in the 1978 law, the most recent reforms tipped the legal scales in favor of individuals filing bankruptcy petitions and more severely limited the amount and kinds of debtors' assets that could be converted into cash for pro rata distribution to banks and other creditors.

Today, a substantial proportion of household assets may be exempt from liquidation in order to help bankrupt individuals recover financially and, eventually, pay off their obligations voluntarily. For example, a married couple may be able to shelter under federal bankruptcy protection up to $40,000 in such personal assets as the equity in a home, household furniture and appliances, jewelry, a car, retirement accounts, and any equipment used in the debtor's job. A few states have passed statutes allowing even more assets to be sheltered from creditors, and federal law permits a debtor filing bankruptcy to switch to state bankruptcy rules where this change would be beneficial. Nearly a third of the states, however, have adopted more conservative rules that shelter fewer debtor assets than does federal law.

The federal bankruptcy code specifies the rules under which a troubled debtor's personal assets can be sold, with the proceeds allocated to the individual's creditors. The Bankruptcy Act directs the courts to approve a repayment plan that allows a debtor to gradually pay off his or her creditors, who may not repossess or foreclose on any of the debtor's assets as long as the court-approved payments are being made. The results are to make bankers more cautious about borderline loan requests and probably to encourage banks to include higher risk premiums in their consumer loan rates, which could price many lower-income borrowers out of the market for household credit.

Concept Checks

19–13. What is home equity lending and what are its advantages and disadvantages for banks?

19–14. What problems do banks face in developing consumer cash management programs?

19–15. How is the changing age structure of the population likely to affect bank consumer loan programs?

19–16. What impact have recent changes in U.S. bankruptcy laws had on consumer lending by banks?

Summary

Lending to consumers and making real estate loans have been among the most popular financial services for bankers in recent years. These forms of credit help the bank diversify its customer base, bringing in consumer deposits and sources of revenue to supplement and offset the risk of its business loans and deposits. Indeed, many banks in recent years have turned increasingly to consumer and real estate loans to escape or reduce the effects of business cycles, which periodically lead to considerable stress for many of the bank's traditional business credit accounts, and to avoid intense competition from foreign banking firms.

Nevertheless, consumer and real estate lending present their own significant challenges for bankers. These loans typically have higher default rates than do most other forms of bank lending, though their gross loan yields also tend to be much higher, making household loans in most years among the most profitable credit accounts a bank can hold. The keys to making good consumer loans lie in judging the character and sense of responsibility of the borrower. A bank can usually judge these elements by examining the borrower's past loan payment record, which in most cases can be obtained from a local or regional credit bureau.

Consumer lending increasingly has been influenced by federal and state laws and regulations. Most of these rules focus upon (1) disclosure to the consumer of all the significant details of a loan agreement and (2) prevention of discrimination on account of age, race, sex, and other factors in granting credit and setting loan rates. These laws and regulations are designed to promote competition, encourage consumers to shop for credit, and aid the individual customer in making an informed credit decision.

Real estate loans are often aimed directly or indirectly at the individual consumer. These loans help to finance the construction of new homes, apartments, shopping centers, office buildings, and other forms of real property. Banks make both short-term real estate credit (usually in the form of interim construction loans) and long-term mortgage credit available to individuals and business firms. The most successful real estate loan programs are generally at those banks possessing a high proportion of longer-term deposits and a staff skilled in the assessment of property values and in real estate law. More than any other type of loan, real estate credit depends heavily on correctly judging the value of and outlook for the loan's collateral—the land or structures whose purchase is being financed by the loan.

Key Terms in This Chapter

Residential mortgage loans
Installment loans
Credit bureau
Cosigner
Right of offset
Credit scoring
Disclosure rules
Antidiscrimination laws
Truth-in-Lending Act
Fair Credit Reporting Act
Fair Credit Billing Act

Fair Debt Collection Practices Act
Equal Credit Opportunity Act
Community Reinvestment Act
Construction loans
Home equity loans

Problems and Projects

1. The Childress family has applied for a $5,000 loan for home improvements, especially to install a new roof and add new carpeting. Bob Childress is a welder at Ford Motor Co., the first year he has held that job, and his wife sells clothing at Wal-Mart. They have three children. The Childresses own their home, which they purchased six months ago, and have an *average* credit rating, with some late bill payments. They have a telephone, but hold only a checking account with the bank and a few bonds. Mr. Childress has a $35,000 life insurance policy with a cash-surrender value of $1,100. Suppose the bank uses the credit scoring system presented in this chapter and denies all credit applications scoring fewer than 36 points. Is the Childress family likely to get their loan?

2. Mr. and Mrs. Napper are interested in funding their children's college education by taking out a home equity loan in the amount of about $24,000. Eldridge National Bank is willing to extend a loan, using the Nappers' home as collateral. Their home has been appraised at $110,000, and the bank has a policy of allowing a customer to use no more than 70 percent of the appraised value of a home as a borrowing base. The Nappers still owe $60,000 on the first mortgage against their home. Is there enough residual value left in the Nappers' home to support their loan request? How could the bank help them meet their credit needs?

   Alternative scenarios:

   (1) Suppose the bank agrees to raise the Nappers' borrowing base to 76 percent of appraised value. Would this help them meet their educational goals?

   (2) If the Nappers could reduce the balance still owed on their first mortgage to $50,000, would this make them eligible for a loan that fully meets their needs?

   (3) Suppose the resale market for homes in the Nappers' local community appears to be headed downward. There are many unsold residences on the market and the average home is taking about nine months to sell. How would this new information affect the bank's decision on this loan? How could the bank adjust the loan's terms to deal with this latest news from the local housing market? Please be specific.

3. Arthur Renfro has just been informed by his bank that he can access a line of credit of no more than $28,000 based upon the equity value in his home. Renfro still owes $30,500 on a first mortgage against his home and $11,500 on a second mortgage claim against the home, which was incurred last year to repair the roof and driveway. If the appraised value of Renfro's residence is $95,000, what percentage of the home's estimated market value is the bank using to determine Renfro's maximum available line of credit?

4. Which federal law or laws applies to each of the situations described below?

   a. A loan officer asks an individual requesting a loan about what race he or she belongs to.

   b. A bill collector called Jim Jones three times yesterday at the latter's work number without first asking permission.

   c. Sixton National Bank has developed a special form to tell its customers the finance charges they must pay to secure a loan.

   d. Consumer Savings Bank has just received an outstanding rating from bank examiners for its efforts to serve all segments of its trade territory.

   e. Presage State Bank must disclose once a year the areas in the local community where it has made home mortgage and home improvement loans.

   f. Reliance Credit Card Company is contacted by one of its customers in a dispute over the amount of charges the customer made at a local department store that accepts the company's credit cards.

g. Amy Imed, after requesting a copy of her credit bureau report, discovers several errors in the report and demands a correction.

5. James Smithern has asked for a $3,500 loan from Beard Center National Bank to repay some personal expenses. The bank uses a credit-scoring system to evaluate such requests, which contains the following discriminating factors along with their associated point weights in parentheses:

> Credit Rating (excellent, 3; average, 2; poor or no record, 0)
> Time in Current Job (five years or more, 6; one to five years, 3)
> Time at Current Residence (more than 2 years, 4; one to two years, 2; less than one year, 1)
> Telephone in Residence (yes, 1; no, 0)
> Holds Account at Bank (yes, 2; no, 0).

The bank generally grants a loan if a customer scores 9 or more points. Mr. Smithern has an average credit rating, has been in his current job for three years, has been at his current residence for two years, has a telephone, but has no account at the bank. Is James Smithern likely to receive the loan he has requested?

6. Singleton Merchants Bank, in reviewing its credit card customers, finds that of those customers who scored 40 points or less on its credit-scoring system, 35 percent (or a total of 10,615 credit customers) turned out to be delinquent credits, resulting in a total loss. This group of bad credit card loans averaged $1,200 in size per customer account. Examining its successful credit accounts Singleton finds that 12 percent of its good customers (or a total of 3,640 customers) scored 40 points or less on the bank's scoring system. These low-scoring but good accounts generated about $1,500 in revenues each. If the bank's credit card division follows the decision rule of granting credit cards only to those customers scoring more than 40 points and future credit accounts

generate about the same average revenues and losses, about how much can the bank expect to save in net losses?

7. The T. Williams family purchased its three-bedroom home for $97,000 on the outskirts of San Francisco 10 years ago. The initial mortgage loan on the house was for $70,500, but has now been paid down to $53,800. Currently, comparable homes in the same neighborhood are selling on the market for about $185,000. What is the family's *borrowing base* that might be drawn upon as collateral for a home equity loan?

Suppose a bank proposes to offer a credit line based upon two-thirds of the home's current appraised value. What is the maximum credit line the bank will make available to the Williams family?

8. The Vaud family needs some extra funds to put their two children through college starting this coming fall and to buy a new computer system for a part-time home business. They are not sure of the current market value of their home, though comparable four-bedroom homes are selling for about $210,000 in the neighborhood. The Van Nuys Federal and Merchants Savings Bank will loan 80 percent of the property's appraised value, but the Vauds still owe $142,000 on their home mortgage and a home improvement loan combined. What maximum amount of credit is available to this family should it elect to seek a home equity credit line?

9. San Carlos Bank and Trust Company uses a credit-scoring system to evaluate most consumer loans that amount to more than $2,500. The key factors used in its scoring system are:

Borrower's length of employment in his/her present job:	
More than one year	6 points
Less than one year	3 points
Borrower's length of time at current address:	
More than 2 years	8 points
One to two years	4 points
Less than one year	2 points

Borrower's current home situation:

Owns home	7 points
Rents home or apartment	4 points
Lives with friend or relative	2 points

Credit bureau report:

Excellent	8 points
Average	5 points
Below average or no record	2 points

Credit cards currently active:

One card	6 points
Two cards	4 points
More than two cards	2 points

Deposit account(s) with bank:

Yes	5 points
No	2 points

The Mulvaney family has two wage earners who have held their present jobs for 18 months. They have lived at their current street address for one year, where they rent on a six-month lease. Their credit report is excellent but shows only one previous charge. However, they are actively using two credit cards right now to help with household expenses. Yesterday, they opened an account at San Carlos and deposited $250. The Mulvaneys have asked for a $4,500 loan to purchase a used car and some furniture. The bank has a cutoff score in its scoring system of 30 points. Would you make this loan for two years, as they have requested? Are there factors not included in the scoring system that you would like to know more about? Please explain.

Selected References

For an analysis of the risks in consumer lending, see the following:

 1. Canner, Glenn B., and Charles A. Luckett. "Home Equity Lending." *Federal Reserve Bulletin,* May 1989, pp. 333–44.

See the following studies for further discussion of real estate lending procedures and practices:

 2. Noon, H. Richard. "Residential Mortgage Lending and Mortgage Loan Warehousing." In *The Bankers' Handbook,* 3rd ed. Homewood, Ill.: Richard D. Irwin, 1989.

 3. Reavis, Charles G., Jr. "Lending on Income Property." In *The Bankers Handbook,* 3rd ed. Homewood, Ill.: Richard D. Irwin, 1989.

For an overview of consumer credit laws and their impact, see the following:

 4. Day, George S., and William K. Brandt. "Consumer Research and the Evaluation of Information Disclosure Requirements: The Case of Truth in Lending." *Journal of Consumer Research,* June 1974, pp. 21–32.

 5. Rose, Peter S. "The Performance of Outstanding CRA-Rated Banks." *Bankers Magazine,* September/October 1994, pp. 53–59.

For a discussion of the role of technology in modern consumer lending, see:

 6. Bruene, Jim. "Online Profitability: Just a Credit Application Away?" *The Journal of Lending and Credit Risk Management,* June 1997, pp. 52–63.

 7. Avery, Robert B., Raphael W. Bostic, Paul S. Calem, and Glenn B. Conner. "Credit Risk, Credit Scoring, and the Performance of Home Mortgages." *Federal Reserve Bulletin,* July 1996, pp. 621–48.

 8. Mester, Loretta J. "What's the Point of Credit Scoring?" *Business Review,* Federal Reserve Bank of Philadelphia, September/October 1997 pp. 3–16.

 9. Conner, Glenn B., Thomas A. Durkin, and Charles A. Luckett. "Recent Developments in Home Equity Lending," *Federal Reserve Bulletin,* April 1998, pp. 241–51.

20 Pricing Consumer and Real Estate Loans

Learning and Management Decision Objectives

The purpose of this chapter is to learn how consumer and real estate loan rates may be determined and to see the options a bank loan officer has today in pricing loans extended to individuals and families.

Introduction

A financial institution prices every consumer loan by setting an interest rate, maturity, and terms of repayment that both the bank and the customer find comfortable. While most consumer loans are short term, stretching over a few weeks or months, long-term loans to purchase automobiles, home appliances, and new homes may stretch from one or two years all the way out to 25 or 30 years. Indeed, in some cases such as with automobile loans consumer loan maturities have been extended in recent years as higher car prices have encouraged lenders to grant longer periods of loan repayment so that consumers can afford the monthly payments on today's high-priced cars. A bank loan officer will usually try to work with the customer, proposing different loan maturities until a repayment schedule is found that, when taking into consideration the consumer's other debt obligations, fits both current and projected household income.

There is usually a negative relationship between the interest rate a consumer is asked to pay and the amount of deposits the consumer is willing to keep with the bank. Customers pledging larger deposits often are granted lower loan rates. Competition among consumer credit suppliers is also a powerful factor shaping consumer loan rates. Where banks face intense competition for consumer loans, interest rates tend to be driven down closer to loan production costs.

Shorter-term cash loans may be unsecured, but longer-term loans to purchase automobiles and other consumer durables are nearly always secured by the assets purchased. For example, with an auto loan the bank will draw up a security agreement and a *chattel mortgage,* giving the bank control over the property if the loan cannot be paid out as planned. Copies of such agreements are usually placed in a public file (such as in the local courthouse or with the secretary of state in the state where the loan is contracted) to alert other lenders that the bank has a claim against the customer's assets.

The Interest Rate Attached to Nonresidential Consumer Loans

Most consumer loans, like most business loans, are priced off some base or cost rate, with a profit margin and compensation for risk added on. For example, the rate on a consumer installment loan may be figured from the cost-plus model:

$$
\begin{array}{l}
\begin{matrix}
\text{Loan rate} \\
\text{paid by the} \\
\text{consumer}
\end{matrix}
=
\begin{matrix}
\text{Bank's cost} \\
\text{of raising} \\
\text{loanable} \\
\text{funds}
\end{matrix}
+
\begin{matrix}
\text{Nonfunds operating} \\
\text{cost (including} \\
\text{wages and salaries} \\
\text{of bank personnel)}
\end{matrix}
\\[3em]
+
\begin{matrix}
\text{Premium for} \\
\text{risk of} \\
\text{customer} \\
\text{default}
\end{matrix}
+
\begin{matrix}
\text{Premium for term} \\
\text{risk with a} \\
\text{longer-term loan}
\end{matrix}
+
\begin{matrix}
\text{Desired} \\
\text{profit} \\
\text{margin}
\end{matrix}
\end{array}
$$

Banks use a wide variety of methods to determine the actual loan rates they will offer to their household customers. The most popular methods for calculating consumer loan rates include the annual percentage rate (or APR), the simple interest method, the discount rate, and the add-on rate method.

Annual Percentage Rate.   Under the terms of the Truth-in-Lending Act, passed in the United States in 1968, the bank must give the individual borrower a statement specifying the **annual percentage rate (APR)** for the proposed loan. The APR is the internal rate of return that equates total payments with the amount of the loan. It takes into account how fast the loan is being repaid and how much credit the customer will actually have use of during the life of the loan.

For example, if a consumer borrows $2,000 for a year, paying off the loan in 12 equal monthly installments, and is assessed $200 in interest cost, the loan rate is not 10 percent (or $200 divided by $2,000), because this borrower has use of much less than $2,000 for a good portion of the coming year. A closer approximation to the true rate on this loan would be 20 percent ($200 ÷ $2,000 ÷ 2) because, over the whole year, the customer has, on average, about $1,000 in credit actually available for use. During the first half of the year, the customer has more than $1,000 at his or her disposal. But in the latter half of the year, the customer will have less than $1,000 available until the loan balance reaches zero at the end of the 12th month.

The Federal Reserve System has prepared rate tables for loan officers to use when the loan rate has been figured by other methods (such as by the simple interest method) in order to convert any given loan rate into the APR. (For an example of these tables, see inside the back cover of this text.) This conversion is clearly of benefit to consumers, because it allows them to compare the loan rate with the loan rates offered by other lenders. The APR encourages individuals to shop around for credit.

For an example of how to use the annual percentage rate (APR) tables (inside the text's back cover) suppose that you, as the loan officer, quote your customer an APR of 12 percent on a one-year loan of $1,000 to be repaid monthly. The customer asks: *how much will I pay in finance charges under this loan?* Checking the "Annual Percentage

Rate Table for Monthly Payment Plans" (inside the back cover) we look down the 12.00% column and across the 12th row (indicating 12 monthly payments). In the table we see that the finance charge per $100 on this loan is $6.62. Because the loan is for $1,000, not $100, the total finance charge to the customer will be

$$\frac{\$1,000}{\$100} \times \$6.62, \text{ or } \$66.20$$

over the life of the loan.

On the other hand, suppose the customer is told he or she must pay $260 in finance charges to get a $2,000 loan for 24 months. This means the customer will pay $260/$2,000/$100 or $13 for every $100 of the $2,000 loan. What APR is this customer being quoted? Checking the APR table inside the text's back cover again, we look across row number 24 for 24 loan payments. In that row the closest figure to $13.00 in finance charges per $100 of loan is $12.98, which lies under the 12.00 percent APR column. Clearly, this customer is being quoted a 12 percent annual percentage loan rate.

Simple Interest.   The **simple interest** approach, like the APR, also adjusts for the length of time a borrower actually has use of the credit he or she is paying for. If the customer is paying off a loan gradually, the simple interest approach first determines the declining loan balance, and that reduced balance is then used to determine the amount of interest owed.

For example, suppose the customer asks for $2,000 for a year at a simple interest rate of 12 percent in order to purchase some furniture. If none of the principal of this loan is to be paid off until the year ends, the interest owed by the customer is as follows:

$$\text{Interest owed} = \text{Principal} \times \text{Rate} \times \text{Time}$$

or

$$I = \$2,000 \times 0.12 \times 1 = \$240$$

At maturity the customer will pay the bank $2,240, or $2,000 in principal plus $240 in interest.

Now assume instead that the loan principal is to be paid off in four quarterly installments of $500 each. The interest owed in each quarter will be:

First quarter: $I = \$2,000 \times 0.12 \times 1/4$
                                   $I = \$60$

Second quarter: $I = \$1,500 \times 0.12 \times 1/4$
                                   $I = \$45$

Third quarter: $I = \$1,000 \times 0.12 \times 1/4$
                                   $I = \$30$

Fourth quarter: $I = \$500 \times 0.12 \times 1/4$
                                   $I = \$15$

Total interest owed: = \$60 + \$45 + \$30 + \$15
                                                 = \$150

Total payments due are as follows:

First quarter:	\$500 + \$60 = \$560
Second quarter:	\$500 + \$45 = \$545
Third quarter:	\$500 + \$30 = \$530
Fourth quarter:	\$500 + \$15 = \$515

Total payments due: \$2,000 + \$150 = \$2,150

Clearly, with simple interest the customer saves on interest as the loan approaches maturity.

The Discount Rate Method. While most consumer loans allow the customer to pay off the interest owed, as well as the principal, gradually over the life of a loan, the **discount rate method** requires the customer to pay interest up front. Under this approach, interest is deduced *first,* and the customer receives the loan amount *less* any interest owed.

For example, suppose the loan officer offers a consumer \$2,000 at a 12 percent loan rate. The \$240 in interest (\$2,000 × 0.12) is deducted from the loan principal; the borrower receives as a deposit available for spending \$2,000 minus \$240, or \$1,760. When the loan matures, however, the customer must pay back the full \$2,000. The borrower's effective loan rate is:

$$\frac{\text{Discount}}{\text{loan rate}} = \frac{\text{Interest owed}}{\text{Net amount of credit received}} = \frac{\$240}{\$1,760} = 0.136, \text{ or } 13.6 \text{ percent}$$

The Add-On Loan Rate Method. One of the oldest loan-rate calculation methods is known simply as the **add-on method** because any interest owed is added to the principal amount of the loan before the customer is told what the required installment payments will be. For example, if the customer requests \$2,000 and is offered a 12 percent add-on interest rate and a repayment plan of 12 equal monthly installments, the total payments due will be \$2,000 in principal plus \$240 in interest, or \$2,240. Each monthly payment will be \$186.67 (\$2,240 ÷ 12), consisting of \$166.67 in loan principal and \$20 in monthly interest. Because the borrower has only about \$1,000, on average, available during the year, the effective loan rate is approximately as follows:

$$\frac{\text{Effective}}{\text{loan rate}} = \frac{\text{Interest owed}}{\text{Average loan amount during year}} = \frac{\$240}{\$1,000} = 0.24, \text{ or } 24 \text{ percent}$$

Only if the loan is paid off in a single lump sum at the end will the add-on rate equal the simple interest rate. Otherwise, the consumer is paying a higher effective loan rate than he or she is being quoted.

Rule of 78s.   A rule of thumb used to determine exactly how much interest income a bank is entitled to accrue at any point in time from a consumer loan that is being paid out in monthly installments is known as the **Rule of 78s.** This is particularly important when a borrower pays off a loan early and may therefore be entitled to a rebate of some of the interest charges associated with the loan. The rule of 78s arises from the fact that the sum of the digits 1 through 12 is 78 (that is, $1 + 2 + 3 + \ldots + 10 + 11 + 12 = 78$). To determine the borrowing customer's interest rebate from early repayment of an installment loan, total the digits for the months remaining on the loan and divide that sum by 78. For example, suppose a consumer requests a one-year loan to be repaid in 12 monthly installments, but is able to repay the loan after only nine months. This customer would be entitled to receive back as an interest rebate:

$$\frac{1+2+3}{1+2+\ldots+11+12} \times 100 = \frac{6}{78} \times 100 = 7.69 \text{ percent}$$

of the total finance charges on the loan. The lender is entitled to keep 92.31 percent of those finance charges.

Compensating Balance Requirements.   Many banks require that a consumer borrowing money from them keep a certain percentage of the loan amount in a deposit account. This so-called **compensating deposit balance** requirement raises the effective cost of a consumer loan because the borrower does not have use of the full amount of the loan. Instead, the borrower only has use of the loan amount minus the required deposit balance. The effective interest return to the bank then rises above the loan rate quoted to the borrower.

For example, suppose $1,000 is borrowed for one year at an interest rate of 8 percent. The lending bank requires that 10 percent of the loan amount, which is $100, be kept on deposit with the bank throughout the life of the loan. This means the borrower will have use of only $900 (or $1,000 less 0.10 × $1,000). With a loan rate of 8 percent the borrower will owe $80 in interest (or $1,000 × 0.08). However, the true or effective loan rate is *not* 8 percent, but rather:

$$\begin{array}{l}\text{Effective} \\ \text{loan rate with} \\ \text{compensating} \\ \text{balance} \\ \text{requirement}\end{array} = \frac{\begin{array}{c}\text{Amount of} \\ \text{interest owed} \\ \text{on the loan}\end{array}}{\begin{array}{c}\text{Total amount} \\ \text{borrowed less} \\ \text{compensating} \\ \text{balance required}\end{array}} = \frac{\$80}{(\$1{,}000 - \$100)} = \begin{array}{c}0.0889, \\ \text{or} \\ 8.89 \\ \text{percent}\end{array}$$

Clearly, the stipulation in a consumer loan agreement that funds must be kept on deposit with the lending bank raises the bank's effective loan yield.

Use of Variable Rates on Consumer Loans

The majority of installment and lump-sum payment loans to families and individuals are made with *fixed* interest rates rather than with floating rates that change with credit

Banker's Insights and Issues

Consumer Loan Rates: Recent Surveys and What They Reveal

Consumer loan rates are among the most interesting interest rates charged for credit in the financial system. Recently the Federal Reserve Board began surveying banks and finance companies for the loan rates they quote (as well as for selected other loan terms, such as loan maturity, loan-to-value ratios, and the average amount financed) for automobile loans and for personal credit. An example of the recent loan terms quoted on these different loan types is shown in the table below.

Type of Loan and Lending Institution	Average Annual Loan Rate	Type of Loan	Survey Item
		Average Maturity of Loans in Months:	
Commercial Banks:			
48-month new car loan	8.92%	New car loans	54.6 months
24-month personal loan	13.46	Used car loans	51.1
Credit cards—all accounts	15.88		
Credit cards—accounts assessed interest	15.13		
Auto Finance Companies:		Loan-to-Value Ratio:	
New car loans	7.44	New car loans	92%
Used car loans	13.08	Used car loans	99
		Amount Financed in Dollars:	
		New car loans	$16,837
		Used car loans	12,202

Source: Survey by the Board of Governors of the Federal Reserve System. See selected monthly issues of the *Federal Reserve Bulletin*, including the November 1997 Issue, Table 1.56, Page A36.

market conditions. However, due to the volatility of interest rates in the 1980s and 1990s, a greater number of floating-rate consumer loans have appeared. One reason for the sparing use of floating rates on most consumer loans is their comparatively short maturities. Then, too, banks find it relatively easy to match the maturities of their deposits to the maturities of their large-volume consumer loans, especially by more aggressively selling CDs in the required maturity range. When floating-rate consumer loans are issued, their contract rates are most often tied to either the prime (commercial) loan rate or to U.S. Treasury bill rates in what is often called *base rate* pricing.

Surveying the table above reveals some interesting associations between consumer loan rates and other terms of a consumer loan, such as maturity, cost, and risk. We notice, for example, that credit card loans, which are among the riskiest loans to make in terms of both loan default and losses due to credit card fraud, tend to carry the highest average interest rates. Automobile loans are generally cheaper ratewise than personal loans (even though the latter tend to have shorter maturities) because auto loans are usually secured by marketable collateral (assets)—the automobile itself—while many personal loans are either unsecured by any specific collateral or have collateral pledged that is more difficult to sell at a relatively stable price.

We note also that new car loan rates tend to be lower than used car loan rates. The newer the vehicle, the easier it generally is to sell should the borrower be unable to repay and bankers find that many new car owners tend to take better care of their vehicles than do many used car owners. However, used cars have been rising rapidly in price due to heavier demand as many new cars have become so expensive. Then, too, car rental companies have tended to keep their fleets for longer periods, so the supply of used cars from this traditional source has diminished in recent years. As a result, many used-car loans are now extended for maturities that equal or exceed new-car loan maturities, and lenders have been willing to extend a larger percentage of a used car's purchase price in the form of a loan, recognizing the generally rising trend in used car market prices.

Overall, there is evidence that consumers have recently become much more sensitive to differences in loan rates on different types of loans offered by different lending institutions. More and more borrowers today are jumping from one credit card, installment, or home mortgage lender to another as competing lenders offer "teaser" low loan rates, refinancing their debt to lower monthly payments. Indeed, even the smallest consumer borrowers with little financial education are now increasingly shopping around and learning to refinance everything from automobile, mobile home, and home mortgage loans to credit card obligations. The result is narrower spreads on consumer loans, lower profits, and greater consolidation among lending institutions.

For example, in March 1995 the majority of the largest U.S. banks were quoting a prime rate of 9 percent. A consumer borrowing to finance a vacation or to repay some medical bills might be quoted an initial rate of:

$$
\begin{array}{l}
\text{Floating} \\
\text{prime-based} \\
\text{consumer} \\
\text{loan rate}
\end{array}
=
\begin{array}{l}
\text{Prime} \\
\text{or base} \\
\text{rate}
\end{array}
+
\begin{array}{l}
\text{Risk} \\
\text{premium}
\end{array}
=
\begin{array}{l}
9 \\
\text{percent}
\end{array}
+
\begin{array}{l}
4 \\
\text{percent}
\end{array}
=
\begin{array}{l}
13 \\
\text{percent}
\end{array}
$$

If the prime rate subsequently moves upward to 10 percent, then the consumer's new loan rate would be:

$$\begin{array}{c}\text{Floating prime-based}\\\text{consumer loan rate}\end{array} = 10 \text{ percent} + 4 \text{ percent} = 14 \text{ percent}$$

Quite obviously, if the lending institution controls the base rate itself, the lender could change the base and the loan rate itself anytime it wishes. Because this could be grossly unfair to borrowers, most bank regulatory agencies insist that the base rate being used *not* be under the lender's direct control. In the example above, the prime rate quoted in *The Wall Street Journal* and other widely read financial news sheets is based on an average of top-quality loan rates quoted by at least 75 percent of the 30 largest banks in the United States. Thus, it would be difficult for any one bank to arbitrarily reset its prime rate irrespective of market conditions simply to jack up the loan rates paid by its customers.

Concept Checks

20–1. What options does a bank loan officer have in pricing consumer loans?

20–2. Suppose a customer is offered a loan at a discount rate of 8 percent and pays $75 in interest at the beginning of the term of the loan. What net amount of credit did this customer receive? Suppose you are told that the effective rate on this loan is 12 percent. What is the average loan amount the customer has available during the year?

20–3. See if you can determine what APR you are charging a consumer loan customer, using the APR table inside the back cover of this text, if you grant the customer a loan for five years, payable in monthly installments, if the customer must pay a finance charge of $42.74 per $100.

20–4. If you quote a consumer loan customer an APR of 16 percent on a $10,000 loan with a term of four years that requires monthly installment payments, what finance charge must this customer pay?

Interest Rates on Home Mortgage Loans

For nearly half a century, stretching from the Great Depression of the 1930s into the 1970s, most home mortgage loans to finance the purchase of new homes were **fixed-rate mortgages (FRMs)**—that is, they carried *fixed* terms, especially a *fixed interest rate* that the borrower could rely upon. In the early 1970s, the pressure of inflation and volatile interest rates gave rise to adjustable-rate home mortgage loans, with several states allowing their state-chartered mortgage lending institutions to offer such loans. Then in 1981, both the Comptroller of the Currency and the Federal Home Loan Bank

Board authorized **adjustable-rate mortgages (ARMs)** for all U.S. federally chartered depository institutions. So rapid has been the growth of ARMs that in recent years roughly as many new mortgage loans have carried adjustable rates as fixed rates. About one-quarter of all home mortgage loans outstanding have adjustable terms today.

The recent upsurge in the popularity of ARMs may be attributed to the aggressive marketing of these loans by bankers seeking to make the yields on their earning assets more responsive to market interest rate movements. Many bankers have offered "teaser rates" that are significantly below loan rates on fixed-rate mortgages (FRMs). Because ARMs often do carry lower initial interest rates than traditional fixed-rate mortgages, they allow more individuals and families to qualify for a home mortgage loan. Many home mortgage lenders have also begun to offer *cap rates* on ARMs. For example, the lender may agree not to raise the loan rate more than two percentage points in any given year or more than five percentage points over the life of the loan, no matter how high other interest rates in the economy go.

Whether a customer takes out an FRM or an ARM, the loan officer must determine what the initial loan rate will be and, therefore, what the monthly payments will be. Each monthly payment on a home mortgage loan reduces a portion of the principal of the loan and a portion of the interest owed on the total amount borrowed. With the majority of mortgage loan contracts today, most monthly payments early in the life of the loan go to pay interest. As the loan gets closer to maturity, the monthly payments increasingly are devoted to reducing the loan's outstanding principal.

A useful formula to help loan officers and customers determine if a mortgage loan is affordable is the following expression for figuring the *required monthly payment,* given the interest rate the bank or other mortgage lender will charge:

$$\text{Customer's monthly loan mortgage payment} = \frac{\text{Amount of loan principal} \times \left(\dfrac{\text{Annual loan rate}}{12}\right) \times \left(1 + \dfrac{\text{Annual loan rate}}{12}\right)^{t \times 12}}{\left[\left(1 + \dfrac{\text{Annual loan rate}}{12}\right)^{t \times 12} - 1\right]}$$

In this case, t is the number of years the loan will cover. The factor 12 is included to restate the loan's term and annual rate of interest in *months.*

To illustrate this formula's use, suppose a customer is interested in securing a 25-year mortgage loan of $50,000 to purchase a new home. The bank has decided that an interest rate of 12 percent is about right for today's market. The required monthly payments would be as follows:

$$\text{Each monthly payment} = \frac{\$50,000 \times \left(\dfrac{0.12}{12}\right) \times \left(1 + \dfrac{0.12}{12}\right)^{25 \times 12}}{\left(1 + \dfrac{0.12}{12}\right)^{25 \times 12} - 1} = \frac{\$9,894.23}{18.7885}$$

$$= \$526.61$$

Thus, with a fixed-rate mortgage (FRM) loan this customer would pay $526.61 monthly for 25 years, which amounts to $107,985 in total interest payments over the life of the loan plus gradual repayment of the principal of $50,000.

The actual monthly payment on the loan just described normally will vary somewhat from year to year even with an FRM due to changes in property taxes, dwelling insurance, and other fees that typically are included in each monthly installment payment on a home mortgage. An easier method for calculating the monthly payment shown above is to use the annual percentage rate (APR) table inside the back cover. To find the mortgage loan's required monthly payment, determine the total finance charge the customer will pay at any given interest rate over the life of the loan. The intersection of the annual interest rate (along the APR table's top row) and the number of payments that must be made between now and the loan's maturity date gives the total finance charge per $100 financed by the bank. If we divide $100 into the total amount of the loan and multiply the resulting figure by the total finance charge per $100 financed, we can determine the total amount of interest the customer must pay by the time the loan runs out. Specifically:

$$\begin{array}{l} \text{Total finance} \\ \text{charge per} \\ \text{\$100 financed} \end{array} = \$215.97$$

$$\begin{array}{l} \text{Total finance} \\ \text{charge on} \\ \text{the amount} \\ \text{of the loan} \end{array} = \frac{\$50,000}{\$100} \times \$215.97 = \$107,985$$

$$\begin{array}{l} \text{Monthly payment} \\ \text{on the home} \\ \text{mortgage} \end{array} = \frac{\left(\begin{array}{cc} \text{Total finance} & \text{Loan} \\ \text{charge} & + \text{amount} \end{array} \right)}{\text{Number of payments}} = \frac{(\$107,985 + \$50,000)}{300}$$

$$= \$526.61$$

Note that this simpler method yields the same monthly payment as does the long formula presented in the preceding paragraph.

In the foregoing example we calculated the required monthly payments on a fixed-rate mortgage (FRM). We can, of course, use the same method to calculate the required monthly payment on an adjustable rate mortgage loan (ARM) by simply plugging in a new interest rate each time that interest rates change. For example, assume that, as in the FRM example above, the initial loan rate for an ARM is also 12 percent. However, after one year (i.e., 12 monthly payments) has elapsed, the mortgage loan rate rises to 13 percent.

In this case the customer's monthly payments would increase to:

$$\begin{array}{l} \text{Each} \\ \text{monthly} \\ \text{payment} \end{array} = \frac{\$49,663 \times \left(\dfrac{0.13}{12} \right) \times \left(1 + \dfrac{0.13}{12} \right)^{24 \times 12}}{\left(1 + \dfrac{0.13}{12} \right)^{24 \times 12} - 1} = \$563.31$$

This example assumes that the loan rate increased to 13 percent beginning with the 13th monthly payment. Note that after one year the principal of the loan (which originally stood at $50,000) had dropped to $49,663 due to the monthly payments made during the first 12 months of the loan. Despite a full year of payments, the principal of the loan dropped only slightly because the bulk of payments early in the life of a mortgage loan go to pay interest charges rather than principal. When considering whether or not to approve a customer's request for an adjustable-rate loan, the loan officer must decide whether a rise in interest rates is likely and whether the customer has sufficient budget flexibility and future earnings potential to handle the varying loan payments that can exist with an adjustable-rate loan.

Charging the Customer Mortgage Points.   Home mortgage loan agreements often require borrowers to pay an additional charge up front called **points.** This extra charge is determined by multiplying the amount of the home mortgage loan by a specific percentage figure. For example, suppose the borrower seeks a $100,000 home loan and the lender assesses the borrower an up-front charge of two points. In this case the home buyer's extra charge would be:

$$\begin{matrix} \text{Dollar amount} \\ \text{of points} \\ \text{charged on} \\ \text{a home} \\ \text{mortgage} \\ \text{loan} \end{matrix} = \begin{matrix} \text{Amount} \\ \text{of the} \\ \text{mortgage} \\ \text{loan} \end{matrix} \times \begin{matrix} \text{Number} \\ \text{of points} \\ \text{charged} \\ \text{by the} \\ \text{lender} \end{matrix} = \$100,000 \times 0.02 = \$2,000$$

By requiring the borrower to pay something extra over and above the interest owed on his or her home loan, a bank can earn a higher effective interest rate on a loan than just the loan rate quoted to the borrower. This extra yield to the bank can be found by deducting from the amount of the mortgage loan the dollar amount of points charged (as determined from the formula above) and by adding the dollar amount of points to the interest owed on the loan. In this instance we would argue that the borrower has available for his or her use, not the full amount of the mortgage loan, but rather the loan amount *less* the points assessed by the bank.

For example, suppose a borrower is assessed two points on a 20-year home mortgage loan amounting to $100,000 and bearing an interest rate of 7 percent. Deducting the $2,000 in points (or $100,000 × 0.02) from the $100,000 loan amount tells us that the borrower has only $98,000 in credit available. This raises the borrower's effective interest rate from 7 percent to about 7.26 percent and thereby generates a higher effective yield for the bank. Points in a home mortgage loan have an impact on a borrower's effective loan rate similar to the impact of a required compensating balance discussed earlier in this chapter.

Summary

Over the years several different methods for determining the interest rates on consumer loans have emerged. Among the most popular are the *simple interest method,* which adjusts for the declining balance on a loan that is paid back in installments over time, the *add-on rate* approach, which charges interest fees based on the full face amount of a loan when the loan begins, and the *discount rate method,* in which interest is paid up front, and the borrower has use only of the net amount remaining after all the interest owed is deducted from the face amount of the note the borrower signs. With so many different interest rate measures used for consumer loans, confusion was bound to occur. Accordingly, the U.S. government and federal bank regulatory agencies require today that consumers be told the *annual percentage rate* (APR) they will have to pay to obtain credit—an actuarial rate that adjusts for the changing balance of a loan and the number of payments a consumer will be required to make in order to obtain the credit he or she needs.

There is a trend today toward more variable (flexible) loan rates in the consumer credit field in order to reduce the interest rate risk faced by consumer lending institutions. A substantial number (though still a minority) of all consumer loans today are tied to some base interest rate (such as the prime lending rate or government bond rate), with the loan rate assessed against the consumer changing with movements in the base rate. This trend toward more flexible loan rates is particularly evident in home mortgage lending where most lenders offer both fixed-rate mortgages (FRMs) and adjustable-rate mortgages (ARMs). In the case of an adjustable-rate loan, bank loan officers must be especially careful in deciding whether a borrowing customer has sufficient budgetary flexibility to be able to adjust to variable loan payments, particularly if it seems likely that market interest rates may rise very high over the life of the loan.

Key Terms in This Chapter

Annual percentage rate (APR)
Simple interest
Discount rate method
Add-on method
Rule of 78s

Compensating deposit balance
Fixed-rate mortgages (FRMs)
Adjustable-rate mortgages (ARMs)
Points

Problems and Projects

1. William Crenshaw, who operates a small retail store in the shopping center adjacent to the bank's branch office, has asked for a personal loan of $4,500. Crenshaw wants to keep the principal of the loan for a full year and pay the interest at that time. However, the bank insists on monthly amortization of the loan, with a 13 percent annual interest rate. Under these terms, how much interest will Crenshaw pay in a year? How much interest would he have paid if he had gotten the loan on his preferred terms?

2. Frank Petrel wants to start his own business, an auto repair shop, located at the corner of Kresick Avenue and Vine Street. He has asked

the bank for a $10,000 new-venture loan. The bank has a policy of making *discount-rate* loans in these cases if the venture looks good, but at an interest rate of prime plus 2. (The prime rate is currently posted at 12.5 percent.) If Mr. Petrel's loan is approved for the full amount requested, what net proceeds will he have to work with from this loan? What is the effective interest rate on this loan for one year?

Alternative scenarios:

(1) Would Mr. Petrel be better off if he were able to get a $10,000 personal loan with a 12.5 percent *add-on rate* for one year? Why or why not?

(2) What happens to the effective rate on Mr. Petrel's loan if the prime rate changes to 10 percent?

(3) How does the effective rate on this loan change if the prime rate increases to 13 percent?

(4) Suppose Mr. Petrel is able to raise personal equity to put into the new business in the amount of $2,500 from his accumulated savings and from a small loan extended by a close friend. The bank then will lend him just $7,500 at a discount rate of prime plus one-and-a-half percentage points (currently prime is 12 percent). What is the effective interest rate on the loan in this case?

3. The Robbins family has asked for a 20-year mortgage in the amount of $60,000 to purchase a home. At a 10 percent loan rate, what is the required monthly payment?

Alternative scenarios:

(1) If the Robbins' home mortgage loan rate is adjustable and rises to 11 percent at the beginning of the loan's second year, what will the required monthly payment be?

(2) Suppose the rate on the Robbins' home mortgage declines to 9 percent at the beginning of the loan's second year. What happens to the required monthly payment?

(3) Would the Robbins family be better off under all of the above scenarios if they took out a 15-year mortgage instead of a 20-year

mortgage? What would they gain and what would they give up with this mortgage loan of shorter maturity?

4. James Alters received a $1,500 loan last month with the intention of repaying the loan in 12 months. However, Alters now discovers he has the cash to repay the loan right now after making just one payment. What percentage of the total finance charge is Alters entitled to receive as a rebate and what percentage of the loan's finance charge is the bank entitled to keep?

5. Constance Homer is planning to start a small business and has asked Slidell Corners State Bank for a $10,000 loan. The bank agrees to Ms. Homer's business proposal and indicates it will give Constance $9,400 when the loan begins and collect $600 in interest up front. What is the effective interest rate on this loan?

6. The Lindal family has been planning a vacation to Europe for the past two years. Stilwater Savings and Credit Bank agrees to advance a loan of $2,500 to finance the trip provided the Lindal's pay the loan back in 12 equal monthly installments during the current year. The bank will charge an add-on loan rate of 12 percent. How much in interest will the Lindal's pay under the add-on rate method? What is the amount of each required monthly payment? What is the effective loan rate in this case?

7. Joseph Nework's request for a three-year automobile loan for $10,000 has been approved. Reston Center Bank will require equal monthly installment payments for 36 months until the loan is fully retired. The bank tells Joseph that he must pay a total of $2,217 in finance charges to receive this loan. What is the loan's APR? (Hint: Be sure to check the APR tables inside the back cover of the text.)

8. Kyle Ellisor has asked for a 30-year mortgage to purchase a home on Long Island. The purchase price is $260,000, of which Ellisor must borrow $225,000 to be repaid in monthly installments. If Kyle can get this loan for an APR of 14 percent, how much in total finance charges must he pay?

9. Suppose that the Quisling family plans to borrow $1,800 at a simple interest rate of 11 percent for one year to acquire new lawn furniture. What amount of interest must the family pay? How much in total must they pay back to the lender?

10. Mary Perland is offered a $1,200 loan for a year to be paid back in equal quarterly installments of $300 each. If Mary is offered the loan at 8 percent simple interest, how much in total interest charges will she pay? Would Mary be better off (in terms of lower interest cost) if she were offered the $1,200 at 6 percent simple interest with only one principal payment when the loan reaches maturity? What advantage would this second set of loan terms have over the first set of loan terms?

11. The Tielman family has asked for a $2,500 loan for one year to complete home repairs. First National Bank will loan the money but insists that the Tielmans move their deposit account to First National from the bank where they used to trade. The loan will carry an interest rate of 8 percent and the Tielmans must keep a minimum $500 balance in their deposit account. What is the effective interest rate on this loan?

12. Bill and Sue Rogers are negotiating with their local bank to secure a mortgage loan in order to buy their first home. With only a limited down payment available to them, Bill and Sue must borrow $80,000. Moreover, the bank has assessed them one-and-a-half points on the loan. What is the dollar amount of points they must pay to receive this loan? How much home mortgage credit will they actually have available for their use?

13. As loan officer you quote Mr. and Mrs. Coldner an APR of 14 percent on a two-year loan to remodel their kitchen. The loan amount is $6,000. Using the APR tables inside the back cover of the text, determine the total finance charge on this loan.

   If the Coldners reject this offer and insist on a 12 percent APR for this two-year loan, how much in income will the bank lose?

14. Dresden Bank's personal loan department quotes Mr. Angelo a finance charge of $6.06 for each $100 in credit the bank is willing to extend to him for a year (assuming the balance of the loan is to be paid off in 12 equal installments). What APR is Mr. Angelo being quoted by the bank? How much would he save per $100 borrowed if he could retire the loan in six months?

15. Would you expect loan interest rates on new cars to be higher than on used cars? Why or why not? Would you expect a personal loan to carry a higher interest rate than an automobile loan? Why or why not? Please give all the reasons you can for your answers to these two questions.

Selected References

For discussions of the pricing and calculation of consumer loan rates, see the following:

1. Federal Reserve Bank of Chicago. *ABCs of Figuring Interest,* 1993.
2. Goodman, John L., and Charles A. Luckett. "Adjustable-Rate Financing in Mortgage and Consumer Credit Markets." *Federal Reserve Bulletin,* November 1985, pp. 825–38.
3. Trainer, Richard D. C. *The Arithmetic of Interest Rates.* Federal Reserve Bank of New York, 1990.

VI THE BANK'S ORGANIZATIONAL STRUCTURE AND SERVICE OPTIONS: CHOOSING A CHANNEL FOR FUTURE GROWTH AND EXPANSION

21 CREATING AND MANAGING BANK SERVICE OUTLETS:

Establishing New Banks, Branches, Electronic and Automated Facilities

Learning and Management Decision Objectives

The purpose of this chapter is to learn how new banks are chartered by state and federal authorities in the United States, to determine what makes a good site for a new branch office, to recognize how the role of branch offices is changing, and to explore the advantages and disadvantages of limited-service automated banking facilities.

Introduction

One of the most important components of bank-provided services is *convenience*. Bank customers want access to their checking or savings accounts and access to loans at a time and place that conveniently answers their financial-service needs. For most of banking's history *convenience* has meant *location*. Businesses and consumers have preferred to buy the services of a bank located in the same community or neighborhood rather than from a bank situated across town, in another state, or from another region or country.

However, customers' views about what is "convenient" about a bank are changing with the growing use of home and office computers, fax machines, automated tellers dispensing cash and accepting deposits, point-of-sale terminals in retail stores allowing a customer to pay electronically for his or her purchases, and credit cards that grant access to an instant loan without requiring bank approval for every purchase made. These new technologies for storing and transmitting financial information have eroded the significance of *physical location* (geography) as the main determinant of which bank a customer chooses today. In today's world *timely access* to banking services, not just the physical location of a bank's service facilities, becomes the key indicator of customer convenience. For example, it may be faster and easier to request a loan via telephone and fax machine from a bank located hundreds of miles away than it is to visit a bank situated only blocks away, but reachable only by weaving your way through traffic jams and crowded parking lots.

However, for some important financial services today—especially checking accounts, small savings deposits, safety deposit boxes, and consumer and small business loans—*physical location* or *physical presence* is still of considerable importance to many bank customers. This is especially true when something goes wrong with a banking service. For example, when a customer discovers that his or her deposit account is overdrawn or when the customer's estimate of an account balance does not agree with the bank's figures and checks begin to bounce, the presence of a nearby bank office often becomes very important. Thus, for many retail deposit and loan services and when special problems arise, the convenient physical location of a bank is still a valued commodity to many users of banking services.

In deciding how they will respond to customers' changing demands for timely access to banking services, bankers today have several options to choose from:

1. *Chartering completely new banks.*
2. *Establishing new full-service branch offices,* offering most or all of the services that are also available at the bank's home office.
3. *Setting up limited-service facilities,* including drive-in and walk-up teller windows, self-service terminals inside bank branches, automated teller machines (both those on bank premises and those situated in remote locations, such as shopping centers, airports, or retail shops), point-of-sale terminals in stores linked to the bank's computer, telephone banking services, home and office computers linked to a bank's computer through the Internet, and other electronic media.

In the sections that follow we examine each of these options for delivering a bank's services conveniently to its customers.

Chartering a New Bank

No one can start a bank in the United States (and in many other nations as well) without the express approval of federal or state authorities. The public's need for a new bank in a particular location must be demonstrated and the honesty and competence of its organizers and proposed management established. Sufficient protection against failure must be provided in the form of equity capital pledged by the founding stockholders. Usually they must supply enough start-up capital (currently in the $2 million to $10 million range) to cover several years (usually at least the initial three years) and show that the proposed new institution will soon achieve adequate levels of profitability.

Why is all this required for new banks? Government chartering agencies believe that banks need special scrutiny for several reasons: (1) they are the principal institutions holding the public's savings, and unregulated chartering activity might result in excessive numbers of poorly capitalized banks that fail; (2) banks are at the heart of the payments process to support trade and commerce, so their failure could disrupt business activity; and (3) banks create more money (immediate spending power) than any other financial institution, which suggests that chartering too many banks might result in excessive money creation and inflation. Although there is considerable debate about the validity of these arguments, they constitute the key rationale for the elaborate structure of cradle-to-grave regulation and restrictions on entry into the industry that characterizes most banking systems today.

The Bank Chartering Process

Only the banking commissions in each of the 50 U.S. states and the **Office of the Comptroller of the Currency** (OCC)—a division of the U.S. Treasury Department—can issue a **charter of incorporation** to start a new U.S. bank. Generally speaking, federal standards for receiving a bank charter are more rigorous than the rules of the **state banking commissions.** However, organizers often seek a federal bank charter for the added prestige it conveys in the minds of customers, especially large depositors. An additional check on the bank chartering policies of the state banking commissions is provided by the **Federal Deposit Insurance Corporation (FDIC).** Most newly formed banks immediately seek FDIC insurance for their deposits in order to strengthen public confidence in the new institution and the banking laws of most states require a new bank to obtain federal deposit insurance certification before the state banking commission will issue its charter of incorporation. The FDIC must be convinced that the new bank is likely to be managed prudently before it will issue a certificate of insurance, which guarantees federal payments of up to $100,000 to each qualified deposit holder if the bank fails and another bank cannot be found to assume responsibility for the failing bank's deposits.

In 1992 the FDIC announced new conditions under which it would grant new banks deposit insurance. These changes were dictated primarily by congressional passage of the Financial Institutions Reform, Recovery, and Enforcement Act of 1989 and the FDIC Improvement Act of 1991. Prior to passage of these two laws, banks receiving federal charters and those securing membership in the Federal Reserve System were automatically granted FDIC insurance coverage. Now *all* new federal and state banks must *apply* for FDIC insurance. Moreover, the FDIC increased initial minimum capitalization requirements for new banks from $750,000 to at least $2 million. Those who own new banks must demonstrate their ability to support their bank's operations and provide the new bank with capital as needed. Initial capitalization for a new bank must be sufficient to provide that institution with an 8 percent ratio of equity capital to assets by the end of its third year of operation. In addition, any stock bonuses or stock option plans granted to a new bank's directors, officers, or other insiders must be fully disclosed to *all* shareholders. New banks must secure an annual independent audit of their books for at least the first five years after insurance coverage is granted.

The chartering process typically begins with a group of people or a bank holding company organization becoming convinced that a new bank is needed in a particular city. Frequently, a group of local businessmen and women who have found the services (especially the loans) of existing banks in the area to be inadequate will come together to fill out a bank charter application. Sometimes the entry of banks from out of town, buying up local banks, stimulates local businessmen and women to come together to organize a new bank more responsive to their personalized service needs. The application forms will be mailed upon request from the Comptroller or from the banking commission of the state where the proposed bank is to be located.

The choice between pursuing a federal or a state bank charter usually comes down to weighing the benefits and costs of each for the particular bank and location the organizers have in mind. The key pros and cons include the following:

Benefits of Applying for a Federal (National) Bank Charter
- It brings added prestige due to stricter regulatory standards, which may help attract corporate and individual deposits.
- In times of trouble the technical assistance supplied to a struggling bank by national bank authorities may be of better quality, giving the troubled bank a better chance of long-run survival.

Benefits of Applying for a State Bank Charter
- It may be easier and less costly to secure a state charter.
- The bank need not join the Federal Reserve System and, therefore, avoids having to buy and hold low-yielding Federal Reserve stock.
- Many states allow a bank to lend a higher percentage of its capital to a single borrower, while national banks can lend unsecured only up to 15 percent of their capital and surplus.
- State-chartered banks may be able to make types of loans (e.g., loans on unimproved land) or offer services (e.g., sales of insurance) that national banks cannot offer.

Concept Checks

21–1. Why is the physical location or physical presence of a bank still important to many bank customers despite recent advances in long-distance communications technology?

21–2. Why is the creation (chartering) of new banks closely regulated?

21–3. What do you see as the principal benefits and costs of government regulation of the number of bank charters issued?

21–4. Who charters new banks in the United States?

21–5. What key role does the FDIC play in the chartering process?

21–6. What are the advantages of having a national bank charter? A state bank charter?

Questions Regulators Usually Ask the Organizers of a New Bank

It is instructive to look at the types of information chartering authorities demand before approving or denying a bank charter application. A sample of the questions asked by the Comptroller of the Currency on applications to charter new national banks is given in the text below. These criteria are often used by bank organizers and government chartering agencies to assess a new bank's prospects for success.

Here are some of the most important questions the Comptroller's office will ask of a new bank's organizers:

1. What are the population and geographic boundaries of the primary service area (PSA) from which the new bank is expected to generate 75 percent or

more of its loans and deposits? The PSA must have enough businesses and households to ensure an adequate customer base for the new bank.

2. How many competing banks, savings and loans, credit unions, finance companies, and insurance companies granting loans are located within the service area of the proposed bank? The organizers must include information on competitor's services, hours of operation, and distances from the proposed bank. The more intense local competition is, the more difficult it is for a new bank to attract customers.

3. What are the number, types, and sizes of businesses in the service area? New banks depend heavily on the demands of businesses for commercial deposit services and for loans to stock their shelves with inventories and to purchase business equipment.

4. The organizers are asked to describe traffic patterns in the proposed bank's service area, the adequacy of its roads and highways, and any geographic barriers to the flow of traffic. Most new banks are situated along major routes of travel for commuters going to work and to shopping areas and schools, providing greater customer convenience.

5. Specifically, what is happening to population growth, incomes, types of occupations represented, educational levels, and the age distribution of residents in the proposed bank service area? The presence of well-educated residents in the local area implies higher incomes and greater use of banking services.

6. The organizers are asked to describe the banking history of the local community, the frequency with which new banks have been added to the area, and their track record of performance. The rapid growth of other banks in the local area and good profitability among these institutions suggests that the proposed bank might also become profitable and experience good growth.

7. The organizers must indicate who is to own any stock issued by the proposed bank, especially the amount to be held by the bank's organizers, directors, officers, and their families. The chartering agency wants to be sure the bank can raise adequate capital to support its future growth and protect its depositors and likes to see evidence of a broad base of support among local residents.

8. What is the business and banking experience of the organizers and senior management of the new bank? Successful businesspeople on the bank's board and staff will help attract new credit and deposit accounts. Many chartering agencies insist on fingerprinting the organizers and managers of new banks to facilitate background checks in order to make sure the individuals involved have clean records.

9. What are the organizers' projections for total deposits, loans, revenues, operating expenses, and net income for the first three to five years of the proposed bank's operation? The quality of these projections will shed light on how much the organizers of a proposed new bank know about the banking business.

The answers to these questions are often supported by a detailed economic analysis of the local market, prepared by an economist or professional business analyst.

Frequently, local businesses and households are surveyed on the possible need for a new bank. If existing banks in the area protest the awarding of a new charter, a public hearing may be held, in which the organizers will submit testimony concerning (1) why there is a public need for the new bank, (2) the likelihood the new bank will be profitable (usually within three years), and (3) whether there is adequate business in the local area to support both the new bank and existing financial institutions without increasing the probability of bank failures.

The organizers usually establish **public need** by pointing out either that local banks are not conveniently located to businesses and residents in the area or that existing banks fail to offer some key services, such as business equipment loans or trust services. However, the public-need factor in bank charter decisions appears to have become somewhat less important in recent years. In 1984 the Comptroller of the Currency announced that, in the future, *less* emphasis would be placed on "public convenience and needs" in evaluating applications for new national bank charters. Under the new feasibility standard used by the Comptroller's office, applicants for a national bank charter are asked for a detailed business plan and are required to demonstrate that skilled management will be hired for the new bank. If the organizers pledge sufficient capital and the business plan and proposed management appear to be adequate, a new charter is likely to be issued.

Opponents of the charter application (which may include local bankers and others with an interest in preserving current industry conditions) usually counter by claiming (*a*) that residents of the area are already adequately served by existing banks and (*b*) that chartering a new bank would threaten the well-being of existing institutions. At times public hearings held to consider bank charter applications become very bitter because so much in time, resources, and future bank earnings are at stake.

Concept Checks

21–7. What kinds of information must the organizers of new national banks provide the Comptroller of the Currency in order to get a charter?

21–8. What is the meaning of *public need* as it applies to the chartering of new banks?

Factors Weighing on the Decision to Seek a New Bank Charter

Filing a bank charter application is a costly process in most of the United States. An attorney with knowledge of banking laws is usually hired, and an economic consultant is often employed to survey local residents and assess the proposed bank's prospects for success. The filing fee ranges from $1,000 or more to file an application for a state charter to $2,500 for a federal charter application. Filling out the formal application and preparing for a public hearing requires the expenditure of thousands of dollars, which the organizers of the proposed bank often supply after endorsing an expense-sharing agreement in which a small group of investors agree to supply in advance a small pro rata share of the total amount of capital they have pledged to support the new bank. Moreover, there is no guarantee of success even after all these monies are spent because the regulatory authorities may refuse to grant a charter (usually alleging that there is insufficient business activity in the service area to support a new bank). Thus, the organizers of a new bank must carefully analyze their business prospects and answer several key questions regarding external and internal factors that might affect the new bank's chances for success. For example:

1. External factors:
   a. *The level of local economic activity.* Is it high enough to generate sufficient deposit and loan demand to support a new bank?
   Economic activity is often measured by the volume of retail sales, personal income, bank debits (i.e., local check volume), and number of households and businesses in the bank's service area.
   b. *Growth of local economic activity.* Is the local market area growing fast enough to generate additional deposits and loans so that the new bank can grow to an efficient size? This is often measured by trends in total deposits and loans, retail sales, bank debits, population growth, construction activity (i.e., number of building permits or housing starts), and school enrollments.
   c. *The need for a new bank.* Has the local population grown or moved into new areas not currently receiving convenient banking services? This is often measured by population per bank or per banking office, recent earnings and deposit growth of existing banks, number and size of new residential construction projects (apartments, single-family homes, etc.).
   d. *The strength and character of local competition in supplying financial services.* How many competing financial institutions accept savings or checkbook funds and loan applications and how aggressive are they in advertising their services? This is often measured by the number of bank offices relative to area population and the number of other financial institutions offering checkable accounts, savings plans, consumer loans, and business credit.

2. Internal factors:
   a. *Qualifications and contacts of the new bank's organizers.* Do the organizers have adequate depth of experience in business affairs and especially in banking? Is their reputation in the local community strong enough to attract customers to the bank?
   b. *Management quality.* Have the organizers been able to find a chief executive officer with adequate training and experience in bank management? Will the organizing group be able to find and pay competent management and staff to fill the bank's key posts?
   c. *Pledging of capital to cover the cost of filing a charter application and getting under way.* Is the net worth position of the proposed bank's organizers strong enough to meet the initial capitalization requirements imposed by regulation and cover consulting and legal fees? Because the chartering process covers many months and may wind up in court before the new bank is allowed to open, do the organizers have sufficient financial strength to see the project through to its completion?

Volume and Characteristics of New Charters

In view of all the foregoing questions and issues and their associated costs and risks, it may come as no surprise that only a fraction of the businesspeople who consider starting a new bank ultimately submit formal applications for new charters, and some banks that do receive charters never open for business due to capital shortages, site preparation problems, or other causes. Yet, surprisingly, the number of new banks being chartered in the United States recently has accelerated, averaging a hundred or more per year, due, in part, to the displacement of many skilled bank officers who lost their jobs when their former banks were merged and to public demand for more personalized service sometimes not available from large, established banks.

Clearly, merely getting charter approval does not end the challenges facing a new bank's organizers and management. Following charter approval, stock can be legally offered to the public through a so-called *offering memorandum* that describes the charter's business plan, management, and the rights and terms of the stock sale. In the United States a Deposit Insurance Application usually must be filed with the FDIC after the charter application is approved. Corporate bylaws must be adopted, operating policies drafted, and bonding and insurance secured for bank employees. Added to these costs are the riskiness of a new venture, the burdens imposed by regulation, and the recent liberalization of state and federal laws permitting branching and interstate banking, which increases the competition new banks must contend with.

Where are most newly chartered banks located? What types of markets do new banks serve?

In answering these questions, we must keep in mind the following point: *The choice of location for a new bank is a capital-budgeting decision subject to the same financial constraints as any other long-term investment decision.* According to the theory of capital budgeting, the location banking entrepreneurs choose for a new charter reflects their desire to maximize their utility by seeking the highest possible rate of return on invested funds compared with the returns on alternative uses of their money. Otherwise, why charter a bank instead of investing in some other kind of business enterprise? Investors will do so only if the new bank is expected to generate higher returns for its stockholders than other investments of comparable risk.

Presumably, the organizers of a new bank will estimate the future net cash flows expected from the proposed bank, projecting future bank revenues less all cash expenses (including salaries and wages, the cost of borrowing funds, and taxes). These cash flow estimates must be compared to the cash outlays required to get the new bank started, including the amount of capital pledged by the stockholders, filing and attorney's fees, rental fees if a temporary structure (such as a mobile home) is used at first as a site, and construction costs. If the expected net return over all costs equals or exceeds the minimum return acceptable to the bank's organizers, they will have an economic incentive to go forward with a new charter or branch office application.

Edwards and Edwards [12] have observed that the desired rate of new entry into the banking system will approach a long-run equilibrium that ensures an adequate supply of banking services to satisfy demand at no more than a normal rate of return on equity capital for bank stockholders. The equilibrium rate of return from bank entry will be higher and the rate at which new bank charters are awarded will be *lower* under regulation than if there were no regulatory restrictions on charter activity. Thus, society pays a price for restricting the number of bank charters awarded each year: *With fewer banks, the public is served less conveniently and there may be less competition to serve the individual bank customer, resulting perhaps in higher prices for banking services and diminished quantity and/or quality of services provided.* However, the likely benefits for society from regulation are a lower rate of bank failures and, perhaps, greater public confidence in the safety and soundness of the banking system.

Analysis of recent charter approvals suggests that most new U.S. banks are chartered in relatively large urban areas where, presumably, expected rates of return on the organizers' investments are the highest. For example, Rose and Fry [5] found that new charter markets had a median population of close to 200,000, and their population growth rate was approximately double the total U.S. population growth rate. A regression model of annual chartering activity by state indicated that population per banking office, growth of bank assets, extent of bank holding company activity, and market concentration explained most of the variation from state to state in bank chartering activity.

In the case of *population per banking office,* as population increases relative to the number of banking organizations operating in a given state, increased numbers of new charters are issued. Presumably, many bank organizers view population growth as a proxy for growth in the demand for banking services. The faster *total bank assets* in a state grow, the greater the probability of chartering new banking institutions there presumably because the success of area banks leads new-bank organizers to expect success when their bank is chartered. In contrast, increases in the *bank concentration ratio* tend to reduce chartering activity in a state by 20 to 30 percent, as do state laws that permit greater branching and holding company activity. This suggests that substantial numbers of bank organizers fear having to take on a dominant bank in their chosen area. Still, no one has found convincing evidence that new banks are overwhelmed by their competition, nor can they be driven from any local market if they are willing to compete.

How Well Do New Banks Perform?[1]

Launching a new banking organization entails considerable risk. There is no guarantee that the new institution will survive and prosper. Deregulation of the financial sector has brought scores of new competitors into traditional banking markets. Moreover, existing banks have a decided advantage over newly chartered institutions in their greater experience, greater size, and well-established reputations. How successful, in general, are new banks?

Research findings are generally optimistic. Most new banks grow, in terms of total deposits, at a moderate to rapid rate, initially attracting funds from their organizers, from business associates of the organizers, and from customers dissatisfied with other banks. In fact, Motter [16] observed in a study of newly chartered national banks that increases

---

[1]Portions of this section are based on the author's article in *The Canadian Banker* [11] and are used with permission.

in loan accounts tended to outstrip gains in deposits as customers denied loans by other banks moved quickly to sound out the credit policies of the new banking institution in town. Despite a track record of loan losses that generally exceeded those of established banks, most new banks were profitable within two years of opening their doors.

However, Austin and Binkert [2] found, in a study of more than 300 banks, that most new institutions do *not* live up to the enthusiastic growth predictions of their organizers. Nearly 70 percent of the new banks they examined still had relatively few deposits two to four years after they opened for business. Research suggests these new banks were well below the minimum size needed for efficient operation, though few of the newly formed institutions experienced actual financial difficulties.

In a review of new banks formed in Massachusetts, Shea [7] found that early monitoring and control of operating expenses are vital for a new bank to be successful. It must carve out a solid niche in the local community that differentiates it from other banks in the minds of customers. Nevertheless, the majority of new banks became profitable in their second or third year of operation.

Research studies suggest that the early performance of a new bank is strongly tied to the experience, financial strength, and market contacts of those who put the organization together. Selby [6], for example, reviewed the progress of new Georgia banks and found that the volume of deposits generated by the banks' first board of directors accounted for a major share of deposits brought in during the initial year of operation. This finding emphasizes the need to find organizers who have successfully operated other businesses, have above-average financial strength, and are actively involved in the local area.

The growth of income in the local market, especially household after-tax income and business sales, appears to be positively related to new bank growth. Moreover, a study by Yeats, Irons, and Rhoades [8] suggests that a greater number of existing banks may generate more competition and thereby slow a new bank's growth. However, a study of 548 newly chartered banks, by Arshadi and Lawrence [1], found that *internal* factors under the control of bank management were at least as important as *external* (market or regulatory) factors in influencing the success achieved by new banks. These internal factors included containment of operating costs (particularly salaries and wages), achievement of adequate bank size, and pricing policies set by management. Demographic factors (such as population growth) and market structure (such as the number of banks serving the same market) turned out to be relatively less important than factors wholly or partially under management control. The authors contend that government chartering authorities should pay more attention to the managerial abilities of a bank's organizers in deciding whether to charter a new bank.

The chartering of new banks has been shown in numerous research studies to have competitive effects that generally serve the public interest. Most such studies (e.g., Fraser and Rose [10], Motter [16], and McCall and Peterson [15]) have looked at small cities and rural communities served by one, two, or three banks in which a new competitor is suddenly chartered by either state or federal authorities. Generally, existing banks in these smaller communities have stepped up their lending activities and become more active in attracting funds through deposit sales after a new bank has entered, suggesting that local residents gained better service. Evidence on whether the prices of financial services were reduced or the yields paid to savings account customers increased is decidedly mixed, however. Most studies find *few* price effects from the entry of new banks. However, a review of the intrusion of New York City banks into neighboring counties, by Motter and Carson [17], uncovered a tendency for loan rates to fall following the entry of a new bank. Most studies find little net earnings impact and no evidence that new entry threatens the survival of existing financial institutions.

Concept Checks

21–9. What are the key factors the organizers of a new bank should consider before deciding to seek a charter?

21–10. Where are most new banks chartered in the United States?

21–11. How well do most new banks perform for the public and for their owners?

Establishing Full-Service Branch Offices: Choosing Locations and Designing New Branches[2]

When an established bank wishes to enter new markets or when its valued customers move, the most important vehicle for market entry in the modern era has been the creation of new **branch offices,** rather than new banks, offering many, if not all, the services that are also available at the bank's home office. Branches are usually much cheaper to establish than chartering whole new banking corporations. Less capital is required, the application for new branch offices in most states is far less detailed than that usually required for a proposed new bank charter, and there is usually much less duplication of staff because a new branch doesn't normally require a full slate of officers and operations personnel as a new bank would. As a result of these advantages, the number of full-service branch offices in the United States has grown from just over 10,000 in 1960 to well over 50,000 in the 1990s.

The location, design, and services offered by a bank branch office depend, first, upon the preferences of bank customers and, secondly, on the preferences of bank management and employees. *Both* customer-friendly and worker-friendly branch offices are needed. Marketing research studies suggest that most bank customers rate an atmosphere of *confidentiality* and *privacy* in carrying out banking transactions as the most important features of bank branch offices. And bank customers and employees seem also to rank *efficiency* high in describing the arrangement of an ideal branch office—service departments and work stations should be easy to find and easily reachable for both customers and employees.

---

[2]Portions of this section are based upon the author's article on bank branching in *The Canadian Banker* [23] and are used with permission.

BancOne of Columbus, Ohio, is an industry leader in designing and testing new ideas for the design of bank branch offices and other customer service facilities. When the customer enters one of its newer branches in Ohio, he or she may be confronted with such eye-catching features as neon lights that highlight what services each department or booth offers and direct customers' attention to daily specials (i.e., merchandising graphics). To further ease customer anxiety, there is an information desk near the entrance to help confused customers find the service counters that best meet their needs. Visually attractive advertisements confront customers waiting in the lobby to meet with financial-service representatives. More recently, BancOne has developed both full-service branches—providing traditional services (such as loans and deposits) and new services (such as travel planning, insurance, real estate brokerage, and financial counseling)—and specialized branches ("boutiques") that supply services specifically geared to their local area (such as savings and investment products for retired customers).

The message of these recent innovations seems reasonably clear—customers, particularly *new* customers, need guidance on where to go and what services are available inside each branch office. Otherwise, they will soon become frustrated with the bank's services (or lack thereof) and go elsewhere. Moreover, unless service options are clearly communicated when a customer enters a branch office, the bank is in danger of losing potential fee income from service sales.

Desirable Sites for New Branches

Among the most desirable sites for full-service branch offices today are those with at least some of the following characteristics:

1. Traffic count is heavy (for example, 30,000 to 40,000 cars per day), indicating a large flow of vehicular traffic (and potential customers) passing near the proposed site, but even at peak times (e.g., on Friday afternoons) customers must be able to easily see and access the office and its drive-in windows.

2. Large numbers of retail shops and stores present in the surrounding neighborhood, which usually generate a substantial volume of loan and deposit business.

3. Local populations that are of above-average age (particularly those individuals 45 years of age and older) who often have substantial amounts of savings the bank can manage for them.

4. The surrounding area contains substantial numbers of business owners, managers, and professional men and women at work or in residence.

5. The number of service facilities operated by other banks and nonbank financial-service competitors is *not* increasing rapidly in the area, leaving a substantial volume of business that a new bank office might be able to attract.

6. Above-average population growth, with more rapid increases in population usually favorable to establishing a branch office in a local area.

7. Above-average population density (i.e., a greater number of persons per square mile around the proposed site).

8. A sufficiently larger number of people in the branch's neighborhood to generate enough customers to reach at least a break-even volume of banking activity. Many bankers establish a target ratio of

$$\begin{array}{c} \text{Population} \\ \text{per bank} \\ \text{office} \end{array} = \frac{\begin{array}{c}\text{Total population in the} \\ \text{area to be served}\end{array}}{\begin{array}{c}\text{Number of branch offices} \\ \text{present in the area} \\ \text{(including the proposed new branch)}\end{array}}$$

In the United States there is an average of about 4,000 people per branch office. However, some other nations have much higher average population-per-branch ratios. For example, Austria and Germany have more than 10,000 people per branch, while Japan has over 8,000 people per bank branch office. The larger the population served by each office, the more deposits and other services are likely to be purchased, expanding bank revenues and enhancing efficiency of operations. However, branches can become too large, thereby operating at excessive cost and failing to provide convenient and personalized customer service.

9. Above-average levels of household income, with higher-income groups usually offering bank branches the opportunity to sell more services.

For branch offices designed primarily to attract *deposits,* the key branch sites to look for are usually neighborhoods with relatively high median individual and family incomes, heavy concentrations of retail stores and shops, older-than-average resident populations, and high proportions of homeowners rather than renters. Banks seeking more *checking accounts* through their branches generally should enter neighborhoods with high levels of individual and family incomes as well as areas where shopping centers and retail stores are concentrated. Higher levels of *savings deposits* are usually to be found in local markets where there is an above-average proportion of older heads of households (including retired individuals and families) and where there is a large proportion of residents who own their own homes.

For branches primarily created to generate *loan demand from household customers,* residential areas with a heavy proportion of young families and substantial new home construction, along with concentrations of retail stores and shopping centers and high traffic flow, are particularly desirable locations. In contrast, *commercial loan demand* is usually centered in central city office locations where the bank's credit analysts, management information systems personnel, and loan approval committees are normally housed.

The decision of whether or not to establish a branch office is a capital-budgeting decision, requiring a large initial cash outflow (cost) to fund the purchase or lease of property and to begin operations. Branches are usually created with the expectation that future net cash inflows (NCF) will be large enough to guarantee the bank an acceptable return, $E(r)$, on its invested capital. That is, the bank can estimate its expected return from the formula:

$$\begin{array}{c}\text{Cash outflow to}\\\text{fund the establishment}\\\text{of a new branch}\\\text{office}\end{array} = \frac{NCF_1}{[1+E(r)]^1} + \frac{NCF_2}{[1+E(r)]^2} + \cdots \qquad (1)$$

$$+ \frac{NCF_n}{[1+E(r)]^n}$$

where a new branch will be judged to be economically viable if its expected return, $E(r)$, equals or exceeds the minimum acceptable return (k) to the bank's stockholders; that is, $E(r) \geq k$. For example, if a new branch office is expected to cost $3 million to acquire the site and install the necessary equipment to begin operations and generate $600,000 in annual cash inflow net of all operating expenses for 10 years, the branch's expected return will be found from:

$$\$3,000,000 = \frac{\$600,000}{[1+E(r)]^1} + \frac{\$600,000}{[1+E(r)]^2} + \cdots + \frac{\$600,000}{[1+E(r)]^{10}}$$

Using the present value and annuity tables in the inside front cover of this book, we find that the proposed branch's expected return, $E(r)$, is 15 percent.

If the shareholders' minimum acceptable rate of return is 10 percent, this branch project appears to be economically viable. Of course, the return the bank actually earns from its investment in each branch depends upon the demand for its services in the communities it serves, the quality of its management and staff, and the cost in capital and other resources necessary to open and operate the branch.

When considering possible locations for new branches, management should consider not only the expected rate of return, $E(r)$, from each new branch location, but also (*a*) the variance around that expected return, $\sigma^2[E(r)]$, which is due mainly to fluctuations in economic conditions in the area served by the branch, and (*b*) the covariance, COV, of expected returns from the proposed new branch, existing branches, and other assets previously established or acquired by the bank $\{COV[E(r_i), E(R_j)]\}$. The impact of a new branch's expected return (R_B) on a bank's overall or total return (R_T) from its existing branches and other assets (R_{OA}) can be found from:

$$E(R_T) = W \times E(R_B) + (1 - W) \times E(R_{OA}) \qquad (2)$$

where W is the proportion of the bank's total resources to be invested in new branch B and $(1 - W)$ is the proportion of the bank's resources invested in all of its other branches and other assets (OA). The marginal impact of a new branch on the bank's overall risk, measured by the variance of its total return (R_T), is:

$$\sigma^2(R_T) = W^2\sigma^2(R_B) + (1 - W)^2\,\sigma^2(R_{OA}) + 2W\,(1 - W)\,COV(R_B, R_{OA}) \qquad (3)$$

where

$$COV(R_B, R_{OA}) = \rho_{B,OA} \times \sigma_B \times \sigma_{OA}$$

with $\rho_{B,OA}$ representing the correlation coefficient between the expected return from the proposed new branch and the returns from other bank branches and assets, σ_B the standard deviation of the proposed new branch's expected return, and σ_{OA} the standard deviation of return from other bank assets.

To see the usefulness of the above formulas let's suppose the following return and risk information is known by a bank's management about a proposed new branch office project:

$$E(R_B) = 15 \text{ percent} \qquad \sigma(R_B) = 3 \text{ percent}$$
$$E(R_{OA}) = 10 \text{ percent} \qquad \sigma(R_{OA}) = 3 \text{ percent}$$

Suppose the proposed new branch would represent 25 percent of the bank's total assets, meaning the bank's other branches and assets must represent the remaining 75 percent of the bank's total assets. That is,

$$W = 0.25$$
$$\text{and}$$
$$(1 - W) = 0.75$$

and the new branch's returns are *negatively* related to the returns from the bank's other assets, specifically:

$$\rho_{B,A} = -0.40$$

Using formula (2), above, the bank's expected return after investing in the new branch B would be:

$$E(R_T) = 0.25 (15 \text{ percent}) + 0.75 (10 \text{ percent}) = 11.25 \text{ percent}$$

The total risk carried by the bank after adding the new branch would be:

$$\sigma^2(R_T) = (0.25)^2 (3 \text{ percent}) + (0.75)^2 (3 \text{ percent})$$
$$+ 2(0.25)(0.75)(-0.40)(3 \text{ percent})(3 \text{ percent})$$

Then,

$$\sigma^2(R_T) = 3.23 \text{ percent}$$

or

$$\sigma(R_T) \approx 1.80 \text{ percent}$$

The foregoing calculations show us that not only would the proposed new branch increase the bank's total rate of return from all of its assets (increasing R_T from 10 percent to 11.25 percent) but the proposed new branch's negative return correlation with the bank's existing branches and other assets also lowers the bank's standard deviation of its total return from 3 percent to 1.80 percent, producing a *diversification effect* that reduces the bank's overall risk exposure.

Thus, it is not always optimal for management to choose only those branch sites offering the highest expected returns to the bank. Risk and the covariance of a proposed new branch's expected return with the expected returns from a bank's other assets must also be considered. If two branches cost about the same to construct and generate about the same expected returns, management would most likely choose that branch location that is situated in a more stable local economy so that the variability about the branch's expected return is lower. Moreover, if two branch sites have similar construction costs, expected returns, and return variances, management is usually better off to select that site whose expected return has a low positive or even a negative covariance with the returns expected from the bank's other branches. Such a choice would tend to lower the overall risk from the bank's whole portfolio of service facilities.

Branch Regulation

Regulation in the United States recently has made it more difficult to close full-service branch offices. The FDIC Improvement Act of 1991, for example, requires a U.S. bank to notify its principal regulatory agency and its customers at least 90 days before a branch office is to be closed and to post a conspicuous notice of the plan to close a branch at the branch site at least 30 days prior to its closing. Moreover, the Community Reinvestment Act of 1977 requires banks to make an effort to reach *all* segments of their communities with services, which often makes it difficult to receive permission to close a branch in neighborhoods where customer volume and deposits may be declining but there are few other bank service outlets available. Organized consumer protests of branch office closings are not uncommon today, and many banks prefer to avoid the negative publicity that branch closings can generate.

The Community Reinvestment Act can also be used by regulators to prevent a bank with a poor community-service record from branching into areas it believes are highly desirable. For example, in February 1993 the Federal Reserve Board denied Farmers and Merchants Bank of Long Beach permission to branch into Cosa Mesa, California, on grounds the bank had a poor community service record and, allegedly, had racked up numerous violations of consumer credit laws.

The Changing Role of Branches

Many bank analysts see the roles played by branch offices evolving in *new* directions today. With a stronger *sales* orientation sweeping through banking, branches today represent the bank's "eyes and ears" in local areas that help the organization identify the largest and potentially most profitable customers and link them to the bank's most profitable services. Also, branches appear to offer the greatest opportunities for *cross-selling,* where each customer is offered a package of financial services that fully meets his or her needs. Most automated facilities do not appear to be as effective at cross-selling multiple services as full-service branch offices are.

This concept of making branches as *sales oriented* as possible explains why a growing number of bank branches today are specially configured to maximize sales opportunities. For example, the low-profit, but heavily used teller stations now are frequently placed at the *rear* of branch office lobbies so that customers going to the teller windows must pass by departments advertising other fee-generating services. Customers waiting in their cars at drive-in windows today are often confronted with signs advertising loans and other services and with loudspeakers that, over a backdrop of soft music, remind them of new service opportunities at the bank. Moreover, branch office hours increasingly are being set, not for bank employees' convenience, but to match local customers' shopping and recreational schedules (including Saturday and Sunday hours). Of course, the new sales-oriented strategy of branch banking assumes that all bank employees in each branch office are trained to know about all the services the bank offers and are taught to look for every opportunity to sell more services to their customers.

Branch offices are coming to be viewed today less as mere deposit gatherers and more as sources of fee-generating service sales and for booking profitable assets. In a sense bank branches are struggling today to become more like other retail stores, where the goal is to sell customers as many products as possible, while minimizing operating costs. Increasingly, this objective has meant the substitution of as much automation as possible in place of personnel, storage, and office space.

One of the keys to branch office profitability is to apply the latest information technology and thereby lower personnel costs, moving operations personnel and those who must review and approve customer loan requests—that is, those personnel not needed for direct selling to the consumer—to a centrally located operations center. Customer self-service terminals are becoming more readily available so that customers themselves can readily obtain price quotations on new services, get copies of bank forms and legal documents, monitor their own accounts, and even schedule appointments with bank staff. However, automation on this scale demands that the bank branches of the future be much larger in size, averaging perhaps $75 million to $100 million in deposits instead of the $10 million to $40 million deposit-size range so prevalent today. In many cases this will require consolidation of smaller branches into fewer large branch offices with fewer and more productive employees serving customers.

In-Store Branching

More bank branches in the future are likely to be located inside shopping centers, supermarkets, and other stores, selling not just deposits and cashing checks, but also marketing a full range of fee-based services through sales-oriented employees (such as the in-store branches operated by Wells Fargo). These **in-store branches** typically are much less costly to build and maintain, costing as little as one-fourth the expense incurred in constructing and operating a stand-alone branch, usually operate over longer hours (including weekends and holidays, which often are more convenient banking times for wealthier customers and those with heavy workweek schedules), and experience more traffic flow than conventional branches as customers enter stores to buy groceries, hardware, and apparel and usually pass right by the bank's service counters. While there is evidence that fewer loans typically arise from in-store branches than from stand-alone branches, deposit volume is often heavier at in-store sites, which frequently attract the store's own deposit of its daily cash receipts and the personal accounts of store employees.

So rapid has been the growth of in-store bank branches that by 1991 approximately 7 percent of U.S. grocery stores and about 10 percent of American chain stores had banking facilities housed within their walls. In 1993 alone supermarket bank branches rose by 26 percent to reach about 2,000 such offices, representing 3 percent of all branches of financial institutions in the United States. Store branch environments present their own challenges and problems, however. For one thing they usually require aggressive marketing strategies in order to get shoppers "in a banking mood." Moreover, in-store branches usually have *no* drive-in windows. To be successful, an in-store branch operation must seek close cooperation with store owners and employees (including joint advertising and promotion activities). It helps greatly if the store mentions the bank in its advertising and if public announcements are made periodically during operating hours, reminding shoppers of the bank's presence in the store. Some retail stores and banks have engaged in cooperative promotional campaigns—for example, offering customers who open a deposit account free merchandise from the store.

Bankers of the future are going to have to be more creative than in the past in seeking out new sites in which to locate profitable branch offices. For example, Harris Trust of Chicago has pioneered branches in apartment complexes, while Phoenix's Valley National Bank (now Bank One) not long ago opened a rent-free branch, operating just a few hours each day, in a senior citizens' retirement home. Other branches have recently appeared in factories and hospitals in an attempt to bring the bank closer to locations where current and potential customers reside, work, or enjoy their leisure time.

Establishing and Monitoring Limited-Service Facilities

The high cost of chartering new banks and of setting up and operating full-service branch offices has led recently to an explosion of limited-service facilities—automated teller machines (ATMs) and ATM networks, point-of-sale terminals, telephone and personal computer service outlets, and drive-in facilities.

Point-of-Sale Terminals.   Computer facilities in retail shops and stores that permit a customer to instantly pay for goods and services electronically by deducting the cost of each purchase directly from his or her deposit account are known as **point-of-sale (POS) terminals.** The customer presents an encoded *debit card,* containing his or her account number and access code, to the store clerk who inserts it into a computer terminal connected to the bank's computer system. The customer's account is charged for the purchase and funds are automatically transferred to the store's bank deposit.

The banking industry is about equally divided between online and offline POS systems. The latter accumulate all of a customer's transactions until day's end and then the total of all transactions is subtracted from the customer's account. In contrast, online systems deduct each purchase as it is made from the customer's account. Costwise, banks would prefer offline POS systems, but online systems appear to reduce the frequency of customer overdrafts and, thus, may be less costly in the long run and more profitable if they allow a bank to safely offer POS services to a wider array of customers.

POS terminals are increasing rapidly all over the world. In the United States the number of POS terminals rose by 66 percent in 1992 alone, climbing from 50,000 to over 80,000. The majority of the recently installed POS terminals have appeared in gasoline stations and supermarkets. Among the market leaders in this field are MasterCard and Visa which sell their point-of-sale systems under the trade names MAESTRO and INTERLINK.

Customer resistance to POS usage appears to be fading and their future growth is expected to be quite rapid. Banks must work to overcome several disadvantages for the customer, such as loss of checkbook float (because loss of funds occurs the same day), computer problems that can generate costly mistakes, and the absence of canceled checks, which give customers handy written receipts for tax purposes. However, checking account fees are on the rise, which eventually may make POS terminals more economically attractive for bank customers.

Automated Tellers (ATMs).   An **ATM** combines a computer terminal, recordkeeping system, and cash vault in one unit, permitting customers to enter the bank's bookkeeping system with either a plastic card containing a personal identification number (PIN) or by punching a special code number into a computer terminal linked to the bank's computerized records 24 hours a day. Once access is gained into the bank's system, cash withdrawals may be made up to prespecified limits, and deposits, balance inquiries, and bill paying may take place. With ATMs taking over more routine services like cashing checks, bank personnel have more time to sell other services and help those customers who have special service needs. The average ATM processes more than 200 transactions per day, though some handle more than 600 customer requests per day.

Where did ATMs begin? The forerunner of all the modern-day machines began operations at a branch office of Britain's Barclays Bank in 1967. This first automatic dispenser could only accommodate customer cash withdrawals, however; no other banking services were provided. Most bankers at the time expected that customers would use this pioneering automated device only when full-service offices were not open. One of the earliest visitors to Barclays new machine was the U.S. entrepreneur B. J. Meredith. When Meredith's own firm showed no immediate interest in producing these new machines, he contacted his famous relative, Don Meredith—former professional football quarterback. Together with other investors the Merediths set up a new firm, Docutel, Inc., to manufacture ATMs. The first Docutel automated teller was set up at Citizens and Southern National Bank in Atlanta. However, it was a competitor, First National Bank of Atlanta, that enjoyed the greatest success with this new technology, aggressively marketing its new machines.

Soon, banks worldwide were asking for these new machines and competing manufacturers, such as Diebold and IBM, became active suppliers to the marketplace. In response to the emerging competition Docutel came out with what was thought to be a significant technical advance, but this newest ATM did not succeed because of operating glitches and the fact that the new device was bigger than the old ATM and, therefore, wouldn't fit into the space most banks had set aside for their original teller machines. Olivetti purchased the company in 1982, but eventually closed down its operations. Soon, strong competitors manufacturing ever-more-sophisticated machines began to offer a growing array of automated service options.

ATMs today frequently offer such diverse services and products as bus and train tickets, sales of postage stamps, passes to athletic events and movies, gift certificates, and paying for purchases made at participating retail shops. Today ATMs are frequently shared by several banks in order to lower costs and are networked with hundreds of other machines (more than 100 shared networks serve the U.S. alone) in order to offer customers full access to their accounts while traveling. Though expensive to purchase and install, ATMs save on employee salaries and benefits, utility bills, and maintenance costs. Diebold, Inc., a world leader in electronic banking, estimates that an ATM costs about $30,000, on average, while the cost of opening a full-service branch averages close to $1 million.

U.S. banks spend over $4 billion a year on ATMs and close to 140,000 are currently operating in the U.S. with thousands more available in Canada, Japan, and Western Europe. Approximately half of all U.S. households possess at least one ATM access card. U.S. ATMs handle about 5 billion financial transactions annually and bring in about $1 billion a year in bank revenues. Access fees, if they exist, are normally cheaper (averaging about 30 cents per cash withdrawal) if a customer uses an ATM owned by his or her bank. However, fees are more common if you use another bank's ATM that is networked to your bank because most depository institutions charge each other an interchange fee. Banks that do assess their customers user fees often employ *conditional pricing schedules*—for example, if the customer's deposit balance drops below $1,000, a fee of 25 to 50 cents may be assessed per ATM transaction; otherwise, customer access may be free.

As Neeley [22] observes, charging an ATM usage fee is highly controversial. Recently the two largest automated teller networks in the United States—PLUS and Cirrus—decided to let the owners of ATMs that are part of their two national networks charge noncustomers a surcharge for ATM use. Several regional systems also began to charge for their ATM services. In part, the higher fees reflect the pattern of ATM usage today—with just over 85 percent of all transactions consisting of cash withdrawals from bank accounts, while deposits into bank accounts represent only about 10 percent of all ATM transactions. Other potential fee-generating uses are almost nil at present even though many ATMs have the capability to dispense theater tickets, postage stamps, mutual fund shares, and traveler's checks. Then, too, because banks belonging to an ATM network pay "interchange fees" (ranging from 50 cents to about $2.00) to the network's owners, these fees often are passed along to bank customers in the form of surcharges. Customers can generally escape these fees only by sticking to their own bank's ATMs or by using human tellers inside the bank lobby or at drive-in windows. However, these surcharge fees may hurt smaller banks that own few machines, encouraging customers seeking to avoid ATM fees to transfer their accounts to the largest banks, which operate more machines in more locations. These fees may be especially damaging to low-income consumers who often have few full-service branch offices in their neighborhoods but may have ATMs nearby.

During the past two decades, many banks have moved to lower their operating costs by adding ATMs onto their full-service branch offices and by simultaneously reducing the number of personnel and the amount of rented space inside each branch office. For example, Zimmerman [27] reports that Manufacturers Hanover Trust in New York City added new ATMs to three of its least profitable branch offices, making them semiautomated branches. The bank was able to cut the number of staff members working in those branches in half and sharply reduce its rental costs. Surprisingly, customer deposit balances almost doubled at these reconfigured branches.

One important consideration with automation, however, is the amount of downtime ATMs often experience. If no human tellers are available and the bank has only one ATM on site and it is not working, customers often become frustrated and may take their business elsewhere. This is why many banks install *multiple* ATMs at the same site and often replace their old machines frequently—for example, every three to five years.

Automated tellers generally rank high in resource efficiency—they call for only a limited commitment of bank resources, particularly bank staff. ATMs process many more transactions per month than human tellers (an average of about 6,400 for ATMs compared to about 4,300 transactions per month per human teller) and do so at lower cost per transaction (automated teller transactions cost an average of about $3.75 per customer per month versus an average of about $4.38 per customer per month for a full-service branch office). On a per-transaction basis the same transaction that costs the bank an average of about 36 cents through an ATM costs about $1.06 through a human teller. This is why some banks (like First Chicago) have, at times, charged service fees if a customer uses a human teller for a transaction that could be handled more cheaply through an ATM.

However, automated tellers and other limited-service facilities do *not* rank high among those customers interested in personalized service (particularly among older customers), nor do they rank high in their ability to sell peripheral services, such as enticing customers to take out a car loan or purchase a savings or retirement plan. Banks that put their ATMs outside or away from branch office lobbies often find that this move sharply diminishes their ability to sell other services. Moreover, many customers view limited-service facilities as less safe due to the frequent incidence of crime—robbery and even murder of bank customers in an effort to steal their cash or to get hold of their personal identification numbers so the thief can access the customer's account at will. Automated facilities frequently attract crime because about three-quarters to two-thirds of all transactions carried out through these machines are cash withdrawals. Video and central station monitoring along with privacy screens, extensive lighting systems, and built-in alarms are popular methods today for increasing ATM safety and security.

How do banks decide whether to add a new ATM to the services they currently offer? The basic answer is that they estimate the cash savings the new machine is likely to generate if customers use the ATM instead of writing a check or going to a human teller, translate the estimated volume of future savings into their present value, and then compare the estimated present value of savings against the cash outlay required to purchase and install the new machine. For example, standard new ATMs today may cost in the range of $40,000 to $50,000 each and may cost another $30,000 to $40,000 to install, depending on location and other factors. Let's suppose the total cash outlay will be $80,000. After analyzing its check-processing costs, the bank estimates that it will save $1.00 for each check that is not written because customers will use the machine instead. Suppose the machine is expected to last for 10 years and handle 30,000 cash transactions per year. At $1.00 in savings per transaction, the total annual volume of savings should be approximately $30,000. The cost of capital the bank will incur to raise new funds to finance the ATM's purchase and installation is estimated to be

14 percent based upon the bank's risk exposure and expected future earnings. Therefore, we have:

$$
\begin{array}{l}
\text{Present value of} \\
\text{stream of cash} \\
\text{savings from the} \\
\text{new ATM}
\end{array}
=
\begin{array}{l}
\text{Present value of} \\
\text{an annuity of} \\
\$30,000 \text{ per year} \\
\text{at a discount rate} \\
\text{of 14 percent}
\end{array}
=
\begin{array}{l}
\$30,000 \times 5.216 \\
\text{(the annuity factor from} \\
\text{the annuity table inside the front} \\
\text{cover for 14 percent and 10 years)}
\end{array}
$$

$$ = \$156,480 $$

Because the new machine will cost just $80,000 to buy and install, this investment will generate a net present value (NPV) of +$76,480 (or $156,480 − $80,000) for the bank, thus adding value to the bank's balance sheet. Management would be likely to proceed with this project.

In closing, however, we must note that ATMs are not necessarily profitable for all banks. For example, because ATMs are available 24 hours a day, customers may use these machines more frequently and for smaller transactions then they would with a human teller. For example, if the customer needs cash for a movie on Friday night and for dinner on Sunday, he or she may access an ATM Friday afternoon for $30 and then drive to the ATM again on Sunday for another $50 to pay for dinner. In contrast, customers may visit a teller in the bank's lobby or drive-in center on Friday and withdraw $80 for the whole weekend. Moreover, customers show little hesitation to use ATMs for their cash withdrawals but then use a human teller when it's time to deposit a payroll check, thus requiring a bank to operate *both* teller machines and have human tellers available during regular business hours. Then, too, the widening use of surcharge fees for ATM use by many banks may cause some customers to reduce their usage of automated tellers in favor of human tellers, pushing up bank costs once again. A recent study conducted at the Federal Reserve Board concluded that the cost of operating ATMs has exceeded the income they generate for a bank by more than $10,000 annually per machine. (See, for example, Kennickell [21].)

Automated Loan Machines (ALMs).   One interesting self-service device being experimented with in the Midwest is an **ALM**—automated loan machine. These computer terminals permit a customer to apply for a loan by inputting certain information into the terminal, such as the customer's Social Security number and driver's license number. The customer may also be asked a series of questions to verify the customer's identity and credit standing. The ALMs may have access to a database that can include the customer's driving record from the state motor vehicle division and the customer's credit bureau report. If the machine grants the loan applied for (which normally ranges from about $500 to perhaps $5,000 to $10,000), the customer may be asked to sign a note on an electronic pad and then either receive a check or have the amount recorded in his or her deposit account.

These loan machines offer the possibility of banks saving substantial amounts of money in making smaller size consumer and business loans. Unfortunately, ALMs do not allow for flexibility in evaluating customers who may have no credit history or past credit problems but are now good-quality credit customers who deserve special consideration. They also do not permit banks to personally interview their customers, make judgments about the customers' character, or maximize the opportunity to sell other services.

Self-Service Terminals.   As the decade of the 1990s began, several banks in New England launched self-service terminals, allowing customers on their own to open new accounts, transfer funds between accounts, order checks, stop payment on checks previously issued, and get information on the terms of other services their banks offer. Some banks have added telephones and video screens so that customers with self-service problems or other questions can dial up a bank employee day or night. Self-service machines linked to bank office personnel offer the prospect of providing fully automated service centers with on-line visual access to bank personnel for special problems around the clock, seven days a week, at substantially lower cost than at traditional fully staffed branches that often needlessly duplicate both personnel and equipment.

Home and Office Banking.   Giving customers access to bank services—via telephone, computer terminals, TV monitors, or other electronic devices from their own home or office or while traveling or shopping, seems to be slowly gaining ground once again after a disappointing start during the 1980s. For example, in 1993 First Chicago Bank announced a deal with Microsoft to launch a new home banking program offering customers several convenient service options.

Many banking experts see home and office banking or banking while in motion as the ultimate end point in the long-term evolution of bank service facilities—that some day, technology permitting, nearly all banking transactions initiated by customers will arise from the customer's own location, be it at home, in an automobile, at work, or in a shopping mall or restaurant, at any hour of the day or night. Systems to allow customers to make computer purchases over the Internet or, alternately, through home television sets are already in place in some areas.

Many banks are developing highly automated telephone centers today that help their customers satisfy their demands for bank services without having to walk inside a branch or even get out of a car or even open a car window to approach an ATM. Some experts argue that the *telephone* will be the key bank delivery channel for the future because so many different services can be marketed, then delivered and, finally, verified via telephone. And with increasing use of cell phones in automobiles and on the street, computer keyboards, drive-in, and walk-up windows have come to look less convenient and efficient than many customers once thought they were.

Bank Facilities of the Future

Despite continually advancing technology, however, most banking experts seem to agree that the total number of bank branches industrywide will probably not decline very much; indeed, the total of all branch facilities may continue to grow in the future (though at a somewhat slower pace) if the population desiring to use banking services

Bank Management in Action

Bankers' Use of the Internet as a Service Delivery Medium

Increasingly, large and small banks are establishing web sites on the global Internet. Several of these institutions have begun to sell selected services via their **Internet service sites** and acquaint customers with the other services that are available from the banks' offices. Some banks include maps on their web sites so customers can not only find where the banks' nearest offices are located, but also what locations within each branch office offer certain services. Several "virtual banks" have recently appeared that exist only on the web and survive from the fees they earn by collecting and dispensing customer funds electronically.

Services Most Commonly Offered Via the Net   These include making payments (especially paying recurring utility bills or employing bill presentment systems where the customer is shown a bill on the computer screen and electronic payment options appear), checking on account balances, moving funds between accounts, and getting access to application forms for loans, deposits, and other services. Most banks currently use the web for advertising rather than service delivery, but this is changing rapidly as the number of home computers grows and the number of Internet users mounts into the millions. For example, Visa and Internet search service company Yahoo! recently announced a joint venture to boost credit card sales on the Net.

> *Advantages for Banks:* The Net is a low-cost source of information and service delivery for a bank, providing availability at any time around the globe; there is a relatively low cost to establish a web site and to maintain that site; using the Net a customer finds the bank rather than the bank searching for its customers; customer use is measurable; and it's easier to get customer feedback on service quality, pricing, and problems.

> *Disadvantages:* Among the toughest problems are protecting customer privacy and heading off crime (such as by using private dial-ups, breaking transactions into small bundles, or using coded data so that thieves have a tougher time breaking in); the Net is not a warm and inviting medium through which a banker can easily get to know and recognize his or her clients; many customers do not yet have compatible electronic systems; and the cost of being able to link up may be prohibitive to some potential customers.

continues to increase. However, the design and function of most branches are likely to evolve into new configurations—more wholly or partially automated facilities with broader self-service capabilities, more service facilities in non-stand-alone locations in or adjacent to other stores, and fewer full-service, fully staffed offices. Branches of the future will probably more closely resemble nonbank retail stores in their appearance and design rather than traditional bank facilities. Indeed, future bank service facilities will include information-access equipment that is so portable, bank facilities will be able to visit the customer rather than the other way around.

Possible Internet Uses by Banks: Banks can use the Internet for advertising, conducting customer surveys, giving customers a detailed description of bank facilities, checking transactions on behalf of a customer and conducting business 24 hours a day, granting speedy access to bank application forms, and promoting conversations between customers and banks to improve services because the Net makes it easier to gather customer complaints and solicit customer evaluation of bank services.

Ways to Promote Bank Customer Internet Use: Banks should use the Net to emphasize safety; promote the bank's home page at every opportunity; revise the home site as often as possible to hold customer interest; survey customers frequently about quality, satisfaction, and availability of the bank's services; allow customers to download the bank's commercials and use as screen savers and to download information about the bank's facilities; promote customer dialogue to resolve problems through E-mail, telephone, etc.

Bankers need to ask themselves several key questions when planning to offer services via the Internet and in designing their web sites and electronic communications systems. For example:

- Is the bank doing a good job describing its service offerings and explaining how a customer can access those services?
- Is the bank really concerned about the customer's security and privacy—concerned enough to take significant steps to protect the customer?
- Does the bank provide a way for the public to get questions answered and problems solved?
- Does it identify someone specifically (by name) that the customer can contact with questions and problems?
- Does the bank give the customer enough information to evaluate the bank's current financial condition (something that would matter especially to large depositors and stockholders)?
- Does the bank provide a way for job seekers to find out about career opportunities with the bank?
- As good as the bank's web site may look, is there room for improvement? What would make the bank's web page look and function even better for the customer?

For example, FoundersBank, near Philadelphia, has recently tested a portable briefcase "office" designed by Bell Atlantic Corporation, allowing a banker to talk directly to a customer in his or her home or office and retrieve information from the bank's files as needed. The use of "digital cash" will permit customers to be their own bank branches for certain transactions, carrying a pocket-size terminal to register payments for goods and services and to transfer funds as needed or a "smart card" (already popular in Europe) which is an electronic purse holding a specified amount of electronic money to spend. When the money is spent, the card can no longer be used until it is "refilled." Those full-service branch offices that remain will likely be specifically geared to the special service needs of the neighborhoods and communities they serve and more oriented toward personal interaction with their customers, helping them plan for the future with the aid of the bank's services and expert advice.

And, more than ever, each full-service branch and limited-service facility will have to prove its worth by generating deposits and fee income that enable the bank's resources and earnings to grow competitively. Banks of the future are likely to follow the lead of many retail stores in evaluating the success of their branch offices and limited-service facilities in terms of profits and costs per square foot. Future bank service facilities will have to combine a retail, sales-oriented environment with customer-friendly automation and still be flexible enough to deal with continuing product innovation. No longer can branches and limited-service facilities be just deposit gatherers; they must also be aggressive fee generators, selling credit, money management, and planning services to businesses and individuals as well as traditional deposit and savings plans. And the roles of branch managers will change as well, with managers having to spend more time on the street generating new business (i.e., becoming highly sales-oriented) by calling regularly on prospective clients and building stronger links to their communities.

Concept Checks

21–12. Why is the establishment of new branch offices usually favored by bankers over the chartering of new banks as a vehicle for delivering banking services?

21–13. What factors do bankers consider in evaluating possible sites for new branch offices?

21–14. What changes are occurring in the design of, and the roles played by, bank branches? Please explain why these changes are occurring.

21–15. What laws and regulations affect the creation of new bank branches and the closing of existing branches? What advantages and what problems can the closing of a bank branch office create?

21–16. What new and innovative sites have been selected for new branch offices in recent years? Why have these sites been chosen by many banks? Do you have any ideas about other new branch sites that you believe bankers should consider?

21–17. What are POS terminals and where are they usually located?

21–18. What services do ATMs provide? What are the principal limitations of ATMs as a bank service provider? Should ATM usage carry fees?

21–19. What are self-service terminals and what advantages do they have for banks and bank customers?

21–20. What services are currently available from banks on the Internet? What problems have bankers encountered in trying to offer Internet services?

21–21. How can banks better promote their Internet service options?

Summary

Convenience—timely access to bank services—is a key factor in determining how customers choose which bank or other financial-service firm to use. Advances in communications technology allow customers to reach banks over great distances so that timely access today does not mean that all banks need to locate their offices in the same neighborhoods and communities where their customers reside. Nevertheless, for many services (especially checking services and loans), the nearby physical presence of a bank office still remains appealing to many customers, especially to households and small businesses.

Banking organizations today use three different types of facilities to serve most of their customers—chartering new banks, building new branch offices, or setting up limited-service facilities such as automated tellers, point-of-sale terminals, Internet service channels, and smart (electronically encoded) cards. Each type of facility has unique advantages and disadvantages and appeals to different customer groups.

If a banking company elects to charter a new bank to serve a newly emerging market, the organizers have the option of applying for a corporate charter from federal authorities (the Office of the Comptroller of the Currency) or from the banking commission of the state where the proposed new bank would be located. Most regulatory authorities require that the new bank's organizers prove a public need for an additional charter, demonstrate that existing banks would not be harmed, and show that the newly chartered institution likely would be profitable within a reasonable time period (normally three years). Ultimately, the FDIC exerts a key influence over both federal and state chartering activity through its power to issue or not issue a certificate of insurance to cover a new bank's deposits. New banks are more likely to appear where population and income growth are faster than average and where the market is not already dominated by a few large banking organizations, although liberal branching laws tend to discourage the chartering of new banks.

More popular than chartering new banks in recent years has been the opening of new full-service branches of existing banks. Opening branches requires less capital and generally incurs lower organizational costs than chartering new banking corporations. Most branches are established in areas where traffic flow is relatively heavy with large numbers of retail shops and stores nearby and where there is an opportunity to attract deposits and loan requests from families and businesses with substantial incomes and sales. Among the most important factors examined by bankers to select sites for new branches are population density, area income and sales levels, and industrial and business development. Most branches are being carefully evaluated today for the service revenues they bring in and their operating costs and more branches are being closed today than in the past due to the rising cost of land, personnel, and equipment. These costs have spurred the development of in-store branches, where construction costs are generally low, and the replacement of branches with automated teller machines, point-of-sale terminals, Internet sites, and other electronic delivery systems that can handle high volume transactions less expensively. Unfortunately, electronic delivery systems cannot cross-sell different bank services as effectively as can bank personnel meeting directly with the customer. Because of the trend toward banks becoming more sales-oriented—reaching out to generate as much fee income as possible by selling each customer multiple financial services—full-service bank branch offices are likely to continue to grow in many areas right alongside automated teller machines (ATMs), customer-accessed computer terminals, and services offered by web sites and electronic cards. However, the branches of the future will probably be larger, more automated, and more marketing-oriented than those of the past.

Key Terms in This Chapter

Office of the Comptroller of the Currency
Charter of incorporation
State banking commissions
Federal Deposit Insurance Corporation (FDIC)
Public need
Branch offices

In-store branches
Point-of-sale terminals
ATM
ALM
Internet service sites

Problems and Projects

1. A group of businessmen and women from the town of Papillon are considering filing an application with the state banking commission to charter a new bank. Due to a lack of current banking facilities within a 10-mile radius of the community, the organizing group estimates that the initial banking facility would cost about $2.5 million to build along with another $700,000 in other organizing expenses and would last for about 20 years. Total revenues are projected to be $210,000 the first year, while total operating expenses are projected to reach $180,000 in year one. Revenues are expected to increase 8 percent annually after the first year, while expenses will grow an estimated 7 percent annually after year one. If the organizers require a minimum of a 10 percent annual rate of return on their investment of capital in the proposed new bank, are they likely to proceed with their charter application given the above estimates?

2. Luvel National Bank is considering the establishment of a new branch office at the corner of Lafayette and Connecticut Avenues. The bank's economics department projects annual operating revenues of $1.25 million from fee income generated by service sales and annual branch operating expenses of $680,000. The cost of procuring the property is $1.66 million and branch construction will total an estimated $2.32 million; the facility is expected to last 16 years. If the bank has a minimum acceptable rate of return on its invested capital of 12 percent, will Luvell likely proceed with this branch office project?

3. Sullivan Bank of Commerce estimates that the building of a new branch office in the newly developed Guidar residential township will yield an annual expected return of 12 percent with an estimated standard deviation of 4 percent. The bank's marketing department estimates that cash flows from the proposed Guidar branch will be mildly positively correlated (with a correlation coefficient of +0.30) with the bank's other sources of cash flow. The expected annual return from the bank's existing facilities and other assets is 11 percent with a standard deviation of 3 percent. The branch will represent just 10 percent of Sullivan's total assets. Will the proposed branch increase Sullivan's overall rate of return? Its overall risk?

4. The following statistics and estimates were compiled by First National Bank of Eastlin regarding a proposed new branch office and the bank itself:

Branch office expected return	= 16%
Standard deviation of return	= 5%
Bank's overall expected return	= 12%
Standard deviation of bank's return	= 2%
Branch asset value as a percentage of total bank assets	= 15%
Correlation of net cash flows for branch and bank as a whole	= +0.35

What will happen to the bank's total expected return and overall risk if the proposed new branch project is adopted?

5. First National Bank of Huron is considering installing three ATMs in its westside branch. The new machines are expected to cost $48,000 apiece. Installation costs will amount to about $32,000 per machine. Each machine has a projected useful life of 10 years. Due to rapid growth in the westside district these three machines are expected to handle 180,000 cash transactions per year. On average, each cash transaction is expected to save 42 cents in check processing costs. If First National has a 12 percent cost of capital, should the bank proceed with this investment project?

6. First State Security Bank is planning to set up its own web page to advertise its location and services on the Internet and to offer customers selected service options, such as paying recurring household bills, verification of account balances, and dispensing deposit account and loan application forms. What factors should First State take into account as it plans its own web page and Internet service menu? How can the bank effectively differentiate itself from other banks currently present on the Internet system? How might the bank be able to involve its own customers in designing its web site and pricing its Internet service package?

Selected References

For information on how new banks perform, see the following studies:

1. Arshadi, Nasser, and Edward C. Lawrence. "An Empirical Investigation of New Bank Performance." *Journal of Banking and Finance* 11(1987), pp. 33–48.
2. Austin, Douglas V., and Christopher G. Binkert. "A Performance Analysis of Newly Chartered Commercial Banks." *The Magazine of Bank Administration,* April 1975, pp. 34–35.
3. Brislin, Patricia, and Anthony M. Santomero. "De Novo Banking in the Third District." *Business Review,* January/February 1991, pp. 3–12.
4. Hunter, William C., and Aruna Srinivasan. "New Banks Control Their Own Future." *Economics Update,* Federal Reserve Bank of Atlanta 3, no. 3 (March 1990), pp. 1–2.
5. Rose, Peter S., and Clifford L. Fry. "Entry into U.S. Banking Markets: Dimensions and Implications of the Charter Process." Paper presented at the Western Finance Association Meetings, Honolulu, Hawaii, June 1976.
6. Selby, Edward. "The Role of Director Deposits in New Bank Growth." *Journal of Bank Research,* Spring 1981, pp. 60–61.
7. Shea, Maurice, P., III. "New Commercial Banks in Massachusetts." *New England Business Review,* Federal Reserve Bank of Boston, September 1967, pp. 2–9.
8. Yeats, Alexander J.; Edward D. Irons; and Stephen A. Rhoades. "An Analysis of New Bank Growth." *The Journal of Business,* April 1975, pp. 199–212.

9. Zimmerman, Gary C. "Small California Banks Hold Their Own." *Weekly Letter,* Federal Reserve Bank of San Francisco, January 26, 1990, pp. 1–2.

For studies of how new banks affect existing institutions, see the following:

10. Fraser, Donald R., and Peter S. Rose. "Bank Entry and Bank Performance." *The Journal of Finance* 27 (March 1972), pp. 65–78.
11. Rose, Peter S. "Competition and the New Banks," *The Canadian Banker and ICB Review* 84, no. 4 (July/August 1977), pp. 61–66.

For a discussion of the reasons for and impact of entry regulation in banking, see these studies:

12. Edwards, Linda N., and Franklin R. Edwards. "Measuring the Effectiveness of Regulation: The Case of Bank Entry Regulation." *Journal of Law and Economics* 17 (October 1974), pp. 445–60.
13. Alton, Gilbert R. "Measures of Potential for *De Novo* Entry in Bank Acquisition Cases: An Evaluation." *Proceedings of the Conference on Bank Structure and Competition,* Federal Reserve Bank of Chicago, 1974, pp. 159–70.
14. Hanweck, Gerald. "Bank Entry into Local Markets; An Empirical Assessment of the Degree of Potential Competition via New Bank Formation." *Proceedings of the Conference on Bank Structure and Competition,* Federal Reserve Bank of Chicago, 1971, pp. 161–72.

15. McCall, Allan S., and Manfred D. Peterson. *The Impact of De Novo Commercial Bank Entry.* Working paper no. 76-7, Federal Deposit Insurance Corporation, 1976.

16. Motter, David C. "Bank Formation and the Public Interest." *The National Banking Review* 2 (March 1967), pp. 299–350.

17. Motter, David C., and Dean Carson. "Bank Entry and the Public Interest: A Case Study." *The National Banking Review* 1 (June 1964), pp. 469–512.

For a review of factors bearing on establishing new branches and limited-service facilities:

18. Fox, R. Gerald. "Future Direction of Branch Banking." *World of Banking* 11, no. 3 (May/June 1992), pp. 4–7.

19. Garry, Michael. "Money in the Bank." *Progressive Grocer,* December 1991, pp. 62–65.

20. Horvitz, Paul M. "ATM Surcharges: Their Effect on Competition and Efficiency." *Journal of Retail Banking Services,* Autumn 1996, pp. 57–62.

21. Kennickell, Arthur B. "Who Uses Electronic Banking? Results from the 1995 Survey of Consumer Finances." Finance and Economic Discussion Series No. 35, Federal Reserve Board, Washington, D.C., 1997.

22. Neeley, Michelle Clark. "What Price Convenience? The ATM Surcharge Debate." *Regional Economist,* Federal Reserve Bank of Boston, July 1997, pp. 5–9.

23. Rose, Peter S. "The Bank Branch: Which Way to the Future?" *The Canadian Banker* 43, no. 6 (December 1986), pp. 40–50.

24. Smith, Rex Lee, III, and James A. Schweikart. "A Better Way to Assess Branch Profitability." *ABA Banking Journal,* April 1992, pp. 54–56.

25. Strunk, Bill. "Branch Banking." *Texas Banking,* June 1988, pp. 20–22.

26. Zdanowicz, John S. "Applying Portfolio Theory to Branch Selection." *Journal of Retail Banking* 13, no. 4, (Fall 1991), pp. 25–28.

27. Zimmerman, Kim. "Automation Helps Struggling Branch Double Deposits." *Bank Systems and Equipment* 25, no. 9 (September 1988), pp. 90–91.

22 BANK MERGERS AND ACQUISITIONS: MANAGING THE ACQUISITION PROCESS

Learning and Management Decision Objectives

The purpose of this chapter is to understand why the banking industry undertakes so many mergers each year and to determine what legal, regulatory, and economic factors should be considered when the management of a bank wants to pursue a merger.

Introduction

In many nations around the globe, a wave of mergers between both large and small banks has been under way for several years.[1] In the United States banking has consistently ranked in the top five of all U.S. industries in the number of merger transactions year after year. More than 6,000 U.S. banks have been absorbed via merger since 1980, including some recent megamergers involving such industry leaders as BankAmerica, Chase Manhattan Bank, Citicorp, BancOne, NationsBank, and other leading banking firms. In Europe a massive merger wave involving leading banks, insurance companies, securities firms, and other financial-service providers is under way in preparation for the formation of the consolidated European Community, when competition among financial firms should become even more intense. In Japan the Bank of Tokyo and Mitsubishi Bank recently combined to form the world's largest bank with more than $750 billion in assets. Moreover, banks in the United States are now mimicking their European counterparts by reaching out to gobble up security brokers and dealers, finance companies, insurance firms, credit card companies, thrift institutions, and other nonbank service providers. (Examples include BancOne's recent acquisition of credit card leader First USA; NationsBank's purchase of Montgomery Securities; Summit Bancorp's purchase of the thrift institution, Collective Bancorp; and Citicorp's proposed merger with Travelers Insurance Corporation.) The current merger

---

[1]This chapter is based, in part, on the author's article in *The Canadian Banker* [14]. Reprinted material is used with the permission of the publisher.

Some of the Largest Mergers in Recent U.S. Banking History*

Acquiring Institution	Acquired Institution	Announced On:	Estimated Total Share Value** (billions)
Nationsbank, North Carolina	Barnett Banks, Florida	August 1997	$15.5
Wells Fargo Bank, California	First Interstate Bancorp, California	January 1996	12.3
Chase Manhattan/Chemical Banking Corp., New York	_____	August 1995	11.4
NationsBank, North Carolina	Boatmen's Bancshares, Missouri	August 1996	9.8
First Bank System, Minnesota	U.S. Bancorp, Oregon	March 1997	9.1

Note: *Recently proposed mergers of (a) NationsBank with BankAmerica are valued at about $60 billion;
(b) BancOne Corp with First Chicago NBD Corp at nearly $30 billion; and (c) Citicorp with Travelers Group Inc.
at close to $83 billion will, if approved, represent the largest banking mergers in history.
**The estimated share value is calculated on the day of announcement of the merger using the acquirer's stock
price and the number of shares the acquirer will issue to shareholders of the acquired institution.

wave in banking and other financial-service industries is unlikely to end soon and its effects will be long lasting. The public will be confronted in the future with fewer, but larger, banking organizations that will pose stronger competition for banks not joining the merger trend. In this chapter, we examine the nature, causes, and effects of mergers in banking. We will look at the laws and regulations that shape bank mergers and the factors that are important in selecting a merger partner for a bank.

The Motives behind the Rapid Growth of Bank Mergers

As Table 22–1 illustrates, bank mergers usually occur because: (1) the stockholders (owners) of the banks involved expect to increase their wealth (value per share of bank stock) or perhaps reduce their risk exposure, thus increasing their welfare; or (2) the management of a bank expects to gain higher salaries and employee benefits, greater job security, or greater prestige from managing a larger banking firm; or (3) both stockholders and management may reap benefits from a bank merger. However, there may be other motives as well. Let's take a closer look at some of the most powerful bank merger motives that appear to have been at work in recent years.

Profit Potential.   To most authorities in the banking field the recent upsurge in bank mergers—averaging 300 to 400 a year in the United States alone—reflects the expectation of the stockholders that **profit potential** will increase once the merger is completed. If the acquiring organization has more aggressive management than the banking firm it acquires, bank revenues may rise as markets are more fully exploited and new services developed. This is especially true of interstate mergers like the affiliation

TABLE 22–1   Possible Motives for Bank Mergers and Acquisitions

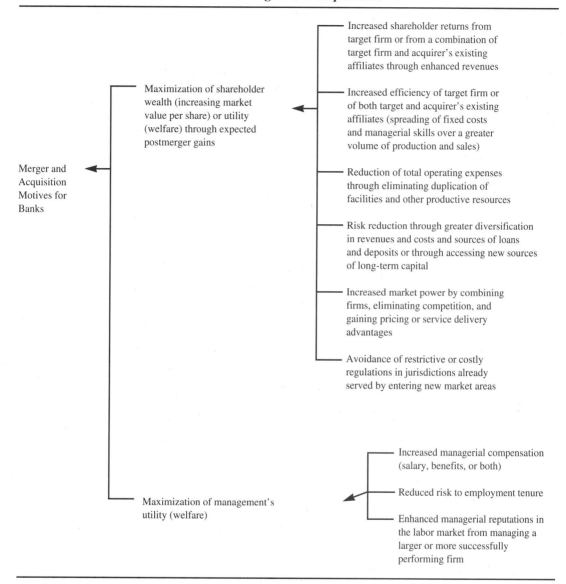

of Wells Fargo Bank with First Interstate Bank or the proposed combination of NationsBank and Bank of America where many new states are entered, opening up much greater new revenue potential. Moreover, if the acquiring bank's management is better trained than the management of the acquired bank, the efficiency of the merged organization may increase, resulting in more effective control over operating expenses. Either way—through reduced expenses or expanded revenues—mergers can improve the profit potential of banking organizations. Other factors held equal, the value of a bank's stock will rise, increasing the welfare of its stockholders.

Risk Reduction.   Alternatively, many partners to merger anticipate reduced **cash flow risk** and reduced **earnings risk** as well. The lower risk may arise from the fact that mergers increase the overall size and prestige of a banking organization, open up new markets with different economic characteristics from markets already served, or make possible the offering of new services whose cash flows are different in timing from the cash flows generated by existing services. Many European bank mergers in recent years (pursued by such leading banks as ABN AMRO and Verenigte Spaarbank) appear to have been motivated by the search for "complementarity" in services—for example, a wholesale-oriented bank pursuing a retail-oriented bank or a bank allying itself with an insurance company—in an effort to broaden the menu of services offered the public, thereby reducing the merging banks' risk exposure from relying upon too narrow a lineup of services (as illustrated in the United States by the proposed merger of Travelers Group of San Francisco and Citicorp of New York).

Therefore, mergers can help to *diversify* the combined banking organization's sources of cash flow and earnings, resulting in a more stable banking firm able to withstand wide fluctuations in economic conditions and in the competitive environment of the industry.

Rescue of Failing Banks.   Many bank mergers have been encouraged by the FDIC and other regulatory agencies as a way to conserve scarce insurance reserves and avoid an interruption of customer service when a bank is about to fail. One of the most prominent examples was the acquisition of First City Bancorporation of Texas in January 1993 by Chemical Bank of New York through its Texas Commerce Bank affiliate. In this case a well-managed and capital-strong banking company saw an opportunity to acquire substantial assets (about $6.6 billion) and deposits (close to $4.4 billion) with only a limited capital investment (less than $350 million). Following passage of the Garn–St Germain Depository Institutions Act (1982) and the Competitive Equality in Banking Act (1987), bank holding companies were allowed to reach across state lines to acquire failing banks and thrifts. Finally, with the enactment of the Financial Institutions Reform, Recovery, and Enforcement Act of 1989 Congress voted to allow bank holding companies to acquire even healthy thrift institutions anywhere inside the United States, subject to regulatory approval.

Tax and Market-Positioning Motives.   Many mergers arise from expected **tax benefits,** especially where the acquired bank has earnings losses that can be used to offset taxable profits of the acquirer [18]. There may also be **market-positioning benefits,** in which a merger will permit the acquiring bank to acquire a base in a completely new market. Acquiring an existing bank, rather than chartering a new banking firm with new personnel, can significantly reduce the cost of positioning in a new market. Further expansion in the form of branching or future mergers can subsequently take place, with the most recently acquired bank as a base of operations. These market-positioning mergers are likely to accelerate in the future now that the Riegle-Neal Interstate Banking Act has become law in the United States and recent banking directives have been passed by the European Economic Community to more freely allow banks to cross state and national boundaries, make acquisitions, and purchase or establish new branch offices. The proposed merger of Travelers Group and Citicorp in the U.S., for example, would drastically alter the market positioning of two giant firms, creating a huge market leader serving more than 100 million customers in more than 100 nations.

A good example of how mergers can be employed to better the market position of acquiring banks occurred in 1991 when federal regulators decided to close the Bank of New England Corp. and place its good assets (estimated at $13 billion) up for bids. Several large bidders—most notably BankAmerica Corp. of San Francisco and Fleet/Norstar Financial Group—saw this potential acquisition as a way to become a major financial services player in the New England region, particularly in Connecticut, Massachusetts, and Maine, where the Bank of New England operated subsidiary banks. The winning bidder proved to be Fleet/Norstar Financial Group of Providence, Rhode Island. As a result of this merger it became the largest bank in New England.

Cost Savings or Efficiency Motive.   The Fleet/New England merger also illustrates the **cost-savings** or **efficiency** motive behind many bank mergers. Fleet's staff estimated that by combining its operations with Bank of New England, it would save about $350 million annually, thereby generating additional earnings of $150 million to $200 million per year. More recently, large-scale staff reductions and savings from eliminating duplicate facilities have followed in the wake of such megamergers as BankAmerica Corp. and Security Pacific Corp., Chemical Bank and Manufacturers Hanover, NCNB and C&S/Sovran Bank (which merged to become NationsBank), and Chase Manhattan and Chemical Bank of New York, and Wells Fargo and First Interstate Bancorp. For example, in April 1992 BankAmerica merged with Security Pacific to create what was then the second largest banking corporation in the United States, holding total assets of almost $200 billion. After the merger close to 500 branch offices were targeted for closure, with projected savings of over a billion dollars. In the Chemical Bank–Manufacturers Hanover merger more than 6,000 employees were laid off through the elimination of duplicate departments and branch offices. Significant layoffs are also expected if Travelers Group and Citicorp are permitted to merge since the combined company will have well over 160,000 employees along with $700 billion in assets.

The search for cost savings (economies of scale) were also uncovered in a survey by Lausberg and Rose [26, 27] of the massive merger wave occurring in European banking during the 1980s and 1990s. Of the 107 European bank merger events examined, the single most important merger motivation was the desire to reduce operating costs followed by a plan to diversify into new markets as part of an internationalization strategy.

Other Merger Motives.   Management may believe a merger will result in increased capacity for growth, maintaining the acquiring bank's historic growth rate. Moreover, a merger enables a bank to expand its loan limit to better accommodate corporate customers. This is a particularly important factor in markets where the bank's principal business customers may be growing more rapidly than the bank itself (as noted by Peek and Rosengren [23]).

Mergers often give smaller banks access to capable new management, which is always in short supply. Large banking companies recruit on college campuses and often hire through employment agencies in major metropolitan areas. Smaller, outlying banks have fewer market contacts to help find managerial talent, and they may not be able to afford top-quality personnel. The same is true of access to costly new electronic banking technology. For example, the proposed merger of First Union Corp of North Carolina and CoreStates Financial Corp. of Pennsylvania appeared to be driven, in part, by CoreStates' need for upgraded computer systems to more efficiently handle its retail consumer accounts and the year 2000 conversion problem.

Merger Motives That Banking Executives Identify.   In a study by Prasad and Prasad [25], senior executives from 25 of the largest banking firms in the United States were asked what factors they consider in choosing target banks to acquire. The most prominent feature mentioned was *quality of management.* Several officers of leading banks said they preferred merger partners whose managements were compatible with their own. Other key factors mentioned in identifying desirable banks to acquire were profitability (especially return on assets), efficiency of operations, and maintenance of market share.

Concept Checks

22–1.   Exactly what is a bank merger?

22–2.   Why are there so many mergers each year in the banking industry?

22–3.   What factors seem to motivate most bank mergers?

Selecting a Suitable Merger Partner

How can management and the owners of a bank decide if a proposed merger is good for the organization? The answer involves measuring *both* the costs and benefits of a proposed merger. Because the acquiring and acquired banks may have different reasons for pursuing a merger, this is not an easy cost–benefit calculation. Even so, the most important goal of any merger should be to increase the *market value* of the surviving firm so that its stockholders receive higher returns on the funds they have invested in the bank. Bank stockholders deserve a return on their investment commensurate with the risks they have taken on.

Thus, a merger is beneficial to bank stockholders in the long run if it *increases a bank's stock price per share.* The value (price) of a bank's stock depends upon:

1. The expected stream of future dividends flowing to the stockholders.

2. The discount factor applied to the future bank stock dividend stream, based on the rate of return required by the capital markets on investments of comparable risk.

Specifically,

$$\text{Market price per share of the bank's stock} = \sum_t \frac{D_t}{(1+c)^t}$$

where annual expected dividends per share are represented by D_t and c is the opportunity cost rate on capital invested in projects that expose investors to comparable risk. Clearly, if a proposed merger increases expected future stockholder dividends or lowers investors' required rate of return from the organization by reducing its risk, or combines the two, the bank's stock will *rise* in price and the stockholders will benefit from the transaction.

How might a merger increase the bank's expected future earnings or reduce its level of risk exposure? One possibility is by *improving operating efficiency*—that is, by reducing operating cost per unit of output. The bank might achieve greater efficiency by consolidating operations and eliminating unnecessary duplication. Thus, instead of two separate planning and marketing programs, two separate auditing staffs, and so forth, the merged bank may be able to get by with just one. Existing resources—land, labor, capital, and management skills—may be utilized more efficiently if new production and service delivery methods (such as automated equipment) are utilized, increasing the volume of services produced with the same number of inputs.

Another route to higher earnings is to enter new markets or offer new services via merger. Entry into new markets can generate *geographic diversification* if the markets entered have different economic characteristics from those the bank already serves. Alternatively, a merger may allow banks with different packages of services to combine their service menus, expanding the service options presented to their customers. This is *product-line diversification.* Both forms of diversification tend to stabilize a banking organization's cash flow and net earnings, presenting the stockholders with less risk and probably increasing the market value of their stock. Ideally, merger-minded bankers want to find an acquisition target whose earnings or cash flow is *negatively* correlated (or displays a low positive correlation) with the acquiring organization's cash flows.

For many bankers, a major consideration in any proposed merger is its probable impact on the earnings per share (EPS) of stock of the surviving firm. Will EPS *improve* after the merger, making the bank's stock more attractive to investors in the financial marketplace? Stockholders of the bank to be acquired are usually asking the same question: If we exchange our stock in the old bank for the stock of the acquiring bank, will our EPS rise?

Generally speaking, the stockholders of *both* acquiring and acquired banks will experience a gain in earnings per share of stock if (*a*) a bank or banking company with a higher stock-price-to-earnings (P-E) ratio acquires a bank or banking company with a lower P-E ratio and (*b*) combined earnings do not fall after the merger. In this instance, earnings per share will rise even if the acquired bank's stockholders are paid a reasonable premium for their shares. For example, suppose the stockholders of Bank A, whose current stock price is $20 per share, agree to acquire Bank B, whose stock is currently valued at $16 per share. If Bank A earned $5 per share of stock on its latest report and B also earned $5 per share, they would have the following P-E ratios:

$$\text{A's P-E ratio} = \frac{\$20 \text{ price per share}}{\$5 \text{ earnings per share}} = 4$$

$$\text{B's P-E ratio} = \frac{\$16 \text{ price per share}}{\$5 \text{ earnings per share}} = 3.2$$

Suppose, too, that these two banks had, respectively, 100,000 shares and 50,000 shares of common stock outstanding and that Bank A reported net earnings of $500,000, while B posted net earnings of $250,000. Thus, their combined earnings would be $750,000 in the most recent year.

If the shareholders of Bank B agree to sell out at B's current stock price of $16 per share, they will receive 4/5 ($16/$20) of a share of stock in Bank A for each share of B's stock. Thus, a total of 40,000 shares of Bank A (50,000 Bank B shares × 4/5) will be issued to the stockholders of Bank B to complete the merger. The combined banking organization will then have 140,000 shares outstanding. If earnings remain constant after the merger, the stockholders' earnings per share will be

$$\frac{\text{Earnings}}{\text{per share}} = \frac{\text{Combined earnings}}{\text{Shares of stock outstanding}} = \frac{\$750,000}{140,000} = \$5.36$$

which is clearly higher than the $5 per share that Bank A and Bank B each earned for their shareholders before they merged.

As long as the acquiring bank's P-E ratio is larger than the acquired bank's P-E ratio, there is room for paying the acquired bank's shareholders at least a moderate **merger premium** to sweeten the deal. A merger premium expressed in percentage terms can be calculated from the formula:

$$\frac{\text{Merger premium}}{\text{(in percent)}} = \frac{\begin{array}{c}\text{Acquired bank's} \\ \text{current stock} \\ \text{price per share}\end{array} + \begin{array}{c}\text{Additional amount} \\ \text{paid by the acquirer} \\ \text{for each share of the} \\ \text{acquired bank's stock}\end{array}}{\text{Acquired bank's current stock price}} \times 100$$

For example, suppose that despite the difference in current market value between Bank A's and Bank B's stock (i.e., $20 versus $16 per share), Bank A's shareholders agree to offer B's shareholders a bonus of $4 per share (i.e., a merger premium of [$16 + $4]/$16 = 1.25, or 125 percent). This means B's stockholders will exchange their stock for Bank A's shares with an **exchange ratio** of 1:1. Therefore, B's shareholders, who currently hold 50,000 shares in Bank B, will wind up holding 50,000 shares in Bank A. The combined organization will have 150,000 shares outstanding. If earnings remain at $750,000 following the merger, the consolidated banking organization will be able to maintain its earnings per share at the current level of $5 (i.e., $750,000/150,000 shares).

Unfortunately, paying merger premiums can get out of hand. In recent years, merger premiums ranging from 150 to 250 percent have become commonplace, and they often yield disappointing results for the stockholders long after these mergers are consummated. For example, suppose B's shareholders are offered a merger premium of 150 percent—that is, they are paid $24 per share for stock currently valued at $16 (or [$16 + $8]/$16 = 1.5). This means B's stockholders will get 6/5 of a share ($24/$20) in the acquiring organization, Bank A, for every share of Bank B's stock they now hold. When the exchange is made on these terms, there will be 60,000 new shares of Bank A (6/5 × 50,000 of B's shares), or a total of 160,000 shares for the combined banking firm. If total earnings do not fall but remain close to $750,000, the merged bank will report the following earnings per share:

$$EPS = \$750,000 \div 160,000 = \$4.69$$

Clearly, the earnings per share of the merged firm will have declined due to the **dilution of ownership** created by offering the acquired bank's stockholders an excessive number of new shares relative to the value of their old shares.

If the ratio of the stock price to the earnings of the bank to be acquired is *greater* than the P-E ratio for the acquiring bank, the combined firm's EPS will *fall* below its original level, a victim of spreading available earnings over more shares of stock— *earnings dilution.* For example, suppose Bank A, with a P-E ratio of 4 (or a $20 price per share/$5 in EPS) and 100,000 shares of stock outstanding, attempts to acquire Bank B, with a P-E ratio of 5 (i.e., $25 share price/$5 in EPS) and 50,000 shares of stock issued. Assume that total earnings after the merger ($750,000) match the banks' combined earnings before the merger. If A's stockholders agree to grant B's owners 1.25 shares ($25 price per share for B's stock ÷ $20 per share for A's stock) in the merged bank for each share of stock they presently hold, the new bank will have 62,500 new shares (i.e., 1.25 × 50,000 of B's shares) added to the 100,000 the acquiring bank already has outstanding. The merged banking firm will then have earnings per share of

$$EPS = \$750,000 \div 162,500 \text{ shares} = \$4.62$$

which is substantially *less* than the $5 in earnings per share Bank A posted before this merger. There is a significant dilution of earnings in this case because of the greater P-E ratio of the acquired bank and because so many new shares were issued to pay the high merger premiums promised to the acquired bank's shareholders.

The financial success of a merger, then, depends heavily on the comparative dollar amounts of earnings reported by the two banking organizations and their relative price-earnings ratios. The immediate change in earnings per share from the merger of Bank A and Bank B depends on this ratio:

$$\frac{\text{Price per share of Bank A's stock}}{\text{Current net earnings of Bank A}} \div \frac{\text{Price per share of Bank B's stock}}{\text{Current net earnings of Bank B}}$$

Of course, even if EPS goes down right after the merger, the transaction may still be worth pursuing if *future earnings* are expected to grow *faster* as a result of the acquisition. If significantly greater efficiency and cost savings result *over the long run,* the effects of paying a higher price (in new stock that must be handed over to the acquired bank's shareholders) will be more than made up eventually. Standard financial management practice calls for analyzing what will happen to the combined organization's EPS under different possible scenarios of future earnings and stock prices. If it takes too long to recover the cost of an acquisition according to the projected path of EPS, management of the acquiring institution should look elsewhere for a merger target.

The Merger and Acquisition Route to Growth

Whatever its motives, each *merger* is simply a financial transaction that results in the acquisition of one or more banks by another banking institution. The acquired bank (usually the smaller of the two) gives up its charter and adopts a new name (usually the name of the acquiring organization). The assets and liabilities of the acquired bank are added to those of the acquiring bank.[2] A merger normally occurs after the managements of the acquiring and acquired organizations have struck a deal. The proposed transaction must then be ratified by the board of directors of each organization and possibly by a vote of each firm's common stockholders.[3]

If the stockholders approve (usually by at least a two-thirds majority), the unit of government that issued the original charter of incorporation must be notified, along with the banking agencies that have supervisory authority over the banks involved. In the United States the federal banking agencies have 30 days to comment on the merger and there is a 30-day period for public comments as well. Public notice that a merger application has been filed must appear three times over a 30-day period, at approximately two-week intervals, in a newspaper of general circulation serving the communities where the main offices of the banks involved are located. The Justice Department can bring suit if it believes competition would be significantly reduced after the merger.

In deciding whether or not to merge, management and the board of directors of the acquiring firm look at many characteristics of the targeted institution. The principal factors examined by most bank merger analysts fall into six broad categories: (1) the bank's history, ownership, and management; (2) the condition of its balance sheet; (3) the bank's track record of growth and operating performance; (4) the condition of its income statement and cash flow; (5) the condition and prospects of the local economy served by the targeted institution; and (6) the competitive structure of the

---

[2]Two or more banks may also *consolidate* their assets to form one bank, with all participating banks giving up their former identities to become parts of a larger organization. Consolidations are much less common in banking than mergers, however.

[3]In a purchase and assumption transaction, two-thirds of the shareholders of the acquired bank must approve; however, usually no shareholder vote of approval is required by stockholders of the acquiring bank, nor is shareholder approval usually required when a bank engages in a partial liquidation of its assets (e.g., selling some branch offices).

market for financial services that the bank operates in (as indicated by any barriers to entry, market shares, and degree of market concentration).

In addition to the foregoing items, many acquirers will look at:

1. The comparative management styles of the merging organizations.
2. The principal customers the targeted bank serves.
3. Current personnel and employee benefits.
4. Compatibility of accounting and management information systems among the merging companies.
5. Condition of the targeted bank's physical assets.
6. Ownership and earnings dilution before and after the proposed merger.

A thorough evaluation of any proposed corporate merger *before* it occurs is absolutely essential, as recent experience has shown.

Methods of Consummating Merger Transactions

Mergers are generally carried out using one of two techniques: (1) purchase of assets or (2) purchase of common stock. With the **purchase-of-assets method,** the acquiring institution buys all or a portion of the assets of the acquired organization, using either cash or its own stock. In purchase-of-assets mergers, the acquired institution usually distributes the cash or stock to its shareholders in the form of a liquidating dividend, and the acquired organization is then dissolved. With some asset purchase deals, however, the institution selling its assets may continue to operate as a separate, but smaller, corporation.

With the **purchase-of-stock method,** on the other hand, the acquired firm ceases to exist; the acquiring firm assumes *all* of its assets and liabilities. While cash may be used to settle either type of merger transaction, banking regulations require that all but the smallest mergers and acquisitions be paid for by issuing additional stock of the acquirer. Moreover, a stock transaction has the advantage of not being subject to taxation until the stock is sold, while cash payments are usually subject to immediate taxation. Stock transactions trade current gains for future gains that are expected to be larger if everything goes as planned.[4]

The most frequent kind of merger in banking today involves **wholesale** (large metropolitan) **banks** merging with smaller **retail banks.** This lets money center banks gain access to relatively low-cost, less-interest-sensitive consumer accounts and channel those deposited funds into corporate loans. Some bank takeovers are friendly—readily agreed to by all parties—while a few are *hostile,* resisted by existing management and stockholders. In the acquisition of Irving Trust by Bank of New York, for example, the management and directors of Irving created obstacle after obstacle, legal and financial, to this corporate marriage before the courts finally cleared it to proceed.

---

[4]Bank merger transactions generally must be accounted for in accordance with Accounting Principles Board Opinion No. 16 (APB No. 16). The difference between the purchase price and the fair value of net assets acquired in mergers should be treated as an intangible asset in accordance with generally accepted accounting principles (GAAP).

Regulatory Rules for Bank Mergers in the United States

Two sets of rules generally govern bank mergers—decisions by courts of law and statutes enacted by legislatures, backed up by specific banking regulations. In the United States, for example, the Sherman Antitrust Act of 1890 and the Clayton Act of 1914 forbid mergers that would result in attempts to monopolize or lessen competition in any industry. Whenever any such merger is proposed, it must be challenged in court by the United States Department of Justice.

In addition, specific laws apply to bank merger transactions. In the United States, the **Bank Merger Act of 1960** requires each merging bank to request approval from its principal federal regulatory agency before a merger can take place. For national banks, this means applying to the Comptroller of the Currency for prior approval. For insured state-chartered banks that are members of the Federal Reserve System, the Fed's approval is required. Insured, state-chartered nonmember institutions must gain approval from the Federal Deposit Insurance Corporation.

Under the terms of the Bank Merger Act, each federal agency must give top priority to the **competitive effects** of a proposed merger. This means estimating the probable effects of a merger on the pricing and availability of banking services in the local community and on the degree of concentration of bank deposits or assets in the largest organizations in the local market. Thus, current merger laws in banking rest on the three premises that: (1) the *cluster of products* offered by a bank is the relevant product line to be considered in a bank merger or acquisition; (2) the relevant market to be concerned about is *local* (counties or metropolitan areas); and (3) the *structure* of the local market (usually measured by degree of concentration) is the principal determining factor in how much competition already exists and how a merger might damage or aid that competition. Where concentration is high—that is, where the largest banking institutions control a dominant share of local deposits or assets—the risk of damaging competition is greater, and the merger is less likely to win regulatory approval unless the merging institutions agree to divest some of their affiliated banks and branches. For example, in 1992 Bank America was allowed to acquire Security Pacific Corp. only after agreeing to divest itself of 213 branch offices in five states holding almost $9 billion in deposits.

Moreover, the *trend* in concentration also comes under close scrutiny from the bank regulatory agencies. Banking markets that have recently experienced increasing concentration ratios or declining numbers of financial-service suppliers are less likely to see mergers approved than are markets where concentration is falling. Other factors that must be weighted include the financial history and condition of the merging banks, the adequacy of their capital, the banks' earnings prospects, strength of management, and the convenience and needs of the community to be served. Mergers with anticompetitive effects cannot go unchallenged by federal authorities unless the applicant banks can show that such combinations would result in significant **public benefits.** Among the possible benefits are providing banking services where none are conveniently available and rescuing a failing bank whose collapse would have damaging effects on the public welfare.

The federal supervisory agencies prefer to approve mergers that will enhance the financial strength of the institutions involved. Regulators repeatedly emphasize the need for improving management skills and strengthening equity capital. The existence of such laws and regulations creates a barrier for any merger that would lead to substantial changes in market share and market concentration, possibly damaging competition in the local (county or metropolitan) market. This creates a dilemma for aggressive banking organizations. Expansion-minded bankers must distinguish proposed combinations that are likely to be challenged by the government, resulting in expensive legal battles, from those that are likely to sail through with few problems. It should be noted that the large majority of bank merger applications filed—usually more than 90 percent—are *approved*. However, this high approval rate reflects a good deal of screening out of unacceptable mergers through informal conferences between merger-minded bankers and regulatory officials.

Justice Department Guidelines

To reduce the legal uncertainties, the U.S. Department of Justice issued formal guidelines for merger applicants in 1968. The initial **Justice Department Merger Guidelines** were quite restrictive. They required firms operating in markets judged to be highly concentrated, with only limited competition, to acquire primarily *foothold businesses* (i.e., those having a small or insignificant market share) or to enter such markets *de novo* (i.e., start a new firm). In June 1982, the Reagan administration authorized more liberal merger guidelines. These rules permitted combinations that would probably have been challenged by the Justice Department under the old guidelines. The Justice Department further modified its merger guidelines in 1992, including the special guidelines for bank mergers that we operate under today.

The degree of *concentration* in a market is measured by the proportion of assets or deposits controlled by the largest banks serving that market. Presumably, if the largest banks control a substantial share of market assets or deposits, anticompetitive behavior (including collusive agreements) is more likely, resulting in damage to the public from excessive prices and poor service quality. The new Justice Department guidelines require the calculation of the **Herfindahl-Hirschman Index** (HHI) as a summary measure of *market concentration.* HHI reflects the proportion of total assets, deposits, or sales accounted for by each firm serving a given market. Each firm's market share is squared, and HHI is calculated as the sum of squared market shares for all firms serving a specific market area. Thus, the Herfindahl index is derived from this formula:

$$HHI = \sum_{i=1}^{k} A_i^{\,2}$$

where A_i represents the percentage of market-area deposits or assets controlled by the ith bank in the market, and there are k banks in total serving the market. We note from the above formula that the Herfindahl index reflects *both* the number of banks in the market and the concentration of deposits or assets in the largest banks and assigns heavier weight (by squaring each bank's market share) to those banks commanding the biggest market shares.

For example, suppose that a small local banking market contains four banks having the deposits and market shares shown below:

Deposits and Market Shares in Edgecroft County

Name of Bank	Deposits in Latest Annual Report	Market Shares of Total Deposits (A_i)	Square of Each Bank's Market Share (A_i^2)
First Security National Bank	**$245 million**	**50.8%**	**2,580.6**
Edgecroft National Bank	$113 million	23.4	547.6
Lincoln County State Bank	$ 69 million	14.3	204.5
Edgecroft State Bank and			
Trust Co.	$ 55 million	11.4	130.0
Totals	**$482 million**	99.9%	3,462.7

In this case:

$$HHI = \sum A_i^2 = 3,462.7 \text{ points}$$

HHI may vary from 10,000 (i.e., 100^2)—a monopoly position, where the leading firm is the market's sole supplier—to near zero for unconcentrated markets. In theory, the smaller the value of HHI, the less one or a few firms dominate any given market and the more equally are market shares distributed among firms. The more nearly firms are equal in size, the more competitive the relevant market is usually assumed to be and the less likely is anticompetitive behavior.

Under the newest Department of Justice guidelines for bank mergers in the United States (revised 1984 and 1992), any merger that would result (*a*) in a postmerger Herfindahl index of less than 1,800 or (*b*) change the value of the Herfindahl index in the relevant market area by less than 200 points would *not* likely be challenged by the U.S. Justice Department because, in the government's view, the merged firm would not gain enough market power to significantly damage the public welfare. However, when a proposed bank merger appears to yield a Herfindahl index exceeding these guidelines (i.e., the HHI in the relevant market is more than 1,800), the Justice Department considers such a market "highly concentrated." Proposed mergers in highly concentrated markets are likely to draw a Justice Department challenge in federal court unless the department's lawyers and economists can find evidence of extenuating circumstances.

Consider the example above in which we calculated the market shares of banks in Edgecroft county, where HHI equaled 3,462.7 points. According to the Justice Department's guidelines, Edgecroft would be a "highly concentrated market" (provided that Justice confined its definition of the relevant banking market to the local county itself and did not bring in surrounding areas that have more banks, as often happens where cities span several counties). The biggest bank in Edgecroft, First Security National, held a 50.8 percent market share. First Security would have a difficult time gaining approval for a merger with any other Edgecroft bank. (The largest bank in the county is more than twice as large as its nearest competitor, and the smallest bank has only an 11 percent market share.) Indeed, it would be difficult for *any* mergers to take place inside the Edgecroft market because of its highly concentrated status and because no matter which two of the four banks might wish to merge with each other, the resulting change in HHI would be relatively large. (As an example, if the two smallest banks merged, their combined market share would be 25.7 percent, which, when squared, is 660.5 points. The HHI for the market would climb more than 300 points, from 3,462.7 to 3,788.7, following the merger.) However, a bank *outside* the Edgecroft market might well be able to merge with one of the Edgecroft banks (in what is known as a *market extension merger*). This would leave the local market's HHI unchanged and would not reduce the number of alternative suppliers of banking services to the public.

Extenuating circumstances are frequently considered in approving those mergers that lead to only moderate increases in market concentration. These mitigating factors may include the ease with which new firms can enter the same market, the conduct of firms already present in the market, the types of products involved and the terms under which they are being sold, and the type and character of buyers in the relevant market area.

In recent years, the Justice Department has liberalized its standards for judging the anticompetitive effects of bank mergers. One device Justice has used to carry out this more liberal attitude is to include *nonbank financial institutions* in the calculation of some concentration ratios for local markets. (The Federal Reserve Board has recently included 50 percent or more of local thrift deposits in calculating the impact of a proposed bank merger on competition in the community where a proposed merger is to take place.) Including the deposits held by savings and loans, credit unions, and other financial institutions in the total deposits of a local market area lowers the market share held by each bank. Thus, fewer bank mergers will appear to damage competition and more mergers will receive federal approval, other factors held equal. However, recent research (see, for example, Kwast, Starr-McCluer, and Wolken [28]) suggests that in most local markets banks continue to be the dominant financial-service provider to households and small businesses, especially for checking and savings services and for credit—a feature that has not changed much over the years despite the appearance of new technology and government deregulation of the financial-services industry.

The Merger Decision-Making Process by U.S. Federal Regulators

U.S. federal bank regulatory agencies must apply the standards imposed by the Bank Merger Act and the Justice Department Merger Guidelines to *all* merger proposals. Each merger application is reviewed (*a*) by staff economists and attorneys working for the federal banking agencies to assess the potential impact of the proposed merger on competition and (*b*) by officials of the agencies' examination and supervision department to assess the merger's probable impact on the financial condition and future prospects of the banks involved.

The Bank Merger Act also requires the federal agency that is the merging banks' principal supervisor to assess the effect of the proposed merger on public convenience and the public's need for an adequate supply of financial services at reasonable prices. The agency involved must review the banks' records to determine if they have made an affirmative effort to serve *all* segments of the population in their trade area without discrimination. This assessment is required under the terms of the Community Reinvestment Act of 1977, which forbids banks from *redlining*—that is, marking off certain neighborhoods within their trade area and declining to extend financial services (especially credit) to residents of those neighborhoods. Compliance with this affirmative action law has become much more important to federal regulators (as indicated, for example, by the Federal Reserve Board's denial in 1989 of an application from Continental Illinois National Bank to acquire the Grand Canyon State Bank of Arizona on grounds that Continental did not have a satisfactory track record in following the CRA's community-service guidelines). As we saw in Chapter 19, federal examiners must review each bank's community service record each time they examine a bank's financial records and award a CRA rating, ranging from "outstanding" down to "substantial noncompliance." Any bank that has a low CRA rating runs the risk of having its proposed merger denied by the federal banking agencies.

Recently an additional regulatory hurdle has been imposed on merging banks in the form of the Home Mortgage Disclosure Act (HMDA). This law requires banks making home mortgage loans to report periodically the geographic distribution and other features of their home loans so that regulatory authorities can look for any evidence of discrimination against individuals and families seeking loans to purchase new homes on the basis of race, ethnic origins, neighborhood location, or other illegal factors. Banks that appear to have practiced discriminatory lending practices face an uphill battle in trying to win approval of a proposed merger.

Making a Success of a Merger

As we will see later in this chapter, when we review recent research studies of the outcomes of bank mergers, many of these mergers simply do not work. A variety of factors often get in the way of bank mergers' success, including poor or ill-prepared management, a mismatch of corporate cultures and styles, excessive prices paid by the acquirer for the acquired bank, a failure to take into account the customers' feelings and concerns, and a lack of strategic "fit" between the combining companies so that nothing really meshes smoothly with minimal friction and the merged bank finds that it cannot move forward as a cohesive and effective competitor.

While there are many keys to truly successful bank mergers, recent experience and research have suggested a few helpful steps that improve the chances for a desirable merger performance outcome. These include:

1. Acquirer, know thyself! Every banking company that is intent on growth through merger must thoroughly evaluate its own financial condition, track record of performance, strengths and weaknesses of the markets it already serves, and strategic objectives. Such an analysis can help management and stockholders identify strengths and weaknesses and clarify whether a merger or series of mergers could really help to magnify the bank's strengths and compensate for its weaknesses.
2. Get organized for a detailed analysis of possible new markets to enter and banks to acquire! Banks that are merger focused should create a management/shareholder team (including outside consultants, such as investment banking specialists) with

the skills needed to successfully evaluate potential new markets, potential acquisitions, and their apparent strengths and weaknesses.

Favorable markets to enter typically show a track record of above-average but stable growth in incomes and business sales, a somewhat older-than-average population with a high proportion of professional workers and business owners and managers, moderate to low inflation with stable currency prices, moderate competition, and a favorable regulatory environment that does not hinder bank expansion or the development of new banking services. Desirable merger targets, on the other hand, show evidence of persistent earnings growth and market acceptance of the services they offer (as measured by the growth of assets and deposits and a rising market share), a strong capital base, facilities and equipment that are functioning well and are up to date, evidence of close monitoring and control over operating costs, and complementary goals and objectives between acquiring and acquired institutions.

3. Establish a realistic price for the target banking firm based on a careful assessment of its projected future earnings discounted by a capital cost rate that fully reflects the risks of the target market and target firm and reflects all prospective costs that will have to be met by the acquiring firm (such as closing or upgrading poorly located or inadequately equipped branches, replacing outdated or incompatible management information systems, educating inadequately trained staff to handle new services, and correcting salary disparities that may exist between the two merging organizations).

4. Once a merger is agreed upon, create a combined management team (with capable managers from both acquiring and acquired firms) that will direct, control, and continually assess the quality of progress toward the consolidation of the two organizations into one effective banking unit.

5. Establish a reporting and communications system between senior management, branch and line managers, and staff that promotes rapid two-way communication of goals, operating problems, and ideas for improved technology and procedures so that employees at all levels feel involved in the merger, are convinced that effort and initiative will be rewarded, and believe they have a contribution to make toward the merger's ultimate success.

6. Create communications channels for both employees and customers to promote (1) understanding of why the merger or acquisition was pursued; and (2) what the consequences are likely to be for both anxious customers and employees who may fear interruption of service, loss of jobs, higher service fees, the disappearance of familiar faces inside the bank, etc. This may require the setting up of customer and employee "hot lines" to calm concerned people and give them the direction and assurances they seek.

7. Set up customer advisory panels to evaluate and comment upon the merged bank's community image, service and marketing effectiveness, its efforts to recognize valued and loyal customers, pricing schedules, and general helpfulness to customers.

The foregoing steps, even if faithfully followed, do not promise successful bank mergers, but they will increase the probability that a merger will proceed more smoothly and possibly achieve its long-range goals.

Concept Checks

22–4. What factors should a bank consider when choosing a good merger partner?

22–5. What factors must the regulatory authorities consider when deciding whether to approve or deny a bank merger?

22–6. When is a banking market too concentrated to allow a merger to proceed? What could happen if a bank merger were approved in an excessively concentrated market area?

22–7. What steps that management can take appear to contribute to the chances for success in a bank merger? Why do you think many bank mergers produce disappointing results?

Research Studies of Bank Mergers

What is the track record of bank mergers? What impact do they have on the public and upon bank stockholders? A number of studies over the years have addressed these questions. In general, their financial results are mixed—some positive and some negative effects. Other challenging problems—such as establishing a solid base in a new market—are often resolved through the merger route, however.

The Financial Impact

For example, a recent study by the author [16], which looked at the earnings impact of approximately 600 national bank mergers, found *no* significant differences in profitability between merging and comparably sized nonmerging banks serving the same local markets. In fact, this study showed that the acquired banks were significantly *more* profitable than their acquirers in the returns earned for their stockholders. However, the acquired institutions were significantly *less* profitable than comparable-size nonmerging banks serving the same markets, perhaps giving rise to the expectation among stockholders and management involved in these mergers that such combinations would help to improve bank earnings.[5]

Studies by Pettway and Trifts [7] and by Darnell [19] tend to confirm this picture of poor profit performance. Darnell found that most acquisitions involved payment by the acquiring banks of substantial premiums over book value to shareholders of the acquired banks. Moreover, these merger premiums tended to rise as more mergers occurred because there were usually fewer remaining banks to buy. The observations of

---

[5]The same study also showed that acquiring national banks were less efficient (measured by employee productivity) than comparable nonmerging institutions, suggesting that expected improvements in *efficiency* may have been an important motivation for these mergers.

Pettway and Trifts and of Darnell suggest the existence of *nonprofit* factors behind many bank mergers.

There is some evidence that the stockholders of interstate banking companies acquiring banks across state lines have scored slightly positive abnormal returns on their stock when such acquisitions have been announced. For example, a study by Millon-Cornett and De [5] examined the impact on stock prices of the announcement of selected interstate bank acquisitions over the 1982–86 period. These researchers found that the shareholders of *both* the acquiring and the acquired banks reaped positive returns that were higher than would be expected from the risk incurred by these stockholders. Moreover, James and Weir [4] also found higher than normal returns to the stockholders of acquiring banking companies for bank mergers taking place within the same state. And, both Millon-Cornett and Tehranian [6] and Spong and Shoenhair [11] found improvements in bank performance after interstate mergers were concluded, including increased earnings, better cost control, greater employee productivity, and faster growth. Rose [10] also found that interstate banks tend to gain greater local and statewide market shares of deposits and loans (but not earnings) when they acquire banks across state lines, but Goldberg and Hanweck [2] found no gains in statewide shares nor any edge in profitability over noninterstate banks.

Do bankers involved in mergers generally regard their efforts as successful? A survey by the author [15] of nearly 600 U.S. bank mergers occurring from 1970 to 1985 asked that very question of the CEOs involved. Overall, no more than two-thirds of these merging institutions believed they had fulfilled their merger expectations. For example, in only about half the cases investigated did profits, growth, market share, or market power actually increase and risk and operating costs fall. Roughly one-third of those seeking more qualified management apparently did not find it. However, CEOs at a substantial majority of the merging institutions (at least 80 percent) believed that their banks' capital base had improved and they were now a more efficient banking organization.

Unfortunately, as another study by the author [8] suggests, there are absolutely no guarantees that any bank merger will be successful, just as there never is any guarantee of benefits from any other type of capital investment. The author's study of 572 U.S. acquiring banking institutions, purchasing nearly 650 other banks over the 1970–88 period, found a nearly *symmetric* distribution of earnings outcomes from these mergers—roughly half registering positive earnings gains (lasting about two years) and about half displaying negative earnings results. Among the banks experiencing earnings gains, lower operating costs, greater employee productivity, faster growth, and greater concentration (perhaps implying less competition) in the markets where the headquarter's offices of banks were located appeared to lead to the greater earnings achieved. Thus, a significant portion of higher postmerger returns to the owners of U.S. banks appeared to be due to increases in postmerger market concentration, which in several cases seemed also to be associated with lower operating efficiency. This latter outcome suggests that, in some cases at least, the public may be paying higher prices and fees for banking services than would prevail in less concentrated (more competitive) markets. If so, bank regulatory agencies need to take a closer look at any proposed mergers for possible evidence of significant changes in the competitive climate within merger-active market areas.

The Public Benefits

In what ways does the public benefit from bank mergers? Most studies that have looked at this issue find few real public benefits. For example, the survey by the author [15] discussed earlier asked the CEOs of acquiring U.S. banks whether there had been any increase in hours of operation in order to provide the public with better access to banking facilities. Fewer than 20 percent of the merging banks reported any increase in hours of operation. About one-third changed their pricing policies, but the most common change was a price *increase* following merger, particularly in checking-account service fees, loan rates, deposit interest rates, and safe-deposit box fees. This result is echoed by Kohn [22], Bacon [1], and Snider [17], who all found that banks absorbed in a merger tend to have their prices changed to match those of the acquiring organization.

On the positive side, there is no convincing evidence that the public has suffered from a decline in service quality or availability following most bank mergers. In fact, Kaufman's study [21] of Elkhart, Indiana, where two of three banks in town merged, found that the majority of businesses and consumers surveyed believed that service quality had gone up following this merger. Kohn [22] found no evidence of a loss of local funding in a study of bank and thrift mergers in New York State, while Jones and Laudadio [20] suggested that mergers may significantly lower the bank failure rate. This notion was reinforced by Rose [9] whose study of 84 large U.S. bank holding companies making interstate acquisitions of banks found that diversifying bank operations into at least four states or two different economic regions of the nation could stabilize asset and equity returns, reduce the chances of insolvency, and lead to lower operating costs.

Concept Checks

22–8.   What does recent research evidence tell us about the impact of most bank mergers?

22–9.   Does it appear that most mergers among banking firms serve the public interest?

Summary

Mergers have been a major vehicle for change in the banking industry for many decades. They have permitted bankers to follow their customers into new markets and to replace outmoded facilities with new ones. Generally, merging is less expensive than establishing new banks or new branch offices. However, despite a large number of bank mergers in recent years, it has not been conclu- sively established that these combinations have benefited either the public or the acquiring banks, though management and stockholders of acquired banks seem to have received some benefits.

All bank mergers in the United States are regu- lated by federal or state authorities or both. The Bank Merger Act of 1960 requires any proposed merger involving a bank to be approved or denied by the bank's principal federal supervisory agency—the Comptroller of the Currency, the Federal Deposit Insurance Corporation, or the Federal Reserve System. Advisory opinions are also requested from other bank regulatory agencies that have jurisdiction over the banks involved. Finally, the effects on competition of each proposed bank merger must be evaluated by the U.S. Department of Justice, which can sue to block the merger if it believes the transaction would adversely affect competition.

Interbank marriages will continue to make the headlines as major banks strive to position themselves in the dynamic, ever-changing financial marketplace. In some cases, bank marriages will be government inspired, as troubled institutions are rescued by healthy, acquisition-minded ones. Others will be based on the search for cost economies and synergistic benefits that improve efficiency. Still others will represent efforts to enter new markets and cross state lines in an attempt to take advantage of recent trends toward liberalizing state and federal banking laws, allowing banks to take advantage of greater geographic diversification and reduce their exposure to risk.

Key Terms in This Chapter

Profit potential	Purchase-of-assets method
Cash flow risk	Purchase-of-stock method
Earnings risk	Wholesale banks
Tax benefits	Retail banks
Market-positioning benefits	Bank Merger Act of 1960
Cost savings (efficiency)	Competitive effects
Merger premium	Public benefits
Exchange ratio	Justice Department Merger Guidelines
Dilution of ownership	Herfindahl-Hirschman Index

Problems and Projects

1. Evaluate the impact of the following proposed mergers upon the *postmerger earnings per share* of the combined banking organization:

   a. The acquiring bank reports that the current price of its stock is $18 per share and the bank earns $6 per share for its stockholders; the acquired bank's stock is selling for $15 per share and that bank is earning $5 per share. The acquiring institution has issued 200,000 shares of common stock, whereas the acquired bank has 100,000 shares of stock outstanding. Stock will be exchanged in this merger transaction exactly at its current market price. Most recently, the acquiring bank turned in net earnings of $1,200,000 and the acquired banking firm reported net earnings of $300,000. Following this merger, combined earnings of $1,600,000 are expected.

   b. The bank to be acquired is currently earning $14 per share, and its acquirer is reporting earnings of $12 per share. The acquired firm's stock is trading in today's market at $24 per share, while the acquiring firm's stock exchanges today for $20 per share. The acquired bank has 75,000 shares outstanding; the acquiring institution, on the other hand, has issued 80,000 shares of common stock. The combined organization is expected to earn $900,000; before the merger, the acquired bank posted net earnings of $400,000 and the acquiring bank tallied net earnings of $600,000. If the stock will be traded at the going market price to effect this merger, what will postmerger earnings per share be?

2. Under the following scenarios, calculate the *merger premium* and the *exchange ratio:*

   a. The acquired bank's stock is selling in the market today at $8 per share, while the acquiring institution's stock is trading at $12 per share. The acquiring bank's stockholders have agreed to extend to shareholders of the target bank a bonus of $4 per share. The acquired bank has 30,000 shares of common stock outstanding, and the acquiring institution has 50,000 common equity shares. Combined earnings after the merger are expected to remain at their premerger level of $1,250,000 (where the acquiring bank earned $1,000,000 and the acquired institution $250,000).

   b. The acquiring banking firm reports that its common stock is selling in today's market at $30 per share. In contrast, the acquired bank's equity shares are trading at $24 per share. To make the merger succeed, the acquired firm's shareholders will be given a bonus of $2 per share. The acquiring bank has 120,000 shares of common stock issued and outstanding, while the acquired institution has issued 40,000 equity shares. The acquiring bank reported premerger annual earnings of $850,000, and the acquired institution earned $150,000. After the merger, earnings are expected to decline to $900,000. Is there any evidence of dilution of ownership or earnings in either merger transaction described above?

   Alternative scenarios:

   (1) Suppose Silverton National Bank's total deposits rise to $910 million, while Silverton County Merchants Bank now posts $596 million in deposits. Commerce National Bank now reports total deposits of $376 million, while Rocky Mountain Trust and Security National report current deposits of $225 million and $118 million, respectively. What happens to HHI in the Silverton metropolitan area? Do you think a merger involving the largest and the third-largest bank in town would be approved by the U.S. Department of Justice? Why or why not?

3. The Silverton metropolitan area is presently served by five large branch banks with total deposits as follows:

	Current Deposits
Silverton National Bank	$854 million
Silverton County Merchants Bank	605 million
Commerce National Bank of Silverton	383 million
Rocky Mountain Trust Company	211 million
Security National Bank and Trust	107 million

Calculate the Herfindahl-Hirschman Index (HHI) for the Silverton metropolitan area. Suppose that Rocky Mountain Trust and Security National Bank propose to merge. What would happen to the HHI in the metropolitan area? Would the U.S. Department of Justice be likely to approve this proposed merger? Would your conclusion change if the Silverton County Merchants Bank and the Rocky Mountain Trust Company planned to merge?

   (2) Suppose the deposits of all banks increase by 12 percent. How would this affect the HHI in the Silverton metropolitan area?

   (3) What if, due to a serious economic recession, all deposits in the metropolitan area fall by 10 percent?

4. Langley Bank and Trust has just received an offer to merge from Courthouse County National Bank. Langley's stock is currently selling for $40 per share. The shareholders of Courthouse County Bank agree to pay Langley's stockholders a bonus of $10 per share. What is the merger premium in this case? If Courthouse County's shares are now trading for $65 per share, what is the exchange ratio between the equity shares of the two banks? Suppose that Langley has 10,000 shares and Courthouse County has 30,000 shares outstanding. How many shares in the merged firm will Langley's shareholders wind up with after the merger? How many total shares will the merged banking company have outstanding?

5. The city of Wanslow is served by three banks which recently reported deposits of $234 million, $182 million, and $67 million, respectively. Calculate the Herfindahl index for the Wanslow market area. If the second and third largest banks merge, what would the postmerger Herfindahl index be? Under the most recent Department of Justice guidelines discussed in the chapter, would the Justice Department be likely to challenge this merger?

6. In which of the situations described below do the stockholders of both acquiring and acquired banks experience a gain in earnings per share of stock as a result of a merger?

	P-E Ratio of Acquiring Bank	P-E Ratio of Acquired Bank	Premerger Earnings of Acquiring Bank	Premerger Earnings of Acquired Bank	Combined Earnings after the Merger
A.	5	3	$750,000	$425,000	$1,200,000
B.	4	6	$470,000	$490,000	$850,000
C.	8	7	$890,000	$650,000	$1,540,000
D.	12	12	$1,615,000	$422,000	$2,035,000

7. Please list the steps that you believe should contribute positively to success in a bank merger transaction. What management decisions or goals? On average, what proportion of bank mergers would you expect would be likely to achieve the goals of management and/or the owners and what proportion would likely fall well short of the mergers' objectives?

Selected References

For analysis of how mergers affect bank perfor-mance, see these studies:

1. Bacon, Peter W. *A Study of Bank Mergers in Marion County, Indiana, 1945 to 1966.* Staff Memorandum, Research Department, Federal Reserve Bank of Chicago, October 1967.
2. Goldberg, L. G., and G. A. Hanweck. "What Can We Expect from Interstate Banking?" *Journal of Banking and Finance* 12 (1988), pp. 51–67.
3. Hunter, William C., and Larry D. Wall. "Bank Merger Motivations: A Review of the Evidence and an Examination of Key Target Bank Characteristics." *Economic Review,* Federal Reserve Bank of Atlanta, September/October 1989, pp. 2–19.
4. James, Christopher, and Peggy Weir. "Returns to Acquirers and Competition in the Acquisitions Market: The Case of Banking." *Journal of Political Economy* 95 (1983), pp. 355–70.

5. Millon-Cornett, M., and S. De. "Common Stock Returns in Corporate Takeover Bids: Evidence of Interstate Bank Mergers." *Journal of Banking and Finance* 15 (1991), pp. 273–95.

6. Millon-Cornett, M., and H. Tehranian. "Changes in Corporate Performance Associated with Bank Acquisitions." *Journal of Financial Economics* 31 (1992), pp. 211–34.

7. Pettway, Richard, and J. W. Trifts. "Do Banks Overbid When Acquiring Failed Banks?" *Financial Management* 14 (Summer 1985), pp. 5–15.

8. Rose, Peter S. "The Distribution of Outcomes from Corporate Mergers: The Case of Commercial Banking." *Journal of Accounting Auditing, and Finance,* X, no. 2 (March 1995).

9. _____. "The Diversification and Cost Effects of Interstate Banking." *The Financial Review* 31, no. 2 (May 1996), pp. 431–52.

10. _____. *The Local and Statewide Market Share Advantages of Interstate Banking Firms,* unpublished paper, Texas A&M University, September 1997.

11. Spong, Kenneth, and J. D. Shoenhair. "Performance of Banks Acquired on an Interstate Basis." *Financial Industry Perspectives,* Federal Reserve Bank of Kansas City, December 1992, pp. 15–23.

These studies treat bank merger regulations and laws:

12. Rhoades, Stephen A. "The Implications of Financial Deregulation, Interstate Banking, and Financial Supermarkets for Bank Merger Policy." *The Magazine of Bank Administration,* November 1983, pp. 48–52.

13. _____. "*Bank Mergers and Industrywide Structure, 1980–94,* Staff Study No. 169, Board of Governors of the Federal Reserve System, January 1996.

14. Rose, Peter S. "Merger Mania, Banking Style." *The Canadian Banker* 90, no. 5 (1984), pp. 38–44.

15. _____. "Improving Regulatory Policy for Mergers: An Assessment of Bank Merger Motivations and Performance Effects." *Issues in Bank Regulation* 9, no. 3 (Winter 1987), pp. 32–39.

16. _____. "The Impact of Mergers in Banking: Evidence from a Nationwide Sample of Federally Chartered Banks." *Journal of Economics and Business* 39, no. 4 (November 1987), pp. 289–312.

17. Snider, Thomas E. "The Effect of Merger on the Lending Behavior of Rural Banks in Virginia." *Journal of Bank Research,* Spring 1973, pp. 52–57.

18. Weston, J. Fred, and Kwang S. Chung. "Do Mergers Make Money?" *Mergers and Acquisitions,* Fall 1983, pp. 40–48.

For an analysis of the terms under which bank mergers take place, see the following:

19. Darnell, Jerome C. "Bank Mergers: The Prices Paid for Merger Partners." *Business Review,* Federal Reserve Bank of Philadelphia, July 1973, pp. 16–25.

For a review of the public interest aspects of bank mergers, see the following:

20. Jones, J. C. H., and L. Laudadio. "Canadian Bank Mergers, The Public Interest, and Public Policy." *Banca Nazionale del Lavoro,* 1973, pp. 109–40.

21. Kaufman, George G. "Customers View a Bank Merger—Before and After Surveys." *Business Conditions,* Federal Reserve Bank of Chicago, July 1989, pp. 5–8.

22. Kohn, Ernest. *Branch Banking, Bank Mergers, and the Public Interest.* New York State Banking Department, 1964.

23. Peek, Joe, and Eric S. Rosengren. "Have Borrower Concentration Limits Encouraged Bank Consolidation?" *New England Economic Review,* Federal Reserve Bank of Boston, January/February 1997, pp. 37–47.

24. Rose, Peter S. "Convenience and Needs: A Survey of Holding Company Bank Services." *Issues in Bank Regulation* 6, no. 3 (Winter 1988), pp. 26–31.

For a discussion of planning for mergers, see:

25. Prasad, Rose M., and S. Benjamin Prasad. "Strategic Planning in Banks: Senior Executives' Views." *International Journal of Management* 6, no. 4 (December 1989), pp. 435–41.

26. Lausberg, Carsten, and Peter S. Rose. "Merger Motives in European Banking: Results of an Empirical Study." *Bank Archiv* 43 no. 3 (1995), pp. 177–86.

27. _____. "Managing Bank Mergers." *Bank Archive* 45 (June 1997), pp. 423–27.

28. Kwast, Myron L., Martha Starr-McCluer, and John D. Wolken. *Market Definition and the Analysis of Antitrust in Banking,* Finance and Economics Discussion Series No. 1997-52, Board of Governors of the Federal Reserve System, Washington, D.C., 1997.

23 INTERNATIONAL BANKING SERVICE OPTIONS

Learning and Management Decision Objectives

The purpose of this chapter is to learn what services international banks offer their customers and to discover the options a bank manager has under law and regulation to organize a multinational bank.

Introduction

Banks have been heavily involved in selling their services across national borders from the industry's very beginnings.[1] The first banks were located principally in global trading centers around the Mediterranean Sea, including Athens, Cairo, Jerusalem, and Rome, aiding merchants in financing shipments of raw materials and goods for sale and exchanging one nation's currency and coin for that of another to assist travelers as well as local merchants. In the colonial period of American history and well into the 19th century, the financing needs of American businesses were met principally by foreign banks.

In the 1950s and 1960s, U.S. banks rapidly expanded their operations abroad, establishing branch offices, subsidiaries, and joint ventures with local firms in hundreds of foreign markets. This period of foreign expansion by U.S. banks was directed mainly at the commercial centers of western Europe, the Middle East, and South and Central America. In the 1970s and 1980s, American banks expanded their presence around the Pacific Rim, especially in Japan, China, Hong Kong, and Singapore. These multinational banks played a key role in investing the huge amounts of funds flowing to oil producers as world oil prices surged upward in the 1970s and in financing the huge trade deficits of the United States.

---

[1]Portions of this chapter are based on the author's 1987 article in *The Canadian Banker* [6]. Reprinted material is used with the permission of the publisher.

However, during the 1980s the torch of leadership in international banking passed to Japanese banks, which established strong beachheads in London, New York City, and other major financial centers. At the same time, international banking institutions in the United States and western Europe experienced a marked slowing in their growth. Intensified competition, spurred on by banking deregulation in Great Britain, the United States, and several other nations and by significant advances in communications technology, forced many international banks to reduce their physical presence in foreign markets in order to cut operating costs. At the same time, many of their major loan customers, especially such Third World countries as Brazil and Mexico, were experiencing severe economic problems, which slowed or stopped repayment of their loans. The result was a slowdown and, in many cases, a retrenchment in banking operations around the globe, though in the 1990s international banking activities began to expand rapidly again as Europe, Asia, and the Americas experienced moderate to strong growth. The torch of banking leadership appeared to pass once again to American and European banks, lead by such giants as Citicorp, BankAmerica, UBS/Swiss Bank, Chase Manhattan, Barclays PLC and HSBC holdings of the United Kingdom, the Netherlands ING Group, and Germany's Deutsche Bank. International banking services today continue to be vitally important sources of revenue and earnings for leading banks throughout the world.

In this chapter, we take a close look at the organizational forms, services, problems, and challenges facing international banking operations today.

Types of Foreign Banking Organizations

In their pursuit of business around the world, banks use a wide variety of *organizational structures* to deliver services to their international customers (as illustrated in Exhibit 23–1).

Representative Offices.   The simplest organizational presence for a bank active in foreign markets is the **representative office**—a limited-service facility that can market the services supplied by the home office and identify new customers, but does not take deposits or book loans. These offices are established to supply support services both to the parent bank and to its customers.

Agency Offices.   Somewhat more complete than the representative office is an **agency office,** which in many jurisdictions does not take deposits from the public (though New York agencies, for example, can take deposits), but does make commitments to make or purchase loans, provide seasonal and revolving credit agreements, issue standby letters of credit, provide technical assistance and advice to customers (primarily corporations and governments), administers their cash accounts, and assists with customer security trading.

Branch Offices.   The most common organizational unit for most international banks is the **branch office,** offering the bank's full line of services. Foreign branches are *not* separate legal entities, but merely the local office that represents a single large banking corporation. They can accept deposits from the public subject to the regulations of the country where they are located and may escape some of the rules for deposit taking faced by branches of the same bank in its home country. For example, the branch offices of U.S. banks overseas do not have to post legal reserve requirements or pay FDIC insurance fees on the deposits they take abroad.

Subsidiaries.   When an international bank acquires majority ownership of a separate, legally incorporated foreign bank, the foreign bank is referred to as a **subsidiary** of the international bank. Because the subsidiary possesses its own charter and capital stock, it will not necessarily close down if its majority owner fails. Similarly, a subsidiary bank can be closed without a substantial adverse effect on the international bank that owns it (as happened in the Philippines when a subsidiary of New York's Citicorp closed). Subsidiaries may be used instead of branches because local regulations may prohibit or restrict branching or because of tax advantages. Also, many international banks prefer to acquire an existing firm overseas that already has an established customer base.

Joint Ventures.   A bank that is particularly concerned about risk exposure in entering a new foreign market, lacks the necessary expertise and customer contacts abroad, or wishes to offer services prohibited to banks alone may choose to enter into a **joint venture** with a foreign firm, sharing both profits and expenses.

Edge Act Corporations.   **Edge Acts** are separate domestic U.S. companies owned by a U.S. bank or by a foreign bank, but located outside the home state of the bank that owns them. These subsidiary corporations are limited primarily to international or foreign business transactions. Federal legislation passed at the end of World War I permitted banks large enough to post the required capital to apply for Edge Act charters from the Federal Reserve Board in Washington, D.C.

Agreement Corporations.   These business corporations are subsidiaries of a bank organized under Section 25 of the Federal Reserve Act and must devote the bulk of their activities to serving international customers and carrying out international transactions, similar to Edge Act corporations.

IBFs.   An **international banking facility (IBF)** is a creation of U.S. banking regulations, first authorized by the Federal Reserve Board in December 1981. IBFs are simply computerized account records that are not a part of the domestic U.S. accounts of the bank that operates the IBF. They must be domiciled inside U.S. territory and their activities must focus upon international commerce. Deposits placed in an IBF are exempt from U.S. deposit reserve requirements and deposit insurance fees. IBFs may be operated by either U.S.-chartered banks or by banks foreign to the United States.

Shell Branches.   In order to escape the burden of regulation, many international banks have established special foreign offices, which look like empty shells, that merely record the receipt of deposits and other international transactions. These **shell branches** often contain little more than a desk and a telephone or FAX machine where deposits from the worldwide Eurocurrency markets are booked to avoid deposit insurance assessments, reserve requirements, and other costs incurred when deposits are accepted by a domestic bank. Many large international banks have operated shell branches for years in such attractive locations as the Bahamas and the Grand Cayman Islands.

Export Trading Companies (ETCs).   In 1982, the U.S. Congress passed the **Export Trading Company Act** (ETCA), which allowed U.S. banking firms and Edge Act Corporations to create **export trading companies** (ETCs). According to Federal Reserve Board regulations, these specialized firms must receive over half of their income from activities associated with exporting goods and services from the United States. Once established, an ETC can offer such services as export insurance coverage, transportation and warehousing of saleable products, trade financing, and research into the possibility of exploiting markets abroad.

Concept Checks

23–1.   What organizational forms do international banks use to reach their customers?

23–2.   Why are there so many different types of international banking organizations?

Regulation of International Banking

International banking activities are closely regulated by both home and host countries all over the globe. However, there is a strong trend today toward deregulation of banking and the related fields of securities brokerage and securities underwriting. An increasing number of nations today recognize the necessity of coordinating their regulatory activities so that, eventually, all banks serving international markets will operate under similar rules (sometimes called *harmonization*).

Goals of International Banking Regulation

International banking activities are regulated for many of the same reasons that shape domestic banking regulations. There is an almost universal concern for *protecting the safety of depositor funds,* which usually translates into laws and regulations restricting bank risk exposure and rules specifying minimum amounts of owners' equity capital to serve as a cushion against operating losses. Regulations frequently limit nonbanking business activities to avoid excessive risk taking and criminal activity, as in the famous Bank of Credit and Commerce International (BCCI) case.[2] Then, too, to the extent that international banks can create money through their lending and deposit-creating activities, international banking activity is regulated to *promote stable growth in money and credit* in order to avoid threats to each nation's economic health.

However, many international banking regulations are unique to the international field itself—that is, they don't apply to most domestic banking activity. For example, *foreign exchange controls* protect a nation against loss of its foreign currency reserves, which might damage its prospects for repaying international loans and purchasing goods and services abroad. Another instance would be rules that *restrict the outflow of scarce capital* that some governments see as vitally necessary for the health of their domestic economies. There is also a strong desire in many parts of the world to *protect domestic financial institutions and financial markets from foreign competition.* Many countries prefer to avoid international entanglements and excessive dependence on other countries for vital raw materials and other goods and services. This isolationist philosophy often leads to outright prohibition of outsiders from entry into full-service banking and may also restrict the international operations of domestic banks.

Regulation of Foreign Bank Activity in the United States

Beginning in the 1970s and continuing to the present day, foreign banks have entered the United States in force, attracted by the huge size of the common market formed by the 50 states, the relative economic and political stability of the United States, and the expansion of foreign banks' own customers inside U.S. territory (e.g., Japanese auto and electronics firms producing and selling products made in America). As noted by Misback [12], there were more than 560 U.S. branch and agency offices operated by

---

[2]See Chapter 2 for a discussion of the details behind the famous BCCI bank case.

close to 300 foreign-owned banks in 1991, and these U.S. offices held more than $400 billion in assets (or about 18 percent of total U.S.-chartered banking assets). By mid-1997 foreign bank offices held more than 21 percent of the total assets claimed by all U.S.-chartered banks, as shown in Table 23–1. In total, their financial assets approached $770 billion, of which nearly half ($362 billion) were loans.

The International Banking Act of 1978.   The expansion of foreign banking activity inside America's borders led to strong pressure on Congress by domestic banking groups and, eventually, to passage of the **International Banking Act** (IBA) of 1978—the first major federal law regulating foreign bank activity in the United States. The IBA's key components were as follows:

- It required branches and agency offices of foreign banks to secure federal licenses for their U.S. operations.
- It restricted foreign bank branching within the United States, requiring each bank to designate a home state and follow that state's branching rules just as American banks must do.

TABLE 23–1   **Foreign Banking Offices in the United States***

	(Dollar Figures in Billions)						
	1991	*1992*	*1993*	*1994*	*1995*	*1996*	*1997***
Total financial assets held by foreign banks in the U.S.	$437.5	$509.3	$542.2	$589.7	$666.3	$713.8	$765.9
Percent of all financial assets held by U.S.-chartered banks	16.5%	18.5%	18.6%	18.9%	20.1%	20.8%	21.4%
Total loans held by foreign banks in the U.S.	$260.0	$281.3	$268.8	$277.7	$303.9	$339.9	$362.3
Percent of total loans held by U.S.-chartered banks	14.3%	15.3%	13.9%	13.2%	13.1%	13.9%	14.1%
Total deposits held by foreign banks in the U.S.	$119.2	$127.7	$126.1	$128.1	$138.2	$193.3	$230.3
Percent of total deposits held by U.S.-chartered banks	6.4%	7.0%	6.9%	6.7%	6.6%	8.4%	9.5%

Note:*Includes branches and agencies of foreign banks, Edge Act and agreement corporations, New York investment companies (until 1996, II), and American Express Bank.
**Through second quarter of 1997.
Source: Board of Governors of the Federal Reserve System, *Flow of Funds Accounts of the United States,* Second Quarter 1997.

- It stipulated that deposits accepted at the U.S. branch or agency offices of foreign banks holding $1 billion or more in consolidated assets are subject to legal reserve requirements as determined by the Federal Reserve Board.

- It made U.S. branches of foreign banks eligible for deposit insurance under stipulated conditions and granted them access to certain Federal Reserve services (such as the ability to borrow from the Federal Reserve banks).

The Foreign Bank Supervision Enhancement Act of 1991. On December 19, 1991, Congress amended the IBA with passage of the **Foreign Bank Supervision Enhancement Act.** The new law, which grew out of a federal investigation of the scandal involving the Bank of Credit and Commerce International (BCCI) of Luxembourg, places tighter controls on foreign bank operations in the United States. Applications from foreign banks to expand their U.S. banking activities must be reviewed and approved by the Federal Reserve Board. Service offerings of foreign banks are basically limited to the same list of banking services that U.S. national banks are permitted to offer. Moreover, no foreign bank can accept retail deposit accounts of less than $100,000 from the public unless they first seek insurance coverage from the FDIC. Any foreign bank desiring to acquire more than 5 percent of the voting shares of a U.S. bank or bank holding company must first seek Federal Reserve Board approval.

Under the 1991 law the Federal Reserve System must also review how thoroughly foreign banks are supervised by their home countries. If the Federal Reserve Board determines that regulation and supervision of a foreign bank by that bank's home nation is inadequate, the Fed can deny that foreign bank permission to establish a branch, agency, or representative office inside United States territory or to start or acquire any U.S. subsidiary firms. Moreover, the Board can terminate the operations of a foreign bank in the United States if it finds the bank violated U.S. laws, engaged in unsafe or unsound banking practices inside U.S. territory, or is not being operated in a manner consistent with the public interest. The 1991 law empowered the Fed to examine the U.S. offices and affiliates of any foreign bank and stipulated that the Federal Reserve Board must be notified a minimum of 30 days in advance if a foreign bank wishes to close any of its U.S. offices.

New Capital Regulations for Major Banks Worldwide

The spread of foreign banks into the United States and of U.S. banks into other nations, coupled with serious international debt problems, soon led to new regulatory standards for the capital that international banks must hold as a buffer against risk. First, in November 1983, the U.S. Congress passed the **International Lending and Supervision Act,** which required federal regulatory agencies to prepare new capital and lending rules for U.S.-supervised banks. Specifically, the 1983 law required U.S. banks to

1. Hold reserves that are charged against current income in a special account, called the Allocated Transfer Risk Reserve (ATRR), against any foreign loans showing evidence of protracted repayment problems.

2. Restrict the size of loan rescheduling fees that could be charged against international borrowers facing problems repaying their loans and require the banks involved in restructuring troubled international loans to amortize any fees assessed over the life of the loans involved.

3. Report the extent of their credit exposure from loans made to foreign borrowers and make public any credit exposures to any single country that exceed the lesser of 15 percent of primary capital or 0.75 percent of total assets.

4. Maintain enough capital to protect the depositors of an international bank against risk exposure.

Soon after these rules were implemented, negotiations began between the United States and other leading nations to determine if international cooperation in banking regulation was possible. Turmoil in international markets, especially a debt crisis involving less-developed countries, delayed this process for several years until preliminary guidelines were announced in December 1987. Finally, on July 15, 1988, representatives of 12 nations announced a final agreement in Basle, Switzerland, on common bank capital standards. The **Basle Agreement,** as we saw earlier in Chapter 15, called for all banks to achieve a minimum total-capital-to-total assets ratio of 8 percent. The announced purpose of the Basle Agreement was twofold: (1) to strengthen international banks, thereby strengthening public confidence in them, and (2) to remove important inequalities in banking regulation between nations that contribute to competitive inequalities between their banks. Relative to banks with lower capital requirements, banking institutions from more conservative, closely regulated banking systems with tougher capital requirements were placed at a disadvantage in pursuing customers and meeting their funding needs. In the wake of the Basle Agreement, many leading banks announced plans to raise new capital and sell off assets to improve their capital-asset ratios.

Concept Checks

23–3. What are the principal goals of international banking regulation?

23–4. What were the key provisions of the U.S. International Banking Act of 1978 and the International Lending and Supervision Act of 1983?

23–5. Explain what the Basle Agreement is and why it is so important.

Customer Services Supplied by Banks in International Markets

Customers active in foreign markets require a wide variety of services, ranging from credit and the execution of payments to the provision of marketing advice and assistance (see, for example, Table 23–2). The variety of services offered by international banks has expanded significantly in response to evolving customer needs and intense international competition.

TABLE 23–2   **Key Customer Services Offered by International Banks**

The International Bank Service Menu

Supplying foreign currencies for customer
   transactions

Hedging against foreign currency risk (currency
   futures and options, forward contracts, and swaps)

Security underwriting for corporate customers
   (bond, note, and stock issues)

Hedging against interest rate risk (interest rate
   swaps, caps, financial futures, and options)

Supplying long- and short-term credit and credit
   guarantees (direct loans, note issuance facilities,
   Europaper, ADRs, etc.)

Payments and cash management services
   (acceptances, letters of credit, and other drafts)

Savings or thrift instruments (CDs, savings
   accounts, pension programs)

Foreign marketing assistance for customers
   (foreign market analysis, insurance,
   and trade financing)

Making Foreign Currencies Available for Customer Transactions

International banks supply foreign currency—**FOREX**—services to their customers. Many of their customers require sizable quantities of spendable currencies to pay for imported goods and raw materials, to purchase foreign securities, and to complete mergers and acquisitions. Other customers may receive on a regular basis large amounts of foreign currency or foreign-currency–denominated deposits from businesses and individuals abroad who buy their products or purchase their securities. These foreign funds must be exchanged for domestic currency to help the customer meet his or her own cash needs. International banks routinely hold working balances of those foreign currencies most in demand by their customers.

Hedging against Foreign Currency Risk Exposure

Customers who receive or dispense large amounts of foreign currencies look to their banks for protection against *currency risk*—the potential for loss due to fluctuations in currency prices (exchange rates). But, customers are not the only ones who face currency risk; international banks themselves also face substantial currency risk which must be dealt with.

Currency risks arise most often in international banking when banks: (*a*) make foreign-currency–denominated loans to their customers; (*b*) issue foreign-currency–denominated IOUs (such as deposits) to raise new funds, (*c*) purchase foreign-issued securities, or (*d*) trade in foreign currencies for a bank's own currency position as well as the currency needs of its customers. The *net exposure* of a bank or of one of its customers to fluctuations in the value of any particular currency can be determined from the following equation:

$$\text{Net exposure to risk from any one currency} = \overbrace{\left[\begin{array}{c} \text{Assets held that are} \\ \text{denominated in the} \\ \text{currency} \end{array} - \begin{array}{c} \text{Liabilities issued in} \\ \text{the currency} \end{array} \right]}^{\text{Net foreign-currency – denominated assets}}$$

Bankers' Insights and Issues

The Big Bang and Japan's Financial Problems

The Japanese banking system, plagued for several years by a troubled domestic economy and serious loan losses, now finds itself in the midst of another source of turmoil and challenge—the so-called Big Bang. This sweeping agenda for regulatory reform, expected to be completed by 2001, will bring about deregulation of many aspects of the Japanese financial system in an effort to reduce the overall size of that nation's banking system, increase competition, and perhaps lead to higher returns for Japanese savers. Many Japanese hope that regulatory reform will also spawn more prudent bank lending policies, more coordinated and enlightened regulatory policies (that pay closer attention to current market developments), and bring more Japan-related financial transactions back to the homeland instead of going to foreign financial centers (such as London and New York), as is often the case today.

Currently banks dominate the Japanese financial system, and government influence over where and how Japanese banks make loans has frequently resulted in making too many loans to troubled industries, resulting in magnified loan losses. Then, too, many Japanese banks and industrial firms share common ownership, which has made monitoring of banks' risk exposure by their stockholders less effective when those same stockholders often represent companies that have outstanding bank loans. Moreover, Japanese consumers often find themselves with few domestic choices on where to place their savings other than at banks or with the government-controlled postal system.

Among the most important changes expected to flow from the Japanese "Big Bang" are:

1. A breakup in the regulatory structure so that new agencies (including the Financial Supervisory Agency [FSA] scheduled to open in July, 1998) other than Japan's Ministry of Finance, which has been relatively slow to change and rigid in many of its regulatory practices, will watch over the

$$+ \overbrace{\left[\begin{array}{c} \text{Volume of the} \\ \text{currency purchased} \end{array} - \begin{array}{c} \text{Volume of the} \\ \text{currency sold} \end{array} \right]}^{\text{Net position in foreign currency}}$$

An international bank or bank customer with a *positive* net exposure in a given foreign currency—that is, whose net foreign-currency–denominated assets plus its net foreign-currency position is greater than zero—is said to be a *net long* in that particular currency. This condition may arise because the bank or its customer has more foreign-currency–denominated assets than liabilities or has purchased more of a foreign currency than it has sold or both. If the currency involved declines in value in the foreign exchange markets relative to the value of the domestic currency, the bank or its customer will suffer a loss due to its net long position in that particular currency.

On the other hand, a bank or bank customer may have a *negative* net exposure in a given foreign currency—indicating that its net foreign-currency–denominated assets

banking, insurance, and securities industries and deal more speedily with failing institutions and bad loans.

2. Foreign financial-service companies (including banks, insurance companies, securities firms, and pension funds) are likely to play a bigger role with more freedom to compete against domestic Japanese financial firms on their own home ground.

3. More freedom to hold financial accounts abroad as well as domestically so that Japanese savers and investors can more easily invest abroad as they search for the highest yields available, while foreign individuals and institutions can more readily move their funds between Japan and other global financial centers.

4. The emergence of a much larger and more flexible government and corporate bond market, which could grow to become a major competitor with banks as a significant source of credit in the Japanese economy.

5. A change in brokerage commissions on stock trading that results in more flexible fees that are primarily market driven.

6. Japanese security companies beginning to look more like banks in being able to offer their customers more different ways to save and execute payments.

7. The derivatives market may expand to embrace not only exchange-traded derivatives but also a much larger market share for over-the-counter derivative contracts.

8. More flexibility in approving mergers among banks and other financial-service companies may be granted by government policymakers so that weaker Japanese financial institutions can more easily be absorbed by stronger ones (with government support and encouragement for merging the weakest institutions), and the benefits of economies of scale in reducing operating costs and increasing efficiency will become more of a reality within the Japanese financial sector.

9. New regulatory approaches to deal with bad loans and troubled financial firms, such as prompt corrective action when troubles first surface, more rapid write-offs of troubled assets, external audits of individual companies' financial statements, closer adherence to international capital standards for banks, and the speedy closing of financial institutions with inadequate capital.

Source: For further discussion of Japan's banking problems and its recent efforts at financial reform see, for example, Michael Hutchison, "Financial Crises and Bank Supervision: New Directions for Japan?" *Economic Letter*, Federal Reserve Bank of San Francisco, No. 97-37 (December 12, 1997), pp. 1–3.

plus net foreign-currency position is less than zero. This may occur because the bank's or the bank customer's liabilities in a given foreign currency are greater than its assets denominated in that same currency, or the volume of the currency sold exceeds the amount purchased or both. In this instance the bank or its customer is said to be in a *net short* position in that particular currency. If the currency involved increases in value against the bank's or the customer's home currency, a loss will occur in a net short position. In general, the more volatile a given currency is, the greater the possibility for scoring gains or for experiencing losses from any given foreign currency position.

Recent research evidence (see, for example, Hopper [13]) suggests that currency exchange rates are not consistently predictable and show no reliable connection to such fundamental factors as money supply growth and output in different countries—two forces that finance theory suggests should help to explain relative currency-price movements. (There is, however, some evidence that the volatilities of currencies tend to cluster around certain intervals of time, suggesting that price volatility patterns might be used to anticipate high daily risk exposures and avoid serious losses on certain days.) Accordingly, international banks typically employ a wide variety of currency-hedging techniques to help shelter their own and their customers' currency risk exposure. The most widely used of these currency-risk management techniques include forward contracts, currency futures contracts, currency options, currency warrants, and currency swaps.

Forward Contracts.   For example, banks may use **forward contracts,** in which a customer anticipating a future need to make currency purchases will work through the bank to negotiate a contract with another party calling for the delivery of currency at a stipulated price on a specific future date. Customers needing currency will agree to accept a specific amount of currency on a given future day for a price set today.

On the other hand, customers expecting to *receive* currency will often seek out contracts to sell that currency at a prespecified price. Because the price is set at the opening of a forward contract, the customer is protected from currency risk no matter which way currency prices go. If the customer is uncertain of the future date and the amount of currency involved, the bank may provide an *option forward contract,* in which the customer receives the right, but not the obligation, to deliver or take delivery of specific currencies on a future date (known as the *value date*) at an agreed-upon exchange rate.

Currency Futures Contracts.   An increasingly popular alternative to the forward contract is a **currency futures contract.** These contractual agreements between buyer and seller promise delivery of stipulated currencies at a specified price on or before a terminal date. The two basic futures contract types are *long hedges* and *short hedges.*

Long hedges in currency futures are designed to protect a bank's customer from increases in the price of the currency the customer must eventually acquire. They are particularly useful for *importers,* because payment for goods received often must be made in the foreign exporter's home currency, and a rise in the exchange rate between the exporter's home currency and the importer's home currency can quickly eliminate any expected profit on the sale of goods. Under a long hedge contract, the customer pledges to take delivery of currency at contract maturity for price X. If currency prices subsequently rise, the customer can go back to the currency futures market and sell similar currency futures contracts at the new higher price, Y. This cancels out the customer's obligation to take delivery of currency and, at the same time, generates a trading profit on each contract equal to the price difference (Y − X) less any commission charged and taxes. Profits made on currency futures help to offset any loss that arises when the customer must actually acquire the currency and pay for the imported goods.

Alternatively, many customers, especially those *exporting* goods, find *short-hedge* futures contracts useful. These agreements require the customer to pledge delivery of a stipulated currency at a guaranteed price, X, to a counterparty on the maturity date. If currency prices subsequently fall, the customer can enter the futures market again on or before the first contract's maturity date and buy similar contracts at the lower price, Y, thus eliminating the responsibility to deliver currency. A profit is earned on each contract first sold and then bought equal to X – Y (minus taxes and transactions costs).

Other Tools for Reducing Currency Risk

Currency Options.   The recent volatility of foreign exchange rates has given rise to an ever-growing volume of new techniques to deal with currency risk. For example, in 1982 a new hedging instrument—the **currency option**—appeared. It gives a buyer the right, though not the obligation, to either deliver or take delivery of a designated currency or foreign-currency–denominated futures contract at a set price any time before the option expires. Thus, unlike the forward market, where delivery must take place on a certain date, actual delivery may not occur in the option market. Currency options include both spot and futures options.

Exchange-traded currency options on futures contracts have been growing rapidly in recent years. These contracts depend for their value on the underlying futures contract, which in turn depends on the price of the currency itself. When the price of a currency rises, the nearest-term currency futures contract also rises in price. A bank holding sizable assets denominated in that currency can reduce the risk of loss from falling currency spot prices by selling currency futures or by buying put options or selling call options for that same currency.

Call currency options give their holder the right to purchase currency or currency futures contracts at a fixed price any time before the option expires. *Put* currency options represent the right to sell currency or currency futures contracts at a specified price on or before the published expiration date. For example, a call on German deutsche mark (DM) futures contracts at a strike price of $0.42 gives the buyer of this call option the right to buy a contract calling for delivery of marks at a price of $0.42 to the buyer. If the market price of mark futures climbs above $0.42 per mark, the call option is said to be "in the money," and its buyer will exercise his or her option and take delivery of deutsche mark futures contracts at a price of $0.42. On the other hand, if mark futures stay below a strike price of $0.42, the call option will go unexercised because the buyer of the call can purchase futures contracts more cheaply in the market; in this case, the call option would be "out of the money." Generally, a put option is needed to protect against a fall in currency prices, whereas call options protect against loss from rising currency prices.

The advantage of the currency option is that it limits downside risk but need not reduce upside profits. The purchase price of a currency option is normally low enough to permit even small firms to participate in currency-hedging activities, and the currency option is a more flexible instrument than most other currency-hedging tools. However, this instrument is available only from a limited number of banks and a few currency exchanges, and it exposes the offering banks to additional risk that may limit this market's future growth.

Currency Swaps.   Finally, currency risk can be reduced with **currency swaps.** Using such a swap, a company or individual that needs to borrow a foreign currency contacts a counterparty who is scheduled to receive the same foreign currency on a convenient future date and is willing to give domestic currency to the borrower in exchange. When the contract matures and the currency must be repaid, the counterparty to the swap receives back the domestic currency from the borrower and pays back the borrowed foreign currency. Where a loan is involved, the borrower is fully hedged by the swap just described. In this case, the borrower receives domestic currency initially by swapping the borrowed foreign currency and then receives the borrowed currency back just in time to pay off its foreign-currency–denominated loan. There is no currency risk, because the foreign currency inflow and outflow exactly offset each other.

Supplying Customers with Short- and Long-Term Credit or Credit Guarantees

International banks are the leading source of credit for multinational corporations and many governmental units at home and abroad. They provide both short- and long-term financing for the purchase of raw materials and for meeting payrolls, constructing buildings, and other important long-term projects.

Note-Issuance Facilities.   Most international bank loans are short-term business credits carrying floating interest rates that are usually tied to some international base rate or reference rate. The most popular rate of this type is LIBOR—the London Interbank Offered Rate on borrowings of short-term Eurodollar deposits between international banks. Increasingly in recent years, however, international banks have provided credit guarantees for their customers' borrowings in the open market. One of the most popular of these is the **note issuance facility,** or **NIF.** Launched in the early 1980s, NIFs are medium-term credit agreements between international banks and their larger corporate and governmental customers. The NIF customer is authorized to periodically issue short-term notes, each of which usually comes due in 90 to 180 days, over a stipulated period (such as five years). The bank pledges to either buy up any notes not bought by other investors or grant supplemental loans based on LIBOR or on some other reference interest rate. In most cases, the customer's notes are denominated in U.S. dollars and are in large denominations (e.g., $1 million or larger).

Europaper.   International banks have also played a key role in the rapidly expanding **Eurocommercial paper (ECP)** market, where multinational corporations raise short-term credit covering weeks or months. This short-term loan market is centered in London's financial district and has attracted international banks and nonfinancial corporations as investors. While few ECP borrowers are based in the United States, a growing cadre of U.S. companies whose credit ratings are not strong enough to crack the U.S. commercial paper market or who need to sell longer-maturity paper are successfully placing their notes in the Europaper market. A recent spur to this market has come from financial deregulation in Japan, which now permits Japanese bank affiliates abroad to underwrite international commercial paper, while both Japanese and non-Japanese firms have recently been allowed to issue and buy yen-denominated commercial paper. International banks are heavy buyers of ECP for themselves and their investing customers and are also among the leading sellers of ECP issues. For example, Citicorp Investment Bank, Ltd., and Swiss Banking Corporation International have accounted for about 30 percent of all international paper sold to investors in recent years.

A related form of assistance provided to selected foreign credit customers by U.S. banks is the **American depository receipt (ADR)**—a receipt issued by a U.S. bank that makes it easier for a foreign business borrower to sell its securities to U.S. investors. In essence, an ADR is a negotiable instrument representing an ownership interest in the stock or other securities of a non-U.S. company. A U.S. bank agrees to hold the securities issued and to sell investors the ADRs as claims against those securities. A prominent example was the issue of ADRs by the Bank of New York against French government bonds in the Fall of 1988.

When the security issuer approves of such an arrangement, the ADR is said to be "sponsored" by the issuer. However, an international bank can simply choose to package any foreign securities that might be of interest to U.S. investors and sell ADRs without issuer approval, resulting in "unsponsored" depository receipts. ADRs may or may not be registered with the U.S. Securities and Exchange Commission (unsponsored ADRs are exempt from registration requirements) and sold on a U.S. securities exchange. One of their main attractions for U.S. investors is the absence of currency risk, since the value of a foreign security represented by an ADR is transformed by this instrument into U.S. dollars. Moreover, American investors can now diversify their portfolios more easily by buying ADRs and usually recover their funds more quickly by liquidating an ADR than by trying to sell a foreign-issued security.

Supplying Payments and Thrift (Savings) Instruments to International Customers

International banks are essential to the functioning of global trade and commerce through the offering of *payments and thrift instruments.* Not only do they provide foreign currencies for a customer making cash payments overseas, but they also can transfer the ownership of deposits through the global correspondent banking system. International banks issue and accept *drafts* in payment for purchases of goods and services across national borders. These irrevocable commitments of a bank to pay may be in the form of *sight drafts,* due and payable upon presentation, or *time drafts,* payable only on a specific future date, usually just long enough for goods to be shipped to another country. Time drafts usually arise when an importer requests its bank to issue a *letter of credit,* guaranteeing that the bank will pay a certain exporter of goods if the importer fails to do so. The exporter may then draw through one of its correspondent banks a bill for payment, which is presented to the importer's bank for acceptance and eventual payment. International banks also issue traveler's checks denominated in foreign currencies and will cable or wire funds anywhere a customer designates.

International banks also encourage *thrift*—short-term and long-term savings—by their customers. Most of these savings instruments are certificates of deposit (CDs)—interest-bearing receipts for funds deposited in a bank. While CDs were developed to be fixed-rate savings instruments, a sizable minority carry floating interest rates tied to movements of a specific base rate (such as LIBOR). The maturity of these instruments is divided into legs, or roll periods, during which the interest rate may change based on what has happened to the base rate over the current roll period. Each day, major international banks post sets of CD rates for the most popular deposit maturities, posting higher or lower rates based on their need for funds.

The tremendous success of this bank funds-raising instrument led to an expansion of the CD concept around the world in the form of the Eurodollar CD—a dollar-denominated deposit sold in million-dollar units, first in London and eventually reaching all major financial centers. Today, most EuroCDs are issued by branches of the largest U.S., Japanese, Canadian, West European, and British clearing banks. Large-denomination EuroCDs traded in the interbank market are often called *tap CDs,* while packages of smaller-denomination EuroCDs sold to a wide range of investors are usually called *tranche CDs.*

While most Eurodollars are fixed-rate deposits, floating-rate CDs (FRCDs) and floating-rate notes (FRNs) appeared in the 1970s to protect investors and borrowers against interest rate risk. These flexible-rate investments tend to be medium- to long-term in maturity, ranging from about 1 year to about 5 years in the case of FRCDs and to about 20 years for FRNs, with the attached interest rates typically adjusted every three to six months to match current interest rate movements.

Underwriting Customer Note and Bond Issues in the Eurobond Market

The development of note issuance facilities (NIFs) by international banks, discussed earlier, is but one example of the growing role of international banks in *underwriting new securities issues* in the open market. Another example is the **Eurobond market**—where borrowers issue bonds outside their home country. One reason for the growth of such a market was the increasing number of U.S. corporations, led by firms the size of Ford Motor Co. and Campbell Soup Co., that decided to tap Eurobonds to fund their overseas ventures. When U.S. interest rates rise, even purely domestic firms may find that Eurobond borrowings look cheaper by comparison. Leading banks active in this market include Lloyds Bank PLC, Chemical Banking Corp., and Citicorp. In an effort to broaden the market's appeal for the future, recent innovations have appeared. Among them are debt securities denominated in European currency units (ECUs), representing the mix of currencies issued by member nations of the European Community (EC).

Protecting Customers against Interest Rate Risk

International banks have been called upon in growing numbers to help protect their customers against *interest rate risk*—the risk of loss due to adverse interest rate movements. Borrowers contract for loans whose interest rates float with changes in market conditions. Thus, rising interest rates increase the customer's borrowing cost and threaten to erode the profit margin on investment projects supported by borrowing. Conversely, the bank's customer may suffer a loss in the event interest rates fall if the customer's funds are invested in deposits with floating interest yields or in other short-maturity investments that must be renewed at lower interest rates. Similarly, a customer with a fixed-rate loan fails to benefit from lower market interest rates unless steps are taken to cover that eventuality.

Interest Rate Swaps.   International banks can help their customers limit interest rate risk exposure by arranging **interest rate swaps.** As described in Chapter 8, these contractual agreements require each party to pay all or a portion of the interest bill owed on the other party's loan. Not only do interest rate swaps usually reduce interest expense for each party, but they also permit each swap partner to more accurately balance cash inflows generated by its assets with cash outflows traceable to its liabilities.

Interest Rate Caps.   International banks also limit the interest rate risk exposure of borrowing customers by imposing caps (maximum rates) on a customer loan in return for a fee. For example, the customer requesting a $100 million loan with an interest rate based on LIBOR may ask for an 11 percent interest rate cap so that a rise in market interest rates does not send the loan rate above 11 percent. Such caps transfer interest rate risk from the borrowing customer to the international bank and often carry a stiff fee to compensate the bank for its added risk exposure. As an illustration, the capped $100 million loan described above required the customer to pay a $3 million fee just to secure the rate cap.

Financial Futures and Options.   International banks are also active in assisting their customers with trading in financial futures and option contracts. For example, if the customer faces substantial loss from a rise in interest rates, then a *short* futures hedge (as described in Chapter 8) can be used to offset any loss due to a higher loan rate; alternatively, a *put* option could be employed. The prospect of customer losses from falling interest rates, on the other hand, could be hedged through a *long* (or buying) futures hedge or through the use of a *call* option.

Helping Customers Market Their Products through Export Trading Companies

An increasingly popular device for aiding customers to sell their goods abroad is the *export trading company* (ETC). The Japanese pioneered this export-promoting organization. Japanese ETCs have been closely intertwined with that nation's manufacturing and banking firms for at least a century and have built up extensive foreign contacts and created enormous foreign marketing opportunities for their affiliated firms. ETCs research foreign markets, identify firms in those foreign markets that could distribute Japanese products, and then provide or arrange the funding, insurance, and transportation needed to move goods to market. Prominent among Japanese trading companies are such familiar firms as Sumitomo, Mitsui, and Mitsubishi. While larger U.S. manufacturers have also developed extensive foreign trading operations, thousands of smaller U.S. firms have not maximized their opportunities in export markets, in part due to a lack of adequate market research or contacts abroad.

ETCs have been developed by leading money center banks in the United States and by dozens of smaller regional and community banks. Leading U.S. institutions launching ETC operations include BankAmerica, Bankers Trust Co., Chase Manhattan Corp., Citicorp, and Fleet Financial Group. Despite widespread interest, however, the growth of export trading activity via ETCs based in the United States has been disappointing thus far. To be sure, external developments have played a major role in limiting ETC activities, particularly the fluctuating value of the U.S. dollar in international markets and the difficulties many less-developed countries have faced in finding resources to pay for imports from the United States and in servicing their international debt. Lack of bank management experience with the ETC form of organization and lack of distribution channels and market data from abroad have proven to be major hurdles, especially for smaller banks.

U.S. banks have also complained of heavy capitalization requirements, regulatory limits on credit extended from banks to their ETC affiliates, and legal restrictions on the proportion of income that must come from exporting activities. For example, at least 51 percent of ETC income must come from U.S. exporting activities, and a U.S. bank can invest no more than 5 percent of its consolidated capital in an ETC nor lend more than 10 percent of its capital to its own ETC.

Concept Checks

23–6.   Describe the principal customer services supplied by banks in international markets.

23–7.   What types of risk exposure do international banks strive to control in order to aid their customers?

23–8.   What is a NIF? An ADR?

23–9.   Of what benefit can NIFs and ADRs be to international banks and their customers?

Future Problems for International Banks

Growing Customer Use of Securities Markets to Raise Funds

International banks today are facing a major challenge to their loan business comparable to what U.S. banks encountered decades ago—growing competition from the securities markets. When many international loans developed severe repayment problems in the 1980s, international banks withdrew substantial resources from the global credit market. Securities houses were quick to seize this opening and provide a conduit for borrower offerings of notes and bonds in the Eurocurrency markets. Later, large insurance companies and other large nonbank financial institutions joined the competition to attract borrowers away from banks and assist them in their access to the open market to sell securities and raise new capital. While international banks have purchased many of these securities themselves, they have been forced to settle for slower growth or even declines in bank credit, with smaller earnings margins on the credit they do extend to international borrowers.

Whether banks can regain their share of global business credit seems doubtful due to the regulations that constrain bank risk-taking worldwide, public fears about bank soundness, and the aggressiveness of securities dealers, insurance companies, and other financial-service providers intent on widening their shares of the lucrative corporate financing market. Indeed, as Table 23–3 reflects, several of the world's largest securities dealers and insurance companies have reached asset sizes and have service menus fully comparable to many of the globe's biggest banks, and there is intense competition worldwide between all three of these key types of financial-service industries. Challenged as never before, international banks today must work hard to find new sources of revenue and capital to meet the potent competition posed by both bank

TABLE 23–3   The Largest International Banks, Insurance Companies, and Securities Brokers and Dealers in Direct Competition for Large Corporate and Governmental Customers around the Globe
(Estimated Consolidated Assets in 1996)

Leading International Banks	*Estimated Consolidated Assets*	*Leading International Insurance Companies*	*Estimated Consolidated Assets*
Bank of Tokyo-Mitsubishi (Consolidated)	$750 Billion	Nippon Life Insurance	$346 Billion
		ZenKyoren Insurance	260
Deutsche Bank AG	575	Dai-Ichi Mutual Life	243
Sumitomo Bank	482	Company	
Dai-Ichi Kangyo Bank	477	Axa/Equitable	218
Fuji Bank	475	Allianz Holding Company	203
Sanwa Bank of Japan	471	Sumitomo Life Insurance	202
ABN Amro Holdings of the Netherlands	445	Metropolitan Life	190
Sakura Bank	437	Compagnie UAP of France	182
Industrial and Commercial Bank of China	435	International Netherlands Goep	104
HSBC Holdings of Great Britain	405	Prudential Insurance Company	180
Norinchukin Bank	401	American International Group	149
Industrial Bank of Japan	400	Meiji Life Insurance of Japan	135
Dresdner Bank AG	390	ITT Hartford	108
Banque Nationale de Paris	359	Netherlands Aegon	105
Societe Generale of France	342	Asahi Mutual of Japan	104
Chase Manhattan/Chemical Bank	336	Zurich Insurance Co.	98
		Cigna	96
Union Bank of Switzerland	325	Aetna Life and Casualty	94
Commerzbank of Germany	321	Travelers Insurance Co.	92
Barclay's Bank	318		
National Westminster Bank	316		
Credit Lyonnais	312		
Citicorp	278		
NationsBank	265		

and nonbank financial-service customers—for example, by selling their superior ability at credit evaluation, at packaging loans and securities for resale, and at creating credit guarantees in support of their customers' global financial-service needs.

Developing Better Methods for Assessing Risk in International Lending

Today the greatest source of risk for most international banks lies in granting foreign loans. Foreign lending is generally more risky than domestic lending because information sources overseas are often less reliable than those at home, it's easier to monitor a

TABLE 23–3   *(concluded)*

Leading International Security Brokers and Dealers	Estimated Consolidated Assets	Leading International Security Brokers and Dealers	Estimated Consolidated Assets
Morgan Stanley/Dean Witter/Discover Card	$132 Billion	Donaldson, Lufkin, and Jenrette	$25 Billion
Merrill Lynch Corp.	129	Prudential Securities Company	15
Credit Suisse-First Boston Corporation	308	Schroders of Great Britain	13
Nomura Securities	41	Charles Schwab	8
Lehman Brothers	75		
Goldman Sachs	74		
Salomon Brothers	122		
Daiwa Securities	96		
Nikko Securities Co.	39		
Bear Stearns Co.	38		
Yamaichi Securities	50		
Smith Barney	26		
Paine Webber Co.	25		
SBC Warburg of Switzerland	26		

loan made nearby rather than one made thousands of miles away, and the court systems needed to enforce contracts and conduct bankruptcy proceedings are often absent in the international arena. This added risk associated with international loans is often called *country risk.* A related and somewhat narrower form of international lending risk—called *sovereign risk*—occurs when a foreign government takes actions that interfere with the repayment of an international loan, such as by repudiating all foreign debt obligations, appropriating private property, or suspending loan payments for a time to conserve the home government's foreign exchange reserves.

Unfortunately, there is no effective international tribunal for lenders to sue foreign governments that pursue policies preventing the full repayment of loans. The result is that banks choosing to lend abroad must analyze *both* the individual borrower and the country and government where the borrower resides.

In the late 1980s, the deteriorating quality of international loans forced many banks to seek new remedies for the risks of international lending, especially for dealing with problem loans. This problem came to widespread public attention in 1982, when Brazil and Mexico declared a moratorium on repayments of loans extended by foreign banks. However, international loan problems were evident to bankers much earlier than this, especially when most loan principal repayments from Mexico and a few other Latin American countries were suspended in the early 1980s.

During the 1990s other crises occurred, first in Latin America when the Mexican peso declined sharply in 1994 and 1995, setting in motion severe economic shock waves that spread out from Mexico to affect other Latin American nations as well until recovery set in during 1996 and 1997. Then in 1997 and 1998 an Asian economic and financial crisis unfolded in several prominent Asian nations, including Indonesia, the Philippines, Thailand, Korea, Hong Kong, and Japan. Asian currency prices fell sharply against the U.S. dollar and banks failed or struggled under the burden of heavy loan losses linked to declining business profits and sales and falling real estate and stock prices. The International Monetary Fund (IMF) and leading industrial countries in the West rushed to help with international loans, but also urged many of the troubled countries and banking systems to set in motion or accelerate economic reforms. Asian bankers were urged to more carefully assess the true economic potential of their borrowing customers rather than simply making loans based upon historic relationships or political pressure. Governments were urged to move more rapidly toward privatization of their economic systems and to rely more heavily in their policies and decision-making upon the signals sent by international markets rather than dictatorial government rules and to stop subsidizing inefficient firms and industries.

One popular solution to international debt problems faced recently by several nations, particularly among such leading U.S. banks as Citicorp, Chase Manhattan, and Security Pacific (later merged with BankAmerica), has been the development of **debt-for-equity swaps.** Under these debt-for-stock arrangements, international banks have received an equity interest (common or preferred stock) in some foreign projects in lieu of customers paying back their loans. Debt-for-equity swaps have been used in Argentina, Chile, Mexico, the Philippines, and Venezuela, among other nations. However, these exchanges have raised a number of serious bank management issues. First, debt-for-stock swaps are often tightly regulated by bank supervisory authorities. For example, U.S. banks can only be passive equity investors and must hold less than 20 percent of the equity issued by a nonfinancial firm, which means that most U.S. banks essentially are limited to buying controlling shares of only financial-service firms abroad. Another problem is the danger of a borrowing nation reneging on the debt-equity swap if the lending institution appears to be entangling itself in the country's internal affairs in order to protect its interests. Fearing this development, some nations have forbidden equity investments in key industries. For example, Brazil has restricted foreign investment in its data processing industry.

Troubled international loans may also be *restructured* so that a new loan agreement is put together to replace the old loan agreement. The new loan usually assesses the borrower a lower interest rate and grants a longer maturity until final payment in return for a restructuring fee paid to the lender. The net cost (or *concessionality*) of such a loan to the lender is usually measured by the difference in present value of the original loan versus the (usually lower) present value of the newly restructured loan. Alternatively, a troubled loan can be sold in the secondary market for international loans which has grown up since the early 1980s, and is centered around commercial banks and security dealers in New York and London. Many banks have found buyers for discounted international loans among large corporations, other banks, and wealthy investors seeking speculative investments with prospectively high returns. Selling international loans removes these credits from the balance sheet, provides funding for new assets, and may raise the value of the selling bank's stock.[3]

Still another method used by international banks to deal with troubled international credits is to write off all or a portion of a foreign loan, recognizing that loan as a

---

[3]See Chapter 9 for a full discussion of the potential benefits and costs of loan sales off bank balance sheets.

probable loss. The result is a credit against taxes that, in effect, shares the loan loss between the bank's shareholders and the government. Another alternative, used recently in attempts to deal with troubled loans from Brazil and Mexico, is for banks to accept *exit bonds* in lieu of loan repayments. These debt securities are typically valued below the loans they replace and usually require lower or longer-term debt-service payments. Exit bonds may be backed by government securities or other acceptable collateral. For example, in January 1990, the U.S. Treasury Department announced plans to sell zero-coupon U.S. government bonds to Mexico at prices below their market value in order to support a refinancing agreement worked out between Mexico and leading international banks. These bonds, issued as part of the so-called Brady Plan, could be used by Mexico to pay off exit bonds issued to banks lending to that nation. Other nations, including Argentina, Brazil, and the Philippines, converted some of their loans into Brady bonds bearing longer maturities and lower interest rates than the original bank loans. These swaps of Brady bonds for loans were frequently supported by the central bank of the country where the borrower resides, providing a high-quality loan guarantee. Recently, the credit ratings of several nations using the Brady Plan have so improved that these countries are reaching the international capital markets and borrowing on their own without the need of Brady Plan support.

Finally, an even older "solution" to international bank debt problems is the *buy-back agreement,* in which indebted governments or private firms agree to repurchase their own debt, though at a deeply discounted price. Recent examples of debt buy-backs have come from Chile and Bolivia. The result is a tax loss for the bank based on the difference between the troubled loan's original value and its buy-back cash price. These agreements are viewed as a last-ditch alternative for countries or firms that have virtually no hope of repaying their debt.

In most cases, a *combination* of remedies for troubled international loans has been used, including restructuring of delinquent loans and rescheduling their interest and principal payments, supplemental support by the International Monetary Fund (IMF), stimulation of exports, and reduction of imports by indebted nations in an effort to buy time so these countries can move toward debt retirement and a stronger domestic economy. Unfortunately, only limited progress has been made to date in resolving these debt problems, much of it by banks forgiving or discounting a substantial portion of their troubled debt. So serious did this problem become in the late 1980s and 1990s that the World Bank announced plans to create a Multilateral Investment Guarantee Agency to insure foreign investments in developing countries.

There is little argument today with the proposition that banks engaged in international lending need to develop improved methods for analyzing the quality and soundness of international loans before they are made and better methods for monitoring international borrower performance after the loans are granted. Several risk evaluation systems are in use today.

For example, the *checklist approach* lists economic and political factors believed to be significantly correlated with loan risk—such as military or civil conflicts, balance-of-payments deficits, and rising unemployment. Comparative weights may be applied to each factor on the list, or all may be equally considered in the international loan evaluation process. The weights may take the form of statistical or mathematical probabilities, leading to the calculation of an index value for default risk. Changes in the index value then become part of an early warning loan evaluation system. The listed items may be supplemented by field reports from bank personnel with firsthand knowledge of the debtor country.

An alternative approach, which uses expert opinion in making a determination, is the *Delphi method.* Business analysts, economists, and experts in international law are assembled, and their separate, independently derived risk evaluations of a country are compiled and shared with each member of the expert panel. Panel members are then given an opportunity to revise their earlier assessments of a country's risk exposure. The final report is prepared as a consensus view of the amount of an individual country's risk exposure.

One serious problem with both of these approaches is timeliness. Significant changes in default-risk exposure may occur well before any of the calculated indices or group opinion surveys pick it up. More recently, advanced statistical methods (including discriminant analysis) have been applied to country risk problems (as noted by Melvin and Schlagenhauf [2]). Linear modeling techniques have been constructed that attempt to classify international loans into those that will be successfully repaid versus those that will require debt rescheduling or will be defaulted outright based upon key preselected predictor variables.

Among the most popular predictor variables to measure the risk exposure of loans to a particular country include growth of the domestic money supply (an indicator of possible future inflation and currency devaluations), the ratio of real investment to gross national or gross domestic product (which measures a nation's future ability to be productive), the ratio of interest and debt amortization payments to total exports (which compares required debt payments to the principal source for generating foreign exchange reserves to repay debt—a nation's exports), and the ratio of total imports to a nation's foreign exchange reserves (which measures a country's spending abroad relative to the availability of foreign exchange reserves to pay for that spending). However, controversy has continued to swirl around the usefulness of these advanced statistical models due to delays in the reporting of key data, the importance of hard-to-capture random events (such as labor strikes or political revolutions), and instability over time in the relative importance of the different predictor variables used in country-risk models.

Recently published country-risk indicators have become popular aids for bank loan officers trying to evaluate an international loan. One such widely used indicator is the *Euromoney Index,* published by *Euromoney* magazine. *Euromoney's* country risk index is based upon a variety of economic and political variables, including access to bank and open-market financing sources, credit ratings, and the international borrower's default history. Another popular indicator of country risk today is the *Institutional Investor Index* (III), published twice a year by *Institutional Investor* magazine. The III is derived from a survey of loan officers who work for multinational banks and submit their rankings of each nation as to its probability of default.

Credit-quality indicators like those supplied by *Euromoney* and *Institutional Investor* are often supplemented by market price information arising from sales of international loans. The prices of debt (loans or bonds) issued by various countries and

Bankers' Insights and Issues

Opportunities and Risks for Bankers Entering Mexico in the Wake of the NAFTA Agreement

Before the North American Free Trade Agreement (NAFTA) was finally ratified by all three member nations—Canada, Mexico, and the United States—in 1993 many bankers from Canada, the United States, and other nations were very hesitant to conduct a significant volume of business inside Mexico. For one thing, federal and state laws there prohibited most full-service banking offices operated by foreign banks with the exception of those foreign banking firms (like Citicorp) who had entered Mexico before these restrictions were passed into law. Foreign-owned banks and other international investors also faced severe currency (FOREX) risk due to the recent volatility of the Mexican peso, the risk of adverse political developments (such as the Chiapas rebellion), and cultural barriers for bankers not well informed about Mexico's history, language, and customs.

The implementation of NAFTA has helped with some of the above barriers to expansion into Mexico, but not all. Recent modifications in NAFTA have permitted foreign investors to own up to 30 percent of a Mexican bank and an even larger percentage, particularly if a Mexican bank is in danger of failing, with government approval. The Mexican government has also gradually increased the percentage of total capital foreign investors as a whole can commit to the Mexican banking system—up to as much as 15 percent by the year 2001. U.S. and other foreign banks were also granted the possibility of setting up separately capitalized banking subsidiaries inside Mexico to offer full-service banking, but as of yet cannot establish full-service branch offices of the bank back home.

Despite the high capital requirements and the risks, many foreign banks have recently entered Mexico or submitted applications to the Mexican government for future entry. Among the most prominent of recent entrants are large U.S. and Spanish money-

traded in New York and London's secondary market for international debt provide a daily barometer of how the market as a whole views the risk exposure from each borrowing country. Major international dealers, such as Salomon Brothers, provide the latest price quotes on those foreign loans currently available for sale.

Adjusting to New Market Opportunities Created by Deregulation and New International Agreements

International financial markets are passing through dramatic change as deregulation in one nation after another and international treaties open up new financial-service opportunities. In the United States 49 of the 50 states passed legislation permitting interstate banking in the 1980s and 1990s. Then the federal government moved in 1994 to allow nationwide acquisitions of American banks by holding companies as well as opening up the opportunity for interstate branch banking. These same interstate privileges were extended to foreign banks, making the United States a more attractive market for expanding center banks, which have entered either by merger and acquisition or by setting up *de novo* subsidiaries. The inefficiencies in the current Mexican banking system and the generally older technology still employed by many Mexican banks appear to offer strong business opportunities for well-capitalized and technologically advanced foreign banking organizations.

Unfortunately a number of problems remain as potential traps for unwary foreign bankers. One of the most significant centers upon the risks of lending to businesses and consumers in Mexico for those foreign bankers not familiar with Mexico's legal and judicial system. Mexico's commercial code differs substantially from business laws in the United States and Canada, for example. Inside Mexico bankers attempting to enforce the terms of a loan agreement against a borrower who refuses or is unable to pay may run into several difficulties, including long court delays and low standing in the courts relative to other claimants against the borrower's assets.

For example, Mexican law generally grants higher priority to holders of claims against real property and to the claims of laborers and lower priority to the claims of lending institutions against such typical borrower's assets as inventory, accounts receivable, and other movable types of property. Moreover, court decisions may be so long delayed that the assets lenders seek to recover may have already lost much of their value. Foreign bankers have learned how to deal with some of these problems by using such devices as asking borrowers to pledge dollar-denominated assets behind their loans or to prove they have access to U.S.-dollar income sources in order to service loans that are going to be used inside Mexico. Foreign bankers may also ask well-capitalized Mexican banks to provide standby credit guarantees of loans granted to Mexican businesses or consumers or find other banks to participate in peso-related loans in an effort to share the risks involved.

international banks, as well as for international security dealers, insurance companies, and other global financial-service providers.

Opportunities Created by NAFTA.   In November 1993 the United States government gave final approval to the North American Free Trade Agreement (NAFTA), setting in motion a gradual opening up of Mexico's financial system to outside entry by banks and other financial-service firms from Canada and the United States. The Mexican banking market has become particularly attractive for outside entry as the year 2000 approaches because Mexico's banks and nonbank service firms have not moved aggressively to serve such important customer groups as small businesses and households, in part because they are still recovering from the stultifying effects of government ownership, which began in 1982 and lasted for more than a decade. The government's earlier seizure of the banking system seriously retarded the modernization of Mexico's banks. However, NAFTA permits only *gradual* entry through separately capitalized subsidiaries into Mexico by banks and nonbank financial-service companies, carrying over into the 21st century in an

Bankers' Insights and Issues

The Emerging European Monetary Union and Its Implications for Bankers

The coming together and ultimate political and economic consolidation of Europe has been a lengthy historical drama following centuries of war and political and economic turmoil. Finally, in 1951 Belgium, France, Germany, Italy, Luxembourg, and the Netherlands established the first major cooperative economic framework when the European Coal and Steel Community was created, followed by the Treaty of Rome in 1957, forming the EEC—European Economic Community, which by 1968 had eliminated virtually all tariff barriers among these six nations of western Europe. In 1973 the United Kingdom, Ireland, and Denmark were added to the EEC, followed by Greece in 1981, Spain and Portugal in 1986, and Austria, Sweden, and Finland in 1985. By 1987 EEC countries were ready to approve the Single European Act to promote better political and economic coordination of their policies.

Then, the Maastricht Treaty on European Union was adopted after considerable debate and swirling controversy in 1992. Among the most controversial of its provisions was a call for the creation of a single European currency (the Euro), for a common central bank (the ECB), and for the integration of foreign policies, judicial and legal systems, and domestic affairs. Ultimately, Maastricht set in motion the rules for each nation to become a member state of the European Community (EC), provided it could jump over the tough hurdles Maastricht laid down. Among its most stringent requirements were the following:

1. Moderate and sustainable government budget deficits and a cap on the overall size of the public debt of each member state.
2. Relatively stable exchange rates between European and other currencies.
3. Relatively low rates of inflation (general price stability).
4. Relatively low long-term market interest rates.

Unfortunately, many of these hurdles to EC membership are not well defined and it is not clear how strictly these requirements will be enforced, keeping some nations out while allowing others to enter at an early phase of the community-formation process. (Initially 11 of 15 potential member states are expected to convert to a common currency.) It seems almost certain at this point that the creation of the EC with a common money and financial system will be a fairly drawn-out and difficult process before *all* potential member states are allowed to come aboard. Indeed, even now talks have begun to bring a few former East bloc countries eventually into the EC.

By the opening of the 21st century the new European Monetary Union is supposed to be: (*a*) operating under fixed currency exchange rates; (*b*) subject to the money and credit management policies of a common European Central Bank (ECB); (*c*) exchanging Europe's 17 billion paper notes and nearly 80 billion coins spread across several different national currencies for a common European monetary unit (the Euro) as the new legal tender for buying goods and services anywhere in the EC, resulting in the reduction of foreign exchange risk and lower transactions costs (with savings of about $300 million a year) for those individuals and institutions trading in Europe and using the new common currency unit. Hopefully at least, the result will be a more efficient allocation of capital in a highly competitive European marketplace. Overall, a united Europe would become the globe's second-largest unified financial system after the United States and would have a larger population than the U.S. (about 300 million compared to about 270 million) and a larger share of global trade. Moreover, competition is increasing in Europe; inflation and unemployment are falling as economic conditions on the continent appear to be strengthening.

The planned new European Central Bank will be designed to promote stable prices and low inflation, but won't be able to control directly member governments' spending habits or their capacity to borrow money. Moreover, no one knows yet how stable or volatile a currency the new Euro is likely to be because the economic and political policies of individual European nations will no longer simply impact the value of their currencies alone. Rather, each member nation will have some impact on the Euro's market value in world currency markets.

The potential benefits for European banks and for banks from other corners of the globe that choose to serve European markets are many. With one common currency the risk of currency price fluctuations should be both lower and less complicated to deal with. Moreover, contracts and financial statements should all eventually be converted to the same monetary unit, promoting standardization of accounting practices and making it easier for bank loan officers to evaluate and monitor the financial performance of their borrowing customers. Bankers should find it easier to geographically diversify their loan portfolios and sources of funding and reach out to a broader and deeper marketplace for financial services, rivaling the United States in size and customer diversity. More capital may flow into Europe from other parts of the globe in search of what appear now to be greater marketing opportunities, boosting the level of economic activity.

Bank customers, however, should also find it easier to compare the prices of financial services from financial institution to institution, increasing competition among financial-service providers. Inefficient financial-service companies may be driven out of business or forced into mergers with stronger competitors. Indeed, this process of European financial consolidation has been well under way since the mid-1980s, with many hundreds of mergers occurring among banks, insurance companies, and securities firms. These organizations are trying to gain greater size and greater expertise in order to counter an expected increase in tough international competition, not only with financial-service firms from neighboring European nations but from American and Asian financial-service providers as well. In fact, entrepreneurs from all over the globe may see renewed economic promise in a consolidating European economic and financial system, resulting in a shift of economic and political leadership with European nations coming to play a larger role in world affairs.

attempt to protect domestic financial-service providers from being overwhelmed by heavyweight Canadian, U.S., European, and Asian financial companies before the Mexican firms are strong enough to fight their own battles. Meanwhile, NAFTA may be on the verge of expanding to include Chile and other member nations, granting still more marketing opportunities for leading international banks.

Opportunities in the EC and in Eastern Europe.   An even larger and more challenging expansion opportunity lies in the continuing integration of the European Community (EC) and the opening up of Eastern Europe and the nations from the former Soviet Union to privatization of property, new businesses, and free markets. Trade barriers are due to be eliminated among the member nations of the EC as the 20th century ends and the new century unfolds, under the leadership of a unified European central bank and a common monetary unit (provided all the economic, fiscal, and trade problems Europe still faces can be resolved). When combined with now independent eastern Europe the combined eastern and western European regions boast a population that is significantly larger than the United States.

There is still great uncertainty, however, concerning what trade barriers the EC group itself may impose upon outside entrants. The European Community is likely to permit full-scale outside penetration of its trade area only to those nations that fully open their own borders to European firms. U.S. and Japanese companies, in particular, are vying for footholds in this expanded free-trade zone, but both face real challenges due to Europe's greater diversity in cultures across the continent and its unique attitude toward foreign firms. For example, marketing success across the European continent as a whole appears to demand a significant local presence throughout Europe. Merely setting up an exporting firm without building a local network of distributors carries little chance of long-term success, particularly in wresting market share from resident competitors and from U.S. firms that have had a significant presence there for many years.

The Need for Careful Planning.   These international marketing challenges will demand careful planning, particularly the formulation of global long-range investment strategies. These plans must take into account subtle differences in language, customs, and legal systems. Above all else, there must be *organizational flexibility* that permits rapid response to new opportunities as new local markets open up and early recognition of developing problems when existing markets deteriorate or new regulatory barriers appear.

Concept Checks

23–10.   This chapter focuses on three major problem areas that international banks must deal with in the future. What are these three areas?

23–11.   What different approaches to country risk evaluation have been developed by international banks in recent years?

Summary

International banking techniques have been practiced for centuries in the Middle East and western Europe. In this century, both U.S. and Japanese banks have come to play dominant roles in international markets, particularly for large corporate and economic development loans. Despite its venerable age, international banking has recently passed through some of the most tumultuous events in its long history. Economic and political problems have buffeted the global system as world oil prices and inflation soared and then oil and other commodity prices plummeted, bringing many less-developed nations to the brink of bankruptcy. Slower growth at home and in world trade as well as problems with loans to less-developed countries have plagued U.S. banks, which began to scale back their international operations. Meanwhile, Japanese banks catapulted into global banking leadership, due in part to the long-term rise in the value of the yen in international currency markets, a stronger Japanese economy, and innovative Japanese management techniques. More recently, the Japanese banking system has experienced the stresses of a fluctuating economy as a deep economic recession has dampened demand for loans and deregulation has created greater international competition.

As in the past, organizational forms used by international banks have continued to evolve in response to changing market conditions and improvements in transportation and communications techniques. Traditional organizational forms include representative offices, agencies, branches, affiliated companies, and subsidiaries. More recently, as the risks of international banking operations have increased, joint ventures and other interlocking relationships between banks themselves and between banks and other financial-service companies have grown in importance.

International banking services today cover a wide range of customer financial needs, such as supplying foreign currencies, hedging to deal with fluctuating currency prices and interest rates, loans and credit guarantees for trade and capital expansion, cash management services, and export marketing support. One of the most dynamic banking service areas is assistance with foreign mergers and acquisitions and with exploiting opportunities to enter new markets and develop new products more akin to foreign customer needs. There has been a trend toward deregulation of financial services in the United States, Canada, Japan, Great Britain, Australia, and many other nations as well, stimulating the growth of competition in global financial markets.

Unfortunately, the confluence of added competition and the severe economic and trading problems of some less-developed nations has resulted in new types of international banking regulations, especially cooperative regulation of banking capital and the maintenance of reserves against troubled international loans. Continuing problems with troubled foreign loans will require international banks in the future to pay much more attention to maintaining acceptable levels of long-term capital in order to promote greater public confidence in the international banking system. Global-oriented banks will also need to develop new ways to lure back some of their largest borrowing customers, who have increasingly learned how to bypass their banks and raise funds directly from the international capital markets or with the help of nonbank service providers led by security dealers, insurance companies, and other leading financial firms.

An added challenge is the opening of major new market areas to bankers. The most prominent are the European Community (EC), Asia (particularly Japan, Taiwan, Singapore, Hong Kong, China, and South Korea), and North and South America (especially Canada, Mexico, and the United States as a result of passage in 1993 of the North American Free Trade Agreement, or NAFTA). These developing markets will demand new services and a greater understanding of foreign cultures. All of this must be accomplished within the constraints of preserving public confidence and winning the approval of an increasingly integrated international regulatory community. Truly, international banking faces one of the most challenging eras in its long history.

Key Terms in This Chapter

Representative office
Agency office
Branch office
Subsidiary
Joint venture
Edge Acts
International banking facility (IBF)
Shell branches
Export Trading Company Act
Export trading companies
International Banking Act
Foreign Bank Supervision Enhancement Act
International Lending and Supervision Act

Basle Agreement
FOREX
Forward contracts
Currency futures contract
Currency option
Currency swaps
Note issuance facility (NIF)
Eurocommercial paper (ECP)
American depository receipt (ADR)
Eurobond market
Interest rate swaps
Debt-for-equity swaps

Problems and Projects

1. Pacific Trading Company purchased Canadian dollars yesterday in anticipation of a purchase of electric equipment through a Canadian supply house. However, Pacific was contacted this morning by a Japanese trading company that says equipment closer to its specifications is available in 48 hours from an electronics manufacturer in Osaka. A phone call to Pacific's bank this morning indicated that another of the bank's customers, a furniture importer located in San Francisco, purchased a comparable amount of yen in order to pay for an incoming shipment from Tokyo, only to discover that the shipment will be delayed until next week. Meanwhile, the furniture company must pay off an inventory loan tomorrow that it received 30 days ago from Toronto-Dominion Bank.

    Which of the instruments described in this chapter would be most helpful to these two companies? Construct a diagram that illustrates the transaction you, as a banker, would recommend to these two firms to help solve their current problem.

2. Nelson Sporting Goods has ordered a shipment of soccer equipment from a manufacturer and

    distributor in Munich. Payment for the shipment (which is valued at $3.5 million U.S.) must be made in deutsche marks that have changed in value in the last 30 days from 1.9268DM/$ to 1.9502DM/$. If this trend is expected to continue, would you as Nelson's banker recommend that this customer use a currency futures hedge? Why or why not?

    Alternative scenario:

    Suppose the deutsche mark changed within the last week from 1.7981DM/$ to 1.7870 DM/$ and a similar change is expected during the time Nelson must pay for the shipment of soccer equipment. What would you recommend for Nelson? What kind of currency futures contract might be advisable and why?

3. U.S. Signal Q Corporation will import new wooden toys from a French manufacturer this week at a price of 200 francs per item for eventual distribution to retail stores. The current franc-dollar exchange rate is 5.92 francs per U.S. dollar. Payment for the shipment will be made by Signal Q next month, but French francs are expected to appreciate significantly against the dollar. Signal Q asks its bank, Southern

Merchants Bank, N.A., for advice on what to do. What kind of futures transaction could be used to deal with this problem faced by Signal Q Corporation? Futures contracts calling for delivery of francs next month are priced currently at 5.95 francs per dollar (or 16.81 U.S. cents per franc) and are expected to be priced next month at 5.90 francs per dollar (or 16.95 U.S. cents per franc).

4. Maesen Hardware Manufacturing Corporation regularly ships tools to the United States to retail hardware outlets from its shipping warehouse in Stuttgart, Germany. Its normal credit terms call for full payment in U.S. dollars for the hardware it ships within 90 days of the shipment date. However, Maesen must convert all U.S. dollars received from its customers into marks in order to compensate its local workers and suppliers. Maesen has just made a large shipment to retail dealers in the United States and is concerned about a forecast just received from its local bank that the U.S. dollar–German mark exchange rate will fall sharply over the next month. The current mark–U.S. dollar exchange rate is 1.75 marks per dollar (or 57.14 U.S. cents per mark). However, the local bank's current forecast calls for the exchange rate to climb to 60.20 U.S. cents per mark (or 1.66 marks per dollar), so that Maesen will receive substantially less in marks for each U.S. dollar it receives in payment for its tools. Please explain how Maesen Corporation with the aid of its bank could use currency futures to offset at least a portion of its projected loss due to the expected change in the mark-dollar exchange rate.

5. Hilgarde International Mercantile Guaranty Corporation has made a $15 million investment in a stamping mill located in northern Germany and fears a substantial decline in the mark's current spot price from $0.58 to $0.50, lowering the value of the firm's capital investment. Hilgarde's principal U.S. bank advises the firm to use an appropriate option contract to help reduce Hilgarde's risk of loss due to currency risk.

What currency option contract would you recommend to deal with this situation? Explain why the option contract you have selected would help to reduce the firm's currency risk exposure.

6. Sogo International Bank of Japan holds U.S.-dollar denominated assets of $394 million and dollar-denominated liabilities of $587 million, has purchased U.S. dollars in the currency markets amounting to $66 million, and sold U.S. dollars totaling $24 million. What is Sogo's *net* exposure to risk from fluctuations in U.S. dollar prices relative to the bank's domestic currency? Under what circumstances could Sogo lose if dollar prices change relative to the yen?

7. Suppose that Westminster Bank has a net long position in U.S. dollars of $8 million, dollar-denominated liabilities of $115 million, U.S. dollar purchases of $268 million, and dollar sales of $173 million. What is the current value of the bank's dollar-denominated assets? Suppose the U.S. dollar's exchange value rises against the pound. Is Westminster likely to gain or lose? Why?

Selected References

For excellent discussions of assessing risk in international lending, see the following:

1. Denison, Daniel R. "A Pragmatic Model for Country Risk Analysis." *Journal of Commercial Bank Lending,* March 1984, pp. 29–37.
2. Melvin, Michael, and Don Schlagenhauf. "A Country Risk Index: Econometric Formulation and an Application to Mexico." *Economic Inquiry,* 1984, pp. 601–19.

For an analysis of the recent activities of U.S. banks in international markets, see these studies:

3. Corrigan, E. Gerald. "Coping with Globally Integrated Financial Markets." *Quarterly Review,* Federal Reserve Bank of New York, Winter 1987, pp. 1–5.
4. Houpt, James V. *International Trends for U.S. Banks and Banking Markets.* Staff Study no. 156, Board of Governors of the Federal Reserve System, May 1988.
5. Pardee, Scott E. "Internationalization of Financial Markets." *Economic Review,* Federal Reserve Bank of Kansas City, February 1987, pp. 3–7.
6. Rose, Peter S. "The Quest for Funds: New Directions in a New Market." *The Canadian Banker* 94, no. 5 (September/October 1987), pp. 46–55.

For an analysis of the rapid expansion of Japanese banking abroad, see:

7. Frankel, Allen B., and Paul B. Morgan, "Deregulation and Competition in Japanese Banking." *Federal Reserve Bulletin,* August 1992, pp. 579–93.
8. Rose, Peter S. *Japanese Banking and Investment in the United States: An Assessment of Their Impact upon U.S. Markets and Institutions.* New York: Quorum Books, 1991.
9. Zimmer, Steven A., and Robert N. McCauley. "Bank Cost of Capital and International Competition." *Quarterly Review,* Federal Reserve Bank of New York, Winter 1991, pp. 33–59.

These studies discuss the international debt crisis and currency hedging tools:

10. Truman, Edwin M. "U.S. Policy on the Problems of International Debt." *Federal Reserve Bulletin,* November 1989, pp. 727–35.
11. Kawaller, Ira G. "Options on Currency Futures." *The Bankers Magazine,* January/February 1987, pp. 20–22.

For an explanation of U.S. regulations on foreign banks see:

12. Misback, Anan E. "The Foreign Bank Supervision Enhancement Act of 1991." *Federal Reserve Bulletin,* January 1993, pp. 1–10.

For an analysis of banking and financial problems in Europe and Asia, see:

13. Hopper, Gregory P. "What Determines the Exchange Rate: Economic Factors or Market Sentiment?" *Business Review,* Federal Reserve Bank of Philadelphia, September/October 1997, pp. 17–29.
14. Huh, Chan. "Banking System Developments in the Four Asian Tigers." *Economic Letter,* Federal Reserve Bank of San Francisco, No. 97-22 (August 8, 1997), pp. 1–3.
15. Kashyap, Anil K., and Jeremy C. Stein. "The Role of Banks in Monetary Policy: A Survey with Implications for the European Monetary Union." *Economic Perspectives* 21, no. 5 (September/October 1997), pp. 2–17.
16. Spiegel, Mark M. "Fiscal Constraints in the EMU." *Economic Letter,* Federal Reserve Bank of San Francisco, No. 97-23 (August 15, 1997), pp. 1–3.

account party   The customer who requests a standby letter of credit from a bank or other lender of funds.

add-on method   A procedure for calculating a consumer's loan rate in which interest is assigned on the full principal of an installment loan.

adjustable-rate mortgages (ARMs)   Loans against real property whose interest rate periodically adjusts to changes in market interest rates.

affiliated banks   Banks whose stock has been acquired by a bank holding company.

agency offices   International banking offices that provide credit and other nondeposit services.

agricultural loans   Credit extended to farm and ranch operations to assist in planting and harvesting crops and to care for and market livestock.

ALMs   Automated loan machines that allow a customer to enter selected bits of information and receive a loan of cash if the machines' programmed credit standards are met.

American depository receipt (ADR)   A receipt issued by a U.S. bank that makes it easier for a foreign business borrower to sell its securities in the United States.

annual percentage rate (APR)   Interest rate on a loan required to be quoted to a consumer seeking a loan in the United States.

annuities   An investment product sold by many banks today in which the customer invests his or her savings under the terms of a contract that promises a stream of income in the future (either fixed or variable in amount).

antidiscrimination laws   Legislation that prevents the grouping of loan customers into categories according to their age, sex, race, national origin, location of residence, religious affiliation, or receipt of public assistance and that prohibits the denial of a loan to anyone solely because of membership in one or more of these groups.

asset-based loans   Loans secured by a business firm's assets, particularly accounts receivable and inventory.

asset-liability management   The process of decision making in order to control a bank's exposure to interest rate risk.

asset liquidity management   A strategy for meeting liquidity needs, used mainly by smaller banks, in which liquid funds are stored in readily marketable assets that can be quickly converted into cash as needed.

asset management   A bank management strategy that regards the volume and mix of a bank's sources of funds as determined largely by the wishes of its customers and calls for management to concentrate on controlling assets, rather than on managing liabilities, in order to meet a bank's liquidity needs and other goals.

asset utilization   The ratio of a bank's total operating revenues to its total assets, measuring the bank's average yield on all of its assets.

assignments   A form of loan sale in which ownership of a loan is transferred to the loan buyer who then has a direct claim against the borrower.

ATM   Automated teller machine through which a bank customer can access his or her deposit account, make loan payments, or obtain information and other services.

balanced liquidity management The combined use of both asset management and liability management to cover a bank's liquidity needs.

bank The financial intermediary that offers the widest range of financial services—especially credit, savings, and payment services—and performs the widest range of financial functions of any business firm in the economy.

bank discount rate The method by which yields on Treasury bills and other money market securities are calculated which uses par value and a 360-day year to determine the appropriate discount rate or yield.

bank holding company A corporation chartered for the purpose of holding the stock (equity shares) of one or more banks.

Bank Holding Company Act Legislation in the United States that brought bank holding company organizations under comprehensive federal regulation.

Bank Merger Act of 1960 A law passed by the U.S. Congress that requires each merging bank to notify its principal federal regulatory agency of a pending merger and requests federal approval before the merger can be completed.

bank profitability An important indicator of bank performance, it indicates the rate of return a bank has been able to generate from using the resources at its command in order to produce and sell services.

bankers' acceptance A bank's written promise to pay the holder of the acceptance a designated amount of money on a specific future date.

bankers' banks Regional service firms, often created as joint ventures by groups of banks, in order to facilitate the delivery of certain customer services, such as the rapid transfer and investment of customer funds and the execution of orders to buy or sell securities.

basic (lifeline) banking Low-cost deposits and other services that are designed to meet the banking needs of customers of limited means.

Basle Agreement A negotiated agreement between bank regulatory authorities in the United States, Canada, Great Britain, Japan, and eight other nations in western Europe to set common capital requirements for all banks under their jurisdiction.

below-prime pricing Interest rates on loans are set below the prevailing bank prime rate, usually based on the level of key money market interest rates (such as the current market rate on Federal funds or commercial paper).

beneficiary The party who will receive payment under a financial guarantee if certain events occur, such as default on a loan.

board of directors The committee elected by the stockholders (owners of the bank) to set policy and oversee the bank's performance.

Board of Governors The center of authority and decision making within the Federal Reserve System; the board must contain no more than seven persons, each selected by the president of the United States and confirmed by the U.S. Senate for a term not exceeding 14 years.

branch banking An arrangement in which a bank offers a full range of services from multiple locations, including a head office and one or more branch offices.

branch offices Full-service units operated by a bank that is headquartered in another location.

business risk The probability that the economy in a bank's market area will turn down into a recession, with reduced demand for loans, deposits, and other bank services.

call risk The danger that an investor in loans or securities will experience a lower-than-expected rate of return due to the issuer of the loans or securities calling in these instruments and retiring them early before they reach maturity.

CAMELS rating A system that assigns a numerical rating to a bank based on examiner judgment regarding the bank's capital adequacy, asset condition, management quality, earnings record, liquidity position, and sensitivity to market risk.

cap rate An upper limit on a loan's contract interest rate so that a customer's loan rate can rise no higher than the cap, regardless of the future course of market interest rates.

capital Long-term funds contributed to a bank primarily by its owners, consisting mainly of stock, reserves, and retained earnings.

capital market instruments Investment securities that reach maturity over periods longer than one year.

cash This term is one of the six Cs of credit which loan officers should review in any loan application, referring to the generation of income or cash flow by a borrowing customer.

cash flow Usually measured by the net income plus noncash expenses (such as depreciation) of a business loan customer.

cash flow risk The danger that cash flows from a banking organization may fluctuate widely due to economic conditions, service mix, and other factors; a merger may help to reduce this risk by combining banking organizations and service packages that have different cash flow patterns over time.

cash management services A service in which a bank agrees to handle cash collections and cash disbursements for a business firm and to invest any temporary cash surpluses in interest-bearing securities until those funds are needed.

certificate of deposit (CD) An interest-bearing receipt for the deposit of funds in a bank or nonbank thrift institution for a specified period of time.

charter of incorporation A license to open and operate a commercial bank, issued by either the banking commission of the state where the bank is to be located or the Comptroller of the Currency (for federally chartered banks) inside the United States.

clearing balances Deposits held with the Federal Reserve banks by depository institutions to help clear checks for payment and collection and that allow the banks using Federal Reserve services to earn interest credits on these balances in order to help offset the cost of Fed services.

collateral A borrower's possession of adequate net worth, quality assets, or other items of value that give added support to his or her ability to repay a loan.

commercial and industrial loans Credit granted to businesses to help cover purchases of inventory, plant, and equipment and to meet other operating expenses.

commercial paper Short-term, unsecured IOUs offered to investors in the money market by major corporations with the strongest credit ratings.

commercial paper market Market where short-term notes with maturities ranging from three or four days to nine months are traded, issued by well-known banking and nonbanking companies for the purpose of raising working capital.

common stock Type of bank capital measured by the par value of all common equity shares outstanding that pays a variable return to its owners after all expenses and other claims are met.

Community Reinvestment Act Federal law passed in 1977 requiring covered depository institutions to make "an affirmative effort" to serve all segments of their trade territory without discrimination.

compensating deposit balances Required deposits a customer must keep with a bank as a condition for getting a loan.

competitive effects The aspect of a merger or acquisition between two or more banks that will have an impact on interfirm rivalry, either reducing or increasing competition in the markets served by the firms involved; this impact of a bank merger or acquisition is, under current federal law, the most important factor federal regulatory agencies must weigh in deciding to approve or deny any proposed acquisitions or mergers.

Competitive Equality in Banking Act Legislation that authorized recapitalization of the Federal Savings and Loan Insurance Corporation to deal more effectively with failing savings and loan associations, required banks to provide more information to their customers on when credit is given for deposited funds and placed a moratorium on the creation of nonbank banks and the offering of insurance, securities, and real estate services by commercial banks operating inside the United States.

Comptroller of the Currency (or Administrator of National Banks) The federal government agency, a part of the U.S. Treasury Department, that awards charters for new national banks in the United States and also supervises and regularly examines all existing national banks.

construction loans Short-term loans designed to fund the building of new structures and then be paid off and replaced with a longer-term mortgage loan once the construction phase of the project has ended.

contingent liabilities Debt obligations that will not come due unless certain events occur (such as borrower default or the exercise of product warranties).

contingent obligation A financial instrument whose issuer pledges to pay if certain events (such as default on a loan) occur; for example, federal deposit insurance is a contingent obligation of the government, payable if a bank fails.

core capital Permanent capital of a bank, consisting mainly of common stock, surplus, retained earnings, and equity reserves.

core deposits A stable and predictable base of deposited funds (usually supplied by households and smaller businesses) that is not highly sensitive to movements in market interest rates but tends to remain loyal to the bank.

corporate bonds Debt securities issued by private corporations with original maturities longer than five years.

corporate notes Debt securities issued by private corporations with original maturities of five years or less.

correspondent banking A system of formal and informal relationships among large and small banks established to facilitate the exchange of certain services, such as the clearing of checks and the exchange of information between banks.

cosigner A person obligated to support the repayment of a loan by a borrower who either has no credit record or has such a poor track record of repaying loans that he or she cannot get a loan without the support of the cosigner.

cost-benefit loan pricing A method for pricing loans that adds all costs of making a loan and compares those costs to all expected revenues generated by a loan.

cost-plus loan pricing Figuring the rate of interest on a loan by adding together all interest and noninterest costs associated with making the loan plus margins for profit and risk.

cost-plus-profit deposit pricing Charging customers for the full cost or a significant portion of the total cost of any deposit services they use.

cost savings (efficiency) A motivation for bank mergers that rests on the possibility that by combining two or more banks together, overall operating expenses will be reduced, creating the possibility of a rise in net income for the combined (merged) institution.

credit availability risk The possibility that lenders may not have the funds to loan or be willing to accommodate every qualified borrower when credit is requested.

credit bureau A business firm that keeps data files on people who have borrowed money, indicating their previous record of loan repayments.

credit default swaps Financial agreements that permit a bank or other lender to protect itself against credit (default risk) by receiving compensation from a counterparty to help offset excessive loan losses or excessive fluctuations in loan revenue.

credit derivatives Financial contracts that are designed to protect a bank or other lending institution against loss due to defaults on its loans or security holdings.

credit enhancement A contract in which a bank or other institution promises to back up the credit of another firm.

credit life insurance An insurance policy that guarantees repayment of a loan if a borrower dies or is disabled before his or her loan is paid off.

credit option An agreement between a bank or other lending institution and an option writer that is designed to protect a lender against possible loss due to declines in the value of some of its assets or is designed to prevent a significant rise in borrowing costs should the borrower's credit rating be lowered or other events occur that result in higher fund-raising costs.

credit risk The probability that the issuer of a loan or security will fail and default on any promised payments of interest or principal or both.

credit scoring The use of a discriminant equation to classify loan applicants according to the probability of their repaying their loans, based on customer characteristics (such as their credit rating or length of employment).

credit swap A financial contract designed to reduce the risk of default on loans by having two lending institutions exchange a portion of their expected loan payments with each other.

crime risk The danger of fraud, embezzlement, robbery, or other crimes that could result in loss for a bank.

currency exchange Trading one form of currency (such as dollars) for another (such as francs or pesos) in return for a fee; one of the first services offered by banks when the banking industry began centuries ago.

currency futures contract Agreement between a buyer and a seller of foreign currencies that promises delivery of a stipulated currency at a specified price on a specific date in the future.

currency option Contract giving the option holder the right, but not the obligation, to deliver or take delivery of a specific currency at a set price on or before the contract's expiration date.

currency swaps Agreements between two or more parties who need to borrow foreign currency that help to protect them against changes in currency prices by agreeing to exchange payments denominated in different currencies.

customer profitability analysis A method for evaluating a customer's loan request that takes into account all bank revenues and expenses associated with serving that particular customer and calculates an expected net return over all costs incurred from serving the customer.

customer relationship doctrine   The bank management strategy whose first priority is making loans to all those customers who meet the bank's quality standards and from whom the bank expects to receive positive earnings.

debt-for-equity swaps   Financial device used for some troubled international loans in which lenders agree to accept shares of stock in exchange for the debt securities of borrowing countries having trouble repaying their debts.

demand deposit   Checking account services that permit depositors to write drafts in payment for goods and services which the bank involved must honor immediately upon presentation.

de novo bank   A newly chartered banking corporation.

deposit fee schedules   Establishing minimum-size account balances and charging a lower or even zero fee if the customer's deposit balance climbs *above* that required minimum but a higher fee if the average balance falls *below* the required minimum amount.

Depository Institutions Deregulation and Monetary Control Act   Legislation which legally mandated that federal interest rate ceilings on deposits sold to the public be phased out so that deposit interest rates could more closely reflect prevailing market conditions; it also authorized the offering of NOW accounts throughout the United States, which pay an explicit interest return to the customer and have third-party payment powers.

dilution of ownership   The degree to which the proportionate share of ownership held by the current owners of a banking firm is reduced when additional equity shares are issued to new stockholders or to the shareholders of a banking firm that is being acquired.

disclosure rules   Laws and regulations that mandate telling the consumer about financing costs and other essential terms of a loan or lease agreement.

discount brokerage services   A bank service to assist customers with purchases and sales of securities at relatively low brokerage fees.

discount rate method   The procedure used to assess interest on a loan in which interest is deducted up front at the beginning of the loan and the customer receives for his or her use the full principal of the loan less the interest assessed.

discount window   Department within each Federal Reserve bank that lends legal reserves to banks for short periods of time.

discounting commercial notes   The process of making loans to local merchants who use IOUs received from their customers as collateral to borrow from a bank.

dual banking system   A system of banking regulation in which both federal and state authorities have significant regulatory powers and supervisory responsibilities over the activities of commercial banks.

duration   A present-value weighted measure of the maturity of an individual security or portfolio of securities in which the timing and amount of *all* expected cash flows expected from the security or portfolio of securities is considered.

duration gap   The difference between the duration of a bank's assets and the duration of its liabilities.

earnings risk   The danger that earnings for a banking organization may fluctuate widely due to changes in economic conditions, demand for services, mix of services offered, or other factors; a merger between two or more banking organizations may dampen this form of risk by bringing together different revenue sources with different cash flow patterns over time.

Edge Acts   Subsidiary companies of a banking organization that must devote the majority of their activities to transactions involving international trade and commerce; establishment of these subsidiaries must be approved by the Federal Reserve Board.

efficiency   An indicator of how well a bank's management and staff have been able to keep the growth of its revenues and income ahead of rising operating costs.

Equal Credit Opportunity Act   Legislation passed by the U.S. Congress in 1974 that prohibits lenders from asking certain questions of a borrowing customer, such as his or her age, race, or religion, and from denying a loan based solely upon a credit applicant's age, race, religion, ethnic origins, receipt of public assistance, or similar characteristics.

equipment leasing services   The purchase of equipment on behalf of a bank customer in order to lease the equipment to that customer in return for a series of lease payments.

equity commitment notes Type of bank capital in the form of debt securities that is repayable only from the future sale of bank stock.

equity multiplier The ratio of a bank's total assets to its total equity capital.

equity reserves Type of bank capital representing funds set aside for contingencies such as losses on assets, legal action against the bank, and other extraordinary events, as well as providing a reserve for dividends expected to be paid out to stockholders but not yet declared and a sinking fund to be used to retire stock or debt capital instruments in the future.

Eurobond market An institution that brings together sellers of bonds issued outside their home country and interested buyers in one or more other nations.

Eurocommercial paper (ECP) Short-term notes issued by multinational corporations and sold to investors in one or more countries that permit these corporations to borrow funds for a few days, weeks, or months.

Eurocurrency deposit Deposits denominated in a currency different from the currency of the home country of the bank where they are created.

events of default A section contained in most loan agreements listing what actions or omissions by a borrower would represent a violation of the terms of the agreement and what action the bank is legally authorized to take in response.

exchange ratio The number of shares of stock in the acquiring firm that stockholders of the acquired firm will receive for each share they hold.

exchange risk The probability of loss to a bank because of fluctuating currency prices in international markets.

Export-Import Bank A lender of funds created by the U.S. government to aid with export-import financing and to make loans that support the development of overseas markets.

export trading companies (ETCs) Organizational devices to aid bank customers in selling their goods abroad, particularly the products of smaller businesses, by creating a subsidiary firm to help with foreign marketing and the financing of exports.

Export Trading Company Act Law passed by the U.S. Congress in 1982 that allowed U.S. banks to make direct investments in export trading companies to help their U.S. business customers sell goods and services abroad.

factoring Sale of the shorter-term assets of a business firm that are expected to roll over into cash in the near term, such as accounts receivable and inventory, in order to raise more working capital.

Fair Credit Billing Act Legislation enacted by the U.S. Congress in 1974 that permits consumers to dispute alleged billing errors committed by a merchant or credit card company and requires that consumers receive a prompt investigation of any billing disputes under penalty of forfeiture of at least a portion of the amount billed.

Fair Credit Reporting Act Legislation that authorizes U.S. consumers to review their credit records, as reflected in the files of a credit bureau, for accuracy and to demand the investigation and correction of any inaccuracies.

Fair Debt Collection Practices Act Legislation passed by the U.S. Congress limiting how far a creditor can go in pressing a loan customer to pay up.

FDIC Improvement Act A law passed by the U.S. Congress in 1991 to recapitalize the Federal Deposit Insurance Corporation and exercise closer regulation over troubled banks.

federal agency securities Marketable notes and bonds sold by agencies owned by or started by the federal government, such as the Federal National Mortgage Association (FNMA) or the farm credit agencies.

Federal Deposit Insurance Corporation (FDIC) The U.S. government agency that guarantees the repayment of the public's deposits in U.S. banks up to a maximum of $100,000 and assesses insurance premiums that must be paid by banks offering federally insured deposits.

Federal funds market A domestic source of reserves in which a bank can borrow the excess reserves held by other banks; also known as *same-day money* because these funds can be transferred instantaneously by wire from the lending institution to the borrowing institution.

Federal Open Market Committee (FOMC) Composed of the members of the Federal Reserve Board and the presidents of the Federal Reserve banks, the FOMC sets money and credit policies for the Federal Reserve System and oversees the conduct of open market operations, the Federal Reserve's chief policy tool.

Federal Reserve Bank A quasi-public institution created in 1913 by the Federal Reserve Act that provides financial services (such as check clearing) to depository institutions in the region served by each individual Federal Reserve Bank.

Federal Reserve System The federal agency that serves as a "lender of last resort" for banks in need of temporary loans and is charged by the U.S. Congress to monitor and control the growth of money and credit and stabilize credit market conditions and the economy.

fiduciary relationship An agreement between a bank and its customer in which the bank becomes responsible for managing the customer's funds or other property.

financial advisory services A range of services offered by banks that may include investment advice, the preparation of tax returns, and help with recordkeeping; business customers often receive aid in checking on the credit standing of prospective customers unknown to them and assistance in evaluating marketing opportunities abroad.

financial boutiques Banks and other financial-service companies that offer a limited set of services to selected customer groups.

financial futures Contracts calling for the delivery of specific types of securities at a set price on a specific future date.

financial guarantees Instruments used to enhance the credit standing of a borrower in order to help lower the borrower's credit costs by pledging to reimburse a lender if the borrower fails to pay.

financial institution loans Both long- and short-term credit extended to banks, insurance companies, and other financial institutions.

Financial Institutions Reform, Recovery, and Enforcement Act U.S. legislation, passed in 1989, that authorized bank holding companies to acquire healthy savings and loan associations and restructured the FDIC, dividing its insurance fund into a Bank Insurance Fund (BIF) to cover U.S. commercial bank deposits and a Savings Associations' Insurance Fund (SAIF) to insure the deposits of U.S.-based savings and loan associations.

fiscal policy Changes in government spending and taxation that are designed to contribute to the nation's economic goals.

fixed-rate mortgages (FRMs) Loans against real property whose rate of interest does not change during the life of the loan.

Foreign Bank Supervision Enhancement Act U.S. law, passed in 1991, giving the Federal Reserve Board greater regulatory powers over foreign banks operating in the United States, including the power to close a foreign bank's U.S. facilities if found to be inadequately supervised or operated in an unsafe manner.

FOREX Foreign currencies and foreign-currency–denominated deposits offered by international banks to aid their customers who trade and travel abroad.

forward contracts Agreements that can be used when a customer anticipates a future need to acquire foreign currency or expects to receive foreign currency; a bank negotiates a contract with another party on behalf of its customer, fixing the price at which currency is exchanged and specifying a date on which the currency will be delivered.

full-service branch A branch office of a bank that offers all or most of the same services that the bank's head office also offers.

full-service interstate banking The establishment of banks or bank branches across state lines by individual banking organizations that offer a complete menu of banking services.

Funds-Flow Statement A financial statement that shows where a bank's funds have come from and how they have been used over a specific time period.

funds gap The difference between current and projected credit and deposit flows that creates a need for raising additional bank reserves or for profitably investing any excess reserves that may arise.

funds management Combining asset and liability management strategies in order to achieve a bank's goals and meet its liquidity needs more effectively.

Garn–St Germain Depository Institutions Act A deregulation bill, passed in 1982, that permitted nonbank thrift institutions to become more like commercial banks in the services they could offer and allowed all federally regulated depository institutions to offer deposits competitive with money market mutual fund share accounts.

geographic diversification Spreading out a bank's credit accounts and deposits among customers located in different communities, regions, or countries in order to reduce the overall risk of loss to a bank.

Glass-Steagall Act Legislation passed by the U.S. Congress in 1933 that legally mandated the separation of commercial and investment banking, imposed interest rate ceilings on bank deposits, authorized the creation of the Federal Deposit Insurance Corporation, and granted federally chartered banks the power to branch throughout a state, provided that state grants similar powers to its own state-chartered banks.

Herfindahl-Hirschman Index   A summary measure of market concentration used by the U.S. Justice Department, in which the assets of each firm serving a given market are squared and the squared market shares of all firms are then summed to derive a single index number reflecting the degree of concentration of assets in the largest firms.

holding period yield (HPY)   A rate of discount bringing the current price of a security into line with its stream of expected cash inflows and its expected sale price at the end of the investor's holding period.

home equity loans   Credit extended to an individual or family on the basis of the spread or gap between the estimated market value of a home and the amount of mortgage loans outstanding against the property.

inflation risk   The probability that the prices of goods and services (including the interest rate on borrowed funds and the cost of personnel and other productive resources) the bank must purchase will rise or that the value of a bank's assets will be eroded due to rising prices, lowering its expected returns on invested capital.

insurance policies   Contracts that guarantee payment if the customer dies, becomes disabled, or suffers loss of property or earning power.

installment loans   Credits that are repayable in two or more consecutive payments, usually on a monthly or quarterly basis.

in-store branches   Bank branches located in a grocery store or other retail outlet.

interest rate cap   Ceiling interest rate imposed on a loan designed to protect the borrower from an unacceptable rise in the interest cost of a loan.

interest rate collar   A combination of an interest rate cap and an interest rate floor; puts brackets around the movement of a loan rate so that it cannot rise above the cap or fall below the floor.

interest rate floor   Minimum interest rate below which the interest cost of a loan normally cannot fall, thus protecting the lender from additional lost revenue if market interest rates move lower.

interest rate option   A contract that either (1) grants a holder of securities or loans the right to place (put) those instruments with another investor at a specified exercise price before the option expires or (2) allows an investor to take delivery of securities or other financial instruments (call) from another investor at a specified price on or before the option's expiration date.

interest rate risk   The probability that rising or falling interest rates will adversely affect the bank's margin of interest revenues over interest expenses or result in decreasing the value of a bank's net worth.

interest rate swaps   Agreements that enable two different borrowers of funds to aid each other by exchanging some of the most favorable features of their loans; usually the two participating institutions exchange interest rate payments in order to reduce their borrowing costs and better balance their inflows and outflows of funds.

interest sensitive   A bank asset or liability item that can be repriced as market interest rates change.

interest-sensitive gap management   Management techniques that usually require a bank to perform a computer analysis of the maturities and repricing opportunities associated with its interest-bearing assets, deposits, and money market borrowings in order to determine when and by how much it is exposed to interest rate risk.

interim construction loan   Secured short-term lending to support the construction of homes, apartments, office buildings, shopping centers, and other permanent structures.

internal capital growth rate   The rate of growth of net earnings that remain inside a bank rather than being paid out to its stockholders; this growth rate depends on a bank's return on equity and its dividend policies.

International Banking Act   Law passed by the U.S. Congress in 1978 that brought foreign banks operating in the United States under federal regulation for the first time; it required foreign banking offices taking deposits from the public to post reserve requirements and allowed them to apply for federal deposit insurance coverage.

international banking facility (IBF)   Computerized account records that are kept separate from a U.S. bank's domestic accounts and that keep track primarily of international or overseas transactions.

International Lending and Supervision Act   Legislation passed by the U.S. Congress in 1983 that requires U.S. banks to hold stipulated minimum amounts of capital and that sets standards for making and evaluating overseas loans.

Internet service sites   Computer files or pages set up on the World Wide Web by banks to advertise their services or offer selected service options to web users.

investment banking services   A bank's offer to underwrite a corporate or institutional customer's securities in order to aid that customer in raising funds.

joint venture Cooperative service production and delivery between banks or between banks and nonbank firms in order to provide a wider array of customer services at a profit.

Justice Department Merger Guidelines Standards for evaluating the impact of a proposed merger on the concentration of assets or deposits in a given market area; the Justice Department uses these standards to help it decide whether to sue to block a proposed merger that might damage competition.

lagged reserve accounting (LRA) An accounting system begun by the Federal Reserve in 1984 for calculating each bank's legal reserve requirement, in which the reserve computation and reserve maintenance periods for transaction deposits overlap but are not exactly the same.

LBOs (leveraged buyouts) Contractual agreements in which a company or small group of individual investors purchases a business or buys a portion of a business firm's assets with heavy use of debt and relatively little equity capital and relies on increased earnings after the business is taken over to retire the debt.

legal reserves Assets that by law must be held behind a bank's deposits or other designated liabilities; in the United States, these assets consist of vault cash and deposits at the Federal Reserve banks.

letter of credit A legal notice in which a bank or other institution guarantees the credit of one of its customers who is borrowing from another institution.

liability management Use of borrowed funds to meet a bank's liquidity needs, in which a bank attracts the volume of liquidity it needs by raising or lowering the rate of interest it is willing to pay on borrowed funds.

LIBOR The London Interbank Offered Rate on short-term Eurodollar deposits, which is used as a common basis for quoting loan rates to corporations and other large borrowers.

liquid asset Any asset that meets three conditions: (1) price stability, (2) ready marketability, and (3) reversibility.

liquidity Access to sufficient immediately spendable funds at reasonable cost exactly when those funds are needed.

liquidity gap The amount by which the sources and uses of liquidity for a bank do not match.

liquidity indicators Certain bellwether financial ratios (e.g., total loans outstanding divided by total assets) that are used to estimate a bank's possible liquidity needs and to monitor changes in its liquidity position.

liquidity risk The probability that a bank will be unable to raise cash precisely when cash is needed at reasonable cost and in the volume required.

loan commitment agreements Promises by a bank to provide credit to a customer in the future, provided certain conditions are met.

loan option A device to lock in the amount and cost of borrowing for a designated time period by allowing a customer to borrow at a guaranteed interest rate, regardless of any subsequent changes in market interest rates, until the option expires.

loan participation Agreement under which a bank will share a large loan with one or more other lenders in order to provide the borrower with sufficient funds and reduce risk exposure to any one lending institution.

loan review A process of periodic investigation of all outstanding loans on a bank's books to make sure each loan is paying out as planned, all necessary documentation is present, and the bank's loan officers are following the institution's loan policy.

loan sales A form of investment banking in which the banker trades on his or her superior ability to evaluate the creditworthiness of borrowers and sells some of the loans the bank has made to other investors who value the bank's expertise in assessing credit quality.

loan strip The sale of a portion of a large loan for a short period of time, usually for a period less than the loan's remaining time to maturity.

loan workouts Activity within a bank that focuses on delinquent loans and that tries to develop and implement strategies designed to recover as much of the bank's funds as possible from troubled borrowers.

loans to individuals Credit extended to households to finance the purchase of automobiles and appliances, medical and personal expenses, and other household needs.

market risk The potential for loss due to rising or falling interest rates; the danger that changing interest rates may force a bank to accept substantial losses on any assets that must be sold or acquired or on any funds that must be borrowed or repaid.

market-penetration deposit pricing   Offering high interest rates (often well above current market levels) or charging low or zero customer fees in order to bring in as many new deposit customers as possible.

market-positioning benefits   A motive for conducting a merger between two or more banking firms, in which the banks involved anticipate gaining access to important new markets not previously served or securing a stronger foothold in markets currently served.

McFadden-Pepper Act   Legislation passed by the U.S. Congress in 1927 that allows national banks to branch within the city where they are headquartered if the laws of the state involved do not forbid such branches.

member bank   A commercial bank that has joined the Federal Reserve System and is subject to its rules and regulations; includes all national banks as well as state-chartered banks that elect to join the Federal Reserve System.

merchant banks   Banks that provide not only all the consumer and commercial services a regular bank provides but also offer credit, investment, and consulting services in an attempt to satisfy all the financial-service needs of their clients; usually these banks invest a substantial share of their own equity capital in a customer's commercial project.

merger premium   A bonus offered to the shareholders of a banking firm to be acquired, consisting of an amount of cash or stock in the acquiring bank that exceeds the current market value of the acquired bank's stock.

minority interest in consolidated subsidiaries   Partial ownership interest that a bank holds in other business firms.

monetary policy   The Federal Reserve's primary job, which involves making sure that the banking and financial system functions smoothly and that the supply of money and credit from that system contributes to the nation's economic goals.

money market deposit accounts (MMDAs)   Short-maturity deposits having a term of only a few days, weeks, or months and on which the bank can pay any competitive interest rate over designated short intervals of time; these deposits may also have limited checking account powers.

money market instruments   Investment securities that reach maturity within one year and are noted for their low credit risk and ready marketability.

money position manager   Managerial position within a bank that is responsible for ensuring that the institution maintains an adequate level of legal reserves to meet its reserve requirements as set by law and also has access to sufficient quantities of reserves to accommodate customer demand and meet other cash needs.

mortgage-backed bond   A debt instrument representing a claim against the interest and principal payments generated by a pool of mortgage loans.

mortgage banking companies   Financial-service firms that acquire mortgage loans for eventual resale to longer-term lenders (e.g., insurance companies and pension funds).

multibank holding companies   A type of bank holding company that holds stock in more than one bank.

municipal bonds   Debt obligations issued by states, cities, counties, and other local governmental units.

mutual funds   Investment companies that attract savings from the public which are invested in a pool of stocks, bonds, and other financial instruments, with each saver receiving a share of the earnings generated by the pool of financial instruments.

national nonreciprocity   A state law that allows banks or bank holding companies from any other state in the nation to enter a particular state without the state entered requiring other states to extend the same entry privileges to its banks.

national reciprocity   A state law that allows banks or bank holding companies from any other state in the nation to enter a particular state with new service facilities or through acquisition, provided banks from that state are granted the same entry privilege by other states in the nation.

negotiable CD   A type of interest-bearing deposit that may be sold to other investors in the secondary market any number of times before it reaches maturity.

networking   The sharing of facilities for the movement of funds and financial information between banks.

net interest margin   The spread between the interest income and interest expense of a bank, divided by either its total assets or its total earning assets.

net liquidity position   The difference between the volume of liquid funds available to a bank and the demand for liquid funds that the bank faces.

net profit margin   The ratio of a bank's net income after taxes divided by its total operating revenues.

nonbank banks Financial-service firms that either offer checking account services or grant commercial loans, but not both.

nondeposit investment products Bank sales of mutual funds, annuities, and other nondeposit instruments offered through the bank's service delivery facilities, either with the aid of an affiliate of the bank or offered by an unrelated financial-services company but sold through the bank's service facilities.

noninterest margin The spread between noninterest income and noninterest expenses of a bank, divided by its total assets or total earning assets.

note A written contract between a borrowing customer and a bank describing the responsibilities of both parties.

note issuance facility (NIF) A medium-term credit agreement between an international bank and its larger corporate and governmental credit customers, where the customer is authorized to periodically issue short-term notes, each of which usually comes due and is retired in 90 to 180 days, over a stipulated contract period (such as five years), with the bank pledging to buy any notes the customer cannot sell to other investors.

NOW accounts Savings deposits against which a customer can write negotiable drafts (checks) but that reserve the bank's right to insist on prior notice before the customer withdraws his or her funds.

Office of the Comptroller of the Currency See **Comptroller of the Currency.**

open market operations (OMO) Purchases and sales of securities—in most cases, direct obligations of the government—that are designed to move bank reserves and interest rates toward levels desired by a central bank (such as the Federal Reserve System).

operating risk The danger of loss due to fluctuating earnings and cash flows from a bank's business operations.

opportunity cost Forgone income that is not earned because idle funds have not been invested in earning assets; also, the yield available on the next best alternate use of the bank's funds.

organizational forms The structure of operations, facilities, and personnel within a bank that enables it to produce and deliver financial services; it includes such organizational forms as unit banks, branch banks, and holding companies.

participation loans Purchases of loans by a third party, not part of the original loan contracts.

passbook savings deposits Accounts sold to household customers in small denominations along with a small booklet or computer statement showing the account's current balance, interest earnings, deposits, and withdrawals.

pledging Backing bank deposits owed to the federal government and local units of government by requiring the banks holding those deposits to hold designated high-quality (low-risk) assets (usually government securities of various types) that could be sold to recover government funds if the bank fails.

point-of-sale terminals Computer equipment in stores to allow electronic payments for goods and services.

points An up-front fee often charged a borrower taking on a home mortgage which is determined by multiplying the loan amount by the number of percentage points assessed the borrower.

portfolio diversification Spreading out a bank's credit accounts and deposits among a wide variety of customers, including many large and small businesses, different industries, and households, in order to reduce the bank's risk of loss.

portfolio immunization An interest-rate hedging device that permits a bank to reduce loss in the value of its assets or in the value of its net worth due to changing interest rates by equating the average duration of the bank's assets to the average duration of its liabilities.

portfolio shifting Selling selected securities, often at a loss, to offset taxable income from other sources and to restructure a bank's asset portfolio to one that is more appropriate for current market conditions.

preferred stock Type of bank capital measured by the par value of any shares outstanding that promise to pay their owners a fixed rate of return or (in the case of variable-rate preferred) a rate determined by an agreed-upon formula.

prepayment risk A risk carried by many securitized assets in which some of these assets (usually loans) are paid off early and the investor receiving those prepayments may be forced to reinvest the prepaid funds at lower current market yields, resulting in a lower than expected overall return from investing in securitized assets.

price leadership A method for setting loan rates that looks to leading banks in the industry to set the base loan rate.

primary capital   The sum of total equity capital, the allowance for possible loan losses, mandatory convertible debentures, and minority interests in consolidated subsidiaries, minus intangible assets other than purchased loan-servicing rights.

prime rate   An administered interest rate on loans quoted by leading banks and usually set by a vote of each bank's board of directors; the interest rate that is usually thought by the public to be the best (lowest) rate for loans and that a bank quotes to its biggest and best customers (principally large corporations).

product-line diversification   Offering multiple financial services in order to reduce the risk associated with declining revenues and income from any one service offered by a bank.

project loans   Credit designed to finance the construction of fixed assets associated with a particular investment project that is expected to generate a flow of revenue in future periods sufficient to repay the loan and turn a profit.

profit potential   A motive for carrying out a merger, in which the shareholders of either the acquiring banking firm, the acquired firm, or both anticipate greater profits due to greater revenues or lower operating costs after the merger is completed.

public benefits   Aspect of a bank merger or holding-company acquisition application in which merging or acquiring banks must show how the transaction will improve the quality, availability, or pricing of banking services offered to the public.

public need   One of the criteria used by governmental agencies to determine whether a new bank or branch should be approved for a charter, which focuses on whether or not an adequate volume and variety of financial services are available conveniently in a given market area.

purchase-of-assets method   A method for completing a merger in which the acquiring institution buys all or a portion of the assets of the acquired organization, using either cash or its own stock to pay for the purchase.

purchase-of-stock method   A method for carrying out a merger in which the acquired firm usually ceases to exist because the acquiring firm assumes all of its assets and liabilities.

real estate brokerage services   A service that assists bank customers in finding homes and other properties for sale or for rent.

real estate loans   Credit secured by real property, including short-term credit to support building construction and land development, and longer-term credit to support the purchase of residential and commercial structures.

regional reciprocity   A type of state law that allows only banks or bank holding companies from selected other states in the same region of the nation to enter a particular state's territory with new service facilities or through acquisition, provided banks from the state entered receive similar privileges for entry into other states located in the same region.

relationship pricing   Basing fees charged a customer on the number of services and the intensity of use of those services that the customer purchases from a bank.

Report of Condition   A bank's balance sheet, which lists the assets, liabilities, and equity capital (owners' funds) held by or invested in the bank at any single point in time; reports of condition must be filed periodically with bank regulatory agencies.

Report of Income   A bank's income statement, which indicates how much revenue has been received and what expenses have been incurred over a specific period of time; reports of income must be filed periodically with bank regulatory agencies.

representative office   The simplest organizational presence for a bank in foreign markets, consisting of limited-service facilities that can market services supplied by the home office and identify new customers but usually cannot take deposits or make decisions on the granting of loans.

repurchase agreement (RP)   A money market instrument that involves the temporary sale of high-quality assets (usually government securities) accompanied by an agreement to buy back those assets on a specific future date at a predetermined price or yield.

reserve computation period   A period of time established by the Federal Reserve System for certain depository institutions over which the daily average amounts of various deposits are computed to determine each institution's legal reserve requirement.

reserve maintenance period   According to federal law and regulation, a period of time spanning two weeks, during which a bank must hold the daily average amount of legal reserves it is required by law to hold behind its deposits and other reservable liabilities.

residential mortgage loans   Credit to finance the purchase of homes or fund improvements on private residences.

retail banks Consumer-oriented banks that sell the majority of their services to households and smaller businesses.

retail credit Smaller-denomination loans extended to individuals and families as well as to smaller businesses.

restrictive covenants Parts of a loan agreement, specifying actions the borrower must take or must not take for a loan agreement to remain in force.

retirement plans Financial plans offered by banks that accumulate and manage the savings of customers until they reach retirement age.

revolving credit line A financing arrangement that allows a business customer to borrow up to a specified limit, repay all or a portion of the borrowing, and reborrow as necessary until the credit line matures.

Riegle Community Development and Regulatory Improvement Act Federal law passed in 1994 that loosens regulations on bank reporting and provides funds for promoting the economic development of depressed communities.

Riegle-Neal Interstate Banking and Branching Efficiency Act Federal law passed in 1994 that permits bank holding companies to acquire banks nationwide and authorizes interstate branching beginning June 1, 1997.

right of offset The legal authority of a bank that has extended a loan to one of its customers to seize any checking or savings deposits the customer may hold with the bank in order to recover the bank's funds.

ROA Return on the total assets of a bank as measured by its ratio of net income after taxes to total assets.

ROE Return on equity capital invested in a bank by its stockholders, measured by after-tax net income divided by total equity capital.

Rule of 78s A method for calculating rebates of interest payments to be returned to a customer if a loan is retired early.

safekeeping A bank's practice of holding precious metals, securities, and other valuables owned by its customers in secure vaults.

savings deposits Interest-bearing funds left with banks for a period of weeks, months, or years (with no minimum required maturity under U.S. regulations).

secondary capital The sum of all forms of temporary capital for a bank, including limited-life preferred stock, subordinated notes and debentures, and mandatory convertible debt instruments not eligible to be counted as primary capital.

security brokerage Banks offering their customers a channel through which to buy stocks, bonds, and other securities at low transactions cost instead of having to go through a security broker or dealer.

securitization Setting aside a group of income-earning assets and issuing securities against them in order to raise new funds.

securitized assets Loans placed in an income-generating pool against which securities are issued in order to raise new funds.

self-liquidating loans Business loans, usually to support the purchase of inventories, in which the credit is gradually repaid by the borrowing customer as inventory is sold.

service differentiation Creating perceptions in the minds of a bank's customers that its services are of better quality, are more conveniently available, or differ in some other significant way from similar services offered by competitors.

servicing rights Rights retained by a bank selling a loan in which the bank, for a fee, continues to collect interest payments from the borrower and monitors the borrower's compliance with loan terms on behalf of the purchaser of the loan.

shell branches Booking offices located offshore from the United States that record international transactions (such as taking deposits) and escape many regulatory restrictions that limit the activities of domestic bank offices.

simple interest A method for calculating the interest rate on a loan that adjusts for the declining balance on a loan and uses a formula, principal times interest times time, to determine the amount of interest owed.

solvency risk The probability or chance that a bank or one of its borrowing customers will fail.

sources and uses of funds method Approach developed for estimating a bank's liquidity requirements that examines the expected sources of liquidity (for a bank, principally its deposits) and the expected uses of liquidity (principally its loans) and estimates the net difference between funds sources and uses over a given period of time in order to aid liquidity planning.

Sources and Uses of Funds Statement Financial reports on a business customer showing changes in assets and liabilities over a given period of time.

standby letter of credit (SLC) Popular type of financial guarantee in which the issuer of the letter guarantees the beneficiary of the letter that a loan he or she has made will be repaid.

state banking commissions Boards or commissions appointed by governors or legislators in each of the 50 states that are responsible for issuing new bank charters and supervising and examining state-chartered banks.

Statement of Stockholders' Equity A financial statement that shows what changes have occurred in a bank's capital account (where the owners have invested their funds) over a specified time period.

stockholders The owners of a bank who hold one or more shares of common and/or preferred stock issued by their banking corporation and elect its board of directors.

stripped security A debt security whose promised interest payments and promised repayments of principal are separated from each other; each of these promised payment streams becomes the basis for issuing new securities in the form of interest-only (IO) and principal-only (PO) discount obligations.

structure of funds method Method of estimating a bank's liquidity requirements that depends on a detailed analysis of a bank's deposit and loan customers and how the levels of their deposits and loans are likely to change over time.

subordinated debentures (or notes) Type of bank capital represented by debt instruments whose claim against the bank legally follows the claims of depositors but comes ahead of the bank's stockholders.

subsidiary A corporation operated by international banks that is used to sell bank and nonbank services overseas and is often set up or acquired because bank branch offices may be prohibited in some foreign markets or because of tax advantages or other factors.

Super NOWs Savings accounts that usually promise a higher interest return than regular NOW accounts but often impose restrictions on the number of drafts (checks) or withdrawals the depositor is allowed to make.

supplemental capital Secondary forms of bank capital, such as debt securities and limited-life preferred stock, that usually have a definite maturity and are not, therefore, perpetual funding instruments.

surplus Type of bank capital representing the excess amount above each share of stock's par value paid in by a bank's stockholders when they purchased their shares.

sweep accounts Contracts executed between a bank and some of its deposit customers that allow the bank to transfer funds (usually overnight) out of the customers' checking accounts into their savings deposits or into other types of deposits that do not carry legal reserve requirements.

tax benefits Ways to save on a bank's tax obligation by investing in tax-exempt earning assets, incurring tax-deductible expenses, or accruing income losses that help offset taxable income from loans or other income sources.

tax swapping A process in which lower-yielding securities may be sold at a loss that is deductible from a bank's ordinary taxable income, usually to be replaced by securities bearing more favorable returns.

term loans Credit extended for longer than one year and designed to fund longer-term business investments, such as the purchase of equipment or the construction of new physical facilities.

thrift deposits Accounts whose principal purpose is to provide an interest-bearing outlet for customer savings—that is, a place for the customer to store liquid purchasing power at interest until needed.

Tier 1 capital Core capital for a banking firm that includes common stock, undivided profits, selected preferred stock and intangible assets, and minority interest in subsidiary businesses.

Tier 2 capital Supplemental long-term funds for a bank including allowance for loan and lease losses, subordinated debt capital, selected preferred stock, and equity notes.

time deposits Interest-bearing accounts with stated maturities, which may carry penalties in the form of lost interest earnings or reduction of principal if early withdrawal occurs.

trade associations Informal groups to which individual banks or bankers belong in order to promote the industry's viewpoint with the public and to educate bankers on the latest trends affecting the industry.

transaction deposit A bank deposit service in which checks or drafts against the deposit may be used to pay for purchases of goods and services.

Treasury bill A direct obligation of the U.S. government that must mature within one year from date of issue.

Treasury bonds The longest-term U.S. Treasury debt securities, with original maturities beyond 10 years.

Treasury notes Coupon instruments issued by the U.S. government, with original maturities from more than 1 year to a maximum of 10 years, which promise investors a fixed rate of return.

trust services Management of property and other valuables owned by a customer under a contract (the trust agreement) in which the bank serves as trustee and the customer becomes the trustor during a specified period of time.

Truth-in-Lending Act Legislation passed by the U.S. Congress in 1968 that promotes the informed use of credit among consumers by requiring full disclosure of credit terms and costs.

Truth-in-Savings Act Legislation passed by the U.S. Congress in 1991 that requires depository institutions to fully disclose the prices and other terms offered on deposit services so that customers can more easily compare deposit plans offered by different service providers.

underwriting Buying new securities from the businesses that issued them and attempting to resell those securities at a profit to other investors.

undivided profits Type of bank capital representing the net earnings of a bank that have been retained in the business rather than being paid out as dividends to the bank's stockholders.

Uniform Bank Performance Report (UBPR) A compilation of financial and operating information, periodically required to be submitted to the federal banking agencies, that is designed to aid regulators and financial analysts in analyzing a U.S. bank's financial condition.

unit banks Banks that offer the full range of their services from one office, though a small number of services (such as taking deposits or cashing checks) may be offered from limited-service facilities (such as drive-in windows and ATMs).

upscale target pricing The use of carefully designed deposit advertising programs and deposit pricing schemes to appeal to customers with higher levels of income or net worth, such as business owners and managers, doctors, lawyers, and other professionals.

warranties A section within a loan agreement in which a borrower affirms to the lender that the information he or she supplies is true and correct.

wholesale banks Large metropolitan banks that offer financial services, mainly to corporations and other institutions.

wholesale lenders Banks that devote the bulk of their credit portfolios to large-denomination loans extended to corporations and other relatively large business firms and institutions.

working capital The current assets of a business firm (consisting principally of cash, accounts receivable, inventory, and other assets normally expected to roll over into cash within a year); some authorities define working capital as equal to current assets minus current liabilities.

working capital loans Loans that provide businesses with short-term credit lasting from a few days to one year and that are often used to fund the purchase of inventories in order to put goods on shelves or to purchase raw materials.

yield curve A graphic picture of how interest rates vary with different maturities of securities as viewed at a single point in time.

yield to maturity (YTM) The expected rate of return on a debt security held until its maturity date is reached, based on the security's purchase price, promised interest payments, and redemption value at maturity.

CASE 1

CHASE MANHATTAN CORPORATION: THE MAKING OF AMERICA'S LARGEST BANK*

In mid-August 1995, Walter Shipley, chairman and CEO of Chemical Banking Corporation, was preparing to leave the bank's Manhattan headquarters building after a long day. For the past four weeks he and other senior Chemical managers had been in intensive negotiations with their counterparts at Chase Manhattan Corporation, including that bank's chairman and CEO Thomas Labrecque. At issue was whether the two banks would agree to merge in a friendly transaction. If completed, the merger would produce the largest commercial bank in the United States, and the fourth largest bank in the world, with total assets of nearly $300 billion and over 74,000 employees.

Shipley believed the merger would create value in two ways. First, it would allow the banks to realize substantial savings in operating and overhead costs. The banks' businesses overlapped in many areas, and they both maintained extensive retail branch networks in the Downstate New York area. In addition, both banks were headquartered in Manhattan, and maintained elaborate trading floors in both Manhattan and London. Cost savings of up to $1.5 billion were deemed possible, but this would require reducing the banks' combined workforce by 12,000 employees and closing over 100 branches.

The second benefit of the merger, in Shipley's view, was that as a larger bank with significant product and market leadership positions, Chemical-Chase would enjoy significantly higher revenue growth. Larger banks with leadership positions in each business could more easily enter new markets and develop new products; they could better satisfy the complex needs of large corporate customers; and they could better afford the large-scale investments in new technology that would be required to take a financial services firm into the twenty-first century.

Important issues had to be resolved before the merger could proceed. It would be necessary to set an exchange ratio for the transaction—the number of shares of Chemical stock that would be swapped for each share of Chase stock. It would also be necessary to decide how, and by whom, the new entity would be managed, as well as how the two complex organizations would be integrated.

Shipley also had more fundamental concerns. Chemical was currently profitable, and was under no immediate pressure to merge or change its present course. And less than four years earlier, Chemical had merged with Manufacturers Hanover to form the second-largest bank in the U.S., with combined shareholders' equity of $7.3 billion. The full integration of these two banks had only recently been completed. This raised a number of important questions. Did a merger with Chase—or any bank—make sense at this time? If the merger did go forward, would it be possible to achieve the proposed cost savings without damaging the bank's long-term competitiveness, or its ability to keep up with the rapid pace of change in the financial services industry? And would the stock market give the bank full credit for the value created by the merger?

---

*Casewriter note: For expositional purposes this case study portrays events surrounding the merger mainly from the perspective of Chemical Bank's management, and therefore does not fully reflect the active involvement and participation of Chase management in the design and execution of the merger.

Professor Stuart C. Gilson and Research Associate Cedric X. Escalle prepared this case as the basis for class discussion rather than to illustrate either effective or ineffective handling of an administrative situation. Mitchell Madison Group (New York) provided various background materials that were used in this case.

Chemical Banking Corporation

The Chemical Banking Corporation was founded in 1824 by three New York City merchants as a division of a chemical manufacturing company. Twenty years later, the chemical business was liquidated and the company was reincorporated as a bank. Over the next century, the bank rapidly expanded, and developed a reputation for sound, conservative management. During the 1930s, Chemical's business prospered, and its deposits rose by 40%, even while 8,000 other banks failed.

The postwar era was a period of spectacular growth for Chemical. From 1946 to 1972, the bank's assets increased from $1.35 billion to $15 billion. It aggressively acquired other banks, and expanded into in a variety of new product and geographic markets. Starting in the late 1950s, Chemical greatly expanded its international business, forming numerous overseas subsidiaries, and opening up its first full-service branch in London in 1959. Over the next two decades the bank established offices in key financial centers around the world, including Frankfurt, the Bahamas, Zurich, Brussels, Paris, Tokyo, Milan, Taiwan, and Singapore. As part of this growth, the bank also diversified into a variety of different banking products and services, and decentralized its organizational structure. It had two objectives in doing this: to increase the proportion of its earnings that were derived from fee-based service businesses (thereby reducing its exposure to fluctuations in interest rate spreads), and to acquire a reputation for being innovative.

Still lacking a clear niche in the industry, however, and with its financial performance lagging, starting in the early 1980's Chemical restructured its non-consumer banking businesses, and undertook a series of aggressive acquisitions. In 1982 Chemical secured a future presence in the profitable Florida market by acquiring a stake in Florida National Banks. In 1986 it entered into a deferred merger agreement with New Jersey–based Horizon Bancorp (the merger was consummated in 1989). And in 1987 it acquired Texas Commerce Bankshares (TCB) in what was then the largest interstate bank merger in U.S. history. These acquisitions were made either in anticipation of, or in response to, agreements between various States to allow interstate banking, which had previously been prohibited. In the banking industry as a whole, the number of such acquisitions increased dramatically in response to these regulatory changes.

Although Chemical continued to grow in size, by the late 1980s and early 1990s its financial performance began to suffer under the strain of a U.S. recession, mounting real estate losses, and increasing loan defaults by sovereign borrowers, especially in Latin America. In 1991, $1 billion of loans in Chemical's $6.7 billion real estate portfolio was in default.

The Merger with Manufacturers Hanover.　In late 1991 Chemical Banking Corp. merged with Manufacturers Hanover Corporation. This transaction was the first major bank merger "among equals." (At the time Chemical and Manufacturers Hanover were, respectively, the sixth- and ninth-largest banks in the United States.) With total assets of $135 billion, the bank was second-largest in the United States, after Citicorp.

The chief executives of the two banks—Walter Shipley at Chemical and John McGillicuddy at Manufacturers Hanover—conceived the merger as an opportunity to realize substantial cost savings, through approximately 6,000 employee layoffs and the closing of 80 branches (especially in the New York City area where both banks were headquartered). To reflect the costs of merger-related workforce reductions and bank office consolidations, Chemical took a pre-tax restructuring charge of $625 million in 1991 (later, in 1993, it took an additional charge of $158 million). Also, in January 1992—less than one month after the 1991 merger became effective—the bank sold 57.5 million shares of new common stock in a massive public offering, netting proceeds of $1.52 billion. The issue was, at the time, the largest equity offering ever by a U.S. bank.

The merger was subsequently judged a success by Chemical management and most market analysts. By 1995, management believed, the merger had enabled the bank to reduce its pretax non-interest expense by almost $750 million a year. This amount represented 36% of Manufacturer Hanover's total non-interest expense, or 19% of the two banks' combined non-interest expense, before the merger. Annual corporate overhead expense alone had been reduced by nearly 30% since the merger. Chemical's efficiency ratio, which stood at 75% in 1990, had fallen to 58% by 1993.[1]

---

[1]The efficiency ratio, a standard measure of operating efficiency used in the banking industry, equals total non-interest expense per dollar of "revenue," where revenue is defined as the sum of (1) non-interest income and (2) *net* interest income (i.e., gross interest income *minus* gross interest expense).

Despite the financial benefits of the merger, however, by late 1994 the bank had fallen to fourth place in terms of total size, as the U.S. banking industry was consumed by a wave of merger activity and other huge banks were formed. And near the end of 1994, Chemical launched a major initiative aimed at reducing expenses and selectively investing for revenue growth, called the "Margin Improvement Program." Under this initiative the bank would seek an additional $440 million in annual expense reductions by restructuring and rationalizing its operations; and it would reinvest about half of these savings in selected areas, including its national consumer and investment banking businesses. In 1994 Chemical took a pretax restructuring charge of $308 million for the costs of implementing the program. The program was fully implemented by mid-1995.

The Chase Manhattan Corporation

Chase Manhattan Corporation was formed in 1955 as the merger of two New York–based banks, Chase National Bank and the Bank of Manhattan. Both of these banks had colorful histories. The company that was to become the Bank of Manhattan was formed in 1799 to supply water to New York City residents during a yellow fever epidemic, but its real purpose was to be a bank, and in less than a year this is what it became. By 1955 the bank had grown to become one of the nation's most profitable and well-regarded regional banks. Most of its business was in retail banking, and it operated 67 branches in New York City. Chase National Bank was one of the largest banks in the world, following decades of high growth. This growth was fueled both by acquisitions (during the 1920s and 1930s it had acquired seven of the largest banks in New York City) and by aggressive development of new markets and products (especially in corporate banking). The bank had extensive international operations, and it was the first bank to open up branches in Germany and Japan after World War II.

A driving force behind the merger was David Rockefeller, and he became chairman of Chase in 1969. The Rockefeller family was one of the most important families in American business and politics. Rockefeller travelled extensively, and he developed close ties to business and government leaders around the world. Through size and political connections, Chase became a major power broker in international affairs. By the end of the 1970s, Chase was the third largest bank in the United States, with 226 branches in New York City. It was truly a global bank: two-thirds of its income came from foreign operations, and it operated 34 subsidiaries outside the United States.

In the 1980s, however, Chase encountered significant difficulties. The bank found itself holding hundreds of millions of dollars in bad real estate loans; and it had one of the largest exposures to defaulted Third World debt of any U.S. bank. In May 1987 Chase added $1.6 billion to its loan loss reserves, and for the year it reported a record loss of $895 million; for 1989 and 1990 it had a combined loss of one billion dollars.

The bank's response to this crisis was to reduce its workforce by 10% between 1986 and 1988, and to replace the chairman and CEO, Willard Butcher, with Thomas Labrecque (David Rockefeller had retired in 1981). Labrecque had started with Chase as a trainee in 1964, and had steadily advanced through the management ranks. Under Labrecque, Chase took further steps to address its problems. By the end of 1991 the workforce was reduced by another 6,000, and several subsidiaries were sold. The bank scaled back its foreign operations by eliminating many of its overseas branches. And it eliminated all of its domestic branches that were located outside the New York area. Going forward, Chase would focus its energies in three areas: regional banking in the New York/Tri-State region; national consumer operations (e.g., credit cards, home mortgages, and automobile loans); and international investment banking.

These initiatives seemed to work, and Chase returned to profitability in 1991 when it reported net income of $520 million. Earnings continued to be positive for the next three years, reaching $1.1 billion in 1994. The bank's stock price remained weak, however, and many analysts felt that Chase was vulnerable to being taken over by a stronger bank.

Takeover speculation intensified in April 1995, when money manager Michael Price acquired a 6.1% stake in Chase and became its largest shareholder. Price, who had a reputation as a shareholder activist, publicly called on Chase management to consider ways to increase the stock price. He especially favored actions that would allow the bank to achieve greater business focus, including divestitures or spinoffs of non-core businesses. He told the press: "Chase's activities are so sprawling that Wall Street is having trouble evaluating the bank's worth."[2]

Chase management agreed that the bank was undervalued, but believed the problem was not in being too

---

[2]*The New York Times,* April 7, 1995, p. D1.

diversified; indeed, it felt that "the company's large reach was the very essence of its value."[3] In June 1995, the bank responded by announcing a restructuring program that was code-named "Focus." Under this program the bank would reduce its workforce by an additional three to six thousand people, and, by 1997, reduce its annual non-interest costs by $400 million (pretax). One banking analyst, however, commented that "Chase's biggest problem isn't one of expense reduction but revenue growth. In an era of rapid bank consolidation, product innovation and cutthroat competition, Chase hasn't been aggressive enough in pursuing new business opportunities."[4] Major initiatives under the program had not yet started when final merger negotiations with Chemical commenced in mid-July 1995.

Restructuring in the Banking Industry

Merger and Consolidation.   The 1990s witnessed a number of significant changes in the U.S. banking industry. Having worked through most of its problems in 1990 and 1991, the industry entered a period of record profitability. Between 1991 and 1995, U.S. commercial banks experienced a near quadrupling of their total pretax earnings from $20 billion to $80 billion. This growth represented a dramatic turnaround from the late-1980s, which had seen a record number of bank failures.

There had also been a dramatic upsurge in bank mergers. During 1988–1990 the total value of bank equity acquired in acquisitions had been $4.5 billion a year on average; since 1991 the average had been over $15 billion, $25.5 billion for the first eight months of 1995 alone.[5] This trend reflected both an increase in the number of transactions as well as an increase in average transaction size; the most recent mergers had been of unprecedented size (**Exhibit 1**). One consequence of this merger activity was a decline in the number of banks. In 1980 there were 15,300 commercial banks in the United States; by 1995 there were fewer than 10,000. The banking industry had also become

more concentrated, with the top 50 banks now holding 65% of total bank assets, up from 53% in 1985.

Bank industry analysts recognized two distinct types of bank mergers: in-market mergers and market extension mergers. In an in-market merger, the acquiring bank and target bank did business in the same geographic markets. Elimination of duplication and overlap between the banks' activities allowed them to realize potentially significant savings in operating and overhead expenses. A market extension merger, in contrast, was a merger between banks that did business in distinct, non-overlapping markets. These mergers produced fewer expense reduction opportunities, but also more opportunities to enter new markets, diversify income streams, and grow revenues. Both types of mergers allowed banks to achieve scale economies in certain back office operations, for example those that supported a credit card or mortgage servicing business.

The 1991 merger of Chemical and Manufacturers Hanover had been an in-market merger, as was the February 1995 merger between New England–based Fleet Bank and Shawmut Bank. In-market mergers typically produced pretax cost savings equal to 30%–40% of the target bank's total non-interest expense before the merger.

In contrast, the June 1995 merger of First Union (based in Charlotte, North Carolina) and First Fidelity (based in Newark, New Jersey) was a market extension merger. With a value of $5.4 billion, this was the largest bank merger to date; the resulting bank was the sixth-largest in the United States, with $124 billion in assets and 1,970 branches located all the way from Florida to Connecticut. The banks' branch networks only overlapped in Maryland, so cost savings were expected to be relatively modest (5% of the two banks' combined non-interest expense).[6] **Exhibit 2** shows the principal geographic markets served by the top 50 U.S. banks.

Forces for Change.   According to some observers, the high level of restructuring by commercial banks could be traced to powerful economic forces that were dramatically

[3]*The New York Times,* April 7, 1995, p. D1.

[4]*The Wall Street Journal,* 27 June, 1995, p. 3.

[5]Source: Investment banking analysis prepared for Chemical Bank (excludes transactions under $35 million).

[6]One analysis of bank mergers showed that average cost savings varied substantially across different functional areas of the bank. For market extension mergers, cost savings relating to the merging banks' branch networks were found to be roughly equal to 5% of the acquired bank's total non-interest expense, on average. For cost savings related to staff and to systems and operations, the corresponding percentage was 20%. These percentages were significantly higher for in-market mergers: 35% for branch networks, and 40% for staff and systems/operations (Source: Mitchell Madison Group).

EXHIBIT 1 Major Bank Mergers Announced in 1995 (through August)

Acquiror/Acquiree	Transaction Value ($ billion)	Price to Book	Price to Market[a]	Buyer Rationale	Seller Rationale
First Union/First Fidelity	5.4	1.9x	1.3x	Geographic expansion Revenue enhancements	Limited growth prospects Margin compression 30% shareholder
First Chicago/NBD	5.3	1.5	1.1	Merger of equals–defensive move Achieve scale Preserve Chicago headquarters Preserve name	Achieve scale Consolidate Midwestern position
Fleet/Shawmut	3.7	1.8	1.5	Achieve size Market consolidation Cost reduction	Limited growth prospects Margin compression Limited acquisition opportunities Weak stock price Defensive move
PNC/Midlantic	3.0	2.0	1.3	Strengthen New Jersey franchise Revenue enhancements Cost savings	Importance of size/scale Weak competitive position
US Bancorp/West One	1.6	2.0	1.4	Geographic expansion Achieve scale	Achieve scale Attractive social issues
NAB/Michigan National	1.5	1.9	1.2	Market entry vehicle Opportunities for further acquisitions	Defensive move
Boatmen's/Fourth Financial	1.2	1.8	1.1	Strong position in Oklahoma and Kansas Achieve scale	Limited growth prospects Margin compression Limited acquisition opportunities

[a]Based on price one day prior to announcement.
Source: Company documents.

EXHIBIT 2 Geographic Markets Served by the Top 50 U.S. Banks, by Assets (billions of dollars)

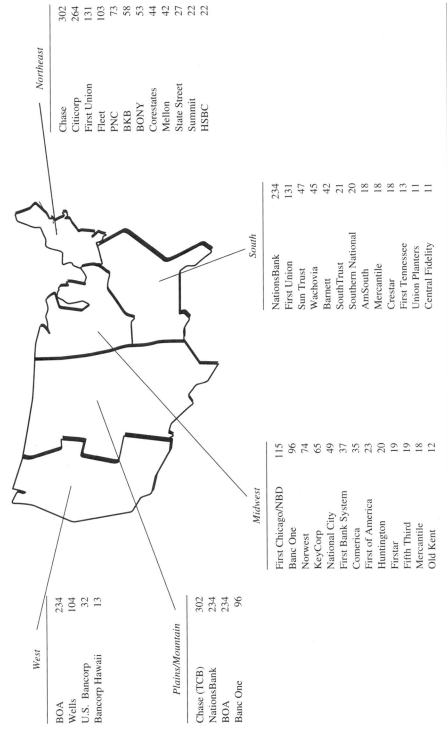

West

BOA	234
Wells	104
U.S. Bancorp	32
Bancorp Hawaii	13

Plains/Mountain

Chase (TCB)	302
NationsBank	234
BOA	234
Banc One	96

Midwest

First Chicago/NBD	115
Banc One	96
Norwest	74
KeyCorp	65
National City	49
First Bank System	37
Comerica	35
First of America	23
Huntington	20
Firstar	19
Fifth Third	19
Mercantile	18
Old Kent	12

South

NationsBank	234
First Union	131
Sun Trust	47
Wachovia	45
Barnett	42
SouthTrust	21
Southern National	20
AmSouth	18
Mercantile	18
Crestar	18
First Tennessee	13
Union Planters	11
Central Fidelity	11

Northeast

Chase	302
Citicorp	264
First Union	131
Fleet	103
PNC	73
BKB	58
BONY	53
Corestates	44
Mellon	42
State Street	27
Summit	22
HSBC	22

Source: Mitchell Madison Group.

altering the profitability and structure of the entire financial services industry.[7]

Traditionally, government regulation had imposed severe limits on the product and geographic markets in which a given financial institution could legally do business. For example, the 1933 Glass-Steagall Act prohibited commercial banks from underwriting corporate securities, and the 1927 McFadden Act and the 1956 Bank Holding Company Act restricted interstate branch banking. As a result, the financial services industry tended to be organized along institutional lines, with different financial institutions—commercial banks, savings and loans, insurance companies, mutual funds, and pension funds—each providing a distinct set of products and services.

With the recent trend towards deregulation of the financial services industry, however, many of these barriers were breaking down. For example, in 1994 congress passed the Riegle-Neal Interstate Banking and Branching Efficiency Act, which provided for nationwide banking by October 1995. And since the late 1980s, commercial banks had, on a restricted basis, been allowed to underwrite certain corporate securities.[8] More recently, banks had received the right to sell mutual funds, in direct competition with mutual fund complexes like Fidelity and Vanguard.

While these trends clearly benefited banks, deregulation had also given non-bank financial institutions increased access to the banks' traditional markets. For example, mutual fund companies could now offer their shareholders check-writing privileges, providing the banks' customers with a direct substitute for bank checking accounts. As a result of these and related developments, U.S. households had allocated an increasing fraction of their savings to non-bank institutions. In 1994, for example, only 35% of households' financial assets were held in conventional bank deposits, down sharply from 49% in 1980. **Exhibit 3** shows market share information for selected products and services offered by commercial banks.

These trends were reinforced by the sharp decline in the cost of computing technology. This development enabled non-banks to develop a cost advantage in providing certain products and services through increased specialization, and compete directly with banks in their traditional markets. In corporate lending, institutions like General Motors Acceptance Corporation and General Electric Credit Corporation now provided U.S. businesses with hundreds of billions of dollars of financing (much of it secured by certain specialized assets). In the consumer credit card business, non-bank institutions now accounted for 40% of all credit card outstandings, up from 25% in 1992. And the mortgage servicing business was now dominated by non-bank institutions, although some banks—including Chemical and Chase—continued to have a significant presence in this market.

The impact of technology was not one-sided, however. Advances in technology and computing power, while allowing non-bank institutions to intrude on the banks' traditional businesses, also provided banks with their own opportunities to develop new markets and products. One potentially promising area was "on-line" or "home" banking. Some expected the growth of this market to be huge (**Exhibit 4**). Significant investments in new technology would be necessary to develop this business, however. And growth in home banking could be limited by the increasing availability and popularity of ATMs. (In 1990 there were 80,200 ATMs installed in the United States; by 1995 there were 122,700.)

Taking all of these factors into account, the current level of profitability in the U.S. banking sector might therefore be difficult to sustain. For 1995, total pretax earnings for all U.S. banks were expected to be around $75 billion, implying a return on shareholders' equity of 14.7%.[9] But increasing competition for banks' traditional

---

[7]The following section draws heavily on Robert C. Merton, "The Financial System and Economic Performance," *Journal of Financial Services Research,* December 1990; Dwight B. Crane and Zvi Bodie, "Form Follows Function: The Transformation of Banking," *Harvard Business Review,* March–April 1996, pp. 109–117; and Dwight B. Crane *et al., The Global Financial System* (Boston: Harvard Business School Press, 1996).

[8]Following a Supreme Court Ruling in July 1988, commercial banks were permitted to conduct nonbanking activities such as securities underwriting and trading through a special ("Section 20") subsidiary. As of August 1995, revenue from the underwriting business was legally capped at 10% of the subsidiary's gross revenue, but many industry observers expected this percentage—and the list of securities banks could underwrite—to grow.

[9]This figure includes a deduction for banks' aggregate loan losses, which in 1995 were equal to 30 basis points on total bank assets of $4.2 trillion. This was below the previous 10-year average loan loss rate of 55 basis points.

businesses from non-bank institutions—who could provide the same products and services at lower cost—meant that banks had to find ways to cut their costs if they were to avoid future declines in profitability or market share. **Exhibit 5** reports relative interest rates earned or charged by banks and competing financial institutions.

Restructuring Analysis

The decision to pursue a merger of Chemical and Chase was the product of a lengthy, much more general debate that had been proceeding independently at each bank for several years. Management at each bank was keenly aware of the powerful forces that were reshaping the financial services industry, potentially threatening the long-term profitability of commercial banks.

A merger with a bank or other financial institution represented one important option for dealing with these pressures, but the issues here were complicated. Under a traditional in-market merger, elimination of redundant retail branch offices and other "hard" assets made it possible to achieve significant reductions in operating expenses. Participants in this debate recognized, however, that it was becoming increasingly difficult to measure the extent of a bank's retail business in terms of "bricks and mortar." For many products—for example, credit cards and consumer mortgage loans—the relevant markets were national in scope, yet a merger of these businesses could also create significant expense reduction opportunities.

A market extension merger, which would allow a bank to grow revenues and enter new markets, represented another competitive response. This option also raised a number of difficult questions. As with in-market mergers, market extension mergers could be differentiated by the "closeness" of the merging banks' businesses. Both Chemical and Chase management recognized that a market extension merger could be used either to strengthen and grow existing product lines, or to acquire new products and enter entirely new businesses. (An example of the latter option would be a merger between a bank and a full-service brokerage house, although such a combination would not have been permitted under then-existing regulations.)

Other issues were debated as well. One was the mix of retail and wholesale business that was most appropriate for each bank; this mix would clearly be affected by the choice of merger partner. Another issue was whether it made more sense to expand in multiple markets at once by acquiring a multi-line bank, or instead to concentrate on growing certain selected businesses individually, for example, by acquiring a consumer credit card company. Chemical and Chase had both recently acquired, or were in the process of acquiring, consumer mortgage loan companies.

A critical consideration in any merger decision would be the opportunity to realize economies of scale and scope by expanding the size of the bank, thereby strengthening the market and product positions of the combined institutions. At Chemical, Shipley felt strongly that larger institutions with market leadership enjoyed a distinct competitive advantage.

For one thing, larger banks could better afford the massive investment in new information technology that was needed to provide the level of service and breadth of product offerings that retail and corporate customers were increasingly demanding. Chemical believed it would have to invest billions of dollars in new technology over the next few years to respond to these pressures.

Shipley had argued this point several years earlier when Chemical merged with Manufacturers Hanover:

> If it's important for the United States to have large, globally competitive automobile companies, globally competitive chemical companies, globally competitive computer companies, it's important to have large globally competitive banks as well. There is a certain point where the scale of your operations does become important, in terms of profitability and ability to serve your customers efficiently and effectively, and your ability to invest in new products and services. It is very hard for a small bank to keep up with the technology development expenses.[10]

Shipley also perceived scale economies in the discretionary outlays that Chemical would have to make in its various businesses over time to stay competitive, as new products were introduced, and existing products were improved. For example, a new innovation in the credit card business might require an up-front investment of $100 million, regardless of the number of credit cards issued or the dollar value of card receivables managed by the bank.

Finally, Shipley believed that larger banks enjoyed a distinct comparative advantage in attracting new business, especially from corporate clients. If a company needed bank financing for a new investment or acquisition, for example,

---

[10]*The Record,* September 8, 1991, p. B1.

EXHIBIT 3   Comparative Market Share Data: Tri-State Regional Banking
(Top Five Rankings for 1994)

| | Downstate New York Middle Market | | | | New York 9 County Consumer Share | | |
| | Relationship Share | | Lead Share | | Deposit Share | | |
	Rank	*Share[a]*	*Rank*	*Share*	*Branches*	*Rank*	*Share*
Chemical	1	55%	1	29%	282	1	14%
Chase	3	30%	2	12%	184	3	6%
Citicorp	4	29%	4	7%	212	2	13%
Bank of New York	2	31%	5	7%	237	4	4%
NatWest	N.R.	N.R.	3	7%	131	5	3%
Merrill Lynch	5	23%	N.R.	N.R.	N.R.	N.R.	N.R.

N.R. = not ranked in top five.

[a]Gives credit for each banking relationship and therefore adds to more than 100%.

Source: Claritis, The Nilsson Report, *National Mortgage News,* Lipper Analytical Services, Inc., Loan Pricing Corporation Gold Sheets.

Comparative Market Share Data: National Consumer Business
(dollar amounts in $ billions)

Top Credit Card Issuers (1994)	*Rank*	*Cards*	*Outstandings*
Citibank	1	34.0	$39.0
Discover Card	2	42.6	20.9
MBNA	3	16.0	17.6
AT&T Universal	4	22.0	12.3
First Chicago	5	18.3	12.2
First USA	6	8.8	11.0
Household Bank	7	15.0	10.8
Chase	8	13.3	10.4
Chemical	9	9.8	8.9
American Express	10	25.3	8.1

Mortgage Originations (first half 1995)	*Rank*	*Originations*	*Share*
Countrywide	1	$13.1	4.5%
Norwest	2	12.3	4.2
Prudential	3	5.7	2.0
Fleet	4	5.5	1.9
Chase	5	5.3	1.8
Chemical	6	4.9	1.7
NationsBank	7	4.1	1.4
Great Western Bank	8	4.0	1.4
BankAmerica	9	3.9	1.3
GMAC Mortgage	10	3.3	1.1

EXHIBIT 3 (*concluded*) Comparative Market Share Data: National Consumer Business

(dollar amounts in $ billions)

Mortgage Servicing (June 30, 1995)	*Rank*	*Servicing*
Countrywide	1	$121.2
GE Mortgage	2	109.4
Norwest	3	100.5
Fleet	4	99.8
Prudential	5	77.8
NationsBank	6	77.5
Chase	7	73.6
BankAmerica	8	57.1
Chemical	9	51.9
Home Savings	10	49.5

Bank Mutual Fund Assets under Management (March 31, 1995)	*Rank*	*Servicing*
Mellon	1	$68.0
PNC Bank	2	22.4
NationsBank	3	14.7
Wells Fargo	4	10.6
Chase	10	7.0
Chemical	13	5.7

Loan Syndications— Agent Only (first-half 1995)	*Rank*	*Agent Volume*	*Number of Deals*	*Share*
Chemical	1	$132	162	24%
J. P. Morgan	2	68	73	12
Citicorp	3	56	101	10
BankAmerica	4	52	115	9
Chase	5	46	94	8
NationsBank	6	27	94	5
First Chicago	7	22	62	4
Bank of New York	8	22	38	4
Bankers Trust	9	22	59	4
Bank of Nova Scotia	10	11	20	2

EXHIBIT 4 Projected Growth in Online Banking

Lower Cost + Greater Power + Shifting Demand = Rapid Adoption

Online Banking

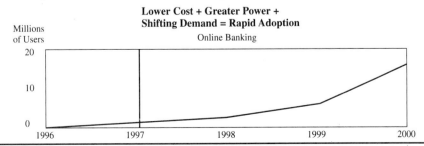

Source: Company documents.

EXHIBIT 5   **1995 Interest Rate Comparisons**

	Aggregate Amount Outstanding for Banks ($ billions)	Average U.S. Rates Paid or Charged	
		Banks	Main Competitors
Deposit rate[a]	$453	2.71%	5.05%
Credit card loan rate	240	16.0%	14.0%
Small business loan rate spread[b]	300	6.0%	3.0%

[a]Represents money market demand accounts for banks, and money market mutual funds with check-writing privileges for main competitors.

[b]Spread for "Main Competitors" represents estimated future spread given the likely impact of increasing competition in this market.

Source: Mitchell Madison Group, FDIC, analyst reports.

a large bank would be better positioned to underwrite the loan and provide the needed funds. A large bank would also have the depth of management and the financial wherewithal to offer a broad range of products and services to its corporate clients, in essence offering them "one-stop shopping." Being larger, and better capitalized, would also make a bank more competitive in derivatives market-making. Finally, some banking industry observers reckoned that treasurers and chief financial officers at larger (e.g., *Fortune* 500) firms preferred to conduct their business with larger banks, which as large institutions themselves better understood the needs of a large corporation.

Summing up these arguments, Shipley noted:

(M)arket leadership across the board (will) materially (enhance) our ability to deploy resources for maximum return. We will be able to finance our growth businesses, including nationwide consumer products and services, private banking, trading, securities underwriting, and information and transaction services, without penalizing other businesses that are solid, but where the potential for growth is not as large. We will have the resources to create new and better products, build closer linkages among our products and provide greater convenience and choice for customers, leading to above average revenue growth.[11]

Chemical management believed that the 1991 merger with Manufacturers Hanover had produced material revenue enhancements and scale economies, resulting in additional revenues in the range $150–200 million a year since the merger. Management believed this increase was

in large part made possible by the bank's $1.52 billion equity issue immediately following the merger, which significantly improved its credit quality.

Not all bank executives shared Shipley's vision of the industry, however. A number of banks appeared to have developed profitable niches in relatively narrow or specialized product lines. For example, Boston-based BayBank had achieved success by emphasizing consumer banking and small business lending, building an extensive branch-ATM network and emphasizing convenience for the customer. Ohio-based Banc One had also chosen to focus on traditional retail banking and middle-market corporate lending (although its markets were much broader geographically). At the other extreme, State Street Bank & Trust Company specialized in providing financial services like asset custody and investment management for institutions and wealthy individuals, and had little presence in traditional banking activities like deposit-taking or lending. Similarly, New York–based J. P. Morgan had grown to become one of the largest banks in the United States largely on the strength of its wholesale banking business, which included corporate lending and securities underwriting, financial derivatives, and sales and trading; it did not operate retail bank branches, or have a presence in any national consumer lending business (such as credit cards or mortgage loans). Bankers Trust had also completely exited from retail banking.

More generally, in recent years scores of industrial companies had chosen to increase their business focus,

[11]Source: Company 1995 annual report of shareholders.

and become much smaller, through downsizing, spin-offs, and asset divestitures—effectively undoing the diversification programs they had pursued years before. Such increases in focus were often rewarded with an increase in the firm's stock price; one study, for example, estimated that firms announcing spinoffs increased their stock price by 3%, on average.[12]

Benefits of a Chemical/Chase Merger.   At Chemical, a more focused inquiry into the benefits of merging with another bank began in early 1995. This effort, like the more general strategic discussion that preceded it, was initially led by a small group of senior managers that included the three members of the Office of the Chairman, supported by Peter Tobin and Dina Dublon (respectively, the chief financial officer and corporate treasurer of Chemical). The group's goal was to think broadly about the kinds of combinations that might make sense for the bank. A long list of potential merger partners was considered, that included BankAmerica, Chase, Nations-Bank, First Union, Banc One, and J. P. Morgan, among others. **Exhibit 6** shows financial and descriptive information for these banks. **Exhibit 7** shows estimates of the potential cost savings that might be achieved if Chemical were to merge with these banks, based on the experience of recent bank mergers.

As the analysis moved forward, and the bank's choices were vigorously debated, a consensus began to emerge that the interests of Chemical would be best served through a merger with Chase.

From Chemical's perspective, Chase was an attractive merger partner for several reasons. It had a globally recognized brand name. It had strong wholesale businesses, and was a leading provider of foreign exchange products. These product lines were complemented by the bank's state-of-the-art trading operations. It was the largest custodian in the world (with $1.8 trillion in total trust and custody assets), and a leader in the international money transfer business. Chase also had competitive strengths in private banking, credit cards, and mortgage banking. Finally, it was a leading provider of retail and middle market corporate banking services in New York State (especially in Downstate New York, which included Manhattan and the nearby metropolitan areas).

A merger of Chemical and Chase would also create significant expense reduction opportunities. Chemical and Chase operated in a number of common businesses. Geographically, the retail and middle market banking activities of both banks were concentrated in the Tri-State area (New York, New Jersey, and Connecticut). Both banks were headquartered in Manhattan, and both maintained technologically sophisticated sales and trading operations in Manhattan and London.

Management's analysis showed that a Chemical-Chase merger could eventually produce $1.5 billion of annual cost savings. Implementing the "merger saves" would take time, however, so in the first and second year after the merger, anticipated savings would be $600 million and $1.05 billion, respectively. **Exhibit 8** shows a breakdown of anticipated expense reductions under the merger.

To achieve these cost savings, it would be necessary to close redundant retail branch offices, reduce the size of the banks' combined workforces, and otherwise eliminate excess capacity that would be created by the merger. For example, it would make sense to keep only one trading floor in operation in Manhattan. As many as 100 retail branches might have to be closed. **Exhibit 9** shows the location of Chemical and Chase retail bank branches in the Downstate New York area.

It would also be necessary to let go of approximately 12,000 employees. The banks hoped to achieve up to two-thirds of these workforce reductions, or "saves," through retirements and attrition, with the rest coming from layoffs. The reductions would be staged over several years.

While announcements of in-market bank mergers were generally well-received by the stock market, some observers felt that aggressive cost cutting entailed certain risks. As one bank executive commented: "Once you get (a bank's efficiency ratio) down much further than 55%, what I am afraid happens is that you get a trade-off for service. And if your service slips, that's going to impact your revenue side."[13]

Beyond the anticipated cost savings, the merger would also produce a much larger bank, and therefore allow shareholders to realize the potential benefits of increased scale and scope that Shipley envisioned. A merged Chemical-Chase would be the largest commercial bank in the United States, and the fourth-largest bank in the world. On a pro forma basis, as of June 30,

---

[12]See Patrick J. Cusatis, James A. Miles, and J. Randall Woolridge, "Restructuring Through Spinoffs: The Stock Market Evidence," *Journal of Financial Economics,* vol. 33, 1993.

[13]Gerry Cameron, CEO of U.S. Bancorp, quoted in *The American Banker,* January 8, 1996, p. 6a.

EXHIBIT 6 Comparables Analysis, December 31, 1994 (dollar amounts in $millions)

	Chemical	Chase	BankAmerica	Nationsbank	First Union	Banc One	J.P. Morgan
Income Statement Data							
Interest income	9,088	8,134	12,384	10,529	5,095	6,437	8,379
Non-interest income	3,597	3,053	4,147	2,597	1,159	1,420	3,536
Interest expense	4,414	4,445	4,842	5,318	2,061	2,249	6,398
Non-interest expense[a]	5,509	4,472	7,512	4,942	2,677	3,847	33,692
Net income	1,294	1,205	2,176	1,609	925	1,005	1,215
EPS	4.64	5.87	5.33	6.12	5.22	2.42	6.02
Performance Ratios							
Return on average assets	0.78%	1.01%	1.08%	1.02%	1.27%	1.15%	0.70%
Return on average common equity	12.32%	15.79%	13.20%	16.10%	17.04%	13.35%	12.90%
Efficiency ratio	63.00%	66.33%	64.27%	62.54%	62.47%	64.60%	66.92%
Non-performing assets as % of total assets	0.66%		1.03%	0.67%	0.72%	0.52%	0.14%
Balance Sheet Data							
Total assets	171,423	114,038	215,475	169,604	77,314	88,923	154,917
Total loans	78,767	63,038	137,222	103,371	53,051	61,096	20,949
Total deposits	96,506	69,956	154,394	100,470	58,958	68,090	43,085
Total liabilities (total debt)	160,711	105,679	196,584	158,593	71,916	81,358	145,349
Risk-based capital ratio —Tier 1	8.20%	8.30%	7.27%	7.43%	7.76%	9.93%	9.60%
—Total	12.35%	12.78%	11.69%	11.47%	12.94%	13.33%	14.20%
Market Data							
Common stock—High	42.13	40.00	50.25	57.38	47.63	44.73	79.38
Price —Low	33.63	30.38	38.38	43.38	39.38	24.13	55.13
Number shares, year end (in millions)	244.5	181.2	371.2	276.4	176.0	396.9	187.7
Market value/share	35.88	34.38	39.50	45.13	41.38	25.38	56.13
Book value/share	37.88	39.28	42.63	39.43	30.66	18.43	46.73
Market-to-book ratio	94.72%	87.51%	92.66%	114.44%	134.95%	137.71%	120.10%
Other							
Headquarters (City/State)	New York, NY	New York, NY	San Francisco, CA	Charlotte, NC	Charlotte, NC	Columbus, OH	New York, NY
Employees	42,130	35,774	98,600	61,484	31,858	48,800	17,055

[a]Non-interest expense reported in this exhibit includes nonrecurring charges; non-interest expense net of nonrecurring charges is reported in Exhibit 11.
Source: Companies' Annual Reports.

EXHIBIT 7   Estimated Impact of Merger between Chemical and Selected Banks

| Target Bank | Estimated Reduction in Noninterest Expense | | Chemical's Ownership at Current Market Price of Common Stock[a] | Impact on Chemical's EPS[b] | Impact on Target's EPS[b] |
	$ Millions	As % of Target's Premerger Expenses			
Chase	$1,500	34%	59%	31%	44%
BankAmerica	655	13	40	8	12
NationsBank	539	10	45	9	10
First Union[c]	185	7	60	3	7
Banc One	350	10	51	(1)	18
J.P. Morgan	587	15	50	(2)	34

[a]Assumes Chemical's common stock price is $53.50.

[b]1995 pro forma full-year impact of expense reductions based on consensus analyst EPS forecasts.

[c]Shown before consolidation of First Fidelity.

Source: Casewriter estimates.

EXHIBIT 8   Targeted Merger Saves, Pre-Tax (dollar amounts in $ millions)

Business Unit	Planned Saves as Percent of Combined Expense Base[a]	Forecasted Dollar Savings	Reduction In FTEs[b]
Global Bank	19%	$560	3,600
Global Services	12%	$150	1,400
Tri-State Regional	16%	$250	2,600
National Consumer	16%	$280	2,700
TCB (Texas)	0%	0	0
Total Regional & National Consumer Business	13%	$530	5,300
Central Information Technology & Operations	25%	$240	1,000
Corporate Functions	29%	$190	1,200
Miscellaneous		$30	
Total	**18%**	**$1,700[c]**	**12,500**
Saves as Percent of Smaller Base (Chase)	38%		
One-Time Pre-Tax Restructuring Charges		$1,650	
Related Expenses		$250	
Total		$1,900	

[a]Combined Expense Base equals the sum of total non-interest expense for Chemical and Chase.

[b]Stands for Full-Time Equivalent employees.

[c]This figure reflects a $200 million positive adjustment that management later made to the initial $1.5 billion estimate of merger savings.

EXHIBIT 9 Location of Chemical and Chase Branches Prior to Any Closings

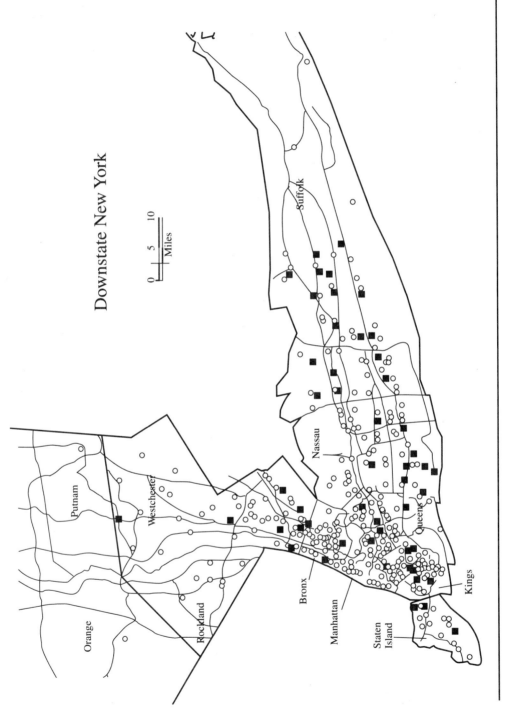

Downstate New York

0 5 10
Miles

Orange

Putnam

Rockland

Westchester

Bronx

Manhattan

Staten
Island

Queens

Kings

Nassau

Suffolk

Source: Company documents.

EXHIBIT 10   1995 Forecast Revenues by Business Line

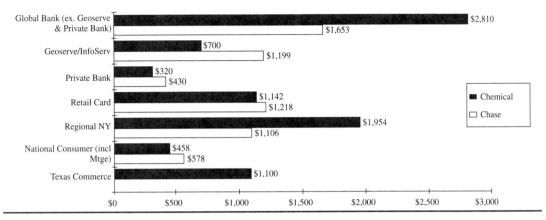

Casewriter note: Geoserve and Infoserv offer operational and information technology support services to wholesale customers.
Source: Company documents.

1995, the banks would have combined total assets of $297.3 billion (surpassing Citicorp with $257 billion in assets) and a total stock market capitalization of $22.9 billion (book value of $20.0 million). Chemical-Chase would have total loans outstanding of $148.9 billion, and total deposits of $163.2 billion.

Shipley's goal was for the merged bank to become the leader in nearly every business in which it operated, including credit cards, mortgage banking, branch banking, national consumer banking, syndicated loan financing, and global capital markets. **Exhibit 10** shows 1995 revenue forecasts for the two banks by line of business. The benefits of increased size, he believed, would eventually translate into higher revenues, especially in the bank's operating services, global wholesale banking, and international private banking businesses. Given the many factors and events that could affect revenues, however, coming up with a precise estimate of the potential revenue enhancements would be extremely difficult. Based on an extremely conservative analysis, the bank estimated that revenues could increase by $20 million in the second year of the merger, and $120 million a year thereafter—but actual revenue increases could be substantially higher than this.

A number of analysts who had recently speculated about a possible Chemical-Chase merger also believed that the merged bank's increased size and diversity would enable it to get a better credit rating, thus lowering the cost of borrowing. Currently Chemical and Chase

were each rated A by *Standard and Poors,* but the analysts believed a merger might raise this to at least AA–.

Over the short-term, however, management recognized that the merger would place some stress on the banks' combined earnings. Revenues would decline to some extent due to overlap of the banks' businesses and client bases in some areas, such as credit cards, deposits, and middle market and corporate lending. Revenue could also be adversely affected by the disruptions that would occur as the banks undertook to integrate their computer systems and ATM networks, temporarily inconveniencing customers. Management estimated that the incremental negative impact of these factors on revenue could be $125 million in the first year of the merger.

In addition, the merged bank would incur a one-time restructuring charge. Management estimated that the total charge would be $1.5 billion. This included $550 million for severance payments, $550 million for real estate–related restructuring costs, and $400 [million] for other costs. Employees that were laid off would be paid severance equal to three weeks' salary for each year of service, plus an additional 26 weeks of pay if they had been with the bank for more than 25 years. Each departing employee would also receive a $2,500 grant to pay for retraining programs.

Ultimately, to justify the merger it would be necessary to show that the banks' stockholders would be made better off. Given the size and complexity of the banks' operations, and the massive changes that were still taking place in the industry, valuing the merger could be difficult. Wall Street analysts currently valued commercial banks using a price-earnings multiple of about 8 times, although a higher multiple could be justified for banks with above-average growth prospects. **Exhibit 11** presents stand-alone financial projections for Chemical and Chase.

Challenges

The new bank would be called the Chase Manhattan Bank, to capitalize on the stronger name recognition that Chase enjoyed internationally. Actually making the merger work presented a number of significant challenges.

Setting the Merger Terms.   Chemical planned to finance its merger with Chase by swapping its common stock for Chase's at a predetermined ratio, as it had also done in its 1991 merger with Manufacturers Hanover. Choosing an appropriate exchange ratio—the number of shares of the acquiring bank offered in exchange for each share of the target bank—involved certain trade-offs. In bank mergers where the acquiring bank was clearly dominant, the exchange ratio would typically be set to give a 30% premium to target bank shareholders (that is, target bank shareholders would be given stock in the acquiring bank worth 30% more in market value than the shares they gave up). In some recent mergers involving a dominant bank the premium had reached 40%. In its recent merger with First Fidelity, First Union had paid a 32% premium above market value to acquire First Fidelity's shares.

In contrast, the premium paid in a "merger of equals" was generally much smaller—as low as 5%—although the acquiring bank would be less well off in the sense of having to relinquish more management control to the target bank. In merging with Manufacturers Hanover, Chemical had paid a premium of only 10% above Manufacturers Hanover's pre-merger announcement stock price.

In the current merger negotiations, setting the exchange ratio turned out to be a complicated, and emotional, issue. The desire of senior management at both Chemical and Chase was to structure the deal so that shareholders and employees of the two banks would share equally in both the rewards and the risks of the merger. Shipley believed that a lower acquisition premium made it easier for management to be objective in deciding which people and assets to retain when the banks were put together; it would also facilitate more equitable sharing of management control.

In general, the exchange ratio in a bank merger was the product of negotiation between the merging banks. The healthier and better capitalized bank, or the bank that made the greater contribution to the merger benefits, would be negotiating from a position of greater strength. The exchange ratio would therefore likely reflect a number of characteristics of the two banks, including size, profitability, asset quality, and the contribution to total cost savings or revenue growth projected under the merger. **Exhibit 12** shows the stock price history of Chemical and Chase, and **Exhibit 13** shows ten-year financial summaries for the two banks.

Merger Integration.   The task of integrating the two banks would pose a major challenge. First, it would be necessary to decide which of the two banks' distinct systems and technologies should be retained for the merged bank. For example, each bank's retail branch network had its own particular check-clearing system, but only one of these systems could be used once the two branch networks were merged. Similar choices had to be made with respect to deposits systems, bank statements, ATMs, and literally hundreds of other systems. The integration of these systems would have to proceed smoothly to avoid inconveniencing the banks' customers. (The bank adopted the motto: "This is our merger, not our customers' merger.")

It would also be necessary to decide how the planned layoffs, branch closings, back office eliminations, and asset disposals should be divided between the two banks. The decision was complicated. On the one hand, the goal of producing a more competitive bank would be best served by retaining only the best people and the best assets. On the other hand, one bank could not appear to be dominant in this process if this were truly to be a "merger of equals," and in many cases the choice would not be obvious (as, for example, when a Chase branch and a Chemical branch both occupied the same city block). Shipley believed it would be very difficult to cut costs and grow revenues according to plan if employees of the acquired bank felt inferior or "second-class."

The integration would be overseen by Chemical's senior vice-chairman, Ed Miller, with the primary support of the bank's chief administrative officer, Joseph Sponholz. The process would take place in several stages, starting with the formation of "mapping" teams—groups of managers from both banks who would collect information necessary to plan the integration. The integration process would be tracked closely using a computer software program called the Merger Overview Model ("MOM"). This model would provide a precise timetable for implementing the proposed merger saves and system integrations.

MOM was extraordinarily complex. Each key event or "milestone" that was planned as part of the integration was precisely noted on a timeline that stretched from August 1995 through December 1998. MOM contemplated more than 3,300 major milestones in all, and planned to complete three-quarters of them by the end of 1996. MOM also explicitly recognized the thousands of "interdependencies" that were present in the integration plan. For example, the banks' ATM machines could not be fully integrated until a single software system was adopted for processing ATM transactions. Similarly, retail branch offices could not be combined until the banks agreed on a uniform check-clearing system. Given such interdependencies, if a single milestone were missed, the entire integration schedule could be disrupted. **Exhibit 14** shows a condensed graphical representation of MOM.

It would also be necessary to integrate senior management of the two banks. Shipley would be appointed chairman and chief executive officer of the new bank, while Labrecque would become president and chief operating officer. Other senior management appointments also had to be decided.

Some industry observers felt that merging Chemical and Chase would be more challenging than merging Chemical and Manufacturers had been. Chemical and Chase had been competitors for over 200 years and they had distinct corporate cultures.

Impact on Employees.   The merger could create morale problems. Both banks had downsized their workforces over the past three years, and the prospect of additional workforce reductions could generate anxiety and ill will among employees.

A merger would affect the well-being of Chemical and Chase employees in another important way. In 1994, both banks had adopted broad-based stock option plans for all of their full- and part-time employees. Approximately 20 million options had been granted initially under Chemical's plan, at an exercise price of $40.50, and 32.5 million such options were outstanding at the end of 1994, with exercise prices ranging from $30.77–$40.50. Under Chase's option plan, 13.2 million options were outstanding at the end of 1994, with exercise prices ranging from $32.00–$38.50. These two plans would have to be integrated somehow if the banks merged.

Given the size of the merger, and the public's interest in corporate downsizing, it was likely that any layoffs would be very closely scrutinized by the news media.

Other Issues.   There were a number of other issues that had to be addressed as well.

If the merger cost savings and revenue enhancements materialized as forecasted, the bank would accumulate significant cash in excess of regulatory capital requirements over the next few years. Management therefore had to decide what to do with this cash. One possibility was to finance a stock buyback program.

If management wished to account for the merger as a nontaxable "pooling" transaction, however, SEC rules limited the number of shares that could be repurchased (by Chemical or Chase) in the two years prior to the merger and 180 days after the merger. Management estimated that the merged bank could repurchase up to 10 percent of the shares issued in the deal without violating pooling rules. If the merger did not qualify for pooling treatment, then it would have to be accounted for as a "purchase" transaction, and the difference between the acquisition price and the book value of Chase stock acquired would have to be amortized over 25 years as "goodwill."

The merger would have to be approved by various regulatory agencies, including the Federal Reserve Board and the New York State Banking Department.

The merger could also meet with resistance from some community activists. Under the 1977 Community Reinvestment Act, banks were required to meet the credit needs of the communities that they served. Some community activist groups were critical of Chase's lending record with low-income and minority customers, and could seek to legally block a merger. To meet the concerns of these groups, Chemical and Chase were prepared to commit up to $20 billion for community investment if they merged.

Finally, it was necessary to decide what information about the anticipated merger benefits should be disclosed to Wall Street analysts and investors. In the earlier merger with Manufacturers Hanover, management had provided a fairly detailed breakdown of anticipated expense reductions and revenue enhancements by product line and business. At the time, it had been management's hope that by providing this level of disclosure, the benefits of the merger would be reflected more quickly (and accurately) in the bank's stock price.

EXHIBIT 11 Stand-Alone Financial Projections: Chemical (millions of dollars, except per share amounts)

	1994	1995	1996	1997	1998	1999	2000
Total Revenues	**8,272**	**8,404**	**8,800**	**9,394**	**9,936**	**10,510**	**11,119**
Expenses excluding ORE	5,159	4,959	4,943	5,185	5,433	5,698	5,953
Income Before Provision	**3,113**	**3,445**	**3,858**	**4,209**	**4,503**	**4,821**	**5,166**
Provision	550	500	650	750	800	850	900
ORE	41	(12)	17	17	17	17	17
NEBT	2,522	2,957	3,191	3,442	3,686	3,954	4,249
Taxes	1,046	1,141	1,244	1,340	1,438	1,542	1,657
Operating Income	**1,476**	**1,816**	**1,946**	**2,099**	**2,248**	**2,412**	**2,592**
Extraordinary	(180)	(11)	0	0	0	0	0
Reported Income	**1,296**	**1,805**	**1,946**	**2,099**	**2,248**	**2,412**	**2,592**
Preferred dividends	138	100	100	100	100	100	100
Net Income Applicable to Common	**$1,158**	**$1,705**	**$1,846**	**$1,999**	**$2,148**	**$2,312**	**$2,492**
Common equity[a]	$9,262	$10,730	$11,930	$13,229	$14,626	$16,128	$17,748
Period-end assets	171,423	178,655	188,655	198,655	208,588	219,017	229,968
Period-end loans	78,767	88,000	94,000	102,000	106,774	111,780	117,016
Average shares[a]	249.3	260.9	260.9	260.9	260.9	260.9	260.9

[a]Assumes constant fully diluted shares of 261 million and no dividend reinvestment plan.
Source: Casewriter analysis based on various analysts' estimates.

EXHIBIT 11 (*concluded*) Stand-Alone Financial Projections: Chase (millions of dollars, except per share amounts)

	1994	1995	1996	1997	1998	1999	2000
Total Revenues	**6,659**	**6,525**	**7,014**	**7,434**	**7,880**	**8,351**	**8,856**
Expenses excluding Savings and ORE	4,308	4,457	4,600	4,768	4,943	5,124	5,313
Focus savings	0	0	(400)	(400)	(400)	(400)	(400)
Net expenses	4,308	4,457	4,200	4,368	4,543	4,724	4,913
Income Before Provision	**2,351**	**2,068**	**2,814**	**3,067**	**3,336**	**3,627**	**3,943**
Provision	500	360	450	500	525	546	567
ORE	7	(30)	0	0	0	0	0
NEBT	1,844	1,738	2,364	2,567	2,811	3,081	3,376
Taxes	589	695	945	1,026	1,124	1,234	1,351
Operating Income	**1,255**	**1,043**	**1,419**	**1,542**	**1,687**	**1,847**	**2,025**
Extraordinary	(50)	(240)	0	0	0	0	0
Reported Income	**1,205**	**803**	**1,419**	**1,541**	**1,687**	**1,847**	**2,025**
Preferred dividends	127	123	123	123	123	123	123
Net Income Applicable to Common	**$1,078**	**$680**	**$1,296**	**$1,419**	**$1,564**	**$1,724**	**$1,902**
Common equity[a]	$6,959	$7,649	$8,491	$9,413	$10,430	$11,550	$12,787
Period-end assets	114,038	127,007	134,922	142,462	150,385	158,777	167,674
Period-end loans	63,038	66,639	70,446	74,471	78,725	83,222	87,977
Average shares[a]	183.6	189.9	189.9	189.9	189.9	189.9	189.9

[a]Assumes constant fully diluted shares of 261 million and no dividend reinvestment plan.

Source: Casewriter analysis based on various analysts' estimates.

EXHIBIT 12   Common Stock Price Histories

Month-End	Chemical	Chase
Jan 94	39.500	36.130
Feb 94	37.250	32.630
Mar 94	36.380	32.250
Apr 94	34.750	34.000
May 94	38.380	37.750
Jun 94	38.500	38.250
Jul 94	38.380	36.880
Aug 94	38.750	37.750
Sept 94	35.000	34.630
Oct 94	38.000	36.000
Nov 94	36.380	35.630
Dec 94	35.880	34.380
Jan 95	39.000	33.130
Feb 95	40.130	35.880
Mar 95	37.750	35.630
Apr 95	41.750	43.750
May 95	46.130	46.250
Jun 95	47.250	47.000
Jul 95	51.630	53.630

Source: Company documents.

The Decision

Shipley believed that a Chemical-Chase merger made good strategic sense, but the stakes involved were enormous, and he was prepared to call the merger off if an acceptable set of deal terms could not be reached. Intensive negotiations between the two banks had been going on for several weeks. Even though both banks had considerable experience in bank mergers, the decisions that had to be made were complicated.

As he drove home, Shipley reviewed the many questions that had come up during the day's discussions. How should the exchange ratio be set? Were the targeted cost savings achievable? How would the layoffs, branch closings, and other expense reductions impact the two banks? How would the merger affect the banks' combined stock prices—and what could the banks do to ensure that Wall Street understood the value that the merger would create?

More fundamentally, was Chase truly the best merger partner for Chemical? From Chemical's perspective, one option was simply to wait. The bank was not under any immediate pressure to cut costs, and its recent financial performance had been solid. Moreover, the task of implementing the earlier merger with Manufacturers Hanover had, over the past four years, placed non-trivial demands on management's time and on the bank's resources. Undertaking a new merger at this time—on a much larger scale than the first—might impose a significant strain on the organization. Finally, the pace of merger activity and consolidation in the U.S. banking industry had been quite high during the past year, and this had put upward pressure on acquisition premiums paid in bank mergers.[14] On the other hand, as more and more large banks were acquired, fewer attractive merger opportunities would remain for Chemical if it chose to wait. Chase might even merge with some other bank if Chemical did not proceed with its own bid; recently, the chief financial officer of NationsBank had publicly expressed some interest in Chase as a potential merger partner.

---

[14]In 1995, the average price paid to acquire one share of common stock in a target bank was about 15.7 times the bank's earnings-per-share for the most recent twelve months, up from 14.4 times in 1994.

EXHIBIT 13   Chemical, Ten-Year Financial Summary, 1985–1994 (dollar amounts in $millions)

	1994	1993	1992	1991[a]	1990	1989	1988	1987	1986	1985
Income Statement Data										
Interest Income	9,088	8,403	9,148	11,282	6,511	6,823	6,220	5,470	4,520	4,883
Non-interest Income	3,597	4,024	3,026	2,846	1,456	1,404	1,424	1,285	968	768
Interest Expense	4,414	3,767	4,550	7,169	4,460	4,806	3,913	3,500	2,850	3,311
Non-interest Expense	5,509	5,293	4,930	5,324	2,623	2,740	2,460	2,476	1,708	1,532
Provision for loan losses	550	1,259	1,365	1,345	537	1,135	364	1,492	439	281
Net Income	1,294	1,604	1,086	154	291	(482)	754	(854)	402	390
Restructuring charge	308	158	0	625	52	0	11	135	0	0
EPS (incl. extraordinary income and charges)	4.64	5.63	3.90	0.11	2.38	(8.29)	12.02	(16.68)	7.57	7.33
Performance Ratios										
Return on Average Assets	0.78%	1.11%	0.78%	0.11%	0.37%	n.m.	0.99%	n.m.	0.70%	0.70%
Return on Average Common Equity	12.32%	16.66%	12.36%	0.33%	7.08%	n.m.	27.74%	n.m.	14.22%	15.06%
Efficiency Ratio	63%	58%	61%	65%	75%	80%	66%	76%	65%	65%
Non-performing assets as % of total assets	0.66%	2.35%	4.36%	4.43%	4.50%	4.59%	n.a.	n.a.	n.a.	n.a.
Balance Sheet Data										
Total Assets	171,423	149,888	139,655	138,930	73,019	71,513	67,349	78,189	60,564	56,990
Total Loans	78,767	75,381	82,010	84,237	45,131	44,512	41,590	49,800	39,425	39,096
Total Deposits	96,506	98,277	94,173	92,950	48,951	50,151	47,966	55,509	39,055	34,505
Total Liabilities (Total Debt)	160,711	138,724	129,084	131,649	69,112	67,808	63,382	75,186	63,382	75,186
Market Data										
Common Stock Price, Year-End	35.88	40.13	38.63	21.25	10.75	29.88	31.00	21.38	42.25	45.38
Other										
Employees	42,130	41,567	39,687	43,169	26,689	29,139	27,225	28,597	20,993	19,691

n.m. = ratio is not meaningful because earnings are negative.

n.a. – data are not available.

[a]Chemical merged with Manufacturers Hanover in December 1991. Financials for prior years shown in the exhibit have not been restated for the effects of the merger.

Source: Company annual reports.

EXHIBIT 13 (*concluded*) **Chase, Ten-Year Financial Summary, 1985–1994 (dollar amounts in $millions)**

	1994	1993	1992	1991	1990	1989	1988	1987	1986	1985
Income Statement Data										
Interest Income	8,134	8,468	8,705	9,638	11,572	11,959	10,112	8,839	7,717	8,418
Non-interest Income	3,053	2,949	2,420	2,202	2,100	1,945	2,252	1,906	1,743	1,316
Interest Expense	4,445	4,605	5,141	6,293	8,384	8,934	6,850	5,858	4,721	5,669
Non-interest Expense	4,472	4,520	3,939	3,818	4,119	3,702	3,431	3,455	3,301	2,732
Provision for loan losses	500	1,561	1,220	1,085	1,300	1,737	750	2,150	595	435
Net Income	1,205	966	639	520	(334)	(665)	1,059	(895)	585	565
Restructuring charge	0	205	0	0	220	38	48	63	30	0
EPS (incl. extraordinary income and charges)	5.87	4.79	3.46	3.12	(3.31)	(7.94)	11.55	(11.56)	6.63	6.39
Performance Ratios										
Return on Average Assets	1.01%	0.94%	0.64%	0.52%	n.m.	n.m.	1.11%	n.m.	0.65%	0.65%
Return on Average Common Equity	15.79%	14.59%	11.14%	10.49%	n.m.	n.m.	27.75%	n.m.	13.29%	13.64%
Efficiency Ratio	66.33%	66.35%	65.83%	68.83%	77.89%	74.49%	62.22%	70.69%	69.65%	67.21%
Non-performing assets as % of total assets	0.6%	1.0%	4.0%	4.4%	4.6%	33.6%	4.2%	4.3%	2.0%	2.33%
Balance Sheet Data										
Total Assets	114,038	102,103	95,862	98,197	98,064	107,369	97,455	99,206	94,838	87,685
Total Loans	63,038	60,493	62,558	67,785	74,727	76,692	69,602	67,979	66,220	61,931
Total Deposits	69,956	71,509	67,224	71,517	70,713	69,073	64,057	68,578	66,003	61,353
Total Liabilities (Total Debt)	105,679	93,981	89,298	92,820	93,279	102,371	92,495	95,220	89,822	83,227
Market Data										
Common Stock Price, Year-End	34.38	33.88	28.50	17.25	10.50	34.75	28.63	22.13	35.63	36.31
Other										
Employees	35,774	34,390	34,540	36,210	38,470	41,610	41,570	42,390	47,480	46,450

n.m. = ratio is not meaningful because earnings are negative.

n.a. – data are not available.

Source: Company annual reports.

EXHIBIT 14   Merger Overview Model

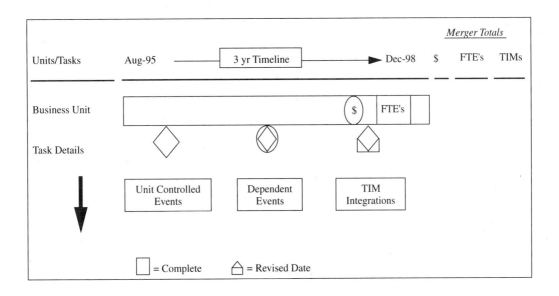

Source: Company documents.

CASE 2
BANC ONE CORPORATION ASSET AND LIABILITY MANAGEMENT

[Derivatives are] simply another Wall Street-developed house of cards.

—Representative Joseph Kennedy[1]

You can call it [the use of derivatives] whatever you want, but in my book it's gambling.

—Representative Henry Gonzalez
Chairman, House Banking Committee[2]

Our use of derivatives is just one more step in the evolution of banking.

—John B. McCoy
Chairman and CEO, Banc One Corporation

On November 15, 1993, Dick Lodge, Banc One Corporation's (Banc One's) chief investment officer (CIO), gathered his notes and headed for a meeting with John B. McCoy, Banc One's chairman and CEO. On the way, he recalled the lunchtime conversation on the golf course six weeks earlier, during which McCoy had first voiced concern over Banc One's falling share price—from a high of $48 3/4 in April 1993 to just $36 3/4 (see **Exhibit 1**). McCoy attributed the decline to investor concern over Banc One's large and growing interest rate derivatives portfolio. During their discussion in September, McCoy had asked Lodge, who was responsible for managing the bank's investment and derivatives portfolio, to think about ways to deal with this problem.

McCoy had been prompted into action not only by the continued price decline, but also by the comments of equity analysts who covered Banc One:

"The increased use of interest rate swaps is creating some sizable distortions in reported earnings, reported earning assets, margins, and the historical measure of return on assets . . . Were Banc One to include [swaps] in reported earning assets, the adjusted level would be 26% higher than is currently reported . . . Given its large position in swap[s], Banc One overstates its margin by 1.31% [and its] return on assets in excess of 0.20% . . . Adjusted for [swaps], Banc One's tangible equity-to-asset ratio would decline by 1.55%."[3]

"Banc One's investors are uncomfortable with so much derivatives exposure. Buyers of regional banks do not expect heavy derivatives involvement . . . Heavy swaps usage clouds Banc One's financial image [and is] extremely confusing . . . It is virtually impossible for anyone on the outside to assess the risks being assumed."[4]

What made this situation more perplexing was that Banc One already had attempted to preempt concern over its growing derivatives portfolio. Along with its second-quarter results, it distributed a booklet detailing its asset and liability management policies and describing its derivatives portfolio, which had grown during the quarter from $23.4 billion to $31.5 billion in notional

Professors Ben Esty and Peter Tufano and Research Assistant Jonathan S. Headley prepared this case as the basis for class discussion rather than to illustrate either effective or ineffective handling of an administrative situation.
Copyright © 1994 by the President and Fellows of Harvard College. To order copies, call (617) 495–6117 or write the Publishing Division, Harvard Business School, Boston, MA 02163. No part of this publication may be reproduced, stored in a retrieval system, used in a spreadsheet, or transmitted in any form or by any means—electronic, mechanical, photocopying, recording, or otherwise—without the permission of Harvard Business School.

[1]As quoted by Barbara A. Rehm, "Regulators Try to Reassure Lawmakers on Swaps," *American Banker,* October 29, 1993, p. 3.
[2]Ibid.
[3]David N. Pringle, "Swaps Revisited, or, How I Learned to Stop Worrying and Love the Derivative," Lazard Frères Equity Research, October 26, 1993, pp. 4–14.
[4]George Salem, "Rating for Banc One Reduced to Hold from Buy Based on Confusion from Heavy Exposure to Interest Rate Swaps," Prudential Securities, November 1993, p. 2, as quoted by First Call.

EXHIBIT 1   Banc One Corporation, Common Stock Price and the Price of Other Regional Bank Stocks, January 4, 1993, through November 14, 1993

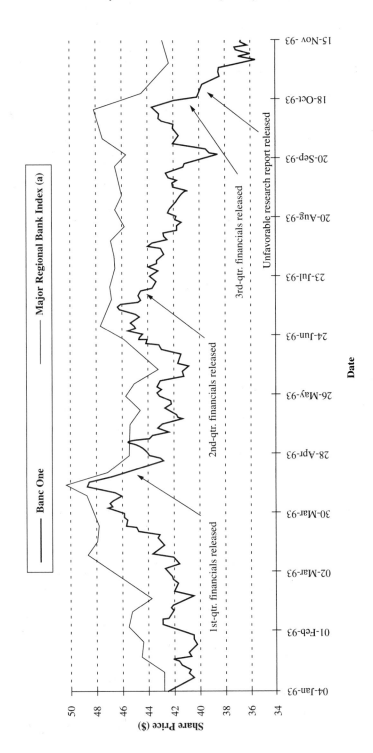

(a) The major regional bank index is an equal-weighted index of 17 banks including Banc One.

Sources: Datasheet, Standard & Poor's Corporation.

principal.[5] Lodge and others believed that the information in the booklet would help assuage any investor's concerns. Yet, given these kinds of comments from the analysts, the message was clearly not getting through.

In Lodge's mind, there was a simple explanation for the large size of Banc One's derivatives portfolio: swaps were attractive investments that lowered the bank's exposure to movements in interest rates. Why the market was penalizing Banc One for something that *reduced* its exposure to risk remained a mystery to him. Earlier in the year, Lodge had expressed his puzzlement to a reporter: "Why in the world more banks don't look at interest rate swaps . . . I don't know. It's not an esoteric phenomenon anymore."[6] Nevertheless, he knew that McCoy attributed the decline to the derivatives portfolio and wanted to discuss alternatives for dealing with the situation.

Banc One Corporation[7]

Banc One Corporation, headquartered in Columbus, Ohio, truly epitomized the spirit of regional banking. With $76.5 billion in assets, it was the largest bank holding company based in Ohio and the eighth largest in the country. Unlike the more traditional bank holding company structure, in which the parent corporation controlled subsidiary banks, Banc One had a three-tiered organizational structure operating across 12 states. The parent, Banc One Corporation, controlled 5 state bank holding companies (in Arizona, Indiana, Ohio, Texas, and Wisconsin), which in turn owned 42 subsidiary banks, or "affiliates." Through its Regional Affiliate Group, Banc One owned another 36 subsidiary banks— for a total of 78 banking affiliates. In addition to its banking affiliates, Banc One controlled 10 nonbanking organizations in various business ranging from insurance to venture capital to data processing.

For its banking business, Banc One had a very well defined, three-pronged strategy: concentrate on retail and middle-market commercial customers; use technology to enhance customer service and to assist in the management of banking affiliates; and grow rapidly by acquiring profitable banks.

Since 1969, it had completed 76 acquisitions involving 139 banks. In just the 10 years since 1982, it had completed 50 acquisitions, making it one of the top 10 corporate acquirers in the country.[8] As of November 1993, Banc One had ten pending acquisitions that would bring an additional $9 billion in assets to the corporation. One of the largest pending acquisitions was Liberty National Bancorp, a bank holding company in Louisville, Kentucky with $4.7 billion in assets.

This deal highlighted many of the principles that guided Banc One's acquisitions. The target, Liberty National, had a strong retail focus, had a solid management team, and was the market leader. In addition, the deal was structured like most of its previous acquisitions: it would be accounted for as a pooling of interests, be paid for with stock, and consist of a tiered offer that depended on the value of Banc One's stock price. The terms of the Liberty National Bancorp deal were as follows:

Banc One's stock price	Ratio of Banc One's shares to Liberty National's shares
under $41.57	0.8421
$41.57 to $44.00	$35.00 worth of stock
above $44.00	0.7954

As of mid-November, Banc One's stock was trading near the "walkaway" price of $34.55. If it was below $34.55 in the second quarter of 1994, when the deal was expected to be consummated, one of two things would happen. Either Liberty National would cancel the deal or Banc One would end up using stock that it felt was undervalued to pay for the deal. Thus, a low stock price would either bring Banc One's acquisition program to a halt or cause it to violate one of its cardinal rules of acquisitions: acquisitions should not be dilutive. According to John McCoy, Banc One has "very strong pricing

---

[5]"Notional" referred to the fictional principal amount on which swap payments were based. For example, if a swap counterparty paid a fixed 7% rate on a swap with a notional value of $100 million, its payment would be $7 million. Likewise, the party paying a floating rate would multiply the prevailing floating-rate index by the notional amount to calculate its payment.

[6]Steven Lipin, "Many Banks Change Strategies to Manage Rate Risk," *The Wall Street Journal,* February 10, 1993, p. B4.

[7]See the HBS cases "Banc One Corporation 1989" (390–029), "Banc One Corporation 1989 (Abridged)" (390–208), and "Banc One Corporation 1991" (392–018) for details on the management and history of Banc One.

[8]Grimm's Mergerstat Review.

discipline. We just don't do dilutive acquisitions."[9] William Boardman, an Executive Vice President at Banc One, elaborated: "When we talk to prospects, we tell them we want the deal to be non-dilutive when we do it, but that we also want it to be non-dilutive next year, and the year after that. Basically, what that means is that you have to grow your earnings at the same rate we're [Banc One] growing our earnings."[10]

While a strict set of principles guided Banc One's acquisition strategy, another well-defined set of principles guided its operating strategy. Internally, the operating strategy was known as the "uncommon partnership," which described the relationship among the affiliate banks and the various parts of the corporation. According to this partnership, the corporation decentralized the "people" side of the business and centralized the "paper" side. To capture the local knowledge of customers and markets, Banc One retained existing management in acquisitions and gave affiliate managers complete autonomy in running their banks. In contrast, Banc One centralized all of the affiliates' data processing, record keeping, and back office operations. This centralization fit well with Banc One's growth strategy. According to Boardman, "Growing just to become larger is not part of our strategy. Growing our economies of scale is."[11] The centralization of operations also capitalized on Banc One's vast experience with computer systems.

Over the years, Banc One had invested heavily in technology and information systems to support the uncommon partnership. Starting at the top with John B. McCoy, there was the belief that information was critical to running such a decentralized organization. One of the most important jobs of Banc One was to gather information from and disseminate it to the affiliates using the Management Information and Control System (MICS). This database tracked financial, productivity, and performance data for all affiliates. Every month, affiliates entered into the database their results and their revised budgets. In return, all affiliate presidents received a one-inch-thick report containing comparative statistics ranking all affiliates. The objective of this system was to encourage friendly competition among banking affiliates and to encourage managers to share information about effective banking products and practices.

Although it was an extremely complicated and highly decentralized organization, Banc One had one of the best financial track records of any bank in the country. Compared with the financial performance of the country's 25 largest bank holding companies in the decade since 1982, it had the highest average return on assets, the highest average return on equity, and the highest ratio of common equity to assets. Even more incredible was that Bank One had a string of 24 years of increasing earnings per share; none of the other large banks had a string of more than 7.[12]

Exhibit 2 summarizes Banc One's operating results and financial performance during the period 1983 to 1992.

Asset and Liability Management

A typical U.S. bank's liabilities consisted of floating-rate liabilities (such as federal funds borrowings) and long-term fixed-rate liabilities (such as certificates of deposit, or CDs). Assets included floating-rate assets (such as variable-rate mortgages and loans, as well as floating-rate investments) and long-term fixed-rate assets (such as fixed-rate mortgages and securities.) Asset and liability management involved matching the economic characteristics of a bank's inflows and outflows. For example, a bank could match the maturity of its assets and liabilities. It also could look at the duration, the contractual fixed/floating nature of its commitments, or an estimate of the period in which its commitments would be repriced in response to changes in market rates as the basis upon which to judge just how well it was matched.

Banks' needs to match assets to liabilities arose from their strategic decisions regarding interest rate exposure. If their assets and liabilities were perfectly matched, then a rise or fall in interest rates would have equal and offsetting impacts on both sides of the balance sheet. In principle, perfect matching would leave a bank's earnings or market value unaffected by changes in interest rates. Alternatively, a bank could adjust its portfolio of assets and liabilities to profit when rates rose, but lose when they fell. It could also position itself to make the opposite bet.

In practice, banks typically had relatively more long-term fixed-rate liabilities (such as CDs) than they had

[9]Steve Cucheo, "What's So Good about Banc One?" *ABA Banking Journal* (July 1991): 57.

[10]J. Christopher Svare, "Acquiring for Growth and Profit: The Banc One Experience" *Bank Management* (November 1990): 24.

[11]Cucheo, op. cit.

[12]Banc One Corporation 1992 Annual Report, p. 2.

Exhibit 2 Banc One Corporation, Financial Performance, 1983 through 1992

	Total Assets ($ millions)	Net Income ($ millions)	Net Income Per Share	Return on Average Assets	Return on Common Equity	Stock Price	Total Market Capital ($ millions)	Average Common Equity to Assets	Net Interest Margin (a)	Credit Rating on Senior Debt
1983	$ 6,153	$ 83	$1.16	1.35%	18.42%	$10.66	$802	7.06%	5.78%	AA
1984	8,088	108	1.31	1.33	17.84	11.67	929	7.10	6.30	AA
1985	9,539	130	1.51	1.37	17.77	17.59	1,491	7.37	6.22	AA
1986	16,299	200	1.60	1.23	16.49	17.19	2,082	7.23	5.73	AA
1987	17,538	209	1.64	1.19	15.12	18.04	2,360	7.82	5.80	AA
1988	23,484	340	2.15	1.45	17.69	18.39	2,876	8.12	5.42	AA
1989	25,518	363	2.29	1.42	16.79	26.76	4,239	8.41	5.20	AA
1990	27,654	423	2.51	1.53	16.24	25.23	4,408	9.36	5.33	AA
1991	33,861	530	2.91	1.56	16.58	47.85	8,833	9.16	6.09	AA-
1992	58,249	781	3.28	1.34	16.26	53.13	12,331	8.04	6.22	AA-
1993 1Q	73,868	287	0.83	1.58	18.94	46.20	11,956	8.18	6.57	AA-
2Q	73,686	282	0.81	1.53	17.91	45.00	12,278	8.44	6.30	AA-
3Q	74,226	285	0.82	1.52	17.43	41.50	11,323	8.60	6.22	AA-

(a) Net interest income on a fully taxable equivalent basis expressed as a percentage of average earning assets.

Source: Banc One Corporation.

long-term fixed-rate assets (such as loans). To make up for this shortfall, banks that wished to match assets and liabilities complemented their loan portfolios with fixed-rate investments commonly called balancing assets, such as Treasury securities. By adjusting the characteristics of the balancing assets, a bank could better match its assets to its existing liabilities.

As chief investment officer of Banc One, Dick Lodge managed the firm's portfolio of balancing assets. His staff of approximately 100 people, with 12 engaged in asset and liability management activities, measured the degree to which the bank's assets and liabilities were matched and made profitable investments consistent with the bank's policy of managing its interest rate exposure. Specifically, they had an official mandate to (1) invest funds in conventional investments and derivatives to conserve the funds' principal value yet provide a reasonable rate of return; (2) keep enough funds in liquid investments to allow the bank to react quickly to demands for cash; (3) control the exposure of Banc One's reported earnings to swings in interest rates; and (4) achieve these objectives without unnecessarily increasing the bank's capital requirements.[13]

In carrying out this mandate, Banc One used investments and derivatives as substitutes for one another. For example, if it wanted to increase its share of fixed-return investments, it could sell a floating-rate investment (or borrow at a floating rate) and use the proceeds to buy a three-year fixed-rate Treasury note. The initial net outflow of these two transactions would be zero, but the transactions would increase the relative magnitude of the bank's fixed-rate portfolio. Alternatively, Banc One could enter into an interest rate swap in which it paid a floating rate of interest and received a fixed rate in return. The initial net outflow of such a swap also would be zero. As in the first example, such a transaction would increase the bank's fixed-rate inflows and reduce its periodic net floating-rate inflows. Because the security transactions and the swap produced similar interest rate exposure, they had to be compared on other dimensions, such as yield, credit risk, capital requirements, transaction costs, and liquidity.

Defining and Measuring Interest Rate Exposure.
Banc One, like other banks, defined its exposure to interest rate risk by calculating its earnings sensitivity, or the impact of interest rate changes on reported earnings. For example, if a gradual 1% upward shift in interest rates during the year increased that year's base earnings by 5%, the bank would have an earnings sensitivity of 5%. If earnings sensitivity was positive, the bank was said to be *asset sensitive* (i.e., the interest rate on assets reset more quickly than liabilities, resulting in increased income if rates rose). If earnings sensitivity was negative, the bank was said to be *liability sensitive* (i.e., liabilities reset more quickly than assets, resulting in a decrease in income if rates rose). If the bank had a 0% earnings sensitivity, then an upward or downward shift in interest rates would have no effect on its earnings.

Like many banks, Banc One's basic portfolio (excluding its balancing assets) was asset sensitive. Its asset sensitivity arose because a large proportion of its assets, such as commercial loans, were indexed to the prime rate and therefore varied contractually with market rates. However, the bank's liabilities included mostly fixed-rate items such as fixed-rate CDs as well as "sticky-fixed" savings and demand deposits whose rates changed much more slowly than market indices. Banc One's relative overabundance of fixed-rate liabilities would make its earnings increase as rates rose. This natural asset-sensitivity was exacerbated by its acquisition program because many of the banks it acquired were highly asset sensitive.

Over the years, Banc One's evolving program to measure interest rate risk mirrored best practice in the U.S. banking industry. Prior to the 1980s, the bank did not precisely measure its exposure to changes in interest rates. Instead, it generally avoided investing in longer-maturity securities, feeling that these investments could add undue risk to the liquidity of its investment portfolio. By the early 1980s, it had become clear to Banc One's management that measuring interest rate risk was a critical task. The second oil shock of the 1970s had increased the level and volatility of interest rates. For example, the prime rate soared to more than 20% in late 1980, twice

---

[13]U.S. regulation demanded that banks hold capital against a fraction of their risk-adjusted assets. In principle, capital requirements, as set out by law, differed by riskiness of investments. For example, Banc One was required to hold no capital against its investments in U.S. Treasury securities, but 50¢ on each dollar invested in municipal revenue bonds. The U.S. risk-based capital regulation was consistent with the Basel Accord, a 1988 agreement among the major industrialized nations.

the average for the 1970s and four times as large as the average in the 1960s. In 1980 alone, the prime rose to 19.8% in April, fell to 11.1% in August and rebounded to more than 20% at the close of the year. To determine the bank's exposure to interest rate movements in this new, more volatile interest rate environment, Banc One began measuring its *maturity gap* in 1981.

Maturity gap analysis compared the difference in maturity between assets and liabilities, adjusted for their repricing interval. Repricing interval referred to the amount of time over which the interest rate on an individual contract remained fixed. For example, a three-year loan with a rate reset after year one would have a repricing-adjusted maturity of one year. Banc One grouped its assets and liabilities into categories, or "buckets," on the basis of their repricing-adjusted maturities (less than 3 months, 3 to 6 months, 6 to 12 months, and more than 12 months.) The maturity gap for each category was the dollar value of assets less liabilities. If the bank made short-term floating-rate loans funded by long-term fixed-rate deposits, it would have a large positive maturity gap in the shorter categories and a large negative maturity gap in the longer periods.

The maturity gaps could then be used to predict how the bank's net interest margin (the difference between the weighted average interest rate received on assets and the weighted average interest rate paid on liabilities)—and therefore earnings—would be affected by changes in interest rates. For example, if interest rates dropped sharply, a large positive maturity gap for the short maturity buckets would predict a drop in interest income and therefore earnings, because the bank would immediately receive lower rates on its loans while still paying higher fixed rates on its deposits.

Unfortunately, implementing the initial maturity gap measurement program was extremely time consuming. By the time each gap report was collected from the affiliates, consolidated, and analyzed, the information was dated. Lodge himself constructed the first gap management report in 1981, and it took almost a year to complete.

In 1984, Banc One began using asset and liability simulations as a more accurate method to measure its exposure to interest rates. By using exact asset and liability portfolios rather than grouping each asset or liability according to its repricing interval, Banc One was able to measure how interest rate changes would affect

earnings. To do so, it created an "on-line balance sheet" that contained up-to-date information on its assets and liabilities, which complemented the MICS process. The key features of each contract, including principal amounts, interest rates, maturity dates, and any amortization schedules of assets and liabilities, were recorded. Then, Banc One used historical data to estimate such items as the maturity of demand-deposit (checking) accounts, the speed with which its bank managers would reprice deposits and loans in response to interest rate shifts, and the rate at which its borrowers might refinance fixed-rate loans if rates dropped.

Once the model was complete, Banc One could simulate how any shift in interest rates would affect its balance sheet and earnings, as well as run sensitivity analyses on its assumptions. Although the model had been refined since 1984, it served as the basis for measuring the bank's interest rate risk and senior management reviewed its predictions monthly. In 1993, this on-line balance sheet was redesigned to include a monthly down-load of each of over 3 million loans or deposits, that is, a discrete asset and liability database on each customer that included prepayment, optionality, and convexity estimates.[14]

Investments for Managing Interest Rate Exposure. Banc One's evolving sophistication in managing interest rate exposure mirrored its sophistication in measuring it. In the early 1980s, it managed its exposure to interest rate risk by adding balancing assets to its investment portfolio until it felt it had enough fixed-rate investments to offset its fixed-rate liabilities. In 1981, 13% and 21% of Banc One's earning assets were money market investments and longer-term securities, respectively. Initially, Banc One invested in short- and medium-term U.S. Treasuries and high-quality municipal bonds. Municipal bonds were an especially attractive investment because prior to 1986, banks could deduct 80% of the interest expense incurred on monies raised to buy them. Because the income earned on the bonds was free of state and federal taxes, banks could enjoy a large after-tax spread on their leveraged municipal bond investments.

In 1983, Banc One began using interest rate swaps as part of its investment portfolio. Originally, swaps were used to lock in high after-tax yields on municipal securities. By buying the municipal bonds, Banc One received an after-tax yield of 9.50%. By then entering

---

[14]All three estimates were merely tools for predicting how the core characteristics (such as maturity, interest rate, etc.) of each of the assets and liabilities would change with any shift in market interest rates.

into an interest rate swap in which it paid a fixed rate of 7.00% and received the London Interbank Offered Rate (LIBOR), a commonly used floating-rate index, it ended up with a net position of receiving LIBOR + 2.50%. The bank's net cash flow from the investment and swap resembled a floating-rate investment with an above-market yield. During the course of 1983 and 1984, Banc One became increasingly comfortable with the use of swaps as a tool to tailor individual investments to suit its needs.

In 1986, Congress passed the Tax Reform Act, which eliminated for banks the deduction of interest expense on the financing for municipal bond investments.[15] Banks turned to other investments that would provide the same high yield they had grown accustomed to receiving. Banc One replaced many of its municipal investments with mortgage-backed securities (MBSs), which were fixed-income investments whose payment stream was backed by pools of mortgage loans and which were typically guaranteed by the federal government. MBSs provided a slightly lower promised after-tax yield than did municipal bonds and carried an additional risk of prepayment. If interest rates fell, borrowers typically refinanced their mortgages by prepaying their existing mortgages. The owner of a pool of mortgages was forced to reinvest precisely when market yields were relatively low and was left with a submarket yield when rates rose.

In 1983, Wall Street created a new type of mortgage security: the CMO, or collateralized mortgage obligation. CMOs took a pool of mortgage loans and carved the principal and interest outflows into a set of different securities, or tranches. The tranches differed from one another only in their priority for repayments of principal. For example, the first tranche of a CMO would receive all of the mortgage prepayments until its principal was returned to its holders. At that point, the second tranche would begin to receive prepayments until its principal was fully paid out, and so on. With a large pool of mortgages, investors could statistically estimate the likely speed of prepayment and therefore the likely time at which each tranche would be fully paid down and stop paying interest. Each tranche paid a different yield to compensate for the various amount of prepayment risk a buyer faced, as well as for the different average life of the investments. By investing in CMOs, Banc One could still receive the high yields associated

with mortgage securities, assuming it was comfortable with the prepayment risk it would bear. In 1993, Banc One had $4.5 billion invested in CMOs, or about a third of their investment portfolio. Earlier in the 1980s, as much as two-thirds of their investment portfolio was held in CMOs.

Swaps as Synthetic Investments.   After using swaps in the mid-1980s to tailor cash flows of individual municipal investments, Banc One realized that it could also use swaps as a proxy for some of its conventional fixed-rate investments. Instead of investing in medium-term U.S. Treasury obligations, it could simply enter into a medium-term receive-fixed swap and put its money into short-term floating-rate cash equivalents. There were several advantages of this "synthetic investment" over conventional investments.

First, the swap greatly improved the bank's liquidity. Banks need cash to accommodate customer withdrawals and to repay existing liabilities, such as CDs, as they mature. Investing in long-dated securities could increase a bank's yield, but if the bank needed to raise cash suddenly, these investments might not be easily liquidated or their liquidation might expose the bank to a large loss in principal. With a swap, the bank could invest in short-term, highly liquid securities with stable principal values. By layering a receive-fixed swap onto this investment, the bank could obtain the economics of the longer-term investment, while still enjoying the high liquidity of the short-term instrument.

Second, unlike investments and borrowings, swaps were off-balance-sheet transactions. If Banc One were to buy a fixed-rate bond and sell a floating-rate security, both would appear on its balance sheet, and the spread between the two would appear as income. However, if it was to enter into a receive-fixed swap with the same cash flow implications, the swap would not appear as either an asset or liability, but would be disclosed only in footnotes to the financial statements. Yet the current net income or loss from the swap transaction still would appear on its income statement. This accounting treatment would tend to overstate traditional profitability measures such as a bank's return on assets in comparison to the identical securities transactions.

Finally, in comparison to a conventional securities investment, swaps could also reduce the amount of capital needed to meet regulatory requirements. These minimum

---

[15]For individuals, the interest paid on debt incurred to purchase tax-exempt obligations was never deductible.

capital requirements grew out of an international agreement, the Basel Accord, signed by the central bankers of the major industrialized countries. In agreement with the Accord, U.S. banking regulators implemented risk-based capital standards beginning in December 1990. The new regulations dictated the amount of capital banks needed to hold as a function of their total risk-based assets.[16] As of year-end 1992, U.S. regulators raised the minimum capital levels and strengthened their power to close institutions that failed to meet these minimums.

Stricter capital standards led banks to prefer assets with lower capital requirements, all else being equal. Some observers attributed the rising growth in bank investments in Treasury securities to their zero risk weighting in the calculation of risk-adjusted assets. Under the capital guidelines, swaps contributed little to the risk-adjusted assets against which the bank had to hold capital.[17] Were a bank to create exposure similar to the swap using securities (other than U.S. Treasury securities), its need to hold capital would be 20% to 100% of the principal value of the assets.[18]

During the late 1980s, Banc One began replacing many of its maturing conventional investments with synthetic investments. As part of this trend, it began to investigate whether it could create a synthetic CMO, which would have the advantages of other swaps, yet deliver the risk/return characteristics of CMO investments. Specifically, a synthetic CMO would allow Banc One to enjoy high yields in exchange for taking on prepayment risk. After a few false starts and discussions with various investment banks, Banc One and its counterparties developed a product called Amortizing Interest Rate Swaps (AIRS).[19]

Because AIRS replicated investments in mortgage securities, they needed to have similar prepayment features. With low interest rates, consumers prepay their mortgages, and mortgage investors receive back their principal. In the AIRS, the notional amount of the swap would be reduced or amortized if interest rates fell. As interest rates declined, the AIRS would amortize faster, thereby leaving the bank to reinvest just when market yields were low. Likewise, when interest rates increased, the maturity of an AIRS would end up longer than expected, thereby leaving the bank with a below-market yield on its investment. In early AIRS, the amortization of the notional principal balance was tied to the performance of a particular pool of actual mortgages, but with later AIRS, the amortization schedule was set by a formula. **Exhibit 3, panel A,** gives the terms for the latter type of AIRS.

As synthetic investments, AIRS produced attractive yields. In these transactions, Banc One would receive a fixed rate of interest and pay LIBOR. In 1993, this fixed rate, called a swap spread, was perhaps 120 basis points over a Treasury security of the same maturity. In comparison, the bank could buy a comparable CMO and receive a yield of 100 basis points over Treasuries. If Banc One was to enter into a standard (nonamortizing) swap of the same term, it might receive a fixed rate of 20 basis points over Treasuries.

With Banc One's mortgage portfolio as well as its investments in CMOs and AIRS, prepayment risk complicated the task of measuring interest rate risk. The embedded options that Banc One sold to its mortgage borrowers, certain depositors, and to its swap counterparties made its earnings sensitivity nonlinear. With a rise in rates, the earnings from its fixed-rate

---

[16]The regulations assigned each asset and some off-balance sheet items a risk weighting from 0% to 100%. The product of the risk weighting times the dollar value of assets in the class determined the dollar value of risk-adjusted assets.

[17]For interest rate swaps with maturities of more than one year, the bank was required to hold capital equal to the swap's market value (if positive) plus .5% of its notional principal times a factor reflecting the counterparty of the swap. This factor was .5 for corporate counterparties and .2 for banks. Thus, if it had a two-year swap with a bank counterparty, with a notional principal amount of $100 million and a current market value of $20,000, Banc One would have to count as risk-adjusted assets [$20,000 + .005($100 million)]*.2, or $104,000.

[18]The risk-adjusted weightings set by the 1992 guidelines included the following:

Cash and U.S. government obligations	0%
Municipal general obligation bonds and agency securities	20%
Municipal revenue bonds	50%
CMOs, mortgage pass-through, and mortgage whole loans	50%
Other loans and other balance sheet assets	100%
Standby letters of credit	100%

[19]These swaps are known also as index amortizing rate swaps.

EXHIBIT 3   Representative Swap Transactions

Panel A: Amortizing Interest Rate Swap (AIRS), September 1993

Notional amount	$500 million
Final maturity (if not amortized early)	3 years
Payment frequency	Quarterly
Banc One pays	3-month LIBOR (3.25% at initiation of swap)
Banc One receives	4.5%
Lockout period	1 year

   (During the lockout period, there is no amortization of the swap.)

Cleanup provision	10% of original notional amount

   (If the notional amount falls to $50 or less through amortization, the swap is canceled.)

Amortization schedule: Each quarter, after the lockout period, the notional principal of the swap is reduced by the following amount for the following quarter, depending on the level of interest rates:

If 3-month LIBOR	Notional Principal Amount	Average Life of Swap
Stays at 3.35% or falls	Completely amortized	1.25 years
Rises to 4.35%	Reduced by 31%	1.75 years
Rises to 5.35%	Reduced by 10.5%	2.5 years
Rises to 6.35 or higher	Not reduced	3.25 years

Panel B: LIBOR-Prime Basis Swap

Notional amount	$200 million
Final maturity	4 years
Payment frequency	Quarterly
Banc One pays	Daily average prime rate—270 basis points (At initiation, prime was 6%)
Banc One receives	3-month LIBOR (subject to caps) (At initiation, 3-month LIBOR was 3.375%)
Caps	In no quarterly period can the rate Banc One receives exceed 25 basis points over the rate received the prior quarter.

Source: Banc One Corporation.

---

investments would not change. However, a drop in rates which precipitated prepayments of mortgages or amortization of the AIRS forced the bank to reinvest the early repayment of principal at the lower market rates. Furthermore, steep rate drops typically increased the rates of prepayment or amortization. For example, though earnings might drop 1% for a 1% increase in rates, a 2% increase in rates might reduce earnings by 3% or 4%, not 2%.

Swaps as a Tool for Risk Management.   Banc One had a long-standing stated policy of "minimizing the impact of fluctuating interest rates on earnings and market values,"[20] and in 1986, its senior management adopted guidelines for allowable earnings sensitivity. This first policy stated that earnings could not change more than 5% for a 1% immediate change in interest rates. Because Banc One was more asset sensitive than its policy would permit, the bank considered

---

[20]Banc One Corporation Third Quarter Report, September 1993, p. 12.

alternatives for adjusting its earnings sensitivity, finally using swaps as its solution.

Although in the past the bank had entered into pay-fixed swaps to transform the cash flows on its municipal investments, the exact opposite swap was required to shift it away from an asset-sensitive position and toward more liability sensitivity. By entering into an interest rate swap in which it paid a floating rate and received a fixed rate in return, it was as if the bank was incurring a floating-rate liability while investing in a fixed-rate asset. This combination would move the bank toward a liability-sensitive (or negative earnings-sensitive) position. Were interest rates to rise, the floating-rate payments on the swaps would increase the bank's interest expense while interest income remained constant, thus reducing earnings and producing liability sensitivity. As Banc One gradually enlarged its interest rate swap portfolio in the mid-1980s, its earnings sensitivity moved to within the specified 5% boundary. See **Exhibit 4** for historical information on Banc One's investment portfolio, swap portfolio, maturity gap, and earnings sensitivity during the period 1988 through 1992.

Because the swaps were designed to adjust the bank's **earnings** sensitivity, the greater its earnings, the more swaps it would need. Also, the more its natural earnings sensitivity strayed from the policy guidelines, the more swaps it would need. Both of these factors contributed to the subsequent growth in its swap portfolio. For example, in 1989, Banc One acquired banks with $12 billion in assets from MCorp, a failed Texas bank. These banks were 23.4% asset sensitive when they were bought, far outside Banc One's policy target range and well above its then-slight liability sensitivity. To bring the new banks in line, Lodge had to enter into a large notional volume of swaps. The bank's continued acquisition strategy, as well as its earnings growth, would increase its need for swaps.[21]

Managing Basis Risk. Though synthetic investments reduced Banc One's earnings sensitivity to overall shifts in interest rates, they created a heightened sensitivity to mismatches *between* floating-rate interest rates, or basis risk. Most of Banc One's floating-rate assets were based on the prime rate. However, most conventional interest rate swaps as well as its AIRS used three-month LIBOR

as an index for floating-rate payments. LIBOR was an actively traded global market rate that changed daily. In contrast, the prime rate was an administered U.S. or local rate that changed infrequently at bankers' discretion. Because of these differences, the spread between the two rates changed dramatically over time. (see **Exhibit 5** for a graph of prime and three-month LIBOR.)

For example, assume the bank entered into a swap in which it received 7% and paid LIBOR. Ignoring the difference between prime and LIBOR, it would effectively transform its prime-based floating-rate assets into fixed-rate investments paying 7%. However, if three-month LIBOR increased 150 basis points but prime was unchanged, Banc One would have transformed its prime-based floating-rate asset into a fixed-rate asset paying not 7% but 5.5%, and it would have created basis risk through its exposure to swings in the prime-LIBOR spread.

To counter this basis risk, Banc One entered into basis swaps that reduced the floating-rate mismatch (see **Exhibit 3, panel B,** for typical basis swap terms). In a basis swap, Banc One would pay a floating rate based on the prime rate and receive a floating rate based on three-month LIBOR. This contract would offset the spread differential between prime and three-month LIBOR. Using a basis swap in conjunction with an AIRS in which it paid LIBOR, Banc One could confidently transform prime-based floating-rate assets to fixed-rate investments.

Managing Counterparty Risk. The credit risk of investing in swaps differed from that of traditional investments. If Banc One bought a U.S. Treasury bond, for example, it would face no credit risk. However, if it entered into a swap transaction in which it received the fixed rate, it would be exposed to the default of its counterparty.

This credit risk was mitigated in three ways. First, the positive swap spread (i.e., yields on swaps were higher than on Treasury securities) gave the bank a higher return to compensate for its credit risk. Second, in an investment, the bank's entire principal was at risk (if the issuer was not the U.S. government), whereas in a swap, only the net payment (fixed less floating) was at risk of default. Third, Banc One established strict policies for managing its counterparty exposure.

---

[21]To meet its anticipated need for swaps, because of expected earnings increases as well as the maturing of existing swap obligations, Banc One began using forward interest rate swaps in the early 1990s. A forward swap contract merely set the terms for a swap contract that would become effective at some future date.

EXHIBIT 4 Banc One's Investment Portfolio and Interest Rate Sensitivity, 1988 through 1992 ($ in millions)

| | Investments | | | | | | | Swaps (a) | | | |
| | Amount Outstanding | | | | Gross Income Received | | | | | | |
	Earning Assets	Loans	Short-term Investments	Securities	Loans	Short-term Investments	Securities	Amount Outstanding	Gross Income Received (b)	Maturity Gap Measure (c)	Earnings Sensitivity
1988	$22,531	$17,325	$ 581	$ 4,625	$1,876	$28	$368	N/A	N/A	-6.67%	-1.00%
1989	23,568	17,909	525	5,133	2,167	39	446	$ 3,299	$291	-3.59%	-1.00%
1990	26,680	20,363	628	5,272	2,303	58	441	3,231	292	-10.07%	-1.55%
1991	41,482	31,168	2,324	7,989	2,747	61	484	11,214	887	-7.33%	-2.30%
1992	54,766	39,142	1,740	13,884	3,872	86	870	10,492	766	-15.70%	-2.60%
1993:Q1	61,807	45,361	1,382	15,064	1,159	11	231	14,132	240	-2.34%	-2.50%
1993:Q2	66,796	48,845	1,978	15,973	1,173	9	235	17,280	275	-2.65%	-2.60%
1993:Q3	68,116	50,105	1,217	16,794	1,189	10	216	22,515	335	-3.64%	-3.30%

(a) Includes only receive-fixed swaps.

(b) Notional volume of outstanding receive-fixed swaps multiplied by average fixed rate received on such swaps.

(c) Maturity gap over the first one-year horizon as a percentage of earning assets, where maturity gap is defined as total assets with adjusted maturity of one year or less minus total liabilities with adjusted maturity of one year or less.

Sources: Banc One Corporation, Annual Reports, 10-Ks.

EXHIBIT 5 Interest Rates and Spreads, 1983 through 1993

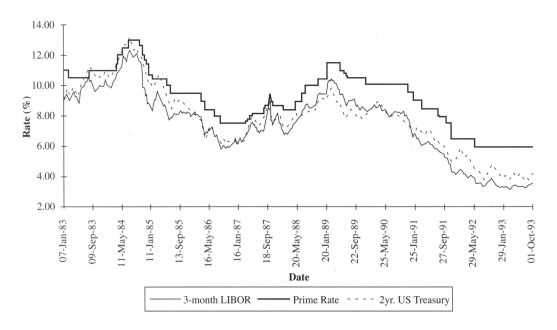

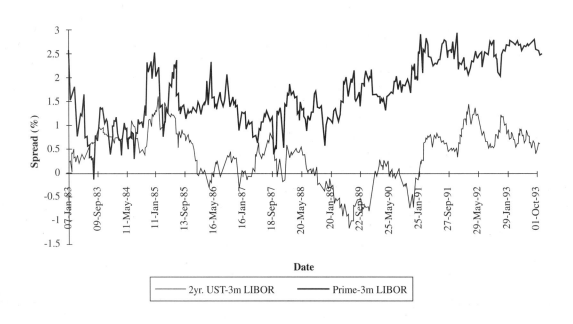

Sources: Citibase, IDC Datasheet, Banc One Corporation.

EXHIBIT 6   **Banc One's Exposure to Its Major Swap Counterparties, October 31, 1993 ($ in millions)**

	Notional Amount	Average Maturity	Mark-to-Market Exposure (a)	Collateral Posted (b)	Net MTM Exposure (c)	Potential Exposure (d)	Net Credit Exposure (e)
Bankers Trust	$12,142	1.77	$123	$132	($9)	$68	$59
Union Bank of Switzerland	$6,976	1.87	$49	$49	$0	$92	$92
Goldman Sachs	$6,163	1.57	$58	$122	($64)	$26	($38)
Lehman Brothers	$4,058	2.32	$16	$81	($65)	$26	($39)
Merrill Lynch	$3,347	2.17	$59	$104	($45)	$10	($35)

(a) Mark-to-market exposure measured as the market value of swap positions with counterparty. A positive exposure indicates that Banc One's swaps have a market value greater than zero.

(b) Collateral is posted in the form of cash or bank-eligible securities. A positive number indicates that Banc One's counterparties have deposited collateral with Banc One.

(c) Represents mark-to-market exposure less collateral posted by Banc One's counterparties.

(d) The bank estimated its potential exposure if it experienced a large movement in interest rates relative to historical experience. Specifically, using historical data, it calculated the distribution of interest rate moves over 30 days. It then calculated how much it could lose, if rates moved against Banc One's favor, and if the size of the rate move was equal to a three-standard-deviation change in rates. Ninety-nine percent of all rate moves would be within three standard deviations, so this potential exposure was considered a conservative estimate of the bank's exposure.

(e) Represents Banc One's potential exposure less the collateral it currently has on hand.

Source: Banc One Corporation.

In all instances, its counterparties were rated no lower than single-A. To understand its potential exposure, Banc One continually monitored its mark-to-market exposure to each counterparty. Its total exposure to any entity, whether through derivatives or direct lending, was limited by clear policy guidelines. In addition, to protect itself against the default of a swap counterparty, Banc One required its counterparties to post collateral, in the form of bank-eligible securities or cash, against the bank's exposure.[22] Investment bank counterparties posted collateral at the initiation of the swap equal to Banc One's possible losses from an extreme one-month move in interest rates.[23] All counterparties were required to post additional collateral as the market value of the swap changed over time.[24] This practice meant that Banc One was not exposed to swap payments for which it did not have collateral, and were the swap to default, the mark-to-market collateral would allow the bank to enter into a new swap that was economically identical to the one that had defaulted. Banc One's counterparties—and its exposures to

each—are shown in **Exhibit 6.** Banc One's collateral requirements were unique, as most large money-center banks and commercial banks were extremely reluctant to post any kind of collateral for swaps, regardless of the counterparty. Yet, because of the magnitude of its derivatives portfolio and because of its solid credit rating, Banc One was almost always able to secure such collateral agreements, even from AAA-rated counterparties.

Controlling the Asset and Liability Management Process. Banc One's careful handling of the counterparty risk was indicative of its long-standing, well-defined investment policies. In late 1993, the investment policies of many banks (including Banc One), and especially their use of derivatives portfolios, came under public scrutiny.

In mid-1993, a consortium of leading financial service firms, known as the Group of Thirty, released a report in which it recommended a set of practices that all derivatives dealers and users follow to ensure that these

---

[22]Bank eligible securities are liquid securities for which the market value can be easily ascertained, and would include a wide range of Treasury securities, bank deposits, and CMOs.

[23]Banking regulations prohibited commercial banks from posting collateral in advance.

[24]Banc One would deliver collateral to its counterparties if the market value of the swap was negative.

instruments were used prudently. This report was commonly seen as a proactive effort at self-regulation to fend off governmental regulation of derivatives. Later that year, in October, the U.S. Comptroller of the Currency, the regulator of national banks, issued its own set of guidelines for the use of swaps. The guidelines focused on the role of senior management and boards of directors in ensuring that users of swaps acted safely. The report charged banks with managing market risk, counterparty credit risk, liquidity risk, and operations and systems risk while remaining mindful of the impact of swaps on the banks' capital base and accounting. Politicians seized on the issue and made their own statements concerning the swap market. The statements of the industry, regulators, and politicians pushed the banking sector's use of derivatives onto the front pages of leading newspapers and made the issue one of general interest.

This newfound interest in the management of derivatives positions came as no surprise to Banc One. For years, senior management had made the prudent use of derivatives and other investments, as well as management of its assets and liabilities, a top priority. Its Asset and Liability Management Committees (ALCOs) were responsible for establishing and implementing policies relating to asset and liability management. The process was governed by a 70-page policy document, updated in April 1993, which outlined an exact system of control and oversight of the bank's asset and liability management policies, including its management of swaps, an integral part of its investment portfolio. The ALCO process was a system for consistently managing interest rate risk, credit risk, funding risk, and capital adequacy. A committee of the most senior bank executives reviewed and ratified major investment decisions, recommended changes to existing policy, and monitored compliance with policy guidelines.

The ALCO process consisted of regular meetings at several levels of the bank. Affiliate banks reviewed their cash position and funds management activities daily. For each state, asset and liability committees were established to monitor that state's activities. At the corporate level, three committees met weekly or monthly to monitor and oversee the overall asset and liability system: the corporate funds management activity committee; the working ALCO committee, which included Lodge, McCoy, and many other senior executives; and the corporate ALCO committee, which included the working ALCO as well as the chairmen of Banc One's holding companies and its chief credit officer. The operation of the MICS system made timely and appropriate information available to each committee.

All policy decisions regarding Banc One's earnings sensitivity were made at the corporate level. Furthermore, the firm's investment activities, including both securities and swaps, were executed at the corporate level by CIO Dick Lodge and his group. Thus, the affiliate and state ALCO groups monitored local deposit and lending activities and their impact on the units' liquidity and interest rate exposure. Corporate ALOC activities overlaid investments and derivatives onto the aggregated activities of the local banks in order to manage the bank's overall exposure.

When it was established in 1986, the bank's policy was to stay within a 5% earnings sensitivity boundary for an *immediate* 1% shock to interest rates. However, Lodge had recently persuaded the working ALCO committee that such a shock was unrealistic. He believed the committee should instead focus on the impact of a *gradual* 1% [change] in the level of interest rates during the year (i.e., rates would slowly rise 1%, so that on average they would have risen 1/2%). The working ALCO committee agreed to this change, and it also set a new boundary for the bank at 4% sensitivity. In addition, the committee set other guidelines:

Earnings Sensitivity	Policy	Nov. 1993 Banc One Position
1st-year impact for a +1% rate change	(4.00)%	(3.30)%
1st-year impact for a +2% rate change	(9.00)%	(8.00)%
1st-year impact for a +3% rate change	(15.00)%	(13.20)%
2nd-year impact for a +1% rate change	(4.00)%	(1.30)%
2nd-year impact for a +2% rate change	(9.00)%	(7.90)%
1st-year impact for a −1% rate change	(4.00)%	4.00%

Within these strategic guidelines, Lodge was permitted, with the working ALCO group's approval, to make tactical decisions on exactly what the bank's earnings sensitivity should be. Although there were several guidelines and Lodge had to comply with each one, both he and the ALCO groups focused mainly on the first-year impact of a gradual 1% change in rates because, historically, it had been rare for interest rates to change much more than 1% in any given year.

In November 1993, if it did not have its $12 billion in fixed-rate investments and $22 billion in receive-fixed swaps, the bank would have been 13% asset sensitive. With them, it was positioned to be 3.3% liability sensitive. This conscious decision to be modestly liability sensitive was the bank's strategic exposure to interest rates. As Lodge explained, "Banks are paid to be liability sensitive," meaning that the yield curve was almost always upward-sloping. By having a controlled amount of long-term fixed-rate income-producing assets exceeding its short-term floating-rate liabilities, the bank could earn the interest differential as long as the yield curve remained upward-sloping and did not shift up dramatically. However, this net position left the bank liability sensitive as a rise in rates would reduce its income.

Although a sudden rise in rates would depress the bank's earnings, the investment portfolio was set up so that this exposure was controlled. Specifically, the swaps in place were level over the next year, but would virtually all mature within two years. Thus, if the bank did not add new swaps to its position, its existing swaps would fall to $17.5 billion by year-end 1994 and $3.6 billion by year-end 1995. Its projected earnings sensitivity would drop to −.2% by the end of 1994, effectively making its earnings unaffected by interest rate swings, and the bank would be asset sensitive by 1995. See **Exhibit 7.**

Although the bank focused primarily on the impact of interest rates on its earnings, the ALCO committee also examined the effect of interest rates on the value of the firm and its common equity. The asset and liability database allowed it to measure the duration[25] of assets and liabilities. Lodge's figures for the bank's key duration measures, as of September 30, 1993, were 1.73 years for on- and off-balance sheet assets and 1.51 years for its liabilities. Because the difference between assets and liabilities was a residual equity account, Lodge could also calculate a rough duration of equity (by weighting each category by its total dollar amount). As of September 30, residual equity had a duration of +4.00 years. For each 1% rise in rates, this duration measure suggested that Banc One's equity value would drop by 4.0%. As interest rates rose, its slightly longer-duration asset base would decline in value faster than its shorter-duration liabilities, leading to a magnified drop in the market value of its equity.

As of September 30, Banc One had $37.7 billion in notional volume of interest rate swaps on its books. Both Lodge and McCoy felt that the bank had drawn some of its unwanted attention because its swap portfolio had grown so dramatically. One analyst identified Banc One as having the second-largest growth in an existing swap portfolio of all regional banks. At the end of 1990, Banc One had only $4.7 billion in swaps on its books. This figure had grown to $13.5 billion at the end of 1991 and $21.0 billion at the end of 1992. Looking forward, Banc One saw continued growth in its swap portfolio as long as its earnings grew, it continued to acquire banks that were more asset sensitive than itself, and the yield curve remained upward-sloping.

Disclosure.   As of November 1993, the Financial Accounting Standards Board (FASB) required minimal disclosure of the details of a company's swap portfolio because swaps were classified as off-balance-sheet items. Generally, the total notional volume of swaps was reported as a footnote to reported financial statements. Under accounting guidelines, though, notional volume had to include *all* swaps, regardless of their purpose or whether they offset one another. Thus, if Banc One entered into a $100 million receive-fixed swap and then a $100 million basis swap to adjust the floating-rate index it paid, the swaps would be reported as $200 million of notional amount, even though they economically replicated only $100 million of a fixed-rate investment. Likewise, if it entered into a $100 million pay-fixed swap and then entered into an exactly offsetting receive-fixed swap, it would report $200 million in swaps.

Even though FASB required minimal swap disclosure, Banc One had voluntarily disclosed additional information, consistent with its reporting policies. In addition to reporting the total notional volume of swaps on its books, it reported the unrealized net gain or loss on its swap portfolio. Banc One's disclosures of its swaps activities for 1993 are shown in **Exhibit 8.**

---

[25]Duration can be defined as the change in value of an asset or liability due to a given small parallel shift in interest rates or, alternatively, as the weighted average time until repayment of the asset or liability. The duration of a portfolio of assets or liabilities measures the net change in value of the entire portfolio due to movements in interest rates or, alternatively, the weighted average time until repayment of the entire portfolio. Because duration assumed a linear response between interest rate shifts and value over a small change in rates, it had to be interpreted with caution for instruments with embedded options as well as for large interest rate movements.

EXHIBIT 7   Banc One's Recent Swap Portfolio and Projected Swap Portfolio if No New Positions Added, October 1993

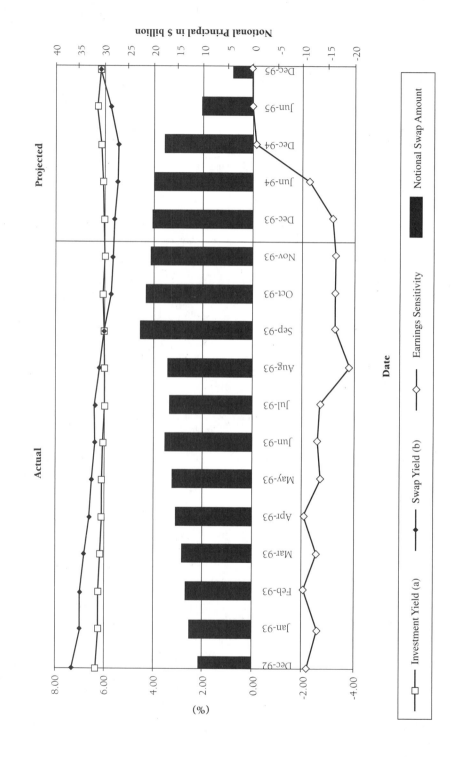

(a) Average yield received on investment portfolio (excluding swaps). For projected period, assumes no new investments made.
(b) Average rate received on receive-fixed swap portfolio. For projected period, assumes no new positions added.
Source: Banc One Corporation.

EXHIBIT 8   Banc One's 1993 Disclosure of Its Interest Rate Management Activities (10-Q filings)

Panel A: 1993 First Quarter

BANC ONE manages interest rate sensitivity within a very small tolerance through the use of off-balance sheet interest rate swaps and other instruments, thereby minimizing the effect of interest rate fluctuations on earnings and market values. The use of swaps resulted in BANC ONE being slightly liability-sensitive at March 31, 1993, countering the natural tendency to be asset-sensitive. The use of swaps to manage interest rate sensitivity increased interest income by $54 million and $50 million, and decreased interest expense by $47 and $34 million in the first quarter of 1993 and 1992, respectively. The notional amount of swaps increased from $8.3 billion to $23.4 billion from March 31, 1992 to March 31, 1993.

Panel B: 1993 Second Quarter

BANC ONE manages interest rate sensitivity within a very small tolerance through the use of off-balance sheet interest rate swaps and other instruments, thereby minimizing the effect of interest rate fluctuations on earnings and market values. The use of swaps resulted in BANC ONE being slightly liability-sensitive at June 30, 1993, adjusting the natural tendency to be asset-sensitive. Swaps increased interest income by $59 million and $113 million for the three and six month periods ending June 30, 1993 as compared to $46 million and $95 million for the same periods in 1993. Swaps decreased deposit and other borrowing cost by $48 million and $96 million for the three and six month periods ended June 30, 1993, compared to decreases of $45 million and $80 million for the same periods in 1992. The notional amount of swaps increased to $31.5 billion from $20.8 billion and $18.4 billion at December 31, and June 29, 1992, respectively. Accruing fixed rate swaps represented $17.4 billion, $10.5 billion and $11.2 billion for the same respective periods.

Panel C: 1993 Third Quarter

The following information supplements Management's Discussion and Analysis in Part 1. The notional amount of swaps shown below represents an agreed upon amount on which calculations of interest payments to be exchanged are based. BANC ONE's credit exposure is limited to the net difference between the calculated pay and receive amounts on each transaction which are generally netted and paid quarterly. BANC ONE's policy is to obtain sufficient collateral from swap counterparties to secure receipt of all amounts due. At September 30, 1993, the market value of interest rate swaps and the related collateral was approximately $536 million and $623 million, respectively. As indicated below, the notional value of the interest rate swap portfolio increased from $21 billion to $38 billion during the nine months ended September 30, 1993. This increase was primarily associated with swaps acquired to replaced fixed rate, on- and off-balance sheet instruments which have or will mature or amortize and to manage interest rate risk in newly acquired affiliates. These new affiliates did not use swaps to manage their exposure to interest rate risk to as great a degree as BANC ONE. Exposure to interest rate risk is determined by simulating the impact of prospective changes in interest rates on the results of operations. Management seeks to insure that over a one-year horizon, net income will not be impacted by more than 4 percent and 9 percent by a gradual change in market interest rates of 1 percent and 2 percent, respectively. At December 31, 1992, a 2.3 percent reduction in forecasted earnings would have resulted from a gradual 1 percent increase in market rates. Due to the increase in the notional value of the swap portfolio noted above, the sensitivity to such

---

Along with the second quarter report, Banc One made available to its investors a 10-page brochure entitled *Banc One Corporation Asset and Liability Management*. This brochure described how the corporation uses swaps and other derivatives to maintain its strong capital position, manage its liquidity, and manage the bank's interest rate exposure.

The Meeting

As Banc One's earnings grew, so too did its swap position. With its growing swap portfolio, it caught the attention of bank analysts. Some applauded the bank's use of swaps to manage its interest rate exposure. Other—more vocal—analysts, were critical, accusing Banc One of using swaps to inflate earnings, inflate capital ratios, and offset declines elsewhere in the bank. These critics

saw the rapidly growing swap positions as heading out of control. One analyst was quoted as saying of the bank's swap activities, "Does that look like hedge activity? They use this stuff to keep the game going." A few analysts had downgraded the stock.

Though it was impossible to pin the recent decline in Banc One's stock price solely on its growing derivatives portfolio, both insiders and outsiders felt that the $10 drop in its stock price was due in large part to the

Exhibit 8 *(concluded)*

a rate increase changed to 3.8 percent at September 30, 1993. BANC ONE believes that both on-balance sheet securities and off-balance sheet derivatives may be used interchangeably to manage interest rate risk to an acceptable level. Various factors are considered in dciding the appropriate mix of such securities and derivatives including liquidity, capital requirements and yield.

During the nine months ended September 30, 1993, BANC ONE entered into $3.8 billion notional amount of basis swap contracts where payments based on the prime rate and LIBOR are exchanged. The variable rate used in the non-basis swap contracts entered into by BANC ONE is based on LIBOR, while many of the variable rate assets being synthetically altered are based on the prime rate. Basis swap contracts, therefore, improve the degree to which the swap portfolio acts as a hedge against the impact of changes in rates on BANC ONE's results of operations.

The table below summarizes by notional amounts the activity for each major category of swaps. For all periods presented, BANC ONE had no deferred gains or losses relating to terminated swap contracts. The terminations shown in the following table

$(millions)	Receive Fixed	Pay Fixed	Basis	Forward Starting	Total
Balance, December 31, 1990	**$3,114**	**$937**	**$550**	**$117**	**$4,719**
Additions	9,797	509			10,306
Maturities/Amortizations	(1,171)	(322)			(1,493)
Terminations	(3,102)				(3,102)
Forward Starting-Becoming Effective	117			(117)	
Acquisitions and Other (net)	2,764	277			3,041
Balance, December 31, 1991	**11,519**	**1,401**	**550**		**13,470**
Additions	2,002	501		11,656	14,159
Maturities/Amortizations	(6,059)	(182)	(350)		(6,591)
Terminations					
Forward Starting-Becoming Effective	3,201	1,005		(4,206)	
Acquisitions and Other (net)	289	(296)			(7)
Balance, December 31, 1992	**10,952**	**2,429**	**200**	**7,450**	**21,031**
Additions	4,428	1,237	3,800	12,000	21,465
Maturities/Amortizations	(3,545)	(861)	(204)		(4,610)
Terminations	(250)	(250)			(500)
Forward Starting-Becoming Effective	10,480			(10,480)	
Acquisitions and Other (net)	450	15	20	(150)	335
Balance, September 30, 1993	**$22,515**	**$2,570**	**$3,816**	**$ 8,820**	**$37,721**

market's reaction to the bank's use of derivatives. One analyst supportive of the company wrote:

> One likely reason for the price weakness is a recent focus on Banc One's liberal use of derivatives to achieve its asset/liability management goals. Since derivatives are relatively new financial instruments, and since their use requires a high degree of financial sophistication and quantitative expertise, there is an understandable aversion to them on the part of many investors . . . Although (Banc One's swap position) is a large notional amount for a regional bank, we think Banc One's use of derivatives has been prudent.[26]

As the meeting began, McCoy voiced his concern about Banc One's falling stock price. From his perspective, he and Lodge faced a dilemma. On the one hand, he felt that swaps were hurting shareholder value because the

---

[26]K. F. Puglisi, "Banc One Corporation," unpublished analyst report, The Chicago Corporation, October 29, 1993.

for the year ended December 31, 1991 resulted in losses of $1.8 million which were recognized during that year in accordance with BANC ONE's accounting policy at that time. The terminations in 1993 related to swaps which had been carried at market value and, therefore, resulted in no deferred gain or loss at termination.

The table below summarizes expected maturities and weighted average interest rates to be received and paid on the swap portfolio at September 30, 1993. A key assumption in the preparation of the table is that rates remain constant at September 30, 1993 levels. To the extent that rates change, both the periodic maturities and the variable interest rates to be received or paid will change. Such changes could be substantial. The maturities change when interest rates change because the swap portfolio includes $23.6 billion of amortizing swaps. Amortization is generally based on certain interest rate indices.

Expected Maturity

$(millions)	4th Quart. 1993	1994	1995	1996	1997	1998	All Other	Total
Receive Fixed Swaps								
Notional Amount	$2,436	$ 9,096	$ 8,880	$1,050	$ 90	$ 46	$917	$22,515
Weighted Average:								
Receive Rate	7.58%	6.00%	5.34%	6.02%	7.24%	6.22%	6.81%	5.95%
Pay Rate	3.28	3.28	3.23	3.36	3.24	3.19	3.54	3.28
Pay Fixed Swaps								
Notional Amount	$ 627	$ 970	$ 318	$ 272	$ 267	$109	$ 7	$ 2,570
Weighted Average:								
Receive Rate	3.25%	3.39%	3.33%	3.26%	3.44%	3.41%	3.31%	3.34%
Pay Rate	6.64	5.86	5.00	5.76	6.07	5.30	8.82	5.96
Basis Swaps								
Notional Amount	0	0	0	$2,200	$1,600	$ 16	0	$ 3,816
Weighted Average:								
Receive Rate	0.00	0.00	0.00	3.22%	3.27%	3.20%	0.00	3.24%
Pay Rate	0.00	0.00	0.00	3.33	3.34	4.80	0.00	3.34
Forward-Starting*								
Notional Amount	$ 500	$ 100	$ 6,720	$1,500	0	0	0	$ 8,820
Weighted Average:								
Receive Rate	7.20%	5.74%	4.98%	5.68%	0.00	0.00	0.00	5.24%
Pay Rate	3.38	3.38	3.38	3.38	0.00	0.00	0.00	3.38
Total	**$3,563**	**$10,166**	**$15,918**	**$5,022**	**$1,957**	**$171**	**$924**	**$37,721**
	6.77%	5.75%	5.15%	4.54%	3.47%	4.14%	6.78%	5.33%
	3.88	3.53	3.33	3.48	3.71	4.69	3.58	3.49

*All receive-fixed swaps.

Source: Banc One Corporation.

investment community did not understand how they were being used. On the other hand, he believed that they were an invaluable tool in managing risk. Given the distance between his beliefs and what he was hearing from the market, he wondered what, if anything, the bank should do.

In an attempt to answer this question, McCoy and Lodge discussed three possible options. First, they could do nothing and hope that Banc One's stock price would recover over time as investors realized that derivatives were actually helping the bank manage interest rate and basis risk. Second, they could abandon or severely limit their derivatives portfolio. Third, they could attempt to

educate investors about how they used derivatives. Their most recent quarterly disclosure gave the market a great deal of data on the bank's swap portfolio, but perhaps even more information might dispel the misconceptions. What information would the market want to see? And how could Banc One credibly present it so as to convince its skeptics and educate swap novices? Perhaps analysts would understand Banc One's ALCO process and use of swaps if they could compare the bank to a hypothetical Banc One that had no swaps or no investments. In preparation, they had created a set of analyses showing this comparison (see the **Appendix**).

$ in billions	Banc One (Stylized)	Twin A (Swaps on balance sheet)	Twin B (No investment activities)
Balance Sheet			
Assets			
Floating-rate assets			
Variable-rate loans	$33.8	$33.8	$33.8
Additional money market assets	0	0	31.8
Fixed-rate Assets			
Fixed-rate loans	18.6	18.6	18.6
Fixed-rate investments	13.4	13.4	0
Additional Treasury securities	0	18.4	0
Other assets	8.4	8.4	8.4
Total Assets	$74.2	$92.6	$92.6
NOTE: Earning Assets (1)	65.8	84.2	84.2
Liabilities and Equity			
Floating-rate liabilities			
Retail deposits	19.3	19.3	19.3
Wholesale deposits (2)	8.8	8.8	8.8
Additional wholesale deposits (3)	0.0	18.4	18.4
Fixed-rate liabilities			
Fixed core deposits (4)	23.8	23.8	23.8
Large time deposits	2.3	2.3	2.3
Other liabilities	13.4	13.4	13.4
Total liabilities	67.6	86.0	86.0
Preferred shares	0.3	0.3	0.3
Common shares	6.4	6.4	6.4
Total	$74.2	$92.6	$92.6
Off-balance-sheet items			
Swaps (5)	$18.4	$0.0	$0.0

(1) Earning assets include loans and investments.

(2) "Wholesale" deposits represent liabilities to other financial institutions, e.g., federal funds borrowings.

(3) For both twin banks, additional needs for funds would be met by borrowing from other financial institutions.

(4) Fixed core deposits are the "sticky-fixed" deposits. Their rates may change with market rates (at bank management's discretion), but they are relatively stable in volume as rates change.

(5) Represents only the swaps in which Banc One receives fixed rates. Does not include its basis swaps or the relatively small amount of other interest rate derivatives in its portfolio.

None of the alternatives was riskless. Doing nothing might give the impression that the bank was hiding something, thereby confirming investors' worst suspicions. If it caused Banc One's stock price to stay low or fall even further, the bank's ability to continue its stock acquisitions would be jeopardized. Eliminating its derivatives portfolio would leave the bank with greater interest rate exposure and few tools to manage it. Disclosing even more information was not a guaranteed solution. In drawing even greater attention to its derivatives portfolio, the bank might raise investors' concerns or increase their confusion.

Appendix: Modeling Banc One's Performance under Alternative Investment Policies.

In preparation for his meeting with McCoy, Dick Lodge asked his staff to prepare a simplified set of Banc One financials that could communicate the essence of the bank's financial statements and the underlying economics of their business. This stylized set of financials would show the basic earnings sensitivity faced by the bank, and how it used swaps to solve this problem. The simplified model would also demonstrate the impact of the bank's derivative activities on its accounting ratios, such as its net interest margin as well as its returns on assets and equity. Moreover, the simplified books would show how swaps affected the bank's dependence on large short-term borrowings as well as demonstrate how the bank's swap portfolio affected the amount of risk-adjusted capital it held.

In order to explain the role that swaps played at Banc One, Lodge and his staff felt it might be instructive to

$ in billions		Banc One (Stylized)	Twin A (Swaps on balance sheet)	Twin B (No investment activities)
Income Statement				
	Rate			
Interest Income from				
Variable-rate loans	7.32%	$2.47	$2.47	$2.47
Additional money market assets	3.50%	0.00	0.00	1.11
Fixed-rate loans	11.13%	2.07	2.07	2.07
Fixed-rate investments	6.88%	0.92	0.92	0.00
Additional Treasury securities	4.30%	0.00	0.79	0.00
Total interest income		5.47	6.26	5.66
Interest expense from:				
Retail deposits	3.27%	0.63	0.63	0.63
Wholesale deposits	3.09%	0.27	0.27	0.27
Additional wholesale deposits	3.09%	0.00	0.57	0.57
Fixed core deposits	3.57%	0.85	0.85	0.85
Large deposits	3.57%	0.08	0.08	0.08
Total interest expense		1.83	2.40	2.40
Income from Swaps (6)	2.50%	0.46	0.00	0.00
Net interest		4.09	3.85	3.25
Non-interest expense		2.37	2.37	2.37
Taxable earnings		1.72	1.48	0.88
Taxes	34.00%	0.59	0.50	0.30
Net income		1.14	0.98	0.58
Performance Measures				
Net interest margin (7)		6.22%	4.58%	3.86%
Net interest margin (excluding swaps) (8)		5.52%	4.58%	3.86%
Return on assets		1.53%	1.06%	0.63%
Equity/Assets (9)		8.56%	6.86%	6.86%
Return on Equity (10)		17.89%	15.42%	9.19%
Dependence on large liabilities (11)		15.0%	33.5%	−5.4%
Risk-adjusted assets (12)		$63.2	$63.1	$74.7
Tier I capital/risk-adjusted assets (13)		10.4%	10.5%	8.8%
Earnings sensitivity (14)		−3.30%	−3.30%	12.88%
Summary				
Earnings		High	Better	Low
Capital		High	Low	Low
Risk Capital		Good	High	Low
Liquidity		Good	Low	High
Earnings Sensitivity		Liability Sensitive	Liability Sensitive	Very Asset Sensitive

(6) Represents the difference between the fixed rate that Banc One receives and the current floating rate. Does not include Banc One's basis swaps.

(7) Net interest (including income from swaps) divided by earning assets.

(8) Net interest (excluding income from swaps) divided by earning assets.

(9) Common equity/assets.

(10) Return to common equity.

(11) Equals (large time deposits + wholesale deposits − money market assets)/(earning assets − money market assets). Represents an estimate of the liabilities that the bank might be called on to honor immediately, net of its assets that could be liquidated immediately.

(12) Calculated by applying the BIS capital weights to each asset category.

(13) Banc One's equity divided by its risk-adjusted assets.

(14) Represents the percentage change in the coming year's net income in response to a gradual 1% rise in interest rates over the coming year. In this model, a gradual 1% rise in rates is the same as an immediate .5% increase in rates. The earnings sensitivity for a 2% or 3% rise in rates would not be merely two or three times the sensitivity for a 1% rise. This is because of the amortization schedule of the bank's swap contract as well as the nature of the other bank assets and liabilities. Furthermore, a 1% fall in rates would not necessarily produce the same earnings sensitivity. Banc One estimated that a 1% drop in rates would lead to a 4.0% increase in earnings, as compared to a 3.3% decline in earnings for a 1% rate increase.

compare Banc One with two hypothetical twin banks whose investment policies differed from its own. The first twin was like Banc One in all regards but one. This hypothetical bank brought its swaps onto the balance sheet by replacing the notional principal of its receive-fixed swaps with investments in fixed-rate securities[27] funded by variable-rate borrowings. Because Banc One's receive-fixed swaps were similar to an investment in fixed-rate securities funded by floating-rate borrowings, this twin would have similar interest rate exposure to Banc One. However, it would differ in its accounting performance, dependence on large liabilities, and capital levels.

A second twin would follow yet another investment strategy. In place of Banc One's fixed-rate investments, this twin would invest in floating-rate loans and investments. In place of Banc One's swaps, it would invest in floating-rate assets financed by floating-rate deposits. The second twin more closely resembles a bank that did not manage its interest rate sensitivity.

The hope was that these simple projections would demonstrate to investors how the bank's investment activities, but especially its derivatives activities, affected its earnings sensitivity, accounting results, liquidity, and capital needs.

---

[27]For this model, it was assumed that the swaps were replaced with investments in Treasury securities financed by floating-rate borrowing. The AIRS that make up the bulk of the bank's swap portfolio would be comparable more to investments in CMOs (with prepayment risk) funded by floating-rate borrowings.

ANNUAL PERCENTAGE RATE TABLE FOR MONTHLY PAYMENT PLANS

Annual Percentage Rate
(Finance Charge Per $100 of Amount Financed)

Number of Payments	10.00%	10.50%	11.00%	11.50%	12.00%	12.50%	13.00%	13.50%	14.00%	14.50%	15.00%	15.50%	16.00%	16.50%	17.00%	17.50%	18.00%
1	0.83	0.87	0.92	0.96	1.00	1.04	1.08	1.12	1.17	1.21	1.25	1.29	1.33	1.37	1.42	1.46	1.50
2	1.25	1.31	1.38	1.44	1.50	1.57	1.63	1.69	1.75	1.82	1.88	1.94	2.00	2.07	2.13	2.19	2.26
3	1.67	1.76	1.84	1.92	2.01	2.09	2.17	2.26	2.34	2.43	2.51	2.59	2.68	2.76	2.85	2.93	3.01
4	2.09	2.20	2.30	2.41	2.51	2.62	2.72	2.83	2.93	3.04	3.14	3.25	3.36	3.46	3.57	3.67	3.78
5	2.51	2.64	2.77	2.89	3.02	3.15	3.27	3.40	3.53	3.65	3.78	3.91	4.04	4.16	4.29	4.42	4.54
6	2.94	3.08	3.23	3.38	3.53	3.68	3.83	3.97	4.12	4.27	4.42	4.57	4.72	4.87	5.02	5.17	5.32
7	3.36	3.53	3.70	3.87	4.04	4.21	4.38	4.55	4.72	4.89	5.06	5.23	5.40	5.58	5.75	5.92	6.09
8	3.79	3.98	4.17	4.36	4.55	4.74	4.94	5.13	5.32	5.51	5.71	5.90	6.09	6.29	6.48	6.67	6.87
9	4.21	4.43	4.64	4.85	5.07	5.28	5.49	5.71	5.92	6.14	6.35	6.57	6.78	7.00	7.22	7.43	7.65
10	4.64	4.88	5.11	5.35	5.58	5.82	6.05	6.29	6.53	6.77	7.00	7.24	7.48	7.72	7.96	8.19	8.43
11	5.07	5.33	5.58	5.84	6.10	6.36	6.62	6.88	7.14	7.40	7.66	7.92	8.18	8.44	8.70	8.96	9.22
12	5.50	5.78	6.06	6.34	6.62	6.90	7.18	7.46	7.74	8.03	8.31	8.59	8.88	9.16	9.45	9.73	10.02
18	8.10	8.52	8.93	9.35	9.77	10.19	10.61	11.03	11.45	11.87	12.29	12.72	13.14	13.57	13.99	14.42	14.85
24	10.75	11.30	11.86	12.42	12.98	13.54	14.10	14.66	15.23	15.80	16.37	16.94	17.51	18.09	18.66	19.24	19.82
30	13.43	14.13	14.83	15.54	16.24	16.95	17.66	18.38	19.10	19.81	20.54	21.26	21.99	22.72	23.45	24.18	24.92
36	16.16	17.01	17.88	18.71	19.57	20.43	21.30	22.17	23.04	23.92	24.80	25.68	26.57	27.46	28.35	29.25	30.15
42	18.93	19.93	20.93	21.94	22.96	23.98	25.00	26.03	27.06	28.10	29.15	30.19	31.25	32.31	33.37	34.44	35.51
48	21.74	22.90	24.06	25.23	26.40	27.58	28.77	29.97	31.17	32.37	33.59	34.81	36.03	37.27	38.50	39.75	41.00
54	24.59	25.91	27.23	28.56	29.91	31.25	32.61	33.98	35.35	36.73	38.12	39.52	40.92	42.33	43.75	45.18	46.62
60	27.48	28.96	30.45	31.96	33.47	34.99	36.52	38.06	39.61	41.17	42.74	44.32	45.91	47.51	49.12	50.73	52.36
66	30.41	32.06	33.73	35.40	37.09	38.78	40.49	42.21	43.95	45.69	47.45	49.22	51.00	52.79	54.59	56.40	58.23
72	33.39	35.21	37.05	38.90	40.76	42.64	44.53	46.44	48.36	50.30	52.24	54.21	56.18	58.17	60.17	62.19	64.22
78	36.40	38.40	40.41	42.45	44.49	46.45	48.64	50.74	52.85	54.98	57.13	59.29	61.46	63.66	65.86	68.09	70.32
84	39.45	41.63	43.83	46.05	48.28	50.54	52.81	55.11	57.42	59.75	62.09	64.46	66.84	69.24	71.66	74.10	76.55
90	42.54	44.91	47.29	49.70	52.13	54.58	57.05	59.54	62.05	64.59	67.14	69.72	72.31	74.93	77.56	80.22	82.89
96	45.67	48.22	50.80	53.40	56.03	58.68	61.35	64.05	66.77	69.51	72.28	75.06	77.88	80.71	83.57	86.44	89.34
102	48.84	51.59	54.36	57.16	59.98	62.83	65.71	68.62	71.55	74.51	77.49	80.50	83.53	86.59	89.67	92.76	95.91
108	52.05	54.99	57.96	60.98	63.99	67.05	70.14	73.26	76.40	79.58	82.78	86.01	89.27	92.56	95.87	99.21	102.57
114	55.30	58.43	61.61	64.81	68.05	71.32	74.63	77.96	81.33	84.73	88.15	91.61	95.10	98.62	102.17	105.74	109.35
120	58.58	61.92	65.30	68.71	72.17	75.65	79.17	82.73	86.32	89.94	93.60	97.29	101.02	104.77	108.56	112.37	116.22
180	93.43	98.97	104.59	110.27	116.03	121.85	127.74	133.70	139.71	145.79	151.93	158.12	164.37	170.67	177.02	183.42	189.88
240	131.61	139.61	147.73	155.94	164.26	172.67	181.18	189.77	198.44	207.20	216.03	224.93	233.90	242.94	252.03	261.19	270.39
300	172.61	183.25	194.03	204.94	215.97	227.11	238.35	249.69	261.13	272.65	284.25	295.92	307.67	319.47	331.34	343.26	355.23
360	215.53	229.31	242.64	256.50	270.30	284.21	298.23	312.35	326.55	340.84	355.20	369.63	384.11	398.65	413.24	427.88	442.55

SOURCE: Federal Reserve Bank of New York.